OKANAGAN UNIV/COLLEGE LIBRARY
D0635869

HANDBOOK OF

ADOLESCENT PSYCHOLOGY

SECOND EDITION

EDITED BY

RICHARD M. LERNER
LAURENCE STEINBERG

JOHN WILEY & SONS, INC.

This book is printed on acid-free paper. ♾

Published by John Wiley & Sons, Inc., Hoboken, New Jersey.
Published simultaneously in Canada.

For general information on our other products and services please contact our Customer Care Department within the United States at (800) 762-2974, outside the United States at (317) 572-3993 or fax (317) 572-4002.

Wiley also publishes its books in a variety of electronic formats. Some content that appears in print may not be available in electronic books. For more information about Wiley products, visit our web site at www.wiley.com.

Library of Congress Cataloging-in-Publication Data:

Lerner, Richard M.
Handbook of adolescent psychology / Richard M. Lerner and Laurence Steinberg.—2nd ed.
p. cm.
Includes bibliographical references and index.
ISBN 0-471-20948-1 (cloth)
1. Adolescent psychology. I. Steinberg, Laurence D., 1952– II. Title.
BF 724.L367 2004
155.5—dc21
2003049664

Printed in the United States of America.
10 9 8 7 6 5 4 3 2 1

Contents

PART TWO SOCIAL RELATIONSHIPS AND SOCIAL CONTEXTS IN ADOLESCENCE

PART THREE ADOLESCENT CHALLENGES, CHOICES, AND POSITIVE YOUTH DEVELOPMENT

Contributors

Manuel Barrera, Jr.
Arizona State University

Peter L. Benson
Search Institute

Robert W. Blum
University of Minnesota

Jeanne Brooks-Gunn
Teachers College, Columbia University

B. Bradford Brown
University of Wisconsin-Madison

Nancy A. Busch-Rossnagel
Fordham University

Laurie Chassin
Arizona State University

W. Andrew Collins
University of Minnesota

Bruce E. Compas
Vanderbilt University

Lisa M. Diamond
University of Utah

Jacquelynne S. Eccles
University of Michigan

Nancy Eisenberg
Arizona State University

David P. Farrington
University of Cambridge

Thaddeus Ferber
Forum for Youth Investment

Celia B. Fisher
Fordham University

Constance A. Flanagan
Pennsylvania State University

Ulla G. Foehr
Stanford Unversity

Nancy L. Galambos
University of Alberta

Julia A. Graber
University of Florida

Beatrix Hamburg
Weill Medical College

David Hamburg
Carnegie Corporation of New York

Mary Agnes Hamilton
Cornell University

Steven F. Hamilton
Cornell University

Penny Hauser-Cram
Boston College

Lisa Henriksen
Stanford University School of Medicine

Andrea Hussong
University of North Carolina Chapel Hill

Daniel P. Keating
University of Toronto

Mary Wyngaarden Krauss
Brandeis University

Reed Larson
University of Illinois,
Urbana/Champaign

Brett Laursen
Florida Atlantic University

Richard M. Lerner
Tufts University

Tama Leventhal
Teachers College, Columbia University

Marc Mannes
Search Institute

Brooke S. G. Molina
University of Pittsburgh Medical Center

Amanda Sheffield Morris
University of New Orleans

Jeylan T. Mortimer
University of Minnesota

Kristin Nelson-Mmari
University of Minnesota

Jari-Erik Nurmi
University of Jyvaskyla

Karen Pittman
Forum for Youth Investment

Jennifer Ritter
Arizona State University

Donald F. Roberts
Stanford University

Alan Rogol
University of Virginia

Ritch C. Savin-Williams
Cornell University

Elizabeth S. Scott
University of Virginia

Lonnie R. Sherrod
Fordham University

Jeremy Staff
University of Minnesota

Laurence Steinberg
Temple University

Elizabeth J. Susman
The Pennsylvania State University

Ryan Trim
Arizona State University

Christopher Uggen
University of Minnesota

Suzanne Wilson
University of Illinois,
Urbana/Champaign

Jennifer L. Woolard
Georgetown University

Foreword

Like snapshots of a growing family (and I use the metaphor "family" rather than "child" because fields of study band together multiple personalities), subsequent editions of a scholarly handbook can reveal phenomenal changes. Imagine family photographs taken 25 years apart. You might hardly recognize the group as the same family. In the case of adolescent study, the 25-year period between Handbook editions has caused transformations every bit as consequential as those we would see in a human family during a similar time span. From my reading of this splendid current Handbook, the changes have been entirely to the good.

As the editors correctly note, the term *adolescence* has been with us for centuries, but the systematic examination of it for scientific purposes really began with G. Stanley Hall in the early 1900s. Hall was a man of immense dedication to the healthy development of young people. He convinced America to create playgrounds for its youth; he helped build the new discipline of development psychology; and he trained many of its early leaders. Yet Hall's own pioneering writings on adolescence bent that young branch in ways that would misdirect the field, and much of its public audience, for most of the ensuing century.

Hall's influences were 19th-century *Bildungsromanen* whose authors wrote romantically of youthful *Sturm und Drang,* a brilliant young "psych-analyist" Sigmund Freud whom Hall introduced to America (and who had been reading those same German novels), and trendy evolutionary theories that confused the ontogenesis of individuals and species. The latter set of influences were so far-fetched and ultimately inflammatory that scientists soon came to ignore this entire line in Hall's writings. But his vision of adolescence as a turbulent, trouble-ridden period that was at best a transition to something saner—if the youngster did not first self-destruct—foreshadowed what was to become the society's dominant view of youths as walking problems. That vision was to be elaborated in numerous ways beyond any imaginings that Hall could have had. These ways led to ill-founded scientific studies as well as poor public policy advice.

The present Handbook is a world apart, for reasons both sensible and profound. For one thing, it is refreshing to read a collection of studies portraying adolescence as a full-colored, rich experience in itself, rather than only as a transition *toward* something or *away* from something. There are many highpoints in the collective portrayal of youth embodied in this Handbook, and I do not mean to slight any of them by mentioning others, but I was especially struck by the lush array of interests, capacities, and meaningful youthful activities that emerges from many of the chapters in this handbook. From the cognitive to the moral, from the academic to the civic, in relations with peers, parents, and society on its most global level, adolescents in this Handbook are shown as active and able players in the world. They are not seen as unwitting pawns of their own uncontrollable desires or helpless victims of external forces beyond their control. The young people in this Handbook reason powerfully; make their own choices about their social and sexual relationships; adapt to their schools in a manner consistent with their own motives and concerns; navigate the complexity of influences that they encounter in their families, neighborhoods, mass media, and legal system; and end up forging their own judgments about who they are and what they believe in. Sometimes their judgments work for the better, sometimes for the worse. There are real risks and casualties associated with this age period, and the Handbook examines several of the most prominent ones. This we have long known. But there is also an infinite promise and positive excitement associated with youth. This, too, has long been known but perhaps was put out of mind too often in our initial century of adolescent research. The current Handbook merits our thanks for bringing the more positive, and accurate, characterization back to the fore.

A few years ago, the Society of Research in Adolescence indulged itself by arranging its biennial conference in sunny San Diego. An effect of the climate was that, at any time during the conference, large numbers of prominent adolescent researchers could be found seated around the hotel swimming pool. Perhaps as an excuse to hang out there myself—but also, I must admit, due to my sincere puzzlement about the matter—I took the opportunity to conduct an informal survey on the following question: What is adolescence?

Notably, none of the 20-or-so researchers whom I collared settled upon a demarcated age period (say, "twixt twelve and twenty") as their final answer. (Here I should probably tweak the present editors for their designation of "the second decade of life" in their Preface, although I am sure that this was not meant to be their considered scientific definition of the term.) Intead, the answers noted benchmark experiences that bounded the period in a developmental sense. The designated benchmarks varied among researchers, but there were commonalities in the responses. Most common of the initiating benchmarks was puberty. The closing benchmark was harder to capture in a word or phrase: it was experiential in nature, and it often touched on the Eriksonian notion of psychosocial identity—my own translation would be something like "a stable personal commitment to an adult role." Now I do not believe that this amalgam—the period between the advent of puberty and a stable commitment to an adult role—would hold up long as a scientific definition, at least without lots of further definitional work on both ends. Yet it is not a bad place to start, and I have found myself using it in public lectures whenever anyone puts to me the pesky question of "What is adolescence?"

I mention this here because puberty is exactly where the substantive set of chapters in this Handbook begins, and the acquisition of social roles in its most important sense—citizenship and civic engagement—is about where the book ends. In between, we have the whole glorious parade of exploration and growth, challenge and struggle, risk and progress. It is another indicator to me of this Handbook's validity—and its value to anyone who wishes to gain a deeper understanding of this most memorable and formative period of live.

William Damon

Preface

According to most social scientists, a generation is about 25 years in length. By that measure, this second edition of the *Handbook of Adolescent Psychology* represents a generational shift, for it was fully 25 years ago that the first edition of this volume was published. A cursory glance at this edition's table of contents will show just how broadly the field has grown in that period of time, and a careful reading of the volume's chapters will reveal that the generational shift has been as deep as it has been broad.

When the first edition of the Handbook was published in 1980, the empirical study of adolescence, by our calculation, was barely 5 years old. Much of what was prepared for that Handbook was, of necessity, theoretical because there was very little empirical work on which contributors could draw. In addition, much of the theorizing was psychoanalytic in nature, because through the mid-1970s that had been the dominant worldview among those who thought about adolescence. Now, it is fair to say that the field has reached full maturity, or at least a level of maturity comparable to that found in the study of any other period of development. Indeed, as we note in the first chapter of the volume, in which we review and reflect on the development of the scientific study of adolescence, research on the second decade of life often serves as a model for research on other stages of development. As the contributions to this volume clearly illustrate, the science of adolescent psychology is sophisticated, interdisciplinary, and empirically rigorous. Interestingly enough, grand theories of adolescence, whether psychoanalytic or not, have waned considerably in their influence.

Other generational changes can also be discerned by comparing the second and first editions of the Handbook. First, the study of adolescent difficulty and disturbance has taken a backseat to the study of processes of normative development. Accordingly, although the current edition includes several chapters on the development of psychological problems in adolescence, they by no means dominate the volume's contents. Second, our knowledge about the ways in which processes of adolescent development are shaped by interacting and embedded systems of proximal and distal contextual forces has made the study of adolescence less purely psychological in nature and far more interdisciplinary. While psychology continues to be the primary discipline reflected in the contents (and, of course, the title) of this Handbook, it is not the only one. Contributors to the volume have drawn on a wide array of disciplines, including sociology, biology, education, neuroscience, and law. Third, the growth in applied developmental science over the past decade has led to a more explicit focus on the ways in which empirically based knowledge about adolescence can be used to promote positive youth development. Several contributions to this volume reflect this emphasis.

This edition of the *Handbook of Adolescent Psychology* is concerned with all aspects of development during the second decade of life, with all the contexts in which this development takes place and with a wide array of social implications and applications of the scientific knowledge gained through empirical research. This edition is divided into three broad sections: foundations of adolescent development, the contexts of adolescent development, and special challenges and opportunities that arise at adolescence. These sections are preceded by a foreword (by William Damon) and followed by an afterword (by Beatrix and David Hamburg), which locate the Handbook's contribution within the history of the field of adolescent development.

The first section of the Handbook examines the foundations of the scientific study of individual development in adolescence. Following an introductory chapter that overviews the past history and future prospects of adolescent psychology as a scientific enterprise (Lerner and Steinberg), contributions in this section examine puberty and its impact on psychological development (Susman and Rogol), cognitive and brain development (Keating), the development of the self (Nurmi), academic motivation and achievement in school settings (Eccles), morality and prosocial development (Eisenberg and Morris), sexuality and sexual relationships (Savin-Williams and Diamond), gender and gender role development (Galambos), and processes of risk and resilience (Compas). Taken together, these chapters illustrate the ways in which biological, intellectual, emotional, and social development unfold and interact during the second decade of the life span.

The second section focuses on the immediate and broader contexts in which adolescent development takes place. The chapters in this section situate adolescent development across history, cultures, and regions of the world (Larson and Wilson); within the family, and especially in the context of the parent-child relationship (Collins and Laursen); within the interconnected and nested contexts of peer relationships, including friendships, romantic relationships, adversarial relationships, cliques, and crowds (Brown); in relationships with adult mentors at work and in the community (Hamilton and Hamilton); in the settings of work and leisure (Staff, Mortimer, and Uggen); in neighborhood contexts (Leventhal and Brooks-Gunn); within the contexts defined by mass media and technology (Roberts, Henriksen, and Foehr); and within the law (Scott and Woolard). Consistent with the ecological perspective on human development that has dominated research on adolescence for the past two decades, these contributions show how variations in proximal, community, and distal contexts profoundly shape and alter the developmental processes, trajectories, and outcomes associated with adolescence.

The final section of the Handbook examines a variety of challenges and opportunities that can threaten or facilitate healthy development in adolescence and explores the ways in which maladaptive as well as positive trajectories of youth development unfold. The first set of contributions in this section considers threats to the well-being of adolescents, including physical illness, examined from an international perspective (Blum and Nelson-Mmari); internalizing problems, including depression, anxiety, and disordered eating (Graber); externalizing problems, including conduct disorder, aggression, and delinquency (Farrington); substance use and abuse, including the use and abuse of tobacco, alcohol, and other drugs (Chassin, Hussong, Barrera, Molina, Trim, and Ritter); and developmental disabilities, including autism, cerebral palsy, epilepsy, mental retardation, and other neurological impairments (Hauser-Cram and Krauss). The second set of contributions in this concluding section examines three sorts of opportunities with the potential to promote health and well-being in adolescence: the promotion of volunteerism and civic engagement among youth (Flanagan); the application of developmental science to facilitate healthy adolescent development (Sherrod, Busch-Rossnagel, and Fisher); and the development of policies and programs explicitly designed to promote positive youth development (Benson, Mannes, Pittman, and Ferber).

There are numerous people to thank for their important contributions to the Handbook. First and foremost, we owe our greatest debt of gratitude to the colleagues who wrote the chapters, foreword, and afterword for the Handbook. Their scholarly excellence and leadership and their commitment to the field are the key assets for any contributions that this Handbook will make both to the scientific study of adolescence and to the application of knowledge that is requisite for enhancing the lives of diverse young people worldwide.

We appreciate as well the important support and guidance provided to us by the members of the editorial board for the Handbook. We thank Peter L. Benson, Dale A. Blyth, Jeanne Brooks-Gunn, B. Bradford Brown, W. Andrew Collins, William Damon, Jacquelynne Eccles, David Elkind, Nancy Galambos, Robert C. Granger, Beatrix Hamburg, Stuart Hauser, E. Mavis Hetherington, Reed Larson, Jacqueline V. Lerner, David Magnusson, Anne C. Petersen, Diane Scott-Jones, Lonnie R. Sherrod, Margaret Beale Spencer, and Wendy Wheeler for their invaluable contributions.

We are very grateful to Karyn Lu, managing editor in the Applied Developmental Science Institute in the Eliot-Pearson Department of Child Development at Tufts University. Her impressive ability to track and coordinate the myriad editorial tasks associated with a project of this scope, her astute editorial skills and wisdom, and her never-diminishing good humor and positive attitude were invaluable resources throughout our work.

We are also appreciative of our publishers and editors at John Wiley & Sons: Peggy Alexander, Jennifer Simon, and Isabel Pratt. Their enthusiasm for our vision for the Handbook, their unflagging support, and their collegial and collaborative approach to the development of this project were vital bases for the successful completion of the Handbook.

We also want to express our gratitude to the several organizations that supported our scholarship during the time we worked on the Handbook. Tufts University and Temple University provided the support and resources necessary to undertake and complete a project like this. In addition, Richard M. Lerner thanks the National 4-H Council, the William T. Grant Foundation, and the Jacobs Foundation, and Laurence Steinberg thanks the John D. and Catherine T. MacArthur Foundation, for their generous support.

Finally, we want to dedicate this Handbook to our greatest sources of inspiration, both for our work on the Handbook and for our scholarship in the field of adolescence: our children, Blair, Jarrett, Justin, and Ben. Now all in their young adulthood, they have taught us our greatest lessons about the nature and potentials of adolescent development.

R.M.L.
L.S.
March 2003

Chapter 1

THE SCIENTIFIC STUDY OF ADOLESCENT DEVELOPMENT

Past, Present, and Future

Richard M. Lerner and Laurence Steinberg

In the opening sentence of the preface to the first edition of his classic *A History of Experimental Psychology,* Edwin G. Boring (1929) reminded readers that "psychology has a long past, but only a short history" (p. ix), a remark he attributed to the pioneer of memory research, Hermann Ebbinghaus. A similar statement may be made about the study of adolescents and their development.

The first use of the term *adolescence* appeared in the 15th century. The term was a derivative of the Latin word *adolescere,* which means to grow up or to grow into maturity (Muuss, 1990). However, more than 1,500 years before this first explicit use of the term both Plato and Aristotle proposed sequential demarcations of the life span, and Aristotle in particular proposed stages of life that are not too dissimilar from sequences that might be included in contemporary models of youth development. He described three successive, 7-year periods (infancy, boyhood, and young manhood) prior to the person's attainment of full, adult maturity. About 2,000 years elapsed between these initial philosophical discussions of adolescence and the emergence, within the 20th century, of the scientific study of the second decade of life.

The history of the scientific study of adolescence has had two overlapping phases and is, we believe, on the cusp of a third. The first phase, which lasted about 70 years, was characterized by three sorts of Cartesian splits (see Overton, 1998) that created false dichotomies that in turn limited the intellectual development of the field. With respect to the first of these polarizations, "grand" models of adolescence that purportedly pertained to all facets of behavior and development predominated (e.g., Erikson, 1959, 1968; Hall, 1904), but these theories were limited because they were either largely all nature (e.g., genetic or maturational; e.g., Freud, 1969; Hall, 1904) or all nurture (e.g., McCandless, 1961). Second, the major empirical studies of adolescence during this period were not primarily theory-driven, hypothesis-testing investigations but were atheoretical, descriptive studies; as such, theory and research were split into separate enterprises (McCandless, 1970). Third, there was a split between scholars whose work was focused on basic developmental processes and practitioners whose focus was on community-based efforts to facilitate the healthy development of adolescents.

The second phase in the scientific study of adolescence arose in the early- to mid-1970s as developmental scientists began to make use of research on adolescents in elucidating developmental issues of interest across the entire life span (Petersen, 1988). At the beginning of the 1970s, the study of adolescence, like the comedian Rodney Dangerfield, "got no respect." Gradually, however, research on adolescent development began to emerge as a dominant force in developmental science. By the end of the 1970s the study of adolescence had finally come of age.

To help place this turning point in the context of the actual lives of the scientists involved in these events, it may be useful to note that the professional careers of the editors of this Handbook began just as this transition was beginning to take place. Across our own professional lifetimes, then, the editors of this volume have witnessed a sea change in scholarly regard for the study of adolescent development. Among those scholars whose own careers have begun more recently, the magnitude of this transformation is probably hard to grasp. To those of us with gray hair, however, the change has been nothing short of astounding. At the beginning of our careers, adolescent development was a minor topic within developmental science, one that was of a level of importance to merit only the publication of an occasional research article within prime developmental journals or minimal representation on the program of major scientific meetings. Now, three decades later, the study of adolescent development is a distinct and major field within developmental science, one that plays a central role in informing, and, through vibrant collaborations with scholars having other scientific specialties, being informed by, other areas of focus.

The emergence of this second phase of the study of adolescence was predicated in part on theoretical interest in healing the Cartesian splits (Overton, 1998) characteristic of the first phase and, as such, in exploring and elaborating developmental models that reject reductionist biological or environmental accounts of development and instead focus on the fused levels of organization constituting the developmental system and its multilayered context (e.g., Sameroff, 1983; Thelen & Smith, 1998). These developmental systems models have provided a metatheory for adolescent developmental research and have been associated with more midlevel (as opposed to grand) theories—models that have been generated to account for person-environment relations within selected domains of development.

Instances of such midlevel developmental systems theories are the stage-environment fit model used to understand achievement in classroom settings (Eccles, Wigfield, & Byrnes, 2003), the goodness of fit model used to understand the relation of temperamental individuality in peer and family relations (Lerner, Anderson, Balsano, Dowling, & Bobek, 2003), and models linking the developmental assets of youth and communities in order to understand positive youth development (Benson, 1997; Damon, 1997). For instance, Damon (1997; Damon & Gregory, 2003) forwarded a new vision and vocabulary about adolescents that was based on their strengths and potential for positive development. Damon explained that such potential could be instantiated by building new youth-community relationships predicated on the creation of *youth charters,* agreements that codified community-specific visions and action agendas for promoting positive life experiences for adolescents.

Generally speaking, the study of adolescence in its second phase was characterized by an interest in developmental plasticity, in diversity, and in the application of science to real-world problems. This phase also was marked by the development and use of more nuanced and powerful developmental methods aimed at providing sensitivity to the collection and analysis of longitudinal data pertinent to the multiple levels.

More than a quarter century ago, Bronfenbrenner (1974) explained the importance of a science of development that involved the full and bidirectional collaboration between the producers and consumers of scientific knowledge. In turn, D. A. Hamburg (1992; D. A. Hamburg & Takanishi, 1996) proposed that the quality of life of adolescents, and their future contributions to civil society, could be enhanced through collaboration among scholars, policy makers, and key social institutions, for instance, community-based youth-serving organizations (e.g., 4-H, Boys and Girls Clubs, scouting), schools, and the media. In our view, D. A. Hamburg's (1992; D. A. Hamburg & Takanishi, 1996) vision has been actualized. We are now at the cusp of the emergence of a third phase in the history of the scientific study of adolescence, one that we hope will be marked by the publication of this Handbook. This phase involves the emergence of the field of adolescent development as an exemplar of the sort of developmental science that can be used by policy makers and practitioners in order to advance civil society and promote positive development (Lerner, Fisher, & Weinberg, 2000). The contributors to this volume provide much evidence that the field of adolescence may be entering a phase of its development wherein such a scientist–policy maker–practitioner collaboration may be a central, organizing frame.

THE FIRST PHASE OF THE SCIENTIFIC STUDY OF ADOLESCENCE

In 1904 G. Stanley Hall, with the publication of his two-volume work *Adolescence,* initiated the scientific study of adolescence. He launched the field as one steeped in a split and nativist view of development, one that was and linked to a biologically based, deficit view of adolescence.

Fancying himself as the "Darwin of the mind" (White, 1968), Hall sought to translate the ideas of Ernst Haeckel (e.g., 1868, 1891), an early contributor to embryology, into a theory of life span human development. Haeckel advanced the idea of recapitulation: The adult stages of the ancestors comprising a species' evolutionary (phylogenetic) history were repeated in compressed form as the embryonic stages of the organism's ontogeny. Hall extended Haeckel's idea of recapitulation beyond the prenatal period in order to fashion a theory of human behavioral development. To Hall, adolescence represented a phylogenetic period when human ancestors went from being beastlike to being civilized. Hall (1904) saw adolescence as a period of storm and stress, as a time of universal and inevitable upheaval.

Although other scholars of this period (e.g., Thorndike, 1904) quickly rejected Hall's recapitulationism on both empirical and methodological grounds (e.g., see Lerner, 2002, for a discussion), other theorists of adolescent development used a conceptual lens comparable to Hall's, at least insofar as his biological reductionism and his deficit view of adolescence were concerned. Anna Freud (1969), for instance, saw adolescence as a biologically based and universal developmental disturbance. Erik Erikson (1950, 1959) viewed the period as one in which an inherited maturational ground plan resulted in the inescapable psychosocial crisis of identity versus role confusion. Even when theorists rejected the nature-based ideas of psychoanalysts or neopsychoanalysts, they proposed nurture-oriented ideas to explain the same problems of developmental disturbance and crisis. For example, McCandless (1961, 1970) presented a social-learning, drive-reduction theory to account for the developmental phenomena of adolescence (e.g., regarding sex differences in identity development) that Erikson (1959) interpreted as being associated with maturation (see Lerner & Spanier, 1980, for a discussion).

Although the developmental theory of cognition proposed by Piaget (1960, 1969, 1970, 1972) involved a more integrative view of nature and nurture than did these other models, the predominant focus of his ideas was on the emergence of formal logical structures and not on the adolescent period per se. The absence of concern in Piaget's theory with the broader array of biological, emotional, personality, social, and societal concerns that had engaged other theorists' discussions of adolescence did not stop a relatively minor and historically transitory interest in Piaget's ideas as a frame for empirical understanding of the adolescent period (Steinberg & Morris, 2001). However, as Steinberg and Morris explained, only a short while after this period of heightened interest in using the onset of formal operations as an explanation for everything adolescent, the influence of Piaget's theory on mainstream empirical work in the study of adolescence would become as modest as that associated with the other grand theories of the period, such as those authored by Erikson or McCandless.

The divergence between the so-called grand theories of the adolescent period and the range of research about adolescence that would come to characterize the field at the end of the 20th century actually existed for much of the first phase of the field's development. The classic studies of adolescence conducted between 1950 and 1980 were not investigations derived from the theories of Hall, Anna Freud, McCandless, Piaget, or even Erikson (work associated with the ideas of Marcia, 1980, notwithstanding). Instead, this research was directed to describing (note, not *explaining;* McCandless, 1970; Petersen, 1988) patterns of covariation among pubertal timing, personal adjustment, and relationships with peers and parents (e.g., Jones & Bayley, 1950; Mussen & Jones, 1957), both within and across cultural settings (e.g., Mussen & Bouterline Young, 1964); the diversity in trajectories of psychological development across adolescence (e.g., Bandura, 1964; Block, 1971; Douvan & Adelson, 1966; Offer, 1969); and the influence of history or temporality (i.e., as operationalized by time of testing- or cohort-related variation) on personality development, achievement, and family relations (e.g., Elder, 1974; Nesselroade & Baltes, 1974). Petersen (1988, p. 584) described the quality of the classic empirical work on adolescence by noting that most "research fell into one of two categories: (a) studies on behavioral or psychological processes that happened to use adolescent subjects, or (b) descriptive accounts of particular groups of adolescents, such as high school students or delinquents."

Despite its separation from the grand theories of adolescence that dominated the field during its first phase of scientific development, this body of early research, as well as the subsequent scholarship it elicited (e.g., see reviews by Lerner & Galambos, 1998; Petersen, 1988; Steinberg & Morris, 2001), made several important contributions to shaping the specific character of the scientific study of adolescence between the early-1980s and late-1990s. As elaborated later, this character involved the longitudinal study of individual-context relations among diverse groups of youth and the use of such scholarship for purposes of both elucidating basic developmental processes and applying developmental science to promote positive youth development (B. Hamburg, 1974; Lerner, 2002).

These contributions also advanced the study of adolescence because scholarship about the second decade of life acted synergistically with broader scholarly activity within developmental science pertinent to the theoretical, methodological, and applied features of the study of human development across the life span. For instance, a classic paper by B. Hamburg (1974) did much to provide the foundation for this integration, in that it made a compelling case for viewing the early adolescent period as a distinct period of the life course and one that provided an exemplary ontogenetic window for understanding key person-context processes involved in coping and adaptation. Based on such evidence, Petersen (1988, p. 584) noted,

> Basic theoretical and empirical advances in several areas have permitted the advance of research on adolescence. Some areas of behavioral science from which adolescence researchers have drawn are life-span developmental psychology, life-course sociology, social support, stress and coping, and cognitive development; important contributing areas in the biomedical sciences include endocrinology and adolescent medicine. The recent maturation to adolescence of subjects in major longitudinal studies . . . has also contributed to the topic's empirical knowledge base.

The emergence of the relationship between the specific study of adolescence and more general scholarship about the overall course of human development provided the bridge to the second phase in the study of adolescent development. Indeed, about a decade after this second phase had begun, Petersen (1988, p. 601) predicted, "Current research on adolescence will not only aid scientific understanding of this particular phase of life, it also may illuminate development more generally." Future events were consistent with Petersen's prognostication.

THE SECOND PHASE OF THE SCIENTIFIC STUDY OF ADOLESCENCE

From the late 1970s through this writing the adolescent period has come to be regarded as an ideal *natural ontogenetic laboratory* for studying key theoretical and methodological issues in developmental science (Lerner, 2002; Steinberg & Morris, 2001). There are several reasons for the special salience of the study of adolescent development to understanding the broader course of life span development. First, although the prenatal and infant period exceeds adolescence as an ontogenetic stage of rapid physical and physiological growth, the years from approximately 10 to 20 not only include the considerable physical and physiological changes associated with puberty but also mark a time when the interdependency of biology and context in human development is readily apparent (Susman & Rogol, this volume). Second, as compared to infants, the cognizing, goal-setting, and relatively autonomous adolescent can, through reciprocal relations with his or her ecology, serve as an active influence on his or her own development, and the study of adolescence can inform these sorts of processes more generally (Lerner, 2002). Third, the multiple individual and contextual transitions into, throughout, and out of this period, involving the major institutions of society (family, peers, schools, and the workplace), engage scholars interested in broader as well as individual levels of organization and also provide a rich opportunity for understanding the nature of multilevel systemic change. Finally, there was also a practical reason for the growing importance of adolescence in the broader field of developmental science: As noted by Steinberg and Morris (2001), the longitudinal samples of many developmental scientists who had been studying infancy or childhood had aged into adolescence. Applied developmental scientists were also drawn to the study of adolescents, not just because of the historically unprecedented sets of challenges to the healthy development of adolescents that arose during the latter decades of the 20th century (Dryfoos, 1990; Lerner, 1995) but also because interest in age groups other than adolescents nevertheless frequently involved this age group (e.g., interest in infants often entailed the study of teenage mothers, and interest in middle and old age frequently entailed the study of the "middle generation squeeze," wherein the adult children of aged parents cared for their own parents while simultaneously raising their own adolescent children).

The Emerging Structure of the Field of Adolescent Development

This scholarly activity at the close of the 1970s was both a product and a producer of a burgeoning network of scholars from multiple disciplines. In 1981 the late Herschel Thornburg launched a series of biennial meetings (called the Conference on Adolescent Research) at the University of Arizona. During these meetings (which occurred also in 1983 and 1985), the idea for a new scholarly society, the Society for Research on Adolescence (SRA), was born. The first meeting of SRA was held in Madison, Wisconsin, in 1986, and Thornburg was elected the first president of the organization. Across the next two decades, with biennial conventions in Alexandria, Virginia (1988), Atlanta (1990), Washington (1992), San Diego (1994), Boston (1996), again in San Diego (1998), Chicago (2000), New Orleans (2002), and Baltimore (2004), and through the leadership of the SRA presidents who succeeded Thornburg—John P. Hill, Anne C. Petersen, E. Mavis Hetherington, Sanford M. Dornbusch, Jeanne Brooks-Gunn, Stuart T. Hauser, Laurence Steinberg, W. Andrew Collins, Jacquelynne Eccles, and Elizabeth Susman—the organization and the field it represented flourished. Between 1986 and 2002, attendance at SRA biennial meetings more than quadrupled. The SRA launched its own scholarly journal in 1991, the *Journal of Research on Adolescence* (Lerner, 1991); grew from approximately 400 members in 1986 to more than 1,200 members in 2002; and attracted disciplinary representation from scholars and practitioners with expertise in psychology, sociology, education, family studies, social work, medicine, psychiatry, criminology, and nursing.

Impetus to this growth in scholarly interest in the study of adolescence also was stimulated by the publication in 1980 of the first handbook for the field. Edited by Joseph Adelson (1980), the *Handbook of Adolescent Psychology* was published as part of the Wiley series on personality processes. The volume reflected the emerging multidisciplinary interest in the field (with chapters discussing levels of organization ranging from biology through history, including an interesting historical chapter on youth movements), the growing interest in systems models of adolescent development (e.g., in the chapters by Elder, 1980, and by Petersen & Taylor, 1980), the importance of longitudinal methodology (Livson & Peskin, 1980), and the increasing interest in diversity (i.e., there was a five-chapter section titled "Variations in Adolescence"). It is important to note that through several chapters pertinent to the problems of adolescence there was still ample representation in the volume of the deficit view of adolescence. Nevertheless, the 1980 Handbook included information pertinent to normative development and developmental plasticity, and several chapters discussed the positive individual and social features of youth development.

The publication of a handbook, the organization of a successful scholarly society, and the initiation of that society's scholarly journal all underscored the growing interest in and the scientific maturity of research on adolescent development. This intellectual milieu and the scholarly opportunities it provided attracted a broad range of scholars to the field, some for reasons that had little to do with adolescence per se, but others because they came to see themselves as experts on the second decade of life. By the mid-1980s a growing cadre of scientists would identify themselves as adolescent developmentalists.

The Study of Adolescence as a Sample Case for Understanding Plasticity and Diversity in Development

Scholars interested primarily in the instantiation of developmental processes within other periods of the life span (e.g., infancy, Easterbrooks & Graham, 1999; adult development and aging, Brim, 1966; Nesselroade & Baltes, 1974) or in disciplines other than developmental psychology (e.g., life course sociology; Burton, 1990; Elder, 1974, 1980) became adolescent developmentalists as well. This attraction inheres in the window that the period provides to understanding how development at any point across the life span involves the relations of diverse and active individuals and diverse, active, and multitiered ecologies (Bronfenbrenner, 1979; Bronfenbrenner & Morris, 1998; Lerner, 2002).

As suggested by Steinberg and Morris (2001), the scientific concern that arguably was most significant in transforming the field of adolescent development beyond a focus on this single developmental period into an exemplar for understanding the breadth of the human life span was the emerging focus within developmental science on the ecology of human development (e.g., Bronfenbrenner, 1979, 2001; Bronfenbrenner & Morris, 1998). The integrated designed and natural ecology was of interest because its study was regarded as holding the key to (a) understanding the system of relations between individuals and contexts that is at the core of the study of human development and (b) providing evidence that theories about the character of interacting developmental system (e.g., Collins, Maccoby, Steinberg, Hetherington, & Bornstein, 2000; Gottlieb, 1997, 1998; Horowitz, 2000; Thelen & Smith, 1998) are more useful in accounting for the variance in human ontogeny than are theories whose grounding is either exclusively in nature (e.g., behavioral genetic or sociobiological; e.g., Plomin, 2000; Rowe, 1994; Rushton, 2000) or exclusively in nurture (e.g., social learning or functional analysis; Gewirtz & Stingle, 1968; McCandless, 1970).

A second set of broader issues that engaged developmental science in the study of adolescence pertained to understanding the bases, parameters, and limits of the plasticity of human development. As implied earlier, this plasticity legitimated an optimistic view about the potential for interventions into the course of life to enhance human development, encouraged growth in scientific activity in the application of developmental science to improve life outcomes, and gave impetus to the idea that positive development could be promoted among all people (Lerner, Fisher, & Weinberg, 2000). Moreover, plasticity meant that the particular instances of human development found within a given sample or period of time were not necessarily representative of the diversity of development that might potentially be observed under different conditions.

Third, developmentalists pursuing an interest in the developmental system and the plasticity in ontogenetic change that it promoted recognized the need to develop and deploy methods that could simultaneously study changes in (at least a subset of) the multiple levels of organization involved in the development of diverse individuals and contexts. Accordingly, multivariate longitudinal designs were promoted as key to the study of the relatively plastic developmental system, as were the development of empirical tools, such as change-sensitive measures, sophisticated data analysis techniques, and strategies such as triangulation of observations within and across both quantitative and qualitative domains of inquiry.

Defining Features of the Study of Adolescence During Its Second Phase

Four defining features of the second phase of the science of adolescent development are worth noting. First, during its second phase of life, the empirical study of adolescence emerged as a *relational* field of inquiry. That is, it became an area of scholarship in which implicitly (e.g., Block, 1971; Mussen & Bouterline-Young, 1964) or, at times, explicitly (e.g., Nesselroade & Baltes, 1974) the key unit of analysis in understanding the development of the person was his or her relation with both more molecular (e.g., biological) and more molar (social group, cultural, and historical) levels of organization (Overton, 1998). In such a relational frame, no one level of organization was seen as the prime mover of development.

A second distinctive feature of the field of adolescence within this second phase derived from its relational character. The confluence of the multiple levels of organization involved in the developmental system provides the structural and functional bases of plasticity and of the inevitable and substantively significant emergence of systematic individual differences; that is, such individuality serves as a key basis of the person's ability to act as an agent in his or her own development (Brandtstädter, 1998; Lerner, 2002). Accordingly, the field of adolescence has become the exemplar within the broader study of human development for the substantive study of diversity and for the person-centered approach to research on human development (Magnusson, 1999a, 1999b; Magnusson & Stattin, 1998).

Third, although there remains a focus within the contemporary adolescent literature on problems of this developmental period (Steinberg & Morris, 2001), the focus on plasticity, diversity of development and people, and individual agency—and thus the strength or capacity of an adolescent to influence his or her development for better or for worse—means that problematic outcomes of adolescent development are now just one of a larger array of outcomes that may characterize the relatively plastic relations between adolescents and their contexts (e.g., B. Hamburg, 1974; D. A. Hamburg, 1992).

Indeed, this plasticity provides the theoretical basis of the view that all young people possess strengths, or, more simply, the potential for positive development (Damon, 1997; Damon & Gregory, 2003).

The idea that the adolescent period provides the ideal time within life to study the bases of positive human development frames what has become a fourth defining feature of the field. The study of adolescent development is now characterized by a synthetic interest in basic and applied concerns about youth development. One's basic understanding of how relational processes within the developmental system provide a basis for diverse developmental trajectories across adolescence can be tested by assessing whether changes in individual and ecological variables within the system combine to actualize the strengths of youth. Benson (1990, 1997; Benson, Mannes, Pittman, & Ferber, this volume) termed these individual and ecological variables *developmental assets.* Such tests of developmental theory, when implemented within the actual ecology of human development, are interventions into the course of adolescent development. Depending on their target level of organization, these actions constitute policies or programs, and in this context basic research in adolescence is also applied developmental science (Bronfenbrenner & Morris, 1998; Lerner, 2002). As a consequence of this trend, the field has come to place a premium on community-based, change-oriented methods, both to study development and to evaluate the efficacy of programs and policies designed to alter the course of adolescent life for the better.

CONCLUSIONS: ADOLESCENCE AS A FIELD OF SCIENTIST–PRACTITIONER–POLICY MAKER COLLABORATION

The chapters in this Handbook both reflect and extend the emphases on individual-context relations, developmental systems, plasticity, diversity, longitudinal methodology, and application that were crystallized and integrated within the second phase of the development of the scientific study of adolescence. As evident within each of the chapters in this Handbook, and as underscored in both the foreword and the afterword to the volume, the study of adolescence today represents the exemplar within developmental science wherein excellent conceptual and empirical work is undertaken with a collaborative orientation to making a contribution both to scholarship and to society. Arguably more so than in scholarship pertinent to other periods across the life span, within the study of adolescence the vision of Bronfenbrenner (1974) and D. A. Hamburg (1992; D. A. Hamburg & Takanishi, 1996) of a developmental science involving reciprocal collaborations among researchers, practitioners, and policy makers is being actively pursued, if not yet completely realized.

The future of civil society in the world rests on the young. Adolescents represent at any point in history the generational cohort that must next be prepared to assume the quality of leadership of self, family, community, and society that will maintain and improve human life. Scientists have a vital role to play to make in enhancing, through the generation of basic and applied knowledge, the probability that adolescents will become fully engaged citizens who are capable of, and committed to, making these contributions. The chapters in this Handbook demonstrate that high-quality scientific work on adolescence is in fact being generated at levels of study ranging from the biological through the historical and sociocultural. Above all, this volume demonstrates that the study of adolescent development at its best both informs and is informed by the concerns of communities, practitioners, and policy makers. It is our hope that we have assembled the best information possible to be used to promote and advocate for the healthy and positive development of young people everywhere.

REFERENCES

Adelson, J. (Ed.). (1980). *Handbook of adolescent psychology.* New York: Wiley.

Bandura, A. (1964). The stormy decade: Fact or fiction? *Psychology in the School, 1,* 224–231.

Benson, P. L. (1990). *The troubled journey: A portrait of 6th–12th grade youth.* Minneapolis, MN: Search Institute.

Benson, P. L. (1997). *All kids are our kids: What communities must do to raise caring and responsible children and adolescents.* San Francisco: Jossey-Bass.

Block, J. (1971). *Lives through time.* Berkeley, CA: Bancroft.

Boring, E. G. (1929). *A history of experimental psychology.* New York: Century.

Brandtstädter, J. (1998). Action perspectives on human development. In W. Damon (Series Ed.) & R. M. Lerner (Vol. Ed.), *Handbook of child psychology: Vol. 1. Theoretical models of human development* (5th ed., pp. 807–863). New York: Wiley.

Brim, O. G., Jr. (1966). Socialization through the life cycle. In O. G. Brim, Jr., & S. Wheeler (Eds.), *Socialization after childhood: Two essays* (pp. 1–49). New York: Wiley.

Bronfenbrenner, U. (1974). Developmental research, public policy, and the ecology of childhood. *Child Development, 45,* 1–5.

Bronfenbrenner, U. (1979). *The ecology of human development: Experiments by nature and design.* Cambridge, MA: Harvard University Press.

Bronfenbrenner, U. (2001). The bioecological theory of human development. In N. J. Smelser & P. B. Baltes (Eds.), *International encyclopedia of the social and behavioral science.* Oxford: Elsevier.

Bronfenbrenner, U., & Morris, P. A. (1998). The ecology of developmental process. In W. Damon (Series Ed.) & R. M. Lerner (Vol. Ed.), *Handbook of child psychology: Vol. 1. Theoretical models of human development* (5th ed., pp. 993–1028). New York: Wiley.

Burton, L. M. (1990). Teenage childbearing as an alternative life-course strategy in multigeneration black families. *Human Nature, 1*(2), 123-143.

Collins, W. A., Maccoby, E. E., Steinberg, L., Hetherington, M. E., & Bornstein, M. H. (2000). Contemporary research on parenting: The case for nature and nurture. *American Psychologist, 55,* 218–232.

Damon, W. (1997). *The youth charter: How communities can work together to raise standards for all our children.* New York: Free Press.

Damon, W., & Gregory, A. (2003). Bringing in a new era in the field of youth development. In R. M. Lerner & P. L. Benson (Eds.), *Developmental assets and asset-building communities: Implications for research, policy, and practice* (pp. 47–64). Norwell, MA: Kluwer Academic.

Douvan, J. D., & Adelson, J. (1966). *The adolescent experience.* New York: Wiley.

Dryfoos, J. G. (1990). *Adolescents at risk: Prevalence and prevention.* New York: Oxford University Press.

Easterbrooks, M. A., & Graham, C. A. (1999). Security of attachment and parenting: Homeless and low-income housed mothers and infants. *American Journal of Orthopsychiatry, 69,* 337–346.

Eccles, J., Wigfield, A., & Byrnes, J. (2003). Cognitive development in adolescence. In R. M. Lerner, M. A. Easterbrooks, & J. Mistry (Eds.), *Handbook of psychology: Vol. 6. Developmental psychology* (pp. 325–350). New York: Wiley.

Elder, G. H. (1974). *Children of the Great Depression.* Chicago: University of Chicago Press.

Elder, G. H. (1980). Adolescence in historical perspective. In J. Adelson (Ed.), *Handbook of adolescent psychology* (pp. 3–46). New York: Wiley.

Erikson, E. H. (1950). *Childhood and society.* New York: Norton.

Erikson, E. H. (1959). Identity and the life cycle. *Psychological Issues, 1,* 18–164.

Erikson, E. H. (1968). *Identity, youth, and crisis.* New York: Norton.

Freud, A. (1969). Adolescence as a developmental disturbance. In G. Caplan & S. Lebovici (Eds.), *Adolescence* (pp. 5–10). New York: Basic Books.

Gewirtz, J. L., & Stingle, K. G. (1968). Learning of generalized imitation as the basis for identification. *Psychological Review, 75,* 374–397.

Gottlieb, G. (1997). *Synthesizing nature-nurture: Prenatal roots of instinctive behavior.* Mahwah, NJ: Erlbaum.

Gottlieb, G. (1998). Normally occurring environmental and behavioral influences on gene activity: From central dogma to probabilistic epigenesis. *Psychological Review, 105,* 792–802.

Hall, G. S. (1904). *Adolescence: Its psychology and its relations to physiology, anthropology, sociology, sex, crime, religion, and education* (Vols. 1 & 2). New York: Appleton.

Haeckel, E. (1868). *Natürliche Schöpfungsgeschichte.* Berlin: Reimer.

Haeckel, E. (1891). Anthropogenie oder Entwickelungsgeschichte des Menschen (4th rev. and enlarged ed.). Leipzig: Engelmann.

Hamburg, B. (1974). Early adolescence: A specific and stressful stage of the life cycle. In G. Coelho, D. A. Hamburg, & J. E. Adams (Eds.), *Coping and adaptation* (pp. 101–125). New York: Basic Books.

Hamburg, D. A. (1992). *Today's children: Creating a future for a generation in crisis.* New York: Times Books.

Hamburg, D. A., & Takanishi, R. (1996). Great transitions: Preparing American youth for the 21st century—The role of research. *Journal of Research on Adolescence, 6,* 379–396.

Horowitz, F. D. (2000). Child development and the PITS: Simple questions, complex answers, and developmental theory. *Child Development, 71,* 1–10.

Jones, M. C., & Bayley, N. (1950). Physical maturing among boys as related to behavior. *Journal of Educational Psychology, 41,* 129–148.

Lerner, R. M. (1991). Editorial: Continuities and changes in the scientific study of adolescence. *Journal of Research on Adolescence, 1,* 1–5.

Lerner, R. M. (1995). *America's youth in crisis: Challenges and options for programs and policies.* Thousand Oaks, CA: Sage.

Lerner, R. M. (2002). *Concepts and theories of human development* (3rd ed.). Mahwah, NJ: Erlbaum.

Lerner, R. M., Anderson, P. M., Balsano, A. B., Dowling, E. M., & Bobek, D. L. (2003). Applied developmental science of positive human development. In R. M. Lerner, M. A. Easterbrooks, & J. Mistry (Eds.), *Handbook of psychology: Vol. 6. Developmental psychology* (pp. 535–558). New York: Wiley.

Lerner, R. M., Fisher, C. B., & Weinberg, R. A. (2000). Toward a science for and of the people: Promoting civil society through the application of developmental science. *Child Development, 71,* 11–20.

Lerner, R. M., & Galambos, N. (1998). Adolescent development: Challenges and opportunities for research, programs, and policies. In J. T. Spence (Ed.), *Annual review of psychology* (Vol. 49, pp. 413–446). Palo Alto, CA: Annual Reviews.

Lerner, R. M., & Spanier, G. B. (1980). *Adolescent development: A life-span perspective.* New York: McGraw-Hill.

Livson, N., & Peskin, H. (1980). Perspectives on adolescence from longitudinal research. In J. Adelson (Ed.), *Handbook of adolescent psychology* (pp. 47–98). New York: Wiley.

Magnusson, D. (1999a). Holistic interactionism: A perspective for research on personality development. In L. A. Pervin & O. P. John (Eds.), *Handbook of personality: Theory and research* (2nd ed., pp. 219–247). New York: Guilford Press.

Magnusson, D. (1999b). On the individual: A person-oriented approach to developmental research. *Euorpean Psychologist, 4,* 205–218.

Magnusson, D., & Stattin, H. (1998). Person-context interaction theories. In W. Damon (Series

Ed.) & R. M. Lerner (Vol. Ed.), *Handbook of child psychology: Vol. 1. Theoretical models of human development* (5th ed., pp. 685–759). New York: Wiley.

Marcia, J. E. (1980). Identity in adolescence. In J. Adelson (Ed.), *Handbook of adolescent psychology* (pp. 159–187) New York: Wiley.

McCandless, R. R. (1961). *Children and adolescents.* New York: Holt, Rinehart, & Winston.

McCandless, B. R. (1970). *Adolescents.* Hinsdale, IL: Dryden Press.

Mussen, P. H., & Bouterline Young, H. (1964). Personality characteristics of psychically advanced and retarded adolescents in Italy and the United States. *Vita Humana, 7,* 186–200.

Mussen, R. H., & Jones, M. C. (1957). Self-conceptions, motivations, and interpersonal attitudes of late- and early-maturing boys. *Child Development, 28,* 242–256.

Muuss, R. E. (1990). *Adolescent behavior and society: A book of readings* (4th ed.). New York: McGraw-Hill.

Nesselroade, J. R., & Baltes, P. B. (1974). Adolescent personality development and historical changes: 1970–72. *Monographs of the Society for Research in Child Development, 39*(154).

Offer, D. (1969). *The psychological world of the teen-ager.* New York: Basic Books.

Overton, W. F. (1998). Developmental psychology: Philosophy, concepts, and methodology. In W. Damon (Series Ed.) & R. M. Lerner (Ed.), *Handbook of child psychology: Vol. 1. Theoretical models of human development* (5th ed., pp. 107–187). New York: Wiley.

Petersen, A. C. (1988). Adolescent development. In M. R. Rosenzweig (Ed.), *Annual review of psychology* (Vol. 39, pp. 583–607). Palo Alto, CA: Annual Reviews.

Petersen, A. C., & Taylor, B. (1980). The biological approach to adolescence: Biological change and psychological adaptation. In J. Adelson (Ed.), *Handbook of adolescent psychology* (pp. 117–155). New York: Wiley.

Piaget, J. (1960). *The child's conception of the world.* Paterson, NJ: Littlefield, Adams.

Piaget, J. (1969). The intellectual development of the adolescent. In G. Caplan & S. Lebovici (Eds.), *Adolescence: Psychosocial perspective* (pp. 22–26). New York: Basic Books.

Piaget, J. (1970). Piaget's theory. In P. H. Mussen (Ed.), *Carmichael's manual of child psychology* (3rd ed., Vol. 1, pp. 703–723). New York: Wiley.

Piaget, J. (1972). Intellectual evolution from adolescence to adulthood. *Human Development, 15,* 1–12.

Plomin, R. (2000). Behavioural genetics in the 21st century. *International Journal of Behavioral Development, 24,* 30–34.

Rowe, D. C. (1994). *The limits of family influence: Genes, experience, and behavior.* New York: Guilford Press.

Rushton, J. P. (2000). *Race, evolution, and behavior* (2nd Special Abridged Ed.). New Brunswick, NJ: Transaction.

Sameroff, A. J. (1983). Developmental systems: Contexts and evolution. In W. Kessen (Ed.), *Handbook of child psychology: Vol. 1. History, theory, and methods* (pp. 237–294). New York: Wiley.

Steinberg, L., & Morris, A. S. (2001). Adolescent development. In S. T. Fiske, D. L. Schacter, & C. Zahn-Waxler (Eds.), *Annual Review of Psychology* (Vol. 52, pp. 83–110). Palo Alto, CA: Annual Reviews.

Thelen, E., & Smith, L. B. (1998). Dynamic systems theories. In W. Damon (Series Editor) & R.M. Lerner (Vol. Ed.), *Handbook of child psychology: Vol. 1. Theoretical models of human development* (5th ed., pp. 563–633). New York: Wiley.

Thorndike, E. L. (1904). The newest psychology. *Educational Review, 28,* 217–227.

White, S. H. (1968). The learning-maturation controversy: Hall to Hull. *Merrill-Palmer Quarterly, 14,* 187–196.

Part One

FOUNDATIONS OF THE DEVELOPMENTAL SCIENCE OF ADOLESCENCE

Chapter 2

PUBERTY AND PSYCHOLOGICAL DEVELOPMENT

Elizabeth J. Susman and Alan Rogol

INTRODUCTION

Puberty is one of the most profound biological and social transitions in the life span. It begins with subtle changes in brain-neuroendocrine processes, hormone concentrations, and physical morphological characteristics and culminates in reproductive maturity. The onset and trajectory of the hormone and physical changes that characterize puberty are well documented. Puberty as a social construction is a more complicated concept and entails definitional ambiguity regarding the onset and offset of puberty; social-role passages into new reference groups; perceptions of body, self, and sexual image; and expectations for independent and mature behavior (Alsaker, 1995). Puberty as an integrated biological and social construction has intrigued scholars, artists, parents, and adolescents alike for centuries, and cultures have ritualized puberty to varying degrees. The biological changes of puberty are universal, but the timing and social significance of these changes to adolescents themselves, societies, and scientific inquiry vary across historical time and cultures. Nonetheless, there is widespread agreement on the profound biosocial complexity of puberty and its essential role as a period beginning with reproductive-function awakening and culminating in sexual maturity.

The evolution of puberty occurred in such a way as to maximize the probability for successful procreation. Puberty-related mutations across generations have favored biological qualities that foster survival in particular geographic and cultural settings. One perspective is that individuals have evolved to be sensitive to features of their early childhood environment (Draper & Harpending, 1982). Therefore, changes in pubertal processes are considered a response to shifting environmental demands. Shifting environmental circumstances are conjectured to be a factor in the downward trend in the age of onset of puberty. This shift reflects secular environmental trends rather than an evolutionary process. Nonetheless, genes that become expressed as a function of environmental demands may favor earlier or later timing of puberty in subsequent generations.

In contrast to the evolutionary and physical-developmental adaptive properties of puberty, the social component of puberty historically was perceived as a major transition contributing to the turbulence and stress experienced by some adolescents. Adolescence as a period of storm and stress is an early- to mid-20th century conception of adolescence (Blos, 1962; Freud, 1958; Hall, 1904) that was viewed as universal and biological in origin. Contemporary empirical-based findings support the view that storm and stress are neither a universal phenomenon nor a biologically based aspect of development. The majority of adolescents enjoy at least some aspects of pubertal development, principally, increased height. Accordingly, the storm and stress perspective has been revised to represent a more balanced view of adolescence as a period of development characterized by biological, cognitive, emotional, and social *reorganization* with the aim of adapting to cultural expectations of becoming an adult. This *revisionist* perspective suggests that adolescence is a period when specific types of problems are more likely to arise than in other periods of development (Arnett, 1999) yet that these problems are not universal. Behavioral reorganization occurs in the service of accommodating to changing social roles, and it is important to note that adolescents change social roles, thereby influencing their social environment. It also implies that the majority of adolescents experience neither maladjustment nor notable undesirable behaviors.

PUBERTY: AN INTEGRATED BIOSOCIAL PERSPECTIVE

The myriad molecular-biological, molar-psychological, and social changes that characterize puberty engender scientific interests that span the biomedical, behavioral, and social sciences. Hence, interdisciplinary perspectives necessarily are required to characterize adolescent development (Lerner, 1998; Magnusson, 1999; Susman, 1997). Research foci on pubertal development now include genetic and neuroendocrine mechanisms that initiate puberty; influences from the molecular to the social contextual; the significance of timing of puberty; and the dynamic interactive processes among physical growth changes, emotions, problem behavior, cognition, and risky sexual activity (but these latter studies remain relatively rare). Given the diversity and magnitude of pubertal changes, an integrative theory is essential for understanding the fragmented findings regarding pubertal development. This chapter presents a review of puberty as a biopsychosocial transition that initiates psychological changes and that simultaneously initiates changes in the social contexts in which adolescents find themselves. This theoretical approach is referred to as *dynamic integration* and refers to the essential fusion of processes across psychological, biological, and contextual levels of functioning.

The absence of an integrated biosocial perspective on puberty has historically been problematic. Puberty as a biological event that deterministically modifies behavior was derived from evolutionary (Parker, 2000) and psychodynamic (Freud, 1958; Hall, 1904) theories that dominated the early 20th century. The perceptual salience of sexual maturation was considered to heighten the psychological significance of biological pubertal changes (Brooks-Gunn & Petersen, 1984). In the last three decades, behaviorism, contextualism, and learning theory supplanted theories of development and evolution. Empirical research came to reflect a dominant interest in contextual influences (e.g., peers and schools) on development (e.g., Simmons & Blyth, 1987). Social contextualism gave rise to the social constructionist viewpoint that the psychological significance of puberty is derived from how others view puberty-related changes. Pubertal changes were considered more graphic to others than to the adolescents themselves. The biological-deterministic and social constructionist views of adolescence disregarded the dynamic integration of biological, psychological, and contextual levels of analysis.

The integration of biological and psychological processes experienced a renaissance with the publication of Petersen's perspective on puberty and psychological development (Petersen & Taylor, 1980). Shortly thereafter, the publication of *Girls at Puberty* (Brooks-Gunn & Petersen, 1983) and a special issue of the *Journal of Youth and Adolescence* on timing of puberty (Brooks-Gunn, Petersen, & Eichorn, 1985) brought to scientific consciousness an integrated perspective that considered the multiple levels of development. This emerging biopsychosocial perspective simultaneously began to be articulated in theoretical models that focused on the centrality of interactions between biological, psychological, and contextual processes (Lerner, 1987). Coincident with the articulation of these biopsychosocial theories, empirical studies assessing the relationships between physical growth and pubertal hormone levels and psychological development began to appear in the literature. These studies addressed issues of family interaction (Steinberg & Hill, 1978), adjustment (Nottelmann et al., 1987), aggressive behavior (Susman et al., 1987), emotions (Brooks-Gunn & Warren, 1989) and sexuality (Udry, Billy, & Morris, 1986; Udry, Billy, Morris, Groff, & Raj, 1985; Udry & Talbert, 1988). The theoretical constructs inherent in the new theoretical perspectives include developmental contextualism (Lerner, 1998), reciprocal interaction and bidirectionality (Cairns, 1997), and holistic interactionism (Magnusson, 1999). We refer to these concepts collectively as within a model of *dynamic integration.* This concept is evoked to replace the concept of interaction, which connotes a specific statistical approach.

Contextualism

The interest in the influence of contexts (as conceptualized in peer, family, and neighborhood)—developmental contextualism (Lerner, 1998)—parallels life span developmental theory. The life span perspective consists of a composition of ideas about the nature of human development from birth to death. It is concerned with the embeddedness of evolution and ontogeny, of consistency and change, of human plasticity, and of the role that developing persons play in their own development (Lerner, 1987). Thus, a life span perspective played a formative role in the genesis of contextualism, a concept that integrates biological and psychological levels with the contextual levels of analysis.

Reciprocal Interaction and Bidirectionality

The systems, or configural and bidirectional, perspective views processes from different levels as having equal potencies in development (Cairns, 1997; Lerner, 1998; Magnusson, 1999; Susman, 1997, 1998). The biological changes that transpire both influence and reciprocally are influenced by psychological, behavioral, and social influences.

Plasticity

Plasticity is inherent to the concept of dynamic integration, as plasticity evolves from the notion that the potential for change exists in the multiple levels of organization that characterize the developing human (Lerner, 1998). Developmental plasticity at puberty has constraints imposed from both endogenous (e.g., genetic) and exogenous (e.g., nutrition) sources. The degree of plasticity in pubertal processes is influenced by genes, neuroendocrine systems, experiential history, and the multiple contexts of development. However, plasticity is relative because all developmental modifications are neither desirable nor possible and the normative age of onset of puberty is narrow.

Interactionism

Magnusson (1999) brought together the concepts of contextualism, reciprocal interaction, and bidirectionality in his metamodel of holistic interactionism. A basic proposition of an interactionism framework is that the individual is an active, intentional part of an integrated, complex, continuous, dynamic, reciprocal, and adaptive person-environment system from the fetal period until death (Magnusson, 1999; Magnusson & Cairns, 1996). Novel patterns of functioning arise during ontogeny, and differences in the rates of development, like differences in timing of puberty, may produce unique organization and configuration of psychological functions that are extremely sensitive to the environmental circumstances in which they are formed (Magnusson & Cairns, 1996). Until the last few decades the role of the environment on modulating puberty-related neuroendocrine processes at puberty was rarely considered.

Dynamic Integration

Dynamic integration embodies the notion that biological processes depend on and simultaneously are dependent on the psychological and social contextual levels of functioning. Consistent with the holistic interactionism perspective, the developmental integration model views development at puberty as the merging of levels of functioning. A fundamental premise is that development proceeds through *integration* rather than compartmentalization of psychological, biological, and contextual processes. For instance, genes no longer are considered deterministic influences on development. Rather, genes are viewed as requiring a specific environment in which to be expressed. Furthermore, genetic influences are not static but change expression across development. Genes responsible for pubertal development, such as gonadotropin releasing hormone (GnRH) genes, begin to stimulate mRNA in late childhood, leading to a cascade of hormonal and physical growth changes. Thus, the physical and hormonal manifestations of puberty are a product of a species genotype. Nonetheless, genetic expression is proposed to be integrated with the experiential history of adolescents and the contexts for social interactions to change behavior at puberty. The physical changes are integrated with the adolescent's psychological attributes, experiences, the timing of the change relative to peers, and the social context in which puberty occurs, which give meaning to puberty. Thus, a dynamic integration perspective focuses on the simultaneous integration among these levels of analysis, such as the integration of hypothalamic, pituitary, and gonadal hormones to bring about physical change, as well as the integration of psychological processes and social contexts to produce psychological development.

An integrated model does not imply that all aspects of puberty are considered simultaneously. Rather, the developmental integration model, as is the case for the developmental contextual and holistic interaction models, acts as a guide for selecting constructs and measures. Within this perspective, developmental processes are accessible to systematic scientific inquiry because they occur in a specific way within organized structures and are guided by specific principles. Critical to integration models is the interpretation of findings at one level of functioning in relation to levels above and below the level of empirical verification.

BIOLOGY OF PUBERTY

Puberty (Latin, *pubertas,* from *pubes, puber,* of ripe age, adult) can be defined as "the state of physical development at which persons are first capable of begetting or bearing children" (*Webster's New Universal Unabridged Dictionary,* 1979). This strictly *event*-driven definition is clearly the culmination of a process that began much earlier and encompasses many parallel processes (as discussed later). Puberty in the human is a unique and integrated transition from childhood to young adulthood that culminates in the attainment of fertility. It marks the time of greatest growth and sexual development since the fetal stages, and it is marked by development of the secondary sexual characteristics for each gender as well as major alterations in linear growth, body composition, and the regional distribution of body fat. All are subserved by qualitative and quantitative alterations in multiple hypothalamic-pituitary end organ axes, especially those for the gonad and the growth hormone (GH)/insulin-like growth factors-1 (IGF-I) axis.

Puberty is the process of physical maturation manifested by an impressive acceleration of linear growth in middle to late childhood and the appearance of secondary sexual characteristics. The secondary sexual characteristics are a result of androgen production from the adrenals in both sexes (adrenarche or pubarche), testosterone (T) from the testes in the male, and estrogens from the ovaries in females (gonadarche). These processes are separate and distinct in origin and timing. Although the rapid growth spurt had previously been attributed to the rising concentrations of gonadal steroid hormones, it is an indirect effect that is mediated through altered growth hormone release and in which insulin-like growth factor I (IGF-I) predominates (Veldhuis, Roemmich, & Rogol, 2000).

The traditional ages of the beginning of normal pubertal development have been 8 years for girls and 9 years for boys. The external manifestations of this onset have been considered the development of breast tissue in the girls and testicular enlargement in boys. The processes leading to these physical signs begin several years earlier, and recent advances in the ability to measure gonadal and adrenal steroid hormones show that several years before the physical signs there is evidence for the reawakening of the hypothalamic-pituitary-gonadal (HPG) and hypothalamic-pituitary-adrenal (HPA) axes. More recent data in girls suggest that breast development (thelarche) and pubic hair development (adrenarche) are being noted even earlier, and thus the definition of precocious development likely should be considered a year or more earlier (Herman-Giddens et al., 1997; Kaplowitz, Oberfield, et al., 1999). The more recent data for boys has not shown any trend toward earlier maturation (Biro, Lucky, Huster, & Morrison, 1995).

Secondary Sexual Characteristics

The method of Tanner (stages 1–5) is the most commonly used throughout the world to assess sexual maturation (Tanner, 1962). A similar rating scale is utilized for pubic hair.

Although pubic hair may be the first external sign of puberty in some boys, reddening and thinning of the scrotum and increased testicular size are the first physical findings of gonadarche (puberty). During puberty in the male the larynx, cricothyroid cartilage, and laryngeal muscles enlarge; the voice breaks at approximately 13.9 years, and the adult voice is attained by approximately 15 years (Karlberg & Taranger, 1976), a welcome relief for boys.

The appearance of breast buds is normally the first external sign of pubertal development (gonadarche) in girls. The growth spurt (discussed later) occurs earlier in the sequence of puberty in girls than in boys and often occurs with minimal breast development. The pace of pubertal development correlates with the levels of sex steroid hormones during early puberty (DeRidder et al., 1992). In girls the duration of puberty is usually 3 to 3.5 years, but puberty may be completed within 2 years or take up to 5 to 6 years to complete (Zacharias, Wurtman, & Shatzoff, 1970). Menarche is a late sign of pubertal development and occurs approximately 2.5 years after thelarche.

Growth

One of the hallmarks of pubertal development is an acceleration in linear growth velocity, or the adolescent growth spurt. As puberty approaches, the growth velocity reaches a minimum (the preadolescent dip) before it accelerates during midpuberty. The timing of the pubertal growth spurt occurs earlier in girls (typically at Tanner breast stage 3) and does not reach the magnitude that it does in boys. Girls average a peak height velocity of 9 cm/yr at age 12 and a total gain in height of 25 cm during pubertal growth (Marshall & Tanner, 1969). Boys attain a mean peak height velocity of 10.3 cm/yr, on average 2 years later than the girls, during Tanner genital stage 4, and gain 28 cm in height (Marshall & Tanner, 1970). The longer duration of pubertal growth in combination with a greater peak height velocity results in the average adult height difference of 13 cm between men and women (Tanner, 1989). Following a period of decelerating height velocity, growth virtually ceases due to epiphyseal fusion, typically at a skeletal age of 15 years in girls and 17 years in boys.

Puberty is also a time of significant weight gain: 50% of adult body weight is gained during adolescence. In boys, peak weight velocity occurs at about the same time or slightly later than peak height velocity (age 14 years) and averages 9 kg/year. In girls, the peak weight velocity lags behind the peak height velocity by approximately 6 months and reaches 8.3 kg/yr at about age 12.5 years (Barnes, 1975; Tanner, 1965). The rate of weight gain decelerates in a fashion similar to height velocity during the latter stages of pubertal development.

Marked changes in body composition, including changes in the relative proportions of water, muscle, fat, and bone, occur during pubertal development and result in the typical male-female physiques. Under the influence of the gonadal steroid hormones and the hormones of the growth hormone IGF-I axis, increases in bone mineral content and muscle mass occur, and the deposition of fat is maximally sexually dimorphic. The changes in the distribution of body fat (central vs. peripheral, subcutaneous vs. visceral, and upper vs. lower body) result in the typical *android* and *gynecoid* patterns of the older adolescent and adult (van Lenthe, van Mechelen, Kemper, & Twisk, 1998).

Differential growth of the shoulders and the pelvis and differences in lean tissue accrual between males and females are also prominent.

Under the influence of T, boys have a significant increase in bone and muscle growth with a simultaneous loss of fat in the limbs (Malina & Bouchard, 1991). The maximal loss of fat and increase in muscle mass in the upper arms correspond to the time of peak height velocity. The significant increase in lean body tissue exceeds the total weight gain due to the simultaneous loss of body fat. As height velocity slows, fat accumulation resumes in both genders but is twice as rapid in girls than in boys (Malina & Bouchard, 1991). Adult men have 1.5 times the lean body mass as the average female and twice the number of muscle cells. The increases in the skeleton and in muscle mass underlie the increased strength of the male. Both androgens and estrogens promote deposition of bone mineral, and more than 90% of the peak skeletal mass is present by age 18 years in adolescents who have progressed through pubertal development at the usual ages. In girls, nearly one third of the total skeletal mineral is deposited in bone during the 3- to 4-year period immediately after the onset of pubertal development (Bonjour, Theintz, Buchs, Slosman, & Rizzoli, 1991; Slemenda et al., 1994). Adolescents with delayed puberty or secondary amenorrhea may fail to accrue bone mineral density normally and take a reduced peak bone mineral content into the rest of their life span, with obvious implications for osteoporosis and bony fractures later in development.

Hormonal Control of Puberty

The hormonal regulation of growth becomes increasingly complex just before and with the onset of puberty. Adequate levels of thyroid hormone and cortisol continue to be prerequisites for normal growth, but the gonadal steroid hormones now play an increasingly major role. There is also a dramatic activation of the GH/IGF-I axis. During adolescence the gonadal steroid hormones and the GH/IGF-I axis continue to exert independent effects on growth, but the *interaction* between them underlies the dramatic alterations in linear growth velocity and body composition, including the regional distribution of body fat.

Pulsatile gonadotropin secretion occurs at all ages, but puberty is heralded by an increase in the amplitude of luteinizing hormone (LH) and follicle-stimulating hormone (FSH) secretion, detectable even before the first external signs of pubertal development are evident. This stage represents a reawakening of the state of the gonadal axis operative during the late fetal and very early neonatal stages. Initially, biologically relevant surges of LH occur predominantly at night, resulting in elevations of gonadal steroid hormone concentration early in the morning. These then wane during the day as these small but relevant levels of gonadal steroids reduce the levels of the gonadotropins because the negative feedback remains operative at the very sensitive prepubertal stage. With continuing maturation of the HPG axis (i.e., becoming relatively less sensitive to the negative feedback of the gonadal steroid hormones), enhanced pulsatile LH release occurs throughout the waking hours as well, resulting in more stable elevations of the gonadal steroid hormones. The rising levels of these hormones promote the development of secondary sex characteristics and the changes in body composition and the regional distribution of body fat noted during pubertal development. Gonadal steroid hormones, primarily estradiol in both genders, also enhance bone mineral accrual and affect adult height by promoting epiphyseal fusion.

A dramatic activation of the GH/IGF-I axis occurs during early- to midpuberty. The rise in the mean 24-hour GH levels results from an increase in the maximal GH secretory rate (pulse amplitude) and in the mass of GH secreted per secretory burst (Veldhuis et al., 2000). The differential increase in GH secretion between boys and girls at puberty follows the pattern of change in growth velocity. Girls show a significant rise in circulating GH levels beginning at Tanner breast stage 2, with the highest levels found at Tanner breast stage 3–4. An increase occurs later in boys, peaking at Tanner genital stage 4 (Martha, Gorman, Blizzard, Rogol, & Veldhuis, 1992). During midpuberty the day-night rhythm is obscured because of a greater rate of rise in secretory amplitude during the day than the night (Martha et al., 1992). By the time adolescent development is complete, the levels of GH and IGF-I decrease to nearly prepubertal levels in both genders.

Clinical observations have shown that both GH and sex steroid hormones must be present for normal pubertal growth. Individuals with a selective deficiency of either hormone (e.g., hypogonadotropic hypogonadism or isolated GH deficiency) have an attenuated pubertal growth spurt (Aynsley-Green, Zachmann, & Prader, 1976; Liu, Merriam, & Sherins, 1987). Many of the growth-promoting actions of the gonadal steroid hormones are mediated through the estrogen rather than androgen receptor, either by direct secretion of estrogen or conversion of androgens to estrogens by peripherally located aromatase. Individuals with complete androgen insensitivity demonstrate that androgens are not necessary to support normal adolescent growth or to achieve pubertal levels of GH and IGF-I if sufficient levels of estrogen are present (Zachmann et al., 1986). Estrogens are responsible for skeletal maturation and fusion of the epiphyseal plates.

Adrenarche

Adrenarche refers to the activation of adrenal androgen production from the zona reticularis. These androgens produce pubic and axillary hair (pubarche) as well as body odor, oily skin, and acne. Adrenarche stems from a poorly understood activation of the HPA axis for androgen production, separate and distinct from the usual activation of the HPA axis for cortisol production. There is a progressive increase in circulating levels of dehydroepiandrosterone (DHEA) and its sulfated form (DHEAS) in both boys and girls beginning by age 7 or 8 years and continuing throughout early adulthood before declining with advancing age.

The exact mechanism responsible for the onset of adrenarche is controversial, although recent evidence suggests that adrenocorticotropic hormone (ACTH; Weber, Clark, Perry, Honour, & Savage, 1997) and/or 3-hydroxysteroid dehydrogenase play a significant role in the regulation of adrenarche (Gell et al., 1998). Adrenarche only recently began to be studied in relation to psychological development (Dorn, Hitt, & Rotenstein, 1999), as discussed later.

Leptin and Puberty

Discovery of the hormone leptin led to the theory that it may be a signal allowing for the initiation of and progression toward puberty (Mantzoros, Flier, & Rogol, 1997). An alternative perspective is that leptin is implicated in the onset of puberty but may not be the cause of the onset. Leptin is 16-kDa adipocyte-secreted protein, a product of the obesity (ob) gene. Serum leptin levels reflect mainly the amount of energy stores but are also influenced by short-term energy imbalance as well as several cytokines (indices of immune system function) and hormones. Leptin is implicated in the initiation of puberty, energy expenditure, normal menstrual cycles, fertility, maintenance of pregnancy, and nutrition. Specifically, leptin may well be one of the messenger molecules signaling the adequacy of the fat stores at puberty for reproduction and maintenance of pregnancy (Kiess et al., 1999). The possible mechanism involves leptin as a hormone that serves to signal the brain with information on the critical amount of fat stores that are necessary for luteinizing hormone-releasing hormone (LHRH) secretion and activation of the HPA axis. Moreover, circadian and ultradian variations of leptin levels are also associated with minute-to-minute variations of LH and estradiol in normal women (Mantzoros, 2000). The mechanisms by which leptin regulates body weight, adiposity, and the hormones that increase at puberty (e.g., testosterone and estrogen) are not yet known.

Leptin is higher in girls than in boys controlling for adiposity (Blum et al., 1997). At the initiation of puberty, circulating leptin concentrations diverge in boys and girls. In boys, leptin concentrations increase and then markedly decrease to prepubertal concentration levels in late puberty. In contrast, in girls there are increasing concentrations at puberty (Roemmich & Rogol, 1999). The increase in leptin is believed to result from different alterations in the regional distribution of body fat in boys and girls at puberty. Overall, sex differences in leptin concentrations are accountable to differences in the amounts of subcutaneous fat in girls and greater androgen concentrations in boys (Roemmich, Clark, Berr, et al., 1998). The biological effects of leptin in adult humans are still to be determined, but reports show that congenital leptin deficiency leads to hyperphagia and excessive weight gain from early infancy onward as well as failure of pubertal onset in adolescence (Ong, Ahmed, & Dunger, 1999). Leptin concentrations have not yet been examined in relation to behavior changes at puberty, but leptin provides a promising biological probe for understanding pubertal processes and problems of body image.

PUBERTY AND BEHAVIOR, EMOTIONS, AND COGNITION

Until the last two decades, studies of pubertal processes considered primarily physical morphological characteristics or menarche in assessing the relationship between biological changes and psychological development. These studies now are enriched by assessment of biological substances—specifically, hormones—that are essential for pubertal development.

Pubertal Status and Pubertal Timing

The literature linking puberty and psychological development includes assessment that considers both pubertal status and timing of puberty. *Pubertal status* refers to the degree of physical maturation on indicators that include breast, genital, and pubic hair development and hormone levels. *Timing of puberty* refers to pubertal status relative to same-age peers.

Pubertal Status: Hormones

The use of hormones to assess degree of pubertal development is a relatively new undertaking. In the following section, hormone levels are examined in relation to their contribution to behavior, emotions and cognition.

Testosterone and Estrogen: Antisocial Behavior "A focus on either social or biological factors can yield only part of the story of aggressive and violent behaviors: integrative investigations are essential to complete the picture" (Cairns & Stoff, 1996, p. 338). Relative to other domains, the integration of biological and psychological processes in relation to antisocial behavior has been evident for some time. Increases in antisocial behavior (physical aggression, relational aggression, conduct disorder symptoms, behavior problems, delinquent and violent behavior, and early and risky sexual activity and arrests) have been attributed to changes in hormones, physical maturation, altered reactivity to life stressors, and, most recently, brain changes during puberty. An unresolved issue is whether antisocial behavior existed prior to puberty but became transformed to more annoying or more serious problems at puberty or whether problems emerge de novo at puberty.

The links between the biology of puberty and problem behavior have been extensively reviewed elsewhere (Brain & Susman, 1997; Buchanan, Eccles, & Becker, 1992). Major advances in relating pubertal status and psychological parameters partially result from advances in hormone assay technologies, whereby hormones can reliably and sensitively be measured in small quantities of blood and saliva.

The steroid hormone testosterone (T) is implicated in physical aggression in animals and antisocial behavior in humans (Brain & Susman, 1997; Mazur & Booth, 1998). The relationship between T and problem behavior is hypothesized to derive from pre- and early postnatal organizational effects of hormones on brain development and later activational influences when T begins to rise at puberty. The argument is that because males are exposed to higher concentrations of androgens than females during pre- and postnatal development and onward, and because males tend to express more physical aggression than females, androgens must be implicated in aggressive behavior and dominance in males (Mazur & Booth, 1998). Because T rises at puberty and externalizing behavior problems also rise at puberty, it follows that T is hypothesized to influence antisocial behavior.

Evidence for the relationship between T and aggressive behavior is derived from a few correlational and experimental studies. In boys in the later stages of pubertal development, Olweus, Mattson, Schalling, and Low (1988) examined the causal pathway between T and provoked and unprovoked aggression and reported that T exerted a direct causal path on provoked aggressive behavior. T appeared to lower the boys' frustration tolerance. For unprovoked aggressive behavior (starting fights and verbal aggression), the findings were somewhat different. T had no direct effects on unprovoked aggressive behavior, but there was an indirect effect of T with low frustration tolerance as a mediator of aggressive behavior. The authors concluded that higher levels of T made the boys more impatient and irritable, in turn increasing readiness to engage in unprovoked aggressive behavior.

Higher levels of T appear to affect observable behavior in subtle ways. Adolescent boys' perceptions of dominance were reflected in peers' T concentrations (Schaal, Tremblay, Soussignan, & Susman, 1996). T was significantly higher in peer-perceived leaders than in nonleaders. In addition, T levels and body mass additively predicted social dominance (Tremblay et al., 1998). It is not yet evident whether social dominance leads to higher T levels or whether higher T and greater body mass lead to higher social dominance.

The relationship between T and antisocial behavior is far from consistent across studies. T was positively related to substance use (Bauman, Foshee, Koch, Haley, & Downton, 1989; Martin et al., 2001), coitus in females (Halpern, Udry, & Suchindran, 1997), and sexual activity in males (Halpern, Udry, & Suchindran, 1998), but there was a negative relationship between T and behavior problems in healthy young boys (Susman et al., 1987). Similarly, there was no relationship between a diagnosis of conduct disorder problems and T in 4- to 10-year-old children (Constantino et al., 1993). In girls, T was not related to aggressive or dominance behaviors in three studies that included early-puberty girls (Brooks-Gunn & Warren, 1989; Inoff-Germain et al., 1988; Susman et al., 1987). It is noteworthy that the associations between antisocial behavior and T are less apparent in girls and in male children and younger adolescents (Brooks-Gunn & Warren, 1989; Constantino et al., 1993; Nottelmann et al., 1987; Susman et al., 1987) than in older adolescents (Olweus et al., 1988) and adults (Mazur & Booth, 1998). These developmental inconsistencies should be expected given the different constructs assessed across studies. Questionnaires that assess the molar aspects of aggressive behavior may not have adequate sensitivity for capturing subtle differences in the behavior of adolescents that covary with T levels. The relatively inconsistent links between T and antisocial behavior in adolescents compared to adults indicates that elevated T and antisocial behavior may be a consequence of aggressive behavior (Constantino et al., 1993). However, a causal influence for T in behavior should be considered. Boys who consistently displayed disruptive behavior problems and were anxious across six years were significantly lower on T than were boys who were not disruptive and anxious (Schaal et al., 1996). These disruptive and anxious boys were also later in their pubertal development. The effect of antisocial behavior on suppression of gonadal steroids may be mediated by stressors and related hormones.

Experimental studies are the preferred approach for establishing the cause-effect relationship between hormones and antisocial behavior. To examine this cause-effect relationship, T or estrogen was administered to delayed-puberty boys and girls in a placebo-controlled, randomized, double-blind, crossover design study. The boys and girls were being treated with physiological doses of T (boys) or conjugated estrogens (girls) (Finkelstein et al., 1997; Liben et al., 2002; Schwab et al., 2001; Susman et al., 1998). Each 3-month treatment period was preceded and followed by a 3-month placebo period. The doses of gonadal steroids were calculated to simulate concentrations in blood in normal early (low dose), middle (middle dose), and late (high dose) pubertal adolescents. Significant increases in aggressive impulses and physical aggression against peers and adults were seen in boys but only at the middle dose. In contrast, significant increases in self-reported aggressive impulses and in physical aggression against both peers and adults were seen in girls at the low and middle dose but not at the high dose of estrogen (Finkelstein et al., 1997). In brief, experimental treatment with T and estradiol resulted in changes in aggressive behavior, suggesting a causal role for these hormones.

The effects of estrogen are less frequently examined in relation to antisocial behavior than are those of T. In the few studies that have examined estrogen, the relationship between T and aggressive behavior in girls mimics the relationship between T and aggressive behavior in boys (Inoff-Germain et al., 1988). The lack of progression of research on estrogen and antisocial behavior reflects two issues. First, only males were included in the majority of studies on hormones and antisocial behavior, as physically aggressive behavior and violence occur more frequently in men and aggressive and violent behavior in girls rarely comes to the attention of the judicial system. Second, the logic of the arguments regarding T, aggressive behavior, and brain development does not take into account the empirical findings on the different forms of aggressive behavior in males and females. Females tend to show higher levels of relational aggression than do boys. Therefore, the relationship between female phenotypic aggressive behavior and hormones requires reconsideration. In human adolescents, dominance may be a productive area to consider for establishing the dynamic integration between hormones and social hierarchies as these hierarchies are established and dissolve rapidly in adolescent peer groups.

Emotions The role of pubertal status in emotions is of sustained interest given that depression symptoms begin to rise during the middle to late pubertal years (Lewinsohn, Clarke, Seeley, & Rohde, 1994; Nolen-Hoeksema & Girgus, 1994). The stressful change hypothesis suggests that girls experiencing the pubertal transition will manifest higher levels of distress than will pre- or postpubertal girls (Ge, Conger, & Elder, 2001b). This hypothesis is based on the assumption that puberty is a stressful transition that requires reorganization of adaptive coping strategies (Caspi & Moffitt, 1991). Some researchers have argued that it is the novelty of a situation, rather than the magnitude of the stressor, that leads to emotional distress in adolescents (Susman, Dorn, Inoff-Germain, Nottelmann, & Chrousos, 1997). This perspective leads to the prediction that given the novel nature of the hormonal and physical growth changes, puberty constitutes a stressful adolescent transition.

In those studies that examine hormones and emotion, there are group differences for depression in girls at different stages of puberty but a larger effect for T than for stage of pubertal development (Angold, Costello, Erkanli, & Worthman, 1999). When Tanner stage and hormones were entered simultaneously into a statistical model, the effect for Tanner stage became nonsignificant, but the effect for T and estradiol remained unchanged. In a parallel study, girls were grouped by pubertal breast stages and four stages of estradiol secretion (Warren & Brooks-Gunn, 1989). The hormonal stages revealed a significant curvilinear trend for depressive affect (increase, then decrease), impulse control (decrease, then increase), and psychopathology (increase, then decrease), indicating significant differences in these indexes during times of rapid increases in hormone levels. In the clinical trial study just described, adolescents with delayed puberty treated with physiological doses of T or estrogen showed few changes in emotions as a result of treatment, with the exception of increased withdrawn behavior in girls (Susman et al.,

1998). Collectively, the studies with adolescents who are progressing normally through puberty demonstrate an association between pubertal status and depression.

Adrenal Androgens and Cognition The role of hormones in cognition has not received much attention in the last decade. In a recent study, maturational status as indexed by T was related to better spatial abilities (Davison & Susman, 2001). As T increased, there was a corresponding increase in spatial ability in boys, and to a lesser extent in girls. In an experimental sex hormone treatment study, spatial performance showed traditional sex differences but did not vary with levels of actively circulating sex steroids (Liben et al., 2002). Further longitudinal research is required to resolve the question of how pubertal hormones and cognition change in an integrated fashion.

Adrenal Androgens

Adrenal androgens represent a class of hormones that traditionally received little attention in relation to behavior. The adrenal androgens DHEA, DHEAS, and Δ4-A are secreted by the adrenal glands and begin to rise during adrenarche.

Adrenal Androgens and Problem Behavior In the last two decades reports began to appear showing relationships between adrenal androgens and antisocial behavior in adolescents. In healthy pubertal-age girls, DHEAS correlated negatively with aggressive affect (Brooks-Gunn & Warren, 1989), and the interaction between negative life events and DHEAS and aggressive affect also was significant. Girls with lower concentrations of DHEAS who experienced negative life events had more aggressive affect than did girls with fewer negative life events. In a study that included healthy 9- to 14-year-old boys and girls, there was a relatively consistent pattern of higher DHEA and Δ4-A and lower DHEAS and problem behaviors (Nottelmann et al., 1987; Nottelmann, Inoff-Germain, Susman, & Chrousos, 1990; Susman, Dorn, & Chrousos, 1991; Susman et al., 1987). Adrenal androgens also were correlated with dominance in girls while interacting with their parents (Inoff-Germain et al., 1988). The links between adrenal androgens and problem behavior extended to sexual behavior as well. Higher levels of adrenal androgens were related to sexual behavior and activities during adolescence (Udry et al., 1985; Udry & Talbert, 1988). In addition, youth with conduct disorder (CD) had significantly higher levels of DHEA and DHEAS than did non-CD youth and reported higher intensity of aggression and delinquency (van Goozen, Matthys, Cohen-Kettenis, Thijssen, & van Engeland, 1998). Support for the links between adrenal androgens and behavior problems was reported in girls with early adrenarche. These girls had higher levels of adrenal androgens and more behavior problems than did the on-time girls (Dorn, Susman, Nottelmann, Inoff-Germain, & Chrousos, 1999). Higher levels of adrenal androgens may be an etiological process in the higher incidence of behavior problems in premature-adrenarche girls.

Adrenal Androgens and Emotions There is a relatively consistent pattern of high adrenal androgens associated with negative affect (Nottelmann et al., 1990; Nottelmann et al., 1987; Susman et al., 1991; Susman et al., 1987). DHEAS levels interact with timing of puberty and depression in girls. Girls with high levels of DHEAS and early maturation had the highest emotional arousal and depressive affect scores (Graber, Brooks-

Gunn, & Warren, in press). Girls with premature adrenarche, who also have higher levels of adrenal androgens, were more anxious than were their peers with on-time adrenarche (Dorn et al., 1999). In addition, higher levels of DHEA predicted the onset of the first episode of major depression during adolescence (Goodyer, Herbert, Tamplin, & Altham, 2000). As is the case for sex steroids, the described associations do not imply causality. Variations in levels of hormones may arise from more distal genetic or experiential origins than recent life events and behavior.

Pubertal Status: Physical Maturation

The relationship between pubertal status (i.e., degree of physical development) and psychological development is hypothesized to result from changing social roles, including increasing family and peer pressures, and cultural expectations for mature behavior. The assumption is that problem behavior and negative emotions will increase with advancing physical development independent of age.

Antisocial Behavior Indeed, more advanced pubertal status contributed significantly to predicting female delinquency (Flannery, Rowe, & Gulley, 1993), symptoms of attention-deficit/hyperactive disorder (ADHD), oppositional disorder (ODD), and conduct disorder (CD; Ge, Brody, Conger, Simons, & Murry, 2002). More advanced pubertal development provides adolescents with opportunities to become involved with older and deviant peers.

Emotions Tanner stage had a larger effect on depression than did age, suggesting that biological change rather than a specific age is related to depression in both boys and girls (Angold, Costello, & Worthman, 1998; Ge et al., 2001b; Ge et al., 2002). Additionally, the association between pubertal status and internalizing distress is stable over time. Pubertal status in 7th grade was significantly related to both internalized distress and hostility assessed at Grades 8 and 10, respectively, and to externalized hostility at Grade 9 (Ge, Conger, & Elder, 2001a). Overall, more advanced stages of physical development favored more negative emotions.

Family The classic study by Steinberg and Hill (1978) showed that family-adolescent interactions are moderated by pubertal development. Conflict between mothers and sons was highest during midpuberty. The same findings emerged in African American adolescents whose parents reported having more verbal aggression with sons during midpuberty than during early or late puberty (Sagrestano, McCormick, Paikoff, & Holmbeck, 1999). The sons reported more "hot" issues and having hot discussions when they were more physically developed. However, the importance of midpubertal status in family conflict is not consistent across studies. Later as opposed to midpubertal status also was associated with more conflict and diminished closeness with parents (Crockett & Petersen, 1987; Savin-Williams & Small, 1986). The lack of consensus regarding pubertal status, conflict, and family interactions is not surprising given the variation in methods for assessing family interaction.

Cognition Cognitive maturation normatively advances with chronological age rather than pubertal maturation. For instance, spatial ability was associated with chronological age but not with pubertal stage in a sample of healthy young adolescents (Davison & Susman, 2001). As discussed earlier, pubertal status in delayed-puberty adolescents was not associated with spatial ability (Liben et al., 2002) and thus denotes consistency across studies.

Psychopathology Pubertal status was associated with a sharp increase in rates of unipolar depression (Angold & Worthman, 1993). Girls begin to have higher rates of both diagnosed depressive disorders and subclinical levels of depressive symptoms than do boys in early to middle adolescence (Angold et al., 1998; Ge, Conger, Lorenz, & Simons, 1994; Laitinen-Krispijn, van der Ende, & Verhulst, 1999). In prepubertal children (Tanner stage 1) disorders with hypomanic-manic symptomatology (Schrauf-nagel, Brumback, Harper, & Weinberg, 2001) and seasonal affective disorders (Swedo et al., 1995) were more common, whereas in pubertal-age adolescents (Tanner stages 3-5) there was a predominance of depressive symptomatology. Other studies found no association between prepubertal and early-adolescent bipolar disorder (Geller et al., 2000). Overall, results are inconclusive regarding the connections between puberty and psychopathology. A major deficit in the literature is that few longitudinal studies of adolescent psychopathology employ state-of-the-art indexes of pubertal development, such as Tanner stage and hormone concentrations.

PUBERTAL TIMING AND ADJUSTMENT

The question of whether timing of puberty influences psychological development is one of the most frequently examined problems in research on adolescents. This interest originates from the wide range of physiologic variations in age of activation of the HPG and growth axes and normal growth at puberty. These variations are a result of genetic, environmental, and nutritional factors, such as self-induced restriction of energy intake and heavy exercise training (Rogol, Clark, & Roemmich, 2000). The importance of timing of puberty effects is based on findings that timing of physical maturational is a potent predictor of adolescent mental health and adult lifestyle health status. In adulthood, earlier maturing girls were likely to interact with deviant peers, bear children earlier, have more children and more abortions, hold lower positions in employment, and have fewer years of education than were later maturers (Stattin & Magnusson, 1990). The importance of including timing of puberty is that considering only pubertal status and chronological age in interpreting findings can be misleading given the wide age range in timing of puberty.

The classic Berkeley, Oakland (Block, 1971), and Fels (Kagan & Moss, 1962) growth studies provided the initial longitudinal findings on the links between timing of maturation and development. Among boys, early maturation tended to be advantageous, with boys being rated as more popular, relaxed, good natured, attractive to peers, and poised (Jones, 1965; Jones & Bayley, 1950). Early maturation in girls tended to be disadvantageous (Jones, Bayley, & Jones ,1948), although the results across studies where not always consistent. These inconsistent findings laid the foundation for a sustained history of contradicting findings related to the effect of timing of puberty on adolescent development.

Theoretical Perspectives on Timing of Puberty

Beginning in the 1980s, two predominant perspectives were articulated to explain the effect of the timing of physical maturation on psychological development. The *maturational deviance hypothesis* (e.g., Brooks-Gunn et al., 1985; Caspi & Moffitt, 1991; Petersen & Taylor, 1980) suggests that adolescents who are off time (earlier or later) in their pubertal development experience more stress than do on-time adolescents. Earlier or later timing of puberty can generate high emotional arousal because being off time means being a minority in relation to peers (Simmons & Blyth, 1987). This *transitional stress* is hypothesized to increase vulnerability to adjustment problems (Caspi & Moffitt, 1991). Being an off-time maturer also may result in a lack of the usual coping strategies and family and social supports that characterize on-time maturers.

The *early-maturational* or *early timing hypothesis* (e.g., Brooks-Gunn et al., 1985; Caspi & Moffitt, 1991; Petersen & Taylor, 1980) posits that being an early developer is especially disadvantageous for girls (Stattin & Magnusson, 1990). The disadvantage may result from a missed opportunity for achieving age-relevant psychosocial tasks of middle childhood (Brooks-Gunn et al., 1985). Early maturation disrupts the normal course of development such that early maturers have less time and are less experienced (stage termination) at solving the challenges imposed by having an adult appearance too early in adolescence (Petersen & Taylor, 1980). However, early maturers face social pressure to adopt adult norms and behavior; to be more socially, emotionally, and cognitively precocious; and to engage in adult behaviors as earlier maturing adolescents appear more physically mature than their chronological age.

The *maturational deviance* and *early-maturational* hypotheses now are enriched by three potential mechanisms to explain timing of maturation and psychological development. First, the *individual diathesis-stress model* (Caspi & Moffitt, 1991; Dorn & Chrousos, 1997; Richters & Weintraub, 1990; Susman, Dorn, & Schiefelbein, 2002) suggests that psychosocial vulnerability factors that exist prior to adolescence accentuate the probability of increases in emotional distress and problem behaviors among adolescents particularly in interaction with the transitional stress of timing of puberty (Caspi & Moffitt, 1991). Second, *transitional stress* refers to the *direct and indirect hormonal influence hypothesis* (Petersen & Taylor, 1980) and predicts that an increase in adrenal and gonadal hormones (direct effects; Susman, 1997) and physical maturation (indirect effects) leads to an increase in emotional distress, substance use, and behavior problems (Angold et al., 1999; Dorn & Chrousos, 1997). Major structural brain changes that may change coping capabilities are occurring as well (Giedd et al., 1999). Third, *contextual amplification* proposes that experiencing the pubertal transition in an opportunistic or deviant context (deviant peers, adverse parenting, or dangerous neighborhoods), increases the probability of behavior problems and emotional distress at puberty (Caspi, Lynam, Moffitt, & Silva, 1993; Stattin & Magnusson, 1990). Both the maturational deviance and early maturational hypotheses generally are considered within the same theoretical model.

Behavior Problems

The early-maturational hypothesis predicts that early-maturing girls engage in more acting-out behavior than do on-time or later maturing peers (Ge et al., 2001b). Early-maturing girls tend to be characterized by more behavior problems and adjustment difficulties than do their later maturing peers (Caspi & Moffitt, 1991). Early maturation was moderated by a history of vulnerability. Early maturers with a history of behavior problems experienced more behavior problems than did on-time or late maturers without a history of behavior problems. Of note is that early-maturing girls with no history of behavior problems experienced fewer behavior problems than did girls with a history of behavior problems who matured on time.

Substance Use

As is the case for other forms of antisocial behavior, substance use is more prevalent in early-maturing boys and girls (Dick, Rose, Kaprio, & Viken, 2000; Orr & Ingersoll, 1995; Wilson, Killen, & Hayward, 1994). Specifically, early timing of maturation is related to increased smoking (Martin et al., 2001). Early maturation was reported in East and West German youths with more frequent cigarette and alcohol use (Wiesner & Ittel, 2002). Neither on-time nor late maturation was associated with substance use. Similarly, in Norwegian and Swedish youths, early maturation was associated with alcohol use, alcohol intoxications, onset of drunkenness, and number of units consumed (Andersson & Magnusson, 1990; Wichstrøm, 2001). Youth substance use may lower resistance to peer pressure, thereby increasing other antisocial behavior and health-compromising behaviors.

Emotions

Early-maturing girls reported more negative emotions than did on-time or later maturing peers (Hayward et al., 1997). Ge et al. (2001a) reported that 7th-grade girls who experienced menarche at younger ages subsequently experienced a higher level of depressive symptoms than did their on-time and late-maturing peers. The significant gender differences disappeared when pubertal transition variables (pubertal status and menarche) were included in the statistical model. This finding is important because it indicates that the pubertal transition per se may explain the often-reported gender difference in depressive symptoms. The effects of early maturation are apparent in boys as well as in girls. Early-maturing boys reported higher levels of externalized hostile feelings and internalized distress symptoms than did on-time and late-maturing boys (Ge et al., 2001b). The negative effects of early maturation for boys are inconsistent with the early findings on the positive effects of early timing of puberty. The transitional stress of early puberty in the current culture may be experienced similarly by boys and girls.

Later maturation is not as consistently related to negative emotions as is earlier maturation. However, later maturation in boys was related to depressed mood (Siegel, Yancy, Aneshensel, & Schuler, 1999), lower achievement (Dubas, Graber, & Petersen, 1991), lower self-esteem or confidence, and less happiness (Crockett & Petersen, 1987). Other studies show no effects of pubertal timing in relation to emotions (Angold et al., 1998; Brooks-Gunn & Warren, 1989). In addition, in one of the few studies on timing of puberty in minority youth, adolescent reports of depressed mood varied by racial and ethnic status (Siegel et al., 1999). The complexity of the interactions between emotions, timing of puberty, and social role change supports the development of theories that integrate biological and psychological mechanisms as proposed earlier.

Body Image

Early-maturing girls are not satisfied with their appearance (Williams & Currie, 2000), height and weight, body image, or body characteristics (Brooks-Gunn et al., 1985; Brooks-Gunn & Warren, 1989; Petersen & Crockett, 1985; Stattin & Magnusson, 1990; Williams & Currie, 2000). In contrast, early-maturing German girls had a more positive body image than did late-maturing girls (Silbereisen, Petersen, Albrecht, & Kracke, 1989). In other studies, early- and late-maturing girls were satisfied with their height (Duncan, Ritter, Dornbusch, Gross, & Carlsmith, 1985). In another case, however, on-time American girls were more satisfied with their bodies (Gargiulo, Attie, Brooks-Gunn, & Warren, 1987). Early-maturing boys have usually been found to be more satisfied with their height than have later-maturing boys (Simmons & Blyth, 1987) but to have poor body image (Siegel et al., 1999).

When the racial and ethnic status of adolescents was considered, the findings of previous studies were further qualified regarding timing of puberty and self-image (Siegel et al., 1999). For Hispanics, girls felt most satisfied with their body if they developed at the same time as did everyone else. However, boys felt less satisfied with their bodies if they matured later than if they matured on time or early. Among African American youth, both boys and girls reported less satisfaction with body image if they were late maturers. Asian American and European American youth reported no effect of timing of puberty on body image. The findings regarding body image lead to one definitive conclusion: Timing of puberty does affect self- and body image in some youth. The moderating influence of racial and ethnic status on timing of puberty and body image adds an exciting new arena for generating valid findings for the large population of racial and ethnic youth.

Psychopathology

Both earlier and later maturation is associated with onset or escalation of psychopathology. Early timing of puberty in girls and late timing in boys were related to a higher incidence of psychopathology and depressed mood (Graber, Lewinsohn, Seeley, & Brooks-Gunn, 1997). Early maturation also was associated with schizotypy syndromes in later adolescence (Kaiser & Gruzelier, 1999). Later maturation was associated with later ages at both the first psychotic symptoms and the first hospitalization (Cohen, Seeman, Gotowiec, & Kopala, 1999). Other studies show no relationship between timing of puberty and psychopathology (Angold et al., 1998; Angold & Worthman, 1993; Geller et al., 2000; Ruiz, Blanco, Santander, & Miranda, 2000). The discrepancies across findings are especially difficult to interpret because the studies use measures that tap both psychiatric diagnoses and affective states.

Cognition

The relationship between timing of maturation and cognition received moderate attention in the 1960s and 1970s but has received little attention since then. In boys, early maturers had the highest grades followed by on-time and then late maturers (Dubas et al., 1991). For girls, late maturers had the highest grades, followed by early maturers and then on-time maturers. Orientation toward achievement also was different for early and later maturers. For boys and girls, on-time and late maturers were higher than early maturers on vocational and educational goals.

As in the case of social developmental factors, the effects of timing of puberty on brain development extended into adulthood. Timing of puberty was related to later EEG coherence and evoked potential P3 latency as putative measures of brain development in adults (Kaiser & Gruzelier, 1999). Late-maturing males showed increased left-hemispheric coherence compared to early-maturing males. In females, P3 latency was shorter in late versus early maturers, whereas there was no difference in males. The findings are consistent with an exaggeration of normal maturational changes in slower maturing individuals. Given that the assessments were done in adulthood, it is not possible to determine what factors other than timing of maturation may have contributed to the pattern of neuropsychological functioning.

Contexts of Development

In keeping with the developmental models just discussed, attention is warranted as to how contexts moderate the links between pubertal status and timing and psychological processes. Reactions to the biological changes of puberty vary systematically with the social context in which they occur (Petersen & Taylor, 1980). Contexts may (a) amplify or attenuate the effects of timing of puberty and (b) influence the onset and progression of puberty. Contexts operate via different social and institutional structures, principally family, peers, and neighborhood.

Family

In a unique study of political change, the effects of family structure on timing of menarche were examined by comparing continuity in parental and filial contexts. Contextual continuity was defined as living in a stable (West Germany) versus an unstable (East Germany) political context (Chasiotis, Scheffer, Restemeier, & Keller, 1998). Mother's age at menarche predicted daughter's age at menarche only under the condition of contextual continuity between generations, which was the case for the West German mothers and daughters. The sensitivity of onset of menarche to contextual variation is likely a reflection of stable nutritional and higher standards of living.

Family interaction also moderates timing of puberty, with early maturation having a stronger effect on externalizing behavior among children with harsh and inconsistent caretakers (Ge et al., 2002). In African American families, interactions were characterized by hot discussions with daughters who matured early or late and daughters who matured early (Sagrestano et al., 1999). The physical stimulus of early maturation is likely a signal to parents to monitor closely the adolescent's opportunity for risk-taking behavior. In turn, monitoring and imposing constraints are likely to lead to parent-adolescent tensions.

Family structure and related experiences are considered a mechanism involved in timing of puberty. Belsky, Steinberg, and Draper (1991) proposed an evolutionary model of family ecology and psychosocial influences to explain timing of puberty. Girls from families characterized by father absence and discordant male-female relationships are hypothesized to perceive males as nonessential to family relationships with the consequence of early sexual activity, unstable pair bonding, and father absence. Empirical tests of this hypothesis have received mixed support. Conflict in the family did predict earlier menarche, and girls in father-absent homes tend to reach puberty earlier than do girls reared in father-present homes (Moffitt, Caspi, Belsky, & Silva, 1992; Surbey, 1990; Wierson, Long, & Forehand, 1993). In a retrospective study of college-age girls, earlier menarche was related to family stress in late childhood (ages 7–11), conflict with mother and anxiousness and internalizing symptoms (anxiousness and depression) in early childhood (birth to age 6), and earlier age at dating boys and more boyfriends (Kim & Smith, 1998). Other studies report that greater marital and family conflict is associated with primarily early timing of puberty in girls (Ellis & Garber, 2000; Graber, Brooks-Gunn, & Warren, 1995). Studies of family functioning and timing of puberty in males are more rare.

A primary criticism of the family stress and early timing hypothesis is that the physiology of the stress system involves mechanisms that should attenuate, rather than accelerate, timing and progression of puberty (see Susman et al., 2003). In stressful circumstances, corticotropin releasing hormone (CRH) is secreted by the hypothalamus, ACTH by the pituitary, and cortisol from the adrenal glands. These components of the stress system downregulate the reproductive HPG axis hormones, thus delaying puberty. For instance, cortisol exerts inhibitory effects at the levels of the GnRH neuron, the pituitary gonadotroph (responsible for secreting luteinizing hormone and follicle stimulating hormone), and the gonad itself, thereby suppressing sex steroids (T and estrogen) and delaying maturation of reproductive function and physical growth. To resolve the controversy regarding family stress and timing of menarche, longitudinal studies are needed to integrate components of the physiology of stress and of reproduction with specific aspects of family stress.

Peers

The composition of the peer network is a powerful moderator of timing of puberty and problem behavior (Ary et al., 1999). Early-maturing boys and girls report more interactions with peers who were deviant (Caspi et al., 1993; Ge et al., 2002; Silbereisen et al., 1989; Wichstrøm, 1999), and early maturers, as well as later maturers, reported a wider range of delinquency, including crime, school opposition behavior, and greater frequency of delinquent activities (Flannery et al., 1993; Williams & Dunlop, 1999). Early-maturing girls with a high prevalence of problem behaviors also associate with older peers (Stattin & Magnusson, 1990). Older or deviant peers engage in behaviors that are normative for their age but not for the early-maturing girls themselves (Stattin & Magnusson, 1990). By associating with older peers, girls match their behavior with older peers' behavior with the eventual outcome of making an earlier transition to adulthood (Ge et al., 2002). In the case of girls, the negative effects of early maturation may be mediated exclusively via interaction with older boys. Thus, a purely social-contextual peer-mediated explanation has been proposed to explain the relationship between timing of puberty and problem behavior.

Schools

Simmons and Blyth (1987) reported that girls who matured early and who began to date early had poorer self-image if their transition to 7th grade involved a shift from a K–6 elementary school into a junior high school than if they remained in a K–8 school. The interpretation was that girls' vulnerability in 7th grade stems from the social and sexual pressures exerted by older boys in junior high. Differences between the culture of schools and pubertal development also were evident in girls enrolled in a national ballet company school compared to girls in a regular school setting (Brooks-Gunn & Warren, 1985; Gargiulo et al., 1987). Among the dancers, on-time maturing dancers experienced significantly more self-image problems than did later maturing girls. However, among the nondancers there were no effects for timing of puberty. In this unique sample, the school context moderated the effects of timing of maturation, likely through weight and physical activity.

The gender composition of the school also moderates how puberty is experienced. In their Dunedin study, Caspi et al. (1993) demonstrated that pubertal timing effects vary systematically depending on whether girls are in same- or mixed-sex school contexts. Consistent with their prediction, early-maturing girls in mixed-sex school settings, where they were exposed to deviant peers, engaged in more norm-violating behavior than did girls who were attending all-girl schools. School policy is not oriented toward considering timing of puberty and its implications for social development; thus, an opportunity is lost for promoting positive youth development by scrutinizing opportunities for socially valued as opposed to deviant peer activities.

Neighborhood

Diverse circumstances in the neighborhood, including socioeconomic status (Obeidallah, Brennan, Brooks-Gunn, Kindlon, & Earls, 2000), consistently have been linked to adolescent behavior problems (Ge et al., 2002). The theory behind these findings is an association between ambient levels of violence and crime on stress levels along with association with deviant peers committing delinquent acts in disadvantaged neighborhoods. Ge et al. reported that early-maturing African American children who live in disadvantaged neighborhoods affiliate more with deviant peers and engage in more externalizing behavior problems at high, average, and low levels of neighborhood disadvantage. Early timing of puberty also is influenced by degree of density of the neighborhood. Early-maturing girls who lived in urban settings, but not those who lived in rural areas, were more likely to use illegal substances (Dick et al., 2000). As was the case for schools, neighborhoods are ill equipped to integrate timing of puberty issues with recreational and positive youth development activities.

THEORETICAL AND METHODOLOGICAL ISSUES

The studies reviewed show both major consistencies and inconsistencies regarding the relationship among pubertal status, timing of puberty, and psychological development. The inconsistencies in findings across studies of pubertal status and pubertal timing emerge for conceptual and methodological reasons. A major theoretical focus has been on the effects of earlier timing of puberty, given societal concerns with the potential consequences of early maturation: precocious sexuality, substance use, and deviance. In most studies, timing of puberty is assessed at one point in time reflecting a deterministic perspective that timing is a stable and enduring quality of an adolescent, rather than a dynamic process with effects that change with age, variations in the tempo of puberty, and contextual factors.

The chronological age when adolescents are assessed for pubertal status or timing will likely influence problem behaviors or emotions. The behaviors that are related to timing of puberty at an earlier age, like externalizing problems, may disappear by later adolescence when adult behavior is required. Nonetheless, the longer term implications of timing of puberty may emerge as transformed manifestations of early problems: substance use, poor marital quality, and health problems in adulthood. A much needed emphasis in future research is identifying whether existing findings, based primarily on European American samples, are valid for adolescents of different ethnic and racial groups as race and ethnic status moderated the effects of timing of puberty in a few previous studies.

The measure of timing of puberty (age of menarche, pubertal stage, or hormone levels) may yield large discrepancies across studies in the relationship between pubertal status and timing and current functioning. To a large degree, timing of puberty has been assessed utilizing a self-report measure of puberty (e.g., pubertal stage or age at menarche). Other studies use objective measures of physical development: the gold standard of Tanner criteria (Marshall & Tanner, 1969, 1970) or hormone concentrations. Each method of assessing pubertal status has strengths and weaknesses. A major problem in the literature is that self-reports of stage of physical development are considered reliable as they correlate with physicians' ratings of stage of pubertal development. However, high rank-order correlations do not signify excellent interrater agreement. The lack of reliability in self-reports of pubertal status (Dorn, Susman, Nottelmann, Inoff-Germain, & Chrousos, 1990) and age of menarche (Dorn et al., 1999) is a major source of error variance in assessing the multiple connections between timing of puberty and psychological functioning. A theoretical and methodological approach that considers the dynamic changing aspects of timing of puberty most assuredly will lead to results with implications for promoting positive development at puberty.

New Horizons

Scholars of adolescent development have accepted the importance of the integration of biological, psychological, and contextual processes long before it was fashionable in other areas of developmental science. The theoretical frameworks discussed in this chapter are consistent with emerging perspectives that processes of development can only be understood by considering the multiple systems that function at multiple levels of development, from the genetic, molecular, and cellular to the societal (Magnusson, 1999). Given these complexities, the following principles might guide research in the future (Susman et al., 2002).

1. Models that consider multiple biological, psychological, and contextual levels of functioning will be interdisciplinary, bringing together the expertise of diverse scientists. An example of such an interdisciplinary effort is the integration of findings from the human genome project, which offers a myriad of possibilities for linking patterns of genes to complex behaviors in specific contexts. This goal cannot be achieved in the immediate future given the complexity of gene-environment relations. Nonetheless, given that

experiences modulate timing of puberty and that specific genes are responsible for the initiation of puberty, future research has the potential for identifying genes that link experience and the onset of puberty.

2. The complexity of integrating multiple levels of analysis necessarily implies that the scale and scope of investigations will be larger than in the past. Nonetheless, it is critically important to continue to pursue hypothesis-driven, small-scale studies at specific levels of analysis. In studies that focus on one level of analysis, such as the biological level, it is critical to acknowledge the contribution of mediators and moderators at contextual levels as well.

3. The integration of biology and behavior is possible given the advances in statistical models in the last decade. The dynamic and changing nature of physical maturation, hormones, and psychological characteristics at puberty now can be captured in longitudinal statistical models using estimates of how changes in one domain (hormones) can lead to changes in another domain (behavior). In addition, other person-oriented approaches like longitudinal cluster analysis and latent transition analysis will allow for examining patterns or configurations in biopsychosocial processes.

4. The variance accounted for by pubertal status or pubertal timing is small. Pubertal status, pubertal timing, and hormones are not sufficient to explain the processes that are involved in complex behaviors. The combination of variables at the biological, individual-psychological, and contextual levels is warranted. An integrated, multilevel model will accrue a larger amount of variance than previous models and will provide integrated knowledge about the holistic properties of individuals.

REFERENCES

Alsaker, F. D. (1995). Timing of puberty and reactions to pubertal changes. In M. Rutter (Ed.), *Psychosocial disturbances in young people: Challenges for prevention* (pp. 37–82). Cambridge, UK: Cambridge University Press.

Andersson, T., & Magnusson, D. (1990). Biological maturation in adolescence and the development of drinking habits and alcohol abuse among young males: A prospective longitudinal study. *Journal of Youth and Adolescence, 19,* 33–42.

Angold, A., Costello, E. J., Erkanli, A., & Worthman, C. (1999). Pubertal changes in hormone levels and depression in girls. *Psychological Medicine, 29,* 1043–1053.

Angold, A., Costello, E. J., & Worthman, C. W. (1998). Puberty and depression: The role of age, pubertal status, and pubertal timing. *Psychological Medicine, 28,* 51–61.

Angold, A., & Worthman, C. W. (1993). Puberty onset of gender differences in rates of depression: A developmental, epidemiological and neuroendocrine perspective. *Journal of Affective Disorders, 29,* 145–158.

Arnett, J. J. (1999). Adolescent storm and stress, reconsidered. *American Psychologist, 54,* 317–326.

Ary, D. V., Duncan, T. E., Biglan, A., Metzler, C. W., Noell, J. W., & Smolkowski, K. (1999). Development of adolescent problem behavior. *Journal of Abnormal Child Psychology, 27,* 141–150.

Aynsley-Green, A., Zachmann, M., & Prader, A. (1976). Interrelation of the therapeutic effects of growth hormone and testosterone on growth in hypopituitarism. *Journal of Pediatrics, 89,* 992.

Barnes, H. B. (1975). Physical growth and development during puberty. *Medical Clinics of North America, 59,* 1305–1317.

Bauman, K. E., Foshee, V. A., Koch, G. G, Haley, N. J., & Downton, M. I. (1989). Testosterone and cigarette smoking in early adolescence. *Journal of Behavioral Medicine, 12,* 425–433.

Belsky, J., Steinberg, L., & Draper, P. (1991). Childhood experience, interpersonal development, and reproductive strategy: An evolutionary theory of socialization. *Child Development, 62,* 647–670.

Biro, F. M., Lucky, A. W., Huster, G. A., & Morrison, J. A. (1995). Pubertal staging in boys. *Journal of Pediatrics, 127,* 100–102.

Block, J. (1971). *Lives through time.* Berkeley, CA: Bancroft Books.

Blos, P. (1962). *On adolescence: A psychoanalytical interpretation.* New York: Free Press.

Blum, W. F., Englaro, P., Hanitsch, S., Juul, A., Hertel, N. T., Muller, J., Skakkebaek, M. L., Heinman, M., Birkett, A. M., Attanasio, W., Kiess, W., & Rascher, W. (1997). Plasma leptin levels in healthy children and adolescents: Dependence on body mass index, body fat mass, gender, pubertal stage, and testosterone. *Journal of Clinical Endocrinology and Metabolism, 82,* 2904–2910.

Bonjour, J., Theintz, G., Buchs, B., Slosman, D., & Rizzoli, R. (1991). Critical years and stages of puberty for spinal and femoral bone mass accumulation during adolescence. *Journal of Clinical Endocrinology and Metabolism, 73,* 555–563.

Brain, P., & Susman, E. J. (1997). Hormonal aspects of antisocial behavior and violence. In D. M. Stoff, J. Breiling, & J. D. Maser (Eds.), *Handbook of antisocial behavior* (pp. 314–323). New York: Wiley.

Brooks-Gunn, J., & Petersen, A. C. (1983). *Girls at puberty: Biological and psychosocial perspectives.* New York: Plenum Press.

Brooks-Gunn, J., & Petersen, A. C. (1984). Problems in studying and defining pubertal events. *Journal of Youth and Adolescence, 13,* 181–196.

Brooks-Gunn, J., Petersen, A. C., & Eichorn, D. (1985). The study of maturational timing effects in adolescence. *Journal of Youth and Adolescence, 14,* 149–161.

Brooks-Gunn, J., & Warren, M. P. (1985). Measuring physical status and timing in early adolescence: A developmental perspective. *Journal of Youth and Adolescence, 14,* 163–189.

Brooks-Gunn, J., & Warren, M. P. (1989). Biological and social contributions to negative affect in young adolescent girls. *Child Development, 60,* 40–55.

Buchanan, C. M., Eccles, J. S., & Becker, J. B. (1992). Are adolescents the victims of raging hormones: Evidence for activational effects of hormones on moods and behavior at adolescence. *Psychological Bulletin, 111,* 62–107.

Cairns, R. B. (1997). Socialization and sociogenesis. In D. Magnusson (Ed.), *The lifespan development of individuals: Behavioral, neurobiological and psychosocial perspectives: A synthesis* (pp. 277–295). New York: Cambridge University Press.

Cairns, R. B., & Stoff, D. M. (1996). Conclusion: A synthesis of studies on the biology of aggression and violence. In D. M. Stoff & R. B. Cairns (Eds.), *Aggression and violence: Genetic, neurobiological and biosocial perspectives.* Mahwah, NJ: Erlbaum.

Caspi, A. M., Lynam, D., Moffitt, T. E., & Silva, P. A. (1993). Unraveling girls' delinquency: Biological, dispositional, and contextual contributions to adolescent misbehavior. *Developmental Psychology, 29,* 19–30.

Caspi, A. M., & Moffitt, T. E. (1991). Individual differences are accentuated during periods of social change: The sample case of girls at puberty. *Journal of Personality and Social Psychology, 61,* 157–168.

Chasiotis, A., Scheffer, D., Restemeier, R., & Keller, H. (1998). Intergenerational context discontinuity affects the onset of puberty: A comparison of parent-child dyads in West and East Germany. *Human Nature, 9,* 321–339.

Cohen, R. Z., Seeman, M. V., Gotowiec, A., & Kopala, L. (1999). Earlier puberty as a predictor of later onset of schizophrenia in women. *American Journal of Psychiatry, 156,* 1059–1064.

Constantino, J. N., Grosz, D., Saenger, P., Chandler, D. W., Nardi, R., & Earls, F. J. (1993). Testosterone and aggression in children. *Journal of the American Academy of Child and Adolescent Psychiatry, 32,* 1217–1222.

Crockett, L. J., & Petersen, A. C. (1987). Pubertal status and psychosocial development: Findings from the Early Adolescence Study. In R. M. Lerner & T. T. Foch (Eds.), *Biological-psychosocial interactions in early adolescence* (pp. 173–188). Hillsdale, NJ: Erlbaum.

Davison, K., & Susman, E. J. (2001). Are hormone levels and cognitive ability related during early adolescence? *International Journal of Behavioral Development, 25,* 416–428.

DeRidder, C. M., Thissen, J. H., Bruning, P. F., Van den Brande, J. L., Zonderland, M. L., & Erich, W. B. (1992). Body fat mass, body fat distribution and pubertal development: A longitudinal study of physical and hormonal sexual maturation in girls. *Journal of Clinical Endocrinology and Metabolism, 75,* 442–446.

Dick, D. M., Rose, R. J., Kaprio, J., & Viken, R. (2000). Pubertal timing and substance use: Associations between and within families across late adolescence. *Developmental Psychology, 36,* 180–189.

Dorn, L. D., & Chrousos, G. P. (1997). The neurobiology of stress: Understanding regulation of affect during female biological transitions. *Seminars in Reproductive Endocrinology, 15,* 19–35.

Dorn, L. D., Hitt, S. F., & Rotenstein, D. (1999). Biopsychological and cognitive differences in children with premature vs. on-time adrenarche. *Archives of Pediatrics and Adolescent Medicine, 153*(2), 137–146.

Dorn, L. D., Susman, E. J., Nottelmann, E. D., Inoff-Germain, G. I., & Chrousos, G. P. (1990). Perceptions of puberty: Adolescent, parent, and health care personnel. *Developmental Psychology, 26,* 322–329.

Dorn, L. D., Susman, E. J., Nottelmann, E. D., Inoff-Germain, G. I., & Chrousos, G. P. (1999). Variability in hormone concentrations and self-reported menstrual histories in young adolescents: Menarche and an integral part of a developmental process. *Journal of Youth and Adolescence, 28,* 283–304.

Draper, P., & Harpending, H. (1982). Father absence and reproductive strategy: An evolutionary perspective. *Journal of Anthropological Research, 58,* 255–273.

Dubas, J. S., Graber, J. A., & Petersen, A. C. (1991). The effects of pubertal development on achievement during adolescence. *American Journal of Education, 99,* 444–460.

Duncan, P. D., Ritter, P. L., Dornbusch, S. M., Gross, R. T., & Carlsmith, J. M. (1985). The effects of pubertal timing on body image, school behavior, and deviance. *Journal of Youth and Adolescence, 14,* 227–235.

Ellis, B. J., & Garber, J. (2000). Psychosocial antecedents of variation in girls' pubertal timing: Maternal depression, stepfather presence, and marital and family stress. *Child Development, 71,* 485–501.

Finkelstein, J. W., Susman, E. J., Chinchilli, V., Kunselman, S. J., D'Arcangelo, M. R., Schwab, J., Demers, L. M., Liben, L., Lookingbill, M. S., & Kulin, H. E. (1997). Estrogen or testosterone increases self-reported aggressive behavior in hypogonadal adolescents. *Journal of Clinical Endocrinology and Metabolism, 82,* 2433–2438.

Flannery, D. J., Rowe, D. C., & Gulley, B. L. (1993). Impact of pubertal status, timing and age on adolescent sexual experience and delinquency. *Journal of Adolescent Research, 8,* 21–40.

Freud, A. (1958). Adolescence. *Psychoanalytic Study of the Child, 15,* 255–278.

Gargiulo, J., Attie, I., Brooks-Gunn, J., & Warren, M. P. (1987). Girls' dating behavior as a function of social context and maturation. *Developmental Psychology, 23,* 730–737.

Ge, X., Brody, G. H., Conger, R. D., Simons, R. L., & Murry, V. (2002). Contextual amplification of pubertal transitional effect on African American children's problem behaviors. *Developmental Psychology, 38,* 42–54.

Ge, X., Conger, R. D., & Elder, G. H. (2001a). Pubertal transition, stressful life events, and the emergence of gender differences in depressive symptoms during adolescence. *Developmental Psychology, 37,* 404–417.

Ge, X., Conger, R. D., & Elder, G. H. (2001b). The relation between puberty and psychological distress in adolescent boys. *Journal of Research on Adolescence, 11,* 49–70.

Ge, X., Conger, R. D., Lorenz, F. O., & Simons, R. L. (1994). Parents' stressful life events and adolescent depressed mood. *Journal of Health and Social Behavior, 35,* 28–44.

Gell, J. S., Carr, B. R., Sasano, I. I., Atkins, B., Margarf, L., Mason, J. I., & Rainey, W. E. (1998). Adrenarche results from development of a 3-beta-hydroxysteroid dehydrogenase-deficient adrenal reticularis. *Journal of Clinical Endocrinology and Metabolism, 83,* 3695–3701.

Geller, B., Zimerman, B., Williams, M., Bolhofner, K., Craney, J. L., Delbello, M. P., & Soutullo,

C. A. (2000). Diagnostic characteristics of 93 cases of a prepubertal and early adolescent bipolar disorder phenotype by gender, puberty and comorbid attention deficit hyperactivity disorder. *Journal of Child and Adolescent Psychopharmacology, 10,* 157–164.

Giedd, J. N., Blumenthal, J., Jeffries, N. O., Rajapakse, J. C., Vaituzis, A. C., Liu, H., Berry, Y. C., Tobin, M., Nelson, J., & Castellanos, F. X. (1999). Development of the human corpus callosum during childhood and adolescence: A longitudinal MRI study. *Progress in Neuro-Psychopharmacology and Biological Psychiatry, 21,* 1185–1201.

Goodyer, I. M., Herbert, J., Tamplin, A., & Altham, P. M. (2000). First-episode major depression in adolescents: Affective, cognitive and endocrine characteristics of risk status and predictors of onset. *British Journal of Psychiatry, 176,* 142–149.

Graber, J. A., Brooks-Gunn, J., & Warren, M. P. (1995). The antecedents of menarcheal age: Heredity, family environment, and stressful life events. *Child Development, 66,* 346–359.

Graber, J. A., Brooks-Gunn, J., & Warren, M. P. (in press). Pubertal effects on adjustment in girls: Moving from demonstrating effects to identifying pathways. *Journal of Youth and Adolescence.*

Graber, J. A., Lewinsohn, R. M., Seeley J. R., & Brooks-Gunn, J. (1997). Is psychopathology associated with the timing of pubertal development? *Journal of the American Academy of Child and Adolescent Psychiatry, 36,* 1768–1776.

Hall, G. S. (1904). *Adolescence.* New York: Appleton.

Halpern, C. T., Udry, J. R., & Suchindran, C. (1997). Testosterone predicts initiation of coitus in adolescent females. *Psychosomatic Medicine, 59,* 161–171.

Halpern, C. T., Udry, J. R., & Suchindran, C. (1998). Monthly measures of salivary testosterone predict sexual activity in adolescent males. *Archives of Sexual Behavior, 27,* 445–465.

Hayward, C., Killen, J. D., Wilson, D. M., Hammer, L. D, Lift, I. F., Kraemer, H. C., Haydel, F., Varady, A., & Taylor, C. B. (1997). Psychiatric risk associated with early puberty in adolescent girls. *Journal of the American Academy of Child and Adolescent Psychiatry, 36,* 255–262.

Herman-Giddens, M. E., Slora, E. J., Wasserman, R. C., Bourdony, C. J., Bhapkar, M. V., Koch, G. G., & Hasemeier, C. M. (1997). Secondary sexual characteristics and menses in young girls seen in office practice: A study from the Pediatric Research in Office Settings network. *Pediatrics, 99,* 505–512.

Inoff-Germain, G., Arnold, G. S., Nottelmann, E. D., Susman, E. J., Cutler, G. B., Jr., & Chrousos, G. P. (1988). Relations between hormone levels and observational measures of aggressive behavior of early adolescents in family interactions. *Developmental Psychology, 24,* 129–139.

Jones, M. C. (1965). Psychological correlates of somatic development. *Child Development, 36.*

Jones, M. C., & Bayley, N. (1950). Physical maturing among boys as related to behavior. *Journal of Educational Psychology, 41,* 129–148.

Jones, M. C., Bayley, N., & Jones, H. E. (1948). Physical maturing among boys as related to behavior. *American Psychologist, 3,* 264.

Kagan, J., & Moss, H. A. (1962). *Birth to maturity.* New York: Wiley.

Kaiser, J., & Gruzelier, J. H. (1999). Timing of puberty and syndromes of schizotypy: A replication. *International Journal of Psychophysiology, 34,* 237–247.

Kaplowitz, P. B., Oberfield, S. E., & Drug and Therapeutics and Executive Committees of the Lawson Wilkins Pediatric Endocrine Society. (1999). Reexamination of the age limit for defining when puberty is precocious in girls in the United States: Implications for evaluation and treatment. *Pediatrics, 104,* 936–941.

Karlberg, P., & Taranger, J. (1976). The somatic development of children in a Swedish urban community. *Acta Paediatrica Scandinavica Supplement, 258,* 1–48.

Kiess, W., Reich, A., Meyer, K., Glasow, A., Deutscher, J., Klammt, J., Yang, Y., Muller, G., & Kratzsch, J. (1999). A role for leptin in sexual maturation and puberty? *Hormone Research, 51,* 55–63.

Kim, K., & Smith, P. K. (1998). Childhood stress, behavioural symptoms and mother-daughter pubertal development. *Journal of Adolescence, 21,* 231–240.

Laitinen-Krispijn, S., van der Ende, J., & Verhulst, F. C. (1999). The role of pubertal progress in the development of depression in early adolescence. *Journal of Affective Disorders, 54,* 211–215.

Lerner, R. (1987). A life-span perspective for early adolescence. In R. M. Lerner & T. T. Foch (Eds.), *Biological-psychological interactions in early adolescence* (pp. 1–34). Hillsdale, NJ: Erlbaum.

Lerner, R. M. (1998). Theories of human development: Contemporary perspectives. In W. Damon (Ed.), *Handbook of child psychology* (pp. 1–24). New York: Wiley.

Lewinsohn, P. M., Clarke, G. N., Seeley, J. R., & Rohde, P. (1994). Major depression in community adolescents: Age at onset, episode duration, and time to recurrence. *Journal of Child and Adolescent Psychiatry, 33,* 809–818.

Liben, L. S., Susman, E. J., Finkelstein, J. W., Chinchilli, V. M., Kunselman, S., Schwab, J., Dubas, J. S., Demers, L. M., Lookingfill, G., Dariangelo, M. R., Krogh, H. R., & Kulin, H. E. (2002). The effects of sex steroids on spatial performance: A review and an experimental clinical investigation. *Developmental Psychology, 38*(2), 236–256.

Liu, L., Merriam, G. R., & Sherins, R. J. (1987). Chronic sex steroid exposure increases mean plasma growth hormone concentration and pulse amplitude in men with isolated hypogonadotropic hypogonadism. *Journal of Clinical Endocrinology and Metabolism, 64,* 651.

Magnusson, D. (1999). Holistic interactionism: A perspective for research on personality development. In L. A. Pervin & O. P. John (Eds.), *Handbook of personality: Theory and research* (2nd ed., pp. 219–247). New York: Guilford Press.

Magnusson, D., & Cairns, R. B. (1996). Developmental science: Toward a unified framework. In R. B. Cairns, G. Elder, & J. Costello (Eds.), *Developmental science* (pp. 7–30). New York: Cambridge University Press.

Malina, R. M., & Bouchard, C. (1991). *Growth maturation and physical activity.* Champaign, IL: Human Kinetics Press.

Mantzoros, C. S. (2000). Role of leptin in reproduction. *Annals of the New York Academy of Sciences, 900,* 174–183.

Mantzoros, C. S., Flier, J. S., & Rogol, A. D. (1997). A longitudinal assessment of hormonal and physical alterations during normal puberty in boys: V. Rising leptin levels may signal the onset of puberty. *Journal of Clinical Endocrinology and Metabolism, 82,* 1066–1070.

Marshall, W. A., & Tanner, J. M. (1969). Variations in patterns of pubertal change in girls. *Archives of Disease in Childhood, 44,* 291–303.

Marshall, W. A., & Tanner, J. M. (1970). Variations in patterns of pubertal changes in boys. *Archives of Disease in Childhood, 45,* 15–23.

Martha, P. M., Jr., Gorman, K. M., Blizzard, R. M., Rogol, A. D., & Veldhuis, J. D. (1992). Endogenous GH secretion and clearance rates in normal boys, as determined by deconvolution analysis: Relationship to age, pubertal status, and body mass. *Journal of Clinical Endocrinology and Metabolism, 74,* 336–344.

Martin, C. A., Logan, T. K., Portis, C., Leukefled, C. G., Lynam, D., & Staton, M. (2001). The association of testosterone with nicotine use in young adult females. *Addictive Behaviors, 26,* 279–283.

Mazur, A., & Booth, A. (1998). Testosterone and dominance in men. *Behavioral and Brain Sciences, 21,* 353–397.

Moffitt, T. E., Caspi, A., Belsky, J., & Silva, P. A. (1992). Childhood experience and onset of menarche: A test of a sociobiological model. *Child Development, 63,* 47–58.

Nolen-Hoeksema, S., & Girgus, J. S. (1994). The emergence of gender differences in depression during adolescence. *Psychological Bulletin, 115,* 424–443.

Nottelmann, E. D., Inoff-Germain, G., Susman, E. J., & Chrousos, G. P. (1990). Hormones and behavior at puberty. In J. Bancroft & J. M. Reinisch (Eds.), *Adolescence and puberty* (pp. 88–123). New York: Oxford University Press.

Nottelmann, E. D., Susman, E. J., Inoff-Germain, G. E., Cutler, G. B., Jr., Loriaux, D. L., & Chrousos, G. P. (1987). Developmental processes in American early adolescence: Relations between adolescent adjustment problems and chronologic age, pubertal stage and puberty-related serum hormone levels. *Journal of Pediatrics, 110,* 473–480.

Obeidallah, D. A., Brennan, R. T., Brooks-Gunn, J., Kindlon, D., & Earls, F. (2000). Socioeconomic status, race, and girls' pubertal maturation: Results from the Project on Human Development in Chicago Neighborhoods. *Journal of Research on Adolescence, 10,* 443–464.

Olweus, D., Mattsson, A., Schalling, D., & Low, H. (1988). Circulating testosterone levels and aggression in adolescent males: A causal analysis. *Psychosomatic Medicine, 50,* 261–272.

Ong, K. K., Ahmed, M. L., & Dunger, D. B. (1999). The role of leptin in human growth and puberty. *Acta Paediatr Supplement, 88,* 95–98.

Orr, D. P., & Ingersoll, G. M. (1995). The contribution of level of cognitive complexity and pubertal timing to behavioral risk in young adolescents. *Pediatrics, 95,* 528–533.

Parker, S. T. (2000). Comparative developmental evolutionary biology, anthropology, and psychology. In S. T. Parker, J. Langer, & L. M. McKinney (Eds.), *Biology, brain, and behavior* (pp. 1–24). Sante Fe, NM: Sar Press.

Petersen, A. C., & Crockett, L. (1985). Pubertal timing and grade effects on adjustment. *Journal of Youth and Adolescence, 14,* 191–206.

Petersen, A. C., & Taylor, B. (1980). The biological approach to adolescence: Biological change and psychosocial adaptation. In J. Adelson (Ed.), *Handbook of adolescent psychology* (pp. 117–155). New York: Wiley.

Richters, J. E., & Weintraub, S. (1990). Beyond diathesis: Toward an understanding of high-risk environments. In J. E. Rolf, A. S. Masten, D. Cicchetti, K. H. Nuechterlein, & S. Weintraub (Eds.), *Risk and protective factors in the development of psychopathology* (pp. 67–96). New York: Cambridge University Press.

Roemmich, J. N., Clark , P. A., Berr, S. S., Mai, V., Mantzoros, C. S., Flier, J. S., Weltman, A., & Rogol, A. D. (1998). Gender differences in leptin levels during puberty are related to the subcutaneous fat depot and sex steroids. *American Journal of Physiology, 275,* E543–551.

Roemmich, J. N., Clark, P. A., Mai, V., Berr, S. S., Weltman, A., Velduis, J. D., & Rogol, A. D. (1998). Alterations in growth and body composition during puberty: III. Influence of maturation, gender, body composition, body fat distribution, aerobic fitness and total energy expenditure on nocturnal growth hormone release during puberty. *Journal of Clinical Endocrinology and Metabolism, 83,* 1440–1447.

Roemmich, J. N., & Rogol, A. D. (1999). Role of leptin during childhood growth and development. *Endocrinology and Metabolism Clinics of North America, 28,* 749–764.

Rogol, A. D., Clark, P. A., & Roemmich, J. N. (2000). Growth and pubertal development in children and adolescents: Effects of diet and physical activity. *American Journal of Clinical Nutrition, 72,* 521S–528S.

Ruiz, A., Blanco, R., Santander, J., & Miranda, E. (2000). Relationship between sex differences in onset of schizophrenia and puberty. *Journal of Psychiatric Research, 34*(4–5), 349–353.

Sagrestano, L. M., McCormick, S. H., Paikoff, R. L., & Holmbeck, G. N. (1999). Pubertal development and parent-child conflict in low-income, urban, African American adolescents. *Journal of Research on Adolescence, 9,* 85–107.

Savin-Williams, R. C., & Small, S. A. (1986). The timing of puberty and its relationship to adolescent and parent perceptions of family interactions. *Developmental Psychology, 22,* 342–347.

Schaal, B., Tremblay, R., Soussignan, B., & Susman, E. J. (1996). Male pubertal testosterone linked to high social dominance but low physical aggression: A 7 year longitudinal study. *Journal of the American Academy of Child Psychiatry, 35,* 1322–1330.

Schraufnagel, C. D., Brumback, R. A., Harper, C. R., & Weinberg, W. A. (2001). Affective illness in children and adolescents: Patterns of presentation in relation to pubertal maturation and family history. *Journal of Child Neurology, 16*(8), 553–561.

Schwab, J., Susman, E. J., Finkelstein, J. W., Chinchilli, V. M., Kunselman, S. J., D'Arcangelo, R. M., Demers, L. M., Lookingbill, G., & Kulin, H. E. (2001). The role of sex hormone replacement therapy on self-perceived competence in adolescents with delayed puberty. *Child Development, 72,* 1439–1450.

Siegel, J. M., Yancey, A. K., Aneshensel, C. S., & Schuler, R. (1999). Body image, perceived pubertal timing and adolescent mental health. *Journal of Adolescent Health, 25,* 155–165.

Silbereisen, R. K., Petersen, A. C., Albrecht, H. T., & Kracke, B. (1989). Maturational timing and the development of problem behavior: Longitudinal studies in adolescence. *Journal of Early Adolescence, 9,* 247–268.

Simmons, R. G., & Blyth, D. (1987). *Pubertal maturation in female development.* New York: De Gruyter.

Slemenda, C. W., Reister, T. K., Hui, S. L., Miller, J. Z., Christian, J. C., & Johnston, C. C. (1994). Influence on skeletal mineralization in children and adolescents: Evidence for varying effects of sexual maturation and physical activity. *Journal of Pediatrics, 125,* 201–207.

Stattin, H., & Magnusson, D. (1990). *Pubertal maturation in female development.* Hillsdale, NJ: Erlbaum.

Steinberg, L. D., & Hill, J. P. (1978). Patterns of family interaction as a function of age, the onset of puberty, and formal thinking. *Developmental Psychology, 14,* 683–684.

Surbey, M. K. (1990). Family composition, stress, and the timing of human menarche. In T. E. Ziegler & F. B. Bercovitch (Eds.), *Socioendocrinology of primate reproduction* (pp. 11–32). New York: Wiley-Liss.

Susman, E. J. (1997). Modeling developmental complexity in adolescence: Capturing the future of biology and behavior in context. *Journal of Research in Adolescence, 7,* 283–306.

Susman, E. J. (1998). Biobehavioural development: An integrative perspective. *International Journal of Behavioral Development, 22,* 671–679.

Susman, E. J., Dorn, L. D., & Chrousos, G. P. (1991). Negative affect and hormone levels in young adolescents: Concurrent and predictive perspectives. *Journal of Youth and Adolescence, 20,* 167–190.

Susman, E. J., Dorn, L. D., Inoff-Germain, G., Nottelmann, E. D., & Chrousos, G. P. (1997). Cortisol reactivity, distress behavior, behavior problems, and emotionality in young adolescents: A longitudinal perspective. *Journal of Research on Adolescence, 7,* 81–105.

Susman, E. J., Dorn, L. D., & Schiefelbein, V. L. (2003). Puberty, sexuality, and health. In R. M. Lerner, M. A. Easterbrooks, & J. Mistry (Eds.), *The comprehensive handbook of psychology* (Vol. 6, pp. 295–324). New York: Wiley.

Susman, E. J., Finkelstein, J. W., Chinchilli, V. M., Schwab, J., Liben, L. S., D'Arcangelo, M. R., Meinke, M. S., Demers, L. M., Lookingbill, G., & Kulin, H. E. (1998). The effect of sex hormone replacement therapy on behavior problems and moods in adolescents with delayed puberty. *Journal of Pediatrics, 33,* 521-525.

Susman, E. J., Inoff-Germain, G., Nottelmann, E. D., Cutler, G. B., Loriaux, D. L., & Chrousos, G. P. (1987). Hormones, emotional dispositions, and aggressive attributes in early adolescents. *Child Development, 58,* 1114–1134.

Swedo, S. E., Pleeter, J. D., Richter, D. M., Hoffman, C. L., Allen, A. J., Hamburger, S. D., & Turner, E. H. (1995). Rate of seasonal affective disorder in children and adolescents. *American Journal of Psychiatry, 152,* 1016–1019.

Tanner, J. M. (1962). *Growth at adolescence.* Springfield, IL: Thomas.

Tanner, J. M. (1965). The relationship of puberty to other maturity indicators and body composition in man. *Symposia of the Society for the Study of Human Biology, 6,* 211.

Tanner, J. M. (1989). *Fetus into man: Physical growth from conception to maturity.* Cambridge: Harvard University Press.

Tremblay, R. E., Schaal, B., Boulerice, B., Arseneault, L., Soussignan, R. G., Paquette, D., & Laurent, D. (1998). Testosterone, physical aggression, dominance, and physical development in early adolescence. *International Journal of Behavioral Development, 22,* 753–777.

Udry, J. R., Billy, J. O. G., & Morris, N. M. (1986). Biosocial foundation for adolescent female sexuality. *Demography, 23,* 217–227.

Udry, R. J., Billy, J. O. G., Morris, N. M., Groff, T. R., & Raj, M. H. (1985). Serum androgenic hormones motivate sexual behavior in adolescent boys. *Fertility and Sterility, 43,* 90–94.

Udry, R. J., & Talbert, L. M. (1988). Sex hormone effects on personality at puberty. *Journal Personality and Social Psychology, 54,* 291–295.

van Goozen, S. H. M., Matthys, W., Cohen-Kettenis, P. T., Thijssen, J. H. H., & van Engeland, H. (1998). Adrenal androgens and aggression in conduct disorder prepubertal boys and normal controls. *Biological Psychiatry, 43,* 156–158.

van Lenthe, F. J., van Mechelen, W., Kemper, H. C., & Twisk, J. W. (1998). Assessment of a central pattern of body fat with blood pressure and lipoproteins from adolescence into adulthood. *American Journal of Epidemiology, 147,* 686–693.

Veldhuis, J. D., Roemmich, J. N., & Rogol, A. D. (2000). Gender and sexual maturation-dependent contrasts in the neuroregulation of growth hormone secretion in prepubertal and late adolescent males and females. *Journal of Clinical Endocrinology and Metabolism, 85,* 2385–2394.

Warren, M. P., & Brooks-Gunn, J. J. (1989). Mood and behavior at adolescence: Evidence for hormonal factors. *Clinical Endocrinology & Metabolism, 69,* 77–83.

Weber, A., Clark, A. J. L., Perry, L. A., Honour, J. W., & Savage, M. O. (1997). Diminished adrenal androgen secretion in familial glucocorticoid deficiency implicates a significant role for ACTH in the induction of Adrenarche. *Clinical Endocrinology, 46,* 431–437.

Webster's New Universal Unabridged Dictionary (2nd ed.). (1979). New York: Simon and Schuster.

Wichstrøm, L. (2001). The impact of pubertal timing on adolescents' alcohol use. *Journal of Research on Adolescence,* 131–150.

Wierson, M., Long, P. J., & Forehand, R. L. (1993). Toward a new understanding of early menarche: The role of environmental stress in pubertal timing. *Adolescence, 28,* 913–924.

Wiesner, M., & Ittel, A. (2002). Relations of pubertal timing and depressive symptoms to substance use in early adolescence. *Journal of Early Adolescence, 22*(1), 5–23.

Williams, J. M., & Currie, C. (2000). Self-esteem and physical development in early adolescence: Pubertal timing and body image. *Journal of Early Adolescence, 20,* 129–149.

Williams, J. M., & Dunlop, L. C. (1999). Pubertal timing and self-reported delinquency among male adolescents. *Journal of Adolescence, 22,* 157–171.

Wilson, D. M., Killen, J. D., & Hayward, C. (1994). Timing and rate of sexual maturation and the onset of cigarette and alcohol use among teenage girls. *Archives of Pediatric Adolescent Medicine, 148,* 789–795.

Zacharias, L., Wurtman, R. J., & Shatzoff, M. (1970). Sexual maturation in contemporary American girls. *American Journal of Obstetrics Gynecology, 108,* 833–846.

Zachmann, M., Prader, A., Sobel, E. H., Crigler, J. F., Jr., Ritzen, E. M., Atares, M., & Ferrandez, A. (1986). Pubertal growth in patients with androgen insensitivity: Indirect evidence for the importance of estrogens in pubertal growth of girls. *Journal of Pediatrics, 108,* 694.

Chapter 3

COGNITIVE AND BRAIN DEVELOPMENT

Daniel P. Keating

THE ADOLESCENT MIND: BUILDING AN INTEGRATED MODEL

The 1958 publication in North America of Inhelder and Piaget's classic work, *The Growth of Logical Thinking from Childhood to Adolescence* (following its 1955 publication in France as "De la logique de l'enfant à la logique de l'adolescent: Essai sur la construction des structures opératoires formelles") is widely recognized as having launched the systematic study of adolescent cognitive development. The introduction to an English-language audience of a comprehensive model for understanding the cognitive transition from childhood to adolescence inspired a generation of researchers to undertake intensive investigations. The echoes reverberate still, even though direct assessment of Piaget's theoretical claims regarding formal operations has become less frequent (Bond, 1998; Keating, 1990a; Moshman, 1998).

Some appreciation of the impact can be gleaned from a simple count of publications on the topic before and after this watershed event. Using a comprehensive search engine (PsychInfo, Cambridge Scientific Abstracts) and crossing the terms *adolescent* or *adolescence* with *cognition, cognitive development,* or *thinking,* fewer than a dozen empirical articles from 1872 (the earliest date for indexing) to 1960 were identified. In succeeding decades, an exponential growth pattern in such publications is apparent, from the low hundreds in the 1960s up to the low thousands in the 1990s. In contrast, this new emphasis virtually displaced publications on psychometric research specific to adolescence, a trend astutely noted at its cusp by Ausubel and Ausubel (1966). Crossing *adolescent* or *adolescence* with *intelligence* or *mental ability* yielded over 1,000 titles in the earliest period, but fewer than 100 in the 1990s.

The shift from a psychometric focus on intelligence and mental ability toward underlying cognitive structure and process reflected larger trends in psychology generally and cognitive science in particular from the early 1960s onward. In addition to the primary goal of rescuing cognitive activity as a legitimate area of inquiry from the behaviorist hegemony of the earlier period, a major scientific goal of the cognitive revolution (Gardner, 1985; Johnson & Erneling, 1997; Pribram, 1986) has been to understand the underpinnings of complex cognitive performance in the most elementary terms possible.

The study of cognitive development in adolescence fit comfortably within this larger trend. The search for the essential elements of cognitive activity in adolescents yielded several prime candidates, each of which spawned a substantial line of research. There were several commonalities among these models. Each sought to identify the driver of adolescent cognitive activity, producing what can be viewed as *single-device accounts* (Keating, 2001a). In so doing, each also sought to answer the perennial question, "What develops?" (Siegler, 1978). Each also sought to demonstrate that there were specifically adolescent features of cognitive development.

Three major theoretical approaches to the core of adolescent cognitive development during this initial efflorescence can be identified: cognition as reasoning, cognition as processing, and cognition as expertise. These major accounts were not unrelated and indeed arose sequentially in response to each other (Keating, 1980, 1990a). In computational terms, one can view these as focusing, respectively, on developments in the design of the operating system, on additions to the speed and/or capacity of the system, or on changes in the size or structure of the database that the system has available.

A major theme of this review is that claims for *independent* developments in these various aspects of adolescent cognition have not been supported by the weight of evidence, even though important developments are clearly evident in each aspect of the overall cognitive system. For example, Demetriou, Christou, Spanoudis, and Platsidou (2002), using individual growth curve modeling from late childhood to adolescence, found that more advanced levels of reasoning arise in part from bottom-up changes in processing efficiency and working memory, but they also found that these lower order elements are reciprocally affected from the top down. This interdependence has complicated the search for the core of what develops—that is, identifying the fundamental driver of adolescent cognitive development independent of other potentially confounding cognitive shifts.

A Central Paradox

The inability to identify a single dominant source that explains what develops in adolescent cognition has contributed to a central paradox. Despite the absolute growth in the number of studies dealing with adolescent cognitive development just noted, and despite the centrality of the questions that animated the major approaches, there is a paradoxical (but widespread) view that there has been relatively little progress on these central themes: "The study of cognitive development in adolescence has been moribund for some time now, replaced by studies of adolescent decision making and judgment" (Steinberg & Morris, 2001, p. 101). Compounding the paradox is an equally widespread view that there are fundamental shifts in adolescent cognition and that these changes are readily observable in important, broadly defined aspects of adolescent thinking (Keating, 1990a; Moshman, 1998). The power of this paradox is further reinforced by the emerging understanding of the dramatic nature and long reach of pubertal events (Angold, Costello, Erkanli, & Worthman, 1999; Angold, Costello, & Worthman, 1998; Susman & Rogol, this volume), which sustains the belief that there should be large and readily identifiable shifts in both cognitive and brain development.

Can this paradox be resolved? To begin to answer this difficult challenge, we need to attend to the subsequent trajectories of research that originated in the different theoretical perspectives noted earlier (Keating, 2001a). This is of more than historical interest. As these approaches have pursued their largely separate paths, they have encountered highly similar dilemmas. Indeed, they are similar not only by analogy, but also as homology. Each has confronted, I argue, the core problem of all single-device accounts. The greater the refinement of parameters to measure the theoretically targeted developmental mechanism, the less these parameters are able to account for broad changes that the theories were designed to explain (Keating, 1996b; Keating, List, & Merriman, 1985).

In short, researchers have long sought to explain the readily apparent and broad changes in adolescent thinking by identifying the underlying mechanism of "what develops" (Siegler, 1978). In pursuing this agenda, it is logical to identify and measure parameters of the targeted mechanism as precisely as possible: pure logic, pure processing efficiency, pure capacity, and so on. As the evidence reviewed in this chapter demonstrates, this research agenda has yielded much new knowledge about adolescent cognition but has encountered significant problems in answering the original question.

To the extent that the strategy has succeeded in purifying the parameters of specific underlying mechanisms, it has been at the cost of explaining variance in the broader cognitive shifts. Moreover, in studies where multiple mechanisms have been examined, especially in longitudinal designs (e.g., Demetriou et al., 2002), there is strong evidence for interdependence among them. It seems increasingly unlikely that any single-device explanation of the major shifts in adolescent cognition will suffice. Confronting these recurring limitations, lines of research have bifurcated and branched, yielding a burgeoning complexity of questions and paradigms that focus on adolescent cognition.

As Steinberg and Morris (2001) accurately noted, this has redirected much of the research attention away from the original questions about the core of adolescent cognitive development toward a search for answers to specific practical questions. These have been more typically addressed by an applied cognitive science with a more context-specific focus on pathways to expertise, on the role of teaching and learning in the acquisition of expertise, and on the development of judgment and decision making (e.g., Keating, 1990b; Klaczynski, Byrnes, & Jacobs, 2001; Kokis, Macpherson, Toplak, West, & Stanovich, 2002; Kuhn, Garcia-Mila, Zohar, & Andersen, 1995; Kuhn & Pearsall, 2000; Kwon & Lawson, 2000; Kwon, Lawson, Chung, & Kim, 2000; Lawson et al., 2000). In pursuing these more applied questions, the dilemmas of interdependence and insufficiency of single-device accounts reemerge for the same reasons and in the same way.

More provocatively, this paradox—of major shifts that are not explained by any single developmental mechanism—can be viewed as a strong indication that a more integrative theoretical account is needed. If one adopts this position, as this review does, we then need to ask what shape such an integrative account might take, what evidence may be available to support such an account, and what would constitute an effective research agenda to probe an integrated model. The prospects for an integrative account have been substantially enhanced by recent major advances in the neurosciences (e.g., Casey, Giedd, & Thomas, 2000; Giedd et al., 1999; Johnson, 2001; Luna et al., 2001; Nelson, 1999; Paus et al., 1999; Sowell, Delis, Stiles, & Jernigan, 2001; Sowell, Trauner, Gamst, & Jernigan, 2002; Steingard et al., 2002), in comparative neuroanatomy across closely related primate species that illuminate core issues of human cognitive evolution (Donald, 2001; Rilling & Insel, 1999), in the increasing sophistication of analyses of longitudinal data and individual growth curves (Demetriou et al., 2002; McArdle, Ferrer-

Caja, Hamagami, & Woodcock, 2002), and in a deepened understanding of the critical role of culture and context in the shaping of cognitive and brain development (Donald, 2001; Francis, Diorio, Plotsky, & Meaney, 2002).

An Emergent Resolution

Drawing on these various sources, the nature of an integrated account has begun to emerge. It is sketched in this introductory section and elaborated in subsequent sections. What lies at the core of adolescent cognitive development is not likely to be any single device that drives it. Rather, it is the attainment of a more fully conscious, self-directed, and self-regulating mind that characterizes the adolescent transition. This is achieved principally through the assembly of an advanced executive suite of capabilities (Donald, 2001), rather than through specific advancement in any one of the constituent elements. This represents a major shift in prevailing views of cognition, going beyond the search for underlying elements (or hidden "demons"; Dennett, 1991) that are formed and operate largely outside awareness. Such coordination of cognitive elements resonates with contemporary work on metacognitive and metastrategic development. In describing the core difference between young and mature scientists, for example, Kuhn and Pearsall (2000) noted that both seek to coordinate theory and evidence, but that in the latter, "the coordination of theory and evidence is carried out under a high degree of conscious control" (p. 115).

Recent advances in developmental neuroscience, propelled by dramatic advances in imaging technologies, point toward a similar resolution. A broad outline of the most significant and cognitively relevant developments in the adolescent brain has begun to coalesce very recently (Casey et al., 2000; Johnson, 2001). Much of the underlying action is focused on specific developments in the prefrontal cortex, but with an equally significant role for rapidly expanding linkages to the whole brain (Donald, 2001; Luna et al., 2001; Newman & Grace, 1999). This complex process of assembly is supported by increasingly rapid connectivity (through continued myelination of nerve fibers), particularly in communication among different brain regions, and by significant and localized synaptic pruning, especially in frontal areas that are crucial to executive functioning (Giedd et al., 1999; Sowell et al., 2001, 2002; Steingard et al., 2002).

It is noteworthy that the most marked differences between adult humans and nonhuman primates (Rilling & Insell, 1999) occur precisely in those features of brain development that emerge most strikingly during adolescence: differentially greater increases in neocortical volume (beyond the expected increase owing to larger brain volume overall); differentially greater gyrification of the prefrontal cortex, indicating a more convoluted design that affords both more capacity for central coordination and more rapid communication; and a greater relative increase in cerebral white matter relative to neocortical gray matter, "suggesting that axonal connections between neocortical neurons may increase faster than the number of neurons as brain size increases" (p. 222). The prefrontal cortex is thus among the latest brain systems to develop, both phylogenetically and ontogenetically, especially the dorsolateral prefrontal cortex (Fuster, 2000). Its importance for adolescent cognitive development can be inferred from this convergence but is more directly evident from its integrative functions.

The prefrontal lobes have long been seen as central to the coordination of cognitive activity (Case, 1992; Stuss, 1992), whose function is to sustain "many high-level metacognitive operations, such as self-evaluation, long-term planning, prioritizing values, maintaining fluency, and the production of appropriate social behavior" (Donald, 2001, p. 198). The reach and complexity of the prefrontal cortex has been further emphasized in recent work identifying important details of its structure and function (Barbas & Hilgetag, 2002; Fuster, 2000; Fuster, Van Hoesen, Morecraft, & Semendeferi, 2000; Watanabe, 2002). In particular, the temporal integration of retrospective memory and preparatory set in the dorsolateral prefrontal cortex (Fuster, 2000) creates the conditions for a broader, more fully conscious control of cognition and behavior. In other words, the narrow window of active awareness that is the focus of much of experimental cognitive science, which seems to undermine assertions of a broader consciousness with significant agency in decision making and planning, captures too little of the important cognitive action (Donald, 2001). In addition, the close connection and communication among regions of the prefrontal cortex that are more cognitive with those that have important linkages with emotional processing, especially the orbitofrontal cortex (Barbas & Hilgetag, 2002), support the view of the prefrontal cortex as a more general synthesizer of experience and governor of action. Thus the role of the prefrontal cortex as not only an integrator of cognitive functions, but also a governing regulator of emotion, attention, and behavior, takes on special importance during adolescence in three ways.

First, patterns of individual differences in how cognition, emotion, and behavior become integrated during adolescence may well have a long reach with respect to the development of psychopathology (Steinberg et al., in press) and to normative habits of mind (Keating, 1996b, 1996c) that influence trajectories of competence and coping. Second, the pubertal influences on many hormonal and neuroendocrine systems are dramatic (Angold et al., 1998, 1999; Susman & Rogol, this volume), entailing the cascading reorganization of body and brain systems. Third, recent evidence from animal models demonstrated the partial reversibility of damage acquired during early development, at both the behavioral and the physiological levels, as a function of enriched environments during puberty (Francis et al., 2002). In combination, this evidence points strongly toward both enduring (but not limitless) neural plasticity and the critical role of developmental experience in shaping future developmental trajectories in cognition and behavior (Nelson, 1999; Nelson, Bloom, Cameron, Amaral, Dahl, & Pine, 2002).

Recent research directions thus point toward the distinct possibility that adolescence may be a sensitive or critical developmental period, much like early development in its ability to shape future trajectories and in the biological embedding of developmental experiences as the principal method through which this occurs (Boyce & Keating, in press; Keating & Hertzman, 1999; Meaney, 2001). The major changes during adolescence just outlined form the essential substrate for adolescence to function as a critical developmental period: the interdependence and developmental coordination of numerous cognitive elements, and of cognition with emotion and behavior; the role of puberty in a fundamental restructuring of many body systems; the apparent concentration of changes in the adolescent brain in the prefrontal cortex (which serves as a governor of cognition and action) together with the enhanced interregional communication between the prefrontal cortex and other brain regions; and in the evidence for substantial synaptic pruning and for nontrivial physiological reversibility of behavioral and neuroendocrine patterns arising from early developmental experiences.

Brain, Culture, and the Centrality of Consciousness

The reemergence of consciousness and its development as a legitimate area of scientific inquiry (Chalmers, 1996; Dennett, 1996; Donald, 2001; Ferrari, Pinard, & Runions, 2001; Searle, 1997) has increased the probability that adolescence may be a critical developmental period for cognitive development and for the myriad ways that cognition plays a role in emotion and action. The late development of the prefrontal cortex in phylogeny and ontogeny, as well as its central integrative function, provides a crucial starting point for understanding the distinctive features of human cognition generally and adolescent cognition specifically.

As McGinn (1999) noted, "Consciousness is hard to miss but easy to avoid, theoretically speaking" (p. 44). The classic subject-object and mind-body problems in epistemology (and philosophy more generally) drove consciousness out of scientific scrutiny in two directions, either by explaining it away through reductionist accounts that allowed it to exist only as an epiphenomenon resting on the actions of more fundamental cognitive automata (Dennett, 1991), or, alternately, by awarding it a privileged position beyond objectifying scientific inquiry, to be understood by largely phenomenological methods. But as McGinn (1999) observed, consciousness just won't go away, posing again the question: "How does consciousness fit into the scientific world picture. . . ?" (p. 44).

Ferrari et al. (2001) argued that Piaget (for whom, they noted, the scientific study of consciousness never became unrespectable) proposed a solution that should be revisited. Specifically, the physiological "rules" that enable cognitive activity and the (psycho)logical "rules" that govern conscious awareness coevolved in a "sophisticated form of parallelism" (p. 195) that exhibits substantial isomorphism and leads toward an "integrative monism" (p. 195) that may never actually arrive.

A Piagetian anecdote about his encounter with Soviet psychologists (in a new translation by Ferrari et al., 2001, p. 199), while revealing heavy ideological baggage, emphasizes the convoluted epistemological and philosophical argumentation that the scientific study of consciousness confronts. In the anecdote, Piaget is cleared of the charge of being an idealist on the grounds that he grants primacy to the preexistence of objects before a knower, even though he maintains a strong stance that the origin of knowing lies in the first actions upon objects. What the Soviets were probing is the essential (but creative) tension at the heart of the Piagetian project (Keating, 1990d, pp. 312–315), between the specification of closed structures with the definable end point of formal reasoning (an idealist position despite the Soviet acquittal), and the identification of an open-system, constructivist process that codevelops iteratively through action on the world (sufficiently objectivist to satisfy his interlocutors on that occasion). As I have previously argued (Keating, 1990d), it is the former position, the closed structure with defined end points, that was initially more amenable to cognitive developmental investigation, and hence defined the limits of much of the research on adolescent cognition. The open systems view, more compatible with much intervening theoretical work, supports the identification of Piaget as a root theorist of the development of consciousness (Ferrari et al., 2001).

Relying more heavily on recent evidence in human evolution and neuroscience, and thus eschewing many of the ideological issues, Donald (2001) proposed a framework that is compatible with these Piagetian arguments that are based in the method of genetic epistemology. Donald's (2001) core argument is that the evolution of the human brain, especially as it branched from the broader primate lineage, was quintessentially social: "The key to understanding the human intellect is not so much the design of the individual brain as the synergy of many brains. We have evolved an adaptation for living in culture, and our exceptional powers as a species derive from the curious fact that we have broken out of one of the most critical limitations of traditional nervous systems—their loneliness, or solipsism" (p. xiii).

It is important to distinguish this notion of the fundamentally social nature of human mind from the line of research in organizational behavior launched by Janis's (1972) seminal work on *groupthink.* That theoretical construct has focused on the mechanisms by which ineffective or poor decision making can occur in the context of (usually small) group dynamics (Flippen, 1999; Jones & Roelofsma, 2000; Park, 2000; Turner & Pratkanis, 1998), such as failure of monitoring, premature concurrence, failure to consider unconventional options, or perceived risk of excluding oneself from the group through disagreement (Baumeister & Leary, 1995). The fundamentally social nature of cognition and consciousness may be a necessary condition for groupthink, but the multifaceted nature of social or collective mind cannot be accurately characterized as groupthink. It is interesting to note, however, that despite a substantial line of research on how peers may influence individual decision making during adolescence (Ormond, Luszcz, Mann, & Beswick, 1991; Payne, 2002; Steinberg & Silverberg, 1986), there is little research on groupthink among adolescents. This is somewhat surprising given the group context that often underlies immaturity of decisions (Cauffman & Steinberg, 1995; Dishion, Eddy, Haas, Li, & Spracklen, 1997) and the salience of the sense of belonging that is an important aspect of the adolescent self (Marshall, 2001). There is a real tension between the formative role of society in essential cognitive development and the need to develop an autonomously critical habit of mind (Keating, 1996c), and clearly this tension is a key dynamic in adolescent cognition.

Donald (2001) proposed three major transitions as levels of consciousness beyond the episodic awareness that we share with our nonhuman primate cousins. Each rests on continuing development and refinement of the "executive suite" that is concentrated in the prefrontal cortex (including its interregional connectivity): "(1) more precise and self-conscious control of action in mimesis; (2) richer and faster accumulation of cultural knowledge, in speech; and (3) much more powerful and reflective cultures, driven by symbolic technology" (p. 262). Note that each of these proceeds as a coevolution of brain and culture; indeed, the signal species characteristic of *Homo sapiens* can be thought of as cultural mind sharing that activates individual minds (whose brains have been designed, as it were, by evolution to participate in just such activity). In this light, there is an essential concordance on the centrality of interactive constructionism between Vygotsky's (1979) cognitive socialization and Piaget's (1965) "internal interactionism" (Ferrari et al., 2001, p. 198).

The implication of these convergences is that there exist potentially homologous qualitative transitions in the evolution of the human brain, the nature of primate group interaction (episodic, mimetic, mythic, and theoretic; Donald, 2001), and adolescent cognitive and brain development. The essence of the homology lies in the nature of human consciousness, including its phylogeny, ontogeny, and inseparability from culture and context. Fully attained human consciousness is thus potentiated by key developments in the brain that are late arrivals in evolutionary history and become fully available for assembly in individual ontogeny only during the adolescent transition. But this potential assembly becomes actual only in close interplay with the surrounding cultural and cognitive web, in which the individual adolescent experiences culture not passively as an external entity, but rather as an active force (Swidler, 1986) that can be used to both define and achieve goals, and serves simultaneously as a fundamental coconstructor of cognition and consciousness.

Understanding how adolescence may function as a critical developmental period will be a major challenge. The necessity of incorporating the multiple interactions of brain-biology, behavior-cognition, and culture-context implies a level of complexity that is daunting. This poses two risks to a productive research agenda that can advance our understanding. First, the complexity may be overwhelming, leading instead toward continued fragmentation and inattention to core questions—the central paradox described earlier. Second, the need for coherence may lead to an overly facile acceptance that the mere proposal of a global homology centered on the emergence of consciousness fully resolves the paradox. It does not, because consciousness emerges (phylogenetically, historically, and ontogenetically) not as one thing, but as the assembly of many things (Donald, 2001). Each of its many subsystems retains some degree of ongoing modular independence in the context of increasing systemic interdependence. Their coordination into a more centrally governed metasystem is unlikely to be smooth developmentally or uniform in execution. Indeed, the individual and developmental anomalies of assembly are readily apparent as performance or procedural intrusions that muddy the waters of what might otherwise be observed as a clear progression to fundamental logical competence (Overton, 1990).

To summarize, the initial stages of research on adolescent cognitive development focused logically and necessarily on isolating key cognitive components. The recent emergence (or reemergence) of consciousness as a legitimate and necessary focus of cognitive research (Donald, 2001) has been driven by a need to understand how those components get assembled into a complex, coordinated cognitive system. The accumulating evidence is particularly relevant to adolescent cognitive development, reflecting the broader movement in cognitive science as it comes to terms with cognitive, cognitive-affective, and developmental neuroscience. In this light, understanding adolescent cognitive development will have to play a central role in understanding human consciousness more generally, as research in a number of related fields points with increasing specificity to this period of development as the one in which the processes of assembly are at their peak.

Contemporary evidence also supports the view that adolescents are biologically susceptible to the embedding of experience in brain and body systems. Thus, a comprehensive research agenda will require a much more detailed understanding of the ways in which context organizes the salient experiences of adolescents (see chapters in Part

II of this volume, especially that by Larson & Wilson). If the adolescent mind is co-constructed by the potentiation of developing cognitive capacities through active engagement with culturally embedded knowledge and meaning systems, then the specific ways in which adolescents engage their cognitive universe become crucial. In contrast, identifying the most salient aspects of early development in order to understand how they may become biologically embedded in the infant and young child may be relatively easier than in the adolescent, with the increased complexity of the relevant contexts and the increased ability for individual choice in the selection of contexts.

The principal goal of this review is thus to examine closely (but not exhaustively, given the breadth of the extant literatures) the major research efforts on adolescent cognitive and brain development, to identify common themes and findings that cut across the disparate research agendas, and to situate those themes with respect to an emergent theoretical perspective that integrates them. To move this research agenda forward productively, emerging methodologies that support interdisciplinary cross-fertilization will be essential. Wilson (1998) argued for an innovative methodological approach that seeks *consilience* of evidence among biological, social, and human sciences. Although hard to achieve, the understanding of adolescent cognitive development requires such an integration, and the evidence reviewed in this chapter suggests that the prospects are promising.

Following this first section, in which the overall argument has been outlined, the balance of the review is organized as follows. In the second part, a more detailed consideration of the major lines of research on adolescent cognitive development is provided, and their theoretical and empirical implications for an integrated model are identified. In the third part, the prospects for grounding adolescent cognitive development in underlying biological and brain development are discussed further, with a particular focus on emerging evidence from the neurosciences that supports (or even requires) an integrated model. In the fourth and final part, the role of context in adolescent cognitive development is addressed in light of these newly emerging perspectives. In contrast to conventional approaches that sought to partial out or control for context in order to identify purely cognitive parameters, arguments for the role of enculturation as an active, integral, and endogenous feature of adolescent thinking are reviewed (Donald, 2001; Keating, 1996b, 1996c; Keating & Sasse, 1996).

ELEMENTS OF COGNITION AND THE EMERGENCE OF CONSCIOUSNESS

As noted earlier, systematic research on adolescent cognitive development started with operationalizing the claims put forward by Inhelder and Piaget (1958), using for the most part the tasks described in that work. The starting point for this line of research is, of course, Piaget's identification of the form of reasoning as the essential element in cognitive transitions. For adolescence, the key transition is from concrete to formal operations. Specifically, the shift from a class-based logic system to a formal propositional logic system was theorized as fundamental, although each system was reflective of an even more basic set of logical operations, the coordination of the relation between affirmation and negation (Keating, 1980; Moshman, 1998). These efforts produced robust findings on age differences in performance but generated less persuasive evidence that the transitions in logical form were the most fundamental level of adolescent cognitive development, a central issue elaborated later (Keating, 1980, 1990a, 1990d; Koslowski, 1996; Kuhn, Amsel, & O'Loughlin, 1988; Markovits & Barrouillet, 2002; Moshman, 1998).

The rising interest in human information processing approaches in the early 1970s generated interest in computational models that would explain changes in logic as changes in processing (e.g., Bryant & Trabasso, 1971; Trabasso, Isen, Dolecki, McLanahan, Riley, & Tucker, 1978). A competing account was also based in cognitive processing but sought to integrate this approach with Piaget's more centralized model. These neo-Piagetian models focused on improvements in capacity as the driver of cognitive development, either as expansion of available working memory (Pascual-Leone, 1978) or in the ability to manipulate increasing numbers of dimensions within working memory through the development of more sophisticated central conceptual structures (Case, 1991; Case & Okamoto, 1996).

A challenge to both the reasoning- and the processing-based accounts arose initially from the increasingly frequent observation that performance on both types of tasks was highly sensitive to both the content of the task performance and the context in which the cognitive performance was being assessed or (less often) observed (Chi, Glaser, & Rees, 1982; Chi, Hutchinson, & Robin, 1989; Koslowski, 1996; Kuhn et al., 1988). This posed a methodological challenge to the reasoning and processing accounts because their claims were rooted in the purity of the theoretical parameters. The intent was not that the paradigms designed to look for underlying patterns of reasoning and processing would be confounded by exogenous factors such as content or context.

Many aspects of this broad trend from logic to processing to expertise have been reviewed elsewhere (Keating, 1980, 1990a, 1990d; Moshman, 1998), and space does not permit a complete overview of all the relevant empirical literature. Each of the main theoretical accounts (reasoning, processing, expertise) has continued to generate substantial new findings bearing on the central theoretical issues. Within each of these topics, a more focused review is presented that updates the state of the question and illustrates key issues by more detailed consideration of representative investigations.

What emerged from the history of logic to processing to expertise is that single-device accounts that hoped to uncover the central pinnacle of adolescent cognitive functioning did not succeed. These can be read as a series of interlocking theoretical moves that attempted to deal with perceived limitations of preceding formulations. Two subsequent moves are reviewed, although neither of them undertook the broad questions that initially animated the field. The first of these is the move from the study of formal reasoning to the study of judgment and decision making, which was rooted in important developments in cognitive science more generally. Many of the issues are closely allied with the study of reasoning per se, and this research is examined just after the review of the reasoning literature. The second is the proliferation of studies of development or acquisition of specific domains of knowledge, skill, or expertise. Again, answers to broad theoretical questions are typically not the goal of these efforts, and they are derivative of the more general work on expertise. Accordingly, that work is considered within the section on cognition as expertise. Finally, it is appropriate to view the emergent integrated model that is described in this review as a distinctly different type of theoretical move, one that explicitly attempts to revisit the original broad questions with the intervening theoretical and empirical work in mind.

Cognition as Reasoning

An early and continuing line of experimental inquiry has probed the logical reasoning of children and adolescents within this framework, both supportively and critically (Bond, 1998; Foltz, Overton, & Ricco, 1995; Markovits & Barrouillet, 2002; Mueller, Sokol, & Overton, 1999). The essential cognitive shift has been characterized as a "developmental advancement" from inductive reasoning (moving from specific observations to a hypothesis, which is verified by further observation) to deductive reasoning (working from a hypothesis to generate logically necessary and testable inferences), and its hallmark is the "systemic availability of deductive competence" (Foltz et al., 1995, p. 183).

The identification of hypothetico-deductive reasoning as the signal feature of adolescent cognitive maturity has been criticized on a number of grounds, including the assertion of its universal epistemological primacy (Keating, 1990d; Markovits & Barrouillet, 2002), the problem of transferability from experimentally decontextualized performance to real-world contexts and content (Keating, 1990a; Klahr, Fay, & Dunbar, 1993; Kuhn et al., 1988), and the insufficiency of empirical confirmation of the Inhelder and Piaget (1958) formulations (Keating, 1980, 1990a).

This last point has been rebutted from a Piagetian perspective, notably by Gray (1990) and by Bond and his colleagues (Bond, 1995a, 1995b, 1998; Bond & Bunting, 1995; Bond & Jackson, 1991; Noelting, Rousseau, Coude, Bond, & Brunel, 2000). This line of rebuttal focuses on the appropriateness of specific empirical probes of the theoretical claims about formal operations. Gray (1990) asked why the manifestations of formal operations in observed performance have been so rare and proposed a distinction between exogenous knowledge and endogenous construction of knowledge. In the former category are manipulations of formal reasoning tasks that make them less abstract and typically show enhanced performance by both adolescents and adults (although many adults still do not show formal reasoning on adapted tasks; Kuhn et al., 1988). Gray argued that these do not constitute true tests of Piaget's claims, in that they may be solved by appeal to knowledge. True tests thus seem to require the observation of endogenous knowledge construction. Gray argued that these are in fact rare because there are few external environments that actually require formal operations. The implication seems to be that formal operations are rarely observed because they are in fact rare in human cognitive activity. In this view, formal operational reasoning is a potential development rather than a normative adolescent transition, and manipulations of content and context that purport to show its attainment by a higher percentage of adults and by younger subjects are diluted tests of the theory of formal operations. This rigorous purification of the measure of formal operations seems to exclude it as a major driver of adolescent cognitive development, in contrast with Inhelder and Piaget's (1958) claims.

It does raise the question of what would constitute sufficient evidence in support of those claims. Two continuing lines of research on formal reasoning have carried the supportive argument forward. The first line of work compares scales of task difficulty theoretically derived from the Piagetian model with empirically obtained scales of performance using measurement models. The second evaluates age differences in judgments of logical determinacy, that is, whether logical arguments alone are sufficient to answer specific problems. A close examination of a substantive study of each type illustrates the nature of this research. Following this examination, the issue of what constitutes an adequate test of the theoretical claims is revisited.

Bond (1998) argued that due to some "commonly held misconceptions about formal operational thought . . . some key criticisms . . . do not meet the criteria of being sufficiently attentive to the issues raised by Inhelder and Piaget" (p. 221). Whereas Keating (1980) focused on the ways in which the claims had been operationalized by a range of researchers, Bond (1998) focused on specific empirical instantiations that are more tightly linked to the theory. The work by Bond and colleagues employed measurement scaling (Rasch-like scaling analyses) to assess empirically their compatibility with empirical data. Close correspondence between the theory-driven (unidimensional) scales and the empirically derived scaling is regarded as confirmation of the theory (Bond, 1998; Mueller, Sokol, & Overton, 1999).

In the Mueller et al. (1999) study, children at 7, 9, 11, and 13 years of age were presented with a series of logical problems that were arrayed in the following theoretical sequence from class reasoning to propositional reasoning: class inclusion ("Are there more apples or more bananas?" "Are there more apples or more fruit?" "Are there more apples or more fruit in the whole world?"); vicariant inclusion ("Are there more balls that are red or more balls that are not green?"); double complementation ("Are there more balls that are not yellow or more balls that are not blue?"); the law of duality ("In the whole world, are there more things that are not eagles or more things that are not birds?"); logical implication (evaluating the accuracy of reality-based syllogistic arguments of all four forms: modus ponens, denial of antecedent, affirmation of consequent, modus tollens); and propositional reasoning (estimating the truth value of competing statements from multiple sources, requiring the coordination of possibilities).

Mueller et al. (1999) reported substantial confirmation of the theoretical ordering of scale difficulty for both the class reasoning and the prepositional reasoning items. On the class reasoning tasks, only one task is out of sequence in the empirically derived (Rasch) scale, and only one subject does not fit the predicted sequence (about 35% of subjects are excluded from this analysis owing to floor or ceiling effects). On the other hand, the issue of how close a correspondence is required in order to claim verification of the theoretical sequence does arise. Excluding the preoperational items that are uniformly passed (the subclass, counting task), there are five levels of significant differences within the predicted concrete operations level (across seven items; Mueller et al., 1999, Table 1, p. 88), and two of the five designated formal operations tasks are not significantly different from the two most difficult concrete operations tasks. The ordering of the propositional reasoning tasks showed no out-of-sequence items, although there are several significant differences among items that are at the same predicted level of difficulty (Table 4, p. 93). The conjoint Rasch scaling of all items (Table 7, p. 97) yielded a similar pattern of predicted sequence (across a broader span of overall difficulty), along with a number of significant differences among items at a similar level. The authors argued that this represents a strong degree of concordance between the predicted and observed scaling of item difficulty. They were less persuaded that even correct task solutions were fully indicative of the presence of formal operational thinking, based on the reasoning that the participants were asked to provide. Specifically, they were often unable to articulate the logical implications on the basis of pure possibilities, referring instead to their perceptions of truth values based in empirical reality.

This detailed study of transitions in reasoning from childhood to adolescence raises a number of classically problematic issues. Mueller et al. (1999) tested two central claims of the theory of formal operations. The first is that the sequence of task difficulty derived from the theory would be captured in a scaling of actual performance. Several criteria are implied by this claim. Do the predicted and observed sequences correspond? Mueller et al. (1999) answered yes, based on the few occurrences of out-of-sequence items. As noted, however, there are significant differences among tasks at the same predicted level. How close a correspondence is theoretically acceptable is not defined and thus somewhat arbitrary, and lies in the eye of the beholder.

Confirming the empirical match to a theory-driven scale is, however, only one test of the theory. Another test is a specificity criterion: Could other theories generate the same task order, such as those arising from processing demands, linguistic complexity, or alternative models of reasoning (Keating, 1996a; Markovits & Barrouillet, 2002)? Another way of stating this point is to ask, How does one get to the specific scaling prediction? If the theoretical scaling is tested against data arising from large age ranges and large task difficulty differences in general, the more likely it is that the empirical scaling from measurement models will match a range of possible theories. On their face, the more difficult items in Mueller et al. (1999) appear more difficult in ways other than their logical demands, most notably in their increasing linguistic complexity and their demands on working memory.

A more persuasive test than correspondence of an obtained scale with a predicted one would be a contrasting test of different orderings based on competing theoretical accounts. Should it prove impossible to generate theoretically differentiated orderings between, say, logical demands and working memory demands, it would be problematic to ascribe an obtained empirical ordering to a unique source. In addition to the correspondence and the specificity criteria, it is appropriate to note that these are age-difference findings rather than developmental findings. We do not know on this (or other similar) evidence whether these patterns emerge in the specified sequence for individuals across the course of development.

The second central claim evaluated by Mueller et al. (1999) was whether the justifications of even successful performance indicated the presence of formal operational thinking. Their conclusions echoed Gray's (1990) observations: "The finding that even children who are capable of generating all possible truth value assignments may still fail to work out their implications points to the critical role that the differentiation and hierarchical integration of the levels of possibility and reality plays in achieving formal operational thought" (p. 101). In other words, even those who successfully solved the task were unable to focus fully on "pure possibilities" (p. 101) and to resist the intrusion of reality. In this formulation, it is easy to detect the resurgence of epistemological privilege favoring the closed-structure model of formal logical reasoning (Keating, 1990d). A more generous interpretation of these adolescents' performance, in line with the integrative model described earlier, is that they are drawing on multiple sources of world knowledge. As they find themselves on increasingly unfamiliar terrain, they tread cautiously as they leave reality behind.

Using the ability to reason in the realm of pure possibilities or of counterfactual logic (Keating, 1990a) as a litmus test of formal operational thinking appears to have the consequence of relegating it to the realm of expert skill, rather than regarding it as the normative acquisition that seems apparent in the original Inhelder and Piaget (1958) formulation. Empirically, such purification of the parameter of formal operational thinking has contributed to the impression of its rarity (consistent with Gray, 1990). At a minimum, the role of pure formal reasoning as a key driver of adolescent cognitive development cannot be sustained from this perspective.

At the same time, it is clear that adolescents are generally more likely to deploy deductive reasoning than are children. Morris and Sloutsky (2001) tested this in a paradigm that required children and adolescents to judge whether a particular claim needed to be tested in the real world or could be solved using logic alone (logically indeterminate versus logically determinate, respectively). They reported that early adolescents (11- and 12-year-olds) were significantly less likely than were children (8- and 9-year-olds) to seek empirical confirmation of predictions that could be solved with logic alone ("logically determinate" problems; Morris & Sloutsky, 2001, Table 2, p. 916). On the other hand, the early adolescents were also less likely to recognize that empirical verification was necessary on logically indeterminate problems, where it is required. This pattern is most striking for young children (4- and 5-year-olds), among whom there is zero variance—empirical verification is always seen as necessary, regardless of the logical frame. One way to interpret this pattern is that early adolescents are much more likely to recognize logical necessity but also tend to overgeneralize this strategy when it is relatively new to them. About 25% of the time, they failed to request empirical verification when it was in fact necessary (compared with only 11% of the children, and none of the youngest children). This may be attributable to the anomalous developmental pattern for "can't tell" responses that has been reported with some regularity (cf. Keating, 1990a), which appears to be similarly overgeneralized during the early phase of acquisition. It also reflects the relatively long acquisition period for the ability to coordinate theory and evidence fully (Koslowski, 1996; Kuhn & Pearsall, 2000).

Morris and Sloutsky (2001) also analyzed intraindividual patterns with respect to accuracy (defined as 75% correct) on three criteria: distinguishing logically determinate from indeterminate problems; correctly evaluating evidence in logically determinate problems; and correctly evaluating evidence in indeterminate problems. The three criteria were combined to yield four patterns of individual responding. The dominant pattern for early adolescents was to meet all three criteria (about 63% of 11- and 12-year-olds), and for younger children to meet none of them (less than 10% showing any pattern other than erroneous or random). For 8- and 9-year-olds, the dominant pattern (50%) was to fail to make the distinction that evidence is required for logically indeterminate problems but not for logically determinate problems, but also to evaluate incorrectly the outcomes of logically determinate predictions.

These incorrect evaluations of evidence most often resulted from lack of attention to both halves of a proposition (which are termed *cuts* in that only one part of the proposition is attended to). For example, one tautological proposition is "The ball will land in red, or it will not land in red." This is logically determined as a correct proposition, for which empirical verification (does it actually land in red or not?) is irrelevant. When the empirical outcome is subsequently shown as not landing in red, children compared to adolescents are more likely to say that the prediction was "wrong" when it is in fact "right" from logical reasoning alone. Morris and Sloutsky (2001) interpreted such cuts as arising from processing limitations, in that the children attended only to the first statement ("land in red") and viewed the empirical outcome as disconfirming. The contradiction condition is similar, with the proposition being logically wrong ("The ball will land in red and will not land in red"), but when paired with the empirical outcome of landing in red, it leads to significant errors among children, who judge it as confirming the proposition.

Another (and not mutually exclusive) interpretation is that the children, compared to adolescents, have greater difficulty inhibiting their response to the observed outcome, whose salience is strong enough to connect affirmatively to at least one of the statements in the proposition. Yet a third interpretation noted by Morris and Sloutsky (2001) is that the linguistic unfamiliarity of such prepositional statements is more problematic for children than for early adolescents. They dismiss this interpretation on the grounds that it is equally unfamiliar to both, although an empirical test of this assertion would be welcome.

Although these data support the general claim that early adolescents give more credence to the logical structure of propositions, the attribution of all the variance to this source seems unwarranted. The use of the "can't tell" response to the predictions is not specifically analyzed. As noted earlier and emphasized by Morris and Sloutsky (2001), less than a third of the early adolescents attempted to solve logical problems empirically, but they do not emphasize as strongly that a quarter of the early adolescents' responses were erroneous attempts to solve empirical problems on the basis of logic alone.

A more comprehensive interpretation might take note of the increased propensity to deploy logical strategies, but note as well that this deployment is too broadly applied during the early stages of its use. There are a number of reasons why this could be true, and several of them may apply to any given instance: insufficient capacity to process the full proposition; lack of inhibitory control that renders the observed outcome highly salient and pushes the response toward the "matching" statement in the proposition; or confusion arising from syntactic decoding difficulties for unfamiliar forms. Bringing all these skills into a coordinated system under conscious control is a difficult achievement that likely requires improvement in each of the constituent pieces as well as improved coordination among the skills.

Recognizing the interpenetrability of various factors that impinge on adolescents' performance on logical tasks generates alternate interpretations of other results as well. For example, Foltz et al. (1995) found that more advanced reasoners (as measured by performance on another task) among fifth to eighth graders were able to use fewer moves to detect whether a test figure matched a sample figure, when the test figure could be matched by selecting successive pieces of it to reveal. Foltz et al. (1995) interpreted this pattern as showing a developmental progression from inductive to deductive reasoning because the more advanced reasoners showed a preference for disconfirming choices, compared to the less advanced reasoners, who preferred confirmatory choices and thus selected more cards to reveal. There were no age differences in performance.

Foltz et al. told the participants to prove whether the test matched the sample in the fewest moves possible, but also to be absolutely certain. Under these instructions, the assertion that the deductive approach is unequivocally a developmental advance seems less convincing. If one focuses more heavily on the second instruction, "to be absolutely certain," then the pursuit of confirmatory evidence seems less obviously immature, even if it is at the cost of making more moves. There are ready analogues to real-world circumstances where confirmatory testing is routine and sensible; redundant testing of water purity or medical diagnoses leap quickly to mind. This is not to argue that the results are not in part attributable to the more advanced reasoners' ability to identify the most economical testing strategy in terms of moves, although of course it is less cognitively economical than ignoring the "fewest moves" constraint and moving directly to empirical testing. It is to argue, however, that the inference of more advanced (i.e., deductive) logic among the more advanced reasoners is not self-evident and that other decision-making criteria may well play a role.

The issues raised in this consideration of research addressed to test claims about the development of formal reasoning will be familiar to those who have followed the debates launched by Inhelder and Piaget (1958). Nonetheless, some of the larger issues regarding construct validity (Cook & Campbell, 1979; Shadish, Cook, & Campbell, 2002) identified by Keating (1980, 1990a) have not been fully addressed: stage change associated with reasoning differences specifically, coordinated emergence of hypothesized changes in longitudinal trajectories, and generalizability across content and context. There may be disagreements on what constitutes an appropriate set of tests for the broad theoretical claims, but the large causal hypotheses of the original formulation cannot be effectively tested by isolated theoretical probes. It remains fair to say, despite specific objections (e.g., Bond, 1998), that the claim for an unequivocal shift in the structure of logic at adolescence has not been supported by the weight of evidence, and a fortiori for the claim that such a shift is a primary driver of adolescent cognitive development. There are undoubtedly shifts in performance on logical tasks, and these remain important to understand. Attributing them to changes purely in logical structure, however, requires more comprehensive evidence than has been reported to date.

What has emerged instead is a picture of generally advancing understanding of how to coordinate theory and evidence, with a substantial amount of interpenetrability between them. The presumed superiority of abstract reasoning in all circumstances is hard to support epistemologically (Keating, 1990d) as well as in terms of how conceptual development proceeds in ontogeny or in science (Klahr, 2000; Koslowski, 1996; Kuhn & Pearsall, 2000).

Recognizing the many limitations that have emerged in the study of adolescent reasoning, Moshman (1998) advanced a framework that acknowledged several distinct types of reasoning and argued for a pluralistic approach to different types of reasoning. This is an explicit attempt to preserve the value of rationality (under attack from skepticism, belief in the epistemological equivalence of any approach, etc.) while acknowledging the limits of the formal operational reasoning model. Moshman identified three general types: case-based, law-based, and dialectical. There are three subtypes of case-based reasoning: analogical, precedent-based, and legal. Both rely on precedent, although they differ in how constraining the precedent is, and there is little adolescent research focusing on either type. A well-known complication in such reasoning, of course, lies in the selection of the precedent and the extraction of what the relevant similarities and differences actually are (Keating & Sasse, 1996), and Moshman (1998) proposed that these processes are likely to reflect important developments during adolescence, although they are "largely unexplored" (p. 955). The second broad type of reasoning is law-based, and it has four subtypes: logical, rule-based, principled, and scientific. Moshman noted similar issues regarding formal reasoning described earlier and concluded that the "transition from logical inference to logical reasoning may have less to do with logical structure than with the thinker's metacognitive attitude toward the proposition under consideration" (p. 957). Rule-based reasoning includes elements not typically found in descriptions of logical reasoning, including pragmatic reasoning; the hallmark is that the reasoner is consciously applying justifiable rules. Principled reasoning attains when a set of guiding principles are adopted and applied. Scientific reasoning is more inclusive in that it values confirmatory as well as disconfirmatory evidence. Dialectical reasoning invokes the issues of reflection and argumentation, embedding reasoning in a continuing discourse. In all instances, Moshman applied a criterion of self-awareness of engaging in an effort to be rational. This typically has two dimensions: a metacognitive understanding and a recognition that reasoning has as a goal the coordination of theory and evidence.

This leads Moshman (1998) to a conclusion that resonates with Keating (1990d) in that there is "little reason to think that advanced cognitive development can be understood as progress along a single developmental pathway toward a general structural endpoint" (p. 970). His project can be read as an effort to rescue the open systems aspect of Piagetian constructivism from its premature closure in fixed structures, leading him to conclude that "what emerges at about age 11 may not be a better logic, but a deeper level of reflection about the nature of logic, theory, and evidence" (Moshman, 1998, p. 972). What emerges from many decades of research on the Piagetian structural project on formal operations is a burgeoning literature on reasoning more broadly construed than in the original formulation, a renewed theoretical interest in the open systems concepts regarding constructivism and consciousness, and a rich repository of cognitive developmental findings that can be productively linked with a rapidly growing and complementary field of developmental neuroscience.

Cognition as Judgment and Decision Making: Dual Process Models

Many of the issues that became the focus of the adolescent reasoning literature have important counterparts in the rapidly growing literature on adolescent judgment and decision making. This is unsurprising in that many of the questions and paradigms derive more or less directly from that source. Initially focused on the ways in which adolescents make practical decisions, the research topic has grown to include a wide range of questions and approaches (Klaczynski, Byrnes, & Jacobs, 2001). In an introduction to a special issue on the topic, Klaczynski et al. identified four major questions: What is good decision making? What is the role of noncognitive performance variables in decision making? What is the influence of social factors in adolescent decision making? With respect to each of these questions, what develops?

The characteristics of good decision making have been a focus of much research beyond the study of adolescence, and much of that work is reflected in core issues of adolescent decision making (Klaczynski, 2001a, 2001b; Kokis et al., 2002). The core insight is that most decisions, whether by adults or adolescents, do not follow logical rules in any formal sense and are rarely even processed analytically. Actual decision making more often takes a heuristic path, relying on general or specific knowledge, similarities to past decisions, untested assumptions about the issue to be decided, and so on. This has been studied as a contrast of analytic versus heuristic processing, in what have been termed *dual process* models (Klaczynski, 2001a, 2001b; Kokis et al., 2002; Stanovich, 1999). The standard paradigm for this research is to identify logical problems for which there is a correct response that can be generated by an analytic approach but that has an appealing bias that a heuristic approach will tend to grasp. Although more often incorrect (at least in these paradigms), heuristic processing is often preferred because it is "cognitively economical, generally produces useful judgments, and is highly contextualized. These judgments are not consciously generated and thus seem to 'pop' into consciousness and 'feel' intuitively correct" (Klaczynski, 2001b, p. 292). There is a nontrivial overlap of these features with the inductive-deductive reasoning differences in the standard logical reasoning paradigms, and thus similar issues often arise (Kokis et al., 2002).

Examples of fallacious heuristic reasoning include (from Klaczynski, 2001b) denominator neglect (in selecting a winning lottery ticket, I prefer a pool with 10 winners out of 100 rather than 1 winner out of 10), the if-only fallacy (I regret a dent to my car more keenly if I chose a particular parking space for some irrelevant reason, even though the a priori probability of harm was equal across those choices), and the sunk-cost fallacy (I persist in an undesirable activity longer if I have made a bigger investment in that activity, even if the investment cannot be recovered). In comparing the performance of early adolescents, middle adolescents, and young adults, Klaczynski (2001b) found significant age differences on all three tasks. In contrast, the frequency of the typical nonnormative responses (i.e., the usual fallacies) did not show age trends. Instead, better, more normative responses replaced atypical errors.

One way of conceptualizing the dual process model is to focus on the decontextualized nature of analytic processing and the highly contextualized nature of heuristic processing. The route to avoiding fallacies, in this framework, is to ignore the context (the 10 winning tickets, the actual dent in the car, the nonrecoverable investment) and focus instead on the logical links (the .10 winning probability is equal, etc.). Three issues arise in this respect. First, most actual, meaningful decisions are made in information-rich rather than information-impoverished environments, and thus sensitivity to context is likely desirable on many (most) occasions. Second, the automaticity aspect of heuristic processing requires deeper probing. The characterization of automaticity as the function of unconscious biases cannot be accepted at face value. They may have been built in as consciously self-constructed patterns (Kokis et al., 2002, footnote 5). Indeed, the ability to build one's own cognitive "demons" may be one of the major accomplishments of the conscious mind (Donald, 2001). Third, moving from the contextualized to the decontextualized is fraught with its own pitfalls. It is not always self-evident which aspects of a decision-making situation are meaningful and which are not. It would thus seem important to model such decision making in circumstances that do not so clearly favor an analytic approach.

Other recent research confirms these basic trends (Klaczynski, 2001a; Kokis et al.,

2002). Kokis et al. reported additional findings that illuminate the nature of dual process models. First, they found that cognitive ability was a stronger predictor of analytic processing (when contrasted with heuristic processing) than was age, and indeed age was not significant in a regression when entered after cognitive ability. They argued that this reflects that the core feature of individual differences (whether age-related or not) is computational capacity, although they argued also for a substantial role of inhibitory control in avoiding the prepotent heuristic tendency. Second, they reported a significant unique contribution of a composite cognitive style variable called *actively open-minded thinking,* suggesting a significant role for noncomputational aspects of cognition.

This finding is consistent with recent work by Byrnes (1998) that emphasizes a self-regulatory dimension of decision making, by Jacobs and Ganzel (1993) that focuses on motivational components, by Ormond et al. (1991) on the metacognitive aspects of decision making, and by Galotti (1999) on the role of naive beliefs and emotions. The development in adolescence of effective real-world decision making is interdependent with a wide range of other factors, including noncognitive aspects of development, the content of the decision, and the context in which decisions are made. Practical recommendations to use analytic processing may be hard for adolescents to implement, especially under circumstances where there is socioemotional pressure (Klaczynski et al., 2001). There may be more to gain from encouraging analytic preprocessing if the products can be captured for later use as heuristics, but this possibility remains a topic for future investigation. In summary, however, the research on adolescent decision making arrives at a similar point to the work on adolescent reasoning, in that the ability to exercise conscious control over processing, in the face of competing demands, becomes more available by adolescence. The integrative function across these demands emerges again as a central issue, reinforced by contemporary neural models of decision making (Krawczyk, 2002, as discussed later).

Cognition as Processing

As noted earlier, much of the initial impetus to address changes in processing speed and capacity during adolescence arose from two independent sources. The first was a general interest in developmental and individual differences in processing, rooted in the larger agenda of human information processing (e.g., Keating & Bobbitt, 1978). The second was an effort to explain higher order differences in reasoning by reducing them to lower order processing differences (e.g., Bryant & Trabasso, 1971).

As this research agenda was pursued, many issues arose (which were addressed earlier), including the purity of processing parameters and their ability to explain higher order cognitive performance (Keating, List, & Merriman, 1985). Three interesting lines of research, however, have been pursued in recent years that contribute to our understanding of adolescent cognitive development, and each is briefly considered here.

Case and Okamoto (1996) assembled an impressive array of evidence on the growth of thinking from childhood to adolescence. It is an extension and revision of the less differentiated capacity arguments that characterized the earlier version of this neo-Piagetian theory (Case, 1991). The trajectory from thinking that is predimensional to unidimensional, to bidimensional, and to integrated bidimensional is demonstrated in several different content domains. In contrast to both formal logical shifts and pure capacity increases, these trajectories represent the growth of central conceptual structures (i.e., organizers of content knowledge) that are argued to be coordinated across different domains. One of the major differences between this and previous theoretical formations is that content knowledge is incorporated inside the system, rather than as an exogenous factor (Keating, 1996a).

Some major challenges remain. First, can explicit translation rules be identified on how to assign the dimensionality of a given task? To the extent that dimensionality is partly dependent on empirical evidence, the independence of the theoretical claims is hard to declare with certainty. Similar to the Mueller et al. (1999) critique mentioned earlier, it is important also to ascertain whether the theoretical sequences are theoretically specific or whether other ways of calibrating difficulty would do as well. Second, the correlated emergence of dimensional shifts across domains is substantial but far from uniform. The discrepancies are sensibly addressed, but it is unclear how much lack of coordination can be explained away before the claim is threatened. Third, and not unique to this research program, the developmental evidence is in fact age-difference evidence, and thus we do not know whether these dimensional shifts occur as predicted for individuals across time.

A second line of neo-Piagetian research has also generated intriguing new findings (Demetriou et al., 2002). In a longitudinal, cross-sequential study of 8-, 10-, 12- , and 14-year-olds who were followed twice more at yearly intervals, the researchers studied the intraindividual patterns of change in processing efficiency (including both speed and control in a Stroop-like task), working memory (including short-term memory and executive memory), and problem solving (including verbal, quantitative, and spatial reasoning). Not unexpectedly, they found substantial developmental shifts in each aspect of cognitive functioning across this age range. More interestingly, they analyzed the relationships among the multiple trajectories to examine directions of influence. The results are complex in that they looked both at growth modeling and at logistic equations to capture nonlinear patterns. From the growth curve modeling, the general picture that emerged was, surprisingly, that overall "growth as such in each of the abilities is not affected by the state of the others at a given point in time" (Demetriou et al., 2002, p. 97). Rather than as fundamental drivers of change, processing efficiency and working memory instead "open possibilities for growth in other abilities. In other words, changes in these functions may be necessary but not sufficient for changes in functions residing at other levels of the mental architecture. . . . [The] realization of these possibilities lies in agents external to these drivers (such as environmental opportunities, individual interests, self-regulatory processes)" (p. 97). The parenthetical comments are particularly relevant to the integrated model advanced in this review. There is no single driver of cognitive change in this age range; rather, cognitive changes arise as a necessary interaction among multiple internal and external features.

The results from the nonlinear (dynamic) logistic growth models revealed a more nuanced but similar portrait. All cognitive functions show a growth pattern that is robust earlier and begins to asymptote as it reaches the older ages (14- to 16-year-olds, in this study). By examining the relative contributions of the different cognitive functions across development, it became clear that processing efficiency has a strong effect on working memory, and working memory has a strong effect on problem solving (reasoning). But there are reciprocal, top-down effects as well, such that improvements in problem solving enhance the function of processing efficiency and working memory.

In sum, the evidence from linear and nonlinear growth parameters leads to the conclusion that as processing efficiency increases, so does working memory capacity. Problem solving (reasoning) is potentiated by increases in both processing efficiency and working memory, such that higher levels of working memory nested within varying levels of processing efficiency lead to higher levels of reasoning. Demetriou et al. (2002) emphasized the central role of executive functions in these patterns and postulated a probable reciprocal interplay of the cognitive functions studied here with self-awareness and self-regulation across development.

The final line of research to be considered in this section (Markovits & Barrouillet, 2002; Markovits & Savary, 1992) could have been included in the section on reasoning, in that its focus is on the development of performance in conditional reasoning tasks. In the theoretical account, which includes a thorough review of the relevant empirical work, Markovits and Barrouillet (2002) made a strong case that developmental differences in reasoning play a marginal role in performance on conditional reasoning tasks. Rather than undertake actual reasoning, most subjects on most occasions deploy a mental model (Johnson-Laird, 1983) of the content of the premises and relations among them. The inability of classic rule-based approaches to account successfully for variations in performance as the content changes is a launching point for mental model accounts. By including content in the process from the beginning, Markovits and Barrouillet argued that they are able to account more readily for a wide range of empirical findings. The primary features that account for developmental variability are the capacity of working memory, the range of knowledge available, the ability to access that knowledge online, and the ability to inhibit information that is not appropriate to the logical problem. They noted especially that the "idea that most reasoners are able to use content-free reasoning procedures in any systematic way appears highly unlikely" (Markovits & Barrouillet, 2002, p. 32).

There is striking convergence in the current state of understanding of the central features of adolescent cognition among these three otherwise distinct lines of research: central conceptual structures (Case & Okamoto, 1996), a mental processing account (Demetriou et al., 2002), and a mental model account (Markovits & Barrouillet, 2002). The areas of convergence include the emphasis on content as integral to cognitive processing and structure, the necessity of coordination among cognitive components, the emergence of more complete coordination around the time of the adolescent transition, and the role of executive function in the development of such coordination. The similarity between this set of core issues and those arising from a review of the development of reasoning offers further support for the potential validity and utility of an integrated account focusing on the emergence of conscious control and coordination as the signal feature of the adolescent cognitive transition.

Cognition as Expertise: Knowledge, Skill, and Conceptual Development

Although some early work on the development of expertise was designed to find alternate explanations for presumed processing differences, the rapidly expanding literature on expertise was not solely a methodological challenge. Rather, it represented a different approach to understanding cognitive development (Chi et al., 1982, 1989; Keating, 1990b; Koslowski, 1996; Kuhn et al., 1988). The key argument of this approach was that the acquisition of knowledge and skills in specific domains is the driving force of cognitive development. More knowledge and greater ability to transfer knowledge across domains are the keys to developmental advancement. From this perspective, measures of better reasoning, faster processing, or greater mental capacity are derivative of the core progress in knowledge acquisition.

Almost by definition, the study of expertise and its development is specific to particular knowledge domains. Moreover, the focus is on the acquisition of expertise through experience, rather than on age or developmental differences in themselves. Indeed, the early demonstrations that young experts could outperform older novices were central to the argument from expertise (Chi et al., 1982). Consequently, the focus of this work has not been on developmental changes that are specific to any given developmental period, including adolescence. Nonetheless, interesting and generalizable findings from this work bear on some of the major issues in adolescent cognitive and brain development.

One general trend in the work on expertise has been a growing recognition of the importance of deep conceptual understanding to the building of expertise (Case, 1999; Chi, Slotta, & deLeeuw, 1994). Although one hallmark remains the acquisition of automaticity that affords an ever-increasing range of performance, their interconnections in a conceptual framework are increasingly recognized as a powerful mechanism for conceptual change and expanding expertise. Such work has also "begun to examine such general properties as conceptual coherence and organization, and to postulate the existence of top-down processing and/or some form of reflexive abstraction" (Case, 1999, p. 792). The valuable role that self-explanation plays in the acquisition of expertise seems in accord with this trend (Chi, 2000), as does the central role of consciously controlled coordination of theory and evidence noted earlier (Kuhn & Pearsall, 2000).

A second general finding is the extremely long period of time that is required to attain high levels of performance in any field. Ericsson and Charness (1999) estimated this duration to be at a minimum of a decade to achieve top-level performance in the modern competitive world. But this applies to premodern expertise acquisition as well. Walker, Hill, Kaplan, and McMillan (2002) studied life span changes in hunting ability among the Ache (a tribal group in Eastern Paraguay) and found that peak success in hunting occurs substantially later than does peak strength. "Given that Ache start hunting around the ages of 12–15, it takes nearly 30 years for hunters to reach their prime" (p. 652). They also noted the evolutionary implications of this as well, which are consistent with the arguments of Donald (2001) and Rilling and Insell (1999): "If hunting was an important economic activity of early hominids, the learning curve for hunting success may partially explain why humans have big brains, long learning periods, and long lifespans" (Walker et al., 2002, p. 654). Two further aspects of the long duration of expertise acquisition merit attention. The first is the crucial role of deliberate practice (Ericsson, 2002; Ericsson & Charness, 1999). The second, noted earlier with regard to heuristic thinking, is the deliberate construction of automatized subroutines that enable much more complex performance. Both observations clearly imply the operation of a consciously guided self-regulatory effort.

These aspects of expertise do not operate only at the level of top performance. The operation of metacognitive oversight and metastrategic knowledge contributes substantially to ordinary expertise in many domains (Kuhn et al., 1995; Kuhn & Pearsall, 2000). Acquiring such metacognitive awareness also appears to enhance performance. Williams, Blythe, White, Li, Gardner, and Sternberg (2002) trained middle school students in five different aspects of metacognitive awareness and observed significant performance enhancements over a 2-year period.

Even though the work on expertise has not focused on adolescent cognitive development in itself, the general findings still yield considerable insight into familiar features of adolescent cognition (Chi, Glaser, & Farr, 1988). The importance of conceptual coordination, conscious control of acquisition, and metacognitive awareness, taken together, emphasizes the role of conscious coordination. The accumulating evidence on cognitive and brain development points to adolescence as a peak period for acquiring such coordination.

In addition to these general trends, there is substantial research on adolescent cognitive development in important practical arenas other than learning and instruction, such as the nature of moral understanding (Chandler, Sokol, & Wainryb, 2000), the balance between self-determination and nurturance rights (Ruck, Abramovitch, & Keating, 1998; Ruck, Keating, Abramovitch, & Koegl, 1998), social exclusion and social-political thinking (Horn, 2003; Torney-Purta, 1991), and identity development (Bosma & Kunnen, 2001). It seems likely that as research in these and other important domains of adolescent thinking moves ahead, the theme of conscious coordination will become an increasing focus.

Cognition as Consciousness: Assembling the Components

This review of the major historic and recent trends in the study of adolescent cognitive development has identified striking convergence. From logic to processing to decision making to expertise, the longstanding search for the primary driver of cognition has had to confront evidence that there is no single driver. Instead, three areas of more complex functioning have been repeatedly observed in the context of the adolescent transition: reciprocal interaction among different cognitive subsystems; mutual influence between cognitive systems and affective, social, and personality dimensions; and a central role for metacognitive features such as self-awareness, self-regulation, and conscious control in the direction of cognitive activity.

The evidence also supports the view that these levels of added complexity make possible, but do not guarantee, the assembly of multiple cognitive developments into an integrated, reflective consciousness. Such assembly requires consciously guided effort. In the absence of such effort, the likely outcome is reliance on unreflective heuristics, algorithms based on shallow conceptual frameworks, and reactive rather than self-regulated emotion and behavior. A productive research agenda on adolescent cognitive development will need to build on these insights, with a greater emphasis in the future on tracking developmental trajectories, including multiple cognitive subsystems in such trajectory analyses, and further exploration of the mutual influence of cognitive and noncognitive factors. In pursuing this renewed research agenda on adolescent cognitive development, much greater attention to the grounding of cognitive activity in biology and to the fundamental role of context in shaping cognitive growth will be essential.

BIOLOGICAL GROUNDING

Even before the systematic study of adolescent development, the biological changes of puberty were self-evident and, moreover, were frequently used as markers in premodern and traditional societies for initiation rites or other social practices that indicated a recognition of their importance. It is thus commonplace to note the importance of biology in the adolescent transition. As we move toward specificity in trying to understand the links between biological changes and adolescent cognitive development, however, conceptual clarity becomes crucial.

Three categories of biological changes can be identified, although it is important to note that they are substantially interdependent. The first is the highly complex suite of physical changes that have been grouped together under the general category of puberty (Angold et al., 1998, 1999; Susman & Rogol, this volume). Within the broad category of pubertal changes, two have special relevance to adolescent cognitive development: developments in brain structure or function that are initiated or catalyzed by pubertal processes; and the cascade of endocrine and neuroendocrine changes that dramatically alter many bodily functions, including emotional and motivational systems (Steinberg et al., in press). The second is the broad set of changes in the brain, with a particular focus as noted earlier on the prefrontal cortex and cortico-cortical interconnectivity. Although there is a set of changes to the brain that largely cooccur with pubertal changes, it is not the case that all changes in the brain at this developmental period are caused by pubertal changes. Given the complexity of both systems and the sparse longitudinal data that examine them conjointly, we know relatively little about how these two systems are connected developmentally or functionally. The third set of changes includes those that are shaped, sculpted, or altered by developmental experience. Both the neural and neuroendocrine-endocrine systems are susceptible to fundamental changes that arise from interactions with the environment (experience-dependent brain development). In this section, aspects of change within each of the first two categories that are relevant to adolescent cognitive development are described and illustrated with selected studies. Literature relevant to the possibility of experience-based brain development is reviewed in the final section of the chapter.

Pubertal Changes

Few direct links from puberty to specific brain or cognitive shifts have been reported, probably because of the complex developmental patterns of each system (puberty, brain, cognition) and the difficulty of including assessments of all three systems in single studies (Keating & Shapka, 1998). One area that has been explored in a number of studies is the development of spatial ability, especially with respect to gender differences in hormonal changes at puberty and potential associations with hemispheric laterality differences (Hassler, 1991; Linn & Petersen, 1985; Newcombe, Semon Dubas, & Baenninger, 1989; Waber, Mann, Merola, & Moylan, 1985). The pattern of results across these studies is inconsistent.

In a recent study that aimed to synthesize the earlier literature, Davison and Susman (2001) tested three hypothesized models (testosterone, estrogen, and ratio) in a longitudinal study of 9- to 14-year-old boys and girls. The pattern of findings was complex, but they concluded that there was support only for a testosterone model, strongly for boys but only weakly for girls. There are competing explanations for the processes that may generate this pattern of results, but the results seem to be inconsistent with a simple or direct link from pubertal to cognitive changes.

This is consistent with studies that have looked for general correlations between physical maturation or pubertal markers and cognitive changes but have not discovered substantial relationships (Orr, Brack, & Ingersoll, 1988; Waber et al., 1985). One-to-one correspondences may thus be quite rare, owing to the complexity of each system. As the models of puberty and of more general changes in the brain become more precise, and if we are able to explore both in longitudinal studies, it is possible and perhaps likely that relationships will emerge. The search for such relationships will be aided by specific hypotheses that increase the focus of the questions, whereas correlations of global measures are likely to be relatively uninformative.

Brain Changes in Adolescence

The goal of identifying the links between change in the brain and changes in cognitive functioning need to be understood against the backdrop of the enormous complexity of brain-behavior links in general (Albright, Jessell, Kandel, & Posner, 2000), multiplied by the added complexity introduced by an understanding of neural plasticity (Nelson, 1999). Against this backdrop, we stand at the edge of very exciting new research developments as new neuroimaging technologies come online, but at present we are groping in the dark in many respects. This brief overview identifies some of the major themes that may illuminate that work in the future, but with a healthy understanding of its provisional nature.

Much of the work is quite recent, representing the application of the new technologies to the study of development. The work on adolescent development is particularly recent. The explosive growth of new technologies for studying the brain make it likely that information about brain development will increase exponentially in the near future: "It is clear that innovative methods like fMRI together with MRI-based morphometry and pharmacologic probes will transform our current understanding of human brain development" (Casey et al., 2000, p. 254).

Most of the recent research on adolescent brain development has used magnetic resonance imaging (MRI) for detailed examinations of anatomical structure (Durston et al., 2001; Giedd et al., 1999; Paus et al., 1999; Schmithorst, Wilke, Dardzinski, & Holland, 2002; Sowell et al., 2001, 2002; Sowell, Thompson, Holmes, Batth, Jernigan, & Toga, 1999a; Sowell, Thompson, Holmes, Jernigan, & Toga, 1999b) and/or functional MRI (fMRI) for observations of the brain as it engages in tasks that illuminate its activity (Casey et al., 2000; Luna et al., 2001). MRI and fMRI are excellent and improving technologies for noninvasive (excluding their use in conjunction with pharmacologic probes) mapping of the brain, in repose or in action. Their temporal resolution is not as sharp as their spatial resolution. The reverse is found in the event-related potentials (ERPs) that are produced by changes in electrical potentials on the scalp that indicate underlying cortical activity, although new techniques are rapidly increasing the spatial resolution of ERP (Luu, Collins, & Tucker, 2000; Luu, Tucker, Derryberry, Reed, & Poulsen, 2003; Oades, Dittmann-Balcar, & Zerbin, 1997; Segalowitz, Unsal, &

Dywan, 1992). In addition to neuroimaging, we are also learning more about adolescent functioning with techniques that have been in use for some time, such as neuropsychological assessment (Kwon & Lawson, 2000; Kwon et al., 2000; Luciana & Nelson, in press) and hormonal assays (Francis et al., 2002). The remainder of this section focuses on major themes that have emerged from this recent work, as it relates to cognitive development.

The prefrontal cortex has been a major focus of interest in neurodevelopment for some time, largely due to its significant role in executive function (Case, 1992; Stuss, 1992) and to its late anatomical development as observed in autopsy studies (Huttenlocher, 1994). More recent work has both reinforced and refined our understanding of its importance (Barbas & Hilgetag, 2002; Durston et al., 2001; Fuster, 2000; Krawczyk, 2002; Watanabe, 2002). Its late arrival in both phylogenetic (Donald, 2001; Rilling & Insel, 1999) and ontogenetic (Fuster et al., 2000; Segalowitz et al., 1992) development make it a prime candidate for special attention in relation to adolescent cognitive development. There is evidence that myelination, an indicator of greater conductivity and thus connectivity, continues to develop prefrontally through the adolescent period: "Maturation of the frontal white matter continues into the second decade of life. The time course of prefrontal maturation makes it possible that myelination is a basis for the gradual development of prefrontal functions" (Klingberg, Vaidya, Gabrieli, Moseley, & Hedehus, 1999, p. 2817).

The continuing development of myelination (not only prefrontally) through this developmental period has been known for some time, and it continues to receive empirical support using newer imaging techniques: "White matter maturation assessed at different ages involves increases in both white matter density and organization during childhood and adolescence" (Schmithorst et al., 2002, p. 212). Paus et al. (1999) reported similar findings on white matter (myelination) associated with corticospinal and frontotemporal pathways. Sowell et al. (2001, 2002) found an inverse relationship between decreased gray matter (evidence of synaptic pruning) and increased white matter (evidence of enhanced connectivity), after controlling for total brain volume, in the adolescent and postadolescent period. Giedd et al. (1999) reported a preadolescent increase in gray matter, followed by a decline as noted earlier. The particular importance of this finding is that if "the increase is related to a second wave of overproduction of synapses, it may herald a critical stage of development when the environment or activities of the teenager may guide selective synapse elimination during adolescence" (Giedd et al., 1999, p. 863). Using ERPs to detect age-by-topography interactions among 10- to 21-year-olds, Oades et al. (1997) reported evidence that is consistent with the MRI findings on prefrontal development, including substantial changes in prefrontal latencies in the 10- to 14-year-old period and an attentional feature (N2 amplitude) developing a frontal focus by age 17.

The rapidly accumulating evidence on adolescent brain development is adding much new information at many levels of analysis. It is likely that this picture will grow more complex and more detailed in the very near future. With respect to adolescent cognitive development, as we have seen it unfold across a number of research traditions, three broad findings can be emphasized. The first is that there is substantial development in adolescence in the prefrontal cortex. The second is that in adolescence there is substantial evidence for enhanced connectivity and organization as seen in increased myelination (white matter) in specific regions. The third is that synaptic pruning (relative decreases in gray matter) is evident during the adolescent period, with perhaps the most significant occurring prefrontally. Neuroimaging is of course not a solution in itself for increasing our understanding of adolescent development, cognitively or otherwise. It will require thoughtful integration with behavioral and cognitive probes, which themselves will need to become increasingly precise.

Johnson (2001) reviewed three different ways in which links between brain and cognitive changes could occur, noting that they are not mutually exclusive: maturation, skill acquisition, and interactive specialization based on interregional interaction. This last is potentially of great importance given the anatomical evidence of special growth during adolescence of the white matter that supports such interregional communication and because of links to cognitive evidence of increased coordination via the prefrontal cortex. Sowell et al. (2001) reported links between thinning of frontal gray matter and performance on verbal and visuospatial memory tasks in 7- to 16-year-olds.

On a behavioral inhibition task, Luna et al. (2001) reported substantial differences in patterns of brain activation across children, adolescents, and adults that were related to the level of voluntary control of eye movement. This fMRI study attributed the ability to initiate and suppress behavior voluntarily to the "maturation of integrated function among the neocortex, striatum, thalamus, and cerebellum" (p. 791). Adolescents, who performed better than did children on this task, apparently recruited different brain systems than did adults to accomplish this. Specifically, the adolescents, compared to adults, showed substantially *more* activity in the dorsolateral prefrontal cortex (DLPFC), "indicating their greater reliance on executive prefrontal behavioral control systems" (p. 791). In contrast, adults showed the pattern of integrated function noted earlier and required significantly less DLPFC activity. This is consistent with the notion of a complex assembly of mechanisms of conscious control during the adolescent transition, which leads to more automatic and less effortful governance by the prefrontal cortex with maturity. It also emphasizes the effortful nature of conscious control, which plays a significant role in any economy of cognitive activity.

This last point merits a more detailed unpacking. One of the hallmarks of expertise, as noted earlier, is the relatively high degree of automaticity of execution among experts compared with novices (Keating, 1990b). This automaticity can be misconstrued as evidence that expertise is built in a connectionist fashion among self-organizing automata for which a governing consciousness is unnecessary. But if automaticity is fully self-organizing through recruitment of more elementary automata, why would effort (in this example, DLPFC activity) be expended to achieve this goal? Regarding automaticity instead as a product of effortful conscious activity—"building one's own [cognitive] demons" in Donald's (2001) evocative phrase—seems more consistent with general developmental progressions (Keating, 1990b) and with the specific fMRI evidence on voluntary control reported by Luna et al. (2001).

Imaging technologies are highly informative but also expensive, logistically demanding, and consequently not readily available for addressing many questions of theoretical and practical importance for adolescent cognitive development. For the foreseeable future, this will impose a moderately strict scientific economy on how to link cognitive and brain development. One consequence of this economy is that sample sizes are generally quite low, making it difficult to generalize easily to populations or subpopulations (Keating, 2001b). Another consequence is that conceptual clarity on the questions that are asked becomes even more important.

Assessment of brain function that is more readily available and has fewer technical constraints is a potentially valuable option. Validation of standard neuropsychological assessments as tools to evaluate specific functions, especially if collected in a standardized fashion, is one promising route: "What is needed in this context is a battery of tests that reliably reflects specific types of neural activity in individuals throughout the lifespan" (Luciana & Nelson, in press, p. 2). In an initial validation study of an automated neuropsychological assessment battery (using laptop computers), Luciana and Nelson reported that on two key frontal functions, planning (Tower of London) and spatial working memory, 12-year-olds had not yet attained adult levels of functioning. This is consistent with the neuroimaging evidence just described, indicating that prefrontal cortex development proceeds well into adolescence.

Kwon and Lawson (2000), Kwon et al. (2000), and Lawson et al. (2000) argued for a critical role of development in the prefrontal lobes in concept acquisition. They used standard neuropsychological testing to assess the level of frontal lobe development (inhibition, planning, disembedding, and working memory). Performance on these frontal lobe tasks was correlated with performance on a scientific reasoning test (a paper-and-pencil measure of Piagetian hypothetico-deductive reasoning) and with gains in a concept acquisition instructional experiment. In the Kwon et al. (2000) study, it is interesting to note that all the prefrontal tasks correlated with proportional reasoning more consistently than with each other, which lends support to the notion that several different prefrontal functions are recruited in order to perform highly demanding cognitive tasks.

There are several additional promising areas of research that may be quite informative for central issues in adolescent cognitive development, but these have not yet been investigated developmentally. For example, a better understanding of the neural basis of decision making as the integration of several different prefrontal functions (Krawczyk, 2002) may point in fruitful directions. In a pattern that echoes recent neuroscience evidence just described, decision making appears to reside in part on the integration of several discriminable functions of the prefrontal cortex:

> The orbitofrontal and ventromedial areas are most relevant to deciding based on reward values and contribute affective information regarding decision attributes and options. (2) Dorsolateral prefrontal cortex is critical in making decisions that call for the consideration of multiple sources of information, and may recruit separable areas when making well defined versus poorly defined decisions. (3) The anterior and ventral cingulate cortex appear especially relevant in sorting among conflicting options, as well as signaling outcome-relevant information. (Krawczyk, 2000, p. 631)

For most of the important decisions that adolescents are called on to make, especially in the heat of the moment, as it were, the coordination of these functions is likely required. Using developmental neuroscience to ground our understanding of how these functions develop and work together, and what developmental experiences are most influential in shaping them, researchers may find new opportunities for studying the specifics of online decision making in adolescence. Within a self-regulatory framework advanced by Byrnes (1998), for example, the role of the anterior cingulate cortex as a conflict monitor and error recognition system becomes of central interest (Bush, Luu, & Posner, 2000; Holroyd & Coles, 2002; Luu et al., 2000, 2003; van Veen & Carter, 2002). When adolescents find themselves in risky situations, perhaps through inadequate advance planning, the importance of knowing that things may be going wrong becomes a critical checking mechanism. Similarly, the interplay of the DLPFC (which may invoke more analytic processing) and the orbitofrontal cortex (which may invoke more gist-like, emotionally valent, heuristic processing) in making decisions where the identification of the relevant information is not self-evident raises important considerations for the specificity of dual process models (Klaczynski, 2001a, 2001b; Kokis et al., 2002).

In a more speculative vein, it may be that significant and specific brain changes are also central to the construction of self during adolescence. Recent theoretical work linking particular neural circuitry to the functioning of the dialogical self (Lewis, 2002) and to awareness of other minds (Frith, 2002) suggests the potential richness of a biological grounding for previously hard-to-specify but crucial developments in higher order thinking and reflection.

In seeking common ground, or consilience, across cognitive-behavioral and neurodevelopmental approaches, two cautions already noted can be usefully recalled here: Cognition and behavior are not reducible to their neural substrate, and the rapid accumulation of evidence arising from new neuroimaging techniques means that the portrait of the brain, both functionally and structurally, is likely to undergo many rapid iterations—and this is even more true of developmental neuroimaging, for which the evidence is even more recent and thus provisional.

On the other hand, the convergences across several lines of both cognitive and neurodevelopmental research on adolescents are striking. The emergence of a more fully conscious cognitive actor is evident from both sets of data and thus is mutually reinforcing. If this convergence in fact reflects some important homologies, then the necessary approach to future research will be interdisciplinary (Wilson, 1998). Of special note is the evidence on synaptic pruning through adolescence, which raises the probability that experience-based brain development also continues through the adolescent period. This implies the crucial importance of the culture and context within which adolescents assemble this potentially powerful tool for conscious control and awareness. Donald (2001) argued that consciousness gets assembled only in the cultural context and thus is inevitably shaped by that context. The biological embedding of experience (Boyce & Keating, in press; Keating & Hertzman, 1999) in adolescence would thus be a potentially significant sensitive or critical developmental period, in that it would shape the consciousness that individuals carry forward into adulthood. This implies in turn the necessity of developing a more refined conceptual framework for context and culture, especially as they impinge on adolescents' emerging consciousness.

CULTURE INTO BIOLOGY: THE MAKING OF THE ADOLESCENT MIND

From the review of adolescent cognitive and brain development, an integrated account has begun to emerge. Based on both lines of evidence, it is clear that adolescence is an important period for the coordination of a wide array of cognitive and brain systems into a self-aware, self-guided, and self-monitoring system of conscious control. It may in fact be a critical period for such developments (Giedd et al., 1999) in that synaptic pruning guided by developmental experiences may influence how such coordination takes place.

An important general rule of brain development, first articulated by Hebb (1949), is that neuronal cells that fire together, wire together (FTWT): "When an axon of cell A is near enough to excite cell B repeatedly or consistently takes part in firing it, some growth or metabolic change takes place in one or both cells such that A's efficiency, as one of the cells in firing B, is increased." Bi and Poo (2001) reviewed research that updates this classic and important observation, including new evidence on the temporal and spatial specificity of FTWT. It is clear that the general rule continues to be confirmed but that the more precise the probe, the more complex it becomes to define what constitutes firing together.

We have by now a reasonably clear picture of the mechanisms by which this occurs in early development (Boyce & Keating, in press; Cynader & Frost, 1999; Meaney, 2001), at least compared with the clarity of the picture of adolescent development. Moreover, the evolutionary purpose of experiential shaping in early development is relatively easy to imagine. For regularly expected features of the environment (e.g., visual input), it makes evolutionary sense to encode a relatively simple program genetically that will be tuned as it encounters that expected environment (Cynader & Frost, 1999). Where environmental variation is probable (e.g., the availability or quality of parental care under conditions of varying hardship), it makes evolutionary sense to have a system with different levels of set points and regulatory function that are activated by the actual experience of the organism (Meaney, 2001).

An equivalent evolutionary story for adolescent consciousness will be far more speculative, largely because the primary features that define the higher levels of consciousness have a single example (*Homo sapiens sapiens*). This can be informed speculation, however, drawing on contemporary comparisons of human and nonhuman primates and on historical and prehistoric evidence (Donald, 2001; Rilling & Insel, 1999). Three possible, nonexclusive bases of evolutionary selection for consciousness have some support and special relevance for the adolescent transition. The first is the long learning curve for the acquisition of expertise, especially when such acquisition requires deliberate, consciously guided effort (Ericsson, 2002; Walker et al., 2002).

The second involves the recruiting function of the prefrontal cortex, pulling together a wide array of cognitive and other systems in the service of conscious goals. This implies a level of cognitive flexibility and niche-picking that would afford survival in a wide array of environments. Retaining neural plasticity while allowing more modular systems to develop so that they can be subsequently recruited would be an evolutionary strategy well suited to maximizing purposeful flexibility.

The third is related to the major physical reorganization that is occasioned by puberty. As noted earlier, we do not know whether the pubertal and brain changes are related directly, indirectly, or coincidentally. We do know that there are major hormonal shifts, some of which have the effect of heightening some aspects of socioemotional life, especially those with a sexual component. Cognitive-affective interactive systems are thus directly impacted. This combination of emerging consciousness and heightened arousal makes it a prime target for socialization experiences that secure the individual's attachment to the group and ensure that the group's goals are undertaken by its upcoming members. Initiation rites appear to serve this purpose of capturing the passion of the youthful members of the group.

Taken together, given the neural evidence that the adolescent brain is primed for a critical period during which environments and activities will shape function, especially prefrontal functions (Giedd et al., 1999), the cognitive evidence that such metalevel reorganization is occurring in concert with these changes in the brain (see the previous main section), and the evolutionary evidence that consciousness is formed in the intersection of the individual and the social mind (Donald, 2001), it is reasonable to conclude that deep attention to the way in which the culture and context operate with respect to adolescent development should be a prime concern for anyone interested in their, and our, well-being.

Beyond speculation and a proposed consilience of evidence, we may well ask whether evidence of such biological embedding (Boyce & Keating, in press; Keating & Hertzman, 1999) exists for the adolescent transition. Is there anything comparable to the dramatic physiological and behavioral effects of stressful early rearing (Meaney, 2001)? Using animals that had experienced a deprived early environment, Francis et al. (2002) explored the potential for reversibility of effect through peripubertal enrichment. Animals in the experimental group were moved at puberty to a more complex and stimulating social and physical environment: "Animals in the enrichment condition were housed in groups of eight animals within a series of large 60 × 30 × 60 cm cages interconnected with a burrow system and filled with toys that were replaced regularly. Standard laboratory conditions were defined as two animals housed in a 20 × 40 × 30 cm clear plastic cage" (Francis et al., 2002, p. 7841). The results provide the first clear evidence on fundamental reversibility of behavioral and physiological damage, although the physiological reversibility was only partial. Francis et al. (2002) described the recovery as more compensatory in nature, creating a physiological work-around to counter the worst effects of early deprivation. The implications of this research for viewing adolescence as a critical period are profound, suggesting that adolescence also provides an opportunity for recovery of function compromised by early experience.

Some findings from research with human subjects are consistent with this evidence in that they show covariation between aspects of context and a pattern of individual differences. In population data on adolescent achievement, there are substantial differences across societies, not only in mean performance but also in the gradient of achievement across socioeconomic status (SES). The replicated finding of interest, termed a *gradient effect* (Keating & Hertzman, 1999), is that where there are steeper gradients (i.e., larger differences in achievement as one moves along the SES scale), there tend to be lower overall means. Conversely, in societies where the differences in developmental outcomes are less stark across levels of SES, the means tend to be higher. Thus, there is evidence for a context effect (societal or cultural) on developmental outcomes in adolescence. Until these gradient effects can be unpacked through (increasingly available) comparative-longitudinal evidence, however, we cannot know whether these contextual effects arose in adolescence or earlier. We also need further evidence to identify which aspects of context influence the gradient effect (Boyce & Keating, in press).

The substantial role of culture in thinking about identity and decision making is evident in Chandler's (2000) contrast of Euro-American and Canadian First Nations adolescents. The essentialist thought of the former is argued as fundamentally different from the self-referential narrative approach of the latter. The broader issue of how to judge competing knowledge claims has more often been investigated among young adults as epistemic development (Moshman, 1998), but these issues may be later appearances of a recursive pattern that begins earlier in development to shape epistemological beliefs (Chandler, Hallett, & Sokol, 2002).

A major difficulty in exploring the ways in which culture and context shape the adolescent mind in this critical period lies in the relative dearth of theory about context as it can be used productively in research, although there are some promising developments in this regard (Boyce, Frank, Jensen, Kessler, Nelson, & Steinberg, 1998; Bronfenbrenner, 1999). Productive theories of context will need to incorporate a notion of "culture in action" (Swidler, 1986) rather than as a static, exogenous feature. In this regard, the ultimate models are likely to have properties of dynamic systems, with recursive feedback built in (Keating, 1990c). In addition, such approaches will need to include many different methods to account for the variety of the adolescent experience.

Significant methodological developments in recent years may afford a rich enough depiction of adolescent experience to enable brain-behavior-context research to proceed. Comparative epidemiological studies can provide a portrait of how adolescents fare in different societies, although as noted we will need to unpack those population patterns in order to get at underlying mechanisms (Keating, 2001b). The construct of social capital may be useful for describing at several levels of detail how the everyday lives of adolescents vary and how that is linked to diverse developmental outcomes. Studies of neighborhood effects using multilevel analyses (Sampson, Morenoff, & Gannon-Rowley, 2002), of social ecologies using ethnographic methods (Anderson, 1998), of adolescents' participation in civil society using survey data (Flanagan, Bowes, Jonsson, Csapo, & Sheblanova, 1998), and of the everyday activities and feelings of adolescents in their families, with their peers, and on their own, using experience sampling methodology (ESM; Larson, 1995; Larson, Richards, Moneta, Holmbeck, & Duckett, 1996), each offer a window onto the features of the adolescent context that may provide multiple opportunities to link differences in context to differences in multiple aspects of adolescents' emerging consciousness. Longitudinal studies of the connections between these areas of context and adolescent outcomes will be essential if we are interested in understanding their influence.

In pursuing these connections, it will be important to view context and culture not as static, exogenous entities that impact on adolescents, but rather as the cognitive and social web that is characterized by the felt connections to one's group. The core of self-regulation and self-knowledge lies in relationships and thus is closely connected to the social mind (Bell & Calkins, 2000; Swidler, 1986; Tice & Bratslavsky, 2000).

In general terms, it seems likely that the route by which culture and context influence cognition and consciousness during the critical adolescent transition will typically be interpersonal and relational, through varying agencies (family, peers, teachers, media, etc.). From a societal perspective, this creates a serious challenge. To the extent that social and cultural practices do not provide the opportunities (or societal affordances; Keating, 2001b) for purposeful engagement that will lead toward self-aware, flexible conscious control, the alternatives may be less productive for adolescents and for the larger society—alienation, reactive dogmatism, cynicism, and skepticism come to mind. On the other hand, creating the conditions for the development of a conscious and critical habit of mind (Keating, 1996c) may yield substantial payoffs for everyone. Better understanding of the links among brain development, cognitive development, and their embeddedness in culture and context would represent a significant step toward that larger societal goal.

REFERENCES

Albright, T. D., Jessell, T. M., Kandel, E. R., & Posner, M. I. (2000). Neural science: A century of progress and the mysteries that remain. *Cell, 100,* S1–S55.

Anderson, E. (1998). The social ecology of youth violence. In M. Tonry & M. Moore (Eds.), *Youth violence* (pp. 63–104). Chicago: University of Chicago Press.

Angold, A., Costello, E. J., Erkanli, A., & Worthman, C. M. (1999). Pubertal changes in hormone levels and depression in girls. *Psychological Medicine, 29,* 1043–1053.

Angold, A., Costello, E. J., & Worthman, C. M. (1998). Puberty and depression: The roles of age, pubertal status and pubertal timing. *Psychological Medicine, 28,* 51–61.

Ausubel, D. P., & Ausubel, P. (1966). Cognitive development in adolescence. *Review of Educational Research, 36,* 403–413.

Barbas, H., & Hilgetag, C. C. (2002). Rules relating connections to cortical structure in primate prefrontal cortex. *Neurocomputing, 44–46,* 301–308.

Baumeister, R. F., & Leary, M. R. (1995). The need to belong: Desire for interpersonal attachments as a fundamental human motivation. *Psychological Bulletin, 117,* 497–529.

Bell, K. L., & Calkins, S. D. (2000). Relationships as inputs and outputs of emotion regulation. *Psychological Inquiry, 11,* 160–163.

Bi, G., & Poo, M. (2001). Synaptic modification by correlated activity: Hebb's postulate revisited. *Annual Review of Neuroscience, 24,* 139–166.

Bond, T. G. (1995a). Piaget and measurement: I. The twain really do meet. *Archives de Psychologie, 63*(245), 71–87.

Bond, T. G. (1995b). Piaget and measurement: II. Empirical validation of the Piagetian model. *Archives de Psychologie, 63*(246), 155–185.

Bond, T. G. (1998). Fifty years of formal operational research: The empirical evidence. *Archives de Psychologie, 66*(258), 221–238.

Bond, T. G., & Bunting, E. (1995). Piaget and measurement: III. Reassessing the -I methode clinique. *Archives de Psychologie, 63*(247), 231–255.

Bond, T. G., & Jackson, I. (1991). The Gou protocol revisited: A Piagetian contextualization of critique. *Archives de Psychologie, 59*(228), 31–53.

Bosma, H. A., & Kunnen, E. S. (2001). Determinants and mechanisms in ego identity development: A review and synthesis. *Developmental Review, 21,* 39–66.

Boyce, W. T., Frank, E., Jensen, P. S., Kessler, R. C., Nelson, C. A., & Steinberg, L. (1998). Social context in developmental psychopathology: Recommendations for future research from the MacArthur Network on Psychopathology and Development. *Development and Psychopathology, 10*(2), 143–164.

Boyce, W. T., & Keating, D. P. (in press). Should we intervene to improve childhood circumstances? In D. Kuh & Y. Ben-Shlomo (Eds.), *A life course approach to chronic disease epidemiology.* Oxford, England: Oxford University Press.

Bronfenbrenner, U. (1999). Environments in developmental perspective: Theoretical and operational models. In S. L. Friedman & T. D. Wachs (Eds.), *Measuring environment across the life span: Emerging methods and concepts* (pp. 3–28). Washington, DC: American Psychological Association.

Bryant, P. E., & Trabasso, T. (1971). Transitive inferences and memory in young children. *Nature, 232*(5311), 456–458.

Bush, G., Luu, P., & Posner, M. I. (2000). Cognitive and emotional influences in anterior cingulate cortex. *Trends in Cognitive Sciences, 4,* 215–222.

Byrnes, J. P. (1998). *The nature and development of decision making: A self-regulation model.* Mahwah, NJ: Erlbaum.

Case, R. (1991). *The mind's staircase.* Hillsdale, NJ: Erlbaum.

Case, R. (1992). The role of the frontal lobes in the regulation of cognitive development. *Brain and Cognition, 20,* 51–73.

Case, R. (1999). Conceptual development. In M. Bennett (Ed.), *Developmental psychology: Achievements and prospects* (pp. 36–54). Philadelphia, PA: Psychology Press.

Case, R., & Okamoto, Y. (1996). The role of central conceptual structures in the development of children's thought. *Monographs of the Society for Research in Child Development, 61*(1–2, Serial No. 246), v–265.

Casey, B. J., Giedd, J. N., & Thomas, K. M. (2000). Structural and functional brain development and its relation to cognitive development. *Biological Psychology, 54,* 241–257.

Cauffman, E., & Steinberg, L. (1995). The cognitive and affective influences on adolescent decision making. *Temple Law Review, 68,* 1763–1789.

Chalmers, D. J. (1996). *The conscious mind: In search of a fundamental theory.* New York: Oxford University Press.

Chandler, M. J. (2000). Surviving time: The persistence of identity in this culture and that. *Culture and Psychology, 6,* 209–231.

Chandler, M. J., Hallett, D., & Sokol, B. W. (2002). Competing claims about competing knowledge claims. In B. K. Hofer & P. R. Pintrich (Eds.), *Personal epistemology: The psychology of beliefs about knowledge and knowing* (pp. 145–168). Mahwah, NJ: Erlbaum.

Chandler, M. J., Sokol, B. W., & Wainryb, C. (2000). Beliefs about truth and beliefs about rightness. *Child Development, 71,* 91–97.

Chi, M. T. H. (2000). Self-explaining: The dual processes of generating inference and repairing mental models. In R. Glaser (Ed.), *Advances in instructional psychology: Educational design and cognitive science* (Vol. 5, pp. 161–238). Mahwah, NJ: Erlbaum.

Chi, M. T. H., Glaser, R., & Farr, M. J. (Eds.). (1988). *The nature of expertise.* Hillsdale, NJ: Erlbaum.

Chi, M. T. H., Glaser, R., & Rees, E. (1982). Expertise in problem solving. In R. J. Sternberg (Ed.), *Advances in the psychology of human intelligence* (Vol. 1, pp. 7–75). Hillsdale, NJ: Erlbaum.

Chi, M. T. H., Hutchinson, J. E., & Robin, A. F. (1989). How inferences about novel domain-related concepts can be constrained by structured knowledge. *Merrill-Palmer Quarterly, 35,* 27–62.

Chi, M. T. H., Slotta, J. D., & de Leeuw, N. (1994). From things to processes: A theory of conceptual change for learning science concepts. *Learning and Instruction, 4,* 27–43.

Cook, T. D., & Campbell, D. T. (1979). *Quasi-experimentation: Design and analysis issues for field settings.* Chicago: Rand-McNally.

Cynader, M. S., & Frost, B. J. (1999). Mechanisms of brain development: Neuronal sculpting by the physical and social environment. In D. P. Keating & C. Hertzman (Eds.), *Developmental health and the wealth of nations: Social, biological, and educational dynamics* (pp. 153–184). New York: Guilford Press.

Davison, K. K., & Susman, E. J. (2001). Are hormone levels and cognitive ability related during early adolescence? *International Journal of Behavioral Development, 25,* 416–428.

Demetriou, A., Christou, C., Spanoudis, G., & Platsidou, M. (2002). The development of mental processing: Efficiency, working memory, and thinking. *Monographs of the Society for Research in Child Development, 67*(1, Serial No. 268).

Dennett, D. C. (1991). *Consciousness explained.* Cambridge, MA: Bradford/MIT Press.

Dennett, D. C. (1996). *Kinds of minds: Toward an understanding of consciousness.* New York: Basic Books.

Dishion, T. J., Eddy, J. M., Haas, E., Li, F., & Spracklen, K. (1997). Friendships and violent behavior during adolescence. *Social Development, 6,* 207–223.

Donald, M. (2001). *A mind so rare: The evolution of human consciousness.* New York: Norton.

Durston, S., Hulshoff, P., Hilleke, E., Casey, B. J., Giedd, J. N., Buitelaar, J. K., & van Engeland, H. (2001). Anatomical MRI of the developing human brain: What have we learned? *Journal of the American Academy of Child and Adolescent Psychiatry, 40,* 1012–1020.

Ericsson, K. A. (2002). Attaining excellence through deliberate practice: Insights from the study of expert performance. In M. Ferrari (Ed.), *The pursuit of excellence through education* (pp. 21–55). Mahwah, NJ: Erlbaum.

Ericsson, K. A., & Charness, N. (1999). Expert performance: Its structure and acquisition. In S. J. Ceci & W. M. Williams (Eds.), *The nature–nurture debate: The essential readings* (pp. 199–255). Malden, MA: Blackwell.

Ferrari, M., Pinard, A., & Runions, K. (2001). Piaget's framework for a scientific study of consciousness. *Human Development, 44,* 195–213.

Flanagan, C. A., Bowes, J. M., Jonsson, B., Csapo, B., & Sheblanova, E. (1998). Ties that bind: Correlates of adolescents' civic commitments in seven countries. *Journal of Social Issues, 54,* 457–475.

Flippen, A. R. (1999). Understanding groupthink from a self-regulatory perspective. *Small Group Research, 30,* 139–165.

Foltz, C., Overton, W. F., & Ricco, R. B. (1995). Proof construction: Adolescent development from inductive to deductive problem-solving strategies. *Journal of Experimental Child Psychology, 59,* 179–195.

Francis, D. D., Diorio, J., Plotsky, P. M., & Meaney, M. J. (2002). Environmental enrichment reverses the effects of maternal separation on stress reactivity. *Journal of Neuroscience, 22,* 7840–7843.

Frith, C. (2002). Attention to action and awareness of other minds. *Consciousness and Cognition, 11,* 481–487.

Fuster, J. M. (2000). The prefrontal cortex of the primate: A synopsis. *Psychobiology, 28,* 125–131.

Fuster, J. M., Van Hoesen, G. W., Morecraft, R. J., & Semendeferi, K. (2000). Executive systems. In B. S. Fogel, R. B. Schiffer, & S. M. Rao (Eds.), *Synopsis of neuropsychiatry* (pp. 229–242). Philadelphia, PA: Lippincott Williams & Wilkins.

Galotti, K. M. (1999). Making a "major" real-life decision: College students choosing an academic major. *Journal of Educational Psychology, 91,* 379–387.

Gardner, H. (1985). *The mind's new science: A history of the cognitive revolution.* New York: Basic Books.

Giedd, J. N., Blumenthal, J., Jeffries, N. O., Castellanos, F. X., Liu, H., Zijdenbos, A., Paus, T., Evans, A. C., & Rapoport, J. L. (1999). Brain development during childhood and adolescence: A longitudinal MRI study. *Nature Neuroscience, 2,* 861–863.

Gray, W. M. (1990). Formal operational thought. In W. F. Overton (Ed.), *Reasoning, necessity, and logic: Developmental perspectives* (pp. 227–253). Hillsdale, NJ: Erlbaum.

Hassler, M. (1991). Maturation rate and spatial, verbal, and musical abilities: A seven-year longitudinal study. *International Journal of Neuroscience, 58,* 183–198.

Hebb, D. O. (1949). *The organization of behavior.* New York: Wiley.

Holroyd, C. B., & Coles, M. G. H. (2002). The neural basis of human error processing: Reinforcement learning, dopamine, and the error-related negativity. *Psychological Review, 109,* 679–709.

Horn, S. S (2003). Adolescents' reasoning about exclusion from social groups. *Developmental Psychology, 39,* 71–84.

Huttenlocher, P. R. (1994). Synaptogenesis, synapse elimination, and neural plasticity in the human cerebral cortex. In C. A. Nelson (Ed.), *Minnesota symposium on child psychology: Vol. 27. Threats to optimal development: Integrating biological, psychological, and social risk factors* (pp. 35–54). Hillsdale, NJ: Erlbaum.

Inhelder, B., & Piaget, J. (1958). *The growth of logical thinking from childhood to adolescence: An essay on the construction of formal operational structures.* Oxford, England: Basic Books.

Jacobs, J. E., & Ganzel, A. K. (1993). Decision making in adolescence: Are we asking the wrong question? *Advances in Motivation and Achievement, 8,* 1–31.

Janis, I. L. (1972). *Victims of groupthink: A psychological study of foreign-policy decisions and fiascoes.* Oxford, England: Houghton Mifflin.

Johnson, M. H. (2001). Functional brain development in humans. *Nature Reviews Neuroscience, 2,* 475–483.

Johnson, D. M., & Erneling, C. E. (Eds.). (1997). *The future of the cognitive revolution.* New York: Oxford University Press.

Johnson-Laird, P. N. (1983). *Mental models: Towards a cognitive science of language, inference, and consciousness.* Cambridge: Harvard University Press.

Jones, P. E., & Roelofsma, P. H. M. P. (2000). The potential for social contextual and group biases in team decision-making: Biases, conditions and psychological mechanisms. *Ergonomics, 43,* 1129–1152.

Keating, D. P. (1980). Thinking processes in adolescence. In J. Adelson (Ed.), *Handbook of adolescent psychology* (pp. 211–246). New York: Wiley.

Keating, D. P. (1990a) Adolescent thinking. In S. Feldman & G. Elliott (Eds.), *At the threshold: The developing adolescent* (pp. 54–89). Cambridge, MA: Harvard University Press.

Keating, D. P. (1990b). Charting pathways to the development of expertise. *Educational Psychologist, 25,* 243–267.

Keating, D. P. (1990c). Developmental processes in the socialization of cognitive structures. *Entwicklung und Lernen: Beiträge zum Symposium anläßlich des 60. Geburtstages von Wolfgang Edelstein [Development and learning: Proceedings of a symposium in honour of Wolfgang Edelstein on his 60th birthday].* Berlin: Max Planck Institut für Bildungsforschung.

Keating, D. P. (1990d). Structuralism, deconstruction, reconstruction: The limits of reasoning. In W. F. Overton (Ed.), *Reasoning, necessity, and logic: Developmental perspectives* (pp. 299–319). Hillsdale, NJ: Erlbaum.

Keating, D. P. (1996a). Central conceptual structures: Seeking developmental integration. *Monographs of the Society for Research in Child Development, 61*(1–2, Serial No. 246), 276–282.

Keating, D. P. (1996b). Habits of mind: Developmental diversity in competence and coping (Reply: Human developmental diversity: A learning society perspective, pp. 211–215). In D. K. Detterman (Ed.), *Current topics in human intelligence: Vol. 5. The environment* (pp. 31–44). Norwood, NJ: Ablex.

Keating, D. P. (1996c). Habits of mind for a learning society: Educating for human development. In D. R. Olson & N. Torrance (Eds.), *Handbook of education and human development: New models of learning, teaching and schooling* (pp. 461–481). Oxford: Blackwell.

Keating, D. P. (2001a, April). *Adolescent development: Old questions, new answers.* Paper presented at the biennial meeting of the Society for Research in Child Development, Minneapolis, MN.

Keating, D. P. (2001b). Definition and selection of competencies from a human development perspective. In *Additional DeSeCo expert opinions* (pp. 1–44). Paris: Organisation for Economic Co-operation and Development.

Keating, D. P., & Bobbitt, B. (1978). Individual and developmental differences in cognitive-processing components of mental ability. *Child Development, 49,* 155–167.

Keating, D. P., & Hertzman, C. (Eds.). (1999). *Developmental health and the wealth of nations: Social, biological, and educational dynamics.* New York: Guilford Press.

Keating, D. P., List, J. A., & Merriman, W. E. (1985). Cognitive processing and cognitive ability: A multivariate validity investigation. *Intelligence, 9,* 149–170.

Keating, D. P., & Sasse, D. K. (1996). Cognitive socialization in adolescence: Critical period for a critical habit of mind. In G. Adams, R. Montemayor, & T. Gullotta (Eds.), *Psychosocial development during adolescence* (pp. 232–258). Thousand Oaks, CA: Sage.

Keating, D. P., & Shapka, J. D. (1998). *Pubertal change, cognitive change, and the development of psychopathology in adolescence: Vol. 1. The report.* Prepared for the MacArthur Foundation Research Network on Psychopathology and Development.

Klaczynski, P. A. (2001a). Analytic and heuristic processing influences on adolescent reasoning and decision making. *Child Development, 72,* 844–861.

Klaczynski, P. A. (2001b). Framing effects on adolescent task representations, analytic and heuristic processing, and decision making: Implications for the normative/descriptive gap. *Applied Developmental Psychology, 22,* 289–309.

Klaczynski, P. A., Byrnes, J. P., & Jacobs, J. E. (2001). Introduction to the special issue: The development of decision making. *Applied Developmental Psychology, 22,* 225–236.

Klahr, D. (2000). *Exploring science: The cognition and development of discovery processes.* Cambridge: MIT Press.

Klahr, D., Fay, A. L., & Dunbar, K. (1993). Heuristics for scientific experimentation: A developmental study. *Cognitive Psychology, 25,* 111–146.

Klingberg, T., Vaidya, C. J., Gabrieli, J. D. E., Moseley, M. E., & Hedehus, M. (1999). Myelination and organization of the frontal white matter in children: A diffusion tensor MRI study. *Neuroreport, 10,* 2817–2821.

Kokis, J. V., Macpherson, R., Toplak, M. E., West, R. F., & Stanovich, K. E. (2002). Heuristic and analytic processing: Age trends and associations with cognitive ability and cognitive styles. *Journal of Experimental Child Psychology, 83,* 26–52.

Koslowski, B. (1996). *Theory and evidence: The development of scientific reasoning.* Cambridge, MA: MIT Press.

Krawczyk, D. C. (2002). Contributions of the prefrontal cortex to the neural basis of human decision making. *Neuroscience and Biobehavioral Reviews, 26,* 631–664.

Kuhn, D., Amsel, E., & O'Loughlin, M. (1988). *The development of scientific thinking skills.* San Diego, CA: Academic Press.

Kuhn, D., Garcia-Mila, M., Zohar, A., & Andersen, C. (1995). Strategies of knowledge acquisition. *Monographs of the Society for Research in Child Development, 60*(4, Serial No. 245).

Kuhn, D., & Pearsall, S. (2000). Developmental origins of scientific thinking. *Journal of Cognition and Development, 1,* 113–129.

Kwon, Y.-J., & Lawson, A. E. (2000). Linking brain growth with the development of scientific reasoning ability and conceptual change during adolescence. *Journal of Research in Science Teaching, 37,* 44–62.

Kwon, Y.-J., Lawson, A. E., Chung, W.-H., & Kim, Y.-S. (2000). Effect on development of proportional reasoning skill of physical experience and cognitive abilities associated with prefontal lobe activity. *Journal of Research in Science Teaching, 37,* 1171–1182.

Larson, R. (1995). Secrets in the bedroom: Adolescents' private use of media. *Journal of Youth and Adolescence, 24,* 535–550.

Larson, R. W., Richards, M. H., Moneta, G., Holmbeck, G., & Duckett, E. (1996). Changes in adolescents' daily interactions with their families from ages 10 to 18: Disengagement and transformation. *Developmental Psychology, 32,* 744–754.

Lawson, A. E., Clark, B., Cramer-Meldrum, E., Falconer, K. A., Sequist, J. M., & Kwon, Y.-J. (2000). Development of scientific reasoning in college biology: Do two levels of general hypothesis-testing skills exist? *Journal of Research in Science Teaching, 37,* 81–101.

Lewis, M. D. (2002). The dialogical brain: Contributions of emotional neurobiology to understanding the dialogical self. *Theory and Psychology, 12,* 175–190.

Linn, M., & Petersen, A. (1985). Emergence and characterization of sex differences in spatial ability: A meta-analysis. *Child Development, 56,* 1479–1498.

Luciana, M., & Nelson, C. A. (in press). Neurodevelopmental assessment of cognitive function using the Cambridge Neuropsychological Testing Automated Battery (CANTAB): Validation and future goals. In J. Rumsey & M. Ernst (Eds.), *The foundation and future of functional neuroimaging in child psychiatry.* Cambridge: Cambridge University Press.

Luna, B., Thulborn, K. R., Munoz, D. P., Merriam, E. P., Garver, K. E., Minshew, N. J., Keshavan, M. S., Genovese, C. R., Eddy, W. F., & Sweeney, J. A. (2001). Maturation of widely distributed brain function subserves cognitive development. *Neuroimage, 13,* 786–793.

Luu, P., Collins, P., & Tucker, D. M. (2000). Mood, personality, and self-monitoring: Negative affect and emotionality in relation to frontal lobe mechanisms of error monitoring. *Journal of Experimental Psychology: General, 129*(1), 43–60.

Luu, P., Tucker, D. M., Derryberry, D., Reed, M., & Poulsen, C. (2003). Electrophysiological responses to errors and feedback in the process of action regulation. *Psychological Science, 14,* 47–53.

Markovits, H., & Barrouillet, P. (2002). The development of conditioned reasoning: A mental model account. *Developmental Review, 22,* 5–36.

Markovits, H., & Savary, F. (1992). Pragmatic schemas and the selection task: To reason or not to reason. *Quarterly Journal of Experimental Psychology: Human Experimental Psychology, 45A,* 133–148.

Marshall, S. K. (2001). Do I matter? Construct validation of adolescents' perceived mattering to parents and friends .*Journal of Adolescence, 24,* 473–490.

McArdle, J. J., Ferrer-Caja, E., Hamagami, F., & Woodcock, R. W. (2002). Comparative longitudinal structural analyses of the growth and decline of multiple intellectual abilities over the life span. *Developmental Psychology, 38,* 115–142.

McGinn, C. (1999, June). Can we ever understand consciousness? *New York Review of Books,* 44.

Meaney, M. J. (2001). Maternal care, gene expression, and the transmission of individual differences in stress reactivity across generations. *Annual Review of Neuroscience, 24,* 1161–1192.

Morris, B. J., & Sloutsky, V. (2001). Children's solutions of logical versus empirical problems: What's missing and what develops? *Cognitive Development, 16,* 907–928.

Moshman, D. (1998). Cognitive development beyond childhood. In D. Kuhn & R. S. Siegler (Eds.), *Handbook of child psychology: Vol. 2. Cognition, perception, and language* (pp. 947–978). New York: Wiley.

Mueller, U., Sokol, B., & Overton, W. F. (1999). Developmental sequences in class reasoning and prepositional reasoning. *Journal of Experimental Child Psychology, 74,* 69–106.

Nelson, C. A. (1999). Neural plasticity and human development. *Current Directions in Psychological Science, 8,* 42–45.

Nelson, C. A., Bloom, F. E., Cameron, J. L., Amaral, D., Dahl, R. E., & Pine, D. (2002). An integrative, multidisciplinary approach to the study of brain-behavior relations in the context of typical and atypical development. *Development and Psychopathology, 14,* 499–520.

Newcombe, N., Semon Dubas, J., & Baenninger, M. (1989). Associations of timing of puberty, spatial ability, and lateralization in adult women. *Child Development, 60,* 246–254.

Newman, J., & Grace, A. A. (1999). Binding across time: The selective gating of frontal and hippocampal systems modulating working memory and attentional states. *Consciousness and Cognition, 8,* 196–212.

Noelting, G., Rousseau, J. P., Coude, G., Bond, T., & Brunel, M.-L. (2000). Can qualitative stage characteristics be revealed quantitatively? *Archives de Psychologie, 68*(266–267), 259–275.

Oades, R. D., Dittmann-Balcar, A., & Zerbin, D. (1997). Development and topography of auditory event-related potentials (ERPs): Mismatch and processing negativity in individuals 8–22 years of age. *Psychophysiology, 34,* 677–693.

Ormond, C., Luszcz, M. A., Mann, L., & Beswick, G. (1991). A metacognitive analysis of decision making in adolescence. *Journal of Adolescence, 14,* 275–291.

Orr, D. P., Brack, C. J., & Ingersoll, G. (1988). Pubertal maturation and cognitive maturity in adolescents. *Journal of Adolescent Health, 9,* 273–279.

Overton, W. F. (1990). Competence and procedures: Constraints on the development of logical reasoning. In W. F. Overton (Ed.), *Reasoning, necessity, and logic: Developmental perspectives* (pp. 1–32). Hillsdale, NJ: Erlbaum.

Park, W.-W. (2000). A comprehensive empirical investigation of the relationships among variables of the groupthink model. *Journal of Organizational Behavior, 21,* 873–887.

Pascual-Leone, J. (1978). Compounds, confounds, and models in developmental information processing: A reply to Trabasso and Foellinger. *Journal of Experimental Child Psychology, 26*(1), 18–40.

Paus, T., Zijdenbos, A., Worsley, K., Collins, D. L., Blumenthal, J., Giedd, J. N., Rapoport, J. L.,

& Evans, A. C. (1999). Structural maturation of neural pathways in children and adolescents: In vivo study. *Science, 283,* 1908–1911.

Payne, M. A. (2002). Adolescent decision-making: A comparison of adult and teenage perspectives in New Zealand. *International Journal of Adolescence and Youth, 10,* 277–295.

Piaget, J. (1965). *Sagasse et illusions de la philosophie (Wisdom and illusions of philosophy).* Paris: Presses Universitaires de France.

Pribram, K. H. (1986). The cognitive revolution and mind/brain issues. *American Psychologist, 41*(5), 507–520.

Rilling, J. K., & Insel, T. R. (1999). The primate neocortex in comparative perspective using magnetic resonance imaging. *Journal of Human Evolution, 37,* 191–223.

Ruck, M. D., Abramovitch, R., & Keating, D. P. (1998). Children's and adolescents' understanding of rights: Balancing nurturance and self-determination. *Child Development, 64,* 404–417.

Ruck, M. D., Keating, D. P., Abramovitch, R., & Koegl, C. (1998). Adolescents' and children's knowledge about rights: Some evidence for how young people view rights in their own lives. *Journal of Adolescence, 21,* 275–289.

Sampson, R. J., Morenoff, J. D., & Gannon-Rowley, T. (2002). Assessing "neighborhood effects": Social processes and new directions in research. *Annual Review of Sociology, 28,* 443–478.

Schmithorst, V. J., Wilke, M., Dardzinski, B. J., & Holland, S. K. (2002). Correlation of white matter diffusivity and anisotropy with age during childhood and adolescence: A cross-sectional diffusion-tensor MR imaging study. *Radiology, 222,* 212–218.

Searle, J. R. (1997). *The mystery of consciousness.* London: Granta Books.

Segalowitz, S. J., Unsal, A., & Dywan, J. (1992). Cleverness and wisdom in 12-year-olds: Electrophysiological evidence for late maturation of the frontal lobe. *Developmental Neuropsychology, 8,* 279–298.

Shadish, W. R., Cook, T. D., & Campbell, D. T. (2002). *Experimental and quasi-experimental designs for generalized causal inference.* Boston: Houghton-Mifflin.

Siegler, R. S. (Ed.). (1978). *Children's thinking: What develops?* Hillsdale, NJ: Erlbaum.

Sowell, E. R., Delis, D., Stiles, J., & Jernigan, T. L. (2001). Improved memory functioning and frontal lobe maturation between childhood and adolescence: A structural MRI study. *Journal of the International Neuropsychological Society, 7,* 312–322.

Sowell, E. R., Thompson, P. M., Holmes, C. J., Batth, R., Jernigan, T. L., & Toga, A. W. (1999a). Localizing age-related changes in brain structure between childhood and adolescence using statistical parametric mapping. *NeuroImage, 9,* 587–597.

Sowell, E. R., Thompson, P. M., Holmes, C. J., Jernigan, T. L., & Toga, A. W. (1999b). In vivo evidence for post-adolescent brain maturation in frontal and striatal regions. *Nature Neuroscience, 2,* 859–861.

Sowell, E. R., Trauner, D. A, Gamst, A., & Jernigan, T. L. (2002). Development of cortical and subcortical brain structures in childhood and adolescence: A structural MRI study. *Developmental Medicine and Child Neurology, 44*(1), 4–16.

Stanovich, K. E. (1999). *Who is rational? Studies of individual differences in reasoning.* Mahwah, NJ: Erlbaum.

Steinberg, L., Dahl, R., Keating, D. P., Kupfer, D. J., Masten, A., & Pine, D. (in press). The study of developmental psychopathology in adolescence: Integrating affective neuroscience with the study of context. In D. Cicchetti (Ed.), *Handbook of developmental psychopathology.* New York: Wiley.

Steinberg, L., & Morris, A. S. (2001). Adolescent development. *Annual Review of Psychology, 52,* 83–110.

Steinberg, L., & Silverberg, S. B. (1986). The vicissitudes of autonomy in early adolescence. *Child Development, 57,* 841–851.

Steingard, R. J., Renshaw, P. F., Hennen, J., Lenox, M., Cintron, C. B., Young, A. D., Connor, D. F., Au, T. H., & Yurgelun-Todd, D. A. (2002). Smaller frontal lobe white matter volumes in depressed adolescents. *Journal of Biological Psychiatry, 52,* 413–417.

Stuss, D. T. (1992). Biological and psychological development of executive functions. *Brain and Cognition, 20,* 8–23.

Swidler, A. (1986). Culture in action: Symbols and strategies. *American Sociological Review, 51,* 273–286.

Tice, D. M., & Bratslavsky, E. (2000). Giving in to feel good: The place of emotion regulation in the context of general self-control. *Psychological Inquiry, 11*(3), 149–159.

Torney-Purta, J. (1991). Recent psychological research relating to children's social cognition and its implications for social and political education. In I. Morriset & A. M. Williams (Eds.), *Social/political education in three countries* (pp. 91–111). Boulder, CO: Social Sciences Education Consortium.

Trabasso, T., Isen, A. M., Dolecki, P., McLanahan, A. G., Riley, C. A., & Tucker, T. (1978). How do children solve class-inclusion problems? In R. S. Siegler (Ed.), *Children's thinking: What develops?* (pp. 151–180). Hillsdale, NJ: Erlbaum.

Turner, M. E., & Pratkanis, A. R. (1998). Twenty-five years of groupthink theory and research: Lessons from the evaluation of a theory. *Organizational Behavior and Human Decision Processes, 73,* 105–115.

van Veen, V., & Carter, C. S. (2002). The anterior cingulate as a conflict monitor: fMRI and ERP studies. *Physiology and Behavior, 77,* 477–482.

Vygotsky, L. S. (1979). *Mind in society.* Cambridge, MA: Harvard University Press.

Waber, D. P., Mann, M. B., Merola, J., & Moylan, P. M. (1985). Physical maturation rate and cognitive performance in early adolescence: A longitudinal examination. *Developmental Psychology, 21,* 666–681.

Walker, R., Hill, K., Kaplan, H., & McMillan, G. (2002). Age-dependency in hunting ability among the Ache of Eastern Paraguay. *Journal of Human Evolution, 42,* 639–657.

Watanabe, M. (2002). Integration across multiple cognitive and motivational domains in monkey prefrontal cortex. In D. T. Stuss & R. T. Knight (Eds.), *Principles of frontal lobe function* (pp. 326–337). London: Oxford University Press.

Williams, W. M., Blythe, T., White, N., Li, J., Gardner, H., & Sternberg, R. J. (2002). Practical intelligence for school: Developing metacognitive sources of achievement in adolescence. *Developmental Review, 22,* 162–210.

Wilson, E. O. (1998). *Consilience: The unity of knowledge.* New York: Knopf.

Chapter 4

SOCIALIZATION AND SELF-DEVELOPMENT

Channeling, Selection, Adjustment, and Reflection

Jari-Erik Nurmi

INTRODUCTION

Adolescence is a crossroads from childhood to adulthood. Childhood experiences and biological characteristics are transformed into interests, competencies, and self-beliefs and begin to play an increasingly important role as the adolescent starts to make his or her way toward adult life. This development is channeled by a variety of opportunities and constraints in the adolescent's social and institutional environments: Not all is possible, but many things are. Out of these alternative pathways the adolescent has to select the ones that appeal to him or her, or, in some cases, to significant others. Not everything is attained, and surprises are part of the game. Therefore, ways to deal with problems and unexpected events are developed. Along with these efforts and adventures, adolescents begin to know themselves and to make reflections about who they are. Young people are not alone in their efforts. Most of them live with their parents but spend increasing amounts of time with their peers and friends. In these relations, advice is given, interests raised, goals negotiated, solutions compared, and outcomes evaluated. The aim of this chapter is to review what is currently known about the ways in which adolescents make their ways into adulthood.

Adolescents face two broad challenges during the transition from childhood to adult life: the entrance into production and reproduction fields of the culture and society. Entrance into production includes becoming an economically independent individual who is able to make his or her living in the society and economic system. This developmental trajectory consists typically of a complex set of decisions concerning schooling, education, and career. In turn, entrance into the reproduction domain includes a pattern of sequential commitments to romantic relationships, building up intimate relations, founding a family, and taking care of children. Although there is a lot of variation in how these two broad challenges are approached, dealt with, and solved, these seem to be the key challenges in all cultures and societies. The reasons for this are simple. When adolescents

The author would like to thank Kaisa Aunola, Terry Honess, and Katariina Salmela-Aro for their valuable comments on the earlier versions of the manuscript and Rakel Nurmi, Maura Nurmi, and Katriina Aho-Nurmi for secretarial assistance.

participate in these two processes, they become the agents in the reproduction of the society, its economy, and its way of life (Nurmi, 1993). Moreover, working through these two general challenges builds up a basis for the adolescent's individuation from his or her childhood family, as well as for his or her entrance into adult life and identity.

An increasing amount of research has been carried out on adolescence during the past two decades. The majority of the studies has focused on examining adolescents' behavioral characteristics, parental behaviors, or some other seemingly objective features of adolescence. This research has provided important information about how adolescents behave in many environments and about how this behavior changes with age. Much less research has been carried out on how the adolescent's mind works and the kinds of consequences this adolescent psychology has for young people's further development. There are, however, a few relevant topics examined in the field of adolescent research, such as self-concept, aspirations, coping, and identity. Some more recent topics that are becoming popular in personality and social psychology are personal goals, social strategies, problem solving, causal attributions, and identity narratives. These topics have also begun to gain increasing attention in adolescent research.

In this chapter I review research on how adolescents' minds work as they move to adulthood, that is, what they think and feel about their lives as adolescents, what kinds of interests they have, the kinds of tools they develop to deal with the challenges of adolescence, and the ways in which they make stories about themselves later on. When reviewing this research I used a few principles to make scientific generalizations of the empirical research. The first principle is that before we make any generalization about the findings, they should be replicated. Second, the source of the information on which the results are based is considered. In some cases, such as parenting, information from both parents and adolescents is a valid source of information. However, when the interest is in a particular person's thinking, such as the mother's educational goals for their child, the ways in which the adolescent perceives his or her mother's goals is a secondary type of information. Finally, the direction of influence is the key issue in developmental psychology. However, it is difficult to deal with because experimental research and intervention studies are rare. The major way to get evidence for the causality in developmental processes is to use cross-lagged longitudinal data, which makes it possible to control the previous level of the dependent variable before examining the later impacts of the independent variables on the dependent variable.

A typical approach in review chapters such as this is to focus on one particular well-defined research area and to exclude other topics. This approach may be problematic for two reasons. The first is that researchers typically develop different kinds of conceptualizations to deal with more or less the same phenomenon. Focusing on one conceptualization only would mean, in fact, that not all important findings for a particular phenomenon will be reviewed. Consequently, the aim of this chapter is to search for the similarities across a variety of conceptualizations rather than to concentrate on analyzing differences. Second, when focusing on one relatively narrow phenomenon and a related research paradigm, there is a danger of losing sight of adolescent development as a whole. In this chapter I make an effort to integrate research on adolescence under a few umbrella concepts in order to provide a more holistic view of the young person.

In order to attain this goal, I first present a view in which adolescents' socialization is described in terms of four mechanisms: channeling, selection, adjustment, and reflection. Then, research on a variety of more traditional concepts, such as future-orientation, occupational aspirations, identity exploration, coping, causal attribution, self-concept, and identity formation, are reviewed under these four headings. A few topics, however, are excluded, such as academic motivation and achievement goals because other chapters in this Handbook focus on them. The role of family and peers as the interpersonal context for adolescent development is also considered. Finally, a few future research directions and methodological issues are discussed.

CHANNELING, SELECTION, ADJUSTMENT, AND REFLECTION

During the adolescent years, an individual moves from being a member of the parents' family to a full member of society. This development is characterized by four key mechanisms (Figure 4.1): First, adolescents grow up in changing environments that *channel* their developmental trajectories. A variety of sociocultural factors like cultural beliefs, institutional structures, and historical events form such environments, which also change rapidly from one age period to another (Nurmi, 1991). Such sociocultural and institutional structures define an opportunity space for the adolescent that channels his or her future-oriented motivation, thinking, and behavior. Second, as suggested by life span theorists (Brandstädter, 1984; Lerner, 1983), adolescents are not passive targets of environmental influences; rather, they *select* their developmental environments and future life paths. Many psychological mechanisms are responsible for this selection: Motives, interests, and personal goals direct adolescents' exploration, planning, decision making, and commitments and lead them to specific educational tracks, peers groups, and leisure activities. Third, as a consequence of their efforts to select the direction of their lives, adolescents end up having specific outcomes and receive feedback about their successes and failures. Feedback about developmental outcomes, particularly about failures and negative events, requires that young people *adjust* their goals, plans, and thinking in order to cope successfully with the future challenges of their developmental trajectories. Many psychological mechanisms, such as reconstruction of goals, coping, and causal attributions, are responsible for this adjustment. Finally, after receiving information about the outcomes of their efforts and ending up in a particular life situation and social position, adolescents typically *reflect* about a variety of issues concerning themselves and their lives: They construct conceptualizations about themselves and tell stories to their parents and peers aimed at building up a coherent personal identity (Figure 4.2).

Channeling: Developmental Tasks, Role Transitions, and Institutional Careers

Adolescents grow up in environments that consist of a variety of social expectations set by their parents, teachers, and peers; many demands and standards are defined by so-

Channeling ⟹ Selection ⟹ Adjustment ⟹ Reflection

Figure 4.1 Channeling, selection, adjustment, and reflection.

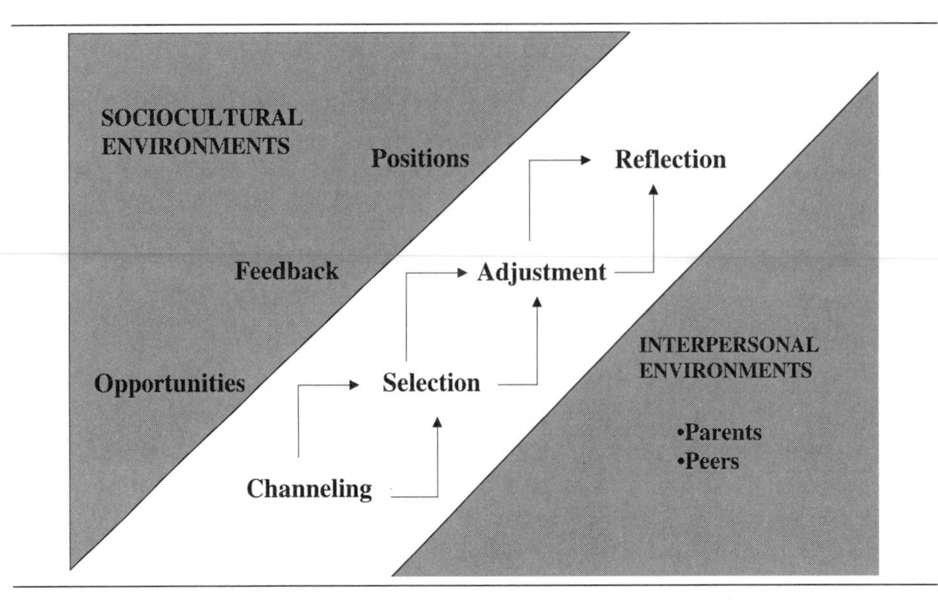

Figure 4.2 Channeling, selection, adjustment, and reflection in sociocultural and interpersonal environments.

cial and institutional sources, such as school curriculums, coaches, and classmates; and a variety of opportunities is created by educational systems and the economy (Figure 4.2). It has been suggested that these age systems are important for adolescent development because they create predictable, socially recognized road maps for human lives (Hagestad & Neugarten, 1985).

One major feature of such environments is that they are closely related to a person's age. Parental expectations, educational standards at school, and opportunities for educational decisions, for example, change from one age to another. Although these kinds of age-graded environments are in most part similar to adolescents of a particular age living in a certain society, they also differ along many factors, such as gender, social stratum, ethnic background, and family characteristics. Perhaps because, by definition, psychologists interested in adolescence have been committed to individuals' thinking and behavior, they have often overlooked the role of such environmental structures.

These age-graded differences in individuals' developmental environments have been described in the life span theory of human development in a variety of conceptualizations. These are discussed next.

Developmental Tasks

The first concept used to describe age-graded contexts was that of the developmental task. The concept was introduced by Havighurst (1948), who defined it as "a task which arises at or about a certain period of time in the life of an individual, successful achievement of which leads to his happiness and success with later tasks, while failure leads to unhappiness in the individual, disapproval by the society and difficulty with later tasks" (p. 2). Havighurst's original conceptualization of the origins of developmental tasks was broad. He saw them as motivated by normative demands, physical maturation, and personal values and aspirations.

According to Havighurst (1948), developmental tasks consist of normative expectations and requirements to do or achieve something at a certain age. Even though key themes of these tasks, such as work, human relationships, and ideology, are the same across the life span, different life stages are characterized by different tasks. Developmental tasks also include beliefs about appropriate behavior and about outcomes that are interpreted as a successful way of handling a specific task. Similarly, these tasks consist of beliefs about inappropriate behavior that is evaluated as a failure. The influence of developmental tasks on individual thinking is mediated by the behavior of and feedback from other people, such as parents, peers, and teachers.

Typical developmental tasks for adolescence include achieving mature relationships with peers and forming a sex-role identity, preparing for marriage and family life, achieving emotional independence from parents, and preparing for an economic career, including planning education. Tasks for early adulthood include finding an occupation, selecting a partner and starting a family, rearing children, and finding a congenial social group (Havighurst, 1948). Although Western societies have changed substantially during the last few decades, more recent descriptions of developmental tasks are very similar to those of Havighurst (e.g., Strough, Berg, & Sansone, 1996).

Social Constraints and Role Transitions

In the decades since Havighurst's (1948) theory, similar conceptualizations have arisen. For example, Neugarten, Moore, and Lowe (1965) considered how age norms and social constraints indicate a prescriptive timetable for ordering major life events. According to them, these sociocultural patterns operate in a society as a system of social controls. On the basis of these normative beliefs, people's behaviors at a certain age can be described as early, late, or on time. Two decades later, similar ideas were put forward, such as role transitions and developmental standards (Elder, 1985). The conceptual differentiation between normative and nonnormative life events suggested by Baltes, Reese, and Lipsitt (1980) also emphasizes the importance of age-graded life-course patterns.

Institutional Careers

Most of the conceptualizations concerning age-graded environments have focused on normative structures and cultural beliefs in certain societies. By doing so, they have overlooked the fact that age-graded changes in institutional patterns also play an important role. For example, schooling and educational systems form age-related tracks that influence individuals' behavior and decisions at a specific age. These types of changes have been described earlier in terms of institutional careers (Mayer, 1986), tracks (Klaczynski & Reese, 1991), and action opportunities (Grotevant, 1987). The major feature that distinguishes these concepts from developmental tasks and role transitions is that they are based on specific institutional and organizational, or even legal, structures, rather than on cultural beliefs. During adolescence individuals are faced with many institutional transitions, particularly in the domain of education and work.

Selection: Goal Construction, Planning, Exploration, and Commitments

Adolescence is characterized by many challenges, demands, and options (Caspi, 2002). Because of this variety of opportunities and restricted individual resources, such as

Table 4.1 Channeling, Selection, Adjustment, and Reflection Mechanisms in Terms of Previous Research

Channeling	Selection	Adjustment	Reflection
Developmental tasks	Personal goals	Coping	Identity
Role transitions	Cognitive strategies	Goal reconstruction	Self-concept
Institutional careers	Problem solving	Causal attributions	Self-esteem
Anticipations of life span transitions	Explorations		Narratives
	Commitments		

time and energy, adolescents must focus on dealing with some of the future challenges available for them. This selection process (Baltes & Baltes, 1990) has been described in previous literature in terms of a variety of psychological mechanisms (Table 4.1).

Goal Construction

One of the key psychological mechanisms responsible for how an adolescent directs his or her development and selects from a variety of environments is motivation (Nurmi, 1993, 1997). On one hand, a young person has individual motives that are based on his or her earlier life history and experiences and on a variety of individual characteristics, such as personality traits and temperament. On the other, he or she is faced with a "space of opportunities" defined by the developmental tasks and by institutional tracks (Poole & Cooney, 1987). An individual constructs personal goals by comparing his or her individual motivation to the opportunities available in his or her environment (Nurmi, 1991; Nuttin, 1984). Such comparison provides a basis for realistic and attainable goals. Personal goals then help the individual to move to a direction that would satisfy his or her individual motivation (Salmela-Aro, Nurmi, Saisto, & Halmesmäki, 2000).

Previous research on adolescents' and young adults' motivation and personal goals arose from three different theoretical frameworks. One is personality psychology, in which many researchers have recently conceptualized motivation in terms of self-articulated personal goals. For example, Little (1983) described motivation in terms of personal projects, Markus and Nurius (1986) as possible selves, and Nurmi (1991) as future goals. Despite the differences in terminology, all these concepts refer to personal goals that (a) are based on more abstract individual motives (Nuttin, 1984), (b) exist within a system of hierarchically organized superordinate and subordinate motivational structures (Leontjev, 1977), (c) refer to some culturally defined task (Cantor, 1990; Nurmi, 1991), and (d) are realized by constructing different means-end structures (Nuttin, 1984). In this framework, personal goals are typically analyzed according to the domains of life they concern, such as education, work-career, family-marriage, leisure activities, property, and self-related–existential types of goals (Little, 1983; Nurmi, 1991).

Another line of research on motivation originates from research on adolescents' future orientation and time perspective (Nurmi, 1991). Thinking about the future is assumed to be of particular importance during the adolescent years because young people must deal with a variety of challenges concerning the transition into adulthood. Besides interest in the contents of adolescent goals, hopes, and fears concerning the future, this framework has typically examined how far into the future adolescents goals, interests, and concerns extend. In addition, the ways in which adolescents think and feel about their goals have been a focus of research (Nurmi, 1989a; Trommsdorff & Lamm, 1980).

The third line of research on adolescent motivation originates in more applied types of work that have focused on interests, aspirations, and expectations that young people have concerning one particular life domain. Typical life domains on which these studies have focused include education (Wilson & Wilson, 1992), occupation (Roisman, 2000), and family (Jenkins Tucker, Barber, & Eccles, 2001).

Strategy Construction, Planning, and Problem Solving

Besides personal goals and motivation, selection, to be completed, requires other psychological mechanisms to come into work. For example, adolescents' educational goals need to be complemented by planning and strategy construction (Nurmi, 1989a). Similarly, fulfilling one's interests in peer groups and intimate relationships requires strategic thinking (Eronen & Nurmi, 1999). When people are faced with a challenge or problem about which they have some experience, they typically apply some personal skills that they have previously developed (Markus & Wurf, 1987). However, when people are faced with new demands and challenges, they need to devise new strategies (Cantor, 1990; Nurmi, 1989a). This strategy construction consists of setting a goal as an anticipated representation of a hoped-for situation and activation of the schemata concerning a particular domain of life, searching for alternative means for goal attainment by means of planning, investing effort in the realization of these plans, regulating the behavior toward goal attainment, and evaluating the behavioral outcomes.

Two major frameworks have examined this planning and strategy construction among adolescents. The first approach focused on investigating the degree to which young people are involved in decision making and planning in a particular life domain, such as education (Klaczynski & Reese, 1991) and future career (Blustein, Devenis, & Kidney, 1989). Some studies have even examined adolescents' planning simultaneously in several domains (Malmberg, 1996). These studies have typically relied on straightforward self-report instruments.

Another approach has included efforts to identify the kinds of cognitive and behavioral patterns that individuals use in different situations. For example, Cantor (1990) described two types of strategies among young people who were successful in college environments. An optimistic strategy was characterized by straightforward striving for success based on high-outcome expectations and positive past experiences and on the desire to enhance already-strong images of competence. Typical of students using a defensive pessimist strategy was to have defensively low expectations and to feel anxious before performance. These negative expectations do not become self-fulfilling prophecies but serve as a protective attributional cover and motivator of the behavior leading to successful outcomes. Other types of strategies have been associated with poor performance. For example, Berglas and Jones (1978) described self-handicappers who are typically concerned about potential failure in a particular task and therefore concentrate on active task-avoidance in order to create excuses for the feared failure. Another prototypical maladaptive strategy is learned helplessness (Abramson, Seligman, & Teasdale, 1978). Because helpless people lack belief in personal control, they end up passively avoiding the new challenges and demands that they are facing.

Exploration and Commitments

Besides construction of goals and strategies, selection of a particular developmental trajectory includes also searching for information and making personal decisions. For example, process-oriented theories of identity development have described identity formation in terms of two mechanisms: exploration and commitments. Bosma (1985) and Grotevant (1987) both suggested that adolescents engage in a variety of explorational activities and related commitments that reflect their personal values and needs. Exploration and commitments may also progress differently in different life domains, such as education, intimate relationships, and ideology. In this approach, identity exploration and commitments are typically measured as continuous variables in different life domains.

Exploration and commitment are widely used concepts also in research focusing on adolescents' educational and occupational development. For example, vocational choice consists of several subsequent stages, such as exploration, crystallization, choice, implementation, and commitment (Harren, 1979). The major interest in this area of research has been to identify factors that influence such career-related exploration (Kracke & Schmitt-Rodermund, 2001), decision making, and commitments (Phillips, 1982).

Adjustment: Coping, Reconstruction of Goals, and Causal Attributions

In the course of the selection process, adolescents may attain the goals to which they were aiming. However, this is not always the case. In many situations, adolescents fail to reach their goals or do not succeed to the extent they expected. Young people may also face unexpected events that endanger some important aspects of their future lives. When adolescents face problems in goal attainment, they need to *adjust* some of their previous goals, cognitions, or behaviors (Figure 4.1). This adjustment process has been described in terms of many psychological mechanisms (Table 4.1).

Coping

When adolescents face problems in goal attainment, they try to find new ways of dealing with them, to avoid the difficult situation, or to avoid related information. These kinds of efforts have been described previously in terms of coping strategies (Folkman, Lazarus, Pimley, & Novacek, 1987). There are several ways to conceptualize coping. According to Seiffge-Krenke (1993), for example, functional coping refers to efforts to manage a problem by actively seeking support, undertaking concrete actions to solve a problem, or reflecting on possible solutions. A dysfunctional coping includes withdrawing from or denying the existence of the problem, avoiding active seeking of solutions, and attempting to regulate the emotions (Seiffge-Krenke, 1993). Understandably, the characteristics of the situation are important in the kind of coping an individual chooses to use. For example, effective coping in changeable situations consists of a greater use of problem-focused coping, whereas in an unchangeable situation effective coping involves a greater use of emotion-focused coping (Compas, Banez, Malcarne, & Worsham, 1991; Folkman et al., 1987). Consistent with this proposition, Blanchard-Fields, Jahnke, and Camp (1995) found that the use of problem-focused coping decreased, whereas passive-dependent coping increased, in use with greater emotional salience.

Research on coping shares similarities with research on strategy construction. Because strategies are typically described as a way to attain a goal, they are here summarized under the selection process. In turn, coping is often described as a way to deal with goal nonattainment or with an unexpected event, and therefore it is discussed under adjustment.

Goal Reconstruction

One further way for an adolescent to adjust to the negative outcomes he or she is facing is to reconstruct personal goals. When people fail to actualize their goals for a specific developmental trajectory, they are likely to modify their previous goals or to disengage from them and engage in new kinds of goals as a part of accommodative strategies (Brandtstädter & Renner, 1990). Doing this reconstruction helps the adolescent, after a failure, to keep motivated, stay on a realistic level of functioning, and maintain positive developmental perspectives when facing the next challenging life situation.

Goal reconstruction may lead to either positive or negative developmental changes. For example, not succeeding in a particular sport may lead to a decision of trying another kind of sport, which, in the long run, may result in a person's finding a lifelong hobby. In turn, having problems at school may lead to increasing interest in social activities with peers, which may further increase low achievement. Goal reconstruction on the basis of feedback from goal attainment is one key mechanism of motivational development (Nurmi, Salmela-Aro, & Koivisto, 2002).

Causal Attributions

One mechanism that plays an important role in the adjustment to a failure in goal attainment is an adolescent's interpretation of events afterward. According to Weiner (1986), after the event is interpreted as success or failure, an individual begins to search for the possible reasons for this event. Such causal attributions typically refer to one's own effort, abilities, or skills; alternatively, they refer to the situation, other people, or luck.

Most people apply self-protecting causal attributions in their efforts to deal with negative outcomes in particular (Taylor & Brown, 1988; Zuckerman, 1979); that is, they take credit for success but blame other people and situational factors for failure. The function of this defensive thinking is to cope with negative feedback concerning their self. Lack of such self-protective attributional bias has been shown to increase the likelihood of depressive symptoms. The problem with the use of attributional bias is that it leads to behavioral patterns that do not promote high effort in challenging situations (Berglas & Jones, 1978).

An alternative approach to causal attributions is to conceptualize them from the point of how functional they are for individual behavior. For example, Glaskow, Dornbusch, Troyer, Steinberg, and Ritter (1997) suggested that dysfunctional attributional style implies lack of faith in one's performance capacities and a reluctance to assume responsibility for one's behavior and the outcomes it may generate. Their definition of dysfunctional causal attribution included references to luck, teacher bias, task difficulty for either success and failure, and lack of ability in response to failure. Functional causal attributions refer to ability and effort after success, and effort attribution for a failure.

Reflection: Identity, Narratives, and Self-Concept

One psychological mechanism that plays a particularly important role during adolescence is the way in which individuals perceive and *reflect* their individual characteristics, behavioral outcomes, and social positions as a way to construct self-concept and identity (Figure 4.1; Erikson, 1959; Harter, 1990). Three different conceptualizations that have been used to describe this self-reflection process (Table 4.1) are discussed in the next sections.

Identity

The ways in which an adolescent perceives him- or herself across time and space have been described as identity (Baumeister & Muraven, 1996; van Hoof, 1999). One major assumption of the original identity theory was that the particular social position or the role the adolescent has adopted has consequences for his or her identity (Erikson, 1959). During adolescence, individuals explore different alternatives and end up in specific adult roles. Perceiving oneself then in a particular role helps an individual to construct an identity of who he or she is (Baumeister & Muraven, 1996; van Hoof, 1999).

Although identity, by definition, refers to the self-structures of an individual, the vast majority of research in the field has relied on Marcia's (1980) identity status paradigm, which focuses on the processes that are assumed to lead to identity formation rather than identity contents per se. Marcia originally operationalized Erikson's (1959) theory of identity formation in terms of four identity statuses. These were defined in terms of the presence and absence of crises and commitment related to important life decisions: identity diffusion (no current crisis or commitment); moratorium (current crisis, no commitment); foreclosure (commitment, no apparent former crisis); and identity achievement (commitment, previous crisis resolved).

Narratives

Individuals also construct narratives and tell stories about themselves as a way to create an identity (McAdams, 1999). Because one main feature of human cognition is that its contents can be shared by language, telling stories is an important means to increase self-coherence, to support positive self-concept and high self-esteem, to relate one's identity to those of significant others, and to create prototypic identity narratives as a member of a particular culture.

According to McAdams (1999), it is on the brink of adulthood that a person begins to construe his or her life in narrative terms. The implicit goal of this is to create an internalized story of the self that binds together the reconstructed past, perceived present, and anticipated future in a way that confers upon life a sense of unity and purpose. Although identity narratives vary in regard to content and structural features, agency and communion are their typical themes, and they are often situated to a specific moral or ideological setting (McAdams, 1999).

Self-Concept and Self-Esteem

Adolescents receive a substantial amount of feedback concerning their skills and competencies during selection and adjustment processes. For example, how well an adolescent is doing at school and the kinds of feedback he or she receives from peers and parents have consequences for what a person thinks about him- or herself (Harter, 1990). This self-concept has been among the most popular research fields in adolescent psychology.

Although the concept of self has been expanded to refer to a wide variety of mechanisms, the definition of self-concept is straightforward: It refers to relatively stable schemata of oneself that are generalized to the extent that they refer to an individual's view of him- or herself across different situations. A person has a self-concept to the extent that he or she has a coherent structure within which the multitude of self-relevant thoughts and feelings achieve organization (Nowalk, Tesser, Vallacher, & Borkowski, 2000). By contrast, self-esteem is typically defined as the ways in which individuals evaluate themselves according to normative or self-related standards. For example, positive self-esteem might be assumed, by definition, to be caused by having more success than expected, and negative self-esteem stems from having less success than expected.

CODEVELOPMENT: PARENTS AND PEERS

Although socialization and self-development, as evidenced in channeling, selection, adjustment, and self-reflection processes, are often described as an individual development, they are closely embedded in the adolescent's interpersonal relationships (Nurmi, 2001). When thinking about their future life and related decisions, young people often negotiate with, ask advice from, or reject information given by their parents and teachers. Similarly, they model their peers and discuss their future lives with their friends (Figure 4.2).

Three topics are particularly interesting in this context. First, to what extent is adolescent socialization directed by parents, or do the outcomes of the adolescent socialization activate certain kinds of parenting? Second, to what extent are adolescents influenced by their peers, or do they rather select a peer group according to their own interests and characteristics? Third, how are adolescents' relationships to their parents and peers related in the process of socialization into adulthood?

Adolescents and Parents: Cause or Effect?

Parent-adolescent relationships have been among the most examined topics in adolescent development (Steinberg, 2001). Although family relationships have been theoretically conceptualized as bidirectional interaction between the adolescent and his or her parent (Bell, 1979; Lerner, 1982), empirical researchers seem to make a strong presumption that it is parenting that influences adolescent development (Crouter, MacDermid, McHale, & Perry-Jenkins, 1990; Jacobson & Crockett, 2000). This seems to be the case even for most recent research even though many researchers have challenged this view and suggested that children also impact their parents' child-rearing patterns (Harris, 1995; Kerr, Stattin, Biesecker, & Fedder-Wreder, in press; Lerner, 1982; Lerner & Spanier, 1978).

This issue of the extent to which parents' attitudes, behaviors, and child-rearing patterns influence their adolescents' development, or whether it is children's thinking and behaviors that have an impact on their mothers' and fathers' parenting, is of key importance for this chapter. On the one hand, there are good reasons to assume that parents influence the ways in which their adolescent children deal with the transition into adulthood. There are at least three possible ways: First, parents may direct the development of their children's interests, goals, and values by communicating expectations and setting normative standards; second, they may influence the ways in which their adolescent child deals with various developmental demands by acting as role models and providing tutoring; and finally, they may contribute to the ways in which adolescents evaluate their success in dealing with these demands by providing support and feedback (Nurmi, 1991). On the other hand, the adolescent's success in dealing with the key demands of his or her age-graded environments may well influence his or her parents' expectations concerning their child's future; adolescents' competencies and coping skills may evoke the use of certain parenting styles among the parents; and adolescents' behavior may cause extra stress for parents, which then influence their thinking, behavior, and even well-being (Figure 4.2).

Adolescents and Peers: Selection or Causation?

Aside from parents, peers and friends are involved in the ways in which adolescents deal with the transition into adulthood (McGuire et al., 1999). Adolescents in a particular peer group exhibit many similarities compared with adolescents in other groups. Such homophily of the peer groups has been reported in many characteristics, such as aspirations (Kandel, 1978), school work (Cohen, 1977), and problem behavior (Urberg, Degirmenciogly, & Pilgrim, 1997). Two major mechanisms have been suggested to be responsible for this homophily. First, peer groups may be important socialization agents in adolescents' development. In this case, adolescents become similar to their peers because peers provide role models, feedback, and a platform for social comparisons (Ryan, 2001). Second, adolescents may select peer groups having members who share similar characteristics and interests with those they have themselves, or they may leave groups that do not fit with their characteristics or motivation (Cohen, 1977). Overall, selection and socialization into peer groups might be assumed to play an important role in the ways in which adolescents deal with the transition into adulthood (Figure 4.2).

Parents or Peers

Starting from early adolescence, children spend increasing amounts of time with their peers both at school and after school (Larson & Richards, 1991), whereas they spend less time with their parents (Collins & Russell, 1991). Some researchers have suggested that children's decreasing closeness to their parents is associated with their increased orientation toward the peers. For example, Steinberg and Silverberg (1986) suggested that the transition from childhood to adolescence is marked more by a trading of dependency on parents for dependency on peers rather than a straightforward growth in autonomy.

Parents and peers play different roles in individuals' attempts to negotiate their ways through adolescence. For example, Tao Hunter (1985) found that adolescents discussed with their parents particularly topics that related to adolescents' social and economic functioning in adulthood (i.e., academic, vocational, and social-ethical issues). By contrast, they discussed with their friends particularly issues concerning interpersonal relations. Another important issue is the extent to which adolescents' relationships with their parents and peers are associated. Fuligni and Eccles (1993) found that adolescents who perceived high parental strictness and little opportunity for decision making were higher in extreme peer orientation. In the following literature review I also examine what is known about the role of parents and peers in adolescents' socialization to adulthood.

RESEARCH ON SOCIALIZATION INTO ADULTHOOD

Earlier in this chapter, adolescent development into adulthood was described in terms of four processes (Table 4.1). In the following sections I review the research on what we know about the channeling, selection, adjustment, and reflection processes among adolescents. For each process, the research on the nature of the processes, the developmental changes, major antecedents and consequences, and the role of family and peers are reviewed.

Channeling: Anticipations of Developmental Tasks and Transitions

Age-graded developmental tasks, role transitions, and institutional tracks were expected to channel the ways in which adolescents direct their future development and select their environments. Previous research supports this by showing that adolescents have relatively detailed conceptions of their age-related developmental environments (i.e., the timing of a variety of developmental tasks, role transitions, turning points, and institutional tracks; Crockett & Bingham, 2000; Nurmi, 1989b). They also anticipate their future lives as a sequence of transitions in which school completion is followed by job entry, and then by marriage and parenthood. Moreover, their anticipations of the major turning points is in accordance with the statistics of the median age at which individuals go through these transitions in a particular society (Crockett & Bingham, 2000; Nurmi, Poole, & Kalakoski, 1996). This is not surprising because the cognitive ability to make such estimations has been shown to develop well before the adolescent years, by the age of 8 to 9 years (Friedman, 2000).

Research on how far into the future adolescents' thinking and personal goals extend gives a similar view. Nurmi (1989b, 1991), for example, showed that young people's thinking about the future extends to the end of the second and to the beginning of the third decade of life: Adolescents expected their education-related goals to be actualized, on average, at about the age of 18 to 19, occupation-related goals to be actualized at the age of 22 to 23, and goals related to family at the age of 25 to 26. Adolescents' life course anticipations are also predictive of their subsequent life course events, particularly in the family domain (Hogan, 1985).

Research has also shown gender differences in the life span anticipations. Girls tend to anticipate forming a partnership, establishing a family, and having children earlier than do boys (Malmberg, 1996), which again is in accordance with the statistics.

Among girls, the anticipations of the timing of educational and occupational transition are closely connected to the anticipations of family formation (Crockett & Bingham, 2000). This finding is thought to reflect the fact that girls take into account the role conflicts of these two domains more than boys do (Hogan, 1985).

The Role of Family

Family characteristics are associated with adolescents' anticipations of their life span transitions. For example, high parental education contributes to a later expected age for all major transitions (Crockett & Bingham, 2000; Hogan, 1985). Similarly, adolescents who have grown up in homes of lower socioeconomic standing expect earlier youth-to-adult transitions. In addition, parents' values are associated with their children's expectations: parents who have liberated sex-role attitudes have daughters who expect to leave the parental household earlier than do the daughters of parents with more conservative attitudes (Hogan, 1985).

Moreover, parents' views of their adolescent child's future transitions contribute to the child's future life. Hogan (1985) found in a longitudinal study that mothers' educational aspirations for their daughters predicted the timing of the daughters' marital transitions. Moreover, daughters of mothers who emphasized traditional sex roles were more likely to marry as adolescents compared with other young women. By contrast, daughters of mothers who emphasized the importance of career-preparatory education tend to delay marriage and family.

Selection

Goal Construction

One mechanism that plays an important role in how an adolescent directs his or her development and selects from a variety of environments is the kind of personal goals he or she constructs. Such goals are important, because they help the young person to move to a direction that would satisfy his or her personal motivation.

Transitions and Institutional Tracks One of the key assumptions of this chapter is that adolescents construct their goals by comparing their individual motives to the opportunity space created by their age-graded sociocultural environments. When adolescents are asked about their future hopes and interests, they typically report topics that focus on their personal future lives, such as education, occupation, family, leisure activities, travel, and self-related issues (Nurmi, 1991; Salmela-Aro, 2001). It is interesting to note that there is little variation across societies and cultures in such hopes and interests (for a review, see Nurmi, 1991). During adolescence, individuals become increasingly interested in future occupation, education, and family (Nurmi, 1989b). By contrast, adolescents' interest in leisure activities decreases with age. The majority of the research on developmental changes is based on age-group comparisons, although similar results have been found in longitudinal studies (Nurmi, 1989b).

These results are in accordance with the life span theory of adolescent development (Nurmi, 1991, 1993): A substantial proportion of adolescents' future hopes and interests focus on the major developmental tasks of this period. The finding that adolescents become increasingly interested in these topics with age may reflect the fact that as the transitions come closer, they increasingly motivate adolescents' thinking (Nurmi, 1989a).

Young people not only construct goals that are in accordance with age-graded developmental tasks and role transitions, but they also continuously reconstruct their personal goals to match the specific stages of a particular transition they are experiencing. For example, Salmela-Aro et al. (2000) showed that women who were facing a transition to parenthood not only had goals that reflected this particular transition overall but also reconstructed their goals to match with the specific stages of this transition: Womens' personal goals changed from achievement-related topics to pregnancy, then to the birth of a child, and finally to taking care of the child and motherhood. Moreover, Heckhausen and Tomasik (2002) found that vocational goals become more sober and less glorious when the actual vocational transition moves closer.

A variety of institutional transitions and tracks also provide a basis for adolescents' future-oriented goals. For instance, Klaczynski and Reese (1991) found that college-preparatory high school students held more career-oriented values and educational goals, and projected their future goals further in the future, compared with vocational school students. By contrast, vocational school students' goals focused more on preparation for adulthood and attainment of adult status than did those of college-preparatory high school students. Similar results have been found for the interpersonal domain of life. Salmela-Aro and Nurmi (1997) found that young adults' life situation, such as being married and having children, predicted their subsequent family-related goals. By contrast, being single predicted turning to self-focused, existential goals.

Consequences Individual motivation and personal goals were assumed to play an important role in the ways in which adolescents select their future environments and direct their lives. Along this assumption, Schoon and Parsons (2002) found that adolescents' aspirations at the age of 16 predicted their occupational aspirations during young adulthood. Moreover, Nurmi et al. (2002) found that the more young adults emphasized the importance of work-related goals and the more they thought they progressed in the achievement of such goals, the more likely they were to find work that was commensurate with their education and the less likely they were to be unemployed after graduation. Furthermore, concrete college goals have also been found to predict subsequent college attendance (Pimentel, 1996). Similarly, young adults' family-related goals predict their subsequent moving toward marriage or living in cohabitation relationships (Salmela-Aro & Nurmi, 1997), as well as the actual age of cohabitation and marriage (Pimentel, 1996). By contrast, young adults' self-focused, existential types of goals have been shown to predict subsequent negative life events, such as breaking up of an intimate relationship.

Optimism and Control Beliefs In order to be active agents in the selection of their future developmental trajectories, adolescents' personal goals need to be evidenced in their positive thinking about the future and belief in personal control. The research suggests not only that a majority of adolescents show much interest in their future but also that they are relatively optimistic about it and believe in their personal control (e.g.,

Brown & Larson, 2002; Nurmi, 1989a). Moreover, adolescents construct the view of their personal future in ways that support their optimism. For example, they do consider negative life events, such as divorce (Blinn & Pike, 1989), alcoholism, and unemployment (Malmberg & Norrgård, 1999), to be less likely in their own future life than in that of other people.

In addition, adolescents' beliefs concerning the future become more internal and optimistic with age (Nurmi, 1989a). However, present institutional environments are associated with the ways in which adolescents attribute causes for their behavioral outcomes. For example, Klaczynski and Reese (1991) found that college-preparatory high school students made more internal attributions for positive educational outcomes than did vocational school students. Moreover, Malmberg and Trempala (1998) showed that vocational school students were less optimistic about their success in the future than were secondary school students.

Adolescents' Fears Adolescents also have fears and worries about their future that are typically concerned with three major topics (Nurmi, 1991). First, young people typically report concerns related to dealing with normative developmental tasks, such as becoming unemployed, failing at school, and facing a divorce (Solantaus, 1987). Second, some adolescents are concerned about possible negative life events that may happen to their parents and family members, such as health problems and divorce. The third class of adolescents' fears concern society-level events, such as nuclear war (Solantaus, 1987) or environmental problems (Poole & Cooney, 1987). These differences in adolescents' fears and concerns reflect the historical time and topics that are discussed in the mass media and in public during a particular era (Nurmi, 1991). For example, the high rates of concerns related to nuclear war were typical in Western Europe in the early 1980s, whereas concerns about global issues such as pollution have been reported in subsequent decades (Nurmi, Salmela-Aro, & Ruotsalainen, 1994).

Personal Goals as Interpersonal Negotiation The construction of personal goals is not solely the outcome of individual cognitive processing but is shared by other people, such as parents, friends, and peers (Nurmi, 2001). For example, Meegan and Berg (2001) found that college students appraised the majority of their goals as either directly or indirectly shared, whereas only a minority of their goals were considered purely as their own. When Malmberg (1996) asked adolescents about the key sources of information concerning future education, occupation, and family life, parents were reported as the most used sources followed by peers, school friends, the mass media, and schools.

The Role of the Family The kinds of goals adolescents have for their own future and the kinds of goals parents overall have for their adolescent child's future are closely similar: Both adolescents' and parents' goals concerning adolescents' future lives typically concern education, occupation, family, and leisure activities, whereas the fears of both groups concern health-related issues, education, and work (Lanz, Rosnati, Marta, & Scabini, 2001). Similarly, parents and their adolescent child share similar kinds of educational goals (Trusty & Pirtle, 1998), educational aspirations (Bandura, Barbaranelli, Caprara, & Pastorelli, 2001), occupational aspirations (Jodl, Michael, Malanchuk, Eccles, & Sameroff, 2001), and values overall (Kasser, Ryan, Zax, & Sameroff, 1995). In addition, mothers and fathers play a similar role in adolescents' future-oriented goals (Trusty & Pirtle, 1998).

Research has also shown that parental characteristics, beliefs, and parenting practices are associated with the kinds of goals adolescents have. High level of education among parents, involvement in adolescents' school programs (Wilson & Wilson, 1992), high levels of parental advice (Jenkins Tucker et al., 2001), close identification with the parent (Jodl et al., 2001), low levels of parental control and positive family interaction (Glasgow et al., 1997), and nurturance (Kasser et al., 1995) are associated in adolescence with high educational aspirations, interest in future education and occupation, and internality and optimism concerning the future.

Unfortunately, the vast majority of this research is based on cross-sectional data. Consequently, we cannot be sure that it is parents who contribute to the kinds of goals their adolescent children have. Although parents' goals and values may provide a basis for those of adolescents by means of modeling, advice, and negotiating (Nurmi, 2001), there are several alternative explanations. First, both parents' and adolescents' goals may be influenced by the same sources, such as socioeconomic background and related cultural values. Second, it is possible that adolescents' aspirations, such as emphasizing the importance of education and subsequent high achievement, are reflected also in parents' aspirations concerning their children. Third, it is possible that the kinds of aspiration and goals adolescents have concerning education, for instance, influence their parents' child-rearing patterns. In addition, siblings also play a role in the ways in which adolescents think about their future (Jenkins Tucker, Barber, & Eccles, 1996).

Role of Peers Adolescents report that the peer group is an important context in which future-related issues are discussed (Malmberg, 1996). Young people and their peers share similar kinds of goals and aspirations (Hallinan & Williams, 1990; Kandel & Lesser, 1969). Particularly intimate friends and those of the same gender share similar goals (Hallinan & Williams, 1990; Kandel & Lesser, 1969). There is also evidence that parental relationships may moderate the association between adolescents' and their peers' goals. For example, Fuligni and Eccles (1993) showed that adolescents who perceived few opportunities to be involved in decision making at home tended to seek more advice from their peers concerning the future compared with those who had more opportunities. Because these studies were cross-sectional, we cannot be sure whether adolescents are influenced by their peers or whether young people select the peers who have similar aspirations as they have themselves.

Well-Being The life span theory of motivation suggests that personal goals that match with the age-graded developmental tasks of a particular age are adaptive and that they subsequently contribute to individual well-being (Nurmi, 1993, 2001). Both cross-sectional research (Emmons, 1991) and longitudinal studies (Salmela-Aro & Nurmi, 1997) have shown that young adults who report interpersonal and family-related goals show also a higher level of well-being and lower levels of depressive symptoms than do other young people. Moreover, Salmela-Aro, Nurmi, Saisto, and Halmesmäki (2001) found that the reconstruction of personal goals to match with the particular stage-specific demands of a certain transition promote young peoples' well-being. Women who were facing a transition to parenthood, and who adjusted their personal goals to match with the particular stage-specific demands of this transition, such as topics related to family, spouse, and the birth of the child, showed a decrease in depressive symptoms; those who disengaged from such goals showed an increase in depressive symptoms

There is a strong consensus that thinking about self- and identity-related issues is not only a natural part of adolescence and young adulthood but also one developmental task of this life period (Bosma & Kunnen, 2001; Erikson, 1959; Marcia, 1980). From this point of view, it is surprising that one of the most often replicated findings in the research literature is that self-focused, existential kinds of goals are associated with low well-being (Salmela-Aro et al., 2001). Moreover, there is a transactional pattern between well-being and self-focused goals: An increase in self-focused goals leads to an increase in depressive symptoms, whereas a high level of depressive symptoms increases the focus on self-related goals (Salmela-Aro & Nurmi, 1997; Salmela-Aro et al., 2001). However, there seems to be one exception to these results. Self-focused goals lead to high well-being when people are in a kind of moratorium situation in which they are faced with several alternative trajectories. Nurmi and Salmela-Aro (2002) found that although self-related goals predicted a high level of depressive symptoms among those who had just made a transition from school to a new job, self-focused goals decreased the level of depressive symptoms among those who were continuing their studies in another institution or who were at home with their children.

Norm-Breaking Behavior Stattin and Kerr (2001) found that adolescents who reported self-focused values (personal satisfaction and enjoyment) were more likely in later periods to become engaged in risky behaviors, such as norm breaking, risky sex, smoking, and drinking, and to associate with delinquent friends, compared with adolescents who have other-focused values (concern for others' well-being and the common good). Oyserman and Markus (1990) found that although delinquent adolescents had as much as other young people goals concerning future occupation and education, the majority of their concerns reflected a fear of becoming a criminal. These results suggest that adolescents have realistic anticipations of the dangers of their future.

Planning and Strategy Construction

Another mechanism that plays an important role in the selection of specific developmental trajectories during adolescence is the kinds of tools young people develop to attain their goals.

Development Planning skills increase with age during childhood (Pea & Hawkins, 1987). Although most children have acquired basic planning skills by the age of 10 to 11 years (Oppenheimer, 1987), such skills continue to develop up to the early 20s (Dreher & Oerter, 1987; Pasupathi, Staudinger, & Baltes, 2001). In addition, future-related knowledge and complexity of strategies increase with age (Nurmi, 1989b).

The Kinds of Strategies Määttä, Stattin, and Nurmi (2002) made an effort to identify naturally occurring subgroups of adolescents on the basis of the kinds of strategies they deploy in achievement contexts. They were able to identify four kinds of patterns by use of clustering by cases analysis: the users of an optimistic strategy, those deploying defensive pessimism, self-handicappers, and those showing helplessness. Not only did these match well with the strategies described in previous literature, but individuals deploying them also differed along a variety of well-being and outcome measurements, such as academic achievement, academic adjustment, self-esteem, and well-being, according to theoretical hypotheses. Similarly, Eronen, Nurmi, and Salmela-Aro (1997) identified three kinds of strategies in interpersonal contexts. They were planning-oriented, avoidant, and impulsive strategies.

Antecedents of Strategy Use A few cross-lagged longitudinal studies show that academic achievement and related feedback provide a basis for the strategies that young people deploy at later points in academic contexts. For example, a low level of academic achievement and dissatisfaction with grades predict increases in failure expectation and task avoidance (Nurmi, Aunola, Salmela-Aro, & Lindroos, 2002). They also predict turning to the use of self-handicapping (Eronen, Nurmi, & Salmela-Aro, 1998). Similarly, research in social contexts suggests that success in dealing with previous interpersonal challenges contributes to the kinds of strategies individuals deploy later in life. For example, frequent peer contacts and good social adjustment increase the use of a planning-oriented and impulsive social strategy, whereas less frequent peer contacts and loneliness lead to the use of an avoidant social strategy (Eronen et al., 1997; Nurmi & Salmela-Aro, 1997).

Role of Family There is little research on the ways in which parents contribute to adolescents' strategy construction. Aunola, Stattin, and Nurmi (2000b) showed that adolescents from authoritative families applied high levels of adaptive achievement strategies; in turn, adolescents from neglectful families applied maladaptive strategies to a greater extent. Moreover, perceived secure attachment to parents and positive family interaction are associated with active problem solving and planning (Greenberger, McLaughlin, & Caitlin, 1998), whereas lack of parental care is associated with a high level of self-handicapping (Greaven, Santor, Thompson, & Zuroff, 2000).

Because these findings are based on cross-sectional data, we do not know whether family characteristics and parenting have an impact on adolescents' strategy construction or vice versa. However, Rueter and Conger (1998) found in a cross-lagged longitudinal study a reciprocal relationship between parenting and adolescent problem-solving behavior. On the one hand, negative parental behavior predicted a decline in adolescents' flexible problem solving, whereas nurturant parenting increased it. On the other hand, adolescents' disruptive and inflexible behavior decreased subsequent nurturant parenting.

Consequences of Strategy Use Research in university environments has shown that the deployment of optimistic and defensive pessimistic strategies increases the individual's academic satisfaction, whereas the deployment of a self-handicapping strategy predicts low academic achievement and academic dissatisfaction (Eronen et al., 1998; Nurmi et al., 2002). Similarly, Elliott, Godshall, Shrout, and Witty (1990) found that self-appraised problem solving was predictive of grade point average among college students. Moreover, the deployment of maladaptive strategies, such as passive avoidance, leads to problems in dealing with the transition from school to work, such as unemployment (Määttä, Nurmi, & Majava, 2002).

There is similar evidence in affiliate situations. For example, young people with a planning-oriented and impulsive social strategy later reported frequent peer contacts and social adjustment, whereas those who showed pessimistic and avoidant social strategies had less frequent peer contacts and high levels of loneliness (Eronen et al., 1997; Nurmi & Salmela-Aro, 1997). Eronen and Nurmi (1999) showed further that the impact of social strategies on young people's popularity and unpopularity was mediated through their social behavior and person perception.

Well-Being The kinds of strategies that individuals deploy have been found to be associated with their well-being. For example, Määttä, Stattin, et al. (2002) showed that adolescents who reported the use of optimistic or defensive pessimistic strategies in achievement contexts reported lower levels of depressive symptoms than did those who deployed self-handicapping and helpless patterns. D'Zurilla and Sheedy (1991) found that general problem-solving ability was associated with a low level of subsequent psychological stress. In addition, Rudolph, Lambert, Clark, and Kurlakowsky (2001) found that maladaptive self-regulatory beliefs increased school-related stress and depressive symptoms. There is also evidence of a cumulative recursive pattern. For instance, Davila, Hammen, Burge, Paley, and Daley (1995) found in a longitudinal study that functional interpersonal problem solving decreased depressive symptoms. In turn, high depression also led to the use of less functional problem solving.

Problem Behavior It has been assumed that the use of maladaptive strategies would lead to low achievement and other kinds of problems at school (Nurmi, 1993). Consistent with this idea, underachieving adolescents have been found to apply a self-handicapping type of achievement strategy (Nurmi, Onatsu, & Haavisto, 1995). Moreover, adolescents who had serious problems in socialization in terms of dropping out of vocational education and being unemployed deployed a maladaptive strategy characterized by expecting failure, active task-avoidance, and lack of self-protective causal attributions (Nurmi, Salmela-Aro, & Ruotsalainen, 1994). Määttä, Stattin, et al. (2002) reported that adolescents who deploy either self-handicapping or helplessness strategies in achievement contexts also show higher levels of norm-breaking behavior than do those who reported the use of optimistic or defensive-pessimistic strategies. The results, however, are based on cross-sectional data.

Exploration and Commitments

Exploring information about the future and making commitments are important parts of the selection mechanism. Research indicates that the major foci of adolescents' explorations and commitments pertain to major age-graded developmental tasks. For example, Bosma (1985) found that school, occupation, leisure activities, friendship, and parents were among the most important topics of adolescents' identity exploration and commitment.

Age Differences Research has shown that compared to younger age groups, older adolescents report higher levels of exploration in educational, occupational, and relational domains of life (Kalakoski & Nurmi, 1998; Meilman, 1979; Nurmi, Seginer, & Poole, 1995). There is also a similar trend for the level of commitment, although the results are not as clear. Kalakoski and Nurmi (1998) found that the amount of exploration and commitments that adolescents reported reflected the timing of upcoming educational transitions: Young people who were about to face an educational transition reported higher levels of exploration and commitment related to future education than did those who had a longer time before the same transition.

The Role of the Family Only a few studies have researched the role of the family in exploration and commitments. Kracke (1997) found that parental authoritativeness, openness to adolescent issues, and concern with promoting career exploration were positively associated with career exploration of their adolescent children. Moreover, Blustein, Walbridge, Friedlander, and Palladino (1991) found that adolescents' positive attachments to both parents were positively related to progress in commitment to career choice. Kracke and Schmitt-Rodermund (2001) found that child-centered parenting increased adolescents' occupational exploration.

Adjustment

Coping

One assumption of this chapter is that when adolescents face problems in goal attainment or unexpected events, they try to find new ways of dealing with the situation. This process has been conceptualized in terms of coping (Folkman et al., 1987).

Age Differences Previous research suggests that as adolescent age, they deploy a broader range of coping strategies (Compas, Connor-Smith, Saltzman, Harding Thomsen, & Wadsworth, 2001; Williams & McGillicuddy-DeLisi, 2000). However, results on the developmental changes in the kinds of coping adolescents use is less clear. Although most studies show that emotion-focused coping increases with age (Compas, Malcarne, & Fondacaro, 1988; Seiffge-Krenke, 1993), not all studies agree (Stern & Zevon, 1990). Similarly, some studies suggest that problem-focused coping increases with age during adolescence (Seiffge-Krenke, 1993), whereas others have not found such change (Blanchard-Fields et al., 1995; Compas et al., 1988). Recent reviews of the topic present contradictory conclusions as well (Compas, 1987; Hauser & Bowls, 1990). One reason for these mixed findings may be that the coping modes that adolescents deploy are closely associated with the kinds of situations they are facing. If the situations that adolescents face as they grow older vary across their developmental environments, this may explain the different patterns of age differences that have emerged in different studies.

Antecedents One major antecedent of coping is individuals' temperament. For example, highly reactive individuals have a lower threshold of initial response, are slower in recovery, and display greater reactivation of stress after repeated exposure to it (Compas et al., 2001). However, most research on the topic has been carried out among children. It has also been suggested that a number of other individual differences, such as self-efficacy, self-esteem, and intelligence (Compas, 1987; Hauser & Bowls, 1990), provide a basis for the kinds of coping young people deploy. However, little research has been carried out on the topic.

Consequences There is considerable cross-sectional research about the possible consequences of coping, for example in academic settings. However, results are contradictory. For example, Compas et al. (2001) suggested in a literature review that problem-focused coping is associated with high levels of competence, whereas Zeidner (1995) forwarded a more pessimistic conclusion suggesting that there is no consensus about which coping strategy is most effective and adaptive in promoting academic outcomes.

Family There is some evidence suggesting that authoritative and positive parenting is associated with problem-focused coping, whereas more negative parenting is related to emotion-focused coping. For example, Stern and Zevon (1990) found that a negative perception of the family environment was associated with the use of emotionally based coping strategies, whereas positive perceptions of family climate were related to the use of more problem-focused coping. Dusek and Danko (1994) found that adolescents who perceived their parents as more authoritative and indulgent used more problem-focused coping, whereas perceiving parents as more firm and monitoring was associated with emotion-focused coping. This evidence, however, is based on cross-sectional findings and therefore should be interpreted cautiously.

Peers Little research has been carried out on the role of peers in adolescents' coping. In one study among Chinese students, Tao, Dong, and colleagues (Tao, Dong, Pratt, Husberger, & Pancer, 2000) found that the students' use of problem-focused coping patterns was positively, and the use of emotion-focused coping pattern was negatively, associated with peer support.

Well-Being The majority of the research on the consequences of coping has focused on internalizing and externalizing problem behavior. Following a review of the literature, Compas et al. (2001) suggested that emotion-focused and disengagement coping were associated with poorer psychological adjustment, whereas problem-focused and engagement coping were associated with better psychological adjustment (see also Compas et al., 1988; Recklitis & Noam, 1999). Muris, Schmidt, Lambrichs, and Meesters (2001) found also that passive coping was associated with high levels of depressive symptoms, and active coping with low levels of them. Because this research was based on cross-sectional studies, it is hard to know whether it is a certain kind of coping that leads to low adjustment or vice versa.

Goal Reconstruction

Research on how adolescents reconstruct their goals based on their previous successes and failures is almost absent. In one of the few studies, Nurmi and colleagues (Nurmi & Salmela-Aro, 2002; Nurmi et al., 2002) found that young adults reconstructed their personal goals to suit their current life situation following their successes and failures in dealing with the transition from school to work. For example, those who were successful in dealing with the transition showed a decreasing interest in goals that were no longer adaptive in their current life situation, such as educational goals. By contrast, young adults who had problems in finding work decreased their focus on the goals in this particular life domain and turned to other kinds of goals, such as educational and self-focused goals (Nurmi & Salmela-Aro, 2002). Moreover, young adults who found work that was commensurate with their education appraised their work-related goals later on in life as increasingly achievable and as arousing positive emotions; those who had become unemployed showed a reverse pattern (Normi et al., 2002).

Nurmi and Salmela-Aro (2002) found further that the ways in which young adults reconstructed their goals after certain outcomes contributed to their subsequent well-being. For example, high focus on work-related goals decreased depressive symptoms among those who had received a job, whereas the same goal pattern increased depressive symptoms among those who had not been able to find a job. Among the latter group, lack of work-related goals but high interest in education-related goals seemed to lead to high well-being. These results emphasize the importance of reconstructing one's goals to match with the particular life situation by disengaging from previous goals that are no longer adaptive.

Causal Attributions

The ways in which adolescents attribute the causes of their successes and failures might be assumed to have consequences for their well-being, self-concepts, and behaviors in future situations. Despite the importance of the topic, relatively little research has been carried out on it.

Antecedents The feedback young people receive from their previous efforts to deal with a particular task has consequences for the causal attributions they subsequently make. For example, Georgiou (1999) found that a high level of achievement among young adolescents was associated with attributing success to one's own effort and ability, whereas low achievement was related to attributing it to external factors. Moreover, Määttä, Nurmi, et al. (2002) found in a cross-lagged longitudinal study that young adults' problems in dealing with the transition from school to work decreased their use of self-protecting causal attributions. There is also evidence that positive self-concept is associated with the use of self-protecting attributions. For instance, Marsh (1984) found that preadolescents with positive self-concept were likely to internalize responsibility for success but not for failure.

Consequences There is considerable research showing that the lack of self-protecting causal attributions is associated with problems at school (e.g., Määttä, Nurmi, et al., 2002) and after finishing school (e.g., Nurmi et al., 1994). Glasgow et al. (1997) found in a cross-lagged longitudinal study that dysfunctional causal attributions lowered adolescents' willingness for classroom engagement and for doing homework. Nurmi et al. (2002) found that ability attributions after success predicted subsequent academic achievement among young adults.

The Role of the Family There is evidence suggesting that parents have an impact on adolescents' use of self-protecting causal attributions. For example, Greenberger et al. 1998) found that secure attachment to parents was associated with a tendency to explain successes and failures in self-enhancing ways. Similarly, Aunola et al. (2000b) found that adolescents from authoritative or permissive families reported higher levels of self-protecting causal attributions than did those from authoritarian or neglected families.

Well-Being One key assumption in the literature is that individuals deploy self-protecting causal attributions as buffers against negative feedback in a particular task. The few cross-sectional studies in the field show that deployment of negative attributional style or lack of the use of self-protecting attributions is associated with depression (Joiner & Wagner, 1995). In one longitudinal study, Määttä, Nurmi, et al. (2002) found not only that young adults' problems in dealing with the transition from school to work decreased their use of self-serving causal attributions but also that, if this happened, it had a negative impact on their well-being.

Reflection

Identity

During the socialization process adolescents enter into certain adult roles and positions that have consequences for the ways in which they reflect themselves in terms of identities and self-structures. The vast majority of research on identity has relied on Marcia's (1980) identity status paradigm, in which identity formation is operationalized in terms of four identity statuses (i.e., identity diffusion, moratorium, foreclosure, and identity achievement).

Age Differences The main idea of Marcia's original theory was that adolescents proceed from less advanced identity statuses to more advanced ones. On the basis of reanalysis of several empirical data sets, Waterman (1999) suggested that the findings support Marcia's theory: The largest proportion of early adolescents seems to be in identity diffusion or identity foreclosure statuses, and their proportion was lower in older age groups. By contrast, few preadolescents were reported to be in the identity achievement status, but the proportion of the individuals in this group was higher among older adolescents. The percentage of adolescents in moratorium status seems to peak at the age of 17 to 19, after which it decreases. Meeus, Iedema, Helsen, and Vollebergh (1999) came to a similar conclusion in their review. In a longitudinal study using identity statuses as continuous variables, Streitmatter (1993) found that foreclosure and diffusion scores decreased across a 2-year period of high school, whereas moratorium scores increased. No change in achievement scores was found.

Other reviews of the research on identity development have been more critical about the identity status paradigm. For example, in her extensive review of the few cross-lagged longitudinal studies that exist in this area, van Hoof (1999) concluded that progressive changes in the identity statuses are small. She suggested that this lack of change occurred because identity statuses seem to be very stable across time. She also pointed to other findings that do not fit well with Marcia's (1980) theory. For example, one fourth of college and adult respondents are typically still in a diffuse status of identity, which theoretically should be a starting point rather than an end point in identity development.

Although identity, by definition, refers to the ways in which an individual perceives him- or herself, surprisingly little research has been carried out on the relationships between identity statuses and self-concept. In one study, Makros and McCabe (2001) found that adolescents in the foreclosed and achievement statuses had lower levels of self-belief discrepancy than did those in the moratorium and diffused statuses. Dunkel and Anthis (2001) found that identity exploration was positively correlated with the number of possible selves. Moreover, identity commitment was associated with the consistency in hoped-for selves across time. These are interesting findings because they show that different identity statuses are associated with the ways in which adolescents perceive themselves. Some studies have also examined the mechanisms that are involved in identity formation and constructions of self-knowledge. For instance, Kerpelman and Lamke (1997) found that women who were highly certain about their future career identity engaged more in self-verification than did women who were uncertain.

Role of the Family Very little is known about the antecedents of identity formation. The major finding is that adolescents in the foreclosure identity status have the closest relationships with their parents, whereas adolescents in the moratorium and achievement statuses are more critical toward their parents (Waterman, 1982). Moreover, moratorium and identity-achievement adolescents perceived their relationships with their parents as being more independent and encouraging than did diffused or foreclosed youths (Samuolis, Layburn, & Schiaffino, 2001). Because all these findings come from cross-sectional studies, the associations may well stem from the fact that adolescents' explorations and commitments influence their parental relations rather than vice versa.

Consequences Research on the consequences of identity formation on individuals' later development is practically absent. In one study, Wallace-Broscious, Serafica, and Osipow (1994) found that identity achievement status was positively associated with career decidedness and planning, whereas moratorium and diffusion statuses were negatively related to career planning and decision making.

Well-Being In a literature review, Meeus et al. (1999) suggested that moratorium is the identity status with the lowest level of well-being, whereas foreclosed and identity achievers show the highest levels of well-being. However, because these results are based on cross-sectional data, there is no way to know whether reaching a particular identity status contributes to adolescents' well-being or whether adolescents' well-being contributes to identity status.

Self-Concept and Self-Esteem

The ways in which young people perceive themselves, and the kinds of attitudes they have about themselves, have been among the most popular research topics in adolescent psychology (Harter, 1990).

Development In her extensive review, Harter (1990) suggested first that self-concept development during adolescence is characterized by developmental shifts from relatively concrete descriptions of one's social and behavioral exterior in childhood to more abstract self-portraits that depict one's psychological interior; this change may also mean that self-concept becomes less dependent on concrete feedback to a person. Second, there is an increase in differentiation of self-concept across social roles and contexts in early adolescence, although not all evidence supports this conclusion (Marsh, 1984). Third, there is an increasing integration of self-related concepts in later adolescence (Harter, 1990). Montemayor and Eisen (1977) found that there was an increase across the adolescent years in self-descriptions referring to occupational role and to existential and ideological topics, as well as decreases in reference to citizenship, territoriality, possessions, and the physical self. These results are in accordance with the notion that expected entrance into adult roles begins to play an increasingly important role in how adolescents perceive themselves.

Findings on the development of self-esteem are contradictory (Baldwin & Hoffman, 2000). Some findings suggest that self-esteem increases during adolescence (e.g., O'Malley & Bachman, 1983), whereas other studies have shown a decrease (Marsh, 1989). One reason for these inconsistent findings may be that self-esteem trajectories are individual and influenced by many contextual factors. For example, Baldwin and Hoffmann (2002) found that adolescents' self-esteem fluctuates significantly and that the developmental pattern of such fluctuations varied among individuals.

Antecedents There is a general consensus that self-concept is influenced by the attitudes of significant others, particularly concerning physical appearance, peer acceptance, and scholastic and athletic competence (Harter, 1990). Some more recent studies have shown that institutional transitions and life events also influence self-concept and self-esteem. In an extensive longitudinal study, for example, Cole et al. (2000) found that the transition to middle school involved a drop in the mean and stability of academic and sports self-concept; academic self-concept further increased after moving out of the middle school environment; and finally, in later adolescence, self-concept began to become increasingly stable. Moreover, school grades (Zimmerman, Copeland, Shope, & Dielman, 1997), as well as stressful life events (Baldwin & Hoffmann, 2002), have been shown to have an impact on adolescents' self-esteem.

The Role of the Family There is considerable evidence that parents contribute to adolescents' self-conceptions and attitudes. For example, being a member of a cohesive family is associated with increased self-esteem over time (Baldwin & Hoffmann, 2002). Moreover, Frome and Eccles (1998) found that parents' perception of their adolescent child's abilities was more highly associated with the child's self-concept of ability than were the actual grades.

CONCLUSIONS

Adolescents' socialization into adulthood and related self-development were conceptualized in terms of four mechanisms: First, it was assumed that the age-graded developmental tasks, role transitions, and institutional tracks define an opportunity space that channels young people's future-oriented motivation, thinking, and behavior. Second, the kinds of motives and personal goals adolescents construct, and the ways in which they explore, plan, construct strategies, and enter into commitments were assumed to be responsible for the ways in which adolescents direct their future development and select their developmental environments. Third, as a consequence of their efforts, adolescents attain outcomes, either successes or failures, which requires them to adjust their previous efforts in terms of goal reconstruction, coping, and the use of self-protective causal attributions. Finally, after ending up in a particular social position and related life situation, adolescents construct reflections and tell stories about who they are.

Socialization and Self-Development

A review of previous research suggested, first, that adolescents have relatively detailed conceptions of their age-graded developmental environments (i.e., the timing and sequential structure of the transitions and tracks they are facing in the future). It was therefore no surprise that such age-graded structures *channel* adolescents' personal goals and interests: Young people's future hopes and interests were found to focus typically on the major developmental tasks of their own age period. Young people also continuously reconstruct their personal goals to match with the specific stages of a particular transition through which they are going, as well as the institutional tracks in which they are involved.

Both the personal goals adolescents have and the cognitive strategies they deploy, which were assumed to be the major mechanisms in the selection process, were found to contribute to the developmental trajectories they face subsequently, as well as how well they are able to deal with the related challenges and demands. Clear evidence was found from longitudinal studies that adolescents' motives and personal goals predict how their lives will proceed in educational, occupational, and family-related trajectories. Similarly, the kinds of plans and strategies that adolescents apply have consequences for their success in dealing with major challenges at school, at work, and also in interpersonal relationships. However, adolescents become interested in forthcoming developmental tasks and transitions as they grow older, and the tools they have for dealing with these demands and challenges develop rapidly during early adolescence in particular. Although the majority of adolescents deploy adaptive strategies, such as optimistic and task-focused patterns, some of them deploy avoidant strategies as a way to deal with a fear of failure or anxiety.

This review showed also that adolescents whose goals focus on major age-graded developmental tasks have higher well-being than do those who have other kinds of goals, perhaps because such goals help them to deal with the major demands and challenges they are facing. Although it has been assumed that thinking of self-related issues is a part of adolescents' lives, strong evidence was found that self-focused, existential type of goals are detrimental to young people's well-being. Moreover, the deployment of adaptive strategies led not only to higher levels of success in academic and interpersonal domains of life but also, in the longer run, to higher well-being.

There is also considerable evidence that parents and their adolescent children share similar kinds of goals concerning the adolescent's future. Moreover, positive and authoritative parenting is associated not only with adolescents' high level of interest in major developmental tasks, such as education and occupation, but also with adolescents' use of adaptive strategies, particularly in achievement contexts.

After adolescents have received feedback about the outcomes of their efforts to deal with the major developmental challenges and demands, they have to adjust their previous efforts in terms of coping, reconstruction of goals, and making causal attributions.

Surprisingly, much less research has been conducted on the antecedents and consequences of this adjustment compared with those of selection processes. Research on coping showed that problem-focused coping and engagement coping are associated with higher levels of psychological adjustment, whereas emotion-focused coping seems to lead to maladjustment. However, there was little evidence that coping has clear consequences for individual success in dealing with particular kinds of tasks. Authoritative and positive parenting was shown to be associated with problem-focused coping, whereas more negative parenting is related to emotion-focused coping.

Very little research has been carried out on how adolescents reconstruct their personal goals based on their previous successes and failures. The few studies suggest that adolescents reconstruct their goals on the basis of the feedback they receive concerning goal attainment and that such goal reconstruction contributes to their well-being.

Similarly, little research has been carried out on the role that causal attributions have in the situations in which young people have had problems in dealing with previous demands. The few studies that exist show that problems in dealing with major transitions decrease the use of self-protective causal attributions, which then leads to an increase in depressive symptoms. Dysfunctional causal attributions also lower adolescents' active engagement in school activities, and subsequently their academic achievement.

It was also assumed that entrance into certain roles and social positions has consequences for the identities or self-concepts that adolescents construct. Although the studies suggest that younger adolescents more frequently report less developed identity statuses than do older adolescents, relatively little is know about the developmental antecedents or consequences of these developments.

By contrast, we know much, on a descriptive level, about how self-concept and self-esteem develop during adolescence. However, some of the recent findings have challenged previous theories by suggesting a more dynamic view according to which adolescents' self-concepts fluctuate significantly and follow, in many cases, individual developmental trajectories. This fluctuation has been found to reflect many changes in the individual's development environments, such as school transitions, grades, and a variety of stressful life events.

Socialization in Place: Different Developmental Environments

In this chapter adolescent socialization and self-development were conceptualized in terms of four mechanisms that are responsible for the transaction between the developing adolescent, on the one hand, and his or her age-graded sociocultural environment, on the other. It can also be assumed that the substantial amount of variation across societies and cultures in the developmental environments in which adolescents grow up (Brown, Larson, & Saraswathi, 2002; Hurrelmann, 1994) channels their subsequent development in many ways. One key factor that contributes to this variation is education: There are many differences in the educational systems that are reflected in adolescents' thinking and lives across the world (Hurrelmann, 1994; Nurmi, Seginer, et al., 1995; Scnabel, Alfeld, Eccles, Köller, & Baumert, 2002). For example, in many European countries and the United States, streaming in education based on academic achievement begins relatively early (Hurrelmann, 1994), which also influences adolescents' subsequent opportunities. In some other societies, such as Scandinavian countries, adolescents receive comprehensive education until the age of fifteen without any streaming (Nurmi & Siurala, 1994). These differences in educational transition then cooccur with those of occupational life. For example, a large proportion of young British youths leave school and enter the labor force at the age of 16, which is very different compared to countries that aim at long education for a whole cohort, such as the United States and Scandinavian countries.

There are also many cross-national differences in the transitions related to interpersonal life, such as the age of first marriage and the patterns of starting family life, that influence adolescents' socialization into adulthood in many ways (cf. Martínez, de Miguel, & Fernández, 1994; Roe, Bjurström, & Förnäs, 1994). One further factor along which developmental environments vary is the relative importance of parents and peers in adolescents' lives. Although peers are an important part of adolescents lives in most parts of the world, in some contexts (e.g., in India and in Arab countries) peer groups play a relatively minor role, particularly for girls (Brown et al., 2002).

Besides cross-national differences, adolescents' developmental environments vary also within societies along many factors, such as ethnicity and socioeconomic status. Young people who come from diverse backgrounds face different opportunity structures, age-related normative demands, and standards and are provided different role models and parental tutoring. Such differences then have consequences for the ways in which adolescents direct their lives in the domains of education, occupation, and interpersonal relations; for how they adjust to the outcomes of their efforts; and for the kinds of reflections they construct about themselves during the transition from adolescence to adulthood. For example, in the United States the percentage of adolescents who had completed high school and the percentage of those who have a bachelor degree vary substantially according to ethnicity: Whites show the highest percentages, followed by Blacks, while Latinos show the lowest educational attainment (Kerckhoff, 2002). Such differences are important because they are also reflected in an individual's occupational career and problems with it, such as unemployment.

Another important factor that influences the challenges, opportunities, and standards that adolescents face is the socioeconomic status of their family, which consists of a number of interrelated variables, such as family income and values, parental education, and membership in particular subcultures and communities. For example, family income is a foremost factor in differentiating the paths taken through the transition from adolescence to adulthood in many countries (Mortimer & Larson, 2002). As adolescents have relatively detailed conceptions of their age-graded developmental environments (Crockett & Bingham, 2000), they are probably also conscious of how their social background will influence them. The impact of socioeconomic status is reflected not only in the opportunity structure but also in parents' values and aspirations, which have been shown to influence adolescents' subsequent life paths (Hogan, 1985).

Because the key assumption in this chapter is that adolescents' age-graded developmental environments provide a basis for the ways in which adolescents direct their development and adjust to developmental outcomes, this variation in adolescents' environments across and within countries can be expected to be reflected in many ways in the channeling, selection, adjustment, and reflection processes. For example, Scnabel et al. (2002) showed that academic achievement was predictive of adolescents' career decisions both in Germany and the United States, whereas social background influences were more pronounced in Germany. Moreover, Nurmi, Seginer, et al. (1995) found that due to earlier and shorter educational transitions, Australian adolescents showed higher levels of exploration and commitments, both in the domain of future education and work, compared with their Israeli and Finnish counterparts. They also expected their goals and hopes related to future education and work to be realized earlier in their lives than did young Finns and Israelis.

Overall, these results are important because they suggest that the different environments in which adolescents grow up produce substantial amounts of variation in their subsequent life paths. Consequently, one must be careful in making generalizations from results found in one sociocultural context to other environments. However, this variation provides researchers with an interesting option to examine the extent to which their theories and findings generalize across different developmental environments.

Socialization in Time: Historical Changes

It is only during the past 100 years that adolescence emerged as an independent and extended life period, mainly due to the extended period of education (Hurrelman, 1994). Moreover, adolescence, as well as how it is defined by society and culture, shows continuous change. Herdandez (1997) summarized the trends in the United States during the past 150 years. According to him, the major changes in the developmental context of children and adolescents during the century before the second world war included the shift to nonfarm work by fathers, a drastic constriction of family size, and enormous increases in educational attainments. After the half century that followed, the key changes have included the increase of labor force participation by mothers, the rise of single parenthood, and a large decline and then substantial rise in child poverty. Although the timing of these historical changes has varied from one country to another, the general patterns are more or less the same in industrialized countries. Moreover, some of the recent changes in developing countries resemble the changes that happened in industrialized societies several decades ago (Brown et al., 2002). The importance of these analyses for adolescent research is that they help us to understand that how things appear in young people's lives at a given moment is not a consequence of unchangeable general laws but rather is influenced by many historical and societal developments.

A few recent trends also modify adolescent development. First, gender differences in adolescents' thinking and interests seem to be changing in industrialized countries. Although girls continue to be more interested in future family and human relationships and boys in material aspects of life, comparisons of research findings across the past 30 years suggest that girls' interests in education and occupation began to exceed those of boys (Nurmi, 2001). These results accord well with the statistics that in many countries the proportion of girls in higher education exceeds that for boys. However, in less industrialized countries the experiences and opportunities of adolescents boys and girls have remained markedly different (Brown & Larson, 2002).

Another still-continuing change is a move from rural areas to urban environments. It has been suggested that living in urban versus rural living environments, along with related differences in the opportunity structures, is reflected in young people's motivation and thinking in many ways. For example, Nurmi et al. (1994) found that adolescents' exploration and commitments related to education and occupation increased with age in urban environments but not in rural environments. This difference was suggested to be due to the fact that rural environments provide less educational choices than do urban contexts.

The third developmental trend that influences adolescents' lives in most parts of the world is globalization (Brown & Larson, 2002). Besides a move from rural to urban environments and increasing length of education, globalization refers also to the important role of a uniform youth culture as reflected in standard elements of dress, music taste, and entertainment. This development is closely connected to the increasing importance of new information technologies and worldwide media business.

One recent change in adolescents' lives in industrialized countries consists of an increase in so-called turbulences in the transition into job markets. Many young people start their occupational careers in jobs that both they and their employer expect to be temporary. Although it has been suggested that this trend is due to the educational system of the United States (Kerckhoff, 2002), a similar trend is evident in many European countries. The problem of this development is that it may also postpone other transitions during young adulthood, such as gaining independence from parents and starting one's own family.

The final important recent change in adolescent life is the increase in divorce and single parenthood. If this trend continues, it may lead to many changes in adolescent socialization. For example, as most of the single parents are women, increasing amounts of adolescents are living in a situation in which they lack advice and support from their fathers (Jenkins Tucker et al., 2001). This may cause particular problems in adolescent socialization into the adult world, particularly for boys.

Methodological Implications

This chapter summarized the results of research about adolescents' socialization and self-development. Unfortunately, many parts of the literature review concluded that the research included serious methodological limitations.

One typical feature of the reviewed studies was that the direction of influence was presupposed on the basis of cross-sectional findings. This problem was particularly true for the research that focused on the role of parent and peer relations in adolescents development. Consequently, there is a need to enhance the quality of data when examining any developmental mechanisms. One way to do this is to use cross-lagged longitudinal data in which the same variables are repeatedly measured across time. This means that the time for easy solutions to conduct adolescent research is over: Cross-sectional procedures in the examination of developmental processes are in many cases wastes of time and money.

Another way to test the direction of effects is to use intervention studies. This approach has not been typical in the research on adolescents socialization, perhaps because it is not clear what should be targeted in interventions. In the case of problem behaviors, such as criminality and drug abuse, this, of course, is not a problem.

One assumption in this chapter is that adolescent development consists of interactions between the developing individual and his or her changing age-graded environments. The major idea is that age-graded environments channel adolescents motives and interests, and feedback concerning their efforts in dealing with a variety of transitions and challenges leads to the adjustment of previous strategies and goals and the formation of reflections concerning oneself. Examination of such mechanisms requires at least two features of the data.

First, as the processes included in socialization might be assumed to change rapidly, there is a need for intensive measurements, such as every half year or even less. The problem with traditional longitudinal studies is, namely, that they may not be intensive enough to reach the critical developmental changes. Examination of developmental processes should be preceded by theoretical analysis of the time range during which major developmental processes take place, and this time range should then be applied to define the length of the time intervals between the measurements (Aunola, Leskinen, Onatsu-Arvilommi, & Nurmi, 2002).

The second requirement for the successful examination of processes such as socialization is that studies focus on periods of adolescent development during which key developmental processes take place. It might be assumed that the times when adolescents are facing some major transitions in their lives are such important periods. During early adolescence such transitions are typically scheduled by the individual's age. During late adolescence, they may appear more independently from age, which may require less traditional research designs. One additional aspect of such studies on critical transitions is that if a group of individuals is followed only across a particular transition, the phenomena under focus can be measured intensively.

In sum, the results reviewed in this chapter indicate that we know much about how age-graded sociocultural environments channel adolescent development, as well as about the mechanisms by which adolescents select their developmental environments. There are also data depicting how adolescents reflect themselves as a consequence of these adventures. However, less is known about how adolescents try to adjust their previous efforts as a means to deal with negative feedback and failures. Moreover, the fact that only a few cross-lagged longitudinal studies have been conducted on the role that parents and peers play in adolescent socialization and self-development limits our possibilities to understand the processes taking place in these interpersonal settings.

REFERENCES

Abramson, L. Y., Seligman, M. E. P., & Teasdale, J. D. (1978). Learned helplessness in humans: Critique and reformulation. *Journal of Abnormal Psychology, 87,* 49–74.

Aunola, K., Leskinen, E., Onatsu-Arvilommi, T., & Nurmi, J.-E. (2002). Three methods for studying developmental change: A case of reading skills and self-concept. *British Journal of Educational Psychology, 72,* 343–360.

Aunola, K., Stattin, H., & Nurmi, J.-E. (2000a). Adolescents' achievement strategies, school adjustment, and externalizing and internalizing problem behaviors. *Journal of Youth and Adolescence, 29,* 289–306.

Aunola, K., Stattin, H., & Nurmi, J.-E. (2000b). Parenting styles and adolescents' achievement strategies. *Journal of Adolescence, 23,* 205–222.

Baldwin, S. A., & Hoffmann, J. P. (2002). The dynamics of self-esteem: A growth-curve analysis. *Journal of Youth and Adolescence, 31,* 101–113.

Baltes, P. B., & Baltes, M. M. (1990). Psychological perspectives on successful aging: The model of selective optimization with compensation. In P. B. Baltes & M. M. Baltes (Eds.), *Suc-*

cessful aging: Perspectives from behavioral sciences (pp. 1–34). Cambridge: Cambridge University Press.

Baltes, P. B., Reese, H. W., & Lipsitt, L. P. (1980). Life-span developmental psychology. *Annual Review of Psychology, 31,* 65–100.

Bandura, A., Barbaranelli, C., Caprara, G. V., & Pastorelli, C. (2001). Self-efficacy beliefs as shapers of children's aspirations and career trajectories. *Child Development, 72,* 187–206.

Baumeister, R. F., & Muraven, M. (1996). Identity as adaptation to social, cultural, and historical context. *Journal of Adolescence, 19,* 405–416.

Bell, R. Q. (1979). Parent, child, and reciprocal influences. *American Psychologist, 34,* 821–826.

Berglas, S., & Jones, E. E. (1978). Drug choice as a self-handicapping strategy in response to noncontingent success. *Journal of Personality and Social Psychology, 36,* 405–417.

Blanchard-Fields, F., Jahnke, H. C., & Camp, C. (1995). Age differences in problem-solving style: The role of emotional salience. *Psychology and Aging, 10,* 173–180.

Blinn, L. M., & Pike, G. (1989). Future time perspective: Adolescents' predictions of their interpersonal lives in the future. *Adolescence, 24,* 289–301.

Blustein, D. L., Devenis, L. E., & Kidney, B. A. (1989). Relationship between the identity formation process and career development. *Journal of Counseling Psychology, 36,* 196–202.

Blustein, D. L., Walbridge, M. M., Friedlander, M. L., & Palladino, D. E. (1991). Contributions of psychological separation and parental attachment to the career development process. *Journal of Counseling Psychology, 38,* 39–50.

Bosma, H. A. (1985). *Identity development in adolescence. Coping with commitments.* Groningen, Netherlands: Rijksuniversiteit Te Groningen.

Bosma, H. A., & Kunnen, E. S. (2001). Determinants and mechanisms in ego identity development: A review and synthesis. *Developmental Review, 21,* 39–66.

Brandtstädter, J. (1984). Personal and social control over development: Some implications of an action perspective in life-span developmental psychology. In P. B. Baltes & O. G. Brim Jr. (Eds.), *Life-span development and behavior* (Vol. 6, pp. 1–32). New York: Academic Press.

Brandtstädter, J., & Renner, G. (1990). Tenacious goal pursuit and flexible goal adjustment: Explication and age-related analysis of assimilative and accommodative strategies of coping. *Psychology and Aging, 5,* 58–67.

Brown, B. B., & Larson, R. W. (2002). Kaleidoscope of adolescence: Experiences of the world's youth at the beginning of the 21st century. In B. B. Brown, R. W. Larson, & T. S. Saraswathi (Eds.), *The world's youth: Adolescence in eight regions of the globe* (pp. 1–20). Cambridge, MA: Cambridge University Press.

Brown, B. B., Larson, R. W., & Saraswathi, T. S. (Eds.). (2002). *The world's youth: Adolescence in eight regions of the globe.* Cambridge, MA: Cambridge University Press.

Cantor, N. (1990). From thought to behavior: "Having" and "doing" in the study of personality and cognition. *American Psychologist, 45,* 735–750.

Caspi, A. (2002). Social selection, social causation and developmental pathways: Empirical strategies for better understanding how individuals and environments are linked across the life course. In L. Pulkkinen & A. Caspi (Eds.), *Paths to successful development. Personality in the life course* (pp. 281–301). Cambridge, UK: Cambridge University Press.

Cohen, J. M. (1977). Sources of peer group homogeneity. *Sociology of Education, 50,* 227–241.

Cole, D. A., Maxwell, S. E., Martin, J. M., Peeke, L. G., Seroczynski, A. D., Tram, J. M., Hoffman, K. B., Ruiz, M. D., Jacquez, F., & Maschman, T. (2001). The development of multiple domains of child and adolescent self-concept: A cohort sequential longitudinal study. *Child Development, 72,* 1723–1746.

Collins, W. A., & Russell, G. (1991). Mother-child and father-child relationships in middle childhood and adolescence: A developmental analysis. *Developmental Review, 11,* 99–136.

Compas, B. E. (1987). Coping with stress during childhood and adolescence. *Psychological Bulletin, 101,* 393–403.

Compas, B. E., Banez, G. A., Malcarne, V., & Worsham, N. (1991). Perceived control and coping with stress: A developmental perspective. *Journal of Social Issues, 47,* 23–34.

Compas, B. E., Connor-Smith, J. K., Saltzman, H., Harding Thomsen, A., & Wadsworth, M. E. (2001). Coping with stress during childhood and adolescence: Problems, progress, and potential in theory and research. *Psychological Bulletin, 127,* 87–127.

Compas, B. E., Malcarne, V. L., & Fondacaro, K. M. (1988). Coping with stressful events in older childhood and young adolescents. *Journal of Consulting and Clinical Psychology, 56,* 405–411.

Crockett, L. J., & Bingham, C. R. (2000). Anticipating adulthood: Expected timing of work and family transitions among rural youth. *Journal of Research on Adolescence, 10,* 151–172.

Crouter, A. C., MacDermid, S. M., McHale, S. M., & Perry-Jenkins, M. (1990). Parental monitoring and perceptions of children's school performance and conduct in dual- and single-earner families. *Developmental Psychology, 26,* 649–657.

Davila, J., Hammen, C., Burge, D., Paley, B., & Daley, S. E. (1995). Poor interpersonal problem solving as a mechanism of stress generation in depression among adolescent women. *Journal of Abnormal Psychology, 104,* 592–600.

Dreher, M., & Oerter, R. (1987). Action planning competencies during adolescence and early adulthood. In S. H. Friedman, E. Kofsky Scholnick, & R. R. Cocking (Eds.), *Blueprints for thinking. The role of planning in cognitive development* (pp. 321–355). Cambridge, MA: Cambridge University Press.

Dunkel, C. S., & Anthis, K. S. (2001). The role of possible selves in identity formation: A short-term longitudinal study. *Journal of Adolescence, 24,* 765–776.

Dusek, J. B., & Danko, M. (1994). Adolescent coping styles and perceptions of parental child rearing. *Journal of Adolescent Research, 9,* 412–426.

D'Zurilla, T. D., & Sheedy, C. F. (1991). Relation between social problem-solving ability and subsequent level of psychological stress in college students. *Journal of Personality and Social Psychology, 61,* 841–846.

Elder, G. H., Jr. (1985). Perspectives on the life course. In G. H. Elder Jr. (Ed.), *Life course dynamics* (pp. 23–49). Ithaca, NY: Cornell University Press.

Elliot, T. R., Godshall, F., Shrout, J. E., & Witty, T. E. (1990). Problem-solving appraisal, self-reported study habits, and performance of academically at-risk college students. *Journal of Counseling Psychology, 2,* 203–207.

Emmons, R. A. (1991). Personal strivings, daily life events and psychological and physical well-being. *Journal of Personality, 59,* 455–472.

Erikson, E. H. (1959). *Identity and the life cycle.* New York: International Universities Press.

Eronen, S., & Nurmi, J.-E. (1999). Social reaction styles, interpersonal behaviours and person perception: A multi-informant approach. *Journal of Social and Personal Relationships, 16,* 315–333.

Eronen, S., Nurmi, J.-E., & Salmela-Aro, K. (1997). Planning-oriented, avoidant, and impulsive social reaction styles: A person-oriented approach. *Journal of Research in Personality, 31,* 34–57.

Eronen, S., Nurmi, J.-E., & Salmela-Aro, K. (1998). Optimistic, defensive-pessimistic, impulsive and self-handicapping strategies in university environments. *Learning and Instruction, 8,* 159–177.

Folkman, S., Lazarus, R. S., Pimley, S., & Novacek, J. (1987). Age differences in stress and coping processes. *Psychology and Aging, 2,* 171–184.

Friedman, W. J. (2000). The development of children's knowledge of the times of future events. *Child Development, 71,* 913–932.

Frome, P. M., & Eccles, J. S. (1998). Parents' influence on children's achievement-related perceptions. *Journal of Personality and Social Psychology, 74,* 435–452.

Fuligni, A. J., & Eccles, J. S. (1993). Perceived parent-child relationships and early adolescents' orientation toward peers. *Developmental Psychology, 29,* 622–632.

Georgiou, S. N. (1999). Achievement attributions of sixth grade children and their parents. *Educational Psychology, 19,* 399–412.

Glasgow, K. L., Dornbusch, S. M., Troyer, L., Steinberg, L., & Ritter, P. L. (1997). Parenting styles, adolescents' attributions, and educational outcomes in nine heterogeneous high schools. *Child Development, 68,* 507–529.

Greaven, S. H., Santor, D. A., Thompson, R., & Zuroff, D. C. (2000). Adolescent self-handicapping, depressive affect, and maternal parenting styles. *Journal of Youth and Adolescence, 29,* 631–646.

Greenberger, E., McLaughlin, C. S., & Caitlin, S. (1998). Attachment, coping, and explanatory style in late adolescence. *Journal of Youth and Adolescence, 27,* 121–139.

Grotevant, H. D. (1987). Toward a process model of identity formation. *Journal of Adolescent Research, 2,* 203–222.

Hagestadt, G. O., & Neugarten, B. L. (1985). Age and the life course. In R. H. Binstock & E. Shanas (Eds.), *Handbook of aging and the social sciences* (pp. 35–61). New York: Van Nostrand Reinhold.

Hallinan, M. T., & Williams, R. A. (1990). Students' characteristics and the peer influence process. *Sociology of Education, 63,* 122–132.

Harren, V. A. (1979). A model of career decision making for college students. *Journal of Vocational Behavior, 14,* 119–133.

Harris, J. R. (1995). Where is the child's environment? A group socialization theory of development. *Psychological Review, 102,* 458–489.

Harter, S. (1990). Self and identity development. In S. S. Feldman & G. R. Elliott (Eds.), *At the threshold: The developing adolescent* (pp. 388–413). Cambridge: Harvard University Press.

Hauser, S. T., & Bowls, M. (1990). Stress, coping and adaptation. In S. S. Feldman & G. R. Elliott (Eds.), *At the threshold: The developing adolescent* (pp. 352–387). Cambridge: Harvard University Press.

Havighurst, R. J. (1948). *Developmental tasks and education* (3rd ed.). New York: McKay.

Heckhausen, J., & Tomasik, M. J. (2002). Get an apprenticeship before school is out: How German adolescents adjust vocational aspirations when getting close to a developmental deadline. *Journal of Vocational Behavior, 60,* 199–219.

Hernandez, D. J. (1997). Child development and social demography of childhood. *Child Development, 68,* 149–169.

Hogan, D. P. (1985). Parental influences on the timing of early life transitions. *Current Perspectives on Aging and the Life Cycle, 1,* 1–59.

Hurrelmann, K. (Ed.). (1994). *International handbook of adolescence.* Westport, CT: Greenwood Press.

Jacobson, K. C., & Crockett, L. J. (2000). Parental monitoring and adolescent adjustment: An ecological perspective. *Journal of Research on Adolescence, 10,* 65–97.

Jenkins Tucker, C., Barber, B. L., & Eccles, J. S. (1996). Advice about life plans and personal problems in late adolescent. *Journal of Youth and Adolescence, 26,* 63–76.

Jenkins Tucker, C., Barber, B. L., & Eccles, J. S. (2001). Advice about life plans from mothers, fathers, and siblings in always-married and divorced families during late adolescence. *Journal of Youth and Adolescence, 30,* 729–747.

Jodl, K. M., Michael, A., Malanchuk, O., Eccles, J. S., & Sameroff, A. (2001). Parents' roles in shaping early adolescents' occupational aspirations. *Child Development, 72,* 1247–1265.

Joiner, T. E., Jr., & Wagner, K. D. (1995). Attributional style and depression in children and adolescents: A meta-analytic review. *Clinical Psychology Review, 15,* 777–798.

Kalakoski, V., & Nurmi, J.-E. (1998). Identity and educational transitions: Age differences in adolescent and commitment related to education, occupation, and family. *Journal of Research on Adolescence, 8,* 29–47.

Kandel, D. B. (1978). Homophily, selection, and socialization in adolescent friendships. *American Journal of Sociology, 84,* 427–436.

Kandel, D. B., & Lesser, G. S. (1969). Parental and peer influences on educational plans of adolescents. *American Sociological Review, 34,* 213–223.

Kasser, T., Ryan, R. M., Zax, M., & Sameroff, A. (1995). The relations of maternal and social environments to late adolescents' materialistic and prosocial values. *Developmental Psychology, 31,* 907–914.

Kerckhoff, A. C. (2002). The transition from school to work. In J. T. Mortimer & R. W. Larson (Eds.), *The changing adolescent experience: Societal trends and the transition to adulthood* (pp. 52–87) Cambridge, MA: Cambridge University Press.

Kerpelman, J. L., & Lamke, L. K. (1997). Anticipation of future identities: A control theory approach to identity development within the context of serious dating relationships. *Personal Relationships, 4,* 47–62.

Kerr, M., Stattin, H., Biesecker, G., & Fedder-Wreder, L. (in press). Parents and peers as developmental context. In R. M. Lerner, M. A. Easterbrooke, & J. Mistry (Eds.), *Comprehensive handbook of psychology: Vol. 6. Developmental psychology.* New York: Wiley.

Klaczynski, P. A., & Reese, H. W. (1991). Educational trajectory and "action orientation": Grade and track differences. *Journal of Youth and Adolescence, 20,* 441–462.

Kracke, B. (1997). Parental behaviors and adolescents' career exploration. *Career Development Quarterly, 45,* 341–350.

Kracke, B., & Schmitt-Rodermund, E. (2001). Adolescents' career exploration in the context of educational and occupational transition. In J.-E. Nurmi (Ed.), *Navigating through adolescence: European perspectives* (pp. 141–168). New York: Routledge Falmer.

Lanz, M., Rosnati, R., Marta, E., & Scabini, E. (2001). Adolescents' future: A comparison of young people's and their parents' views. In J.-E. Nurmi (Ed.), *Navigating through adolescence: European perspectives* (pp. 169–198). New York: Routledge Falmer.

Larson, R., & Richards, M. H. (1991). Daily companionship in late childhood and early adolescence: Changing developmental contexts. *Child Development, 62,* 284–300.

Leontjev, A. N. (1977). *Toiminta, tietoisuus, persoonallisuus* (Action, cognition, and personality). Helsinki: Kansankulttuuri.

Lerner, R. M. (1982). Children and adolescents as producers of their development. *Developmental Review, 2,* 242–320.

Lerner, R. M. (1983). A "goodness of fit" model of person-context interaction. In D. Magnusson & V. L. Allen (Eds.), *Human development: An interactional perspective* (pp. 279–294). New York: Academic Press.

Lerner, R. M., & Spanier, G. B. (Eds.). (1978). *Child influences on marital and family interaction. A life-span perspective.* New York: Academic Press.

Little, B. R. (1983). Personal projects: A rationale and method for investigation. *Environment and Behavior, 15,* 273–309.

Määttä, S., Nurmi, J.-E., & Majava, E.-M. (2002). Young adults' achievement and attributional strategies in the transition from school to work: Antecedents and consequences. *European Journal of Personality, 16,* 295–311.

Määttä, S., Stattin, H., & Nurmi, J.-E. (2002). Achievement strategies at school: Types and correlated. *Journal of Adolescence, 25, 31–46.*

Makros, J., & McCabe, M. P. (2001). Relationships between identity and self-representations during adolescence. *Journal of Youth and Adolescence, 30,* 623–639.

Malmberg, L.-E. (1996). How do Finnish students prepare for their future in three school types? The relation between content of plans, information gathering and self-evaluations. *British Journal of Educational Psychology, 66,* 457–469.

Malmberg, L.-E., & Norrgård, S. (1999). Adolescents' ideas of normative life-span development and personal future goals. *Journal of Adolescence, 22,* 33–47.

Malmberg, L.-E., & Trempala, J. (1998). Future planning both at school and in other contexts: The case of Finnish and Polish general-secondary and vocational-school students. *Scandinavian Journal of Educational Research, 42,* 207–226.

Marcia, J. E. (1980). Identity in adolescence. In J. Adelson (Ed.), *Handbook of adolescent psychology* (pp. 159–187). New York: Wiley.

Markus, H., & Nurius, P. (1986). Possible selves. *American Psychologist, 41,* 954–969.

Markus, H., & Wurf, E. (1987). The dynamic self-concept: A social psychological perspective. *Annual Review of Psychology, 38,* 299–337.

Marsh, H. W. (1984). Relations among dimensions of self-attribution, dimensions of self-concept, and academic achievements. *Journal of Educational Psychology, 76,* 1291–1308.

Martínez, R.-A., de Miguel, M., & Fernández, S. (1994). Spain. In K. Hurrelmann (Ed.), *International handbook of adolescence* (pp. 360–373). Westport, CT: Greenwood Press.

Mayer, K. U. (1986). Structural constraints on the life course. *Human Development, 29,* 163–170.

McAdams, D. (1999). Personal narratives and the life story. In L. A. Perwin & O. P. John (Eds.), *Handbook of personality: Theory and research* (pp. 478–500). New York: Guilford Press.

McGuire, S., Manke, B., Saudino, K. J., Reiss, D., Hetherington, E. M., & Plomin, R. (1999). Perceived competence and self-worth during adolescence: A longitudinal behavioral genetic study. *Child Development, 70,* 1283–1296.

Meegan, S. P., & Berg, C. A. (2001). Whose life task is it anyway? Social appraisal and life task pursuit. *Journal of Personality, 69,* 363–389.

Meeus, W., Iedema, J., Helsen, M., & Vollebergh, W. (1999). Patterns of adolescent identity development: Review of literature and longitudinal analysis. *Developmental Review, 19,* 419–461.

Meilman, P. (1979). Cross-sectional age changes in ego identity status during adolescence. *Developmental Psychology, 15,* 230–231.

Montemayor, R., & Eisen, M. (1977). The development of self-conceptions from childhood to adolescence. *Developmental Psychology, 13,* 314–319.

Mortimer, J. T., & Larson, R. W. (2002). Macrostructural trends and reshaping adolescence . In J. T. Mortimer & R. W. Larson (Eds.), *The changing adolescent experience: Societal trends and the transition to adulthood* (pp. 1–17). Cambridge, MA: Cambridge University Press.

Muris, P., Schmidt, H., Lambrichs, R., & Meesters, C. (2001). Protective and vulnerability factors of depression in normal adolescents. *Behavior Research and Therapy, 39,* 555–565.

Neugarten, B. L., Moore, J. W., & Lowe, J. C. (1965). Age norms, age constraints, and adult socialization. *American Journal of Sociology, 70,* 710–717.

Nowalk, A., Tesser, A., Vallacher, R. R., & Borkowski, W. (2000). Society of self: The emergence of collective properties in self-structure. *Psychological Review, 107,* 39–61.

Nurmi, J.-E. (1989a). Adolescents' orientation to the future: Development of interests and plans, and related attributions and affects, in the life-span context. *Commentationes Scientiarum Socialium, 39.* Helsinki: Finnish Society for Sciences and Letters.

Nurmi, J.-E. (1989b). Development of orientation to the future during early adolescence: A four-year longitudinal study and two cross-sectional comparisons. *International Journal of Psychology, 24,* 195–214.

Nurmi, J.-E. (1991). How do adolescents see their future? A review of the development of future orientation and planning. *Developmental Review, 11,* 1–59.

Nurmi, J.-E. (1993). Adolescent development in an age-graded context: The role of personal beliefs, goals and strategies in the tackling of developmental tasks and standards. *International Journal of Behavioral Development, 16,* 169–189.

Nurmi, J.-E. (1997). Self-definition and mental health during adolescence and young adulthood. In J. Schulenberg, J. Maggs, & K. Hurrelmann (Eds.), *Health risks and developmental transitions during adolescence* (pp. 395–419). Cambridge: Cambridge University Press.

Nurmi, J.-E. (2001). Adolescents' self-direction and self-definition in age-graded sociocultural and interpersonal contexts. In J.-E. Nurmi (Ed.), *Navigating through adolescence: European perspectives* (pp. 229–250). New York: Routledge Falmer.

Nurmi, J.-E., Aunola, K., Salmela-Aro, K., & Lindroos, M. (2002). Success expectation, task avoidance and academic performance and satisfaction: Three studies on antecedents, consequences and correlates. *Contemporary Educational Psychology, 28,* 59–90.

Nurmi, J. -E., Onatsu, T., & Haavisto, T. (1995). Underachievers' cognitive and behavioral strategies: Self-handicapping at school. *Contemporary Educational Psychology, 20,* 188–200.

Nurmi, J.-E., Poole, M. E., & Kalakoski, V. (1993). Age differences in adolescent future-oriented goals, concerns, and related temporal extension in different sociocultural contexts. *Journal of Youth and Adolescence, 23,* 471–487.

Nurmi, J.-E., Poole, M. E., & Kalakoski, V. (1996). Age differences in adolescent identity exploration and commitment in urban and rural environments. *Journal of Adolescence, 19,* 443–452.

Nurmi, J.-E., & Salmela-Aro, K. (1997). Social strategies and loneliness: A prospective study. *Personality and Individual Differences, 23,* 205–215.

Nurmi, J.-E., & Salmela-Aro, K. (2002). Goal construction, reconstruction and depressive symptoms in a life-span context: The transition from school to work. *Journal of Personality, 70,* 385–420.

Nurmi, J.-E., Salmela-Aro, K., & Koivisto, P. (2002). Goal importance and related achievement beliefs and emotions during the transition from vocational school to work: Antecedents and consequences. *Journal of Vocational Behavior, 60,* 241–261.

Nurmi, J.-E., Salmela-Aro, K., & Ruotsalainen, H. (1994). Cognitive and attributional strategies among unemployment adults: A case of the failure-trap strategy. *European Journal of Personality, 8,* 135–148.

Nurmi, J.-E., Seginer, R., & Poole, M. E. (1995). Searching for the future in different environments. A comparison of Australian, Finnish and Israeli adolescents' future orientation, explorations and commitments. In P. Noack, M. Hofer, & J. Youniss (Eds.), *Psychological responses to social change: Human development in changing environments* (pp. 219–238). Berlin: de Gruyter.

Nurmi, J.-E., & Siurala, L. (1994). Finland. In K. Hurrelmann (Ed.), *International handbook of adolescence* (pp. 131–145). Westport, CT: Greenwood Press.

Nuttin, J. R. (1984). *Motivation, planning, and action. A relational theory of behavior dynamics.* Hillsdale, NJ: Erlbaum.

O'Malley, P., & Bachman, J. G. (1983). Self-esteem: Change and stability between ages 13 and 23. *Developmental Psychology, 19,* 257–268.

Oppenheimer, L. (1987). Cognitive and social variables in the plan of action. In S. H. Friedman, E. Kofsky Scholnick, & R. R. Cocking (Eds.), *Blueprints for thinking: The role of planning in cognitive development.* Cambridge: Cambridge University Press.

Oyserman, D., & Markus, H. R. (1990). Possible selves and delinquency. *Journal of Personality and Social Psychology, 59,* 112–125.

Pasupathi, M., Staudinger, U. M., & Baltes, B. P. (2001). Seeds of wisdom: Adolescents' knowledge and judgement about difficult life problems. *Developmental Psychology, 37,* 351–361.

Pea, R. D., & Hawkins, J. (1987). Planning in a chore-scheduling task. In S. H. Friedman, E. Kofsky Scholnick, & R. R. Cocking (Eds.), *Blueprints for thinking: The role of planning in cognitive development* (pp. 273–302). Cambridge, MA: Cambridge University Press.

Phillips, S. D. (1982). Career exploration in adulthood. *Journal of Vocational Behavior, 20,* 129–140.

Pimentel, E. F. (1996). Effects of adolescent achievement and family goals on the early adult transition. In T. T. Mortimer & M. D. Finch (Eds.), *Adolescents, work, and family: An intergenerational developmental analysis*: Vol. 6. Understanding Families (pp. 191–220). Thousand Oaks, CA: Sage.

Poole, M. E., & Cooney, G. H. (1987). Orientations to the future: A comparison of adolescents in Australia and Singapore. *Journal of Youth and Adolescence, 16,* 129–151.

Recklitis, C. J., & Noam, G. G. (1999). Clinical and developmental perspectives on adolescent coping. *Child Psychiatry and Human Development, 30,* 87–101.

Roisman, G. (2000). Infant attachment security as a discriminant predictor of career development in late adolescence. *Journal of Adolescent Research, 15,* 531–545.

Rudolph, K. D., Lambert, S. F., Clark, A. G., & Kurlakowsky, K. D. (2001). Negotiating the transition to middle school: The role of self-regulatory processes. *Child Development, 72,* 929–946.

Rueter, M. A., & Conger, R. D. (1998). Reciprocal influences between parenting and adolescent problem-solving behavior. *Developmental Psychology, 34,* 1470–1482.

Ryan, A. M. (2001). The peer group as a context for the development of young adolescent motivation and achievement. *Child Development, 72,* 1135–1150.

Salmela-Aro, K. (2001). Personal goals during the transition to young adulthood. In J.-E. Nurmi (Ed.), *Navigating through adolescence: European perspectives* (pp. 59–84). New York: Routledge Falmer.

Salmela-Aro, K., & Nurmi, J.-E. (1997). Goal contents, well-being, and life context during transition to university: A longitudinal study. *International Journal of Behavioral Development, 20,* 471–491.

Salmela-Aro, K., Nurmi, J.-E., Saisto, T., & Halmesmäki, E. (2000). Women's and men's personal goals during the transition to parenthood. *Journal of Family Psychology, 14,* 171–186.

Salmela-Aro, K., Nurmi, J.-E., Saisto, T., & Halmesmäki, E. (2001). Goal reconstruction and depressive symptoms during the transition to motherhood: Evidence from two cross-lagged longitudinal studies. *Journal of Personality and Social Psychology, 81,* 1144–1159.

Samuolis, J., Layburn, K., & Schiaffino, K. (2001). Identity development and attachment to parents in college students. *Journal of Youth and Adolescence, 30,* 373–384.

Schoon, I., & Parsons, S. (2002). Teenage aspirations for future careers and occupational outcomes. *Journal of Vocational Behavior, 60,* 262–288.

Scnabel, K. U., Alfeld, C., Eccles, J. S., Köller, O., & Baumert, J. (2002). Parental influence on students' educational choices in the United States and Germany: Different ramifications—same effect? *Journal of Vocational Behavior, 60,* 178–198.

Seiffge-Krenke, I. (1993). Coping behavior in normal and clinical samples: More similarities than differences? *Journal of Adolescence, 16,* 285–303.

Solantaus, T. (1987). Hopes and worries of young people in three European countries. *Health Promotion, 2,* 19–27.

Stattin, H., & Kerr, M. (2001). Adolescents' values matter. In J.-E. Nurmi (Ed.), *Navigating through adolescence: European perspectives* (pp. 21–58). New York: Routledge Falmer.

Steinberg, L. (2001). We know some things: Parent-adolescent relationships in retrospect and prospect. *Journal of Research on Adolescence, 11,* 1–19.

Steinberg, L., & Silverberg, S. (1986). The vicissitudes of autonomy in early adolescence. *Child Development, 57,* 841–851.

Stern, M., & Zevon, M. A. (1990). Stress, coping, and family environment: The adolescent's response to naturally occurring stressors. *Journal of Adolescent Research, 5,* 290–305.

Streitmatter, J. (1993). Gender differences in identity development. *Adolescence, 28,* 55–66.

Strough, J., Berg, C. A., & Sansone C. (1996). Goals for solving everyday problems across the life span: Age and gender differences in the salience of interpersonal concerns. *Developmental Psychology, 32,* 1106–1115.

Tao, S., Dong, Q., Pratt, M., Husberger, B., & Pancer, M. (2000). Social support: Relations to coping and adjustment during the transition to university in the people's republic of China. *Journal of Adolescent Research, 15,* 123–144.

Tao Hunter, F. (1985). Adolescents' perceptions of discussions with parents and friends. *Developmental Psychology, 21,* 433–440.

Taylor, S. E., & Brown, J. (1988). Illusion and well-being: A social psychological perspective on mental health. *Psychological Bulletin, 103,* 193–210.

Trommsdorf, G., & Lamm, H. (1980). Future orientation of institutionalized and noninstitutionalized delinquents and nondelinquents. *European Journal of Social Psychology, 10,* 247–278.

Trusty, J., & Pirtle, T. (1998). Parents' transmission of educational goals to their adolescent children. *Journal of Research and Development in Education, 32,* 53–65.

Urberg, K., Degirmencioglu, S., & Pilgrim, C. (1997). Close friend and group influence on adolescent cigarette smoking and alcohol use. *Developmental Psychology, 33,* 834–844.

van Hoof, A. (1999). The identity status field re-reviewed: An update of unresolved and neglected issues with a view on some alternative approaches. *Developmental Review, 19,* 497–556.

Wallace-Broscious, A., Serafica, F. C., & Osipow, S. H. (1994). Adolescents career development: Relationships to self-concept and identity status. *Journal of Research on Adolescence, 4,* 127–149.

Waterman, A. S. (1982). Identity development from adolescence to adulthood: An extension of theory and a review of research. *Developmental Psychology, 28,* 341–358.

Waterman, A. S. (1999). Issues of identity formation revisited: United States and the Netherlands. *Developmental Review, 19,* 462–497.

Weiner, B. (1986). *An attributional theory of motivation and emotion.* New York: Springer-Verlag.

Williams, K., & McGillicuddy-DeLisi, A. (2000). Coping strategies in adolescents. *Journal of Applied Developmental Psychology, 20,* 537–549.

Wilson, P. M., & Wilson, J. R. (1992). Environmental influences on adolescent educational aspirations. *Youth and Society, 24,* 52–70.

Zeidner, M. (1995). Adaptive coping with test situations: A review of the literature. *Educational Psychologist, 30,* 123–133.

Zimmerman, M. A., Copeland, L. A., Shope, J. T., & Dielman, T. E. (1997). A longitudinal study of self-esteem: Implications for adolescent development. *Journal of Youth and Adolescence, 26,* 117–141.

Zuckerman, M. (1979). Attribution of success and failure revised, or: motivational bias is alive and well in attributional theory. *Journal of Personality, 47,* 245–287.

Chapter 5

SCHOOLS, ACADEMIC MOTIVATION, AND STAGE-ENVIRONMENT FIT

Jacquelynne S. Eccles

From the time individuals first enter school until they complete their formal schooling, children and adolescents spend more time in schools than in any other place outside their homes. Exploring all of the possible ways in which educational institutions influence motivation and development during adolescence is beyond the scope of a single chapter. In this chapter I discuss the ways in which schools influence adolescents' social-emotional and behavioral development through organizational, social, and instructional processes ranging from those based in the immediate, proximal relation between students and the tasks they are asked to perform to the role that principals and the school boards play in setting school-level and district-level policies, which in turn influence the social organization of the entire school community. I discuss at length three examples of the ways in which these multiple organizational levels interact synergistically to influence adolescent development through their impact on the daily experiences that adolescents in the United States encounter as they move through the American school system. The first example focuses on the role of school transitions, the second on the role of curricular tracking, and the third on extracurricular activities. Few of these processes have been studied in countries other than the United States. I assume similar processes are true in other countries, but this remains to be demonstrated empirically.

A DEVELOPMENTAL VIEW OF THE IMPACT OF SCHOOLS ON DEVELOPMENT

Understanding the impact of schools on adolescent development requires a conceptual framework for thinking simultaneously about schools as contexts in which development takes place and about the changing developmental needs of students as they move through the school system. My colleagues and I have been working on such a framework for the last 20 years. In the late 1980s Carol Midgley and I proposed our model of stage-environment fit to guide research on the impact of school transitions on adolescent development (see Eccles & Midgley, 1989; Eccles et al., 1993). We argued that individuals have changing emotional, cognitive, and social needs and personal goals as they mature. Drawing on ideas related to person-environment fit and self-determination theory (e.g., Deci & Ryan, 1985), we argued that schools need to change in developmentally appropriate ways if they are to provide the kind of social context that will continue to motivate students' interest and engagement as the students mature. To the extent that this does not happen, we predicted that students would disengage first psychologically and then physically from school as they matured into and through adolescence. This should be particularly true as the adolescents acquired more incentives and more power to control their own behavior. I say more about both of these psychological perspectives on the impact of classroom experiences later.

More recently, Robert Roeser and I (see Eccles & Roeser, 1999) proposed a framework for thinking about school influences that dissected the school context into a series of hierarchically ordered, interdependent levels of organization beginning at the most basic level of the classroom and then moving up in complexity to the school as an organizational system embedded in a larger cultural system. In adopting this heuristic, we assumed that (a) schools are systems characterized by multiple levels of regulatory processes (organizational, social, and instructional in nature); (b) these processes are interrelated across levels of analysis; (c) such processes are usually dynamic in nature, sometimes being worked out each day between the various social actors (e.g., teachers and students); (d) these processes change as children move through different school levels (elementary, middle, and high school); and (e) these processes regulate children's and adolescents' cognitive, social-emotional, and behavioral development. In this chapter I focus on the interface between these theoretical frameworks. I begin with a summary of Eccles and Roeser's multilevel description of school contexts.

AN ECOLOGICAL VIEW OF SCHOOLS AND THEIR IMPACT ON DEVELOPMENT DURING ADOLESCENCE

From the location of the school within macroregulatory systems characterized by national, state, and school district laws and educational policies to the miniregulatory systems that involve the minute-to-minute interactions between teachers and individual students, schools are a system of complex, multilevel, regulatory processes. Eccles and Roeser (1999) described these different levels of the school environment in terms of their hierarchical ordering—moving from the student in a classroom, to the school building itself, then to the school district, and finally to the larger communities in which school districts are located. Within each of these levels, we discussed those beliefs and practices that affect students' experiences on a daily basis. At the classroom level, we focused attention on teacher beliefs and instructional practices, teacher-student relationships, the nature and design of tasks and instruction, and the nature and structure of classroom activities and groups. At the level of the school building, we focused attention on organizational climate and such schoolwide practices as academic tracking, school start time, and the provision of extracurricular activities. At the level of the school district, we focused on the between-school grade configurations that create particular school-transition experiences for students. Finally at the level of schools embedded in larger social systems, we discussed such issues as school resources, as well as the linkages of schools with parents and with the labor market.

Eccles and Roeser (1999) further assumed that in any given school setting these multilevel processes are interwoven with one another. Relations between different levels of organization in the school may be complementary or contradictory and may influence students either directly or indirectly. For instance, a principal may decide that all of his or her teachers should use a particular practice such as cooperative learning. However, the impact of such a decision on the daily experiences of students depends on how well this practice is actually implemented at the classroom level. If done well, students should be seen working successfully in groups on complex, authentic problems. Such a well-implemented school policy is likely to produce gains in self-esteem, interethnic relationships, and achievement among students, especially those of low ability or status (Slavin, 1990). In contrast, if done poorly, chaos can result, leading to far less positive outcomes at the student level. How such a schoolwide instructional policy is implemented depends on many factors including the morale within the school, the relationships between the principal and the teachers, the teachers' understanding and endorsement of the new instructional practice, the way in which the policy change was decided upon, the provision of adequate in-service training, the provision of adequate supports for implementation of new strategies, and the students' willingness to go along with the new practice. Recent debates about the likely impact of national standards testing provide another example of the complex ways in which a new policy—this time a state- or national-level policy—can affect the daily experiences of teachers and students in the classroom and in the school building.

Eccles and Roeser (1999) also assumed that the processes associated with the different levels of school interacting dynamically with each other, rather than static resources or characteristics of the curriculum, teachers, or school per se, influence adolescents' development. In addition, adolescents' own constructions of meaning and interpretations of events within the school environment are critical mediators between school characteristics and students' feelings, beliefs, and behavior.

Finally, in keeping with the stage-environment perspective proposed by Eccles and Midgely (1989), Eccles and Roeser (1999) assumed that these different school-related processes change across the course of children's and adolescents' development as they progress through elementary, middle, and high school. That is, not only are children and adolescents developing, but so too is the whole nature of the schools that they attend. For example, the organizational, social, and instructional processes in schools change as children move from elementary to middle school. Eccles and Midgley argued that these changes are often associated with declines in many adolescents' motivation and behavior. Understanding the interaction of different school features with the developmental needs of adolescents is critical to understanding the role of schooling in young people's development (see Eccles & Midgley, 1989). In the next sections I discuss those characteristics of each level likely to be most important for understanding the impact of schools on adolescent development. I also discuss how school characteristics at each level may also influence group differences in adolescent development, paying particular attention to gender and ethnic group differences within the United States.

LEVEL 1: CLASSROOMS

The most immediate educational environment to the student is the classroom. This is also the level that has received the most attention from educational psychologists. In this section I review what we know about teacher beliefs, classroom climate, the nature of the academic work itself, and experiences of racial/ethnic discrimination.

Teacher Beliefs

Teacher beliefs have received much attention in educational psychology. In this section I focus on two types of beliefs: Teachers' general sense of their own teaching efficacy and teachers' expectations for specific students in their class.

Teachers' General Sense of Efficacy

When teachers hold high general expectations for student achievement and students perceive these expectations, students learn more, experience a greater sense of self-worth and competence as learners, feel more connected to their teacher and their school, and resist involvement in problem behaviors (Eccles et al. 1993; Lee & Smith, 2001; Roeser, Eccles, & Sameroff, 1998; Rutter, 1983; Weinstein, 1989). Similarly, teachers who feel they are able to reach even the most difficult students and who believe in their ability to affect students' lives communicate such positive expectations and beliefs to their students. Thus, a high sense of general teacher efficacy can enhance students' own confidence in their ability to master academic material, thereby promoting effort investment and achievement as well as a positive emotional relationship with their teacher and greater engagement in school as a social institution (Ashton, 1985; Midgley, Feldlaufer, & Eccles, 1989b). Alternatively, teachers who have low confidence in their teaching efficacy often engage in behaviors that reinforce feelings of incompetence and alienation in their students, increasing the likelihood that their students will develop learned helpless responses to failure in the classroom, depressive affect, anger, and disengagement (see Cole, 1991; Roeser, Eccles, & Freedman-Doan, 1999). Lee and Smith (2001) stressed this aspect of teachers' general beliefs as a critical component for secondary school reform (see also Jackson & Davis, 2000).

As I discuss in more detail later, the prevalence of teachers with a low sense of personal teaching efficacy is higher in junior high and middle schools than in elementary schools and higher in schools that serve high proportions of ethnic minority and poor adolescents than in schools that serve more affluent and higher achieving adolescents (Darling-Hammond, 1997; Eccles, Wigfield, & Schiefele, 1998). This fact alone provides a possible explanation for both average levels of declining school engagement during early to middle adolescence and for social class and ethnic group differences in school engagement.

Differential Teacher Expectations

Equally important are the differential expectations teachers often hold for various individuals within the same classroom and the differential treatments that sometimes accompany these expectations. Beginning with the work by Rosenthal (1969), many researchers have shown that undermining teacher-expectancy effects depend on how teachers structure activities differently, as well as interact differently with, high- and low-expectancy students and on how the students perceive these differences (Brophy, 1985; Cooper, 1979; Eccles & Wigfield, 1985; Weinstein, 1989). Most concerns have been raised over behaviors that create a self-fulfilling prophecy by undermining the learning and well-being of those students for whom the teachers hold the lowest expectations.

Much work on teacher expectancy effects has focused on differential treatment related to gender, race/ethnic group, and/or social class. Most of this work has documented the small but fairly consistent undermining effects of low teacher expectations on girls (for math and science), on minority children (for all subject areas), and on children from lower-social-class family backgrounds (again for all subject areas) (see Eccles & Wigfield, 1985; Ferguson, 1998; Jussim, Eccles, & Madon, 1996; Valencia, 1991). In addition, Jussim et al. (1996) found that even though these effects are typically quite small, young women, African American adolescents, and students from poorer homes are more subject to both the positive and negative teacher expectancy effects than are other students.

Researchers such as Steele (1992) have linked this form of differential treatment, particularly for African American students, to school disengagement and disidentification (the separation of one's self-esteem from all forms of school-related feedback). Steele argued that African American students become aware of the fact that teachers and other adults have negative stereotypes of African Americans' academic abilities. This awareness (labeled *stereotype threat* by Steele and his colleagues) increases their anxieties, which in turn lead them to disidentify with the school context to protect their self-esteem. It is interesting that recent studies using the same theoretical notions and experimental techniques have shown that Asian students believe that teachers and adults expect them to perform very well and that this belief leads Asian students to perform better on tests when their ethnic identity is made salient (Shih, Pittinsky, & Ambady, 1999). Thus, the psychological processes associated with stereotype threat can either undermine or facilitate performance on standardized tests depending on the nature of commonly held stereotypes about the intellectual strengths and weaknesses of different social groups.

Classroom Climate

Classroom climate refers to the more general character of the classroom and teacher-student relationships within the classroom. In this section I focus on the following aspects of classroom climate: Teacher-student relationships, classroom management, and motivational climate.

Teacher-Student Relationships

Teacher-student relationships are a key component of classroom climate: High-quality teacher-student relationships facilitate academic motivation, school engagement, academic success, self-esteem, and more general socioemotional well-being (Deci & Ryan, 1985; Eccles et al., 1998; Goodenow, 1993; Midgley et al., 1989b; Roeser, Midgley, & Urdan, 1996). Teachers who trust, care about, and are respectful of students provide the social-emotional support that students need to approach, engage, and persist on academic learning tasks and to develop positive achievement-related self-perceptions and values. Feeling emotionally supported is one of the most important characteristics of contexts that support positive development. Correlational studies with adolescents show that students' perceptions of caring teachers enhance their feelings of self-esteem, school belonging, and positive affect in school (Roeser & Eccles, 1998; Roeser et al., 1996).

Declines in both adolescents' perception of emotional support from their teachers and in the adolescents' sense of belonging in their classrooms are quite common as adolescents move from elementary school into secondary schools (Eccles et al., 1998). This shift is particularly troublesome in our highly mobile society in which teachers represent one of the last stable sources of nonparental role models for adolescents. In addition to teaching, teachers in mobile societies such as the United States can provide guidance and assistance when social-emotional or academic problems arise. This role is especially important for promoting developmental competence when conditions in the family and neighborhood cannot or do not provide such supports (Eccles, Lord, & Roeser, 1996; Simmons & Blyth, 1987).

Classroom Management

Work related to classroom management has focused on two general issues: orderliness/predictability and control/autonomy. With regard to orderliness and predictability, the evidence is quite clear: Student achievement and conduct are enhanced when teachers establish smoothly running and efficient procedures for monitoring student progress, providing feedback, enforcing accountability for work completion, and organizing group activities (e.g., Eccles et al., 1998; Pintrich & Schunk, 1996). Unfortunately, such conditions are often absent, particularly in highly stressed and underfunded schools with inexperienced teachers (Darling-Hammond, 1997).

In addition, research on international comparisons of instruction suggest that American teachers are often more lax in their classroom management and provide less systematic and rigorous control over the instructional sequences (Stevenson & Stigler, 1992). Furthermore, this research suggests that these differences in teachers' control-related practices could be a partial explanation for the relatively poor performance of many American youth on international standardized tests of math and science achievement (Schmidt, McKnight, & Raizen, 1997).

Motivational Climate

Several teams of researchers have suggested that teachers engage in a wide range of behaviors that create a pervasive motivational climate in the classroom. For example, Rosenholtz and Simpson (1984) suggested a cluster of general teaching practices (e.g., individualized vs. whole-group instruction, ability grouping practices, and publicness of feedback) that should affect motivation because these practices make ability differences in classrooms especially salient to students (see Mac Iver, 1988). They assumed that these practices affect the motivation of all students by increasing the salience of extrinsic motivators and ego-focused learning goals, leading to greater incidence of social comparison behaviors and increased perception of ability as an entity state rather than an incremental condition. All of these changes reduce the quality of students' motivation and learning. The magnitude of the negative consequences of these shifts, however, should be greatest for low-performing students: As these students become more aware of their relative low standing, they are likely to adopt a variety of ego-protective strategies that unfortunately undermine learning and mastery (Covington, 1992).

More recently, researchers interested in goal theory have proposed a similar set of classroom characteristics (Ames, 1992; E. M. Anderman, & Maehr, 1994; Maehr & Midgley, 1996; Pintrich & Schunk, 1996; Roeser, Midgley, & Maehr, 1994). Goal theorists propose two major achievement goal systems: mastery-oriented goals and performance-oriented goals. Students with mastery-oriented goals focus on learning the material and on their own improvement over time. Students with performance-oriented goals focus on doing better than other students in their class. Goal theorists further argue that a mastery orientation sustains school engagement and achievement better than does a performance orientation (see Ames, 1992; Maehr & Midgley, 1996; Midgley, 2002). Evidence is quite strong for the first prediction and more mixed for the second: The desire to do better than others often has positive rather than negative consequences, whereas the fear of failing (performance-avoidance goal orientation) undermines school performance (see Midgley, 2002). Finally, these theorists suggest that the publicness of feedback, particularly social comparative feedback, and a classroom focus on competition between students undermine mastery motivation and increase performance motivation. The school-reform work of Midgley, Maehr, and their colleagues has shown that social reform efforts to reduce these types of classroom practices, particularly those associated with performance feedback, social comparative grading systems, and ego-focused, competitive motivational strategies have positive consequences for adolescents' academic motivation, persistence on difficult learning tasks, and socioemotional development (e.g., Maehr & Midgley, 1996).

The work on understanding group differences in achievement and achievement choices is another example of an attempt to identify a broad set of classroom characteristics related to motivation. The work on girls and math is one example of this approach. There are sex differences in adolescents' preference for different types of learning contexts that likely interact with subject area to produce sex differences in interest in different subject areas (Eccles, 1989; Hoffmann & Haeussler, 1995). Females appear to respond more positively to math and science instruction if it is taught in a cooperative or individualized manner rather than a competitive manner, if it is taught from an applied or person-centered perspective rather than a theoretical or abstract perspective, if it is taught using a hands-on approach rather than a book-learning approach, and if the teacher avoids sexism in its many subtle forms. The reason given for these effects is the fit between the teaching style, the instructional focus, and females' values, goals, motivational orientations, and learning styles. The few relevant studies support this hypothesis (Eccles & Harold, 1993; Hoffmann & Haeussler, 1995). If such classroom practices are more prevalent in one subject area (e.g., physical science or math) than another (e.g., biological or social science), one would expect sex differences in motivation to study these subject areas. In addition, however, math and physical science do not have to be taught in these ways; more girl-friendly instructional approaches can be used. When they are, girls, as well as boys, are more likely to continue taking courses in these fields and to consider working in these fields when they become adults.

The girl-friendly classroom conclusion is a good example of person-environment fit. Many investigators have suggested that students are maximally motivated to learn in situations that fit well with their interests, current skill level, and psychological needs, so that the material is challenging, interesting, and meaningful (e.g., Csikszentmihalyi, Rathunde, & Whalen, 1993; Eccles et al., 1993; Krapp, Hidi, & Renninger, 1992). Variations on this theme include aptitude by treatment interactions and theories stressing cultural match or mismatch as one explanation for group differences in school achievement and activity choices (e.g., Fordham & Ogbu, 1986; Suarrez-Orozco & Suarrez-Orozco, 1995; Valencia, 1991). For example, Valencia (1991) concluded that a mismatch of both the values of the school and the materials being taught contributed to the poor performance and high dropout rates among Latino youth in the high school they studied. Deyhle and LeCompte (1999) made a similar argument in their discussion of the poor performance of Native American youth in traditional middle school contexts. The misfit between the needs of young adolescents and the nature of junior high school environments is another example of these person-environment fit dynamics.

The Nature of Academic Work

Academic work is at the heart of the school experience. Two aspects of academic tasks are important: the content of the curriculum and the design of instruction. The nature of academic content has an important impact on students' attention, interest, and cognitive effort. Long ago, Dewey (1902/1990) proposed that academic work that is meaningful to the historical and developmental reality of students' experiences will promote sustained attention, high investment of cognitive and affective resources in learning, and strong identification with educational goals and aims. In general, research supports this hypothesis: Content that provides meaningful exploration is critical given that boredom in school, low interest, and perceived irrelevance of the curriculum are associated with poor attention, diminished achievement, disengagement, and alienation from school (e.g., Finn, 1989; Jackson & Davis, 2000; Larson & Richards, 1989). Curricula that represent the voices, images, and historical experiences of traditionally underrepresented groups are also important (Valencia, 1991). Choosing materials that provide an appropriate level of challenge for a given class, designing learning activities that require diverse cognitive operations (e.g., opinion, following routines, memory, comprehension), structuring lessons so that they build on each other in a systematic fashion, using multiple representations of a given problem, and explicitly teaching students strategies that assist in learning are but a few of the design features that scaffold learning and promote effort investment, interest in learning, and achievement (Blumenfeld, 1992; Deci & Ryan, 1985; Eccles et al., 1998).

Unfortunately, American secondary schools have problems providing each of these types of educational experiences. Recent work by Larson and his colleagues has documented the fact that adolescents are bored most of the time that they are in secondary school classrooms (Larson, 2000; Larson & Richards, 1989). Culturally meaningful learning experiences are rare in many American secondary schools (Fine, 1991; Valencia, 1991). The disconnection of traditional curricula from the experiences of these groups can explain the alienation of some group members from the educational process, sometimes eventuating in school dropout (Fine, 1991; Sheets & Hollins, 1999). Appropriately designed tasks that adequately scaffold learning are also rare in many inner-city and poor schools (Darling-Hammond, 1997).

In addition, from a developmental perspective, there is evidence that the nature of academic work too often does not change over time in ways that are concurrent with the increasing cognitive sophistication, diverse life experiences, and identity needs of adolescents as they move from the elementary into the secondary school years (Carnegie Council, 1989; Lee & Smith, 2001). As one indication of this, middle school students report the highest rates of boredom when doing schoolwork, especially passive work (e.g., listening to lectures) and in particular classes such as social studies, math, and science (Larson & Richards, 1989). There is also evidence that the *content* of the curriculum taught in schools does not broaden to incorporate either important health or social issues that become increasingly salient as adolescents move through puberty and deal with the identity explorations associated with adolescence (Carnegie Council, 1989). Further, academic work sometimes becomes less, rather than more, complex in terms of the cognitive demands as adolescents move from elementary to junior high school (Eccles et al., 1998). It may be that declines in some adolescents' motivation during the transition to secondary school in part reflect academic work that lacks challenge and meaning commensurate with adolescents' cognitive and emotional needs (Eccles & Midgley, 1989). Recent efforts at middle school reform support this hypothesis: motivation is maintained when middle schools and junior high schools introduce more challenging and meaningful academic work (Jackson & Davis, 2000). I discuss this in more detail later.

Experiences of Racial-Ethnic Discrimination

Researchers interested in the relatively poor academic performance of adolescents from some ethnic/racial groups have suggested another classroom-based experience as critical for adolescent development, namely, experiences of racial/ethnic discrimination (Essed, 1990; Feagin, 1992; Fordham & Ogbu, 1986; Garcia Coll et al., 1996; Rosenbaum, Kulieke, & Rubinowitz, 1988; Ruggiero & Taylor, 1995; Taylor, Casten, Flickinger, Roberts, & Fulmore, 1994; Wong, Eccles, & Sameroff, in press). Two types of discrimination have been discussed: (a) anticipation of future discrimination in the labor market, which might be seen as undermining the long-term benefits of education (Fordham & Ogbu, 1986), and (b) the impact of daily experiences of discrimination on one's mental health and academic motivation (Essed, 1990; Wong et al., in press). Both types are likely to influence adolescent development, but research on these issues is in its infancy. Wong et al. (in press) found that anticipated future discrimination leads to increases in African American youth's motivation to do well in school, which in turn leads to increases in academic performance. In this sample, anticipated future discrimination appeared to motivate the youth to do their very best so that they would be maximally equipped to deal with future discrimination. In contrast, daily experiences of racial discrimination from their peers and teachers led to declines in school engagement and confidence in one's academic competence and grades, along with increases in depression and anger.

Level 1: Summary

The studies of classroom-level influences suggest that development is optimized when students are provided with challenging tasks in a mastery-oriented environment that also provides good emotional and cognitive support, meaningful material to learn and master, and sufficient support for their own autonomy and initiative. Connell and Wellborn (1991), as well as Deci and Ryan (1985), suggested that humans have three basic needs: to feel competent, to feel socially attached, and to have autonomous control in their lives. Further, they hypothesized that individuals develop best in contexts that provide opportunities for each of these needs to be met. Clearly, the types of classroom characteristics that emerge as important for both socioemotional and intellectual development would provide such opportunities.

LEVEL 2: SCHOOL BUILDINGS

Schools are formal organizations and, as such, have characteristics and features that are superordinate to classroom characteristics. These aspects of the whole school environment should impact on adolescents' intellectual, social-emotional, and behavioral development. Important school-level organizational features include school climate and sense of community (Goodenow, 1993; Rutter, 1983) and the relationships among the students themselves. School organizational features also include such schoolwide practices as curricular tracking, start and stop times, and the availability of extracurricular activities.

General Social Climate

Researchers have become interested in the social climate of the entire school. These researchers suggest that schools vary in the climate and general expectations regarding student potential and that such variations affect the development of both teachers and students in very fundamental ways (e.g., Bandura, 1994; Bryk, Lee, & Holland, 1993; Mac Iver, Reuman, & Main, 1995; Rosenbaum et al., 1988; Rutter, Maughan, Mortimore, & Ouston, 1979). For example, in their analysis of higher achievement in Catholic schools, Bryk et al. (1993) discussed how the culture within Catholic schools is fundamentally different from the culture within most public schools in ways that positively affect the motivation of students, parents, and teachers. This culture (school climate) values academics, has high expectations that all students can learn, and affirms the belief that the business of school is learning. Similarly, Lee and Smith (2001) showed that between-school differences in teachers' sense of their own personal efficacy as well as their confidence in the general ability of the teachers at their school to teach all students accounted, in part, for between-school differences in adolescents' high school performance and motivation. Finally, Bandura (1994) documented between-school differences in the general level of teachers' personal efficacy beliefs and argued that these differences translate into teaching practices that undermine the motivation of many students and teachers in the school.

Maehr, Midgley, and their colleagues argued that just as classroom practices give rise to certain achievement goals, so too do schools through particular policies and practices. A school-level emphasis on different achievement goals creates a schoolwide psychological environment that affects students' academic beliefs, affects, and behaviors (e.g., Maehr & Midgley, 1996; Roeser et al., 1996). For example, schools' use of public honor rolls and assemblies for the highest achieving students, class rankings on report cards, differential curricular offerings for students of various ability levels, and so on all emphasize relative ability, competition, and social comparison in the school and create a school-level ability rather than mastery/task focus. In contrast, through the recognition of academic effort and improvement, rewards for different competencies that extend to all students, and through practices that emphasize learning and task mastery (block scheduling, interdisciplinary curricular teams, cooperative learning), schools can promote a school-level focus on discovery, effort and improvement, and academic mastery. The academic goal focus of a school also has important implications for students' mental health. In a series of studies, Roeser and Eccles found that students' belief that their school is ability-focused leads to declines in students' educational values, achievement, and self-esteem and increases in their anger, depressive symptoms, and school truancy as they move from seventh to eighth grade (Roeser & Eccles, 1998; Roeser et al., 1998). Fiqueira-McDonough (1986) reported similar findings in a study of two high schools that were similar in intake characteristics and achievement outcomes but differed in their academic orientation and rates of delinquent behavior. The high school characterized by a greater emphasis on competition and high grades (ability orientation) had higher delinquency rates, and the students' grades were a major correlate of students' involvement in delinquent behavior (low grades predicted increased delinquent behavior). In contrast, in the school that had more diverse goals and greater interest in non-academic needs, school attachment (valuing of school, liking teachers) was greater on average, and those students with high school attachment engaged in the least delinquent activity.

One final note on school-level academic goal emphases: They are strongly correlated with adolescents' perceptions of the school's social climate. Adolescents who perceive a task orientation in their school also report that their teachers are friendly, caring, and respectful. These factors in turn predict an increased sense of belonging in school among adolescents (see also Goodenow, 1993). In contrast, perceptions of a schoolwide ability orientation are negatively correlated with adolescents' perceptions of caring teachers (Roeser et al., 1996). From the adolescents' perspective, a deemphasis on comparison and competition and an emphasis on effort and improvement are intertwined with their view of caring teachers.

Academic Tracks and Curricular Differentiation

Another important school-level feature relates to academic tracks or curriculum differentiation policies. These terms refer to the regularities in the ways in which schools structure the learning experiences for different types of students (Oakes, Gamoran, & Page, 1992). The practice of providing different educational experiences for students of different ability levels is widespread in American schools. Tracking takes different forms at different grade levels. It includes within-class ability grouping for different subject matters or between-class ability grouping in which different types of students are assigned to different teachers. Within-classroom ability grouping for reading and math is quite common in elementary school. In secondary school, between-class tracking is more widespread and is often linked to the sequencing of specific courses for students bound for different post–secondary school trajectories (e.g., the college prep, general, or vocational tracks). Differentiated curricular experiences for students of different ability levels influence school experiences in two major ways: First, tracking determines the quality and kinds of instruction each student receives (Rosenbaum, 1976, 1980; Oakes et al., 1992), and second, it determines exposure to different peers and thus, to a certain degree, the nature of social relationships that youth form in school (Fuligni, Eccles, & Barber, 1995).

Despite years of research on the impact of tracking practices, few strong and definitive answers have emerged (see Fuligni et al., 1995; Gamoran & Mare, 1989; Kulik & Kulik, 1987; Slavin, 1990). The results vary depending on the outcome assessed, the group studied, the length of the study, the control groups used for comparison, and the specific nature of the context in which these practices are manifest. The best justification for these practices, derived from a person-environment fit perspective, is the belief that students are more motivated to learn if the material is adapted to their current competence level. There is some evidence to support this view for students placed in high ability and gifted classrooms, high within-class ability groups, and college tracks (Dreeben & Barr, 1988; Fuligni et al., 1995; Gamoran & Mare, 1989; Kulik & Kulik, 1987; Pallas, Entwisle, Alexander, & Stluka, 1994).

The results for adolescents placed in low-ability and noncollege tracks are usually inconsistent with this hypothesis. By and large, the effects found for this group of students are negative (Dreeben & Barr, 1988; Pallas et al., 1994; Rosenbaum, 1976, 1980; Rosenbaum et al., 1988; Vanfossen, Jones, & Spade, 1987). Low-track placement predicts poor attitudes toward school, feelings of incompetence, and problem behaviors both within school (nonattendance, crime, misconduct) and in the broader community (drug use, arrests); it also predicts lower educational attainments (Oakes et al., 1992). These negative effects reflect the fact that students placed in the lower tracks are often provided with inferior educational experience and support.

Ability grouping also has an impact on students' peer groups: Between-classroom ability grouping and curricular tracking increase the extent of contact among adolescents with similar levels of achievement and engagement with school. For those doing poorly in school, tracking is likely to facilitate friendships among students who are similarly alienated from school and are more likely to engage in risky or delinquent behaviors (Dryfoos, 1990). Dishion, McCord, and Poulin (1999) showed experimentally how such collecting of alienated adolescents increases their involvement in problem behaviors. This collecting of adolescents with poor achievement or adjustment histories also places additional discipline burdens on the teachers who teach these classes (Oakes et al., 1992), making such classes unpopular with the teachers as well as the students and decreasing the likelihood that the teachers with the most experience will allow themselves to be assigned to these classes.

Concerns have also been raised about the way students get placed in different classes and how difficult it is for students to change tracks once initial placements have been made. These issues are important both early in a child's school career (e.g., Entwisle & Alexander, 1993) and later in adolescence, when course placement is linked directly to the kinds of educational options that are available to the student after high school. Minority youth, particularly African American and Latino boys, are more likely to be assigned to low-ability classes and non-college-bound curricular tracks than are other groups; furthermore, careful assessment of the placements has shown that many of these youth were incorrectly assigned to these classes (Dornbusch, 1994; Oakes et al.,

1992). The consequences of such misassignment are great. It has long-term consequences for students' ability to go to college once they complete secondary school.

Extracurricular Activities

There is growing interest in the role of extracurricular activities in adolescent development. Some people are interested because these activities can fill time and thus decrease the time available for adolescents to get in trouble. For example, in communities where few structured opportunities for after-school activities exist (especially poor urban communities), adolescents are most likely to be involved in high-risk behaviors such as substance use, crime, violence, and sexual activity during the period between 2 and 8 P.M. Providing structured activities either at school or within community organizations after school when many adolescents have no adults at home to supervise them is an important consideration in preventing adolescents from engaging in high-risk behaviors (Carnegie Council, 1989; Eccles & Gootman, 2001).

Others are interested in the potential benefits of such activities for adolescent development (Carnegie Corporation of New York, 1992; Eccles & Gootman, 2001). There is a positive link between adolescents' extracurricular activities and both educational outcomes (e.g., high school completion, adult educational attainment, occupation, and income) and positive youth development (better mental health and lower rates of involvement in delinquent activities), even after controlling for social class and ability (Barber, Eccles, & Stone, 2001; Eccles & Barber, 1999; Larson & Kleiber, 1993; Mahoney & Cairns, 1997; McNeal, 1995; Otto & Alwin, 1977). Participation in sports, in particular, has been linked to lower likelihood of school dropout, higher rates of college attendance, greater educational attainment by age 25, and higher occupational attainment at least through the 20s (Barber et al., 2001; Deeter, 1990; Eccles & Barber, 1999; McNeal, 1995), especially among low-achieving and blue-collar male athletes (Holland & Andre, 1987). Participation in school-based extracurricular activities has also been linked to increases on such positive developmental outcomes as high school GPA, strong school engagement, and high educational aspirations (Eccles & Barber, 1999; Lamborn, Brown, Mounts, & Steinberg, 1992; Newmann, Wehlage, & Lamborn, 1992). Similarly, participation in high school extracurricular activities and out-of-school volunteer activities predicts high levels of adult participation in the political process and other types of volunteer activities, continued sport engagement, and better physical and mental health (Glancy, Willits, & Farrell, 1986; Youniss, McLellan, & Yates, 1997; Youniss, Yates, & Su, 1997).

In contrast to these positive associations, sports has also been linked to increased rates of school deviance and drug and alcohol use (e.g., Eccles & Barber, 1999; Lamborn, Brown, Mounts, & Steinberg, 1992). These results suggest that participation in organized extracurricular activities can have both positive and negative effects. Why?

Several investigators have offered explanations for the positive results associated with participation: Rehberg (1969) suggested the importance of association with academically oriented peers, exposure to academic values, enhanced self-esteem, generalization of a high sense of personal efficacy, and superior career guidance and encouragement. Coleman (1961) stressed the values and norms associated with the different peer clusters engaged in various types of extracurricular activities. Otto and Alwin (1977) added skill and attitude acquisition (both interpersonal and personal) and increased membership in important social networks.

More recently, investigators have focused on the links among peer group formation, identity formation, and activity involvement (Eccles & Barber, 1999). For example, Eckert (1989) explored the link between the peer group identity formation and both in- and out-of-school activity involvement. As one moves into and through adolescence, individuals become identified with particular groups of friends or crowds (see also Brown, 1990). Being a member of one of these crowds helps structure both what one does with one's time and the kinds of values and norms to which one is exposed. Over time, the coalescence of one's personal identity, one's peer group, and the kinds of activities one participates in as a consequence of both one's identity and one's peer group can shape the nature of one's developmental pathway into adulthood.

This strong link between activity participation and peer group membership also provides an explanation for the negative influences of sports participation on drug and alcohol use. Knowing what an adolescent is doing often tells us a lot about who the adolescent is with: It is very likely that participation in organized activity settings directly affects adolescents' peer groups precisely because such participation structures a substantial amount of peer group interaction. One's coparticipants become one's peer crowd. And such peer crowds often develop an activity-based culture, providing adolescents with the opportunity to identify with a group having a shared sense of style and commitment. Involvement in a school organization or sports links an adolescent to a set of similar peers, provides shared experiences and goals, and can reinforce friendships between peers. In turn, these experiences should influence identity formation as well as other aspects of adolescent development.

What is important from a school-building perspective is that schools differ in the extent to which they provide positive extracurricular activities for their students. Researchers who study the advantages of small schools often point to the fact that more students get to participate in extracurricular activities in small schools because there are fewer bodies to fill all of the available slots (Elder & Conger, 2000). Large schools have an overabundance of students to fill all of the available activity slots. The situation is even worse in poor, large secondary schools that have had to cut extracurricular activities to stay within their budgets. Recently, federal and state initiatives have emerged to help increase the availability of after-school programs that are housed in school buildings. Unfortunately, most of this money is going to elementary school and middle school programs rather than high schools (Eccles & Gootman, 2001).

Summary of School-Level Effects

In this section I reviewed the impact of several features of the whole school on adolescent development. These features included school climate, curricular tracking practices, and the availability of extracurricular activities. There is very strong evidence that each of these schoolwide characteristics impacts adolescent development. Often, between-school variations on these characteristics result from school district policies or financial constraints that are beyond the control of the building's principal and staff. Reform efforts, however, have shown that changes can be created in each of these domains and that such changes can have a positive impact on the development of the adolescents attending the reformed school.

LEVEL 3: SCHOOL DISTRICTS AND SECONDARY SCHOOL TRANSITIONS

School transitions are an excellent example of how the multiple levels of schools interact to affect development. All school districts must decide how they will group the grade levels within the various school buildings. One common arrangement is to group children in kindergarten through 6th grade in elementary schools, young adolescents in grades 7 through 9 in junior high schools, and older adolescents in grades 10 through 12 in senior high schools. Another common arrangement places the transitions after grades 5 and 8, creating elementary schools, middle schools, and senior high schools. The third popular arrangement groups young people in grades K–8 in one school and then grades 9–12 in a high school. In each of these arrangements the students typically move to a new and often larger building at each of the major transition points. These move typically also involve increased bussing and exposure to a much more diverse student body. In this section I discuss two of these transitions: the transition from elementary to middle or junior high school and the transition from middle or junior high school to high school. Because most of the empirical work has focused on the junior high–middle school transition, I emphasize this transition.

The Middle-Grades School Transition

There is substantial evidence of declines in academic motivation and achievement across the early-adolescence years (approximately ages 11–14; E. M. Anderman & Maehr, 1994; Eccles & Midgley, 1989; Eccles et al., 1993; Maehr & Midgley, 1996). These declines often coincide with the transition into either middle school or junior high school. For example, there is a marked decline in some early adolescents' school grades as they move into junior high school (Simmons & Blyth, 1987). Similar declines occur for such motivational constructs as interest in school (Epstein & McPartland, 1976), intrinsic motivation (Harter, 1981), self-concepts/self-perceptions and confidence in one's intellectual abilities (Wigfield, Eccles, Mac Iver, Reuman, & Midgley, 1991), mastery goal orientation (E. M. Anderman & Midgley, 1997), and a sense of belonging at school (L. H. Anderman, 1999). There are also increases in test anxiety (Wigfield & Eccles, 1989), focus on self-evaluation rather than task mastery (Nicholls, 1990), focus on performance goals (E. M. Anderman & Midgley, 1997), and both truancy and school dropout (Rosenbaum, 1976). Although these changes are not extreme for most adolescents, there is sufficient evidence of declines in various indicators of academic motivation, behavior, and self-perception over the early adolescent years to make one wonder what is happening (see Eccles & Midgley, 1989). Further, although few studies have gathered information on ethnic or social-class differences in these declines, academic failure and dropout are especially problematic among some ethnic groups and among youth from communities and families of low socioeconomic status. It is probable then that these groups are particularly likely to show these declines in academic motivation and self-perception as they move into and through the secondary school years.

Several explanations have been offered for these seemingly negative changes in academic motivation: Some point to the intrapsychic upheaval associated with young adolescent development (see Arnett, 1999). Others point to the simultaneous occurrence of several life changes. For example, Simmons and Blyth (1987) attributed these declines, particularly among females, to the coincidence of the junior high school transition with pubertal development. Still others point to the nature of the junior high school environment itself rather than the transition per se.

Extending person-environment fit theory (see Hunt, 1975) into a developmental perspective (stage-environment fit theory), Eccles and Midgley (1989) proposed that these negative developmental changes result from the fact that traditional junior high schools do not provide developmentally appropriate educational environments for young adolescents. The authors suggested that different types of educational environments are needed for different age groups to meet developmental needs and foster continued developmental growth. Exposure to the developmentally appropriate environment would facilitate both motivation and continued growth; in contrast, exposure to developmentally inappropriate environments, especially developmentally regressive environments, should create a particularly poor person-environment fit, which should lead to declines in motivation as well as detachment from the goals of the institution. What is critical to this argument is that the transition itself is *not* the cause of the declines; instead, it is the nature of the school into which the students move. Within this framework, the right kinds of middle school reforms can be quite effective at reducing these declines.

Two approaches have been used to study the middle school transition: one focused on more global school-level characteristics such as school size, degree of departmentalization, and extent of bureaucratization and the other on more specific classroom and motivational dynamics.

The first type is best exemplified by the work of Simmons and Blyth (1987). They pointed out that most junior high schools are substantially larger than elementary schools and that instruction is more likely to be organized departmentally. As a result, junior high school teachers typically teach several different groups of students, making it very difficult for students to form a close relationship with any school-affiliated adult precisely at the point in development when there is a great need for guidance and support from nonfamilial adults. Such changes in student-teacher relationships are also likely to undermine the sense of community and trust between students and teachers, leading to a lowered sense of efficacy among the teachers, an increased reliance on authoritarian control practices by the teachers, and an increased sense of alienation among the students. Finally, such changes are likely to decrease the probability that any particular student's difficulties will be noticed early enough to get the student necessary help, thus increasing the likelihood that students on the edge will be allowed to slip onto negative motivational and performance trajectories, leading to increased school failure and dropout.

The latter is best exemplified by the work of Eccles and Midgley and by the studies on middle school reform initiated by the Carnegie Foundation after their report *Turn-*

ing Points (Carnegie Council, 1989; Jackson & Davis, 2000). These scholars have looked at several specific aspects of the classroom and school environment and have shown that negative changes in these aspects of student' experiences at school as they make the middle or junior high school transition are linked to the declines in school motivation and engagement. They have also shown that changing these aspects of the middle school environment can be effective in reducing the declines in school engagement often associated with this school transition (E. M. Anderman, Maehr, & Midgley, 1999; Maehr & Midgley, 1996).

Grade-Related Differences in Teacher Beliefs

Differences in all types of teacher beliefs have been shown in studies comparing elementary and middle grades teachers. For example, junior high school teachers on average have lower confidence in their own teaching efficacy than do elementary school teachers (i.e., their ability to teach and influence all of the students in their classes; Feldlaufer, Midgley, & Eccles, 1988; Midgley, Feldlaufer, & Eccles, 1989a). An equally troubling difference occurs for teachers' views of their roles in their students' lives. For example, Roeser and Midgley (1997) found that with increasing grade level, middle school (6th to 8th grades) teachers are less likely to endorse the notion that students' mental health concerns are part of the teacher role. Thus, at a time when adolescents need academic and social-emotional guidance and support from both parents and nonparental adults (i.e., during early adolescence), teachers appear less likely to be able to provide such support given the number of students they teach, their educational training, and the size of secondary schools. This creates holes in the safety net available to adolescents at a time when they are in particularly acute need of adult support and guidance (Simmons & Blyth, 1987). It is not surprising that the most at-risk youth often fall through these holes.

Grade-Related Differences in Authority Relationships

Despite the increasing maturity of students, junior high school teachers place a greater emphasis on teacher control and discipline and provide fewer opportunities for student decision making, choice, and self-management than do elementary school teachers (e.g., Feldlaufer et al., 1988; Midgley & Feldlaufer, 1987). Both stage-environment fit theory (Eccles et al., 1993) and self-determination theory suggest that these practices will create a mismatch between young adolescents' desires for autonomy and control and their perceptions of the opportunities in their learning environments; this mismatch is predicted to lead to a decline in the adolescents' intrinsic motivation and interest in school. Evidence supports this prediction (Mac Iver & Reuman, 1988).

Grade-Related Differences in Affective Relationships

Junior high and middle school classrooms are often characterized by a less personal and positive teacher-student relationship than are elementary school classrooms (Feldlaufer et al., 1988; Midgley, Feldlaufer, & Eccles, 1988). Given the association of classroom climate and student motivation reviewed earlier, it should not be surprising that moving into a less supportive classroom leads to a decline in these young adolescents' interest in the subject matter being taught in that classroom, particularly among the low achieving students (Midgley et al., 1988).

Grade-Related Differences in Grading Practices

There is no stronger predictor of students' self-confidence and efficacy than the grades they receive. If academic marks decline with the junior high or middle school transition, then adolescents' self-perceptions and academic motivation should also decline. In fact, junior high school teachers do use stricter and more social comparison–based standards than do elementary school teachers to assess student competency and to evaluate student performance, leading to a drop in grades for many young adolescents as they make the transition to junior high school (Eccles & Midgley, 1989; Finger & Silverman, 1966; Simmons & Blyth, 1987). It is interesting that this decline in grades is not matched by a decline in the adolescents' scores on standardized achievement tests, suggesting that the decline reflects a change in grading practices rather than a change in the rate of the students' learning (Kavrell & Petersen, 1984). Imagine what such a decline in grades might do to young adolescents' self-confidence and motivation. Although Simmons and Blyth (1987) did not look at this specific question, they did document the impact of this grade drop on subsequent school performance and dropout. Even after controlling for a youth's performance prior to the school transition, the magnitude of the grade drop following the transition into either junior high school or middle school was a major predictor of leaving school early in both studies (see also Roderick, 1993).

Grade-Related Differences in Motivational Goal Context

Several of the changes just noted are linked together in goal theory. Classroom practices related to grading practices, support for autonomy, and instructional organization affect the relative salience of mastery versus performance goals that students adopt as they engage in the learning tasks at school. Given changes associated with these practices, it is not surprising that both teachers and students think that their school environment is becoming increasingly focused on competition, relative ability, and social comparison as the young adolescents progress from elementary to middle or junior high school (Midgley, Anderman, & Hicks, 1995; Roeser, Midgley, & Maehr, 1994). The types of changes associated with the middle-grades school transition should precipitate greater focus on performance goals. In support of this prediction, Midgley et al. (1995) found that both teachers and students indicated that performance-focused goals were more prevalent and task-focused goals were less prevalent in the middle school classrooms than in the elementary school classrooms. In addition, the elementary school teachers reported using task-focused instructional strategies more frequently than did the middle school teachers. Finally, at both grade levels the extent to which teachers were task-focused predicted the students' and the teachers' sense of personal efficacy. Thus, it is no surprise that personal efficacy was lower among the middle school participants than among the elementary school participants.

Anderman, Maehr, and Midgley (1999) extended this work by comparing two groups of young adolescents: a group who moved into a middle school that emphasized task-focused instructional practices and a group who moved into a middle school that emphasized more traditional performance/ability-focused instructional practices. Although these two groups of students did not differ in their motivational goals prior to the school transition, they did after the transition. As predicted, the adolescents who moved into the first type of middle school were less likely to show an increase in their extrinsic motivational and performance-oriented motivational goals.

Summary

Changes such as those just reviewed are likely to have a negative effect on many children's motivational orientation toward school at any grade level. However, Eccles and Midgley (1989) argued that these types of school environmental changes are particularly harmful at early adolescence given what is known about psychological development during this stage of life. Evidence from a variety of sources suggests that early adolescent development is characterized by increases in desire for autonomy, peer orientation, self-focus and self-consciousness, salience of identity issues, concern over heterosexual relationships, and capacity for abstract cognitive activity (see Brown, 1990; Eccles & Midgley, 1989; Keating, 1990; Simmons & Blyth, 1987; Wigfield, Eccles, & Pintrich, 1996). Simmons and Blyth (1987) argued that adolescents need safe, intellectually challenging environments to adapt to these shifts. In light of these needs, the environmental changes often associated with transition to junior high school are likely to be especially harmful in that they emphasize competition, social comparison, a performance-goal orientation rather than a mastery-goal orientation, and self-assessment of ability at a time of heightened self-focus; they decrease decision making and choice at a time when the desire for control is growing; and they disrupt the opportunity for a close relationship between students and teachers at a time when adolescents may be in special need of close adult relationships outside of the home. The nature of these environmental changes, coupled with the normal course of individual development, is likely to result in a developmental mismatch so that the fit between the young adolescent and the classroom environment is particularly poor, increasing the risk of negative motivational outcomes, especially for adolescents who are having difficulty succeeding in school academically.

The High School Transition

Although there is less work on the transition to high school, the existing work suggests quite similar problems (Coleman & Hoffer, 1987; Jencks & Brown, 1975; Wehlage, Rutter, Smith, Lesko, & Fernandez, 1989). For example, high schools are typically even larger and more bureaucratic than are junior high schools and middle schools. Bryk, Lee, and Smith (1989) provided numerous examples of how the sense of community among teachers and students is undermined by the size and bureaucratic structure of most high schools. There is little opportunity for students and teachers to get to know each other, and, likely as a consequence, there is distrust between them and little attachment to a common set of goals and values. There is also little opportunity for the students to form mentor-like relationships with nonfamilial adults, and little effort is made to make instruction relevant to the students. Such environments are likely to undermine further the motivation and involvement of many students, especially those not doing particularly well academically, those not enrolled in the favored classes, and those who are alienated from the values of the adults in the high school. These hypotheses need to be tested.

The few available studies provide initial support (see Lee & Smith, 2001). For example, Fine (1991) documented how secondary school practices cumulate to drive out students who are not doing very well academically. Similarly, studies of ethnic minority youth provide extensive evidence that alienating and noninclusive high school practices undermine the school engagement and achievement of students of color (e.g., Darling-Hammond, 1997; Deyhle & LeCompte, 1999; Ferguson, 1998; Jackson & Davis, 2000; Lee, Bryk, & Smith, 1993; Suarrez-Orozco & Suarrez-Orozco, 1995; Taylor et al., 1994; Valencia, 1991).

Recent work by Midgley and her colleagues provides additional support. In a longitudinal study of adolescents from elementary school to high school, they were able to look at the impact of both the middle school and the high school transition. They found less evidence of negative changes in school experiences as the students moved into the middle school than when they moved into the high school. As one would expect with the stage-environment fit theory, they found that the motivational declines were associated with the high school rather than the middle school transition (see chapters in Midgley, 2002). They concluded that middle school reform efforts have been effective in changing the middle school environment in ways that support rather than undermine the young adolescents' school engagement and motivation. Further, they concluded that reform is now needed at the high school level. These reforms look very much like the reforms that were advocated for the middle school years.

Most large public high schools also organize instruction around curricular tracks that sort students into different groups. As a result, there is even greater diversity in the educational experiences of high school students than of middle grades students; unfortunately, this diversity is often associated more with the students' social class and ethnic group than with differences in the students' talents and interests (Lee & Bryk, 1989). As a result, curricular tracking has served to reinforce social stratification rather than foster optimal education for all students, particularly in large schools (Dornbusch, 1994; Lee & Bryk, 1989). Lee and Bryk (1989) documented that average school achievement levels do not benefit from this curricular tracking. Quite the contrary—evidence comparing Catholic high schools with public high schools suggests that average school achievement levels are increased when all students are required to take the same challenging curriculum. This conclusion is true even after one has controlled for student selectivity factors. A more thorough examination of how the organization and structure of our high schools influence cognitive, motivational, and achievement outcomes is needed.

Summary

In this section I summarized the evidence related to the impact of school transitions on development. As one would expect, given what we now know about the ecological nature of the junior high school transition, many early adolescents, particularly the low achievers and the highly anxious, experience great difficulty with this transition. In many ways, this transition can be characterized as a developmentally regressive shift in one's school context. Consistent with our stage-environment fit perspective, such a shift has negative consequences for many youth's school engagement and performance. Also consistent with our stage-environment fit perspective, there are now an increasing number of intervention studies showing that the junior high school transition does not have to yield negative consequences for vulnerable youth. Educational institutions for the middle grades can be designed in a developmentally progressive manner; when they are, the majority of early adolescents gain from this school transition. Finally, emerging evidence on the senior high school transition suggests that reforms are badly needed at this level.

LEVEL 4: SCHOOLS AS EMBEDDED ORGANIZATIONS IN LARGER COMMUNITY

The most distal aspect of school influence on adolescent development lies in the fact that schools are embedded in much larger social systems. Characteristics of the communities and the nations in which schools are placed influence everything about what goes on in the school building itself. Discussing all of the macro influences is beyond the scope of a single chapter. In this section I focus on two macro characteristics: school resources and the link of schools to the labor market.

School Resources

Certainly student composition issues such as the number of low-ability students or the percent of minority students can affect both the internal organization and the climate of the school, which, in turn, can impact the educational and behavioral outcomes of the students (e.g., Rutter et al., 1979). School resources in terms of adequate materials, a safe environment, and continuity of teaching staff are also important for adolescents' learning and well-being. School district–level variations in such school resources are likely a major contributor to the continuing inequity in educational outcomes for several minority groups in the United States.

About 37% of African American youth and 32% of Latino youth, compared to 5% of European American and 22% of Asian youth, are enrolled in the 47 largest city school districts in this country; in addition, African American and Latino youth attend some of the poorest school districts in this country. In turn, 28% of the youth enrolled in city schools live in poverty, and 55% are eligible for free or reduced-cost lunch, suggesting that class may be as important (or more important) as race in the differences that emerge. Teachers in these schools report feeling less safe than do teachers in other school districts, dropout rates are highest, and achievement levels at all grades are the lowest (Council of the Great City Schools, 1992). Finally, schools that serve these populations are less likely than schools serving more advantaged populations to offer either high-quality remedial services or advanced courses and courses that facilitate the acquisition of higher order thinking skills and active learning strategies. Even adolescents who are extremely motivated may find it difficult to perform well under these educational circumstances.

Link to the Labor Market

I end this discussion of schools with a very brief discussion of the links between school and the labor market. In the United States this link is typically part of what we call vocational education. Reviewing this very extensive field is beyond the scope of one chapter, but it is important in a chapter focused on the impact of schools on adolescent development to acknowledge the role schools play in preparing youth to make the transition from school into the labor market.

Several scholars have recently refocused attention on this issue. These scholars include Stephen and Mary Agnes Hamilton, James Rosenbaum, and Jeylan Mortimer. By explicitly comparing the American vocational-educational systems with the German systems, the Hamiltons have highlighted the inadequacies of the former (Hamilton & Hamilton, 1999). The American vocational-educational system is often not well connected to the labor market; in contrast, the German vocational-educational system has been very well connected, making it much easier for non-college-bound youth in Germany to move directly into well-paying career-ladder jobs once they have finished their educational training. A well-connected apprenticeship experience is one of the most distinguishing features of the German system (see Heinz, 1999, for fuller discussion). In the United States, junior colleges sometimes provide the bridge between secondary school and work (Grubb, 1999; Rosenbaum, 1999). In addition, some youth in the United States are able to piece together an informal apprenticeship-like experience that helps them make a smoother transition (Mortimer & Johnson, 1999).

What we are missing, however, is a well-designed national policy regarding the role that secondary schools should play in helping non-college-bound youth make a successful transition to the labor market. Consequently, many American youth leave high school poorly trained for jobs that can provide wages high enough to support a family (Grubb, 1999; Rosenbaum, 1999; William T. Grant Commission, 1988).

SUMMARY AND CONCLUSIONS

I have outlined many ways in which schools affect the development of adolescents and stressed the need to take both a systems-level and a developmental perspective on schools. I began by pointing out how the multiple levels of school organization interact to shape the day-to-day experiences of adolescents and teachers. I also stressed the interface of schools as complex changing institutions with the developmental trajectories of individuals. To understand how schools influence development, one needs to understand change at both the individual and the institutional level. Stage-environment fit theory provides an excellent example of the linking of these two developmental trajectories. Imagine two trajectories: one at the school level and one at the individual level. Schools change in many ways over the grade levels. The nature of these changes can be developmentally appropriate or inappropriate in terms of the extent to which they foster continued development toward the transition into adulthood and maturity. Youth travel through this changing context as they move from grade to grade and from school to school. Similarly, youth develop and change as they get older. They also have assumptions about their increasing maturity and the privileges it ought to afford them.

Optimal development is most likely when these two trajectories of change are in synchrony with each other—that is, when the changes in the context mesh well with, and perhaps even slightly precede, the patterns of change occurring at the individual level.

I also discussed the many ways in which experiences at school are influenced by the larger cultural and social milieu in which schools are nested. Culturally shared beliefs influence how we fund our schools, what and how we teach, and how we design school policy at all levels. These policies, in turn, influence the types of connections that schools have with families, communities, higher educational institutions, the labor market, and the daily experiences of youth in the schools they attend. On some levels, our schools are succeeding very well in supporting both learning and positive youth development for many groups of people. At other levels, schools are not supporting optimal learning or preparation for adult development for many young people. Adolescents of color, particularly African Americans, Latinos, and Native Americans, still perform less well than European Americans and some groups of Asian Americans (for discussions see, e.g., Jencks & Phillips, 1998; Steinberg, Dornbusch, & Brown, 1992; Suarrez-Orozco & Suarrez-Orozco, 1995; Valencia, 1991).

REFERENCES

Ames, C. (1992). Classrooms: Goals, structures, and student motivation. *Journal of Educational Psychology, 84,* 261–271.

Anderman, E. M., & Maehr, M. L. (1994). Motivation and schooling in the middle grades. *Review of Educational Research, 64,* 287–309.

Anderman, E. M., Maehr, M. L., & Midgley, C. (1999). Declining motivation after the transition to middle school: Schools can make a difference. *Journal of Research and Development in Education, 32,* 131–147.

Anderman, E. M., & Midgley, C. (1997). Changes in achievement goal orientation, perceived academic competence, and grades across the transition to middle level schools. *Contemporary Educational Psychology, 22,* 269–298.

Anderman, L. H. (1999). Classroom goal orientation, school belonging and social goals as predictors of students' positive and negative affect following the transition to middle school. *Journal of Research and Development in Education, 32,* 90–103.

Arnett, J. J. (1999). Adolescent storm and stress, reconsidered. *American Psychologist, 54,* 317–326.

Ashton, P. (1985). Motivation and the teacher's sense of efficacy. In C. Ames & R. Ames (Eds.), *Research on motivation in education: Vol. 2. The classroom milieu* (pp. 141–171). Orlando, FL: Academic Press.

Bandura, A. (1994). *Self-efficacy: The exercise of control.* New York: W. H. Freeman.

Barber, B. L., Eccles, J. S., & Stone, M. R. (2001). Whatever happened to the Jock, the Brain, and the Princess? Young adult pathways linked to adolescent activity involvement and social identity. *Journal of Adolescent Research, 16,* 429–455.

Blumenfeld, P. C. (1992). Classroom learning and motivation: Clarifying and expanding goal theory. *Journal of Educational Psychology, 84,* 272–281.

Brophy, J. (1985). Teachers' expectations, motives, and goals for working with problem students. In C. Ames & R. Ames (Eds.), *Research on motivation in education: Vol. 2. The classroom milieu* (pp. 175–213). New York: Academic Press.

Brown, B. B. (1990). Peer groups and peer culture. In S. S. Feldman & G. R. Elliott (Eds.), *At the threshold: The developing adolescent* (pp. 171–196). Cambridge, MA: Harvard University Press.

Bryk, A. S., Lee, V. E., & Holland P. B. (1993). *Catholic schools and the common good.* Cambridge, MA: Harvard University Press.

Bryk, A. S., Lee, V. E., & Smith, J. B. (1989, May). *High school organization and its effects on teachers and students: An interpretative summary of the research.* Paper presented at the invitational conference on Choice and Control in American Education: Robert M. La Follette of Public Affairs, University of Wisconsin-Madison, Madison, WI.

Carnegie Corporation of New York. (1992). *A matter of time: Risk and opportunity in the non school hours.* New York: Author.

Carnegie Council on Adolescent Development. (1989). *Turning points: Preparing American youth for the 21st century.* New York: Carnegie Corporation.

Cole, D. A. (1991). Preliminary support for a competency-based model of depression in children. *Journal of Abnormal Psychology, 100,* 181–190.

Coleman, J. S. (1961). *The adolescent society.* New York: Free Press.

Coleman, J. S., & Hoffer, T. (1987). *Public and private high schools: The impact of communities.* New York: Basic Books.

Connell, J. P., & Wellborn, J. G. (1991). Competence, autonomy, and relatedness: A motivational analysis of self-system processes. In R. Gunnar & L. A. Sroufe (Eds.), *Minnesota symposia on child psychology* (Vol. 23, pp. 43–77). Hillsdale, NJ: Erlbaum.

Cooper, H. M. (1979). Pygmalion grows up: A model for teacher expectation communication and performance influence. *Review of Educational Research 49*(3), 389–410.

Council of the Great City Schools. (1992). *National urban education goals: Baseline indicators, 1990–91.* Washington, DC: Author.

Covington, M. V. (1992). *Making the grade: A self-worth perspective on motivation and school reform.* New York: Cambridge University Press.

Csikszentmihalyi, M., Rathunde, K., & Whalen, S, (1993). *Talented teenagers: The roots of success and failure.* New York: Cambridge University Press.

Darling-Hammond, L. (1997). *The right to learn: A blueprint for creating schools that work.* San Francisco: Jossey-Bass.

Deci, E. L., & Ryan, R. M. (1985). *Intrinsic motivation and self determination in human behavior.* New York: Plenum Press.

Deeter, T. E. (1990). Remodeling expectancy and value in physical activity. *Journal of Sport and Exercise Psychology, 12,* 83–91.

Dewey, J. (1990). *The child and the curriculum.* Chicago: University of Chicago Press. (Original work published 1902)

Deyhle, D., & LeCompte, M. (1999). Cultural differences in child development: Navaho adolescents in middle schools. In R. H. Sheets & E. R. Hollins (Eds.), *Racial and ethnic identity in school practices: Aspects of human development* (pp. 123–140). Mahwah, NJ: Erlbaum.

Dishion, T. J., McCord, J., & Poulin, F. (1999). When interventions harm: Peer groups and problem behavior. *American Psychologist, 54*(9), 755–764.

Dornbusch, S. M. (1994). *Off the track.* Presidential address at the biennial meeting of the Society for Research on Adolescence, San Diego, CA.

Dreeben, R., & Barr, R. (1988). Classroom composition and the design of instruction. *Sociology of Education, 61,* 129–142.

Dryfoos, J. G. (1990). *Adolescents at risk: Prevalence and prevention.* Oxford: Oxford University Press.

Eccles, J. S. (1989). Bringing young women to math and science. In M. Crawford & M. Gentry (Eds.), *Gender and thought: Psychological perspectives* (pp. 36–57). New York: Springer-Verlag.

Eccles, J. S., & Barber, B. L. (1999). Student council, volunteering, basketball, or marching band: What kind of extracurricular involvement matters? *Journal of Adolescent Research, 14,* 10–43.

Eccles, J. S., & Gootman, J. (2001). *Community programs to promote youth development.* Washington, DC: National Academy Press.

Eccles, J. S., & Harold, R. D. (1993). Parent-school involvement during the early adolescent years . *Teachers' College Record, 94,* 568–587.

Eccles, J. S., Lord, S., & Roeser, R. (1996). Round holes, square pegs, rocky roads, and sore feet: The impact of stage/environment fit on young adolescents' experiences in schools and families. In D. Cicchetti & S. L. Toth (Eds.), *Rochester Symposium on Developmental Psychopathology: Vol. 8. Adolescence: Opportunities and challenges* (pp. 47–93). Rochester NY: University of Rochester Press.

Eccles, J. S., & Midgley, C. (1989). Stage/environment fit: Developmentally appropriate classrooms for early adolescents. In R. Ames & C. Ames (Eds.), *Research on motivation in education* (Vol. 3, pp. 139–181). New York: Academic Press.

Eccles, J. S., Midgley, C., Wigfield, A., Buchanan, C. M., Reuman, D., Flanagan, C., & MacIver, D. (1993). Development during adolescence: The impact of stage-environment fit on adolescents' experiences in schools and families. *American Psychologist, 48,* 90–101.

Eccles, J. S., & Roeser, R. (1999). School and community influences on human development. In M. Bornstein & M. Lamb (Eds.), *Developmental psychology: An advanced textbook* (4th ed., pp. 503–554). Mahwah, NJ: Erlbaum.

Eccles, J. S., & Wigfield, A. (1985). Teacher expectations and student motivation. In J. B. Dusek (Ed.), *Teacher expectations* (pp. 185–217). Hillsdale, NJ: Erlbaum.

Eccles, J. S., Wigfield, A., & Schiefele, U. (1998). Motivation. In N. Eisenberg (Ed.), *Handbook of child psychology: Vol. 3. Social, emotional, and personality development.* (5th ed., pp. 1017–1095). New York: Wiley.

Eckert, P. (1989). *Jocks and burnouts: Social categories and identity in the high school.* New York: Teacher College Press.

Elder, G. H., Jr., & Conger, R. D. (2000). *Children of the land.* Chicago: Chicago University Press.

Entwisle, D. R., & Alexander, K. L. (1993). Entry into school: The beginning school transition and educational stratification in the United States. *Annual Review of Sociology, 19,* 401–423.

Epstein, J. L., & McPartland, J. M. (1976). The concept and measurement of the quality of school life. *American Educational Research Journal, 13,* 15–30.

Essed, P. (1990). *Everyday racism: Reports from women of two cultures.* Claremont, CA: Hunter House.

Feagin, J. R. (1992). The continuing significance of racism: Discrimination against Black students in White colleges. *Journal of Black Studies, 22,* 546–578.

Feldlaufer, H., Midgley, C., & Eccles, J. S. (1988). Student, teacher, and observer perceptions of the classroom environment before and after the transition to junior high school. *Journal of Early Adolescence, 8,* 133–156.

Ferguson, R. F. (1998). Teachers' perceptions and expectations and the Black-White test score gap. In C. Jencks & M. Phillips (Eds.), *The Black-White test score gap* (pp. 273–317). Washington, DC: Brookings Institute Press.

Fine, M. (1991). *Framing dropouts: Notes on the politics of an urban public high school.* Albany: State University of New York Press.

Finger, J. A., & Silverman, M. (1966). Changes in academic performance in the junior high school. *Personnel and Guidance Journal, 45,* 157–164.

Finn, J. D. (1989). Withdrawing from school. *Review of Educational Research, 59,* 117–142.

Fiqueira-McDonough, J. (1986). School context, gender, and delinquency. *Journal of Youth and Adolescence, 15,* 79–98.

Fordham, S., & Ogbu, J. U. (1986). Black students' school success: Coping with "the burden of 'acting white.'" *Urban Review, 18,* 176–206.

Fuligni, A. J., Eccles, J. S., & Barber, B. L. (1995). The long-term effects of seventh-grade ability grouping in mathematics. *Journal of Early Adolescence, 15*(1), 58–89.

Gamoran, A., & Mare, R. D. (1989). Secondary school tracking and educational inequality: Compensation, reinforcement, or neutrality? *American Journal of Sociology, 94,* 1146–1183.

Garcia Coll, C. T., Crnic, K., Hamerty, G., Wasik, B. H., Jenkins, R., Vazquez Garcia, H., & McAdoo, H. P. (1996). An integrative model for the study of developmental competencies in minority children. *Child Development, 20,* 1891–1914.

Glancy, M., Willits, F. K., & Farrell, P. (1986). Adolescent activities and adult success and happiness: Twenty-four years later. *Sociology and Social Research, 70,* 242–250.

Goodenow, C. (1993). Classroom belonging among early adolescent students: Relationships to motivation and achievement. *Journal of Early Adolescence, 13*(1), 21–43.
Grubb, W. N. (1999). The subbaccalaureate labor market in the United States: Challenges for the school-to-work transition. In W. R. Heinz (Ed.), *From education to work: Cross national perspectives* (pp. 171–193). Cambridge: Cambridge University Press.
Hamilton, S. F., & Hamilton, M. A. (1999). Creating new pathways to adulthood by adapting German apprenticeship in the United States. In W. R. Heinz (Ed.), *From education to work: Cross national perspectives* (pp. 194–213). Cambridge: Cambridge University Press.
Harter, S. (1981). A new self-report scale of intrinsic versus extrinsic orientation in the classroom: Motivational and informational components. *Developmental Psychology, 17,* 300–312.
Heinz, W. R. (Ed.). (1999). *From education to work: Cross national perspectives.* Cambridge: Cambridge University Press.
Hoffmann, L., & Haeussler, L. (1995, April). *Modification of interests by instruction.* Paper presented at Annual AERA Meeting, San Francisco.
Holland, A., & Andre, T. (1987). Participation in extracurricular activities in secondary school: What is known, what needs to be known? *Review of Educational Research, 57,* 437–466.
Hunt, D. E. (1975). Person-environment interaction: A challenge found wanting before it was tried. *Review of Educational Research, 45,* 209–230.
Jackson, A. W., & Davis, G. A. (2000). *Turning points 2000: Educating adolescents in the 21st century.* New York: Teachers College Press.
Jencks, C. L., & Brown, M. (1975). The effects of high schools on their students. *Harvard Educational Review, 45,* 273–324.
Jencks, C. L., & Phillips, M. (Eds.). (1998). *The Black-White test score gap.* Washington DC: Brookings Institute Press.
Jussim, L., Eccles, J. S., & Madon, S. (1996). Social perception, social stereotypes, and teacher expectations: Accuracy and the quest for the powerful self-fulfilling prophecy. In L. Berkowitz (Ed.), *Advances in experimental social psychology* (pp. 281–388). New York: Academic Press.
Kavrell, S. M., & Petersen, A. C. (1984). Patterns of achievement in early adolescence. In M. L. Maehr (Ed.), *Advances in motivation and achievement* (pp. 1–35). Greenwich, CT: JAI Press.
Keating, D. P. (1990). Adolescent thinking. In S. S. Feldman & G. R. Elliott (Eds.), *At the threshold: The developing adolescent* (pp. 54–89). Cambridge, MA: Harvard University Press.
Krapp, A., Hidi, S., & Renninger, K. A. (1992). Interest, learning and development. In K. A. Renninger, S. Hidi, & A. Krapp (Eds.), *The role of interest in learning and development* (pp. 3–25). Hillsdale, NJ: Erlbaum.
Kulik, J. A., & Kulik, C. L. (1987). Effects of ability grouping on student achievement. *Equity and Excellence, 23,* 22–30.
Lamborn, S. D., Brown, B. B., Mounts, N. S., & Steinberg, L. (1992). Putting school in perspective: The influence of family, peers, extracurricular participation, and part-time work on academic engagement. In F. M. Newmann (Ed.), *Student engagement and achievement in American secondary schools* (pp. 153–181). New York: Teachers College Press.
Larson, R. W. (2000). Toward a psychology of positive youth development. *American Psychologist, 55*(1), 170–183.
Larson, R. W., & Kleiber, D. (1993). Free time activities as factors in adolescent adjustment. In P. Tolan & B. Cohler (Eds.), *Handbook of clinical research and practice with adolescents* (pp. 125–145). New York: Wiley.
Larson, R. W., & Richards, M. (Eds.). (1989). The changing life space of early adolescence (Special issue). *Journal of Youth and Adolescence, 18,* 501–626.
Lee, V. E., & Bryk, A. S. (1989). A multilevel model of the social distribution of high school achievement. *Sociology of Education, 62,* 172–192.
Lee, V. E., Bryk, A. S., & Smith, J. B. (1993). The organization of effective secondary schools. In L. Darling-Hammond (Ed.), *Review of research in education* (Vol. 19, pp. 171–267). Washington, DC: American Educational Research Association.

Lee, V. E., & Smith, J. (2001). *Restructuring high schools for equity and excellence: What works.* New York: Teacher's College Press.

Mac Iver, D. J. (1988). Classroom environments and the stratification of pupils' ability perceptions. *Journal of Educational Psychology, 80*(4), 1–40.

Mac Iver, D. J., & Reuman, D. A. (1988, April). *Decision-making in the classroom and early adolescents' valuing of mathematics.* Paper presented at the annual meeting of the American Educational Research Association, New Orleans.

Mac Iver, D. J., Reuman, D. A., & Main, S. R. (1995). Social structuring of school: Studying what is, illuminating what could be. In *Annual review of psychology* (Vol. 46, pp. 375–400). Palo Alto, CA: Annual Reviews.

Maehr, M. L., & Midgley, C. (1996). *Transforming school cultures to enhance student motivation and learning.* Boulder, CO: Westview Press.

Mahoney, J. L., & Cairns, R. B. (1997). Do extracurricular activities protect against early school dropout? *Developmental Psychology, 33,* 241–253.

McNeal, R. B. (1995). Extracurricular activities and high school dropouts. *Sociology of Education, 68,* 62–81.

Midgley, C. (2002). *Goals, goal structures, and patterns of adaptive learning.* Mahwah, NJ: Erlbaum.

Midgley, C., Anderman, E., & Hicks, L. (1995). Differences between elementary and middle school teachers and students: A goal theory approach. *Journal of Early Adolescence, 15,* 90–113.

Midgley, C., & Feldlaufer, H. (1987). Students' and teachers' decision-making fit before and after the transition to junior high school. *Journal of Early Adolescence, 7,* 225–241.

Midgley, C., Feldlaufer, H., & Eccles, J. S. (1988). The transition to junior high school: Beliefs of pre- and post-transition teachers. *Journal of Youth and Adolescence, 17,* 543–562.

Midgley, C. M., Feldlaufer, H., & Eccles, J. S. (1989a). Changes in teacher efficacy and student self- and task-related beliefs during the transition to junior high school. *Journal of Educational Psychology, 81,* 247–258.

Midgley, C. M., Feldlaufer, H., & Eccles, J. S. (1989b). Student/teacher relations and attitudes toward mathematics before and after the transition to junior high school. *Child Development, 60,* 981–992.

Mortimer, J. T., & Johnson, M. K. (1999). Adolescent part-time work and postsecondary transition pathways in the United States. In W. R. Heinz (Ed.), *From education to work: Cross national perspectives* (pp. 111–148). Cambridge: Cambridge University Press.

Newmann, F. M., Wehlage, G. G., & Lamborn, S. D. (1992). The significance and sources of student engagement. In F. M. Newmann (Ed.), *Student engagement and achievement in American secondary schools* (pp. 11–39). New York: Teachers College Press.

Nicholls, J. G. (1990). What is ability and why are we mindful of it? A developmental perspective. In R. J. Sternberg & J. Kolligian (Eds.), *Competence considered* (pp. 11–40). New Haven, CT: Yale University Press.

Oakes, J., Gamoran, A., & Page, R. N. (1992). Curriculum differentiation: Opportunities, outcomes, and meanings. In P. Jackson (Ed.), *Handbook of research on curriculum* (pp. 570–608). New York: MacMillan.

Otto, L. B., & Alwin, D. (1977). Athletics, aspirations and attainments. *Sociology of Education, 50,* 102–113.

Pallas, A. M., Entwisle, D. R., Alexander, K. L., & Stluka, M. F. (1994). Ability-group effects: Instructional, social, or institutional? *Sociology of Education, 67,* 27–46.

Pintrich, P. R., & Schunk, D. H. (1996). *Motivation in education: Theory, research, and application.* Englewood Cliffs, NJ: Prentice Hall.

Rehberg, R. A. (1969). Behavioral and attitudinal consequences of high school interscholastic sports: A speculative consideration. *Adolescence, 4,* 69–88.

Roderick, M. (1993). *The path to dropping out: Evidence for intervention.* Westport, CT: Auburn House.

Roeser, R. W., & Eccles, J. S. (1998). Adolescents' perceptions of middle school: Relation to longitudinal changes in academic and psychological adjustment. *Journal of Research on Adolescence, 88,* 123–158.

Roeser, R. W., Eccles, J. S., & Freedman-Doan, C. (1999). Academic functioning and mental health in adolescence: Patterns, progressions, and routes from childhood. *Journal of Adolescent Research, 14,* 135–174.

Roeser, R. W., Eccles, J. S., & Sameroff, J. (1998). Academic and emotional functioning in early adolescence: Longitudinal relations, patterns, and prediction by experience in middle school. *Development and Psychopathology, 10,* 321–352.

Roeser, R. W., & Midgley, C. M. (1997). Teachers' views of aspects of student mental health. *Elementary School Journal, 98*(2), 115–133.

Roeser, R. W., Midgley, C. M., & Maehr, M. L. (1994, February). *Unfolding and enfolding youth: A development study of school culture and student well-being.* Paper presented at the Society for Research on Adolescence, San Diego.

Roeser, R. W., Midgley, C. M., & Urdan, T. C. (1996). Perceptions of the school psychological environment and early adolescents' psychological and behavioral functioning in school: The mediating role of goals and belonging. *Journal of Educational Psychology, 88,* 408–422.

Rosenbaum, J. E. (1976). *Making inequality: The hidden curriculum of high school tracking.* New York: Wiley.

Rosenbaum, J. E. (1980). Social implications of educational grouping. *Review of Research in Education, 7,* 361–401.

Rosenbaum, J. E. (1999). Institutional networks and informal strategies for improving work entry for youths. In W. R. Heinz (Ed.), *From education to work: Cross national perspectives* (pp. 235–259). Cambridge: Cambridge University Press.

Rosenbaum, J. E., Kulieke, M. J., & Rubinowitz, L. S. (1988). White suburban schools' responses to low-income Black children: Sources of successes and problems. *Urban Review, 20,* 28–41.

Rosenholtz, S. J., & Simpson, C. (1984). The formation of ability conceptions: Developmental trend or social construction? *Review of Educational Research, 54,* 301–325.

Rosenthal, R. (1969). Interpersonal expectations effects of the experimenter's hypothesis. In R. Rosenthal & R. L. Rosnow (Eds.), *Artifact in behavioral research* (pp. 192–279). New York: Academic Press.

Ruggiero, K. M., & Taylor, D. M. (1995). Coping with discrimination: How disadvantaged group members perceive the discrimination that confronts them. *Journal of Personality and Social Psychology, 68,* 826–838.

Rutter, M. (1983). School effects on pupil progress: Research findings and policy implications. *Child Development, 54,* 1–29.

Rutter, M., Maughan, B., Mortimore, P., & Ouston, J. (1979). *Fifteen thousand hours: Secondary schools and their effects on children.* Cambridge: Harvard University Press.

Schmidt, W. H., McKnight, C. C., & Raizen, S. (1997). *A splintered vision: An investigation of U.S. science and math instruction.* Boston: Kluwer Academic.

Shih, M., Pittinsky, T. L., & Ambady, N. (1999). Stereotype susceptibility: Identity salience and shifts in quantitative performance. *Psychological Science, 10,* 80–83.

Simmons, R. G., & Blyth, D. A. (1987). *Moving into adolescence: The impact of pubertal change and school context.* Hawthorn, NY: de Gruyter.

Sheets, R. H., & Hollins, E. R. (Eds.). (1999). *Racial and ethnic identity in school practices: Aspects of human development.* Mahwah, NJ: Erlbaum.

Slavin, R. E. (1990). Achievement effects of ability grouping in secondary schools: A best-evidence synthesis. *Review of Educational Research, 60,* 471–499.

Steele, C. M. (1992). Race and the schooling of Black Americans. *The Atlantic, 269*(4), 68–72.

Steinberg, L., Dornbusch, S., & Brown, B. (1992). Ethnic differences in adolescents achievements: An ecological perspective. *American Psychologist, 47,* 723–729.

Stevenson, H. W., & Stigler, J. W. (1992). *The learning gap: Why our schools are failing and what we can learn from Japanese and Chinese education.* New York: Summit Books.

Suarrez-Orozco, M., & Suarrez-Orozco, C. (1995). *Transformations: Immigration, family life, and achievement motivation among Latino adolescents.* Stanford, CA: Stanford University Press.

Taylor, R. D., Casten, R., Flickinger, S., Roberts, D., & Fulmore, C. D. (1994). Explaining the school performance of African-American adolescents. *Journal of Research on Adolescence, 4,* 21–44.

Valencia, R. R. (Ed.). (1991). *Chicano school failure and success: Research and policy agendas for the 1990s.* London: Falmer Press.

Vanfossen, B. E., Jones, J. D., & Spade, J. Z. (1987). Curriculum tracking and status maintenance. *Sociology of Education, 60,* 104–122.

Wehlage, G., Rutter, R., Smith, G., Lesko, N., & Fernandez, R. (1989). *Reducing the risk: Schools as communities of support.* Philadelphia: Falmer Press.

Weinstein, R. (1989). Perceptions of classroom processes and student motivation: Children's views of self-fulfilling prophecies. In C. Ames & R. Ames (Eds.), *Research on motivation in Education: Vol. 3. Goals and cognitions* (pp. 13–44). New York: Academic Press.

Wigfield, A., & Eccles, J. S. (1989). Test anxiety in elementary and secondary school students. *Educational Psychologist, 24,* 159–183.

Wigfield, A., Eccles, J. S., Mac Iver, D., Reuman, D., & Midgley, C. (1991). Transitions at early adolescence: Changes in children's domain-specific self-perceptions and general self-esteem across the transition to junior high school. *Developmental Psychology, 27,* 552–565.

Wigfield, A., Eccles, J. S., & Pintrich, P. R. (1996). Development between the ages of eleven and twenty-five. In D. C. Berliner & R. C. Calfee (Eds.), *The handbook of educational psychology* (pp. 148–185). New York: MacMillan.

William T. Grant Commission on Work, Family, and Citizenship. (1988). *The forgotten half: Pathways to success for America's youth and young families.* Washington, DC: Author.

Wong, C. A., Eccles, J. S., & Sameroff, A. (in press). Ethnic discrimination and ethnic identification: The influence on African-Americans' school and socio-emotional adjustment. *Journal of Personality.*

Youniss, J., McLellan, J. A., & Yates, M. (1997). What we know about engendering civic identity. *American Behavioral Scientist, 40,* 619–630.

Youniss, J., Yates, M., & Su, Y. (1997). Social integration: Community service and marijuana use in high school seniors. *Journal of Adolescent Research, 12,* 245–262.

Chapter 6

MORAL COGNITIONS AND PROSOCIAL RESPONDING IN ADOLESCENCE

Nancy Eisenberg and Amanda Sheffield Morris

From the late 1960s through the 1980s, research on moral judgment flourished, especially work influenced by Kohlberg's (1981, 1984) influential cognitive developmental approach to moral judgment. In addition, there was a marked upsurge in empirical research on prosocial development from the early to mid-1970s until approximately a decade ago. Much of the early research on moral judgment included adolescent study participants; moreover, in recent years there has been an inordinate amount of research on adolescents' aggression and antisocial behavior. Nonetheless, as noted by Hoffman in 1980 and Eisenberg in 1990, studies of the prosocial aspects of moral development during adolescence have been limited in quantity. Indeed, in 1987 Hill commented that "capability for relatedness, connectedness, communion, and for what Gilligan has termed 'caring morality' have . . . been little studied" (p. 24). Perhaps the relative dearth of research on adolescents' prosocial tendencies is not surprising, given that social science researchers and the popular press have tended to emphasize the negative aspects of adolescence, painting a picture of this developmental period as one of emotional turmoil, hormones, and delinquency (Steinberg & Morris, 2001).

Nonetheless, there is a body of research on adolescent moral reasoning and prosocial behavior that is informative for researchers and practitioners interested in adolescent development. In this chapter we review findings on adolescents' moral reasoning or attributions and prosocial behaviors and emotional reactions (e.g., empathy and sympathy). We begin with a brief discussion of some of the reasons why one would expect morality to continue to develop in adolescence. Next, findings on moral cognitions (e.g., moral judgment and attributions) are discussed, including those pertaining to justice-oriented and prosocial issues. Then data on adolescents' prosocial behavior (including volunteer and civic activities) and empathy-related responding are reviewed. Normative development (i.e., age-related changes) and variables related to individual differences in moral development are considered. Research conducted with children in late elementary school and high school is emphasized in this chapter, rather than work with college students. Moreover, more recent findings and trends in conceptual and empirical work often are highlighted; readers can access earlier reviews for detailed summaries of prior work (e.g., Hoffman, 1980; Eisenberg, 1990).

Work on this chapter was supported by a grant from the National Institutes of Mental Health (1 R01 MH 60838) and the National Institute of Drug Abuse (DA05227).

THE FOUNDATIONS FOR MORAL COGNITIONS AND PROSOCIAL DEVELOPMENT IN ADOLESCENCE

During the preschool and elementary school years, major advances are evident in moral judgment and in regard to the frequency of some types of morally relevant behaviors (e.g., some positive behaviors; Eisenberg & Fabes, 1998; Rest, 1983). Nonetheless, there are reasons to expect further change in moral cognitions and prosocial tendencies in adolescence. First, moral judgment and prosocial behaviors such as helping, sharing, and comforting have been linked both conceptually and empirically with perspective-taking skills (Eisenberg, 1986; Kohlberg, 1981, 1984), which continues to develop in adolescence. For example, it is not until preadolescence (ages 10–12) that individuals are "aware of the infinite regress (I know that you know that I know that you know, etc.) characteristic of dyadic relations; that each person is simultaneously aware of his own and others' subjective abilities . . . [and begins] to view his own interactions with and subjective perspectives of others from a third person perspective" (Selman, 1975, p. 40). Moreover, later in adolescence, the individual may become aware that in taking another's perspective, "the mutuality of perspectives includes a view of both self and other as complex psychological systems of values, beliefs, attitudes, etc. [and the] . . . further awareness that the mutuality of understanding of each other's point of view can take place at different qualitative levels—for example, persons can 'know' each other as acquaintances, friends, closest friends, lovers, etc." (p. 40). Selman (1980) reported a linear pattern of change in social perspective taking from childhood to adulthood, including advances for many individuals from adolescence into adulthood. Given the conceptual importance of understanding another's perspective for sympathy, other-oriented prosocial behaviors, and higher level moral reasoning, advances in perspective-taking skills in adolescence would be expected to be associated with further development of these capabilities during the same period (Colby, Kohlberg, Gibbs, & Lieberman, 1983; Eisenberg, 1986; Kohlberg, 1984).

Similarly, the advances in social problem-solving skills and interpersonal negotiation skills noted during adolescence (e.g., Berg, 1989; Brion-Meisels & Selman, 1984) would be expected to contribute to the development of other-oriented social interaction, as would advances in conceptions of friendship and relationships (Brown & Gilligan, 1992; Rubin, Bukowski, & Parker, 1998; Selman, 1980) and in the ability to make accurate attributions about others' motives (Crick & Dodge, 1994; see also Eisenberg, 1986). In addition, changes in conceptions of the self from childhood into adolescence likely promote moral and prosocial development. In childhood, the self is defined primarily in terms of nonmoral properties (e.g., bodily properties, material possessions, or typical behavior); in contrast, by late adolescence, the self is defined in terms of social and psychological aspects of the self, and morality is the major regulator of social interactions, whereas belief systems are central to characterizing the psychological self (see Damon & Hart, 1988; Harter, 1999).

Finally, changes in the quality of moral reasoning and in the likelihood of sympathetic responding during adolescence that are discussed in this chapter have been conceptually linked to the development of altruistic tendencies (e.g., Eisenberg, 1986; Eisenberg & Fabes, 1998). For example, Hoffman (2000) argued that the ability to sympathize with the distresses of others who are abstract (i.e., are not in the immediate situation) and with the chronic distress of others (including disadvantaged social groups) develops in late childhood or early adolescence, based on early adolescents' newfound ability to view others as having continuing personal identities and life experiences beyond the immediate situation. This change in sympathy is believed to promote adolescents' willingness to assist abstract individuals or groups (who are not immediately present).

In brief, during late childhood and adolescence there are significant changes in sociocognitive skills and affective responses that are believed to foster the development of moral reasoning and altruistic tendencies (i.e., high-level prosocial responding). Therefore, adolescence would be expected to be a period of growth for moral and prosocial dispositions, cognitions, and behaviors.

MORAL REASONING

As mentioned previously, one reason to expect change in moral behavior in adolescence is that moral reasoning continues to mature during adolescence and into adulthood. Moral reasoning (or judgment), depending on its conceptualization, reflects the structure and content of an individual's reasoning about hypothetical or real-life moral dilemmas—that is, how an individual justifies his or her moral decisions (Eisenberg, 1986; Kohlberg, 1981; Rest, 1979). In some studies, scores of moral reasoning may reflect the actual decision made by a person as much or more than its reasoning (e.g., Piaget, 1932/1965).

Time does not permit an in-depth review of the basic findings on the development of moral reasoning and recent changes in its measurement (see Rest, Narvaez, Bebeau, & Thoma, 1999a, 1999b; Walker, in press). Rather, focal issues in recent research on adolescents' moral judgment are briefly summarized. These include findings on adolescents' level of moral reasoning and its structure and the relations of moral reasoning to adolescents' adjustment, social competence, and risky behaviors, as well as to socialization correlates.

The Nature of Adolescents' Moral Reasoning

Justice Reasoning

The type of moral reasoning that has received the most empirical attention is Kohlberg's (1981) justice-oriented reasoning. According to Colby et al. (1983), although Stage 2 (individualism, instrumental purpose, and exchange) reasoning is predominant in early adolescence, at about age 13, and throughout adolescence, Stage 3 (mutual interpersonal expectations, relationships, and interpersonal conformity reasoning) moral reasoning is the most common, dominant mode of moral reasoning. In this type of reasoning, the "right" includes living up to what is expected by people close to you or what others generally expect of people in your role (as son, wife, etc.). "Being good" is important and is reflected in having good motives, showing concern for others, and maintaining mutual relationships through trust, loyalty, respect, and gratitude (Colby et al., 1983). At this stage, the focus in moral reasoning shifts from self-interest (Stage 2) to fulfilling others' expectations and concern with one's position in others' eyes, as well as maintaining positive interpersonal relationships with others. Stage 4 (social system and conscience) reasoning also is used by some adolescents, but generally only infrequently. Stage 4 reasoning increases with age from early adolescence into adulthood. Stage 4 reasoning emphasizes fulfilling the duties to which you agreed, upholding laws except in extreme cases in which they conflict with other fixed social duties, and contributing to the society, group, or institution (Colby et al., 1983).

Recent research is consistent with earlier findings (e.g., Dawson, 2002; Walker, Gustafson, & Hennig, 2001; Pratt, Arnold, Pratt, & Diessner, 1999; see also Narvaez, 1998) in regard to the nature of adolescents' moral reasoning. However, it has been argued that what has been coded as Stage 3 might actually be two different stages (Dawson, 2002) or that there are really only three developmental schemas or levels: personal interest (Stages 2 and 3), maintaining norms (Stage 4), and postconventional (Stages 5 and 6; Rest, Narvaez, Bebeau, & Thoma, 1999b). Thus, there is currently no consensus on the nature of moral stages in adolescence.

In recent years there has been a considerable amount of research in which adolescents have been asked to reason about real-life rather than hypothetical moral dilemmas. Walker, Pitts, Hennig, and Matsuba (1995) found that there was no significant difference between 16- to 19-year-olds' (senior high school students') moral reasoning about real-life moral conflicts (coded using Kohlberg's stages) and 18- to 25-year-olds' (undergraduates') reasoning, although 35- to 48-year-olds and 65- to 84-year-olds reasoned at higher levels than did the two younger groups. Thus, change in moral reasoning in late adolescence about real-life moral dilemmas (as well as hypothetical dilemmas) appears to be relatively gradual.

Consistent with Kohlberg's theory (1981), it also appears that for justice reasoning, at least as traditionally coded, there is a cycle of consolidation and then transition upward from stage to stage (with a mix of reasoning—especially higher level reasoning and one's modal level of reasoning during the transition). These findings support a structural model in which moral reasoning during late childhood and adolescence advances from lower to more mature levels, with periods of apparent disequilibrium between them (Walker et al., 2001). In addition, it appears that both adolescents and adults are more likely to use alternative ethical systems (other than Kohlberg's) such as religious prescriptions, community norms, professional codes, and care reasoning when they are in a period of transition between stages (Thoma & Rest, 1999).

Prosocial Reasoning

As was acknowledged by Thoma and Rest (1999), individuals sometimes use moral reasoning that is not well represented in Kohlberg's (1981) justice-oriented moral reasoning. One type of reasoning used by adolescents is care-oriented reasoning (Perry & McIntire, 1995; Skoe et al., 1999). According to Gilligan (1982), the focus of care reasoning is on not turning away from others rather than not treating others unfairly (i.e., justice concerns). Gilligan's care reasoning is similar to the stages of prosocial moral reasoning delineated by Eisenberg (1986), who defines prosocial moral reasoning as reasoning about moral dilemmas in which one person's needs or desires conflict with those of others in a context in which the role of prohibitions, authorities' dictates, and formal obligations is minimal.

In the last decade, Eisenberg and colleagues (Eisenberg, Miller, Shell, McNalley, & Shea, 1991; Eisenberg, Carlo, Murphy, & Van Court, 1995) have followed children through adolescence into early adulthood to delineate the development of their prosocial moral reasoning. In general, they have found that some self-reflective and internalized modes of moral reasoning (e.g., reasoning pertaining to role taking; positive or negative affect based on the consequences of behavioral choices; positive affect related to living up to internalized values; internalized norm, rule, and law reasoning; generalized reciprocity) increased in use, whereas stereotypic reasoning (e.g., references to expected or normative behavior, e.g., "it's nice to help") continued to decrease in use from childhood until the late teens. The linear increases in references to positive affect and values about consequences and negative affect about consequences was not found until late adolescence. However, hedonistic reasoning (i.e., reasoning in which the justification is one's own desires, e.g., "She wouldn't help because she would rather go to the party"), which had decreased from childhood into early midadolescence, increased modestly in midadolescence and then again in late adolescence, primarily for males. Moreover, direct reciprocity and approval-oriented reasoning, which had begun to decline in midadolescence, showed little evidence of declining in the late teens (and even increased somewhat). Although there was a linear increase in overall level of reasoning throughout adolescence (see also Eisenberg-Berg, 1979), moral reasoning at age 19 to 20 was not predicted from moral reasoning at earlier points in adolescence, apparently because of substantial declines in reasoning (due to increases in direct reciprocity and hedonistic reasoning) for some people and substantial increases in reasoning due to the use of higher level categories of reasoning for some others. In contrast, there was some continuity in moral reasoning from age 13 to 14 years to 17 to 18 years.

Somewhat similar findings have been obtained by other researchers using a variety of methods (Carlo, Eisenberg, & Knight, 1992). For example, in a study of Israeli 12- to 13-, 14- to 15-, and 16- to 17-year-olds' self-reported motives for their own volunteering to help, reports of altruistic motives (i.e., personal willingness to assist without any expectation of reward or approval, and without reference to compliance) increased with age (Bar-Tal & Nissim, 1984). Further, in work on attributions about the value of others' prosocial actions, investigators have found that from early adolescence into early adulthood, students increasingly devalue prosocial actions done for self-related reasons (e.g., tangible rewards, returning a favor), approval, or praise or to avoid criticism and punishment and increasingly value prosocial actions done out of empathy (see Eisenberg, 1986, 1990, for reviews).

In one of the few cross-cultural studies on the topic, Boehnke, Silbereisen, Eisenberg, Reykowski, and Palmonari (1989) examined German, Polish, Italian, and American elementary, junior, and high school students' attributions for why story characters engaged in prosocial actions. Interest in others was a relatively favored motive at all ages, whereas self-focused motives were chosen infrequently by the preadolescents and junior and senior high school students. Conformity-related reasons decreased with age in Italian, German, and Polish samples across grades 6, 9, 10, and 12, whereas task-oriented reasons (i.e., pragmatic concerns related to the completion of a task) increased. In another sample of German students in grades 5–6 or 7–9, preference for hedonistic motives (i.e., motives related to an individual's feelings of physical well-being but not other aspects of self-interest) decreased with age, and preference for task-oriented motives (e.g., "because I know if I helped, the work would get done more quickly") increased. For American children in grades 2–3, 5–6, and 7–8, selection of hedonistic motives decreased with age in early adolescence (Boehnke et al., 1989). Thus, adolescents preferred other-oriented or task-oriented motives for assisting, and conformity and hedonistic motives were somewhat less preferred with age. The lack of an age-related change in other-oriented motives may have been due to the format of the measure.

Gilligan (1982) argued that care-related moral reasoning is somewhat more common among females, and there is some support for this assertion. In a meta-analysis, Jaffee and Hyde (2000) found a small sex difference in care-related reasoning (broadly defined) favoring females (effect size = .28). Of particular interest, this difference was much larger in adolescents (.53) than in children (.08), university students (.18), or young adults who were not university students (.33). However, in adolescence, whether girls score higher than boys in care-related reasoning may depend on the country or culture. For example, in a study with young adolescents, a sex difference was found in Canada but not in Norway (Skoe et al., 1999). In the United States, however, the sex difference favoring females' higher use of care-oriented reasoning was replicated in a study of African American seventh graders' reasoning about dating dilemmas (Weisz & Black, 2002).

In regard to prosocial moral reasoning, Eisenberg et al. (1987) found that a sex difference in types of reasoning reflecting an other-orientation seemed to emerge in early adolescence and generally was maintained throughout adolescence for at least some higher level modes of other-oriented moral reasoning and for the overall level of prosocial moral reasoning (Eisenberg et al., 1991, 1995). Similarly, Boehnke et al. (1989) found modest evidence of females providing more other-oriented and less self-interested reasons for hypothetical story characters' prosocial actions.

Thus, in general, investigators have found that moral reasoning and attributions regarding motives for prosocial behavior tend to stabilize or become more other-oriented and higher level with age during the adolescent years and that females tend to express more of such reasoning and attributions than do males.

Relations of Higher Level Moral Reasoning to Adolescents' Adjustment and Social Competence

Adolescents' levels (and type) of moral reasoning are important in part because they relate to differences in their behavior (or attitudes toward various behaviors), including externalizing problems, prosocial behaviors, adjustment, and risky behaviors. Moreover, adolescents' moral reasoning has been linked to their political attitudes and tolerance of others.

Externalizing Problems

Adolescents' moral reasoning has been relatively consistently related to their antisocial behavior. In reviews a decade apart, Nelson, Smith, and Dodd (1990) and Jurkovic (1980) found that juvenile delinquents use less mature moral reasoning than do their nondelinquent peers. Additional studies not in those reviews generally are consistent with their conclusions (e.g., Aleixo & Norris, 2000; Carlo, Koller, & Eisenberg, 1998; Trevethan & Walker, 1989), although self-reported offending was not related to justice-related moral reasoning within a group of convicted young male offenders (Aleixo &

Norris, 2000). Similarly, adolescents who score lower on moral judgment are more aggressive (for boys but not girls; Schonert-Reichl, 1999), hold more positive attitudes toward violent groups (Sotelo & Sangrador, 1999), and are more likely to perceive intentionally injurious sport actions as legitimate (Bredemeier, 1985). Acting out preadolescent and adolescent males are also more accepting in their judgments about others' aggressive actions (Sanvitale, Saltzstein, & Fish, 1989; see also Berkowitz, Mueller, Schnell, & Padberg, 1986). Further, gains in moral reasoning due to an intervention with delinquents have been linked to lower recidivism in adolescents (although the gains in moral reasoning due to the intervention were not significant; Gibbs, Potter, Barriga, & Liau, 1996).

Conversely, adolescents who reason at more mature levels are more prosocial and socially competent. For example, higher level and other-oriented prosocial moral judgments generally have been positively related to humanitarian political attitudes (Eisenberg-Berg & Mussen, 1978), as well as self- and other-reported prosocial tendencies and sympathy across the teen years (Carlo, Eisenberg, & Knight, 1992; Eisenberg et al., 1991, 1995, 2002). Moreover, measures of moral reasoning tapping a justice orientation more than a care orientation have been associated with Italian adolescents' involvement in volunteer activities (Comunian & Gielen, 1995) and with 10- to 13-year-old Canadian girls' (but not boys') prosocial nominations by peers (Schonert-Reichl, 1999), as well as with tolerance of others' views or lifestyles (Breslin, 1982; Raaijmakers, Verbogt, & Vollebergh, 1998). In regard to social competence, level of justice-oriented moral reasoning has been related to pre- and young adolescents' peer sociometric status and peer nominations for leadership (girls only). Socially withdrawn behavior or shyness with peers has been negatively related to the level of justice-related moral reasoning for boys in early adolescence (Schonert-Reichl, 1999) and for emotionally disturbed individuals in early and midadolescence (Sigman & Erdynast, 1988; Sigman, Ungerer, & Russell, 1983). Further, justice-related moral judgment has been linked to higher level social-problem-solving skills in 14- to 18-year-old inner city youth (Kennedy, Felner, Cauce, & Primavera, 1988) and with mature ego functioning (inter- and intrapersonal strategies for coping; Matsuba & Walker, 1998). Mature ego defense mechanisms at ages 13–14 and 16–18 also have been associated with higher level justice-reasoning 10 to 20 years later (sometimes even when controlling for moral reasoning in adolescence; Hart & Chmiel, 1992). Thus, although the findings have not always been significant and the percent of variance accounted for by these relations is generally modest, adolescents who are more advanced in their moral reasoning appear to be not only more moral in their behavior but also better adjusted and higher in social competence.

The Relation of Moral Judgments to Adolescents' Attitudes About Risky Behavior

A special concern in adolescence is with the rise in risky behaviors such as drug use, sexual activity, and suicide. Although very limited, there is some evidence of links between cognitions about morality and adolescents' tendencies to endorse or engage in such behaviors.

Some investigators have examined the relation of level of moral judgment to adolescents' risky behavior. There appear to be weak but not very consistent relations between the two (Berkowitz et al., 1995). For example, in a study of undergraduates, Hubbs-Tait and Garmon (1995) found that risk taking during sexual intercourse (i.e., lower likelihood of using condoms) was inversely related with level of justice-related moral reasoning (on Rest's, 1979, defining issues test, or DIT). In contrast, in a study of sexually active teenage girls, Jurs (1984) found no relation between moral reasoning (also on the DIT) and the responsible use of birth control, getting pregnant, and the decision to abort (although adolescents reasoning at higher levels were more likely to have taken a sex education course).

However, whether an individual considers a given risky behavior to be a moral issue may moderate the relation of moral judgment to risky behaviors. Some investigators have examined adolescents' tendencies to categorize risky behaviors as involving moral, social-conventional, personal, or prudential decisions. *Moral* judgments involve categorical and prescriptive judgments of right and wrong about interpersonal issues such as harm and justice. *Social-conventional* issues pertain to customs or regulations intended to ensure social coordination and social organization, such as choices about modes of dress, table manners, and forms of greeting. *Personal* choices refer to issues of private behavior that impinge primarily on the self. For example, within Western culture, the choice of friends or recreational activities usually is considered a personal choice, whereas *prudential* issues involve actual or potential self-harm (but do not involve others' welfare; Nucci, Guerra, & Lee, 1991; Tisak, Tisak, & Rogers, 1994).

Many high school students consider the use of legal drugs such as nicotine, caffeine, and alcohol, as well as premarital sex, as a personal or prudential choice (especially the latter, if assessed) rather than a behavior that should be controlled by authorities or as a moral issue (Killen, Leviton, & Cahill, 1991; Kuther & Higgins-D'Alessandro, 2000; Nucci et al., 1991). In contrast, the use of illegal drugs such as cocaine, crack, and marijuana is less likely to be viewed as an issue under personal jurisdiction and is more likely to be viewed as wrong, regardless of authority or laws (Killen et al., 1991). Risky behaviors are seldom viewed as social-conventional issues (Killen et al., 1991; Nucci et al., 1991; see Tisak et al., 1994, for data on adolescents' views on the legitimacy of parents' attempts to prohibit contact with drug-using friends). Of importance, students who are higher in the use of drugs are more likely than are their low-using students to view the drug use as a personal choice (Kuther & Higgins-D'Alessandro, 2000), and less likely to view it as harmful and a prudentially unacceptable choice (wrong only because it hurts the self; Nucci et al., 1991). High drug users also are more likely to view themselves as the only authority with regard to the choice to use drugs and are less likely than are their peers to view parents or the law as legitimate authorities (Nucci et al., 1991). Moreover, in one study, adolescents' views about the nature of decisions regarding drug use were found to moderate the relation of the level of justice-related moral reasoning to drug use. When adolescents considered drug use a moral decision, a higher degree of substance use was related to lower level justice-oriented moral reasoning, whereas moral reasoning was unrelated to the use of drugs for adolescents who considered it to be a personal decision (similar findings were not obtained for sexual behavior or suicide; Kuther & Higgins-D'Alessandro, 2000). Findings such as these suggest that moral reasoning is related to some risky behaviors, but only for adolescents who view them as having moral relevance. However, it is not clear whether moral reasoning actually affects risky behavior or participation in risky behavior affects how adolescents categorize risky behaviors.

Socialization of Moral Reasoning

Parental Influences

Socialization by parents typically has been assigned a circumscribed role in moral development by cognitive developmental theorists such as Kohlberg (Walker & Hennig, 1999). Thus, it is not surprising that the contributions of parenting to the development of moral reasoning have not been studied extensively. Some aspects of socialization that have received the most attention in studies with adolescents are parental moral reasoning, parental warmth, and aspects of parent-child discussions that might stimulate perspective taking or autonomous moral thinking.

Based on cognitive developmental theory, one would expect parenting practices that create cognitive conflict about moral issues to be linked to higher level moral judgment. Somewhat consistent with this notion, there is evidence that a Socratic style of discussion (encouraging the child to form opinions and to use reasoning) between parents and children, combined with other variables (such as parental support) is most conducive to the development of justice-related moral reasoning in late childhood and adolescence. Based on studies in which parents and their child discussed hypothetical and real-life moral dilemmas (sometimes one in the child's life) and attempted to reach a consensus, Walker and Hennig (1999) concluded that

> parents who engage in cognitively challenging and highly opinionated interactions, who are hostile, critical, and interfering, and who display poor ego functioning (defensiveness, rigidity, rationalization, insensitivity, inappropriate emotional expression) provide a context that hinders children's opportunities to move toward more mature moral understandings. In contrast, effective parents are more child-centered and scaffold their child's development by eliciting the child's opinions, drawing out the child's reasoning with appropriate probing questions, and checking for understanding; all in the context of emotional support and attentiveness and with the challenging stimulation of advanced moral reasoning. (pp. 370, 372)

In Walker's studies, parent behaviors such as critiquing and directly challenging the child (especially in a hostile manner), presenting of counterconsiderations, and simply providing information were not associated with children's moral growth. Direct challenges to the child's reasoning may have been viewed as hostile by the child and, consequently, may have been counterproductive, whereas simple provision of information may have been viewed as lecturing (Walker & Hennig, 1999; Walker, Hennig, & Krettenauer, 2000; see Walker & Taylor, 1991). Similar findings in regard to style of interactions have been found in other studies of preadolescents or adolescents, although there are some inconsistencies in the literature. Buck, Walsh, and Rothman (1981) examined the relation of parental behaviors during a discussion with their 10- to 13-year-old boys' moral reasoning of how to handle sons' aggression. Boys with higher moral reasoning had parents who considered their son's view and tended to encourage their son to express his views. Similarly, Holstein (1972) found that parents who encouraged their children's participation in discussion and decision making were more likely to have children who reasoned at relatively high levels. In contrast to Walker and Hennig

(1999), Pratt et al. (1999) observed that fathers' tendencies to extend, challenge, or clarify the reasoning of their adolescents were positively related to adolescents' concurrent moral reasoning and reasoning two years later. Similar findings were not obtained for mothers, although mothers' tendencies to consider their children's perspectives when recalling socialization encounters were related to higher level moral reasoning at the 2-year follow-up.

Other investigators besides Walker and Hennig (1999) have obtained associations between parental warmth or involvement and high-level moral reasoning in adolescents (e.g., Buck et al., 1981; McDevitt, Lennon, & Kopriva, 1991; Palmer & Hollin, 1996; Powers, 1988; Speicher, 1992). In some relevant studies, researchers found relations between parental nurturance and moral reasoning for one parent or for one group of children (e.g., age or sex group) but not the other (e.g., Bakken & Romig, 1994; Hart, 1988). Inconsistencies may occur because parental warmth by itself probably is not sufficient to stimulate higher level moral reasoning. As noted by Hoffman (2000), parental warmth provides an optimal environment for socialization because children are more likely to attend to parents and care about pleasing them when the relationship generally is supportive. Thus, parental warmth may not have a direct effect on children's moral reasoning but may moderate the effectiveness of other parental practices in fostering the growth of moral reasoning. A combination of warmth and other productive parental practices such as using a Socratic method in discussions and holding high standards for children may be necessary to foster adolescents' moral reasoning. In support of this premise, authoritative parenting (which includes support, demands for appropriate behavior and control, and practices such as induction) has been linked to higher level moral judgment in adolescents (Boyes & Allen, 1993; Pratt et al., 1999), although democratic parenting has not always been associated with adolescents' moral reasoning (Speicher, 1992).

Consistent with the relation of authoritative parenting to higher level moral reasoning, there appears to be a modest relation between parental use of inductions (reasoning) during discipline and older children and adolescents' moral judgment (Janssen, Janssens, & Gerris, 1992), although such relations often vary across parent, social class, or age group (e.g., Eisikovits & Sagi, 1982; Parikh, 1980; see Eisenberg & Valiente, 2002, for more detail). Moreover, parental emphasis on prosocial behavior has been associated with higher level prosocial moral reasoning (McDevitt et al., 1991). Further, agreement between parents in regard to child-rearing practices, attitudes, and values at age 3 has predicted higher moral reasoning for 14-year-old males (but not females; Vaughn, Block, & Block, 1988).

In summary, higher level reasoning in adolescence is related to parenting that is supportive and stimulates adolescents to question and expand on their reasoning, as well as with an authoritative parenting style (including inductive discipline). However, findings are limited in number and sometimes inconsistent (e.g., Leahy, 1981; see Eisenberg & Valiente, 2002). Although infrequently examined, it is possible that the parenting behaviors and characteristics associated with adolescents' moral judgment vary across adolescence. For example, based on her finding that moral judgment was predicted by reports of comfort with and frequency of family moral and political discussions in later adolescence and early adulthood, but not earlier adolescence, Speicher (1992) suggested that the quality of interpersonal family relationships may be more important for the development of moral reasoning in early adolescence, whereas aspects of the family environment related to cognitive stimulation and perspective taking may be important at an older age. Currently, there are too few data to test such a prediction. Moreover, because all the extant data with adolescents are correlational, it is unclear to what degree parental behaviors actually cause changes in adolescents' moral reasoning; indeed, variations in adolescents' moral reasoning may elicit different parenting styles and practices (and some other factor such as genetics may affect both parenting and adolescents' moral judgment). In addition, it is unclear whether the findings just reviewed generalize to non-Western countries; little of this work was conducted in non-Western societies, and there is debate regarding the degree to which systems for coding moral judgment developed in the United States accurately represent the development of moral judgment in non-Western, nonindustrialized countries.

Peer Influences

Cognitive-developmental theorists have argued that interactions with peers are a more important influence on moral development than are interactions with parents or other adults because peer relations are more egalitarian and provide opportunities for social interaction among equals. The equal status in peer interactions is viewed as encouraging peers to cooperate and deal with moral conflicts by balancing self-interest and others' interests at comparable levels (Piaget, 1932/1965; Kohlberg, 1969). Moreover, interactions with peers also may provide opportunities for self-exploration and allow adolescents to discuss identity issues, such as beliefs and aspirations, among a supportive group of equals, which might affect their moral identity. In general, research indicates that peers do play a role in the development of adolescents' moral reasoning, although most relevant work has been conducted with children rather than adolescents.

Of the studies that have examined peer influences on moral reasoning, most find that moral discussions with peers do have a positive effect on moral development. At least one study found that peers may even have a greater influence than parents. Using an experimental design, Kruger (1992) found that girls in a peer-adolescent conflict discussion had higher levels of moral development on a posttest compared to girls in a parent-adolescent discussion. Similarly, Walker et al. (2000) examined parent and peer effects on moral reasoning by having parent-adolescent and friend-adolescent dyads discuss moral conflicts. The sample included a group of adolescents in late childhood and midadolescence, and moral reasoning was assessed yearly over four years using Kohlberg's Moral Justice Interview (MJI). Walker et al. found evidence for both parent and peer influences on moral reasoning, but patterns of influence differed. For peers, they found that friends' interfering speech (which interfered with discussion and indicated negative affect) was associated with higher levels of moral development; this finding is in line with the cognitive-developmental notion that some degree of conflict among peers supports moral development. Contrary to this idea and to previous findings (Berkowitz & Gibbs, 1983), Walker et al. also found that peers' high-powered, dominant challenges to moral thinking (coded as highly operational speech that operates on the reasoning of another, e.g., critiques or competitive clarification) were related to minimal moral development. This contradiction in Walker et al.'s findings suggests that a moderate degree of conflict in discussion with a friend may promote moral development, as long as the conflict is not overly challenging and dominant (see also Schonert-Reichl, 1999). Walker et al. hypothesized that the difference between their findings and those of Berkowitz and Gibbs, who found positive relations between operational-challenging conversation and moral reasoning among peers, likely was due to the nature of the peers used in the two studies. In the Berkowitz and Gibbs study, the peer was an unacquainted peer; in the Walker et al. study, the peer was a friend.

Walker et al. (2000) also found that for both parent and peer dyads, a Socratic style of discussion predicted moral development. In contrast, for both parents (as mentioned previously) and peers, highly informative interactions (sharing opinions, agreement, or disagreement), which may have been perceived as intrusive and lecturing, were associated with lower levels of moral reasoning.

The quality of peers' relationships may also play a role in adolescent moral development. Schonert-Reichl (1999) examined associations of peer relationships and friendship quality to adolescent moral reasoning in youth aged 10 through 13. Adolescents completed sociometric measures of peer acceptance, questionnaires about their friendships, and Kohlberg's moral reasoning measure. Having a greater number of close friends, being perceived as a leader, and peer nominations for prosocial behavior were associated with higher levels of moral reasoning.

Moreover, Schonert-Reichl's (1999) findings suggested that time spent with friends and the quality of such interaction was linked to moral reasoning, although findings differ for males and females. For example, females' socializing and agentic activities with friends were both associated with higher levels of moral reasoning, indicating that more interaction with peers in general has a positive impact on moral judgment. In contrast, for boys, those who did not resolve conflicts with friends quickly and easily were higher in moral reasoning, again highlighting the importance of some level of conflict in the development of moral judgment.

In summary, research findings are consistent with the view that peers influence adolescents' moral reasoning through friendship, peer group qualities, and dialogue about moral conflicts. It also appears that a moderate degree of conflict among friends may be associated with higher levels of moral reasoning, perhaps due to challenges to the adolescents' thinking. However, because most relevant studies are correlational in design (or could not control the quality of peer interactions), it is difficult to ascertain the direction of effects.

PROSOCIAL BEHAVIOR

Prosocial behavior is defined as voluntary behavior intended to benefit another (e.g., Eisenberg, 1986; Staub, 1979). Prosocial behaviors based on moral emotions and values rather than factors such as self-interest or the desire for approval usually are labeled as altruistic. Unfortunately, it is often impossible to know whether a person's motives for performing prosocial behaviors are altruistic.

In this section we examine age-related changes in prosocial behavior from childhood into adolescence. Then we review the consistency of prosocial tendencies in adolescence, followed by a discussion of gender differences in adolescents' prosocial behavior. Next, other correlates of prosocial behavior in adolescence are briefly discussed, including personality or personal characteristics (e.g., regulation, social competence, and adjustment) and characteristics of the family or parental practices. Finally, correlates and possible consequences of adolescents' involvement in voluntary and civic activities are reviewed, and the possible role of adolescents' volunteering or civic service in their prosocial development is examined.

Age Trends in Prosocial Behavior and Empathy-Related Responding

If adolescents' moral reasoning is more sophisticated and other-oriented than is that of younger children, one would expect prosocial behavior to increase with age throughout childhood and into adolescence. According to a recent meta-analysis (Eisenberg & Fabes, 1998), prosocial behavior does increase across childhood, and adolescents tend to be higher in prosocial behavior than preschoolers (on a variety of measures of prosocial behavior, mostly observed measures) and children aged 7 to 12 (on sharing and donating but not instrumental helping or comforting). Adolescents and children did not differ in their self-reported prosocial behavior; however, they differed on observations of prosocial behavior and on others' reports thereof. Differences between adolescents and both preschoolers and young children held for comparison of early adolescents (age 13–15) and older adolescents (age 16–18; Fabes, Carlo, Kupanoff, & Laible, 1999). However, there was limited evidence of an increase in prosocial responding across adolescence (from age 12 to 17 or 18), although prosocial behavior did increase in adolescence in experimental-structured studies (but not naturalistic-correlational studies) and when the recipient of aid was a child rather than an adult (Eisenberg & Fabes, 1998). Thus, although adolescents exhibit more prosocial behavior than do younger children, change in adolescence was noted only for particular recipients or types of studies. However, the number of studies that compared older and younger adolescents was surprisingly small (11), so the findings must be viewed as merely suggestive.

In the meta-analysis, prosocial behavior directed toward adults did not change with age in adolescence. This may be particularly true in the family setting. Eberly and Montemayor (1998) found that adolescents' reports of prosocial behaviors directed at parents (e.g., helping with various tasks) were higher in 8th graders than either 6th or 10th graders (who did not differ from one another); there were no age-related differences in parents' reports of helpfulness. In a 2-year follow-up of the same sample, adolescents' self-reported prosocial behavior directed toward their parents did not change for 6th graders who became 8th graders, declined over the two years for 8th graders who became 10th graders, and increased for 10th graders who became 12th graders. Thus, there seemed to be a sort of regression to the mean; 8th graders, who initially were high in self-reported helpfulness, declined over the two years whereas 10th graders, who were low, increased. In contrast, parents' reports of adolescents' helpfulness did not change. Self-reported prosocial behavior directed toward fathers increased over the two years; their helpfulness toward their mothers (and parent-reported helpfulness to each parent) did not change (Eberly & Montemayor, 1999). In another study of 5th to 9th graders, parents generally reported a decline in helpfulness with age (Eberly, Montemayor, & Flannery, 1993). Moreover, Keith, Nelson, Schlabach, and Thompson (1990) found no change with age among a sample of 10- to 14-year-olds in their family responsibilities (e.g., doing chores for the family). Thus, there seems to be no clear pattern of change in adolescence in helping of parents. Perhaps the inconsistencies in the literature are partly due to the fact that many adolescents spend less time at home than when younger, and this variable has not been considered in analyses of helpfulness directed at parents (Larson & Richards, 1991).

As was mentioned previously, empathy-related responding has been linked theoretically and empirically to prosocial behavior. Based on Hoffman's theory, one would expect an age-related increase in empathy-related responding, especially in situations in which empathy or sympathy is toward abstract groups (e.g., needy individuals). Eisenberg and Fabes (1996) reported an age-related increase in empathy-related responding (empathy or sympathy); however, they did not break down the findings by age. In early studies of empathy-related responding (before about 1986), findings regarding age trends in empathy-related responding in adolescence were inconsistent, although there was some evidence of an increase from childhood into adolescence (Eysenck, Easting, & Pearson, 1984; Saklofske & Eysenck, 1983; see Lennon & Eisenberg, 1987). More recently, there has been additional evidence of an increase in empathy-related responding, especially for sympathy. For example, in a longitudinal study of 9th and 10th graders, Davis and Franzoi (1991) found an increase in sympathy and a decline in personal distress over two years. In a cross-sectional study of 6th to 12th graders, Olweus and Endresen (1998) found an increase in girls' empathic distress (likely primarily personal distress), whereas boys' empathy did not change. Girls' sympathetic concern toward male and female targets increased with age, as did boys' sympathy with female targets; however, males' sympathy toward male targets declined somewhat with age, particularly between grades 8 and 9 (also see Szagun, 1992). In another cross-sectional study, Strayer and Roberts (1997) found that both self-reported empathic sadness and concerned facial reactions to evocative videotapes increased with age (although there was no age difference in affective matching of the emotion in the film). In contrast, in a cross-sectional study of 8th and 11th graders in Israel, Karniol, Gabay, Ochion, and Harari (1998) found no change in self-reported sympathy or personal distress, and empathy with fantasy stimuli (e.g., films, books) declined with age. In general, then, there seems to be a modest increase in sympathy with age (which may vary with the recipient), whereas the few findings for personal distress were inconsistent. The fact that such change apparently is modest is consistent with the lack of consistent change in prosocial behavior during adolescence, although as discussed shortly, researchers have found that volunteering does increase from childhood to adolescence.

Consistency in Prosocial Responding

There is considerable evidence that individual differences in preadolescents' and adolescents' prosocial behavior and empathy-sympathy show modest to moderate consistency across contexts (e.g., Dlugokinski & Firestone, 1973; Small, Zeldin, & Savin-Williams, 1983; Zeldin, Williams, & Small, 1984; see Eisenberg, 1990; cf. Payne, 1980) and two years or more time (e.g., Bar-Tal & Raviv, 1979; Davis & Franzoi, 1991; Eberly & Montemayor, 1999; Eisenberg et al., 1995; cf. Murphy, Shepard, Eisenberg, Fabes, & Guthrie, 1999). Eisenberg et al. (1999) found that consistency in prosocial behavior from the preschool years until adolescence and early adulthood was partially mediated by individual differences in sympathy; it is likely that consistency across adolescence is also partly due to the stability of sympathetic responding. The consistency in prosocial tendencies in adolescence suggests that individual differences in prosocial values, goals, and/or self-schema are fairly stable by adolescence (Eisenberg et al., 2002).

Because moral behavior seems to be more consistent if it is based on higher level moral values and orientations (Rholes & Lane, 1985), one would expect more consistency in prosocial behavior in adolescence than at younger ages. Unfortunately, although consistency in prosocial tendencies appears to be higher in adolescence than at younger ages (Caprara, Barbaranelli, Pastorell, Bandura, & Zimbardo, 2000; Eisenberg & Fabes, 1998), the degree of consistency across age groups has not been systematically compared.

Gender Differences in Prosocial Behavior and Empathy-Related Responding

The common stereotype is that females are more caring, other-oriented, and helpful than are males. Clearly this stereotype is not entirely accurate; prosocial behavior in childhood and adulthood appears to vary with the degree to which a prosocial action is consistent with gender roles (e.g., Eagly & Crowley, 1986; Zarbatany, Hartmann, Gelfand, & Vinciguerra, 1985). Nonetheless, there appears to be a kernel of truth to the stereotype, at least in childhood and adolescence. In a meta-analysis of gender differences in prosocial behavior, Eisenberg and Fabes (1998) found that across childhood and adolescence, females were higher on prosocial behavior, and this difference held to varying degrees across types of prosocial behavior, the method of data collection and the study design, and the target of prosocial behavior (e.g., a child or an adult). The biggest gender difference was for kind-considerate behavior; differences were considerably smaller for sharing/donating, instrumental help, and comforting. The size of the gender difference increased with age but was reduced to nonsignificance when the effects of other study qualities were controlled in the analyses (correlational-naturalistic studies increased with age, and stronger gender differences were obtained in them than in structured-experimental contexts). Further analysis of these studies indicated that the sex difference was significantly stronger in early (13–15 years) and late (16–18 years) adolescence than in early or middle childhood (Fabes et al., 1999). Whether this pattern held when controlling for study characteristics was not reported.

Findings in recent studies generally have been consistent with the conclusion that there is a gender difference favoring females in prosocial behavior (e.g., Estrada, 1995). For example, in a study of 7- to 13-year-olds in Italy, Caprara, Barbaranelli, and Pastorelli (2001) found that children rated girls in their grade as more prosocial (e.g., helpful, likely to share, likely to try to cheer up a sad person) than boys at ages 11, 12, and 13, but not at ages 7 to 10; teachers rated girls as more prosocial at ages 9, 10, 11, and 13. In both childhood and early adolescence, females reported more prosocial behavior. In addition, some investigators (e.g., Jones & Dembo, 1989), but not all (e.g., Berndt & Perry, 1986), have found that females are more prosocial in intimate friendship-relationships. Adolescent females, in comparison to adolescent males, reported more helpful or caring activities at both home and work (Call, Mortimer, & Shanahan, 1995), although reports of helpfulness directed toward adolescents' parents sometimes have (Eberly et al., 1993), and sometimes have not (Eberly & Montemayor, 1998, 1999), differed by sex of the adolescent. Female adolescents do more traditionally female household tasks whereas males do more masculine tasks (Keith et al., 1990), and it is likely that many females tasks (e.g., caring for younger children, helping in the kitchen or with laundry) are considered to be more prosocial than masculine tasks such as working in the yard or washing the car. More generally, female adolescents (and young adults), in comparison to males, report that it is more important to help others (the difference seemed to hold across close and distant relationships; Killen & Turiel, 1998) and have been found to engage in more volunteer activities (Keith et al., 1990).

Similarly, gender differences have been found in empathy-related responding in childhood and adolescence. In their meta-analysis, Eisenberg and Fabes (1998) found that the difference in self-reported empathy and sympathy was significant for self-reported and observational measures of empathy-related responding (including combined behavioral and facial reactions) but not for nonverbal facial and physiological measures. The gender difference in self-reported empathy and sympathy increased with age across childhood and adolescence (there are few studies using other methods in adolescence). Other relatively recent work using self-report measures is consistent with prior research with adolescents in finding that female adolescents report more sympathy (Eisenberg et al., 1995; Estrada, 1995; Karniol et al., 1998; Olweus & Endresen, 1998; Strayer & Roberts, 1997) and personal distress (Eisenberg et al., 1995; Olweus & Endresen, 1998) than do males, are viewed as more sympathetic by adults (Murphy et al., 1999), and also show more facial empathy (matching of emotions; Strayer & Roberts, 1997).

Thus, it appears that in adolescence, females view themselves as more prosocial and empathic-sympathetic and also enact more prosocial, caring behaviors than do males. This difference may be partly due to the types of prosocial behaviors measured in adolescence and the characteristics of the studies; the sex difference is smaller when experimental studies of instrumental helping (especially on masculine tasks) are examined (Eisenberg & Fabes, 1996). However, in adolescence, both parents (Power & Shanks, 1989) and adolescents (McDevitt et al., 1991) report that parents (or just mothers; McDevitt et al., 1991) emphasize prosocial behavior more with daughters than sons. For example, in a large study of 18-year-olds in seven countries (Australia, United States, Sweden, Hungary, Czech Republic, Bulgaria, and Russia), Flannagan, Bowes, Jonsson, Csapo, and Sheblanova (1998) found that females in all countries reported higher levels of families' encouragement of an ethic of social responsibility than did males (and they volunteered more in five of the seven countries). Thus, prosociality and caring are likely more basic to females' self-image and values. Individual differences in femininity have been found to account for the sex difference in sympathy in adolescence (Karniol et al., 1998), and emotional expressiveness and caring behavior are part of the feminine stereotype (and most measures of femininity). Thus, even if males and females both experience empathic emotion, females may be more likely than males to interpret it as sympathy and link it to prosocial goals and values. Moreover, because females in early adolescence have been found to have a more prosocial self-schema than males, one would expect these schema to heighten their prosocial responding, at least if the schema are made salient to them in the situation (see Froming, Nasby, & McManus, 1998) or perhaps when the situation offers opportunities for assisting in ways that are consistent with a feminine gender role.

The Relation of Adolescents' Dispositional Characteristics to Their Prosocial Responding

Prosocial behavior in adolescence has been related to a variety of other aspects of functioning, including empathy-related responding, moral behavior, social competence, level of social cognition, and academic performance. There are, however, relatively few studies on most correlates of prosocial responding, and often the data are all self-reported. Thus, many of the findings require further verification, although the fact that they generally are consistent with findings for children and adults supports their veracity.

Consistent with theory (Eisenberg, 1986; Hoffman, 2000; Staub, 1979), adolescents' empathy-related responding, especially sympathetic concern, has been positively related to measures of prosocial goals, attitudes, and behavior for both self-report and occasionally behavioral or other-report measures (Eisenberg et al., 1991, 1995; Estrada, 1996; Krevans & Gibbs, 1996; see Eisenberg & Fabes, 1998). Moreover, adolescents' (and preadolescents') personal distress tends to be unrelated or negatively related to empathy-related responding (Eisenberg et al., 1991, 1995; Estrada, 1996). Conversely, empathy or sympathy (Carlo, Roesch, & Melby, 1998; Cohen & Strayer, 1996; Murphy et al., 1999) and prosocial behavior (Caprara et al., 2000; Rigby, 1993; not Carlo et al., 1998) usually have been negatively related to measures of delinquency, bullying, and externalizing problems, as well as to dispositional anger and negative emotionality (Carlo et al., 1998; Murphy et al., 1999). These findings are relatively consistent and sometimes based on behavioral measures or multiple reporters (e.g., Caprara et al., 2001; Cohen & Strayer, 1996). Sympathetic young adolescents also are viewed as well regulated by parents and teachers (Murphy et al., 1999).

Prosocial behavior and empathy-related responding have not been consistently related to sociability (Carlo et al., 1998) or social withdrawal (Schonert-Reichl, 1999); rather, extroverted and introverted early adolescents tend to differ in the degree to which their prosocial behaviors are affected by the presence of other people (Suda & Fouts, 1980). Prosocial adolescents tend to be well liked (Caprara et al., 2000), and popular adolescents tend to engage in more helping involving peers, whereas less popular adolescents tend to help in situations that do not involve interaction with peers (Hampson, 1984). Similarly, teachers' reports of early adolescents' sympathy have been correlated with prior peer nominations of high social status and with teachers' antecedent and concurrent ratings of socially competent and appropriate behavior at school (Murphy et al., 1999). There is limited and mixed evidence that prosocial and sympathetic adolescents are more mature in their social cognition, such as perspective taking (Eisenberg et al., 1991; Estrada, 1996; cf. Emler & Rushton, 1974; Marsh, Serfica, & Barenboim, 1981), means-end thinking (Marsh et al., 1981), and moral reasoning (see prior review and Eisenberg, 1986). Preadolescents who are viewed as prosocial by their peers also are less likely than are less prosocial peers to attribute hostile intent to others (an attribution style generally associated with low aggression) or to feel distressed in provocative situations, tend to evaluate aggressive responses to provocation more negatively (and prosocial responses more positively), and are more likely to endorse relational rather than instrumental goals for dealing with peer provocation (Nelson & Crick, 1999).

Prosocial adolescents also have been found to be high in self-esteem (Johnson, Beebe, Mortimer, & Snyder, 1998) but not especially high in dominant behavior (Small et al., 1983). Prosocial behavior predicts concurrent grades, intrinsic motivation toward school, and educational aspirations (Johnson et al., 1998), as well as future grades at school (Caprara et al., 2000).

Situational Factors

Of course, adolescents' sympathy and prosocial behavior are affected by situational factors, as well as by dispositional characteristics. However, there is little systematic research on any given situational variable. One that has received attention is the target of a potential prosocial action. Young adolescents are more likely to share with or assist friends than acquaintances and disliked peers (Berndt, 1985; Buhrmester, Goldfarb, & Cantrell, 1992) and perceive friends as more supportive than nonfriends (Berndt & Perry, 1986). This is not surprising given the importance to adolescents of intimacy and helping one another in friendships (e.g., Youniss, 1980). Moreover, there likely is an interaction between personality and situational factors in terms of which situations evoke prosocial responding from which individuals. For example, as already noted, popular and less popular 8th graders prefer to help in different situations (Hampson, 1984), as do extroverted and introverted 6th graders (Suda & Fouts, 1980).

The Socialization of Prosocial Behavior and Empathy-Sympathy

Family Influences

In the larger literature on the socialization of prosocial behavior in childhood, high levels of prosocial behavior and empathy-sympathy have been related to supportive parenting, especially in combination with parental modeling of prosocial, caring behavior, and parental discipline that is not punitive but involves the use of inductions (reasoning) and the setting of high standards for children (Eisenberg & Fabes, 1998). The limited findings in studies with adolescents generally are consistent with this pattern. For example, although findings often were statistically significant for only one sex or the other, parental use of inductive discipline (usually reported by parents or their adolescent children) has been related to preadolescents' or adolescents' prosocial behavior (e.g., Bar-Tal, Nadler, & Blechman, 1980; Hoffman & Saltzstein, 1967; Krevans & Gibbs, 1996) and empathy-sympathy (Krevans & Gibbs, 1996), especially for individuals with a history of inductive discipline (Dlugokinski & Firestone, 1974). In contrast, power-assertive discipline (e.g., punishment or threats thereof) has been negatively related to young adolescents' sympathy-empathy and prosocial behavior (Krevans & Gibbs, 1996). Moreover, adolescents' prosocial behavior has been correlated with parental emphasis on autonomy (Bar-Tal et al., 1980), as well as adolescents' reports of parent-adolescent interdependency (i.e., shared time, engaging in mutual activities, and strength of parental influence; Eberly & Montemayor, 1998). Consistent with findings on the modeling of prosocial behavior and the importance of parental expectations for prosocial-moral behavior, adolescent exemplars of prosocial commitment have been found to have identities that incorporate parental-related representations (e.g., "what my mother is like, what I am like with my father", "what my mother expects me to be"; Hart & Fegley, 1995). Because adolescents report that they share values with their parents (Hill, 1987), it is likely that parents' prosocial values contribute to adolescents' prosocial tendencies.

Consistent with the relation between adolescents' prosocial tendencies and their interdependency with parents, supportive parenting has been positively related to prosocial characteristics in adolescence in some studies (Bar-Tal et al., 1980; Eberly & Montemayor, 1993, 1998; Mussen, Harris, Rutherford, & Keasey, 1970), although findings in other studies have been nonsignificant or inconsistent (Carlo et al., 1998; Eberly & Montemayor, 1999). Adolescents who report prosocial tendencies also tend to describe their parents in positive terms and report positive relationships with parents (Rigby, 1993). Supportive parenting may set an affective climate that moderates the degree to which adolescents are responsive to parental discipline, demands, values, and teachings (Hoffman, 2000). Thus, parental support may be positively related to prosocial development only when parents use inductions, model prosocial tendencies, or have high expectations regarding prosocial or moral behavior (Eisenberg & Fabes, 1998).

It is also possible that siblings contribute to adolescents' development. For example, Tucker, Updegraff, McHale, and Crouter (1999) found that older early-adolescent (ages 10–12) female siblings' empathy was positively related to their younger (2–3 years younger) sisters' empathy. The authors posited that younger sisters may model or identify with older sisters; however, it should be noted that findings are correlational and not longitudinal, so causality could go both ways. Findings also varied for sister-brother relationships (see Tucker et al., 1999) but nevertheless support the idea that siblings may have an influence on moral development.

Unfortunately, most of the research on the socialization of adolescents' prosocial tendencies is correlational, and much is based solely on adolescents' reports (although some include parents' reports; e.g., Eberly & Montemayor, 1993, 1998, 1999; Krevans & Gibbs, 1996). In addition, much of the existing research has been conducted with young adolescents. Thus, we know relatively little about the socialization correlates of prosocial behavior in older adolescents.

Peer Influences

There is very little research on the relation of prosocial behavior to peer interactions. It has been found that popular, well-adjusted peers tend to be more prosocial than do rejected peers (e.g., Coie, Dodge, & Kupersmidt, 1990; Wentzel & Caldwell, 1997). Whereas it is likely that prosocial behavior affects peer acceptance, it is not known if the quality of peer relationships affects prosocial behavior. Wentzel and McNamara (1999) posited that peers may affect prosocial behavior both directly and through their influence on emotional functioning. Children who are accepted by peers would be expected to have opportunities to learn and practice prosocial skills. Moreover, adolescents in a supportive emotional environment may be less likely to experience emotional distress, thus leading to more positive, prosocial behavior. In a study of 6th graders, Wentzel and McNamara found that peer acceptance, not family cohesion, was associated with prosocial behavior and that adolescent emotional distress mediated concurrent relations between perceived support from peers and prosocial behavior. These findings support their hypotheses, although it is also possible that prosocial early adolescents were more likely to garner peer acceptance and support and that this fact affected their emotional distress.

VOLUNTEERING AND COMMUNITY SERVICE

Another important prosocial behavior that has received a great deal of attention in the last decade is volunteering and community service (see also Flannagan, this volume). Adolescence is a time when youth are beginning to engage in adult-like activities and behaviors that reflect adult society. Community service is one type of activity in which many teens participate; indeed, approximately half of all adolescents engage in some type of community service or volunteer activity (see Yates & Youniss, 1996a). Involvement in such activities, which provide meaningful exposure to adult society, creates an opportunity for adolescents to explore their identities and potential roles in the community and greater society (Youniss, McLellan, Su, & Yates, 1999; Youniss & Yates, 1997).

Individual Characteristics Associated With Volunteering

Adolescent volunteers tend to share certain characteristics, such as extraversion, a commitment to others, and a high degree of self-understanding. Some of these characteristics exist prior to adolescence; however, many may become solidified during this developmental period in conjunction with identity development (Yates & Youniss, 1996a). Moreover, developmental characteristics (e.g., cognitive development) and background characteristics (e.g., parental education and gender) also are related to adolescents' propensities to engage in community service.

Similar to findings for prosocial behavior more generally, gender differences in volunteering behavior have been examined in several studies. Studies indicate that females tend to volunteer more than males, and adolescents from families with higher levels of socioeconomic status are also more likely to volunteer (Nolin, Chaney, Chapman, & Chandler, 1997; Youniss, McLellan, Su, et al., 1999; cf. Johnson et al., 1998; also see Flannagan, this volume). In one of the few studies to examine sex differences associated with the effects of volunteering, Stukas, Switzer, Dew, Goycoolea, and Simmons (1999) examined 7th grade students who were involved in a mandatory service-learning program (e.g., tutors for younger students, volunteers at a senior center) as part of their school curriculum. Girls felt more positively than did boys about volunteering and were more likely to report wanting to help in the future as a result of the program. The authors suggested that these variations may have been due to socialization differences between boys and girls that emphasize females' focus on prosocial goals of the program, whereas males might have focused more on the mandatory nature of the program (see Miller, 1994).

In regard to personality characteristics, in contrast to some other types of prosocial behavior, individuals who volunteer tend to be more extraverted and social compared with nonvolunteers (e.g., Knapp & Holzberg, 1964), which makes sense because of the social interaction involved in most volunteer activities. Similarly, individuals (e.g., college students) involved in community service tend to be involved in a variety of clubs and activities (e.g., 4-H, YMCA, church; Fitch, 1987). There is also evidence suggesting that community service participation actually lowers adolescents' levels of alienation and isolation (Calabrese & Schumer, 1986) and that volunteers tend to have a greater desire to help others and a strong sense of social responsibility (Magen & Aharoni, 1991; see also Yates & Youniss, 1996a).

Identity Development

Adolescence has traditionally been viewed as a developmental period in which youth struggle to establish their own identities separate from their parents. Researchers studying volunteering and community service often link identity development to civic involvement (see Yates & Youniss, 1996a; see also Youniss, McLellan, Su, et al., 1999; Youniss & Yates, 1997). In a review of 44 articles on community service, Yates and Youniss (1996a) emphasized three components of identity development that are associated with volunteer behavior: *agency,* which emphasizes Erikson's (1968) concept of industry reflecting an individuals' self-concept of ability and future capabilities, and *social relatedness* and *moral-political awareness,* which refer to individuals' understandings of the self in relation to sociohistorical context.

Studies on agency indicate that volunteering is associated with increased self-understanding and higher levels of perceived competence and self-esteem (Yates & Youniss, 1996a). For example, Serow (1990) found that GPA, measures of mastery, and the number of goal-oriented activities were associated with volunteering behavior. Similarly, Johnson et al. (1998) found that adolescents involved in volunteer activities have higher educational plans and aspirations, grade point averages, academic self-esteem, and intrinsic motivation toward school work. In addition, adolescent volunteers tend to have higher levels of internal locus of control (Bensen et al., 1980).

Moreover, self-understanding has been related to prosocial volunteering behavior. For example, Hart and Fegley (1995) studied teens nominated by community leaders as care exemplars (individuals committed to the care of others in the community). Compared to matched controls, care exemplars were more likely to describe themselves in terms of moral goals and personality characteristics and were more likely to have self-concepts involving the importance of personal beliefs. Moreover, care exemplars were more likely to express a close connection between their actual and ideal selves, indicating that care exemplars were more driven by their ideals and beliefs. It is interesting that controls did not differ from the care exemplars in moral judgment or cognitive complexity, suggesting that differences in self-understanding and self-concept were more related to volunteering and moral behavior.

Studies examining *social relatedness and moral political-awareness* suggest that, in general, adolescents who volunteer provide moral reasons for their behavior and are more likely to engage in political and civic activities in adulthood (see also Flannagan, this volume; Fendrich, 1993; Yates & Youniss, 1996b). There also is some evidence that community service actually enhances adolescents' thinking about societal values and social order. For example, Yates and Youniss (1998) examined the narratives of Black adolescents who participated in a soup kitchen for the homeless. They found that over time, adolescents' narratives reflected more transcendence (values that supersede the family and self and have historical continuity), suggesting that the youths became more aware of values such as justice and social responsibility as a result of their experience.

The Socialization of Volunteering and Community Service

The socialization of volunteering and community service likely occurs in the home, peer group, and religious institutions. Indeed, research indicates that parents, peers, and community institutions, such as a church or synagogue, all are associated with adolescent volunteering. However, many studies are correlational, so it is difficult to determine causality.

Parental Influences

Despite increases in peer influence during adolescence, research suggests that parents also have an important impact on adolescents during this developmental period (Collins, Maccoby, Steinberg, Hetherington, & Bornstein, 2000). Parents influence adolescent volunteering in a variety of ways. Mechanisms of influence could include, but are not limited to, the transmission of socioeconomic status, modeling and setting an example, the transmission of values, and active recruitment into community service (Janoski & Wilson, 1995). Moreover, parents have the ability to demonstrate and teach youth that service can be a meaningful part of life that impacts others in important ways (Yates & Youniss, 1996a).

Consistent with the notion that parental modeling influences adolescents' service-related activities, youth who participate in community service tend to have one or both parents involved in community service (e.g., Keith et al., 1990). There also is some evidence suggesting that parental volunteering is more closely linked to girls' than to boys' volunteering. Stukas et al. (1999) found that adolescent girls with parents involved in volunteering and community service were more likely to have altruistic self-images compared to girls without parents involved in volunteering. There was no effect of parental volunteering on boys' altruistic self-images. Nevertheless, both boys and girls who had parents engaged in some form of community service were more likely to perceive themselves as engaging in volunteer work in the future compared to adolescents without parents involved in community service.

Parenting styles also may contribute to volunteering or community service. Gunnoe, Hetherington, and Reiss (1999) found that authoritative parenting was positively related to adolescents' social responsibility, measured as a composite of prosocial behavior, concern for right and wrong, and responsibility for actions. In addition, parental religiosity had direct and indirect effects (through authoritative parenting) on adolescent social responsibility (Gunnoe et al., 1999).

Peer Influences

Although there is not much research on peer influences specifically on volunteering behavior, peers may play an important role in adolescent community service. Involvement in most types of extracurricular activities—many of which involve peers—is linked to adolescent community service (e.g., Youniss, McLellan, Su, et al., 1999). Youniss, McLellan, Su, et al. (1999) hypothesized that this effect is due to peer group influences and to the fact that many groups and clubs engage in community service as a part of their group activities.

In one study examining the effects of peer crowd on adolescent volunteering, teens in *school* crowds (e.g., value achievement and involved in school clubs) were more likely to volunteer than were fun-crowd (e.g., popular) members. School, all around, and average crowd members were more likely to report the intention to be involved in future community service compared to disengaged and fun-crowd members (Youniss, McLellan, & Mazer, 2001).

Pugh and Hart (1999) explored adolescents' peer group orientation and their expectations regarding future community service. They found that increased studying and decreased orientation toward peer group informal reward (i.e., valuing a fun or delinquent subculture) were related to higher levels of expected future volunteerism. There was no relation between formal peer group orientation/identity (which reflects a commitment to being well-rounded and participating in extracurricular activities and valuing academics) and perceptions of future volunteering. Nevertheless, adolescents' perceptions of the activities that they engage in with peers may have some influence on moral identity development.

Religious Influences

The social institution that has been most often associated with volunteering is the church or synagogue (Youniss, 1993). In general, adolescents who view religion as important, compared to adolescents who do not, are more likely to engage in volunteering and community service (Marris et al., 2000; Youniss, McLellan, & Yates, 1999). Volunteers tend to attend church more frequently (e.g., Bensen et al., 1980) and score higher on measures of religiosity (e.g., Fitch, 1991). One large-scale study of 5th through 9th graders (N = 8,165; Bensen et al., 1980) found that volunteering was predicted by adolescents' intrinsic religious orientation, which reflects an open, flexible religious system in which internalized values guide behavior, suggesting that religious identity and community service are somewhat intertwined. Youniss, McLellen, and Yates (1999) argued that religiosity affects youth volunteering because religious organizations typically sponsor service, and the act of service and good will is grounded in most religious belief systems.

Outcomes Associated With Volunteering and Community Service

Regardless of the empirical evidence, many individuals believe that involvement in community service inherently is associated with positive youth development. Indeed, state and federal laws have been passed that encourage youth volunteering based on this underlying assumption (e.g., the National Community Service Trust Act of 1993). For example, the state of Maryland now requires service hours for high school graduation. Moreover, judicial systems often require youth who have been convicted of a crime to participate in community service programs. Do these types of programs affect adolescent adjustment? There is evidence suggesting that these programs do make a difference.

For example, adolescents who volunteer in high school are more likely to volunteer later in life and value the need for community service (Janoski, Musick, & Wilson,

1998). Of course, correlational studies cannot prove causal relations. However, as a step toward firmer inferences about causality, some studies examining the effects of volunteering and service have used a prepost design with volunteering as the intervening factor. Of these studies, few have used random assignment (for an exception see Allen, Philliber, Herrling, & Kuperminc, 1997), but most have included a comparison control group and a prepost design (even though it is often not random; see Moore & Allen, 1996; Yates & Youniss, 1996a). For example, using a prepost test design, researchers have found that community service is associated with increases in adolescents' self-esteem (Conrad & Hedin, 1982), self-confidence (Cognetta & Sprinthall, 1978), self-image (Switzers, Simmons, Dew, Regalski, & Wang, 1995), and personal responsibility and competence (Conrad & Hedin, 1982; Hamilton & Fenzel, 1988). In a panel design of youth volunteers and nonvolunteers in which a variety of initial levels of variables correlated with volunteering were taken into account, volunteering was related with gains in subsequent intrinsic work values, anticipated importance of career, and anticipated importance of community involvement (Johnson et al., 1998). There is also evidence that service participation is related to decreases in truancy, deviant school behavior, disciplinary problems, and lower rates of pregnancy (Allen et al., 1997; Calabrese & Schumer, 1986; Switzer et al., 1995; see also Yates & Youniss, 1996a). Similarly, involvement in prosocial activities such as church and volunteer activities is associated with higher educational trajectories and lower levels of risky behavior (Eccles & Barber, 1999). Moreover, studies using a prepost, control-group design also indicate that working with marginalized populations may increase levels of empathy (Hobfoll, 1980) and tolerance (Riecken, 1952). In a comprehensive review of volunteering programs aimed at intervention, many of which were mentioned earlier, Moore and Allen (1996) concluded that volunteer programs for adolescents reduce rates for course failure, suspension from school, school dropout, and teen pregnancy and improve reading skills, self-concept, and attitudes toward society. However, the authors noted that the quality of the program (e.g., allowing adolescents autonomy and choice), length of the program (programs 12 weeks or more tend to be more successful than shorter programs), and age of adolescents (in some programs older youth benefited more) affect potential benefits of volunteering.

In most relevant studies, the volunteers and nonvolunteers vary in a number of personal characteristics. However, involvement in community service has been associated with prosocial and deviant behavior in expected directions, even when controlling for background characteristics such as socioeconomic status and gender. For example, in a study of 13,000 high school seniors discussed previously, Youniss, McLellan, Su, et al. (1999) reported that service was positively associated with conventional political orientation (e.g., voting) and conventional religious orientation (church attendance and judging religion as an important part of life) among adolescents. In contrast, service was negatively associated with marijuana use. Service was also associated with unconventional political acts such as boycotting and demonstrating, suggesting that community service does not merely reflect an adherence to adult societal norms.

Unfortunately, nearly all research on volunteering and community service has been correlational or used a prepost design without random assignment, and many of the samples are too small to provide adequate power for detecting effects (Moore & Allen, 1996). Moreover, it is possible that in many of the studies volunteers differ from nonvolunteers not only in their characteristics but also in their ongoing developmental trajectories. To assess better the effects of participating in service, studies are needed in which adolescents who wish to volunteer are assigned to groups that do so or engage in some other, less prosocial activity.

CONCLUSIONS AND FUTURE DIRECTIONS

Although there is an accumulating database on adolescents' moral reasoning and prosocial behaviors and emotion, it is meager compared to that for preadolescent children. Thus, many of the findings presented in this chapter have not been replicated, and some of the conclusions are based on only one or a few studies. Clearly, there is much to be learned. In regard to moral reasoning, there is not yet consensus on the stages of moral reasoning and the degree to which they are qualitative in nature. This is a larger issue in the moral reasoning research, as findings differ for different content domains and methods of coding. Moreover, although work using real-life (rather than hypothetical) moral dilemmas seems particularly appropriate for adolescents, we do not yet know much about factors that affect reasoning about real-life moral dilemmas that have already occurred. In addition, although there sometimes is a relation between moral reasoning and behavior, we know little about variables that moderate the degree of this relation. It also is possible that any relation between moral judgment (or labeling a behavior as moral) and behavior is due to post hoc construction of moral reasoning based on the adolescents' justifications of their own behavior (Haidt, 2001). A valuable approach is to see if successful moral reasoning interventions also influence adolescents' risky behaviors, as well as their amoral or antisocial behavior.

Relatively little is known about the socialization of moral reasoning in adolescence, both in the family and outside of it. Due to the increasing role of peers and other extrafamilial individuals in adolescents' lives (Larson & Richards, 1991), it would be useful to know more about the ways in which extrafamilial influences combine with familial factors to affect moral cognitions, and whether familial influences change in magnitude with age in adolescence (or change in a nonlinear manner). It is likely that peers and involvement in extrafamilial activities influence adolescents' moral development in both positive and negative ways, but it is difficult to disentangle the extent to which these factors actually shape adolescents' moral development and to discover whether adolescents self-select into peer groups and activities that are consistent with their moral values and behavior.

There is somewhat more work (especially in the last decade) on adolescents' prosocial behavior (including volunteering and civic involvement) and empathy-related responding than on their moral cognitions. However, little is known about how the context (social or otherwise), including the peer group, affects adolescents' prosocial tendencies. Given the importance of identity formation in adolescence, it also would be useful to know if prosocial predispositions, which seem to be relatively stable across adolescence, undergo further change or consolidation in late adolescence. Similarly, it is possible that changes in identity, values, or perspective taking in middle or late adolescence affect people's tendencies to sympathize with others, although little is known about the development of sympathy in adolescence.

Much of the work reviewed in this chapter has been correlational, so few firm conclusions can be drawn in regard to causality. Alternative explanations—including ones involving heredity—often are possible. Even in many of the studies involving prepost tests, it is possible that factors other than the targeted variables (e.g., volunteer experience) account for effects. For example, adolescents who choose to be volunteers may have a number of personal and background characteristics that could account for positive developmental changes over time. More experimental and longitudinal research across the adolescent years is an obvious need.

As is true in much of the moral development research, most of the data involving adolescents have been collected in North America or perhaps Europe. Little is known about the generalizability of many of the findings to ethnic minorities or other cultures. Especially for morality, culture is likely to be an important influence on development, and this may be especially true for adolescents, who are preparing for entry into their adult culture.

Finally, unlike in the past, there is no grand theory (e.g., psychoanalytic or social learning theory) that adequately ties together work on moral development. Although grand theories likely cannot account for the complexity of moral development, often minitheories are not available to guide our thinking about adolescents' moral development (see, however, Hoffman, 2000). Clearly, some of the central issues in adolescence, such as the development of identity, the importance of adolescents' obtaining some psychological autonomy while still retaining a strong connection to socializers (Allen, Hauser, Eickholt, Bell, & O'Connor, 1994), and the central role of peers in adolescents' development, require additional conceptual (as well as empirical) attention in work on moral development. Moreover, additional emphasis on mediating processes, factors that moderate the nature of relations between moral functioning and other variables, and developmental trajectories of different aspects of moral responding would deepen our understanding of adolescents' moral development. Thus, there is much work to be done if we are to grasp the nature of adolescents' moral thought and behavior and to develop ways to prevent and ameliorate deficits in moral development.

REFERENCES

Aleixo, P. A., & Norris, C. E. (2000). Personality and moral reasoning in young offenders. *Personality and Individual Differences, 28,* 609–623.

Allen, J. P., Hauser, S. T., Eickholt, C., Bell, K. L., & O'Connor, T. G. (1994). Autonomy and relatedness in family interactions as predictors of expressions on negative adolescent affect. *Journal of Research on Adolescence, 4,* 535–552.

Allen, J. P., Philliber, S., Herrling, S., & Kuperminc, G. P. (1997). Preventing teen pregnancy and academic failure: Experimental evaluation of a developmentally based approach. *Child Development, 64,* 729–742.

Bakken, L., & Romig, C. (1994). The relationship of perceived family dynamics to adolescents' principled moral reasoning. *Journal of Adolescent Research, 9,* 442–457.

Bar-Tal, D., Nadler, A., & Blechman, N. (1980). The relationship between Israeli children's helping behavior and their perception on parents' socialization practices. *Journal of Social Psychology, 111,* 159–167.

Bar-Tal, D., & Nissim, R. (1984). Helping behavior and moral judgment among adolescents. *British Journal of Developmental Psychology, 2,* 329–336.

Bar-Tal, D., & Raviv, A. (1979). Consistency in helping-behavior measures. *Child Development, 50,* 1235–1238.

Bensen, P., Dehority, J., Garman, L., Hanson, E., Hochschwender, M., Lebold, C., Rohr, R., & Sullivan, J. (1980). Intrapersonal correlates of nonspontaneous helping behavior. *Journal of Social Psychology, 110,* 87–95.

Berg, C. A. (1989). Knowledge of strategies for dealing with everyday problems from childhood through adolescence. *Developmental Psychology, 25,* 607–618.

Berkowitz, M. W., Begun, A. L., Zweben, A., Giese, J. K., Mulry, G., Horan, C., Wheeler, T., Gimenez, J., & Piette, J. (1995). Assessing how adolescents think about the morality of substance use. *Drugs and Society, 8,* 111–124.

Berkowitz, M. W., & Gibbs, J. C. (1983). Measuring the developmental features of moral discussion. *Merrill-Palmer Quarterly 29,* 399–410.

Berkowitz, M. W., Mueller, C. W., Schnell, S. V., & Padberg, M. T. (1986). Moral reasoning and judgments of aggression. *Journal of Psychology and Social Psychology, 51,* 885–891.

Berndt, T. J. (1985). Prosocial behavior between friends in middle childhood and early adolescence. *Journal of Early Adolescence, 5,* 307–317.

Berndt, T. J., & Perry, T. B. (1986). Children's perceptions of friendships as supportive relationships. *Developmental Psychology, 22,* 640–648.

Boehnke, K., Silbereisen, R. K., Eisenberg, N., Reykowski, J., & Palmonari, A. (1989). The development of prosocial motivation: A cross-national study. *Journal of Cross Cultural Psychology, 20,* 219–243.

Boyes, M. C., & Allen, S. G. (1993). Styles of parent-child interaction and moral reasoning in adolescence. *Merrill-Palmer Quarterly, 39,* 551–570.

Bredemeier, B. J. (1985). Moral reasoning and the perceived legitimacy of intentionally injurious sport acts. *Journal of Sport Psychology, 7,* 110–124.

Breslin, A. (1982). Tolerance and moral reasoning among adolescents in Ireland. *Journal of Moral Education, 11,* 112–127.

Brion-Meisels, S., & Selman, R. L. (1984). Early adolescent development of new interpersonal strategies: Understanding and intervention. *School Psychology Review, 13,* 278–291.

Brown, L. M., & Gilligan, C. (1992). *Meeting at the crossroads: Women's psychology and girls' development.* Cambridge, MA: Harvard University Press.

Buck, L. Z., Walsh, W. F., & Rothman, G. (1981). Relationship between parental moral judgment and socialization. *Youth and Society, 13,* 91–116.

Buhrmester, D., Goldfarb, J., & Cantrell, D. (1992). Self-presentation when sharing with friends and nonfriends. *Journal of Early Adolescence, 12,* 61–79.

Calabrese, R. L., & Schumer, H. (1986). The effects of service activities on adolescent alienation. *Adolescence, 21,* 675–687.

Call, K. T., Mortimer, J. T., & Shanahan, M. J. (1995). Helpfulness and the development of competence in adolescence. *Child Development, 66,* 129–138.

Caprara, G. V., Barbaranelli, C., & Pastorelli, C. (2001). Prosocial behavior and aggression in childhood and pre-adolescence. In A. C. Bohart & D. J. Stipek (Eds.), *Constructive and destructive behavior: Implications for family, school, and society* (pp. 187–203).Washington, DC: American Psychological Association.

Caprara, G. V., Barbaranelli, C., Pastorelli, C., Bandura, A., & Zimbardo, P. G. (2000). Prosocial foundations of children's academic achievement. *Psychological Science, 11,* 302–306.

Carlo, G., Eisenberg, N., & Knight, G. P. (1992). An objective measure of adolescents' prosocial moral reasoning. *Journal of Research on Adolescence, 2,* 331–349.

Carlo, G., Koller, S., & Eisenberg, N. (1998). Prosocial moral reasoning in institutionalized delinquent, orphaned, and noninstitutionalized Brazilian adolescents. *Journal of Adolescent Research, 13,* 363–376.

Carlo, G., Roesch, S. C., & Melby, J. (1998). The multiplicative relations of parenting and temperament to prosocial and antisocial behaviors in adolescence. *Journal of Early Adolescence, 18.*

Cognetta, P. V., & Sprinthall, N. A. (1978). Students as teachers: Role taking as a means of promoting psychological and ethical development during adolescence. In N. A. Sprinthall & R. L. Mosher (Eds.), *Value development . . . As the aim of education.* Schenectady, NY: Character Research Press.

Cohen, D., & Strayer, J. (1996). Empathy in conduct-disordered and comparison youth. *Developmental Psychology, 32,* 988–998.

Coie, J. D., Dodge, K. A., & Kupersmidt, J. B. (1990). Peer group behavior and social status. In S. R. Asher & J. D. Coie (Eds.), *Peer rejection in childhood* (pp. 17–59). Cambridge, UK: Cambridge University Press.

Colby, A., Kohlberg, L., Gibbs, J., & Lieberman, M. (1983). A longitudinal study of moral judgment. *Monographs of the Society for Research in Child Development, 48*(1–2, Serial No. 200).

Collins, W. A., Maccoby, E., Steinberg, L., Hetherington, E. M., & Bornstein, M. (2000). Contemporary research on parenting: The case for nature *and* nurture. *American Psychologist, 55,* 218–232.

Conrad, D., & Hedin, D. (1982). The impact of experiential education on adolescent development. In D. Conrad & D. Hedin (Eds.), *Youth participation and experiential education.* New York: Haworth Press.

Comunian, A. L., & Gielen, U. P. (1995). Moral reasoning and prosocial action in Italian culture. *Journal of Social Psychology, 135,* 699–706.

Crick, N. R., & Dodge, K. A. (1994). A review and reformulation of social information-processing mechanisms in children's social adjustment. *Psychological Bulletin, 115,* 74–101.

Damon, W., & Hart, D. (1988). *Self-understanding in childhood and adolescence.* Cambridge, UK: Cambridge University Press.

Davis, M. H., & Franzoi, S. L. (1991). Stability and change in adolescent self-consciousness. *Journal of Research in Personality 25,* 70–87.

Dawson, T. L. (2002). New tools, new insights: Kohlberg's moral judgment stages revisited. *International Journal of Behavioral Development, 26,* 154–166.

Dlugokinski, E., & Firestone, I. J. (1973). Congruence among four methods of measuring other-centeredness. *Child Development, 44,* 304–308.

Dlugokinski, E. L, & Firestone, I. J. (1974). Other centeredness and susceptibility to charitable appeals: Effects of perceived discipline. *Developmental Psychology, 10,* 21–28.

Eagly, A. H., & Crowley, M. (1986). Gender and helping behavior: A meta-analytic review of the social psychological literature. *Psychological Bulletin, 100,* 283–308.

Eberly, M. B., & Montemayor, R. (1998). Doing good deeds: An examination of adolescent prosocial behavior in the context of parent-adolescent relationships. *Journal of Adolescent Research, 13,* 403–432.

Eberly, M. B., & Montemayor, R. (1999). Adolescent affection and helpfulness toward parents: A 2-year follow-up. *Journal of Early Adolescence, 19,* 226–248.

Eberly, M. B., Montemayor, R., & Flannery, D. J. (1993). Variation in adolescent helpfulness toward parents in a family context. *Journal of Early Adolescence, 13,* 228–244.

Eccles, J. S., & Barber, B. L. (1999). Student council, volunteering, basketball, or marching band: What kind of extracurricular involvement matters? *Journal of Adolescent Research, 14,* 10–43.

Eisenberg, N. (1986). *Altruistic emotion, cognition, and behavior.* Hillsdale, NJ: Erlbaum.

Eisenberg, N. (1990). Prosocial development in early and mid adolescence. In R. Montemayor, G. R. Adams, & T. P. Gullotta (Eds.), *From childhood to adolescence: A transitional period? Advances in adolescence* (Vol. 2, pp. 240–269). Newbury Park, CA: Sage.

Eisenberg, N., Carlo, G., Murphy, B., & Van Court, P. (1995). Prosocial development in late adolescence: A longitudinal study. *Child Development, 66,* 1179–1197.

Eisenberg, N., & Fabes, R. A. (1998). Prosocial development. In W. Damon (Series Ed.) & N. Eisenberg (Vol. Ed.), *Handbook of child psychology: Vol. 3. Social, emotional, and personality development* (5th ed., pp. 701–778). New York: Wiley.

Eisenberg, N., Guthrie, I., Cumberland, A., Murphy, B. C., Shepard, S. A., Zhou, Q., & Carlo, G. (2002). Prosocial development in early adulthood: A longitudinal study. *Journal of Personality and Social Psychology, 82,* 993–1006.

Eisenberg, N., Miller, P. A., Shell, R., McNalley, S., & Shea, C. (1991). Prosocial development in adolescence: A longitudinal study. *Developmental Psychology, 27,* 849–857.

Eisenberg, N., Shell, R., Pasternack, J., Lennon, R., Beller, R., & Mathy, R. M. (1987). Prosocial development in middle childhood: A longitudinal study. *Developmental Psychology, 24,* 712–718.

Eisenberg, N., & Valiente, C. (2002). Children's prosocial and moral development. In M. Bornstein (Ed.), *Handbook of parenting* (2nd ed, Vol. 5, pp. 111–142). Mahwah, NJ: Erlbaum.

Eisenberg-Berg, N. (1979). The development of children's prosocial moral judgment. *Developmental Psychology, 15,* 128–137.

Eisenberg-Berg, N., & Mussen, P. (1980). Correlates of political liberalism and conservatism in adolescence. *Journal of Genetic Psychology, 137,* 165–177.

Eisikovits, Z., & Sagi, A. (1982). Moral development and discipline encounter in delinquent and nondelinquent adolescents. *Journal of Youth and Adolescence, 11,* 217–246.

Emler, N. P., & Rushton, J. P. (1974). Cognitive-developmental factors in children's generosity. *British Journal of Social and Clinical Psychology, 13,* 277–281.

Erikson, E. H. (1968). *Identity: Youth and crisis.* New York: W. W. Norton.

Estrada, P. (1995). Adolescents' self-reports of prosocial responses to friends and acquaintances: The role of sympathy-related cognitive, affective, and motivational processes. *Journal of Research on Adolescence, 5,* 173–200.

Eysenck, S. B. G., Easting, G., & Pearson, P. R. (1984). Age norms for impulsiveness: Venturesomeness and empathy in children. *Personality and Individual Differences, 5,* 315–321.

Fabes, R. A., Carlo, G., Kupanoff, K., & Laible, D. (1999). Early adolescence and prosocial/moral behavior: I. The role of individual processes. *Journal of Early Adolescence, 19,* 5–16.

Fendrich, J. (1993). *Ideal citizens.* Albany: State University of New York Press.

Fitch, R. T. (1987). Characteristics and motivations of college students volunteering for community service. *Journal of College Student Personnel, 28,* 424–431.

Flannagan, C. A., Bowes, J. M., Jonsson, B., Csapo, B., & Sheblanova, E. (1998). Ties that bind: Correlates of adolescents' civic commitment in seven countries. *Journal of Social Issues, 54,* 457–475.

Froming, W. J., Nasby, W., & McManus, J. (1998). Prosocial self-schemas, self-awareness, and children's prosocial behavior. *Journal of Personality and Social Psychology, 75,* 766–777.

Gibbs, J. C., Potter, G. B., Barriga, A. Q., & Liau, A. K. (1996). Developing the helping skills and prosocial motivation of aggressive adolescents in peer group programs. *Aggression and Violent Behavior, 1,* 283–305.

Gilligan, C. (1982). *In a different voice: Psychological theory and women's development.* Cambridge, MA: Harvard University Press.

Gunnoe, M. L., Hetherington, E. M., & Reiss, D. (1999). Parental religiosity, parenting style, and adolescent social responsibility. *Journal of Early Adolescence, 19,* 199–225.

Haidt, J. (2001). The emotional dog and its rational tail: A social intuitionist approach to moral judgment. *Psychological Review, 108,* 814–834.

Hamilton, S. F., & Fenzel, L. M. (1988). The impact of volunteer experience on adolescent social development: Evidence of program effects. *Journal of Adolescent Research, 3,* 65–80.

Hampson, R. B. (1984). Adolescent prosocial behavior: Peer-group and situational factors associated with helping. *Journal of Personality and Social Psychology, 46,* 153–162.

Hart, D. (1988). A longitudinal study of adolescents' socialization and identification as predictors of adult moral judgment development. *Merrill-Palmer Quarterly, 34,* 245–260.

Hart, D., & Chmiel, S. (1992). Influence of defense mechanisms on moral judgment development: A longitudinal study. *Developmental Psychology, 28,* 722–730.

Hart, D., & Fegley, S. (1995). Altruism and caring in adolescence: Relations to self-understanding and social judgment. *Child Development, 66,* 1346–1359.

Harter, S. (1999). *The cognitive and social construction of the developing self.* New York: Guilford Press.

Hill, J. P. (1987). Research on adolescents and their families: Past and prospects. *New Directions in Child Development, 37,* 13–31.

Hobfoll, S. E. (1980). Personal characteristics of the college volunteer. *American Journal of Community Psychology, 8,* 503–506.

Hoffman, M. L. (1980). Moral development in adolescence. In J. Adelson (Ed.), *Handbook of adolescent psychology* (pp. 295–343). New York: Wiley.

Hoffman, M. L. (2000). *Empathy and moral development: Implications for caring and justice.* Cambridge, UK: Cambridge University Press.

Hoffman, M. L., & Saltzstein, H. D. (1967). Parent discipline and the child's moral development. *Journal of Personality and Social Psychology, 5,* 45–57.

Holstein, C. (1972). The relation of children's moral judgment level to that of their parents and to communication patterns in the family. In R. C. Smart & M. S. Smart (Eds.), *Readings in child development and relationships.* New York: Macmillan.

Hubbs-Tait, L., & Garmon, L. C. (1995). The relationship of moral reasoning and AIDS knowledge to risky sexual behavior. *Adolescence, 30,* 539–564.

Jaffee, S., & Hyde, J. S. (2000). Gender differences in moral orientation: A meta-analysis. *Psychological Bulletin, 126,* 703–726.

Janoski, T., Musick, M., & Wilson, J. (1998). Being volunteered? The impact of social participation and pro-social attitudes on volunteering. *Sociological Forum, 13,* 495–519.

Janoski, T., & Wilson, J. (1995). Pathways to volunteerism: Family socialization and status transmission models. *Social Forces, 74,* 271–292.

Janssen, A. W. H., Janssens, J. M. A. M., & Gerris, J. R. M. (1992). Parents' and children's levels of moral reasoning: Antecedents and consequences of parental discipline strategies. In J. M. A. M. Janssens & J. R. M. Gerris (Eds.), *Child rearing: Influence on prosocial and moral development* (pp. 169–196). Amsterdam: Swets and Zeitlinger.

Johnson, M. K., Beebe, T., Mortimer, J. T., & Snyder, M. (1998). Volunteerism in adolescence: A process perspective. *Journal of Research on Adolescence, 8,* 309–332.

Jones, G. P., & Dembo, M. H. (1989). Age and sex role differences in intimate friendships during childhood and adolescence. *Merrill-Palmer Quarterly, 35,* 445–462.

Jurkovic, G. J. (1980). The juvenile delinquent as a moral philosopher: A structural-developmental perspective. *Psychological Bulletin, 88,* 709–727.

Jurs, J. (1984). Correlation of moral development with use of birth control and pregnancy among teenage girls. *Psychological Reports, 55,* 1009–1010.

Karniol, R., Gabay, R., Ochion, Y., & Harari, Y. (1998). Is gender or gender-role orientation a better predictor of empathy in adolescence? *Sex Roles, 39,* 45–59.

Keith, J. G., Nelson, C. S., Schlabach, J. H., & Thompson, C. J. (1990). The relationship between parental employment and three measures of early adolescent responsibility: Family-related, personal, and social. *Journal of Early Adolescence, 10,* 399–415.

Kennedy, M. G., Felner, R. D, Cauce, A., & Primavera, J. (1988). Social problem solving and adjustment in adolescence: The influence of moral reasoning level, scoring alternatives, and family climate. *Journal of Clinical Child Psychology, 17,* 75–83.

Killen, M., Leviton, M., & Cahill, J. (1991). Adolescent reasoning about drug use. *Journal of Adolescent Research, 6,* 336–356.

Killen, M., & Turiel, E. (1998). Adolescents' and young adults' evaluations of helping and sacrificing for others. *Journal of Research on Adolescence, 8,* 355–375.

Knapp, R. H., & Holzberg, J. D. (1964). Characteristics of college students volunteering for service to mental patients. *Journal of Consulting Psychology, 28,* 82–85.

Kohlberg, L. (1969). Stage and sequence: The cognitive-developmental approach to socialization. In D. A. Goslin (Ed.), *Handbook of socialization theory and research* (pp. 347–480). Chicago: Rand McNally.

Kohlberg, L. (1981). *The philosophy of moral development: Moral stages and the idea of justice.* San Francisco, CA: Harper and Row.

Kohlberg, L. (1984). *Essays on moral development: Vol. 2. The psychology of moral development.* San Francisco: Harper and Row.

Krevans, J., & Gibbs, J. C. (1996). Parents' use of inductive discipline: Relations to children's empathy and prosocial behavior. *Child Development, 67,* 3263–3277.

Kruger, A. C. (1992). The effect of peer and adult-child transactive discussions on moral reasoning. *Merrill-Palmer Quarterly, 38,* 191–211.

Kuther, T. L., & Higgins-D'Alessandro, A. (2000). Bridging the gap between moral reasoning and adolescent engagement in risky behavior. *Journal of Adolescence, 23,* 409–422.

Larson, R., & Richards, M. H. (1991). Daily companionship in late childhood and early adolescence: Changing developmental contexts. *Child Development, 62,* 284–300.

Leahy, R. L. (1981). Parental practices and the development of moral judgment and self-image disparity during adolescence. *Developmental Psychology, 17,* 580–594.

Lennon, R., & Eisenberg, N. (1987). Gender and age differences in empathy and sympathy. In N. Eisenberg & J. Strayer (Eds.), *Empathy and its development* (pp. 195–217). New York: Cambridge University Press.

Magen, Z., & Aharoni, R. (1991). Adolescents' contributing toward others: Relationship to positive experiences and transpersonal commitment. *Journal of Humanistic Psychology, 31,* 126–143.

Marris, J. S., Jagers, R. J., Hatcher, C. A., Lawhon, G. D., Murphy, E. J., & Murray, Y. F. (2000). Religiosity, volunteerism, and community involvement among African American men: An exploratory analysis. *Journal of Community Psychology, 28,* 391–406.

Marsh, D. T., Serfica, F. C., & Barenboim, C. (1981). Interrelations among perspective taking, interpersonal problem solving, and interpersonal functioning. *Journal of Genetic Psychology, 138,* 37–48.

Matsuba, M. K., & Walker, L. J. (1998). Moral reasoning in the context of ego functioning. *Merrill-Palmer Quarterly, 44,* 464–483.

McDevitt, T. M., Lennon, R., & Kopriva, R. J. (1991). Adolescents' perceptions of mothers' and fathers' prosocial actions and empathic responses. *Youth and Society, 22,* 387–409.

Miller, F. (1994). Gender differences in adolescents' attitudes toward mandatory community service. *Journal of Adolescence, 17,* 381–393.

Moore, C. W., & Allen, J. P. (1996). The effects of volunteering on the young volunteer. *Journal of Primary Prevention, 17,* 231–258.

Murphy, B. C., Shepard, S. A., Eisenberg, N., Fabes, R. A., & Guthrie, I. K. (1999). Contemporaneous and longitudinal relations of young adolescents' dispositional sympathy to their emotionality, regulation, and social functioning. *Journal of Early Adolescence, 19,* 66–97.

Mussen, P., Harris, S., Rutherford, E., & Keasey, C. (1970). Honesty and altruism among preadolescents. *Developmental Psychology, 3,* 169–194.

Moore, C. W., & Allen, J. P. (1996). The effects of volunteering on the young volunteer. *Journal of Primary Prevention, 17,* 231–259.

Narvaez, D. (1998). The influence of moral schemas on the reconstruction of moral narratives in eight graders and college students. *Journal of Educational Psychology, 90,* 13–24.

Nelson, J. R., Smith, D. J., & Dodd, J. (1990). The moral reasoning of juvenile delinquents: A meta-analysis. *Journal of Abnormal Child Psychology, 19,* 231–239.

Nelson, D. A., & Crick, N. R. (1999). Rose-colored glasses: Examining the social information-processing of prosocial young adolescents. *Journal of Early Adolescence, 19,* 17–38.

Nolin, M. J., Chaney, B., Chapman, C., & Chandler, K. (1997). *Student participation in community service.* Washington, DC: U.S. Department of Education.

Nucci, L., Guerra, N., & Lee, J. (1991). Adolescent judgments of the personal, prudential, and normative aspects of drug usage. *Developmental Psychology, 27,* 841–848.

Olweus, D., & Endresen, I. M. (1998). The importance of sex-of-stimulus object: Age trends and sex differences in empathic responsiveness. *Social Development, 7,* 370–388.

Palmer, E. J., & Hollin, C. R. (1996). Sociomoral reasoning, perceptions of own parenting, and self-reported delinquency. *Personality and Individual Differences, 21,* 175–182.

Palmer, E. J., & Hollin, C. R. (1998). A comparison of patterns of moral development in young offenders and non-offenders. *Legal and Criminological Psychology, 3,* 225–235.

Parikh, B. (1980). Development of moral judgment and its relation to family environment factors in Indian and American families. *Child Development, 51,* 1030–1039.

Payne, F. D. (1980). Children's prosocial conduct in structural situations and as viewed by others: Consistency, convergence and relationships with person variables. *Child Development, 51,* 1252–1259.

Perry, C. M., & McIntire, W. G. (1995). Modes of moral judgment among early adolescents. *Adolescence, 30,* 707–715.

Piaget, J. (1965). *The moral judgment of the child.* New York: Free Press. (Original work published 1932)

Power, T. G., & Shanks, J. A. (1989). Parents as socializers: Maternal and paternal views. *Journal of Youth and Adolescence, 18,* 203–220.

Powers, S. I. (1988). Moral judgment development within the family. *Journal of Moral Education, 17,* 209–219.

Pratt, M. W., Arnold, M. L., Pratt, A. D., & Diessner, R. (1999). Predicting adolescent moral reasoning from family climate: A longitudinal study. *Journal of Early Adolescence, 19,* 148–175.

Pugh, M. J., & Hart, D. (1999). Identity development and peer group participation. *New Directions in Child and Adolescent Development, 84,* 55–70.

Raaijmakers, Q. A. W., Verbogt, T. F. M. A., & Vollebergh, W. A. M. (1998). Moral reasoning and political beliefs of Dutch adolescents and young adults. *Journal of Social Issues, 54,* 531–546.

Rest, J. R. (1979). *Development in judging moral issues.* Minneapolis: University of Minnesota Press.

Rest, J. R. (1983). Morality. In P. Mussen (Ed.), *Handbook of child psychology: Vol. 3. Cognitive development* (pp. 556–629). New York: Wiley.

Rest, J. R., Narvaez, D., Bebeau, M. J., & Thoma, S. J. (1999a). A neo-Kohlbergian approach: The DIT and schema theory. *Educational Psychology Review, 11,* 291–324.

Rest, J. R., Narvaez, D., Bebeau, M. J., & Thoma, S. J. (1999b). *Postconventional moral thinking: A neo-Kohlbergian approach.* Mahwah, NJ: Erlbaum.

Rholes, W. S., & Lane, L. W. (1985). Consistency between cognitions and behavior: Cause and consequence of cognitive moral development. In J. B. Pryor & J. D. Day (Eds.), *The development of social cognition* (pp. 97–114). New York: Springer-Verlag.

Riecken, R. W. (1952). *The volunteer work camp: A psychological evaluation.* Cambridge: Addison-Wesley.

Rigby, K. (1993). School children's perceptions of their families and parents as a function of peer relations. *Journal of Genetic Psychology, 154,* 501–513.

Rubin, K. H., Bukowski, W., & Parker, J. G. (1998). Peer interactions, relationships, and groups. In W. Damon (Series Ed.) & N. Eisenberg (Vol. Ed.), *Handbook of child psychology: Vol. 3. Social, emotional, and personality development* (5th ed., pp. 619–700). New York: Wiley.

Saklofske, D. H., & Eysenck, S. B. G. (1983). Impulsiveness and venturesomeness in Canadian children. *Psychological Reports, 52,* 147–152.

Sanvitale, D., Saltzstein, H. D., & Fish, M. (1989). Moral judgments by normal and conduct-disordered preadolescent and adolescent boys. *Merrill-Palmer Quarterly, 35,* 463–481.

Schonert-Reichl, K. A. (1999). Relations of peer acceptance, friendship adjustment, and social behavior to moral reasoning during early adolescence. *Journal of Early Adolescence, 19,* 249–279.

Selman, R. L. (1975). Level of social perspective taking and the development of empathy in children: Speculations from a social-cognitive viewpoint. *Journal of Moral Education, 5,* 35–43.

Selman, R. L. (1980). *The growth of interpersonal understanding: Developmental and clinical analysis.* New York: Academic Press.

Serow, R. C. (1990). Volunteering and values: An analysis of participation in community service. *Journal of Research and Development in Education, 23,* 198–203.

Sigman, M., & Erdynast, A. (1988). Interpersonal understanding and moral judgment in adolescents with emotional and cognitive disorders. *Child Psychiatry and Human Development, 19,* 36–44.

Sigman, M., Ungerer, J. A., & Russell, A. (1983). Moral judgment in relation to behavioral and cognitive disorders in adolescents. *Journal of Abnormal Child Psychology, 11,* 503–512.

Skoe, E. A., Hansen, K. L., Morch, W-T., Bakke, I., Hoffmann, T., Larsen, B., & Aasheim, M. (1999). Care-based moral reasoning in Norwegian and Canadian early adolescents: A cross-national comparison. *Journal of Early Adolescence, 19,* 280–291.
Small, S. A., Zeldin, R. S., & Savin-Williams, R. C. (1983). In search of personality traits: A multimethod analysis of naturally occurring prosocial and dominance behavior. *Journal of Personality, 51,* 1–16.
Sotelo, M. J., & Sangrador, J. L. (1999). Correlations of self-ratings of attitude towards violent groups with measures of personality, self-esteem, and moral reasoning. *Psychological Reports, 1999,* 558–560.
Speicher, B. (1992). Adolescent moral judgment and perceptions of family interaction. *Journal of Family Psychology, 6,* 128–138.
Staub, E. (1979). *Positive social behavior and morality: Vol. 2. Socialization and development.* New York: Academic Press.
Steinberg, L., & Morris, A. S. (2001). Adolescent development. *Annual Review of Psychology, 52,* 83–110.
Strayer, J., & Roberts, W. (1997). Facial and verbal measures of children's emotions and empathy. *International Journal of Behavioral Development, 20,* 627–649.
Stukas, A. A., Switzer, G. E., Dew, M. A., Goycoolea, J. M., & Simmons, R. G. (1999). Parental helping models, gender, and service-learning. *Journal of Prevention and Intervention in the Community, 18,* 5–18.
Suda, W., & Fouts, G. (1980). Effects of peer presence on helping in introverted and extroverted children. *Child Development, 51,*1272–1275.
Switzer, G. E., Simmons, R. G., Dew, M. A., Regalski, J. M., & Wang, C. (1995). The effect of a school-based helper program on adolescent self-image, attitudes, and behavior. *Journal of Early Adolescence, 15,* 429–455.
Szagun, G. (1992). Children's understanding of the feeling experience and causes of sympathy. *Journal of Child Psychology and Psychiatry, 33,* 1183–1191.
Thoma, S. J., & Rest, J. R. (1999). The relationship between moral decision making and patterns of consolidation and transition in moral judgment development. *Developmental Psychology, 35,* 323–334.
Tisak, M. S., Tisak, J., & Rogers, M. J. (1994). Adolescents' reasoning about authority and friendship relations in the context of drug usage. *Journal of Adolescence, 17,* 265–282.
Trevethan, S. D., & Walker, L. J. (1989). Hypothetical versus real-life moral reasoning among psychopathic and delinquent youth. *Development and Psychopathology, 1,* 91–103.
Tucker, C. J., Updegraff, K. A., McHale, S., & Crouter, A. C. (1999). Older siblings as socializers of younger siblings' empathy. *Journal of Early Adolescence, 19,* 176–198.
Vaughn, B. E., Block, J. H., & Block, J. (1988). Parental agreement on child rearing during early childhood and the psychological characteristics of adolescents. *Child Development, 59,* 1020–1033.
Walker, L. J. (in press). The model and the measure: An appraisal of the Minnesota approach to moral development. *Journal of Moral Education.*
Walker, L. J., Gustafson, P., & Hennig, K. H. (2001). The consolidation/transition model in moral reasoning development. *Developmental Psychology, 37,* 187–197.
Walker, L. J., & Hennig, K. H. (1999). Parenting style and the development of moral reasoning. *Journal of Moral Education, 28,* 359–374.
Walker, L. J., Hennig, K. H., & Krettenauer, T. (2000). Parent and peer contexts for children's moral reasoning development. *Child Development, 71,* 1033–1048.
Walker, L. J., Pitts, R. C., Hennig, K. H., & Matsuba, M. K. (1995). Reasoning about morality and real-life moral problems. In M. Killen & D. Hart (Eds.), *Morality in everyday life* (pp. 371–407). Cambridge, UK: Cambridge University Press.
Walker, L. J., & Taylor, J. H. (1991). Family interactions and the development of moral reasoning. *Child Development, 62,* 264–283.
Weisz, A. N., & Black, B. M. (2002). Gender and moral reasoning: African American youth respond to dating dilemmas. *Journal of Human Behavior in the Social Environment, 5,* 35–52.

Wentzel, K. R., & Caldwell, K. C. (1997). Friendships, peer acceptance, and group membership: Relations to academic achievement in middle school. *Child Development, 68,* 1198–1209.

Wentzel, K. R., & McNamara, C. C. (1999). Interpersonal relationships, emotional distress, and prosocial behavior in middle school. *Journal of Early Adolescence, 19,* 114–125.

Yates, M., & Youniss, J. (1996a). A development perspective on community service in adolescence. *Social Development, 5,* 85–111.

Yates, M., & Youniss, J. (1996b). Community service and political-moral identity in adolescents. *Journal of Research on Adolescence, 6,* 271–284.

Yates, M., & Youniss, J. (1998). Community service and political identity development in adolescence. *Journal of Social Issues, 43,* 495–512.

Youniss, J. (1980). *Parents and peers in social development: A Sullivan-Piaget perspective.* Chicago: University of Chicago Press.

Youniss, J. (1993). Integrating culture and religion into developmental psychology. *Family Perspective, 26,* 171–188.

Youniss, J., McLellan, J. A., & Mazer, B. (2001). Voluntary service, peer group orientation, and civic engagement. *Journal of Adolescent Research, 16,* 456–468.

Youniss, J., McLellan, J. A., Su, Y., & Yates. M. (1999). The role of community service in identity development: Normative, unconventional, and deviant orientations. *Journal of Adolescent Research, 14,* 248–261.

Youniss, J., McLellan, J. A., & Yates, M. (1999). Religion, community service, and identity in American Youth. *Journal of Adolescence, 22,* 243–253.

Youniss, J., & Yates, M. (1997). *Community service and social responsibility in youth.* Chicago: University of Chicago Press.

Zarbatany, L., Hartmann, D. P., Gelfand, D. M., & Vinciguerra, P. (1985). Gender differences in altruistic reputation: Are they artifactual? *Developmental Psychology, 21,* 97–101.

Zeldin, R. A., Savin-Williams, R. C., & Small, S. A. (1984). Dimensions of prosocial behavior in adolescent males. *Journal of Social Psychology, 123,* 159–168.

Chapter 7

SEX

Ritch C. Savin-Williams and Lisa M. Diamond

> All adolescents have sex lives, whether they are sexually active with others, with themselves, or seemingly not at all. The question is whether they are going to have healthy experiences, at any or every level of sexual activity. (Ponton, 2000, p. 2)

> In America today, it is nearly impossible to publish a book that says children and teenagers can have sexual pleasure and be safe too, . . . [yet sex] is a vehicle to self-knowledge, love, healing, creativity, adventure, and intense feelings of aliveness. (Levine, 2002, pp. xix, 225)

These two popular books question accepted wisdom regarding the role of sexuality in adolescents' lives. Over one quarter of a century ago one of the first systematic studies of adolescent sexuality echoed these concerns, asking researchers and educators to help adolescents to "integrate the biological, social, and psychological aspects of their sexuality into all aspects of their lives" so that they could "realize their potential as whole human beings" (Chilman, 1978, p. 1). This goal remains unrealized, perhaps because nearly 80% of U.S. adults believe teenage sex is always or almost always wrong (Laumann, Gagnon, Michael, & Michaels, 1994, p. 322) and because adolescent sexual activity is commonly associated with a host of negative by-products, including pregnancy, sexually transmitted diseases (STDs), abortions, substance abuse, delinquency, AIDS, and bad grades. Scare tactics are widespread, with the expressed purpose of convincing adolescents to avoid sex. Paradoxically, however, ubiquitous and often exploitative depictions of sexuality are common in an American culture that "advertises [erotic] ecstasy but denies safety" to its adolescent members (Gullotta, 1993, p. vii).

Contemporary sexuality research reflects these contradictory perspectives. Although developmental researchers have amassed an incredible amount of data on when and with whom adolescents initiate sex, which youth pursue sexual activity, the type and number of specific acts they engage in, how often they use protection against pregnancy and STDs, and how many have abortions, researchers have shied away from collecting in-depth information on the *qualitative* aspects of adolescents' developing sexual desires and early sexual experiences. Consequently, we know little about how adolescents *develop* their conceptualizations of sex, what makes someone a sex partner, how youth negotiate between conflicting motivations for and against different sexual activities, how they experience and interpret their sexual thoughts and fantasies, and how the subjective and symbolic meaning of sexuality is shaped by their culture and social-cognitive-biological maturation. Thus, even after decades of research on adolescent sexuality, many fundamental questions about normative sexual development from prepubescence to young adulthood remain unanswered. Di Mauro (1997, p. 4) concluded, "We have very little understanding of what constitutes sexual health, what motivates sexual behavior, how sexual norms are developed and sustained, and how these evolve over time."

It is with these caveats that we offer the present review. Of course, it is impossible to cover adolescent sexuality comprehensively in a single chapter and still maintain a point of view. We therefore begin by calling attention to the implicit and explicit conceptual frameworks shaping the questions asked, the methods used, and hence the answers offered about adolescent sexuality. We then review the most reliable contemporary data on the who, what, and when of teenage sexuality, highlighting overarching themes, emerging trends, and underinvestigated questions. Our review follows a rough trajectory from inside to outside, beginning with a youth's internal sexual desires and motivations, moving to solitary and then partnered sexual activities, and finally addressing in a more limited fashion the diverse array of individual and contextual factors that moderate adolescent sexual expression. In the interests of space, a number of areas are *not* addressed that have established their own extensive literatures. These include competing theoretical perspectives on the role of sexuality in adolescent development (Downs & Hillje, 1993; Miller & Benson, 1999; Moore & Rosenthal, 1993), historic and cultural variations in adolescent sexuality (Brumberg, 1997; Downs & Hillje, 1993; Schlegel & Barry, 1991), legal aspects of adolescent sexuality (Levesque, 2000), romantic relationships (Florsheim, 2003; Furman, Brown, & Feiring, 1999), the biology of sexual maturation (Brooks-Gunn & Reiter, 1990), the influence of contextual factors (e.g., family characteristics, friendships, peer norms, and community size and milieu) and demography (e.g., social class, region, and ethnicity) to explain variations in the timing and frequency of sex (Manlove, Terry-Humen, Papillo, Franzetta, Williams, & Ryan, 2001; Moore & Rosenthal, 1993), and sexual abuse and coercion (Laumann et al., 1994; Saywitz, Mannarino, Berliner, & Cohen, 2000; Schwartz, 1999). Our intent is to delineate where we are in the study of adolescent sexuality and where we have yet to go in our continuing attempts to build sound, scientific, sophisticated models of adolescent sexual development that capably represent its variety, complexity, and meaning.

RISK FACTORS AND PROBLEM BEHAVIORS

Contemporary Western culture considers teenage sexual expression a dangerous activity that should be delayed until greater maturity is achieved, or prevented until marriage, rather than as a normative aspect of development with the potential to promote growth and well-being. For example, a recent sex advice columnist warned about the "treacherous territory" of adolescent sexuality: "I don't care how far exactly it goes; that kind of behavior means moving into an intimacy that kids are simply not prepared for . . . and most experts believe that kids under 16 do not have the psychological and neurological development necessary to satisfactorily manage these feelings" (Pinsky, 2002, p. 6). Research mirrors this perspective, generally adopting a medicalized, reductionist, and implicitly moralizing view of adolescent sexuality as *risk behaviors* that threaten social welfare and public health by exacerbating a host of personal and social problems (Carpenter, 2001; Leitenberg & Saltzman, 2000; Sonenstein, Ku, & Pleck, 1997). Indeed, the primary motivation for investigating adolescent sex is to intervene and prevent the following array of negative outcomes linked with early sexual initiation:

- Teenage pregnancies and abortions (Alan Guttmacher Institute, 1994; Laumann et al., 1994; Miller & Moore, 1990)
- Transmission and acquisition of STDs (Alan Guttmacher Institute, 1994; Miller & Moore, 1990)
- Frequent sexual activity and multiple sex partners (Davis & Lay-Yee, 1999; Seidman, Mosher, & Aral, 1994)
- Decline in school attendance and performance and in educational aspirations (Costa, Jessor, Donovan, & Fortenberry, 1995; Crockett, Bingham, Chopak, & Vicary, 1996; Halpern, Joyner, Udry, & Suchindran, 2000; Kirby, 2002; Leitenberg & Saltzman, 2000; Manlove et al., 2001; Miller et al., 1997; Resnick, Bearman, Blum et al., 1997)
- Smoking, drinking, substance use, and illegal or deviant behavior (Costa et al., 1995; Crockett et al., 1996; Dorius, Heaton, & Steffen, 1993; R. Jessor & Jessor, 1977; S. L. Jessor & Jessor, 1977; Leitenberg & Saltzman, 2000; Lynch, 2001; Miller et al., 1997; Paul, McManus, & Hayes, 2000; Rosenthal, Smith, & de Visser, 1999; Whitbeck, Yoder, Hoyt, & Conger, 1999)

The notion that *some* types and contexts of adolescent sexual activity might be more strongly associated with these negative outcomes than others is insufficiently addressed, and thus intervention often consists of one solution: delaying *all* adolescent sexual activity as long as possible, with the hope that social, cognitive, and moral maturity will allow youth to manage more successfully the complexities and risks of sexual interactions (Dittus, Jaccard, & Gordon, 1997; Gardner & Wilcox, 1993). In fact, adolescent sex is considered so intrinsically and uniformly dangerous that some have characterized sexually inexperienced youth as "virgin *survivors*" (Costa et al., 1995, emphasis added), blessed because they have somehow succeeded in resisting the poisonous lure of sexual gratification and its inevitable negative repercussions (de Gaston, Jensen, & Weed, 1995).

Notably, this negative emphasis applies not only to research on adolescents but also to sexual behavior throughout the life course (di Mauro, 1997), manifested in our culture's longstanding anxiety with regard to *childhood* sexuality. Although many researchers readily acknowledge that prepubertal children experience and enjoy sexual feelings and engage in sexual exploration and stimulation, research ethics and cultural norms essentially preclude the collection of data on such experiences (Okami, Olmstead, & Abramson, 1997). Even when parents are willing to allow researchers to conduct sensitive, scientific assessments of prepubertal sexual development, those who fund research show reticence (Brooks-Gunn & Reiter, 1990). Instead, studies of child development emphasize biological maturation and sex-role development, ignore sexual feelings and behavior, and typically treat puberty as the starting point of sexual development (Gullotta, Adams, & Montemayor, 1993; Ponton, 2000).

Overall, the negative cast of research on adolescent sexuality can be interpreted as exemplifying the general tendency to portray sexuality as a source of problems rather than an integral aspect of human development (di Mauro, 1997). For example, after reviewing the literature on adolescent sexuality, Katchadourian (1990, pp. 348–349) concluded that insufficient attention had been devoted to sexual behavior as "part of the normal process of becoming an adult physically and psychosocially. . . . Sex must take its rightful place among other bodily functions and human experiences." In recent years, an increasing number of thoughtful and constructive critiques has assumed this position (Ehrhardt, 1996; Savin-Williams, 2001; Tolman, 2002; Tolman & Diamond, 2001; Wright, 1998). This move away from a negative focus reflects an emerging trend in psychological research toward greater emphasis on positive dimensions of human experience, such as optimism (Aspinwall & Taylor, 1997) and positive emotions (Fredrickson, 1998), rather than on psychological deficits and pathologies (Seligman & Csikszentmihalyi, 2000). This change is signaled to some extent in the growing attention to youth resiliency and developmental assets rather than risk factors (Cicchetti & Garmezy, 1993; Cowen, Wyman, Work, & Parker, 1990; Galambos & Leadbeater, 2000). Research on adolescent sexuality would profit from a similarly expanded approach—a topic we revisit at the end of this chapter.

This refocusing, however, might be a particularly thorny battle. As scholars have long noted, national politics often dictates the kind of scientific research deemed worthy of receiving public support and funding. Given cultural squeamishness about adolescent sexuality, political support for adolescent sex research is generally predicated on the necessity of averting or ameliorating public health problems such as STDs and teenage pregnancy (Brumberg, 1997; Carpenter, 2001; di Mauro, 1997; Sonenstein et al., 1997). Studies of positive, normative sexual experience not only have difficulty meeting this standard but often are condemned as implicitly condoning adolescent sexual behavior. Even when comprehensive investigations of sexual development are framed around public health concerns—such as Rindfuss and Udry's 1988 American Teen Study, which proposed to estimate the prevalence and correlates of risky sexual behaviors in different cohorts—political support remains tenuous (see discussion in Gardner & Wilcox, 1993). Despite positive peer review by the National Institutes of Health, funding was canceled, reflecting the reality that any and all investigations of adolescent sexuality are considered suspicious and politically dangerous. Understandably, some researchers have adopted an alarmist stance that warns of a public health disaster if adolescent sex is not prevented or reduced.

Not only does this perspective restrict our range of knowledge regarding normative adolescent sexual development, but it also hampers the very aim of sexual risk reduction and health promotion. Wright (1998) reviewed numerous reasons why conventional safer sex research inadvertently works against the identification and promotion of strategies for reducing adolescents' risks for pregnancy and STDs. Most notably, he argued that "as a result of reducing human sexuality to a small number of behaviors and measurable elements, researchers have run the risk of pathologizing normal behavior . . . [which] can lead to intense feelings of shame and guilt when one has unprotected sex, making it that much more difficult to have an open dialogue with one's partners and social network about one's questions and concerns regarding safer sex" (pp. 9–10). Similar conclusions emerge from research on erotophobia, the tendency to respond negatively to sexual cues. Erotophobic individuals have difficulty talking openly about sex, learning about and using information about contraception, and taking responsibility for their sexual and reproductive health (W. A. Fisher & Fisher, 1998). Thus, although the denigration of adolescent sexuality has been predicated on protecting health and well-being, it might actually do more harm than good.

Thus, critics such as Erhardt (1996) and Wright (1998) have called on researchers to shift their focus toward normalizing and contextualizing adolescents' sexual feelings, giving youth the safety to consider multiple ways of expression (including celibacy), and emphasizing sexual responsibility. Wright (1998) specifically argued that to promote sexual health effectively, sex researchers must jettison conceptualizations of sexual behavior as the product of rational decision making and instead acknowledge that sexuality has "its own rationality" (p. 14) and symbolic meaning; treat the sexual dyad rather than the individual as the unit of research and intervention; acknowledge the dynamic, changing nature of individuals' sexual needs and opportunities, rather than treating individuals and their predispositions as static; and give greater attention to the social-cultural context of sexual interactions. Wright (1998) noted that European researchers have begun to adopt these changes; it remains to be seen whether American researchers will follow suit.

As it stands now, conventional adolescent sex research has a host of methodological shortcomings that work against the correctives Wright recommended. Understanding the nature and implications of these limitations is critical for evaluating and interpreting contemporary data on adolescent sexuality.

METHODOLOGICAL ISSUES

A considerable cottage industry has developed around methodological issues in sex research, particularly on adolescents (Bancroft, 1997; Catania, 1999; Catania, Gibson, Chitwood, & Coates, 1990; Goodson, Evans, & Edmundson, 1997; Moore & Rosenthal, 1993; Schwarz, 1999; Wiederman, 1999). One chief critique is the paucity of empirical data on the reliability and validity of techniques assessing the development and prevalence of adolescent sexual behavior (Catania et al., 1990). Another problem is that research designs are often simplistic, rarely taking advantage of the more complex perspectives afforded by multimethod, cross-disciplinary collaborations, and rarely attempting to integrate findings across multiple disciplines (di Mauro, 1997; Sonenstein et al., 1997). In addition to these fairly broad shortcomings, researchers have identified a number of more specific problems: *what* is studied, *who* is studied, and *how* it is studied.

What Is Studied? The Definition and Meaning of Sex

When researchers use the term *sex,* they nearly always mean sexual intercourse—more specifically, penile-vaginal intercourse. Despite the obvious fact that this is only one among many forms of adolescent sexual expression, researchers often adopt the larger culture's preoccupation with this form of sexual activity (Schwartz, 1999), ostensibly because it is the riskiest (Schuster, Bell, & Kanouse, 1996). This, of course, is a matter of perspective. If youth are less likely to refrain from noncoital activities or to use protection during such activities because they are perceived as safer, then such behaviors introduce greater rather than lesser risk.

But the problem runs deeper. The widespread, unquestioned equation of penile-vaginal intercourse with sex reflects a failure to examine systematically "whether the respondent's understanding of the question matches what the researcher had in mind" (Schwarz, 1999, p. 94). The full pragmatic and erotic meaning of the youth's sexual world is not elicited by the simple question, "Have you had sex?" As Reinisch and Sanders (1999, p. 1918) noted, answers to this question depend on (unmeasured) factors such as "consent, cohort, the potential costs and benefits of labeling a behavior, socioeconomic status, subculture, geography, and the demands of polite society." A number of feminist scholars have questioned the gender neutrality of the sex-as-intercourse equation, believing the parallel is more in the minds of males than females (Peplau & Garnets, 2000; Rodríguez Rust, 2000; Rose, 2000; Rothblum, 2000). In reality, researchers rarely disclose how they define sex or even whether they resolved potential discrepancies in definitions of sex. Thus, it is common to encounter statements such as, "The majority of the students reported having sex at least once a month" (Prince & Bernard, 1998, p. 17), without knowing just what respondents meant by "having sex." Other studies use the even vaguer term "sexually active." To researchers' credit, their hands are often tied by school officials, parents, funding agencies, and institutional review boards that require that sex questions avoid explicit terminology and descriptions of specific sex acts (Crockett et al., 1996).

Substantial evidence indicates that contemporary adolescents do not have uniform conceptualizations of sex and sexual activity. Based on surveys of college students from the U.S. Midwest (Sanders & Reinisch, 1999), the United Kingdom (Pitts & Rahman, 2001), and the Internet (Mustanski, 2002), practically all youth consider penile-vaginal intercourse to be sex, but they disagree regarding other sex acts. For example, Sanders and Reinisch (1999) found that 81% of respondents considered penile-anal intercourse to be sex, and approximately 20% counted manual and oral stimulation. Notably, these proportions varied by sex, with males generally adopting more flexible definitions of sex. In a qualitative study of 15- to 19-year-old boys (Sonenstein et al., 1997), one respondent claimed that touching a female breast counted as having sex, whereas another said that sex involved going on a date and kissing. Some boys asserted that the term *sex* was reserved for any and all sexual activities pursued within an emotionally invested relationship.

Definitions also vary according to sexual identity status. Whereas male and female sexual-minority (i.e., nonheterosexual) youth generally viewed penile-anal intercourse, oral stimulation, oral-anal contact, and use of sex accessories as sex, heterosexual youth were significantly less likely to agree (Mustanski, 2002; Sanders & Reinisch, 1999). For some behaviors (e.g., kissing and touching breasts), sexual-minority males adopted broader definitions of sex than did sexual-minority females; for other behaviors (e.g., oral and manual stimulation of genitals), sexual-minority females espoused the broader definitions (Mustanski, 2002).

The question of orgasm raises new issues. Researchers (Bogart, Cecil, Wagstaff, Pinkerton, & Abramson, 2000; Mustanski, 2002) have detected variability in the degree to which orgasm is considered essential to definitions of sex. The perceived importance of orgasm appears to depend on situational factors, such as the relational context and "who does what to whom." Bogart et al. (2000) found that many heterosexual college students only viewed penile-anal intercourse (between a man and woman) as sex for the man if he had an orgasm. Similar to Sanders and Reinisch (1999), respondents were more likely to count oral stimulation as sex if the recipient experienced orgasm than if he or she did not. In contrast, the giver of oral stimulation was rarely considered to have had sex because he or she was presumed not to have achieved orgasm.

Studies of so-called virginity loss also shed light on the multiplicity of sex definitions. One early study (Berger & Wenger, 1973) found that college students generally agreed that a woman loses her virginity when her vagina is fully penetrated by a man; interestingly, however, over one third believed that a woman who brought herself to orgasm and ruptured her hymen was no longer a virgin. Over half agreed that a man who penetrated a female's vagina without ejaculating had lost his virginity; considerably less thought that giving or receiving manual stimulation to climax or even ejaculating by self-stimulation should be considered virginity loss. Carpenter's (2001) qualitative study found that one quarter of young adults counted oral sex as virginity loss, and more than half counted heterosexual anal intercourse. A majority construed same-sex activity as virginity loss, especially for individuals who identified as lesbian, gay, or bisexual.

As these diverse findings attest, adolescents use no single standard to certify particular activities as sex. Consequently, two different adolescents with identical sexual histories might check different boxes on a questionnaire asking whether they had "had sex." This methodological conundrum was lucidly critiqued by Frye (1990), who emphasized the impossibility of comparing heterosexual and lesbian respondents' answers to the seemingly simply question, "How often do you have sex?"

> [Some lesbians] might have counted a two- or three-cycle evening as one "time" they "had sex"; some might have counted it as two or three "times." Some may have counted as "times" only the times both partners had orgasms; some may have counted as "times" occasions on which at least one had an orgasm; those who do not have orgasms or have them far more rarely than they "have sex" may not have figured orgasms into the calculations; perhaps some counted as a "time" every episode in which both touched the other's vulva more than fleetingly and not for something like a health examination. . . . But this also raises the questions of how heterosexuals counted their sexual acts. By orgasm? By whose orgasms? If the havings of sex by heterosexual married couples did take on the average eight minutes, my guess is that in a very large number of those cases the women did not experience orgasms. (p. 244)

In response to such problems, some have called for more systematic specificity in survey language (Schwarz, 1999), whereas others have argued that quantitative tabulations of specific sexual acts be supplemented with qualitative interview data assessing how youth define and give meaning to different forms of sexual expression (Tolman, 2002). Although numerous researchers have, in fact, accepted the challenge of conducting nuanced and labor-intensive interviews with youth about their subjective experiences and interpretations of sexual desires, fantasies, and behaviors (Fine, 1988; Savin-Williams, 1998, 2003b; Thompson, 1995; Tolman, 2002), such research receives far less attention than do large-scale surveys of sexual activity and contraceptive use because no "hard data" about risky and problematic behavior are generated that preoccupy policy makers and media outlets. Nonetheless, such qualitative data are critical for translating information on adolescents' sexual acts into meaningful, multifaceted models of adolescent sexual experience that productively inform efforts to promote psychological and sexual health from childhood to adulthood.

The diverse and multifaceted meanings that adolescents attach to their sexual feelings and behaviors have also been largely uninvestigated, save for general observations about the greater attention to affectional components of sexuality among women than men (Diamond, 2003b). Savin-Williams's (1998) qualitative study of sexual-minority young men illustrates the importance of assessing the meanings attached to behaviors. As children and early adolescents, most were not troubled by their pursuit of same-sex activities because they attributed them to simple curiosity and pleasure seeking. Although some had a nagging feeling that they were more into the same-sex encounters than they ought to be, it was primarily during adolescence proper that same-sex experiences began to mean something about their sexual identity. Clearly, simple tabulation of isolated behaviors reveals relatively little about the changing meanings of these behaviors for psychosocial development.

Perhaps the most critical contribution of investigating sexual meanings is that in addition to pinpointing discrepancies in adolescents' conceptualizations of sexual activity, such research helps reveal the sources of these conceptualizations, which in turn provide indispensable information on how different youth reason about sexual activity, the numerous factors impinging on their symbolic interpretations of sexuality, and the multilayered web of sexual cognitions shaping their affective responses to sexual interactions. For example, what constellation of personal, social, and cultural factors renders one youth's interpretation of pleasurable same-sex activity—and its ramifications for sexual identity—different from another's perspective? Whereas prior sex research has been overwhelmingly preoccupied with the onset and progression of specific behaviors, it is also clearly important to investigate the onset and progression of adolescents' cognitive conceptions and affective responses to different forms of sexual expression, and how these trajectories of sexual meaning are moderated by sex, ethnicity, relationship status, sexual orientation, and family background.

Who Is Studied? Target Populations, Sampling Problems, and Missing Data

Another problem facing researchers concerns which adolescents constitute the research samples. At the broadest level, we lack systematic cross-cultural data on adolescent sexuality that would provide important correctives to ill-informed speculations about which behaviors and developmental timetables are natural for adolescents. In this regard, Schlegel and Barry's (1991) compilation of cross-cultural data culled from a diverse array of ethnographies is particularly valuable and unique. Their review highlights the incredible variability in adolescent sexual behavior across different cultures, as well as the remarkable diversity in adults' expectations regarding adolescent sexuality. Whereas some societies forestall adolescent heterosexual experimentation altogether by segregating the sexes as soon as they reach puberty, others permit and even encourage noncoital experimentation, as long as pregnancy is avoided. Clearly, numerous ways exist to conceptualize and manage adolescent sexuality, many of which can be legitimately considered normal and natural. However, little contemporary research and discourse on adolescent sexuality takes such variability into account.

Within U.S. culture, identification of study populations is additionally problematic. In a notable contrast to virtually all other areas of research on adolescence, investigations of adolescent sexuality (especially studies of sexual decision making, contraception, and safer sex) have focused disproportionately on girls—particularly poor girls and girls of color (Fordham, 1993; Tolman & Higgins, 1996), reflecting the widespread notion that girls are the gatekeepers of adolescent sexuality and are therefore the primary sites for investigations of sexual risk and intervention (Thompson, 1995; Tolman, 2002) and that sexuality is more of a problem for poor and ethnic-minority youth than for privileged European American youth. Although data suggest that these groups do, in fact, often pursue riskier sexual trajectories than do wealthy European American youth, the reductionist nature of most sex research precludes sensitive analyses of the multiple mechanisms mediating this association. Thus, the pathways through which subsets of adolescents track different patterns of sexual behavior remain insufficiently elaborated, leaving only broad-based stereotypes about race, poverty, and sex, as well as ill-informed assumptions about which adolescents need intervention.

Systematic inattention to sexual-minority adolescents has been another persistent problem. Note that we use the phrase *sexual minority* rather than *lesbian, gay,* or *bisexual,* reflecting our view that adolescents with desires for or experiences with same-sex partners deserve systematic attention regardless of how they label their sexual identity. Nonetheless, few studies of adolescent sexuality bother to ask respondents about same-sex behavior, orientation, and identity, and some distinctly exclude youth with same-sex attractions or relationships on the basis that their experiences cannot be meaningfully compared with those of heterosexuals (regarding romantic relationships, see Savin-Williams, 2003a). In reality, we have little empirical basis on which to make such presumptions. Although research on sexual-minority youth has increased dramatically during the past two decades, few investigators have systematically compared the normative social-developmental experiences of sexual-minority and heterosexual youth, and few have integrated what is known about adolescent same-sex sexuality with what is known about adolescent cross-sex sexuality (Diamond, 2002). Rather, research programs have progressed on parallel, independent tracks, as if these populations are so fundamentally distinct from one another as to render any comparisons meaningless. In reality, research increasingly suggests that boundaries between gay and straight are relatively plastic, and this may be particularly true during the adolescent years (Diamond, 2002, 2003a, 2003b). Unless researchers systematically ask heterosexual-identified youth about same-sex experiences and lesbian-, gay-, and bisexual-identified youth about cross-sex experiences, our understanding of both phenomena will remain impoverished.

Across many samples, adolescents who are uncomfortable with discussing sexual matters or self-conscious about their pattern of sexual experience—whether they view it as too much, too little, too early, too late, or too weird—self-select themselves out of such studies, or their parents do it for them by denying parental consent (Trivedi & Sabini, 1998; Wiederman, 1999). Thus, accurate snapshots of the full range of contemporary adolescents' sexual lives are exceedingly difficult to obtain. Fortunately, we can systematically examine sampling-problems bias by comparing findings from smaller studies with large-scale investigations, such as the National Longitudinal Study of

Adolescent Health, or Add Health (www.cpc.unc.edu/projects/addhealth), a random, representative survey of American adolescents. A notable strength of this study is that it asks *all* youth to report on attractions and romantic relationships with females and males.

Even in the largest, most representative studies, however, missing data present a substantial problem. As every researcher knows, respondents frequently skip questions they do not understand or feel uncomfortable answering, and different investigators handle this problem in different ways. Some delete data of all respondents providing incomplete responses; others select by question, so that analyses are conducted with different subsets of the total sample. When the amount of missing data is small and not systematically related to key variables of interest, differences between these strategies are likely to have little import. In sexuality research, however, it is not uncommon to have sizable missing data on the most sensitive and important information. Imputation of missing data is typically recommended in such cases (Tabachnick & Fidell, 2001), and computer programs for validly conducting such imputations have become increasingly sophisticated and easy to use (Schafer & Graham, 2002). However, few adolescent researchers use such techniques or test whether missing data are disproportionately likely among younger versus older respondents, males versus females, or those with less versus more sexual experience. Given the sensitivity of questions about sexual matters, missing data are likely to be a more significant and systematic problem than for most other areas of social scientific research, yet the extent to which the data problem has systematically biased extant research findings on adolescent sexuality remains unknown.

How Is Sex Studied?

The overwhelming majority of sex research relies on self-reports of sexual feelings and behaviors, and the limitations of this methodology are well known (Schwarz, 1999). In addition to problems with vaguely worded questions about "having sex" and the underutilization of in-depth, qualitative interviews, is the straightforward problem of validity: How do we know whether reports of sexual behavior are accurate? Several investigators have used longitudinal assessments to examine the veracity of adolescent reports of sexual behavior. Based on the first two waves of Add Health data, only 22% of sexually experienced youth reported the same date of first sex (Upchurch, Lillard, Aneshensel, & Li, 2002). Most revised the date to an older age. Over one in ten reclaimed virginity status with Asian Americans of both sexes most likely to "become" virgins. Newcomer and Udry (1988) found that during the second wave of data collection, 10% of respondents reported having misrepresented their behavior at Time 1. Specifically, boys tended to overreport the amount of sex they had, whereas girls tended to say that they were virgins when they were not. Similar sex differences have been reported in other studies. Siegel, Aten, and Roghmann (1998) found that 8% of high school girls understated their sexual experience, whereas 14% of boys overstated their sexual experience. This reflects an awareness that sexual behavior means something about them in the eyes of peers, parents, and society at large (Catania, 1999; Schwarz, 1999). Boys may exaggerate sexual activity to measure up to perceived standards of sexual prowess, whereas girls minimize sexual experiences so as not to appear irresponsible or promiscuous (Catania, 1999; Siegel et al., 1998).

Further complicating matters is the fact that responses to questions about sexual behavior vary according to methods used to ask those questions. A comparison of the 1990 and 2000 national surveys of British sexual behavior (Copas et al., 2002) found that use of a computer-assisted self-interviewing format (CASI) elicited higher reports of sensitive sexual behavior than did face-to-face interviews. Adult women's reports of same-sex behavior increased from 7% to 9.7% and men's from 6.7% to 8.4% when CASI was used in lieu of interviews. Among adolescents, reports of same-sex manual stimulation, oral stimulation, and receptive anal sex were all substantially higher with CASI than with self-administered questionnaires (Turner, Miller, & Rogers, 1997). We are not advocating the elimination of questionnaires, but they should be modified to accentuate ease of response, clarity, nonjudgmental wording, and assurances of confidentiality. In studies employing these modifications, girls are more likely to disclose sexual activity and boys to admit that they are virgins (Catania, 1999).

Irregularities in self-reports are also influenced by qualities of the adolescents and their environments. Youth of different cohorts and educational levels or with different types of family, community, economic, and cultural backgrounds might have remarkably different motives for concealing and revealing aspects of their sexual lives (Catania, 1999; Oliver & Hyde, 1993). Older adolescents are generally more embarrassed than are younger adolescents about being virgins—and thus more likely to misrepresent this fact (Carpenter, 2001). With regard to ethnicity, Latina female adolescents might feel pressure to adhere to *simpatía,* which involves pleasing others and being likable, and might therefore underestimate sexual activities that violate family or peer expectations. A Latino male adolescent, by contrast, might feel pressure to conform to *machismo,* involving hypermasculine appearance, stalwart rejection of homosexuality, and grandiose assessments of heterosexual behavior.

It is important to note, however, that not all inaccuracies stem from dishonesty or willful misrepresentation. Some youth believe they are being accurate but have memory errors due to the length of time over which they are asked to recollect, or their responses merely represent individual differences in cognition or socioemotional development that impinge on the capacity for contemporaneous or recollected self-reflection (Catania, 1999). Others, owing to variations in personal meanings and definitions assigned to sexual activity, might simply misunderstand the questions asked of them (Goodson et al., 1997).

Finally, practically every study conducted on adolescent sexuality has treated the individual as the unit of analysis (Wright, 1998), even though partnered sexual interactions are inherently dyadic phenomena (see reliability data in Ochs & Binik, 1999). Thus, in attempting to predict an adolescent's pattern of sexual activity from his or her personality, motives, environment, or personal history, we are effectively assuming that sexual partners are blank slates without personalities, motives, environments, or personal histories of their own. Of course, the well-known problem of statistical nonindependence between reports of partners in a dyad has historically made it difficult to conduct valid and interpretable dyadic analyses (Gable & Reis, 1999). In recent years, however, techniques for analyzing dyadic and other forms of nested data, such as structural equation modeling and hierarchical linear modeling, have become more widely accessible. Such techniques make it possible, for example, to test hypotheses about the degree to which each adolescent's personal characteristics contribute to characteristics of the sexual dyad (e.g., latency to begin sexual activity within a particular relationship). Greater attention to these sophisticated and informative analyses is likely to become increasingly important in sex research.

One of these personal characteristics that requires investigation is the degree of sexual desire, which might well interact with a partner's characteristics. For example, Pat's religiosity might moderate the influence of Chris's sexual motivation on their joint sexual activity. Although sexual desire is obviously a critical component of sexuality, researchers studying child and adolescent sexual development have devoted scant attention to it (Tolman & Diamond, 2001).

SEXUAL DESIRE

Sexual desire is often presumed to be a fairly uniform experience propelling adolescents toward a diverse array of sexual behaviors, much the same way that hunger is presumed to be a uniform experience propelling one toward a diverse array of foods. This presumption has circumscribed the types of questions asked about adolescents' desires and the manner in which they are asked. Thus, although data are available on first sexual desire, we do not have sufficiently detailed information on the subjective quality of this experience for systematically modeling trajectories of sexual motivation from childhood to young adulthood or to understand their links to sexual behavior.

Such blind spots reflect the tendency for developmental researchers to emphasize the nuts and bolts of sexual maturation at the expense of investigating the experiential aspects of this process (Brooks-Gunn & Paikoff, 1997). They also expose society's deep-seated ambivalence regarding early manifestations of sexuality and the need to control and monitor sexual behavior rather than promote positive sexual self-concepts (Fine, 1988). If the overarching goal of research is simply to prevent risky sexual behaviors, then questions about the subjective quality of a youth's desires might appear to be irrelevant. We, of course, disagree. A brief review of what is and is not known about the development of sexual desire suggests that this may be one of the most promising areas for future research on adolescent sexuality.

What Is Desire and When Does It Start?

Although a considerable debate rages regarding how to define sexual desire, most investigators subscribe to a conceptualization resembling the following: "an interest in sexual objects or activities or a wish, need, or drive to seek out sexual objects or to engage in sexual activities" (Regan & Berscheid, 1995, p. 346). Note, however, that this definition combines two phenomena that are not entirely equivalent: an *interest* in sexual objects and a drive to *seek* sexual objects. This subtle but critical distinction is well known to those familiar with the sexual behavior of nonhuman primates (Hrdy, 1987), but it rarely receives substantive attention in discussions of human sexuality (Bancroft, 1989; H. E. Fisher, 1998; Wallen, 1995). These two types of sexual desires are denoted *proceptivity,* the basic urge to seek and initiate sexual activity, and *receptivity* (arousability), the capacity to become interested in sex when encountering certain eliciting stimuli (Bancroft, 1989; Beach, 1976; Wallen, 1995). It is important to note that although variability in proceptive sexual desire is tightly linked to variability in gonadal hormones (specifically, testosterone in men and both testosterone and estrogen in women), variability in arousability is not (reviewed in Tolman & Diamond, 2001).

This difference might explain the fact that although sharp increases in pubertal gonadal hormone levels correspond to sharp increases in the frequency and intensity of self-reported sexual desires (Halpern, Udry, Campbell, & Suchindran, 1993; Udry & Billy, 1987; Udry, Talbert, & Morris, 1986), this is not the onset of sexual desire. Children report first awareness of sexual desires and attractions as early as 9 years, perhaps linked to the maturation of the adrenal gland (McClintock & Herdt, 1996), and some experiment with self-stimulation as early as 6 (Friedrich, Grambsch, Broughton, Kuiper, & Beilke, 1991). Perhaps these early childhood experiences of desire (and occasionally sexual behavior) stem from hormone-independent arousability, whereas the classic pubertal surges in self-reported sexual desire reflect the hormonally mediated development of proceptivity. If so, this supports McClintock and Herdt's (1996) argument that sexuality does not suddenly turn on at puberty but develops over the course of childhood and adolescence through a subtle and gradual intertwining of erotic and social experiences. Specifically, the existing literature on distinctions between arousability and proceptivity suggests that although young children might become aroused in response to erotic stimuli, they seldom experience strong urges to act on those feelings until puberty.

It is difficult to test this model because so little information is available on how early sexual feelings are experienced. In fact, we cannot even be sure that adolescents are describing the same thing when they talk about sexual desire, given that few studies provide participants with an operationalization of desire or solicit qualitative descriptions of these feelings and the contexts in which they were experienced. Correspondingly, little is known about whether developmental changes exist in subjective experiences of desire and whether such transitions have implications for understanding developmental transitions in sexual behavior.

Sex Differences in Desire

Such information might be particularly valuable for understanding well-documented sex differences in sexuality. As reviewed by Baumeister, Catanese, and Vohs (2001), empirical data (as well as conventional wisdom) have long suggested that women experience less frequent and insistent sexual desires than do men. Although the vast majority of this research has focused on adults, data indicate that these differences are also observed during childhood and adolescence. For example, regardless of sexual orientation, boys become aware of their sexual interests and impulses several years earlier than girls do (Knoth, Boyd, & Singer, 1988; Savin-Williams & Diamond, 2000), and boys report more frequent sexual arousal (several times a day versus once a week). Boys also report their sexual arousal to be more intense and distracting than do girls (Knoth et al., 1988).

The origin of such differences remains a topic of active debate. Are there, in fact, biologically mediated sex differences in the objective strength and intensity of sexual desires, perhaps stemming from differences in circulating androgen levels, or is it simply that sociocultural norms discourage women from acknowledging or attending to their experiences of sexual arousal? Research using physiological measures of genital blood flow has found that women often show distinct discrepancies between their degree of physical arousal and their subjective feelings of arousal (Heiman, 1975). This is consistent with the finding that less than 50% of female teenagers report that they can always detect their sexual arousal, compared to 90% of male teenagers (Knoth et al., 1988).

Of course, sex differences in sexual desire might have both biological and sociocultural origins (Tolman & Diamond, 2001). For example, Wallen's (1995) review of nonhuman primate behavior suggested that because of fluctuating estrogen levels, arousability (rather than hormone-dependent proceptivity) may play a greater role in structuring female than male sexuality. If this model holds for humans as well, it might explain why situation and context appear to play a greater role in structuring women's than men's sexual desires and behaviors. In his review of the literature, Baumeister (2000) found considerable empirical evidence suggesting that female sexuality is more malleable and mutable than male sexuality, meaning that it is more responsive to cultural and social factors, more subject to change in response to external circumstances, and more variable within the life course of any particular woman. Among the voluminous evidence he marshaled in support of this view were data indicating that women show less consistency between their sexual attitudes and behaviors (because women's sensitivity to situational context leads them to act in ways that contradict their attitudes) and evidence that women show greater temporal and developmental variation than men in what they desire (type of sex partner and activity), their degree of desire (frequency of sex and fantasy), and the way they express their desires (patterns of sexual activity). Adolescent girls are thus more likely to have sexual experiences contrary to their sexual orientation, to alter and enjoy different kinds of sexuality, and to change sexualities (*fluidity;* Diamond, 1998, 2000a, 2003a).

The notion that female sexuality is more contextual than male sexuality—and particularly dependent on interpersonal relationships—has reached the status of conventional wisdom. When college students were asked what they thought "caused" sexual desire (Regan & Berscheid, 1995), the most widely endorsed causes of male sexual desire were biological processes and a physical need for sex. By contrast, the most widely endorsed causes of female sexual desire were interpersonal experiences related to romantic love. Similarly, more sexual-minority women than men reported that first awareness of same-sex desires occurred in the context of strong emotional bonds (Diamond, 2003b). Perhaps such differences reflect both the cultural pressures on women to restrict sexual activity to affectional contexts and women's heightened sensitivity to situational aspects of sexual experience. Longitudinally tracking experiences of both proceptive and receptive sexual desires from childhood to adulthood would provide a fruitful means to investigate this possibility.

Such research would also allow for systematic investigation of within-sex variability in desire, another topic that has been woefully understudied in developmental research on sexuality. Although numerous studies have focused on within-sex variability in the timing of pubertal maturation, variability in the outcomes of maturation—at least with respect to sexual urges and arousability—has received scant attention. As noted earlier, this reflects the implicit (but incorrect) presumption that sexual desire is a relatively uniform substrate for sexuality that is simply turned on at puberty. Nevertheless, some adolescents have more frequent and intense sexual desires and fantasies than do other same-sex peers (Udry, 1990); far too little is known about the origin of such interindividual differences, their longitudinal stability, and their implications for sexual behavior over the life course. Investigating such questions requires longitudinal assessments of links between children's changing hormone levels, social experiences, sociocultural environments, and the quality and context of sexual feelings. Such data might be difficult (if not impossible) to collect in the face of the political, financial, and logistical obstacles that continue to hinder developmental research on adolescent sexuality.

SEXUAL MOTIVES

Sexual desire is one thing; behavior is quite another. Numerous reasons exist for why adolescents do or do not pursue sexual activity, and understanding these motivations, as well as the factors that facilitate or obstruct them, is critical to a systematic analysis of adolescent sexual development. Quite tellingly, sexual *intentions* are among the strongest predictors of an adolescent's future sexual *behavior* (Kinsman, Romer, Furstenberg, & Schwartz, 1998). Furthermore, intraindividual and interindividual differences in adolescents' motives for pursuing sex are systematically related to the *types* of sexual contact pursued with committed versus casual partners, with few versus many partners, with planned versus unplanned sex, and with protected versus unprotected sex (Cooper, Shapiro, & Powers, 1998; Levinson, Jaccard, & Beamer, 1995).

Perhaps the most obvious motive for sexual activity is sexual desire. As noted, although pubertal hormonal changes do not create sexual desire and arousal de novo, they do imbue sexual feelings with newfound force and impetus. In addition, postpubertal adolescents receive multiple social cues from parents, peers, and the media that they are now supposed to desire and seek sexual activity. They may consequently become increasingly attuned to the vicissitudes in their own states of sexual arousal. Thus, straightforward sexual release is clearly a salient motive for adolescent sexual activity. Masturbation can also provide such release, without incurring risks associated with partnered sexual activity. However, sex educators and youth advocates are generally wary of making this argument publicly—after all, in 1994 former United States Surgeon General Joycelyn Elders lost her job for doing so.

Obviously, however, sexual desire is not the only reason adolescents seek sexual activity. Another important motivation, particularly with regard to the initial forays of youth into sexual behavior, is straightforward curiosity, fueled in part by the heavy emphasis and tolerance for progressively more explicit depictions and discussions of sexuality in mainstream films, television shows, and the Internet (Brown, 2002). Other than friends and parents, the media are often sources for how adolescents learn about sexuality (Sutton, Brown, Wilson, & Klein, 2002). Although the media provide considerable and increasing exposure to adolescents about sex, little is known about how the media actually affect adolescent sexual behavior (Brown, 2002). Ward and Rivadeneyra (1999) found that television likely shapes adolescent sexual behavior indirectly, by first depicting permissible sexual attitudes, normative expectations, and a view of sexual reality. Media may also trigger sexual curiosity at progressively earlier ages—if everybody is talking about it and apparently doing it, it must be pretty incredible!

Different cultures cope with this sexual curiosity in a variety of ways (Schlegel &

Barry, 1991). Some ensure that pubertal boys and girls have no contact whatsoever with each other, effectively preventing curiosity and desire from spilling over into actual sexual contact. Others provide safe spaces for youth to experiment with noncoital sexual activity, while enforcing strict prohibitions on premarital coitus. Schlegel and Barry (1991) noted that contemporary American society attempts a tricky balance between these two approaches, permitting extensive unsupervised contact among adolescents while simultaneously denouncing the sexual experimentation that inevitably arises under such circumstances.

The achievement of social status is another important motive for adolescent sexual contact, signaling to oneself and others the realization of a much-desired adult sexual status (O'Sullivan, Meyer-Bahlburg, & Watkins, 2000; Paikoff, 1995). Notably, among girls it is often not just sexual activity that confers popularity and mature status, but the entire complex of relationship phenomena that sex is associated with, such as having a boyfriend and being in love (O'Sullivan & Meyer-Bahlburg, 2003; Simon, Eder, & Evans, 1992). Thus, regardless of whether adolescents encounter implicit or explicit peer pressure to engage in sex, they may be motivated to pursue such activity simply to stay on course with what they perceive to be the normative sexual-developmental schedule. For example, urban 6th grade students who initiated sexual intercourse during the school year were disproportionately likely to believe that most of their friends were already experienced and to associate sexual activity with social gains (Kinsman et al., 1998). Having sex might also function to establish independence from parents or to signal rejection of parental, religious, or community norms. In such cases, the strength or frequency of sexual desires might be a nonissue.

Romantic relationships also provide numerous motives and opportunities for sexual activity. Perhaps most obviously, romantic relationships afford frequent occasions to become sexually aroused and to act on those desires, consistent with the fact that the earlier and more frequently youth date, the earlier and more frequently they engage in sexual activity (Bearman & Bruckner, 1999; Blum et al., 2000; Halpern, Joyner, et al., 2000; Whitbeck et al., 1999). In addition, the more emotionally committed an adolescent's romantic relationship, the more likely he or she is to pursue a range of sexual behaviors with the partner (Miller & Benson, 1999). However, it is difficult to determine whether the emotional feelings that youth experience in these relationships are themselves sexual motivators or whether they simply provide an appropriate context in which to act on sexual feelings. Although it is commonly expected in U.S. culture that romantic and affectionate feelings precede thinking about and pursuing sex with a partner (Miller & Benson, 1999; Smith, 1994), little systematic data exist on the extent to which this is true, reflecting the overall dearth of research on the psychological and biobehavioral links between experiences of emotional affection and sexual desire (Diamond, 2003b). Miller and Benson (1999) argued that the role of emotional intimacy as a motivator for sex is changing and that, conversely, adolescents are increasingly using body-centered sexual experiences as a means of establishing intimacy. Although no systematic research on this hypothesis exists, paradoxically, youth view sexual activity at an early age to be more acceptable within a serious than a casual relationship but *in practice* engage in sexual activity earlier within casual than serious relationships (Feldman, Turner, & Araujo, 1999).

Romantic relationships are particularly critical for understanding adolescent girls' sexual activity. Young women are more likely than young men to describe love and affection as causes of sexual desire (Regan & Berscheid, 1995) and intimate relationships as providing a more motivating context for their sexual activity. For example, Zani (1991) found that the vast majority of Italian girls had their first coitus with a boy they were dating for approximately 8 months; few followed the boys' pattern of having first coitus as an episode with a casual partner. Studies of both heterosexuals and sexual minorities indicate that young women are more likely than young men to associate sexual activity with relationship phenomena, such as love and commitment (Blumstein & Schwarz, 1983; Oliver & Hyde, 1993; Peplau & Garnets, 2000; Rodríguez Rust, 2000; Rose, 2000; Rothblum, 2000), to report that emotional involvement is a prerequisite for sex (Carroll, Volk, & Hyde, 1985), and to engage in sex in order to enhance emotional intimacy (Brigman & Knox, 1992). Boys, too, perceive sex as a relationship-building activity but are more likely to emphasize the role of its physical pleasure (Frazier & Esterly, 1990).

Some have argued that these sex differences are increasingly narrowing (Smith, 1994). For example, both male and female teenagers report seeking both physical pleasure and emotional intimacy from sexual activity (Kalof, 1995). Feldman et al. (1999, p. 46) argued that relationships may be more important motivators for younger rather than older girls because "with age and experience, women may become comfortable with their sexuality and no longer need to justify sexual activity by referring to an important or serious relationship." Perhaps conversely, boys are more likely to emphasize relationship motives for sexual activity as they mature, as both the novelty of sexual contact and its implications for social status wane and as they become more adept at forming and maintaining intimate romantic relationships.

Finally, research suggests that many adolescents pursue sexual activity as an emotion-regulating mechanism that attenuates or distracts them from negative emotions and helps them cope with troublesome events (Brigman & Knox, 1992; Levinson et al., 1995). Although such motives are not as common as intimacy- or pleasure-based motives for sexual activity, they deserve substantive attention given that adolescents with emotion-regulation motives are less likely to pursue sexual activity within committed relationships and tend to have a greater number of sexual partners and riskier sexual practices (Cooper et al., 1998). Emotion-regulating motives for sex are particularly important when considering the well-established correlations between compromised family and community environments and problematic adolescent sexual behavior (Miller et al., 1997). Specifically, adolescents whose environments have provided them with few opportunities to master emotion regulation skills, or whose exposure to environmental stressors regularly overwhelms their emotion regulation capacities, might be particularly likely to turn to sexual activity (as well as other mood-regulating behaviors such as substance use) to manage day-to-day negative emotions. Female youth with inadequate emotional support might construe both early sex *and* early motherhood—whether consciously or unconsciously—as routes to emotional closeness and nurturance (Musick, 1993).

With the multiple interacting underpinnings of sexuality more clearly in focus, we can more capably interpret the extant data on what contemporary adolescents are actually *doing* sexually, as well as the numerous factors that influence their sexual behavior—from autoerotic activity to same-sex sexuality—from childhood through young adulthood.

THE STATE OF ADOLESCENT SEX

A *New York Times* headline announcing "More in High School Are Virgins" (Lewin, 2002) advertises recent views of virginity's comeback. During the last decade, the proportion of adolescents who report sexual intercourse dropped from 51% to 43% among girls and from 57% to 49% among boys, and the linear decrease was notable at all grade levels (Centers for Disease Control, 2002). However, the methodological problems noted earlier, the incorporation of other sexual behaviors in lieu of coitus, and the progressive decoupling of sex and marriage likely attenuate virginity's resurgence. Indeed, far more sexual activity appears to be taking place between today's teenagers than ever before. Reiss (1967) argued that sexual attitudes and behavior have shifted from an emphasis on premarital abstinence toward embracing a standard of permissiveness with affection (i.e., sexual activity between adolescents is acceptable if they like or love each other). Overall, many social institutions—from families to churches to schools to governments—have become more tolerant of adolescent sexual behavior and have reduced sanctions against it. These attitudinal changes have been accompanied by social structural changes concerning sex equality, constructions of the family, and reductions in parental supervision (Hopkins, 2000).

When contemplating sexual behavior, it is critical to consider the sexes separately. In general, adolescent boys are more likely than girls to have sexually permissive attitudes, to be sexually experienced at earlier ages, to have more sex (including same-sex behavior), to have had sex more recently, to count more sex partners, and to have a variety of comparatively unusual sexual experiences (Browning, Kessler, Hatfield, & Choo, 1999; Centers for Disease Control, 2002; Manlove et al., 2001). Although mean age differences between the sexes have decreased, the proportion of adolescent boys with sexual experience is generally equal to that of girls one year older (Alan Guttmacher Institute, 1994). Young women report more guilt about sex and more often endorse the old-fashioned double standard of sexual behavior. No consistent sex differences have been reported for sexual satisfaction and many noncoital behaviors. Furthermore, sex differences are decreasing in many aspects of sexual behavior, including premarital sex attitudes, number of sex partners, frequency of sexual intercourse, and masturbation (Oliver & Hyde, 1993; Sawyer & Smith, 1996).

Although research on these historic changes and their implications for adolescent health and development has focused on sexual intercourse, it is important to consider the full range of sexual behaviors that youth pursue from childhood through adolescence, their developmental context, and the ways in which they are interpreted and experienced. This broad perspective is particularly valuable given recent discussions regarding whether the encouragement of noncoital sexual activity might be an effective strategy for helping adolescents delay coitus and therefore reduce risks for pregnancy and STDs (Genius & Genius, 1996; Kegan, 1996). We therefore begin with a discussion of autoerotic activity in childhood and adolescence and then discuss noncoital partnered activity, coitus, and same-sex behavior.

Autoerotic Activity

Exceptionally little is known about prepubertal solitary sexual activities, making it difficult to determine what a normative developmental trajectory of autoerotic behavior looks like from childhood through puberty and young adulthood. The limited empirical data available suggest that children of both sexes and all sexual orientations exhibit a variety of solitary sexual behaviors, often at relatively high frequencies. A retrospective study of Swedish high school seniors (Larsson & Svedin, 2002) found that by age 12, more than three fourths reported that they had engaged in autoerotic activities, including self-examination, self-stimulation, and viewing sexually explicit pictures or videos. Nearly twice as many boys than girls had masturbated and reached orgasm. Studies of U.S. children have found fewer instances of autoerotic activity, perhaps because of methodological differences. Relying on mothers' reports of sexual behavior (Friedrich et al., 1991), 11% of 6- to 12-year-olds had masturbated by hand or object, although a much larger percentage (36% of boys and 18% of girls) had "touched their sex parts at home."

Despite this evidence, most adolescents and adults believe that the normative and acceptable time to initiate such activities is puberty (Bauserman & Davis, 1996). Certainly, rates of masturbation increase with age. In a representative sample of 8th to 10th graders, Udry (1988) found that 32% of boys and 26% of girls reported masturbation; among 18- to 24-year olds, these figures rose to 61% of men and 36% of women (Laumann et al., 1994). However, prevalence estimates vary considerably, with respondents far more likely to report adolescent masturbation when asked about it retrospectively. For example, one study (Halpern, Udry, Suchindran, & Campbell, 2000) found that less than one third of 13-year-old boys reported masturbating. When these boys were reinterviewed as young adults, however, more than twice as many admitted having masturbated during early adolescence. Adolescents are more likely to skip or give inconsistent responses to questions about masturbation than about any other sexual activity, reflecting the pervasive stigma attached to this activity (Rodgers, Billy, & Udry, 1982). Indeed, nearly 60% of young adults felt guilty after masturbation (Laumann et al., 1994), and over 80% of adolescents in another study viewed masturbation as a harmful activity (Halpern et al., 1993). One of the worst insults a Greek adolescent can hurl at another is to say the equivalent of "you masturbate" (Papadopoulos, Stamboulides, & Triantafillou, 2000).

We do not know exactly why youth hold these attitudes, although some youth believe that admitting to masturbation means that they are not having real sex, are oversexed, or are out of control (Halpern, Udry, et al., 2000)—or whether these attitudes are related to the messages parents give children (implicitly or explicitly) about masturbation. Without such information, it is difficult to interpret the relevance of these behaviors and variations in their onset and frequency for adolescents' developing sexual self-concepts. However, one consistent pattern with a long history that has emerged is that more boys than girls, from childhood through young adulthood, report masturbating (Kinsey, Pomeroy, & Martin, 1948; Kinsey, Pomeroy, Martin, & Gebhard, 1953; Laumann et al., 1994). In their review of the literature on sexual behavior, Oliver and Hyde (1993) noted that sex differences in masturbation were among the largest and most reliable in the empirical literature. In one study of college students (Schwartz, 1999), 15% of males reported never having masturbated, compared with 63% of females (see also Larsson & Svedin, 2002; Weinburg et al., 1995). Notably, these studies found few or no sex differences in rates of partnered noncoital activities, such as kissing and oral sex. These findings suggest that women's sexual drives are just as strong and persistent as men's and that their lower rates of masturbation reflect the fact that this activity is disproportionately stigmatized for women. One might argue instead that women's low rates of masturbation do in fact reflect their generally weaker sex drives (Baumeister et al., 2001) but that adolescent girls tend to go along with what their partners want regarding partnered sexual activity.

Research has found that pubertal increases in sexual thoughts and masturbation (but not coitus) are associated with increases in female levels of the adrenal androgens dehydroepiandrosterone (DHEA) and delta-4 androstenedione (D4AD; Udry et al., 1986), suggesting that girls' rates of masturbation are at least partially attributable to their hormonally mediated sexual motivation. Without systematic qualitative data on adolescents' sexual motives and experiences of autoerotic activity, however, it is impossible to interpret the extent to which variations in these activities reflect individuals' personal desires versus social controls and norms.

Partnered, Noncoital Activity

Similar to solitary sexual activities, partnered sexual activities prior to adolescence are common but seldom documented. Okami et al. (1997) reported that almost half of young adult women and men had engaged in interactive sexual activities (excluding solitary masturbation) prior to age 6. In another sample, three quarters of both sexes had engaged in sex before age 12 (Larsson & Svedin, 2002). The most frequent activities included talking about sex, kissing and hugging, watching or reading pornography (primarily boys), and humping or feigning intercourse. Masturbating with a friend was reported by 14% of boys and 7% of girls. Even less common were showing one's genitals, watching others in a sexual way, having another child touch one's genitals, and exploring another child's genitals. The most sexually explicit activities—vaginal, anal, oral, and object intercourse—were reported by less than 5% of children.

What is the meaning and developmental relevance of these activities? Limited empirical evidence suggests that if an early onset of partnered sexual contact (whether with the same or other sex) is not experienced as abusive or coercive, then it has a positive impact on adolescent and adult sexual arousal, pleasure, satisfaction, and acceptance of various sexual behaviors for self and others (Bauserman & Davis, 1996; Rind, 2001; Sandfort, 1992; Savin-Williams, 1998, 2003b). Of course, given the degree of sex negativity in U.S. culture, not all adults view these as desirable outcomes. As for general social adjustment, little evidence suggests that childhood sex is associated with either developmental benefits or deficits (Okami et al., 1997), yet this topic has received little systematic study.

Clearly, to understand the role of childhood sex in adolescent sexual and social development, we need data on which children engage in such activities, the context in which they are pursued, and the personal meanings of these activities for the children involved. Given the difficulties conducting research on childhood sexuality, it may be some time before answers are obtained. Until that time, data reviewed by Okami et al. (1997) advise caution in interpreting children's sexual activity. Although it seems intuitive to view such behaviors as rehearsals for pubertal sexual behavior, no direct empirical support exists for this interpretation. An alternative possibility is that childhood sexual activity is an altogether different phenomenon than pubertal sexual activity, with developmentally specific motives, qualities, and functions corresponding to children's social, cognitive, and biological maturation.

As for adolescent noncoital sexual activity, the scant research suggests that it is fairly widespread: One study found that over 80% of youth had participated in noncoital, partnered sexual activities (typically mutual masturbation and oral-genital contact) before age 16 (Bauserman & Davis, 1996). Over 60% of such activities were pursued with partners of roughly the same age, and 92% were heterosexual in nature. Do adolescents engage in such behaviors as a lead-up to intercourse? This has certainly been a longstanding assumption among both researchers and adolescents alike. Empirical data directly addressing this question are contained in the Add Health survey for first incidences of various behaviors, which suggest the following sequence: holding hands, kissing, necking (kissing for a long time), feeling breasts over clothes, feeling breasts under clothes or with no clothes on, feeling a penis over clothes, feeling a penis under clothes or with no clothes on, feeling a vagina over clothes, feeling a vagina under clothes or with no clothes on, and engaging in penile-vaginal intercourse (Halpern, Joyner, et al., 2000). Whether this progression characterizes a particular encounter or represents a series of unfolding activities across many encounters is undocumented.

In addition, this sequence may not be complete. Most notably missing, but included in other sequences, are oral sex (Rosenthal & Smith, 1997; Weinberg, Lottes, & Shaver, 1995) and anal contact (Ochs & Binik, 1999). Weinberg et al. (1995) found that over 70% of undergraduates had engaged in active and receptive oral sex, and 16% had engaged in heterosexual anal intercourse. Some variability exists in whether adolescents consider oral sex to be more or less advanced than or simply a safer alternative to coitus. Some studies have found that adolescents' first participation in oral sex *follows* first coitus (Weinberg et al., 1995), whereas others find the opposite pattern (Schwartz, 1999). Overall, the temporal gap among sexual behaviors at the end of the sequence is small. For example, mutual masturbation, oral sex, and coitus were all pursued at around age 17 for men and 16 for women (Weinberg et al., 1995). Bear in mind, however, that data on the latest appearing, most sensitive behaviors are the most susceptible to inconsistent responses or nonresponses on surveys (Rodgers et al., 1982).

Other than the fact that so-defined late-starting and African American adolescents tend to skip earlier behaviors in the sequence, it is unclear whether the onset, duration, or content of this normative progression varies systematically as a function of personal or social factors (Halpern, Joyner, et al., 2000; Rosenthal & Smith, 1997; Weinberg et al., 1995). Adolescents with earlier timetables tend to be disproportionately likely to believe in early autonomy, to use sexually explicit media, and to abuse substances (Rosenthal & Smith, 1997), but such data do not reveal whether such factors lead to or result from early sexual trajectories. Another important unanswered question concerns how youth understand and interpret these trajectories. Where do they acquire their notions of which behaviors are more or less intimate or advanced? How do they negotiate this sequence with their partners? What are the repercussions of progressing too quickly or too slowly? The earlier youth participate in noncoital sexual activity, the earlier they participate in coitus (Bauserman & Davis, 1996), but research has not investigated the extent to which adolescents continue to pursue noncoital activities after their first coital experience (an issue with substantial implications regarding risks for pregnancy and STDs) and whether systematic differences exist in relative preferences of youth for noncoital versus coital activity. More qualitative, experiential research would help to elucidate the multiple meanings attached to noncoital activity among contemporary adolescents.

Coitus

The most reliable data, with some cross-cultural validity, suggest a historic trend—more pronounced among girls than boys—toward progressively earlier initiation of coitus (Centers for Disease Control, 2002; Davis & Lay-Yee, 1999; DeLamater & Friedrich, 2002; Laumann et al., 1994), such that by the time youth are between 18 and 24 years old, 12% of men and 6% of women have not had intercourse (Laumann et al., 1994). Although young women consistently initiate coitus at later ages than young men across various cohorts, ethnicities, geographies, socioeconomic statuses, and religious affiliations (Centers for Disease Control, 2002), this sex difference has been progressively shrinking as women's age of coital initiation has dropped. Currently, women's sexual debut averages age 17; men's, age 16 (Alan Guttmacher Institute, 1994; Baumeister, 2000; Centers for Disease Control, 2002; Davis & Lay-Yee, 1999; DeLamater & Friedrich, 2002; Hopkins, 2000; Sprecher & Hatfield, 1996). Other notable historic changes concern marital status. In the early 1950s, slightly more than half of all female teenagers were unmarried when they experienced first coitus; by the late 1980s, nearly all (95%) girls had their sexual debut before marriage (Alan Guttmacher Institute, 1994).

These dramatic changes in female coital behavior provide a partial explanation for the fact that their sexuality has been more consistently problematized than has male adolescent sexuality (Tolman & Diamond, 2001). A key factor driving this concern is the high rate of unplanned pregnancy among contemporary American adolescents (Alan Guttmacher Institute, 1994). Notably, although rates of adolescent coitus in the United States are comparable to rates in other industrialized nations, our teenage birthrate is considerably higher: twice the rate in Great Britain, seven times the rate in Denmark and the Netherlands, and fifteen times the rate in Japan (United Nations, 1991). Furthermore, although the adolescent birthrate has actually declined in the United States since the 1960s, from 89.1 births per 1,000 teens in 1960 to 56.8 births per 1,000 teens in 1995, the proportion of these births occurring among unmarried adolescents has increased, from 15% of teen births in 1960 to 75% in 1995 (U.S. Department of Health and Human Services, 1995). Thus, the focus on delaying adolescent coitus stems from efforts to prevent the negative socioeconomic, educational, health, and social consequences associated with nonmarital adolescent pregnancy, along with the obvious dangers of STDs (Blum, 2002). Contraceptives ameliorate some risk, but rates of consistent and correct use of contraceptives remain low among adolescents, despite intensive and pervasive safer sex campaigns in the United States and other industrialized Western nations (Abma, Chandra, Mosher, Peterson, & Piccinino, 1997; Tyden, Olsson, & Bjorkelund-Ylander, 1991; Weisman, Plichta, Nathanson, Ensmiger, & Robinson, 1991).

Nonetheless, longitudinal research on other problem behaviors associated with early coitus (e.g., substance use, disrupted family relationships, and delinquency) suggests that interventions aimed specifically at delaying coitus would likely have little effect on these phenomena. Bingham and Crockett (1996) followed a group of adolescents from a single school district in a rural community from 9th through 12th grade. No negative psychosocial outcomes were associated with early coitus after prior psychosocial adjustment had been statistically controlled. In other words, to the extent that consistent associations are observed between early coitus and adolescent problem behaviors, these associations are likely due to preexisting characteristics of the adolescents rather than to the experience of early coitus itself.

Even so, coitus has demonstrable health implications for adolescents (Bingham & Crockett, 1996), and thus considerable effort has been aimed at disentangling the multiple factors that predict when adolescents initiate coital activity. Some of the best research has involved longitudinal observations of pubertal changes in hormones, sexual activity, and social-attitudinal factors such as friends' participation in sexual activity, peer popularity, grades, sexual permissiveness, future orientation, parents' education, and locus of control (Udry, 1988, 1990; Udry, Kovenock, Morris, & Vandenberg, 1995; Udry et al., 1986). Maturational changes in free testosterone levels were directly related to initiation of coitus for European American males, to the exclusion of all social variables save for popularity among cross-sex friends. The pattern of results was the opposite among European American girls: Hormones had no direct effect on first coitus (although they were significantly related to sexual thoughts and fantasies), but *every* social variable significantly influenced initiation of first intercourse, and most of these factors operated independently of one another. It is significant that different patterns were observed for African American girls: The strongest predictor of sexual behavior was the observable level of pubertal maturation—whether they looked mature to peers.

A number of additional studies (reviewed in Halpern, 2003) across cultures and cohorts have yielded similar findings regarding the greater sensitivity of young women than men to social and environmental influences on intercourse. For example, among Chinese adolescents, early maturation predicted an early onset of dating and coitus among boys, but not among girls (Lam, Shi, Ho, Stewart, & Fan, 2002). The authors speculated that boys are freer to express their hormonal state because of parental monitoring and supervision of girls once they begin puberty. The consistency of this sex difference is particularly noteworthy given that during the past 50 years, cultural changes in sexual norms and attitudes have been far more pronounced with regard to female than to male sexuality.

Another important factor to consider, according to Udry et al. (1986), is that although adolescent boys face a nearly uniformly positive environment with regard to sexual behavior (which should ostensibly clear the way for hormonally mediated sexual motivation to predict coital onset straightforwardly), adolescent girls face inconstant, highly differentiated environments that send an array of conflicting and confusing messages about the desirability and costs of sexual behavior. Thus, it should not be surprising that under such circumstances, girls' hormonal maturation predicts changes in their sexual thoughts and motivation, but not coital onset.

In recent years, an increasing number of researchers and educators have argued that promoting noncoital sexual behavior among adolescents (e.g., mutual masturbation and oral sex) might be a more effective route to reduce pregnancy and STDs than advocating either abstinence or use of contraceptives and condoms. If adolescents view orgasm rather than intercourse as the end point of sexual arousal, they might not feel as compelled (both personally and by peers) to move from noncoital to coital activity (Kegan, 1996). Currently, no reliable empirical data testing whether this is true are available (Genius & Genius, 1996). Research on adult couples using noncoital sexual activity to avoid pregnancy reports annual failure rates as high as 47% (Genius & Genius, 1996). However, it might be harder for coitally experienced adults to abstain from intercourse than coitally inexperienced adolescents, given that the symbolic distinction between virgin and nonvirgin status might provide an additional incentive for youth to abstain from coitus. It is likely that research and discussion of various sexual health education strategies will increase in the ensuing years.

Clearly, multiple factors lead one adolescent to seek exclusively noncoital behavior with multiple partners beginning at an early age and another to pursue early coitus with one partner at a time in a series of serious dating relationships. In general, the more bonds an adolescent has to conventional society, the less likely she or he is to transition to sexual intercourse. A longitudinal study of junior high school students found that an "unconventional lifestyle" predicted transition to nonvirginity among European American and Latino youth (Costa et al., 1995; for high school students, see S. L. Jessor & Jessor, 1975). Similarly, among British males ages 16 to 25 (Kupek, 2001), the number of sex partners and sexually permissive attitudes were both predicted by the rejection of traditional values, such as educational attainment and abstaining from smoking and drinking. Social control appears to work more convincingly on girls than boys, perhaps because male sexual behavior is considered less deviant (Crockett et al., 1996). One social bond, religiosity, has consistently been associated with a decrease in sexual initiation, especially for girls (Crockett et al., 1996; Halpern, Joyner, et al., 2000; Miller et al., 1997; Manlove et al., 2001; Resnick et al., 1997; Seidman et al., 1994).

We now turn to a topic often underappreciated or minimized in adolescent sex research: same-sex behavior. Such behavior can be experimental, part of the sequence that leads to coitus, or the end point of adolescent sexual expression.

Same-Sex Behavior

Practically all research on same-sex behavior has been conducted with youth who self-identify as lesbian, gay, or bisexual, even though such youth comprise only a small subset of the total number of adolescents with same-sex attractions, fantasies, romances, or sexual activities (Savin-Williams, 2001). Furthermore, these various components of same-sex sexuality do not necessarily coincide. Quite simply, not all adolescents who experience same-sex desires are lesbian, gay, or bisexual, and not all of these individuals engage in same-sex activities during adolescence (Diamond, 2000a, 2003a; Golden, 1996; Savin-Williams, 1998; Weinberg, Williams, & Pryor, 1994). Given our primitive understanding of how sexual orientation and sexual behavior link up with regard to etiology and experience (Diamond, 2003b), we can learn more about their nature and long-term significance by assessing and interpreting them separately than by implicitly treating one as a proxy for the entire complex. Even if youth with same-sex attractions never act on them, never identify as gay, and never come out to friends or family, it is quite likely that their development follows notably different trajectories than does that of youth who never experience such feelings.

How many such youth are there? Among respondents to the random, representative, confidential Add Health survey, over 8% of boys and 6% of girls reported experiencing either same-sex attractions or a same-sex relationship (Russell & Joyner, 2001). For comparison, Laumann et al.'s (1994) similarly random, representative survey of American adults found that 10% of men and nearly 9% of women reported same-sex attractions or behaviors. However, fewer than 2% of adolescents identify as lesbian, gay, or bisexual (Garofalo, Wolf, Wissow, Woods, & Goodman, 1999; Remafedi, Resnick, Blum, & Harris, 1992). In terms of same-sex behavior, proportions have been difficult to ascertain because of stigma attached to such behaviors. One study of junior high school students (Halpern et al., 1993) found that despite a confidential questionnaire, only a handful of youth reported same-sex contact by age 16. Among Greek (Papadopoulos et al., 2000) and British (Copas et al., 2002) young adults, about 3% reported same-sex activities, compared with nearly 4% of adolescent respondents to the Massachusetts 1995 Youth Risk Behavior Survey (YRBS; Garofalo et al., 1999). Age and sexual experience might be important factors when interpreting differential rates of behavior. The fraction of adolescent boys reporting same-sex sexual contact was .4% at age 12 but nearly 3% by age 18 (Remafedi et al., 1992). In a Vermont study (DuRant, Krowchuk, & Sinal, 1998), the proportion of youth reporting same-sex contact rose from 1% to nearly 9% of young men and 5% of young women when the sample was restricted to youth who had heterosexual coitus.

Developmental researchers might presume that adolescents who engage in same-sex contact are simply experimenting and will eventually identify as heterosexual. For example, Maccoby (1998, p. 191), among others (Katchadourian, 1990), asserted that "a substantial number of people experiment with same-sex sexuality at some point in their lives, and a small minority settle into a life-long pattern of homosexuality." Indeed, although one of the best predictors of an eventual same-sex identity is childhood and adolescent same-sex behavior (Bell, Weinberg, & Hammersmith, 1981), the majority of adolescent same-sex behavior occurs among youth who currently consider themselves heterosexual. Half of youth reporting same-sex behavior on the Massachusetts YRBS (Garofalo et al., 1999) were heterosexually identified, and a study of Minnesota public school students found that over 60% reporting same-sex behavior identified as heterosexual (Remafedi et al., 1992). Note, as well, that many sexual-minority young adults who pursued same-sex behavior in childhood and adolescence reported that their partners were "likely" heterosexual (Savin-Williams, 1998). Similar discrepancies between behavior and identity have emerged from studies of adults. Although only about 2% to 3% of adults identified as lesbian, gay, or bisexual, three times as many reported having had same-sex experiences since puberty (Laumann et al., 1994). These data do not imply that heterosexually identified youth with same-sex behavior are necessarily heterosexual by sexual orientation. For example, in the Minnesota study, twice as many youth reported same-sex fantasies as identified as lesbian, gay, or bisexual, and four times as many reported that they were primarily attracted to the same sex as identified as a sexual minority.

Given cultural heterocentric assumptions and active sexual prejudice against sexual minorities (Herek, 2000), it should not be surprising that most adolescents with same-sex contact claim to be heterosexual. With the dearth of longitudinal research on sexual orientation, behavior, and identity, it is impossible to know for certain what proportion of adolescent same-sex behavior represents experimentation and what proportion represents a precursor of adult same-sex sexuality. The only prospective study of female sexual-minority youth (Diamond, 2000b, 2003a, in press) found that over a 5-year period, 13% who had previously considered themselves to be nonheterosexual reclaimed a heterosexual label. Notably, however, only one young woman called her previous sexual-minority identification a phase, and all reported that they still experienced sexual attractions to women. Typically, however, the relative infrequency of same-sex attractions, often coupled with a serious and satisfying heterosexual relationship, led such women to identify as heterosexual, despite acknowledging their ongoing potential for same-sex sexuality.

Retrospective data collected from adults (Laumann et al., 1994) suggest notable sex differences in patterns of adolescent same-sex behavior. Among adult male respondents who had ever had same-sex contact, 42% engaged in such contact during adolescence *only*. In other words, nearly half of their same-sex behavior represented teenage "experimentation." In stark contrast, practically all female respondents with adolescent same-sex contact pursued such contact into adulthood, indicating that adolescent same-sex behavior was a better predictor of adult same-sex sexuality among women than among men. However, this does not suggest that same-sex behavior is always a marker of lesbianism or bisexuality among women; rather, when heterosexual women pursue same-sex behavior, they do so at later ages, often in college rather than high school. This may reflect the historic fact that women have had fewer opportunities and social license to experiment sexually during their adolescent years (Gagnon & Simon, 1973).

Are there any factors that researchers might use to distinguish experimental same-sex behavior from that which signals an underlying same-sex orientation? One possibility is that youth with an underlying same-sex orientation pursue such behavior more consistently than do heterosexual youth and that they choose it over opportunities for other-sex contact (although this is less true of bisexual youth). In the Vermont YRBS study, over half of males with a same-sex experience reported having had more than four different male partners, and most of these individuals also reported never having had sex with a female (DuRant et al., 1998). This might be construed as a prehomosexual trajectory, but at the current time no direct evidence exists to confirm or disconfirm this possibility. In her longitudinal study of young women, Diamond (2000b, 2003a, in press) found that factors such as age of first same-sex attractions, first sexual questioning, and first same-sex contact failed to distinguish women who relinquished their sexual-minority identities from those who did not. The only significant predictor of future identity 5 years later was initial greater relative proportions of same-sex to other-sex attractions.

Complicating these matters are cultural considerations. For example, paradoxical attitudes toward male-male sexual exploits are common in many Latino cultures. Carballo-

Diéguez (1997) noted that across interancestry variations, Latin cultures tend to permit males to choose other males as sex partners providing that it is a private choice undertaken solely to satisfy sexual urges, rather than a public acknowledgment of a gay identity encompassing both sex and love. Furthermore, strong links are perceived between men's behavioral roles in same-sex activity and their sexual and gender identity. A Latino man can pursue same-sex activity without threatening his heterosexual identity if he assumes the inserter role in oral and anal sex, maintains a highly masculine demeanor, and expresses no tender feelings toward his partner (no kissing). On the other hand, men who allow themselves to be penetrated are considered intrinsically effeminate and are ridiculed as *jotos* (faggots; Carrier, 1995).

Of course, investigations into the diverse meanings that adolescents attach to their same-sex behavior and the degree of emotional and physical satisfaction they experience in these interactions relative to cross-sex interactions might predict future identification. However, such investigations have not been undertaken because it is sufficiently difficult for researchers to find heterosexually identified adolescents who report same-sex behavior, much less answer detailed questions about why they engage in such behavior and how satisfying these experiences are. Perhaps the best strategy is to pose such questions retrospectively. The combination of greater maturity and the cessation of same-sex behavior might render such respondents more willing to speak openly and honestly about their prior same-sex experiences.

In regard to youth who identify as lesbian, gay, or bisexual, the average age of first same-sex activity for females ranges from 14 (Rosario, Meyer-Bahlburg, Hunter, Exner, Gwadz, & Keller, 1996) to 18 (Diamond, 1998); for males, the range is narrower, usually averaging between ages 13 and 15 (D'Augelli, in press; Herdt & Boxer, 1993; Rosario et al., 1996; Savin-Williams, 1998). The typical context of a sexual-minority youth's first same-sex experience varies according to its timing. One retrospective study (Savin-Williams, 1998) found that prepubertal same-sex contact among boys often occurred during play activities with a same-age friend or relative; if during early adolescence, also with close friends but now less playful and more explicitly sexual; and if during the high school years, often with a notably older partner, a stranger, or a dating acquaintance. Among girls, close friends were common first partners at all ages, and young women rarely had their first same-sex contact with a stranger or passing acquaintance, but rather within the context of a full-fledged love affair (Savin-Williams, 2003b). Some of these began as ambiguously passionate, platonic friendships that spilled over into sexual desire and activity (Diamond, 2000a).

Over half of gay and bisexual men and about 80% of lesbian and bisexual women also have cross-sex experiences during adolescence. Herdt and Boxer (1993) reported that more lesbian and bisexual adolescent girls had cross-sex *before* same-sex sexual activity, whereas boys followed the opposite pattern. This finding has been replicated in some (D'Augelli, in press; Savin-Williams, 1998, 2003b) but not all (Rosario et al., 1996) studies. Given that a sexual-minority youth's cross-sex activities usually take place within the context of a dating relationship, this might reflect greater social pressures on teenage girls to date (Weinberg et al., 1994), the greater incidence of girls as invitee rather than inviter in adolescent dating, or the greater likelihood that sexual-minority women are authentically attracted to both sexes (Baumeister, 2000; Diamond, in press). Many male and female sexual-minority youth report that their cross-sex relationships are deeply satisfying—sometimes only emotionally, but sometimes both emotionally and physically (Diamond, 1998; Savin-Williams & Diamond, 2000). Of course, some youth report that cross-sex activities were pursued because of obligation rather than desire (Savin-Williams, 1998, 2003b), which surely characterizes some heterosexuals' cross-sex activities as well.

The sexes also differ regarding the sequencing of same-sex behavior and a sexual identification. Whereas same-sex activity typically occurs 1 to 2 years prior to a gay or bisexual identification among males (Herdt & Boxer, 1993; Rosario et al., 1996; Savin-Williams & Diamond, 2000), sexual-minority females are more likely to have their first same-sex contact after identifying as lesbian or bisexual (Diamond, 1998; Savin-Williams & Diamond, 2000). As noted, this might stem from the greater sexual license granted to adolescent boys than girls, which appears to be fading as sexual-minority boys question their sexuality at earlier ages and adopt a gay or bisexual label before having same-sex contact. One recent investigation found that sexual-minority young men were more likely than an older cohort (56% versus 38%) to have their first same-sex experience after identifying as gay or bisexual (Dubé, 2000). In interpreting such sequences, it bears noting that, consistent with research on heterosexual youth (Udry & Billy, 1987; Udry et al., 1986), interpersonal and situational factors appear to exert a greater press on sexual-minority women's than men's psychosexual development (Diamond, 2003b).

THE CONTEXT OF ADOLESCENT SEX: SEXUAL PARTNERS AND RELATIONSHIPS

Although clear variability exists in the sexual pursuits of adolescents, one factor is notably consistent: The vast majority initiates sex with partners near their own age (DeLamater & Friedrich, 2002; Larsson & Svedin, 2002; Leitenberg & Saltzman, 2000; Savin-Williams, 1998, 2003b). In one study, 93% of youth reported that their first sexual partner was within 2 years of their age (Larsson & Svedin, 2002). Among heterosexuals, the age differential was greatest when the initiation of sexual intercourse was early (Leitenberg & Saltzman, 2000); among sexual-minority young men, the opposite was found with regard to first genital contact (Savin-Williams, 1998).

As for the relationship between partners, if a youth's first sexual encounter is during childhood, the partner is likely to be a friend, although occasionally a cousin or sibling. Only rarely do children pursue sexual activity with unacquainted peers or adults (Larsson & Svedin, 2002; Savin-Williams, 1998, 2003b). Among older youth, a sex divide exists. The majority of adolescent girls, across sexual orientation and demographic categories, reported initiating sexual activity with someone they were dating seriously or were in love with, whereas boys' first sexual partners were typically girls they had just met or girls they knew well but were "just dating" (de Gaston et al., 1995; Papadopoulos et al., 2000; Weinberg et al., 1995; Zani, 1991). Laumann et al. (1994) found that 75% of young adult women had first sex with a spouse or someone they loved, compared with 41% of young men, who were more likely than women to report that their first partner was someone they knew well but did not love (37% versus 17%) or someone they did not know well, had just met, or had paid (21% versus 7%). Of course, these findings directly reflect aforementioned sex differences in the extent to which interpersonal relationships and emotional feelings—in contrast to straightforward sexual desires—function as motivators for adolescents' sexual activity.

Sex differences also exist in expectations regarding coital timing within an ongoing relationship. As Maccoby (1998) noted, girls typically want to prolong the early stages of dating and to delay intercourse, whereas boys typically want to accelerate the pace at which sexual intimacy progresses. This is consistent with research on adults: Within an ongoing relationship, men tend to push for sex while women set limits (Browning et al., 1999). One study found that college men expected sex at about the 10th date, whereas women expected sex after the 16th date (Cohen & Shotland, 1996). Both sexes believed that men wanted sex irrespective of physical attraction or emotional involvement and that women did not. In reality, both men and women expected sex only when they were attracted to the person, although men were more likely to expect sex in the absence of emotional closeness.

A common research focus concerns the overall number of sexual partners. Conflicting findings have been reported; some studies report that the average high school senior has had more than one intercourse partner (Alan Guttmacher Institute, 1994), whereas others report that the majority of youth have had only one partner by the end of high school (de Gaston et al., 1995; Prince & Bernard, 1998). Findings of sex differences, however, have been more consistent, with young men reporting more partners than young women. National data (Centers for Disease Control, 2002) indicate that 17% of high school boys but just 11% of high school girls have had more than four partners over their lifetime. One study found that undergraduate men had about three sex partners in the past year and seven over their lifetime, whereas women had about two and five, respectively (Weinberg et al., 1995). By contrast, Laumann et al. (1994) found that 55% of women and 44% of men between the ages of 18 and 24 had thus far had only one partner. Sex differences in partner number are observed across cohorts and cultures and are generally larger in more restrictive, traditional societies (Laumann et al., 1994; Papadopoulos et al., 2000; Prince & Bernard, 1998). However, it is important not to conflate the number of coital partners with overall frequency of sexual activity. Because young women are more likely than men (73% vs. 38%) to report that their current sexual relationship is an ongoing relationship (de Gaston et al., 1995), they tend to report higher rates of sexual activity, albeit with the same person, whereas young men have more infrequent sex with a variety of different individuals (Prince & Bernard, 1998).

In general, an earlier onset of sexual behavior is associated with larger numbers of sex partners (Kupek, 2001; Moore & Rosenthal, 1993; Seidman et al., 1994), and this pattern persists over time. The number of cross-sex partners an individual recalls before age 18 mirrors the number she or he has in subsequent years (Laumann et al., 1994). Similar to declines in age of first coitus among girls, changes in partner number reflect historic transformations in attitudes and norms regarding female sexuality. In previous eras, having sex *at all*—especially with multiple partners—would have been scandalous for any girl hoping eventually to marry, as it would have labeled her a slut. Although having multiple partners is still less acceptable for girls than for boys, the stigma attached to such behavior has significantly declined. This is particularly true if a girl's multiple sexual relationships are full-fledged, committed romances, rather than casual liaisons or hook-ups.

THE EVALUATION OF SEXUAL EXPERIENCES

Given the tremendous buildup that sex receives, it is bound to disappoint some youth when it finally happens. However, little is known concerning how adolescents evaluate their sexual experiences, and most of the available data focus exclusively on intercourse. One notable exception is the research of Larsson and Svedin (2002), who examined the autoerotic and noncoital sexual activities of 11- to 12-year-olds. The most prevalent evaluations were extremely positive, including "pleasant body sensations," "excitement," "natural feeling," "silly," and "sexually stimulated." Less than 5% evaluated their sexual experiences as "frightening," "bad," "unpleasant body sensation," or "angry." Feelings of guilt were rare, although slightly more common among girls than boys. When followed up as high school seniors, over 90% described their earlier sexual experiences as "normal" or "good," and all but 4% said they had either a positive or a neutral effect on them. Notably, the exceptions were often individuals who had coercive early experiences.

Intercourse, however, is another matter, particularly for girls. Moore and Rosenthal (1993) concluded in a review of the extant literature that first coitus is often not pleasurable for adolescent girls. For example, Italian adolescent girls were often so disappointed by their first sexual experiences that they refrained from sexual activity altogether for lengthy periods of time (Zani, 1991). Adolescent boys evaluated their early intercourse experiences more positively, and data collected from young adults indicate that young men were more likely than women to have consistent orgasms with their primary partner (Laumann et al., 1994). Although 70% rated sexual intercourse as highly appealing, young men were more likely than women to evaluate a variety of other sexual activities as appealing, such as watching one's partner undress (50% and 31%), receiving oral sex (47% and 35%), and giving oral sex (32% and 15%). It is interesting to consider the degree to which the young women's dissatisfaction might be moderated by their partners' experience, considerateness, and familiarity with the female body; such factors (or at least a youth's perceptions of them), however, have not been studied systematically.

Another potential moderator of a youth's sexual satisfaction might be simultaneous feelings of guilt, shame, or regret about sexual activity, which are more common among young women than among men (Benda & DiBlasio, 1994; Crockett et al., 1996; de Gaston et al., 1995). Such feelings appear to be an inevitable consequence of the ways in which girls are socialized to think about their sexuality. As Gagnon (1972) noted, from early childhood girls are trained for love, romance, and marriage rather than libidinal sexual behavior, and thus the entire course of their sexual development is culturally policed. Fine (1988) argued that schools and sex education curricula further dampen female sexuality by teaching girls that they are continually at risk for victimization and danger. As a result, young women appear disproportionately sensitive to the risks presented by sexual behavior, whereas young men are more sensitive to the rewards associated with sex (Benda & DiBlasio, 1994; Crockett et al., 1996). Such factors likely play a critical role in shaping the subjective quality of adolescents' early sexual experiences.

The relational context of an adolescent's sexual activity also plays an important evaluative role. Adolescent girls are more likely to have a positive experience if sex occurs within the confines of a steady relationship, particularly one characterized by good communication (Donald, Lucke, Dunne, & Raphael, 1995) and high intimacy and engagement (Thompson, 1995). Relational contexts are important for boys, as well. One study of Swedish and American youth found that over 90% of both young men and women expressed greater happiness, more satisfaction, and less guilt about their most recent sexual intercourse when it was pursued within the context of a significant relationship (Weinberg et al., 1995; see also Zani, 1991). Nonetheless, the difference between the perceived quality of relationship sex and nonrelationship sex was greater for women. Note, too, that despite their lower rates of orgasm frequency, the young adult women in Laumann et al.'s (1994) study were just as likely as were their male counterparts to describe their current sexual relationship as emotionally *and* physically satisfying.

Adolescent girls are also more likely than boys—by a factor of seven—to report feeling pressured to have sex in their romantic relationships (de Gaston et al., 1995). Notably, these girls nonetheless described their relationships as providing valuable emotional reassurance and protection, perhaps giving them a strong motive to give in to sexual pressure in order to preserve the relationship. Overall, however, practically all boys and the majority of girls reported *wanting* their first intercourse (Laumann et al., 1994; Zani, 1991). Another category are those who did not want their first intercourse experience but were not forced into it: 25% of women but only 8% of men in one study (Laumann et al., 1994). This liminal category—not wanted, but not forced—is a fascinating one that receives little attention in research on contemporary adolescents. How do young men experience this ambivalence, given that they receive strong and persistent cultural messages telling them that they should want any and all sexual activity?

Despite the stigma placed on their same-sex activities, sexual-minority youth of both sexes reported that they thoroughly enjoyed their prepubertal and adolescent same-sex activities (Savin-Williams, 1998, 2003b). Although similar to heterosexuals, boys were more likely than were girls to report such childhood activities. Some, however, felt considerable unease or shame about enjoying such activities too much. Others worried about whether their parents would catch them and punish them, although such concerns did not generally dampen the eroticism of these early encounters. Young men who waited until high school or college for their first same-sex encounter typically reacted with more distress, largely because their enjoyment confirmed their long-denied worst fear: "I'm gay!"

Sexual-minority youth (especially bisexuals) who pursued cross-sex relationships often experienced them as both emotionally and physically ("Sex is sex!") gratifying, even if they would have preferred same-sex partners (Diamond, 1998; Savin-Williams & Diamond, 2000). For some, however, sexual interactions with these partners evoked guilt if they were not as pleasurable as they thought they should be. Others, especially those whose cross-sex activities were motivated primarily by curiosity or direct pressure from boy- or girlfriends, went along with the sexual activity in an effort to please their partner and to keep the relationship intact (motives also common among heterosexual female youth). This lack of passion and fulfillment in cross-sex encounters highlighted and reinforced for some youth their emerging same-sex interests (Savin-Williams, 1998, 2003b). Although the sex that some young sexual-minority women pursued with boys was characterized as bad, it was not always clear whether this was because of their sexual orientation or because of their partners' fumbling inexperience (Savin-Williams, 2003b).

These cases highlight the extent to which adolescents' evaluations of early sexual experiences depend on their initial expectations as well as on the context in which they occur. Those who naively assume that all sexual activities, and sexual intercourse in particular, will be as uniformly satisfying as they appear to be in the media are bound to be let down by reality. Nevertheless, parents rarely communicate to their children that good sex is a skill to be learned like any other and that it often takes time to master. Youth who appreciate this fact will have more realistic expectations about the satisfaction they can expect from their initial sexual experiences and will therefore be in a better position to evaluate how positive or negative sexual experiences bear on their self-concept, current relationships, and sexual identity.

POSITIVE SEXUAL DEVELOPMENT

Most researchers attest to the dramatic changes in age of coital onset, number of sex partners, and frequency of sexual intercourse, as well as to the tolerance—if not acceptance—of diverse sexual behaviors and identities (Browning et al., 1999; Feldman et al., 1999; Miller & Benson, 1999). In reviewing the historic record, Maccoby (1998) concluded that the legendary sexual revolution involved a realization by youth that they have a right to sexual pleasure and fulfillment, a decline in the influence of earlier generations' dictates concerning good versus bad sexual behavior, and an increase in the visibility of explicit sexuality in daily life. Although the availability of contraceptives fueled the changes, Feldman et al. (1999, p. 46) argued that in addition, "the feminist movement, with its insistence that women's sexual desire and gratification be recognized, together with media representation of women's overt sexuality, have succeeded in permitting women to openly acknowledge their sexuality in a way similar to men." Traditional sex roles and morality were challenged, and sex for women became less shameful, less mysterious, and more a personal than a family decision (Hopkins, 2000). Reproductive sex was replaced by recreational sex, giving license for girls to behave in the way that boys always have (Levine, 2002).

Although permissiveness with affection and commitment is the prominent contemporary standard, sex differences in sexual behavior still persist, and some would argue that the total eradication of such differences is neither justifiable nor ideal (Weinberg et al., 1995). After all, despite the historic changes in conceptions of female sexuality, adolescents continue to judge a girl's sexual behavior more harshly than a boy's (Maccoby, 1998; Milhausen & Herold, 1999; Weinberg et al., 1995). Thus, female sexual adventurousness and promiscuity exact a heavy price in social condemnation and peer derision (Maccoby, 1998). Within this context, it is difficult to discern what a positive, empowering, and healthy model of female sexual development should look like. Certainly, questions of female sexual pleasure and entitlement are missing from current agendas for adolescent sex education. As Fine (1988) noted, young women are consistently reminded of the negative consequences of sexuality, especially sexual behavior pursued outside the context of a serious relationship. They have been indoctrinated to believe that it is *their* job to suppress sexual desire, to serve as sexual gatekeepers, and to avoid the physical, emotional, moral, reproductive, and financial costs of rape, disease, and pregnancy. According to this perspective, there is no positive model of female adolescent sexuality. Only adult woman are granted sexual agency.

Tolman (1994, 2000; Tolman, Spencer, Harmon, Rosen-Reynoso, & Striepe, in press) and O'Sullivan (O'Sullivan & Meyer-Bahlburg, 2003; O'Sullivan, Meyer-Bahlburg, & Watkins, 2001) have illustrated and expanded Fine's points in interviews with adolescents. Taught to inhibit, censure, or deny sexual desire, arousal, and pleasure, young adolescent girls reported relinquishing sexual agency. We encourage boys to explore their sexuality fully; we leave girls mystified about what it means when they feel sexual desire or pleasure (O'Sullivan et al., 2000). Tolman's (2000, p. 70) radical corrective was to adopt and communicate to adolescents a normative expectation that girls "can and should experience sexual desire—not that they should or will necessarily act on these feelings, but that they should be able to recognize and acknowledge what is a part of the self."

It is important to recognize that some argue that the aforementioned sex differences are not as inevitable and pervasive as they are portrayed. Girls are more sexually oriented and boys more romantically oriented than previous research might indicate. Kalof (1995) reported that teenagers of both sexes seek both physical and emotional pleasure from their sexual activity, disputing the myth that young women participate in sex only to achieve closeness and not because of desire. Indeed, a recent *New York Times* article, "She's Got to Be a Macho Girl" (Kuczynski, 2002), quoted one teenage boy as reporting that girls are now the sexual aggressors: "They [girls] have more attitude. They have more power. And they overpower guys more. I mean, it's scary." In addition, emotional intimacy and self-disclosure are as important for some young men as they are for young women. Tolman et al. (in press) echoed these sentiments in interviews with young men. Heterosexual initiation was more than belt notches, more than raging hormones bent on one objective. Similar to girls, adolescent boys also desire romance, companionship, sharing, and trust, and they ably distinguish romantic from recreational sex.

In scholarly circles, however, these longings must appear surprising. Given the impetus to avert or forestall the so-called treacherous sexual activities of adolescents, research addressing how adolescent sexuality can be positive and growth promoting is nearly absent from the empirical literature. Although some studies show that adolescents who engage in early or frequent sexual activities have some positive as well as negative characteristics, the positive traits themselves might be considered controversial. For example, adolescents who pursue early and frequent sex are less conventional, more independent, more autonomous, and less religious; they view themselves as attractive and successful in forming romantic relationships and have less traditional attitudes toward sex roles (Costa et al., 1995; Crockett et al., 1996; Davis & Lay-Yee, 1999; S. L. Jessor & Jessor, 1975; McLaughlin, Chen, Greenberger, & Biermeier, 1997; Moore & Rosenthal, 1993; Rosenthal et al., 1999). Some adults view such traits as precursors to the development of an empowered, agentic, creative, and adventurous adult, whereas others view these traits as harbingers of rebelliousness, deviance, and risk.

With regard to the relationship between self-evaluative traits and sexual behavior, research has been mixed. Youth with high self-esteem report high sexual restraint (Lynch, 2001; Paul et al., 2000), yet sex during childhood and adolescence among gay youth is not associated with lower self-esteem (Rind, 2001; Savin-Williams, 1998); indeed, one study of heterosexual boys found that early sexual debut was associated with *higher* levels of self-esteem (S. L. Jessor & Jessor, 1975). Perhaps high self-esteem buffers some boys against the risk of sexual rejection, rendering them more likely to seek or respond to sexual opportunities; furthermore, success with gaining a sex partner is socially rewarding and might raise a youth's self-regard over time (Paul et al., 2000). For girls, engaging in casual sex might decrease her self-worth if she views it as violating social expectations. Overall, it appears misguided to view early coitus uniformly as a cause of psychosocial maladjustment; to the contrary, well-adjusted, socially competent youth might be the most successful at finding sexual partners (Crockett et al., 1996).

These findings support former Surgeon General Elders's call to end the "conspiracy of silence" about adolescent sexuality and her advocacy for teaching children and teenagers self-respect and sexual self-esteem by reducing misinformation, scare tactics, and hysteria. Elders argued that "treating sex as dangerous is dangerous in itself" (Levine, 2002, p. x). Similarly, Carpenter (2001, p. 128) noted that "sexuality constitutes a central feature of identity: individuals are to a great degree defined by themselves and others, both socially and morally, in terms of their sexuality." However, the vast majority of scholarly research on adolescence, intent on reducing sexual behavior, ignores this aspect of sexuality altogether.

Several popular books, quoted at the outset of this review, remind scholars of the growth potential and exhilarating possibilities of adolescent sexuality (Levine, 2002; Ponton, 2000). If teenagers are physically but not emotionally or cognitively ready for sex, this is due in large part to the failure of adults to prepare them. O'Sullivan et al. (2001, p. 288) noted that parents "rarely acknowledged the positive aspects of sexuality outside the context of harm. It appears that their communication efforts ultimately deter their daughters from confiding in them about their sexual interest or participation." The impact among their African American and Latina families was straightforward: Girls turned increasingly to others, not parents, for advice on psychosexual issues central for making wise healthy sexual choices.

Finally, we agree with Tolman (1994), who noted that research on adolescent sexuality has been almost exclusively defined as sexual intercourse and nonvirginity status, rather than in terms of the diverse meanings that sexuality has for the individual. She advocated unhitching sexuality from pregnancy and deviance and reconceptualizing adolescent sexuality to encompass not only sexual intercourse but also multiple forms of sexual and affectional ideation and experience. Our goal should be to encourage adolescents "to know their sexuality as feelings as well as actions, feelings to which they are entitled, feelings that are in fact not necessarily the same as actions" (p. 268). Extending Tolman's (2000, p. 78) mandate to boys, we are further obliged to teach adolescents not only of "the physical and emotional risks of sexuality, but also of the ways in which our sexuality can make us more resilient and more alive and about our entitlement to an erotic voice." If we want to guide adolescent sexual development along the most positive trajectories possible, total denial is as untenable as total freedom. Rather, we should help adolescents develop the cognitive, emotional, and interpersonal skills necessary for them to assess appropriately the pleasures and dangers of sexuality so that they can make informed sexual choices that keep them safe and foster positive sexual self-concepts.

REFERENCES

Abma, J., Chandra, A., Mosher, W., Peterson, L., & Piccinino, L. (1997). Fertility, family planning, and women's health: New data from the 1995 National Survey of Family Growth. *Vital Health Statistics* (Vol. 23). Hyattsville, MD: National Center for Health Statistics.

Alan Guttmacher Institute. (1994). *Sex and America's teenagers.* Washington, DC: Author.

Aspinwall, L. G., & Taylor, S. E. (1997). A stitch in time: Self-regulation and proactive coping. *Psychological Bulletin, 121,* 417–436.

Bancroft, J. H. (1989). Sexual desire and the brain. *Sexual and Marital Therapy, 3,* 11–27.

Bancroft, J. H. (Ed.). (1997). *Researching sexual behavior: Methodological issues.* Bloomington: Indiana University Press.

Baumeister, R. F. (2000). Gender differences in erotic plasticity: The female sex drive as socially flexible and responsive. *Psychological Bulletin, 126,* 247–374.

Baumeister, R. F., Catanese, K. R., & Vohs, K. D. (2001). Is there a gender difference in strength of sex drive? Theoretical views, conceptual distinctions, and a review of relevant evidence. *Personality and Social Psychology Review, 5,* 242–273.

Bauserman, R., & Davis C. (1996). Perceptions of early sexual experiences and adult sexual adjustment. *Journal of Psychology and Human Sexuality, 8,* 37–59.

Beach, F. A. (1976). Sexual attractivity, proceptivity, and receptivity in female mammals. *Hormones and Behavior, 7,* 105–138.

Bearman, P. S., & Bruckner, H. (1999). *Power in numbers: Peer effects on adolescent girls' sexual debut and pregnancy.* Washington, DC: National Campaign to Prevent Teen Pregnancy.

Bell, A. P., Weinberg, M. S., & Hammersmith, S. K. (1981). *Sexual preference: Its development in men and women.* Bloomington: Indiana University Press.

Benda, B. B., & DiBlasio, F. A. (1994). An integration of theory: Adolescent sexual contacts. *Journal of Youth and Adolescence, 23,* 403–420.

Berger, D. G., & Wenger, M. G. (1973). The ideology of virginity. *Journal of Marriage and the Family, ,* 666–676.

Bingham, C. R., & Crockett, L. J. (1996). Longitudinal adjustment patterns of boys and girls experiencing early, middle, and late sexual intercourse. *Developmental Psychology, 32,* 647–658.

Blum, R. W. (2002). *Mothers' influence on teen sex: Connections that promote postponing sexual intercourse.* Center for Adolescent Health and Development, University of Minnesota, Minneapolis.

Blum, R. W., Beuhring, T., Shew, M. L., Bearinger, L. H., Sieving, R. E., & Resnick, M. D. (2000). The effects of race/ethnicity, income, and family structure on adolescent risk behaviors. *American Journal of Public Health, 90,* 1879–1884.

Blumstein, P., & Schwarz, P. (1983). *American couples: Money, work, sex.* New York: Morrow.

Bogart, L. M., Cecil, H., Wagstaff, D. A., Pinkerton, S. D., & Abramson, P. R. (2000). Is it "sex"? College students' interpretations of sexual behavior terminology. *Journal of Sex Research, 37,* 108–116.

Brigman, B., & Knox, D. (1992). University students' motivations to have intercourse. *College Student Journal, 26,* 406–408.

Brooks-Gunn, J., & Paikoff, R. (1997). Sexuality and developmental transitions during adolescence, part II. In J. Schulenberg, J. Maggs, & K. Hurrelmann (Eds.), *Health risks and developmental transitions during adolescents* (pp. 190–219). London: Cambridge University Press.

Brooks-Gunn, J., & Reiter, E. (1990). The role of pubertal processes. In S. S. Feldman & G. E. Elliott (Eds.), *At the threshold: The developing adolescent* (pp. 16–23). Cambridge, MA: Harvard University Press.

Brown, J. D. (2002). Mass media influences on sexuality. *Journal of Sex Research, 39,* 42–45.

Browning, J. R., Kessler, D., Hatfield, E., & Choo, P. (1999). Power, gender, and sexual behavior. *Journal of Sex Research, 36,* 342–347.

Brumberg, J. J. (1997). *The body project: An intimate history of American girls.* New York: Random House.

Carballo-Diéguez, A. (1997). Sexual research with Latino men who have sex with men. In J. Bancroft (Ed.), *Researching sexual behavior: Methodological issues* (pp. 134–144). Bloomington: Indiana University Press.

Carpenter, L. M. (2001). The ambiguity of "having sex": The subjective experience of virginity loss in the United States. *Journal of Sex Research, 38,* 127–139.

Carrier, J. (1995). *De los ostros: Intimacy and homosexuality among Mexican men.* New York: Columbia University Press.

Carroll, J. L., Volk, K. D., & Hyde, J. S. (1985). Differences between males and females in motives for engaging in sexual intercourse. *Archives of Sexual Behavior, 14,* 131–139.

Catania, J. A. (1999). A framework for conceptualizing reporting bias and its antecedents in interviews assessing human sexuality. *Journal of Sex Research, 36,* 25–38.

Catania, J. A., Gibson, D. R., Chitwood, D. D., & Coates, T. J. (1990). Methodological problems in AIDS behavioral research: Influences on measurement error and participation bias in studies of sexual behavior. *Psychological Bulletin, 108,* 339–362.

Centers for Disease Control. (2002, September 27). Trends in sexual risk behaviors among high school students—United States, 1991–2001. *Mortality and Morbidity Weekly Review, 51*(38), 856–859.

Chilman, C. S. (1978). *Adolescent sexuality in a changing American society: Social and psychological perspectives.* Bethesda, MD: National Institutes of Health.

Cicchetti, D., & Garmezy, N. (1993). Prospects and promises in the study of resilience. *Development and Psychopathology, 5,* 497–502.

Cohen, L. L., & Shotland, R. L. (1996). Timing of first sexual intercourse in a relationship: Expectations, experiences, and perceptions of others. *Journal of Sex Research, 33,* 291–299.

Cooper, M. L., Shapiro, C. M., & Powers, A. M. (1998). Motivations for sex and risky sexual behavior among adolescents and young adults: A functional perspective. *Journal of Personality and Social Psychology, 75,* 1528–1558.

Copas, A. J., Wellings, K., Erens, B., Mercer, C. H., McManus, S., Fenton, K. A., Korovessis, C., Macdowall, W., Nanchahal, K., & Johnson, A. M. (2002). The accuracy of reported sensitive sexual behaviour in Britain: Exploring the extent of change 1990–2000. *Sexual Transmission and Infection, 78,* 26–30.

Costa, F. M., Jessor, R., Donovan, J. E., & Fortenberry, J. D. (1995). Early initiation of sexual intercourse: The influence of psychosocial unconventionality. *Journal of Research on Adolescence, 5,* 93–121.

Cowen, E. L., Wyman, P. A., Work, W. C., & Parker, G. R. (1990). The Rochester Child Resilience Project: Overview and summary of first year findings. *Development and Psychopathology, 2,* 193–212.

Crockett, L. J., Bingham, C. R., Chopak, J. S., & Vicary, J. R. (1996). Timing of first sexual intercourse: The role of social control, social learning, and problem behavior. *Journal of Youth and Adolescence, 25,* 89–111.

D'Augelli, A. R. (in press). Developmental and contextual factors and mental health among lesbian, gay, and bisexual youths. In A. Omoto & H. Kurtzman (Eds.), *Recent research on sexual orientation.* Washington, DC: American Psychological Association Press.

Davis, P., & Lay-Yee, R. (1999). Early sex and its behavioral consequences in New Zealand. *Journal of Sex Research, 36,* 135–144.

de Gaston, J. F., Jensen, L., & Weed, S. (1995). A closer look at adolescent sexual activity. *Journal of Youth and Adolescence, 24,* 465–479.

DeLamater, J., & Friedrich, W. N. (2002). Human sexual development. *Journal of Sex Research, 39,* 10–14.

Denny, N. W., Field, J. K., & Quadagno, D. (1984). Sex differences in sexual needs and desires. *Archives of Sexual Behavior, 13,* 233–245.

Diamond, L. M. (1998). Development of sexual orientation among adolescent and young adult women. *Developmental Psychology, 34,* 1085–1095.

Diamond, L. M. (2000a). Passionate friendships among adolescent sexual-minority women. *Journal of Research on Adolescence, 10,* 191–209.

Diamond, L. M. (2000b). Sexual identity, attractions, and behavior among young sexual-minority women over a two-year period. *Developmental Psychology, 36,* 241–250.

Diamond, L. M. (2002). "Having a girlfriend without knowing it": The relationships of adolescent lesbian and bisexual women. *Journal of Lesbian Studies, 6,* 5–16.

Diamond, L. M. (2003a). Was it a phase? Young women's relinquishment of lesbian/bisexual identities over a 5-year period. *Journal of Personality and Social Psychology, 84,* 352–364.

Diamond, L. M. (2003b). What does sexual orientation orient? A biobehavioral model distinguishing romantic love and sexual desire. *Psychological Review, 110,* 173–192.

Diamond, L. M. (in press). What we got wrong about sexual identity development: Unexpected findings from a longitudinal study of young women. In A. Omoto & H. Kurtzman (Eds.), *Recent research on sexual orientation.* Washington, DC: American Psychological Association.

Diamond, L. M., & Savin-Williams, R. C. (2000). Explaining diversity in the development of same-sex sexuality among young women. *Journal of Social Issues, 56,* 297–313.

Di Mauro, D. (1997). Sexuality research in the United States. In J. Bancroft (Ed.), *Researching sexual behavior: Methodological issues* (pp. 3–8). Bloomington: Indiana University Press.

Dittus, P. J., Jaccard, J., & Gordon, V. V. (1997). The impact of African American fathers on adolescent sexual behavior. *Journal of Youth and Adolescence, 26,* 445–465.

Donald, M., Lucke, J., Dunne, M., & Raphael, B. (1995). Gender differences associated with young people's emotional reactions to sexual intercourse. *Journal of Youth and Adolescence, 24,* 453–464.

Dorius, G. L., Heaton, T. B., & Steffen, P. (1993). Adolescent life events and their association with the onset of sexual intercourse. *Youth and Society, 25,* 3–23.

Downs, A. C., & Hillje, L. S. (1993). Historical and theoretical perspectives on adolescent sexuality: An overview. In T. P. Gullotta, G. R. Adams, & R. Montemayor (Eds.), *Adolescent sexuality* (pp. 1–33). Newbury Park, CA: Sage.

Dubé, E. M. (2000). Sexual identity and intimacy development among two cohorts of sexual-minority men. The role of sexual behavior in the identification process of gay and bisexual males. *Journal of Sex Research, 37,* 123–132.

DuRant, R. H., Krowchuk, D. P., & Sinal, S. H. (1998). Victimization, use of violence, and drug use at school among male adolescents who engage in same-sex sexual behavior. *Journal of Pediatrics, 132,* 113–118.

Ehrhardt, A. A. (1996). Our view of adolescent sexuality: A focus on risk behavior without the developmental context. *American Journal of Public Health, 86,* 1523–1525.

Feldman, S. S., Turner, R. A., & Araujo, K. (1999). Interpersonal context as an influence on sexual timetables of youths: Gender and ethnic effects. *Journal of Research on Adolescence, 9,* 25–52.

Fine, M. (1988). Sexuality, schooling, and adolescent females: The missing discourse of desire. *Harvard Educational Review, 58,* 29–53.

Fisher, H. E. (1998). Lust, attraction, and attachment in mammalian reproduction. *Human Nature, 9,* 23–52.

Fisher, W. A., & Fisher, J. D., (1998). Understanding and promoting sexual and reproductive health behavior: Theory and method. *Annual Review of Sex Research, 9,* 39–76.

Florsheim, P. (Ed.). (2003). *Adolescent romantic relations and sexual behavior: Theory, research, and practical implications.* Mahwah, NJ: Erlbaum.

Fordham, S. (1993). "Those loud black girls": (Black) women, silence, and gender "passing" in the academy. *Anthropology and Education Quarterly, 24,* 3–32.

Frazier, P. A., & Esterly, E. (1990). Correlates of relationship beliefs: Gender, relationship experience and relationship satisfaction. *Journal of Social and Personal Relationships, 7,* 331–352.

Friedrich, W. N., Grambsch, P., Broughton, D., Kuiper, J., & Beilke, R. L. (1991). Normative sexual behavior in children. *Pediatrics, 88,* 456–464.

Frye, M. (1990). Lesbian "sex." In J. Allen (Ed.), *Lesbian philosophies and cultures.* Albany: State University of New York Press.

Furman, W., Brown, B. B., & Feiring, C. (Eds.). (1999). *The development of romantic relationships in adolescence.* New York: Cambridge University Press.

Gable, S. L., & Reis, H. T. (1999). Now and then, them and us, this and that: Studying relationships across time, partner, context, and person. *Personal Relationships, 6,* 415–432.

Gagnon, J. H. (1972). The creation of the sexual in early adolescence. In J. Kagan & R. Coles (Eds.), *Twelve to sixteen: Early adolescence* (pp. 231–257). New York: W. W. Norton.

Gagnon, J. H., & Simon, W. (1973). *Sexual conduct: The social sources of human sexuality.* Chicago: Aldine.

Galambos, N. L., & Leadbeater, B. J. (2000). Trends in adolescent research for the new millennium. *International Journal of Behavioral Development, 24,* 289–294.

Gardner, W., & Wilcox, B. L. (1993). Political intervention in scientific peer review: Research on adolescent sexual behavior. *American Psychologist, 48,* 972–983.

Garofalo, R., Wolf, R. C., Wissow, L. S., Woods, E. R., & Goodman, E. (1999). Sexual orientation and risk of suicide attempts among a representative sample of youth. *Archives of Pediatrics and Adolescent Medicine, 153,* 487–493.

Genius, S. J., & Genius, S. K. (1996). Orgasm without organisms: Science or propaganda? *Clinical Pediatrics, 35,* 10–17.

Golden, C. (1996). What's in a name? Sexual self-identification among women. In R. C. Savin-Williams & K. M. Cohen (Eds.), *The lives of lesbians, gays, and bisexuals: Children to adults* (pp. 229–249). Fort Worth, TX: Harcourt Brace.

Goodson, P., Evans, A., & Edmundson, E. (1997). Female adolescents and onset of sexual intercourse: A theory-based review of research from 1984 to 1994. *Journal of Adolescent Health, 21,* 147–156.

Gullotta, T. P. (1993). Preface. In T. P. Gullotta, G. R. Adams, & R. Montemayor (Eds.), *Adolescent sexuality* (pp. vii–viii). Newbury Park, CA: Sage.

Gullotta, T. P., Adams, G. R., & Montemayor, R. (Eds.). (1993). *Adolescent sexuality.* Newbury Park, CA: Sage.

Halpern, C. T. (2003). Biological influences on adolescent romantic and sexual behavior. In P. Florsheim (Ed.), *Adolescent romantic relations and sexual behavior: Theory, research, and practical implications.* Mahwah, NJ: Erlbaum.

Halpern, C. T., Joyner, K., Udry, J. R., & Suchindran, C. (2000). Smart teens don't have sex (or kiss much either). *Journal of Adolescent Health, 26,* 213–225.

Halpern, C. T., Udry, J. R., Campbell, B., & Suchindran, C. (1993). Testosterone and pubertal development as predictors of sexual activity: A panel analysis of adolescent males. *Psychosomatic Medicine, 55,* 436–447.

Halpern, C. J. T., Udry, J. R., Suchindran, C., & Campbell, B. (2000). Adolescent males' willingness to report masturbation. *Journal of Sex Research, 37,* 327–332.

Heiman, J. R. (1975). The physiology of erotica: Women's sexual arousal. *Psychology Today, 8,* 90–94.

Herdt, G., & Boxer, A. M. (1993). *Children of Horizons: How gay and lesbian teens are leading a new way out of the closet.* Boston: Beacon Press.

Herek, G. M. (2000). The psychology of sexual prejudice. *Current Directions in Psychological Science, 9*(1), 19–22.

Hopkins, K. W. (2000). Testing Reiss's autonomy theory on changes in non-marital coital attitudes and behaviors of U.S. teenagers: 1960–1990. *Scandinavian Journal of Sexology, 3,* 113–125.

Hrdy, S. B. (1987). The primate origins of human sexuality. In R. Bellig & G. Stevens (Eds.), *The evolution of sex* (pp. 101–132). San Francisco: Harper & Row.

Jessor, R., & Jessor, S. L. (1977). *Problem behavior and psychosocial development: A longitudinal study of youth.* New York: Academic Press.

Jessor, S. L., & Jessor, R. (1975). Transition from virginity to nonvirginity among youth: A social-psychological study over time. *Developmental Psychology, 11,* 473–484.

Kalof, L. (1995). Sex, power, and dependency: The politics of adolescent sexuality. *Journal of Youth and Adolescence, 24,* 229–249.

Katchadourian, H. (1990). Sexuality. In S. S. Feldman & G. R. Elliott (Eds.), *At the threshold: The developing adolescent* (pp. 330–351). Cambridge, MA: Harvard University Press.

Kegan, R. (1996). Neither "safe sex" nor "abstinence" may work—now what? Toward a third norm for youthful sexuality. In D. Cicchetti & S. L. Toth (Eds.), *Adolescence: Opportunities and challenges. Rochester symposium on developmental psychopathology* (Vol. 7, pp. 125–147). Rochester, NY: University of Rochester Press.

Kinsey, A. C., Pomeroy, W. B., & Martin, C. E. (1948). *Sexual behavior in the human male.* Philadelphia: W. B. Saunders.

Kinsey, A. C., Pomeroy, W. B., Martin, C. E., & Gebhard, P. H. (1953). *Sexual behavior in the human female.* Philadelphia: W. B. Saunders.

Kinsman, S. B., Romer, D., Furstenberg, F. F., & Schwartz, D. F. (1998). Early sexual initiation: The role of peer norms. *Pediatrics, 102,* 1185–1192.

Kirby, D. (2002). The impact of schools and school programs upon adolescent sexual behavior. *Journal of Sex Research, 39,* 27–33.

Knoth, R., Boyd, K., & Singer, B. (1988). Empirical tests of sexual selection theory: Predictions of sex differences in onset, intensity, and time course of sexual arousal. *Journal of Sex Research, 24,* 73–89.

Kuczynski, A. (2002, November 3). She's got to be a macho girl. *New York Times,* Section 9, pp. 1, 12.

Kupek, E. (2001). Sexual attitudes and number of partners in young British men. *Archives of Sexual Behavior, 30,* 13–27.

Lam, T. H., Shi, H. J., Ho, L. M., Stewart, S. M., & Fan, S. (2002). Timing of pubertal maturation and heterosexual behavior among Hong Kong Chinese adolescents. *Archives of Sexual Behavior, 31,* 359–366.

Larsson, I., & Svedin, C. G. (2002). Sexual experiences in childhood: Young adults' recollections. *Archives of Sexual Behavior, 31,* 263–273.

Laumann, E. O., Gagnon, J. H., Michael, R. T., & Michaels, S. (1994). *The social organization of sexuality: Sexual practices in the United States.* Chicago: University of Chicago Press.

Leitenberg, H., & Saltzman, H. (2000). A statewide survey of age at first intercourse for adolescent females and age of their male partners: Relation to other risk behaviors and statutory rape implications. *Archives of Sexual Behavior, 29,* 203–215.

Levesque, R. J. R. (2000). *Adolescents, sex, and the law: Preparing adolescents for responsible citizenship.* Washington, DC: American Psychological Association.

Levine, J. (2002). *Harmful to minors: The perils of protecting children from sex.* Minneapolis: University of Minnesota Press.

Levinson, R. A., Jaccard, J., & Beamer, L. (1995). Older adolescents' engagement in casual sex: Impact of risk perception and psychosocial motivations. *Journal of Youth and Adolescence, 24,* 349–364.

Lewin, T. (2002, September 29). More in high school are virgins, study finds. *New York Times.*

Lynch, C. O. (2001). Risk and protective factors associated with adolescent sexual activity. *Adolescent and Family Health, 2,* 99–107.

Maccoby, E. E. (1998). *The two sexes: Growing up apart and coming together.* Cambridge, MA: Belknap Press.

Manlove, J., Terry-Humen, E., Papillo, A. R., Franzetta, K., Williams, S., & Ryan, S. (2001). *Background for community-level work on positive reproductive health in adolescence: Reviewing the literature on contributing factors.* Washington, DC: Child Trends.

McClintock, M. K., & Herdt, G. (1996). Rethinking puberty: The development of sexual attraction. *Current Directions in Psychological Science, 5,* 178–183.

McLaughlin, C. S., Chen, C., Greenberger, E., & Biermeier, C. (1997). Family, peer, and individual correlates of sexual experience among Caucasian and Asian American late adolescents. *Journal of Research on Adolescence, 7,* 33–53.

Milhausen, R. R., & Herold, E. S. (1999). Does the sexual double standard still exist? Perceptions of university women. *Journal of Sex Research, 36,* 361–368.

Miller, B. C., & Benson, B. (1999). Romantic and sexual relationship development during adolescence. In W. Furman, B. B. Brown, & C. Feiring (Eds.), *The development of romantic relationships in adolescence* (pp. 99–121). New York: Cambridge University Press.

Miller, B. C., Christopherson, C. R., & King, P. K. (1993). Sexual behavior in adolescence. In T. P. Gullotta, G. R. Adams, & R. Montemayor (Eds.), *Adolescent sexuality* (pp. 57–76). Newbury Park, CA: Sage.

Miller, B., & Moore, K. (1990). Adolescent sexual behavior, pregnancy, and parenting: Research through the 1980's. *Journal of Marriage and the Family, 52,* 1025–1044.

Miller, B. C., Norton, M. C., Curtis, T., Hill, E. J., Schvaneveldt, P., & Young, M. H. (1997). The timing of sexual intercourse among adolescents: Family, peer, and other antecedents. *Youth and Society, 29,* 54–83.

Moore, S., & Rosenthal, D. (1993). *Sexuality in adolescence.* New York: Routledge.

Musick, J. S. (1993). *Young, poor, and pregnant: The psychology of teenage motherhood.* New Haven, CT: Yale University Press.

Mustanski, B. (2003). *Semantic heterogeneity in the definition of "having sex" for homosexuals.* Manuscript submitted for publication.

Newcomer, S., & Udry, J. R. (1988). Adolescents' honesty in a survey of sexual behavior. *Journal of Adolescent Research, 3,* 419–423.

Ochs, E. P., & Binik, Y. M. (1999). The use of couple data to determine the reliability of self-reported sexual behavior. *Journal of Sex Research, 36,* 374–384.

Okami, P., Olmstead, R., & Abramson, P. R. (1997). Sexual experiences in early childhood: 18-year longitudinal data from the UCLA family lifestyles project. *Journal of Sex Research, 34,* 339–347.

Oliver, M. B., & Hyde, J. S. (1993). Gender differences in sexuality: A meta-analysis. *Psychological Bulletin, 114,* 29–51.

O'Sullivan, L. F., & Meyer-Bahlburg, H. F. L. (2003). African American and Latina inner-city girls' reports of romantic and sexual development. *Journal of Social and Personal Relationships, 20,* 221–238.

O'Sullivan, L. F., Meyer-Bahlburg, H. F. L., & Watkins, B. X. (2000). Social cognitions associated with pubertal development in a sample of urban, low-income, African-American and Latina girls and mothers. *Journal of Adolescent Health, 27,* 227–235.

O'Sullivan, L. F., Meyer-Bahlburg, H. F. L., & Watkins, B. X. (2001). Mother-daughter communication about sex among urban African American and Latino families. *Journal of Adolescent Research, 16,* 269–292.

Paikoff, R. L. (1995). Early heterosexual debut: Situations of sexual possibility during the transition to adolescence. *American Journal of Orthopsychiatry, 65,* 389–401.

Papadopoulos, N. G., Stamboulides, P., & Triantafillou, T. (2000). The psychosexual development and behavior of university students: A nationwide survey in Greece. *Journal of Psychology and Human Sexuality, 11,* 93–110.

Paul, E. L., McManus, B., & Hayes, A. (2000). "Hookups": Characteristics and correlates of college students' spontaneous and anonymous sexual experiences. *Journal of Sex Research, 37,* 76–88.

Peplau, L. A., & Garnets, L. D. (2000). A new paradigm for understanding women's sexuality. *Journal of Social Issues, 56,* 329–350.

Pinsky, D. (2002, August 23–25). The sex lives of kids. *USA Weekend* (pp. 6–7).

Pitts, M., & Rahman, Q. (2001). Which behaviors constitute "having sex" among university students in the UK? *Archives of Sexual Behavior, 30,* 169–176.

Ponton, L. (2000). *The sex lives of teenagers: Revealing the secret world of adolescent boys and girls.* New York: Penguin Putman.

Prince, A., & Bernard, A. L. (1998). Sexual behaviors and safer sex practices of college students on a commuter campus. *Journal of American College Health, 47,* 11–21.

Regan, P. C., & Berscheid, E. (1995). Gender differences in beliefs about the causes of male and female sexual desire. *Personal Relationships, 2,* 345–358.

Reinisch, J. M., & Sanders, S. A. (1999). Attitudes toward and definitions of having sex: In reply. *Journal of the American Medical Association, 282*(20), 1918–1919.

Reiss, I. (1967). *The social context of premarital sexual permissiveness.* New York: Holt, Rinehart & Winston.

Remafedi, G., Resnick, M., Blum, R., & Harris, L. (1992). Demography of sexual orientation in adolescents. *Pediatrics, 89,* 714–721.

Resnick, M. D., Bearman, P. S., Blum, R. W., Bauman, K. E., Harris, K. M., Jones, J., Tabor, J., Beuhring, T., Sieving, R. E., Shew, M., Ireland, M., Bearinger, L. H., & Udry, J. R. (1997). Protecting adolescents from harm, findings from the national longitudinal study on adolescent health. *Journal of American Medical Association, 278,* 823–832.

Rind, B. (2001). Gay and bisexual adolescent boys' sexual experiences with men: An empirical examination of psychological correlates in a nonclinical sample. *Archives of Sexual Behavior, 30,* 345–368.

Rodgers, J. L., Billy, J. O. G., & Udry, J. R. (1982). The rescission of behaviors: Inconsistent responses in adolescent sexuality data. *Social Science Research, 11,* 280–296.

Rosario, M., Meyer-Bahlburg, H. F. L., Hunter, J., Exner, T. M., Gwadz, M., & Keller, A. M. (1996). The psychosexual development of urban lesbian, gay, and bisexual youths. *Journal of Sex Research, 33,* 113–126.

Rose, S. (2000). Heterosexism and the study of women's romantic and friend relationships. *Journal of Social Issues, 56,* 315–328.

Rosenthal, D. A., & Smith, A. M. A. (1997). Adolescent sexual timetables. *Journal of Youth and Adolescence, 26,* 619–636.

Rosenthal, D. A., Smith, A. M. A., & de Visser, R. (1999). Personal and social factors influencing age at first sexual intercourse. *Archives of Sexual Behavior, 28,* 319–333.

Rothblum, E. D. (2000). Sexual orientation and sex in women's lives: Conceptual and methodological issues. *Journal of Social Issues, 56,* 193–204.

Rodríguez Rust, P. C. (2000). Bisexuality: A contemporary paradox for women. *Journal of Social Issues, 56,* 205–221.

Russell, S., & Joyner, K. (2001). Adolescent sexual orientation and suicide risk: Evidence from a national study. *American Journal of Public Health, 91,* 1276–1281.

Sanders, S. A., & Reinisch, J. M. (1999). Would you say you 'had sex' if . . . ? *Journal of the American Medical Association, 281,* 275–277.

Sandfort, T. G. M. (1992). The argument for adult-child sex: A critical appraisal and new data. In W. O'Donohue & J. H. Geer (Eds.), *The sexual abuse of children: Vol. 1. Theory and research* (pp. 38–48). Hillside, NJ: Erlbaum.

Savin-Williams, R. C. (1998). *". . . and then I became gay": Young men's stories.* New York: Routledge.

Savin-Williams, R. C. (2001). A critique of research on sexual-minority youths. *Journal of Adolescence, 24,* 15–23.

Savin-Williams, R. C. (2003a). Are adolescent same-sex romantic relationships on our radar screen? In P. Florsheim (Ed.), *Adolescent romantic relations and sexual behavior: Theory, research, and practical implications* (pp. 325–336). Mahwah, NJ: Erlbaum.

Savin-Williams, R. C. (2003b). *Sexual-minority youth.* Unpublished manuscript.

Savin-Williams, R. C., & Diamond, L. M. (2000). Sexual identity trajectories among sexual-minority youths: Gender comparisons. *Archives of Sexual Behavior, 29,* 419–440.

Sawyer, R. G., & Smith, N. G. (1996). A survey of situational factors at first intercourse among college students. *American Journal of Health Behavior, 20,* 208–217.

Saywitz, K. J., Mannarino, A. P., Berliner, L., & Cohen, J. A. (2000). Treatment of sexually abused children and adolescents. *American Psychologist, 55,* 1040–1049.

Schafer, J. L., & Graham, J. W. (2002). Missing data: Our view of the state of the art. *Psychological Methods, 7,* 147–177.
Schlegel, A., & Barry, H., III. (1991). *Adolescence: An anthropological inquiry.* New York: Free Press.
Schuster, M. A., Bell, R. M., & Kanouse, D. E. (1996). The sexual practices of adolescent virgins: Genital sexual activities of high school students who have never had vaginal intercourse. *American Journal of Public Health, 86,* 1570–1576.
Schwartz, I. M. (1999). Sexual activity prior to coital initiation: A comparison between males and females. *Archives of Sexual Behavior, 28,* 63–69.
Schwarz, N. (1999). Self-reports: How the questions shape the answers. *American Psychologist, 54,* 93–105.
Seidman, S. N., Mosher, W. D., & Aral, S. O. (1994). Predictors of high-risk behavior in unmarried American women: Adolescent environment as risk factor. *Journal of Adolescent Health, 15,* 126–132.
Seligman, M. E. P., & Csikszentmihalyi, M. (2000). Positive psychology: An introduction. *American Psychologist, 55,* 5–14.
Siegel, D. M., Aten, M. J., & Roghmann, K. J. (1998). Self-reported honesty among middle and high school students responding to a sexual behavior questionnaire. *Journal of Adolescent Health, 23,* 20–28.
Simon, R. W., Eder, D., & Evans, C. (1992). The development of feeling norms underlying romantic love among adolescent females. *Social Psychology Quarterly, 55,* 29–46.
Smith, T. W. (1994). Attitudes towards sexual permissiveness: Trends, correlates, and behavioral connections. In A. S. Rossi (Ed.), *Sexuality across the life course* (pp. 63–97). Chicago: University of Chicago Press.
Sonenstein, F. L., Ku, L., & Pleck, J. H. (1997). Measuring sexual behavior among teenage males in the United States. In J. Bancroft (Ed.), *Researching sexual behavior: Methodological issues* (pp. 87–105). Bloomington: Indiana University Press.
Sprecher, S., & Hatfield, E. (1996). Premarital sexual standards among U.S. college students: Comparison with Russian and Japanese students. *Archives of Sexual Behavior, 25,* 261–288.
Sutton, M. J., Brown, J. D., Wilson, K. M., & Klein, J. D. (2002). Shaking the tree of knowledge for forbidden fruit: Where adolescents learn about sexuality and contraception. In J. D. Brown, J. R. Steele, & K. Walsh-Childers (Eds.), *Sexual teens, sexual media* (pp. 25–55). Mahwah, NJ: Erlbaum.
Tabachnick, B. G., & Fidell, L. S. (2001). *Using multivariate statistics* (4th ed.). Needham Heights, MA: Allyn & Bacon.
Thompson, S. (1995). *Going all the way: Teenage girls' tales of sex, romance and pregnancy.* New York: Hill and Wang.
Tolman, D. L. (2002). *Dilemma of desire: Teenage girls and sexuality.* Cambridge, MA: Harvard University Press.
Tolman, D. L. (2000). Object lessons: Romance, violation, and female adolescent sexual desire. *Journal of Sex Education and Therapy, 25,* 70–79.
Tolman, D. L. (1994). Adolescent girls' sexuality: Debunking the myth of the urban girl. In B. J. R. Leadbeater & N. Way (Eds.), *Urban girls: Resisting stereotypes, creating identities* (pp. 255–271). New York: New York University Press.
Tolman, D. L., & Diamond, L. M. (2001). Desegregating sexuality research: Combining cultural and biological perspectives on gender and desire. *Annual Review of Sex Research, 12,* 33–74.
Tolman, D. L., & Higgins, T. (1996). How being a good girl can be bad for girls. In N. B. Maglin & D. Perry (Eds.), *Good girls/bad girls: Women, sex, violence and power in the 1990s* (pp. 205–225). New Brunswick, NJ: Rutgers University Press.
Tolman, D. L., Spencer, R., Harmon, T., Rosen-Reynoso, & Striepe, M. (in press). Getting close, staying cool: Early adolescent boys' experiences with romantic relationships. In N. Way & J. Y. Chu (Eds.), *Adolescent boys in context.* New York: New York University Press.
Trivedi, N., & Sabini, J. (1998). Volunteer bias, sexuality, and personality. *Archives of Sexual Behavior, 27,* 181–195.

Turner, C. F., Miller, H. G., & Rogers, S. M. (1997). Survey measurement of sexual behavior: Problems and progress. In J. Bancroft (Ed.), *Researching sexual behavior: Methodological issues* (pp. 37–60). Bloomington: Indiana University Press.

Tyden, T., Olsson, S., & Bjorkelund-Ylander, C. (1991). Female university students in Sweden: Sex, contraception and STDs. *Advances in Contraception, 7,* 165–171.

Udry, J. R. (1988). Biological predispositions and social control in adolescent sexual behavior. *American Sociological Review, 53,* 709–722.

Udry, J. R. (1990). Hormonal and social determinants of adolescent sexual initiation. In J. Bancroft & J. M. Reinisch (Eds.), *Adolescence and puberty* (pp. 70–87). New York: Oxford University Press.

Udry, J. R., & Billy, J. O. G. (1987). Initiation of coitus in early adolescence. *American Sociological Review, 52,* 841–855.

Udry, J. R., Kovenock, J., Morris, N. M., & Vandenberg, B. J. (1995). Childhood precursors of age at first intercourse for females. *Archives of Sexual Behavior, 24,* 329–337.

Udry, J. R., Talbert, L. M., & Morris, N. M. (1986). Biosocial foundations for adolescent female sexuality. *Demography, 23,* 217–230.

United Nations. (1991). *Demographic yearbook.* New York: Author.

Upchurch, D. M., Lillard, L. A., Aneshensel, C. S., & Li, N. F. (2002). Inconsistencies in reporting the occurrence and timing of first intercourse among adolescents. *Journal of Sex Research, 39,* 197–206.

U.S. Department of Health and Human Services. (1995). *Report to Congress on out-of-wedlock childrearing.* Hyattsville, MD: Author.

Wallen, K. (1995). The evolution of female sexual desire. In P. R. Abramson & S. D. Pinkerton (Eds.), *Sexual nature/sexual culture* (pp. 57–79). Chicago: University of Chicago Press.

Ward, L. M., & Rivadeneyra, R. (1999). Contributions of entertainment television to adolescents' sexual attitudes and expectations: The role of viewing amount versus viewer involvement. *Journal of Sex Research, 36,* 237–249.

Weinberg, M. S., Lottes, I. L., & Shaver, F. M. (1995). Swedish or American heterosexual college youth: Who is more permissive? *Archives of Sexual Behavior, 24,* 409–437.

Weinberg, M. S., Williams, C. J., & Pryor, D. W. (1994). *Dual attraction: Understanding bisexuality.* New York: Oxford University Press.

Weisman, C. S., Plichta, S., Nathanson, C. A., Ensmiger, M., & Robinson, J. C. (1991). Consistency of condom use for disease prevention among adolescent users of oral contraceptives. *Family Planning Perspectives, 23,* 71–74.

Whisman, V. (1996). *Queer by choice: Lesbians, gay men, and the politics of identity.* New York: Routledge.

Whitbeck, L. B., Yoder, K. A., Hoyt, D. R., & Conger, R. D. (1999). Early adolescent sexual activity: A developmental study. *Journal of Marriage and the Family, 61,* 934–946.

Wiederman, M. W. (1999). Volunteer bias in sexuality research using college student participants. *Journal of Sex Research, 36,* 59–66.

Wright, M. T. (1998). Beyond risk factors: Trends in European safer sex research. *Journal of Psychology and Human Sexuality, 10,* 7–18.

Zani, B. (1991). Male and female patterns in the discovery of sexuality during adolescence. *Journal of Adolescence, 14,* 163–178.

Chapter 8

GENDER AND GENDER ROLE DEVELOPMENT IN ADOLESCENCE

Nancy L. Galambos

Sex and gender. Although both of these words have simple and objective definitions, they are associated with powerful and sometimes conflicting images. These two words have a plethora of personal meanings that can evoke an array of unexpected emotions. The associations that people make when they consider the meaning of sex and gender run the gamut from jokes and embarrassment to serious concerns about power imbalances and inequalities, from angry thoughts related to the battle of the sexes, to happy recognition of the intimate bonds of romantic love, and from arguments about the division of household labor to expressions about the joys of parenting.

In the scholarly literature, the following objective definitions are common: *sex* indicates the biological status of male or female, whereas *gender* is a label used to indicate characteristics that are believed to be learned and acquired by males or females as a result of social experience. As such, use of the word *sex* to describe differences between males and females in their development can imply that these differences are biologically based. Reference to gender implies that observed differences between males and females are experientially based (Lippa, 2002; Ruble & Martin, 1998). In this chapter I use the term *gender* to refer to most of the constructs that are discussed, both for the purpose of consistency and in recognition that human development is undeniably a social as well as a biological phenomenon. In adolescence, the biological, cognitive, and social changes that transform girls and boys into women and men bring to the fore the issue of gender differences and highlight gender as an issue critical to understanding adolescent development.

The purpose of this chapter is to review current theory and research pertinent to the development of gender differences and gender socialization in adolescence. I begin by defining important constructs pertaining to gender roles and discuss the construct of gender identity, which, arguably, is a core influence on the developmental paths that adolescents follow. I then present overviews of the major theories of and approaches to the sources and development of gender differences. This discussion is followed by an explanation of the gender intensification hypothesis, which pertains specifically to the divergence of gender roles in adolescence. I also explore evidence for gender differences in characteristics and behaviors that may be seen in adolescence. Because gender develops as a function of the many contexts in which the adolescent is a part, selected contexts for the socialization of gendered characteristics and behaviors are also explored. These contexts include the family (parents and siblings), school, peers, and the media.

Finally, throughout this chapter I point to emerging directions of research in the study of gender in adolescence and make suggestions for areas in which research is needed. Although much has been learned about gender and gender role development, it will become clear that issues of sex and gender in adolescence are still as fascinating and mystifying as ever.

GENDER ROLE CONSTRUCTS

The scholarly literature on gender roles is replete with constructs related to gender, sometimes with different terms used to refer to the same quality and different definitions applied to the same term. Moreover, operationalizations of gender-related constructs differ from study to study (Liben & Bigler, 2002; Signorella, Bigler, & Liben, 1993). To avoid confusion, terms that are used frequently in this chapter are defined here. To begin, the term *gender role* typically refers to shared cultural expectations about appropriate behaviors for the sexes (Spence & Helmreich, 1978). *Gender typing* is the process by which individuals develop the attributes that are consistent with their gender roles. The products of this process are seen in *gender-typed attributes,* for example, gender-typed behaviors, personality characteristics, beliefs, preferences, and attitudes. Of course, the products of gender typing consist of numerous covert and overt attributes, making the concept of gender-typed attributes necessarily multidimensional (Huston, 1983). The term *gendered behavior* is a contemporary term frequently used to denote behavior that is gender typed. The term *gender development* or *gender role development* is typically used to refer to intraindividual change in any or all of the many gender-typed attributes that may appear, disappear, become magnified or diminished, or change form or expression across any portion of the life span.

One core dimension or outcome of gender typing is labeled *gender identity* (sometimes called gender role identity or gender role orientation). Originally conceived as simply knowing that one is male or female, gender identity is established in early childhood (Kohlberg, 1966). Applied to older individuals, however, the concept of gender identity is much more complex. Gender identity has been defined as the extent to which individuals see themselves as masculine and feminine (Bem, 1974; Spence & Helmreich, 1978). *Masculinity* may be demonstrated by the possession of instrumental traits such as showing leadership, athleticism, and independence, whereas *femininity* is captured in expressive traits such as compassion, sensitivity, and cheerfulness (Holt & Ellis, 1998; Spence & Helmreich, 1978). From this perspective, masculine males and feminine females are regarded as having a gender-typed identity. Some individuals, however, are androgynous, showing high levels of both masculinity and femininity, or undifferentiated, with low levels of both (Bem, 1974). Bem (1981) later theorized that masculine males and feminine females are *gender schematic* (viewing themselves and the world through a gendered lens) but others (nonmasculine males and nonfeminine females) are *gender aschematic* (non-gender-typed).

Spence (1993; Spence & Hall, 1996) has challenged the value of the gender identity construct as it has been conceived, arguing that gender-related self-perceptions are complex and multifactorial, showing heterogeneity across individuals of the same sex as well as heterogeneity within individuals. Spence and Hall (1996) claimed that "the heterogeneous collection of self-perceptions, beliefs, and behaviors that distinguish between males and females do not contribute to a single factor or even to two factors, but instead are multifactorial. . . . Knowledge of a person's standing on one set of gender-related measures cannot automatically be assumed to yield information about their standing on another set" (p. 663). Indeed, research on adolescents shows that their masculine and feminine personality attributes and their observed behavior in laboratory-based situations are not necessarily correlated (Katz & Walsh, 1991; Kolaric & Galambos, 1995). Increasingly, researchers are employing multidimensional definitions of gender identity. As an example, Egan and Perry (2001) construed gender identity as consisting of many elements including perceived compatibility with one's gender group (including feelings of gender typicality and contentment with one's gender), perceived pressure to conform to one's gender role, and attitudes toward gender groups. Liben and Bigler (2002) argued that it is important to distinguish and examine the relations between gender typing of self in terms of one's activities, traits, and occupations, and gender typing of others (i.e., attitudes toward and stereotypes about what males and females can or should do).

Another construct of some consequence in the literature is *gender role flexibility.* Gender role flexibility has been discussed as the capability of changing one's behavior, regardless of gender, to meet the demands of the context. The adoption of behaviors consistent with one's gender role may restrict the individual's life choices, but gender role flexibility opens more avenues to behaviors and choices and hence is thought to be associated with more optimal psychological health (Bem, 1975; Hefner, Rebecca, & Oleshansky, 1975; Worell, 1981).

How is gender role flexibility measured? Although there is no single operationalization of gender role flexibility, a lower level of gender typing on indexes of gender-typed attributes (e.g., those who are gender aschematic) might mean that the individual is more behaviorally flexible (Bem, 1974; Worell, 1981). Thus, those individuals who see a wide variety of behaviors and personality traits as open to males and females, who feel comfortable in pursuing interests and careers that may not be a part of their prescribed gender roles, and who describe themselves as both masculine and feminine may be most likely to be among the people who show behavioral flexibility (Bem, 1975). Katz and Ksansnak (1994) argued that there are two aspects of gender role flexibility: one's own preferences and one's tolerance toward flexibility in others. Their cross-sectional study spanning middle childhood through adolescence found that gender role flexibility was higher in females and increased in both sexes with age. Moreover, the authors found that gender role flexibility was associated with increased cognitive flexibility as well as exposure to socialization environments (i.e., parents and friends) that are flexible.

Another dimension or outcome of gender typing may be seen in the individual's *gender role attitudes,* which are feelings of approval or disapproval toward gender roles (Huston, 1983; Spence & Helmreich, 1978). Galambos, Petersen, Richards, and Gitelson (1985) reported that young adolescent girls with gender role attitudes that favored equality of the sexes were more likely to have positive self-images than were girls who approved of the gender-based division of roles. *Gender stereotypes* are also frequently measured in research on gender roles; these are defined as an individual's beliefs about the characteristics associated with males and females. Using a combined cross-sectional and longitudinal design, Alfieri, Ruble, and Higgins (1996) examined whether there were age differences and change in gender stereotypes in the period from middle childhood through middle adolescence (Grades 4 through 11). The results, which were similar for the cross-sectional and longitudinal comparisons, showed that flexibility with respect to gender stereotypes decreased during adolescence but also showed a temporary increase immediately following the transition to junior high school (in either 7th or 8th grade). Thus, the temporary increase in flexibility concerning gender stereotypes seemed to be occasioned by school transitions in which young adolescents were likely exposed to a wider range of peers and personalities (Alfieri et al., 1996).

THEORIES OF GENDER DEVELOPMENT

Large bodies of literature are devoted to a range of theories that attempt to explain how gendered characteristics and behaviors develop. It is beyond the scope of this chapter to present these theories in detail, but it is important to review briefly the principles of several current theoretical perspectives on gender that are relevant to research on adolescence. Contemporary orientations to understanding gender development fall into three broad categories: biological, social learning (socialization), and cognitive theories. Moreover, a fourth theoretical orientation, the developmental systems approach, is discussed as a superordinate perspective that may be able to integrate elements of biological, social learning, and cognitive theories and to guide future research on gender development in adolescence.

Biological Theories

Biological approaches to gender assume that biological factors (e.g., genes, hormones) are the basis of male-female differences in behavior. Evolutionary theory is an example of a biological approach in which the operative principles for the determination of social behavior are natural selection and the transmission of one's genetic material (Ruble & Martin, 1998). As such, evolutionary theory focuses on gender differences in mate preference (younger partners for males and older partners for females), sexual behavior (more interest in sexual activity among males), and parental investment in children (higher in females). Gender differences in these behaviors are believed to promote fertility and ensure the survival of children (Kenrick & Luce, 2000; Lippa, 2002). Moreover, the tenets of evolutionary theory are consistent with other gender differences in behavior, such as higher rates of aggression among males than females. Homicide, for instance, may be a strategy to limit competition for sexual partners (Kenrick & Luce, 2000; Lippa, 2002).

Biological theories draw attention to the impact of genes on human development. Genes influence the presence and levels of hormones such as testosterone, which in turn are believed to have an impact on behavior (see Susman & Rogol, this volume). Prenatal levels of hormones are thought to organize the central nervous system and brain structures (with higher levels of testosterone "masculinizing" these structures), whereas the increases in hormones at puberty are assumed by some to activate reproductive and gender-typical behavior (Lippa, 2000; Udry, 2000). Evidence in support of a hormone-behavior connection comes from studies linking prenatal levels of androgens to gender-typed behaviors and interests in childhood, adolescence, and adulthood. For example, Berenbaum (1999; Berenbaum & Snyder, 1995) found that prenatal exposure to relatively high levels of androgens in girls is associated in childhood and adolescence with gender-atypical (i.e., masculine) interests and activities, even though these girls identified with and were raised as females. Similarly, Udry (2000) reported a link between prenatal exposure to high levels of testosterone and females' gender-atypical behavior 30 years later. Biological theories have been criticized for not taking into account variability in gender differences across culture, for neglecting the role of experience in shaping gendered behavior throughout the life course, for overgeneralizing results from animals to humans, and for using counterfactual models of genetic action (Bussey & Bandura, 1999; Kennelly, Merz, & Lorber, 2000; Lerner, 2002; Lippa, 2002).

Some contemporary proponents of biological theories promote biopsychosocial models of hormone-behavior associations that avoid a strong stance on biological determinism by acknowledging that biological factors interact with cultural or environmental factors to influence gendered behavior (Kenrick & Luce, 2000; Susman, 1997; Susman & Rogol, this volume). For example, Udry (2000) argued for an integrated model of gendered behavior that has biological foundations but is open to some influence of socialization. Indeed, his study comparing the gender-typed behavior of young women with higher or lower levels of prenatal exposure to androgens showed a significant positive relationship between their feminine behavior as adults and their perceptions of their mothers as encouraging femininity in childhood. The effect of mothers' encouragement was limited, however, to young women who were not exposed prenatally to high levels of androgens (Udry, 2000). In a behavior-genetic study designed to examine genetic and environmental influences on gender-typed behaviors and attitudes in male and female adolescents, Cleveland, Udry, and Chantala (2001) found that 25% of the variance in males' and 38% of the variance in females' gender-typed characteristics were attributable to genetic influences. The remaining 75% and 62% of the variance (for males and females, respectively) was accounted for by nonshared environmental influences (e.g., peers, teachers, media) and measurement error. The effect of shared environments (i.e., parents) was negligible.

Social Learning (Socialization) Theories

Evidence for environmental influences on gender differences in development (e.g., Cleveland et al., 2001) draws attention to the importance of considering how socialization experiences shape gender development. Early social learning approaches highlighted the roles of observation, modeling, imitation, and reinforcement in the emergence of gender differences (Mischel, 1966). Most social learning approaches assume that parents, teachers, peers, siblings, and the mass media provide models for how to behave and shape gendered behavior through the punishment of gender-atypical activities and reward for gender-typical activities. There is a large body of literature on children providing support for the social learning approach (Lippa, 2002).

Later social learning approaches expanded to include a consideration of cognitive and psychological factors that also play a role in gender differentiation, for example, the social cognitive theory of gender development (Bandura, 1986; Bussey & Bandura, 1999). Bussey and Bandura (1999) reviewed evidence for their complex sociocognitive model of *triadic reciprocal causation,* in which elements of the triad are the personal (cognitive, motivational, affective, self-regulatory), behavioral (gender-linked activity patterns), and environmental (social influences in everyday life). These elements or subsystems are believed to interact with and influence one another. Biological influences are downplayed, as most gender differences are seen to be cultural in origin. Emphasized in this model is the self as agent. The individual is seen as an active processor and interpreter of gender-related information, which feeds into decisions on how to conduct oneself. Another important aspect of social cognitive theory is that triadic reciprocal causation is presumed to operate throughout the life course. The learning of gender-typical or gender-atypical behaviors, roles, and characteristics is not limited to early parts of the life span but can develop throughout life (Bussey & Bandura, 1999). This assumption can help to spur research on gender roles during the period of adolescence, as much more empirical attention has been paid to gendered behavior in childhood. With respect to developmental research on gender roles in adolescence, it is probably safe to say that more studies than not have been guided roughly by a social learning perspective on gender differences.

Cognitive Theories

A chapter by Kohlberg (1966) heralded the cognitive approach to understanding the development of gender differences. Largely focused on explaining gender development in the childhood years, Kohlberg asserted that children are active processors of information and that they categorize individuals (including themselves) according to gender. Critical to his theory is the development of gender identity (which was defined as knowing that one is male or female) and gender stability (understanding that gender is maintained over time) in early childhood. This understanding allows the child to seek out information concerning the appropriate behaviors for males and females and to behave accordingly (in a gender-typed manner) to achieve consistency between the self and the environment (Martin, 2000; Ruble & Martin, 1998).

Kohlberg's theory paved the way for other cognitive theories, including Bem's (1981) gender schema theory. Bem argued that individuals develop gender schemas, or naive theories about gender, through which they view the world and themselves. Gender schemas are beliefs, cognitions, and ideas related to male-female differences and to masculinity and femininity. These schemas organize the way that people, situations, and events are interpreted and can influence and bias behavior (Martin, 2000). Bem (1981) proposed individual differences in the gender schemas that people hold. Gender-schematic individuals see the world and themselves in terms of gender stereotypes; that is, males should be and act masculine, whereas females should be and act feminine. Gender-aschematic individuals, on the other hand, are less attuned to noticing and interpreting their own and others' behavior in gendered terms.

More recently, the cognitive perspective has been expanded to include dynamic and multifaceted gender schemas. It is recognized that there are many different gender-related constructs (e.g., gender identity, gender role attitudes). These constructs and others should be identified, measured, and examined together with behavior in individuals at different ages and across time and situations in order to acquire a better understanding of gender differences in development (Martin, 2000).

Developmental Systems Orientation

Considering the past several decades of theorizing and research on gender development, the biological, social learning, and cognitive approaches generally have become more complex and more considerate of the probability of multiple, interactive influences from many levels of analysis (both within and outside of the individual) on gender-related behavior. Indeed, in some cases, proponents of one approach have acknowledged and incorporated elements of other approaches in their own evolving views of influences on gender development. For example, whereas a strict social learning perspective places primary emphasis on the acquisition of gendered behavior through the imitation of models, reinforcement, and punishment, the sociocognitive model of Bussey and Bandura (1999) identified as equally important individual characteristics such as cognitive, attentional, perceptual, and self-regulatory skills and processes. Similarly, after examining data on gender-typed characteristics in 5- to 12-year-old children, Serbin, Powlishta, and Gulko (1993) concluded that both the socialization and cognitive perspectives received support. Moreover, they developed a model of gender typing that included cognitive and socialization influences. Similarly, Susman's (1997; Susman & Rogol, this volume) biopsychosocial model of influences on adolescent behavior eschews biological determinism in favor of multiple, reciprocally related factors involving both the adolescent and his or her context. These examples demonstrate movement toward developmental systems models for understanding the determinants of gendered behavior in adolescence.

The developmental systems approach is an orientation to the study of human development that has several key assumptions (Lerner, 2002). First, developmental systems models recognize the embeddedness of the individual in multiple, interrelated contexts. In other words, the adolescent experience is shaped by involvement in and exposure to contexts such as the family, school, peers, community, and culture. These contexts are interdependent, each having an influence on the other. Second, developmental systems models acknowledge reciprocal or bidirectional relations between the individual and the contexts of which he or she is a part. That is, the adolescent both influences and is influenced by people and events in different contexts. Third, the adolescent is considered as an active producer of his or her development, an individual who brings a host of characteristics (e.g., physical, cognitive, emotional, personality), understandings, desires, and needs to the interactions that he or she has with the environment. Therefore, the changing relations between adolescents and their interdependent and changing contexts are responsible for determining adolescents' developmental trajectories (Lerner, 2002; Lerner, Lerner, De Stefanis, & Apfel, 2001).

Applied to the study of gender development, the developmental systems approach leads us to consider the influences of many levels of organization, including broad sets of biological, cognitive, and social attributes. That is, the acquisition and expression of gender-typed characteristics and behaviors cannot fully be understood without measuring the changing and interrelated qualities of the active adolescent as well as multiple and changing features of the context. This focus necessitates multivariate studies (including many variables), multilevel research (focusing on biological, cognitive, and social aspects of gender development), and longitudinal designs that can capture change in the adolescent and in the context (Lerner, 2002). In essence, the developmental systems approach moves beyond the biological, cognitive, and socialization perspectives by calling for the careful study, consideration, and integration of themes from each one.

THE GENDER INTENSIFICATION HYPOTHESIS

With the biological, cognitive, emotional, and social changes that occur during the period of adolescence, it is reasonable to view adolescence as a primary transition point during which gendered behaviors may be enacted, questioned, changed, or solidified. Indeed, considering the period of adolescence, Hill and Lynch (1983) argued that with the onset of puberty, boys and girls experience an intensification of gender-related expectations. This *gender intensification hypothesis* posits that behavioral, attitudinal, and psychological differences between adolescent boys and girls increase with age and are the result of increased socialization pressures to conform to traditional masculine and feminine gender roles. Hill and Lynch (1983) proposed that puberty plays a role in the differentiation of masculine and feminine characteristics by serving as a signal to socializing others (parents, teachers, peers) that the adolescent is beginning the approach to adulthood and should begin to act accordingly, that is, in ways that resemble the stereotypical male or female adult.

Galambos, Almeida, and Petersen (1990) suggested that empirical support for gender intensification would be provided if (a) a pattern of increasing differentiation between boys and girls was shown on characteristics that already exhibited gender differences prior to early adolescence and (b) the intensification of gender-related attributes was greatest for those adolescents who had entered puberty. To test the gender intensification hypothesis, Galambos et al. (1990) examined longitudinal data on adolescents followed from the 6th through the 8th grades. The pattern of mean-level change in three gender-related attributes was observed: self-reported masculinity, femininity, and gender role attitudes. The results indicated that initial gender differences on masculinity (with boys higher than girls) and on gender role attitudes (with girls exhibiting more egalitarian attitudes than boys) increased from 6th to 8th grade. However, pubertal timing was unrelated to this gender divergence. Thus, there was partial support for the gender intensification hypothesis.

Crouter, Manke, and McHale (1995) examined whether there was evidence for gender intensification in family socialization experiences and whether the family context (parents' division of labor, sex of younger sibling) played a role in these experiences. At two points across a 1-year period in early adolescence, they observed adolescents' participation in masculine and feminine household chores and adolescents' involvement in dyadic activities with mothers and fathers (with girls expected to become more involved with mothers and boys expected to become more involved with fathers). The results showed that adolescent girls in families with a traditional parental division of labor (i.e., the mother performed most household chores) and with a younger brother maintained a high level of participation in feminine household tasks, whereas participation of the rest of the sample in feminine tasks declined. Boys in families with a traditional parental division of labor increased their performance of masculine household tasks compared to other adolescents. Concerning dyadic activities, boys' involvement with their fathers increased over the year, whereas girls' involvement with their mothers increased over the same time. This pattern of differentiation in dyadic activities with parents was strongest, however, in boys with younger sisters and girls with younger brothers. Thus, the results provided some support for gender intensification in family socialization experiences, dependent on selected aspects of the family context.

Another study examined self-competence in math, language arts, and sports in a sample of children first recruited in Grades 1 through 4 and followed for 8 years (Jacobs, Lanza, Osgood, Eccles, & Wigfield, 2002). Because boys typically rate their abilities as higher than girls in math and sports and girls rate their competence as higher than boys in language arts (e.g., English; Eccles et al., 1993), the investigators were able to examine the gender intensification hypothesis by exploring developmental trajectories of gender-typed academic attributes across the period of childhood through adolescence. Using growth curve analysis techniques, the authors found that there was not an increased gender differentiation in self-competence in math, language arts, and sports during adolescence. Rather, the gender difference in math competence (with boys feeling more competent) was largest in Grade 1, and by Grade 12 girls and boys reported similar levels of competence in math. With respect to language arts, girls and boys started out at similar levels, but by Grade 6 there was a dramatic gender difference favoring girls, which narrowed somewhat by Grade 12. The growth curve for competence in sports demonstrated a significant gender difference in Grade 1 (favoring boys) that continued through to Grade 12. Self-rated competence in all domains declined on average over the period of the study. The investigators did not examine whether puberty was related to differences in developmental trajectories of self-rated competence.

What is the validity of the gender intensification hypothesis? It is both surprising and interesting that the gender intensification hypothesis was not supported in the Jacobs et al. (2002) study. This is an excellent example of research covering a large age range and a long span of time in which to observe whether and when gender differences emerge or escalate. As such, this may be the only study explicitly speaking to the gender intensification hypothesis that has covered so large an age span. A rigorous test of the gender intensification hypothesis can be conducted only in the context of such longitudinal data. Other longitudinal studies finding some support for gender intensification were short-term (Crouter et al., 1995; Galambos et al., 1990). The Jacobs et al. (2002) study raises the possibility that when considered across the period of childhood and adolescence, gender intensification is not as strong or as wide-ranging a phenomenon as was first assumed. Of course, the breadth of gender-related constructs that have been studied for gender intensification in adolescence is quite small. Growth trajectories in gender-related constructs differ by domain; even within the area of achievement, patterns of change in gender differences vary according to the specific subject of study (e.g., math vs. language arts; Jacobs et al., 2002). Therefore, considering the many aspects of gender-related development that could be observed, the gender intensification hypothesis has not yet been subjected to a fair test.

In general, the jury is not yet in on the validity of the gender intensification hypothesis, but it is unlikely that gender intensification will apply uniformly to the many aspects of gender identity and gender-related constructs. In addition to the need for more longitudinal research on multiple gender-related constructs covering the period of childhood through adolescence, further study should be undertaken of the process of puberty as it relates to gender differentiation. Examination of the links between social transitions (e.g., Alfieri et al., 1996) and contexts (e.g., Crouter et al., 1995) and gender differentiation would also be helpful in charting the developmental trajectories of girls and boys in the domains of gender-related attitudes, expectations, beliefs, and behaviors.

GENDER DIFFERENCES IN ADOLESCENCE

Underlying efforts to understand gender development in adolescence is the observation of differences between adolescent girls and boys. What is the evidence for such differences in adolescence? How wide-ranging are these differences? Many variables have been assessed for gender differences—more than can possibly be reviewed in these pages. Thus, in this section I examine evidence for gender differences in domains selected because they have received much empirical attention in adolescence, they should command the resources of more researchers, or they are emerging areas of interest with exciting potential. These domains include research on gender-related constructs, educational and occupational achievement, self-esteem, depression, aggression, problem and risk-taking behavior, positive youth development, peer relations and intimacy, and verbal and nonverbal behavior.

Gender-Related Constructs

Compared with adolescent girls, adolescent boys hold less egalitarian gender role attitudes (Galambos et al., 1985, 1990) and identify themselves as having more masculine and less feminine personality traits and interests (Galambos et al., 1990; Kenny & Gallagher, 2002; Updegraff, McHale, & Crouter, 2000). Adolescent girls do more feminine household work, whereas adolescent boys engage in more masculine household chores (McHale, Bartko, Crouter, & Perry-Jenkins, 1990). Although gender role flexibility (the acquisition of both feminine and masculine qualities) is seen as desirable by researchers (Bem, 1975; Hefner et al., 1975), research suggests that from the perspective of the adolescent boy's psychosocial well-being, having masculine attributes may be more important than is having feminine attributes (Markstrom-Adams, 1989). In adolescent boys, high masculinity, but not high femininity, is related to high self-esteem and peer acceptance. The results for girls point to the advantages of gender role flexibility. High levels of masculinity *and* femininity in girls are significantly related to self-esteem and peer acceptance; femininity alone is not associated with high adjustment (Lamke, 1982; Massad, 1981). Moreover, having masculine personality characteristics and less traditional gender role attitudes is related in girls to lower levels of weight concerns and disordered eating (Edwards-Leeper & Allgeier, 2002; McHale, Corneal, Crouter, & Birch, 2001). Masculinity in girls is also connected to better performance on a national test of cognitive abilities (Lippa, 1998).

Some authors have speculated that pressures on boys to engage in behavior consistent with their gender role are stronger than pressures on girls to do so, and the consequences for resisting such pressure are more severe (e.g., Huston, 1983). Indeed, Polce-Lynch, Myers, Kliewer, and Kilmartin (2001) found in a cross-sectional study that gender differences in self-reported emotional expression (the extent to which one outwardly displays emotion) were nonexistent in Grade 5, significant in Grade 8, and even larger in Grade 12. Whereas girls increased in their emotional expressiveness, boys became more restrictive; these results are congruent with the gender intensification hypothesis (Polce-Lynch et al., 2001). Berndt and Heller (1986) reported that in a cross-sectional sample of individuals ranging from kindergarten to college age, participants found it more acceptable for girls than for boys to behave in a manner inconsistent with their gender role. This study also showed that girls developed flexible gender stereotypes for girls (i.e., finding it acceptable for girls to choose masculine activities) sooner than boys did.

In general, studies examining gender-related constructs in adolescence (e.g., gender identity, gender role attitudes, gender stereotypes) seem to be less numerous today than in the 1980s. In fact, Ruble and Martin (1998) showed that for all age groups combined and for children specifically, articles on gender-related constructs dropped off after 1985. However, articles on gender differences in characteristics remained high and consistent from 1985 to 1993. The focus in adolescence now seems to be on gender differences in domains such as achievement, aggression, and depression.

Educational and Occupational Achievement

Nowhere are gender differences more apparent than in the work that males and females do. One has only to look around to see that many occupations are dominated by one sex more than the other (e.g., males in engineering, females in nursing). This might not be so interesting if the financial rewards and the benefits associated with male-dominated occupations did not typically exceed those of many female-dominated occupations. However, when it comes to financial well-being, females are at a distinct disadvantage.

Despite women's increased participation in the labor force, the influence of the women's movement, and weakening gender roles (Holt & Ellis, 1998), the career choices of many teens of both sexes reflect relatively traditional, gender-related occupational aspirations (Schulenberg, Goldstein, & Vondracek, 1991). The roots of gender differences in occupational trajectories are undoubtedly complicated, but one source of influence is in course selection and achievement in high school. During adolescence, for instance, boys gain an advantage over girls in certain domains of mathematics achievement (Linn & Petersen, 1986), although this gender gap is closing (Marsh & Yeung, 1998). Compared to boys, girls in secondary school and beyond have less interest in math and science, more often drop out of or elect not to take math and science courses, and avoid educational and career paths that require these courses (Kavrell & Petersen, 1984). Gender differences in academic achievement and in career preferences are not attributable to differences in ability, but rather to factors such as girls' and parents' attributions about the sources of girls' success. That is, girls (and their parents) are more likely than boys (and their parents) to attribute girls' success to external factors and effort rather than to ability (Eccles et al., 1993; Li & Adamson, 1995; Lightbody, Siann, Stocks, & Walsh, 1996; Tenenbaum & Leaper, 2003). Thus, girls may be limited in their eventual occupational attainment by how they and others see themselves during the high school years. One aspect of self-perception that might be important for girls is their self-esteem.

Self-Esteem

One of the sources for the gender intensification hypothesis was research suggesting that during adolescence, girls' self-esteem drops relative to boys' (Hill & Lynch, 1983). Research had shown that in early adolescence, girls are more self-conscious and hold themselves in lower esteem than do males (Rosenberg & Simmons, 1975). A classic study by Simmons, Blyth, Van Cleave, and Bush (1979) found that a decline in girls' self-esteem coincided with the transition from an elementary to a junior high school environment. Moreover, this decrease was strongest in girls who had experienced menarche and had started dating. Simmons, Burgeson, Carlton-Ford, and Blyth (1987) also reported declines in self-esteem among adolescent girls, but they tied the magnitude of the decline to the number of life transitions (e.g., moving to a new neighborhood, experiencing a family disruption). A larger number of transitions may tax the resources of the adolescent, who has difficulty coping with all of the new demands. This, in turn, may be associated with more negativity in feelings about the self. The popular press has latched on to the issue of gender differences in self-esteem in adolescence, characterizing the loss of girls' self-esteem as precipitous and dramatic (e.g., Pipher, 1994). How accurate is this picture?

A recent meta-analysis examining gender differences in global self-esteem (the overall regard held for the self) puts claims of dramatic losses of self-esteem in adolescent girls into perspective (Kling, Hyde, Showers, & Buswell, 1999). Kling et al. aggregated over 200 reports containing data on gender differences in global self-esteem, representing over 97,000 research participants from the ages of 7 to over 60 years. The results were that with all ages combined, there was an overall gender difference; males showed higher self-esteem than did females. The effect was a small one, however ($d = .21$). Comparisons across age demonstrated that the gender difference peaked in late adolescence (ages 15 to 18), with an effect size that was moderate ($d = .33$). The gender difference was negligible by age 60. Kling et al. (1999) also conducted analyses of gender differences in self-esteem in several large national data sets available in the United States, which covered the ages from 13 to 32 years. The finding of an overall small gender difference in self-esteem favoring males was replicated in this set of analyses. The gender differences were relatively stable across age in these data sets, except for one in which the gender difference was highest for participants in Grade 8 ($d = .24$) compared to those in Grades 10 and 12 ($d = .15$ and $.16$, respectively).

The authors also examined whether gender differences were moderated by ethnicity (African American and European American samples), with mixed results. One analysis found that the gender difference in self-esteem did not pertain to African Americans, whereas the other found no moderator effect of ethnicity (Kling et al., 1999). Overall, the results suggest that there may be some decline in self-esteem for girls in adolescence, but the magnitude of the decline cannot be considered to be dramatic.

In addition to the life transitions noted in the Simmons et al. (1987) study, decreases in self-esteem in adolescence may be connected with pubertal changes, increased weight gain, the importance of physical appearance, and body dissatisfaction (Tobin-Richards, Boxer, & Petersen, 1983). Adolescent girls are significantly more dissatisfied with their bodies than are adolescent boys (Barker & Galambos, 2003; Richards, Boxer, Petersen, & Albrecht, 1990; Rosenblum & Lewis, 1999). In early adolescence, boys with more advanced pubertal development feel more attractive and more satisfied with their bodies than do girls with more advanced pubertal development (Tobin-Richards et al., 1983). Moreover, the weight gains of puberty seem to have a more negative impact on girls' body satisfaction, depression, self-esteem, and perceived romantic competence than on boys' (McHale, Corneal, et al., 2001; Richards et al., 1990; Barker & Galambos, 2003). Thus, it appears that girls' self-perceptions in general are related in part to the physical changes that occur in adolescence.

Depression

During adolescence, more girls than boys show depressive symptoms and become clinically depressed. This gender difference appears to emerge after age 13 and is maintained throughout adulthood, with about twice as many females as males evidencing depression (Galambos, Leadbeater, & Vitunski, 2002; Ge, Lorenz, Conger, Elder, & Simons, 1994; Klerman & Weissman, 1989). One of the most challenging contemporary research questions is: Why more girls? (Petersen, Sarigiani, & Kennedy, 1991).

Three alternative explanations have been offered for the emergence of gender differences in depression in adolescence (Nolen-Hoeksema & Girgus, 1994). These explanations assert that adolescent girls are more likely to manifest depression for the following reasons. First, they experience more stresses than do boys *beginning in adolescence,* and this higher prevalence of stresses leads to their higher rates of depression. Second, there are different risk factors leading to depression in girls and boys (e.g., social difficulties for girls and athletic incompetence for boys), and early adolescence exposes girls to more of their risk factors. Third, girls are exposed to more risk factors for depression *before adolescence* (e.g., concern for others and low assertiveness), and this early risk combines with new challenges of adolescence (e.g., puberty and dating) to produce depression.

With respect to the first explanation, adolescent girls do seem to be exposed to more stressors, such as early puberty, sexual abuse, difficulties with family members, and negative life events (Ge et al., 1994; Gore, Aseltine, & Colten, 1993). At least one study has clearly linked stressful events in girls' lives to increases in their depressive symptoms (Ge et al., 1994). The validity of this first explanation is an open question awaiting further research. The second explanation seems to be countered by the available evidence; generally, the risk factors for the development of depression in girls are similar to the risk factors for boys. When they exist, difficulties in social relationships (with peers or parents), ruminative coping, body dissatisfaction, feelings of helplessness, and low school achievement are all correlated with increased depressive symptoms in both sexes (Nolen-Hoeksema & Girgus, 1994). The third explanation for gender differences in adolescent depression may offer the most promise. Risk factors such as having a cooperative rather than aggressive interpersonal style, use of a ruminative coping style, and vulnerability to the stresses encountered by significant others are more prevalent in girls before adolescence; these early risk factors probably combine with the typically greater challenges of adolescence for girls to produce substantial differences in depression in adolescence (Leadbeater, Blatt, & Quinlan, 1995; Nolen-Hoeksema & Girgus, 1994; Petersen et al., 1993). More research is needed, however, to provide evidence for this explanation.

Aggression

Meta-analytic studies find that aggression is higher in male than in female adults, reaching overall effect sizes in the .20s (Bettencourt & Miller, 1996; Eagly & Steffen, 1986). Gender differences in physical aggression emerge early in childhood, are historically present in virtually all cultures, are found in many other species, and are related in men to higher levels of testosterone. Thus, it is likely that biological influences play an important role in gender differences in aggression (Lippa, 2002). Although rates of serious forms of aggression (i.e., violence) are significantly higher in adolescent males than in females, an emerging trend in research focuses on the origins, correlates, and sequelae of violence perpetrated by adolescent females (Artz, 1998; Moretti & Odgers, 2002). Some of this research suggests that pathways to violence for girls may be different from those for boys (Moretti & Odgers, 2002).

It is not news that males are more physically aggressive than females, but it may be surprising to some that females engage in as much or more aggression as males—at least of the relational variety. That is, Crick and colleagues (Crick & Grotpeter, 1995; Crick et al., 1998) distinguished between overt and relational types of aggression. Overt, or physical-verbal, types of aggression enable the domination of others through physical and verbal means (e.g., threatening). Relational (covert) aggression is defined as harm of others through deliberate manipulation and damage to their peer relationships. Relational aggression consists of acts such as spreading rumors, telling tales or revealing secrets about one's friends, shunning or excluding friends from a social circle, and engaging in silent treatment. Whereas rates of overt aggression are higher among males than females, the reverse is true for rates of relational aggression (Crick et al., 1998). In studies of preschool through school-age children, relational and physical aggression are positively correlated. Moreover, as with overt aggression, children who engage in relational aggression tend to score higher on measures of internalizing symptoms and social maladjustment (Crick, Casas, & Ku, 1999; Crick & Grotpeter, 1995). Crick et al. (2001) argued that in adolescence, forms of relational aggression become more complex and sophisticated. In a sample of adolescents referred for assessment because of aggression and delinquency problems, negative self-representations (portraying one's attributes in a negative manner) and perceived negative representations by peers (believing that peers have a negative view of oneself) were linked positively with reports of relational aggression in girls but not boys. Self-negativity predicted overt aggression in both girls and boys (Moretti, Holland, & McKay, 2001). Therefore, negative views of the self may play a role in girls' relational aggression.

Problem and Risk-Taking Behavior

The concept of problem behavior has been increasingly used as a way of grouping together many adolescent activities that have the potential to create problems or difficulties for the adolescent or for others. Problem behavior may be defined as "behavior that departs from familial or social standards, that poses some risk to the individual or to society" (Maggs & Galambos, 1993, p. 79). It may include explicitly illegal acts such as shoplifting and status (underage) offenses such as drinking, as well as some seemingly less serious behaviors like disobeying the rules of parents or school authorities. Gender differences in problem behaviors have frequently been observed. Girls, for instance, are less often engaged in problem behaviors than are boys and are likely to terminate their involvement in such behaviors sooner than are boys (Ensminger, 1990; Petersen, Richmond, & Leffert, 1993).

A recent meta-analysis of 150 studies on gender differences in risk-taking behavior (which overlaps to some extent with problem behavior but may also be broader, including categories of intellectual risks and risk taking in physical skills) found an interesting pattern of results (Byrnes, Miller, & Schafer, 1999). Whereas the overall average effect size was significant but small, with males taking more risks than females ($d = .13$), the size of the difference depended on the category of risk taking as well as on the age of the participants (classified into five groups ranging from 3- to 9-year-olds to over 21 years). A gender difference in drinking and using drugs was found only in 18- to 21-year-olds and in those over age 21. More college-age males (18 to 21 years) reported drinking and drug use ($d = .17$), whereas more females over age 21 reported drinking and drug use ($d = -.15$). A gender gap in reckless driving, with males reporting more of it, was strongest in 18- to 21-year-olds ($d = .37$) and in those over age 21 ($d = .85$) compared to 14- to 17-year-olds ($d = .16$). The only age group in which there was a significant gender difference in smoking was among 18- to 21-year-olds (higher in females). Finally, more males than females engaged in risky sexual activities in early adolescence (ages 10 to 13; $d = .60$), in middle adolescence (ages 14 to 17; $d = .22$), and at college age ($d = .18$), but in those over 21, more females engaged in risky sex ($d = -.11$). The authors reported that overall the gender gap seems to be diminishing over time (Byrnes et al., 1999).

What explains differential rates of problem behaviors or risk taking in males and females? Many theories abound (Byrnes et al., 1999). For example, Arnett (1992) referred to higher propensities of sensation-seeking desires (probably biologically based) in males relative to females as well as to cultural factors and gender roles that shape the behaviors considered appropriate for males and females. Nell (2002) argued that reckless driving in young males is an evolutionary adaptation that is reinforced by myths and narrative forms (e.g., James Bond movies) that promote feelings of invulnerability and immortality. Moffitt, Caspi, Rutter, and Silva (2001) presented longitudinal evidence that gender differences in adolescents' and adults' antisocial behavior (including conduct disorder, delinquency, and violence) may be attributed to males' higher exposure to risk factors such as neurocognitive deficits, undercontrolled temperaments, poor impulse control, and hyperactivity in early childhood. It is likely that the processes by which males and females come to engage in different levels of problem behaviors and risk taking involve a variety of predispositional, cognitive, emotional, situational, and sociocultural factors.

Positive Youth Development

An emerging trend in the literature on adolescence is an increasing focus on understanding positive youth development (Galambos & Leadbeater, 2000; Lerner & Galambos, 1998). Scales, Benson, Leffert, and Blyth (2000) identified seven indicators of positive youth development (or *thriving outcomes*), including school success, leadership, helping others, maintenance of physical health, delay of gratification, valuing diversity, and overcoming adversity. Although it is common to assume that one sex or the other possesses more positive qualities (e.g., girls are thought to be more helpful and altruistic), there is a dearth of empirical research examining sex differences in positive youth development. In a study of over 6,000 adolescents in an ethnically diverse sample, girls were significantly more likely than boys to report more school success and greater ability to resist dangerous situations. Boys, on the other hand, were more likely than girls to be engaged in leadership activities (Scales et al., 2000). It could be the case that certain indicators of positive youth development have more important consequences for one sex than for the other. Gore, Farrell, and Gordon (2001), for example, suggested that girls' involvement in team sports activities counteracted the negative effect of a low grade point average on depressed mood. Although it is too soon to say whether there are generalizable and systematic gender differences in specific aspects of positive youth development, such differences are worth exploring in future research.

Peer Relations and Intimacy

There is much research in the area of adolescence showing differences in males' and females' experiences of friendships. Girls' friendships typically are more numerous, deeper, and more interdependent than are those of boys; moreover, in their friendships girls reveal more empathy, a greater need for nurturance, and the desire for and ability to sustain intimate relationships. Boys, in contrast, tend to place relatively more emphasis on having a congenial companion with whom they share an interest in sports, hobbies, or other activities, and they are also more directive and controlling (Bukowski, Newcomb, & Hoza, 1987; Connolly & Konarski, 1994; DuBois & Hirsch, 1993; Noack, Krettek, & Walper, 2001; Updegraff et al., 2000; Youniss & Smollar, 1985).

The greater intimacy in peer relationships that girls experience extends to their romantic associations. In a study of Israeli adolescents, girls reported that their romantic relationships lasted longer than did boys', and they reported higher levels of affective intensity in these relationships. Attachment and care were seen more by girls than by boys to be among the advantages of dating, whereas more boys saw romantic relationships in terms of game-playing love (i.e., keeping her guessing; Shulman & Scharf, 2000). Another study showed that from Grade 8 to Grade 12, girls more than boys increased the amount of time they spent with a boy, as well as the amount of time they spent thinking about a boy (Richards, Crowe, Larson, & Swarr, 1998). An analysis of gender differences in adolescent reactions to heartbreak (i.e., breaking up with a partner) revealed that more girls than boys cried, approached friends for solace, reported insomnia and feelings of isolation, and thought about suicide. More boys than girls reported verbal and physical violence, going out more often, using alcohol or drugs, and turning to sex and a new relationship (Drolet, Lafleur, & Trottier, 2000). The pattern of findings pertaining to the characteristics of adolescent friendships, romantic relationships, and reactions to heartbreak mesh well with current understanding of the feminine and masculine gender roles. That is, females are viewed as expressive, nurturant, and empathetic and attached to others. Males, on the other hand, are viewed as strong, aggressive, and able to stand alone.

Verbal and Nonverbal Behavior

Among the many gender-related dimensions that can be studied are observable, gender-typed behaviors. One aspect of conformity to one's gender role is how people behave in social situations (Huston, 1983; Leaper, 2000). Indeed, Deaux and Major (1987) argued that gender is constructed in the process of social interaction. Hundreds of studies of gender differences in the verbal and nonverbal behaviors of adult females and males, and some of children, show that females and males behave differently on some dimensions. For example, women more often than men ask questions, smile and laugh, and gaze at their partners, whereas men more often interrupt, spend more time speaking, and offer facts (Hall & Halberstadt, 1986; West & Zimmerman, 1985). Such studies of adolescents, however, are rare. One observational study that examined gender differences in the interactions of adolescents (ages 11–14) enrolled in a summer camp found that boys were more assertive and argumentative whereas girls were more complimentary and advice seeking and giving (Savin-Williams, 1979).

In a study designed to examine gender differences in the verbal and nonverbal behaviors of adolescents, Kolaric and Galambos (1995) videotaped 30 unacquainted mixed-sex dyads composed of 15-year-olds. With respect to verbal behaviors, girls and boys were more similar than different. They did not differ in questions, interruptions, or showing uncertainty. Amount of speaking time was higher for boys when the topic of the discussion was a masculine task (i.e., changing oil) but higher in girls when the topic was a feminine task (i.e., babysitting). With respect to nonverbal behaviors, girls engaged in more smiling, coy smiling, hair flipping, and appearing smaller compared to boys, whereas boys did more chin touching. There were no gender differences, however, in gestures, head-facial touching, gazing, and head tilts. The authors speculated that girls were engaged in nonverbal display behaviors that communicated their femininity. It is interesting, however, that girls' and boys' views of themselves as masculine or feminine were not significantly related to their verbal and nonverbal behaviors (Kolaric & Galambos, 1995). In a similar study, girls were found to engage in more hair stroking, coy smiles, and eyebrow lifts with smiles, whereas boys, again, did more chin touching (Tilton-Weaver, 1997). A meta-analysis of gender differences in smiling showed that the largest difference was present in adolescents, compared to young, middle-aged, and older adults (La France, Hecht, & Levy Paluck, 2003). This understudied area of research has much potential to shed light on adolescents' gender-typed behaviors.

SOCIALIZATION CONTEXTS

The learning of gendered behavior is likely the result of the adolescent's participation in multiple contexts in which there are models for and pressures to behave in gender-typed ways. In this section, evidence for the effects of several prominent contexts on the learning of gendered behaviors is presented. These contexts include the family, peers, school, and the mass media.

Family

The family has received more attention than any other context in research on gender development in adolescence. The influence of parents in particular has a long history of research. The relationship between family structure and gender-typed behavior and characteristics was examined in early studies of mothers' employment, as researchers found that adolescent girls with employed mothers were less gender typed than were those with nonemployed mothers (Gold & Andres, 1978; Hoffman, 1974). Other studies indicated that boys were less gender typed if they came from single-mother households rather than two-parent homes (Russell & Ellis, 1991; Stevenson & Black, 1988). There is a large body of literature on how the quality and content of interactions between parents and children is related to gendered characteristics in children. One of the questions has been whether mothers and fathers treat daughters and sons differently (McHale, Crouter, & Whiteman, 2003). A meta-analysis by Lytton and Romney (1991) indicated gender-differential socialization by parents in one domain: encouraging gender-typed activities in their children. Another meta-analysis found that parents with more gender-schematic identities and attitudes were more likely to have offspring with gender-typed cognitions, attitudes, and interests than were gender-schematic parents (Tenenbaum & Leaper, 2002).

McHale et al. (2003) pointed to ways in which parents might influence adolescents' gender role development. Specifically, parents serve as instructors and opportunity providers, may model gendered behaviors in marital relationships, and may have personality characteristics, leisure interests, and gender role attitudes that reflect more or less gender role flexibility. One study showed that boys' participation in masculine and feminine household tasks may be linked to family structure and to fathers' own involvement in these tasks. Specifically, in single-earner families, there were positive correlations between fathers' and sons' engagement in masculine household tasks and in feminine tasks. Moreover, boys in single-earner families who were more highly involved in feminine tasks felt less competent and more stressed by their responsibilities compared to boys in dual-earner families who were so involved (McHale et al., 1990). These results pointed to the possible importance of congruence between the traditionality of the family context and tasks performed by boys for boys' psychosocial adjustment. Examining parents' gender role attitudes and girls' weight concerns, McHale, Corneal, et al. (2001) found that weight concerns were higher in adolescent girls whose mothers expressed more traditional gender role attitudes. Fathers' gender role attitudes were not linked with their daughters' concerns about weight.

An interesting short-term (2-year) longitudinal study investigated predictors of tomboy activities in girls who started the study in Grades 4/5 or 9/10/11 (McHale, Shanahan, Updegraff, Crouter, & Booth, 2002). Tomboyism was defined as the time spent in masculine play and leisure activities (e.g., competitive sports) relative to feminine play and leisure activities (e.g., dance). The researchers examined to what extent parents' gender-typed characteristics (gender role attitudes, masculinity, femininity, and gender-typed leisure interests), girls' gender-typed characteristics (gender role attitudes, masculinity, femininity, and gender-typed leisure interests), and parents' and girls' testosterone levels were linked to changes in tomboyism over time. In preadolescence, change in girls' tomboy activities was predicted only by the girls' earlier interests in such activities. In early adolescence, in addition to previous levels of tomboyism, mothers' masculine interests and fathers' more egalitarian gender role attitudes were linked with girls' increasing involvement in tomboy activities. In middle adolescence, girls' previous level of tomboyism and their fathers' masculine personality and masculine interests predicted increases in girls' tomboyism. Moreover, there was evidence that in middle childhood, mothers' and girls' higher levels of testosterone were linked to tomboy activities. Another set of analyses found that girls who engaged in tomboy activities reported more social competence with peers, better relationships with their parents, and an internal locus of control (McHale et al., 2002). These results as a whole are informative in that they clearly link some aspects of parents' gender-related characteristics to their daughters' behavior.

There is evidence that siblings also play a role in gender socialization (McHale, Crouter, & Tucker, 1999) and in some instances may be even more important than parents. McHale, Updegraff, Helms-Erikson, and Crouter (2001) found that over a 2-year period in early adolescence, younger siblings became more like their older siblings with respect to gender role attitudes, gender-typed personality qualities (i.e., masculinity, femininity), and masculine leisure activities. These results held even after controlling for the effect of parents' gender-typed characteristics on adolescents. In contrast, older siblings became less like their younger siblings. The authors concluded that the results were consistent with a social learning process for younger siblings, in which older siblings served as models. On the other hand, older siblings seemed to be engaged in a deidentification process, which involved differentiating themselves from their siblings (McHale, Updegraff, et al., 2001).

Updegraff et al. (2000) extended this research on sibling influences by examining the relationship between the gender composition of firstborn-secondborn sibling dyads (same- vs. mixed-sex) and the qualities of adolescents' same-sex friendships. The authors predicted that having a sister or a brother might be linked to intimacy (higher in girls' relationships) and control (higher in boys' relationships) in close friendships and to friends' masculine and feminine leisure interests and personality qualities. The results showed that adolescents with brothers, compared to those with sisters, were more controlling in their close friendships and also had friends who were more controlling. These findings are consistent with a social learning perspective in which siblings may learn more controlling behaviors from their brothers. On the other hand, brothers did not seem to learn intimacy from their sisters. This study adds to evidence that siblings are an important part of the gender socialization experience.

Peers

Beginning in early childhood and evident in many cultures, boys and girls segregate themselves into same-sex peer groups, continuing until about age 12 (Maccoby, 1990). Within these same-sex groups, girls form dyadic or triadic friendships, whereas boys form larger friendship networks. The quality of girls' and boys' same-sex interactions in these groups differs as well, with competition and conflict present in the all-male groups and nurturance and empathy characterizing the all-girl groups. The intimacy that is present in girls in adolescence may have a basis in these earlier all-girl groups. Maccoby (1990, 2002) argued that gender-typed behavior is observed, learned, and reinforced in these groups. It is not clear, however, to what extent peer groups in adolescence form a context for and shape gendered behaviors.

The void in empirical work on peer influences on gender-typed behavior in adolescence is deep. It is evident from studies conducted of adults, however, that this void could be filled with interesting and relevant research. For example, research on dyadic interactions in young adults demonstrates that gender-typed behaviors may be more noticeable in same- compared to mixed-sex dyads (Carli, 1989) and in dyads discussing masculine-oriented issues (Dovidio, Brown, Heltman, Ellyson, & Keating, 1988). A study of young children found that girls' expression of their own perspectives was significantly higher in all-girl playgroups than in playgroups in which boys were present (Benenson, Del Bianco, Philippoussis, & Apostoleris, 1997). It would be interesting to see observational studies of the behaviors of male and female adolescents in interaction with same- and other-sex peers. The enactment of gender roles could come alive (or not) in these situations. In addition, the kind of pressures to which adolescents are exposed to conform to gender roles could be documented. Given that the gender intensification hypothesis assumes that peers are important socializing agents for gender-typed behavior, it is surprising that researchers have not picked up on the need to document whether, to what extent, and by which processes peers influence gender-related behavior.

School

Much of the difference in girls' lower interest in math and science has been attributed not to the abilities of girls (who perform comparably to boys when they have equivalent backgrounds and academic experiences), but to teacher and parent expectations for girls' lower achievement and interest in these subjects (Parsons, Kaczala, & Meece, 1982; Parsons, Adler, & Kaczala, 1982). In addition, boys are given greater time, attention, and encouragement in the classroom (Mullis & Jenkins, 1988). These findings point to schools as sources of gender differences in academic interests.

One study provided tantalizing evidence that all-girl schools could reduce the academic disadvantages that girls can experience. Using data from the large-scale High School and Beyond study, Lee and Bryk (1986) compared the experiences of over 1,800 girls and boys enrolled in similarly constituted coeducational and single-sex private Catholic schools as they moved from Grade 10 through Grade 12. They investigated a wide variety of student outcomes including academic and social attitudes, school-related behaviors, course enrollment, academic achievement, educational aspirations, self-concept, and gender role attitudes. After carefully adjusting for family background and school variables, the results were consistently in favor of girls who attended all-girl schools. Relative to girls in coeducational schools, girls in single-sex schools did more homework, associated more with academically oriented peers, expressed more interest in math and English, took more math courses, made more gains in reading and science achievement across the 2-year period, had higher educational aspirations, rated their schools and teachers more positively, and became increasingly more egalitarian in their gender role attitudes from Grade 10 to Grade 12. Boys in single-sex schools also experienced advantages relative to their coeducational counterparts (e.g., they enrolled in more math and science courses and had higher achievement scores in some areas), but the differences were weaker, and on most variables (educational aspirations, self-concept, and gains in achievement) there were no school differences at all.

On a different note, studies have indicated that early maturation in girls is a risk factor for their involvement in delinquency (e.g., Stattin & Magnusson, 1990). Caspi, Lynam, Moffitt, and Silva (1993) compared the effects of early, on-time, and later maturation in a sample of adolescent girls attending either mixed-sex or all-girl secondary schools in New Zealand. As in previous research, early maturation was associated with higher levels of delinquency at ages 13 and 15 and more association with peers who engaged in such behavior. (On-time and late maturation were not linked with delinquency.) The association between early maturation and delinquency, however, was found only among girls who attended mixed-sex schools. The authors concluded that "at least two factors are necessary for the initiation and maintenance of female delinquency: puberty and boys" (Caspi et al., 1993, p. 26).

Both of these studies point to the important role that the school context can play in the gender socialization of adolescents. Studies of the differences between single-sex and coeducational schools highlight the concern that North American schools in general (because most are coeducational) may to some extent perpetuate gender stereotypes. These results also suggest the importance of looking within schools to determine what practices and experiences increase or diminish gender differences. Naturally, teacher behavior and attitudes, school climate, and the endorsement of gender stereotypes and pressures for conformity by classmates are among the school variables that likely contribute to gender socialization.

Mass Media

The mass media, including movies, television, and magazines, have come under fire from academics and members of the public for their sexualization of young girls, the portrayal of violence, and the perpetuation of gender stereotypes and unrealistic expectations for body weight and appearance. Because of its pervasiveness, television has received special attention as a purveyor of messages containing gender stereotypes. Research on the content of television programming demonstrates that television consistently underrepresents women as a proportion of the population, glorifies youth and beauty, presents unrealistic and stereotyped images of women's and men's bodies, and portrays women and men in stereotyped roles and occupations. Moreover, these images are present in situation comedies, children's programs, music videos, and commercials. And despite the negative publicity that this issue has received, the content with respect to gender stereotyping has remained remarkably stable over the last 30 to 50 years (Signorielli, 2001).

In an interesting content analysis of 28 situation comedies on television, Fouts and Burggraf (1999) coded the body weights, dieting behaviors, and verbal behaviors directed at the bodies or weights of 52 female characters who were central to the shows. In line with the literature in general (Signorielli, 2001), underweight females were overrepresented (33% of the characters) and overweight females (7%) underrepresented relative to the U.S. population. Nearly half of the female characters received positive comments about their bodies from other male characters; 21% received such comments from other female characters. The thinner the female character was, the more positive were the comments bestowed on her by male characters. There was no relationship between thinness of the character and negative comments directed at her. However, the more the female character engaged in dieting activities, the more she made negative comments about herself. In a similar study, Fouts and Burggraf (2000) found a positive relation between female characters' body weight and male characters' negative comments about her weight or body. Moreover, an examination of reactions of the audience to the negative comments indicated that 80% of these comments were greeted by laughter, giggles, and "oohs." Another study examining the weights of central male characters found that above-average weights were underrepresented, that male characters rarely received negative comments about their bodies from female characters, and that when they did, the audience did not respond. Males who were heavier, however, made more negative comments about their bodies, and this was reinforced with audience laughter (Fouts & Vaughan, 2002b). Findings such as these illustrate the distortion of reality (e.g., overrepresenting thin females) that is present in television sitcoms and the perpetuation of gender stereotypes such as "thinner is better." Naturally, the social learning perspective leads us to worry about the possible harm to viewers who receive and internalize these messages.

In general, research has shown an association between television viewing and the possession of gender-typed views and attitudes for all segments of the life span (Signorielli, 2001). It is difficult, however, to document the causal effects of television viewing on gender roles and gendered behavior. Correlational studies cannot determine whether individuals with more traditional gender role attitudes, for instance, have those attitudes because they watch more television or whether they watch more television because they already had more traditional gender role attitudes. Combined with the results of natural experiments, longitudinal studies can help to illuminate the direction of effects (Ruble & Martin, 1998).

With respect to adolescence in particular (a period for which there are few relevant studies), there is a positive relationship between the amount of television watched and more traditional gender role attitudes and stereotypes (Morgan, 1982, 1987). In a longitudinal study of adolescents, higher levels of television viewing predicted increases in girls' gender stereotyping across a 1-year period (Morgan, 1982). Another study found that 10- to 17-year-old girls who had an external locus of control combined with relatively high amounts of television watching were most at risk for reporting symptoms of eating disorders (Fouts & Vaughan, 2002a). Girls perceive higher levels of influence from the media on their body images compared to boys (Polce-Lynch et al., 2001). Anderson, Huston, Schmitt, Linebarger, and Wright (2001), however, reported that higher levels of entertainment television viewing were linked to poorer body images in adolescent girls and boys.

ETHNIC DIVERSITY IN GENDER DEVELOPMENT

The study of gender development in adolescence has been largely restricted to European American samples of middle-class adolescents (see Kulis, Marsiglia, & Hecht, 2002, for an exception). Thus, what we think we know about gender development may not necessarily be generalizable to other ethnic groups. For example, Basow and Rubin (1999) suggested that the socioeconomic conditions experienced by African American women lead them to take on both masculine and feminine behaviors and roles. In essence, then, these women may be ahead of their European American counterparts in gender role flexibility (Binion, 1990).

In early adolescence, African American girls have higher self-esteem compared with

European American girls. In addition, African American girls barely register a decline in self-esteem in early adolescence compared with that seen in European American girls. Latinas, on the other hand, have high self-esteem prior to early adolescence but show a steep drop beginning in high school (American Association of University Women, 1992). African American and Asian American girls and women also report lower levels of eating disordered symptoms and body dissatisfaction compared with European Americans (Akan & Grilo, 1995). A study of 4th-, 6th-, and 8th-grade African American and European American girls and boys found that African American girls, compared with all others, believed that girls were more competent than were boys in all academic domains (Feagans, Rowley, Kurtz-Costes, & Mistry, 2002). On the other hand, with respect to academic self-esteem, African American girls may start out high but seem to lose their confidence across the adolescent years (American Association of University Women, 1992). A strong self-esteem in African American girls and Latinas has been linked to a strong ethnic identity (Phinney & Alipuria, 1990; Phinney & Chavira, 1992).

Basow and Rubin (1999) concluded that it is important to consider minority-group status when studying gender development. Furthermore, they pointed out not only that gender development should be considered in ethnically diverse samples but also that investigations should include different religious and sexual minorities. These areas represent virtually unexplored territory that could shed light on the ways in which gender development differs by ethnic, religious, and sexual background and experience.

SUMMARY AND CONCLUSIONS

How and why do girls and boys differ? It is easy to conclude after reading the results of many studies that adolescent girls and boys differ dramatically. It is important to remember, though, that gender differences in characteristics and behavior do not mean that all males are one way and all females are another. Rather, many males and females are both masculine and feminine, and results of meta-analyses show that where there are gender differences, few are large in effect. Thus, gender differences should not be exaggerated.

At the same time, it is difficult to get a handle on the breadth and depth of the gender difference. Part of this difficulty may stem from personal experiences with both sexes. We all walk in this world, making observations that lead many of us at one time or another to draw sweeping conclusions about gender differences. Undoubtedly, these personal experiences also color our reading of the literature on gender roles. Part of the difficulty in understanding exactly how boys and girls differ arises also from the complex multidimensionality of gender role constructs and of behavior in general. Whereas we might note a gender difference in one behavior, there might not be one in a related behavior. Or whereas we might observe what we think is a gender-typed quality in someone we know, other dimensions of his or her behavior may strike us as distinctly not gender typed. Matters become more complicated when we consider that gender role development does not stop at a young age. Across time, as individuals mature and become exposed to other people, contexts, and places, their visions of themselves and of gender roles may change. It would be interesting to learn what the wisdom of old age brings to our own personal construction of gender.

As for the question of why there are differences between girls and boys, the answer is equally difficult. What the literature tells us is that there seems to be truth to all of the theories that have been offered to explain gender development. Biology may not be destiny, but it announces to the world that with respect to some internal and external physical attributes, girls and boys are different. Moreover, the external physical attributes are impossible to ignore in adolescence when gender differences in size and shape increase exponentially. Cognitive perspectives on gender and role development also have something to offer in terms of understanding why girls and boys might be different. Gains in cognitive development that occur in infancy through adolescence undoubtedly shape the individual's evolving gender schemas, which become more complex with age and show interindividual variability. These schemas, including the many aspects of gender identity, help to explain individual differences in gender-typed behavior. Finally, there is evidence for gender socialization in many contexts, including the family, peers, school, and mass media. Differential treatment of girls and boys occurs to some extent in each of these contexts, but it depends, of course, on who is in that context and what behaviors they show toward the adolescent.

A developmental systems approach to gender development leads us to consider biology, cognition, and socialization as interrelated and important influences on adolescent behavior. If we accept that adolescent girls and boys are different in some ways, then we can attribute those differences to a complexity of changing and interwoven influences. Trying to understand the exact nature of gender differences and the myriad of influences on gender development, however, remains a most fascinating and challenging task.

REFERENCES

Akan, G. E., & Grilo, C. M. (1995). Sociocultural influences on eating attitudes and behaviors, body image, and psychological functioning: A comparison of African-American, Asian American, and Caucasian college women. *International Journal of Eating Disorders, 18,* 181–187.

Alfieri, T., Ruble, D. N., & Higgins, E. T. (1996). Gender stereotypes during adolescence: Developmental changes and the transition to junior high school. *Developmental Psychology, 32,* 1129–1137.

American Association of University Women. (1992). *The AAUW report: How schools shortchange girls.* Washington, DC: Author.

Anderson, D. R., Huston, A. C., Schmitt, K. L., Linebarger, D. L., & Wright, J. C. (2001). Early childhood television viewing and adolescent behavior: The recontact study. *Monographs of the Society for Research in Child Development, 66*(1, Serial No. 264).

Arnett, J. (1992). Reckless behavior in adolescence: A developmental perspective. *Developmental Review, 12,* 339–373.

Artz, S. (1998). *Sex, power, and the violent school girl.* Toronto: Trifolium Books.

Bandura, A. (1986). *Social foundations of thought and action: A social cognitive theory.* Englewood Cliffs, NJ: Prentice-Hall.

Barker, E. T., & Galambos, N. L. (2003). Body dissatisfaction of adolescent girls and boys: Risk and resource factors. *Journal of Early Adolescence, 23,* 141–165.

Basow, S. A., & Rubin, L. R. (1999). Gender influences on adolescent development. In N. G. Johnson, M. C. Roberts, & J. P. Worell (Eds.), *Beyond appearance: A new look at adolescent girls* (pp. 25–52). Washington, DC: American Psychological Association.

Bem, S. L. (1974). The measurement of psychological androgyny. *Journal of Consulting and Clinical Psychology, 42,* 155–162.
Bem, S. L. (1975). Sex role adaptability: One consequence of psychological androgyny. *Journal of Personality and Social Psychology, 31,* 634–643.
Bem, S. L. (1981). Gender schema theory: A cognitive account of sex typing. *Psychological Review, 88,* 354–364.
Benenson, J. F., Del Bianco, R., Philippoussis, & Apostoleris, N. H. (1997). Girls' expression of their own perspectives in the presence of varying numbers of boys. *International Journal of Behavioral Development, 21,* 389–405.
Berenbaum, S. A. (1999). Effects of early androgens on sex-typed activities and interests in adolescents with congenital adrenal hyperplasia. *Hormones and Behavior, 35,* 102–110.
Berenbaum, S. A., & Snyder, E. (1995). Early hormonal influences on childhood sex-typed activity and playmate preferences: Implications for the development of sexual orientation. *Developmental Psychology, 31,* 31–42.
Berndt, T. J., & Heller, K. A. (1986). Gender stereotypes and social inferences: A developmental study. *Journal of Personality and Social Psychology, 50,* 889–898.
Bettencourt, B. A., & Miller, N. (1996). Gender differences in aggression as a function of provocation: A meta-analysis. *Psychological Bulletin, 119,* 422–447.
Binion, V. J. (1990). Psychological androgyny: A Black female perspective. *Sex Roles, 22,* 487–507.
Bukowski, W. M., Newcomb, A. F., & Hoza, B. (1987). Friendship conceptions among early adolescents: A longitudinal study of stability and change. *Journal of Early Adolescence, 7,* 143–152.
Bussey, K., & Bandura, A. (1999). Social cognitive theory of gender development and differentiation. *Psychological Review, 106,* 676–713.
Byrnes, J. P., Miller, D. C., & Schafer, W. D. (1999). Gender differences in risk taking: A meta-analysis. *Psychological Bulletin, 125,* 367–383.
Carli, L. L. (1989). Gender differences in interaction style and influence. *Journal of Personality and Social Psychology, 56,* 565–576.
Caspi, A., Lynam, D., Moffitt, T. E., & Silva, P. A. (1993). Unravelling girls' delinquency: Biological, dispositional, and contextual contributions to adolescent misbehavior. *Developmental Psychology, 29,* 19–30.
Cleveland, H. H., Udry, J. R., & Chantala, K. (2001). Environmental and genetic influences on sex-typed behaviors and attitudes of male and female adolescents. *Personality and Social Psychology Bulletin, 27,* 1587–1598.
Connolly, J. A., & Konarski, R. (1994). Peer self-concept in adolescence: Analysis of factor structure and of associations with peer experience. *Journal of Research on Adolescence, 4,* 385–403.
Crick, N. R., Casas, J. F., & Ku, H.-C. (1999). Relational and physical forms of peer victimization in preschool. *Developmental Psychology, 35,* 376–385.
Crick, N. R., & Grotpeter, J. K. (1995). Relational aggression, gender, and social-psychological adjustment. *Child Development, 66,* 710–722.
Crick, N. R., Nelson, D. A., Morales, J. R., Cullerton-Sen, C., Casas, J. F., & Hickman, S. E. (2001). Relational victimization in childhood and adolescence: I hurt you through the grapevine. In J. Juvonen & S. Graham (Eds.), *Peer harassment in school: The plight of the vulnerable and victimized* (pp. 196–214). New York: Guilford Press.
Crick, N. R., Werner, N. E., O'Brien, K. M., Nelson, D. A., Grotpeter, J. K., & Markon, K. (1998). Childhood aggression and gender: A new look at an old problem. In D. Bernstein (Ed.), *Nebraska symposium on motivation: Vol. 45. Gender and motivation* (pp. 75–141). Lincoln: University of Nebraska Press.
Crouter, A. C., Manke, B. A., & McHale, S. M. (1995). The family context of gender intensification in early adolescence. *Child Development, 66,* 317–329.
Deaux, K., & Major, B. (1987). Putting gender into context: An interactive model of gender-related behavior. *Psychological Review, 94,* 369–389.
Dovidio, J. F., Brown, C. E., Heltman, K., Ellyson, S. L., & Keating, C. F. (1988). Power displays between women and men in discussions of gender-linked tasks: A multichannel study. *Journal of Personality and Social Psychology, 55,* 580–587.

Drolet, M., Lafleur, I., & Trottier, G. (2000). Differential analysis of adolescent heartbreak: Do males and females react differently? *Canadian Social Work, 2,* 30–40.

DuBois, D. L., & Hirsch, B. J. (1993). School/nonschool friendship patterns in early adolescence. *Journal of Early Adolescence, 13,* 102–122.

Eagly, A. H., & Steffen, V. J. (1986). Gender and aggressive behavior: A meta-analytic review of the social psychological literature. *Psychological Bulletin, 100,* 309–330.

Eccles, J. S., Jacobs, J. E., Harold, R. D., Yoon, K. S., Arbreton, A., & Freedman-Doan, C. (1993). Parents and gender-role socialization during the middle childhood and adolescent years. In S. Oskamp & M. Costanzo (Eds.), *Gender issues in contemporary society* (pp. 59–83). Newbury Park, CA: Sage.

Edwards-Leeper, L., & Allgeier, E. R. (2002, April). *The relationship between disordered eating and gender role identity/egalitarianism in adolescent females and their parents.* Paper presented at the Biennial Meeting of the Society for Research on Adolescence, New Orleans, LA.

Egan, S. K., & Perry, D. G. (2001). Gender identity: A multidimensional analysis with implications for psychosocial adjustment. *Developmental Psychology, 37,* 451–463.

Ensminger, M. E. (1990). Sexual activity and problem behaviors among black, urban adolescents, *Child Development, 61,* 2032–2046.

Feagans, L. A., Rowley, S., Kurtz-Costes, B., & Mistry, R. S. (2002, April). *Children's stereotypes: Beliefs about gender, race, and social class differences in ability.* Paper presented at the Biennial Meeting of the Society for Research on Adolescence, New Orleans, LA.

Fouts, G., & Burggraf, K. (1999). Television situation comedies: Female body images and verbal reinforcement. *Sex Roles, 40,* 473–481.

Fouts, G., & Burggraf, K. (2000). Television situation comedies: Female weight, male negative comments, and audience reactions. *Sex Roles, 42,* 925–952.

Fouts, G., & Vaughan, K. (2002a). Locus of control, television viewing, and eating disorder symptomatology in young females. *Journal of Adolescence, 25,* 307–311.

Fouts, G., & Vaughan, K. (2002b). Television situation comedies: Male weight, negative references, and audience reactions. *Sex Roles, 46,* 439–442.

Galambos, N. L., Almeida, D. M., & Petersen, A. C. (1990). Masculinity, femininity, and sex role attitudes in early adolescence: Exploring gender intensification. *Child Development, 61,* 1905–1914.

Galambos, N. L., & Leadbeater, B. M. (2000). Trends in adolescent research for the new millennium. *International Journal of Behavioral Development, 24,* 289–294.

Galambos, N. L., Leadbeater, B. M., & Barker, E. T. (in press). Gender differences in and risk factors for depression in Canadian adolescents: A four-year longitudinal study. *International Journal of Behavioral Development.*

Galambos, N. L., Petersen, A. C., Richards, M., & Gitelson, I. B. (1985). The Attitudes toward Women Scale for Adolescents (AWSA): A study of reliability and validity. *Sex Roles, 13,* 343–356.

Ge, X., Lorenz, F. O., Conger, R. D., Elder, G. H., Jr., & Simons, R. L. (1994). Trajectories of stressful life events and depressive symptoms during adolescence. *Developmental Psychology, 30,* 467–483.

Gold, D., & Andres, D. (1978). Comparisons of adolescent children with employed and nonemployed mothers. *Merrill-Palmer Quarterly, 24,* 243–253.

Gore, S., Aseltine, R. H., Jr., & Colten, M. E. (1993). Gender, social-relational involvement, and depression. *Journal of Research on Adolescence, 3,* 101–125.

Gore, S., Farrell, F., & Gordon, J. (2001). Sports involvement as protection against depressed mood. *Journal of Research on Adolescence, 11,* 119–130.

Hall, J. A., & Halberstadt, A. G. (1986). Smiling and gazing. In J. S. Hyde & M. C. Linn (Eds.), *The psychology of gender: Advances through meta-analysis* (pp. 136–158). Baltimore: Johns Hopkins University Press.

Hefner, R., Rebecca, M., & Oleshansky, B. (1975). Development of sex-role transcendence. *Human Development, 18,* 143–158.

Hill, J. P., & Lynch, M. E. (1983). The intensification of gender-related role expectations during early adolescence. In J. Brooks-Gunn & A. C. Petersen (Eds.), *Girls at puberty: Biological and psychosocial perspectives* (pp. 201–228). New York: Plenum.

Hoffman, L. W. (1974). Effects of maternal employment on the child: A review of the research. *Developmental Psychology, 10,* 204–228.

Holt, C. L., & Ellis, J. B. (1998). Assessing the current validity of the Bem Sex-role Inventory. *Sex Roles, 39,* 929–941.

Huston, A. C. (1983). Sex-typing. In M. Hetherington (Ed.), *Handbook of child psychology: Vol. 4. Socialization, personality, and social development* (pp. 387–467). New York: Wiley.

Jacobs, J. E., Lanza, S., Osgood, D. W., Eccles, J. S., & Wigfield, A. (2002). Changes in children's self-competence and values: Gender and domain differences across grades one through twelve. *Child Development, 73,* 509–527.

Katz, P. A., & Ksansnak, K. R. (1994). Developmental aspects of gender role flexibility and traditionality in middle childhood and adolescence. *Developmental Psychology, 30,* 272–282.

Katz, P. A., & Walsh, P. V. (1991). Modification of children's gender-stereotyped behavior. *Child Development, 62,* 338–351.

Kavrell, S. M., & Petersen, A. C. (1984). Patterns of achievement in early adolescence. In M. L. Maehr & M. W. Steinkamp (Eds.), *Women and science.* Greenwich, CT: JAI Press.

Kennelly, I., Merz, S. N., & Lorber, J. (2000). What is gender? *American Sociological Review, 65,* 598–605.

Kenny, M. E., & Gallagher, L. A. (2002). Instrumental and social/relational correlates of perceived maternal and paternal attachment in adolescence. *Journal of Adolescence, 25,* 203–219.

Kenrick, D. T., & Luce, C. L. (2000). An evolutionary life-history model of gender differences and similarities. In T. Eckes & H. M. Trautner (Eds.), *The developmental social psychology of gender* (pp. 35–63). Mahwah, NJ: Erlbaum.

Klerman, G. L., & Weissman, M. M. (1989). Increasing rates of depression. *Journal of the American Medical Association, 261,* 2229–2235.

Kling, K. C., Hyde, J. S., Showers, C. J., & Buswell, B. N. (1999). Gender differences in self-esteem: A meta-analysis. *Psychological Bulletin, 15,* 470–500.

Kohlberg, L. (1966). A cognitive-developmental analysis of children's sex-role concepts and attitudes. In E. E. Maccoby (Ed.), *The development of sex differences* (pp. 82–173). Stanford, CA: Stanford University Press.

Kolaric, G. C., & Galambos, N. L. (1995). Face-to-face interactions in mixed-sex adolescent dyads: Do girls and boys behave differently? *Journal of Early Adolescence, 15,* 363–382.

Kulis, S., Marsiglia, F. F., & Hecht, M. L. (2002). Gender labels and gender identity as predictors of drug use among ethnically diverse middle school students. *Youth and Society, 33,* 442–475.

La France, M., Hecht, M. A., & Levy Paluck, E. (2003). The contingent smile: A meta-analysis of sex differences in smiling. *Psychological Bulletin, 129,* 305–334.

Lamke, L. K. (1982). The impact of sex-role orientation on self-esteem in early adolescence. *Child Development, 53,* 1530–1535.

Leadbeater, B. J., Blatt, S. J., & Quinlan, D. M. (1995). Gender-linked vulnerabilities to depressive symptoms, stress, and problem behaviors in adolescents. *Journal of Research on Adolescence, 5,* 1–29.

Leaper, C. (2000). The social construction and socialization of gender during development. In P. H. Miller & E. Kofsky Scholnick (Eds.), *Toward a feminist developmental psychology* (pp. 127–152). Florence, KY: Taylor & Francis/Routledge.

Lee, V. E., & Bryk, A. S. (1986). Effects of single-sex secondary schools on student achievement and attitudes. *Journal of Educational Psychology, 78,* 381–395.

Lerner, R. M. (2002). *Concepts and theories of human development* (3rd ed.). Mahwah, NJ: Erlbaum.

Lerner, R. M., & Galambos, N. L. (1998). Adolescent development: Challenges and opportunities for research, programs, and policies. In J.T. Spence (Ed.), *Annual review of psychology* (Vol. 49, pp. 413–446). Palo Alto, CA: Annual Reviews.

Lerner, R. M., Lerner, J. V., De Stefanis, I., & Apfel, A. (2001). Understanding developmental systems in adolescence: Implications for methodological strategies, data analytic approaches, and training. *Journal of Adolescent Research, 16,* 9–27.

Li, A. K. F., & Adamson, G. (1995). Motivational patterns related to gifted students' learning of mathematics, science, and English: An examination of gender differences. *Journal for the Education of the Gifted, 18,* 284–297.

Liben, L. S., & Bigler, R. S. (2002). The developmental course of gender differentiation: Conceptualizing, measuring, and evaluating constructs and pathways. *Monographs of the Society for Research in Child Development, 67*(2, Serial No. 269).

Lightbody, P., Siann, G., Stocks, R., & Walsh, D. (1996). Motivation and attribution at secondary school: The role of gender. *Educational Studies, 22,* 13–25.

Linn, M. C., & Petersen, A. C. (1986). A meta-analysis of gender differences in spatial ability: Implications for math and science achievement. In J. S. Hyde & M. C. Linn (Eds.), *The psychology of gender: Advances through meta-analysis* (pp. 67–101). Baltimore, MD: Johns Hopkins University Press.

Lippa, R. A. (1998). Gender-related individual differences and National Merit Test performance: Girls who are "masculine" and boys who are "feminine" tend to do better. In L. E. Ellis & L. Ebertz (Eds.), *Males, females, and behavior: Toward biological understanding* (pp. 177–193). Westport, CT: Praeger.

Lippa, R. A. (2002). *Gender, nature, and nurture.* Mahwah, NJ: Erlbaum.

Lytton, H., & Romney, D. M. (1991). Parents' differential socialization of boys and girls: A meta-analysis. *Psychological Bulletin, 109,* 269–297.

Maccoby, E. E. (1990). Gender and relationships: A developmental account. *American Psychologist, 45,* 513–520.

Maccoby, E. E. (2002). Gender and group process: A developmental perspective. *Current Directions in Psychological Science, 11,* 54–58.

Maggs, J. L., & Galambos, N. L. (1993). Alternative structural models for understanding adolescent problem behavior in two-earner families. *Journal of Early Adolescence, 13,* 79–101.

Markstrom-Adams, C. (1989). Androgyny and its relation to adolescent psychosocial well-being: A review of the literature. *Sex Roles, 21,* 325–340.

Marsh, H. W., & Yeung, A. S. (1998). Longitudinal structural equation models of academic self-concept and achievement: Gender differences in the development of math and English constructs. *American Educational Research Journal, 35,* 705–738.

Martin, C. L. (2000). Cognitive theories of gender development. In T. Eckes & H. M. Trautner (Eds.), *The developmental social psychology of gender* (pp. 91–121). Mahwah, NJ: Erlbaum.

Massad, C. M. (1981). Sex role identity and adjustment during adolescence. *Child Development, 52,* 1290–1298.

McHale, S. M., Bartko, W. T., Crouter, A. C., & Perry-Jenkins, M. (1990). Children's housework and psychosocial functioning: The mediating effects of parents' sex-role behaviors and attitudes. *Child Development, 61,* 1413–1426.

McHale, S. M., Corneal, D. A., Crouter, A. C., & Birch, L. L. (2001). Gender and weight concerns in early and middle adolescence: Links with well-being and family characteristics. *Journal of Clinical Child Psychology, 30,* 338–348.

McHale, S. M., Crouter, A. C., & Tucker, C. J. (1999). Family context and gender role socialization in middle childhood: Comparing girls to boys and sisters to brothers. *Child Development, 70.*

McHale, S. M., Crouter, A. C., & Whiteman, S. D. (2003). The family contexts of gender development in childhood and adolescence. *Social Development, 12,* 125–148.

McHale, S. M., Shanahan, L., Updegraff, K. A., Crouter, A. C., & Booth, A. C. (2002). *Tomboy behavior and gender development in middle childhood and adolescence.* Poster presented at the Biennial Meeting of the Society for Research in Adolescence, New Orleans, LA.

McHale, S. M., Updegraff, K. A., Helms-Erikson, H., & Crouter, A. C. (2001). Sibling influences on gender development in middle childhood and early adolescence: A longitudinal study. *Developmental Psychology, 37,* 115–125.

Mischel, W. (1966). A social-learning view of sex differences in behavior. In E. E. Maccoby (Ed.), *The development of sex differences* (pp. 57–81). Stanford, CA: Stanford University Press.

Moffitt, T. E., Caspi, A., Rutter, M., & Silva, P. A. (2001). *Sex differences in antisocial behaviour:*

Conduct disorder, delinquency, and violence in the Dunedin Longitudinal Study. Cambridge: Cambridge University Press.

Moretti, M. M., Holland, R., & McKay, S. (2001). Self-other representations and relational and overt aggression in adolescent girls and boys. *Behavioral Sciences and the Law, 19,* 109–126.

Moretti, M. M., & Odgers, C. (2002). Aggressive and violent girls: Prevalence, profiles and contributing factors. In R. R. Corrado, R. Roesch, D. S. Hart, & J. K. Gierowski (Eds.), *Multi-problem and violent youth: A foundation for comparative research on needs, interventions, and outcomes* (pp. 116–129). Amsterdam: IOS Press.

Morgan, M. (1982). Television and adolescents' sex-role stereotypes: A longitudinal study. *Journal of Personality and Social Psychology, 43,* 947–955.

Morgan, M. (1987). Television, sex-role attitudes, and sex-role behavior. *Journal of Early Adolescence, 7,* 269–282.

Nell, V. (2002). Why young men drive dangerously: Implications for injury prevention. *Current Directions in Psychological Science, 11,* 75–79.

Noack, P., Krettek, C., & Walper, S. (2001). Peer relations of adolescents from nuclear and separated families. *Journal of Adolescence, 24,* 535–548.

Nolen-Hoeksema, S., & Girgus, J. S. (1994). The emergence of gender differences in depression during adolescence. *Psychological Bulletin, 115,* 424–443.

Parsons, J. E., Adler, T., & Kaczala, C. M. (1982). Socialization of achievement attitudes and beliefs: Parental influences. *Child Development, 53,* 310–321.

Parsons, J. E., Kaczala, C. M., & Meece, J. L. (1982). Socialization of achievement attitudes and beliefs: Classroom influences. *Child Development, 53,* 322–339.

Petersen, A. C., Richmond, J. B., & Leffert, N. (1993). Social changes among youth: The United States experience. *Journal of Adolescent Health, 14,* 632–637.

Petersen, A. C., Sarigiani, P. A., & Kennedy, R. E. (1991). Adolescent depression: Why more girls? *Journal of Youth and Adolescence, 20,* 247–271.

Pipher, M. (1994). *Reviving Ophelia: Saving the selves of adolescent girls.* New York: Ballantine Books.

Phinney, J. S., & Alipuria, L. L. (1990). Ethnic identity in college students from four ethnic groups. *Journal of Adolescence, 13,* 171–183.

Phinney, J. S., & Chavira, V. (1992). Ethnic identity and self-esteem: An exploratory longitudinal study. *Journal of Adolescence, 15,* 271–282.

Polce-Lynch, M., Myers, B. J., Kliewer, W., & Kilmartin, C. (2001). Adolescent self-esteem and gender: Exploring relations to sexual harassment, body image, media influence, and emotional expression. *Journal of Youth and Adolescence, 30,* 225–244.

Richards, M. H., Boxer, A. M., Petersen, A. C., & Albrecht, R. (1990). Relations of weight to body image in pubertal girls and boys from two communities. *Developmental Psychology, 26,* 313–321.

Richards, M. H., Crowe, P. A., Larson, R., & Swarr, A. (1998). Developmental patterns and gender differences in the experience of peer companionship during adolescence. *Child Development, 69,* 154–163.

Rosenberg, F. R., & Simmons, R. G. (1975). Sex differences in the self-concept in adolescence. *Sex Roles, 1,* 147–159.

Rosenblum, G. D., & Lewis, M. (1999). The relations among body image, physical attractiveness, and body mass in adolescence. *Child Development, 70,* 50–64.

Ruble, D. N., & Martin, C. L. (1998). Gender development. In W. Damon (Series Ed.) & N. Eisenberg (Vol. Ed.), *Handbook of child psychology: Vol. 3. Social, emotional, and personality development* (5th ed., pp. 933–1016). New York: Wiley.

Russell, C. N., & Ellis, J. B. (1991). Sex-role development in single parent households. *Social Behavior and Personality, 19,* 5–9.

Savin-Williams, R. C. (1979). Dominance hierarchies in groups of early adolescents. *Child Development, 50,* 923–935.

Scales, P. C., Benson, P. L., Leffert, N., & Blyth, D. A. (2000). Contribution of developmental assets to the prediction of thriving among adolescents. *Applied Developmental Science, 4,* 27–46.

Schulenberg, J., Goldstein, A. E., & Vondracek, F. W. (1991). Gender differences in adolescents' career interests: Beyond main effects. *Journal of Research on Adolescence, 1,* 37–61.
Serbin, L. A., Powlishta, K. K., & Gulko, J. (1993). The development of sex typing in middle childhood. *Monographs of the Society for Research in Child Development, 58*(2, Serial No. 232).
Shulman, S., & Scharf, M. (2000). Adolescent romantic behaviors and perceptions: Age- and gender-related differences, and links with family and peer relationships. *Journal of Research on Adolescence, 10,* 99–118.
Signorella, M. L., Bigler, R. S., & Liben, L. S. (1993). Developmental differences in children's gender schemata about others: A meta-analytic review. *Developmental Review, 13,* 147–183.
Signorielli, N. (2001). Television's gender role images and contribution to stereotyping: Past, present, future. In D. G. Singer & J. L. Singer (Eds.), *Handbook of children and the media* (pp. 341–358). Thousand Oaks, CA: Sage.
Simmons, R. G., Blyth, D. A., Van Cleave, E. F., & Bush, D. M. (1979). Entry into early adolescence: The impact of school structure, puberty, and early dating on self-esteem. *American Sociological Review, 44,* 948–967.
Simmons, R. B., Burgeson, R., Carlton-Ford, S., & Blyth, D. A. (1987). The impact of cumulative change in early adolescence. *Child Development, 58,* 1220–1234.
Spence, J. T. (1993). Gender-related traits and gender ideology: Evidence for a multifactorial theory. *Journal of Personality and Social Psychology, 64,* 624–635.
Spence, J. T., & Hall, S. K. (1996). Children's gender-related self-perceptions, activity preferences, and occupational stereotypes: A test of three models of gender constructs. *Sex Roles, 35,* 659–691.
Spence, J. T., & Helmreich, R. L. (1978). *Masculinity and femininity: Their psychological dimensions, correlates, and antecedents.* Austin: University of Texas Press.
Stattin, H., & Magnusson, D. (1990). *Pubertal maturation in female development.* Hillsdale, NJ: Erlbaum.
Stevenson, M. R., & Black, K. N. (1988). Paternal absence and sex-role development: A meta-analysis. *Child Development, 59,* 793–814.
Susman, E. J. (1997). Modeling developmental complexity in adolescence: Hormones and behavior in context. *Journal of Research on Adolescence, 7,* 283–306.
Tenenbaum, H. R., & Leaper, C. (2002). Are parents' gender schemas related to their children's gender-related cognitions? A meta-analysis. *Developmental Psychology, 38,* 615–630.
Tenenbaum, H. R., & Leaper, C. (2003). Parent-child conversations about science: The socialization of gender inequities? *Developmental Psychology, 39,* 34–47.
Tilton-Weaver, L. C. (1997). *Adolescent perceptions of nonverbal displays in mixed-sex encounters.* Unpublished masters thesis, University of Victoria.
Tobin-Richards, M. H., Boxer, A. M., & Petersen, A. C. (1983). The psychological significance of pubertal change: Sex differences in perceptions of self during early adolescence. In J. Brooks-Gunn & A. C. Petersen (Eds.), *Girls at puberty: Biological and psychosocial perspectives* (pp. 127–154). New York: Plenum.
Udry, J. R. (2000). Biological limits of gender construction. *American Sociological Review, 65,* 443–457.
Updegraff, K. A., McHale, S. M., & Crouter, A. C. (2000). Adolescents' sex-typed friendship experiences: Does having a sister versus a brother matter? *Child Development, 71,* 1597–1610.
West, C., & Zimmerman, D. H. (1985). Gender, language, and discourse. In T. A. VanDijk (Ed.), *Handbook of discourse analysis* (pp. 103–124). London: Academic Press.
Worell, J. (1981). Life-span sex roles: Development, continuity, and change. In R. M. Lerner & N. A. Busch-Rossnagel (Eds.), *Individuals as producers of their development: A life-span perspective* (pp. 313–347). New York: Academic Press.
Youniss, J., & Smollar, J. (1985). *Adolescent relations with mothers, fathers, and friends.* Chicago: University of Chicago Press.

Chapter 9

PROCESSES OF RISK AND RESILIENCE DURING ADOLESCENCE

Linking Contexts and Individuals

Bruce E. Compas

Adolescents traverse two distinct pathways through the second decade of life. On the one hand, most adolescents navigate this developmental period successfully without encountering significant psychological, social, or health problems. On the other hand, adolescence marks the increase in the incidence of a number of mental health problems and threats to physical health. Several psychiatric disorders increase significantly in incidence and prevalence during adolescence, including depression, conduct disorder, and eating disorders. Threats to health through smoking, substance abuse, and unprotected sex increase dramatically during this period. The prediction of which individuals will follow a successful path versus those who will encounter significant problems during adolescence is critical for preventing psychopathology and illness and promoting successful development.

Processes of risk and resilience are at the center of our understanding of adaptive and maladaptive paths of development during adolescence. Understanding risk factors and processes of risk is central to the identification of those adolescents most in need of early intervention, whereas clarification of protective factors and processes of resilience can inform interventions to strengthen those at greatest risk. In the pursuit of these goals, risk and resilience have been examined at two disparate levels: broad social contextual processes and individual psychological and biological processes. Furthermore, some important sources of risk and resilience precede adolescence and are linked to processes that begin in childhood and continue into adolescence, whereas others arise in adolescence, and their effects either may be limited to adolescence or continue into adulthood. Integration of these different levels of analysis and developmental trajectories is essential for a truly adolescent model of risk and resilience (Steinberg, 2002).

There is now a large body of evidence on contextual and individual sources of risk and resilience in adolescence, and a comprehensive review of this work would be valuable. At this point in the development of the field, however, it is more important to highlight some of the central issues that have prevented the construction of a comprehensive, integrated perspective on adolescent risk and resilience (Luthar, Cicchetti, & Becker, 2000). To accomplish this, exemplars from risk and resilience research can be used to mark progress that has been made and identify areas in need of further research. Poverty and economic adversity represent an important example of broad contextual sources of risk. In contrast, temperament and biological development are salient examples of individual-level risk factors. These two areas of research are useful to highlight the state of research and theory on adolescent risk and resilience and to generate directions for future work.

A major impediment to increasing our understanding of risk and resilience has been the failure to integrate contextual and individual levels of analysis. Research on social contextual factors such as poverty has not been coupled with methods to measure individual processes of development in adolescents faced with significant economic adversity. Similarly, research on temperament and related development during adolescence has often ignored the broader context in which development occurs. A comprehensive understanding of risk and resilience during adolescence requires an integration of multiple levels and methods of analysis of contextual and individual factors (Cicchetti & Dawson, 2002). Moreover, concepts are needed that can provide linkages across these different levels. I propose that stress and the ways that individuals respond to and cope with stress are unifying processes that can facilitate a multilevel approach to adolescent risk and resilience. Proximal stressors, especially stressors within the family, mediate the effects of distal contextual risk factors. The effects of proximal stressors are further mediated by the ways that adolescents respond to and cope with stress. And both automatic stress responses and effortful coping responses may be influenced by individual development, including temperament and biological developmental processes, during adolescence.

DEFINING KEY TERMS AND CONCEPTS

A number of concepts and terms are used to describe processes of risk and resilience. This terminology is important beyond the level of semantics, as it conveys important differences regarding the nature of who will develop problems and disorders during adolescence and who will survive relatively unscathed. However, confusion over the definitions of key terms and over the sheer number of different terms that have been employed has been problematic.

Risk

The term *risk* refers to the increased probability of a negative outcome in a specified population (Kraemer et al., 1997). Thus, risk (or *degree of risk*) is a quantitative concept that is reflected as either an odds ratio when outcomes are measured categorically or as some variant of a regression weight when the outcomes are continuous or quantitative. For example the odds of developing a mood disorder (major depressive disorder or dysthymic disorder) or a disruptive behavior disorder (oppositional defiant disorder or conduct disorder) can be calculated as a function of characteristics of the individual (e.g., age, gender), family factors (e.g., harsh parenting, parental psychopathology), and neighborhood characteristics (e.g., violence, inadequate housing). A *risk factor* is an agent or characteristic of the individual or the environment that is related to the increased probability of a negative outcome. For example, Rolf and Johnson (1990) defined risk factors as variables that "have proven or presumed effects that can directly increase the likelihood of a maladaptive outcome" (p. 387). The degree of risk associated with a given risk factor can be calculated at various levels, including the degree of risk for an individual person, a family, a classroom, a school, or a community. When outcomes are dichotomous, a risk factor can be used to divide the population into two groups, high risk and low risk, that comprise the total population (Kraemer et al., 1997). Quantitative measures of risk distinguish individuals along a continuum from high to low.

In addition to distinguishing levels of risk, temporal precedence must be established between risks and outcomes; that is, the presence of or exposure to the risk factor must precede evidence of the development of the outcome. Kraemer et al. (1997) addressed the issue of temporal precedence within a typology of risk factors. If a factor is simply associated with an outcome at a single point in time, it is identified as a *correlate.* A correlate that has been shown to precede the outcome is a *risk factor,* and a risk factor that can be changed is a *variable risk factor.* Finally, if manipulation of the risk factor changes the outcome, it is a *causal risk factor.* Thus, the final step in risk research is likely to involve preventive interventions designed to change established risk factors in order to determine their possible causal role.

Cumulative risk refers to the cooccurrence of more than one risk factor for a given individual or within a population (Rutter, 1987a, 1987b). As the number of risk factors increases, the mental and physical health and development of adolescents decline (Friedman & Chase-Lansdale, 2002). For example, poverty and economic hardship are associated with multiple additional risks, including neighborhood crime and violence, lack of access to quality schools, single parenthood, and family conflict. Similarly, parental psychopathology, another important risk factor throughout childhood and adolescence, is linked with family conflict and discord and possible genetic risks for psychopathology (Friedman & Chase-Lansdale, 2002). Negative outcomes increase additively or exponentially as the number of risk factors increases.

A concept closely related to risk is that of *vulnerability* (e.g., Blum, McNeely, & Nonnemaker, 2002). However, vulnerability differs from risk in that it implies a focus on differences in the degree to which risk factors are associated with negative outcomes for specific individuals. That is, vulnerability addresses the question of why some individuals who are exposed to risk are more likely to develop a negative outcome. For example, it is clear that negative psychological outcomes ensue for some but certainly not all adolescents who experience parental divorce (Wolchik et al., 2000). Individual differences in vulnerability to parental divorce are related to child characteristics (e.g., age and gender) and to the level of conflict and hostility between the parents, even after separation and divorce have occurred. Thus, vulnerability factors or markers encompass those factors that exacerbate the negative effects of the risk condition.

Resilience

Similar attention has been given to defining the concept of *resilience.* Luthar and Cicchetti (2000) defined resilience as a "dynamic process wherein individuals display positive adaptation despite experiences of significant adversity or trauma" (p. 858). Similarly, Masten (2001) defined resilience as "a class of phenomena characterized by good outcomes in spite of threats to adaptation or development" (p. 228). Resilience does not merely imply a personality trait or an attribute of the individual; rather, it is intended to reflect a process of positive adaptation in the presence of risk that may be the result of individual factors, environmental factors, or the interplay of the two (Luthar & Cicchetti, 2000). Resilience research is concerned with identifying mechanisms or processes that might underlie evidence of positive adaptation in the presence of risk. Masten (2001) distinguished among several models of resilience. Variable-focused models of resilience test relations among quantitative measures of risk, outcomes, and potential characteristics of the individual or the environment that may serve a protective function against the adverse effects of risk. Within this approach, researchers can test for mediators and moderators of risk that can provide evidence of protection or resilience. Person-focused models of resilience examine individuals in an attempt to identify and compare those who display patterns of resilience (as evidenced by positive outcomes) and those who succumb to risk (as reflected in negative outcomes).

Closely related to the concept of resilience are *protective factors,* which are conceptualized as aspects of the individual or the environment that are related to resilient outcomes. In one of the original conceptualizations, Garmezy (1983) defined protective factors as "those attributes of persons, environments, situations, and events that appear to temper predictions of psychopathology based on an individual's at-risk status" (p. 73). In this sense, protective factors are the converse of vulnerability factors: Protective factors are characteristics of the individual or the environment that are associated with positive outcomes in the face of risk, whereas vulnerability factors are associated with negative outcomes in at-risk individuals.

Risk and Resilience

Although there is merit to distinguishing between risk and resilience (and between vulnerability and protective factors), there are challenges in the conceptualization of these two sets of factors and processes. Foremost is the difficulty of determining whether risk and resilience are distinct constructs or whether they exist on a continuum whose bipolar ends represent risk and resilience. In some instances, high levels of a factor protect individuals from risk whereas low levels of the same factor amplify risk. For example, high IQ serves a protective function in the face of socioeconomic adversity, but low IQ also increases the potency of the effects of poverty (Sameroff, 1999). Thus, IQ both increases (a vulnerability factor) and decreases (a protective factor) risk associated with socioeconomic hardship. In other instances, high levels of a factor are protective, but low levels are neutral or benign in relation to the source of risk. For example, the temperamental characteristics of negative affectivity and positive affectivity, respectively, are risk and resilience factors for emotional problems (Compas, Connor-Smith, & Jaser, in press). However, these two traits are orthogonal, as low negative affectivity does not denote positive affectivity. Thus, low negative affectivity indicates the absence of this vulnerability factor, but it does not serve as a protective factor.

To address some of the confusion between risk and protective factors, Sameroff (2000) used the term *promotive factors* to refer to those characteristics of individuals and environments that are associated with positive outcomes irrespective of risk; that is, they are associated with positive outcomes in both high- and low-risk populations

(Gutman, Sameroff, & Eccles, 2002; Sameroff, 2000). Protective factors would be expected to have no effect in low-risk populations or to be magnified in the presence of high risk (Gutman et al., 2002; Rutter, 1987a, 1987b).

The situation is further complicated in that some risk and protective factors are stable, whereas others change with development. For example, some temperamental characteristics emerge in infancy and remain stable throughout childhood and adolescence. Stable individual differences in temperament may function as either risk or protective factors in adolescence, depending on the characteristic in question. Similarly, some features of the environment may be stable sources of risk or protection throughout childhood and adolescence (e.g., chronic poverty, a supportive and structured family environment). Other factors may emerge during adolescence as sources of risk and protection and can be defined as developmental risk and protective factors. For example, some aspects of cognitive and brain development change dramatically during early adolescence and mark this as a period of heightened risk for many adolescents (Spear, 2000a, 2000b). Similarly, it appears that the effects of certain types of stressful events are relatively benign during childhood but are much more likely to be associated with negative outcomes during adolescence (Hankin & Abramson, 2001).

Methodological Issues

Research Design

As noted earlier, the temporal precedence of a factor in relation to an outcome must be present in order to establish risk (Kraemer et al., 1997). Thus, true risk research requires the use of prospective longitudinal designs. In reality, however, risk research often unfolds sequentially, beginning with cross-sectional studies that are useful in identifying candidate risk factors that warrant attention in more costly longitudinal studies. Cross-sectional studies are a cost-effective step in the identification of risk and protective factors, as they require much less time, effort, and money than do prospective studies. However, they cannot provide evidence of the role of individual or environmental factors as predictors of negative outcomes (evidence of increased risk) or of positive outcomes in the presence of risk factors (resilience).

Furthermore, the identification of *processes* of risk and resilience, as opposed to the identification of risk or protective *factors,* requires attention to the mediation and moderation of risk and resilience factors. Process research is required to explain *how* specific characteristics of the person or the environment lead to negative outcomes or to positive outcomes that are against the odds. For example, it is clear that growing up in poverty is an enormous risk factor for negative developmental outcomes in adolescence (Friedman & Chase-Lansdale, 2002; McLoyd, 1998). However, process research is needed to identify the mediators of the relation between poverty and negative outcomes. These include neighborhood, school, and family factors that play out in the daily lives of poor adolescents. Similarly, moderators may explain why some adolescents are more vulnerable to the effects of some sources of stress and adversity. For example, gender and personality characteristics have been found to be important moderators of stressful events during adolescence. However, the identification of a moderator may require further research on the mediators that account for observed moderation effects. For example, adolescent girls may be more vulnerable to the effects of interpersonal stress, but the reason is the ways that they appraise and cope with such events and not because of their gender per se (Compas & Wagner, 1991; Hankin & Abramson, 2001).

Measurement

A host of issues and problems arises in the measurement of risk and protective factors, processes of risk and resilience, and positive and negative developmental outcomes. Inherent in the constructs of both risk and resilience is the need to operationalize negative and positive adolescent developmental outcomes, including emotional, psychological, and physical problems as well as disorder, health, and well-being. There are, however, a number of challenges to the conceptualization and measurement of these outcomes.

Definitions of resilience require attention to the nature of positive adaptation, which is typically defined in terms of manifestations of social competence or success at meeting stage-relevant developmental tasks (Luthar & Cicchetti, 2000). Successful adaptation in the face of risk can also be reflected in positive mental health during adolescence, which can be operationalized along two primary dimensions reflecting the skills and capacity to manage adversity and the capacity to involve oneself in personally meaningful activities (Compas, 1993). Thus, positive mental health is reflected in the ability to overcome risk. It is more than this, however, as positive mental health also includes the ability to engage oneself in relationships and activities that are personally meaningful and productive. Positive mental health and positive development are relative concepts and depend on a number factors, including cultural context, developmental level, and differences in the perspective of various interested parties including adolescents, parents, teachers, and health professionals (Compas, 1993).

Resilience may also be manifested in physical health and healthy development, which, like positive mental health, include more than the absence of disease. Health is defined as a state of physical, mental, and social well-being and not merely the absence of disease (Richmond, 1993). Current biopsychosocial models of development consider health in terms of personal experiences of general well-being (quality of life), the capacity to perform developmentally expected roles and tasks (adaptive functioning), and fulfilling one's health potential (Millstein, Petersen, & Nightingale, 1993). Some indicators of poor health in adolescence do not immediately manifest themselves in disease or illness but are linked to later poor health outcomes. For example, obesity during adolescence may not result in any immediate health problems but is a strong risk factor for later cardiovascular disease and adult-onset diabetes. Although not related to disease and illness during adolescence, obesity may be related to impairment in current physical functioning and decreased quality of life. Thus, although obesity is not an illness or a disease, it is also not reflective of a state of health.

The challenges of measuring negative outcomes are even greater than those involved in documenting positive adaptation. Most studies of risk and emotional and behavioral problems in adolescence have relied on measures of negative emotional states or checklists that are used to assess syndromes of emotional and behavioral problems. These have included measures of symptoms associated with specific internalizing problems such as depressive symptoms and anxiety and the broad factors of internalizing and externalizing problems (e.g., Achenbach, 1991; Achenbach & Dumenci, 2001). Risk researchers also use structured diagnostic interviews to assess psychiatric disorders as represented in the *Diagnostic and Statistical Manual of Mental Disorders–Fourth Edition* (*DSM-IV;* American Psychiatric Association, 1994). These two approaches are not incompatible, however, as quantitative variations in symptoms have been shown to be related to categorical diagnoses for several disorders (e.g., Achenbach & Dumenci, 2001; Gerhardt, Compas, Connor, & Achenbach, 1999; Jensen et al., 1996). Furthermore, both elevated scores on dimensional measures of symptoms or syndromes and diagnoses of categorical disorders are associated with significant impairment and problems in functioning (e.g., Gotlib, Lewinsohn, & Seeley, 1995; Lengua, Sadowski, Friedrich, & Fisher, 2001). Therefore, *both* are viable perspectives on psychopathology in young people.

The assessment of symptoms as opposed to categorical diagnoses has implications for the type of research design required, as well as the types of research questions that can be answered. Studies of symptoms or quantitative variations on syndromes of psychopathology are typically used in variable focused studies that are concerned with the linear relation between the level of risk (or resilience) and the number, level, or severity of psychological symptoms. Because symptoms are continuous and quantitative, researchers are not typically concerned with the timing of the onset of symptoms or the point at which symptoms exceed a specific threshold. The focus is on the degree to which changes in levels of risk account for changes in symptoms over time, as tested in variants of multiple regression models (e.g., Bolger, Patterson, Thompson, & Kupersmidt, 1995; Ge, Lorenz, Conger, Elder, & Simons, 1994).

The relation between risk factors and categorical diagnoses of disorder has been tested somewhat less often, in part because of the greater demands involved in the administration of clinical interviews. In addition, when the focus is on categorical diagnoses based on *DSM-IV* criteria, the emphasis is on the onset, duration, and remission of a disorder. Therefore, researchers must carefully document the timing of risk factors in relation to changes in diagnostic status. This requires the use of measures of both risk and psychopathology that are sensitive to timing and duration and research designs that are able to identify the specific timing of the onset of risk factors in relation to the onset or termination of an episode of disorder. Structured interviews are currently the best, albeit most labor-intensive, approach for accomplishing these goals in the assessment both of risk factors, such as stressful experiences, and psychological disorder (e.g., Rudolph & Hammen, 2000).

In addition to consideration of the method used to measure outcomes, it is also critical to account for the source of the data. The relatively low level of concordance in the reports of different informants on child and adolescent maladjustment and psychopathology is widely recognized (Achenbach, McConaughy, & Howell, 1987). Correlations among reports of parents, teachers, and adolescents are typically small to moderate in magnitude, and these correlations are typically lower for internalizing than for externalizing problems (Kazdin, 1994). Although low rates of correspondence are potentially problematic, the general consensus is that different informants provide equally valid perspectives on adolescent problems, with specific perspectives particularly valid for specific types of symptoms (Garber, Keiley, & Martin, 2002). For example, teachers and parents may be better informants of externalizing symptoms, and children and adolescents may be better informants of internalizing symptoms. Most research on adolescent risk has failed to give careful attention to the informant effects in reports of risk factors and outcomes. Several studies have noted, however, that adolescent reports of risk factors are more strongly associated with their own reports of symptoms of psychopathology than with parental reports of symptoms (e.g., Compas et al., 1989). This suggests that common method variance in the assessment of both stressors and symptoms may contribute to the association between these two variables.

The measurement of negative outcomes is further complicated by the tendency of symptoms of psychopathology and psychiatric disorders to cooccur or to be comorbid in adolescence (e.g., Angold & Costello, 1993; Compas & Hammen, 1994). This presents risk researchers with a challenge in their efforts to identify specificity in the association between particular types of stressors and particular psychological problems. When an association is found between a particular risk factor and symptoms of a particular disorder (e.g., depression), this association may not be unique to that disorder. Rather, the risk factor may serve as a relatively nonspecific risk factor for psychopathology because psychopathology often occurs in relatively nonspecific patterns. Thus, researchers need to include broad-based assessments of a range of different types of psychopathology if they are adequately to capture the types of problems that are associated with stressors and to determine the degree to which particular risk factors are specifically related to particular outcomes (Grant, Compas, Thurm, & McMahon, 2003). Specificity requires careful consideration of both contextual factors and individual differences (see Steinberg & Avenevoli, 2000).

Summary

Theory and research on adolescent risk and resilience are fraught with multiple overlapping terms and concepts. At its core, however, this area is characterized by two observations that, regardless of the terms used, are relatively simple and enduring. First, some adolescents suffer poor health and psychological outcomes during this developmental period, and factors associated with a greater likelihood of negative outcomes need to be identified. Second, once predictors of increased risk for negative outcomes have been identified, it is clear that some adolescents evidence positive outcomes despite exposure to known risks. The challenge is in the identification of the processes that lead from risk and protective factors to good and bad outcomes. Perhaps the best source of illumination on these processes comes from a somewhat weathered set of concepts: stress, stress responses, and coping (Compas & Grant, 2002).

STRESS, STRESS RESPONSES, AND COPING: UNIFYING CONCEPTS FOR UNDERSTANDING RISK AND RESILIENCE

Research on exposure to stressful events and circumstances and the ways that adolescents respond to and cope with stress has provided essential information on the linkages between contextual and individual processes of risk and resilience. Specifically, exposure to stressful events and circumstances is a primary pathway through which distal risk factors exert effects on adolescent mental and physical health, including the generation of stressors in neighborhood, school, peer, and family environments. Furthermore, individual differences in automatic and controlled responses to stress are crucial mediators of the effects of both distal and proximal sources of stress. Stress, stress responses, and coping are now considered in detail as they relate to processes of risk and resilience.

Stress

Defining Stress

Stress is an old concept that will neither die nor fade away. In spite of strong criticism of the construct (e.g., Lazarus, 1993), stress remains a centrally important factor in understanding risk factors and processes. Prevailing definitions of stress all include environmental circumstances or conditions that threaten, challenge, exceed, or harm the psychological or biological capacities of the individual. Definitions of stress differ, however, in the degree to which they emphasize psychological processes that are implicated in determining what is and is not stressful to a given individual. On the one hand, transactional approaches posit that the occurrence of stress is dependent on the degree to which individuals *perceive* environmental demands as threatening, challenging, or harmful (Lazarus & Folkman, 1984). Alternatively, environmental perspectives emphasize the importance of *objectively* documenting the occurrence of environmental events and conditions independent of the potential confounds of cognitive appraisals (Cohen, Kessler, & Gordon, 1995).

Although the transactional definition of stress is widely embraced, it poses problems for stress research with adolescents. Research on stress during infancy and early childhood indicates clear negative effects of maternal separation, abuse, and neglect on infants (e.g., Field, 1994; Perry, Pollard, Blakley, Baker, & Vigilante, 1995). Whether or not these events are subjectively experienced as stressful, it is clear that adverse effects can occur in young children without the complex cognitive appraisals that are central to the transactional approach. In addition, preliminary research indicates that cognitive appraisal processes do not interact with stressful events in the prediction of symptoms until late childhood or early adolescence and that appraisals increase in their significance during this period (e.g., Nolen-Hoeksema, Girgus, & Seligman, 1992; Turner & Cole, 1994).

As conceptual models of adolescent developmental psychopathology have become more sophisticated, greater emphasis has been placed on moderating and mediating processes that influence or explain the relation between stress and psychopathology (Cicchetti & Cohen, 1995; Grant, Compas, Stuhlmacher, Thurm, & McMahon, 2003). Models of stress that fail to distinguish psychosocial stressors from mediating and moderating processes, including cognitive appraisal processes, are problematic. To understand fully how stressful experiences, moderating factors, and mediating processes relate to one another in the prediction of psychopathology and adjustment, it is important to define and measure each of these processes clearly. The single essential element of the concept of stress that is conceptually distinct from moderators-mediators, psychological symptoms, and other risk factors is the occurrence of external, environmental threat to the individual (Cohen et al., 1995).

Given the limitations with transactional definitions of stress for research with adolescents, this chapter presents a definition that focuses on external, environmental changes or conditions. Specifically, I adopt Grant et al.'s (2003) definition of stress as "environmental events or chronic conditions that objectively threaten the physical and/or psychological health or well-being of youth of a particular age in a particular society." This definition is consistent with traditional stimulus-based definitions of stress and more recent definitions of stressors and objective stress (e.g., Rudolph & Hammen, 2000). Events or chronic circumstances can threaten the well-being of an individual without leading to a negative outcome. Thus, stressful events and conditions are defined independent of their effects or outcomes. Moreover, this definition allows for positive outcomes in the face of objectively threatening circumstances; that is, it allows for resilience.

In spite of the need for clarity in the definition of stress, in a recent review of stress measurement methods used in research with children and adolescents (Grant et al., 2003), my colleagues and I found wide variability in the ways that stress was conceptualized and measured. Of those researchers utilizing cumulative stress scales or interviews (as opposed to measures of specific stressors such as sexual abuse), fewer than 10% used a well-validated measure. Forty-five percent reported that they developed their own measure, and the remaining authors used one of the approximately 50 currently available measures of cumulative stress (Grant et al., 2003). Psychometric data on most measures were not provided, and few of the authors who developed their own scales provided information about their method of measurement development or the items comprised in their scales (Grant et al., 2003).

One promising method for improving precision in stress research involves the use of structured interviews for the assessment of stressors experienced by adolescents (e.g., Goodyer & Altham, 1991a, 1991b; McQuaid, Monroe, Roberts, Kupfer, & Frank, 2000; Rudolph et al., 2000). Interviews are used to identify stressors that have been encountered and the conditions that surround these events. Probes for each event include a description of what occurred, when it occurred, the context of the event or ongoing circumstances, and the consequences of the event. External raters then evaluate and rate the level of threat associated with each event and condition based on the context of the stressor. For example, the objective threat rating given to the stressor "death of a grandmother" would be higher for an adolescent for whom the grandmother was a primary caretaker than for an adolescent who's grandmother lived far away and was seen only occasionally (Rudolph et al., 2000). Ratings are then summed to form an index of the stressors that each adolescent has encountered.

Stressors and Adolescent Psychopathology

Stressors remain central to current etiological theories of child and adolescent psychopathology. This is evident in that more than 1,500 empirical investigations of the relation between stressors and psychological symptoms among youth have been conducted in the past 15 years alone (Grant et al., 2003). However, the level of interest in the relation between stressors and psychological problems in adolescence has not been matched by progress in the field. As described earlier, variability in the conceptualization and operationalization of stress and stressors has created significant problems (Grant et al., 2003).

Underlying these specific measurement concerns is the broader issue that most studies of the relation between stressors and psychological problems in children and adolescents have not been theory driven beyond the general theoretical notion that stressors pose a risk factor for psychopathology (Grant et al., 2003; Steinberg & Avenevoli, 2000). Grant et al. (2003) proposed a framework to guide research on stress during childhood and adolescence. This general model includes five central hypotheses: (a) Stressors lead to psychopathology; (b) moderators influence the relation between stressors and psychopathology; (c) mediators explain the relation between stressors and psychopathology; (d) relations among stressors, moderators, mediators, and psychopathology are reciprocal and dynamic; and (e) there is specificity in the relations among stressors, moderators, and mediators. These hypotheses reflect many of the core issues and assumptions in research on risk factors, protective factors, and processes of vulnerability and resilience.

The first hypothesis of this model, that stressors lead to negative psychological and health outcomes, provides the conceptual basis for all studies of the relation between stressors and psychological problems in children and adolescents. Nonetheless, comparatively few studies (about 60) have tested this hypothesis using prospective designs. Although the number of prospective studies is disappointing at this stage of research on stress in adolescence, it reflects significant progress from 15 years ago (see Compas, 1987b). Furthermore, in our recent review my colleagues and I found evidence in 53 studies that stressful life experiences predict psychological problems in children and adolescents over time (Grant et al., 2003). Thus, evidence indicates that the cumulative effect of stressful events meets the criterion for a risk factor (Kraemer et al., 1997), and more specifically for cumulative risk.

Potential moderators of the relation between stressors and psychopathology have been examined in numerous studies (Grant et al., 2003). Moderators may be conceptualized as vulnerabilities or protective factors, as they represent preexisting characteristics that increase or decrease the likelihood that stressors will lead to psychopathology. Moderators may also be viewed as the mechanisms that explain why similar processes may lead to various outcomes (multifinality) and varying processes may lead to similar outcomes (equifinality; Cicchetti, & Rogosch, 1999). Potential moderating variables include age, gender, temperament, stress (autonomic) reactivity, the presence of supportive relationships, and stable cognitive styles. Research on moderators and mediators is central to identifying processes of risk and resilience.

Although some variables may serve either a moderating or mediating function, mediators are conceptually distinct from moderators. Whereas moderators are characteristics of adolescents or their social networks prior to stressors, mediators are activated, set off, or caused by the current stressful experience and conceptually and statistically account for the relation between stressors and negative outcomes (Baron & Kenny, 1986; Holmbeck, 1997). Mediators may include variables such as coping responses, cognitive style, and family processes. In our recent review of the literature on mediators of the association between stressors and psychological problems in young people, we found promising evidence of mediating effects, particularly in regard to mediators of the effects of poverty on adolescent outcomes (Grant et al., 2003).

The hypothesis that relations among stressors, moderators, mediators, and health and psychological outcomes are reciprocal and dynamic has received relatively little attention in research on stress during adolescence (Grant et al., 2003). However, those studies that have examined this issue have found evidence that symptoms do predict increases in stressful events over time (e.g., Compas et al., 1989; DuBois, Felner, Meares,

& Krier, 1994; Sandler, Tein, & West, 1994). Thus, some stressful events (referred to as dependent events) during adolescence are generated by symptoms and other characteristics of adolescents themselves. Some of the risk associated with stressful events can be self-generated and contribute to a vicious cycle in which stress may trigger initial behavioral and emotional problems, which in turn lead to more stress.

The final hypothesis in this model is that there is specificity in relations among particular stressors, moderators, mediators, and psychological outcomes. Evidence of specificity requires that a particular type of stressor (e.g., interpersonal rejection) is linked with a particular type of psychological problem (e.g., depression) via a particular mediating process (e.g., ruminative coping) in the context of a particular moderating variable (e.g., female gender, adolescent age). In a recent review, McMahon, Grant, Compas, Thurm, and Ey (2003) failed to identify any studies that had examined a full specificity model including specific mediating and moderating processes in the relation between particular stressors and particular outcomes (see also Steinberg & Avenevoli, 2000). With a few notable exceptions (e.g., Sandler, Reynolds, Kliewer, & Ramirez, 1992), studies capable of examining specificity effects (i.e., studies that included more than one type of stressor and more than one type of psychological outcome) tested only a subset of the features of specificity, and a consistent pattern of specific effects failed to emerge (McMahon et al., 2003). Thus, current evidence indicates that stressful events and circumstances are a general, nonspecific risk for psychopathology. However, this is in part a result of the failure of most studies to include the elements necessary to test for specificity.

Coping and Self-Regulation

A major source of variation in the effects of stress during adolescence is the result of the ways that adolescents react to stress and cope with stress and the degree to which they are able to regulate their emotions, behaviors, thoughts, and physiological responses to stress.

Distinguishing Among Competence, Resilience, and Coping

Although the terms *coping, competence,* and *resilience* are often used interchangeably, they reflect distinct aspects of successful development and adaptation (e.g., Compas, Connor-Smith, Saltzman, Thomsen, & Wadsworth, 2001; Compas & Harding, 1998; Masten & Coatsworth, 1998). The primary distinction is that coping refers to *processes* of adaptation, competence refers to the *characteristics and resources* that are needed for successful adaptation, and resilience is reflected in *outcomes* for which competence and coping have been effectively put into action in response to stress and adversity. Therefore, coping can be viewed as efforts to enact or mobilize competence or personal resources, and resilience as the successful outcome of these actions. Coping includes the behaviors and thoughts that are implemented by individuals when faced with stress without reference to their efficacy, whereas resilience refers to the results of the coping responses of competent individuals who have been faced with stress and have coped in an effective and adaptive manner. However, not all coping efforts represent the enactment of competence, and not all outcomes of coping are reflected in resilience; indeed, some coping efforts fail.

Definitions of Coping

Two challenges are foremost in generating a definition of coping to guide research with adolescents. The first is the need for a definition that reflects the nature of developmental processes. It is unlikely that the basic characteristics or the efficacy of coping are the same for a young child as for an adolescent, and any definition of coping should reflect such changes. Second, it is important to distinguish coping from other aspects of the ways that individuals respond to stress, as the utility of any definition of coping depends in part on the degree of specificity that is conveyed.

In those instances in which coping has been defined in research with adolescents, investigators frequently have drawn on definitions from models of adult coping; conceptualizations of coping that are explicitly concerned with adolescence (and childhood) have emerged only recently. The most widely cited definition is that of Lazarus and Folkman (1984), which is derived from their adult model of stress, cognitive appraisal, and coping. This conceptualization of coping has been the basis for numerous investigations of coping in adolescence (e.g., Compas, Malcarne, & Fondacaro, 1988; Lengua & Sandler, 1996; Steele, Forehand, & Armistead, 1997). Lazarus and Folkman (1984) defined coping as "constantly changing cognitive and behavioral efforts to manage specific external and/or internal demands that are appraised as taxing or exceeding the resources of the person" (p. 141). Coping is viewed as an ongoing dynamic process that changes in response to the changing demands of a stressful encounter or event. Furthermore, coping is conceptualized as purposeful responses that are directed toward resolving the stressful relationship between the self and the environment (problem-focused coping) or toward palliating negative emotions that arise as a result of stress (emotion-focused coping).

Perspectives on coping that are more explicitly concerned with childhood and adolescence include those outlined by Weisz and colleagues (Rudolph, Dennig, & Weisz, 1995; Weisz, McCabe, & Dennig, 1994), Skinner (1995), and Eisenberg and colleagues (e.g., Eisenberg, Fabes, & Guthrie, 1997; see Compas et al., 2001, for a review of these perspectives). A central issue in defining coping during adolescence (and childhood) is whether coping includes all responses to stress, particularly both controlled and automatic responses. Skinner's (1995) definition of coping includes both volitional and involuntary or automatic responses to manage threats to competence, autonomy, and relatedness, and although Eisenberg et al. (1997) acknowledged that coping and emotional regulation are processes that typically involve effort, coping is not always conscious and intentional.

We view coping as one aspect of a broader set of processes that are enacted in response to stress (Compas et al., 2001). Specifically, we define coping as "conscious volitional efforts to regulate emotion, cognition, behavior, physiology, and the environment in response to stressful events or circumstances" (Compas et al., 2001, p. 89). These regulatory processes both draw on and are constrained by the biological, cognitive, social, and emotional development of the individual. An individual's developmental level both contributes to the resources that are available for coping and limits the types of coping responses the individual can enact. Coping is a subset of broader self-regulatory processes, with coping referring to regulatory efforts that are volitionally and intentionally enacted specifically in response to stress. Furthermore, coping is limited to responses that are controlled and volitional and is distinct from automatic stress response processes.

Although coping refers to the ways that an individual attempts to manage and adapt to stress, coping is a process that is embedded in and draws on social relationships. Some coping efforts involve obtaining information, emotional support, tangible forms of help, and guidance from others. Sources of support for adolescents include parents, siblings, peers, teachers, and other significant adults in their lives. Thus, coping is an important process that can lead to resilient outcomes, but it is not limited to the characteristics of individuals; coping is frequently a social process.

Dimensions and Categories of Coping

Coping research has been hindered by confusion and a lack of consensus about the dimensions of categories (Skinner et al., 2003). My colleagues and I proposed that stress responses can be distinguished along two broad dimensions: voluntary (controlled) versus involuntary (automatic) and engagement versus disengagement (Compas et al., 2001; Connor-Smith, Compas, Thomsen, Wadsworth, & Saltzman, 2000). The inclusion or exclusion of automatic stress responses within the definition of coping is to a certain degree one of semantics, as both perspectives recognize the importance of the two broad categories of controlled or voluntary responses and automatic or involuntary responses to stress. However, the degree to which these two components of stress responses are conceptualized and measured as distinct processes and the extent to which the relationship between them is understood are of fundamental importance in understanding processes of adaptation and resilience.

Regardless of how these concepts are mapped onto a definition of coping, it is important to distinguish between volitional and involuntary responses to stress for several reasons. First, this distinction avoids an overly broad and imprecise definition of coping in which coping includes everything that individuals do in response to stress (Lazarus & Folkman, 1984; Rudolph et al., 1995). Second, automatic and controlled processes are experienced as subjectively and qualitatively different: Individuals can distinguish between those aspects of their thoughts and behavior that they experience as under their personal control versus those that are beyond their control (Skinner, 1995). For example, the release of emotions can occur through an involuntary ventilation of emotions (crying) or through a controlled process such as writing, and the effects of these processes on emotions and physiology may be quite different (Pennebaker, 1997). Third, volitional and involuntary responses may emerge differently over the course of development, with involuntary responses present early in development (e.g., Rothbart, 1991), followed by the emergence of volitional responses in early childhood. Fourth, volitional and involuntary processes may differ in the ways they respond to interventions. Psychological interventions are often designed to teach individuals skills in managing those aspects of cognition and behavior that are under personal control, but they can only indirectly increase or decrease responses that are experienced as uncontrollable.

Empirical support for the distinction between controlled or volitional responses and automatic or involuntary responses comes from a wide range of sources, including research on associative conditioning and learning (Shiffrin, 1997; Shiffrin & Schneider, 1977), experimental research on strategic-controlled and automatic cognitive processes in emotions and emotional disorders (Gotlib & Krasnoperova, 1998; Mathews & MacLeod, 1994), research distinguishing some aspects of temperamental characteristics from intentional behavior and cognitive processes (Rothbart, 1991), research on automaticity in social cognition (e.g., Bargh, 1997; Mischel, 1997), and research in cognitive and affective neuroscience that has shown that there are distinct brain structures responsible for these two processes (Davidson, Jackson, & Kalin, 2000; Posner & DiGirolamo, 2000). For example, responses to threatening cues in the environment, which are experienced as stressful and therefore may initiate coping behavior, are processed on both an automatic, uncontrolled level as well as a controlled, strategic level (see Mathews & MacLeod, 1994, for a review of research with adults). Research has recently begun to examine these two levels of processing in children as well (e.g., Daleiden & Vasey, 1997; Vasey, El-Hag, & Daleiden, 1996). For example, using an experimental task to test for automatic attentional biases to threatening cues, Boyer et al. (2003) found that adolescents with a history of recurrent abdominal pain responded to pain and anxiety words that were presented at levels that activated automatic (20 ms) responses but avoided pain and anxiety words presented at a level (1,250 ms) that elicited controlled responses.

My colleagues and I have proposed that both automatic and controlled responses to stress can be further distinguished as engaging with a stressor or one's responses to the stressor, or disengaging from the stressor and one's responses (Compas et al., 2001). The origins of the engagement-disengagement dimension can be found in the concept of the fight (engagement) or flight (disengagement) response (e.g., Cannon, 1933, 1934; Gray, 1991) and in the contrast between approach and avoidance responses (Krohne, 1996). Voluntary or controlled responses (coping) that involve engagement can be further distinguished by their goals—oriented toward achieving primary control or secondary control (Connor-Smith et al., 2000). The goals of achieving either primary or secondary control are fundamental in motivational models of coping and self-regulation (e.g., Weisz, 1990). However, these goals are pursued only as part of controlled efforts to engage with the stressor or one's thoughts, emotions, and physiological reactions to the stressor (Rudolph et al., 1995).

Empirical support for this model comes from confirmatory factor analyses in studies of adolescents from different cultural groups reporting on their responses to different domains of stress (interpersonal stress, economic strain, family conflict; Benson, Compas, & Layne, 2003; Connor-Smith et al., 2000; Wadsworth, Reichman, Benson, & Compas, 2003). A first factor has been labeled primary control engagement coping (Connor-Smith et al., 2000; Rudolph, Dennig, & Weisz, 1995) or active coping (Ayers, Sandler, West, & Roosa, 1996; L. S. Walker, Smith, Garber, & Van Slyke, 1997) and is defined as coping intended to influence objective events or conditions or one's emotional responses to stress. This category includes not only problem solving and other coping efforts directed at changing the stressor but also direct efforts to change one's emotional reactions (Connor-Smith et al., 2000). The second category has been labeled secondary control engagement coping (Connor-Smith et al., 2000; Rudolph et al., 1995) and accommodative coping (Ayers et al., 1997; L. S. Walker et al., 1997) and encompasses coping efforts aimed at maximizing one's fit to current conditions. Examples include acceptance, cognitive restructuring, and distraction. A third category is disengagement (Connor-Smith et al., 2000) or avoidance (Ayers et al., 1997; L. S. Walker et al., 1997) coping, which is defined as an effort to disengage cognitively or behaviorally from the source of stress or one's emotions.

Studies of coping and emotional distress during adolescence suggest that primary control coping is associated with better adjustment in response to stressors that are objectively controllable or are perceived as controllable (Compas et al., 2001). Secondary control coping is better suited for uncontrollable stressors, as indicated by lower levels of symptoms when these strategies are used in uncontrollable situations (Compas et al., 2001). Disengagement or avoidance coping has consistently been found to be associated with poorer adjustment (higher levels of symptoms) regardless of the nature of the stressor.

Coping, Temperament, and Stress Responses

Coping is linked to but also distinct from several aspects of temperament, including the constructs of reactivity (response) and self-regulation (Compas et al., 2001, in press). Reactivity encompasses individual differences in physiological and emotional responses to stress. Physiological reactivity includes the threshold, dampening, and reactivation of autonomic arousal (e.g., Boyce, Barr, & Zeltzer, 1992). Although the characteristics of reactivity may vary across different emotions (e.g., fear vs. anger), highly reactive individuals have a lower threshold of initial response, are slower in recovery or returning to baseline, and display greater reactivation of arousal with repeated exposure to stress. High reactivity is generally associated with inhibited temperament, whereas low reactivity is associated with uninhibited temperament. Individual differences in reactivity and temperament are related to coping, as they affect the individual's initial automatic response to stress and may constrain or facilitate certain types of coping responses (Compas, 1987a). For example, the temperamental characteristics of behavioral inhibition (e.g., Kagan & Snidman, 1991) and attentional control (e.g., Posner & Rothbart, 1994; Rothbart, Posner, & Hershey, 1995) are related to individual differences in reactivity to stress. Behavioral inhibition includes the tendency to experience high levels of arousal in novel, threatening, or stressful situations and may be related to the use of avoidance and withdrawal as coping methods, whereas uninhibited temperament is expected to be related to more active and approach-oriented coping responses. Individual differences in the capacity for attentional control (the ability to sustain attention as well as to shift attention) may be related to the ability to use strategies such as distraction to cope with negative emotions.

As noted earlier, coping is also related to or is an aspect of self-regulation. From infancy, individuals are capable of regulating aspects of their physiological arousal, behavior, and emotions (Gunnar, 1994; Rothbart, 1991). However, regulation is achieved initially through involuntary, biologically based processes (e.g., Blass & Ciaramitaro, 1994). These regulatory capacities are augmented early in development by responses that are acquired through learning and experience but are under the control of contextual cues that elicit and maintain behavior (Rothbart, 1991). Therefore, some important aspects of self-regulation precede the development of the capacity for the conscious volitional efforts that comprise coping. Features of responses to stress in infancy that precede coping include individual differences in self-soothing behaviors (e.g., Gunnar, 1994). These behaviors develop prior to the skills needed for conscious volitional self-regulation, yet they are important aspects of the ways that infants regulate themselves in response to stress. Coping is influenced by the emergence of cognitive and behavioral capacities for regulation of the self and the environment, including the emergence of intentionality, representational thinking, language, metacognition, and the capacity for delay.

RISK AND RESILIENCE: EXEMPLARS FROM RESEARCH ON STRESS AND COPING

Research on sources of risk and resilience during adolescence has addressed an impressive array of contextual and individual factors. To exemplify important issues in adolescent risk and resilience, the focus here is on three exemplars of risk and resilience in adolescence that are linked to stress, stress reactivity, and coping. Poverty is a significant source of stress in the lives of millions of adolescents, and for adolescents who live in poverty it is a stable source of risk throughout childhood and adolescence. Temperamental characteristics represent important individual sources of risk and resilience that are also stable from childhood and into adolescence. There is very little evidence on the stability or developmental changes in coping during childhood and adolescence. However, recent research on brain development during adolescence provides intriguing and provocative evidence for changes in the capacity to cope during early adolescence. These sources of risk and resilience are important in their own right because of the role they play in problems of development during adolescence. They are additionally important, however, because they represent distinct levels of analysis of risk processes and because their integration can serve as a model for comprehensive approaches to adolescent risk and resilience (Cicchetti & Dawson, 2002).

Stable Contextual Risk Factors: Poverty and Economic Adversity

Poverty is the single most important social problem facing young people in the United States. Sixteen percent of America's children under the age of 18 years live in poverty, and 37% of children under 18 live in low-income families, defined as families living within 200% of the poverty line (National Center for Children in Poverty, 2003). Furthermore, 6% of children in America live in extreme poverty (defined in 2000 as an annual income of $6,930 for a family of three). Subgroups of the population are even more likely to live in poverty: 30% of African American children, 28% of Latino children, and 33% of first-generation children of immigrant parents live in poverty. The percentages of America's children living in poverty has shifted over the years from an estimated 27% in 1959 to 14% in 1969 and rose sharply between 1979 and 1984 from 17% to 22% (National Center for Children in Poverty, 2003). The numbers of children living in poverty peaked in 1993, but the rate is likely to rise again in light of recent economic downturns in the early 21st century.

Adolescents in poverty live both in poor families and in poor neighborhoods and are exposed to risks in both of these contexts (e.g., Furstenberg, 2001). Although the effects of poverty are especially pronounced in the development of very young children, poverty is one of the most significant markers of negative outcomes in the mental and physical health of adolescents. Numerous studies have established an association between poverty and psychological problems in youth (e.g., McLoyd, 1998), and adolescents who grow up poor are at heightened risk for a wide range of psychological problems (McLoyd, 1998). Poverty has pronounced effects on children's cognitive development and academic achievement. These effects are evident early in development (as early as preschool measures of cognitive skills), but they continue to be evident during adolescence as reflected in cognitive and verbal skills, achievement test scores, grade retentions, course failures, placement in special education, high school graduation rate, high school dropout rate, and completed years of schooling (Friedman & Chase-Lansdale, 2002; McLoyd, 1998). Poverty is also related to socioemotional development during adolescence as evidenced by the association of poverty and increased rates of internalizing and externalizing problems and disorders. The effects of poverty appear to be stronger on externalizing problems such as delinquency and antisocial behavior, but there are measurable effects on anxiety and depression as well (McLoyd, 1998).

Poverty and economic hardship are also related to increased risk for physical health problems and disease in children and adolescents (Chen, Matthews, & Boyce, 2002). Similar to the socioeconomic status (SES)–health gradient in adults (Adler et al., 1994), there is a direct, linear relationship between SES and health in children and adolescents such that for every decrease in SES there is an associated increase in health risk. The effects of SES on health vary somewhat with age across health outcomes, with the strongest effects in adolescence occurring for smoking and other health risk behaviors. There is also strong evidence to suggest that one of the primary pathways through which economic hardship exerts an effect on physical health is through prolonged arousal of negative emotions and associated physiological arousal (Gallo & Matthews, 2003).

In addition to its potency as a risk factor, poverty is an interesting and important example of risk because persistent poverty, beginning in childhood and lasting through adolescence, has a much more deleterious effect on development than does transient poverty (McLoyd, 1998). Thus, poverty is an example of a stable risk factor that exerts effects early in development, but these effects persist into adolescence and become increasingly more pronounced the longer the duration of exposure to the risk factor. Research has not clarified, however, whether the effects of prolonged poverty increase linearly, whether there are changes in the strength of this relationship with development, or whether there are qualitative changes in the effects of poverty as individuals move from childhood into adolescence. If the association is linear, negative outcomes should increase additively with development. After controlling for age, the number and severity of problems for children living in poverty would be greater in school-age children than in preschool children and greater in adolescents than in school-age children. Changes in the strength of the effects of poverty would be reflected in greater increases in problems associated with poverty as some points in development. For example, there may be a dramatic rise in rates of problems during preschool development, relatively stable rates of problems during middle childhood, and then a second jump in rates of problems in early adolescence. A qualitative shift would be reflected in changes in the nature and types of problems that are produced by poverty during adolescence as compared with early childhood. However, these changes would have to be unique to the types of problems linked to poverty as opposed to qualitative changes in the nature of problems that are linked to development in general. These developmental processes have not been addressed.

Stable Individual Risk Factors: Temperament

Individual differences in behavioral and affective style or temperament emerge in infancy and remain relatively stable throughout childhood and adolescence and are presumed to have an underlying biological basis (Rothbart & Bates, 1998). Temperament is multidimensional in nature, although there is little consensus on what the primary dimensions of temperament are. Furthermore, there has been debate regarding the continuous versus categorical nature of temperament characteristics, with recent research suggesting that at least some temperamental characteristics are categorical rather than continuous in nature (e.g., Woodward, Lenzenweger, Kagan, Snidman, & Arcus, 2000).

Recent research has begun to elucidate some of the biological substrates of specific temperamental characteristics that are related to both automatic and controlled responses to stress. The anterior attention network described by Posner and Rothbart (1998), and perhaps most importantly the anterior cingulate, plays a central role in the effortful (controlled) regulation of attention. For example, attentional processes in infancy are largely regulated by stimulus characteristics. However, the capacity for effortful control over the direction of attention increases throughout early childhood and into the school-age years (Posner & Rothbart). There are strong individual differences in the capacity for effortful, voluntary control of attention, and these differences are reflective of individual differences in temperamental traits. Moreover, patterns of attentional control and attentional shift are related to levels of emotional arousal—specifically to the level of negative emotion that is experienced in response to external stimuli (Posner & Rothbart).

Attentional control and other temperamental characteristics may be related to the ability purposively to employ more complex, voluntary types of coping. For example, in path analyses of parents' reports of children's and adolescents' temperament, coping, and symptoms in a sample of children and adolescents with recurrent abdominal pain, Thomsen, Compas, Colletti, Stanger, and Boyer (2003) found that poor attentional control was related to higher symptoms of anxiety and depression. However, this association was fully mediated by secondary control coping. That is, children and adolescents with temperamentally higher levels of attentional control used more secondary control coping and had lower symptoms of anxiety and depression. Greater control over attentional processes may facilitate the use of more complex cognitive coping processes by allowing children to shift their attention away from their pain, reinterpret the situation in more benign terms, and selectively attend to positive thoughts and stimuli.

Temperament may also be related to the engagement-disengagement dimension of stress responses. Asymmetry in the relative activation of the right and left frontal hemisphere is hypothesized to reflect children's underlying motivational disposition to approach (engage) or withdraw (disengage) from novelty or potential threat—that is, to individual differences in behavioral inhibition (Calkins & Fox, 2002). Infants who display higher levels of negative affect and motor activity at 4 months of age display greater right frontal hemispheric activation, as contrasted with greater left frontal activation in infants who display more positive affect and motor activity (Calkins, Fox, & Marshall, 1996). Furthermore, infants who display high negative affect, motor behavior, and right frontal activation were more likely to exhibit social withdrawal at 4 years of age (Henderson, Fox, & Rubin, 2001).

Several prospective studies have used temperamental traits to predict symptoms of psychopathology during adolescence. For example, individuals showing high levels of negative affectivity as toddlers are more likely to have elevated rates of depressive symptoms and disorders during adolescence and young adulthood (Caspi, Moffitt, Newman, & Silva, 1996; Gjerde, 1995). Windle and Davies (1999) examined the relation between temperament and depressive symptoms and heavy alcohol use in adolescence. They found that a group of adolescents who were characterized by high depressive symptoms only (as compared with those who were high in alcohol use only, high in both depressive symptoms and alcohol use, or low in both) were higher in traits characteristic of difficult temperament, including behavioral inflexibility, lower rhythmicity, greater withdrawal, lower positive mood, and low task orientation (poor concentration). In a related study, Davies and Windle (2001) examined difficult temperament as a source of vulnerability to parental conflict and discord. Depressive symptoms were correlated both within time and across time with poorer task orientation (concentration), low rhythmicity, and low adaptability. Furthermore, higher depressive symptoms were predicted by the interaction of parental marital discord and low task orientation. These studies suggest that depressive symptoms are associated with several temperamental characteristics related to emotionality, attentional control, and general dysregulation of behavior (Compas et al., in press). Thus, individual differences in temperament that emerge early in development may represent stable sources of risk that manifest themselves in negative outcomes in adolescence.

Variable Individual Risk Factors: Brain Development During Adolescence

In addition to aspects of brain function related to temperament that are stable from childhood into adolescence, there are also important changes in brain function at adolescence that are relevant to automatic and controlled responses to stress. Automatic processes are exemplified by the limbic system and its role in basic emotion processes. The limbic system includes the amygdala, which is involved in the identification of threat-relevant cues in the environment; the hippocampus, which is responsible for the storage of emotionally related information and experiences into memory; and the hypothalamus, which, among many other functions, is involved in responses to stress through its downstream connections to the pituitary gland and the adrenal glands. Controlled effortful processes are regulated by the prefrontal cortex, which is responsible for various executive functions involved in the regulation of emotion and goal-directed behavior. Prefrontal cortical structures include the anterior attentional system, which is involved in the controlled regulation of attention and plays a critical role in modulating information input.

Important changes in brain structure and function continue to develop throughout adolescence and into adulthood (e.g., Nelson, Bloom, Cameron, Amaral, Dahl, & Pine, 2002; Spear, 2000a, 2000b; E. F. Walker, 2002). The portions of the brain that are responsible for executive functions, higher order cognitive processes, and effortful control in the prefrontal cortex continue to develop gradually throughout adolescence. In contrast, brain structures and functions related to emotions in the limbic system develop earlier in childhood, but growth in the limbic system may be accelerated by the secretion of sex hormones and sexual maturation associated with puberty. Thus, emotional processes governed by the limbic system, many of which are automatic in nature, may develop more rapidly than and may precede the development of controlled, volitional processes in the prefrontal cortex. This developmental pattern parallels the emergence of temperamental characteristics that are automatic prior to processes of effortful control (Rothbart, 1991).

The asynchrony between development of emotional processes in the limbic system and development in the executive functions of the prefrontal cortex may result in what Nelson et al. (2002) referred to as "starting the engines with an unskilled driver" (p. 515). That is, adolescents may be at increased risk for emotional problems and disorders because the brain systems that activate emotions (including negative emotions such as sadness, anxiety, and anger) are developed before the capacity for volitional, effortful control of these emotions is fully in place. This certainly would seem maladaptive from an evolutionary perspective. However, this asynchrony may be directly related to secular trends in the early onset of pubertal maturation and therefore may be more characteristic of modern adolescence than was true for previous generations.

In addition, aspects of adolescent brain development may predispose adolescents to be vulnerable to both the effects of stress (as represented by heightened levels of negative emotions) and the effects of alcohol as a means of dampening stress-related emotional arousal (Spear, 2000a, 2000b). There is cross-species evidence of transformation and remodeling of certain aspects of brain structure during adolescence that includes changes in the prefrontal cortex in ways that may affect goal-directed behaviors. During adolescence there is a decrease in the amount of input to the prefrontal cortex from certain neurotransmitters that are related to both excitatory (glutamate) and inhibitory (gamma-aminobutyric acid) functions, and concomitantly the input from dopamine in this brain region peaks during adolescence (Spear, 2000a, 2000b). These changes appear to be linked to increased novelty seeking and the motivational value of stimuli, including the reinforcing properties of drugs and alcohol (Spear, 2000a, 2000b). There also may be brain changes that are related to affiliative behavior with peers that may map onto the social reinforcing properties of some high-risk behaviors. Therefore, changes in brain function and structure that are unique to adolescence may predispose adolescents to the biologically reinforcing properties of alcohol, as well as to social (peer) reinforcement for this risky behavior.

Evidence from functional magnetic resonance imaging (fMRI) and electrophysiology studies indicates that some aspects of frontal brain activity are enhanced during adolescence (Casey, Giedd, & Thomas, 2000; E. F. Walker, 2002). This increased activation in the prefrontal cortex may be reflective of advances in executive function and other complex, higher order cognitive processing. This suggests a possible protective mechanism to the extent that enhanced executive function could contribute to increased self-control, self-regulation, and coping. Thus, brain development during adolescence may be simultaneously increasing risk in some ways and enhancing resilience in other ways.

In addition to changes in brain function and structure that may affect automatic and controlled responses to stress, prolonged exposure to stress also changes brain function and structure. Changes (neural plasticity) that occur in response to stress suggest that the brain itself is designed to be resilient (McEwen, 2000). For example, acute stress can enhance the memory of events that are potentially threatening to the organism, thereby preparing the individual to be better able to detect similar threats in the future. Even some forms of chronic stress may cause adaptive plasticity in the brain (McEwen, 2000). Evidence of adaptive plasticity and resilience in the brain notwithstanding, there is also extensive evidence that brain and neuroendocrine responses to chronic stress can be maladaptive. For example, Susman and colleagues (Susman, Dorn, Inoff-Germain, Nottelmann, & Chrousos, 1997) identified individual differences in cortisol reactivity in a challenging situation such that some adolescents increased, some did not change, and others decreased in cortisol level. Adolescents who showed increased cortisol reactivity reported more behavior problems and symptoms of depression a year later than did adolescents who did not change or who decreased in cortisol level. These findings suggest that biological stress responses of some adolescents may increase the adverse effects of stress.

Highly traumatic stress or stress that is chronic and prolonged may actually damage brain structures and functions (Sapolsky, 1996). Evidence from animal and human research indicates that the hippocampus, the portion of the brain that plays a role in encoding experience and information, especially those that involve emotion, into memory, is damaged by prolonged or extreme stress (Sapolsky, 1996). Several recent studies have shown that traumatic experiences and chronic stress can affect brain development, structure, and function in childhood and adolescence. For example, DeBellis et al. (2002) found that compared with controls, children and adolescents with posttraumatic stress disorder (PTSD) related to child abuse and maltreatment had smaller intracranial, cerebral, and prefrontal cortex masses, less prefrontal cortical white matter, smaller right temporal lobe volumes and areas of the corpus callosum and its subregions, and larger frontal lobe cerebrospinal fluid volumes. These findings suggest that maltreatment-related stress is associated with adverse brain development. Damage to the hippocampus can be doubly problematic, as the hippocampus plays an important role in the regulation of the hypothalamic-pituitary-adrenal (HPA) axis (Bratt et al., 2001). Thus, prolonged HPA activation in response to chronic stress may lead to hippocampal damage that may contribute to further HPA-axis dysregulation.

In summary, recent research suggests that exposure to prolonged, chronic stress may lead to dysregulation in automatic stress response processes while simultaneously decreasing the capacity for effortful coping responses. Thus, adolescents who are at-risk because of chronic stress may be the most vulnerable because of the development of maladaptive stress response processes.

Mechanisms of Risk: Mediators and Moderators of Poverty

Proximal Stressors as Mediators of Poverty

Poverty functions as a distal risk factor for health and mental health problems during adolescence. A primary pathway for these effects is through the generation of stressors within the family and associated levels of negative affect within the family (Friedman & Chase-Lansdale, 2002). Specifically, research has examined the quality of parenting and stressful parent-child interactions when parents are under economic stress. Harsh, punitive parenting, interparental conflict, and parent-adolescent conflict are found disproportionately in families under economic pressure, and these factors have been linked to emotional and behavioral problems in poor adolescents (e.g., Conger et al.,

1992, 1993). Similarly, poor neighborhood quality, family violence, and marital separation are associated with behavior problems in adolescents in poor, high-risk, inner-city communities (e.g., Dawkins, Fullilove, & Dawkins 1996; Martinèz & Richters, 1993).

A sufficient number of studies have examined these associations to justify a quantitative review. Based on these studies, my colleagues and I conducted a meta-analysis of family stress as a mediator of the effects of poverty on adolescent development (see Grant et al., 2003). The results of this meta-analysis were then used to test a conceptual model in which family stressors related to negative parenting mediate the relation between poverty and psychological symptoms in children and adolescents. Results of path analyses based on meta-analytic findings generally support a model in which family stressors related to negative parenting mediate the relation between poverty and psychological symptoms in children and adolescents (Grant et al., in press). Thus, poverty places chronic strain on families and creates stress within families that takes a toll on the development and adjustment of adolescents. Although the mediational model was generally supported, the best fit for both the total sample (cross-sectional and prospective studies) and the longitudinal subsample included direct pathways between poverty and psychological symptoms in addition to mediated effects (Grant et al., in press). Unexpectedly, the best fit for the total sample included a direct path between poverty and internalizing symptoms, whereas the best fit for the longitudinal subsample included a direct path between poverty and externalizing symptoms.

These results can be explained in several ways. First, it may be that methodological differences between the two samples (beyond the timeframe of data collection) accounted for these discrepant findings. Although this interpretation cannot be ruled out, we compared methods across the two data sets and did not identify any methodological factors that accounted for this pattern of results (i.e., the measures, sample sizes, sample characteristics, and sources of information were highly variable within each data set but did not differ in any apparent way across the data sets). A second interpretation is that the associations among poverty, negative parenting, and psychological problems change with development. It is possible that poverty exerts both a direct and an indirect effect on internalizing symptoms early in development, whereas the direct effects of poverty on externalizing symptoms emerge in late childhood and adolescence. Previous research has suggested that internalizing symptoms such as anxiety serve as conduits for externalizing symptoms such as aggression (e.g., Barnow, Lucht, & Freyberger, 2001). It is plausible that in some contexts of poverty (e.g., inner city neighborhoods), internalizing symptoms (e.g., PTSD) might emerge first, followed by externalizing symptoms (e.g., aggression). Externalizing symptoms might eventually become the more common psychological response, perhaps even providing some protection in a dangerous environment (Gorman-Smith, Tolan, & Henry, 2000). These interpretations remain speculative at this point, and additional research is needed to test the hypothesis that the relations among poverty, negative parenting, and particular types of psychopathology change with development.

Little evidence emerged for the hypothesis that negative parenting serves as a stronger mediator for internalizing than for externalizing symptoms in poor families. In the longitudinal sample, the best fitting model included an additional direct pathway from poverty to externalizing (but not internalizing) symptoms (Grant et al., 2003). Contradictory evidence emerged for the total sample, however, as a direct path from poverty to internalizing symptoms actually provided a better fit with the data than did a direct path from poverty to externalizing symptoms. Taken together, there is little evidence for a better fit for internalizing symptoms. The lack of support for this specificity hypothesis may simply reflect common pathways leading to high cooccurrence rates for internalizing and externalizing symptoms in young people (McMahon et al., 2003) or suggest that poverty is a nonspecific stressor (Steinberg & Avenevoli, 2000).

Coping and Stress Reactivity as Mediators of Poverty

Family stressors are important mediators of the effects of poverty on adolescent adjustment and development. However, this relationship may be further mediated or moderated by the ways that adolescents cope with and respond to family stress. Tests of coping and stress responses require specification of the source of stress. With regard to poverty, economic strain and family conflict appear to be two important family stress processes that may serve as sources of stress for adolescents. Coping and stress responses may partially determine how well adolescents function during and following these stressors (i.e., as mediators of the association between economic strain and behavior problems). Alternatively, coping and stress responses may serve as moderators by changing the relationship between a stressor and subsequent and concomitant psychological functioning, depending on the relative amount of a particular type of coping the adolescent uses.

There are relatively few studies describing how adolescents themselves cope with economic stress. Leadbeater and Linares (1992) examined relations among life stress, receipt of social support, and depressive symptoms in a sample of low-income adolescent mothers and found that receiving assistance from friends and family predicted fewer depressive symptoms over time for these young mothers. Chase-Lansdale, Brooks-Gunn, and Zamsky (1994) found that the presence of a grandmother in the home of an adolescent mother had important effects on the quality of the mother's parenting skills. However, because most adolescents are generally not responsible for parenting or for managing economic challenges, it is unclear how instrumental social supports like these will be useful for the majority of adolescents. Social support is only one way through which primary control, secondary control, or disengagement coping may be enacted (Compas et al., 2001). Therefore, these studies addressed only a limited range of coping responses.

A recent study by Wadsworth and Compas (2002) tested a broader model of adolescent coping with economic hardship and its effects on adolescent psychological adjustment. Using adolescents' self-reports and objective data on SES, we examined the associations among family SES, perceived economic strain, family conflict, and coping responses in a sample of 364 Euro-American, rural, low-income adolescents. Objective indicators of economic hardship were evident in this sample, as the mean parental employment score was 3.7 on the Hollingshead (1975) 9-point scale (equivalent to laborer or tenant farmer), and 29% of the adolescents were on the subsidized school lunch program. Two theoretical models were tested using structural equation modeling—one testing coping as a mediator of the stress-psychopathology relationship and the other testing coping as a moderator. Consistent with the findings of our recent meta-analysis (Grant et al., in press), the results of this study revealed that family economic hardship was related to both aggression and anxiety-depression primarily through two proximal stressors, perceived economic strain and conflict among family members (Wadsworth

& Compas, 2002). That is, low SES was predictive of increased economic strain and increased conflict within families. These more proximal stressors mediated the association between SES and adolescent aggressive behavior and anxiety-depression.

Adolescents' coping served to mediate further the effects of SES and family stress on their symptoms of aggression and anxiety-depression. These analyses identified two types of coping that are associated with fewer anxiety-depression and aggression problems in the face of these stressors: Both primary control and secondary control engagement coping were associated with fewer adjustment problems. Effects were most pronounced for secondary control coping; greater use of these strategies (acceptance, distraction, cognitive restructuring) was related to lower symptoms of anxiety-depression in response to economic strain and family conflict and to lower aggressive behavior in response to family conflict. Primary control coping (problem solving, emotional expression, emotional modulation) was related to lower anxiety-depression and aggression in response to family conflict. However, neither type of coping mediated the relation between economic strain and aggressive behavior problems. (No evidence was found for the effects for coping as a moderator of the association between family and economic stress and adolescent adjustment problems.)

These findings suggest that resilient adolescents in this sample were those who were able to mobilize and employ primary and secondary control engagement coping responses. This is consistent with the view that coping is an important manifestation of resilience—effective coping is what resilient adolescents do in response to stress. However, the mediational models also showed that as conflict and economic strains within the family increased, adolescents reported using less of these two adaptive forms of coping (Wadsworth & Compas, 2002). That is, adolescents who were under greater stress and who therefore could potentially benefit the most of the use of primary and secondary control coping reported using less of both of these types of coping. This is consistent with research showing that as the load exerted by stressors increases, it interferes with more complex cognitive forms of coping such as those encompassed in primary and secondary control coping (e.g., Matthews & Wells, 1996). This finding is also consistent with evidence that stress has adverse effects on the development of complex cognitive skills that are necessary for coping. Adolescents who were living under greater economic stress (as indicated by lower SES) were faced with more family economic strains and more family conflict, and in turn were less able to cope in ways that would be most adaptive in managing these stressors. Thus, they were faced with cumulative risk across distal (low income) and proximal (family stress) contextual risk factors and the absence of an important protective factor (poor coping) as well. This is the combination that Friedman and Chase-Lansdale (2002) and others have hypothesized to be an especially high-risk scenario.

TOWARD AN INTEGRATIVE MODEL OF STRESS, COPING, RISK, AND RESILIENCE IN ADOLESCENCE

A comprehensive understanding of processes of risk and resilience during adolescence will require multiple levels of analyses of stable and changing aspects of individual adolescents and their environments. The research reviewed in this chapter points to several basic principles about risk and resilience during adolescence and highlights important directions for future research.

1. Processes of risk and resilience operate at multiple levels during adolescence. A comprehensive understanding of who is at risk for negative outcomes and who develops positively in spite of exposure to known levels of risk requires analysis of multiple levels of functioning. Risk and resilience processes include aspects of individuals and their social contexts. Contextual factors include the broad social circumstances in which adolescents develop. A compelling example of contextual risk can be seen in the effects of poverty on adolescent development. However, the effects of distal risk factors such as poverty are the result of factors embedded in the more immediate social environments of adolescents, including disruptions and strains that are evident in families. The multiple levels of context are further complicated by levels of individual functioning, including cognitive, affective, and behavioral responses to stress and efforts to cope with stress. These response processes are affected by underlying biological development and functioning.

In spite of recognition of the need for multiple levels of analysis in risk and resilience research (Cicchetti & Dawson, 2002), there has been little progress in this regard. Most studies continue to focus on one level of analysis, be it molar or molecular. At the greatest extremes, investigations of biological development (including brain development) during adolescence have typically relied on samples of convenience and have not examined these important changes in adolescents who are exposed to greatest risk due to chronic sources of stress and adversity. Similarly, research on distal contextual factors such as poverty has typically failed to examine individual-level processes that may exacerbate or protect adolescents from the effects of broad risk factors. Research is needed that examines how distal environmental risks get into behavior and under the skin. Similarly, studies of individual processes, including brain development and function, need to be conducted on those individuals in greatest need. Much more precise predictions of positive and negative developmental outcomes during adolescence can be made based on multiple levels of analysis.

2. Some processes of risk and resilience are stable from childhood into adolescence. Important sources of risk and protection from risk are in place prior to adolescence. Many sources of adversity in the environment, including chronic poverty, emerge during childhood and continue unabated through adolescence. But there are also enduring resources in families, neighborhoods, and schools that also follow individuals through early development and into adolescence. At the individual level, there are stable characteristics, such as temperament, that serve to make adolescents more vulnerable to or protect them from risk. Therefore, longitudinal research that begins prior to adolescence is needed to understand fully what places some adolescents at risk and what protects others from negative outcomes.

3. Some processes of risk and resilience change with development during adolescence. A model of risk and resilience in adolescence must include processes that emerge during adolescence and that may be unique to this developmental period (Steinberg, 2002). Changes in cognitive, emotional, social, and biological development bring with them a host of increased sources of risk and concomitant increases in protective factors. Some forms of interpersonal stress increase during adolescence, along with changes in cognitive processes that can contribute both to greater vulnerability and protection from stress. Emerging evidence on brain development during adolescence also points to changes in brain function that may shape automatic and controlled responses to stress. Research on these changes is in its earliest phases, however, and is a high priority for future research.

4. *Trajectories of adolescent development are shaped by both stable and developmental sources of risk and resilience.* Healthy and problematic physical and psychological development during adolescence is not static and is best reflected in pathways or trajectories of development and change (Compas, Hinden, & Gerhardt, 1995; Garber et al., 2002; Moffitt & Caspi, 2001). In some instances, these trajectories have their onset well prior to adolescence, and adolescent development reflects the continuation of an increasing or decreasing slope. In other cases, trajectories are changed significantly by contextual and individual development during adolescence. Distinguishing risk and resilience processes that contribute to stable versus changing trajectories is a high priority.

5. *Stress and stress reactivity are important unifying constructs for understanding processes of risk.* After decades of research and thousands of studies, the concepts of stress and stress reactivity continue to play a central role in research on risk processes during adolescence. Stress, or more accurately stressful events and circumstances, operate at multiple levels and are both stable and changing during adolescence. As exemplified in research on the effects of poverty, adolescents who lack economic resources are under chronic stress. However, the stress of poverty is best understood by examining the more proximal sources of stress that are manifested in adolescents' immediate environments.

Individual differences in temperament influence stress processes by shaping automatic physiological, emotional, cognitive, and behavioral responses to stress. Behavioral inhibition, positive and negative affectivity, and attentional control are examples of temperamental characteristics that may shape responses to stress and thereby contribute to vulnerability or protection from stress. Because of problems inherent in retrospective recall of early temperament, longitudinal studies are needed in which temperamental characteristics are measured in childhood and used as predictors of responses to stress and adversity in adolescence.

6. *Coping is an important unifying construct for understanding processes of resilience.* The ways that adolescents cope with stress and adversity represent an essential feature of resilience. This includes the skills that the individual develops to regulate reactions to stress and the social and interpersonal resources that are used to facilitate effective coping. Coping is one of the primary processes through which resilient outcomes are achieved. Therefore, it is essential to develop a detailed accounting of the ways of coping that are associated with positive and negative outcomes in adolescence. The details of effective and ineffective coping form a foundation for interventions to enhance resilience and decrease the adverse effects of stress during adolescence (Compas, Langrock, Keller, Merchant, & Copeland, 2002).

REFERENCES

Achenbach, T. M. (1991). *Integrative guide for the 1991 CBCL/4–18, YSR, and TRF Profiles.* Burlington: University of Vermont.

Achenbach, T. M., & Dumenci, L. (2001). Advances in empirically based assessment: Revised cross-informant syndromes and new DSM-oriented scales for the CBCL, YSR, and TRF: Comment on Lengua, Sadowksi, Friedrich, and Fisher (2001). *Journal of Consulting and Clinical Psychology, 69,* 699–702.

Achenbach, T. M., McConaughy, S. M., & Howell, C. T. (1987). Child/adolescent behavior and emotional problems: Implications of cross-informant correlations for situational specificity. *Psychological Bulletin, 101,* 213–232.

Adler, N. E., Boyce, W. T., Chesney, M. A., Cohen, S., Folkman, S., Kahn, R. L., & Syme, L. (1994). Socioeconomic status and health: The challenge of the gradient. *American Psychologist, 49,* 15–24.

American Psychiatric Association. (1994). *Diagnostic and statistical manual of mental disorders* (4th ed.). Washington, DC: Author.

Angold, A., & Costello, E. J. (1993). Depressive comorbidity in children and adolescents: Empirical, theoretical, and methodological issues. *American Journal of Psychiatry, 150,* 1779–1791.

Ayers, T. S., Sandler, I. N., West, S. G., & Roosa, M. W. (1996). A dispositional and situational assessment of children's coping: Testing alternative models of coping. *Journal of Personality, 64,* 923–958.

Bargh, J. A. (1997). The automaticity of everyday life. In R. S. Wyer (Ed.), *The automaticity of everyday life: Vol. 10. Advances in social cognition* (pp. 1–61). Mahwah, NJ: Erlbaum.

Barnow, S., Lucht, M., & Freyberger, H. J. (2001). Influence of punishment, emotional rejection, child abuse, and broken home on aggression in adolescence: An examination of aggressive adolescents in Germany. *Psychopathology, 34,* 167–173.

Baron, R. M., & Kenny, D. A. (1986). The moderator-mediator variable distinction in social psychological research: Conceptual, strategic, and statistical considerations. *Journal of Personality and Social Psychology, 51,* 1173–1182.

Benson, M. A., Compas, B. E., & Layne, C. (2003). *Measurement of post-war coping and stress responses in Bosnian adolescents.* Manuscript submitted for publication.

Blass, E., & Ciaramitaro, V. (1994). A new look at some old mechanisms in human newborns: Taste and tactile determinants of state, affect, and action. *Monographs of the Society for Research on Child Development, 59*(1, Serial No. 244).

Blum, R. W., McNeely, C., & Nonnemaker, J. (2002). Vulnerability, risk, and protection. *Journal of Adolescent Health, 31,* 28–39.

Bolger, K. E., Patterson, C. J., Thompson, W. W., & Kupersmidt, J. B. (1995). Psychosocial adjustment among children experiencing persistent and intermittent family economic hardship. *Child Development, 66,* 1107–1129.

Boyce, W. T., Barr, R. G., & Zeltzer, L. K. (1992). Temperament and the psychobiology of childhood stress. *Pediatrics, 90,* 483–486.

Boyer, M. B., Compas, B. E., Stanger, C., Colletti, R. B., Konik, B., Morrow, S. B., & Thomsen, A. H. (2003). *Supraliminal and subliminal attentional biases in children with recurrent abdominal pain.* Manuscript submitted for publication.

Brett, A. M., Kelley, S. P., Knowles, J. P., Barrett, J., Davis, K., Davis, M., & Mittlemann, G. (2001). Long-term modulation of the HPA axis by the hippocampus: Behavioral, biochemical, and immunological endpoints in rats exposed to chronic mild stress. *Psychoneuroendocrinology, 26,* 121–145.

Calkins, S. D., & Fox, N. A. (2002). Self-regulatory processes in early personality development: A multilevel approach to the study of childhood social withdrawal and aggression. *Development and Psychopathology, 14,* 477–498.

Calkins, S. D., Fox, N. A., & Marshall, T. R. (1996). Behavioral and physiological antecedents of inhibited and uninhibited behavior. *Child Development, 67,* 523–540.

Cannon, W. (1933). *The wisdom of the body.* New York: Norton.
Cannon, W. (1934). The significance of emotional level. *Scientific Monthly, 38,* 101–110.
Casey, B. J., Giedd, J. N., & Thomas, K. M. (2000). Structural and functional brain development and its relation to cognitive development. *Biological Psychology, 54,* 246–257.
Caspi, A., Moffitt, T. E., Newman, D. L., & Silva, P. A. (1996). Behavioral observations at age 3 predict adult psychiatric disorders: Longitudinal evidence from a birth cohort. *Archives of General Psychiatry, 53,* 1033–1039.
Chase-Lansdale, P. L., Brooks-Gunn, J., & Zamsky, E. S. (1994). Young African American multigenerational families in poverty: Quality of mothering and grandmothering. *Child Development, 65,* 373–393.
Chen, E., Matthews, K. A., & Boyce, W. T. (2002). Socioeconomic differences in children's health: How and why do these relationships change with age? *Psychological Bulletin, 128,* 295–329.
Cicchetti, D., & Cohen, D. (1995). Perspectives on developmental psychopathology. In D. Cicchetti & D. Cohen (Eds.), *Developmental psychopathology: Vol. 1. Theory and methods* (pp. 3–20). New York: Wiley.
Cicchetti, D., & Dawson, G. (2002). Editorial: Multiple levels of analysis. *Development and Psychopathology, 14,* 417–420.
Cicchetti, D., & Rogosh, F. A. (1999). Psychopathology as risk for adolescent substance use disorders: A developmental psychopathology perspective. *Journal of Clinical Child Psychology, 28,* 355–365.
Cohen, S., Kessler, R. C., & Gordon, L. U. (1995). *Measuring stress.* New York: Oxford University Press.
Compas, B. E. (1987a). Coping with stress during childhood and adolescence. *Psychological Bulletin, 101,* 393–403.
Compas, B. E. (1987b). Stress and life events during childhood and adolescence. *Clinical Psychology Review, 7,* 275–302.
Compas, B. E. (1993). Promoting adolescent mental health. In S. G. Millstein, A. C. Peterson, & E. O. Nightengale (Eds.), *Promoting the health of adolescents: New directions for the 21st century.* New York: Oxford University Press.
Compas, B. E., Connor-Smith, J. K., & Jaser, S. S. (in press). Temperament, stress reactivity, and coping: Implications for depression in childhood and adolescence. *Journal of Clinical Child and Adolescent Psychology.*
Compas, B. E., Connor-Smith, J. K., Saltzman, H., Thomsen, A. H., & Wadsworth, M. E. (2001). Coping with stress during childhood and adolescence: Progress, problems, and potential in theory and research. *Psychological Bulletin, 127,* 87–127.
Compas, B. E., & Grant, K. E. (2002). Processes of risk and resilience in adolescence. In R. M. Lerner, F. Jacobs, & D. Wertlieb (Eds.), *Handbook of applied developmental science: Vol. 1. Applying developmental science for youth and families: Historical and theoretical foundations.* Thousand Oaks, CA: Sage.
Compas, B. E., & Hammen, C. L. (1994). Child and adolescent depression: Covariation and comorbidity in development. In R. J. Haggerty, N. Garmezy, M. Rutter, & L. Sherrod (Eds.), *Risk and resilience in children: Developmental approaches* (pp. 225–267). New York: Cambridge University Press.
Compas, B. E., & Harding, A. (1998). Competence across the lifespan: Lessons from coping with cancer. In D. Pushkar and W. M. Bukowski (Eds.), *Improving competence across the lifespan: Building interventions based on theory and research* (pp. 9–26). New York: Plenum.
Compas, B. E., Hinden, B. R., & Gerhardt, C. A. (1995). Adolescent development: Pathways and processes of risk and resilience. *Annual Review of Psychology, 46,* 265–293.
Compas, B. E., Howell, D. C., Phares, V., Williams, R. A., Giunta, C. T., & Ledoux, N. (1989). Risk factors for emotional/behavioral problems in young adolescents: A prospective analysis of adolescent and parental stress and symptoms. *Journal of Consulting and Clinical Psychology, 57,* 732–740.
Compas, B. E., Langrock, A. M., Keller, G., Merchant, M. J., & Copeland, M. E. (2002). Coping with parental depression: Processes of adaptation to chronic stress. In S. H. Good-

man & I. H. Gotlib (Eds.), *Children of depressed parents: Mechanisms of risk and implications for treatment* (pp. 227–252). Washington, DC: American Psychological Association.

Compas, B. E., Malcarne, V. L., & Fondacaro, K. M. (1988). Coping with stressful events in older children and young adolescents. *Journal of Consulting and Clinical Psychology, 56,* 405–411.

Compas, B. E., & Wagner, B. M. (1991). Psychosocial stress during adolescence: Intrapersonal and interpersonal processes. In M. E. Colten & S. Gore (Eds.), *Adolescent stress: Causes and consequences—Social institutions and social change* (pp. 67–85). New York: de Gruyter.

Conger, R. D., Conger, K. J., Elder, G. H., Jr., Lorenz, F., Simons, R., & Whitbeck, L. (1992). A family process model of economic hardship and adjustment of early adolescent boys. *Child Development, 63,* 526–541.

Conger, R. D., Conger, K. J., Elder, G. H., Jr., Lorenz, F., Simons, R., & Whitbeck, L. (1993). A family process model of economic hardship and adjustment of early adolescent girls. *Developmental Psychology, 29,* 206–219.

Connor-Smith, J. K., Compas, B. E., Thomsen, A. H., Wadsworth, M. E., & Saltzman, H. (2000). Responses to stress: Measurement of coping and reactivity in children and adolescents. *Journal of Consulting and Clinical Psychology, 68,* 976–992.

Daleiden, E. L., & Vasey, M. W. (1997). An information-processing perspective on childhood anxiety. *Clinical Psychology Review, 17,* 407–429.

Davidson, R. J., Jackson, D. C., & Kalin, N. H. (2000). Emotion, plasticity, context, and regulation: Perspectives from affective neuroscience. *Psychological Bulletin, 126,* 890–909.

Davies, P. T., & Windle, M. (2001). Interparental discord and adolescent adjustment trajectories: The potentiating and protective role of intrapersonal attributes. *Child Development, 72,* 1163–1178.

Dawkins, M. P., Fullilove, C., & Dawkins, M. (1996). Early assessment of problem behavior among young children in high-risk environments. *Family Therapy, 22,* 133–141.

DeBellis, M. D., Keshavan, M. S., Shifflett, H., Iyengar, S., Beers, S. R., Hall, J., & Moritz, G. (2002). Brain structures in pediatric maltreatment-related posttraumatic stress disorder: A sociodemographically matched study. *Biological Psychiatry, 52,* 1066–1078.

DuBois, D., Felner, R., Meares, H., & Krier, M. (1994). Prospective investigation of the effects of socioeconomic disadvantage, life stress, and social support on early adolescent adjustment. *Journal of Abnormal Psychology, 103,* 511–522.

Eisenberg, N., Fabes, R. A., & Guthrie, I. (1997). Coping with stress: The roles of regulation and development. In J. N. Sandler & S. A. Wolchik (Eds.), *Handbook of children's coping with common stressors: Linking theory, research, and intervention.* New York: Plenum.

Field, T. (1995). Infants of depressed mothers. *Infant Behavior and Development, 18*(1), 1–13.

Friedman, R. J., & Chase-Lansdale, P. L. (2002). Chronic adversities. In M. Rutter & E. Taylor (Eds.), *Child and adolescent psychiatry* (4th ed., pp. 261–276). Oxford, UK: Blackwell Science.

Furstenberg, F. F. (2001). Managing to make it. *Journal of Family Issues, 22,* 150–162.

Gallo, L. C., & Matthews, K. A. (2003). Understanding the association between socioeconomic status and physical health: Do negative emotions play a role? *Psychological Bulletin, 129,* 10–51.

Garber, J., Keiley, M. K., & Martin, N. C. (2002). Developmental trajectories of adolescents' depressive symptoms: Predictors of change. *Journal of Consulting and Clinical Psychology, 70,* 79–95.

Garmezy, N. (1983).

Ge, X., Lorenz, F. O., Conger, R. D., Elder, G. H., Jr., & Simons, R. L. (1994). Trajectories of stressful life events and depressive symptoms during adolescence. *Developmental Psychology, 30,* 467–483.

Gerhardt, C. A., Compas, B. E., Connor, J. K., & Achenbach, T. M. (1999). Association of a mixed anxiety-depression syndrome and symptoms of major depression. *Journal of Youth and Adolescence, 28*(3), 305–323.

Gjerde, P. F. (1995). Alternative pathways to chronic depressive symptoms in young adults: Gender differences in developmental trajectories. *Child Development, 66,* 1277–1300.

Goodyer, I. M., & Altham, P. M. E. (1991a). Lifetime exit events and recent social and family adversities in anxious and depressed school-age children and adolescents: I. *Journal of Affective Disorders, 21,* 219–228.

Goodyer, I. M., & Altham, P. M. E. (1991b). Lifetime exit events and recent social and family adversities in anxious and depressed school-age children and adolescents: II. *Journal of Affective Disorders, 21,* 229–238.

Gorman-Smith, D., Tolan, P. H., & Henry, D. (2000). A developmental-ecological model of the relation of family functioning to patterns of delinquency. *Journal of Quantitative Criminology, 16,* 169–198.

Gotlib, I. H., & Krasnoperova, E. (1998). Biased information processing as a vulnerability factor for depression. *Behavior Therapy, 29,* 603–617.

Gotlib, I. H., Lewinsohn, P. M., & Seeley, J. R. (1995). Symptoms versus a diagnosis of depression: Differences in psychosocial functioning. *Journal of Consulting and Clinical Psychology, 65,* 90–100.

Grant, K. E., Compas, B. E., Stuhlmacher, A., Thurm, A. E., & McMahon, S. D. (in press). Stressors and child/adolescent psychopathology: Moving from markers to mechanisms of risk. *Psychological Bulletin.*

Grant, K. E., Compas, B. E., Thurm, A., & McMahon, S. (2003). *Stressors and child/adolescent psychopathology: Measurement issues and prospective effects.* Manuscript submitted for publication.

Gray, J. A. (1991). The neuropsychology of temperament. In J. Strelau & A. Angleitner (Eds.), *Explorations in temperament: International perspectives on theory and measurement* (pp. 105–128). New York: Plenum Press.

Gunnar, M. (1994). Psychoendocrine studies of temperament and stress in early childhood: Expanding current models. In J. E. Bates & T. D. Wachs (Eds.), *Temperament: Individual differences at the interface of biology and behavior* (pp. 25–38). Washington, DC: American Psychological Association.

Gutman, L. M., Sameroff, A. J., & Eccles, J .S. (2002). The academic achievement of African American students during early adolescence: An examination of multiple risk, promotive, and protective factors. *American Journal of Community Psychology, 30,* 367–400.

Hankin, B. L., & Abramson, L. Y. (2001). Development of gender differences in depression: An elaborated cognitive vulnerability-transactional stress theory. *Psychological Bulletin, 127,* 773–796.

Henderson, H. A., Fox, N. A., & Rubin, K. H. (2001). Temperamental contributions to development. In J. T. Ennes (Ed.), *The development of attention: Research and theory* (pp. 47–66). New York: Elsevier.

Hollingshead, A. B. (1975). *Four-factor index of social status.* Unpublished manuscript, Yale University, Department of Sociology, New Haven, CT.

Holmbeck, G. N. (1997). Toward terminology, conceptual, and statistical clarity in the study of mediators and moderators: Examples from the child-clinical and pediatric psychology literatures. *Journal of Consulting and Clinical Psychology, 65,* 599–610.

Jensen, P. S., Watanabe, H. K., Richters, J. E., Roper, M., Hibbs, E. D., Salzberg, A. D., & Liu, S. (1996). Scales, diagnoses, and child psychopathology: II. Comparing the CBCL and DISC against external validators. *Journal of Abnormal Child Psychology, 24,* 151–168.

Kagan, J., & Snidman, N. (1991). Infant predictors of inhibited and uninhibited profiles. *Psychological Science, 2,* 40–44.

Kazdin, A. (1994). Informant variability in the assessment of childhood depression. In W. M. Reynolds & H. E. Johnston (Eds.), *Handbook of depression in children and adolescents* (pp. 249–270). New York: Plenum Press.

Kraemer, H. C., Kazdin, A. E., Offord, D. R., Kessler, R. C., Jensen, P. S., & Kupfer, D. J. (1997). Coming to terms with the terms of risk. *Archives of General Psychiatry, 54,* 337–343.

Krohne, H. W. (1996). Individual differences in coping. In M. Zeidner & N. S. Endler (Eds.), *Handbook of coping: Theory, research, and application* (pp. 381–409). New York: Wiley.

Lazarus, R. S., & Folkman, S. (1984). *Stress, appraisal and coping.* New York: Springer.

Leadbeater, B., & Linares, O. (1992). Depressive symptoms in Black and Puerto Rican adolescent mothers in the first 3 years postpartum. *Development and Psychopathology, 4,* 451–468.

Lengua, L. J., Sadowski, C. A., Friedrich, W. N., & Fisher, J. (2001). Rationally and empirically derived dimensions of childrens' symptomatology: Expert ratings and confirmatory factor analyses of the CBCL. *Journal of Consulting and Clinical Psychology, 69,* 683–698.

Lengua, L., & Sandler, I. (1996). Self-regulation as a moderator of the relation between coping and symptomatology in children of divorce. *Journal of Abnormal Child Psychology, 24,* 681–701.

Luthar, S. S., & Cicchetti, D. (2000). The construct of resilience: Implications for interventions and social policy. *Development and Psychopathology, 12,* 857–885.

Luthar, S. S., Cicchetti, D., & Becker, B. (2000). The construct of resilience: A critcial evaluation and guidelines for future work. *Child Development, 71,* 543–562.

Martinèz, P., & Richters, J. E. (1993). The NIMH Community Violence Project II: Children's distress symptoms associated with violence exposure. *Psychiatry: Interpersonal and Biological Processes, 56,* 22–35.

Masten, A. S. (2001). Ordinary magic: Resilience processes in development. *American Psychologist, 56,* 227–238.

Masten, A. S., & Coatsworth, J. D. (1998). The development of competence in favorable and unfavorable environments: Lessons from research on successful children. *American Psychologist, 53,* 205–220.

Mathews, A., & MacLeod, C. (1994). Cognitive approaches to emotion and emotional disorders. *Annual Review of Psychology, 45,* 25–50.

Matthews, G., & Wells, A. (1996). Attentional processes, dysfunctional coping, and clinical intervention. In M. Zeidner & N. S. Endier (Eds.), *Handbook of coping: Theory, research, applications* (pp. 573–601). New York: Wiley.

McEwen, B. S. (2000). The neurobiology of stress: From serendipity to clinical relevance. *Brain Research, 886,* 172–189.

McLoyd, V. C. (1998). Socioeconomic disadvantage and child development. *American Psychologist, 53,* 185–204.

McMahon, S. D., Grant, K. E., Compas, B. E., Thurm, A. E., & Ey, S. (2003). Stress and psychopathology in children and adolescents: Is there evidence for specificity? *Journal of Child Psychology and Psychiatry, 44,* 1–27.

McQuaid, J. R., Monroe, S. M., Roberts, J. E., Kupfer, D. J., & Frank, E. (2000). A comparison of two life stress assessment approaches: Prospective prediction of treatment outcome in recurrent depression. *Journal of Abnormal Psychology, 109,* 787–791.

Mischel, W. (1997). Was the cognitive revolution just a detour on the road to behaviorism? On the need to reconcile situational control and personal control. In R. J. Wyer (Ed.), *Advances in social cognition: Vol. 10. The automaticity of everyday life* (pp. 181–186). Mahwah, NJ: Erlbaum.

Moffitt, T. E., & Caspi, A. (2001). Childhood predictors differentiate life-course persistent and adolescent-limited antisocial pathways among males and females. *Development and Psychopathology, 13,* 355–375.

National Center for Children in Poverty (2003). *Low-income children in the United States: A brief demographic profile.* New York: Author.

Nelson, C. A., Bloom, F. E., Cameron, J. L., Amaral, D., Dahl, R. E., & Pine, D. (2002). An integrative, multidisciplinary approach to the study of brain-behavior relations in the context of typical and atypical development. *Development and Psychopathology, 14,* 499–520.

Nolen-Hoeksema, S., Girgus, J. S., & Seligman, M. E. P. (1992). Predictors and consequences childhood depressive symptoms: A 5-year longitudinal study. *Journal of Abnormal Psychology, 101,* 405–422.

Pennebaker, J. (1997). *Opening up: The healing power of expressive emotions* (Rev. ed.). New York: Guilford Press.

Perry, B. D., Pollard, R. A., Blakley, T. L., Baker, W. L., & Vigilante, D. (1995). Childhood trauma, the neurobiology of adaptation, and "use-dependent" development of the brain: How "states" become "traits." *Infant Mental Heath Journal, 16,* 271–289.

Posner, M. I., & DiGirolamo, G. J. (2000). Cognitive neuroscience: Origins and promise. *Psychological Bulletin, 126,* 873–889.

Posner, M. I., & Rothbart, M. K. (1994). Attentional regulation: From mechanism to culture. In P. Bertelson, P. Eelen, & G. d'Ydewalle (Eds.), *International perspectives on psychological science: Vol. 1* (pp. 41–55). Hove, England: Erlbaum.

Posner, M. I., & Rothbart, M. K. (1998). Attention, self-regulation and consciousness. *Philosophical Transactions of the Royal Society of London, 353B,* 1915–1927.

Richmond, J. (1993). Health promotion in historical perspective. In S. G. Millstein, A. C. Petersen, & E. O. Nightingale (Eds.), *Promoting the health of adolescents: New directions for the twenty-first century* (pp. v–vii). New York: Oxford University Press.

Rolf, J., & Johnson, J. (1990). Protected or vulnerable: The challenge of AIDS to developmental psychopathology. In J. Rolf, A. S. Masten, D. Cicchetti, K. H. Nuechterlein, & S. Weinstraub (Eds.), *Risk and protective factors in the development of psychopathology* (pp. 384–404). Cambridge, England: Cambridge University Press.

Rothbart, M. K. (1991). Temperament: A developmental framework. In J. Strelau & A. Angleitner (Eds.), *Explorations in temperament: International perspectives on theory and measurement* (pp. 61–74). New York: Plenum Press.

Rothbart, M. K., & Bates, J. E. (1998). Temperament. In W. Damon (Series Ed.) & N. Eisenberg (Vol. Ed.), *Handbook of child psychology: Vol. 3. Social, emotional, and personality development* (5th ed., pp. 105–176). New York: Wiley.

Rothbart, M. K, Posner, M. I., & Hershey, K. L. (1995) Temperament, attention, and developmental psychopathology. In D. Cicchetti & D. Cohen (Eds.), *Developmental psychopathology: Vol. 1. Theory and methods* (pp. 315–340). New York: Wiley.

Rudolph, K. D., Dennig, M. D., & Weisz, J. R. (1995). Determinants and consequences of children's coping in the medical setting: Conceptualization, review, and critique. *Psychological Bulletin, 118,* 328–357.

Rudolph, K. D., & Hammen, C. (2000). Age and gender determinants of stress exposure, generation, and reactions in youngsters: A transactional perspective. *Child Development, 70,* 660–677.

Rudolph, K. D., Hammen, C., Burge, D., Lindberg, N., Herzberg, D., & Daley, S. E. (2000). Toward an interpersonal life-stress model of depression: The developmental context of stress generation. *Development and Psychopathology, 12,* 215–234.

Rutter, M. (1987a). Psychosocial resilience and protective mechanisms. *American journal of orthopsychiatry, 57(3),* 316–331.

Rutter, M. (1987b). Psychosocial resilience and protective mechanisms. In J. Rolf, A. Masten, D. Cichetti, K. Nuechterlein, & S. Weintraub (Eds.), *Risk and protective factors in the development of psychopathology* (pp. 181–214). New York: Cambridge University Press.

Sameroff, Arnold J. (2000). Developmental systems and psychopathology. *Development & Psychopathology,* 12(3), 297–312.

Sandler, I. N., Reynolds, K. D., Kliewer, W., & Ramirez, R. (1992). Specificity of the relation between life events and psychological symptomatology. *Journal of Clinical Child Psychology, 21,* 240–248.

Sandler, I. N., Tein, J., & West, S. G. (1994). Coping, stress, and psychological symptoms of children of divorce: A cross-sectional and longitudinal study. *Child Development, 65,* 1744–1763.

Sapolsky, R. M. (1996). Why stress is bad for your brain. *Science, 273*(5276), 749–756.

Shiffrin, R. M. (1997). Attention, automatism, and consciousness. In J. D. Cohen & J. W. Schooler (Eds.), *Scientific approaches to consciousness* (pp.). Mahwah, NJ: Erlbaum.

Shiffrin, R. M., & Schneider, W. (1977). Controlled and automatic human information processing: II. Perceptual learning, automatic attending, and a general theory. *Psychological Review, 84,* 127–190.

Skinner, E. A. (1995). *Perceived control, motivation, and coping.* Thousand Oaks, CA: Sage.

Skinner, E. A., Edge, K., Altman, J., & Sherwood, H. (2003). Searching for the structure of coping: A review and critique of category systems for classifying ways of coping. *Psychological Bulletin, 129,* 216–269.

Spear, L. P. (2000a). The adolescent brain and age-related behavioral manifestations. *Neuroscience and Biobehavioral Reviews, 24,* 417–463.

Spear, L. P. (2000b). Neurobehavioral changes in adolescence. *Current Directions in Psychological Science, 9,* 111–114.

Steele, R., Forehand, R., & Armistead, L. (1997). The role of family processes and coping strategies in the relationship between parental chronic illness and childhood internalizing problems. *Journal of Abnormal Child Psychology, 25,* 83–94.

Steinberg, L. (2002). Clinical adolescent psychology: What it is, and what it needs to be. *Journal of Consulting and Clinical Psychology, 70,* 124–128.

Steinberg, L., & Avenevoli, S. (2000). The role of context in the development of psychopathology: A conceptual framework and some speculative propositions. *Child Development, 71,* 66–74.

Susman, E. J., Dorn, L. D., Inoff-Germain, G., Nottelmann, E. D., & Chrousos, G. P. (1997). Cortisol reactivity, distress behavior, and behavioral and psychological problems in young adolescents: A longitudinal perspective. *Journal of Research on Adolescence, 7,* 81–105.

Thomsen, A. H., Compas, B. E., Colletti, R. B., Stanger, C., & Boyer, M. (2003). *Individual differences in coping and temperament in children with recurrent abdominal pain.* Manuscript submitted for publication.

Turner, J. E., Jr., & Cole, D. A. (1994). Developmental differences in cognitive diatheses for child depression. *Journal of Abnormal Child Psychology, 22,* 15–32.

Vasey, M. W., El-Hag, N., & Daleiden, E. L. (1996). Anxiety and the processing of emotionally threatening stimuli: Distinctive patterns of selective attention among high- and low-test-anxious children. *Child Development, 67,* 1173–1185.

Wadsworth, M. E., & Compas, B. E. (2002). Coping with family conflict and economic strain: The adolescent perspective. *Journal of Research on Adolescence, 12,* 243–274.

Wadsworth, M. E., Reickman, T., Benson, M. A., & Compas, B. E. (2003). *Coping and responses to stress in Navajo adolescents: Psychometric properties of the responses to stress questionnaire.* Manuscript submitted for publication.

Walker, E. F. (2002). Adolescent neurodevelopment and psychopathology. *Current Directions in Psychological Science, 11,* 24–28.

Walker, L. S., Smith, C. A., Garber, J., & Van Slyke, D. A. (1997). Development and validation of the Pain Response Inventory for Children. *Psychological Assessment, 9,* 392–405.

Weisz, J. R. (1990). Development of content related beliefs, goals, and styles in childhood and adolescence: A clinical perspective. In J. Rodin, C. Schooler, & K. Warner Schaie (Eds.), *Self-directedness: Cause and effect throughout the life course* (pp. 103–145). Hillsdale, NJ: Erlbaum.

Weisz, J. R., McCabe, M. A., & Dennig, M. D. (1994). Primary and secondary control among children undergoing medical procedures: Adjustment as a function of coping style. *Journal of Consulting and Clinical Psychology, 62,* 324–332.

Windle, M., & Davies, P. T. (1999). Depression and heavy alcohol use among adolescents: Concurrent and prospective relations. *Development and Psychopathology, 11,* 823–844.

Wolchik, S. A., West, S. G., Sandler, I. N., Tein, J. Y., Coatsworth, D., Leugua, L., Weiss, L., Anderson, E. R., Greene, S. M., & Griffin, W. A. (2000). An experimental evaluation of theory-based mother and mother-child programs for children of divorce. *Journal of Consulting and Clinical Psychology, 68,* 843–856.

Woodward, S., Lenzenweger, M. F., Kagan, J., Snidman, N. C., & Arcus, D. (2000). Taxonic structure of infant reactivity: Quantitative evidence from a taxometric perspective. *Psychological Science, 11,* 296–301.

Part Two

SOCIAL RELATIONSHIPS AND SOCIAL CONTEXTS IN ADOLESCENCE

Chapter 10

ADOLESCENCE ACROSS PLACE AND TIME

Globalization and the Changing Pathways to Adulthood

Reed Larson and Suzanne Wilson

As we enter the 21st century, it is clear that the life period of adolescence can no longer be seen as just a Western phenomenon. A transitional life stage between childhood and adulthood is now evident in most societies of the world. Schlegel and Barry (1991) argued that some form of adolescence, often brief, existed across nonindustrial societies. The new adolescences now taking hold across societies, however, are distinguished by a common set of historically recent elements associated with globalization that create a longer, more distinct transitional period. These include longer schooling, earlier puberty, later marriage, and, for many youth, urbanization, removal from the full-time labor force, and greater separation from the world of adults (Caldwell, Caldwell, Caldwell, & Pieris, 1998; Larson, 2002). We use the plural *adolescences* very deliberately to emphasize the diversity in the experience of this life period across societies. The pathway to adulthood—these adolescences—take different forms in different social, cultural, and economic settings. In many societies, for example, this period does not involve the task of psychic separation from parents or carry the connotations of emotional turmoil associated with adolescence in the West (Dasen, 2000).

A common feature across settings is societal change. Adolescence in all parts of the world has been in flux. In the Philippines, a pattern has emerged in which adolescent girls are sent by their families to work and send home their earnings (Peterson, 1990; Santa Maria, 2002). Sexual revolutions have occurred in Japan and parts of Latin America (Stevenson & Zusho, 2002; Welti, 2002). In Islamic nations, significant numbers of rural youth who migrate to cities are attracted to a Muslim fundamentalism that embraces distinct gender roles, veiling of young women, and resistance to Western worldviews (V. Hoffman, 1995). This change and flux, in some cases, creates opportunities for young people to shape lives for themselves that were unimagined by their parents. But change also creates uncertainty and risk. Many youth are taking uncharted pathways that put them at risk for exploitation, for sexual victimization, or, simply, for reaching adulthood ill-prepared for life in the 21st century.

For scholars of adolescence, the emergence of new and diverse adolescences repre-

The work on this paper was partly supported by the William T. Grant Foundation.

sents a major challenge. There are currently over 1 billion youth in the second decade of life, and we know very little about the great majority of them. Most scholars of adolescence are in Western nations, and their research focuses almost entirely on youth in their corners of the globe. However, given increased global interaction and interdependency—including the continued immigration of diverse cultural groups into Western nations—it is essential that the field of adolescence awake from its parochialism and pay attention to the multiplicity of adolescences that make up the world community.

(Note that this paper is addressed to an audience of mostly Western students of adolescence. We periodically employ a Western viewpoint as a frame of reference, not because it is more correct or deserves elevated status, but because in attempting to produce good reader-based prose, we feel it is helpful to begin from the framework most familiar to our readers—a framework we often challenge. Both Western and non-Western scholars have an important role to play in the project outlined here.)

This chapter attempts to articulate this challenge. It is a successor to Glen Elder's (1980) chapter in the first edition of *The Handbook of Adolescence,* which articulated how historical contexts shape adolescent experience. Our goal here is to describe ways in which diverse and changing international contexts do the same. Given the enormous range of world cultures and disparate adolescent topics, it is necessary to focus on only a few issues and illustrations. We have selected five topics, related to adolescents' public image, family relationships, employment, schooling, and gender, and we use these to discuss how frameworks and concepts in adolescent scholarship need to be expanded or reconceived to accommodate a diverse and changing world. As a preparatory step, we first examine the macro societal processes that are leading to the creation of these new adolescences.

THE GLOBAL WORLD: PROCESSES SHAPING ADOLESCENTS' EXPERIENCES

Elder (1998) wrote that students of human development "generally fail to apprehend social structure as a *constitutive force* in development" (p. 944, emphasis added). To understand the ongoing changes in adolescences across the world, we need to understand the structural processes (economic, societal, and cultural) driving these changes. We start with two hot-button concepts, globalization and modernization, which each provide implicit grand theories of the structural changes occurring within societies.

What Is Globalization?

Globalization is a trendy word that can mean everything and nothing. It is used in different contexts to refer to cross-national phenomena in the spheres of economics, culture, government, and communications. A commonality across uses of the term is the thesis that interconnections and interdependencies across the globe are increasing. People on opposite sides of the planet—including adolescents—are connected by greater flow of goods, capital, information, images, fads, and problems (Tomlinson, 1999). This shrinking of the globe brings people on opposite sides of the world into closer contact. Globalization includes top-down changes driven by powerful elites and multinational business and organizations. It also includes bottom-up processes in which new communication media allow ordinary people to be agents on a wider sphere, for example, when Andean craftsmen use the Internet to sell their wares in the United States and when youth activists in China, Peru, and South Africa use fax and e-mail to organize protest movements (Youniss et al., 2002).

Interconnection does not mean only relationships of cooperation and trust. Globalization, as of yet, is not making adults and adolescents from different parts of the world into one happy family. The terrorist attacks of September 11, 2001, and the continuing aftermath of geopolitical dynamics illustrate that this interconnection can take the form of conflict, counterreactions, and ongoing divergent interpretations of the same events. Tomlinson (1999) suggested that the experience of globalization is analogous to living in a crowded "global neighborhood," where we do not choose and may not like our neighbors but are obliged to live alongside them. As a result, the life options and trajectories of adolescents are increasingly interconnected with events outside their nations' borders.

Scholars writing about globalization emphasize that it includes processes of both integration and differentiation (S. Hoffman, 1998). Integration includes not only the growing interconnections just mentioned, but more subtle changes involving increased overlap in the knowledge base and frame of reference among people in different cultures (e.g., knowing how to use a telephone or the outcomes of World Cup games). Differentiation is an opposite and possibly equal force. It includes segmentation within or between societies as a result of economic interests, ethnic tensions, or other differences (Hallack, 2000). Similar to Erikson's (1968) process of negative identity, groups sometimes form values and make decisions in counterreaction to those of other groups. For example, Marty and Appleby (1994) described how the outlook of many current fundamentalist movements (most with large contingents of youth) are formed in direct reaction against dominant values and lifestyles.

A critical implication of this is that globalization does not mean Westernization. As a current dominant economic power, certainly the West has influences, including on adolescents, in many parts of the world. Caldwell et al. (1998) credited the portrayals of love in Western cinema with contributing to the undermining of arranged marriages in Africa. *Time Magazine* reported that the powerful influence of computer and communication culture has led hip young Korean men to adopt "the scruffy, geeky dress of Microsoft chairman Bill Gates" (MacIntyer, 2001, p. B10). But evidence indicates that there are numerous ways in which cultures (and adolescents) around the world are not being Westernized. Extensive psychological research indicates that distinct cultural values endure even as societies change (Inglehart & Baker, 2000; Smith & Schwartz, 1997). Thus, although middle-class youth in India sometimes adopt Western clothing and aspects of Western lifestyles (especially when out with friends), beneath this superficial gloss, unique Indian ways of thinking shape their major decisions (Verma & Saraswathi, 2002). It is important to point out that Western youth, too, readily pick up trends from other cultures, such as the current interest in Latin music and Japanese anime films in the United States and the influence of Nigerian-born youth on London adolescents (Caldwell et al., 1998). But these influences are also often a superficial gloss. Analyses of globalization suggest that the world is shaped by numerous centers of influence that interact but also counterreact and remain distinct (S. Hoffman, 1998; Tomlinson, 1999). We can expect that the adolescences of the future will reflect differing amalgams of local, regional, and global elements.

Modernization: The Other Kind of Development

Modernization is an overlapping, older, and more controversial concept used to describe a set of macro structural changes theorized to be occurring across societies. It is controversial because, as with the concept of globalization, it too has often been conflated with Westernization and biased by Western individualistic and liberal assumptions and values. Parallel to theorists of human development such as Piaget, theorists of societal and economic development have postulated that societies go through an invariant sequence of advances and that Western society represents the most advanced stage in this sequence. Critics of this type of thought have pointed out that Japan has become as technologically modern (and postmodern) as any nation while maintaining distinct Eastern cultural values, business practices, and ways of life (Kağitçibaşi, 1997). China and the state of Kerala in India are examples where long life expectancies and high rates of education—cardinal features of modernization—were achieved without market capitalism, another feature typically linked to modernization (Sen, 1999). As with human development, there is no singular inner dynamic of social and economic development that creates convergence of all societies (nor all adolescences) toward an identical mold.

That said, however, many argue that a loose family of demographic, economic, technological, and social changes is developing across all or most societies of the world (Inglehart, 1997). These changes, which most people refer to as modernization (at least in private company), include

- A demographic transition (longer life span followed by reduced birth rates and smaller families)
- Changes in national economies (capital accumulation, shifts from agrarian to manufacturing and service economies)
- Urbanization (accompanied by erosion of primary communities and traditional village systems of education, social control, and intergenerational transmission)
- Spread of technology, improved health care, and new means of communication
- Development of an information society in which knowledge is a fundamental commodity

This family of changes shapes the elements of what we have called the new adolescences (or could, more daringly, be called modern adolescences). These changes increase the value of education, which leads to longer schooling and youths' removal from the labor force, greater separation from the worlds of adults, and later marriage. As a result, young people across many societies now experience a longer and more distinct transitional life stage than they did in the past.

From Grand to Midrange Theory

Attention-grabbing concepts like modernization and globalization, however, get us only so far before they begin obscuring important variations among societies. These general concepts share the flaws of valuable but overly broad psychological constructs like intelligence, resilience, and the ego. As with human development, the development of societies is partly ideographic, particularistic, and modular. To understand the structural forces driving changes (and constancy) in adolescent experience in particular societies, we need to begin to separate out the specific processes that vary from one society to another, some of which do not fit under the umbrella of globalization or modernization. In attempts to do this, Larson (2002) surveyed recent international literature across the disciplines of social science to see what macro structural processes are being discussed in each field that might be relevant to the future of adolescence (summarized in Table 10.1). Three processes merit particular attention.

First, it has been said that demography is destiny, and this certainly applies to the shaping of adolescent experience. The proportion of young people in a population affects their access to the resources most vital to them, particularly education and jobs. Many poor nations continue to have high birth rates, making it difficult to build enough schools to catch up with their growing numbers of youth; worldwide, 1.9 billion new jobs will need to be created over the next 50 years just to sustain current dismal levels of employment (L. Brown, Garder, & Halweil, 1999). These demographic realities significantly narrow life opportunities for adolescents in these countries. In contrast, in many developed nations birth rates are far below the replacement rate of 2.1 per woman, and thus the proportion of youth in these populations is small and shrinking. As a result, adolescents in Europe, Japan, and Russia are likely to experience much greater access to education and richer job opportunities; however, they also face the burden of supporting a large, growing, and politically powerful elderly population (Fussell, 2002).

A second, interrelated process is that economic stratification is increasing between and within nations. The difference in per capita income between the wealthiest and poorest countries grew by a factor of five between 1870 and 1990, while stratification within many nations also grew (Fussell & Greene, 2002; Guillèn, 2001). The rich have grown richer, and the poor have grown poorer (or failed to advance from abject poverty). For the fortunate youth, increased wealth provides them access to new opportunities for education and leisure. For adolescents among the world's large rural peasant and urban poor populations, limited access to schooling, health care, and employment severely restricts their life pathways.

A third crucial set of processes is that of intergenerational transmission and cultural continuity. Culture might best be understood as the frame of reference that people begin acquiring in infancy and that molds how they think about themselves and others. It is embedded in the language one learns, one's intimate relationships and daily activities, the religion one is taught, and other existential fundamentals, such as when, where, and how one experiences different emotions. Each culture contains its own indigenous psychology, which includes developmental tasks and precepts, as well as postulates of what is "true, beautiful, good, and normal" (Shweder et al., 1998, p. 867). Far from losing

Table 10.1 Summary of Macrostructural Processes Across Disciplinary Areas That Are Influencing Adolescences

Discipline	Major Processes and Changes	Influence on Adolescence
Demography	Demographic transition (longer life span, reduced birth rates)	Reduction in numbers of youth in the population relative to the number of elderly
Geography	Rural to urban migration	Adolescents live in dense urban areas, with less connection to community and more exposure to crime, crowding, and other urban ills
	Migration of family members for employment	Families split up
	Confluence of diverse peoples due to internal and cross-national migration	Adolescents challenged to get along with peers having diverse cultures; need to develop skills for code shifting
Economics	Globalization of markets	New opportunities for families and adolescents; undermining of traditional forms of subsistence
	Widening economic disparities within nations	Wider differences between families in provision of resources and opportunities for young people
	Widening economic disparities between nations	Wider differences in capability of nations to provide education, health care, and other services to adolescents
Anthropology	Intergenerational transmission of cultures, values, and beliefs	Persistence in cultural values and worldviews, including indigenous psychologies of development
	Globalization of culture	Cross-cultural exchange of images and scripts
Political Science	Democratization	Greater voice of adolescents and their parents
	Cross-national influences	More pressure across nations to adhere to standards of international behavior
	Continuing conflicts between groups	Adolescent males recruited as insurgents and soldiers
	Growth of nongovernmental organizations	New sources of resources and opportunities for civic engagement
	Fundamentalist and reactionary movements	Adolescents adapt or form values that are particularistic or deliberately in opposition to those of others

(continued)

Table 10.1 *(Continued)*

Discipline	Major Processes and Changes	Influence on Adolescence
Sociology	Information society	Longer schooling
	Changing social institutions: rationalization, choice, reduction in codification	Families take more varied, voluntary forms; adolescents need skills to function in more diverse and ad hoc settings
	Changing roles of women	More opportunities for girls and young women; greater requirements for independence
Technology and Society	Spread of mass media (radio, TV, & print media)	Exposure to diverse lifestyles, youth culture
	Spread of information and communication technology	Youth gain access to information and communicate and exercise agency across boundaries of age, distance, gender, etc.
	Biotechnology	New options to address asolescents' physical and psychological limits

Source. Based on Larson (2002).

influence with modernization, these distinct cultural frames of reference continue to guide adolescents even as new ideas and images are introduced (B. B. Brown, Larson, & Saraswathi, 2002). Thus, in Niger and other African nations, adolescents come of age in a culture where "fat is beautiful," and young women use steroids or eat cattle feed that is laced with growth hormones in pursuit of the ideal corpulent body type (Onishi, 2001). We live in an era, too, when nationalism and growing value given to cultural identity lead cultural groups deliberately to reassert and adapt cultural systems and values in the face of change (Hechter & Okamoto, 2001; Shweder et al., 1998). In sum, the ways in which adolescents' worldviews are embedded within inherited cultural frameworks should not be underestimated.

Understanding adolescence in a given society, then, is partly a matter of understanding the distinct constellation of demographic, economic, cultural, technological, religious, and other structural factors that are operative in shaping the pathways to adulthood in that society. We have, however, left out an important additional contributor and level of analysis.

Adolescents as Coagents in Shaping Their Experience

Interwoven with these macrostructural processes is the important role that adolescents themselves play. Social science since the 1960s has increasingly acknowledged ways in which the path between macro processes and individuals is a two-way street (Elder & O'Rand, 1995). Adolescents are not passive recipients of change; they respond to and shape it, often in collaboration with their families, peers, and others (Brandstädter & Lerner, 1999; Elder, 1998).

The first point to be made here is that the adolescents play an active role in shaping their lives and, in turn, in shaping society. Adolescents are agents of their own development. They actively select their environments, friends, schools, and romantic partners (Elder & O'Rand, 1995; Lerner & Walls, 1999; Scarr & McCartney, 1983). They create meanings, and they are often planful: They set long-term goals and strive for them (Shanahan & Elder, 2002). By their choices, meaning making, and actions, adolescents in turn shape societal structures and the future pathways of adolescence. Their collective decisions to use contraception or pursue further schooling affect the demographic and economic macroprocesses we just discussed. In some cases, adolescents change a society by deliberately acting together, for example, when youth-led movements have a role in overthrowing governments (Youniss & Ruth, 2002) or their purchasing decisions alter the economy. As Mannheim (1952) argued, each new generation of youth represents an instrument of social change.

It is important to understand, though, that adolescents do not act alone: Agency is distributed. In a collectivist culture this agency and planfulness are often exercised by parents and family elders who make decisions with or on behalf of adolescents (Verma & Saraswathi, 1992). Even in the most individualistic culture, adolescents' choices are influenced by parents, teachers, employers, and friends; and local institutions such as schools and religious organizations make decisions, allocate resources, and set policies that shape the paths available to youth. Of course, these significant others and these local institutions are also being changed by globalization, which affects how they influence adolescents. For example, in most nations mothers' employment outside the home is increasing, family sizes are shrinking, and rates of marital dissolution are rising, all of which influence how parents relate to and guide adolescents (Larson, Wilson, Brown, Furstenberg, & Verma, 2002).

A final point is that the agency of adolescents, their parents, and those around them is constrained by societal circumstances: They experience bounded agency (Shanahan, 2000). Economic conditions, political events, and other historic macrostructural factors may limit individuals' degrees of freedom—or they may create demand conditions or normative imperatives that dictate what choices they make, such as when a war creates an imperative that young men become soldiers (Elder, 1998). Adolescents in poor families generally have fewer alternative pathways because of their limited resources and social capital (Elder, 1998); this is especially true for poor youth in developing countries, where government and social agencies are also poor in resources. Cultural values may also narrow the choices that are considered viable: Societies differ considerably in their allowance for individual deviation from societal norms (Triandis & Suh, 2002) and in the latitude they provide for young people to switch life paths (Hamilton, 1994).

Divergent Pathways to Adulthood

It would be nice if the world were a simpler place. But the interplay of individual agency and macrostructural processes that shapes adolescent experience across societies is complex and idiosyncratic. Multiple layers of systems enter in and shape the contexts in which youth live. These include top-down processes of global integration, differentiation, and modernization, as well as processes of cultural transmission and stability. They also include the bottom-up role that adolescents, their families, and communities play as bounded agents. To understand what is driving changes in adolescents' experience within a given society, one needs to look at the unique interaction of these multiple processes in that society.

How are these factors shaping the new adolescences? How do our paradigms for understanding adolescence need to be expanded or reconfigured for adolescents' experiences across diverse societies? To get a handle on these questions, we now shift to examining specific domains of youth experience. We have chosen issues from within core topic areas of adolescent scholarship, including family relationships, employment, education, and gender, to serve as illustrations. We start by examining how the public's concepts of this age period vary across societies.

SHIFTING CULTURAL REPRESENTATIONS OF ADOLESCENTS AND THE ADOLESCENT AGE PERIOD

Young people's experiences in a society are shaped in part by how that society thinks about them, and these ways of thinking are changing. Cultural representations of the period between childhood and adulthood—how it is named, conceptualized, and rendered in public images—influence the resources and pathways made available to adolescents. Girls among the Gusii of Kenya, for example, are inducted into adulthood by the ordeal of circumcision into the stage of *omoiseke,* a term that means "marriageable girl," namely, someone whose parents await an offer of bride price (Levine, 1980). Male youth among the Sambia of New Guinea are defined as "initiates" and taught that ingestion of semen following fellatio preformed on older men helps prepare them for manhood (Herdt, 1982). Across societies, adolescents are increasingly identified as students, a label that links them to the age-segregated institution of schooling and prioritizes their role as learners of academic knowledge (B. B. Brown & Larson, 2002). Across cultures, adolescence is represented as a time of preparation (Schlegel, 1995), but beyond this, wide variability exists.

Variability occurs not only between but also within cultures. Old and new representations (e.g., initiate and student) may coexist and contend with each other. Aubrun and Grady (2000) found that American adults often toggle between contrasting positive and negative images of youth. At one moment the adults they studied would adopt an empathetic frame that drew on their own experiences during adolescence and portrayed youth sympathetically as struggling, learning, and growing toward a positive adulthood. At other moments, however, they would switch to a negative frame that viewed youth as self-centered, disrespectful, and having lower morals than did their generation. A troubling finding is that American adults toggle to this negative view even when presented with evidence that it is an inaccurate portrayal of the majority of youth (Gilliam & Bales, 2001). Historically, adults' representations of adolescents appear to be more positive when the country needs young people's labor or military participation and more negative when it does not (Enright, Levy, Harris, & Lapsley, 1987).

Similar competing positive and negative images occur in other cultures. In Arabic, the terms *fata* for males and *fatat* for females signify youths in the midst of growth and development. Yet the closest term to adolescence is *murahaqa,* which refers to puberty and invokes an image of this age period as fraught with sexual temptations and disobedience (Booth, 2002). Schlegel and Barry (1991) concluded from an analysis of 175 cultures that virtually all contained positive views of youth, and some but not all also had ambivalent or negative views. Thus the presence of competing representations of adolescents—and the potential for toggling between different frames—appears to be common across many societies.

What is particularly relevant for scholars of adolescence is that in a number of societies, new negative images of youth have been entering the public mind via the new mass media. Indian society has traditionally held very favorable attitudes toward the young (Shukla, 1994), but the image of the delinquent-male "superpredator" has recently been introduced by the media (Thapa, Raval, & Chakravarty, 1999). New, more negative public images are also reported in Africa (Dasen, 2000); and in Brazil the new term *menore* (minor), most often used in reference to poor, minority youth, invokes connotations of delinquency and violence (Pereira & Heringer, 1994).

Societies' conception of the beginning and ending points of adolescence are also changing. In some parts of Africa the age of initiation has been deliberately lowered with the goal of cementing bonds between youth and the local community before youth are lured away by the city (Levine, 1980). In many parts of the world schooling and other factors are delaying transitions that mark the end of adolescence (e.g., school leaving, full-time employment, and marriage; B. B. Brown & Larson, 2002; Caldwell et al., 1998). Arnett (2000) observed that a distinct postteenage but preadult period, which he calls emerging adulthood, is appearing across societies. In Japan a new pattern of women in their 20s continuing to live at home has led to their being labeled "parasite singles," reflecting the society's ambivalence toward a group that has traditionally been expected to sacrifice themselves in care of young children (Orenstein, 2001).

Underneath these shifting representations of adolescence is the negotiation of new realities with traditional cultural foundations. On the one hand, the globalization of media presents the public in different parts of the world with a larger palette of new images to draw upon: adolescents drinking Coke and enjoying themselves, young people in love, and youth as criminals—or suicide bombers. On the other hand, Islamic, Christian, Hindu, Buddhist, and other traditions have systems of values that shape how the young are viewed within specific cultural milieus. Among Hindus, for example, the ancient Dharmashastras, which prescribe a code of conduct for each stage of development, continue to have a strong influence on young people's family behavior (Verma & Saraswathi, 2002). The interplay of old and new images of adolescents results in distinct evolving conceptions of youth in different cultural contexts. For instance, the media image of the American teenager—blue-jean clad, independent, and willful—is viewed across much of the world; and it is both imitated and, in some contexts, invoked as a depiction of what a society does *not* want its youth to become (V. Hoffman, 1995; Salamon, 1995).

Adolescents, of course, are anything but passive in this arbitration of representations of their age period. Maori youth in New Zealand have drawn on the rap music of African Americans to symbolize their separation from mainstream society (Tupuola, 2000). European American youth have drawn on cultural meanings from other cultural groups (African American, Jamaican, Latino) as part of the symbolic negotiation of their own identities. A common pattern is that youth draw discriminately from local and international sources. Arabic girls draw on the images of romance from Indian cinema (S. S. Davis & Davis, 1995). Raï youth music in Algeria and Afro pop in sub-Saharan Africa fuse local folk songs with rhythms, sounds, and themes drawn from Western rock music and other sources.

The central point is that public conceptions of adolescents in many societies are in a critical period of revision. They are, in a sense, up for grabs. The lengthening of adolescence and the new roles associated with it create an opening, in which new images can catch the attention of a national public and compete with the old. These new images are important because they influence the resources and options that adults make available to young people. The increased prevalence of negative images of delinquents within both American and Brazilian society, for example, has contributed to the adoption of harsher, more punitive approaches to juvenile justice (Cullen & Wright, 2002; Diversi, Moraes, & Morelli, 1999). Scholars of adolescence need to be aware of this interplay of old and new images within whatever society they are examining, as well as of how this interplay shapes adolescent pathways. We also need to study the societal processes that shape these representations: Under what conditions are adults most receptive to negative images of adolescents? How might the media or other intervention tools be used to influence the public's images so that they are more accurate and understanding of adolescents' needs (Gilliam & Bales, 2001)?

We turn now to the cultural construction of adolescence within the domain of the family.

ADOLESCENTS' FAMILY RELATIONSHIPS: ALTERNATIVES TO THE DEVELOPMENTAL TASK OF AUTONOMY

To understand adolescents' family experience across societies, it is essential that we look beyond Western conceptions of these relationships. In Western developmental psychology (which is often a frame of reference even for non-Western developmentalists; Saraswathi, 1999b), it is understood that individuation from family is a central task of adolescence (Freud, 1946; Havighurst, 1953). Recent writings have stressed that this process of working toward emotional self-sufficiency does not mean severing connections to family; the task of autonomy is best achieved when there are continuing positive relationships with parents (Grotevant & Cooper, 1986; Hauser, 1991). Nonetheless, evidence from Western samples confirms that a process of behavioral and emotional distancing occurs (Larson, Richards, Moneta, Holmbeck, & Duckett, 1996; Steinberg & Silverberg, 1986); and while there is much discussion about the costs of this distancing and accompanying conflict on the well-being of both parents and adolescents (Steinberg, 2001), the process of emotional separation is generally viewed as inevitable and ultimately beneficial for adolescents.

The Developmental Tasks in Indian Families

The family relationships of adolescents in India illustrate how different expectations, behaviors, and developmental scenarios can be in another society. To illustrate this, we focus here on middle-class, urban adolescents, a group whose material lives are not too dissimilar from middle-class Western adolescents. In an experience sampling study, we found that Indian 8th graders spent 39% of their waking hours with family members, much more than the 23% found for a comparable study of American 8th graders. The Indian adolescents also spent twice as much time talking with their families (Larson, Verma, & Dworkin, in press). Time-budget data from Indian college students suggest that this large quantity of family time does not diminish markedly in late adolescence (Verma, 1995; Verma & Saraswathi, 1992). What is most striking is that these Indian adolescents reported being significantly happier than did the American 8th graders during time with their families (and less happy during time with friends); the Indians reported far fewer occasions of negative emotions in the family context. Furthermore, half of these Indian adolescents reported preferring to spend time with their families, and only 29% preferred to spend time with their peers (Larson et al., in press). Achieving behavioral or emotional separation from family did not appear to be a priority for Indian 8th graders. Kakar (1978) reported that strong emotional interdependency with family continues into adulthood, particularly with mothers.

Anthropological research explains this developmental pattern, showing that Indian culture places ties to the family, including extended family, at the center of people's lives across the life span (Seymour, 1999; Sinha, 1994). Respect, deference, and dependence on older family members is taught to children from an early age (Bharat, 1997); independence is not valued in Indian families and is equated with disobedience (Ramanujam, 1978). In the Indian value system it is a virtue to subordinate one's own individual needs to the needs of the kinship group (Saraswathi, 1999a). This primacy given to family ties is not unique to India but has also been reported among adolescents in Indonesia (French, Rianasari, Pidada, Nelwan, & Buhrmester, 2001), Bangladesh (Stewart, Bond, Abdullah, & Ma, 2000), Morocco (S. S. Davis & Davis, 1989), and Argentina (Facio & Batistuta, 1998). In many collectivist societies, children are given major responsibilities starting at an early age (Gauvain, 1999), but this is a distinct dimension from emotional independence.

Rather than striving for autonomy, Indian adolescents appear to face a different central family developmental task. Based on three decades of anthropological research, Seymour (1999) concluded that the self in Indian society is defined not through differentiation from others but through interdependence with them. One's worth as a person, she concluded, is defined through the development of a "we-self." The psychic task of Indian adolescents is not to become separate but to reduce separation—to work on strengthening emotional bonds and overcoming impulses that create differentiation. A similar lifelong developmental task of breaking down egotistical impulses and harmonizing oneself with the family and community has been described in Confucian cultures (Greenfield, 1994; Wei-Ming, 1976). Greenfield (1994) suggested that this is by no means easy. It goes against fundamental human dispositions that prioritize personal needs. Clearly more research is needed, but it is possible that we will find that the family developmental task of adolescents in cultures that value interdependence is harder and more challenging than is the task of youth in the West.

Cultural Change

Some of our Western students and colleagues have responded to this different Indian family script by seeing it as interesting, but quaint and of limited importance, because everyone knows that in 50 years (or perhaps sooner) adolescence in other countries will be just like it is in the West. This possibility of convergence toward a Western, so-called modern script is also voiced by some Indian scholars who worry that urbanization, mobility, and mothers' employment are weakening family cohesion (Bharat, 1997; Biswas, 1992). Research does suggest several ways in which Indian and Western family relationships have been converging, at least in the middle class. Smaller families and affluence have permitted Indian middle-class parents to become less authoritarian and more responsive to children (Kashyap, 1993; Saraswathi & Ganapathy, 2002). These urban middle-class parents, as compared to rural and lower–socioeconomic status (SES) parents, do not see children as an economic asset but rather value children as a source of love and personal fulfillment (Kapadia & Shah, 1998; Srivastava, 1997).

This shift to more responsive parenting, however, has not altered the centrality that middle-class Indians give to the family or the lifelong interdependency in families. Parents still often choose careers and, in the great majority of cases, spouses for their children (Ramu, 1988; Uplaonkar, 1995). In fact, two thirds of youth in an Indian middle-class sample reported that they preferred having their parents arrange their marriages (Verma & Saraswathi, 2002). Rather than succumbing to a Western mold of modernization, Indian society has selectively integrated facets of modernization into its value system. Thus, although the number of joint extended family households has fallen with urbanization, many have found that it provides a useful adaptation to urban life: Live-in grandparents and adult siblings provide child care and additional sources of emotional support to hurried urban parents and their adolescents (Sharma & Srivastava, 1991). Families increasingly use the media, including the Internet, to identify potential spouses for arranged marriages (Saraswathi, 1999a). In our research with Indian 8th graders, we found virtually no correlation between indicators of family modernization (e.g., women's employment, parents' education, nuclear household) and indicators of family cohesion (Larson et al., in press). The large volume of time that Indian adolescents spend with their families and the positive emotional quality of these relationships may well be a developmental asset that helps young people adjust to modern, urban life.

In sum, the Indian middle-class family is changing, but it would be a serious mistake to think it is becoming Western—that it is only a matter of time before adolescents in this or other collectivist societies will start prioritizing individual needs and begin to break away from their families. Research in different nations has repeatedly shown that the set of economic and societal changes called modernization does not necessarily lead to adoption of individualistic values (Smith & Schwartz, 1997). Middle-class families in these societies are found to become more materially independent—they make functional shifts in orientation to adapt to urban life—but emotional interdependence and mutual responsibility remain (Kağitçibaşi, 1997; Mistry & Saraswathi, 2002). We think it likely that in 50 years Indian adolescents will still be working on the task of strengthening emotional bonds with their parents. In fact, research on immigrant Indian families in the West—who have been highly exposed to the Western model—suggests that their adolescents also work hard at maintaining family cohesion (Gupta, 1999).

As with other sections in this chapter, this one provides only a sketch and unavoidably overlooks many important issues that have yet to be studied in depth. Western research on adolescent family relationships teaches us that as we look closer, these relationships become more complex and multifaceted than was originally thought (Silverberg &

Gondoli, 1996; Steinberg, 2001). Surely the same will be true of research on adolescent relations across diverse non-Western nations.

YOUNG ADOLESCENTS IN THE LABOR FORCE

Broadening the lens of research on adolescent work to include the developing world brings into focus the issues of child labor. One reaction to this topic may be that there is nothing to research: The employment of youth under 15 years of age should be banned. However, this simple sentiment can be counterproductive, as illustrated by the impact of the Harkin Bill (put before the U.S. Congress in the early 1990s), which was intended to combat child labor by prohibiting importation of any goods that used underage workers. In response to just the threat of this bill passing, the garment industry in Bangladesh dismissed 50,000 to 70,000 young workers, most of them young adolescent girls. Although some of these youth entered a schooling program, the great majority found new employment in the domestic, informal, and street economies—working as maids, stone crushers, welders, street hawkers, and prostitutes—where work conditions and human rights violations are much worse and less easily monitored than in the garment industry (Rahman, Khanam, & Absar, 1999). This illustrates how deeply youth employment is entrenched and why it cannot be readily eliminated.

Consider, too, that parents in parts of Africa, India, and Bangladesh see youths' early introduction to an occupation and to making economic contributions to the family as crucial to their socialization (Nieuwenhuys, 1996). Verma (1999) pointed out that young people in India have worked throughout recorded history, laboring with parents in the fields or as apprenticed artisans; child labor is part of the cultural heritage. But she also warned that the conditions of young adolescents' employment are changing. Urbanization, globalization, and modernization have altered the types of employment available to youth, and often move work further from the family hearth. There are important questions, then, to be asked. Some are familiar to research on adolescent employment in the West, such as the influence of employment on schoolwork and the effects of different numbers of work hours. But there are also less familiar issues, including more severe effects on physical health, the conditions of employment in the informal sector, and the differing family dynamics that may result when young adolescents are major breadwinners in the family. We first describe who works and why and then turn to these important questions.

Who Works and Why

We focus on employment among young adolescents because although employment sometimes starts earlier in childhood, there is a large increase in employment rates for this age period. For the world as a whole, the United Nations' International Labour Office (ILO, 2002) estimated that 23% of all 10- to 14-year-olds are economically active—a total of 138 million youth. These rates are estimated at 35% in sub-Saharan Africa, 27% in Asia and the Pacific, 22% in Latin America, and 20% in the Middle East and North Africa. (Although rates are much lower in Europe and the United States, employment of young adolescents occurs there as well. In an average week, almost 70,000 14- and 15-year-olds are estimated to work illegally in the United States; Kruse & Mahony, 2000.) Approximately three fourths of these youth work over 14 hours a week, and half work under conditions that the ILO considers to be hazardous. Over half of these employed youth do not attend school.

The types of employment these young adolescents hold are extremely diverse. They range from apprenticeships and working in a family craft, farm, or business to factory labor, live-in domestic service, and street activities. Much of this work occurs in the informal sector (ILO, 1996) and is not counted in national unemployment statistics or accounts of gross national or gross domestic product. Indeed employment of young adolescents in most nations is illegal, which by default makes it work considered to be part of the informal market. Some youth are entrepreneurial, working as venders or scavengers. Others work in unofficial relationships with family members, a local merchant, a factory foreman, or someone they may be indentured to in another village or city. In some cases these informal arrangements are quite complex, involving linkages between employers, community power brokers, and parents; in addition, youth may simply assist parents at their jobs. Though informal, the conditions of employment can be binding. The ILO (2002) estimated that 5.7 million children and young adolescents are in bonded and forced labor.

There are both push and pull factors that promote young adolescents' work. The most cited push factor is family need (Bachman, 2000). Conditions of extreme poverty often leave no alternative but for young adolescents to work. A survey in Bangladesh found that one third of the surveyed child and adolescent workers contributed between 21% and 30% of the family's total income, another quarter earned between 31% and 50%, and another 7% of the child and adolescent workers earned between 50% and 80% of the family's total income (Rahman et al., 1999). It is important to realize, as we mentioned earlier, that in collectivist societies it is often parents, not adolescents, who make the decisions in young people's lives. Mensch, Bruce, and Greene (1998) stressed that in Southeast Asia it is typically the parents who decide to sell their daughters into prostitution. In addition to poverty, inferior schools and degrading experiences in schools are a push factor in young adolescents' employment. Meyers and Boyden (1998, p. 18) argued these are often "as or more significant than family poverty." A study of working children in Africa, Asia, and Latin America found that children and young adolescents cited abusive treatment as a major reason for preferring work over school (Woodhead, 1999).

Other factors also pull youth into employment. In many settings, work is one of the most critical domains in which adolescents, especially poor youth, integrate themselves into their families and communities; they gain status and respect by becoming family breadwinners (Meyers & Boyden, 1998; Nieuwenhuys, 1996). We discussed in the last section how adolescents in collectivist societies often face the developmental task of strengthening their bonds to their families. By providing economic assistance to the household, young adolescents fulfill filial duties and prove that they belong. Another pull factor is the jobs themselves. Some of the new jobs being created by more liberal international trade policies are particularly attractive. Compared to jobs in agriculture, those in the export industry can provide opportunities to learn a skill, ensure steady and higher income, and offer better working conditions (Rahman et al., 1999; Working Child, 2002).

Developmental Costs and Benefits

This diversity of types and conditions of employment presents a difficult challenge to researchers attempting to evaluate their effects on young people. Research to date shows that employment of young adolescents can have both positive and negative effects, not all of which can be isolated from each other. Most of the existing empirical evidence regarding the impact of work on children and adolescents in the developing world has focused on its physical effects. For example, studies of young workers in India have shown that working in the garment industry or in glass and metal factories can permanently damage adolescents' lungs from breathing toxic fumes and steam (Sundaram, 1995). Studies of young female workers in the Dominican Republic have shown that they suffer from kidney and bladder infections because they are prohibited from using the bathroom for long periods of time (Dunn, 1991). These effects, however, vary across types of employment. Children in some export sectors have better diets and health and are less prone to accidents than are those in other industries largely because of the nature of the working environment (Rahman et al., 1999). Thus far, there is simply not enough reliable data to support the conclusion either that children who work are more likely to be sick or malnourished or that work gives young adolescents access to food and health resources and therefore supports their physical development and well-being (Meyers & Boyden, 1998).

When we shift to examining the psychosocial effects of young adolescent employment, the picture is no less complex; much more research and conceptual work need to be done. Consider, for example, the case of a 13-year-old boy in Cairo, described by Farrag (1995), who had been working in a weaving shop for two years:

> Salem likes his work, and his relationship with his employer encourages him to perform better. He is proud and satisfied with his contribution to the family income. He sees himself as an indispensable part of the family. . . . He is quite sure that one day he'll have a family of his own, and that any father would be proud to give him his daughter in marriage. (p. 243)

Salem is developing skills and strengthening his bond to his family and appears to have a healthy mentoring relationship with his employer. When employed young adolescents are interviewed, some describe their work as a means to develop responsibility, gain self-esteem, and achieve economic autonomy (Woodhead, 1999). In the case of adolescent girls, Mensch et al. (1998) argued that employment can play a vital role in giving young women pride, a sense of agency, and the chance to develop an identity apart from that of daughter and wife. Nonetheless, many youth in the developing world are employed in jobs that are highly repetitive, involve little skill development, and have employers who see them only as a source of cheap docile labor (Rodgers & Standing, 1981). Research is needed that differentiates the effects of the various types and conditions of employment.

A central research issue concerns the pathways that different types of youth employment provide to adult work. Worldwide, studies show that heavy work schedules lower adolescents' school performance and may contribute to school dropout (Meyers & Boyden, 1998; Steinberg & Cauffman, 1995). Work in certain economic activities (e.g., in an engineering or carpenter shop), however, is considered by adolescents and their families to be a valuable opportunity for learning employable skills (Rahman et al., 1999);

to them it can be a preferred alternative to secondary education. Reasonably well-off children in Surat, India, quit school to work in the diamond industry because the entire family believes that the diamond-polishing industry offers long-term prospects for employment at an acceptable wage (Bachman, 2000). Only when investments in education promise greater future returns may families be willing to keep their adolescents in school. On the other hand, youth who drop out of school to work as weavers, wagon makers, potters, or in numerous other traditional crafts may face a future in which their expertise becomes antiquated, leaving them qualified only to work as pedicab drivers or factory laborers.

Under current conditions, the question of whether employment is categorically good or bad for young adolescents is not the right question. The key issue is not whether youth work, but the nature of their work, its physical and developmental impact, and how it relates to other aspects of their lives, especially their family relationships and long-term economic prospects. Mensch et al. (1998, p. 39) argued that "too little attention has been given to the question, 'compared to what?'" Research on adolescent employment needs to make comparisons—not only between young adolescents who work and those who do not, but among those who work in different sectors of the economy and under different conditions. We can expect the costs and benefits of adolescent employment to be moderated by the factors leading adolescents to work, the social and physical conditions of their employment, the skill set they are acquiring, and how likely this skill set is to match the jobs available as economies continue to change.

Adroit policy research is also critical. Adolescent work is embedded in a complex of family needs, cultural assumptions, and community relationships. Culturally sensitive interventions need to be tested that address these multiple layers and involve coordination among governments, nongovernmental organizations, social workers, community leaders, and unions (Rahman et al., 1999; Saraswathi & Larson, 2002). Clearly, efforts should be made to eliminate forms of adolescent employment that are physically harmful and expose youth to unacceptable risks. But how to achieve this is a difficult empirical question. The goal generally needs to be to bring child and adolescent labor under both formal and informal controls. Creative efforts are also needed to find ways for adolescents to work while allowing them to stay in school. It is also vital to determine how schools can provide education that broaden adolescents' opportunities to secure a job in the future.

CHANGING PSYCHOLOGIES OF EDUCATION: INTRINSIC MOTIVATION AND THE EXAMINATION HELL

An imperative that increasingly applies to both poor and middle-class adolescents across the world is that education matters. It matters for adult employment: The global shift to an information economy requires employees (including those in service and working-class jobs) to have capacities to read, write, do math, manipulate symbols, and use computers. Young people who have not obtained these skills face increasing rates of unemployment and falling or stagnant wages, while salaries for youth with college and advanced degrees are rising (Castells, 1996). Education also matters for other domains. The basic demands of adult daily life—obtaining safe food, health care, and shelter for one's family—increasingly require literacy and numeracy to navigate complex knowledge worlds and institutional systems. Greater contact among people from diverse ethnic and religious groups has made it essential that youth obtain multicultural knowledge and communication skills (Larson et al., 2002; Parker, Ninomiya, & Cogan, 1999).

These changes are putting a premium on a psychology of education that can successfully motivate youth through 12, 16, or more years of schooling. This is by no means an easy task, and nations differ in their results. Even in the most educationally successful nations, secondary schools struggle with students' boredom, underachievement, and other factors that lead them to drop out. By *psychology of education* we refer to the indigenous system of beliefs, attitudes, incentives, and supports that mobilize youth to climb this educational ladder. To help youth prepare for the adulthood of the 21st century, it is critical that we better understand the diverse psychologies that propel adolescents' school achievement.

The Indigenous Psychology of American Education

The psychology of education that is familiar to most scholars of adolescence is that of the West, particularly the United States. This model of learning is built around the ideal of a self-motivated individual learner who is nurtured and supported by a student-centered teacher. Popular writings on education celebrate "love of learning" as the Holy Grail of education (e.g., Fried, 2001), and the mission statements of many American schools emphasize giving each student the chance to fulfill her or his potential. Much of the scholarly literature on school motivation—stretching from John Dewey to the present—focuses on intrinsic motivation, autonomy, and various hyphenated "self-constructs" (self-efficacy, self-worth) as essential to effective education (Wigfield & Eccles, 2002). A basic belief is that self-motivated learning is most satisfying to the learner and most effective overall (Markus, Kitayama, & Heiman, 1996). Recently a Vygotskian, collaborative model of distributed learning has entered American educational discourse, particularly for elementary education, but the assumption that students are willing and self-motivated learners remains dominant.

This psychology of education, however, fails for many students. A major gap exists between this motivational ideal and the reality experienced by many American adolescents. Research shows that educational motivation declines for many students as they enter the secondary school years (Eccles, Wigfield, Harold, & Blumenfield, 1993). When signaled at random times during schoolwork, adolescents report high rates of boredom and wanting to be doing something else (Larson, Ham, & Raffaelli, 1989; Larson & Richards, 1991). Far from being intrinsically motivated, large numbers of secondary students, including high achievers, actively resist schooling in both overt and covert ways (Giroux, 1983; MacLeod, 1995). Fifteen percent of high school students drop out of school (Alexander, Entwisle, & Kabbani, 2001), and many more drop out psychologically (Covington & Dray, 2002).

Defenders of this psychology of education argue that American schools have fallen short in providing the right conditions (e.g., Csikszentmihalyi & Larson, 1984). Nonetheless, the reality is that a psychology of intrinsic motivated learning is not working for many students. In tacit admission of defeat, many American politicians are currently promoting mandatory achievement testing—a means to induce achievement based on external rather than internal consequences—as a way to improve the performance of schools and students. But research to date is unclear whether such tests can be successful in spurring a greater number of students to high performance and raises questions as to possible negative consequences, such as stress and anxiety (National Research Council, 1999). Clearly, the United States has a lot to learn to create a psychology of education that will effectively motivate students to acquire what they need for adulthood in the 21st century.

Psychologies of Education in East Asia

The nations of East Asia provide a markedly different indigenous psychology and culture of learning. Education in China, Japan, and other East Asian nations reflects a strong influence of Confucianism, in which education is seen as a central moral life enterprise (Serpell & Hatano, 1997; Wei-Ming, 1976). Interviewed about their conception of learning, a sample of Chinese adults reported that learning requires personal humility, endurance of hardship, and constant and single-minded devotion; they also reported seeing education as the primary pathway to the ideal of moral self-perfection (Li, 2001). Other research in China and Japan corroborates these themes of selfless devotion of intense effort to education (Chinese Cultural Connection, 1987; Cummings, 1997; Rohlen, 1997). What may be most foreign to Westerners is that this devotion to learning is socially rather than individually motivated. For East Asian students, in the words of Markus et al. (1996, p. 882), "the press for achievement [is] experienced as a desire to do what is expected." Whereas self fulfillment is seen as the most satisfying and effective engine of learning in Western indigenous psychology, in East Asia fulfilling the expectations of family members and others is found to be a stronger motivator of achievement. Learning is valued not because it enhances the self but because it deepens connections to the social unit (Heine et al., 2001).

This different psychology of education is related to the distinct patterns of achievement behavior in East Asian adolescents. In controlled laboratory studies by Heine et al. (2001), Japanese adolescents were found to be much more persistent than North Americans following the experience of failure. When they had done poorly on a task, Japanese students worked longer on a follow-up task. The findings of these studies suggest that Japanese students are more readily motivated by desire for self-improvement, which the authors attributed to the importance given to effort in this cultural system and the social obligation youth feel to strive for perfection. Given this robustness to their motivation, it is not surprising that 95% of both Japanese males and females graduate from high school. In international comparisons of knowledge in science and math, Japanese youth (and those from other East Asian nations) are at or near the top, substantially above U.S. students (Stevenson & Zusho, 2002). These findings also provide an explanation as to why the ethno-psychology based on intrinsic motivation and self-affirmation fails for many American adolescents: Their motivation appears to be fragile in conditions where the self is not being affirmed (Heine et al., 2001).

It would be a mistake, however, to overidealize East Asian indigenous psychologies of education. First, it has been argued that the focus of Confucian education on conforming to a cultural standard of perfection, often exemplified in the teacher, leads to less creativity and that it encourages passive, uncritical conformity to a single model

(Serpell & Hatano, 1997; Shields, 1989). Second, East Asian systems of secondary education rely heavily on competitive achievement tests as a means to sort students for continued education and careers, and these create what has been called an "Examination Hell" (Amano, 1989). In Korea, for example, virtually all students in academic high schools aspire to pass the college entrance examination—and they believe that with sufficient effort they can—but only one quarter do. The result is that Korean high school students devote enormous efforts but experience a high degree of situational anxiety, stress, and depression (Lee & Larson, 1996, 2000), a pattern also evident in Taiwan and somewhat less in Japan (Crystal et al., 1994). The strength of the East Asian approach is the pervasive cultural support for education, but a concern is the stress it creates for students who fear they may not measure up.

Educational Motivation Across Cultural Contexts

Other cultures of the world exemplify the varieties of ways in which human motivation is conceived and schoolwork is supported. Markus et al. (1996) observed that cultures differ in locating human agency in spirits, in the balance of various internal and external forces, or in routine scripted social practices. Thus, education in India is motivated in part by the Hindu concept of dharma or duty (Kumar, 2000). Serpell and Hatano (1997) described an Islamic model of education that is based on submission to the authority of elders. Moroccan teachers use the threat of physical punishment to induce learning (S. S. Davis & Davis, 1989). Youth in sub-Saharan Africa learn through indigenous systems rooted in a cultural moral imperative to participate in the family and community (Nsamenang, 2002).

In developing countries the importance of these diverse motivational psychologies is often overshadowed by more daunting social and economic barriers to education. These include absence of schools, inadequate school resources, the needs of poor families for their children's labor, early marriage, and barriers to education for girls or specific cultural groups (Buchmann & Hannum, 2001; Fussell & Greene, 2002). Many postcolonial societies have inherited school systems that promote rote learning of information and skills that are out of tune with local ways of life and job opportunities; indeed, some developing countries are producing large numbers of university graduates with few skills for adult employment (Nsamenang, 2002; Verma & Saraswathi, 2002). Many of these settings also rely on exams to select students for educational advancement, creating examination stress similar to that in East Asia (Booth, 2002; Verma, Sharma, & Larson, 2002). An adequate understanding of adolescent education in these settings cannot ignore these social and economic factors.

As education matters more and more to adulthood, it is essential that we find ways to make certain that all adolescents are engaged in learning. Clearly, no culture or nation has worked out a surefire educational psychology to guarantee that every one of its youth are motivated in school. The Western ethno-psychology of intrinsic motivation leaves behind many youth for whom love of learning dwindles in adolescence or is extinguished by experiences of failure. The Confucian ethno-psychology appears to elicit greater effort across a wider cross section of students, but it is not without shortcomings. Systems throughout the world that give a major role to testing produce costs in the form of overemphasis on rote learning and generation of examination stress. Across cultures there is a need to understand how youth with different talents and learning styles can be matched to learning environments that engage them in acquiring the diverse skills needed for adulthood in the 21st century.

GIRLS' ADOLESCENCE AND BOYS': WORLDS APART

To this point we have given little attention to gender, but across societies gender is a central coordinate of adolescence that cannot be ignored. Consider the following anecdotes:

- A 12-year-old Lebanese girl is forcefully escorted home, slapped in the face, and admonished to behave with dignity by her 19-year-old brother (Joseph, 1994).
- After puberty, a Mexican girl who once shopped for food in the town plaza is no longer allowed to go out alone and is kept under close surveillance, while boys of her age are given new freedoms (Chiñas, 1992).
- A 16-year-old Turkish girl wants someday to own the family business, but it has already been named after her 7-year-old brother (White, 1995).

Adolescent girls in many cultural settings inhabit a world that is distinct from that of boys, as these examples poignantly illustrate. In Western societies, gender differences in life options have been decreasing over the last 100 years, and a dominant frame among Western scholars is to see gender differences in terms of "overlapping bell curves" (Bernstein, 1998). In many regions of the globe, however, girls' and boys' experiences are so dissimilar as to constitute separate adolescences. Societies conceive of the two genders in dramatically different terms, suggesting that the study of adolescent girls and boys almost needs to be conceptualized as distinct enterprises.

Disparate Contexts of Socialization

In most cultures differential treatment of girls is intensified at puberty. Budding sexuality induces deeply rooted cultural concerns and invokes diverging scripts of socialization for girls and boys. In the Middle East and parts of Latin America, Africa, and Asia, families' honor, status, and long-term financial interests (through marriage contracts) are tied to girls' virginity, thus requiring that girls' sexuality be tightly monitored and controlled. In many settings, adolescent girls' mobility outside the home is greatly restricted in order to protect their sexual purity. Girls suspected of sexual coquetry or any premarital heterosexual encounter face social ostracism and may even be victims of family violence (D. A. Davis, 1995; Schlegel & Barry, 1991). In most of the same societies, males' sexual rendezvous tend to be tolerated by adults and admired by peers as affirmations of manhood (World Health Organization, 2000). In cultures where strong patriarchal values persist, this gender role intensification at puberty inducts boys into a world where they gain freedom and mobility, while girls are denied these opportunities (Mensch et al., 1998).

Puberty also intensifies preparation for separate adult family roles, requiring girls and boys to spend their time in distinct daily contexts of socialization. In most of the world, the primary adult role of women is seen to be domestic, and men carry little responsibility for childcare and household labor (UNICEF, 1995). To prepare for their role, girls' time is directed toward an intensive pattern of labor activities in and around the house. In Laos, for example, an adolescent girl may spend up to two and a half hours every day husking, washing, soaking, and steaming rice (Ireson, 1996). In Istanbul, a girl must learn how to serve tea or water with the proper gestures and ceremony, how to cook and clean the house, and how to care for younger children, for she will be required to display these skills when the family of a prospective husband comes to call (White, 1995). By early adolescence, girls' principal developmental agenda is learning how to manage the variety of household and nurturing tasks that will define them as adults.

This combination of sexual control and preparation for domestic roles often means that girls gain less socialization than boys in contexts away from home. Because it is boys who are groomed for adult jobs, girls are less likely to take part in paid employment or apprenticeships (Larson & Verma, 1999). For the same reason, girls in Africa, the Middle East, and South Asia are less likely to be enrolled in secondary school (UNESCO, 1999). In rural regions of China and Laos, continuing to send an adolescent daughter to school—when she could be helping out at home—is considered a bad investment because the skills she would gain will be lost to her natal household once she marries and joins her husband's household (Ireson, 1996). Nonetheless, young women's lack of preparation for adult employment is an increasing liability in the modern world. Women's employment is becoming more essential to the financial well-being (or survival) of two-parent households. In addition, rising rates of abandonment and marital dissolution increase the importance of women's ability to support a family on their own (Larson et al., 2002).

In sum, adolescent girls' and boys' participation in distinct daily worlds translates into marked differences in their developmental experiences. Girls' restricted movement and submission to family control means that they have fewer chances to develop independent thinking; they may even find it difficult to conceptualize any clear notion of their own individual welfare (Mensch et al., 1998; Sen, 1990). In these contexts, girls may face what Erikson (1968) called "identity foreclosure"; their restricted social interactions and culturally imposed identities of wife and mother prohibit them from the exploration and experimentation necessary for the development of agency—a capacity increasingly needed for adulthood in a changing society. (Critical analysis and debate are needed on what constitutes positive development in the context of these differing and contested pathways.) Of course, boys in these settings face their own sets of developmental challenges, which often includes dealing with rigid codes of honor and facing higher risks of mortality due to violence, accidents, and suicide (WHO, 2000).

Cultural Change and Pathways for Girls

Are globalization, modernization, and other factors leading to new adolescences that are reducing the divergence between the worlds of girls and boys? The good news is that over the past 25 years, the creation of public education systems has resulted in increasing numbers of girls attending school, especially secondary school. Girls in East Asia and Southeast Asia have caught up to boys in rates of high school (but not college) enrollment; however, girls still lag behind in Latin America, Africa, the Middle East, and South Asia (UNESCO, 1999). School attendance increases girls' literacy and gives them increased opportunities to interact with same-age peers. For many previously confined young women, the opportunity to attend school has helped break down and undermine some of the taboos and restrictions on girls' behavior and gives them exposure to more diverse contexts and role models outside the family (S. S. Davis & Davis, 1995). Increased education is leading girls (more so than boys) to have more egalitarian gender-role attitudes and expectations (Booth, 2002; Mensch, Ibrahim, Lee, & El-Gibaly, 2000). Most important, education increases young women's life choices. It makes them better prepared for jobs in the emerging information society. Better educated girls also marry later, delay childbearing, and have fewer children, all of which improve their life opportunities (United Nations, 1995).

This good news, however, needs to be qualified. Economic stratification between and within nations perpetuates differential access to education, with girls in poor rural families least likely to have the opportunity to attend school. Furthermore, education does not necessarily conjoin adolescent girls' and boys' worlds. In some settings, education may simply continue to perpetuate existing cultural gender roles. In Bangladesh, for example, a family's motive for sending girls to school is primarily to enhance the family's marriage capital by making girls more competitive in the marriage market (Arends-Kuenning & Amin, 2001, p. 130). In Saudi Arabia boys and girls attend separate schools with different curricula, and the girls' curriculum includes fewer academic subjects and has a heavy domestic science component. In some Turkish middle and high schools, boys are assigned extra time for science labs or field trips and are instructed in crafts such as bookbinding, woodworking, and paper marbling, whereas girls are instructed in modern techniques of housekeeping, including cooking, baking, sewing, and child care (Arat, 1998).

In addition, in many cases girls' school attendance does not reduce their responsibility for performing domestic work. In a study of adolescents in Egypt, Mensch et al. (2000) found that among school-attending 16- to 19-year-old adolescents, 68% of girls, as compared to 26% of boys, reported doing domestic chores. In Kenya, schoolgirls are found to spend an average of almost two hours per day on chores, whereas schoolboys spend less than one hour a day (Mensch et al., 1998). As a result of their domestic responsibilities, girls in many nations continue to have limited opportunities for the learning that comes from leisure and interaction with peers, such as learning mutuality in horizontal relationships (S. S. Davis & Davis, 1995; Mensch et al., 1998). The reality is that gender differences are deeply entrenched, embedded in language, family concepts, and cultural scripts and myths. Modernization and globalization may often lead to only superficial changes in adolescents' daily gender socialization.

Even when cultural change opens new opportunities for young women, we need to be attuned to ways in which these can bring new developmental challenges and threats. In traditional societies, girls' pathway to adulthood, although constrained, was clear. In many contexts girls now must forge new, uncharted routes. As girls make gains in education and social visibility, they are left to navigate their way to adulthood with less help from their mothers, aunts, and grandmothers, whose experiences were from a different era. Furthermore, the new options available are often more restricted than are those available to boys. An uneducated teenage girl seeking employment in Bangkok discovers very limited choices: domestic service, factory work, laboring, or prostitution (Cook, 1998). Even with more education, young women often find themselves in less remunerative jobs than those obtained by young men (Santa Maria, 2002). In addition, complex and chaotic urban environments create new risks of exploitation and victimization, against which women need to be prepared to protect themselves.

Challenges for Research and Policy

In sum, we have an important task: not only to understand these separate worlds but also to keep up with how these worlds are changing. New challenges and risks are emerging for adolescent girls and boys that urgently need to be understood. Our cursory summary did not provide space to consider the role of media images in affecting the experience of gender or the ways in which gender can be a focus for the types of cultural counterreactions we discussed earlier (e.g., as a rallying point for the reassertion of traditional norms by fundamentalist groups). We have also given little attention to the many important issues facing boys, yet research in diverse regions shows that the societal transition from traditional to modern typically brings significant changes in gender socialization and adult gender roles for males as well (Condon & Stern, 1993; McElroy, 1979). Researchers need to track how larger social forces, like urbanization and economic development, are changing, disrupting, or realigning the pathways to adulthood for both boys and girls.

The implications are important also for youth policy. Mensch et al. (1998) argued that youth policy has been weakened by the assumptions, first, that male and female adolescents form a homogeneous group and, second, that girls have control over their lives. Policy for adolescent girls needs to be organized around the distinctive features of their lives within a cultural setting, which may include their lack of agency, their confinement to domestic roles and responsibilities, their restricted mobility, and their lack of education. The task for researchers, nongovernmental organizations, and policy makers is to develop strategies that are sensitive to the distinct worlds of both adolescent girls and boys.

CONCLUSIONS: TOWARD THE GLOBALIZATION OF ADOLESCENT RESEARCH

Early anthropologists such as Margaret Mead (1928) and Ruth Benedict (1939) characterized adolescence in Western nations as a difficult period due to discontinuity in roles between childhood and adulthood. In other societies they had studied, children and youth gradually learned the work and family roles of their parents; in some there were rites of passage that shaped and supported this transition to adulthood. They observed that in Western societies, however, adolescents were required to learn new roles and dispositions and make choices between numerous alternate pathways.

Saraswathi (1999a) argued that similar discontinuity between childhood and adulthood is now coming about in India, and the same might be said of many other nations. Globalization, modernization, and other changes are disrupting and reconfiguring the paths taken from childhood to adulthood. They are creating a longer adolescent period during which more knowledge needs to be acquired to prepare for adulthood and more choices made between alternate pathways. Children are less able simply to follow their parents' footsteps, particularly in preparing for adult work. The fast pace of cultural change also means that the knowledge learned as a child—and the advice parents are able to give in adolescence—may be less helpful to preparing youth for the world they will live in as adults. This is particularly true for youth in a generation that makes the transition from rural to urban residence.

The issues we have focused on in this chapter illustrate some of the ways in which the pathways through adolescence are becoming more complex and discontinuous. In more societies, the media are presenting new negative images of adolescents that set them apart in a distinct marginal social category and may reduce adults' willingness to provide guidance and resources to help them through the transition. In most societies, globalization is changing the types of work that adolescents do. They are less likely to work in family fields, a family craft, or apprenticeships within the community, and they are more likely to work in factories or in the streets where supports are fewer and pathways into adult employment less secure. We have also pointed to the increasing importance of education to adulthood: The skills and knowledge required for many adult jobs demand more years of schooling. Yet no nation has developed a surefire system for motivating all youth to get the education they need. Indeed, the rates of stress and the number of youth who fail to advance in school are high; in some cases, youth successfully complete 12 or 16 years of schooling only to find that the knowledge they learned is poorly suited to the available career choices. In these and other ways, the pathways to adulthood are becoming longer, more labyrinthine, and discontinuous. Adolescence requires young people to achieve longer and bigger leaps between what they are as children and what they need to become as adults.

It would be a mistake, however, to underestimate the ways in which distinct cultures provide adolescents with resources to facilitate these passages. Mead and Benedict saw discontinuity as a contributor to difficulty and stress for Western adolescents, but we should not be too quick to assume that this occurs in all other contexts. At the same time that societies are changing, cultural values are being passed on and adapted that provide supports and continuity to youth. In the United States, adolescents tend to distance themselves from their families during a period when they need family support. In India, however, adolescents do not break away but rather nurture and work on maintaining strong ties to immediate and extended kin, ties that are a source of stability and valuable resources as they make the transition into adulthood. In East Asian Confucian societies, youth acquire a cultural orientation toward education that supports learning and keeps youth going even when they experience failure. Over the last half century this orientation helped a whole generation stay in school longer and acquire skills that lifted Japan, Korea, and Taiwan from the ranks of developing to developed nations (Cummings, 1997). We should also not underestimate young people's resourcefulness and creativity in finding their way and adapting to new opportunities.

The central point we wish to end with is that there is much diversity across societies. They vary both in the pathways available to adolescents and in the types of supports and resources provided to youth. There are different *adolescences*—across parts of the world as well as within societies as a function of social class, gender, ethnicity, and other factors. We have much to learn about this diversity.

REFERENCES

Alexander, K. L., Entwisle, D. R., & Kabbani, N. S. (2001). The dropout process in life course perspective: Early risk factors at home and school. *Teachers College Record, 103,* 760–822.

Amano, I. (1989). The examination hell and school violence: The dilemma of Japanese education today. In J. J. Shields Jr. (Ed.), *Japanese schooling: Patterns of socialization, equality, and political control* (pp. 111–123). University Park: Pennsylvania State University Press.

Arat, Z. F. (1998). Educating daughters of the republic. In Z. F. Arat (Ed.), *Reconstructing images of a Turkish woman* (pp. 157–180). New York: St. Martin's Press.

Arends-Kuenning, M., & Amin, S. (2001). Women's capabilities and the right to education in Bangladesh. *Politics, Culture and Society, 15,* 125–142.

Arnett, J. (2000). Emerging adulthood: A theory of development from the late teens through the twenties. *American Psychologist, 55,* 469–480.

Aubrun, A., & Grady, J. (2000). *How Americans understand teens: Findings from cognitive interviews.* Washington, DC: Frameworks Institute.

Bachman, S. L. (2000). A new economics of child labor: Searching for answers behind the headlines. *Journal of International Affairs, 53*(2), 545–572.

Benedict, R. (1939). Continuities and discontinuities in cultural conditioning. *Psychiatry, 1,* 161–167.

Bernstein, D. (1998). *Nebraska symposium on motivation: Vol. 5. Gender and motivation.* Lincoln: University of Nebraska Press.

Bharat, S. (1997). Family socialization of the Indian child. *Trends in Social Science Research, 4,* 201–216.

Biswas, P. C. (1992). Perception of parental behaviour and adolescents' frustration. *Indian Journal of Social Work, L111,* 669–678.

Booth, M. (2002). Arab adolescents facing the future: Enduring ideals and pressures to change. In B. B. Brown, R. W. Larson, & T. S. Saraswathi (Eds.), *The world's youth: Adolescence in eight regions of the globe* (pp. 207–242). New York: Cambridge University Press.

Brandstädter, J., & Lerner, R. M. (1999). *Action and self-development: Theory and research through the life span.* Thousand Oaks, CA: Sage.

Brown, B. B., & Larson, R. (2002). The kaleidoscope of adolescence: Experiences of the world's youth at the beginning of the 21st century. In B. B. Brown, R. W. Larson, & T. S. Saraswathi (Eds.), *The world's youth: Adolescence in eight regions of the globe* (pp. 1–20). New York: Cambridge University Press.

Brown, B. B., Larson, R., & Saraswathi, T. S. (Eds.). (2002). *The world's youth: Adolescence in eight regions of the globe.* New York: Cambridge University Press.

Brown, L., Garder, G., & Halweil, B. (1999). 16 impacts of population growth. *Futurist, 33,* 36–41.

Buchmann, N. C., & Hannum, E. (2001). Education and stratification in developing countries: A review of theories and research. *Annual Review of Sociology, 27,* 77–102.

Caldwell, J. C., Caldwell, P., Caldwell, B. K., & Pieris, I. (1998). The construction of adolescence in a changing world: Implications for sexuality, reproduction, and marriage. *Studies in Family Planning, 29,* 137–153.

Castells, M. (1996). *The rise of the network society.* London: Blackwell.

Chiñas, B. (1992). *The Isthmus Zapotecs: A matrifocal culture of Mexico* (2nd ed). Fort Worth, TX: Harcourt Brace Jovanovich.

Chinese Cultural Connection. (1987). Chinese values and the search for culture-free dimensions of culture. *Journal of Cross-Cultural Psychology, 18,* 143–164.

Condon, R. G., & Stern, P. R. (1993). Gender-role preference, gender identity, and gender socialization among contemporary Inuit youth. *Ethos, 21,* 384–416.

Cook, N. (1998). "Dutiful daughters," estranged sisters: Women in Thailand. In K. Sen & M. Stivens (Eds.), *Gender and power in affluent Asia* (pp. 250–290). New York: Routledge.

Covington, M. V., & Dray, E. (2002). The developmental course of achievement motivation: A

need-based approach. In A. Wigfield & J. Eccles (Eds.), *Development of achievement motivation* (pp. 33–56). San Diego, CA: Academic Press.
Crystal, D. S., Chen, C., Fuligni, A., Stevenson, H. W., Hsu, C., Ko, H., Kitamura, S., & Kimura, S. (1994). Psychological maladjustment and academic achievement: A cross-cultural study of Japanese, Chinese, and American high school students. *Child Development, 65*(4), 738–753.
Csikszentmihalyi, M., & Larson, R. (1984). *Being adolescent: Conflict and growth in the teenage years.* New York: Basic Books.
Cullen, F. T., & Wright, J. P. (2002). Criminal justice in the lives of American adolescents. In J. Mortimer & R. Larson (Eds.), *The changing adolescent experience: Societal trends and the transition to adulthood* (pp. 88–128). New York: Cambridge University Press.
Cummings, W. K. (1997). Human resource development: The J-Model. In W. K. Cummings & P. G. Altbach (Eds.), *The challenge of Eastern Asian education: Implications for America* (pp. 275–291). Albany, NY: State University of New York Press.
Dasen, P. R. (2000). Rapid social change and the turmoil of adolescence: A cross-cultural perspective. *International Journal of Group Tensions,* 29, 17–49.
Davis, D. A. (1995). Modernizing the sexes: Changing gender relations in a Moroccan town. *Ethos, 23,* 69–78.
Davis, S. S., & Davis, D. A. (1989). *Adolescence in a Moroccan town: Making social sense.* New Brunswick, NJ: Rutgers University Press.
Davis, S. S., & Davis, D. A. (1995). Love conquers all? Changing images of gender and relationship in Morocco. In E. W. Fernea (Ed.), *Children in the Muslim Middle East* (pp. 93–108). Austin: University of Texas Press.
Diversi, M., Moraes, N., & Morelli, M. (1999). Daily reality on the streets of Campinas, Brazil. In *Homeless and working youth around the world: New directions for child and adolescent development* (No. 85, pp. 19–34). San Francisco: Jossey-Bass.
Dunn, L. (1991). Women organising for change in Caribbean free zones: Strategies and methods. *Working paper from sub-series on women, history and development: Themes and issues* (No. 14). The Hague, Netherlands: Institute of Social Studies.
Eccles, J. S., Wigfield, A., Harold, R., & Blumenfield, P. B. (1993). Age and gender differences in children's self- and task perceptions during elementary school. *Child Development, 64,* 830–847.
Elder, G. H. (1980). Adolescence in historical perspective. In J. Adelson (Ed.), *Handbook of adolescent psychology* (pp. 3–46). New York: Wiley.
Elder, G. H., Jr. (1998). The life course and human development. In R. M. Lerner (Ed.), *Handbook of child psychology: Theoretical models of human development* (Vol. 1, 5th ed., pp. 939–991). New York: Wiley.
Elder, G. H., Jr., & O'Rand, A. M. (1995). Adult lives in a changing society. In K. S. Cook, G. A. Fine, & J. S. House (Eds.), *Sociological perspectives on social psychology* (pp. 452–475). Boston: Allyn and Bacon.
Enright, R. D., Levy, V. M., Harris, D., & Lapsley, D. K. (1987). Do economic conditions influence how theorists view adolescents? *Journal of Youth and Adolescence,* 16, 541–559.
Erikson, E. H. (1968). *Identity: Youth and crisis.* New York: Norton
Facio, A., & Batistuta, M. (1998). Latins, Catholics and from the far south: Argentinian adolescents and their parents. *Journal of Adolescence, 21,* 49–67.
Farrag, E. O. (1995). Working children in Cairo: Case studies. In E. W. Fernea (Ed.), *Children in the Muslim Middle East* (pp. 239–249). Austin: University of Texas Press.
French, D. C., Rianasari, M., Pidada, S., Nelwan, P., & Buhrmester, D. (2001). Social support of Indonesian and U.S. children and adolescents by family members and friends. *Merrill-Palmer Quarterly, 47,* 377–394.
Freud, A. (1946). *The ego and the mechanisms of defense.* New York: International Universities Press.
Fried, R. L. (2001). *The passionate learner: How teachers and parents can help children reclaim the joy of discovery.* Boston: Beacon Press.
Fussell, E. (2002). Youth in aging societies. In J. Mortimer & R. Larson (Eds.), *The changing ado-*

lescent experience: Societal trends and the transition to adulthood (pp. 18–51). New York: Cambridge University Press.

Fussell, E., & Greene, M. E. (2002). Demographic trends affecting youth around the world. In B. B. Brown, R. W. Larson, & T. S. Saraswathi (Eds.), *The world's youth: Adolescence in eight regions of the globe* (pp. 21–60). New York: Cambridge University Press.

Gauvain, M. (1999). Everyday opportunities for the development of planning skills: Sociocultural and family influences. In A. Göncü (Ed.), *Children's engagement in the world: Sociocultural perspectives* (pp. 173–201). New York: Cambridge University Press.

Gilliam, F. D., & Bales, S. (2001). Strategic frame analysis: Reframing America's youth. *Social Policy Report, 15*(3), 1–14. Ann Arbor, MI: Society for Research in Child Development.

Giroux, H. A. (1983). Theories of reproduction and resistance in the new sociology of education: A critical analysis. *Harvard Educational Review, 53,* 257–293.

Greenfield, P. M. (1994). Independence and interdependence as developmental scripts: Implications for theory, research, and practice. In P. M. Greenfield & R. R. Cocking (Eds.), *Cross-cultural roots of minority child development* (pp. 1–37). Hillsdale, NJ: Erlbaum.

Grotevant, H. D., & Cooper, C. R. (1986). Individuation in family relationships: A perspective on individual differences in the development of identify and role-taking skill in adolescence. *Human Development, 29,* 82–100.

Guillèn, M. F. (2001). Is globalization civilizing, destructive, or feeble? A critique of five key debates in the social science literature. *Annual Review of Sociology, 27,* 235–260.

Gupta, S. T. (Ed.). (1999). *Emerging voices: South Asian American women redefine self, family and community.* London: Alta Mira Press.

Hallack, J. (2000). Globalisation and its impact on education. In T. Mebrahtu, M. Crossley, & D. Johnson (Eds.), *Globalisation, educational transformation, and societies in transition* (pp. 21–40). Oxford, UK: Symposium Books.

Hamilton, S. (1994). Employment prospects as motivation for school achievement: Links and gaps between school and work in seven countries. In R. K. Silbereisen & E. Todt (Eds.), *Adolescence in context: The interplay of family, school, peers, and work in adjustment* (pp. 267–303). New York: Springer-Verlag.

Hauser, S. T. (with Powers, S. I., & Noam, G. G.). (1991). *Adolescents and their families: Paths of ego development.* New York: Free Press.

Havighurst, R. J. (1953). *Human development and education.* New York: McKay.

Hechter, M., & Okamoto, D. (2001). Political consequences of minority group formation. *Annual Review of Political Science, 4,* 189–215.

Heine, S., Kitayama, S., Lehman, D., Takata, T., Ide, E., Leung, C., & Matsumoto, H. (2001). Divergent consequences of success and failure in Japan and North America: An investigation of self improving motivations and malleable selves. *Journal of Personality and Social Psychology, 81,* 599–615.

Herdt, G. H. (1982). Fetish and fantasy in Sambia initiation. In G. H. Herdt (Ed.), *Rituals of manhood: Male initiation in Papua New Guinea* (pp. 44–98). Berkeley: University of California Press.

Hoffman, S. (1998). *World disorders: Troubled peace in the post-Cold War era.* Lanham, MD: Rowman & Littlefield.

Hoffman. V. (1995). Muslim fundamentalists: Psychosocial profiles. In M. E. Marty & R. S. Appleby (Eds.), *Fundamentalisms comprehended* (pp. 199–230). Chicago: University of Chicago Press.

International Labour Office. (1996). *Child labor: Targeting the intolerable.* Geneva, Switzerland: Author.

International Labour Office. (2002). *Every child counts: New global estimates on child labour.* Geneva, Switzerland: Author.

Inglehart, (1997). *Modernization and postmodernization: Cultural, ecomomic and political change in 43 societies.* Princeton, NJ: Princeton University Press.

Inglehart, R., & Baker, W. (2000). Modernization, cultural change, and the persistence of traditional values. *American Sociological Review, 65,* 19–51.

Ireson, C. J. (1996). *Field, forest, and family.* Boulder, CO: Westview Press.
Joseph, S. (1994). Brother/sister relationships: Connectivity, love, and power in the reproduction of patriarchy in Lebanon. *American Ethnologist, 21,* 50–73.
Kağitçibaşi, C. (1997). Individualism and collectivism. In J. W. Berry, M. H. Segall, & C. Kağitçibaşi (Eds.), *Handbook of cross-cultural psychology: Social behavior and applications* (Vol. 3, 2nd ed., pp. 1–49). Boston: Allyn and Bacon.
Kakar, S. (1978). *The inner world: A psycho-analytic study of childhood and society in India.* New York: Oxford University Press.
Kapadia, S., & Shah, R. (1998). Strengths and weaknesses of the Indian family: An insider's perspective. *Perspectives in Education, 14,* 173–182.
Kashyap, L. D. (1993). Adolescent/youth and family dynamics and development programmes. *Indian Journal of Social Work, 54,* 94–107.
Kruse, D. L., & Mahony, D. (2000). Illegal child labor in the United States: Prevalence and characteristics. *Industrial and Labor Relations Review, 54,* 17–40.
Kumar, N. (2000). *Lessons from schools: The history of education in Banaras.* New Delhi: Sage.
Larson, R. (2002). Globalization, societal change, and new technologies: What they mean for the future of adolescence. *Journal of Research on Adolescence, 12,* 1–30.
Larson, R., Ham, M., & Raffaelli, M. (1989). The nurturance of motivation and attention in the daily lives of adolescents. In C. Ames & M. Maehr (Eds.), *Advances in motivation and achievement* (Vol. 6, pp. 45–80). Greenwich, CT: JAI Press.
Larson, R., & Richards, M. (1991). Boredom in the middle school years: Blaming schools versus blaming students. *American Journal of Education, 91,* 418–443.
Larson, R. W., Richards, M. H., Moneta, G., Holmbeck, G., & Duckett, E. (1996). Changes in adolescents' daily interactions with their families from ages 10 to 18: Disengagement and transformation. *Developmental Psychology, 32,* 744–754.
Larson, R., & Verma, S. (1999). How children and adolescents around the world spend time: Work, play, and developmental opportunities. *Psychological Bulletin, 125,* 701–736.
Larson, R., Verma, S., & Dworkin, J. (in press). Adolescence without family disengagement: The daily family lives of Indian middle class teenagers. In T. S. Saraswathi (Ed.), *Cross-cultural perspectives in human development.* New Delhi: Sage.
Larson, R., Wilson, S., Brown, B. B., Furstenberg, F. F., Jr., & Verma, S. (2002). Changes in adolescents' interpersonal experiences: Are they being prepared for adult relationships in the twenty-first century? *Journal of Research on Adolescence, 12,* 31–68.
Lee, M., & Larson, R. (1996). Effectiveness of coping: The case of Korean examination stress. *International Journal of Behavioral Development, 19,* 851–869.
Lee, M., & Larson, R. (2000). The Korean "examination hell": Long hours of studying, distress, and depression. *Journal of Youth and Adolescence, 29,* 249–272.
Lerner, R. M., & Walls, T. (1999). Revisiting individuals as producers of their development: From dynamic interactionism to developmental systems. In J. Brandstädter & R. M. Lerner (Eds.), *Action and self-development: Theory and research through the life span* (pp. 3–36). Thousand Oaks, CA: Sage.
Levine, R. (1980). Adulthood among the Gusii of Kenya. In *Themes of love and work* (pp. 77–104).
Li, J. (2001). Chinese conceptualization of learning. *Ethos, 29,* 111–137.
MacIntyer, D. (2001, January 22). South Korea wires up. *Time Magazine,* pp. B10, B12.
MacLeod, J. (1995). *Aint' no makin' it: Aspirations and attainment in a low-income neighborhood.* Boulder, CO: Westview.
Mannheim, K. (1952). The problem of generations. In P. Keckskemeti (Ed.), *Essays on the sociology of knowledge* (pp. 276–320). New York: Oxford University Press.
Markus, H. R., Kitayama, S., & Heiman, R. J. (1996). Culture and "basic" psychological principles. In E. T. Higgins & A. W. Kruglanski (Eds.), *Social psychology: Handbook of basic principles* (pp. 857–913). New York: Guilford Press.
Marty, M. E., & Appleby, R. S. (1994). Introduction. In M. E. Marty & R. S. Appleby (Eds.), *Accounting for fundamentalisms: The dynamic character of movements* (pp. 1–9). Chicago: University of Chicago Press.

McElroy, A. (1979). The negotiation of sex-role identity in eastern Arctic culture change. In A. McElroy & C. Matthiasson (Eds.), *Sex roles in changing cultures. Occasional papers in anthropology* (pp. 61–72). Buffalo, NY: Department of Anthropology, SUNY.

Mead, M. (1928). *Coming of age in Samoa.* New York: William Morrow.

Mensch, B. S., Bruce, J., & Greene, M. E. (1998). *The uncharted passage: Girls' adolescence in the developing world.* New York: Population Council.

Mensch, B. S., Ibrahim, B. L., Lee, S. M., & El-Gibaly, O. (2000, March). *Socialization to gender roles and marriage among Egyptian adolescents.* Paper presented at the Annual Meeting of the Population Association of America, Los Angeles.

Meyers, W., & Boyden, J. (1998). *Child labour: Promoting the best interests of working children* (2nd ed.). London: International Save the Children Alliance.

Mistry, J., & Saraswathi, T. S. (2002) Culture and child development. In R. M. Lerner, M. A. Easterbrooks, & J. Mistry (Eds.), *Comprehensive handbook of psychology: Vol. 6. Developmental psychology* (pp. 267–291). NewYork: Wiley.

National Research Council. (1999). *High stakes: Testing for tracking, promotion, and graduation.* Washington, DC: Author.

Nieuwenhuys, O. (1996). The paradox of child labor and anthropology. *Annual Review of Anthropology, 25,* 237–251.

Nsamenang, B. (2002). Adolescence in sub-Saharan Africa: An image constructed from Africa's triple inheritance. In B. B. Brown, R. W. Larson, & T. S. Saraswathi (Eds.), *The world's youth: Adolescence in eight regions of the globe* (pp. 61–104). New York: Cambridge University Press.

Onishi, N. (2001, February 12). On the scale of beauty, weight weighs heavily. *New York Times International,* p. A4.

Orenstein, P. (2001, July 1). Parasites in prêt-à-porter. *New York Times Magazine,* 31–35.

Parker, W. C., Ninomiya, A., & Cogan, J. (1999). Educating world citizens: Toward multinational curriculum development. *American Educational Research Journal, 36,* 117–146.

Pereira, A., & Heringer, R. (1994). Brazil. In K. Hurrelmann (Ed.), *International handbook of adolescence* (pp. 65–76). Westport, CT: Greenwood Press.

Peterson, J. (1990). Sibling exchanges and complementarity in the Philippine highlands. *Journal of Marriage and Family, 52,* 441–451.

Rahman, M. M., Khanam, R., & Absar, N. (1999). Child labor in Bangladesh: A critical appraisal of Harkin's Bill and the MOU-type schooling program. *Journal of Economic Issues, 33*(4), 985–1105.

Ramanujam, B. K. (1978). The Ahmedabad discussions on change: An Indian viewpoint. In. E. J. Anthony & C. Chiland (Eds.), *The child in his family* (pp. 415–419). New York: Wiley.

Ramu, G. N. (1988). *Family structure and fertility.* New Delhi: Sage.

Rodgers, G., & Standing, G. (1981). The economic roles of children: Issues for analysis. In G. Rodgers & G. Standing (Eds.), *Child work, poverty and underdevelopment.* Geneva, Switzerland: International Labour Office.

Rohlen, T. P. (1997). Differences that make a difference: Explaining Japan's success. In W. K. Cummings & P. G. Altbach (Eds.), *The challenge of Eastern Asian education: Implications for America* (pp. 223–248). Albany, NY: State University of New York Press.

Salamon, L. M. (1995). *Partners in public service: Government-nonprofit relations in the modern welfare state.* Baltimore: Johns Hopkins University Press.

Santa Maria, M. (2002). Youth in Southeast Asia: Living within the continuity of tradition and the turbulence of change. In B. B. Brown, R. W. Larson, & T. S. Saraswathi (Eds.), *The world's youth: Adolescence in eight regions of the globe* (pp. 171–206). New York: Cambridge University Press.

Saraswathi, T. S. (1999a). Adult-child continuity in India: Is adolescence a myth or an emerging reality? In T. S. Saraswathi (Ed.), *Culture, socialization and human development* (pp. 213–232). New Delhi: Sage.

Saraswathi, T. S. (1999b). Introduction. In T. S. Saraswathi (Ed.), *Culture, socialization and human development* (pp.1–42). New Delhi: Sage.

Saraswathi , T. S., & Ganapathy, H. (2002). The Hindu world view of child and human development: Reflections in contemporary parental ethnotheories. In H. Keller, Y. Poortinga, & A. Scholmerich (Eds.), *Between biology and culture: Perspectives on ontogenetic development* (pp. 80–88). London: Cambridge University Press.
Saraswathi, T. S., & Larson, R (2002). Adolescence in global perspective: An agenda of social policy. In B. B. Brown, R. W. Larson, & T. S. Saraswathi (Eds.), *The world's youth: Adolescence in eight regions of the globe* (pp. 344–362). New York: Cambridge University Press.
Scarr, S., & McCartney, K. (1983). How people make their own environments: A theory of genotype-environment effects. *Child Development, 54,* 424–435.
Schlegel, A. (1995). A cross-cultural approach to adolescence. *Ethos, 23*(1), 15–32.
Schlegel, A., & Barry, H. (1991). *Adolescence: An anthropological inquiry.* New York: Free Press.
Sen, A. (1990). Gender and cooperative conflict. In I. Tinker (Ed.), *Persistent inequalities: Rethinking assumptions about development and women* (pp. 123–149). New York: Oxford University Press.
Sen, A. (1999). *Development as freedom.* New York: Random House.
Serpell, R., & Hatano, G. (1997). Education, schooling, and literacy. In J. W. Berry, P. R. Dasen, & T. S. Saraswathi (Eds.), *Handbook of cross-cultural psychology: Vol. 2. Basic processes and human development* (2nd ed., 339–376). Boston: Allyn & Bacon.
Seymour, S. C. (1999). *Women, family, and child care in India.* Cambridge: Cambridge University Press.
Sharma, M., & Srivastava, A. (1991). The family, social network and mental health. In S. Bharat (Ed.), *Research on families with problems in India: Issues and implications.* (Vol. 1, pp. 68–78). Bombay: Tata Institute of Social Sciences.
Shanahan, M. J. (2000). Adolescence. In E. Borgatta & R. Montgomery (Eds.), *Encyclopedia of sociology* (pp. 1–18). New York: Macmillan.
Shanahan, M. J., & Elder, G. (2002). History, agency, and the life course. In L. J. Crockett (Ed.), *Nebraska symposium on otivation: 1999* (Vol. 48, pp. 145–186). Lincoln: University of Nebraska Press.
Shields, J. J. (1989). *Japanese schooling.* University Park: Pennsylvania State University Press.
Shukla, M. (1994). India. In K. Hurrelmann (Ed.), *International handbook of adolescence* (pp. 191–206). Westport, CT: Greenwood Press.
Shweder, R. A., Goodnow, J., Hiatano, G., LeVine, R. A., Markus, H., & Miller, P. (1998). The cultural psychology of development: One mind, many mentalities. In W. Damon & R. Lerner (Eds.), *Handbook of child development* (Vol.1, 5th ed., pp. 865–937). New York: Wiley.
Silverberg, S. B., & Gondoli, D. M. (1996). Autonomy in adolescence: A contextualized perspective. In G. R. Adams, R. Montemayor, & T. P. Gullota (Eds.), *Psychosocial development during adolescence: Progress in developmental contextualism* (pp. 12–61). Thousand Oaks, CA: Sage.
Sinha, D. (1994). The joint family in tradition. *Seminar, 424,* 20–23.
Smith, P. B., & Schwartz, S. H. (1997). Values. In J. W. Berry, M. H. Segall, & C. Kağitçibaşi (Eds.), *Handbook of cross-cultural psychology: Social behavior and applications* (Vol. 3, 2nd ed., pp. 77–118). Boston: Allyn and Bacon.
Srivastava, A. K. (1997). The changing place of child in Indian families: A cross-generational study. *Trends in Social Science Research,* 4, 191–200.
Steinberg, L. (2001). We know some things: Parent-adolescent relationships in retrospect and prospect. *Journal of Research on Adolescence, 11,* 1–9.
Steinberg, L., & Cauffman, E. (1995). The impact of employment on adolescent development. *Annals of Child Development, 11,* 131–166.
Steinberg, L., & Silverberg, S. B. (1986). The vicissitudes of autonomy in early adolescence. *Child Development, 57,* 841–851.
Stevenson, H., & Zusho, A. (2002). Adolescence in China and Japan: Adapting to a changing environment. In B. B. Brown, R. W. Larson, & T. S. Saraswathi (Eds.), *The world's youth: Adolescence in eight regions of the globe* (pp. 141–170). New York: Cambridge University Press.

Stewart, S. M., Bond, M. H., Abdullah, A., & Ma, S. (2000). Gender, parenting, and adolescent functioning in Bangladesh. *Merrill-Palmer Quarterly, 46*(3), 540–563.

Sundaram, I. S. (1995). Child labour: Facing the harsh reality. In R. C. Heredia & E. Mathias (Eds.), *The family in a changing world: Women, children and strategies of intervention* (pp. 120–128). New Delhi: Indian Social Institute.

Thapa, V. J., Raval, S., & Chakravarty, S. (1999, January 18). Young men. *India Today,* 52–58.

Tomlinson, J. (1999). *Globalization and culture.* Chicago: University of Chicago Press.

Triandis, J. C., & Suh, E. M. (2002). Cultural influences on personality. *Annual Review of Psychology, 53,* 133–160.

Tupuola, A. M. (2000, April). *Shifting notions of personal identity for Samoan youth in New Zealand.* Paper presented at the Society for Research on Adolescence, Chicago.

United Nations. (1995). *The world's women: Trends and statistics.* New York: Author.

UNESCO. (1999). *UNESCO statistical yearbook.* Lanham, MD: UNESCO Publishing and Bernan Press.

UNICEF. (1995). *A picture of health: A review and annotated bibliography of the health of young people in developing countries.* Geneva, Switzerland: Author.

Uplaonkar, A. T. (1995). The emerging rural youth: A study of their changing values towards marriage. *Indian Journal of Social Work, 56,* 415–423.

Verma, S. (1995). *Expanding time awareness: A longitudinal intervention study on time sensitization in the Indian youth.* Zurich: Johann Jacobs Foundation.

Verma, S. (1999). Socialization for survival: Developmental issues among working street children in India. In M. Raffaelli & R. Larsen (Eds.), *Homeless and working youth around the world: Exploring developmental issues: New directions in child development* (No. 85, pp. 5–34). San Francisco: Jossey-Bass.

Verma, S., & Saraswathi, T. S. (1992). *At the crossroads: Time use by university students.* New Delhi, India: International Development Research Centre.

Verma, S., & Saraswathi, T. S. (2002). Adolescence in India: Street urchins or Silicon Valley millionaires? In B. B. Brown, R. W. Larson, & T. S. Saraswathi (Eds.), *The world's youth: Adolescence in eight regions of the globe* (pp. 105–140). New York: Cambridge University Press.

Verma, S., Sharma, D., & Larson, R. (2002). School stress in India: Effects on time and daily emotions. *International Journal of Behavioral Development, 26,* 500–508.

Wei-Ming, T. (1976). The Confucian perception of adulthood. *Daedalus, 105,* 109–123.

Welti, C. (2002). Adolescents in Latin America: Facing the future with skepticism. In B. B. Brown, R. W. Larson, & T. S. Saraswathi (Eds.), *The world's youth: Adolescence in eight regions of the globe* (pp. 276–306). New York: Cambridge University Press.

White, J. B. (1995). An unmarried girl and a grinding stone: A Turkish girl's childhood in the city. In E. W. Fernea (Ed.), *Children in the Muslim Middle East* (pp. 257–267). Austin, TX: University of Texas Press.

World Health Organization. (2000). *What about boys? A literature review on the health and development of adolescent boys.* Geneva: Author.

Wigfield, A., & Eccles, J. S. (2002). The development of competence beliefs, expectancies for success, and achievement values from childhood through adolescence. In A. Wigfield & J. S. Eccles (Eds.), *Development of achievement motivation* (pp. 91–120). San Diego, CA: Academic Press.

Woodhead, M. (1999). Combating child labour: Listen to what the children say. *Childhood, 6*(1), 27–49.

Working Child (2002). *US move on working children will burden youngsters.* Retrieved May 18, 2002, from www.workingchild.org

Youniss, J., Bales, S., Christmas-Best, V., Diversi, M., McLaughlin, M., & Silbereisen, R. (2002). Youth civic engagement in the twenty-first century. *Journal of Research on Adolescence, 12,* 121–148.

Youniss, J., & Ruth, A. (2002). Approaching policy for adolescent development in the 21st century. In J. Mortimer & R. Larson (Eds.), *The changing adolescent experience: Societal trends and the transition to adulthood* (pp. 250–271). New York: Cambridge University Press.

Chapter 11

PARENT-ADOLESCENT RELATIONSHIPS AND INFLUENCES

W. Andrew Collins and Brett Laursen

No aspect of adolescent development has received more attention from the public and from researchers than the topic of this chapter. Much of the research indicates that despite altered patterns of interaction, parent-child relationships remain important social and emotional resources well beyond the childhood years (for recent reviews, see Grotevant, 1998; Steinberg, 2001; Steinberg & Silk, 2002). The aim of this chapter is to specify the processes of relationships that sustain the centrality of familial relationships amid the extensive changes of adolescence. Like Grotevant (1998), this chapter espouses the view that the content and quality of relationships, rather than the actions of either parent or adolescent alone, determine the nature and extent of parental influences on development in and beyond adolescence.

The chapter reflects three premises that have emerged from the sizable literature on familial influences during adolescence. First, familial relationships have far-reaching implications for adolescents' relations with peers, teachers, and other adults; for romantic relationships; for school performance; and for eventual occupational choice and degree of success. Second, relationships with parents undergo *transformations* that set the stage for less hierarchical interactions when adolescents reach adulthood (Collins, 1995; Grotevant & Cooper, 1986). Third, contextual and cultural variations significantly shape adolescents' familial relationships and experiences and, in turn, affect the course and outcomes of development both during and beyond adolescence (for reviews, see Furstenberg, 2001; Grotevant, 1998; Larson, Wilson, Brown, Furstenberg, & Verma, 2002; McLoyd, 1998).

The chapter is divided into four main sections. The first outlines theoretical views of parent-adolescent relationships and their developmental significance. The second section focuses on interpersonal processes comprising parent-adolescent relationships, with particular attention to the distinctive characteristics of parent-adolescent relationships and how and why these relationships change during adolescence. The third section then considers whether and how parent-adolescent relationships and their transformations are significant for adolescent development. The fourth section focuses on variability in parent-adolescent relationships and their developmental impact as a function of structural and demographic variations among families.

THEORIES OF PARENT-ADOLESCENT RELATIONSHIPS

Conceptual models of parent-adolescent relationships vary in whether their primary focus is on the adolescent or on the relationship (Laursen & Collins, in press). The prevalent perspective for most of the last century was that adolescents' physical, cognitive, and social maturation produced inherently unstable relationships. The implications of this instability varied from one theoretical perspective to another, the common focus being the relative turbulence of relationships during adolescence relative to those of childhood. More recent models emphasize the nature and processes of adaptation in parent-adolescent relationships. These views emphasize continuity and the enduring nature of bonds forged between parents and adolescents on the premise that functional properties of parent-adolescent interaction persist despite adolescent development and alterations in the content and form of interactions.

Models of Individual Change and Their Implications for Parent-Adolescent Relationships

Views on adolescent maturation attribute the destabilization of parent-adolescent relationships to varying features of adolescent maturation. Psychoanalytic theorists (A. Freud, 1958; S. Freud, 1921/1949) assumed that hormonal changes at puberty give rise to unwelcome Oedipal urges that foster impulse control problems and anxiety, as well as rebelliousness and distance from the family. More recent psychoanalytic formulations (Blos, 1979; Erikson, 1968) emphasize adolescent autonomy striving and ego identity development, rather than impulse control. These later models converge on the dual contentions that awareness of parental fallibility (deidealization) and psychic emancipation drive a wedge between parents and children and that inner turmoil produced by adolescent hormonal fluctuations exacerbates relationship difficulties. Although this account implies that heightened conflict and diminished closeness inevitably follow maturational changes, it also assumes that relationship closeness can be reestablished in late adolescence and young adulthood.

Evolutionary views also emphasize the role of puberty in transforming relationships but propose that change processes stem from physical and cognitive advances that enable adolescents to separate from the family in order to seek mates elsewhere. Heightened conflict with and diminished closeness to parents are regarded as inevitable byproducts of this individuation process. Some writers have envisioned a transactional process, proposing that the resulting independence may hasten pubertal maturation, as well as the converse (Belsky, Steinberg, & Draper, 1991). Although evolutionary views stipulate no mechanism for the reestablishment of parent-child closeness among young adult humans, it may be that parental investment in offspring and the warmth experienced in earlier periods provide a foundation of positive affect and regard that enables both parties to transcend the difficulties of adolescence (Gray & Steinberg, 1999).

Other maturational models give cognitive development a more central role in parent-adolescent relationship changes. In these accounts advances in abstract and complex reasoning foster more nuanced appreciation of interpersonal distinctions and an increasingly reciprocal view of parent-child relationships (Kohlberg, 1969; Selman, 1980). As a result adolescents become more likely to assume equal power in their interactions with parents. The same cognitive advances underlie increasing tendencies to consider certain issues as matters of personal volition, even though they previously were under parental jurisdiction (Smetana, 1988). Parents' reluctance to transform the hierarchical relationships established in childhood into more egalitarian ones creates conflict and curtails closeness, prompting renegotiation of familial roles (Collins, 1995; Selman, 1980; Youniss, 1980).

A fourth group of theorists (e.g., Simmons & Blyth, 1987) view physical and cognitive maturation as sources of constraints and demands for adolescents but give equal emphasis to changes in social expectations and the need to adapt to a variety of new situations during age-graded transitions. This social-psychological perspective also recognizes that changes in parents often play a role in the altered interactions of adolescence (Collins, 1995). Parents' developmental issues related to careers, reevaluation of personal goals, or declining hopes for the future can exacerbate the difficulty of the adjustments required in parent-adolescent relationships, especially those involving mothers. A strong orientation toward work roles could also mean that both mothers and fathers view adolescents' movement toward autonomy as positive (Silverberg & Steinberg, 1990).

Maturationist models imply that once the changes of adolescence are mostly completed, relationship roles can be successfully renegotiated. They thus envision that postadolescent relationships will be characterized by relatively infrequent, manageable conflicts, more extensive markers of closeness, and sophisticated patterns of constructive interaction (Collins, 1995; Smetana, 1989).

Models of Relationship Continuity and Transformation

Alternative models of parent-adolescent relationships focus on forces for stability and change within the dyad, rather than on the impact of individual change on the dyad. The most salient example, attachment formulations, emphasizes the strong emotional ties between parents and adolescents. As a mutually regulated system, parents and children work jointly to maintain the relationship in a manner consistent with cognitive representations derived from their history of interactions with significant others (Bowlby, 1969). Thus, the quality of parent-child relationships is presumed to be inherently stable over time (Allen & Land, 1999).

Attachment in adolescence is distinctive from attachment in earlier relationships, both behaviorally and cognitively. Strong emotional ties to parents may be indicated in subtle and very private ways, including friendly teasing and small acts of concern, as well as in more obvious forms of interdependence such as shared activities with fathers and self-disclosure to mothers. Cognitive advances in adolescence make possible an integrated, overarching view regarding experiences that involve caregiving, caretaking, and confidence in the availability of significant others. Consequently, whereas younger children view attachment in terms that are more specific to the parent-child relationship, adolescents are increasingly attuned to both the similarities and the differences between relationships with parents, other significant adults, friends, and eventually romantic partners and offspring (Allen & Land, 1999).

The functions of secure relationships for adolescents, however, are parallel to those for infants. Whereas security facilitates exploration of the immediate environment in infancy, security affords adolescents a sense of confidence in family support for their explorations outside of the family, including the formation of new relationships with peers and other adults. In longitudinal research, caregiver-child attachments in infancy significantly forecast interactions and management of emotions with teachers and peers in early and middle childhood (Sroufe & Fleeson, 1988). Moreover, representations of attachment in earlier life are related to characteristics of relationships with parents in adolescence and young adulthood (Becker-Stoll & Fremmer-Bombik, 1997). A key implication of attachment formulations is that adolescents and parents with a history of sensitive, responsive interactions and strong emotional bonds facilitate adaptation during the transitions of adolescence.

Similar predictions characterize interdependence, or social relations, models. Interdependence is a hallmark of all close relationships and is manifested in frequent, strong, and diverse interconnections maintained over an extended time (Kelley et al., 1983). In an interdependent relationship, partners engage in mutually influential exchanges and share the perception that their connections are reciprocal and enduring (Reis, Collins, & Berscheid, 2000). These enduring interconnections are internalized by participants and organized into mental schemas that shape expectations concerning future interactions. However, cognitive advances give rise to a realization that the rules of reciprocity and social exchange that govern interactions with friends are not fully generalizable to interactions with parents (Youniss, 1980). Greater autonomy offers adolescents the opportunity to influence interactions with parents on the basis of perceived relationship costs and benefits (Laursen & Bukowski, 1997; Laursen & Collins, in press). The amount of change should vary across dyads, depending on the degree to which the relationship is perceived to be equitable. Increased conflict may occur in poor quality relationships, along with a decline in closeness, as adolescents express a growing dissatisfaction with unequal treatment and unfavorable outcomes. High-quality relationships, however, may change little or may even improve as participants build on mutually beneficent patterns of exchange and attempt to adjust for past inequities.

Although most theoretical accounts neglect the dimensions of relationships that manifest continuity, Collins (1995) proposed a model in which both stability and change are inextricably involved in the natural history of relationships, including those involving adolescents. This expectancy violation–realignment model begins with the assumption that interactions between parents and children are mediated by cognitive and emotional processes associated with *expectancies* about the behavior of the other person. In periods of rapid developmental change, such as the transition to adolescence, parents' expectancies often are violated. These violations may generate emotional turmoil and conflict and also may stimulate parents and children to realign their expectancies appropriately. In younger and older age groups, change may occur more gradually, so that discrepancies are both less frequent and less salient than in periods of rapid multiple changes, such as adolescence. Baumrind (1991) and Holmbeck (1996) also have proposed models implying links between individual development and adaptations in parent-adolescent relationships.

Interplay between continuity and discontinuity is a feature of parent-child relationships throughout childhood and adolescence and in early adulthood as well. Later sections of the chapter give particular attention to the ways in which continuities balance and stabilize familial relationship and influence individual development during adolescence.

INTERPERSONAL PROCESSES IN PARENT-ADOLESCENT RELATIONSHIPS

These theoretical views underscore a primary but often neglected point: Despite a long-standing orientation to the impact of parental actions, the significance of relationships with parents derives from the joint action patterns between the two individuals. The meaning of most parental actions depends on the history of interactions between parent and adolescent and the immediate context of the action of each toward the other (Collins & Madsen, 2003; Maccoby, 1992). In this section we first summarize the concepts commonly used to describe these joint patterns of interaction. Second, we address common changes in relationships during adolescence.

Social Interactions and Influence

As is the case in relationships generally, parent-adolescent dyads vary in *content* or kinds of interactions; the *patterning,* or distribution of positive and negative exchanges; *quality,* or the degree of responsiveness that each shows to the other; and the *cognitive and emotional responses* of each individual to events in the relationship. With respect to the latter, although parents and adolescents who consider themselves close also report mostly positive thoughts and feelings (Collins & Russell, 1991; Laursen & Williams, 1997), a minority appear to have highly interdependent and mutually influential relationships comprised predominantly of negative interactions in which one person neither feels positive toward nor close to the other person (Collins & Repinski, 2001; Offer, 1969).

A focus on the impact of the unique joint patterns of interaction, emotion, and cognition between the two persons—rather than the actions, emotions, and thoughts of either one alone—also has led to research on bidirectional influences within relationships. For example, parents' behaviors may train adolescents toward more mature behavior, but adolescents' responsible actions also affect the degree to which parents continue to grant increasing independence, as appropriate (Collins, Gleason, & Sesma, 1997). Later sections of the chapter focus on the implications of this bidirectional flow of influence for individual adolescents.

Closeness and Conflict in Parent-Adolescent Relationships

Describing dyadic adaptations requires attention to properties of both conflict and closeness. These terms refer to distinct but overlapping properties of relationships. Closeness is an umbrella term for the degree to which individuals affect and are affected by each other across time. Commonly invoked indicators include interdependence, intimacy, closeness, trust, and communication (Laursen & Collins, in press). There is considerable continuity, however, between positive features of relationships during adolescence and those in earlier life, despite the altered patterns of interaction, emotion, and cognition (Collins & Russell, 1991).

Conflict, which is ubiquitous in close relationships, is especially prominent between family members. Theories of adolescent development give a central role to increasing conflict in relationships with parents and to increasing closeness with peers and extrafamilial adults (for a review, see Laursen & Collins, 1994). Surveys of adolescents indicate that disagreements are most common with mothers, followed by siblings, friends, and romantic partners, then fathers; angry disputes arise more frequently with family members than with close peers (Laursen, 1995). Some scholars view conflict as shorthand for interpersonal unpleasantness generally, but here conflict is defined in terms of disagreement and overt behavioral opposition in order to distinguish it from other negative interactions (Shantz, 1987; see also Laursen & Collins, 1994). A key implication of research findings is that the content of, and balance between, expressions of closeness and disagreement substantially determines the impact of parent-adolescent relationships on individual development.

Parent-Adolescent Relationships and Parenting Styles

Interactional variations from one parent-adolescent dyad to another have been subsumed in part by the construct of parenting styles (Baumrind, 1991; Darling & Steinberg, 1993; Maccoby & Martin, 1983). Parental *authoritativeness* denotes a complex amalgam of actions and attitudes that give priority to the child's needs and abilities while at the same time implying age-appropriate maturity demands (Baumrind, 1991; Darling & Steinberg, 1993; Maccoby, 1992). By contrast, *authoritarian parenting styles* are typified by interactions implying relative neglect of the child's needs in favor of the parent's agenda, strong demands for child compliance, and forceful methods for gaining compliance and punishing infractions. Interactions associated with *permissive parenting styles* imply low demands from parents related either to child-centered indulgence toward the child's self-direction or parent-centered inattentiveness and neglect of the child (Maccoby & Martin, 1983). These concepts almost certainly subsume and gain their explanatory power from diverse interactions that often are mistakenly attributed to parents alone (Collins & Madsen, 2003). For example, Maccoby and Martin (1983) identified the defining interactions of authoritativeness as those that are high in reciprocity and bidirectional communication, whereas authoritarian and indulgent styles imply relationships in which desirable levels of reciprocity and communication are disrupted by the dominance of parent (in the authoritarian style) and of child (in the indulgent style). These hypothesized links between parenting styles and interaction patterns illustrate the centrality of qualities of parent-child relationships as a context and a force for socialization.

The distinction between the nature of the relationships between parents and children and the actions of parents toward adolescents becomes clearer in Darling and Steinberg's (1993) formulation, in which parental *styles* are global attitudes and emotional stances that influence the quality of relationships with children and parental *practices* are specific strategies for gaining children's compliance, maintaining control, and enforcing expectations. Parental style, the dimension that is most closely related to parent-child relationships, is regarded as having motivational effects on the child's receptiveness to specific practices. For example, authoritative parents' involvement in their children's schooling has a stronger impact on improvement in school performance, compared to the impact of equally involved authoritarian parents (Steinberg, Lamborn, Dornbusch, & Darling, 1992).

Continuity and Change in Relationships with Mothers and with Fathers

In order to maintain relationships in the midst of rapid and extensive changes of adolescence, relationships must be adapted to the new characteristics of individuals. The most obvious pressure on relationships comes from the physical, social, and cognitive changes in adolescents themselves. Furthermore, adolescents have new experiences that often are different from their experiences with family members. As a consequence, the importance of parents in adolescents' lives depends less on their greater physical power and the extent of shared experiences with their children than in earlier years. As children approach adolescence, interactions with parents typically are based more on conversation, negotiation, and joint decision making than on the parents' unilateral control of behavior (Maccoby, 1984). This section briefly summarizes the sizable research literatures on continuity and change in parent-adolescent relationships. The first part of the section focuses on the implications for parent-adolescent closeness. The second part examines evidence on conflict as a feature of relationships.

Continuity and Change in Parent-Adolescent Closeness

There is considerable continuity between positive features of relationships during adolescence and those earlier in life despite the altered patterns of interaction, emotion, and cognition that are normative to adolescence. The generally positive reports of parents and adolescents regarding their relationships are readily evident in results from an epidemiological study of 14-year-olds living on the Isle of Wight in the United Kingdom (Rutter, Graham, Chadwick, & Yule, 1976). Both parents and adolescents reported a high incidence of positive interactions and a very low incidence of relationship problems such as physical withdrawal and communication difficulties.

Continuities in relationships coexist, however, with significant changes in the amount, content, and perceived meaning of interactions; in expressions of positive and negative affect between parents and adolescents; and in their perceptions of each other and their relationship (Collins & Russell, 1991). Closeness during adolescence is manifest in forms that differ from closeness in earlier parent-child relationships. For example, intimacy, as expressed by cuddling and extensive joint interactions, decreases as children mature, whereas conversations in which information is conveyed and feelings are expressed increase (Hartup & Laursen, 1991). These adaptations are appropriate responses to the maturity level and changing needs of the adolescent. Relationships with parents remain the most influential of all adolescent relationships and shape most of the important decisions confronting children, even as parents' authority over mundane details (e.g., attire, hairstyle) wanes (Steinberg, 2001; Steinberg & Silk, 2002).

Developmental changes in closeness are equally well documented. Subjective rankings of closeness and objective measures of interdependence decrease across the adolescent years (Collins & Repinski, 2001; Laursen & Williams, 1997), as does the amount of time parents and adolescents spend together (Larson, Richards, Moneta, Holmbeck, & Duckett, 1996). Relative to preadolescents, adolescents perceive less companionship and intimacy with parents (Buhrmester & Furman, 1987) and report lower feelings of acceptance by parents and less satisfaction with family life (Hill, 1988). Although perceptions of relationships remain generally warm and supportive, both adolescents and parents report less frequent expressions of positive emotions and more frequent expressions of negative emotions when compared with parents and preadolescent children. Not all trends are negative: Friendliness and positive affect typically rebound to preadolescent levels in middle adolescence (Larson et al., 1996).

Descriptive data on age-related declines in closeness may overstate the significance of changes in parent-adolescent relationships, however, because analyses typically focus exclusively on accumulated estimates of change at the group level without considering change at the level of the family. Longitudinal data from the Pittsburgh Youth Study revealed moderate to high levels of stability in parent and child reports of positive and negative relationship qualities. Across childhood and adolescence the relative ordering of families on various dimensions of closeness remained fairly constant from one year to the next, even though the mean level of each variable fell (Loeber et al., 2000). Other findings show that despite decreases across the adolescent years, parents remain second only to friends or romantic partners in closeness, support, and interdependence (Furman & Buhrmester, 1989; Laursen & Williams, 1997). Many changes in parent-adolescent relationships reflect declining dependence on parents, rather than signifying erosion in the importance of these relationships (Allen & Land, 1999, p. 321). The process of change may not be smooth for all, or even most, parents and adolescents. In efforts to find appropriate levels of independence, for example, adolescents often actively avoid parents during stressful periods, rather than using them as a safe haven from other difficulties. The available findings, however, portray a complex dynamic of relationship continuity and change that belies the conventional view of an abrupt descent toward distance and alienation.

Parent and adolescent views of the family are notable for their divergence, particularly during early adolescence. In general, children tend to see the family in terms quite different from parents' assessments. Parents, especially mothers, tend to appraise the family more positively than adolescents do (Laursen & Collins, in press). For example, mothers routinely report more warmth and affection among family members than adolescents do. Some writers have speculated that mothers' views may be an attempt to ward off the decline in maternal life satisfaction that accompanies adolescent detachment (Silverberg & Steinberg, 1990). Discrepant views of parent-child relationship vary developmentally, however. Mismatched perceptions and discrepant expectations are highest at the outset of adolescence, and views gradually converge over time (Collins, 1995; Seiffge-Krenke, 1999).

Closeness varies from one adolescent to another and from one adolescent-parent pair to another. Adolescents spend more time with their mothers and are more likely to share feelings with them. In contrast, adolescents commonly view fathers as relatively distant figures to be consulted primarily for information and material support (Steinberg & Silk, 2002). Sons and daughters have similarly warm relationships with mothers, but sons are typically closer to fathers than daughters are. These trends tend to accelerate across the adolescent years. Pubertal maturation has been linked to diminished relationship closeness, particularly for fathers and daughters (Hill, 1988), and also with decreases in the amount of time sons spend with mothers and fathers (Larson et al., 1996). Some gender differences may have roots in earlier phases of the relationship. One longitudinal study showed that parent involvement during childhood predicted closeness during adolescence, with stronger links between early father involvement and closeness to father at age 16 for girls than for boys (Flouri & Buchanan, 2002).

Little is known about variations in closeness among adolescents and parents who differ in socioeconomic status or ethnic background. One issue in comparing across diverse groups is the best method for equating the degree of closeness associated with different norms and cultural forms of relating. The suggestion that closeness be operationalized as interdependence may provide a partial solution to this quandary by allowing for members of cultural groups to specify and report on the frequency, duration, diversity, and salience of activities that denote closeness in their respective contexts (Reis et al., 2000). More is known, however, about variations associated with family structure. For example, warmth and intimacy appear to be high between mothers and daughters in divorced, single-parent families relative to intact, two-parent families, but this closeness declines somewhat when the parent remarries (Hetherington & Clingempeel, 1992; Hetherington & Stanley-Hagan, 2002).

Families adapt to individual and relationship changes in varying ways. Most families capitalize on greater adolescent maturity by fostering patterns of sustained interaction that promote a psychological closeness that depends less on frequency of interactions than was the case in childhood. They do so by adjusting prior interaction patterns to meet new demands for adolescent autonomy (Collins, 1995; Steinberg & Silk, 2002). Families with a history of sustained frequent, intense interpersonal problems, however, may lack the adaptive patterns needed for new forms of closeness during periods of relative distance and thus may be unable to surmount the barriers to effective relationships during adolescence (Grotevant & Cooper, 1986; Hauser, Powers, & Noam, 1991).

Continuity and Change in Parent-Adolescent Conflict

Disagreements are comprised of discrete components with a sequential structure (Laursen & Collins, 1994). Like plays or novels, conflicts follow scripts consisting of a protagonist and an antagonist (the participants), a theme (the topic), a complication (the initiation), rising action and crisis (the resolution), and a denouement (the outcome or aftermath). Most parent-adolescent disagreements concern mundane topics, famously tagged by Hill (1988) as "garbage and galoshes" disputes. Regardless of the topic, the majority of disagreements between parents and adolescents are resolved through submission or disengagement; compromise is relatively rare (Laursen, 1995). Most conflicts between parents and adolescents have few negative effects on the relationship, although chronic fighting has been linked to adolescent maladjustment (Smetana, 1996). Compared to disagreements between adolescent friends, those between adolescents and their parents follow a more coercive script. For example, disagreements with parents more often involve mundane topics, power-assertive resolutions, neutral or angry affect, and win-lose outcomes (Adams & Laursen, 2001).

Until recently, parent-adolescent conflicts were thought to increase in early adolescence and decline beginning in middle adolescence. Meta-analytic methods now have shown that this presumed inverted U-shaped curve was an artifact of the failure to distinguish the frequency of conflict from its affective quality. Evidence from multiple studies actually reveals linear declines in the frequency of conflict with parents from early adolescence to midadolescence and again from midadolescence to late adolescence. Significantly, however, the anger associated with these conflicts increases from early adolescence to midadolescence, with little change thereafter (Laursen, Coy, & Collins, 1998). No reliable age differences have emerged in either the topics or the outcomes of parent-adolescent conflict, but there is some indication that typical forms of conflict resolution may change across the adolescent years. The frequency with which resolutions involve one person's simply submitting to the other declines across ages, whereas rates of disengagement without common agreement on a solution increases (Smetana & Gaines, 1999).

In contrast to the relatively detailed information available about parent-child conflict during adolescence, it is remarkable how little we know about changes in parent-child conflict from childhood to adolescence and from adolescence to adulthood. Evidence is limited to a single cross-sectional survey indicating that conflicts with mothers and fathers are perceived to be more prevalent during adolescence than during childhood or young adulthood (Furman & Buhrmester, 1989). Laursen and Collins (in press) offered two speculative propositions regarding long-term developmental trends in parent-child conflict: (a) The level of negative affect in parent-child conflict probably is higher during adolescence than during any other age period, except perhaps toddlerhood; and (b) the prevalence of coercion in parent-child conflict (as signified by one person's submitting to the other) gradually declines across successive age periods from toddlerhood to adulthood.

Parents and adolescents are known to experience their relationships in dramatically different terms (Noller, 1994). Less well known, however, is the frequent finding that adolescents appear to have more accurate (or more honest) appraisals of unpleasant aspects of the relationship than do parents. Reports of family conflict from independent observers frequently match those of adolescent children, but neither observer nor adolescent reports accord with parent reports of the same events (Gonzales, Caucé, & Mason, 1996). Although fathers are stereotyped as the family member most likely to have erroneous perceptions, accumulating evidence implies that it is mothers who most often underestimate the incidence of parent-adolescent conflict and overestimate its severity (Steinberg, 2001). Not coincidentally, mothers also report the most negative repercussions from conflicts with adolescent children (Silverberg & Steinberg, 1990). Several explanations have been offered for mothers' more extreme responses. Chief among them is that conflict represents a personal failure for mothers because it is an indictment of their ability to serve as family conciliators and peacemakers (Vuchinich, 1987). Moreover, conflict is the primary vehicle through which adolescents renegotiate their role in the family, which inevitably diminishes maternal (but not necessarily paternal) authority (Steinberg, 1981). The fact that parent and child reports of conflict appear to converge during late adolescence suggests that disagreements, though often unpleasant, play an important role in aligning expectations and facilitating communication among family members (Collins, 1995). Accounts of this process may vary somewhat, depending on whether adolescents' or parents' reports are given greater attention.

The relation between parent-child conflict behavior and developmental changes in adolescents varies with gender and pubertal status. Findings differ depending on whether the focus is the rate of conflict, affective responses to it, or resolution and also on whether the indicator refers to relative level or developmental trend. Rates of conflict and levels of negative affect are higher in mother-daughter relationships than in other parent-child relationships (Laursen & Collins, 1994). In the meta-analysis by Laursen et al. (1998), conflict rates declined more during adolescence in mother-child relationships than in father-child relationships. Although studies of gender differences in affective reactions to conflict are relatively rare, the few existing findings imply that gender does not moderate age-related trends. Conflict resolutions vary as a function of both parent and adolescent gender: Compromise is more common with mothers than with fathers, and disengagement is more typical of conflict with sons than of conflict with daughters (Smetana, Yau, & Hanson, 1991; Vuchinich, 1987). As with studies of affective reactions, studies of conflict resolution yield no reliable evidence that gender moderates patterns of developmental change (Laursen & Collins, 1994; Laursen et al., 1998).

Variation attributed to puberty depends on whether the indicator is pubertal status or pubertal timing. Pubertal status refers to absolute level of sexual maturity. Meta-analytic comparisons yield a small positive linear association between pubertal status and affect, indicating that greater physical maturity is associated with greater negative affect in parent-adolescent conflict (Laursen et al., 1998). No similar association emerged for pubertal status and the rate of conflict. In observational studies of problem-solving interactions among fathers, mothers, and children (e.g., Hill, 1988; Steinberg, 1981), fathers interrupted adolescents during disagreements more in the middle phases of pubertal maturation than in earlier or later phases, successfully signaling their dominant role in family decision making. Adolescents and mothers mutually interrupted each other more often at this same time, as the former challenged the authority of the latter. In later pubertal phases, mothers' opinions matched the outcomes of group decision making less often than their adolescents' opinions did. This tendency was especially marked with regard to sons' decision-making influence.

Pubertal timing is an indicator of adolescents' relative level of maturity. Generally, early maturing sons and daughters experience more frequent and more intense parent-child conflict than do adolescents who mature on time. Several explanations for these findings have been offered, most of which suggest that parents do not agree with adolescents that physical precocity is a sufficient basis for granting greater autonomy. Overall, the effects of pubertal timing on parent-adolescent conflict are larger and more robust than are those for pubertal status (Laursen & Collins, 1994; Laursen et al., 1998).

Characteristics of parent-adolescent dyads also moderate conflict. Although families vary considerably, the extreme forms of conflict implied by the popular impression of storm and stress are neither typical nor inevitable. Reviews of the literature consistently have concluded that turmoil characterizes a small minority of families with adolescent children (Montemayor, 1983; Smetana, 1996; Steinberg, 2001). Relationship difficulties in these households usually have more to do with dysfunctional family systems or individual mental health problems than with the challenges posed by adolescent development (Offer, 1969; Rutter et al., 1976). Recent cluster analyses based on the rate and severity of parent-adolescent conflict yielded three types of families: placid, squabbling, and tumultuous. Of these groups, only the tumultuous families appear to experience serious interpersonal strife, reporting conflicts that are more frequent, angrier, and less likely to be successfully resolved (Smetana, 1996). Conflict outcomes also vary across dyads such that the significance of a disagreement depends on qualities of connectedness in the relationship (Grotevant & Cooper, 1986; Laursen & Collins, 1994). Positive connectedness promotes constructive resolutions that foster growth and insight; in less supportive relationships conflict is considered a hostile attack that may have negative repercussions (Hauser et al., 1991).

Longitudinal evidence thus corroborates the view that family contentiousness during the adolescent years is best forecast by family disharmony and general dysfunction during the preadolescent years. Although many families experience a modest upswing in conflict at the outset of adolescence, disagreements typically are not a threat to relationships in these families. Indeed, conflict during this period actually may strengthen relationships by providing a vehicle for communication about interpersonal issues that require attention. More than any other form of social interaction, disagreements offer parents and adolescents an opportunity to reconsider and revise expectations and renegotiate roles and responsibilities to be consistent with the autonomy typically accorded to youth in their culture (Collins, 1995; Laursen & Collins, 1994). Most families successfully meet this challenge because they are able to draw on healthy patterns of interaction and communication established in response to the challenges of earlier age periods. Families with histories of ineffective relationships before adolescence are at risk for dysfunctional discord as they encounter pressures to realign relationships in response to developmental changes and issues during adolescence.

To summarize, conflict and closeness reflect aspects of parent-adolescent relationships that vary between and within families. Although not entirely independent of one another, neither is inimical to the other: Conflicts occur in close relationships as well as in those that are less close. Defining closeness in terms of the degree and extensiveness of mutual impact between relationship partners allows researchers to examine the conditions under which these coexisting relationship elements vary with respect to one another (Collins, 1995).

PARENT-ADOLESCENT RELATIONSHIPS AND ADOLESCENT DEVELOPMENT

Links between parent-adolescent relationships and the development of individual adolescents have been the focus of most of the research on families as contexts of adolescent development. Because the evidence on this point has been reviewed recently and extensively by Grotevant (1998) and Steinberg (2001; Steinberg & Silk, 2002), this section is selective. It focuses primarily on an analysis of how the recurring action patterns and emotional qualities of parent-adolescent interactions are related, directly and indirectly, to key aspects of psychosocial competence in adolescence. The section is divided into two parts. The first is an overview of findings linking parent-adolescent interactions to three traditional hallmarks of adolescent development: autonomy, identity, and morality. The second outlines illustrative evidence that parent-adolescent relationships also play an important indirect role in adolescent socialization by moderating and mediating the impact of influences in and beyond the family.

Adolescent Outcomes Associated With Parent-Adolescent Relationships

Behaviors that are typical of authoritative families consistently are linked in research findings to behaviors that are generally considered to indicate positive adjustment. Current models (e.g., Darling & Steinberg, 1993; Grotevant & Cooper, 1986; Hauser et al., 1991) posit that the quality of parent-child exchanges and shared decision making, over and above the specific content of parental teaching, contribute to the development of competencies that are compatible with autonomous, responsible behavior (Collins et al., 1997). Among these competencies are role-taking skills and advanced ego development and identity exploration. More mature levels of these competencies are associated with parent-adolescent relationships marked by behaviors that encourage both individuation (holding and expressing autonomous views, being one's own person) and connectedness (feeling a bond with other family members; e.g., Allen, Hauser, Bell, & O'Connor, 1994; Lamborn, Mounts, Steinberg, & Dornbusch, 1991).

This correlational pattern is evident in research findings relating the development of autonomy to Baumrind's (1991) conceptualization of parental patterns of control (e.g., Lamborn et al., 1991; for an overview, see Steinberg, 2001). These studies give primary attention to authoritative parent-child relationships, marked by parents' expectations of mature behavior in combination with interpersonal warmth, accepting attitudes, bidirectional communication, and an emphasis on training social responsibility and concern for the impact of one's action on others. These characteristics of authoritative parent-child relationships are correlated during childhood and adolescence with higher levels of age-appropriate personal maturity and with socially desirable and responsible behavior (Baumrind, 1991; Lamborn et al., 1991). By contrast, patterns characterized as neglectful, consisting of relatively few expectations, low involvement with the child, and a rejecting, unresponsive, parent-centered attitude are associated with relatively higher levels of antisocial delinquency and drug use and with lower levels of personal maturity and achievement (e.g., Lamborn et al., 1991; Steinberg, Lamborn, Darling, Mounts, & Dornbusch, 1994). The association between parent-adolescent relationships and adolescent competence persists over time, as shown in a longitudinal study following high school students over the period of 1 year (Steinberg et al., 1994).

Similar relational correlates are found in research on morality and identity. In studies of moral development and social responsibility, prosocial behavior is correlated with clearly communicated parental expectations for appropriate behavior, combined with warmth and moderate power and presented with reasoning and explanation (for reviews, see Eisenberg, 1990; Grotevant & Cooper, 1998). Relationships in which parents are responsive to adolescents' expressions of discrepant opinions are associated with a sense of identity among the adolescents and mature social-perception skills in adolescents (e.g., Grotevant & Cooper, 1985; Hauser et al., 1991; Walker & Taylor, 1991). These same characteristics of parent-adolescent relationships are associated with two other qualities of mature identity achievement: self-confidence and autonomously chosen values (Bosma & Gerrits, 1985; Quintana & Lapsley, 1987).

Longitudinal studies have shown that high levels of bidirectional communication and acceptance in parent-child relationships during childhood and early adolescence are correlated positively with psychosocial maturity in later adolescence. Allen et al. (1994) found that parents' (especially fathers') behaviors that made it more difficult for family members to discuss their own reasons for preferring one option over others were highly correlated with decreases in adolescents' ego development and self-esteem between the ages of 14 and 16. In a similar study, Walker and Taylor (1991) found that advances in adolescents' moral-reasoning levels over a 2-year period were best predicted by earlier parent-child interactions characterized by supportive, but cognitively challenging, discussions of moral issues (Walker & Taylor, 1991).

Equally strong and consistent findings show that continuously high levels of conflict are associated with psychosocial problems during adolescence and in later life (for a review, see Laursen & Collins, 1994). Moreover, conflicts may lead to continued or escalating difficulties and even deterioration of relationships. The negative emotionality associated with many conflicts undoubtedly plays a central role in these deleterious outcomes. Conflict is not uniformly deleterious, however. Adolescents who report moderate levels of conflict with parents have better school grades and fewer adjustment problems than do adolescents who report no conflict and those who report frequent conflict (Adams & Laursen, 2001). These findings strengthen the conclusion that relationship properties help to determine whether specific experiences, such as conflicts, are detrimental in development.

Correlational findings leave open the question of how associations between variations in family relationships and adolescent adjustment come about. Several possibilities have been proposed. One is that parents' child-rearing behaviors provide models of different patterns of social responsibility and concern for others. Authoritative parents exemplify socially responsible, caring behavior, whereas neglectful parents model self-absorption and low responsibility for the welfare of others (Baumrind, 1991). Older siblings may represent another source of modeling and reinforcement of values endorsed by parents (Amato, 1989).

A second possibility is that different parenting styles engender differentially effective skills for autonomous, responsible behavior. Grotevant and Cooper (1986) and Hauser et al. (1991) proposed that parents who encourage both individuation and connectedness foster the development of capabilities for more socially responsible, competent behavior. In this respect, parent-child relationships may provide continuities between childhood learning and the new demands of adolescence and adulthood that facilitate the integration of past and future roles.

Third, sensitive, responsive parental treatment of children and adolescents may engender positive emotional bonds that make the values and behaviors of parents more salient and attractive to adolescents. Research findings indicate that adolescents' perceptions of warmth and security in relationships with parents are correlated positively with self-confidence, exploration of issues related to identity, and comfort in interactions with others (Jackson, Dunham, & Kidwell, 1990; Kamptner, 1988). Observational studies of parent-adolescent interaction have shown that adolescents from families marked by high encouragement for expressing and developing one's own point of view disproportionately manifested higher levels of identity exploration (Grotevant & Cooper, 1985) and ego development (Allen et al., 1994). Moreover, Stattin and Kerr (2000; Kerr & Stattin, 2000) recently demonstrated that high parental knowledge derived from adolescent disclosures about their activities, which are enhanced by mutual engagement and communication, predicted positive adolescent adjustment more strongly than did parents' control of adolescents' activities through tracking and surveillance. These findings imply that the characteristically warm, accepting relationships in authoritative families may increase the likelihood of positive parental influences on adolescents (Barnes & Olson, 1985; Darling & Steinberg, 1993).

These three possibilities are not mutually exclusive. Indeed, multiple plausible mechanisms imply a more complex, plausible causal process than does a view that emphasizes the simple transmission of parents' values to the next generation (Grusec & Goodnow, 1994; Grusec, Goodnow, & Kuczynski, 2000). Adolescent adjustment clearly is facilitated by certain parental behaviors, but the operative processes almost certainly include dynamic properties of relationships between parent and child that foster the adolescents' desire or willingness to be influenced (Darling & Steinberg, 1993; Grusec et al., 2000). These relational conceptions of individual competence imply that effective socialization is likely to entail a gradual, rather than abrupt, process of developmental change. Maccoby (1984) argued that the development of autonomy moves from parent regulation in early life, to a period of increasingly shared decision making between parent and child in childhood and adolescence, to self-regulation in adulthood. In this view, coregulation provides an essential period of training for effective interdependence, rather than independence. In her words, parenting that is attentive to training for autonomy "inducts the child into a system of reciprocity" (Maccoby, 1992, p. 1013).

Thus, research findings increasingly suggest that hallmark achievements of adolescence, such as autonomy and identity, "are most easily established not at the expense of attachment relationships with parents, but against a backdrop of secure relationships that are likely to endure well beyond adolescence" (Allen & Land, 1999, p. 319). Similarly, adaptations in relationships themselves enhance, rather than threaten, the psychosocial achievements of the adolescent years.

Parent-Adolescent Relationships as Moderators and Mediators of Influence

Contemporary approaches to research on parenting have moved beyond the exclusive reliance on the global analyses of parenting influence that dominated the field in the last century (Collins, Maccoby, Steinberg, Hetherington, & Bornstein, 2000). Among the insights emerging from these more complex models of parenting is the recognition that in addition to their direct impact on adolescent development, relationships with parents also may be significant as intervening mechanisms in the impact of other significant social influences (Grotevant, 1998). In this section we consider instances in which parent-adolescent relationships serve as *moderators* of relations between other aspects of parental behavior and adolescent outcomes and as *mediators* that help to account for or explain why another source of influence is related to the outcome of interest (Baron & Kenny, 1986).

The moderating effect of relationship qualities on the influence of specific parental actions, for example, can be seen in the finding that the degree to which mutual friendship are linked positively to adolescents' psychological well-being depends on the degree to which the adolescent also experiences familial cohesion and adaptability (Gauze, Bukowski, Aquan-Assee, & Sippola, 1996). Similarly, Fuhrman and Holmbeck (1995) found that when parent-adolescent affect was relatively positive, adolescents were more likely to show positive adjustment when emotional autonomy was high than when emotional autonomy was low. The converse was true when parent-adolescent affect was relatively negative. The potential complexity of moderating relationships is evident in research showing that the perceived quality of relationship with parents facilitated adolescents' modeling of parents' substance use. Adolescents who had a relatively good- or moderate-quality relationship with parents tended to follow their parents' example more than if the relationship was relatively poor, implying that positive relationships with antisocial parents sometimes may be a source of risk (Andrews, Hops, & Duncan, 1997).

The quality of parent-adolescent relationships also moderates the impact of extrafamilial stressors. Junior high school students experiencing high levels of school hassles demonstrated more competent functioning and less evidence of psychopathology if they rated their familial relationships as high quality rather than lower quality (Garber & Little, 1999). Moreover, the link between after-school self-care and involvement in problem behaviors was found to be buffered by parental acceptance and firm control, which are the dual hallmarks of relationships in authoritative families (Galambos & Maggs, 1991).

In addition to moderating effects of parent-adolescent relationships, dyadic interactions also often serve as conduits by which outside forces impinging on the family affect adolescent development. A well-known example is the finding that the impact of a family's sudden economic losses on adolescents was mediated by deterioration of nurturant and involved parenting. In fact, the most significant impact of economic hardship was that of undermining parents' abilities to maintain effective relationships with their adolescent offspring (e.g., Conger et al., 1992). Familial conflicts serve a similar mediating role in the link between family economic hardship and adolescent aggression and anxiety-depression (Wadsworth & Compas, 2002).

Findings of mediator effects point to further possible avenues by which parent-adolescent relationships influence individual development. Mediating processes are both dynamic and complex. In a cross-sectional study of 10- to 16-year-old African American adolescents (Connell, Spencer, & Aber, 1994), parents' engagement with their adolescents was inversely related to the degree of their adolescent's disaffected behavior with school. Path analyses revealed that as parents' involvement lessened, adolescents were likely to become even more disaffected, partly because less parental engagement and support are associated with more negative self-appraisals by adolescents. This transactional process eventually can result in further declines in the adolescents' school performance.

These instances broaden simplistic cause-and-effect models of the impact of parent-adolescent relationships. Rather than focusing only on the assumption that parenting styles and practices *cause* the outcomes to which correlational findings have linked them, compelling evidence is now building to show that parent-adolescent relationships contribute to adolescent development by modifying the impact of other sources of influence and by transmitting them to adolescents through moment-to-moment exchanges between parents and children.

THE IMPACT OF CONTEXT ON RELATIONSHIP PROCESSES AND OUTCOMES

Parent-adolescent relationships and influences occur in contexts that extend beyond the confines of their interactions and immediate settings. The impact of often distal forces on families, relationships, and individuals is well established (e.g., Bronfenbrenner & Crouter, 1983). This section provides a brief overview of instances of contextual influences on parent-adolescent relationships and influences. The first concerns the impact of family systems, encompassing marital, sibling-sibling, and parent-sibling dyads, on the parent-adolescent dyads that exist within them. The second focuses on stressful conditions emanating from outside the family systems, as represented by parents' workplace experiences and economic pressures especially. The third addresses adolescents' relationships with individuals outside of the family, such as peers and nonfamilial adult mentors. The fourth considers variations in relationships across ethnic, cultural, and national groups.

Familial Systems as Contexts

Families typically consist of multiple relationships. Adolescents form dyads with mothers, fathers, siblings, and, frequently, with grandparents, aunts, uncles, and cousins. Today, extended family systems also commonly encompass stepparents, stepchildren, and their kin (e.g., Hetherington & Stanley-Hagan, 2002; Smith & Drew, 2002). These multiple relationships often create conditions that enhance, complicate, or compensate for conditions in parent-adolescent relationships.

Mother-Adolescent and Father-Adolescent Relationships

Information about common variations among relationships within the same family comes largely from comparisons of mother-adolescent and father-adolescent dyads. These dyads typically vary in content and patterning of activities (Collins & Russell, 1991). Mother-adolescent and father-adolescent pairs are similar in that both generally involve both work (e.g., chores, caregiving, homework) and recreation. Compared to mother-adolescent pairs, however, a larger proportion of the time that fathers and adolescents spend together is devoted to recreational activities. Though distinctive, mother-adolescent and father-adolescent pairs mutually influence each other. Adolescents interact with their mothers differently when only the two of them are present than when the father or a sibling is present; the same is true for fathers and adolescents and for two siblings (e.g., Vuchinich, Emery, & Cassidy, 1988). The degree and nature of one dyad's influence on another varies from one family to the next. Support for this point comes from Cook (1994), who showed that the degree to which family members reported feeling coerced by another family member varied from one family to another but also varied from one dyad to another within the family. Consequently, observing only one dyad in a family with more than two members provides only part of the picture of an adolescent's family relationships, a point that is frequently noted by critics of the traditional emphasis on mother-child dyads as indicators of family functioning.

In addition to the relations between parent-adolescent dyads, these dyads also are affected in intact families by interactions between the two parents. Evidence documents, for example, links between marital conflicts and parent-adolescent conflicts (e.g., Davis, Hops, Alpert, & Sheeberg, 1998; Noller, Feeney, Sheehan, & Peterson, 2000). Almeida, Wethington, and Chandler (1999) found that marital conflicts and tensions were followed disproportionately by tense interactions with their adolescents.

Relationships With Siblings

Relationships with siblings have received much less attention than relationships with parents, yet adolescents regard their siblings as important sources of companionship, intimacy, and affect. Although siblings experience more conflict with each other than either sibling does with friends or other peers, adolescents' reports of sibling conflicts more clearly coexist with reports of companionship, warmth, and closeness in descriptions of sibling relationships. Moreover, only some sibling conflicts reported by adolescents arose from feelings of unequal treatment by parents, implying a distinction between ordinary disagreements and sibling rivalry (Buhrmester & Furman, 1990).

Positive relationships with siblings have been associated with perceptions of emotional and school-related support, above and beyond the contributions of mother, father, and peer acceptance (Seginer, 1998). These feelings of support may provide inducements for sharing and for coordinating goals, which in turn may foster both prosocial behavior patterns and self-control (Amato, 1989). Research findings show that older siblings also may provide an entrée into relationships with peers, especially in non–European American ethnic groups (Cooper, 1994). The degree and kind of influence of siblings on adolescents' friendships depend on factors such as having a sister versus a brother and coming from a same-sex versus a mixed-sex dyad (Updegraff, McHale, & Crouter, 2000).

Sibling relationships are closely intertwined with relationships between each sibling and parents. Multivariate genetic analyses reveal that similarity between mother-adolescent and sibling relationships are attributable largely to shared environmental influences in the family (Bussell et al., 1999). Differential treatment of siblings by parents has negative implications for sibling relationships, the parent-adolescent relationship, and adolescent adjustment (Anderson, Hetherington, Reiss, & Howe, 1994; Graham-Bermann, Cutler, Litzenberger, & Schwartz, 1994). Although more information is needed about sibling relations during adolescence, the presence of siblings, the qualities of adolescents' relationships with them, and the ways in which each sibling interacts with parents clearly are important aspects of family systems and their impact.

The contributions of parent-adolescent relationships to adolescent development thus are embedded in the network of familial relationships. The conceptual and methodological challenges of studying familial systems are readily apparent (Grotevant, 1998). It is essential, however, to recognize that evidence of influence within parent-adolescent dyads actually may be a proximal indicator of the impact of experiences in multiple relationships with family members.

Structural Transitions and Parent-Adolescent Relationships

Divorce and remarriage have become almost commonplace for adolescents in the United States, but such transitions can further increase stress and emotional perturbation for adolescents, who are already undergoing multiple physical, cognitive, and social changes. In addition to predivorce parental conflict, separation from one parent, and the need to adjust to a stepparent, these transitions often involve economic need; changes in domicile, neighborhoods, and schools; continuing emotional distress in parents; and reorganization of family roles and relationships (Hetherington & Clingempeel, 1992).

Both divorce and remarriage entail temporary disorganization and disruption of parent-adolescent relationships. Mother-adolescent relationships in divorced families manifest higher levels of both conflict and harmony than do relationships in never-divorced families. Divorced mothers monitor their children's activities less closely and demand greater responsibility for family tasks than do married mothers. Divorced mothers also use more peremptory and coercive techniques to discipline and otherwise influence adolescents' behavior. For their part, adolescents in recently divorced families tend to feel anger and moral indignation toward their parents. Some adolescents react by pulling away from the family and behaving with aloofness toward both parents, a withdrawal that seems to help them adjust to the divorce (Hetherington & Clingempeel, 1992; for a review, see Hetherington & Stanley-Hagan, 2002).

Many researchers have estimated that the resulting difficulties in parent-adolescent relationships are most evident in the first two years following divorce, although variations around this implied average are considerable. Whether these relationship perturbations imply higher levels of conflict in divorced than in never-divorced families is unclear. Some researchers have found more conflict in divorced families in the two-year period of adjustment, with a gradual return to levels similar to those of never-divorced families (e.g., Hetherington & Clingempeel, 1992). Others report that initial increased levels are sustained beyond the first two years (e.g., Baer, 1999), and still others actually found fewer arguments in single-parent families than in married households (Smetana, Yau, Restrepo, & Braeges, 1991). One study suggests that overall rates of parent-adolescent conflict in intact two-parent households and divorced single-parent households are similar but that mother-adolescent conflict differs across households because mothers in single-parent households are engaged in disputes that otherwise fall to fathers in two-parent households (Laursen, 1995). Disruptions in relationships with noncustodial fathers appear to be more extensive and long-lasting than the impact on mother-adolescent relationships, showing links to adjustment and relationships of offspring a decade later when they were young adults (Burns & Dunlop, 1998; Hetherington, 1999).

How unique are these implications of apparent disruptions in relationships to recently divorced parents and adolescents? Some evidence suggests that parental conflict and lack of harmony in the family have negative effects much like those observed in many studies of the impact of divorce (Fauber, Forehand, Thomas, & Wierson, 1990). Moreover, the nature and extent of disruptions vary even among divorced families, with more pronounced links for boys than for girls, especially when the mother is the custodial parent (e.g., Hetherington, 1999; Needle, Su, & Doherty, 1990). Adolescents who have experienced divorce tend to be somewhat less well adjusted than those who have not. A meta-analysis of parental divorce and child adjustment revealed modest differences between divorced and intact families in terms of secondary school student outcomes in the domains of academic achievement, conduct, psychological adjustment, self-concept, and parent-child relationships (Amato & Keith, 1991).

Partly because divorce is so common, living in a single-parent family is rapidly becoming the normal childhood experience. According to the U.S. census, 59% of children born in 1983 will live in a single-parent household for some period before reaching the age of 18 (Hodgkinson, 1985). The impact on children and adolescents is difficult to specify. Single-parent families, like two-parent families, vary greatly. Having support from an extended family member, such as a grandparent, is linked to single parents' success in maintaining authoritative parenting practices; extended family support was much less important in the authoritative parenting of married parents (Taylor, Casten, & Flickinger, 1993). Similarly, children in single-parent households who have regular, supportive contact with their noncustodial parent have different experiences than those for whom the noncustodial parent is rarely, if ever, in contact. These variations are exacerbated by differences among families in the recency of divorce and the number of changes that accompany divorce (for a review, see Steinberg & Silk, 2002). Research findings also have revealed some possible advantages to growing up in households headed by single mothers compared to married-parent households (Barber & Eccles, 1992). Adolescents may develop a greater sense of self-esteem and personal responsibility because of the additional contributions required of them in their households. Adolescents also may develop less stereotyped occupational aspirations and family values.

Adjustment to remarriage appears to be more difficult initially for daughters than for sons (e.g., Needle et al., 1990; Vuchinich, Hetherington, Vuchinich, & Clingempeel, 1991; for a review, see Hetherington & Stanley-Hagan, 2002). Sons sometimes benefit from the introduction of a stepfather into the family. Their relations with their mothers often improve, and stepfathers also report more positive relationships with boys than with girls. Nevertheless, in a recent follow-up of adolescents whose mothers had remarried two years previously, both girls and boys still showed little adjustment to the remarriage (Hetherington & Clingempeel, 1992). The implications for adolescents' relationships with both parents and stepparents probably depend on several factors. One is the relationship between the divorced parents. Continuing tensions and conflict between an adolescent's biological mother and father generally make it more difficult for the adolescent to adjust. Adolescents also may consider the stepparent an obstacle to the biological parents' "getting back together." Another factor is the personality and adjustment of the noncustodial parent. Noncustodial parents who put the welfare and adjustment of their children before their own personal difficulties can make it easier for the children to adapt to family transitions. Recent studies show that adolescents who perceive little conflict between their parents and close relationships between themselves and their parents have fewer adjustment problems than do those whose parents are in conflict with one another (e.g., Brody & Forehand, 1990). One reason for this is that adolescents often feel caught between warring parents and have attendant fears of breaching their relationship with each parent (Buchanan, Maccoby, & Dornbusch, 1991).

Economic Status and Employment

Parent-adolescent relationships also reflect the nature of parents' work roles and the stresses associated with them. Kohn (1979) argued that parents whose work requires conformity rather than individual initiative tend to value obedience over initiative in their children's behavior. In addition, parents' work schedules—whether they are required to travel extensively, and even the distance between workplace and home—often influence what adolescents are expected or allowed to do (Gottfried, Gottfried, & Bathurst, 2002; Hoffman & Youngblade, 1999). In addition, the socioeconomic status of the family, especially conditions of economic hardship, accounts for differences among parent-adolescent pairs. In recent years recurring and prolonged economic downturns in many parts of the United States have widened gaps between families in standard of living, and loss of income and social problems often impair parents' relationships with adolescents (Conger et al., 1992, 1993; McLoyd, 1998). These extrafamilial forces thus trickle down to the daily lives of family members, affecting their interactions and the resulting implications for development.

Dual-Career Families

In more than 70% of two-parent families, both parents work outside the home. This figure is 10 percentage points higher than it was in 1980. Research has focused entirely on mothers' employment, and the few differences that have been found appear to be associated with mothers' reasons for working and their job satisfaction. Mothers who are not satisfied with their jobs sometimes have been found to have less positive relationships with their children than those who enjoy their work. Conversely, mothers who stay at home but would prefer to work report that they find it more difficult to control their children and feel less confident in themselves as mothers (Hoffman & Youngblade, 1999). Many studies, however, show no differences in closeness or other qualities of relationships for working and nonworking mothers (e.g., Galambos & Maggs, 1991; Keith, Nelson, Schlabach, & Thompson, 1990). Moreover, both sons and daughters of working mothers appear to have less stereotyped views of masculine and feminine gender roles (Gottfried et al., 2002; Hoffman & Youngblade, 1999). As maternal employment becomes increasingly common, differences between children of mothers who work at home and those who work elsewhere may diminish further.

Work-related stressors, however, may exacerbate such familial difficulties as marital and parent-child conflicts. Almeida et al. (1999) discovered that both parents were more likely to experience tense interactions with their adolescents when they also had experienced work overloads or home demands. Tension spillover was more likely for mothers with adolescents than for mothers with younger children. Other findings have revealed that the link between parents' work pressures and adolescent well-being were mediated by parents' sense of role overload (Crouter, Bumpus, Maguire, & McHale, 1999).

Economic Hardship

Parent-adolescent relationships in families experiencing sudden economic loss often become less engaged, more conflictual, and more negative in emotional tone. Studies in economically depressed farming and industrial regions, for example, show that parents' worries about jobs and family finances often distract them from the problems of children and adolescents (Conger et al., 1992, 1993; Flanagan & Eccles, 1993; Ge et al., 1992). Parents often became less nurturant toward their adolescents and used disciplinary methods that were both inconsistent and rejecting. In these families, adolescents showed higher levels of depression and loneliness and also were more likely to use drugs and to be involved in delinquent activities.

Socioeconomic Status

Long-term disadvantage has similarly deleterious effects on relationships, resulting in parental behavior that is harsher, more depressed, less vigilant, and less consistent with regard to discipline. Moreover, as with couples experiencing sudden economic loss, parents living in chronic poverty experience higher levels of marital conflict than do more advantaged parents (Brody et al., 1994). The greater likelihood of antisocial behavior and school failure of adolescents living in poverty is equally well established

(Bolger, Patterson, Thompson, & Kupersmidt, 1995; Felner et al., 1995). Despite difficult circumstances, economically disadvantaged parents often combine promotive strategies designed to build adolescent competence and restrictive strategies designed to keep adolescents safe in risky environments (Elder, Eccles, Ardelt, & Lord, 1995).

Extrafamilial Relationships

Current views of the development of behavioral regulation incorporate the bidirectional processes between friends and those between parents and children, as well as the interrelations between the two (Patterson, DeBaryshe, & Ramsey, 1989). Although traditional conceptualizations have placed peer influences in opposition to parental values, evidence from research consistently has shown that extrafamilial relationships work in conjunction with parent-adolescent relationships in predicting behavior and adjustment. Brown, Mounts, Lamborn, and Steinberg (1993) posited that particular parenting practices (e.g., emphasis on academic achievement, parental monitoring, and facilitation of joint parent-child decision making) and parenting styles (e.g., variations along dimensions of demandingness and responsiveness) are associated with certain adolescent behaviors and predispositions. These behaviors then guide adolescents into particular peer groups, such as those commonly referred to as brains, jocks, or druggies. Peer-group norms in turn reinforce the behavioral styles that were the impetus for the affiliation. Thus, parents indirectly affect their children's peer-group association through their influence on certain personality traits and behaviors in their children.

Parent-adolescent relationships further predict the degree to which peers influence adolescents' behavior and adjustment. Increasing orientation to peers over time has been found to be a positive function of perceptions of parental strictness and a negative function of opportunities for decision making to affect the self (Fuligni & Eccles, 1993). Furthermore, having friends appears to be more strongly related to social adjustment among early adolescents from noncohesive and nonadaptable families than among children with more positive familial relationships (Gauze et al., 1996).

Some extrafamilial relationships may in turn affect parent-adolescent relationships. For example, adolescents paired with adult mentors to help with schoolwork experienced improved parent-child relationships, as well as fewer unexcused school absences and increased self-perceived competence (Rhodes, Grossman, & Resch, 2000). The authors showed that these links were mediated by the impact of tutoring on global self-worth, value placed on schooling, and improved grades. Improvements in parent-adolescent relationships may partly reflect reduced conflict with parents as mentors take on the task of helping adolescents master school-related tasks and skills.

In summary, although familial influences, especially from parents, have dominated the research on adolescent adjustment, recent findings clearly implicate interrelated contributions of extrafamilial and familial influences. Their significance likely will become even more apparent as other members of adolescents' rapidly expanding social networks become standard considerations in analyses of adolescents' behavior and adjustment. To date, this broader purview has been addressed primarily in studies of antisocial behavior, and research is needed to examine interrelated influences in other aspects of adolescent development.

Ethnic and Cultural Variations

Variations among families also reflect differences in ethnic and cultural heritages. Different cultures foster sometimes contrasting views of parent-child relationships (Feldman & Rosenthal, 1991). For Korean adolescents, strict parental control signifies parental warmth and low neglect, whereas middle-class adolescents in North America typically regard the same behavior from their parents as repressive (Rohner & Pettengill, 1985). Parent-adolescent conflict appears to be more common in both North America and Europe than in Asian countries (Fuligni, 1998). At the same time, cultural comparisons consistently show sizable overlaps among measures of parents, adolescents, and relationships from different cultural groups and equally or even greater diversity *within* ethnic and cultural groups (Harkness & Super, 2002).

Cultural gaps in the interpretation of parent-adolescent interactions may be especially apparent in immigrant families. Greek Australian adolescents reported more tolerance and acceptance of conflict than did Greek adolescents reared in Greece. Greek Australian parents, however, viewed conflict with their children much as the parents still living in Greece did (Rosenthal, Demetriou, & Efklides, 1989). This contrast is one example of the tensions experienced by immigrant families as parents seek to maintain values from their country of origin and their children adopt attitudes more typical of their new country. Numerous other cross-cultural comparisons have documented similar contrasts in perceptions of appropriate parent and child behavior while simultaneously showing diversity within cultural groups (Fuligni, 1998).

In addition, differences among families that result from contrasting cultural heritages and experiences as members of minority groups in the United States affect their responses to the changes and prospects of adolescence and their expectations regarding parent-adolescent interactions. For example, Asian American families in California reported more formal communication with their parents than did either Hispanic American or European American adolescents. These Asian American youth also expressed higher levels of familistic values, emphasizing the importance of respect for and duty toward parents and family (Cooper, 1994). Some cultures foster relatively more attention to duty and filial piety than others (Hofstede, 1980), and these differences may affect the degree to which adolescents evaluate their relationships with parents and siblings in terms of the quality of interaction, rather than in terms of family obligations. By contrast, in research on parent-adolescent conflict, for example, Smetana and Gaines (1999) found patterns for African American families that paralleled the results of studies with European American families.

Despite cultural and ethnic differences in the perceived qualities of relationships, however, several studies demonstrate that characteristics of parental behavior toward adolescents are consistently correlated in very similar ways with adolescents' development. In a multiethnic sample of 10,000 adolescents in California and Wisconsin, adolescents' perceptions that their parents were authoritative, rather than authoritarian or neglectful, were correlated with personal maturity, school achievement, and low levels of behavioral and psychological problems (Lamborn et al., 1991; Steinberg et al., 1994; for an overview, see Steinberg, 2001). This correlation held for African Americans, Hispanic Americans, Asian Americans, and European Americans alike. Similarly, perceptions of parental rejection have been found to be correlated with poor individual outcomes in a number of different cultures (Rohner & Pettingill, 1985; Rohner & Rohner, 1981). In other words, although typical patterns of parental control may vary across cultures, family environments that emphasize mutuality, respect for the child's opinions, and training for maturity seem to be most effective in helping adolescents develop attitudes and behaviors appropriate to their society. A recent study of the impact of racial identity and parent-adolescent relationships on adolescent functioning illustrates the likely complexity of these links. With a sample of 521 African American high-school seniors, Caldwell, Zimmerman, Bernat, Sellers, and Notaro (2002) found that correlations between racial identity and maternal support, on one hand, and depressive symptoms and anxiety, on the other, were mediated by perceived stress.

The direct and indirect influences of relationships with parents thus extend to ethnic-minority families. However, the enterprise of amassing information on variations in the nature of these links is still in its infancy. Knowledge of indirect links is especially meager. The next phase of research incorporating ethnic and cultural diversity must attend to the more complex contemporary models of parenting that encompass multiple possible pathways of influence (e.g., Collins et al., 2000).

CONCLUSIONS

Contemporary research with parents and adolescents challenges traditional theoretical and methodological approaches to adolescent development. Conceptually, the growing body of findings on adolescents' close relationships implies that adolescent development, like many other putatively individual changes, can be understood more fully in the context of relationships with significant others and that relationships with parents remain central to these contexts (Allen & Land, 1999; Collins et al., 1997). Methodologically, the findings imply the need for broadening the construct of adolescent outcomes to incorporate interpersonal competencies and developmental changes in them and also to adopt more complex contemporary models of the processes through which parent-adolescent relationships may have an impact. The key task is to understand not only the developing individual but also the interplay between individual growth and change and the nature and developmental significance of relationships with others. This broader perspective thus may allow for a more comprehensive understanding of the nature and course of adolescent development.

REFERENCES

Adams, R., & Laursen, B. (2001). The organization and dynamics of adolescent conflict with parents and friends. *Journal of Marriage and Family, 63,* 97–110.

Allen, J. P., Hauser, S. T., Bell, K. L., & O'Connor, T. G. (1994). Longitudinal assessment of autonomy and relatedness in adolescent-family interactions as predictors of adolescent ego development and self-esteem. *Child Development, 65,* 179–194.

Allen, J. P., & Land, D. (1999). Attachment in adolescence. In J. Cassidy & P. R. Shaver (Eds.), *Handbook of attachment: Theory, research, and clinical applications* (pp. 319–335). New York: Guilford Press.

Almeida, D. M., Wethington, E., & Chandler, A. L. (1999). Daily transmission of tensions between marital dyads and parent-child dyads. *Journal of Marriage and the Family, 61,* 49–61.

Amato, P. R. (1989). Family processes and the competence of adolescents and primary school children. *Journal of Youth and Adolescence, 18,* 39–53.

Amato, P. R., & Keith, B. (1991). Parental divorce and the well-being of children: A meta-analysis. *Psychological Bulletin, 110,* 26–46.

Anderson, E., Hetherington, E. M., Reiss, D., & Howe, G. (1994). Parents' nonshared treatment of siblings and the development of social competence during adolescence. *Journal of Family Psychology, 8,* 303–320.

Andrews, J. A., Hops, H., & Duncan, S. C. (1997). Adolescent modeling of parent substance use: The moderating effect of the relationship with the parent. *Journal of Family Psychology, 11,* 259–270.

Baer, J. (1999). The effects of family structure and SES on family processes in early adolescence. *Journal of Adolescence, 22,* 341–354.

Barber, B. L., & Eccles, J. S. (1992). Long-term influence of divorce and single parenting on adolescent family- and work-related values, behaviors, and aspirations. *Psychological Bulletin, 111,* 108–126.

Barnes, H., & Olson, D. (1985). Parent-adolescent communication and the circumplex model. *Child Development, 56,* 438–447.

Baron, R., & Kenny, D. (1986). The moderator-mediator variable distinction in social psychological research: Conceptual, strategic, and statistical considerations. *Journal of Personality and Social Psychology, 51,* 1173–1182.

Baumrind, D. (1991). Effective parenting during the early adolescent transition. In P. A. Cowan & M. Hetherington (Eds.), *Family transitions* (pp. 111–163). Hillsdale, NJ: Erlbaum.

Becker-Stoll, F., & Fremmer-Bombik, E. (1997, April). *Adolescent-mother interaction and attachment: A longitudinal study.* Paper presented at the biennial meeting of the Society for Research in Child Development, Washington, DC.

Belsky, J., Steinberg, L., & Draper, P. (1991). Childhood experience, interpersonal development, and reproductive strategy: An evolutionary theory of socialization. *Child Development, 62,* 647–670.

Blos, P. (1979). *The adolescent passage.* New York: International Universities Press.

Bolger, K. E., Patterson, C. J., Thompson, W. W., & Kupersmidt, J. B. (1995). Psychosocial adjustment among children experiencing persistent and intermittent family economic hardship. *Child Development, 66,* 1107–1129.

Bosma, H. A., & Gerrits, R. S. (1985). Family functioning and identity status in adolescence. *Journal of Early Adolescence, 5,* 69–80.

Bowlby, J. (1969). *Attachment and loss: Vol. 1. Attachment* (2nd ed.). New York: Basic Books.

Brody, G., & Forehand, R. (1990). Interparental conflict, relationship with the noncustodial father, and adolescent post-divorce adjustment. *Journal of Applied Developmental Psychology, 11,* 139–147.

Brody, G., Stoneman, Z., Flor, D., McCrary, C., Hastings, L., & Conyers, O. (1994). Financial resources, parent psychological functioning, parent-co-caregiving, and early adolescent competence in rural two-parent African-American families. *Child Development, 65,* 590–605.

Bronfenbrenner, U., & Crouter, A. C. (1983). The evolution of environmental models in developmental research. In P. Mussen (General Ed.) & W. Kessen (Vol. Ed.), *Handbook of child psychology* (4th ed., pp. 357–414). New York: Wiley.

Brown, B. B., Mounts, N., Lamborn, S. D., & Steinberg, L. (1993). Parenting practices and peer group affiliation in adolescence. *Child Development, 64,* 467–482.

Buchanan, C. M., Maccoby, E. E., & Dornbusch, S. M. (1991). Caught between parents: Adolescents' experience in divorced homes. *Child Development, 62,* 1008–1030.

Buhrmester, D., & Furman, W. (1987). The development of companionship and intimacy. *Child Development, 58,* 1101–1113.

Buhrmester, D., & Furman, W. (1990). Perceptions of sibling relationships during middle childhood and adolescence. *Child Development, 61,* 1387–1398.

Burns, A., & Dunlop, R. (1998). Parental divorce, parent-child relations, and early adult relationships: A longitudinal Australian study. *Personal Relationships, 5,* 393–407.

Bussell, D. A., Neiderhiser, J. M., Pike, A., Plomin, R., Simmens, S., Howe, G. W., Hetherington, E. M., Carroll, E., & Reiss, D. (1999). Adolescents' relationships to siblings and mothers: A multivariate genetic analysis. *Developmental Psychology, 35,* 1248–1259.

Caldwell, C. H., Zimmerman, M. A., Bernat, D. H., Sellers, R. M., & Notaro, P. C. (2002). Racial identity, maternal support, and psychological distress among African American adolescents. *Child Development, 73,* 1322–1336.

Collins, W. A. (1995). Relationships and development: Family adaptation to individual change. In S. Shulman (Ed.), *Close relationships and socioemotional development* (pp. 128–154). New York: Ablex.

Collins, W. A., Gleason, T., & Sesma, A., Jr. (1997). Internalization, autonomy, and relationships: Development during adolescence. In J. E. Grusec & L. Kuczynski (Eds.), *Parenting and children's internalization of values: A handbook of contemporary theory* (pp. 78–99). New York: Wiley.

Collins, W. A., Maccoby, E., Steinberg, L., Hetherington, E. M., & Bornstein, M. (2000). Contemporary research on parenting: The case for nature and nurture. *American Psychologist, 55,* 218–232.

Collins, W. A., & Madsen, S. D. (2003). Developmental changes in parenting interactions. In L. Kuczynski (Ed.), *Handbook of dynamics in parent-child relations* (pp. 49–66). Beverly Hills, CA: Sage.

Collins, W. A., & Repinski, D. J. (2001). Parents and adolescents as transformers of relationships: Dyadic adaptations to developmental change. In J. R. M. Gerris (Ed.), *Dynamics of parenting: International perspectives on nature and sources of parenting* (pp. 429–443). Leuven, Netherlands: Garant.

Collins, W. A., & Russell, G. (1991). Mother-child and father-child relationships in middle childhood and adolescence: A developmental analysis. *Developmental Review, 11,* 99–136.

Conger, R. D., Conger, K. J., Elder, G. H., Jr., Lorenz, F. O., Simons, R. L., & Whitbeck, L. (1992). Family process model of economic hardship and adjustment of early adolescent boys. *Child Development, 63,* 526–541.

Conger, R. D., Conger, K. J., Elder, G. H., Jr., Lorenz, F. O., Simons, R. L., & Whitbeck, L. (1993). Family economic stress and adjustment of early adolescent girls. *Developmental Psychology, 29,* 206–219.

Connell, J. P., Spencer, M. B., & Aber, J. L. (1994). Educational risk and resilience in African-American youth: Context, self, action, and outcomes in school. *Child Development, 65,* 493–506.

Cook, W. L. (1994). A structural equation model of dyadic relationships within the family system. *Journal of Consulting and Clinical Psychology, 62,* 500–509.

Cooper, C. R. (1994). Cultural perspectives on continuity and change in adolescents' relationships. In R. Montemayor, G. R. Adams, & T. P. Gullotta (Eds.), *Personal relationships during adolescence* (pp. 78–100). Thousand Oaks, CA: Sage.

Crouter, A. C., Bumpus, M. F., Maguire, M. C., & McHale, S. M. (1999). Linking parents' work pressure and adolescents' well-being: Insights into dynamics in dual-earner families. *Developmental Psychology, 35,* 1453–1461.

Darling, N., & Steinberg, L. (1993). Parenting style as context: An integrative model. *Psychological Bulletin, 113*(3), 487–496.

Davis, B. T., Hops, H., Alpert, A., & Sheeberg, L. (1998). Child responses to parental conflict and their effect on adjustment: A study of triadic relations. *Journal of Family Psychology, 12,* 163–177.

Eisenberg, N. (1990). Prosocial development in early and mid-adolescence. In R. Montemayor, G. Adams, & T. Gullotta (Eds.), *From childhood to adolescence: A transitional period?* (pp. 240–268). Newbury Park, CA: Sage.

Elder, G. H., Jr., Eccles, J. S., Ardelt, M., & Lord, S. (1995). Inner-city parents under economic pressure: Perspectives on the strategies of parenting. *Journal of Marriage and the Family, 57,* 771–784.

Erikson, E. H. (1968). *Identity: Youth and crisis.* New York: Norton.

Fauber, R., Forehand, R., Thomas, A. M., & Wierson, M. (1990). A mediational model of the impact of marital conflict on adolescent adjustment in intact and divorced families: The role of disrupted parenting. *Child Development, 61,* 1112–1123.

Feldman, S. S., & Rosenthal, D. A. (1991). Age expectations of behavioral autonomy in Hong Kong, Australian and American youth: The influence of family variables and adolescents' values. *International Journal of Psychology, 26,* 1–23.

Felner, R., Brand, S., DuBois, D., Adan, A., Mulhall, P., & Evans, E. (1995). Socioeconomic disadvantage, proximal environmental experiences, and socio-emotional and academic adjustment in early adolescence: Investigation of a mediated effects models. *Child Development, 66,* 774–792.

Flanagan, C. A., & Eccles, J. S. (1993). Changes in parents' work status and adolescents' adjustment at school. *Child Development, 64,* 246–257.

Flouri, E., & Buchanan, A. (2002). What predicts good relationships with parents in adolescence and partners in adult life: Findings from the 1958 British birth cohort. *Journal of Family Psychology, 16,* 186–198.

Freud, A. (1958). Adolescence. In R. Eissler, A. Freud, H. Hartman, & M. Kris (Eds.), *Psychoanalytic study of the child* (Vol. 13, pp. 255–278). New York: International Universities Press.

Freud, S. (1949). *Group psychology and the analysis of the ego.* New York: Bantam. (Original work published 1921)

Fuhrman, T., & Holmbeck, G. N. (1995). A contextual-moderator analysis of emotional autonomy and adjustment in adolescence. *Child Development, 66,* 793–811.

Fuligni, A. J. (1998). The adjustment of children from immigrant families. *Current Directions in Psychological Science, 7,* 99–103.

Fuligni, A. J., & Eccles, J. S. (1993). Perceived parent-child relationships and early adolescents' orientation toward peers. *Developmental Psychology, 29,* 622–632.

Furman, W., & Buhrmester, D. (1989). Age and sex differences in perceptions of networks of personal relationships. *Child Development, 63,* 103–152.

Furstenberg, F., Jr. (2001). The sociology of adolescence and youth in the 1990s: A critical commentary. In R. M. Milardo (Ed.), *Understanding families into the new millennium: A decade in review* (pp. 115–129). Minneapolis: National Council on Family Relations.

Galambos, N. L., & Maggs, J. L. (1991). Out-of-school care of young adolescents and self-reported behavior. *Developmental Psychology, 27,* 644–655.

Garber, J., & Little, S. (1999). Predictors of competence among offspring of depressed mothers. *Journal of Adolescent Research, 14,* 44–71.

Gauze, C., Bukowski, W. M., Aquan-Assee, J., & Sippola, L. K. (1996). Interactions between family environment and friendship and associations with self-perceived well-being during early adolescence. *Child Development, 67,* 2201–2216.

Ge, X., Conger, R. D., Lorenz, F. O., Elder, G. H., Jr., Montague, R. B., & Simons, R. L. (1992). Linking family economic hardship to adolescent distress. *Journal of Research on Adolescence, 2,* 351–378.

Gonzales, N. A., Caucé, A. M., & Mason, C. A. (1996). Interobserver agreement in the assessment of parental behavior and parent-adolescent conflict: African American mothers, daughters, and independent observers. *Child Development, 67,* 1483–1498.

Gottfried, A. E., Gottfried, A. W., & Bathurst, K. (2002). Maternal and dual-earner employment status and parenting. In M. Bornstein (Ed.), *Handbook of parenting* (Vol. 2, pp. 207–230). Mahwah, NJ: Erlbaum.

Graham-Bermann, S. A., Cutler, S. E., Litzenberger, B. W., & Schwartz, W. E. (1994). Perceived conflict and violence in childhood sibling relationships and later emotional adjustment. *Journal of Family Psychology, 8,* 85–97.

Gray, M., & Steinberg, L. (1999). Unpacking authoritative parenting: Reassessing a multidimensional construct. *Journal of Marriage and the Family, 61,* 574–587.

Grotevant, H. D. (1998). Adolescent development in family contexts. In W. Damon & N. Eisenberg (Eds.), *Handbook of child psychology: Vol. 3. Social, emotional, and personality development* (5th ed., pp. 1097–1150). New York: Wiley.

Grotevant, H. D., & Cooper, C. R. (1985). Patterns of interaction in family relationships and the development of identity formation in adolescence. *Child Development, 51,* 415–428.

Grotevant, H. D., & Cooper, C. R. (1986). Individuation in family relationships: A perspective on individual differences in the development of identity and role-taking in adolescence. *Human Development, 29,* 82–100.

Grotevant, H. D., & Cooper, C. R. (1998). Individuality and connectedness in adolescent development: Review and prospects for research on identity, relationships, and context. In E. Skoe & A. von der Lippe (Eds.), *Personality development in adolescence: A cross national and life span perspective* (pp. 3–37). London: Routledge.

Grusec, J., & Goodnow, J. J. (1994). The impact of parental discipline methods on the child's internalization of values: A reconceptualization of current points of view. *Developmental Psychology, 30,* 4–19.

Grusec, J., Goodnow, J. J., & Kuczynski, L. (2000). New directions in analyses of parenting contributions to children's acquisition of values. *Child Development, 71,* 205–211.

Harkness, S., & Super, C. (2002). Culture and parenting. In M. Bornstein (Ed.), *Handbook of parenting* (Vol. 2, pp. 253–280). Mahwah, NJ: Erlbaum.

Hartup, W. W., & Laursen, B. (1991). Relationships as developmental contexts. In R. Cohen & A. W. Siegel (Eds.), *Context and development* (pp. 253–279). Hillsdale, NJ: Erlbaum.

Hauser, S. T., Powers, S., & Noam, G. (1991). *Adolescents and their families: Paths of ego development.* New York: Free Press.

Hetherington, E. M. (1999). Social capital and the development of youth from nondivorced, divorced, and remarried families. In W. A. Collins & B. Laursen (Eds.), *Relationships as developmental contexts: The Minnesota symposia on child psychology* (Vol. 30, pp. 177–209). Mahwah, NJ: Erlbaum.

Hetherington, E. M., & Clingempeel, W. G. (Eds.). (1992). Coping with marital transitions: A family systems perspective. *Monographs of the Society for Research in Child Development, 57* (Serial No. 227).

Hetherington, E. M., & Stanley-Hagan, M. (2002). Parenting in divorced and remarried families. In M. Bornstein (Ed.), *Handbook of parenting* (Vol. 3, pp. 287–315). Mahwah, NJ: Erlbaum.

Hill, J. P. (1988). Adapting to menarche: Familial control and conflict. In M. R. Gunnar & W. A. Collins (Eds.), *Development during the transition to adolescence: Minnesota symposia on child psychology* (Vol. 21, pp. 43–77). Hillsdale, NJ: Erlbaum.

Hodgkinson, H. (1985). *All one system: Demographics of education, kindergarten through graduate school.* Washington, DC: Institute of Educational Leadership.

Hoffman, L. W., & Youngblade, L. (1999). *Mothers at work: Effects on children's well-being.* New York: Cambridge University Press.

Hofstede, G. (1980). *Culture's consequences: International differences in work-related values.* Beverly Hills, CA: Sage.

Holmbeck, G. N. (1996). A model of family relational transformations during the transition to adolescence: Parent-adolescent conflict and adaptation. In J. A. Graber, J. Brooks-Gunn, & A. C. Petersen (Eds.), *Transitions through adolescence: Interpersonal domains and contexts* (pp. 167–200). Mahwah, NJ: Erlbaum.

Jackson, E. P., Dunham, R. M., & Kidwell, J. S. (1990). The effects of gender and of family cohesion and adaptability on identity status. *Journal of Adolescent Research, 5,* 161–174.

Kamptner, N. L. (1988). Identity development in late adolescence: Causal modeling of social and familial influences. *Journal of Youth and Adolescence, 17,* 493–514.

Keith, J. G., Nelson, C. S., Schlabach, J. H., & Thompson, C. J. (1990). The relationship between parental employment and three measures of early adolescent responsibility: Family-related, personal, and social. *Journal of Early Adolescence, 10,* 399–415.

Kelley, H. H., Berscheid, E., Christensen, A., Harvey, J. H., Huston, T. L., Levinger, G., McClintock, E., Peplau, L. A., & Peterson, D. R. (1983). *Close relationships.* New York: Freeman.

Kerr, M., & Stattin, H. (2000). What parents know, how they know it, and several forms of adolescent adjustment: Further support for a reinterpretation of monitoring. *Developmental Psychology, 36,* 366–380.

Kohlberg, L. (1969). Stage and sequence: The cognitive-developmental approach to socialization. In D. A. Goslin (Ed.), *Handbook of socialization theory and research* (pp. 347–480). Skokie, IL: Rand-McNally.

Kohn, M. L. (1979). The effects of social class on parental values and practices. In D. Reiss & H. A. Hoffman (Eds.), *The American family: Dying or developing* (pp. 45–68). New York: Plenum.

Lamborn, S. D., Mounts, N. S., Steinberg, L., & Dornbusch, S. M. (1991). Patterns of competence and adjustment among adolescents from authoritative, authoritarian, indulgent, and neglectful families. *Child Development, 62,* 1049–1065.

Larson, R. W., Richards, M. H., Moneta, G., Holmbeck, G., & Duckett, E. (1996). Changes in adolescents' daily interactions with their families from ages 10 to 18: Disengagement and transformation. *Developmental Psychology, 32,* 744–754.

Larson, R. W., Wilson, S., Brown, B. B., Furstenberg, F. F., Jr., & Verma, S. (2002). Changes in adolescents' interpersonal experiences: Are they being prepared for adult relationships in the twenty-first century? *Journal of Research on Adolescence, 12,* 31–68.

Laursen, B. (1995). Conflict and social interaction in adolescent relationships. *Journal of Research on Adolescence, 5,* 55–70.

Laursen, B., & Bukowski, W. M. (1997). A developmental guide to the organisation of close relationships. *International Journal of Behavioral Development, 21,* 747–770.

Laursen, B., & Collins, W. A. (1994). Interpersonal conflict during adolescence. *Psychological Bulletin, 115,* 197–209.

Laursen, B., & Collins, W. A. (in press). Parent-child communication during adolescence. In A. Vangelisti (Ed.), *Handbook of family communication.* Mahwah, NJ: Erlbaum.

Laursen, B., Coy, K. C., & Collins, W. A. (1998). Reconsidering changes in parent-child conflict across adolescence: A meta-analysis. *Child Development, 69,* 817–832.

Laursen, B., & Williams, V. (1997). Perceptions of interdependence and closeness in family and peer relationships among adolescents with and without romantic partners. In S. Shulman & W. A. Collins (Eds.), *Romantic relationships in adolescence: Developmental Perspectives. New Directions for Child Development* (No. 78, pp. 3–20). San Francisco: Jossey-Bass.

Loeber, R., Drinkwater, M., Yin, Y., Anderson, S. J., Schmidt, L. C., & Crawford, A. (2000). Stability of family interaction from ages 6 to 18. *Journal of Abnormal Child Psychology, 28,* 353–369.

Maccoby, E. E. (1984). Middle childhood in the context of the family. In W. A. Collins (Ed.), *Development during middle childhood: The years from six to twelve* (pp. 184–239). Washington, DC: National Academy Press.

Maccoby, E. E. (1992). The role of parents in the socialization of children: An historical overview. *Developmental Psychology, 28,* 1006–1017.

Maccoby, E. E., & Martin, J. A. (1983). Socialization in the context of the family: Parent-child interaction. In P. H. Mussen (Ed.), *Handbook of child psychology* (Vol. 4, pp. 1–101). New York: Wiley.

McLoyd, V. C. (1998). Socioeconomic disadvantage and child development. *American Psychologist, 53,* 185–204.

Montemayor, R. (1983). Parents and adolescents in conflict: All families some of the time and some families most of the time. *Journal of Early Adolescence, 3,* 83–103.

Needle, R. H., Su, S., & Doherty, W. J. (1990). Divorce, remarriage, and adolescent substance use: A prospective longitudinal study. *Journal of Marriage and the Family, 52,* 157–169.

Noller, P. (1994). Relationships with parents in adolescence: Process and outcome. In R. Montemayor, G. Adams, & T. Gullotta (Eds.), *Personal relationships during adolescence* (pp. 37–78). Thousand Oaks, CA: Sage.

Noller, P., Feeney, J. A., Sheehan, G., & Peterson, C. (2000). Marital conflict patterns: Links with family conflict and family members' perceptions of one another. *Personal Relationships, 7,* 79–94.

Offer, D. (1969). *The psychological world of the teenager.* London: Basic Books.

Patterson, G. R., DeBaryshe, B., & Ramsey, E. (1989). A developmental perspective on antisocial behavior. *American Psychologist, 44,* 329–335.

Quintana, S. M., & Lapsley, D. K. (1987). Adolescent attachment and ego identity: A structural equations approach to the continuity of adaptation. *Journal of Adolescent Research, 2,* 393–409.

Reis, H. T., Collins, W. A., & Berscheid, E. (2000). The relationship context of human behavior and development. *Psychological Bulletin, 126,* 844–872.

Rhodes, J., Grossman, J., & Resch, N. (2000). Agents of change: Pathways through which mentoring relationships influence adolescents' academic adjustment. *Child Development, 71,* 1662–1671.

Rohner, R. P., & Pettengill, S. M. (1985). Perceived parental acceptance-rejection and parental control among Korean adolescents. *Child Development, 56,* 524–528.

Rohner, R. P., & Rohner, E. C. (1981). Parental acceptance-rejection and parental control: Cross-cultural codes. *Ethnology, 20,* 245–260.

Rosenthal, D. A., Demetriou, A., & Efklides, A. (1989). A cross-national study of the influence of culture on conflict between parents and adolescents. *International Journal of Behavioral Development, 12,* 207–219.

Rutter, M., Graham, P., Chadwick, O., & Yule, W. (1976). Adolescent turmoil: Fact or fiction? *Journal of Child Psychology and Psychiatry, 17,* 35–56.

Seginer, R. (1998). Adolescents' perceptions of relationships with older sibling in the context of other close relationships. *Journal of Research on Adolescence, 8,* 287–308.

Seiffge-Krenke, I. (1999). Families with daughters, families with sons: Different challenges for family relationships and marital satisfaction? *Journal of Youth and Adolescence, 28,* 325–342.

Selman, R. (1980). *The development of interpersonal understanding.* New York: Academic Press.

Shantz, C. U. (1987). Conflict between children. *Child Development, 58,* 283–305.

Silverberg, S. B., & Steinberg, L. (1990). Psychological well-being of parents with early adolescent children. *Developmental Psychology, 26,* 658–666.

Simmons, R. G., & Blyth, D. A. (1987). *Moving into adolescence: The impact of pubertal change and school context.* New York: de Gruyter.

Smetana, J. G. (1988). Adolescents' and parents' conceptions of parental authority. *Child Development, 59,* 321–335.

Smetana, J. G. (1989). Adolescents' and parents' reasoning about actual family conflict. *Child Development, 60,* 1052–1067.

Smetana, J. G. (1996). Adolescent-parent conflict: Implications for adaptive and maladaptive development. In D. Cicchetti & S. L. Toth (Eds.), *Rochester Symposium on Developmental Psychopathology: Vol. 7. Adolescence: Opportunities and challenges* (pp. 1–46). Rochester: University of Rochester.

Smetana, J. G., & Gaines, C. (1999). Adolescent-parent conflict in middle-class African American families. *Child Development, 70,* 1447–1463.

Smetana, J. G., Yau, J., & Hanson, S. (1991). Conflict resolution in families with adolescents. *Journal of Research on Adolescence, 1,* 189–206.

Smetana, J. G., Yau, J., Restrepo, A., & Braeges, J. L. (1991). Adolescent-parent conflict in married an divorced families. *Developmental Psychology, 27,* 1000–1010.

Smith, P. K., & Drew, L. M. (2002). Grandparenthood. In M. Bornstein (Ed.), *Handbook of parenting* (Vol. 3, pp. 141–171). Mahwah, NJ: Erlbaum.

Sroufe, L. A., & Fleeson, J. (1988). The coherence of family relationships. In R. A. Hinde & J. Stevenson-Hinde (Eds.), *Relationships within families: Mutual influences* (pp. 27–47). Oxford, England: Clarendon Press.

Stattin, H., & Kerr, M. (2000). Parental monitoring: A reinterpretation. *Child Development, 71,* 1072–1085.

Steinberg, L. (1981). Transformations in family relations at puberty. *Developmental Psychology, 17,* 833–840.

Steinberg, L. (2001). We know some things: Adolescent-parent relationships in retrospect and prospect. *Journal of Research on Adolescence, 11,* 1–19.

Steinberg, L., Lamborn, S. D., Darling, N., Mounts, N. S., & Dornbusch, S. M. (1994). Over-time changes in adjustment and competence among adolescents from authoritative, authoritarian, indulgent, and neglectful families. *Child Development, 65,* 754–770.

Steinberg, L., Lamborn, S., Dornbusch, S., & Darling, N. (1992). Impact of parenting practices on adolescent achievement: Authoritative parenting, school involvement, and encouragement to succeed. *Child Development, 63,* 1266–1281.

Steinberg, L., & Silk, J. S. (2002). Parenting adolescents. In M. H. Bornstein (Ed.), *Handbook of parenting* (Vol. 1, pp. 103–134). Mahwah, NJ: Erlbaum.

Taylor, R. D., Casten, R., & Flickinger, S. M. (1993). Influence of kinship social support on the parenting experiences and psychosocial adjustment of African-American adolescents. *Developmental Psychology, 29,* 382–388.

Updegraff, K. A., McHale, S. M., & Crouter, A. C. (2000). Adolescents' sex-typed friendship experiences: Does having a sister versus a brother matter? *Child Development, 71,* 1597–1610.

Vuchinich, S. (1987). Starting and stopping spontaneous family conflicts. *Journal of Marriage and the Family, 49,* 591–601.

Vuchinich, S., Emery, R., & Cassidy, J. (1988). Family members as third parties in dyadic family conflict: Strategies, alliances, and outcomes. *Child Development, 59,* 1293–1302.

Vuchinich, S., Hetherington, E. M., Vuchinich, R., & Clingempeel, W. G. (1991). Parent-child interaction and gender differences in early adolescents' adaptations to stepfamilies. *Developmental Psychology, 27,* 618–626.

Wadsworth, M. E., & Compas, B. E. (2002). Coping with family conflict and economic strain: The adolescent perspective. *Journal of Research on Adolescence, 12,* 243–274.

Walker, L., & Taylor, J. (1991). Family interactions and the development of moral reasoning. *Child Development, 62,* 264–283.

Youniss, J. (1980). *Parents and peers in social development.* Chicago: University of Chicago Press.

Chapter 12

ADOLESCENTS' RELATIONSHIPS WITH PEERS

B. Bradford Brown

Ever since G. Stanley Hall's (1904) seminal work a century ago, peer relationships have been regarded as a central feature of American adolescence. From the early years through the present, researchers have remained decidedly ambivalent about the effects of peers on American adolescents (Berndt, 1999), but few deny the significance of peer relationships and interactions during this stage of life. Do peers comprise a supportive social context that fosters identity and helps to socialize youth into adult roles, or do they form an arena for frivolous and delinquent activity, with patterns of interaction that undermine autonomy and self-esteem? In this chapter I overview some of the major features of peer relations that have occupied researchers' attention over the past 10 or 15 years. Insights emerging from their studies underscore the complexity of adolescent peer relations and clarify the conditions under which peer interactions foster healthy or unhealthy development.

Like other major social arenas for adolescents, the peer context is multifaceted. In fact, one of the hallmarks of adolescent peer relationships is that they increase markedly in intensity and complexity. This is reflected in the diversity of topics that have occupied researchers' attention. Most investigations concentrate on one of four aspects of peer relations. The first involves characteristics of the individual that are expected to affect peer interaction. In addition to demographic characteristics (gender, ethnicity, socioeconomic background), researchers have examined general measures of social skills as well as specific traits or behaviors, such as aggression, shyness, or rejection sensitivity. They have also employed sociometric techniques to assign adolescents to sociometric categories as popular among their peers, rejected, neglected, or controversial (both well liked and highly disliked by peers). One interesting finding, for example, is that youth rated high in aggression by peers tend to be regarded either as very popular or very unpopular during early adolescence—a contrast to the elementary school years, when aggression is more clearly associated with rejected peer status.

Characteristics of relationship partners constitute a second focus of study. This includes the age of friends or romantic partners, as well as their attitudes and behaviors. A common assumption is that the attitudes and activities of close associates rub off on adolescents, prompting parents to be concerned that their child will fall into bad company and be misled into misbehavior. For example, Brendgen, Vitaro, and Bukowski (2000a) reported that friends' level of deviance was significantly associated with rates of internalizing and externalizing behavior among early adolescents. Such findings are commonly taken as evidence of friends' capacity to foster deviant behavior among youth, but as the authors of this study note, there are other explanations for the association.

A third, less common focus of study involves characteristics of relationships (rather than individuals in relationships). Several scholars have proposed a list of characteristics by which friendship can be defined, or features that reflect its quality (see Berndt, 1996; Hartup, 1993). Others have derived measures of these features in order to evaluate how healthy an adolescent's relationships are (e.g., Bukowski, Hoza, & Boivin, 1994) or how friendship features are associated with the young person's social and psychological characteristics (reviewed by Rubin, Bukowski, & Parker, 1998). One intriguing question in this area is whether deviant youth display more inadequate friendships (in terms of intimacy, support, trust, conflict, etc.) than do nondeviant youth. The preponderance of evidence suggests that delinquents manifest many positive features in their friendships, but that they also display more negative features than nondelinquents do (Dishion, Andrews, & Crosby, 1995; Houtzager & Baerveldt, 1999). Another aspect of relationships to which scholars have paid considerable attention is stability: how frequently and easily adolescents change relationship partners. Investigators have become interested not only in simple rates of stability but also in factors that affect it.

A final area, also receiving increasing attention, involves relationship dynamics: what goes on during friendship interactions. Brown, Way, and Duff (1999), for example, offered insights on power dynamics in adolescent girls' relationships, based on conversations with a small sample of urban females. Conflict resolution styles have become an issue of increasing interest (Laursen, 1996, 2001). Classic studies of peer pressure based on laboratory experiments (e.g., Costanzo & Shaw, 1966) or self-report questionnaires (Clasen & Brown, 1985) have given way to more sophisticated analyses of attitude and behavior cuing in observations of interactions among close friends or small groups (Dishion, Spracklen, Andrews, & Patterson, 1996; Eder, Evans, & Parker, 1995).

These four aspects of peer relations, or similar categorical schemes, have been used to organize a review of empirical work on child or adolescent peer relations (Hartup, 1996; Rubin et al., 1998). Likewise, many reviews have focused on a single type of peer relationship or have featured separate sections for each type of relationship. In designing more sophisticated studies, however, investigators are beginning to cut across these categories or consider more than one type of relationship. Berndt (1999), for example, proposed a theory of friend influence based on the combination of the second and third aspects: characteristics of friends and characteristics of friendships. Furman (1999), among many others, assessed the connections between young people's relationships with friends and romantic partners. Considering this, it seems more sensible to focus this review on themes in recent research that cut across traditional categories of study or types of relationships.

There is emerging evidence of substantial variability in adolescent peer relationships across cultural contexts. Some cultures severely restrict adolescent interaction with age mates, whereas others are organized to emphasize peer relationships (see Brown, Larson, & Saraswathi, 2002). Peer interaction is extensive in most Western European and European American contexts. So, too, is the literature about peers, and it is the focus of attention in this chapter. Also, like the research itself, I concentrate on informal relationships—those that are organized by adolescents themselves, rather than by adults or social institutions. I have little to say about kin-based peer relationships (with siblings and cousins) because variability in partners' age and family position make it difficult to discern which of these can be legitimately classified as peer relationships. I also have little to say about sexual relationships and behavior. These topics are addressed in detail in other chapters in this volume.

I begin by sketching the organization of peer relationships during adolescence in order to give readers a sense of the full scope of this social context. This is followed by brief comments about theory and methodology employed in empirical investigations. Then, after overviewing rates of participation in various types of peer relationships, I assess research concerning five major themes apparent in recent research. These themes cut across the categories of investigation already mentioned, as well as the various types and levels of peer interaction that are presented in the next section. Rather than presenting an exhaustive review of research, my intention is to highlight emerging insights and identify important issues to be addressed in subsequent research.

ORGANIZATION OF PEER RELATIONS IN ADOLESCENCE

The world of peers is a challenging social context, especially at adolescence because it grows more complex and layered. Scholars have noted at least three different levels of peer interaction (Brown, 1999a; Furman & Simon, 1998; Rubin et al., 1998). First is the dyadic level, dominated by individual friendships, which individuals negotiate practically from the moment they begin interacting with peers in toddlerhood. Friendships still are the focus of most research on adolescent peer relations. Recently, however, investigators have made us aware of two other important dyadic relationships in this stage: romantic partners and mutual enemies (including bully-victim pairs).

A second level, also apparent prior to adolescence, is comprised of small groups of peers who regularly interact with each other. Sometimes referred to as cliques, these groups involve an interweave of relationships that vary in closeness, duration, and mutual regard or affection. Freed from the close supervision of adults, adolescent groups can congeal around antisocial as well as prosocial behavior patterns. Thus, in adolescence, one can see the emergence of delinquent gangs, along with friendship cliques or special interest groups that are not as oriented toward violating social norms.

A third level of peer interaction is not readily apparent before adolescence. It involves what are frequently referred to as crowds and is contingent on adolescents gathering in such large numbers that it is no longer feasible for everyone to know each other personally. The move from self-contained classrooms in elementary schools to larger secondary schools with a constantly shifting set of peers (from class to class) fosters the emergence of peer crowds in North America and some European nations (see, e.g., Thurlow, 2001). So does the expansion of adolescents' social space beyond the neighborhood to the broader community. Peer groups at this level are more cognitive than behavioral, more symbolic than concrete and interactional (Foley, 1990). They involve identification of adolescents who share a similar image or reputation among peers or who have a common feature such as ethnicity or neighborhood, even if they do not consider each other friends or spend much time interacting with each other. This level is deftly illustrated in a series of popular motion pictures (e.g., *The Breakfast Club, Finding Forrester, Heathers, Ten Things I Hate About You*) that, often in their opening scenes, catalog the different crowds into which adolescents are categorized in a particular school or neighborhood.

At each of these levels, adolescents encounter formal relationships (organized and supervised by adults) as well as informal ones. Formal dyads, for example, would include lab partners or a peer tutor and tutee. These are rarely studied because they tend to be short-lived relationships in which adolescents do not have a strong investment (but see Karcher & Lindwall, in press, for an exception). Formal small groups are best illustrated by sports teams, but they would also include other school- or community-based extracurricular activities, as well as youth groups sponsored by religious or community organizations. Formal relationships at the more abstract level of peer crowds are more difficult to discern. Sometimes, an entire school will earn a reputation that is nurtured by the adults in charge, but such instances are rarely the subject of systematic investigation.

The preponderance of research has been directed at informal peer relations, especially friendships, romantic attachments, cliques, and crowds. Adolescents are accorded much more freedom in initiating and pursuing these affiliations than they encounter in formal relationships. Thus, they may be regarded as a truer manifestation of peer interaction and influence. For this reason, they comprise the focus of attention in this chapter.

Four features of this social system must be emphasized. First, the organization just outlined is contingent on the broader cultural and social context in which adolescents live. Even within the United States there is considerable variability, from community to community, in the degree to which the peer system is fully articulated. Adolescents in small, residentially stable communities may find that crowds never emerge because the peer group remains small enough for everyone to know each other personally. Youth whose families discourage dating may not experience meaningful romantic alliances until late adolescence or emerging adulthood. Traditionally oriented Mexican-American families expect their youth to associate primarily with kin (Falicov, 1996), making it much less likely that they will experience the intense friendships and extensive interaction in (nonkin) friendship groups that are characteristic of most European American adolescents.

Second, within this general organization is a very dynamic peer system. At every level, relationships are constantly changing. Fewer than half of reciprocated best friendships survive over a period of one year, although the two partners may remain close friends (Connolly, Furman, & Konarski, 2000; Degirmencioglu, Urberg, Tolson, & Richard, 1998). Most romantic relationships in early adolescence last a matter of weeks or months (Feiring, 1999). Their average duration does grow across the rest of adolescence, but when teenagers dissolve one romantic tie, it is often months before they begin a new one (Connolly et al., 2000). According to social network researchers (with the exception of Ennett & Bauman, 1996), it is quite unusual for a friendship group to remain completely intact over the space of one year or less. Even using liberal criteria of stability (e.g., at least 50% of the initial group members remain linked to each other, at second testing, in social network analyses), studies indicate that between one third and one half of groups dissolve over the course of an academic year (Cairns & Cairns, 1994; Degirmencioglu et al., 1998; Ryan, 2001). Over the course of 6 months or 1 year, one out of two adolescents experience a change in group status—whether one is a core member of a clique, a peripheral member of two or more groups (liaison), or unconnected to any friendship group (isolate); the liaison status is especially unstable (Ennett & Bauman, 1996).

Crowd types may be somewhat more enduring in that certain prototypic crowds—popular youth, athletically oriented groups, loners or nerds, drug-using or deviantly oriented groups, academically focused youth—are usually found across communities and even historical periods (Brown, 1990). However, other crowd types are more school- or era-specific, and within one community the constellation of groups may shift substantially between middle school and high school (see, e.g., Kinney, 1993). The limited evidence available also suggests that most youth alter their crowd affiliations or orientations across adolescence (Kinney, 1993; Strouse, 1999).

Third, a tacit assumption among researchers is that adolescents form coherent, integrated social networks with peers. This assumption makes it legitimate to ask youth to provide a general assessment of their friends or the group they hang out with on a given dimension. It also justifies the construction of sociograms in which adolescents are assigned a single position within a social network. From my observations working with teenagers, I sense that many have multiple, discrete groups of friends. One group may share an activity interest with the young person, another may serve as the basis for socializing, and yet another can be comprised of teammates in a school sport. Adolescents sometimes resist attempts to integrate these groups. When asked why he did not invite his friends to come to church youth group activities, one teenager whom I know replied, "I don't want my worlds colliding. When I'm here [at youth group] I don't have to be the same person that I am with my school friends; I don't want to mess that up." Indeed, one of the tasks of adolescence is to learn how to manage these disparate spheres of social interaction and influence. This is good preparation for adulthood, when individuals routinely maintain separate networks of relationships with coworkers, neighbors, parents of their children's friends, and so on. Researchers do not yet seem to appreciate this facet of adolescent (and adult) peer relationships.

A final important feature of the peer social system is the degree to which relationships at one level are embedded in or affected by interactions at other levels. Dyadic relationships exist within the context of a larger network of associates, who have the capacity to influence the course of a friendship or romantic tie. Macleod (1995) observed a markedly different tone of conversation between two close friends when they were alone (just with the ethnographer) as opposed to surrounded by other members of their friendship clique. Connolly et al. (2000) discovered that adolescents initiated romantic relationships earlier if their friendship network contained a mix of boys and girls rather than just members of their own gender. Stone and Brown (1998) reported that the characteristics an adolescent associated with a particular crowd varied as a function of the adolescent's own crowd affiliation.

At a broader level, the peer system itself is embedded within other social contexts, such as the school or neighborhood. Tracking systems and the organization of extracurricular activities affect the types of peers to which adolescents are exposed (Schofield, 1981). Drawing students from a broad geographical area, as opposed to the immediate neighborhood, affects the ease with which adolescents maintain school-based peer relationships once the school day is over (DuBois & Hirsch, 1990).

Some of these features and their effects on individuals' peer relationships are reflected in emerging themes that I discuss. First, however, some features of the theory and methodology underlying the research should be considered.

A WORD ABOUT THEORY AND METHOD

In the early portion of the 20th century, following the lead of G. Stanley Hall, most research on adolescence was based on psychoanalytic theory. Freud had little to say about peer relationships. At midcentury, however, one of his followers, Harry Stack Sullivan (1953), offered an elaboration of psychoanalytic theory with much more of a peer focus. According to Sullivan, the intense, emotionally charged, same-sex "chumships" that dominated preadolescence were forerunners of sexually charged, other-sex, romantic relationships in adolescence. This directed researchers to pay most attention to friendships in early adolescence and to sexual liaisons in the later stages of this period. Jean Piaget (1958) added a cognitive perspective on how friendships promoted young people's capacity for social perspective taking. Later, Youniss and Smollar (1985) provided a synthesis of these two theories, illustrating the advantages that equality-based peer relationships offered over the hierarchically organized "relationships of constraint" that young people had with parents and other adults. These theoretical perspectives, especially Sullivan's, dominated the work on peer relations throughout the later 1900s.

In the early 1990s, Wyndol Furman (1993) urged the derivation of a more comprehensive theory to guide research on adolescent peer relations (especially research on friendship). None has yet emerged, but this does not imply a lack of progress in understanding peer relations. In fact, it seems doubtful that a context as diverse and complicated as the world of peers at adolescence can be captured effectively under a single theoretical umbrella. In recent years, investigators have drawn effectively on a variety of conceptual models from various academic disciplines to guide their research in this area. Theories from sociology, social psychology, cognitive psychology, and developmental psychology are readily apparent, underscoring the multidisciplinary approach that is needed to capture the multifaceted features of adolescent peer relationships.

Something similar can be observed with regard to methodological approaches to the topic. Certain methodologies have been especially prominent. Research on popularity and peer status has relied primarily on sociometric techniques of peer nominations or ratings (Cillessen & Bukowski, 2000). These techniques are well suited to studying children in closed peer systems such as self-contained school classrooms, but they are not as effective in the larger and more open system encountered by North American adolescents—especially in large, comprehensive high schools. This is one reason why studies of popularity and peer rejection in adolescence tend to focus on youth in the early phases of this life stage.

Most studies of friendship and romantic relationships are based on self-report data. Because much of the significant interaction in these relationships occurs outside of public view—or at least away from the eyes of adults—it seems necessary to rely on adolescents to tell us what goes on with friends and lovers. Unfortunately, adolescents are not reliable reporters of their experiences in dyadic or group relationships. Often, they distort reports about friends to exaggerate similarity with themselves (Kandel & Andrews, 1987) and portray their status in peer groups in self-aggrandizing ways (Stone & Brown, 1999). Investigators of friendship groups and peer crowds have relied either on ethnographic approaches or social network data. Social network analysis offers a more reliable approach to identifying the full range of groups and individuals' positions within them, but ethnography provides richer detail about the dynamic features of group interaction and changes in membership.

Each of these techniques is still widely used, but they have been supplemented by other approaches. An increasing number of investigators conduct longitudinal studies that can chart more effectively the transformations in group membership and the causal associations among variables of interest. Some laboratory studies, with careful analyses of videotaped interactions, have provided important new insights about interaction processes, especially within dyads (e.g., Dishion et al., 1996). The laboratory can only simulate real-world interaction contexts, however, and it can simulate only a circumscribed range of such contexts. Nonetheless, the laboratory offers opportunities to catch nonverbal cues and other subtleties that cannot be measured effectively through other methodologies.

Studies of group dynamics (cliques or crowds) have been conducted most effectively through ethnographic observation. This approach allows investigators to study groups in situ but features shortcomings as well. It is a time-consuming process that yields information on only a small portion of the peer network in any location. There is no guarantee that youth will act the same way when the ethnographer is around as they do when they are not being observed. Ethnographers often have to face ethical dilemmas, such as passively allowing youth to participate in risky or illegal behavior (or perhaps even contributing to such behavior) in order to build and maintain a trusting bond with the group. One alternative is to have youth nominate friends or name peer groups in order to construct social maps of the group structure (e.g., Cairns & Cairns, 1994; Ennett & Bauman, 1996; Gest & Fletcher, 1996; Stone & Brown, 1999). Multidimensional scaling techniques also occasionally have been applied (Lease & Axelrod, 2001; Stone & Brown, 1999). These alternatives require arbitrary decisions about the boundaries of cliques or crowds that may not be affirmed through observation. However, they are more efficient at capturing the structure within the network as a whole, rather than concentrating on a limited set of groups as most ethnographers do.

As with theories, the key to advances is not settling on one methodology but looking for convergence in findings across approaches. More sophisticated studies will incorporate more than one methodology to foster this sort of convergence of results. A more conscientious effort to combine quantitative and qualitative approaches is sorely needed. Researchers also need to continue working with samples from a variety of cultures and social addresses. Increased sensitivity to sample diversity has helped investigators move away from the White, middle-class bias so obvious in research prior to the 1980s.

ADOLESCENTS' PARTICIPATION IN PEER RELATIONS: SOME BASIC FACTS

The most widely repeated assertions about peer relations during adolescence are that they become increasingly important and occupy an increasing amount of an individual's time. Some teenagers shy away from interactions with peers in favor of relationships with individuals much older or younger than themselves—or with no one at all.

At any point in adolescence, however, about 90 percent of youth can name a peer who is a close friend, and given the opportunity to list an unrestricted number of close friends, the majority of adolescents name at least one person who reciprocates the nomination. In recent years, reciprocated nomination has become the primary criterion for identifying a friendship.

Oddly enough, this criterion of reciprocated nomination is almost never applied to studies of romantic relationships. Because the question is posed in different ways (e.g., "Are you dating someone?" "Do you have a steady romantic partner?" "Do you have a boy/girlfriend?"), it is difficult to establish the rate of participation in romantic relationships. The consensus across studies, however, seems to be that only one quarter to one third of 13- to 15-year-olds claim to have been involved in a romantic relationship, compared to 40% or 50% of 15- to 17-year-olds, and 70% or more of 18- to 20-year-olds (Connolly et al., 2000; Davies & Windle, 2000; Laursen & Williams, 1997). Higher percentages participate in dating or casual cross-gender relationships (Davies & Windle, 2000; Montgomery & Sorell, 1998). At all ages, but less so with advancing age, more girls than boys claim to have (or recently have had) a romantic partner. These numbers could be expected to drop by requiring reciprocal acknowledgment of a romantic tie, but it is difficult to estimate how low they would go.

Analyses of membership in friendship groups require participation of the vast majority of network members to be reliable, so such studies are less common than are assessments of dyadic relations. Using social network analysis, several investigators have charted the cliques that exist within a social system and partitioned adolescents into clique members, liaisons (with ties to two or more cliques but lacking central membership in any one group), and isolates (not tied to any clique, but possibly involved in a reciprocated, dyadic friendship). Ryan (2001) reported that 75% of her multiethnic sample of 7th graders were members of cliques, 15% were classified as isolates, and few were liaisons or tied to just one peer in a dyad.

Rates of peer crowd affiliation are more challenging to specify because, in essence, they assess the degree to which an adolescent's reputation among peers matches the image of a particular crowd. Often, the adolescent's attitudes, activities, and demeanor are not a perfect match to any crowd, just more like one group than another. Nevertheless, peer and self-ratings of crowd affiliation typically require assignment of the target adolescent to just one crowd and do not examine the target's relative affinity for various crowds. Using this approach, investigators assert that 40% to 50% of adolescents are clearly associated with one crowd, one third are associated with two or more crowds, and the rest do not clearly fit into any crowd. There is at present too little evidence to comment on age, gender, or ethnic differences in these figures.

By concentrating on just one level of peer interaction or one type of relationship, most investigations fail to provide a more holistic perspective on a given young person's breadth of participation in the peer system. The numbers just cited imply that whereas most young people participate in peer relationships in each level of the peer system at some point in adolescence, they may not be consistently involved in a given level or type of relationship across adolescence. The degree and consistency of participation across time may, themselves, be important but neglected variables related to social and psychological outcomes for youth.

EMERGING THEMES IN RECENT RESEARCH

The array of types of relationships and levels of interaction within the peer system at adolescence creates a rich domain for scientific study. Within the extensive research in this domain I have selected six themes on which to comment. These themes reflect some of the most prominent questions or ideas that investigators have pursued in recent years. Findings from their work have moved the field well beyond the rather idyllic or generic depictions of friendship that were common in research prior to the 1980s, as well as the simplistic notions embedded in studies of peer influence during the same time frame. They give us a sense of the challenges that adolescents confront in attempting to negotiate peer relations successfully during this stage of life.

Instability of Peer Relations

Because investigators have emphasized adolescents' increased capacity for stable and intimate relationships with peers, people may be surprised by just how *unstable* peer relations are during adolescence. Recent research has shed some light on the causes and consequences of instability throughout the peer system, in sociometric status (level of acceptance or rejection by peers), dyadic relationships, and group affiliations.

Sociometric Status

Peer nominations of most liked and least liked classmates or grade mates or peer ratings of the likability of each peer are usually the basis for determining an adolescent's sociometric status. With such data, individuals can be classified as popular (well liked by classmates and not often disliked), rejected (the opposite), neglected (rarely mentioned as liked or disliked), controversial (frequently mentioned as liked *and* disliked), or average. Studies of sociometric status in childhood indicate that category assignment is reasonably stable over very short periods (a month or so) but not stable over long periods (6 months or more; see Rubin et al., 1998). However, some categories (especially rejected status) are more stable than others (especially neglected and controversial status). Moreover, those who are consistently rated as popular display better social and psychological adjustment over the long term than do other youth, especially those who consistently fall into the rejected category (Cillessen, Bukowski, & Haselager, 2000; Coie, Terry, Zakriski, & Lochman, 1995).

During adolescence, both situational and interpersonal characteristics help determine the direction of change in one's sociometric status. Bukowski and his colleagues examined the stability of sociometric status among early-adolescent youth in Canada. They discovered that transitioning from elementary to middle school can disrupt the consistency of peer acceptance, although youth who were socially rejected prior to the transition tended to retain that status through the transition (Hardy, Bukowski, & Sippola, 2002). As children adjust to the new set of peers and larger peer group that they normally encounter in secondary school, it may take a while for the most widely admired youth to emerge, whereas disliked peers make themselves known quickly through their aversive interactions with others. Sociometric status can be enhanced by friendship patterns. In assessing sociometric status in the fall and spring of 6th grade, Sabongui,

Bukowski, and Newcomb (1998) found that children who associated with (sociometrically) popular classmates tended to increase in popularity more than those who befriended average or rejected classmates.

A word of caution is in order about applying the term *popular* to studies of adolescents because it often has a different meaning among youth than among researchers. Sociometric popularity refers to likability ratings or the frequency with which someone is nominated as a desired friend or playmate. Among teenagers, the term usually refers to one's prestige or status in the peer system (Youniss, McLellan, & Strouse, 1994). Popular youth often have the power to set styles and determine what activities will be undertaken and who will be included. For this, they earn others' envy, but not always their admiration. Eder (1985) deftly illustrated this in her ethnographic study of social dynamics among middle school girls. In this school, there was a basic division between the relatively small, elite group of popular boys and girls (labeled trendies) and the masses of normal or unpopular students (dweebs). Being a cheerleader or friend of a cheerleader was the surest route into the popular clique, and most girls aspired to become members. Once accepted into this inner circle, however, girls discovered that outsiders were especially eager to be their friends. The rest of the trendies looked down on close relationships with outsiders, and the new initiates found it impossible to maintain close relationships with all who wished to become their trusted allies. When trendies ignored or rebuffed others' attempts to become friends, they were regarded as snobs, and their likability ratings fell dramatically—except, of course, among fellow trendies, who regarded this as proof of their allegiance to the trendie clique. Eder labeled this the "cycle of popularity," in which likability ratings rose dramatically on initiation into the popular clique, only to fall as outsiders watched the new members ignore old friends and aspiring new ones.

Cliques and Crowds

Of course, as already mentioned, cliques themselves are unstable over the course of adolescence. One curious feature of the reformulation of cliques that has implications for interventions with deviant youth is that although the specific memberships of cliques may change routinely, there is more stability in the types of individuals who are members. Cairns and Cairns (1994) observed that cliques of deviant youth tended to draw new members from other delinquent youth, so that whereas the specific people who belonged to a clique might rotate, the group retained its deviant orientation. Ennett and Bauman (1994) observed a similar but more complicated pattern with reference to tobacco use in cliques. At both measurement points (one year apart), the majority of cliques were comprised exclusively of nonsmokers or smokers. Nonsmokers tended to depart from cliques in which most members smoked, but smokers did not abandon nonsmoking cliques as readily. The implication of these studies is that even though youth change friendship groups frequently, they seem to remain in contact with peers who share their attitudes and behavior patterns. This has implications for patterns of peer influence, which is addressed in a later section.

To date, there has been little examination of the stability of peer crowd affiliation. In measuring orientations toward crowds (essentially, the match between an individual's attitudes and self-perceived reputation among peers and the prototypical characteristics of major crowd types), Strouse (1999) found that two thirds of a national sample shifted orientations between 10th and 12th grade. Some orientations (all-around and studious) were more stable than others, and shifts between certain types were more common than others, especially among girls. This supports the contention of Brown, Mory, and Kinney (1994) that certain features of the crowd system should make it difficult for youth to achieve radical changes in their reputation among peers. It is more likely, they reasoned, that adolescents will move between crowds with fairly similar reputations—for example, from brains to nerds or from druggies to punks rather than from brains to druggies.

According to one ethnographic study, some youth may find it difficult to change crowds. Merten (1996) traced the efforts of a small set of nonaggressive, socially rejected boys to cope with their reputation as "mels" (short for "Melvins"). The boys were widely derided by classmates from a variety of other crowds and, understandably, sought to escape this derision. Only with great effort, however, was one boy successful in this venture. By persistently violating normative expectations of the mels, the young man was able to force associates to reconsider their opinion of him, leaving him open to pursue friendships with less socially rejected peers and move away from the mel crowd. The move was from the mels to the normals, rather than to a high status crowd, which affirmed Brown et al.'s (1994) contentions about restricted mobility among crowds.

Dyadic Relationships

Romantic relationships are inherently short-lived, especially in early adolescence (Feiring, 1999), so it is not surprising that youth are frequently shifting from having a boyfriend or girlfriend to being without such a relationship (Connolly et al., 2000). Because investigators do not ascertain the reciprocity of romantic affiliations, it is not easy to discern whether a youth who reports being romantically involved at two time points is referring to one long-term relationship or to multiple relationships. This important gap in the literature needs to be addressed so that investigators can identify factors other than age that affect stability of romantic liaisons.

Investigators have paid more attention to the causes and consequences of instability in friendships. A school transition increases the likelihood of disruptions in the friendship network. Even if all of one's friends accompany an adolescent to a new school, the influx of new peers and, possibly, a new structural organization (e.g., moving from self-contained classrooms to a constantly shifting set of peers from class to class) can make it difficult to retain existing friendships. Hardy et al. (2002) found that across the transition to middle school, girls' friendships were less stable than were boys', but girls were also better at forming new friendships with unfamiliar peers (those who had not attended their elementary school). Disruption of the friendship network can be debilitating. Keefe and Berndt (1996) discerned a drop in certain dimensions of self-concept among students who reported a lot of positive features to their fall friendships or reported frequent interactions with friends in the fall and then experienced dissolution of those friendships by the following spring. However, rearranging friendships can also be beneficial. Berndt, Hawkins, and Jiao (1999) found an increase in behavior problems across the transition to middle school for youth who maintained friendships with problem oriented peers; this was not true for peers who ended such affiliations.

Way, Cowal, Gingold, Pahl, and Bissessar (2001) provided an intriguing example of instability in friendship orientations among low-income, urban, ethnic minority youth. They submitted respondents' ratings of their friendships on the seven dimensions of the Network of Relationships Inventory (NRI) to a cluster analysis, deriving four distinct types of friendships. When the procedure was repeated a year later, half of the sample changed friendship types, but shifts were much more common (64%) among those initially in the engaged cluster (displaying high scores on most NRI dimensions) than those in the disengaged cluster (30%), who had markedly low scores on the positive dimensions of the NRI.

It is common to attribute instability in peer relations to features of the person or characteristics of the broader social context (e.g., the different organization of middle schools, as compared to elementary schools), so, naturally, these have been the focus of study. Other factors should be considered, however. For example, especially in middle adolescence when romantic relationships become more common, many cliques appear to be comprised of a core set of members and their "associates of the moment." As core members initiate romantic relationships, they may bring their romantic partners into the clique, and their romantic partner may sharply curtail interactions with members of her or his former clique. Once the romantic relationship ends, however, the partner may be subtly or summarily dismissed from the clique and left to rejoin the former clique or find a new set of friends. Individuals who see each other during the course of a time-limited extracurricular activity (e.g., a team sport) may coalesce into a clique, only to see the clique dissipate once the activity is over. These examples illustrate the dynamic nature of social activity and social relationships in adolescence. Given a constantly shifting set of relationship partners, it becomes important to document what goes on within relationships, rather than concentrating strictly on characteristics of an adolescent's peer associates. Relationship processes constitute a second important theme of recent investigations.

Relationship Processes

The accumulation of evidence linking features of relationships or relationship partners to adolescent outcomes has prompted more interest in *how* peer affiliations affect adolescents. What interaction processes are commonly discerned in peer relationships, and how do they affect the individual?

Managing Conflict

For example, what might account for the fact that youth labeled aggressive by their peers also tend to be rejected as candidates for friendship? One explanation concerns attribution processes in peer interactions. Van Oostrum and Horvath (1997) demonstrated that aggressive adolescents are more likely to read negative intent into the behavior of peers. If someone bumps into them, they are more likely to perceive this as a deliberate act than are nonaggressive youth, and they are more likely to retaliate in turn. The negative interactions that ensue serve to reinforce the adolescent's reputation as unlikable and aggressive. Bowker, Bukowski, Hymel, and Sippola (2000) examined the way that youth from different sociometric statuses responded to social stress. Youth regarded by peers as aggressive tended to use more negative-to-others coping strategies in response to social stressors, whereas youth regarded as withdrawn resorted to more emotion-focused coping (i.e., less provocative and more passive coping responses). Aggressive and socially rejected youth were especially prone to employ negative-to-others strategies, especially if they sensed a high degree of control in the situation. Pro-social youth, on the other hand, are less inclined to infer hostile intent to aggressive behavior and thus are motivated to respond with more conciliatory actions that avoid rifts in relationships (Nelson & Crick, 1999).

Shulman and colleagues have explored interaction processes in two different kinds of dyadic relationships, which they labeled environment-sensitive, or interdependent, and distance-sensitive, or disengaged (Shulman & Laursen, 2002; Shulman, Levy-Shiff, Kedem, & Alon, 1997). Individuals in the former type of bond emphasize mutuality and the best interests of the relationship; those in the latter are more self-oriented, intent on maximizing personal gains from the relationship. Older (but not early) adolescents in interdependent friendships were more likely to take responsibility for initiating the conflict, whereas those in disengaged friendships reported more anger about the conflict. Regardless of age, individuals in interdependent friendships tended to employ compromise and withdrawal to settle the conflict, whereas those in disengaged relationships tended to resort to power assertion and third-party resolution. Strategies more common among youth in disengaged friendships do not heal the wounds of conflict as readily, diminishing the long-term viability of the relationship.

Applying the same classification system to romantic partners, Shulman and Knafo (1997) found that those in interdependent relationships were better able to adopt a spirit of cooperation in their relationships, whereas youth in disengaged relationships tended to adopt more competitive stances with their partners. It is certainly possible that distinctive attributional processes underlie these different approaches to interaction in friendships and romantic relationships, but Shulman and colleagues have not yet investigated this linkage.

Corumination

An intriguing example of how positive relationship features can contribute to unhealthy interaction processes is evident in Rose's (2002) work on corumination. Early adolescents in her sample who displayed comparatively intimate and healthy friendships also tended to ruminate more about these relationships. The intimacy exacerbated corumination, in which both partners obsessed about the relationship, which in turn was associated with internalizing symptoms. This process was more apparent among girls than boys, and stronger among preadolescents than early adolescents.

Peer Pressure or Influence

The relationship process that has spawned the most persistent interest among adults is peer pressure or, more generally, peer influence. What are the specific mechanisms by which peers affect an adolescent's attitudes and activities? The extensive literature on social influence processes in social psychology has not been applied very effectively to studies of adolescent peer relations. In fact, for a considerable period of time, rates of peer influence were overstated by crude and inaccurate measurement strategies. Investigators used to consider the correlation between self-reports of behavior and self-appraisals of the behavior of peers as a valid indicator of peer influence. This approach ignores adolescents' inclination to choose friends or romantic partners who are already similar to themselves, as well as their tendency to inflate similarity between self and close associates. Happily, few recent studies manifest these inferential errors, but accurately measuring influence remains a major challenge.

Modes of Influence

First of all, peers exert influence in multiple ways. *Peer pressure,* or direct, overt, and express efforts to prescribe certain attitudes or activities and proscribe others, has generated the most concern among educators and practitioners. A number of drug and delinquency prevention programs are organized around teaching youth how to resist such pressures. To my knowledge, however, there is no evidence that this is the most common or most effective mode of peer influence. At least three others must be considered. Without necessarily intending to effect changes in others, peers *model* behavior (e.g., Hundleby & Mercier, 1987; Kandel & Andrews, 1987). A more intentional strategy is *normative regulation.* Usually accomplished through gossip or teasing, this involves conversations that reinforce the normative expectations of a group (e.g., Eder et al., 1995; Macleod, 1995). The least recognized and studied mode of influence is *structuring of opportunities,* in which peers provide occasions or contexts for the pursuit of certain behaviors. A common example is throwing a party when parents are away, providing the opportunity for adolescents to engage in drug use, sexual activity, or other behaviors that probably would be restricted under adult supervision.

Some of the best examples of modeling are quite dated (e.g., Costanzo & Shaw; 1966; Dunphy, 1969). More recently, Eckert (1989) recounted how members of one peer crowd, the burnouts, would carefully observe the grooming styles, speech patterns, and activities of another crowd, the jocks, and then strive to do precisely the opposite of that crowd. Her work illustrates how peer models may instigate oppositional rather than conforming behavior (although one could argue that the burnouts were actually conforming to jock norms, just in an oppositional fashion).

Normative regulation is observed most readily in conversations among adolescents, especially friendship groups (see Paxton, Schutz, Wertheim, & Muir, 1999). Eder et al. (1995) described lunchroom exchanges among a group of middle school girls and the peers who happened their way. Through comments about a boy they liked and plans to engage him in a relationship, teasing each other about their opinions and activities, and character assaults on other peers, the girls clarified and reinforced normative behaviors within the group. These mechanisms were so subtle and such routine pieces of daily conversation that it is unlikely any of the girls would have labeled them as peer pressure or influence. According to the investigators, however, they had a profound effect on the young people's attitudes and orientations toward school, gender roles, social interactions, and many other features of their lives.

An equally fascinating but even subtler form of normative regulation was witnessed by Dishion et al. (1996). Over a series of years, the investigators observed members of their target sample (boys at risk for deviant behavior) conversing with peers on a variety of subjects in a laboratory setting. Friends of delinquent youth tended to be more responsive when the conversation focused on deviant behavior: smiling or laughing more, making better eye contact, offering more affirming utterances, and continuing the strain of conversation. These conversation cues in turn predicted rates of deviant behavior among target youths in the ensuing year. Such work underscores just how subtle peer influence can be and how difficult it may be to obtain reliable assessments of such influence through self-report strategies.

Issues Deserving Attention

Despite these advances in our understanding of peer influence processes, a number of facets of peer influence remain to be explored. One of these is identifying the peers who are the strongest sources of influence. A common assumption is that peers will be influenced most by their closest associates or by their most intimate and stable relationships. There is some evidence to support this contention. Urberg (1992), for example, found that smoking behavior was predicted by smoking patterns of best friends much better than patterns within the adolescent's peer group. Kiesner, Cadinu, Poulin, and Bucci (2002) cautioned that adolescents' attention to the norms of peer groups depend on their level of identification with the group. They obtained measures of general problem behavior (based on multiple informants) and more specific and serious delinquent activity (based strictly on self-report) from a sample of Italian youth. Group affiliations were established through sociometric data; the average level of delinquent and problem behavior for each group was calculated by averaging the scores of group members. Respondents also indicated how strongly they identified with their group. Although the group identification score did not moderate the association between group level and individual level of problem behavior, the relation between group and individual scores on delinquency was higher when adolescents identified strongly with their group.

Others, however, argue that adolescents are influenced most by those with whom they *want* to be friends, or groups to which they *aspire* for membership, rather than individuals and groups with whom they have well established relationships. Harter (1999) discerned that self-esteem was affected more by approval or disapproval from classmates in general rather than by close friends. Laursen and Williams (1997) discovered that adolescents rated a romantic partner as the strongest source of influence on their activities (among 12 different types of adult and peer relationships). This was true even for respondents not currently in a romantic relationship. Although this could be attributable to the emotional intensity of such relationships, it might also spring from the short-term nature of romantic ties.

A related question is whether there are specific periods in the course of a relationship when adolescents are most amenable to peer influence. Are peers more persuasive in the formative stages of a relationship, when ties are tenuous and efforts to impress are more concerted, or after a trusting bond has been established? Likewise, is peer influence stronger at certain points in a pattern of behavior? Hartup (1999) speculated that influence is likely to be strongest when base rates of a behavior are near zero (e.g., when individuals are initiating activities such as drug use or sexuality, rather than when they have progressed to higher rates of the behavior). Proper answers to these questions require investigators to assess influence repeatedly at several points in a relationship. As yet, there has been little effort to do so.

Complicating Factors

In fact, the evanescent nature of adolescent peer relations makes this a difficult task. In Dishion et al.'s (1996) laboratory observations of friend interactions, target adolescents tended to bring a different peer to the session each year. One must wonder how strong a source of influence specific friends, romantic partners, or friendship groups can be if they are relatively unstable relationships. A partial answer comes from a longitudinal study by Brendgen, Vitaro, and Bukowski (2000b). The investigators assessed levels of delinquency in a sample of early adolescents at base line, then at follow-ups two and three years later. At each time point respondents also named their best friends, many of whom were also study participants. The level of delinquency reported by an adolescent's friends at base line did not predict the adolescent's own delinquency in the final follow-up (net initial levels of delinquency), but delinquency of friends at the first follow-up *was* predictive of the adolescent's final level of delinquent behavior (one year later). This suggests that friend influences are more immediate than long-term. Because it is likely that many, if not most, respondents nominated different peers as close friends over the course of the study, investigators were probably comparing their target respondents' delinquency to the behavior of different peers at the two time points (base line and follow-up). They did not check or control for this contingency, but their findings suggest that influences of one peer can be washed out by the influences of more recent relationships.

Two other factors complicate assessments of peer influence. First, peer influence is a reciprocal process. Adolescents are at once the recipients and producers of peer influence. To some degree, they influence a friend or friendship group at the same time that they are influenced by their peers. Hartup (1999) cautioned that influence in friendship pairs (or larger groups) can be reciprocal without being equal; some youth are more influential than others. Savin-Williams (1980) deftly demonstrated this years ago in studies of early adolescent peer groups in summer camp, but investigators rarely take these dynamics into account. Another approach to assessing influence—applicable, unfortunately, in stable relationships only—is to treat the dyad or group as a unit of analysis, assessing the degree to which each member's attitudes or behavior moves toward the other's (or the group mean).

A second complicating factor is that at any given time and over any time period, most adolescents confront multiple peer influences from different components of their social networks. Some associates may model a behavior that other associates discourage or deride. It is simply unclear how discrepant the pressures and expectations from peers are for most adolescents. Certainly, however, the degree of discrepancy should be a factor in how closely a teenager will accede to the influence emanating from any one source. To consider or control for multiple sources of influence would be a daunting task, but one that is vital to understanding the dynamics of peer influence among adolescents.

There is one final issue to consider with regard to peer influence. Hartup and Laursen (1999) pointed out that many years ago, Robert Sears depicted a model of relationship interdependence based on reinforcement theory, in which situations that change one individual effect changes in another. It is certainly possible that incidental events in the lives of peer associates constitute one of the most profound sources of peer influence on teenagers. When a close friend has a run-in with a parent or teacher over a certain issue, or when a member of one's friendship group endures an abusive romantic relationship, there may be changes in the way the parents or teachers involved interact with other youth or changes in the friendship group's norms about romantic relationships. Simply by being connected to others, adolescents can be affected by their actions and experiences. The four influence processes that I have stipulated fail to cover the full range of ways that young people can be affected by their peers.

Antagonistic Relations

Most informal peer relationships are voluntary, so it is sensible that youth will choose to initiate and continue relationships only if they are positive experiences. Characteristics considered essential to friendship—reciprocity, mutuality, companionship, security, and intimacy—reflect this positive bias (Bukowski et al., 1994; Hartup & Stevens, 1997). Nevertheless, as researchers explore peer relationships more closely, they discover dyadic and group-level affiliations defined by precisely the opposite of these characteristics.

Antagonistic Dyads

In dyads, research on antagonistic relations has focused on bully-victim pairs (see Juvonen & Graham, 2001). Both members of these pairs tend to be rejected by peers, but unlike victims, bullies are regarded as high in aggression as well. Both individuals contribute to this curious alliance, in that bullies seek out particular peers as victims, and victims make themselves desirable targets. Most studies about bullying and victimization concentrate on young people in childhood or early adolescence; longitudinal studies are rare (but are becoming more common). Being either a bully or victim is associated with numerous internalizing and externalizing symptoms. Long-term effects observed in longitudinal studies do not match concurrent effects reported in cross-sectional studies (Juvonen, Nishina, & Graham, 2000), suggesting that cross-sectional studies may confuse factors that contribute to victimization with consequences of being a victim. Moreover, the consequences are contingent on other characteristics of the individual. For example, Graham and Juvonen (2002) studied aggression and victimization in a multiethnic middle school. They found that African American youth were underrepresented among victims; this ethnic group was also perceived by classmates as relatively more aggressive. However, African American adolescents who *were* victims displayed greater loneliness and lower self-esteem than did victims from other ethnic groups. One possible explanation is that when victimization runs counter to the norms of one's group, the consequences of being a victim are more severe.

With the emergence of peer crowds in adolescence, victimization can become "reified" if victims are identified as a crowd type. In enumerating crowds in their school, it is quite common for American adolescents to include a group that is considered socially immature or inept. The dweebs in Eder's (1985) study, mentioned earlier, are one good example. Such groups, however, are more often pitied or ignored than openly derided. As mentioned earlier, Merten (1996) encountered a small group of boys in one middle school who were known as the mels. They became the target of bullying by a broad array of classmates, especially the more aggressive members of the high-status, popular crowd. Other youth were reluctant to associate with mels for fear that they, too, would be associated with the crowd and subjected to harassment. In fact, even fellow mels avoided each other in a desperate attempt to distance themselves from the crowd type. Merten's observations echo Bukowski and Sippola's (2001) warning that although most research has focused on bully-victim dyads, sometimes adolescents are victimized by a much broader set of peers. More work is needed to determine how victimization is transformed by the emergence of peer crowds in adolescence. If Merten's observations are not unique, then they suggest that bullying can expand in adolescence to include socially accepted as well as rejected youth.

Antagonistic interactions also occur in romantic relationships. In one sample of urban youth (Feiring, Deblinger, Hoch-Espada, & Haworth, 2002), one out of four respondents admitted to perpetrating mild forms of aggression with romantic partners; one in five claimed to be victims of such behavior. Over half said they had been the victim of emotional abuse. More girls than boys exercised physical aggression on partners; emotional abuse was more common among older respondents. Girls (but not boys) who felt little responsibility for actions that harmed others were more likely to report being aggressive with their boyfriends. For boys (but not girls), the tendency to blame others for harmful acts was associated with being physically or sexually aggressive with romantic partners. The incidence of date rape in adolescent relationships is also alarmingly high.

The peer system can feature mutual antipathies with a less clear-cut power differential than in bully-victim relations. Both members of these dyads dislike each other and define their relationship in terms of this antipathy, but one is not the clear and consistent aggressor. In a sample of Dutch youth, Abecassis, Hartup, Haselager, Scholte, and Van Lieshout (2002) found that one out of seven girls and one of five boys reported such relationships with a same-sex peer; about one in seven had a mutual antipathy with an other-sex peer. They were most likely to involve youth from rejected and controversial sociometric categories. Little is known about the basis of these relationships, their durations, or the dynamics of interaction between members. Some antipathies may arise from failed efforts at friendship or romantic ties. Two teens may come to dislike each other when one mistreats the other's best friend in a dating relationship or when a former friendship is ended when one member transitions to a new, higher status peer group. Certainly, the incidence of such relationships is high enough to warrant more research.

Group Antagonisms

More information is available about mutual antipathies at the group (clique or crowd) level. For years, scholars and practitioners have bemoaned the hostile character of interactions between friendship cliques, particularly in early adolescence. Adler and Adler (1998) observed the operations of peer cliques as their subjects transitioned from late childhood into early adolescence. Especially in higher status groups, they found extensive evidence of subjugation both within and between groups. Higher status members ridiculed lower status members, who were more likely to accept the harassment than to move to a different clique because of the status they enjoyed as a result of their membership. All group members tended to make fun of or obviously ignore outsiders—actions that Crick et al. (2001) would label relational aggression. The intent seemed to be to create fear and a sense of inferiority among those outside the group. New members of the high status group were socialized into acting toward outsiders in this fashion. Kinney's (1993) high school respondents recounted similar dynamics as they reflected back on their experience of cliques in middle school.

Sometimes, antagonisms among groups seem to fade as youth enter the more complex social world of high school (Kinney, 1993), but there are cases in which the high school social system is defined in terms of mutual antipathies between crowds. Eckert (1989) depicted the peer crowd system in the suburban, mixed-class American school that she studied as anchored by two groups, the jocks and burnouts. The jocks embraced an upper middle-class, competitive, corporate culture, whereas the burnouts took an oppositional stance rooted in more working class, cooperative values. Each group staked out separate turf within the school, and each consciously avoided the other's turf. School activities that one group embraced were eschewed by the other; cross-group romantic relationships and friendships were avoided. Macleod (1995) offered a similar portrait of distancing and distrust between two crowds of youth (one African American, the other European American) in an inner city neighborhood. Deyhle (1986) described how a group of American Indian youth adopted break dancing as their symbol of opposition to the dominant Anglo culture of other groups (including some fellow Navajos or Utes) in their school in the southwestern United States. Their failure to dress, dance, or socialize like other crowds in the school (e.g., they attended football games but spent the time on the side lines break dancing instead of in the stands watching the game) clarified their distinctive lifestyle, but without the aggressive edge to social relations that Eckert and others described.

Are Antagonisms Unhealthy?

Although these dyadic and group antipathies sound unhealthy—and at least at the dyadic level appear to be associated with problematic behaviors or outcomes—they may possibly serve constructive ends for adolescents in terms of identity enhancement. A basic tenet of social identity theory is that group members will exaggerate the positive features of their in-group and the negative characteristics of out-group members in order to enhance their own social identity (see Stone & Brown, 1998). Conflict can serve constructive functions in dyadic relationships as well. Laursen (1996) discovered that conflict was a daily feature of close relationships among American adolescents. High school students in his study reported an average of nearly 8 conflicts a day with various interaction partners. Disagreements were most frequent with mothers, followed by friends, romantic partners, siblings, and fathers. Common sources or subjects of conflict differed among relationships. The incidence of conflicts diminished across adolescence within friendships but rose in romantic relationships, possibly because the relationships grew more intense and stable (Laursen & Collins, 1994). The impact of conflict on these relationships depended substantially on how it was resolved. In most cases, partners worked to settle disagreements in ways that would avoid disruption or dissolution of the relationship. Compromise and negotiation were employed more often in friendships and romantic alliances than in family relationships (with parents or peers). Curiously, conflicts generally had no effects—for better or worse—in friendships, whereas many adolescents felt that they tended to improve their relationship with romantic partners (Laursen, 1993).

Summary

Despite the voluntary nature of most adolescent peer relations, conflict and antagonism are common components of relationships in the peer system. In moderation, they can serve healthy functions for both relationships and individuals. In some cases, however, antagonism or aggressive behavior becomes the basis for the relationship and fosters or perpetuates undesirable outcomes. Increasing awareness of these distinctions should help investigators and practitioners to design more effective intervention programs for youth caught up in (or vulnerable to) antagonistic relations with peers.

Interconnections and Embeddedness

Although most studies tend to focus on just one facet of the peer social system—one type of relationship or one level of engagement with peers—most investigators appreciate the linkages that exist across relationships and levels. Efforts to understand these linkages have advanced to the point that, based on recent research, several assertions can be made about the interconnections and embeddedness of the peer system in adolescence.

The first assertion is that interpersonal characteristics or competencies predispose individuals to certain types of relationship experiences. This is apparent in the connections that several investigators have noted between sociometric status and affiliation patterns. For example, Bagwell, Coie, Terry, and Lochman (2000) found that preadolescents who were rejected by peers still belonged to peer groups but were less central members. They also tended to participate in smaller cliques populated by other rejected youth. Curiously, youth who were regarded as aggressive were just as likely to be involved in peer groups and just as likely to be central members as were nonaggressive youth, although they tended to coalesce with other, aggressively oriented peers. Hanna and Berndt (1995) examined patterns of interaction and affiliation among adolescents attending a summer camp. Campers who were regarded more positively by peers also reported more positive features in their camp friendships. Those who described their prior friendships (outside of camp) in negative terms were viewed as more antagonistic by fellow campers, even though their camp friendships did not display more negative features than did those of other campers. It is possible, of course, that the camp friendships were still in the formative stage and had not yet progressed to a point at which negative features would be apparent. The general implication is that youth who are not well liked by peers have fewer options for friendship and group associates, and those options are dominated by other rejected youth. This makes it more difficult for them to learn and practice effective social skills within peer relationships, so that their social standing within the larger peer group could improve. Perhaps this explains why rejected peer status is more stable than other sociometric categories. These findings also affirm Buhrmester's (1996) admonition that whereas interpersonal competencies influence the course of friendships, friendships also help to shape a young person's interpersonal competencies. It would be useful, in this regard, to examine how changes in sociometric ratings over time are tied to shifting fortunes in dyadic relationships (the adolescent's success or failure in initiating and in maintaining healthy friendships and romantic ties).

A second assertion is that experiences in one type of peer relationship affect opportunities for and experiences with other types of peer relationships. This is the fundamental principle underlying Sullivan's (1953) hypothesis that intense, emotionally charged preadolescent same-sex chumships prepare young people for the intense, sexually charged romantic relationships of adolescence. Few have been able to connect friendship and romance in precisely the fashion that Sullivan described, but there are indicators of a similar association. Furman (1999), for example, questioned a common assumption from attachment theory that the quality of adolescents' romantic relationships would be best predicted by relationships with parents. Rather, he reasoned, because of the affiliative nature of early to midadolescent romantic relations, they may have more in common with friendships. In a small but ethnically and socioeconomically diverse sample of high school seniors, Furman, Simon, Shaffer, and Bouchey (2002) found that qualities of respondents' friendships significantly predicted features of their romantic relationships, but features of the parent-child bond (especially the nature of attachment to parent) did not. In other words, the affective linkages between friendship and romance are stronger, in the early stages of adolescence, than those between romance and parental attachments.

Longitudinal studies following youth from childhood through middle adolescence indicate that having close, same-sex friendships in middle childhood predicts having romantic relationships in early or middle adolescence (Neeman, Hubbard, & Masten, 1995; Sroufe, Egeland, & Carlson, 1999), as well as healthier romantic affiliations in late adolescence (Collins, 2003; Collins, Hennighausen, & Ruh, 1999). Feiring (1999) found that youth are more likely to be involved with other-sex romantic partners in midadolescence if they have had other-sex friendships in early adolescence.

Connoly et al. (2000) provided a more elaborate analysis of how friendship networks launch adolescents into romantic relationships. Gathering data in three successive years (Grades 9–11) on the composition of friendship network and involvement in romantic relations, the investigators found that high school students were more likely to have a romantic relationship if in the previous year they had been involved in a more mixed-gender friendship group. This, in turn, was predicted by having an other-sex close friend even earlier in high school. In other words, a succession of experiences with other-sex friendships and then peer groups early in high school seemed to prepare youth for romantic relationships by the middle of high school. These findings corroborate Dunphy's (1969) observations of Australian youth half a century earlier, in which there was a metamorphosis from isolated, same-sex cliques to mixed-sex cliques to clusters of mixed-sex groups that aided in socializing members into heterosexual romantic relationships. The progression into romantic relationships is not always a smooth one, however. In Brendgen, Vitaro, Doyle, Markiewicz, and Bukowski's (2002) sample of 7th graders, having a romantic relationship was related to poorer psychological and behavior outcomes for socially rejected youth, whereas associations with outcomes were not significant for more socially accepted adolescents. A complicating issue in that study, however, is the timing of entry into romantic relationships, which is discussed in relation to my fifth and final theme.

Whereas friendships can facilitate the move into romantic relationships, they may also be the victims of an adolescent's success in this realm. Youth who are involved in romantic relationships confess that they spend less time with friends, as well as parents and other relationship partners (Laursen & Williams, 1997; Zimmer-Gembeck, 1999). Particularly for females, this can generate feelings of resentment and abandonment, which are difficult to articulate directly to the offending friend without appearing to be overprotective or perhaps sexually attracted to the friend (Roth & Parker, 2001).

A third, somewhat bolder assertion is that peer relations are embedded within a peer system and are affected by the norms and expectations of that system. Researchers have asserted unequivocally that not all adolescent friendships or romantic relationships are alike. Individual characteristics explain much of the variation, but group dynamics are an issue as well. Cliques and crowds shape the norms and arenas of activity for dyadic relationships. Eder (1985) observed how early adolescent girls' need to remain vigilant about their status in the popular clique forced them to approach friendships cautiously. Recognizing their cliquemates—as well as outsiders—as potential competitors for social status, they carefully censured the information they were willing to share with close associates. Eckert (1989) found sharp distinctions in orientations toward friendship between the two dominant groups in the school in which she conducted her ethnography. Jocks were strategic in choosing friends and cautious about self-disclosure, mindful that even close associates could be competitors for social and academic rewards. Their orientation toward friendship was reminiscent of Shulman and Knafo's (1997) disengaged type of relationship. From their position much further down in the school's status hierarchy, the burnouts felt a strong sense of loyalty to and camaraderie with their friends. Trust and reliability were essential in their associates—much more in keeping with Shulman's interdependent type. Eckert argued that these discrepant patterns emerged from the different socioeconomic circumstances of members of the two crowds but that they became normative features of the crowd regardless of members' social class background. Foley (1990) reported similar dynamics in a study of Texas youth.

It is very likely that the timetable for dating, expectations for sexual intimacy, tolerance for diversity (e.g., cross-race friendships or acceptance of homosexual as well as heterosexual romances), and essential features of friendship all vary considerably among friendship groups or reputational crowds. Researchers have yet to delve into this rich source of variance in adolescent peer relations in any systematic way. In fact, all evidence to date comes from ethnographic investigations; studies using other methodologies are needed to confirm and extend their inferences.

A final assertion is that the peer system itself is embedded in broader social contexts and an adolescent's larger network of social relationships. The extensive literature demonstrating connections between parent-child and peer relations needs to be acknowledged here, even though it cannot be examined in detail. Associations with deviant friends, often cited as one of the strongest correlates of delinquent behavior, seem to follow from problematic relationships with parents (Dishion, Patterson, & Griesler, 1994). Relationships with parents and friends both contribute to the quality and duration of romantic ties (Collins, 2003; Furman, 1999). Parenting styles can moderate the effects of friends on both adaptative and problem behavior (Mounts & Steinberg, 1995). Recent work, however, suggests that adolescents are more active in shaping parental input and parental influence on peer relationships during adolescence than scholars of previous decades have assumed. Parental awareness of adolescents' interactions and relationships with peers comes primarily from the information adolescents voluntarily provide, rather than from vigilant parental monitoring (Kerr & Stattin, 2000), and adolescents consciously screen what they share with parents (Darling, Hames, & Cumsille, 2000). Parents seem more likely to react to problems with peer relations than to try proactively to shape their adolescent child's associations with agemates (Mounts, 2001; Tilton-Weaver & Galambos, in press).

School, family, neighborhood, and community all serve as broader contexts in which peer interactions occur for adolescents. Their capacity to shape the nature and effects of peer relationships can be quite profound. Peshkin (1991) described a community whose norms about racial tolerance promoted interaction across ethnic boundaries, helping to explain the unusual number of cross-ethnic friendships among adolescents and their ease in negotiating these relationships. Nevertheless, cross-ethnic romances were uncommon, partially, Peshkin discovered, because of pressures youth felt from parents to confine dating partners to ethnic peers. The number of peer crowds mentioned by British youth varied considerably among the six schools participating in Thurlow's (2001) study. This may have been a function of both the demographic composition of the student bodies as well as the size or social climate in each school. Early-maturing girls attending single-sex, Australian schools manifested lower levels of delinquency than those in coeducational environments, possibly because of their restricted access to cliques containing older, deviantly oriented boys (Caspi, Lynam, Moffitt, & Silva, 1993).

Summary

These four assertions help to place more circumscribed investigations of adolescent peer relations in proper perspective. It is now common for investigators to be sensitive to the demographic background of their respondents. More attention must be paid, however, to respondents' *interpersonal* backgrounds and the social contexts in which the data are collected. Of course, to some extent adolescents are instrumental in selecting and shaping these contexts, just as they are proactive in censuring parents' awareness of their activities and associations with peers. Nonetheless, researchers should continue to be attentive to the linkages between different components of the peer system, as well as the opportunities and constraints that are imposed from a young person's broader network of social relationships.

Developmental Change in the Character of Peer Relationships

Throughout this chapter I have emphasized the dynamic nature of peer relations in adolescence. Individuals routinely change partners and change friendship groups; they move in and out of various types of relationships; and their reputations among peers can be altered by certain events or associations. The daily dynamics of relationship processes and intergroup interactions are essential components of the peer social context. There is one more dynamic that researchers are beginning to understand better: transformations in the nature of peer relationships or the organization of the peer system that are tied to normative processes of individual development. Adolescence spans a considerable time period in technologically advanced cultures, during which individuals undergo dramatic changes in physical characteristics, cognitive abilities, academic and cultural knowledge, and social maturity. To remain functional, the peer system has to grow with the individual. As Buhrmester (1996, p. 165) noted, "Developing needs and concerns dictate, to a sizable degree, the social provisions and relationship features that are sought in friendship." Research on developmental changes in peer relations is not yet well coordinated and systematic, but there is sufficient evidence to illustrate some of the effects that individual development can have.

Expectations about the basic features of friendship change as individuals progress from late childhood to middle adolescence (Berndt & Perry, 1986). Emphasis on sharing activities declines in favor of more concern with sharing secrets, worries, and ambitions; trust becomes as important as companionship. Later, good friends grow more aware of the full spectrum of relationships that each other is pursuing, thus feeling more comfortable allowing their partner to have social experiences outside of their own relationship. Consistent with these shifting expectations, Shulman, Laursen, Kalman, and Karpovsky (1997) discovered that across adolescence in their sample of Israeli youth, emphasis on individuality increased, whereas control and conformity declined.

No age differences were noted in emotional closeness and self-disclosure. Laursen (1996) cited a broader array of studies showing declines across this life stage in admiration, satisfaction, companionship, and reliable alliance of friends (although, consistent with Shulman et al., there was no evidence of a decline in intimacy). Laursen speculated that the pattern of changes reflected the decline of Sullivan's chumship as romantic relations assumed more importance.

Consistent with Laursen's (1996) inference, the percentage of youth reporting romantic affiliations increases with age, and these alliances last longer among older youth (Davies & Windle, 2000). Intimacy with romantic partners also increases with age, to the point that, in late adolescence, it equals self-disclosure to best friends and surpasses closeness to parents (Buhrmester, 1996). Several scholars have proposed stage theories of the development of romantic relationships, describing how they shift from more public relationships overseen by the friendship group to more private affiliations with a depth of feeling and commitment (Brown, 1999b; Connolly & Goldberg, 1999). Consistent with these theories, Davies and Windle (2000) noted a tendency for adolescents to move forward, across a two-year period, along a trajectory from not dating to casual relationships to having a "steady" romantic partner. Individuals varied in their timing at entry into this sequence and the speed with which they progressed to steady relationships. Those who lingered in a stage featuring multiple casual relationships also displayed more problem behavior than those who moved on to more committed relationships. However, individuals who had intermittent casual relationships, broken by periods of no romantic involvement, were also low in problem behavior. Thus, whereas there was no optimal developmental timetable, some trajectories seemed more adaptive than others.

Developmental shifts in behavior patterns may be accompanied by changes in psychological investments in romantic relationships. Furman and Wehner (1997) outlined a behavioral systems perspective on close relationships in adolescence, describing how relationships can meet individuals' needs in four domains: affiliation, attachment, care giving, and sexual gratification. The transfer of attachment from parents to romantic partners was gradual and incomplete (parental attachments are transformed, not abandoned). Early adolescents were likely to look to dating partners to address affiliative needs. Not until late adolescence did romantic relationships typically deepen to address sexual and attachment issues. The nature of this progression was affected, however, by the quality of attachment to parents, with securely attached adolescents progressing somewhat earlier and more confidently toward integrating several behavioral systems, or views, into their romantic relationships.

Investigators have also seen dramatic transformations in the peer crowd system from early to later adolescence. Self-report data indicate that early adolescents' preoccupation with belonging to a popular crowd fades with age; along with this are declines in derogatory comments directed both within and outside a group (Gavin & Furman, 1989). Crowds grow more permeable as well, and less hierarchically ordered by status or influence. Kinney's (1993) longitudinal ethnography of one crowd system confirmed these trajectories, but Kinney also observed two profound shifts in crowd structure from middle school through late high school. With the transition to senior high school, the rigid authority structure separating the populars from the unpopulars broke down, as youth encountered a broader array of groups, each legitimized by the presence of upperclassmen. Youth shunned by the populars in middle school recovered a stronger sense of identity as they were accepted into these groups and removed from the tight control of the popular elite. By late adolescence, the status ordering had almost collapsed, and youth more easily formed close relationships across crowd boundaries.

Even in the face of these changes, however, peer crowds retain some predictive utility relative to developmental trajectories for youth. Prinstein and La Greca (2002) traced changes in internalizing and externalizing behavior across childhood and adolescence of youth who ultimately associated with different crowds in adolescence. The most startling patterns were those of individuals who ultimately became brains. In childhood, they had the lowest average score of any crowd on depression and loneliness and the highest self-esteem. By midadolescence, all of these advantages had disappeared, apparently reflecting the broader peer group's devaluation of academic achievement across this age span.

Information on normative transitions in dyadic and group or crowd relations set the stage for investigations of nonnormative trajectories. For example, early-maturing youth are more likely than their "on-time" or late-maturing peers to have romantic relationships in early adolescence. Several studies indicate, however, that those who begin dating and romantic activity in early adolescence fare worse on a variety of psychological and behavioral measures. Magnussen's (1988) results from a Swedish study are especially illustrative. He found that early-maturing girls often associated with older boys (presumably because their age peers of the other sex, still far away from puberty, did not share their interest in other-sex relationships), but they tended to fall in with male or mixed-sex cliques that had a delinquent orientation. Although the boys offered an outlet for heterosocial interests, they also pulled the early maturers into deviant and sexual activity for which they may not have been emotionally prepared, threatening their psychological well-being as well as their reputation among adults.

Generally, then, there appears to be a synergy between individual's developmental needs and the organization and operation of the peer system. Across adolescence, the peer system transforms to accommodate shifts in individual's interests and relational capacities. Those who engage in relationships "ahead of schedule," however, may be frustrated by the lack of a supportive structure within the broader peer system. In any event, age or developmental stage is a crucial variable for researchers to consider in their investigations of teenage peer relationships and peer structures.

CONCLUSION

The extensive insights that scholars have gleaned from studies of adolescent peer relations since 1985 are at once fascinating and intimidating. Certainly, they have illuminated a number of features of this complex social context, but they have also underscored the need for continued study that is both conceptually and methodologically sophisticated. Five specific recommendations can be highlighted.

First, multiple approaches to a particular issue often can produce insights that a single methodology fails to reveal. Graham and Juvonen (1998) identified victims of peer abuse in a sample of 6th and 7th graders, relying on both self-attributions and peer nominations. Although the two methods were correlated, they tended to produce distinct lists of respondents high in victimization. Moreover, self-perceived victims were distinctive from nonvictims in their tendency to blame their treatment by peers on their character, rather than their behavior. Self-perceived victimization was correlated with loneliness, anxiety, and low self-worth, but none of these variables correlated significantly with peer-rated victimization. Instead, it was related to sociometric ratings of acceptance and rejection. Gest and Fletcher (1996) derived maps of cliques from respondents' own lists of clique members and from a social-cognitive mapping (SCM) approach (Cairns & Cairns, 1994). Agreement between the two methods was well beyond chance, but self-generated lists tended to include just a subset of the cliques derived by SCM. Youth tended to omit (sociometrically) less popular youth from their lists of clique members. The authors of these studies emphasized that both techniques they used generated valid data, just differing in perspectives. But those differences revealed intriguing features of the phenomena under investigation.

Second, investigators should attend to distal as well as proximal associates. Most studies focus on *close* or *best* friends, *steady* romantic partners, or *fellow members* of one's clique or crowd. Giordano (1995) found a sharp distinction in what close friends as opposed to acquaintances wrote in adolescents' school yearbooks. The latter offered more blunt, "unfettered appraisals" of the book owner's personality, appearance, and behavior. Giordano speculated that such appraisals could be dismissed by the adolescent because they came from a lesser valued source, but they might also be taken to heart as more honest and trustworthy than comments from close friends. Eckert's (1989) study of the burnouts' preoccupation with the jocks (and vice versa) illustrated how adolescents may be affected just as strongly by disliked, out-group members as by members of their own crowd. There is still remarkably little attention given to adolescents' "wider circle of friends" and the ways that they influence psychological and social development.

Third, more attention must be paid to diverse cultural and ethnic groups. Researchers are to be commended for deriving more diverse samples for studies, but now they must look more systematically at variation between as well as variability within different groups. Hamm (2000) found substantial differences across ethnic groups in the characteristics on which best friends were similar; she also noticed that factors moderating similarity between friends differed among groups. For example, the degree of similarity in academic achievement among African American friends depended on their socioeconomic status; similarity on this variable among Asian Americans and their friends was contingent on the target student's own level of achievement. Way et al. (2001) documented a similar degree of variability within and across ethnic groups in their typology of adolescent friendships. The results raise questions about how widely shared certain values and orientations are in friendship, both within and across ethnic or cultural communities of adolescents.

A fourth, related suggestion is to continue to emphasize situated appraisals of adolescent peer relations. Hanna and Berndt (1995) reported that whereas friendship quality seemed to be consistent for youth in school and summer camp settings, sociometric status was not. Studies of friendship patterns across a general sample of adolescents may mask substantial differences occurring among individuals from different cliques or crowds. Having established many of these general patterns, investigators should pay more attention to the contexts—within and beyond the peer social system—that modify such patterns.

Finally, sufficient progress has been made in studying romantic relationships to move beyond the heterosexual bias of most studies in this area. Since Savin-Williams's (1994) fascinating appraisal of the issue, some progress has been made in assessing gay, lesbian, and transsexual youths' negotiation of the peer social system (e.g., Diamond, 2000), but researchers should make a more conscientious effort to include assessments of sexual-minority youth in their examinations of peer relationships at all levels of the peer social system.

The matter is settled, then: Peers are neither an entirely supportive and healthy set of associates for adolescents, nor a social force driving them fervently toward maladaptive outcomes. They have the capacity—if not the inclination—to do both, but this capacity is tempered by the adolescent's own background and behavior. Only by continuing to unravel the complexities of this social context will investigators help parents, educators, and practitioners appreciate the profound significance of peers in adolescents' personal and social development.

REFERENCES

Abecassis, M., Hartup, W. W., Haselager, G. J. T., Scholte, R. H. J., & Van Lieshout, C. F. M. (2002). Mutual antipathies and their significance in middle childhood and adolescence. *Child Development, 73,* 1543–1556.

Adler, P. A., & Adler, P. (1998). *Peer power: Preadolescent culture and identity.* New Brunswick, NJ: Rutgers University Press.

Bagwell, C. L., Coie, J. D., Terry, R. A., & Lochman, J. E. (2000). Peer clique participation and social status in preadolescence. *Merrill-Palmer Quarterly, 46,* 280–305.

Berndt, T. J. (1996). Exploring the effects of friendship quality on social development. In W. M. Bukowski, A. F. Newcomb, & W. W. Hartup (Eds.), *The company they keep: Friendship in childhood and adolescence* (pp. 346–365). New York: Cambridge University Press.

Berndt, T. J. (1999). Friends' influence on students' adjustment to school. *Educational Psychologist, 34,* 15–28.

Berndt, T. J., Hawkins, J. A., & Jiao, Z. (1999). Influences of friends and friendships on adjustment to junior high school. *Merrill-Palmer Quarterly, 45,* 13–41.

Berndt, T. J., & Perry, T. B. (1986). Children's perceptions of friendships as supportive relationships. *Developmental Psychology, 22,* 640–648.

Bowker, A., Bukowski, W. M., Hymel, S., & Sippola, L. K. (2000). Coping with daily hassles in the peer group during early adolescence: Variations as a function of peer experience. *Journal of Research on Adolescence, 10,* 211–243.

Brendgen, M., Vitaro, F., & Bukowski, W. M. (2000a). Deviant friends and early adolescents' emotional and behavioral adjustment. *Journal of Research on Adolescence, 10,* 173–189.

Brendgen, M., Vitaro, F., & Bukowski, W. M. (2000b). Stability and variability of adolescents' affiliation with delinquent friends: Predictors and consequences. *Social Development, 9,* 205–225.

Brendgen, M., Vitaro, F. D., Doyle, A. B., Markiewicz, D., & Bukowski, W. M. (2002). Same-sex peer relations and romantic relationships during early adolescence: Interactive links to emotional, behavioral, and academic adjustment. *Merrill-Palmer Quarterly, 48,* 77–103.

Brown, B. B. (1990). Peer groups and peer cultures. In S. S. Feldman & G. R. Elliott (Eds.), *At the threshold: The developing adolescent* (pp 171–196). Cambridge, MA: Harvard University Press.

Brown, B. B. (1999a). Measuring the peer environment of American adolescents. In S. L. Friedman & T. D. Wachs (Eds.), *Assessment of the environment across the life span* (pp. 59–90). Washington, DC: American Psychological Association.

Brown, B. B. (1999b). "You're going with *who?!*": Peer group influences on adolescent romantic relationships. In W. Furman, B. B. Brown, & C. Feiring (Eds.), *The development of romantic relationships in adolescence* (pp. 291–329) London: Cambridge University Press.

Brown, B. B., Larson, R., & Saraswathi, T. S. (Eds.). (2002). *The world's youth: Adolescence in eight regions of the globe.* New York: Cambridge University Press.

Brown, B. B., Mory, M., & Kinney, D. A. (1994). Casting adolescent crowds in relational perspective: Caricature, channel, and context. In R. Montemayor, G. R. Adams, & T. P. Gullotta (Eds.), *Advances in adolescent development: Vol. 6. Personal relationships during adolescence* (pp. 123–167).

Brown, L. M., Way, N., & Duff, J. (1999). The others in my I: Adolescent girls' friendships and peer relations. In N. Johnson, M. Roberts, & J. Worell (Eds.), *Beyond appearances: A new look at adolescent girls* (pp. 205–225). Washington, DC: American Psychological Association.

Buhrmester, D. (1996). Need fulfillment, interpersonal competence, and the developmental contexts of early adolescent friendship. In W. M. Bukowski, A. F. Newcomb, & W. W. Hartup (Eds.), *The company they keep* (pp. 158–185). New York: Cambridge University Press.

Bukowski, W. M., Hoza, B., & Boivin, M. (1994). Measuring friendship quality during pre- and early adolescence: The development and psychometric properties of the friendship qualities scale. *Journal of Social and Personal Relationships, 11,* 471–484.

Bukowski, W. M., & Sippola, L. K. (2001). Groups, individuals, and victimization: A view of the peer system. In J. Juvonen & S. Graham (Eds.), *Peer harassment in school: The plight of the vulnerable and victimized* (pp. 355–377). New York: Guilford Press.

Cairns, R. B., & Cairns, B. D. (1994). *Lifelines and risks: Pathways of youth in our time.* Cambridge: Cambridge University Press.

Caspi, A., Lynam, D., Moffitt, T. E., & Silva, P. A. (1993). Unraveling girls' delinquency: Biological, dispositional, and contextual contributions to adolescent misbehavior. *Developmental Psychology, 29,* 19–30.

Cillessen, A. H. N., & Bukowski, W. M. (Eds.). (2000). *Recent advances in the measurement of acceptance and rejection in the peer system: New direction for child and adolescent development* (No. 88). San Francisco: Jossey-Bass.

Cillessen, A. H. N., Bukowski, W. M., & Haselager, G. J. T. (2000). Stability of sociometric categories. In A. H. N. Cillessen & W. M. Bukowski (Eds.), *Recent advances in the measurement of acceptance and rejection in the peer system: New direction for child and adolescent development* (No. 88, pp. 75–93). San Francisco: Jossey-Bass.

Clasen, D. R., & Brown, B. B. (1985). The multidimensionality of peer pressure in adolescence. *Journal of Youth and Adolescence, 14,* 451–468.

Coie, J. D., Terry, R., Zakriski, A., & Lochman, J. (1995). Early adolescent social influences on delinquent behavior. In J. McCord (Ed.), *Coercion and punishment in long-term perspectives* (pp. 229–244). New York: Cambridge University Press.

Collins, W. A. (2003). More than myth: The developmental significance of romantic relationships during adolescence. *Journal of Research on Adolescence, 13,* 1–24.

Collins, W. A., Hennighausen, K., & Ruh, J. (1999, April). *Peer competence in middle childhood and behavior in romantic relationships in adolescence and young adulthood.* Paper presented at the biennial meeting of the Society for Research in Child Development, Albuquerque, NM.

Connolly, J., Furman, W., & Konarski, R. (2000). The role of peers in the emergence of heterosexual romantic relationships in adolescence. *Child Development, 71,* 1395–1408.

Connolly, J., & Goldberg, A. (1999). Romantic relationships in adolescence: The role of friends and peers in their emergence and development. In W. Furman, B. B. Brown, & C. Feiring (Eds.), *The development of romantic relationships in adolescence* (pp. 266–290). London: Cambridge University Press.

Costanzo, P. R., & Shaw, M. E. (1966). Conformity as a function of age level. *Child Development, 37,* 967–975.

Crick, N. R., Nelson, D. R., Morales, J. R., Cullerton-Sen, C., Casas, J. F., & Hickman, S. E. (2001). Relational victimization in childhood and adolescence. In J. Juvonen & S. Graham (Eds.), *Peer harassment in school* (pp. 196–214). New York: Guilford Press.

Darling, N., Hames, K., & Cumsille, P. (2000, April). When parents and adolescent disagree: Disclosure strategies and motivations. In. Society for Research on Adolescence, New Orleans.
Davies, P. T., & Windle, M. (2000). Middle adolescents' dating pathways and psychosocial adjustment. *Merrill-Palmer Quarterly, 46,* 90–118.
Degirmencioglu, S. M., Urberg, K. A., Tolson, J. M., & Richard, P. (1998). Adolescent friendship networks: Continuity and change over the school year. *Merrill-Palmer Quarterly, 44,* 231–337.
Deyhle, D. (1986). Break dancing and breaking out: Anglos, Utes, and Navajos in a border reservation high school. *Anthropology and Education Quarterly, 17,* 111–127.
Diamond, L. M. (2000). Passionate friendships among adolescent sexual-minority women. *Journal of Research on Adolescence, 10,* 191–209.
Dishion, T. J., Andrews, D. W., & Crosby, L. (1995). Antisocial boys and their friends in early adolescence: Relationship characteristics, quality, and interactional process. *Child Development, 66,* 139–151.
Dishion, T. J., Patterson, G. R., & Griesler, P. C. (1994). Peer adaptations in the development of antisocial behavior: A confluence model. In L. R. Huesmann (Ed.), *Aggressive behavior: Current perspectives* (pp. 61–95). New York: Plenum.
Dishion, T. J., Spracklen, K. M., Andrews, D. W., & Patterson, G. R. (1996). Deviancy training in male adolescent friendships. *Behavior Therapy, 27,* 373–390.
DuBois, D. L., & Hirsch, B. J. (1990). School and neighborhood friendship patterns of blacks and whites in early adolescence. *Child Development, 61,* 524–536.
Dunphy, D. C. (1969). *Cliques, crowds, and gangs.* Melbourne: Chesire.
Eckert, P. (1989). *Jocks and burnouts: Social categories and identity in the high school.* New York: Teachers College Press.
Eder, D. (1985). The cycle of popularity: Interpersonal relations among female adolescence. *Sociology of Education, 58,* 154–165.
Eder, D., Evans, C. C., & Parker, S. (1995). *School talk: Gender and adolescent culture.* New Brunswick, NJ: Rutgers University Press.
Ennett, S. T., & Bauman, K. E. (1994). The contribution of influence and selection to adolescent peer group homogeneity: The case of adolescent cigarette smoking. *Journal of Personality and Social Psychology, 67,* 653–663.
Ennett, S. T., & Bauman, K. E. (1996). Adolescent social networks: School, demographic, and longitudinal considerations. *Journal of Adolescent Research, 11,* 194–215.
Falicov, C. J. (1996). Mexican families. In M. McGoldrick, J. K. Pearce, & J. Giordano (Eds.), *Ethnicity and family therapy* (2nd ed., pp. 169–182). New York: Guilford Press.
Feiring, C. (1999). Other-sex friendship networks and the development of romantic relationships in adolescence. *Journal of Youth and Adolescence, 28,* 495–512.
Feiring, C., Deblinger, E., Hoch-Espada, A., & Haworth, T. (2002). Romantic relationship aggression and attitudes in high school students: The role of gender, grade, and attachment and emotional styles. *Journal of Youth and Adolescence, 31,* 373–385.
Foley, D. E. (1990). *Learning capitalist culture: Deep in the heart of Tejas.* Philadelphia: University of Pennsylvania Press.
Furman, W. (1993). Theory is not a four-letter word: Needed directions in the study of adolescent friendships. In B. Laursen (Ed.), *Close friendships in adolescence* (pp. 89–103). New York: Cambridge University Press.
Furman, W. (1999). Friends and lovers: The role of peer relationships in adolescent romantic relationships. In W. A. Collins & B. Laursen (Eds.), *The Minnesota symposia on child psychology: Vol. 30. Relationships as developmental contexts* (pp. 133–154). Mahwah, NJ: Erlbaum.
Furman, W., & Simon, V. A. (1998). Advice from youth: Some lessons from the study of adolescent relationships. *Journal of Social and Personal Relationships, 15,* 723–739.
Furman, W., Simon, V. A., Shaffer, L., & Bouchey, H. A. (2002). Adolescents' working models and styles for relationships with parents, friends, and romantic partners. *Child Development, 73,* 241–255.
Furman, W., & Wehner, E. A. (1997). Adolescent romantic relationships: A developmental per-

spective. In S. Shulman & W. A. Collins (Eds.), *Romantic relationships in adolescence: Developmental perspectives* (pp. 21–36). San Francisco: Jossey-Bass.
Gavin, L. A., & Furman, W. (1989). Age differences in adolescents' perceptions of their peer groups. *Developmental Psychology, 25,* 827–834.
Gest, S. D., & Fletcher, A. C. (1996, April). *Concordance between self-reported and consensus-based peer groups as a function of social network status in early adolescence.* Paper presented at the biennial meetings of the Society for Research in Adolescence, Boston.
Giordano, P. C. (1995). The wider circle of friends in adolescence. *American Journal of Sociology, 101,* 661–697.
Graham, S., & Juvonen, J. (1998). Self-blame and peer victimization in middle school: An attributional analysis. *Developmental Psychology, 34,* 587–538.
Graham, S., & Juvonen, J. (2002). Ethnicity, peer harassment, and adjustment in middle school: An exploratory study. *Journal of Early Adolescence, 22,* 173–199.
Hall, G. S. (1904). *Adolescence* (Vols. 1 & 2). New York: Appleton.
Hamm, J. V. (2000). Do birds of a feather flock together? The variable bases for African American, Asian American, and European American adolescents' selection of similar friends. *Developmental Psychology, 36,* 209–219.
Hanna, N. A., & Berndt, T. J. (1995). Relations between friendship, group acceptance, and evaluations of summer camp. *Journal of Early Adolescence, 15,* 456–475.
Hardy, C. L., Bukowski, W. M., & Sippola, L. K. (2002). Stability and change in peer relationships during the transition to middle-level school. *Journal of Early Adolescence, 22,* 117–142.
Harter, S. (1999). *The construction of self: A developmental perspective.* New York: Guilford Press.
Hartup, W. W. (1993). Adolescents and their friends. In B. Laursen (Ed.), *Close friendships in adolescence: New directions for child development* (No. 60, pp. 3–22). San Francisco: Jossey-Bass.
Hartup, W. W. (1996). The company they keep: Friendships and their developmental significance. *Child Development, 67,* 1–13.
Hartup, W. W. (1999). Constraints on peer socialization: Let me count the ways. *Merrill-Palmer Quarterly, 45,* 172–183.
Hartup, W. W., & Laursen, B. (1999). Relationships as developmental contexts: Retrospective themes and contemporary issues. In W. A. Collins & B. Laursen (Eds.), *Minnesota Symposium on Child Psychology: Vol. 30. Relationships as developmental contexts* (pp. 13–35). Mahwah, NJ: Erlbaum.
Hartup, W. W., & Stevens, N. (1997). Friendships and adaptation in the life course. *Psychological Bulletin, 121,* 355–370.
Houtzager, B., & Baerveldt, C. (1999). Just like normal: A social network study of the relationship of petty crime and the intimacy of adolescent friendships. *Social Behavior and Personality, 27,* 177–192.
Hundleby, J. D., & Mercier, G. W. (1987). Family and friends as social environments and their relationship to young adolescents' use of alcohol, tobacco, and marijuana. *Journal of Marriage and the Family, 49,* 151–164.
Juvonen, J., & Graham, S. (Eds.). (2001). *Peer harassment in school: The plight of the vulnerable and victimized.* New York: Guilford Press.
Juvonen, J., Nishina, A., & Graham, S. (2000). Peer harassment, psychological adjustment, and school functioning in early adolescence. *Journal of Educational Psychology, 92,* 349–359.
Kandel, D. B., & Andrews, K. (1987). Processes of adolescent socialization by parents and peers. *International Journal of the Addictions, 22,* 319–342.
Karcher, M. J., & Lindwall, J. (in press). Social interest, connectedness, and challenging experiences: What makes high school mentors persist? *Journal of Individual Psychology.*
Keefe, K., & Berndt, T. J. (1996). Relation of friendship quality to self-esteem in early adolescence. *Journal of Early Adolescence, 16,* 110–129.
Kerr, M., & Stattin, H. (2000). What parents know, how they know it, and several forms of adolescent adjustment: Further support for a reinterpretation of monitoring. *Developmental Psychology, 36,* 366–380.
Kiesner, J., Cadinu, M., Poulin, F., & Bucci, M. (2002). Group identification in early adolescence:

Its relation with peer adjustment and its moderator effect on peer influence. *Child Development, 73,* 196–208.
Kinney, D. A. (1993). From nerds to normals: The recovery of identity among adolescents from middle school to high school. *Sociology of Education, 66,* 21–40.
Laursen, B. (Ed.). (1993). *Close friendships in adolescence.* San Francisco: Jossey-Bass.
Laursen, B. (1996). Closeness and conflict in adolescent peer relationships: Interdependence with friends and romantic partners. In W. M. Bukowski, A. F. Newcomb, & W. H. Hartup (Eds.), *The company they keep* (pp. 186–210). New York: Cambridge University Press.
Laursen, B. (2001) A developmental meta-analysis of peer conflict resolution. *Developmental Review, 21,* 423–449.
Laursen, B., & Collins, W. A. (1994). Interpersonal conflict during adolescence. *Psychological Bulletin, 115,* 197–209.
Laursen, B., & Williams, V. A. (1997). Perceptions of interdependence and closeness in family and peer relationships among adolescents with and without a romantic partner. In S. Shulman & W. A. Collins (Eds.), *Romantic relationships in adolescence: Developmental perspectives* (pp. 3–20). San Francisco: Jossey-Bass.
Lease, A. M., & Axelrod, J. L. (2001). Position in the peer group's perceived organizational structure: Relation to social status and friendship. *Journal of Early Adolescence, 21,* 377–404.
Macleod, J. (1995). *Ain't no makin' it.* Boulder, CO: Westview Press.
Magnusson, D. (1988). *Individual development from an interactional perspective.* Hillsdale, NJ: Erlbaum.
Merten, D. E. (1996). Visibility and vulnerability: Responses to rejection by nonaggressive junior high school boys. *Journal of Early Adolescence, 16,* 5–26.
Montgomery, M. J., & Sorell, G. T. (1998). Love and dating experience in early and middle adolescence: Grade and gender comparisons. *Journal of Adolescence, 21,* 677–689.
Mounts, N. S. (2001). Young adolescents' perceptions of parental management of peer relationships. *Journal of Early Adolescence, 21,* 92–122.
Mounts, N. S., & Steinberg, L. (1995). An ecological analysis of peer influence on adolescent grade point average and drug use. *Developmental Psychology, 31,* 915–922.
Neemann, J., Hubbard, J., & Masten, A. (1995). The changing importance of romantic relationship involvement to competence from late childhood to late adolescence. *Development and Psychopathology, 7,* 727–750.
Nelson, D. A., & Crick, N. R. (1999). Rose-colored glasses: Examining the social information-processing of pro-social young adolescents. *Journal of Early Adolescence, 19,* 17–38.
Paxton, S. J., Schutz, H. K., Wertheim, E. H., & Muir, S. L. (1999). Friendship clique and peer influences on body image concerns, dietary restraint, extreme weight loss behaviors, and binge eating in adolescent girls. *Journal of Abnormal Psychology, 108,* 255–266.
Peshkin, A. (1991). *The color of strangers, the color of friends.* Chicago: University of Chicago Press.
Piaget, J. (1958). *The growth in logical thinking from childhood to adolescence.* New York: Basic Books.
Prinstein, M. J., & La Greca, A. M. (2002). Peer crowd affiliation and internalizing distress in childhood and adolescence: A longitudinal follow-back study. *Journal of Research on Adolescence, 12,* 325–351.
Rose, A. (2002). Co-rumination in friendships of girls and boys. *Child Development, 73,* 1830–1843.
Roth, M. A., & Parker, J. G. (2001). Affective and behavioral responses to friends who neglect their friends for dating partners: Influences of gender, jealousy and perspective. *Journal of Adolescence, 24,* 281–296.
Rubin, K. H., Bukowski, W., & Parker, J. G. (1998). Peer interactions, relationships, and groups, In W. Damon (Ed.), *Handbook of child psychology* (5th ed., 619–700). New York: Wiley.
Ryan, A. M. (2001). The peer group as a context for the development of young adolescent motivation and achievement. *Child Development, 72,* 1135–1150.
Sabongui, A. G., Bukowski, W. M., & Newcomb, A. F. (1998). The peer ecology of popularity: The network embeddedness of a child's friend predicts the child's subsequent popularity. In W. M. Bukowski & A. N. H. Cillessen (Eds.), *Sociometry then and now: Building on six*

decades of measuring children's experiences with the peer group. New directions for child development (No. 80, pp. 83–91). San Francisco: Jossey-Bass.
Savin-Williams, R. C. (1980). Dominance hierarchies in groups of middle to late adolescent males. *Journal of Youth and Adolescence, 9,* 75–85.
Savin-Williams, R. C. (1994). Dating those you can't love and loving those you can't date. In R. Montemayor, G. R. Adams, & T. P. Gullatta (Eds.), *Advances in adolescent development: Vol. 6. Personal relationships during adolescence* (pp. 168–195). Thousand Oaks, CA: Sage.
Schofield, J. W. (1981). *Black and white in school: Trust, tension, or tolerance?.* New York: Praeger.
Shulman, S., & Knafo, D. (1997). Balancing closeness and individuality in adolescent close relationships. *International Journal of Behavioral Development, 21,* 687–702.
Shulman, S., & Laursen, B. (2002). Adolescent perceptions of conflict in interdependent and disengaged friendships. *Journal of Research on Adolescence, 12,* 353–372.
Shulman, S., Laursen, B., Kalman, Z., & Karpovsky, S. (1997). Adolescent intimacy revisited. *Journal of Youth and Adolescence, 26,* 597–617.
Shulman, S., Levy-Shiff, R., Kedem, P., & Alon, E. (1997). Intimate relationships among adolescent romantic partners and same-sex friends: Individual and systemic perspectives. In S. Shulman & W. A. Collins (Eds.), *Romantic relationships in adolescence: Developmental perspectives. New directions for child development* (No. 78, pp. 37–51). San Francisco: Jossey-Bass.
Sroufe, L. A., Egeland, B., & Carlson, E. A. (1999). One social world: The integrated development of parent-child and peer relationships. In W. A. Collins & B. Laursen (Eds.), *The Minnesota symposia on child psychology: Vol. 30. Relationships as developmental contexts* (pp. 241–261). Mahwah, NJ: Erlbaum.
Stone, M. R., & Brown, B. B. (1998). In the eye of the beholder: Adolescents' perceptions of peer crowd stereotypes. In R. E. Muuss &. H. D. Porton (Eds.), *Adolescent behavior and society: A book of readings* (5th ed., pp. 158–169). New York: McGraw-Hill.
Stone, M. R., & Brown, B. B. (1999). Identity claims and projections: Descriptions of self and crowds in secondary school. In J. A. McLellan & M. J. V. Pugh (Eds.), *The role of peer groups in adolescent social identity: Exploring the importance of stability and change* (pp. 7–20). San Francisco: Jossey-Bass.
Strouse, D. L. (1999). Adolescent crowd orientations: A social and temporal analysis. In J. A. McLellan & M. J. V. Pugh (Eds.), *The role of peer groups in adolescent social identity: Exploring the importance of stability and change* (pp. 37–54). San Francisco: Jossey-Bass.
Sullivan, H. S. (1953). *The interpersonal theory of psychiatry.* New York: Norton.
Thurlow, C. (2001). The usual suspects? A comparative investigation of crowds and social-type labeling among young British teenagers. *Journal of Youth Studies 4,* 319–334.
Tilton-Weaver, L., & Galambos, N. (in press). Parents' peer management behaviors: Attempts to influence adolescents' peer relationships. *Journal of Research on Adolescence.*
Urberg, K. (1992). Locus of peer influence: Social crowd and best friend. *Journal of Youth and Adolescence, 21,* 439–450.
van Oostrum, N., & Horvath, P. (1997). The effects of hostile attribution on adolescents' aggressive responses to social situations. *Canadian Journal of School Psychology, 13,* 48–59.
Way, N., Cowal, K., Gingold, R., Pahl, K., & Bissessar, N. (2001). Friendship patterns among African American, Asian American, and Latino adolescents from low-income families. *Journal of Social and Personal Relationships, 18,* 29–53.
Youniss, J., McLellan, J. A., & Strouse, D. (1994). "We're popular but we're not snobs": Adolescents describe their crowds. In R. Montemayor, G. R. Adams, & T. P. Gullotta (Eds.), *Advances in adolescent development: Vol. 6. Personal relationships during adolescence* (pp. 101–122). Newbury Park, CA: Sage.
Youniss, J., & Smollar, J. (1985). *Adolescent relations with mothers, fathers, and friends.* Chicago: University of Chicago Press.
Zimmer-Gembeck, M. J. (1999). Stability, change, and individual differences in involvement with friends and romantic partners among adolescent females. *Journal of Youth and Adolescence, 28,* 419–438.

Chapter 13

CONTEXTS FOR MENTORING: ADOLESCENT-ADULT RELATIONSHIPS IN WORKPLACES AND COMMUNITIES

Stephen F. Hamilton and Mary Agnes Hamilton

Mentor is an elastic term. It is popular in part because people can apply it in a variety of ways. *Telementoring* and *e-mentoring* are used for long-distance relationships in which people never actually meet face-to-face. Programs in which college students are designated as mentors for local youth may be indistinguishable from tutoring programs. Group mentoring matches one mentor with multiple protégés who meet simultaneously rather than in the more typical one-to-one relationship. *Peer mentors* violate the expectation that mentors are older than their protégés. In general, however, mentoring programs attempt to foster a relationship between a younger person and an adult that resembles in some ways and may even substitute for a parent-child relationship, harking back to the original Mentor, Odysseus's friend in whose care he left his son, Telemachus, when he left Ithaca to fight in Troy.

In this chapter we cast a wide net, applying the term *mentoring* to relationships that vary in depth and including mentoring programs and naturally occurring mentoring in various contexts—especially in workplaces. We focus on one-to-one adolescent-adult relationships. Our guiding premise is that mentoring can promote development in all adolescents, not just those who are recruited into programs because they are deemed at risk in some way. Mentoring, like parenting, is a source of support for adolescent development that should be available to all.

The complementary adolescent role in a mentoring relationship is most simply called *mentee.* However, other terms are also appropriate and are more resonant. *Protégé* carries the root connotation of being protected or sponsored. *Apprentice* implies a more instrumental relationship in which learning—originally, learning an occupation is central. We are especially interested in apprenticeship, but in view of its rarity in North America we strive to comprehend a wide range of situations in which adolescents are mentored by adults in apprentice-like roles—not only those formally labeled as such and not only those associated with occupational training. The workplaces that can be contexts for such roles and relationships include both school-related work-based learning (youth apprenticeship, internship, and cooperative education) and youth jobs that are unrelated to school.

If all adolescents can benefit from mentoring, then all adolescents should have the opportunity to be mentees, protégés, apprentices, interns, and so forth. The claim that mentoring is universally valuable cannot be firmly grounded in the empirical literature.

Our assertion that all adolescents should have access to mentoring—like any statement containing a value term such as *should*—cannot be proved empirically, although it can be either substantiated or challenged by research. Our purpose in this chapter is to build a conceptual framework based on theory and research that will advance both research and practice.

What Is a Mentor?

Urie Bronfenbrenner (personal communication, September 1988) proffered what we regard as the most thoughtful and compelling definition of a mentor. He arrived at it in the course of a project studying college students' retrospective accounts of mentoring relationships followed by designing and evaluating a mentoring program for young adolescents. He shared it with us as collaborators on that project following a summer of collaboration and conversations with Japanese colleagues interested in the topic.

> A mentor is an older, more experienced person who seeks to further the development of character and competence in a younger person by guiding the latter in acquiring mastery of progressively more complex skills and tasks in which the mentor is already proficient. The guidance is accomplished through demonstration, instruction, challenge, and encouragement on a more or less regular basis over an extended period of time. In the course of this process, the mentor and the young person develop a special bond of mutual commitment. In addition, the young person's relationship to the mentor takes on an emotional character of respect, loyalty, and identification.

Bronfenbrenner's definition serves as an anchor defining the most intensive and enduring form of apprenticeship. It closely matches the idea embedded in the word's etymology—that of an unrelated adult who functions almost like a parent. However, we believe the term can be usefully and appropriately applied even when all of these conditions are not met.

Bronfenbrenner's emphasis on a younger person's "mastery of progressively more complex skills and tasks" is particularly apposite to our emphasis on work and other goal-directed activities as contexts for mentoring. Note, however, that Bronfenbrenner refers not only to the young person's growing competence but also to character. In our terms, mentoring promotes personal and social competence and technical competence as well. Mentors help their protégés master new skills, and they promote character. Although Bronfenbrenner does not spell out the sequence or relation between these two domains, we suspect that character is influenced more by role modeling than by instruction. The relationship's "emotional character of respect, loyalty, and identification" animate the mentor's function as a role model, which, after all, he or she cannot control. An adult only becomes a role model if a youth chooses to regard that adult as one.

We found a striking echo of Bronfenbrenner's definition in the statement of a mentor in the youth apprenticeship demonstration project we directed (Hamilton & Hamilton, 1997, pp. 48–49).

> One of the things I saw that Don was somewhat slack on was discipline. When I would set up a meeting with Don he thought it was okay to show up late. I know one time for sure he

> showed up late to a meeting and I wouldn't meet with him. I told him he had lost his slot. I told him, "We have a time schedule, and you weren't there." And I said, "Not only were you not there, you didn't call me." I think that was the last time he was late. And I'm hoping that carries over into school, into the next job he might have.
>
> I put it on the table and deal with it, okay? Because I think if I allow him to get away with it here he might have felt going to college he could slip, slide, and skate, or do what I call a Peggy Fleming—try to skate through. And I felt that I needed to be firm with him but at the same time be fair. For the most part I think Don appreciated it. And I could tell he appreciated it because as our relationship evolved and the work relationship evolved I noticed that he was able to share more and more with me some other things that were going on in his life too.

This mentor, in addition to teaching the technical aspects of the work, also taught punctuality, which we categorize as an aspect of personal competence. He made the point that demanding punctuality of his apprentice, far from alienating him, actually created a basis for extending their relationship beyond the workplace into his personal life.

Bronfenbrenner's definition emphasizes the teaching role of a mentor, but also describes what social psychologists call a *primary relationship*—one that endures over time and extends across life domains (personal, occupational, leisure) like family relationships and those among close friends. He also enumerates some of the mentor's behaviors: "demonstration, instruction, challenge, and encouragement."

These behaviors emphasize the instrumental function mentors perform more than they do the psychosocial functions. In practice, instrumental and psychosocial functions often overlap, and Bronfenbrenner's definition includes both, but the conceptual distinction helps to differentiate types of mentors and mentoring programs. Referring to the mentoring of adults in corporate settings, Kram (1985) distinguished mentoring for career development (an instrumental purpose) from psychosocial mentoring. Mentor behavior related to career development includes sponsorship, exposure visibility, coaching, and giving challenging assignments. Psychosocial mentoring behavior includes role modeling, confirmation, counseling, and friendship (Chao, Walz, & Gardner, 1992).

Both the psychosocial and instrumental functions of mentoring vary with the protégé's developmental state and associated needs. The ways in which a workplace mentor aids a high school student's career advancement could include some of those listed by Kram (1985) for rising executives, but they would likely also include conveying such basic information as the educational requirements associated with various occupations and positions, a firm's organizational structure, and the professional hierarchy in an occupational area.

Parents and mentors do many of the same things, probably with similar effects on youth. Our position, however, is that mentors by definition are not parents. We believe that the term loses its utility if parents are considered mentors. The relationship between parents and mentors is another issue to which we return later. Other relatives, such as aunts, uncles, and the older spouses of siblings, are easier to include as mentors. Grandparents pose an even more difficult classification challenge. For present purposes it is sufficient to exclude parents.

Bronfenbrenner eloquently described a quasi-parental, close, and enduring relationship. But must we limit the term *mentor* to a nonparental adult with whom an adolescent has such a relationship? We embrace two sides of this issue. Ideally we would reserve the term for just the kind of person Bronfenbrenner describes. Research cited below supports his claim that close, enduring relationships are especially powerful. However, both practical and theoretical arguments support using the term more broadly. We have already excluded from our use of the term in this chapter e-mentors and volunteers who are actually tutors. But if we applied Bronfenbrenner's definition strictly, what would we call the adult who had just been matched with an adolescent in a mentoring program?

In the youth apprenticeship demonstration project we directed, we used two terms (coach and mentor) to distinguish the coach role (a relatively constrained role), which entails teaching apprentices how to perform job tasks, from the mentor role, which we defined as extending beyond this domain to encompass personal and social competence—character—in personal as well as occupational life. (Note that the mentor whose statement was previously quoted referred to teaching his apprentice the importance of punctuality—a social competence in our terms—as setting the stage for mentoring that extended into his apprentice's personal life.) We argued that a program director can assign coaches but that mentors in Bronfenbrenner's sense must be chosen by youth. However, we found the distinction difficult to sustain, partly because the boundary is unclear, but more because the term *mentor* is so widely used and understood as what we wanted to call *coach.* (See Nettles, 1994, for a constructive use of the term *coach.*)

Another reason exists for allowing a looser definition. In his classic article, "The Strength of Weak Ties," Granovetter (1973, see also 1983) made the case that for some purposes—notably, in learning about job possibilities—the most important relationships are not close but distal. Extrapolating from this well-established principle, we would argue that adults can contribute significantly to adolescents' development even when their relationship is moderately close and of limited duration. Use of the gerund form, mentoring, is one (perhaps overly subtle) way to capture both the close and enduring relationships Bronfenbrenner described and the more fleeting relationships that might nonetheless prove quite critical to adolescents. Mentoring allows for a separation of the function from an individual who is identified as a Mentor. (We capitalize this use of the term hereafter to emphasize the person's uniqueness and importance.) Teachers often do the kinds of things we attribute to mentors without necessarily being identified by youth as their mentors. Other adults may similarly perform mentoring functions without being a nonparental adult that a youth identifies as being important in multiple ways, being emotionally close, and having an enduring relationship. This conception opens the prospect for mentoring from multiple sources—not just over the life course, but at any period. It also reduces somewhat the tension that can arise in adults who feel unready to commit to the kind of relationship Bronfenbrenner described but nonetheless are able and willing to teach and advise youth within more constrained boundaries.

NATURAL MENTORING

Natural mentors assume the role without any formal sponsorship or programmatic support. They are part of a young person's existing social network rather than introduced explicitly as mentors. They might be friends of the family, neighbors, athletic coaches, music or dance instructors, clergy, youth group leaders, bosses, or teachers.

Simply being in a young person's social network does not make such an adult a mentor. That term is reserved for those who at least approach Bronfenbrenner's definition: They must actively seek to promote the youth's development by teaching and giving advice, and the two must share an enduring emotional bond.

Natural mentoring has not been extensively studied, nor does relevant research always use the term. Often such research entails surveys of adolescents or of young adults asked to recall their adolescence, in which a key question is about "important people in your life." Questions typically then probe the nature of the relationships and identify some of the people mentioned as unrelated adult mentors (for an example of this approach, see Hamilton & Darling, 1996).

One important finding from this literature is that most adolescents can name at least one adult outside the family who is important. When asked to name the 10 most important people in their lives before they entered college, 82% of 3rd-year college students named at least one adult outside the family (Hamilton & Darling, 1996; see also Blyth, Hill, & Thiel, 1982). In addition, 56% of seventh and eighth graders in another study said they had asked an unrelated adult for help with a problem (Munsch & Blyth, 1993). When asked to name important adults, nearly all adolescents list their parents, usually first. Some list stepparents and absent biological parents, indicating that parental figures are and remain important even when families divide and recombine. Surprisingly, Japanese youth asked the same question were less likely to list parents (Darling, Hamilton, Toyokama, & Matsuda, 2002).

Adolescents who report close nurturing relations with their parents are more likely to report having an unrelated adult who can be classified a mentor than are adolescents whose parents are less involved with them (Hamilton & Darling, 1996). In other words, natural mentors appear to complement parents more than they substitute for them; the rich get richer, so to speak. We would also hypothesize that nurturing parents help their children connect with potential adult mentors—for example, through family connections and participation in religious or other community organizations. According to Darling, Hamilton, and Hames (2003), adolescents' relations with natural mentors are more instrumental than their relations with either peers or parents. This tendency is especially striking in retrospective accounts; adults looking back on their youth identify as important to them people who made an instrumental difference in their lives (Tatar, 1998, p. 699).

The kinds of people adolescents identify as mentors—their social roles—reflect Bronfenbrenner's emphasis on enduring relationships. Classroom teachers are relatively rare. Family friends and neighbors are the most commonly reported social roles. As Darling et al. (2003) point out, the scarcity of teachers in adolescents' lists probably results from the large numbers of students in classes and the resulting impersonal nature of many of their interactions with students. However, teachers cannot be dismissed as potential mentors as long as even a few adolescents identify them as such.

MENTORING PROGRAMS

Matching a young person with an adult mentor has become a leading strategy in youth development programs and policies (Walker, 2000). The idea of a nonparental adult's assuming a quasi-parental role in relation to a young person has ancient roots and is institutionalized in some cultures. However, the term and the idea gained visibility in the past two decades as women began to move into corporate leadership positions. They discovered that one of the advantages enjoyed by their male colleagues and competitors was easy bonding with senior executives, male almost by definition, who gave them critical information and advice during golf games or over Scotch and cigars and who advocated on their behalf in high-level discussions of performance, promotions, and new assignments (Kanter, 1977). A widely read article in the *Harvard Business Review* claimed, "Everyone Who Makes It Has a Mentor" (Collins & Scott, 1978).

Rising corporate executives obviously require types of advice and encouragement quite different from those required by disadvantaged youth, and the nature of their relationships with mentors differs accordingly. Although the application of the idea to disadvantaged youth was not new, it was boosted by an inspiring story of generosity and hope. Eugene Lang, a New York City businessman and philanthropist, was invited to speak to the graduating class of P.S. 121, the Harlem elementary school he had attended. Speaking to the African American and Hispanic students who now lived in his old neighborhood, he felt the hollowness of his exhortations and in an inspired moment promised to pay for the college education of every one who graduated from high school. What followed demonstrated not only that the promise of financial support was a powerful inspiration, but also that it worked best when joined with regular advice, support, encouragement, and intervention. Lang himself met frequently with the students, but he also hired a social worker to engage them and their families more intensively. This attention proved essential to enabling some of the students to cope with barriers to their academic success, including premature parenthood and, in one case, incarceration. The "Dreamers" (as they were called) who made it through high school were eligible for substantial financial aid from other sources. Mentoring made more of a difference than money.

Twenty years later, 54 of the original class of 61 remained part of the I Have a Dream program, and two thirds of those had completed at least 2 years of higher education, a remarkable level of achievement compared to previous P.S. 121 classes, in which only a quarter graduated from high school. Early reports of the program's impact inspired the creation of numerous similar programs and a national foundation (www.ihad.org).

Most mentoring programs for youth emphasize "psychosocial mentoring." Their goals involve reducing problem behavior and improving school performance. Most programs are aimed at youth of elementary and middle-school age. Mentoring is popular as an approach to improving the prospects for disadvantaged youth in part because it is so viscerally appealing. Eugene Lang's story is unique in its scale, but it is easily understandable, and the personal relationship at its center can be replicated by others who lack his financial resources. Voluntary, one-to-one responses to poverty have a long history in the United States (Freedman, 1993), and they have been especially favored by politicians who seek to reduce government spending. Mentoring draws bipartisan support because it is equally attractive to those who advocate self-help and those who are prepared to devote more tax dollars to reducing poverty. Most adults can think of someone who served as a mentor to them. By volunteering to be a mentor, they feel they are giving back some of what they received (Hamilton & Hamilton, in press).

The only flaw in this rosy portrait is the belief that relying on unpaid mentors makes it cheap. Surveying the mentoring movement, Freedman concluded that the greatest threat is "fervor without infrastructure" (1993, pp. 92–93). Successful programs, he found, invest significant resources into staff who recruit, select, train, and support volunteer mentors. In some cases, staff are actually the people who maintain a relationship with youth who are to be mentored because staff are more readily available and remain with the program longer than do many volunteers, despite their best intentions.

Mentoring programs are artificial means of creating relationships between youth and caring adults that might have occurred naturally, without a program, if youth and adults came into regular contact with each other under circumstances that encourage mentoring. Freedman (1993, p. 111) aptly called such circumstances "mentor-rich environments" and advocated more attention to creating them and lessened reliance on a "super mentor" who single-handedly turns a troubled youth's life around. This suggestion is consistent with our theme of mentoring as a function distributed among multiple adults, not only a single person identified as a Mentor.

Mentoring programs operate on the assumption that if they can create mentoring relationships, they will also achieve the same benefits that naturally occurring mentoring appears to confer. However, it is possible that some of those apparent benefits of natural mentoring are simply preexisting qualities in protégés that make them attractive to mentors in the first place—that is, selection effects may account for differences favoring youth with natural mentors. Young people who are more outgoing and readier to take the initiative, who have winning personalities and know how to ingratiate themselves with adults may recruit mentors successfully. Simply assigning an adult mentor to a youth without these qualities may not achieve the desired effects.

Despite this and other critiques that might be leveled at mentoring programs, such programs hold promise as a means of overcoming society's segregation of young people from adults outside their families. Schools isolate young people from adults for most of the day. Suburban residential patterns encourage the congregation of families at similar life course stages. Elders have their own separate institutions and communities. Long work hours and long commuting distances further separate the ages. Ironically, mentoring program participants frequently encounter the same barriers that kept them apart initially. Busy school and work schedules limit the time available together. When mentors have to travel long distances from their homes or workplaces to the neighborhoods where their protégés live, being a mentor takes extra time and precise scheduling. A few missed appointments can doom a relationship (Hamilton & Hamilton, 1992).

Mentoring programs are located in a range of contexts. Big Brothers/Big Sisters and similar programs operate in the community at large. That is, they recruit both "Bigs" and "Littles" from a given geographic area and then the pairs interact in a variety of settings, including homes, parks, restaurants, and movie theaters. Mentoring relationships can also be created within other types of communities. In some faith communities, for example, young people preparing for full membership are assigned to adult members of the community other than their parents who acts as a sponsors for their first communion, confirmation, bat or bar mitzvah, or other coming-of-age rituals. Mentoring programs are also created for more specific purposes, such as aiding teenage mothers or helping young people avoid delinquent behavior. In these cases, both the eligible population of youth and the source of appropriate mentors are constrained.

The term *corporate mentoring* is used for programs in which corporations encourage their employees to become mentors for youth outside the workplace (Lund, 1992). Although the activity is laudable, the term can be confusing because it implies that mentoring occurs inside the corporation or in the workplace. Corporate mentoring programs tend to emphasize psychosocial goals and school performance rather than acquiring work skills.

WORK AS A CONTEXT FOR MENTORING

Workplaces can be mentor-rich environments, bringing adolescents into regular and sustained contact with adults, some of whom may become Mentors and more of whom may do mentoring. The epitome of workplace mentoring is found in the institution of apprenticeship. Apprentice is an in-between role—combining work with learning, adult-like responsibilities for performing real work with not-yet-adult authorization to be less productive, to ask questions, and to make mistakes. It is, in short, an optimal social role for the life stage of adolescence. Although formal apprenticeship is rare in the United States and almost nonexistent for adolescents, in its idealized form it can serve as a benchmark, a point of comparison for less formal adolescent work as a context for mentoring.

Formal apprenticeship is based on a contract that specifies the responsibilities of both parties. The apprentice is expected to perform productive work and is paid for doing so. The employer is expected to teach knowledge and skills that will enable the apprentice to become progressively more productive and ultimately qualified for a position requiring high skills and paying good wages. Mentoring is the master's obligation.

Apprenticeship never gained the prominence in the United States that it held in Europe from medieval times, nor was it ever as formally codified in this country. Part of the attraction of the new world was freedom from feudal-style bonds that maintained a rigid class system. Apprenticeship was one example of such bonds. The country's most famous apprentice, Benjamin Franklin, represented his fellow colonists' and later citizens' attitude very accurately by running away from his contract as an apprentice to his brother (Rorabaugh, 1986; see Hamilton, 1990, for details on apprenticeship in Germany and the United States).

In the United States, as in most countries with highly developed economies (with the notable exception of the German-speaking countries and parts of central Europe), schooling has displaced apprenticeship. School is where young people learn about the world outside their homes and gain the fundamental knowledge and skills they will need as adult workers and citizens. Schools are reasonably efficient organizations for teaching the cognitive skills required in a contemporary economy. As necessary as they are, however, schools separate adolescents from some important kinds of learning opportunities and relationships.

Coleman pointed out that "the student role is not a role of taking action and experiencing consequences. It is not a role in which one learns by hard knocks. It is a relatively passive role, always preparing for action, but never acting" (1972, p. 434). He contrasted American youth of the 19th century and earlier who were intimately engaged in work and community with today's youth who have ready access to vast quantities of knowledge but opportunity to do comparatively little. School learning is typically quite abstract. Students learn general principles and generic skills, with the expectation that they will be able to apply and build on this knowledge in specific situations.

Resnick (1987) identified additional contrasts between learning in school and mental activity outside school. Schools expect students to do their own work and evaluate them as individuals. Outside of school much work is done in teams. (It should be noted that many schools have begun to incorporate more teamwork in their pedagogy as a result of this critique.) Schoolwork tends to be purely mental and abstract. It is related primarily to symbol manipulation. Outside of schools, thinking and reasoning are closely associated with tool use and deeply embedded in particular contexts. Although abstraction and generalization have their virtues, when they are unanchored, they can result in what Whitehead called "inert ideas" (1929, p. 13)—ideas that are not just detached from application but fundamentally flawed.

The limitations and peculiarities of schools as learning environments are not just intellectual and pedagogical; they are also social. Another limitation Coleman (1972) saw in schools is that adolescents predominate there, whereas in most workplaces adolescents are in the minority, surrounded by adults. This observation was part of the rationale behind the report of the Panel on Youth he chaired that issued the report *Youth: Transition to Adulthood* (1974), which recommended work experience as beneficial to adolescent development, especially as a means of linking them more closely with adults. (This report advanced a theme that Coleman articulated in his classic study, *The Adolescent Society,* 1961, of a growing separation between youth and adults.) This salutary view of work as a context in which adolescents can observe and develop relationships with caring adults was challenged directly by Greenberger and Steinberg's (1986) pathbreaking research on both the impact of adolescent work experience and the nature of that work. They found adolescent work concentrated in a narrow slice of the labor market, typified by fast food restaurants, in which adolescents in fact predominate and even spend much of their time serving adolescent customers. They argued persuasively that typical youth jobs no longer offer the opportunities for learning and socialization through interaction with adults that they might have before the rise of the shopping mall with its chain stores and franchise restaurants.

Recognizing the limits of typical youth jobs as learning environments, policy makers became interested in the potential educational value of school-related work experience in the late 1980s, when a stagnant economy was attributed in part to ineffective schools. This attribution was popularized in the 1983 report, *A Nation at Risk* (National Commission on Excellence in Education), which recommended more rigorous courses and examinations for all students and higher standards for high school graduation; however, other recommendations emerged. The most influential alternatives were articulated in *The Forgotten Half* (1988), which was followed by a series of related publications calling attention to the plight of youth without college diplomas and recommending (among other ideas) the adoption of "youth apprenticeship" as a complement to more rigorous schooling (Hamilton, 1990; Lerman & Pouncy, 1990; National Center on Education and the Economy, 1990; Nothdurft, 1989). Youth apprenticeship gained sufficient political support to be included in legislation proposed by the first President Bush and to become one of candidate Bill Clinton's campaign promises. The School-to-Work Opportunities Act of 1994 fulfilled the promise (20 U.S.C. 6101–6251 2000).

Despite being the bill's inspiration—as is evident both in the historical record and in the language of the legislation—youth apprenticeship was not well served by it for at least two reasons. First, the legislation supported a range of approaches to strengthening connections between school and work, only one of which was youth apprenticeship. Others included field trips, job shadowing, cooperative education (already well established in some vocational fields), and paid and unpaid internships of varying duration and formality. It also called for a range of related activities, including reorienting curricula around what were called career majors and working collaboratively with employers and other organizations. Second, exemplifying the process of reinventing government, which had also been a campaign theme, funding for School-to-Work was restricted for most purposes to a 5-year period. This time period proved hopelessly inadequate. It would have been short for instituting a new program, but the legislation called for the creation of new systems—a goal that was much more elusive and literally impossible to achieve in the time allowed.

Employers' reluctance was another critical barrier to youth apprenticeship achieving substantial scale. (For a contrary view, see Bailey, Hughes, & Barr, 2000.) Employers in the United States are not accustomed to providing extensive training to front-line workers. They invest heavily in training for managers and engineers but much less in training workers without college degrees (Eurich, 1985). They also resist hiring applicants in their teens and early 20s for jobs that include training and offer a career ladder. Investing in training high school students who may or may not become their regular employees would therefore be a major change. The most widespread initiative is in auto repair, a field in which shortages of technicians loom because of the advancing median age in the occupation and because changes in automobile technology have brought demands for new kinds of skills. In response to this need, General Motors created a training program for high school students that was inspired by its CEO's experience with German apprenticeship. It is now supported by 10 automobile manufacturers and known as Automotive Youth Educational Systems (AYES; www.ayes.org). Training is based in high school vocational education programs but also includes an internship provided by a local dealer. Siemens Corporation also made a strong commitment to youth apprenticeship, importing to this country programs and practices from its German base (see Hamilton & Hamilton, 1999, for more information on both these initiatives).

Cooperative occupational education experience (co-op), one of the oldest types of work-based learning in the United States, enrolled approximately 8% of high school juniors and seniors at last report, nearly all of them vocational students (U.S. General Accounting Office, 1991, p. 16). Co-op integrates classroom learning with paid, practical work experience in a field of the student's interest. Skills to be mastered are identified in a formal training plan, which is developed at the beginning of the co-op program by the employer, the teacher-coordinator, and the student. Training plans are crucial for identifying goals, establishing criteria, guiding training and evaluation, and maintaining communication among all partners.

At the worksite, students work directly with a supervisor or mentor over a semester or a year to observe, assist, and accomplish work tasks. Programs are planned and supervised by the school, and students receive academic credit for their work and for attendance at an occupational education class. Like other types of work-based learning, co-op programs differ significantly from one another. Because co-op programs are designed and organized by the school in response to the opportunities available in specific workplaces, they are easily modified to fit the needs of different students and schools.

The term *internship* is used far more casually than either apprenticeship or co-op. There is no generally accepted definition of what an intern is and does. Interns may be paid or unpaid. Like apprenticeships and cooperative education, internships combine work-based learning with school-based learning to enhance occupational and academic education. Interns, co-ops, and youth apprentices typically spend part of their school day at work, where they follow a learning plan while also participating in work tasks. Especially in the first year or two of a youth apprenticeship, an observer watching three students at work might be unable to distinguish the youth apprentice from the co-op student from the intern. However, cooperative education and internship diverge in significant ways from youth apprenticeship.

Cooperative education and internship are distinguished by their flexibility and individualization. Many cooperative education and internship instructors arrange worksites for specific students; that is, they begin with a student and find a placement. Learning plans are often customized for a particular student in a particular site. Length of working time, the duration of the experience, and most other aspects of the program are subject to negotiation.

Youth apprenticeship, in contrast, is both more rigid and more systematic. It is organized to impart competencies determined to meet the needs of an industry. Rather than being individualized, it is standardized—both in the sense of being uniform and in the sense of meeting set standards. Youth apprenticeship lasts longer—up to 4 years—and as a result, it yields more advanced technical skills. When youth apprentices achieve the prescribed standards, their achievement is certified by their employer and this certification serves as a portable credential, something they can carry with them to another employer and another geographic location. Interns and co-ops may take away an employer's recommendation but not a recognized credential. The point of distinguishing among the three is not to identify one as superior. They serve different purposes. All three can be powerful learning experiences, but they do not achieve identical objectives.

Another important type of work-based learning that is often overlooked is service-learning. Service-learning, as the hyphen suggests, combines learning opportunities with doing something for others (see www.servicelearning.org/who/def.htm for more definitions). The term has gained currency as a refinement of community service (Honnet & Poulson, 1989), which is now required by some schools. Adding learning to service emphasizes that in addition to helping others, young people also benefit themselves. Links to classroom learning and the opportunity to reflect on the service experience are critical to making service a learning experience.

Because service-learning is supposed to be an altruistic activity (one reason that required service can be problematic), it is often distinguished sharply from work-based learning, which is seen as preparation for earning a living. However, an unpaid internship in an organization providing human services or an advocacy organization may be impossible to distinguish from service-learning.

High-quality work-based learning of any type depends on mentoring; one or more adults must take responsibility for teaching and advising a young person to assure that the work will contribute to learning. We turn now to the question of how mentoring promotes adolescent development.

HOW DOES MENTORING PROMOTE ADOLESCENT DEVELOPMENT?

Four theoretical perspectives shed light on the question of how mentoring promotes adolescent development: (a) the ecology of human development, (b) social learning theory, (c) resilience, and (d) social capital. We summarize each of these perspectives in turn as a basis for examining research about how mentoring affects adolescent development. (These perspectives are the ones we have found most illuminating; others could also be applied. See, for example, Rhodes', 2002, citations of theory and research on counseling and psychotherapy.)

Ecology of Human Development

Bronfenbrenner's definition of a mentor identifies development with gaining "character and competence." It also specifies how this acquisition occurs. Competence is enhanced by the mentor's assistance in the protégé's "mastery of progressively more complex skills and tasks." Character is a product of the emotional attachment, based on "respect, loyalty, and identification." These outcomes and characteristics of the relationship, however, are also interactive. Bronfenbrenner's definition—especially its emphasis on the regular and enduring quality of the relationship—anticipated and is wholly consistent with his bioecological perspective on human development (Bronfenbrenner & Morris, 1998) featuring four defining properties that influence development interactively.

Process

"Proximal processes are posited as the primary engines of development" (Bronfenbrenner & Morris, 1998, p. 996). Proximal processes occur when people interact face-to-face. "Joint activities" is the term Bronfenbrenner (1979,Ch. 5) previously used for a similar construct, which is influenced by Vygotsky's notion of the "zone of proximal development" (1978)—that is, the arena in which a person can perform certain tasks only with assistance. Learning is demonstrated when the person becomes able to perform the same tasks independently.

Person

Development is affected by the characteristics of the people engaged in proximal processes. The characteristics of both the mentor and youth affect the outcome of the relationship. Some adults are more nurturing than others; some youth are more curious and more outgoing than others.

Context

Environmental contexts (Bronfenbrenner, 1979, pp. 22–26) vary in the opportunities and supports they afford for development. As an agent of her or his own development, the developing person selects and shapes contexts as well as being influenced by them.

The immediate settings in which people act are nested within and interact with a set of broader contexts, including the community, culture, and economy.

Time

By definition, development occurs over time. It is also cumulative; those whose development has been fostered at one time are better able to take advantage of future development-enhancing opportunities. Time also refers to the historical period in which a person develops. Bronfenbrenner stressed that enduring social relationships are most likely to foster development, a point emphasized in his definition of a mentor.

This theoretical orientation explains not only why mentoring would be expected to promote development, but also what conditions are most conducive to development. Adult mentors and their apprentices or protégés engage in proximal processes that entail teaching and learning. These processes occur in workplaces producing goods and services or in other engaging settings, and they persist over time. Caring and competent mentors are likely to be most effective, especially when their apprentices are committed, attentive, and diligent. Bronfenbrenner's conception of *The Ecology of Human Development* (1979) also accounts for differences in the effects of mentoring by pointing to the interactive effects that different settings have on each other. An apprentice, intern, or protégé whose parents are supportive will have an experience different from that of one whose parents are disengaged. A young person who arrives with a strong sense of purpose and direction that is based on temperament and previous experiences will be able to take advantage of the learning opportunities more quickly than will one who is unfocused and lacks confidence.

Social Learning Theory

The term *role model* is often used as a synonym for mentor, and being a role model is surely one of the key functions mentors perform. But the two are not strictly synonymous. A role model may be a distant figure—a sports star or musician, for example—whom the adolescent has never met. Nor is role modeling the only form of modeling. Albert Bandura (1986) has made the most extensive and important contributions to theory and research on modeling, or social learning—the two terms reflecting the perspectives of the teacher and the learner, respectively. Bandura aimed not just to describe learning, narrowly defined, but to account for *The Social Foundations of Thought and Action* (1986). His perspective, also designated social cognitive theory, is comprehensive enough to serve as an alternative to the theoretical formulations of psychodynamics, radical behaviorism, and trait theory for explaining human behavior.

Behaviorism focused much of Bandura's argument. He attempted to incorporate its basic elements—stimulus, response, and reward—but then introduced greater complexity. In particular, he tried to explain how the operations of the mind influence behavior and how the person influences the environment. By conceiving of human beings as both acting on and interpreting the environment's stimuli, he explains phenomena that radical behaviorism cannot explain, such as learning by example, or (in behaviorist terms) responding to stimuli and rewards administered to another person but not directly experienced.

"Models" in Bandura's formulation are teachers (intentional or unintentional); "observers" are learners. Unlike the behaviorists, Bandura attended to patterns of thought as well as behavior, and he posited a cognitive process that mediates between observation and performance. He also contradicted the radical behaviorists, who willfully ignore the existence or operation of anything not immediately observable, by citing his own and his associates' research indicating that

> In observational learning of complex novel actions, persons who simply observe the modeled patterns learn little, whereas those who cognitively transform actions to memorable symbolic codes achieve superior learning and retention of modeled activities. (1986, p. 14)

In emphasizing the essential contribution of the learner's own inferences to the learning process, he echoed Dewey (1938, p. 27), who wrote that reflection is what makes the difference between something that happens to a person and a learning experience.

For Bandura (1986), the key act in learning is observation; in teaching, it is modeling. Modeling in his terms goes far beyond the everyday use of the term as a person demonstrating a skill that an observer learns. It comprehends "physical demonstration, pictorial representation, or verbal description" (p. 70). Even reading printed instructions, then, is a case of observational learning. Furthermore, modeling teaches more than motor skills. In fact, Bandura is concerned about how general rules for thinking and acting are learned by observation. He labeled teaching of such lessons "abstract modeling."

> Through the process of abstract modeling, observers extract the rules underlying specific performances for generating behavior that goes beyond what they have seen or heard. In abstract modeling, judgmental skills and generalizable rules are being learned by observation. (Bandura, 1986, p. 100)

To illustrate this process, he described subjects in a study learning to construct sentences using the passive voice after being exposed to models.

One of Bandura's consistent themes is that unaided learning by trial and error (enactive learning) is highly inefficient. Learning by doing is most effective when it is guided by one who already knows. That person is then able to demonstrate, to explain—to think out loud about what is being demonstrated—and to pass judgment on the learner's performance.

Elaborating on his concern for internal influences on behavior, including the learner's inferences, Bandura identified four subfunctions or subprocesses governing observational learning: attentional processes, retention processes, production processes, and motivational processes (1986, pp. 51–69, 86–92). Failure to learn what has been modeled might be attributed to deficits in any of these subprocesses. In the first two, the learner may not have paid attention to the model or may not have retained what the model taught. In the second two, the learning might have occurred superficially but not been demonstrated in the form of altered behavior (i.e., production) because there is insufficient incentive to apply the lesson. Like Bronfenbrenner, Bandura held that learning depends upon the state of the learner as well as on conditions in the environment such as the skill of the teacher and the nature of the content.

Although Bandura applied his theory across a wide terrain, it seems particularly useful in the context of mentoring, especially workplace mentoring. It calls attention to the complexity of the process but identifies key elements in it that may repay close examination. In particular, the multiple roles he ascribes to the model help to enumerate the different kinds of actions that workplace mentors perform (see following discussions and Hamilton & Hamilton, 2002). Moreover, his account of the learner's functions calls attention to the reciprocal nature of the relationship. A mentor cannot succeed without a protégé's active collaboration. Bandura viewed behavior as mutually interacting with aspects of the person and the environment, a three-way interaction, rather than as determined by the bidirectional interaction of person and environment (1977, pp. 9–10). Hence, the apprentice's or protégé's interest, willingness to learn, and active search for competence are as important as the mentor's skill and dedication.

By bringing cognition into learning rather than accepting behaviorism's exclusive preoccupation with stimulus and reinforcement, Bandura placed the learner's thought and action at the center of the learning process. In addition to learning from the immediate consequences of one's own actions, one learns by observing the consequences of others' actions (vicarious learning) and by creating mental models of how things work that enable one to predict consequences that have not even been seen, much less experienced personally. Bandura contributed to our understanding of mentoring a much more complex idea of modeling than simply that of a role model. The outcome of greatest interest to him was learning, which is consistent with Bronfenbrenner's focus on competence; competence is the product of learning.

Social Capital

The term *social capital* makes an analogy between economic capital—such as money, buildings, and machinery—that enable the owner to engage in productive moneymaking activities and social relations or connections that similarly enable those who possess them to find opportunities to engage in productive activity. One of the best examples of social capital is having personal connections that enable one to find a job. A job seeker whose relatives and acquaintances are unemployed or employed only in low-level positions or one without extensive social connections at all is at a severe disadvantage in the labor market compared to a job seeker with many acquaintances and family members who are employed, especially if they hold decision-making positions. The prospects of finding a job are much higher if people tell a job seeker about openings and if acquaintances are in a position to recommend the person to those who are hiring.

Social capital is not always directly convertible into monetary value. A high school student with many friends has an easier time getting a ride home on a rainy afternoon than does one who is socially isolated. Simply knowing someone who can answer questions about daily needs such as a forgotten homework assignment or what people are wearing to the dance counts as social capital. Social capital inheres in the connections that enable a person to achieve her or his goals more readily.

James Coleman spelled out the differences among physical, human, and social capital:

> Physical capital is wholly tangible, being embodied in observable material form; human capital is less tangible, being embodied in the skills and knowledge acquired by an individual; social capital is even less tangible, for it is embodied in the *relations* among persons. Physical capital and human capital facilitate productive activity, and social capital does so as well. (1990, p. 304)

Coleman emphasized two desirable qualities of social capital. One, "closure," refers to reciprocal communication, obligations, and trust within a social network, as when parents in a neighborhood establish and enforce common behavioral norms for their children and share responsibility for each other's children (1990, pp. 319–320). "Stability" is the second. It can refer both to individuals and to the persistence of a social organization over time, regardless of who occupies positions in it. When social organizations are unstable and when individuals move in and out of a community frequently, residents are less able to form and maintain human capital (1990, p. 320).

For adolescents, social capital is especially important as a source of opportunities for development. Having more social capital does not by itself make an adolescent more highly developed. It can, however, enable an adolescent to gain new competencies and apply them in new situations. Having a mentor constitutes social capital for an adolescent. In addition to teaching new competencies directly (explicitly or implicitly), a mentor also extends a youth's social network, helping to create additional social capital by introducing the youth to other people who can be helpful. A mentor in an auto repair shop who is an expert on automobile transmissions, for example, explained to us that he temporarily assigned his apprentice to learn about air conditioning repair from another technician who is more skilled in that domain.

Another key mentoring function related to social capital is sponsorship or advocacy. A mentor may arrange for a youth to do something that would not otherwise have been possible—attending a concert, for example, or becoming a member of a community planning committee. He or she may encourage a teacher or coach to give the mentee a second chance or serve as a reference for a college or job application. Sponsorship is a unique mentoring function because it does not entail that the mentor him- or herself teaches. Rather, the mentor is helping the protégé to gain access to additional learning opportunities.

Putnam distinguished bridging social capital from bonding social capital (2000, pp. 22–24). Bonding social capital unites a group and excludes outsiders, as in a lodge or sorority. Bridging social capital makes connections among people who are different. A mentor from an adolescent's existing social network, such as a religious organization or neighborhood, can help form a bond with that network and function effectively within it. One who has knowledge of and connections with other networks will be able to introduce the adolescent to new people and possibilities. Both bonding and a bridging mentors can be helpful, but in different ways. Adolescents may need different types of mentors for different purposes and at different times in their lives; for example, a bonding mentor to help to clarify a youth's ethnic identity, whereas a bridging mentor is more useful in assisting career exploration.

Resilience

Werner and Smith's (2001) classic studies of the children of Kauai laid the foundation for much of the continuing work on the resilience phenomenon. In contrast to retrospective studies of people overcome by adversity, they followed a cohort of 698 longitudinally. By age 2, "about 30 percent of the individuals in this cohort encountered a combination of potent biological and psychological risk factors . . ." (p. 56). Two thirds of those identified as at risk had serious problems by age 10 and even more serious problems at age 18. The remaining third, however, overcame the same initial adversity. The resilience framework explicates the mechanisms that allow children and youth to overcome their vulnerability and achieve positive developmental outcomes. Rutter (2000) summarized the factors associated with resilience in Werner's work as including

> temperamental characteristics that elicited positive social responses from other people; a lifestyle of planfulness associated with self-efficacy and self-esteem; the availability of competent caregivers and supportive adults who fostered trust and a sense of coherence; and second-chance opportunities at school, work, church, or in the military that led to new experiences likely to foster competence and self-esteem. (pp. 659–660)

These factors can be categorized as personal characteristics, supportive relationships, and beneficial opportunities. Referring to supportive adults, Werner and Smith (2001) refer to relatives, neighbors, friends' parents, youth group leaders, and leaders and members of faith-based organizations. They noted too that participation in youth organizations (e.g., 4-H, YMCA, YWCA) was a source of emotional support (p. 58). Clearly, participation in these and in faith-based organizations provides access to supportive adults.

Interest in resilience has led to resilience training, efforts to instill resilient behavior in at-risk youth. Luthar and Cicchetti (2000, pp. 862–863) warned against treating resilience as an attribute of an individual, pointing out that the term refers simultaneously to a person and to the conditions in which she or he grows up. Attempting to instill resilience in individual children does not provide them with supportive relationships or beneficial opportunities. Moreover, resilience is not universal; a child who can overcome one threat may be vulnerable to another (Rutter, 2000, pp. 651–652). Nor is there reason to believe that resilience endures. As Luthar and Cicchetti explain, "these attributes are not indelibly implanted in children; rather, they are substantially shaped by life circumstances" (p. 863).

Rutter (2000), noting that some lists of protective factors are simply the antonyms of risk factors (p. 658), reserves the use of resilience to populations that have been exposed to risks. "Resilience cannot be studied satisfactorily in the absence of prior demonstration that the individuals concerned have actually experienced substantial risk" (p. 654). As an illustration, he cited Elder's (1986) finding and confirming studies by others that military experience was beneficial to disadvantaged, especially delinquent youth by giving them opportunities for education, postponing marriage, and improving their self-image, but that it has no such beneficial effects for advantaged youth or young adults who had already established careers and marriages (p. 664).

Clearly the kind of nonparental supportive adult found to be critical to resilience is what we are calling a Mentor. Moreover, the opportunities found to be critical as well are often contexts for mentoring. The connection between resilience and mentoring is strong.

> Research on resilience challenges the field to build a connectedness or sense of belonging, by transforming our families, schools, and communities to become "psychological homes" where youth can find mutually caring and respectful relationships and opportunities for meaningful involvement. (Benard, 1999, p. 271)

Synthesis of Theoretical Perspectives

All of these perspectives are consistent with an emphasis on *competence* as the aspect of development to which mentors contribute. Competence, defined in Bronfenbrenner's terms as the capacity to understand and act upon the environment, is the product of social learning. It enables adolescents to set and achieve goals—what social capital is used for. Resilience is a protective process through which individuals display competence or, in Luthar and Cicchetti's terms, "positive adaptation" (2000, p. 858) over time despite significant stress or adverse conditions.

Competence is not the only shorthand term usable to encompass various aspects of development. The recent National Research Council report on youth development uses personal and social assets for the same purpose (Eccles & Gootman, 2002). The two are compatible; competence seems to us to fit better with both the theoretical perspectives and the relevant research results. In developing a youth apprenticeship demonstration project, we worked with employers and educators to identify three categories of competence that we called technical, personal, and social (www.human.cornell.edu/youthwork/). It is helpful to differentiate components of competence in this way. Character, which Bronfenbrenner paired with competence as the outcomes of development in his definition of a mentor, is accounted for in the three categories of technical, personal, and social competence. Character, or the will to do what is right, is important because people can gain skill at destructive and antisocial behavior, which we would not wish to characterize as positive development.

By our definition, personal competence is manifested in responsible action. Social competence enables participation in an organization through adherence to professional rules and norms, teamwork, and communication. In the workplace context, technical competence includes academic knowledge and skill needed to do a good job. Wanting to a good job reflects character. Note that our definition of competence includes attitudes, emphasizing their expression in behavior.

When applying these categories for present purposes, we find it helpful to add academic competence as a fourth category. It is demonstrated by performing well in school (academically and socially), and learning effectively, including subjects that are not directly employment related. We use these four categories of competence in reviewing research results to identify the effects of mentoring on adolescent development.

Joint activities are important, not just relationships. We take this term from Bronfenbrenner, who elaborated it in terms of proximal processes; simply stated, it highlights the centrality to development of people and activities. The resilience literature affirms this point too, both by identifying beneficial opportunities that are associated with resilience and by listing among the supportive adults who are also associated with resilience several with whom adolescents become acquainted through activities, including youth group leaders and clergy. Both the ecology of human development and resilience recognize the balance that is needed between challenging or stretching an adolescent's capacities on the one hand and providing adequate support on the other.

Activities that foster development are optimally challenging. They entail real responsibility, but it is possible to demand too much responsibility, which can impede development. This point is often attributed in the resilience literature to Elder's (1974) study, *Children of the Great Depression,* finding that responsibility for helping the family was beneficial to those who were adolescents when their families lost income but harmful to those who were younger. Engaging in activities that make a difference to others enhances self-efficacy. Participation in the larger community as a genuine contributor is a particularly powerful example of such activities. Such participation is a means of building social capital by expanding the adolescent's social network.

Joint activities entail reciprocity. Adolescents who are mentored contribute to the mentoring process. As a teacher, the adult mentor models; the adolescent learner, in Bandura's terms, attends to the model, transforms cognitively what is being modeled, and produces—does something with what she or he has learned. Note that producing also entails activity. Protégés are not passive receptacles of oracular wisdom. Bandura (1986, p. 54) stated that models are more effective when they are attractive. One form of activity or agency is simply adolescents' selecting their mentors. Some youth, as the resilience literature tells us, attract mentors. Although people who are connected in a social network are not always equal, reciprocity is inherent in network connections. One cannot build social capital without bringing something of value to others. Social capital is a collective good.

An implication of mentoring's reciprocity is that characteristics of people on both sides of the relationship matter, a basic tenet of Bronfenbrenner's. As a result, mentoring cannot be expected to have the same effects on all adolescents. What might appear from outside to be the same treatment or experience will vary in its developmental impact depending upon what each adolescent brings to it. Dewey (1938) referred to this phenomenon in his principles of interaction and continuity.

Mentoring builds *social networks.* It is more than a face-to-face process. It also entails—as the social capital perspective clarifies—some indirect influences when mentors arrange beneficial opportunities for their protégés in which the mentor does not participate. This concept is consistent with Bronfenbrenner's portrayal of the exosystem, which does not include the developing person. One such influence occurs when the mentor links a youth with someone else who is more knowledgeable about a particular topic. Expanding a youth's social network by putting her or him in touch with people who can teach things the mentor does not know is a way of fostering competence indirectly. An example would be a mentor's setting up an appointment for a protégé with a college admissions counselor.

Sponsorship is another form of indirect mentoring. It means advocating on behalf of one's protégé. Actively seeking to get a job for a protégé would be an example. Both of these functions most likely fall under Putnam's definition of bridging social capital rather than bonding, because the most powerful sponsorship creates opportunities that would not otherwise be accessible. However, bonding social capital in the form of sponsorship within one's own community can also be important, as when a member of a faith-based organization sponsors a youth's transition to adult membership. Adolescents need both types of social capital, and they may find bonding in one mentor and bridging in another. We suspect that they need relatively more bridging social capital as they grow older and begin to consider higher education and careers. The importance of social networks and of indirect as well as direct effects are both prominent themes in the ecology of human development.

Although none of the theoretical perspectives suggests it directly, we find in them support for the distinction we have proposed between *mentoring* and *being a Mentor.*

The ecology of human development and resilience both emphasize the deep, enduring mutual commitment between a young person and an adult in a quasi-parental role. Such a person at least approaches Bronfenbrenner's definition of a Mentor and seems by definition to have a substantial impact on a young person's development or growing competence; however, social learning theory, resilience, and social capital identify what we think of as mentoring functions that are performed by people who do not meet this definition but may contribute in important ways to adolescents' growing competence. Other than referring to the value of a model's attractiveness, Bandura pays much less attention than does Bronfenbrenner to the nature of the relationship between an adult teacher and a youth learner. The metaphor, social capital, encourages us to think of fungibility. A person's social capital comes from multiple sources—parents and a life mentor with whom the youth has an enduring multifaceted relationship—but also from weak ties with a friend of a friend, a workplace supervisor, or a teacher. Referring to the adults in the first category as Mentors or perhaps life mentors might be a useful way to distinguish them and what they contribute to development from mentoring as a function that many different adults might perform, under many circumstances, most often outside of an enduring close relationship.

RESEARCH ON MENTORING AND CONTEXTS FOR MENTORING

The question to which we now turn is whether and to what extent research supports the conception of mentoring derived from these theoretical perspectives. We shall examine research focused on mentoring in programs as well as natural mentoring, and more generally, research on the contexts where mentoring takes place. As we address this question, we differentiate among the four domains of competence identified previously: academic, technical, personal, and social. We ask whether the research provides evidence that mentoring enhances adolescents' competence in these four domains, and, if so, whether that appears to result from the dynamics highlighted by the four theoretical perspectives, especially the combination Bronfenbrenner highlights of engagement in challenging activities in the company of a supportive adult who has already mastered them. We look for findings in the research about the contribution of mentoring to growing competence and whether and how joint activities and social networks are implicated. We also look for evidence to support or challenge the distinction between a Mentor as a single individual and mentoring as a distributed function.

Note that these four constructs do not fit neatly along one dimension. Competence is an outcome, a way to capture the impact of mentoring on adolescent development. Joint activities and social networks refer to the process of mentoring. The constructs are distinct from the developmental assets listed in the report of the National Research Council on youth development; they are more closely related to the features of positive developmental settings (Eccles & Gootman, 2002, pp. 90–91). Indeed, those features can easily be construed as qualities associated with good mentoring. Our distinction between mentoring and being or having a Mentor is conceptual. It is not a proposition open to empirical test. The question, therefore, is merely whether it illuminates the phenomenon, not whether it is true.

Our review of research is highly selective and relies at several points on published syntheses. It is organized around the four constructs, which means that some studies are cited more than once. We digress from reporting research results to describe the design and methods employed in a few important studies.

Competence

The most thorough test of mentoring and the most persuasive evidence of its positive effects on adolescent competence was done with Big Brothers/Big Sisters. Public/Private Ventures (Tierney, Grossman, & Resch, 1995) took advantage of long waiting lists in eight cities' programs to create a true control group. Half of all applicants were randomly selected for matching during an 18-month experimental period, while the other half remained in the control group until after 18 months had passed. The 487 treatment group members and 472 control group members in the final sample were predominantly non-White; fewer than 5% lived with both parents. They ranged in age from 10 to 16; 69% were between 11 and 13 when they entered.

After 18 months, boys and girls in the treatment group, compared to those in the control group (a) were less likely to have begun using drugs and alcohol, (b) were less likely to have hit others, (c) showed improved attitudes toward school, (d) had better grades and attendance, and (e) reported better relations with peers and family members. In our terms, these results indicate advantages in personal, social, and academic competence, linked to mentoring. They are especially impressive because 20% of the young people who were randomly assigned to the treatment group were not actually matched with a Big Brother or Big Sister during the 18-month period.

This study is the most powerful empirical support for the value of mentoring programs. Indeed, it is an exemplar of social program evaluation. However, readers should also be aware of some qualifications. First, the advantage shown by Little Brothers and Sisters over comparable youth without mentors is only relative. The normative age trend in the outcomes measured is negative. Having a mentor retarded the negative trends somewhat but did not reverse them. A more serious limitation is that the measures did not show an impact across the desired outcome domains. Twelve measures of antisocial behavior were collected; statistically significant differences were found in three. Ten measures of academic performance were collected; four showed advantages to youth with mentors, but only two were large—skipping class and skipping school. No differences were found in two of the five outcome domains: self concept and social and cultural enrichment. Overall, the main point is that although positive findings were robust and important, they were somewhat sparse.

DuBois, Holloway, Valentine, and Cooper (2002) have added substantially to our understanding of mentoring programs by conducting a meta-analysis of evaluations of 55 programs, including the Big Brothers/Big Sisters study. They found generally positive outcomes in the domains most often targeted by mentoring programs: emotional-psychological, problem and high-risk behavior, social competence, academic-educational, and career-employment. These outcomes clearly fall into our competence categories. Measures varied and not all evaluations assessed each domain. Moreover, the effect sizes were quite modest, ranging from .14 to .18, depending upon whether effects were assumed to be fixed or random. The authors pointed out that these effect sizes are small by the standards applied in meta-analyses and considerably smaller than effect sizes reported for health, educational, and behavioral interventions by professionals (p. 187).

Research on work experience indicates that it enhances competence, although it does not separate any effect of a workplace mentor. After graduation, young people who worked while in high school are employed more steadily and earn more after graduation than did their classmates who were not employed or who worked fewer hours (Meyer & Wise, 1982; Ruhm, 1997). This finding, which has been replicated many times, can be taken as indirect evidence that adolescents acquire work-related competence via work experience, competence that is subsequently rewarded in the adult labor market. However, the inference is subject to some well-founded challenges. It could be that adolescents who worked more in high school already possessed competencies valued by employers and a psychological predisposition to work and that they merely continued to exercise them as adults, accounting for their greater involvement in and success at work during both periods. An alternative inference is that the post-high school advantage to early work experience results primarily from high school graduates' continuing to work in the same places where they were employed as students, thus avoiding the irregular employment associated with postgraduation job searches, at least in the short term.

Greenberger and Steinberg (1986) led the way in studying the impact of work experience on adolescent development. They subjected to empirical test the conventional wisdom that work is a positive influence and found instead lower school grades among adolescents who work long hours; increased use by employed adolescents of alcohol, tobacco, and marijuana; and more engagement in such behavior as stealing and lying. In other words, work, on balance, has a negative impact on some academic competence and some personal and social competencies. These findings are open to the same methodological critique as the economists' positive finding: differences between workers and nonworkers might have predated work experience (i.e., selection effects). However, statistical controls and analyses of several other longitudinal studies have confirmed the association between long hours of work (20 hours per week or more) by high school students and undesirable behavior (National Research Council/Institute of Medicine, 1998). According to Stern, Finkelstein, Urquiola, and Cagampang (1997), such negative effects of work experience are not evident in research on school-related programs.

Mortimer (2003; see also chapter by Mortimer in this volume) has conducted the longest-running longitudinal study of youth employment. She began with a random sample of 1,010 ninth graders (ages 14 and 15) in St. Paul, MN, in 1987. The most recent data collection reported occurred in 1998 and included nearly 76% of the original sample. Long-term longitudinal data specifically about work experience allowed her to look much more closely at the phenomenon. In her own research and in her review of other studies, Mortimer has demonstrated that the effect of work experience is not uniform. It varies by gender and has different effects in different domains—notably, academic performance, educational attainment, problem behavior, and mental health. Moreover, she has also assessed the differential impact of the patterns of employment resulting from the combination of varying levels of work intensity (i.e., number of hours per week) and duration.

In general, young people who work fewer than 20 hours per week, especially when they combine paid work with extracurricular activities and homework, are most successful in high school and afterwards. Those who work more than 20 hours per week tend to do less well in high school but also to have been less interested and less successful in school in ninth grade. They earned more after graduation than their classmates who were not employed or not employed as much, but this advantage fades as time goes on, and not surprisingly, 7 years after graduation their classmates who have graduated from college do much better.

Newman's (1999) ethnographic study of fast food restaurant employees in Harlem found that even work that is generally considered to be routine and lacking in challenge can help youth gain competence. One of the greatest challenges facing workers in the Burger Barn is the disrespect they are shown by peers and customers. Moreover, to succeed at work, they must cultivate the self-control required to resist retaliating when they are "dissed" (i.e., disrespected, p. 93).

> To some degree, they can call on widely accepted American values that honor working people, values that "float" in the culture at large. But this is not enough to construct a positive identity when the reminders of low status—coming from customers, friends, and the media—are relentless. Something stronger is required: a workplace culture that actively functions to overcome the negatives by reinforcing the value of the work ethic. Managers and veteran employees play a critical role in the reinforcement process. Together they create a cocoonlike atmosphere in the back of the restaurant where they counsel new workers distressed by bad-mouthing. (Newman, 1999, 101–102)

Being able to tolerate disrespect without striking back is part of what we call personal competence, as are having a strong work ethic and self-confidence. Maintaining a high level of customer service under these circumstances is technical competence. Newman found that what we would call mentoring from supervisors and veteran adult workers was critical to gaining these competencies.

In contrast to findings in other research that high school students' work reduces commitment to school and school achievement, Newman (1999, pp. 127–129) found that the Burger Barn tried to promote school achievement among its high school student employees. Supervisors were expected to keep track of grades and, before asking whether a worker could stay late on a school night, to inquire about the impact of late hours on school. An 18-year-old employee explained that Burger Barn would like its employees to say that the company helped them get through school, giving them time to study and earnings. Not only the corporation but also the local franchisees saw it as important to public relations that they support education. As a result, they regularly hosted visits by elementary school classes, sponsored tutoring programs, monitored report cards, and even paid bonuses for good grades and college admission. Acknowledging a selection effect, Newman also pointed out that the applicants hired by Burger Barn were generally more committed to school before they were hired than were unsuccessful applicants.

Increased academic competence has been the most consistent effect found among participants in programs supported by the School-to-Work Opportunities Act of 1994. They have enrolled in postsecondary education at higher rates than have comparison group high school graduates (Hughes, Bailey, & Mechur, 2001). One of the key components in the legislation was systematically creating and sustaining work-based learning opportunities and linking them to education. But work-based learning was not the only component of such programs, nor was it universal; some School-to-Work programs emphasized classroom learning about careers and group projects that simulate employment. As a result, the promising findings reported in the review of School-to-Work research do not by themselves support workplace mentoring. Indeed, the only reference to mentors in the legislation is to a person in the school who gives advice to participants, possibly coordinating work-based learning as well. However, combined with the reviews of research that preceded and informed the School-to-Work Opportunities Act (e.g., Office of Research, U.S. Department of Education, 1994; Stern, Finkelstein, Stone, Latting, & Dornsife, 1994), the evidence supports the claim that school-related work-based learning can be a valuable experience. The contribution of mentoring can only be inferred.

To explore the contribution of mentoring in work-based learning programs to the acquisition of competence by adolescents, we conducted a study of what such mentors teach and how they teach (Hamilton, Hamilton, & Vermeylen, 2002). We interviewed mentors (66 in Phase 1, 89 in Phase 2) and youth (61 and 54, respectively). The interviews elicited from both parties teaching goals and descriptions of specific situations in which mentors taught those lessons. The three categories of technical, personal, and social competence captured the teaching goals. The technical competence most often named was learning how to perform job tasks. Among the most commonly cited personal competencies were drive (taking initiative, suggesting improvements) and career planning. Most frequently mentioned social competencies included learning the rules and norms of the workplace and working as part of a team. These results indicate that workplace mentors, as expected, seek to promote the competence of their interns and apprentices, that adolescents' perceptions of what they are learning are congruent with the mentors' goals, and that both groups' perceptions fit well in our categories.

Our study did not attempt to assess adolescents' growing competence. We chose to focus on teaching goals and teaching behaviors because it is extraordinarily difficult to assess what adolescents learn in workplaces; this is surely a major reason that research findings point to rather indirect effects—postsecondary enrollment—rather than direct measures of learning. One would not expect a one-semester intern in a hospital's phlebotomy unit to learn the same things as a 4-year auto repair apprentice. Furthermore, any measurement would have to begin with pretests to account for competencies participants possessed prior to the experience; all this would have to precede assessment of the mentor's contribution to work-based learning.

Many of the same competencies that can be gained from paid work can be gained at least as surely from service. This assertion is particularly true of personal and social competencies such as punctuality and communication, but it extends to technical competencies such as computer use. Indeed, when young people work together to plan and conduct a community service project (as distinct from serving as helpers or interns in an adult-run organization), they have the chance to learn decision-making and management skills that few employers would offer.

The term *mentor* is not prominent in research on service-learning or its practice. In general, the contributions of the adult supervisor, teacher, or group leader are not examined separately but are simply taken as part of the program or experience as a whole;

this makes it impossible to extract findings from this literature about how mentors in work and service influence adolescents' development. However, the literature does have some clear implications. Opportunities for learning—gaining and exercising new knowledge and skill—are essential. Stukas, Clary, and Snyder (1999) reviewed research on the effects of service-learning and classified the positive effects on students in terms of personal development (sense of efficacy, identity, spiritual growth, moral development), interpersonal development (ability to work well with others, take leadership, communicate), improved cultural and racial understanding, social responsibility and citizenship, and commitment to service, as well as academic learning. These outcomes are consistent with our definition of competence. (See Eyler, Giles, & Gray, 1999, for an annotated bibliography with additional research generally supporting these findings.)

Joint Activities

One dimension of the importance of joint activities is simply that activities provide a context for mentoring. A second is that the quality of those activities makes a difference. After comparing overall findings from evaluations of mentoring programs, DuBois et al. (2002) took a second very valuable step by treating as moderators of effect size a set of program features identified as important in the literature. This step enabled them to search for effects related to program quality. They found that effect sizes are positively correlated with the provision of continuing training for mentors (i.e., beyond initial orientation and training), structured activities, expectations for frequent contact, parent involvement, and staff monitoring. In addition, effect size is greater when pairs are in frequent contact, are emotionally close, and stay together longer (DuBois et al., 2002, pp. 187–188). Favorable outcomes were one quarter to one third of a standard deviation higher for youth in mentoring relationships of greater intensity and quality (p. 186). These program features and relationship characteristics yield effect sizes for mentoring programs that remain small but are more impressive. This analysis suggests that one source of small effect sizes is the aggregation of data from stronger and weaker programs. However, it also indicates that mentoring programs should not be expected to have large effects for most participants.

In our assessment of the endurance of matches in a mentoring program, Linking Up (Hamilton & Hamilton, 1992), we found that mentors in more enduring matches took what we called a more instrumental approach, compared to those in matches that did not endure, who concentrated on having a good time together, believing that this approach would create a foundation for building a relationship. Mentors taking an instrumental approach used goal-directed activities as a context for relationship building. They also tended to focus on building their protégés' character as well as competence. Mentors in matches that did not last tended to limit their engagement with youth to fun activities such as going to movies or having ice cream. The epitome of the instrumental activities was a mentor who invited his protégé to help repair a bicycle so they could plan and take a long ride together. Although we are not aware of empirical data to test the hypothesis, we suspect that goal-directed activities or an instrumental approach is more important for the development of older adolescents.

Mortimer and her colleagues concluded that the critical question to ask about adolescents' work experience is not whether they worked but what was the quality of their work (e.g., Mortimer, Harley, & Aronson, 1999). She found that the effects of work experience can be better understood when the nature of the work is considered.

> During high school, the quality of work experience appears to matter far more than hours of work for the psychosocial outcomes under scrutiny. That is, youth who have more successful experiences in the workplace become more competent, in terms of both a general, global sense of efficacy and efficacy in the economic domain. There is also evidence that high quality work experience involving learning opportunities help adolescents acquire occupational values. Opportunities for learning and advancement on the job, the perception that one is being paid well, and limited stressors at work all appear to have significant psychosocial benefits. (2003, p. 181)

Stern and Nakata (1989) provide corroboration for this claim, finding that adolescents able to use skills at their jobs were more successful than others in their first 3 years after graduating from high school. Hamilton and Hamilton (1997, pp. 81–82) provide a checklist of quality features for work-based learning.

Parallel findings can be found in research on service-learning. Stukas, Clary, and Snyder's (1999) review of service-learning studies found that quality matters. Simply participating in service-learning or being employed does not assure positive development. The nature of the experience, the program's structure and implementation are critical.

A third dimension of the construct of joint activities emphasizes their mutuality, especially the active engagement and participation of the protégé in mentoring. Morrow and Styles (1995) examined a subset of 82 Big Brothers/Big Sisters matches, searching for qualities of relationships that might account for their endurance. They distinguished mentors' approaches as developmental and prescriptive. In a developmental relationship, "the adult volunteers held expectations that varied over time in relation to their perception of the needs of *the youth*" (p. 2). These mentors worked hard to build relationships in the beginning and to keep them going, and they actively involved their youth in deciding what to do together and to talk about. Mentors who took a prescriptive approach set goals for their youth and chose activities unilaterally. They took it as their task to transform the youth; developmental mentors concentrated initially on building their relationship and then, after establishing trust, began working on setting goals with youth, such as improving school performance, and planning to meet those goals. After 9 months, only one third of the prescriptive matches were continuing to meet, compared to 90% of the developmental matches (p. 4), confirming the importance of reciprocity in a mentoring relationship. (Note that what Morrow and Styles called prescriptive is not what we meant by instrumental, explained previously, which referred to a focus on activities as a basis for developing a relationship.)

In our study of workplace mentors (Hamilton & Hamilton, 2002) we drew on Bandura (1986) among others, to categorize teaching behaviors as demonstrating, explaining how, explaining why, monitoring (observing and giving feedback), reflective (Socratic) questioning, and problem solving (engaging the youth in a sustained interaction to achieve something the mentor may not initially know how to achieve). We found the first four teaching behaviors to be universal; nearly all mentors said that they used these behaviors for some purpose at some time, and youth confirmed these reports. The last two are challenging to both mentors and youth. Not all mentors used them, according to both youth and adult interviews, and we expected such behaviors to promote more adaptive learning (Bransford, Brown, Cocking, Donovan, & Pellegrino, 2000)—meaning learning that is more than rote and that can be applied and transformed as conditions change. The challenging teaching behaviors, especially problem solving, illustrate well the reciprocal nature of mentoring. Mentors cannot succeed unless their protégés take an active part in the process.

Bandura's (1986) emphasis on cognitive transformation as an essential process in observational learning is a part of reciprocity. In service-learning, this process is known as reflection, following Dewey (1938). The importance of reflection is perhaps the most firmly established principle of service-learning. Reflection in this context means having the opportunity to think about and discuss the service experience and to relate it to beliefs, values, knowledge, and plans (e.g., Conrad & Hedin, 1982).

Younnis and Yates (1997) provide an extended case study that both affirms the importance of reflection and illustrates how it can be encouraged. They describe in depth a course in a Catholic high school that included a service-learning activity, participation in a Washington, DC soup kitchen. The teacher required students to write essays on their experience and organized the class around the topic of social justice. The combination of becoming personally acquainted with indigent people, reading about the sources of poverty and inequality, and discussing and writing about these experiences and issues had a profound impact on the students. Former students also testified to the course's impact on their lives.

Another aspect of reciprocity is the distinctive qualities that both parties bring to a mentoring relationship, which assure that mentoring has different effects on different adolescents. Mortimer's (2003) research on youth employment is the best illustration of this principle. As noted previously, she found that the effects of working vary by gender and are different for different patterns of engagement in work.

Social Networks

In their study of natural mentoring, Rhodes, Ebert, and Fischer (1992) found that young African American mothers who had natural mentors were less depressed than others like them who did not have mentors, an advantage that did not appear to be attributable to differences predating the mentoring relationships. Their analysis suggests that in addition to having a direct effect on reducing depression, these mentors also enable young mothers to make better uses of their social networks and cope with relationship problems, a finding affirming that mentors not only represent social capital themselves but also help protégés form and maintain relationships with others, indirectly building their social capital.

Another study using the Big Brothers/Big Sisters data set (Rhodes, Grossman, & Resch, 2000) demonstrated that much of the power of the mentoring relationship, especially as it affects school attitudes and performance, is mediated by youths' perceptions of improved relations with parents. Mentors have direct effects, but they also work by affecting youths' relations with their parents. This finding supports the claim that mentors generally complement rather than replace parents. It is also a vivid illustration of Bronfenbrenner's (1979, p. 38) emphasis on indirect influences on human development, as well as the centrality of parents. Although it is not a central theme in social capital research and theory, one could interpret this finding as suggesting that having more social capital in the form of a mentor who can do some of what a parent might be expected to do can reduce the pressure on a parent-adolescent relationship.

Call and Mortimer (2001) found that some work environments provide an "arena of comfort" or protective factors to youth experiencing stress in their families. "Support from supervisors at work is found to moderate the effect of family discomfort on employed adolescents' well-being, self-esteem, and mastery. . . . Work comfort (i.e., low work stress and support from a best friend at work) also was found to moderate the effects of family change stressors (i.e., change in father's employment status and family composition) on self-esteem and well-being" (p. 127).

Newman described the workplace as a community, providing "structure and purpose, humor and pleasure, support and understanding in hard times, and a backstop that extends beyond the instrumental purposes of a fast food restaurant" (1999, p. 121). In other words, the job is a source of social capital.

Burger Barn unintentionally provided another, indirect incentive to continue in school and do well. Most employees quickly realized that they should enhance their credentials to assure that they would qualify for better jobs as adults (Newman, 1999, p. 133). Burger Barn employees made use of their workplace social networks to gain leads on other jobs (pp. 161–174). Most of those leads merely allowed lateral mobility—movement to other jobs of the same type, with no gain in earnings or status. However, having lateral options proved important as a buffer against unemployment. More potent were vertical links enabling workers to move up into more rewarding jobs. One employee, Fernando, benefited from the mentoring given him by his supervisor, who spotted his initiative and responsibility and then taught him the competencies required to become a manager and sponsored his promotion. She also advised him to continue his education to be able to move up the ladder, advice he took by enrolling at a local community college (pp. 176–179).

Mentoring and Being a Mentor

Additional analyses of the Big Brothers/Big Sisters data by Grossman and Rhodes (2002) affirm the importance of an enduring relationship between protégé and Mentor. They examined the effect of the duration of the match, controlling for characteristics of both youth and mentors that might be correlated with duration (e.g., more troubled youth might be less likely to stay in a match). They found that

> . . . youth in relationships that lasted for a year or more reported the largest number of improvements. . . . Those in relationships that terminated within 6 months reported decrements in several indicators of functioning, including significant increases in alcohol use. (Grossman & Rhodes, 2002, p. 9)

Essentially, the real payoff to having a Big Brother or Big Sister comes after 1 year; young people whose matches broke up quickly were actually worse off than those in the control group. Dashed hopes may be worse than unfulfilled hopes. This finding affirms Bronfenbrenner's emphasis on duration as an important aspect of a relationship with a Mentor.

DuBois et al. (2002) added further support, finding that mentoring programs with more of the characteristics associated with best practices in the field had stronger positive effects. Duration and frequency of meetings are qualities of a positive mentoring relationship consistent with the ecology of human development. Both Dubois et al. (2002) and Grossman and Rhodes (2002, p. 9) suggested that modest outcomes in evaluations of mentoring programs may result from the inclusion of both short-term and long-term relationships.

However, these findings relate to programs that designated an adult as a young person's Mentor. We should also examine whether adults who might not be formally designated Mentors and whose relationships might be more limited can also engage in mentoring, doing some of the things Mentors do.

In Mortimer's (2003, p. 66) Youth Development Study, 71% of employed youth (in the third wave of data collection, when most subjects were high school juniors) reported that their supervisors were almost always or often "willing to listen to problems and help find solutions" and 38% reported feeling "extremely or quite close to their supervisors." These results indicate that workplaces can accurately be described as mentor-rich environments, places where adolescents can interact with and build relationships with caring adults. Evidence that work, under proper circumstances, is a learning experience implies that mentoring occurs even in the absence of a Mentor.

Newman's rich case studies contain numerous instances of mentoring in workplaces. A few of the workplace mentors we interviewed appeared to have the kind of deep, multidimensional relationship attributed by Bronfenbrenner to Mentors. Most, however, took a much narrower view of their role and responsibilities. Some strictly limited their teaching and advice to work-related matters. Believing that mentoring is also valuable and that adults will be more effective if they are able to place boundaries around their mentoring relationships, we devised an activity for our training program to help them reflect on their personal boundaries and to make them explicit (www.human.cornell.edu/youthwork/).

The research of McLaughlin, Irby, and Langman (1994) demonstrates the promise of youth organizations as contexts for mentoring. They described in detail the work of six adults who

> . . . have created environments in which youth from the tough streets of inner-city neighborhoods can imagine a positive future. Accomplishing what conventional wisdom has often held impossible, these wizards have fashioned organizations that capture adolescents' attention, time, and loyalty. (p. 6)

Such adults mentor large numbers of adolescents who desperately need their support.

Another context, along with work and service, in which we would expect effective mentoring to occur, is intensive leisure activity. Sports, music, drama, dance, chess, model building, stamp collecting, and other such hobbies and leisure activities are challenging and deeply engaging, in contrast to passive or "relaxed leisure" activities such as watching television or hanging out with friends (Kleiber, Larson, & Csikszentmihalyi, 1986). Some are more solitary than others, but to the extent that they entail regular teaching and coaching over a long period of time, they are optimal contexts for mentoring. A cursory look at the research literature did not reveal any sustained attention to mentoring in this context. The most relevant was the finding of McHale, Crouter, and Tucker (2001, p. 1775) that ". . . free time spent with parents and nonparental adults was related to positive adjustment, whereas time spent alone and in unsupervised peer contexts predicted adjustment problems."

CONCLUSIONS AND RECOMMENDATIONS

Our purpose in this chapter has been to understand mentoring as a contribution to adolescent development that is not limited to mentoring programs but that occurs naturally under many different circumstances. By distinguishing the role of Mentor from the more distributed function of mentoring, we extend the term to a range of adults, not just those who take a quasi-parental role. We have also argued that the nature of mentoring changes with adolescents' developmental level and have sought to locate mentoring for older adolescents in the context of challenging goal-directed activity, especially work. Defined this way, mentoring is important as a way of building all adolescents' competence, not only that of adolescents considered at risk.

Theory and research support the claim that mentoring fosters adolescent development in the sense of contribution to their growing competence. We also found support for viewing mentoring as being embedded in joint activities and as a process in which the protégé plays an active part. Mentoring entails expanding adolescents' social networks, linking them with others who can share in the mentoring function and sponsoring them or advocating on their behalf. These observations will be valuable to the extent that they inform and stimulate research and practice. Our recommendations cross the boundaries between research and practice, reflecting our belief that one of the best ways to learn about mentoring is to try to promote it.

The contribution of mentoring to the developmental affordances of various contexts deserves attention. How and to what extent does mentoring enhance the value of work, service, and leisure activity? Do differences in mentoring account for some of the variation in the effects of such settings? For example, is participation in athletics or music more beneficial when a coach or teacher attends to players' academic, personal, and social competence as well as their technical competence?

Are there differences among adolescents, notably in developmental level and parental support, in their need for a single Mentor rather than mentoring from more than one adult? Do some communities offer adolescents better access to mentoring than others? Can differences in levels of mentoring be found among communities that are similar economically, culturally, or ethnically? How can mentoring be made available to adolescents in the most adverse circumstances, such as poverty, isolation, and exposure to violence?

We believe the functions of mentoring are best understood in the context of other relationships in an adolescent's life. An adolescent with uninvolved or absent parents surely needs a more intense and unlimited relationship than does one growing up in a two-parent family with extended family close by. An adolescent lacking a strong parental figure is more likely to need a close, personal, and enduring relationship with a Mentor, whereas one who already has caring adults may gain most from mentoring that is high on instrumental goals but not necessarily on emotional attachment.

Our research with workplace mentors suggests that although programs like Big Brothers/Big Sisters struggle to recruit (and screen and train) adults willing to become Mentors, many more adults are willing to take on a mentoring role that is bounded in its scope, duration, and responsibility, especially if it can be performed as part of their employment. We would urge those undertaking community-wide youth development initiatives to broaden the definition of mentoring in this way. So defined, mentoring occurs not only in mentoring programs and workplaces, but also in such contexts as community service projects, volunteer work, and youth membership on boards and committees. Intensive leisure activities are another context for mentoring. For example, an avid fisher who would hesitate to volunteer to be a Big Brother might eagerly agree to teach a young person to fish; a serious gardener might welcome the help of a neighboring youth in exchange for instructions in the craft.

When we have asked adult mentors of youth in workplaces to talk about their experiences, one of the strongest themes that emerges is joy and satisfaction at being able to get to know and to foster the development of a young person (Hamilton & Hamilton, in press). Mentoring epitomizes what Erikson (1963) called generativity and identified as the developmental task of middle adulthood. Promoting mentoring benefits adults as well as youth. A community-wide initiative for this purpose entails creating mentor-rich environments in which adults and youth engage jointly in challenging activities. By segregating housing and social institutions such as schools, workplaces, clubs, and community activities by age, we have unwittingly divided the generations. Mentoring is a way to reconnect the generations, a goal that is as daunting as it is compelling.

REFERENCES

Bailey, T. R., Hughes, K. L., & Barr, T. (2000). Achieving scale and quality in school-to-work internships: Findings from two employer surveys. *Educational Evaluation and Policy Analysis, 22,* 41–64.

Bandura, A. (1977). *Social learning theory.* Englewood Cliffs, NJ: Prentice-Hall.

Bandura, A. (1986). *The social foundations of thought and action: A social cognitive theory.* Englewood Cliffs, NJ: Prentice-Hall.

Benard, B. Applications of resilience: Possibilities and promise. In M. D. Glantz & J. L. Hohnson (Eds.), *Resilience and development: Positive life adaptations* (pp. 269–277). New York: Kluwer Academic/Plenum.

Blyth, D. A., Hill, J. P., & Thiel, K. S. (1982). Early adolescents' significant others: Grade and gender differences in perceived relationships with familial and nonfamilial adults and young people. *Journal of Youth & Adolescence, 11*(6), 425–450.

Bransford, J. D., Brown, A. L., Cocking, R. R., Donovan, M. S., & Pellegrino, J. W. (Eds.). (2000). *How people learn: Brain, mind, experience, and school.* Washington, DC: National Academy Press.

Bronfenbrenner, U. (1979). *The ecology of human development: Experiments by nature and design.* Cambridge, MA: Harvard University Press.

Bronfenbrenner, U., & Morris, P. (1998). The ecology of developmental processes. In R. M. Lerner (Ed.), *Handbook of child psychology. Theoretical models of human development* (5th ed., Vol. 1, pp. 993–1028. New York: Wiley.

Call, K. T., & Mortimer, J. T. (2001). *Arenas of comfort in adolescence: A study of adjustment in context.* Mahwah, NJ: Erlbaum.

Chao, G. T., Walz, P. M., & Gardner, P. D., (1992). Formal and informal mentorships: A comparison on mentoring functions and contrast with nonmentored counterparts. *Personnel Psychology, 45,* 619–632.

Coleman, J. (1961). *The adolescent society.* New York: Free Press of Glencoe.

Coleman, J. S. (1972). How do the young become adults? *Review of Educational Research, 42,* 431–439.

Coleman, J. S. (1990). *Foundations of social theory.* Cambridge, MA: Belknap Press of Harvard University.

Collins, E. G., & Scott, P. (1978). Everyone who makes it has a mentor. *Harvard Business Review, 56,* 89–101.

Conrad, D., & Hedin, D. (1982). The impact of experiential education on adolescent development. *Child and Youth Services, 4,* 57–76.

Darling, N., Hamilton, S., & Hames, K. (2003). Relationships outside the family: Unrelated adults. In G. R. Adams & M. D. Berzonsky (Eds.), *Blackwell handbook of adolescence.* Malden, MA: Blackwell.

Darling, N., Hamilton, S. F., Toyokawa, T., & Matsuda, S. (2002). Naturally occurring mentoring in Japan and the United States: Social roles and correlates. *American Journal of Community Psychology, 30,* 245–270.

Dewey, J. (1938). *Experience and education.* New York: Collier.

DuBois, D. L., Holloway, B. E., Valentine, J. C., & Cooper, H. (2002). Effectiveness of mentoring programs for youth: A meta-analytic review. *American Journal of Community Psychology, 30,* 157–197.

Eccles, J., & Gootman, J. A. (Eds.). (2002). *Community programs to promote youth development.* Washington, DC: National Academy Press.

Elder, G. H. (1974). *Children of the Great Depression.* Chicago: University of Chicago Press.

Elder, G. H. (1986). Military times and turning points in men's lives. *Developmental Psychology, 22,* 233–245.

Erikson, E. H. (1963). *Childhood and society.* New York: Norton.

Eurich, N. P. (1985). *Corporate classrooms: The learning business.* Princeton, NJ: The Carnegie Foundation for the Advancement of Teaching.

Eyler, J., Giles, D. E., Jr., & Gray, C. J. (1999). *At a glance: What we know about the effects of service-learning on students, faculty, institutions and communities, 1993–1999.* Unpublished manuscript, Vanderbilt University, Nashville, TN.

Freedman, M. (1993). *The kindness of strangers: Reflections on the mentoring movement.* San Francisco: Jossey-Bass.

Granovetter, M. (1973). The strength of weak ties. *American Journal of Sociology, 78,* 1360–1380.

Granovetter, M. (1983). The strength of weak ties: A network theory revisited. *Sociological Theory, 1,* 201–233.

Greenberger, E., & Steinberg, L. (1986). *When teenagers work: The psychological and social costs of adolescent employment.* New York: Basic Books.

Grossman, J. B., & Rhodes, J. E. (2002). The test of time: Predictors and effects of duration in youth mentoring relationships. *American Journal of Community Psychology, 30*(2), 199–219.

Hamilton, M. A., & Hamilton, S. F. (1997). *Learning well at work: Choices for quality.* Washington, DC: U.S. Government Printing Office.

Hamilton, M. A., & Hamilton, S. F. (2002). Why mentoring in the workplace works. In J. Rhodes (Ed.), *New directions for youth development: A critical view of youth mentoring* (pp. 59–89). San Francisco: Jossey-Bass.

Hamilton, M. A., Hamilton, S. F., & Vermeylen, F. M. (2002, April). *Training workplace mentors to use challenging teaching behaviors.* Paper presented at the American Educational Research Association, AERA Annual Meeting, New Orleans, LA.

Hamilton, S. F., & Hamilton, M. A. (in press). Learning by teaching: How instructing apprentices affects adult workers. In J. Oelkers (Ed.), *Futures of education II: Work, education, and occupation. Essays from an interdisciplinary symposium.* Bern, Switzerland: Peter Lang.

Hamilton, S. F. (1990). *Apprenticeship for adulthood: Preparing youth for the future.* New York: Free Press.

Hamilton, S. F., & Darling, N. (1996). Mentors in adolescents' lives. In K. Hurrelmann & S. F. Hamilton (Eds.), *Social problems and social contexts in adolescence: Perspectives across boundaries* (pp. 199–215). Hawthorne, NY: Aldine de Gruyter.

Hamilton, S. F., & Hamilton, M. A. (1992). Mentoring programs: Promise and paradox. *Phi Delta Kappan, 73,* 546–550.

Hamilton, S. F., & Hamilton, M. A. (1999). *Building strong school-to-work systems: Illustrations of key components.* Washington, DC: National School-to-Work Office.

Honnet E. P., & Poulson, S. J. (1989). *Principles of good practice for combining service and learning.* Racine, WI: The Johnson Foundation.

Hughes, K. L., Bailey, T. R., & Mechur, M. J. (2001). *School-to-work. Making a difference in education: A research report to America.* New York: Institute on Education and the Economy, Teachers College, Columbia University.

Kanter, R. M. (1977). *Men and women of the corporation.* New York: Basic Books.

Kleiber, D. A., Larson, R., & Csikszentmihalyi, M. (1986). The experience of leisure in adolescence. *Journal of Leisure Research, 18,* 169–176.

Kram, K. E. (1985). *Mentoring at work: Developmental relationships in organizational life.* Glenview, IL: Scott, Foresman.

Lerman, R. I., & Pouncy, H. (1990). The compelling case for youth apprenticeships. *The Public Interest, 101,* 62–77.

Lund, L. (1992). *Corporate mentoring in U.S. schools: The outstretched hand* (Rep. No. 1007). New York: The Conference Board.

Luthar, S. S., & Cicchetti, D. (2000). The construct of resilience: Implications for interventions and social policies. *Development and Psychopathology, 12,* 857–885.

McHale, S. M., Crouter, A. C., & Tucker, C. J. (2001). Free-time activities in middle childhood: Links with adjustment in early adolescence. *Child Development, 72,* 1764–1778.

McLaughlin, M., Irby, M., & Langman, J. (1994). *Urban sanctuaries: Neighborhood organizations in the lives and futures of inner-city youth.* San Francisco: Jossey-Bass.

Meyer, R. H., & Wise, D. A. (1982). High school preparation and early labor force experience. In R. B. Freeman & D. A. Wise (Eds.), *The youth labor market problem: Its nature, causes, and consequences* (pp. 277–339). Chicago: University of Chicago Press.

Morrow, K. V., & Styles, M. B. (1995). *Building relationships with youth in program settings: A study of Big Brothers/Big Sisters.* Philadelphia: Public/Private Ventures.

Mortimer, J. T. (2003). *Working and growing up in America.* Cambridge, MA: Harvard University Press.

Mortimer, J., Harley, C., & Aronson, P. (1999). How do prior experiences in the workplace set the stage for transitions to adulthood? In A. Booth, A. C. Crouter, & M. J. Shanahan (Eds.), *Transitions to adulthood in a changing economy: No work, no family, no future?* (pp. 131–159). Westport, CT: Praeger.

Munsch, J., & Blyth, D. A. (1993). An analysis of the functional nature of adolescents' supportive relationships. *Journal of Early Adolescence, 13*(2), 132–153.

National Center on Education and the Economy. (1990). *America's choice: High skills or low wages! The report of the Commission on the Skills of the American Workforce.* Rochester, NY: Author.

National Commission on Excellence in Education. (1983). *A nation at risk: The imperative for educational reform.* Washington, DC: U.S. Government Printing Office.

National Research Council and Institute of Medicine. (1998). *Protecting youth at work: Health, safety, and development of working children and adolescents in the United States.* Washington, DC: National Academy Press.

Nettles, S. M. (1992). *Coaching in community settings: A review* (Report No. 9): Boston MA: Center on Families, Communities, Schools & Children's Learning, Institute for Responsive Education, Boston University.

Newman, K. S. (1999). *No shame in my game: The working poor in the inner city.* New York: Vintage Books and the Russell Sage Foundation.

Nothdurft, W. E. (1989). *SchoolWorks: Reinventing public schools to create the workforce of the future.* Washington, DC: The Brookings Institution.

Office of Research, U.S. Department of Education. (1994). *School-to-work: What does the research say about it?* Washington, DC: Author.

Panel on Youth and the Presidents' National Science Advisory Council. (1974). *Youth: Transition to adulthood.* Chicago: University of Chicago Press.

Putnam, R. D. (2000). *Bowling alone: The collapse and revival of American community.* New York: Simon & Schuster.

Resnick, L. B. (1987). Learning in school and out. *Educational Researcher, 16*(9), 13–20.

Rhodes, J. E. (2002). *Stand by me: The risks and rewards of mentoring today's youth.* Cambridge, MA: Harvard University Press.

Rhodes, J. E., Ebert, L., & Fischer, K. (1992) Natural mentors: An overlooked resource in the social networks of African-American adolescent mothers. *American Journal of Community Psychology, 20,* 445–461.

Rhodes, J. E., Grossman, J. B., & Resch, N. L. (2000). Agents of change: Pathways through which mentoring relationships influence adolescents' academic adjustment. *Child Development, 71,* 1662–1671.

Rorabaugh, W. J. (1986). *The craft apprentice: From Franklin to the machine age in America.* New York: Oxford University Press.

Ruhm, C. J. (1997). Is high school employment consumption or investment? *Journal of Labor Economics, 15,* 735–776.

Rutter, M. (2000). Resilience reconsidered: Conceptual considerations, empirical findings, and policy implications. In J. P. Shonkoff & S. J. Meisels (Eds.), *Handbook of early childhood intervention* (pp. 651–682). Cambridge, England: Cambridge University Press.

School-to-Work Opportunities Act of 1994, 20 U.S.C. § 6101 *et seq.* (2000).

Stern, D., & Nakata, Y. F. (1989). Characteristics of high school students, paid jobs, and employment experience after high school. In D. Stern & D. Eichorn (Eds.), *Adolescence and work: Influences of social structure, labor markets, and culture* (pp. 189–234). Hillsdale, NJ: Erlbaum.

Stern, D., Finkelstein, N., Stone, J. R., III, Latting, J., & Dornsife, C. (1994). *Research on school-to-work transition programs in the United States* (MDS-771). Berkeley, CA: National Center for Research in Vocational Education.

Stern, D., Finkelstein, N., Urquiola, M., & Cagampang, H. (1997). What differences does it make if school and work are connected? *Economics of Education Review, 16,* 213–229.

Stukas, A. A., Jr., Clary, E. G., & Snyder, M. (1999). Service learning: Who benefits and why. *Social Policy Report, 13*(4).

Tatar, M. (1998). Significant individuals in adolescence: Adolescent and adult perspectives. *Journal of Adolescence, 21*(6), 691–702.

Tierney, J. P., Grossman, J. B., & Resch, N. L. (1995). *Making a difference: An impact study of Big Brothers/Big Sisters.* Philadelphia: Public/Private Ventures.

U.S. General Accounting Office. (1991). *Transition from school to work: Linking education and worksite training* (GAO/HRD-91-105). Washington, DC: Author.

Vygotsky, L. S. (1978). *Mind in society: The development of higher educational processes.* Edited by M. Cole, V. John-Steiner, S. Scribner, & E. Souberman. Cambridge, MA: Harvard University Press.

Walker, G. (2000). The policy climate for early adolescent initiatives. In *Youth development: Issues, challenges and directions* (pp. 65–80). Philadelphia: Public/Private Ventures.

Werner, E. E., & Smith, R. S. (2001). *Journeys from childhood to midlife: Risk, resilience, and recovery.* Ithaca, NY: Cornell University Press.

Whitehead, A. N. (1929). *The aims of education.* New York: New American Library.

William T. Grant Commission on Work, Family and Citizenship. (1988). *The forgotten half: Pathways to success for America's youth and young families.* Washington, DC: Youth and America's Future.

Younnis, J., & Yates, M. (1997). *Community service and social responsibility in youth.* Chicago: University of Chicago Press.

Chapter 14

WORK AND LEISURE IN ADOLESCENCE

Jeremy Staff, Jeylan T. Mortimer, and Christopher Uggen

Adolescents spend their time in a broad range of work and leisure activities (Larson & Verma, 1999). Adolescent work activities occur in various contexts—in home, school, and volunteer settings, as well as in paid jobs. Adolescent leisure activities take place in similarly diverse locales; they include both passive media use (watching television, listening to music, reading, and browsing the Internet) and active recreation, such as sports, extracurricular activities, and clubs and organizations at school (Larson & Verma, 1999, pp. 702–703). These active pursuits, as well as some of the more passive ones, are generally considered beneficial or "good" leisure activities because they often provide challenges and learning opportunities for the young person (Csikszentmihalyi & Schneider, 2000).

Many adolescents also engage in less beneficial and socially acceptable behaviors in their discretionary time. These potentially harmful or "bad" leisure activities during adolescence include minor delinquency, sexual activity, and the use of illicit drugs, alcohol, and cigarettes. Although some of these behaviors, such as sexual activity and alcohol use, are acceptable and even prescribed for adults, they are generally discouraged for young people. Rather than attempting to review the voluminous scholarly literatures on adolescent work and leisure, this chapter focuses on the intersection of the two domains: (a) how teenage work, especially paid work, influences both good and bad forms of leisure and (b) how different forms of leisure activities in turn influence the propensity toward paid work.

In the United States, the majority of adolescents are employed at some point during high school (an estimated 80–90%; see the Committee on the Health and Safety Implications of Child Labor, 1998). Most of these youth are employed in the retail and service sectors of the economy. According to the 1996 Current Population Survey, approximately 52% of youth ages 15–17 work in the retail sector (employed in department stores, grocery stores, restaurants, and retail stores) and 26% are employed in the service sector (working in education, recreation, health services, and private households). Cashier is the most common teenage job (16% of employed 15- to 17-year-olds), followed by employment as a cook (7%), stock handler and bagger (7%), and fast food server (5%). The third most common sector of work for young people, agriculture, em-

This chapter highlights findings from the Youth Development Study, which is supported by grants titled "Work Experience and Mental Health: A Panel Study of Youth" from the National Institute of Child Health and Human Development (HD44138) and the National Institute of Mental Health (MH42843).

ploys approximately 8% of 15- to 17-year-olds (Committee on the Health and Safety Implications of Child Labor, 1998, pp. 46–47).

As young people age, their likelihood of employment, as well as the hours or intensity of paid work, also increases. For example, data from the National Longitudinal Study of Adolescent Health reveal that approximately 46% of 12th graders averaged 20 or more hours of employment per week during the school year (compared to just 9% of employed 9th graders). Boys typically average more hours of paid work than do girls, especially in the later years of high school. Recent data from the annual Monitoring the Future surveys suggest that approximately 43% of employed males (compared to 38% of employed females) worked *more* than 20 hours per week in their senior year of high school (Safron, Schulenberg, & Bachman, 2001). Not surprisingly, youth average more hours of work during the months of summer vacation than during the school year (Committee on the Health and Safety of Children, 1988, pp. 38–39).

Especially for intensively employed youth, paid work may limit time for good leisure and unpaid work activities. The first position in the debate over paid work and leisure is that working for pay undermines success in good school-related work and leisure activities as well as encourages bad leisure. Critics of youth work argue that intensively employed adolescents have less time for extracurricular activities and active leisure as well as less time for work that takes place in the contexts of the school, the family, and the community. In addition, young workers spend less time doing homework and are more likely to come to school tired and unprepared than are other students (Greenberger & Steinberg, 1986), although not all research uncovers such adverse correlates of employment (Mortimer & Johnson, 1998a). If adolescents become less attached to school, they may become less likely to engage in leisure activities that are organized by the school and monitored by adults for the benefit of young people, such as playing sports, participating in various clubs and organizations, and attending school-sponsored events and functions.

In addition, working youth may become more attracted to unstructured leisure activities, such as going to parties with friends, using drugs and alcohol, and cruising around in cars, because these activities may be more compatible with their work schedules than are adult-sponsored and school-related leisure activities (Osgood, 1999; Safron et al., 2001). In fact, much evidence suggests that those who work more than 20 hours per week are more likely to engage in bad leisure activities; the number of work hours during adolescence is found to be positively associated with delinquency, substance use, and sexual activity (Greenberger & Steinberg, 1986; Ku, Sonenstein, & Pleck, 1993; McMorris & Uggen, 2000; Mortimer & Johnson, 1998b; Steinberg & Dornbusch, 1991; Steinberg, Fegley, & Dornbusch, 1993).

A second position in this debate poses questions about whether paid employment actually squeezes out the more beneficial, good leisure activities. Recent evidence suggests that most employed adolescents spend just as much time as do nonworking youth participating in extracurricular activities and studying (Mortimer, 2003; Shanahan & Flaherty, 2001), which challenges the zero-sum logic that employed adolescents cannot have a well-rounded lifestyle including successful work, family, and school roles. Proponents of youth employment argue that when youth limit the hours they spend in paid work, they are able to balance their multiple commitments to school, to family, and to their jobs, while at the same time acquiring workplace skills and resources that may help them to make good choices in selecting their future careers. Employment may even promote attachment to and success in school if it promotes time management skills and enables young people to practice what they are learning in school (Mortimer, 2003).

A third position in this controversy is that participation in paid work and engagement in good and bad leisure experiences are common constituents of a syndrome of early adult-like identity formation (Bachman & Schulenberg, 1993; Newcomb & Bentler, 1988). Youth who have less involvement, interest, and success in conventional, age-graded adolescent activities—such as going to school and participating in extracurricular sports, clubs, and organizations—are more likely to invest themselves in paid work and to prefer work over school-related activities. Moreover, prior engagement in bad leisure activities such as drinking, having sex, using drugs, and engaging in minor deviance may predispose some youth to enter work environments that offer fewer social constraints on these behaviors than do school and family (Newcomb & Bentler, 1988). These factors coalesce in a pattern of "precocious maturity" that is characterized by long work hours, school disengagement, early residential independence, premature childbearing, and continued involvement in drinking, drug use, delinquency, and sexual activity.

In this chapter, we elaborate these three positions on the interrelations of paid work and leisure during adolescence and the transition to adulthood. The first section describes each of these perspectives in more detail and considers pertinent evidence from diverse data sources and theoretical traditions. In the second section, we explore the precursors and consequences of adolescent work and leisure pursuits. This section identifies demographic factors and prior orientations that influence work and leisure choices during adolescence. It also examines the consequences of teenage work and leisure for educational investment, character development, deviance and substance use, and the acquisition of full-time work in early adulthood. The third and final section offers some suggestions for future inquiry to further explore the complex interrelations of adolescent work and leisure.

THREE PROPOSITIONS DEFINING THE RELATIONSHIP BETWEEN ADOLESCENT PAID WORK AND LEISURE

Adolescents in the United States, when compared to their European and East Asian counterparts, spend more time in paid jobs and leisure activities and much less time doing homework. In fact, U.S. youth spend approximately 6.5 to 8 hours per day in free time, such as watching television, talking, and participating in sports and other structured leisure activities, which is one of the highest rates among contemporary industrialized countries (Larson & Verma, 1999, p. 725).

The following section details three propositions that specify whether paid jobs in adolescence encourage or displace good and bad leisure activities. We also consider the relationship between paid jobs and school-related work activities (especially homework and study time). We focus much of our attention on paid work because the majority of adolescents are employed outside the family setting and most of these jobs lack clear ties to the school. Thus, paid work may undermine obligations to the school and family, as well as disconnect youth from school-related extracurricular activities.

This zero-sum logic is the foundation of the first proposition—that adolescent paid work detracts from more beneficial leisure and work activities and that it exposes young people to potential dangers arising from adult-like leisure activities.

Proposition 1. Paid Employment in Adolescence Decreases Good Leisure and Work and Increases Bad Leisure Activities

Critics of adolescent work suggest that paid employment during adolescence provides few benefits and imposes large opportunity costs that jeopardize a successful transition to adulthood. This proposition is well articulated in Greenberger and Steinberg's *When Teenagers Work: The Psychological and Social Costs of Adolescent Employment* (1986), a powerful critique of paid employment by young people.

First, paid work is thought to limit the time available for good leisure activities. Although adolescents in the United States spend much time in both active and passive leisure, critics argue that employed youth are unable to take full advantage of valuable school-related leisure activities. Extracurricular activities in the arts, sports, and various academic clubs and organizations provide important opportunities for youth to explore their potential interests and values (Csikszentmihalyi & Schneider, 2000). Engagement in these school-related extracurricular activities, such as participation in the performing arts and sports, fosters positive adjustment in high school and young adulthood (Barber, Eccles, & Stone, 2001; Eccles & Barber, 1999). By this logic, paid employment may constrain adolescents from participation in these good leisure activities with their friends and in school, and it may potentially jeopardize the moratorium youth need from the demands and constraints of the adult world (Erikson, 1968). Indeed, empirical evidence has shown that as youth work more hours, their participation in extracurricular sports decreases (Osgood, 1999). Declining participation in extracurricular athletics may potentially undermine academic success in high school, even though sports may offer less protection from the potentially harmful bad leisure activities such as alcohol and drug use (Crosnoe, 2002).

Second, paid employment can detract from school-related work activities, such as getting help from teachers, completing homework, and studying for examinations. For example, working youth may come to school unprepared and fatigued when they work during the school week, making learning and examinations difficult. Empirical research has generally found little difference, however, in school performance between working and nonworking adolescents (Mortimer & Finch, 1986; Steinberg, Greenberber, Garduque, Ruggiero, & Vaux, 1982). However, intensive work hours (more than 20 hours per week) are found to compromise academic success in high school (Carr, Wright, & Brody, 1996; D'Amico, 1984; Greenberger & Steinberg, 1986; Mortimer & Finch, 1986; Steinberg et al., 1982). High work hours increase school absences (Schoenhals, Tienda, & Schneider, 1998) and the probability of school dropout for White males (D'Amico, 1984). Whether moderate hours of work help or hinder academic performance is still debated (Mortimer, Finch, Ryu, Shanahan, & Call, 1996; Mortimer & Johnson, 1998a; Steinberg & Dornbusch, 1991; Steinberg et al., 1993; Warren, LePore, & Mare, 2000).

Third, paid jobs may facilitate potentially harmful or bad leisure activities such as using drugs and alcohol, having sex, and engaging in minor deviance. Youth working many hours on the job have higher rates of delinquency and substance use than do those who work fewer hours (Agnew, 1986; Greenberger & Steinberg, 1986; Lee, 2002); this is particularly true for adolescents from lower socioeconomic origins (Wright, Cullen, & Williams, 1997). The positive relationship between work intensity and problem behavior is not simply the result of preexisting propensities for deviance by the young workers. After controlling for prior engagement in these bad leisure activities, longitudinal research continues to demonstrate a positive effect of work hours on minor delinquency and substance use (McMorris & Uggen, 2000; Mortimer & Johnson, 1998b; Steinberg & Dornbusch, 1991; Steinberg et al., 1993). Researchers have offered several hypotheses for this robust relationship.

One explanation for the effects of work hours on delinquency is that employed adolescents typically work with and serve their peers in entry-level service and retail jobs. Critics of youth work argue that most adolescent jobs, especially those in fast-food restaurants and retail settings, lack opportunities for adult mentorship because many employed youth are supervised by peers who are approximately the same age as their subordinates (Greenberger, 1988). The absence of adult guardians in the employment setting may foster deviance both within and outside the workplace, especially activities linked to defiance of adult authority and violation of workplace rules (such as giving products or services to friends for free, fabricating hours on time cards, or lying about reasons for being absent or tardy). Adolescents who are employed alongside delinquent coworkers tend to commit more workplace crime (Wright & Cullen, 2000) as well as demonstrate more general deviance than do those who do not work with delinquent peers (Ploeger, 1997). In addition, exposure to adolescents and young adults in the workplace may increase the risk of adult-like leisure activities, such as drinking, smoking, and having sex.

Employed youth who work long hours also have less time for structured leisure activities and may also have less flexibility in their work schedules relative to those whose work is less intensive. As such, work reduces their capacity to engage in good leisure (e.g., sports, extracurricular activities), and they may become correspondingly more attracted to less structured, unsupervised, and potentially deviant activities outside the workplace. In particular, intensively employed youth are more likely to go to parties and bars, date, and ride around in cars for fun than are their peers working fewer hours, activities that may increase the likelihood of bad leisure activities (Osgood, 1999; Safron et al., 2001).

Finally, paid jobs may weaken the informal social controls of the school and family in restraining these bad leisure activities. Social control theory (Hirschi, 1969; Kornhauser, 1978) emphasizes the importance of social bonds, which facilitate socialization and restrain deviant behavior. In adolescence, involvement in school and family activities, as well as attachment and commitment to home and school, are key components of the bond to society. Youth who reject the authority of parents and school are less likely to be controlled by them and more likely to commit delinquent acts. By providing an alternative arena for status and success, early work roles may loosen conventional informal social controls during adolescence. In particular, paid jobs can weaken school and parental controls by providing income and autonomy. The increased propensity for smoking, drinking, riding around in cars, and dating, or what Hirschi called "claims to adult status," could result from the weakening of social controls from age-appropriate institutions such as the family and school (Hirschi, 1969, p. 166). Thus, although steady employment is a negative predictor of crime in adulthood (Sampson & Laub, 1993), paid jobs are unlikely to deter criminal activities among young offenders (Uggen, 2000).

In sum, critics of youth work consider paid jobs detrimental to youth development and adjustment. Youth working more than 20 hours per week are thought to have limited time available for good leisure and work activities and greater freedom to pursue unstructured and potentially harmful bad leisure activities. The next proposition presents an alternative argument—that working youth make time for good leisure and work activities, despite their involvement in paid employment. Furthermore, this perspective suggests that some jobs actually reduce the likelihood of delinquency and substance use among working teens.

Proposition 2. Paid Employment in Adolescence Neither Decreases Good Leisure Nor Promotes Bad Leisure Activities

In 1974, the Panel on Youth of the President's Science Advisory Committee gathered to discuss institutions that would help youth become better adults. Headed by James Coleman, the panel advocated a stronger connection between work and school, thus encouraging young people to acquire paid jobs.

> Educational and work institutions are almost wholly distinct. There were some good reasons for that in the past, but in the present and future there are good reasons for a closer connection. These reasons lie in the second class of objectives for youth, experience with responsibility affecting others, and in the creation of settings that involve closer personal relations between adults and youth. (Coleman et al., 1974, p. 160)

The Panel on Youth report suggested that working adults could mentor youth in preparing for future careers, teach them responsibility and independence, and limit their excess time in leisure. In particular, the committee believed that paid jobs would limit the bad leisure activities characteristic of the generally antiadult "adolescent society." Furthermore, work was not thought to be at odds with the student role because work experiences were expected to impress youth with the practical importance of what they were learning in school.

Consistent with this more positive view, recent evidence suggests that moderate involvement in paid jobs does not decrease time for more beneficial leisure and work activities. Using data from the Youth Development Study (YDS), Shanahan and Flaherty (2001) explored time use patterns in the number of hours youth spend in paid work, homework, extracurricular activities, volunteer work, household work, and leisure time with friends. Although several patterns of time use emerged from a person-centered cluster analysis involving various work and leisure roles, teenagers in the two most prevalent classes (comprising approximately 55% of the total sample) spent almost equal amounts of time doing homework, household chores, volunteer work, and extracurricular activities. However, those in the first class did not work (20% of the sample in the 12th grade), whereas those in the second class (35% of the sample in the 12th grade) spent considerable time in paid work (averaging approximately 20 hours per week in the 12th grade).

Shanahan and Flaherty's analysis suggests that many employed youth make time for good leisure activities as well as for household, school, and volunteer work. For these youth, jobs did not diminish hours of homework or school-related extracurricular activities. Other studies indicate that paid jobs in adolescence may actually support the student role. Limited employment during adolescence (20 hours or less per week during high school) is associated with reduced high school dropout rates (D'Amico, 1984), increased involvement in school activities (Mihalic & Elliott, 1997), and higher grade point averages (Mortimer & Johnson, 1998a). Moreover, some evidence suggests that moderate hours of work during high school do not reduce class rank, nor do they limit time for homework and reading outside of class (D'Amico, 1984; Schoenhals et al., 1998).

Regarding more passive leisure activities such as watching television or browsing the Internet, analyses of the National Education Longitudinal Survey and the Monitoring the Future Surveys suggest that time spent watching television is reduced when young people work more hours (Osgood, 1999; Schoenhals et al., 1998). It is interesting to note that in Shanahan and Flaherty's analysis (2001), time spent with friends in nonstructured leisure activities, considered the most likely to foster bad leisure activities by other investigators (Safron et al., 2001), is remarkably consistent for the various classes of workers and nonworkers (averaging 6–9 hours per week).

Second, some adolescent jobs actually decrease the bad unstructured leisure about which critics of youth work warn; this may be especially likely when adolescents are employed in contexts that connect them to family and school—as in family businesses, on farms, or in school-supervised employment (Hansen, Mortimer, & Krueger, 2001). But even employment in fast-food restaurants or other common teenage jobs may reduce illegal and otherwise problematic leisure activities. For example, Newman (1999), in her observation of more than 150 employees of Burger Barn (a pseudonym for fast-food restaurants) in Harlem for 1 year, found that fast-food jobs provided a way for many teenagers to avoid the danger of street violence and participation in the drug trade. Sullivan (1989), in his ethnographic analysis of teenagers in New York, also observed that poor youth in urban areas may gain greater exposure to conventional, prosocial adults and other young people in their jobs, reducing their risk for future delinquency.

Some recent research suggests that the extrinsic and intrinsic qualities of the work environment, not just employment or its intensity, affect the risk of deviance and substance use. For example, Staff and Uggen (in press) found that more adult-like work conditions were associated with more adult-like bad leisure activities. Adolescents who felt that their jobs gave them greater status among their peers as well as workplace freedom and autonomy experienced higher rates of alcohol use and school-related deviance in the senior year of high school. Concerning more serious deviance, higher wages were associated with a greater likelihood of arrest in the senior year of high school.

In contrast, workplace conditions that fostered a balance between work and school and that provided opportunities to learn useful skills reduced the likelihood of school-related deviance, substance use, and arrest in the 12th grade. Thus, jobs that did not compromise the student role appear to inhibit deviance, net of work hours, prior deviance, and self-selection processes. Similarly, Schulenberg and Bachman (1993) found that when early work experiences were connected to future careers and provided opportunities to learn new skills, youth were less likely to engage in bad leisure activities that are associated with high work hours (using drugs and alcohol).

These studies as well as others find that many employed youth do not substitute bad leisure activities for good leisure. Youth who limit their hours of work (especially to 20 hours per week or less) make time for school-related leisure and work activities. In addition, youth jobs that are compatible with the student role can have positive developmental consequences and may limit involvement in bad leisure activities, especially for youth living in neighborhoods with high rates of crime and poverty.

The final proposition does not argue that paid jobs influence leisure activities positively or negatively. Instead, it suggests that the observed associations between adolescent work and leisure activities are spurious, resulting from prior orientations and demographic background characteristics of the young person.

Proposition 3. The Interrelations Between Paid Jobs and Leisure Activities in Adolescence Reflect a Syndrome of Precocious Development

A diverse set of life changes marks the transition from adolescence to young adulthood; these include school completion, the acquisition of full-time employment, economic and residential independence, family formation, and intimate cohabitation or marriage. Some youth prematurely enter adult roles before they are developmentally and socially mature enough for the responsibilities of adulthood. The various manifestations of this process have been referred to as adolescent "transition proneness" (Jessor & Jessor, 1977), "precocious development" (Newcomb & Bentler, 1988), "hurried adolescence" (Safron, Schulenberg, & Bachman, 2001), and "pseudomaturity" (Greenberger & Steinberg, 1986). Each of these concepts suggests a coalescence of more adult-like leisure and work activities that is influenced by the prior orientations, attitudes, and socioeconomic background of the young person.

Precocious development theory suggests that prior engagement in bad leisure activities influences the propensity for paid work in adolescence. According to precocious development theory (Newcomb & Bentler, 1988), early drug use hastens the transition to adulthood. Early drug use is incompatible with the preadult stage of adolescence, as schools and parents attempt to restrain problem behaviors. Adolescent drug users thus have a higher probability of selecting into adult-like situations that are more compatible with substance use, such as moving into their own apartments, quitting school, and acquiring full-time jobs. According to Newcomb and Bentler, ". . . early drug use may increase interest in self-sufficiency and independence, as afforded by a job" (p. 169). Although the pseudomaturity is reinforced through the admiration of peers who perceive the adolescent as more mature and streetwise (Newcomb & Bentler, 1988), these premature adult roles do not provide adequate social control. Drug and alcohol use subsequently increase for these precocious youth in young adulthood (Krohn, Lizotte, & Perez, 1997).

Drawing on data from 654 adolescents in the Los Angeles area, Newcomb and Bentler (1988) found that teenage drug use increased the risk of early family formation (marriage and children) as well as more adult-like work roles. Other studies (Bachman & Schulenberg, 1993) have found a similar relationship between alcohol use and adolescent work hours. Binge drinking during high school is associated with a syndrome of adult-like behaviors such as intensive work hours, limited involvement in adolescent-centered activities, inadequate sleep, and a poor diet. Evidence from the Youth Development Study also suggests that ninth graders with higher rates of substance use, school-related deviance, and law violations worked more hours in subsequent years of high school (Mortimer, 2003; Staff & Uggen, in press). Thus, the negative effect of paid work on substance use and deviance may arise from an endogenous or reciprocal process because prior engagement in these behaviors influences the decision to work.

Other theories suggest that precocious work roles may simply be a common correlate of bad leisure activities in adolescence because both signify adult-like status. According to problem behavior theory (Jessor & Jessor, 1977), the problem behaviors associated with an early transition to adulthood, such as marijuana use, sexual activity, problem drinking, and general deviance, reflect transition proneness, or the desire to act like an adult:

> . . . many of the behaviors that we have referred to as problem behaviors are normatively age graded, that is, are proscribed for those who are younger but are permitted, and even prescribed, for those who are older; and that, because of this, engaging in such behaviors can serve to mark a transition in status, their occurrence representing a developmental change toward, or a claim upon, a more mature status. (Jessor & Jessor, 1977, p. 41)

Thus, bad leisure activities such as alcohol use, smoking, drug use, and sexual activity assume symbolic significance as claims to adult status. Using a longitudinal sample of middle school students as well as college students from the early 1970s, the Jessors found significant interrelations among marijuana use, sexual intercourse, drinking, problem drinking, and general deviance. These behaviors were negatively correlated with conventional behaviors (e.g., school achievement and church attendance). Jessor and Jessor (1977) concluded that these various transition behaviors represented a syndrome of adult-like activities that were often incompatible with more age-appropriate activities.

While prior involvement in delinquency and substance use encourages early adult-like work patterns, prior orientations towards work and school also influence the motivation to work in adolescence. For instance, empirical evidence from the Monitoring the Future Survey demonstrates that an early desire for youth work (measured before the youth obtained jobs) predicts higher work hours as well as problem behaviors in subsequent years (Bachman, Safron, & Schulenberg, in press). Time-use diaries from a sample of Seattle youth also revealed that orientations toward work predicted subsequent work hours as well as school performance (Warren, 2002). Concerning orientations toward school, those students in the Youth Development Study who had lower educational promise (scored below the mean on educational aspirations, grade point average, and intrinsic motivations toward schoolwork) in the ninth grade worked more intensively in the 10th through 12th grades of high school (Mortimer, 2003).

Finally, the social background of adolescents influences their subsequent involvement in paid work as well as good and bad leisure activities. Youth from families of lower socioeconomic status are likely to enter the labor force at a younger age, work more hours, and have less connection to the educational system than are their more advantaged peers (Kerckhoff, 2002). Although youth from lower socioeconomic backgrounds are less likely to be employed than their more advantaged peers, they usually work more intensively when they are employed (Entwisle, Alexander, & Olson, 2000; Mortimer, 2003; Mortimer, Staff, & Oesterle, 2003). The lack of available jobs in many impoverished neighborhoods makes finding early work more difficult for poor youth (Entwisle et al., 2000; Newman, 1999; Sullivan, 1989).

Taking Stock of the Three Propositions

Juxtaposing these three propositions, it becomes difficult to discern whether paid jobs cause bad leisure activities, whether they insulate youth from bad leisure and encourage well-rounded combinations of both work and good leisure activities, or whether work and leisure occur together because they are common constituents of broader syndromes or configurations of adult-like behaviors. Prior orientations, leisure involvements, and demographic background features influence the decision to work—as well as to engage in deviance—in adolescence. Further complicating the picture, leisure activities may reduce or enhance the capacity to work. One study found that although youth who engaged in problem behavior in the ninth grade were more likely to work long hours, these youth were more likely to have sporadic rather than continuous work careers during high school (Mortimer, 2003). This pattern is suggestive of problems in self-regulation, reflected in problem behavior as well as difficulties in sustaining continuous employment.

Each proposition reviewed, positing a different relationship between paid work and leisure, is supported to some extent by empirical research. Thus, adjudicating between these various propositions becomes exceedingly difficult, as paid jobs precede, follow, and co-occur with involvement in both good and bad leisure activities. Choosing among the three possible relationships becomes even more complex when we differentiate good and bad leisure activities, explore the quality and not just the quantity of early work and leisure experiences, and consider social structural arrangements that may impede or encourage paid work as well as leisure activities.

First, the relationship between paid work and good and bad leisure activities, or more generally whether paid work is beneficial or detrimental to adolescent adjustment, is contingent upon the particular leisure behavior. As one example of the relationship between employment and the many bad leisure activities, a long line of research shows that paid work hours are positively associated with youth substance use. Although some forms of substance use appear to be responsive to work intensity or other employment indicators, the prevalence of hard-core drug use is generally very low among adolescents in the general population. In the 2002 Monitoring the Future study, for example, 5% of 12th graders reported cocaine use in the past year and 1% reported heroin use over the same period (Johnston, O'Malley, & Bachman, 2002). In light of these low base rates, few studies have explored the extent to which adolescent employment affects more serious drug use in the general population. Experimental job programs for youth with a history of arrest or school failure generally show no significant effects on heroin or cocaine use (Hollister, Kemper, & Maynard, 1984). Thus, when we speak of a link between drug use and employment, for most youth this link refers to drugs such as cigarettes and alcohol that are proscribed only for adolescents.

Second, much research suggests that the quality of early work and leisure experiences—not just the hours—is important for determining the relationship between paid jobs and good and bad leisure activities. Again, using the example of paid jobs and adolescent substance use, hours of work are positively correlated with alcohol use. How-

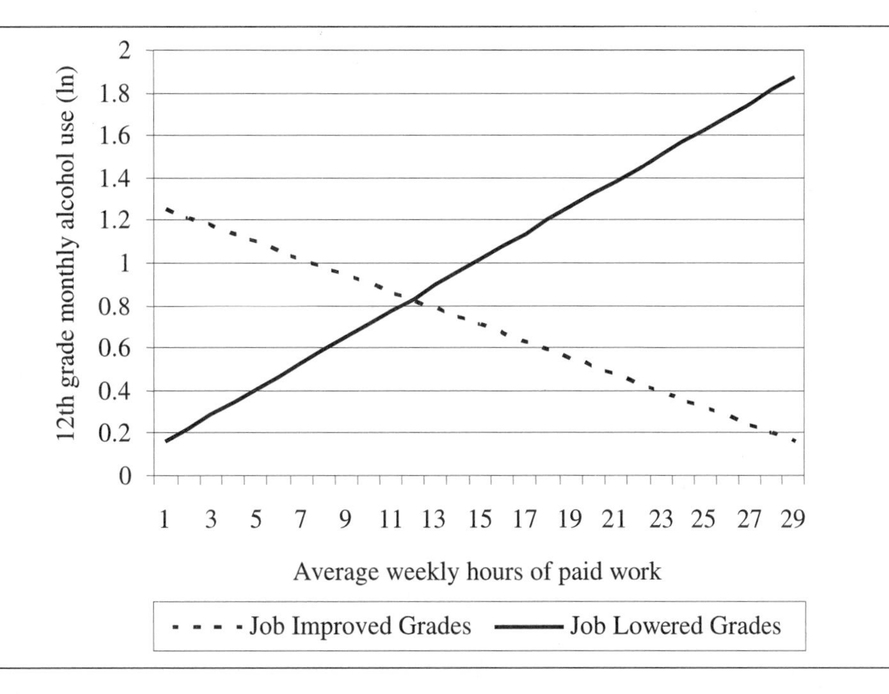

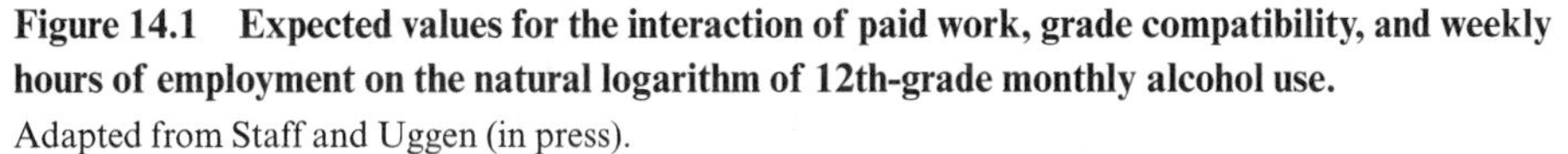

Figure 14.1 Expected values for the interaction of paid work, grade compatibility, and weekly hours of employment on the natural logarithm of 12th-grade monthly alcohol use.
Adapted from Staff and Uggen (in press).

ever, important dimensions of adolescent work interact with work hours in affecting the rate of alcohol use. Certain work dimensions may buffer the effects of high work hours on bad leisure activities. Figure 14.1 displays the relationship between the average weekly hours worked and the compatibility of work with school on 12th-grade alcohol use among YDS respondents. As shown in Figure 14.1, high hours of work decrease alcohol use if work reinforces rather than displaces school roles. When adolescents are unable to balance the role of student and worker and their grades suffer as a result of their jobs, their drinking increases when they work long hours.

Thus, certain types of jobs may be beneficial in reducing bad leisure activities even at high levels of work intensity. In addition, the various interrelations between work hours and specific work dimensions add a further layer of complexity to the relationship between paid jobs and good and bad leisure activities.

Finally, the relationship between paid work and leisure activities may depend on the structural opportunities available to the young people. As mentioned before, poor youth tend to work more hours than do nonpoor youth when they are employed. However, many youth in poor urban neighborhoods face a limited and competitive job market (Newman, 1999). In contrast, youth in more prosperous neighborhoods find a labor market characterized by an abundance of lower-level retail and service jobs, as well as schools with numerous opportunities for more structured leisure activities.

Thus, without many of the opportunities for good leisure activities as well as paid jobs, early work may be a positive experience for youth in poor neighborhoods. Alternatively, the "premature affluence" (Bachman, 1983) associated with work for more advantaged youth may intensify bad leisure activities and limit participation in the many possible school-related good leisure activities that are available. In addition, the abundance of jobs available in more prosperous neighborhoods can sometimes foster negative work attitudes and misbehaviors in young people, such as tardiness, absenteeism, and giving away of goods and services, because more socioeconomically advantaged youth may have ample opportunities to lose and regain work. Thus, the structural opportunities of the young person may influence involvement in paid jobs as well as in both good and bad leisure activities.

A question that we have not yet considered is what the relation between work and leisure in adolescence means for the transition to adulthood. More specifically, what are the consequences of these various interrelations between paid work and good and bad leisure activities for subsequent problem behavior, substance use, and educational and occupational attainment? Do these early work and leisure experiences compromise the future life chances of young people?

WORK AND LEISURE IN THE TRANSITION TO ADULTHOOD

In this section, we explore the long-term implications of adolescent work and leisure for the transition to adulthood. Based on what we know about the relations between paid work and leisure activities and what we know about selection into the various work and leisure patterns, we classify adolescents into two ideal-typical pathways and consider developmental processes in the transition to adulthood. The first pathway characterizes youth who display a hastened or accelerated transition to adult roles.

Pathway 1. The Accelerated Transition to Adulthood

Adolescents on the first pathway are characterized by a precocious maturity with regard to their work and leisure activities. They choose to work more hours during high school, spend less time in school-related good leisure activities, and are more likely to pursue bad leisure that involves using drugs and alcohol, having sex, and engaging in delinquency. As discussed previously, whether these relationships are a consequence (Proposition 1) or merely a correlate (Proposition 3) of paid work is a subject of intense debate.

Nonetheless, intensive involvement in paid labor during high school shapes subsequent educational investment and acquisition of full-time work after high school. Precocious work patterns (more than 20 hours per week throughout high school) have been found to lessen the likelihood of obtaining a 4-year college degree both at age 25 (Mortimer, 2003) and 10 years after high school graduation (Carr, Wright, & Brody, 1991). Moreover, adolescents who pursue intensive work hours engage in more months of full-time work in the years immediately following high school and obtain fewer months of higher education than do their nonworking or moderately working peers (Mortimer, Staff, & Oesterle, 2003).

Furthermore, for youth from lower socioeconomic backgrounds who are more likely to select into intensive work roles in adolescence (Mortimer et al., 2003), the early workplace becomes a viable source of human and social capital. For example, Newman

(1999) found that young people in poor neighborhoods of Harlem worked in fast-food jobs because they offer a viable alternative to the crime and unemployment that characterizes their neighborhoods and because these jobs provide skills and resources that may apply to more prestigious jobs. In his ethnographic analysis of delinquent teens in New York, Sullivan (1989) found that the presence of work in early adolescence may open the door to high-quality work in late adolescence. In addition, Entwisle and her colleagues (2000) found that youth from low socioeconomic backgrounds worked more hours at every grade than did their more economically advantaged peers. The latter authors speculated that early employment (e.g., during middle school) allowed youth with less interest in school an alternative source of social and human capital for future employment. Consistent with these ideas, teenagers in the Youth Development Study who engaged in a more continuous and intensive employment pattern during high school reported more work-related learning opportunities than did those who limited their hours (Mortimer, 2003).

In fact, early adult-like work roles can improve short-term occupational attainment. Intensive work patterns during adolescence have been found to reduce unemployment and increase wages in the years immediately following high school (Stern & Nakata, 1989). Similarly, Carr et al. (1996) found that teenage work has a positive effect on occupational outcomes. Intensive work hours during high school increased wages and employment 10 years later but decreased college attendance, especially the completion of 4 or more years of college. Carr et al. (1996) conclude that "the positive direct effect of teenage work on earnings greatly exceeded its negative indirect effect through educational attainment" in the early career (p. 79). Moreover, teenagers with a lengthy work history (total years employed) have "greater employability" in young adulthood (Mihalic & Elliott, 1997). In the Youth Development Study, those teenagers who worked over 20 hours per week throughout most of their high school years averaged the most months of full-time work in the years immediately following high school (Mortimer et al., 2003). Thus, it appears that an accelerated transition may have positive short-term effects on income and employability but potentially negative effects on educational attainment and possibly long-term occupational attainment. Still, although much evidence links work and short-term occupational attainment, others argue that the effects are spurious due to selection processes (Hotz, Xu, Tienda, & Ahituv, 2002).

But what about the deviance and substance use that accompanies these early work roles? Do they exert independent effects on future deviance, substance use, and attainment? Generally, the higher rates of delinquency and substance use associated with early work roles do not continue into young adulthood. Intensive teenage work roles do not appear to increase adult criminality and substance use, despite the positive relationship between work hours and problem behaviors during adolescence (Mihalic & Elliott, 1997, did find, however, that total years of adolescent work—not work hours—predicted higher rates of alcohol and marijuana use at ages 27 and 28). The preponderance of the evidence indicates that college attendance, rather than adolescent work hours predict high rates of alcohol use in young adulthood (Bachman et al., 2002; McMorris & Uggen, 2000). Youth in the full-time labor force after high school display rates of binge drinking that are lower than those of their college-bound peers (Bachman, Wadsworth, O'Malley, Johnston, & Schulenburg, 1997), a relationship that probably results from the college students' prolonged preadult roles, from their living arrangements (residence in a dormitory, fraternity or sorority), and from positive attitudes toward drug and alcohol use (Bachman et al., 2002).

Yet, some suggest that early problem behaviors may compromise long-term attainment in adulthood. According to Newcomb and Bentler (1988), drug use in adolescence hastens other markers of adult status, such as leaving school and acquiring a full-time job, establishing a residence away from the parental home, and engaging in premarital cohabitation. Although early drug use accelerates a pseudomaturity that is admired by peers, the adolescent is socially and developmentally unprepared to deal with these new adult-like responsibilities:

> . . . Drug users tend to bypass or circumvent the typical maturational sequence of school, work, and marriage, and become engaged in adult roles of jobs and family prematurely, without the necessary growth and development to enhance success with these roles. Thus drug users may develop a pseudomaturity that ill prepares them for the real difficulties of adult life. As a consequence, they will have a greater probability of failing at these roles over time. (pp. 35–36)

This foreshortening of a critical developmental period during adolescence is thus considered to be detrimental to successful adjustment in young adulthood.

To test this perspective, Newcomb and Bentler (1988) sampled 1,634 adolescents in Los Angeles county schools, beginning in 1976. Following 654 adolescents until approximately age 22, they found that adolescent drug use (a latent measure of the frequency of alcohol, cannabis, and hard drug use) decreases job stability and the likelihood of college involvement in young adulthood. Teenage cannabis and hard drug use in particular were associated with several indicators of maladjustment in young adulthood, including unemployment, criminal activities, loneliness, and marital problems. Alcohol use did not predict these deleterious outcomes.

It is interesting to note that teenage drug use (especially cannabis and hard drug use) increased income in young adulthood, which is consistent with other studies finding early drug use to be associated with higher wage rates in young adulthood (Gill & Michaels, 1992; Kaestner, 1991). Newcomb and Bentler (1988) attribute the positive effects of early drug use on attainment to the economic returns of work experience:

> . . . drug use, as a feature of precocious development, propels a teenager into the work force at a younger age and thus this person has gained more work experience and seniority at a job, compared to more conforming and less drug-using youngsters who furthered their education in college. (p. 167)

The bad leisure activities that are such common accompaniments to early work roles thus can have positive short-term economic correlates in the passage to adult status. The short-term gains from an early transition may be fleeting, however. If early drug use diminishes educational attainment, future trajectories of earnings and job prestige may be compromised. Furthermore, young drug users tend to work in jobs that offer high initial wages but limited potential for wage growth (Kandel, Chen, & Gill, 1995). Thus, early transitions and problem behaviors may be beneficial to early career attainment, but they may be detrimental to long-term occupational trajectories and educational attainment.

It should be noted that employment in adolescence—especially for intensively employed youth—has been commonly linked to minor forms of deviance, not major crimes that would attract the attention of the police (Mihalic & Elliott, 1997). Sullivan (1989) found that youth with prior criminal records, especially those from the most economically disadvantaged neighborhoods, had the greatest difficulty in finding work. Official sanctions may embed youth in a more deviant trajectory as they make the transition into adulthood (Hagan, 1993). However, if the minor delinquency associated with working does lead to more serious crime and entanglement in the criminal justice system, these circumstances would adversely affect occupational commitment, economic dependency, and job stability in adulthood, especially for youth from disadvantaged backgrounds. Hagan (1991) found that attitudes favoring delinquency in adolescence diminish occupational prestige in young adulthood only for youth from working-class families.

In summary, youth displaying a precocious maturity in regard to work and leisure activities may experience an accelerated transition to adulthood. During the high school period, these youth are less involved in school-related work and leisure activities, and they are more likely to work high hours in the paid labor force than are their less precocious peers. These youth are also more likely to partake in bad leisure activities such as drinking alcohol, smoking cigarettes, using illicit drugs, having sex, and engaging in minor delinquency.

After high school, precocious youth are more likely to continue with intensive work and to forego higher education. Although more intensive work experience in high school may enhance income and wages in young adulthood, youth in this accelerated pathway typically accrue less education than do youth who limit or moderate their involvement in bad leisure and paid work. Thus, these early work and leisure activities may exert detrimental long-term effects on wages and income. It is interesting to note that the bad leisure associated with early work roles, such as minor delinquency and alcohol use, generally does not continue into adulthood. Still, young people, regardless of whether they are employed, who engage in more serious and persistent problem behaviors will have diminished socioeconomic attainment. The second pathway includes youth who limit or (less commonly) do without early employment experiences in adolescence.

Pathway 2. The Delayed Transition to Adulthood

The second general pathway to adulthood typifies youth who limit their hours of work (a very small percentage of youth do not work at all; see the Committee on the Health and Safety Implications of Child Labor, 1998), maintain active involvement in good leisure activities, and are less likely to partake in the bad leisure activities in high school than are their more precocious peers. Generally, adolescents in the second pathway come from more privileged backgrounds than do those in the first pathway because children from lower socioeconomic backgrounds are at a greater risk for premature work and family roles (Mortimer, 2003).

For these youth not employed in adult-like patterns, early and more limited work is beneficial for the transition to adulthood; these benefits are evident in a diverse set of life domains. For example, early work experiences may help adolescents gain a sense of responsibility, independence, and self-confidence (Aronson, Mortimer, Zierman, &

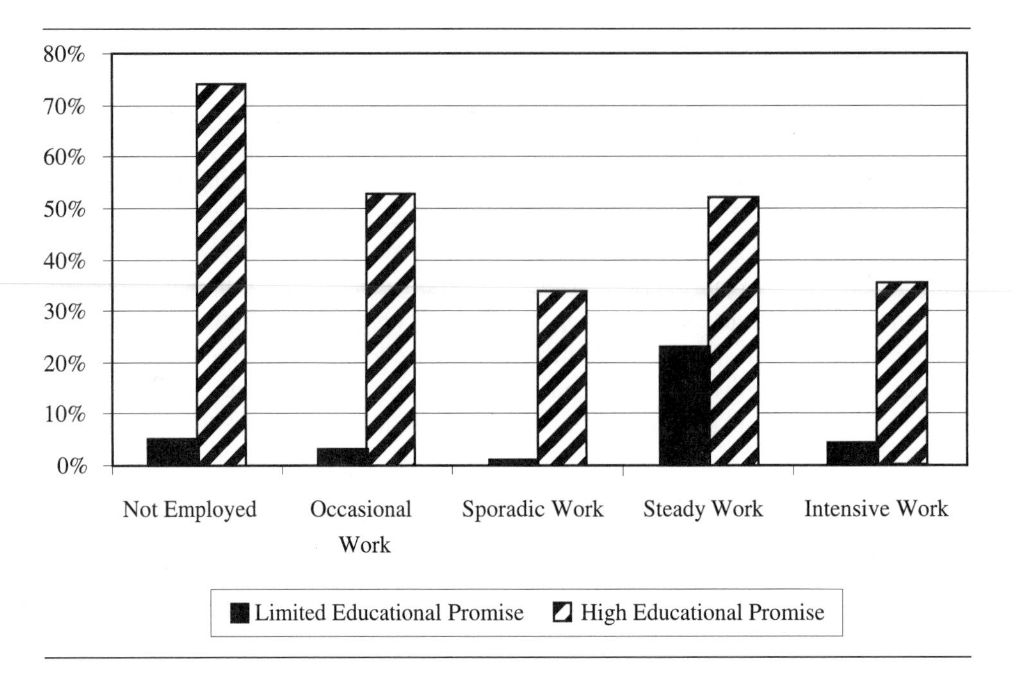

Figure 14.2 B.A. degree receipt by high school paid work investment and educational promise. Adapted from Mortimer, Staff, and Oesterle (2003).

Hacker, 1996; Elder & Rockwell, 1979; Greenberger, 1984; Greenberger & Steinberg, 1986; Phillips & Sandstrom, 1990). In some historical circumstances, work at an early age may be especially valuable for future development. Elder's (1974) study of youth in the Depression era found that early work experiences were associated with more positive mental health and achievement. In this era of economic hardship and stress, youth gained confidence and self-esteem as they contributed to their families through paid jobs and household labor (Elder & Rockwell, 1979).

What are the educational and occupational consequences of moderate work roles for these youth? Using data from the Youth Development Study, Shanahan and Flaherty (2001) found that teenagers who balanced paid jobs, schoolwork, and extracurricular activities were more likely to attend college after their senior year of high school. Not surprisingly, these youth were more likely to receive a 4-year degree than were their highly work-invested and nonworking peers (Mortimer, 2003). Figure 14.2 shows unadjusted mean differences in the receipt of a 4-year bachelor's degree for young people in the Youth Development Study by high school work pattern and educational promise. Adolescents in the intensive work pattern averaged more than 20 hours per week throughout most of high school, while youth in the sporadic work pattern also worked more than 20 hours per week but not continuously. The steady workers, in contrast, limited their paid work to 20 or less hours per week throughout most of high school, while the occasional workers limited both the hours and the duration of their paid work experience. Youth who did not work during the high school period constituted only 7% of the sample.

Not surprisingly, youth who worked intensively (averaging high work hours) during high school—a salient characteristic of the accelerated transition to adulthood—were the least likely to obtain a bachelor's degree. Although most of the small group of youth who did not work had obtained a bachelor's degree by age 27, adolescent employment does not appear to diminish educational trajectories for those who moderated their paid labor in high school. Even youth with low educational promise in the 9th grade (those who scored below the median on grade point average, educational aspirations, and intrinsic motivation toward school) were four times more likely than the intensive workers to receive a 4-year degree if they pursued a more balanced pattern of work during high school (Mortimer et al., 2003). Some evidence also suggests that early work experiences help youth solidify occupational values (Mortimer et al., 1996). This crystallization of work values may be especially beneficial, given the difficulty many young people have in preparing for their future occupations (Rindfuss, Cooksey, & Sutterlin, 1999; Schneider & Stevenson, 1999).

In addition, the bad leisure activities associated with a balanced pattern of work appear to have little consequence for future attainment. For example, Jessor, Donovan, and Costa (1991) found that adolescent problem behaviors (as measured by general deviance and by cigarette, alcohol, marijuana, and illicit drug use) had little effect on occupational prestige, educational attainment, political participation, general health, life satisfaction, self-esteem, or alienation. There was no spillover effect of early problem behavior on young-adult occupational or educational attainment, although youth in this sample had moderate rates of problem behaviors and were mostly from middle-class social origins. In some cases, engagement in these bad leisure activities can enhance attainment in adulthood. Attitudes that favored a "party" subculture in adolescence increased occupational prestige scores in young adulthood for males from non–working-class backgrounds (Hagan, 1991). For these youth, certain bad leisure activities may have enhanced their social capital and thus promoted their future attainment.

Some researchers suggest that for many adolescents, early problem behaviors are limited to adolescence and are generally unlikely to ensnare young people in a long-term trajectory of problem behaviors (Moffitt et al., 2002). Ironically, some of the bad leisure activities associated with intensive work hours in high school become more common in young adulthood for youth who work less intensively during adolescence (McMorris & Uggen, 2000). These youth begin to catch up to their more precocious peers in regard to alcohol use (Bachman et al., 2002) and binge drinking (Bachman et al., 1997). However, those youth who postpone heavy alcohol use (and other drug use) until college also tend to relinquish these activities later as they take on adult work and family roles (Bachman et al., 2002).

We thus find that various types of work and leisure can be consequential for the transition to adulthood. In general, the bad leisure activities associated with less intensive work roles, such as alcohol use and minor deviance, appear to have little consequence for future attainment. The benign consequences of problem behaviors for these young people may result partially from the fact that more economically advantaged youth select into this pathway. Because such youth have greater socioeconomic resources and social capital than do youth in the precocious pathway, their problematic behaviors may receive less scrutiny from the authorities, and they may have greater capacity to compensate for and overcome prior behavioral deficits (Sampson & Laub, 1993).

CONCLUDING COMMENTS

Although great diversity has been demonstrated in work and nonwork activities in adolescence, we focused on the relationship between paid work and good leisure and bad leisure activities. Evidence suggests that paid work—especially highly intensive work—encourages bad leisure activities. When work is limited, allowing balance between employment, school, and other activities, work does not appear to have this negative consequence. In addition, paid work that enhances family relationships or provides a strong link to school may minimize the potential detriments of other paid work. Programs that forge stronger links between school, family, and work—such as cooperative education programs (co-ops)—that provide students with opportunities to be employed as part of their education may be especially protective. Under such conditions, paid work is less likely to crowd out good leisure and encourage bad leisure activities (see Barton, 1996). In addition, teachers could simply have students talk about their work experiences in the classroom, which may help young people deal with work challenges, encourage interest by other students in their jobs, and identify aspects of their work that may benefit them in their future careers (Stone & Mortimer, 1998).

Nonetheless, debates surround the causal efficacy of work activities—are they determinants of good and bad leisure in adolescence? Or, alternatively, do the patterns of both work and leisure activities result from syndromes of behavior attached to prior precocious or conventionally age-graded adolescent identities? First, in coming to terms with this seemingly contradictory literature, it is important to recognize that adolescent agency influences work activity, leisure, and time use more generally. The decisions about whether to work in adolescence and how much to work reflect the young person's social location and prospects for the future—defined by gender, race, parental education, early educational promise, and the adolescent's prior involvement in problematic or deviant behaviors. Given that paid work typically begins prior to high school (about the age of 12), researchers should give greater attention to work histories much earlier in the life course (Entwisle et al., 2001). How do problem behaviors in elementary and middle school influence the decision to work before high school? How does the social class context affect the interrelations of early work and leisure and their consequences?

Second, it is necessary to consider work experience—both paid and unpaid—and leisure jointly, although it is standard practice to separate them. It is difficult to partition the effect of paid work on other types of work and leisure because of their many plausible and empirically strong interrelationships. Analytic techniques that assess the joint occurrence of experiences, such as various clustering procedures and latent class analysis, may help researchers find combinations of work as well as good and bad leisure activities that jointly affect later life outcomes.

Third, research attention needs to be directed to more dynamic processes of work and leisure. Although studies have considered work hours, overall investment in work during high school, and the qualities of jobs, more attention should be directed to patterns of change in work, indicating growth and development over time; that is, some adolescents may stay in the jobs they held early in high school, whereas others advance to jobs that are more challenging and more promotive of vocational development. Similarly, adolescent leisure activities may also change in character, reflecting greater maturity over time or involving greater involvement in serious delinquency and crime.

What are the relationships between these presumably interrelated trajectories? Looking beyond adolescence, fruitful inquiry may be directed to how changes in adolescent work and leisure activity influence trajectories of adult attainment. Are there different adolescent work careers (movements between sequences of jobs) and leisure trajectories, and what are their consequences for career establishment, adult attainment, and other aspects of behavioral and social adjustment? These are the important questions that lie before psychologists and sociologists who strive to better understand the links between these prominent facets of adolescents' and young adults' lives.

REFERENCES

Agnew, R. (1986). Work and delinquency among juveniles attending school. *Journal of Crime and Justice, 9,* 19–41.

Aronson, P. J., Mortimer, J. T., Zierman, C., & Hacker, M. (1996). Generational differences in early work experiences and evaluations. In J. Mortimer & M. Finch (Eds.), *Adolescents, work, and family: An intergenerational developmental analysis* (pp. 25–62). Newbury Park, CA: Sage.

Bachman, J. G. (1983). Premature influence: Do high school students earn too much? *Economic Outlook, USA, 10,* 64–67.

Bachman, J. G., O'Malley, P. J., Schulenberg, J. E., Johnston, L. J., Bryant, A. L., & Merline, A. C. (2002). *The decline of substance use in young adulthood: Changes in social activities, roles, and beliefs.* Mahwah, NJ: Erlbaum.

Bachman, J. G., Safron, D. J., & Schulenberg, J. E. (in press). Wishing to work: New perspectives on how adolescents' part-time work intensity is linked with educational disengagement, drug use, and other problem behaviors. *International Journal of Behavioral Development.*

Bachman, J. G., & Schulenberg, J. (1993). How part-time work intensity relates to drug use, problem behavior, time use, and satisfaction among high school seniors: Are these consequences or merely correlates? *Developmental Psychology, 29,* 220–235.

Bachman, J. G., Wadsworth, K. N., O'Malley, P. M., Johnston, L. D., & Schulenberg, J. E. (1997). *Smoking, drinking and drug use in young adulthood: The impacts of new freedoms and new responsibilities.* Mahwah, NJ: Erlbaum.

Barber, B. L., Eccles, J. S., & Stone, M. R. (2001). Whatever happened to the jock, the brain, and the princess? Young adult pathways linked to adolescent activity involvement and social identity. *Journal of Adolescent Research, 16,* 429–455.

Barton, P. E. (1996). *Co-operative education in high school: Promise and neglect.* Princeton, NJ: Educational Testing Service.

Carr, R., Wright, J., & Brody, C. (1996). Effects of high school work experience a decade later: Evidence from the National Longitudinal Study. *Sociology of Education, 69,* 66–81.

Coleman, J., Bremner, R., Clark, B., Davis, J., Eichorn, D., Griliches, Z., et al. (1974). *Youth: Transition to adulthood.* Chicago: University of Chicago Press.

Committee on the Health and Safety Implications of Child Labor. (1998). *Protecting youth at work.* Washington, DC: National Academy Press.

Csikszentmihalyi, M., & Schneider, B. (2000). *Becoming adult: How teenagers prepare for the world of work.* New York: Basic Books.

Crosnoe, Robert. (2002). Academic and health-related trajectories in adolescence: The intersection of gender and athletics. *Journal of Health and Social Behavior, 43,* 317–335.

D'Amico, R. (1984). Does employment during high school impair academic progress? *Sociology of Education, 57,* 152–164.

Eccles, J., & Barber, B. (1999). Student council, volunteering, basketball, and marching band: What kind of extracurricular involvement matters? *Journal of Adolescent Research, 14,* 10–43.

Elder, G. H., Jr. (1974). *Children of the Great Depression.* Chicago: University of Chicago Press.

Elder, G. H., Jr., & Rockwell, R. C. (1979). Economic depression and postwar opportunity in men's lives: A study of life patterns and health. In R. G. Simmons (Ed.), *Research in community and mental health* (pp. 249–303). Greenwich, CT: JAI Press.

Entwisle, D. R., Alexander, K. L., & Olson, L. S. (2000). Early work histories of urban youth. *American Sociological Review, 65,* 279–297.

Erikson, E. H. (1968). *Identity: Youth and crisis.* New York: Norton.

Gill, A. M., & Michaels, R. J. (1992). Does drug use lower wages? *Industrial and Labor Relations Review, 45,* 419–434.

Greenberger, E. (1984). Children, family, and work. In N. D. Repucci, L. A. Weithorn, E. P. Mulvey, & J. Monahan (Eds.), *Children, mental health, and the law* (pp. 103–122). Beverly Hills, CA: Sage.

Greenberger, E. (1988). Working in teenage america. In J. T. Mortimer & K. M. Borman (Eds.), *Work experience and psychological development through the life span* (pp. 21–50). Boulder, CO: Westview.

Greenberger, E., & Steinberg, L. D. (1986). *When teenagers work: The psychological and social costs of adolescent employment.* New York: Basic Books.

Hagan, J. (1991). Destiny and drift: Subcultural preferences, status attainment, and the risks and rewards of youth. *American Sociological Review, 56,* 567–582.

Hagan, J. (1993). The social embeddedness of crime and unemployment. *Criminology, 31,* 465–491.

Hansen, D., Mortimer, J. T., & Krueger, H. (2001). Adolescent part-time employment in the United States and Germany: Diverse outcomes, contexts, and pathways. In C. Pole, P. Mizen, & A. Bolton (Eds.), *Hidden hands: International perspectives on children's work and labor* (pp. 121–138). London: Routledge Falmer Press.

Hirschi, T. (1969). *Causes of delinquency.* Berkeley: University of California Press.

Hollister, R. G., Jr., Kemper, P., & Maynard, R. A. (1984). *The National Supported Work Demonstration.* Madison: University of Wisconsin Press.

Hotz, V. J., Xu, L. C., Tienda, M., & Ahituv, A. (2002). Are there returns to the wages of young men from working while in school? *The Review of Economics and Statistics, 84,* 221–236.

Jessor, R., Donovan, J. E., & Costa, F. M. (1991). *Beyond adolescence: Problem behavior and young adult development.* Cambridge, NY: Cambridge University Press.

Jessor, R., & Jessor, S. (1977). *Problem behavior and psychosocial development: A longitudinal study of youth.* New York: Academic Press.

Johnston, L. D., O'Malley, P. M., & Bachman, J. G. (2002). Ecstasy use among American teens drops for the first time in recent years, and overall drug and alcohol use also decline in the year after 9/11. Retrieved December 16, 2002, from http://monitoringthefuture.org/pressreleases/02drugpr_complete.pdf

Kaestner, R. (1991). The effects of illicit drug use on the wages of young adults. *Journal of Labor Economics, 9,* 381–412.

Kandel, D., Chen, K., & Gill, A. (1995). The impact of drug use on earnings: A life-span perspective. *Social Forces, 74,* 243–270.

Kerckhoff, A. C. (2002). The transition from school to work. In J. T. Mortimer & R. Larson (Eds.), *The future of adolescent experience: Societal trends and the transition to adulthood* (pp. 52–87). New York: Cambridge University Press.

Kornhauser, R. (1978). *Social sources of delinquency.* Chicago: University of Chicago Press.

Krohn, M. D., Lizotte, A. J., & Perez, C. M. (1997). The interrelationship between substance use and precocious transitions to adult statuses. *Journal of Health and Social Behavior, 38,* 87–103.

Ku, L., Sonenstein, F. L., & Pleck, J. H. (1993). Neighborhood, family, and work: Influences on the premarital behaviors of adolescent males. *Social Forces, 72,* 479–503.

Larson, R., & Verma, S. (1999). How children and adolescents spend time across the world: Work, play, and developmental opportunities. *Psychological Bulletin, 125,* 701–736.

Lee, J. C. (2002, August). *Quality vs. quantity? The relationship between employment and sub-*

stance abuse in high school. Paper presented at the Annual Meeting of the American Sociological Association, Chicago, IL.

Marsh, H. W. (1991). Employment during high school: Character building or subversion of academic goals? *Sociology of Education, 64,* 172–189.

McMorris, B., & Uggen, C. (2000). Alcohol and employment in the transition to adulthood. *Journal of Health and Social Behavior, 41,* 276–294.

Mihalic, S., & Elliott, D. (1997). Short- and long-term consequences of adolescent work. *Youth and Society, 28,* 464–498.

Moffitt, T. E., Capsi, A., Harrington, H., & Milne, B. J. (2002). Males on the life-course-persistent and adolescence-limited antisocial pathways: Follow-up at age 26 years. *Development and Psychopathology, 14,* 179–207.

Mortimer, J. T. (2003). *Work and growing up in America.* Cambridge, MA: Harvard University Press.

Mortimer, J. T., & Finch, M. D. (1986). The effects of part-time work on self-concept and achievement. In K. Borman & J. Reisman (Eds.), *Becoming a worker* (pp. 66–89). Norwood, NJ: Ablex.

Mortimer, J. T., Finch, M. D., Ryu, S., Shanahan, M. J., & Call, K. (1996). The effects of work intensity on adolescent mental health, achievement, and behavioral adjustment: New evidence from a prospective study. *Child Development, 67,* 1243–1261.

Mortimer, J. T., & Johnson, M. K. (1998a). Adolescent part-time work and educational achievement. In K. Borman & B. Schneider (Eds.), *The adolescent years: Social influences and educational challenges* (pp. 183–206). Chicago: National Society for the Study of Education.

Mortimer, J. T., & Johnson, M. K. (1998b). New perspectives on adolescent work and the transition to adulthood. In R. Jessor (Ed.), *New perspectives on adolescent risk behavior* (pp. 425–496). New York: Cambridge University Press.

Mortimer, J. T., Staff, J., & Oesterle, S. (2003). Strategic patterns of adolescent work and early socioeconomic attainment. In J. T. Mortimer & M. Shanahan (Eds.), *Handbook of the life course* (pp. 437–460). New York: Kluwer Academic/Plenum.

Newcomb, M. D., & Bentler, P. M. (1988). *Consequences of adolescent drug use: Impact on the lives of young adults.* Newbury Park, CA: Sage.

Newman, K. S. (1999). *No shame in my game.* New York: Alfred A. Knopf and the Russell Sage Foundation.

Osgood, D. W. (1999). Having the time of their lives: All work and no play? In A. Booth, A. C. Crouter, & M. J. Shanahan (Eds.), *Transitions to adulthood in a changing economy: No work, no family, no future?* (pp. 176–186). Westport, CT: Praeger.

Phillips, S., & Sandstrom, K. L. (1990). Parental attitudes towards youth work. *Youth and Society, 22,* 160–183.

Ploeger, M. (1997). Youth employment and delinquency: Reconsidering a problematic relationship. *Criminology, 35,* 659–675.

Rindfuss, R. R., Cooksey, E. C., & Sutterlin, R. L. (1999). Young adult occupational achievement: Early expectations versus behavioral reality. *Work and Occupations, 26,* 220–263.

Safron, D., Schulenberg, J., & Bachman, J. G. (2001). Part-time work and hurried adolescence: The links among work intensity, social activities, health behaviors, and substance use. *Journal of Health and Social Behavior, 42,* 425–449.

Sampson, R., & Laub, J. (1993). *Crime in the making: Pathways and turning points through life.* Cambridge, MA: Harvard University Press.

Schneider, B., & Stevenson, D. (1999). *The ambitious generation: America's teenagers, motivated but directionless.* New Haven: Yale University Press.

Schoenhals, M., Tienda, M., & Schneider, B. (1998). The educational and personal consequences of adolescent employment. *Social Forces, 77,* 723–762.

Schulenberg, J., & Bachman, J. G. (1993, March). *Long hours on the job? Not so bad for some types of jobs: The quality of work and substance use, affect and stress.* Paper presented at the Biennial Meeting of the Society for Research on Child Development, New Orleans, LA.

Shanahan, M. J., & Flaherty, B. P. (2000, June). *Time use in adolescence and the transition to adulthood.* Paper presented at the Biennial Conference of the European Association for Research on Adolescence, Jena, Germany.

Shanahan, M. J., & Flaherty, B. P. (2001). Dynamic patterns of time use in adolescence. *Child Development, 72,* 385–401.

Staff, J., & Uggen, C. (in press). The fruits of good work: Job quality and adolescent deviance. *Journal of Research in Crime and Delinquency.*

Steel, L. (1991). Early work experience among white and non-white youths: Implications for subsequent enrollment and employment. *Youth and Society, 22,* 419–447.

Steinberg, L. D., & Dornbusch, S. M. (1991). Negative correlates of part-time employment during adolescence: Replication and elaboration. *Developmental Psychology, 27,* 304–313.

Steinberg, L. D., Fegley, S., & Dornbusch, S. M. (1993). Negative impact of part-time work on adolescent adjustment: Evidence from a longitudinal study. *Developmental Psychology, 29,* 171–180.

Steinberg, L. D., Greenberger, E., Garduque, L., Ruggiero, M., & Vaux, A. (1982). Effects of working on adolescent development. *Developmental Psychology, 18,* 385–395.

Stern, D., & Nakata, Y. (1989). Characteristics of high school students' paid jobs and employment experience after graduation. In D. Stern & D. Eichorn (Eds.), *Adolescence and work: Influences of social structure, labor markets, and culture* (pp. 189–233). Hillsdale, NJ: Erlbaum.

Stone, J. R., III, & Mortimer, J. T. (1998). The effect of adolescent employment on vocational development: Public and educational policy implications. *Journal of Vocational Behavior, 53,* 184–214.

Sullivan, M. (1989). *"Getting paid": Youth crime and work in the inner city.* New York: Cornell University Press.

Uggen, C. (2000). Work as a turning point in the life course of criminals: A duration model of age, employment, and recidivism. *American Sociological Review, 67,* 529–546.

Warren, J. R. (2002). Reconsidering the relationship between student employment and academic outcomes: A new theory and better data. *Youth and Society, 33,* 366–393.

Warren, J. R., LePore, P. C., & Mare, R. D. (2000). Employment during high school: Consequences for students' grades in academic courses. *American Educational Research Journal, 37,* 943–969.

Wright, J. P., & Cullen, F. T. (2000). Juvenile involvement in occupational delinquency. *Criminology, 38,* 863–896.

Wright, J. P., Cullen, F. T., & Williams, N. (1997). Working while in school and delinquent involvement: Implications for social policy. *Crime and Delinquency, 43,* 203–221.

Chapter 15

DIVERSITY IN DEVELOPMENTAL TRAJECTORIES ACROSS ADOLESCENCE: NEIGHBORHOOD INFLUENCES

Tama Leventhal and Jeanne Brooks-Gunn

As the 20th century came to a close, numerous researchers marked the occasion by assessing the field of adolescent research, looking back both at the past and towards the future (e.g., Galambos & Leadbeater, 2000; Larson, Brown, & Mortimer, 2002; Steinberg & Morris, 2001). A common theme to emerge from these reviews and reflections was a shift towards viewing adolescent development in social contexts. Specifically, it was acknowledged that at this stage in the life course, social contexts—particularly beyond the family—begin to exert increasing influence on development. Neighborhoods were one such context that received considerable attention (Leventhal & Brooks-Gunn, 2000, 2001). Given general restrictions on adolescents' mobility, neighborhoods provide as well as organize opportunities for social interactions and activities. In addition, neighborhood influences may impinge on other salient social contexts, notably families and schools (Furstenberg, Cook, Eccles, Elder, & Sameroff, 1999; Leventhal & Brooks-Gunn, 2003a; Mayer & Jencks, 1989).

Aside from their apparent developmental significance, interest in neighborhoods as a context for adolescent development was spurred by the confluence of specific historical, theoretical, and empirical forces. Historically, demographic changes in family composition, labor force participation, and residential patterns, as well as the decline of industrialization during the past 50 years drew attention to the increasing concentration of poverty in many urban neighborhoods and to the youth who resided in them (Hernandez, 1993; Massey & Denton, 1993; Wilson, 1987, 1997). Social disorganization theory, which posits that neighborhood structural characteristics—poverty, residential instability, single parenthood, and ethnic heterogeneity—regulate the formation of neighborhood institutions necessary to monitor residents' behavior, especially youth peer groups (Shaw & McKay, 1942), was revisited as a theoretical framework for understanding the multitude of adolescent problem behaviors encountered in many of

The authors would like to thank the National Science Foundation, the National Institute of Child Health and Human Development, and the Spencer Foundation. Additional support was provided by the MacArthur Foundation. We are also grateful to Michelle Neuman and Caroline Israel for assistance with manuscript preparation.

these poor urban neighborhoods (e.g., Bursik, 1988; Kornhauser, 1978; Sampson, 1992; Sampson & Groves, 1989; see also Sampson & Morenoff, 1997, for a review). Alternative theoretical models were conceptualized for considering the negative as well as positive effects that peer behavior and community resources might play in transmitting neighborhood influences to youth (Jencks & Mayer, 1990). At the same time, developmentalists, in general, turned their attention towards ecological models of human development, which stressed examining lives in context (Bronfenbrenner, 1979). Finally, empirical research was fostered by the accessibility of census-based measures of neighborhood sociodemographic characteristics. Studies employing this approach began to provide compelling support for associations among neighborhood structure and adolescent childbearing and educational attainment (Brooks-Gunn, Duncan, Klebanov, & Sealand, 1993; Crane, 1991; Jencks & Mayer, 1990).

Together, these factors served to highlight the importance of neighborhood contexts for the study of adolescent development. Considering their growing conceptual and empirical significance, we conducted a literature review of studies on neighborhood effects on child and adolescent outcomes published from 1990 to 1998; this time frame captured the period since the last major review by Jencks and Mayer in 1990 (Leventhal & Brooks-Gunn, 2001). The field of neighborhood research, however, has continued to expand at an ever-increasing pace since the publication of our review, particularly with respect to adolescent development.

Accordingly, the goal of this chapter is to review the methodological, empirical, and theoretical advances in studying neighborhood contexts and adolescent development. The first section summarizes approaches to studying neighborhood influences, focusing on measurement and study designs. The following section reviews current research findings on neighborhood structural effects on adolescent development by domain—achievement (education and employment), emotional and social well-being (mental health, crime, delinquency, and substance use), and sexual activity and childbearing. The third section considers a taxonomy we developed for addressing the potential pathways through which neighborhood effects might operate on these outcomes (i.e., indirect pathways). The proposed theoretical models include institutional resources (characteristics and range of community resources), relationships and ties (parenting, home environment, and support networks), and norms and collective efficacy (community social structure, peers, and physical threats). Processes most relevant to adolescents are highlighted. Finally, policy implications and future directions for research on neighborhood contexts and adolescence are summarized.

METHODOLOGICAL ISSUES IN STUDYING ADOLESCENT DEVELOPMENT IN NEIGHBORHOOD CONTEXTS

This section presents a brief review of key methodological issues confronting the study of adolescent development in neighborhood contexts, including definitions of neighborhoods, identification and measurement of neighborhood dimensions, study designs, and selection problems. This overview is intended to provide a backdrop for the remaining sections in this chapter (see Leventhal & Brooks-Gunn, 2000, for an expanded discussion).

Neighborhood Definitions

An important question to consider when studying adolescent development in neighborhood contexts is *What is a neighborhood?* Alternative strategies have been used to define the neighborhood unit of analysis. The most frequent approach is to employ data collected from the U.S. Decennial Census compiled from the census forms completed on the first of April during the first year of every decade. A neighborhood is then typically defined as a census tract; tracts contain approximately 3,000–8,000 individuals and are identified with the advice of local communities working under Census Bureau guidelines to reflect prominent physical and social features that signify neighborhoods, such as major streets, railroads, ethnic divisions, and the like. On occasion, even larger census units such as the zip code are employed, which contain approximately 20,000 to 300,000 individuals (depending on whether the locale is rural or urban). Alternatively, researchers have used census block or block groups (census tracts contain one to four block groups), which are smaller units containing about 1,100 individuals per block. Some researchers have combined two to three adjacent or relatively homogenous tracts or block groups into neighborhood clusters (e.g., Brody et al., 2001; Sampson, Raudenbush, & Earls, 1997). Other bureaucratically defined units available from administrative data sources include health districts, police districts, and school districts; these units usually overlap and are employed in conjunction with census data. The smallest neighborhood unit used is the street- or face-block, which includes the two sides of the street facing a person's home. In contrast, most studies do not specify neighborhood boundaries when participant reports of neighborhood conditions are gathered; however, residents' reports of neighborhood boundaries appear to approximate census tracts (or clusters of tracts; Coulton, Korbin, Chan, & Su, 2001; Sampson, 1997).

Neighborhood Dimensions

A critical distinction to make in defining neighborhood dimensions is between neighborhood structure and neighborhood processes. Neighborhood structure entails compositional or sociodemographic attributes, such as median income, employment rate, and racial composition. Neighborhood processes include aspects such as social organization and institutional resources. Although it is thought to be a function of neighborhood structure, neighborhood social organization describes the capacity of residents to work together towards common goals and values and to establish institutions that promote and enforce these goals by regulating behavior (especially that of youth; Sampson, 1992; Shaw & McKay, 1942), and institutional resources involve the presence of services and organizations that promote health, well-being, and general social welfare. Given the accessibility of census data, as noted, census-based measures of neighborhood structural characteristics are employed in a majority of studies (Jencks & Mayer, 1990; Leventhal & Brooks-Gunn, 2000). Neighborhood income or socioeconomic status (SES)—a combination of social and economic indicators—is the most commonly studied structural dimension. Researchers often separate measures of neighborhood SES into high-SES/affluence (e.g., indexing income, percent professionals, and percent college-educated) and low-SES/poverty (e.g., assessing percent poor, percent female-headed households, percent on public assistance, and percent unemployed) because the presence of poor and affluent neighbors may have differential associations with adolescent outcomes (Brooks-Gunn et al., 1993; Jencks & Mayer, 1990). Other structural characteristics frequently considered are racial and ethnic diversity (e.g., percent Black, percent Latino, and percent foreign-born) and residential instability (e.g., percent moved in last 5 years, percent households in current home less than 10 years, and percent homeowners; Brooks-Gunn, Duncan, & Aber, 1997; Sampson et al., 1997). Despite general consistency across studies, specific definitions of these structural dimensions differ somewhat.

Neighborhood social organizational features commonly examined include physical and social disorder, which describes the physical conditions (e.g., abandoned housing and graffiti) and social interactions (e.g., public drinking and prostitution) resulting in part from the content and consensus of values; informal social control, which depicts the degree to which residents monitor the behavior of others in accordance with socially accepted practices; and social cohesion, which refers to the extent of social connections within the neighborhood (measures of informal control and cohesion have been combined to assess what has been called collective efficacy). Institutional resources include the quantity and quality of services, schools, health care facilities, and recreational programs. The census does not directly evaluate neighborhood organization or resources, which are necessary for testing theoretical models (as we subsequently describe). Thus, much research has relied upon parents' or youths' ratings to capture neighborhood processes; these ratings are problematic because they are often confounded with individual-level measures also obtained by means of participant ratings.

Alternative methodologies are required to measure the neighborhood processes described, including systematic social observations, community surveys, neighborhood expert surveys, and administrative data. Systematic social observations or windshield surveys involve trained observers using a structured format to characterize neighborhoods through videotaping, rater checklists, or audiotaping (Kohen, Brooks-Gunn, Leventhal, & Hertzman, 2002; Reiss, 1971; Raudenbush & Sampson, 1999; Spencer, McDermott, Burton, & Kochman, 1997; R. B. Taylor, Gottfredson, & Brower, 1984). Community surveys entail interviewing nonparticipants in the study about their neighborhoods, yielding measures of neighborhoods that are independent from those obtained by study participants (Sampson, 1997; Sampson et al., 1997). Neighborhood expert surveys require interviewing key community leaders such as prominent religious, political, business, and social leaders in the community about their neighborhoods (Earls & Buka, 1997). Finally, alternative administrative data sources are available from city, state, and federal agencies and include vital statistics from health departments, crime reports from police departments, school records from education departments, and child abuse and neglect records from human and social service departments.

Study Designs

Four major designs have been used to study neighborhood effects on adolescent development, including (a) national or multisite studies, (b) city or regional studies, (c) neighborhood-based studies, and (d) experimental or quasi-experimental studies.

National or Multisite Studies

These studies typically have large variation in neighborhood (and family) types and permit estimation of neighborhood effects based on few adolescents per neighborhood. A wide distribution of neighborhood types is preferable because it minimizes multicollinearity among neighborhood dimensions (Duncan, Connell, & Klebanov, 1997; Duncan & Raudenbush, 1999). Although these studies were not designed specifically for examining neighborhood influences, much of the existing neighborhood research had used national data sets, such as the Panel Study of Income Dynamics (PSID; Hill, 1991) and the National Longitudinal Survey of Youth-Child Supplement (NLSY-CS; Baker & Mott, 1989).

City or Regional Studies

These studies focus on a single city or metropolitan area; many are based on school attendance or community-wide surveys (as opposed to neighborhood residence). The range of sampled neighborhoods as well as neighborhood types varies across city and regional studies. Due to these issues, many regional and city studies are comprised of primarily urban, poor, and near-poor neighborhoods. Moreover, the number of youth per neighborhood also varies widely in these studies, making assumptions about independence of observations problematic for standard analytic approaches, such as ordinary least squares regression and the use of hierarchical or multilevel models (Bryk & Raudenbush, 1992)—which account for the nested nature of data—difficult. Well-known examples of city or regional studies include the Pittsburgh Youth Study (Loeber & Wikstrom, 1993) and the Beginning School Study in Baltimore (Entwisle, Alexander, & Olson, 1994).

Neighborhood-Based Studies

These studies incorporate neighborhoods into the study design. The sampling strategy targets certain types of neighborhoods in addition to a range of neighborhood types representative of the population of neighborhoods examined. Sampling is also conducted to ensure an adequate number of adolescents per neighborhood (e.g., approximately 15–30 study participants per neighborhood; Duncan & Raudenbush, 1999) to conduct multilevel analyses. Multilevel analyses provide estimates of variation in outcomes both within and between neighborhoods, yielding more reliable estimates of neighborhood effects on adolescent outcomes. A recent example of a neighborhood-based study is the Project on Human Development in Chicago Neighborhoods in which census data were used to define two stratification variables—SES (three levels) and racial-ethnic composition (seven levels)—that were cross-classified, and then a stratified probability sample of 80 neighborhood clusters was selected for the longitudinal component of the study. Finally, children and youth falling within seven age cohorts were sampled from these 80 neighborhoods; approximately 75 children per neighborhood cluster were interviewed (see Leventhal & Brooks-Gunn, 2003b, for further details). In general, researchers utilizing neighborhood-based designs have found that neighborhoods are internally quite heterogeneous, and typically more variability exists within neighborhoods than across neighborhoods (Cook, Shagle, & Degirmencioglu, 1997; Elliott et al., 1996; Furstenberg et al., 1999).

Experimental or Quasi-Experimental Studies

These studies randomly assign families to live in particular types of neighborhoods. Almost all such studies have utilized housing mobility programs in which low-income families residing in public housing in poor neighborhoods were given the opportunity to relocate to less poor neighborhoods. Because programs cannot serve all eligible or interested families, selection is often random, based on housing availability (i.e., quasi-random), or both. A recent exemplar of an experimental study is the Moving to Opportunity for Fair Housing Demonstration (MTO) sponsored by the U.S. Department of Housing and Urban Development in five cities. The program randomly assigned housing project residents residing in high-poverty neighborhoods to (a) an experimental group, who received housing vouchers and special assistance to move to low-poverty neighborhoods; (b) a comparison group, who received vouchers but no special assistance and no relocation requirements; or (c) a control group, who did not receive vouchers or assistance and remained in public housing (Goering, in press). Experimental designs provide the most valid estimates of neighborhood effects by minimizing selection as a problem.

Selection

Selection or omitted variable bias is the major criticism of the first three study designs outlined (i.e., most existing neighborhood studies). Selection refers to the fact that families have some choice as to the neighborhoods in which they live, and some omitted (or unmeasured) variable associated with neighborhood residence might account for any observed neighborhood effects (Duncan et al., 1997; Tienda, 1991). A common strategy used to minimize selection as a problem is to account for child (e.g., sex and age) and family demographic (e.g., income, parent education, family structure) characteristics in analytic models. Although this approach is preferable (and in our opinion essential) because neighborhood characteristics are defined by family composition, it does not fully overcome the problem of selection. Moreover, many hypothesized omitted variables such as parental depression or motivation are not included in most studies, nor is the direction of bias resulting from the omission of these variables clear. For example, adolescents' parents who have poor mental health may be more likely to stay in disadvantaged neighborhoods than are parents with superior health. Conversely, more organized parents may stay in disadvantaged neighborhoods to conserve funds for recreational and educational activities for their adolescents than do less organized parents. Researchers have used various analytic strategies to address selection issues, including comparisons of siblings or first cousins, instrumental variable analyses, and behavior genetics models (Aaronson, 1997; Caspi, Taylor, Moffitt, & Plomin, 2000; Foster & McLanahan, 1996); however, only experimental designs overcome the selection problem in neighborhood research (although other selection problems may arise).

A REVIEW OF NEIGHBORHOOD STRUCTURAL EFFECTS ON ADOLESCENT DEVELOPMENT

This review builds on a previous summary of the neighborhood research published from 1990 to 1998 (Leventhal & Brooks-Gunn, 2000) by incorporating the work on adolescent development in neighborhood contexts that has appeared since its publication. Following a similar procedure, a review of relevant databases for psychology, sociology, demography, economics, and epidemiology was conducted for articles published between 1998 to 2002. The analysis focused on the three structural dimensions (assessed by the census) most frequently examined—income-SES (affluence/high-SES and poverty/low-SES), racial-ethnic diversity and immigrant concentration, and residential instability. Other neighborhood dimensions are considered in the subsequent section. In both sections, only studies that accounted for individual and family characteristics such as child sex, age, and race-ethnicity; family income and composition; and maternal education, age, and the like in the analysis were included due to potential selection issues.

Three domains of well-being are considered in turn: (a) achievement (test scores, grade failure, high school dropout status, college attendance, years of completed schooling, employment, and earnings), (b) emotional and social well-being (mental health, crime, delinquency, and substance use), and (c) sexual activity (age of initiation, number of partners, and contraception use) and childbearing. Whenever possible, we discriminate between findings for early adolescents (11–15 years old) and late adolescents (16–19 years old) because neighborhoods may have differential effects on outcomes during each developmental period (Aber, Gephart, Brooks-Gunn, & Connell, 1997). For instance, neighborhood influences may increase during late adolescence, when youth are often granted more autonomy than they are at younger ages, resulting in greater exposure to extrafamilial influences such as neighborhoods.

Achievement

Across the studies reviewed, the strongest evidence was found for the association between neighborhood SES and adolescent achievement outcomes (after accounting for child and family background characteristics), particularly the beneficial effects of high-SES neighbors for both younger and older adolescents' achievement. This pattern of findings was supported by both nonexperimental and experimental research. Table 15.1 presents a summary of studies.

The limited research on neighborhood SES effects on young adolescents' achievement drew upon city and regional samples (Connell & Halpern-Felsher, 1997; Dornbusch, Ritter, & Steinberg, 1991; Entwisle et al., 1994; Halpern-Felsher & Connell, 1997). In general, these studies documented a positive association between neighborhood SES-income and various indicators of adolescents' achievement (math achievement, basic skills tests, grade point average, and educational risk score). In addition, studies reported links between neighborhood low-SES and related measures (e.g., male joblessness and female-headed households) and poor educational outcomes (Connell & Halpern-Felsher, 1997; Halpern-Felsher & Connell, 1997). Finally, several of the studies reviewed found that neighborhood SES may have more pronounced effects for

Table 15.1 Summary of Studies Used to Examine Neighborhood Effects on Adolescents' Achievement

Study	Design	Sample	Neighborhood Data	Findings from Published Studies
Adolescent Pathways Project	Longitudinal study of students from low-income schools in New York City, Baltimore, & Washington, DC	669 10–16-year-olds (54% African American)	1980 Census tract data	Halpern-Felsher et al. (1997): Low-SES negative association with European American females' combined reading/math scores.
Beginning School Study in Baltimore	Longitudinal study of youth from 20 randomly selected schools	Approx. 450 8th graders (approx. 50% African American)	1980 Census data; 26 regional planning districts	Entwisle, Alexander, & Olson (1994): Income positive association with boys' math achievement.
California Study	Students drawn from 5 San Francisco Bay Area schools	Approx. 7,000 mostly European American high school students	1980 Census tract data	Dornbusch, Ritter, & Steinberg (1991): SES positive association with reported grades.
Gautreaux Program	Quasi-experimental design	342 African American & Latino families from public housing	Not available	Kaufman & Rosenbaum (1992): Youth who moved to more affluent suburbs more likely to graduate high school, take college prep classes, attend college, be employed, & have higher paying jobs than youth who remained in city.
Moving to Opportunity (Baltimore site evaluation)	Randomized design in 5 cities	1,384 mostly African Americans & Latinos, > 12 year-olds at randomization	1990 Census data	Ludwig, Ladd, & Duncan (2001): Youth who moved to low/middle-income neighborhoods more likely to repeat grade than youth who remained in public housing in high-poverty neighborhoods.
Moving to Opportunity (New York City site evaluation)	Randomized design in 5 cities	588 African American & Latino 6–18-year-olds	1990 Census data	Leventhal & Brooks-Gunn (2002): Male youth aged 11–18 who moved to low-poverty neighborhoods higher reading and math achievement scores than youth who remained in public housing in high-poverty neighborhoods.

Panel Study of Income Dynamics	Nationally representative, longitudinal study	Approx. 3,500 14–22-year-olds (approx. 50% African American)	1970 & 1980 Census tract data	Aaronson (1997): Dropout rate negative association with HSG. Brooks-Gunn, Duncan, Klebanov, & Sealand (1993): Affluence positive association with European Americans' HSG; female headship negative association with HSG. Duncan (1994): Affluence positive association with European Americans' & advantaged African American females' completed schooling & European American males' college attendance; low-income positive association with European American males' & African American females' completed schooling & European American males' college attendance; female headship negative association with African American females' & European American males' completed schooling & African Americans' HSG; female employment rate negative association with females' completed schooling (advantaged African Americans only) & college attendance & positive association with European American males' completed schooling & HSG; percent African American negative association with African Americans' completed schooling (advantaged males only) & college attendance. Foster & McLanahan (1996): Dropout rate negative association with females' HSG. Halpern-Felsher et al. (1997): High-SES positive association with completed schooling (excluding African American males); ethnic diversity positive association with African American males' completed schooling.

(continued)

Table 15.1 *(Continued)*

Study	Design	Sample	Neighborhood Data	Findings from Published Studies
Promoting Academic Competence	Longitudinal, school-based study in Atlanta	346 11- to 16-year-old African Americans	1980 Census tract data	Halpern-Felsher et al. (1997): High-SES positive association with African American females' Iowa Basic Skills scores; male joblessness negative association with African American males' basic skills.
Public Use Microdata Sample	Nationally representative study	92,512 16- to 19-year-olds	1970 15% Neighborhood Characteristics file	Crane (1991): Managerial/professionals positive nonlinear association with HSG; when drop to very few, association stronger for African American males.
Scottish Young People's Survey	Study of 1 educational authority	2,500 young adults	1981 Scottish Census enumeration district data	Garner & Raudenbush (1991): Social deprivation negative association with educational attainment.
Upstate New York Sample	Students drawn from urban school district	1,040 8- to 11-year- olds, 3,406 12–15-year-olds, & 1,797 15–20-year-olds (approx. 75% African American)	1980 Census tract data	Connell & Halpern-Felsher (1997): Neighborhood risk negative association with African American males' HSG. Halpern-Felsher et al. (1997): High-SES negative association with 12–20-year-old European American males' educational risk; male joblessness positive association with 8–15-year-old African American males' & European American females' (12–15 year-old only) educational risk.
Woodlawn Study	Longitudinal study of disadvantaged youth in Chicago	954 African Americans	Average 1970 & 1980 Census tract data; 202 tracts	Ensminger, Lamkin, & Jacobson (1996): Managerial/professionals positive association with males' completed schooling & HSG.

Note. Adapted with permission from *Psychological Bulletin, 126* (pp. 316–317), by T. Leventhal and J. Brooks-Gunn, 2002. Reprinted by permission. HSG = High school graduation. All findings reported are for analyses in which individual and family characteristics were taken into account. Definitions of neighborhood measures are available from authors upon request.

young adolescent boys' achievement than for girls' achievement (Entwisle et al., 1994; Halpern-Felsher & Connell, 1997).

Studies of older adolescents have primarily relied upon national data sets. A number of studies based on the PSID reported associations between neighborhood high-SES/affluence and youths' educational attainment (high school graduation, college attendance, and years of completed schooling); these associations were more salient for European American than for African American youth (Brooks-Gunn et al., 1993; Duncan, 1994; Halpern-Felsher & Connell, 1997). However, one city-based study of African American adolescents found that the presence of managerial and professional neighbors was positively associated with boys' educational attainment (Ensminger, Lamkin, & Jacobson, 1996). In addition, a nonlinear association between this SES measure and youths' chances of completing high school was found in the Public Use Microdata Sample (PUMS), such that when the percentage of professional or managerial workers fell to 5% or fewer (or reached a tipping point), neighborhood effects were more pronounced, especially for African American males (Crane, 1991). Note that most studies cannot test such a premise because of restricted sample sizes; the PUMS sample had over 90,000 youth. Findings from a quasi-experimental study in which low-income, minority youth residing in public housing in poor urban neighborhoods moved to the move affluent suburbs concur with the results of these nonexperimental studies. In a 10-year follow-up, youth who moved to the suburbs were found to be more likely to graduate from high school, take college preparatory classes, attend college, be employed, and earn higher wages than were their peers who remained in the city (Kaufman & Rosenbaum, 1992). Along these same lines, a short-term follow-up of the New York City site of MTO—an experimental study in which low-income families moved from high-poverty to near-poor and low-poverty neighborhoods—found that adolescent boys who moved to low-poverty neighborhoods had higher achievement test scores than did peers who remained in high-poverty neighborhoods (Leventhal & Brooks-Gunn, 2002). A follow-up of the Baltimore MTO site reported that adolescents who move to less poor neighborhoods were more likely to repeat a grade than were youth in high-poverty neighborhoods (Ludwig, Ladd, & Duncan, 2001). Similar to those for young adolescents, findings from several experimental and nonexperimental studies revealed that the beneficial effects of neighborhood high-SES/affluence for educational attainment may be more salient for boys than for girls (Connell & Halpern-Felsher, 1997; Duncan, 1994; Ensminger et al., 1996; Halpern-Felsher & Connell, 1997).

Other measures of neighborhood SES, such as the high school completion rate, percentage of female-headed households, and female employment rate, were found to be associated with educational attainment as well. Almost all of these studies were based on the PSID or other large, national studies (Aaronson, 1997; Brooks-Gunn et al., 1993; Duncan, 1994; Ensminger et al., 1996; Foster & McLanahan, 1996; Garner & Raudenbush, 1991). In the studies presented in Table 15.1, neighborhood SES effects on adolescent achievement were reported when techniques were used to address problems of selection bias, including sibling analyses (Aaronson, 1997; Plotnick & Hoffman, 1999), instrumental variable analyses (Foster & McLanahan, 1996; c.f. Evans, Oates, & Schwab, 1992), and multilevel models (Garner & Raudenbush, 1991).

Two studies based on the PSID reported associations between racial-ethnic diversity and older adolescents' achievement. The first study found that living in a neighborhood with a high percentage of African Americans was negatively associated with African American boys' years of schooling completed and college attendance (Duncan, 1994). However, the other study reported that residing in an ethnically diverse neighborhood (presence of Latinos and foreign-born residents) was positively associated with African American boys' completed schooling (Halpern-Felsher & Connell, 1997). No studies found significant associations between residential stability and adolescents' achievement.

Behavioral and Emotional Outcomes

Growing evidence since our last review concurs with the initial conclusion that neighborhood SES is associated with adolescent behavioral and emotional outcomes (after accounting for background characteristics). In particular, links have been found between low-SES and crime and delinquency (see Table 15.2 for summary of studies). Support was provided from both nonexperimental and experimental studies; however, because research is still somewhat limited, it was difficult to separate out effects for younger and older adolescents.

Only a few studies examined neighborhood SES effects on young adolescents, and most were based on city or regional studies (similar to achievement outcomes). For example, in a rural Iowa sample of European American 8th and 9th graders, neighborhood low SES was positively associated with boys' psychological distress, and the percentage of single-parent families was positively associated with girls' conduct problems (Simons, Johnson, Beaman, Conger, & Whitbeck, 1996). Likewise, among 13- and 16-year-old boys in the Pittsburgh Youth Study, living in low-SES or "underclass" neighborhoods (characterized by poverty, unemployment, male joblessness, female headship, nonmarital childbearing, African American presence, and welfare receipt) was positively associated with youths' delinquent and criminal behavior, and effects were more pronounced for younger than for older adolescents (Loeber & Wikstrom, 1993; Peeples & Loeber, 1994). Studies of older adolescents, using data from a British national study, also found adverse associations between residence in low-SES neighborhoods and adolescents' participation in crime and delinquency (Sampson & Groves, 1989; Veysey & Messner, 1999). Along these same lines, a national study of U.S. 10th graders found that the male joblessness rate was positively associated with drug use; however, the poverty rate was negatively associated with drug use among these same youth (Hoffman, 2002).

Several experimental studies also reported that neighborhood low SES was associated with negative behavioral outcomes. The Boston and New York MTO site evaluations found that for boys, moving to less poor neighborhoods was associated with fewer behavior problems compared with peers who remained in high-poverty neighborhoods (Katz, Kling, & Liebman, 2001; Leventhal & Brooks-Gunn, in press). Among an older sample, male youth in the Baltimore MTO who moved to low-poverty neighborhoods were less likely to be arrested for violent crimes (assessed by administrative records) than were peers who remained in high-poverty neighborhoods (Ludwig, Duncan, & Hirschfield, 2001). Across these three studies, no neighborhood effects were reported for girls.

Four studies found links between racial-ethnic diversity and adolescents' behavioral and emotional problems. Among two cohorts of British youth, neighborhood ethnic

Table 15.2 Summary of Studies Used to Examine Neighborhood Effects on Adolescents' Behavioral and Emotional Outcomes

Study	Design	Sample	Neighborhood Data	Findings from Published Studies
British Crime Survey	National study	Approx. 22,000 youth > 16 years-old from 2 cohorts	1984 British Population Censuses & Surveys; 60 cases per neighborhood	Sampson & Groves (1989): SES negative association with crime & delinquency; ethnic heterogeneity positive association with crime & delinquency; residential stability negative association with crime & delinquency; urbanization positive association with crime. Veysey & Messner (1999): SES negative association with criminal victimization rate; ethnic heterogeneity, family disruption, & urbanization positive association with criminal victimization rate.
National Longitudinal Survey of Youth-Child Supplement	Children born to women in nationally representative study	860 14- to 18- year-olds (26% African American & 9% Latino)	1990 Census tract data	Kowaleski-Jones (2000): Proportion persons lived household past 5 years negative association with risk taking attitudes & aggressive behavior.
Iowa Single Parent Project	Panel study of families in small towns & cities	207 European American 8th & 9th graders	Census data; 104 communities	Simons, Johnson, Beaman, Conger, & Whitbeck (1996): Community disadvantage positive association with males' psychological distress; percent single-parent families positive association with females' conduct problems.
Los Angeles County Study	Community-based survey	877 racially-ethnically diverse 12- to 17- year-olds	1990 Census tract data; 49 tracts	Aneshensel & Sucoff (1996): Conduct disorders high in low-SES, African American neighborhoods & low in low-SES, Latino neighborhoods; oppositional defiant disorders low in low-middle SES, African American neighborhoods & high in middle-SES, European American & Latino neighborhoods; depression high among Latinos except in low-SES, Latino neighborhoods.
Moving to Opportunity (Baltimore site evaluation)	Randomized design in 5 cities	336 mostly African American & Latino 11- to 16- year-olds at randomization	1990 tract Census data	Ludwig, Duncan, & Hirschfield (2001): Male youth who moved to low-poverty neighborhoods less likely to be arrested for violent crimes than youth who remained in public housing in high-poverty neighborhoods.

(continued)

Table 15.2 *(Continued)*

Study	Design	Sample	Neighborhood Data	Findings from Published Studies
Moving to Opportunity (Boston site evaluation)	Randomized design in 5 cities	612 mostly African American & Latino 6- to 15-year-olds	1990 tract Census data	Katz, Kling, & Liebman (2001): Male children & youth who moved to low/middle-income neighborhoods fewer maternal reported behavior problems than peers who remained in public housing in high-poverty neighborhoods.
Moving to Opportunity (New York City site evaluation)	Randomized design in 5 cities	512 African American & Latino 8- to 18-year-olds	1990 Census data	Leventhal & Brooks-Gunn (in press): Male children & youth who moved to low/middle neighborhoods reported fewer anxious/depressive (middle-income only) and dependency problems than peers who remained in public housing in high-poverty neighborhoods.
National Educational Longitudinal Study	Nationally representative, longitudinal study	11,749 10th graders	1990 Census data; 1,784 zip code areas	Hoffmann (2002): Poverty negative association with drug use; male joblessness positive association with drug use.
Pittsburgh Youth Study	Longitudinal study of antisocial behavior with boys drawn from 7 schools	508 13-year-old & 506 16-year-old males (approx. 50% African American)	1980 Census tract data; 88 neighborhoods per Pittsburgh classification (1–7 tracts)	Loeber & Wikstrom (1993): SES negative association with delinquency & offending trajectories, especially for 13-year olds living in inner-city. Peeples & Loeber (1994): Underclass positive association with severity & frequency of delinquency.
Project on Human Development in Chicago Neighborhoods	Longitudinal, neighborhood-based design	1,979 11- to 19- year-olds	1990 Census tract data; 79 neighborhood clusters	Reardon, Brennan, & Buka (2002): Percent African American negative association with onset of cigarette use.

Note. Adapted with permission from *Psychological Bulletin, 126* (p. 319), by T. Leventhal and J. Brooks-Gunn, 2002. Reprinted by permission. All findings reported are for analyses in which individual and family characteristics were taken into account. Definitions of neighborhood measures are available from authors upon request.

heterogeneity was positively associated with adolescents' criminal behavior (personal and property victimization), especially personal victimization (Sampson & Groves, 1989). A replication of this study employing advanced statistical techniques reported similar results (Veysey & Messner, 1999). To the contrary, an investigation of substance use among adolescents 11–19 years of age in the Project on Human Development in Chicago Neighborhoods, a neighborhood-based study, found that living in a neighborhood with few African Americans was associated with earlier onset of cigarette use (Reardon, Brennan, & Buka, 2002). Finally, Aneshensel and Sucoff (1996) examined the effect of neighborhood SES and racial-ethnic diversity simultaneously on the mental health outcomes of 12- to 17-year-olds in Los Angeles. Their results indicated that the prevalence of conduct disorder was highest among adolescents in low-SES, African American neighborhoods and lowest among adolescents in low-SES, Latino neighborhoods. The prevalence of oppositional defiant disorder, on the other hand, was highest among adolescents in middle-SES communities with high concentrations of European Americans and Latinos and lowest among adolescents in low-SES, African American neighborhoods. Latinos displayed more depressive symptoms than did European American and African American youth, except in low-SES neighborhoods with high concentrations of Latinos.

Finally, two studies found associations between neighborhood residential instability and adolescents' externalizing (acting-out and aggressive) behaviors. Among adolescents 14 to 18 years of age in the NLSY-CS, residential stability was negatively associated with risk-taking attitudes and aggressive behavior (Kowaleski-Jones, 2000). Similarly, residential instability had adverse effects on adolescent juvenile delinquency and crime—particularly property crime—in a sample of British youth (Sampson & Groves, 1989).

Sexuality and Childbearing

The most widely studied area in neighborhood research since our last review was adolescent sexual and fertility outcomes (see Table 15.3 for a summary of studies). Almost all studies relied on national data sets and focused on older adolescents, which is not surprising given the nature of the outcomes. A consistent pattern of findings points to associations between neighborhood SES—especially low SES—and adolescents' sexuality and fertility (controlling for individual and family characteristics). In addition, neighborhood employment measures appear to be associated with these outcomes, but the direction of effects was mixed.

Studies using five different national data sets (National Survey of Adolescent Males [NSAM], National Survey of Children [NSC], National Survey of Family Growth [NSFG-III], PSID, and PUMS) reported that indicators of neighborhood SES were associated with adolescent sexual activity. Across these studies, the presence of advantaged socioeconomic conditions such as affluent or professional neighbors was associated with a decreased risk of female adolescents' nonmarital childbearing (Billy & Moore, 1992; Brooks-Gunn et al., 1993; Crane, 1991; South & Crowder, 1999), whereas the absence of such resources, including high poverty and low housing values, was adversely associated with both boys and girls' initiation of sexual intercourse, frequency of intercourse, number of partners, contraceptive use, pregnancy outcomes, and over-

Table 15.3 Summary of Studies Used to Examine Neighborhood Effects on Adolescents' Sexuality and Childbearing

Study	Design	Sample	Neighborhood Data	Findings from Published Studies
Michigan Study	Students drawn from 4 public schools	850 9th graders with low grades (80% African American)	1990 Census tract data	Ramirez-Valles, Zimmerman, & Newcomb (1998): Low-SES positive association with sexual risk behavior (age of initiation, number partners, & frequency condom use). Ramirez-Valles, Zimmerman, & Juarez (2002): Low housing value positive association with African American males' age of first intercourse.
National Survey of Family Growth	Nationally representative study of reproductive behavior	7,969 14–44-year-old females	1980 Census tract data; 1983 County & City Data Book	Billy, Brewster, & Grady (1994): Racial/ethnic composition negative association with 15–19-year-old European Americans engaging in premarital sex; female labor force participation positive association with 15–19-year-olds engaging in premarital sex; adolescent joblessness positive association with 15–19-year-olds African Americans' frequency of intercourse. Billy & Moore (1992): SES negative association with nonmarital childbearing; female unemployment positive association with nonmarital childbearing. Brewster (1994a): Female labor force participation positive association with 14–20-year-old African Americans' noncontracepted first intercourse (urban areas only). Brewster (1994b): Female labor force participation positive association with 15- to 19-year-olds' timing of first intercourse.

				Brewster, Billy, & Grady (1993): Female labor force participation positive association with 14–20-year-old European Americans' contracepted first intercourse; proportion African American & proportion foreign-born negative associations with 14–20-year-old European Americans' age of first nonmarital intercourse & noncontracepted first intercourse; proportion households moved into past 5 years positive association with 14–20-year-old European Americans' age of first nonmarital intercourse, contracepted first intercourse, & noncontracepted first intercourse.
National Survey of Adolescent Males	National survey of never-married males	1,880 15- to 19-year-olds	1980 Census tract & zip code data; 1,494 tracts	Ku, Sonenstein, & Pleck (1993): Poverty positive association with frequency of intercourse & effective contraceptive use & negative association with impregnating someone; unemployment rate positive association with impregnating someone & fathering live birth; percent Latino negative association with number of partners & effective contraceptive use.
National Survey of Children	Nationally representative, longitudinal study of 7–11 year-olds	1,111 18–22-year-olds (20% African American)	1980 Census data; 278 zip code areas	Baumer & South (2001): Low-SES positive association with frequency of sex, number of sexual partners, & unprotected sex. South & Baumer (2001): Low-SES negative association with females' odds of aborting premarital pregnancy. South & Crowder (1999): High-SES negative association with females' odds of premarital birth; low-SES positive association with females' odds of premarital birth.

(continued)

Table 15.3 *(Continued)*

Study	Design	Sample	Neighborhood Data	Findings from Published Studies
Panel Study of Income Dynamics	Nationally representative, longitudinal study	Approx. 3,500 14–22-year-olds (approx. 50% African American)	1970 & 1980 Census tract data	Brooks-Gunn, Duncan, Klebanov, & Sealand (1993): Affluence negative association with European Americans' nonmarital childbearing; managerial/professionals negative association with nonmarital childbearing. South & Crowder (1999): Low-SES positive, nonlinear association with European American females' odds of premarital birth such that odds increase when disadvantage more extreme. Sucoff & Upchurch (1998): For African American females in metropolitan areas, odds of premarital birth higher in both African American, low-SES & African American, middle-SES neighborhoods compared with racially mixed, middle-SES neighborhoods; for those females from affluent families, odds of premarital birth lower in European American, middle-SES neighborhoods compared with racially mixed, middle-SES neighborhoods.
Public Use Microdata Sample	Nationally representative study	92,512 16–19-year-olds	1970 15% Neighborhood Characteristics file	Crane (1991): Managerial-professionals negative nonlinear association with teenage childbearing; when drop to very few, association stronger for African Americans & females in cities.

Note. Adapted with permission from *Psychological Bulletin, 126* (p. 321), by T. Leventhal and J. Brooks-Gunn, 2002. Reprinted by permission. All findings reported are for analyses in which individual and family characteristics were taken into account. Definitions of neighborhood measures are available from authors upon request.

all sexual risk behavior (Baumer & South, 2001; Ku, Sonenstein, & Pleck, 1993; Ramirez-Valles, Zimmerman, & Juarez, 2002; Ramirez-Valles, Zimmerman, & Newcomb, 1998; South & Baumer, 2001; South & Crowder, 1999). Moreover, two studies found nonlinear associations such that female youths' odds of bearing children increased when community disadvantage was most extreme (Crane, 1991; South & Crowder, 1999).

Employment measures were associated with adolescent sexual and fertility outcomes, although the pattern of results was inconsistent. Among adolescent males 15–19 years of age in the NSAM, a high unemployment rate was positively associated with impregnating someone and fathering a child (Ku et al., 1993). Likewise, among females in the NSFG-III, unemployment and joblessness were positively associated with frequency of intercourse and nonmarital childbearing (Billy, Brewster, & Grady, 1994; Billy & Moore, 1992). On the other hand, among these same young women, the percentage of women in the neighborhood (census tract) employed was positively associated with timing of first intercourse and risk of premarital sex (Billy et al., 1994; Brewster, 1994b). In addition, for female youth aged 14–20 in the NSFG-III, female labor force participation was positively associated with noncontracepted first intercourse for African American, urban young women and with contracepted first intercourse for European American young women (Brewster, 1994a; Brewster, Billy, & Grady, 1993). Findings related to female employment may be related to the monitoring and supervision of youth as opposed to socioeconomic resources.

Three studies documented links between racial-ethnic diversity and adolescents' coital and fertility behavior. Among male and European American female adolescents, a high proportion of foreign-born residents, African Americans, or both in the neighborhood was negatively associated with sexual activity (age of first intercourse, premarital sex, number of partners, and contraceptive use; Billy et al., 1994; Brewster et al., 1993; Ku et al., 1993). In addition, one study explored the effect of neighborhood SES and racial-ethnic diversity simultaneously on the fertility outcomes of African American females from metropolitan areas; results indicated that the odds of having a premarital birth were higher in both African American low-SES and African American middle-SES neighborhoods compared with racially mixed, middle-SES neighborhoods (Sucoff & Upchurch, 1998). Finally, a study using data from the NSFG-III found a positive association between residential instability (proportion of households moved into census tract in past 5 years) and sexual initiation among European American 14- to 22-year-old female youth (Brewster et al., 1993).

A FRAMEWORK FOR UNDERSTANDING POTENTIAL PATHWAYS OF NEIGHBORHOOD EFFECTS ON ADOLESCENT OUTCOMES

The research presented in the previous section documents associations between neighborhood structure and adolescent outcomes; however, it does not address the potential pathways through which these neighborhood effects are transmitted to youth. A widely held view among researchers is that neighborhood influences are indirect (or mediated), operating through various processes such as community social organizations, families, peers, and schools. In addition, neighborhood effects are thought to condition (or interact with) other contextual influences—particularly the family environment—

in shaping adolescent development. Despite such expectations, much more theoretical than empirical work has explored mediated and moderated neighborhood effects on adolescent outcomes. Empirical investigations of underlying mechanisms of neighborhood influences have been hindered by the lack of a coherent framework outlined by outcome, age of child, and specific pathways, as well as by methodological limitations—particularly adequate study designs and neighborhood measures. However, over the past several years emerging empirical support concurs with expectations, indicating that neighborhood effects are largely indirect, operating through individual-, family-, and community-level processes.

In this section, three theoretical models for conceptualizing how neighborhoods might influence adolescent development are presented (Leventhal & Brooks-Gunn, 2000, 2001). The first model, institutional resources, posits that the quality, quantity, and diversity of community resources mediate neighborhood effects. The second model, relationships and ties, hypothesizes that parental attributes, social networks, and behavior as well as home environment characteristics transmit neighborhood influences. The final model, norms and collective efficacy, speculates that the extent of community formal and informal institutions present to monitor residents' behavior (especially peer groups) and physical threats to residents accounts for neighborhood effects. These theoretical frames were developed based on a review and analysis of neighborhood studies by Jencks and Mayer (1990), the literature on economic hardship and unemployment (Conger, Ge, Elder, Lorenz, & Simons, 1994; McLoyd, 1990), economic resource perspectives (Haveman & Wolfe, 1994), and work on differential social organization theory (originally social disorganization theory; Sampson, 1992; Sampson et al., 1997; Shaw & McKay, 1942; see Sampson & Morenoff, 1997, for a review).

The theoretical models are intended to be complementary rather than conflicting. For instance, institutional resource mechanisms may be most salient when studying high-SES–achievement links, norms and collective efficacy processes may be most relevant for examining low-SES–delinquency associations, and relationship pathways may be most useful for examining SES–sexual outcome links. In terms of developmental differences, relationship mechanisms might be more relevant for younger than older adolescents because families may exert a greater influence during this period, whereas community norms and processes may be more salient for older than for younger adolescents because of the growing influence of peers during this period. Community institutional resources may play an equally important role in younger and older adolescence, but the specific resource of most relevance may differ for the two age groups. Accordingly, the present review of the theoretical models highlights aspects of each model that are most relevant to adolescents.

Institutional Resources

Economic resource perspectives, focusing typically on the family context, identify resources or opportunities to which children and youth theoretically have access (Brooks-Gunn, Klebanov, & Liaw, 1995; Haveman & Wolfe, 1994). Extrapolating this model to neighborhoods, community resources include the quantity, quality, diversity, and affordability of several types of resources in the community pertinent to adolescents—

schools, health and social services, recreational and social programs, and employment—that could influence well-being (Leventhal & Brooks-Gunn, 2000).

For adolescents, schools are a primary vehicle in which neighborhood effects may operate on adolescents' achievement in particular. Relevant aspects of schools include quality, climate, norms, and demographic makeup. Living in a disadvantaged neighborhood is adversely associated with these school attributes as well as with adolescents' educational outcomes (see Jencks & Mayer, 1990, for a review). Several studies have looked at the intersection of neighborhood context and school norms toward risky behavior. Findings indicate that neighborhood structure is associated with school norms, which, in turn, may be associated with adolescent problem behavior including sexual activity and substance use (Ennett, Flewelling, Lindrooth, & Norton, 1997; Teitler & Weiss, 2000).

The availability, quality, and affordability of medical and social services in the community may be a potential pathway of neighborhood influences, notably on mental and physical health (including sexual risk behavior and pregnancy). Although work examining this resource is scant, access, quality, and variety of health services vary as a function of family SES, with high income generally conferring beneficial effects (Newacheck, Hughes, & Stoddard, 1996; Newacheck, Stoddard, & McManus, 1993). It is likely that the same is true of neighborhood SES (Brooks-Gunn, McCormick, Klebanov, & McCarton, 1998). However, several studies of adolescent sexual behavior found that the availability of family planning and abortion providers in the community was not associated with adolescents' sexual activity, fertility outcomes, or attitudes toward contraceptive use (accounting for neighborhood structure; Brewster et al., 1993; Hughes, Furstenberg, & Teitler, 1995).

Another possible mechanism of neighborhood effects—especially on physical and social development—is the presence of social and recreational activities such as parks, sports programs, art and theater programs, and community centers. A neighborhood-based study of adolescent development in low- to middle-income neighborhoods found that the extent of prosocial activities varied across neighborhoods and was linked to problem behavior (Furstenberg et al., 1999; see also Furstenberg, 2001). Likewise, studies more generally on youth programs and after-school care point to these programs as having beneficial effects on adjustment, particularly for low-income youth (Roth & Brooks-Gunn, 2000; Roth, Brooks-Gunn, Murray, & Foster, 1998; Vandell & Shumow, 1999). Finally, qualitative and quantitative research on families in disadvantaged neighborhoods indicates that when social and recreational programs are not available in families' own communities, parents access resources from the larger surrounding community (Elder, Eccles, Ardelt, & Lord, 1995; Jarrett, 1997).

The last institutional resource most relevant to achievement outcomes and possibly problem behaviors entails the supply of employment opportunities, access to jobs (including transportation), and adolescents' own expectations about available opportunities. Although studies have not examined neighborhood-employment links on adolescent development (most studies focus on young adults), we draw upon research on family-level SES differences in the consequences of adolescent employment (Bachman & Schulenberg, 1993; Gleason & Cain, 1997; Leventhal, Graber, & Brooks-Gunn, 2001; Mortimer, Finch, Ryu, Shanahan, & Call, 1996; Newman, 1999; Steinberg, Fegley, & Dornbusch, 1993; Sullivan, 1989). Extrapolating for this work, the impact of adolescent employment (and available opportunities) on subsequent outcomes may be moderated by neighborhood SES, such that in disadvantaged neighborhoods, the effects of employment may be beneficial because fewer developmentally enhancing outlets beyond employment may exist. In contrast, in more affluent neighborhoods, where learning and social activities may provide more enriching alternatives to employment, the effects of employment may be more detrimental. At the individual level, adolescents' expectations about employment opportunities available to them are likely affected by their neighborhoods (including presence of working role models), and these expectations may be associated with resultant outcomes including educational attainment, substance use, crime, sexual activity, and childbearing (Billy et al., 1994; Ogbu, 1991; Paulter & Lewko, 1987; Willis, 1977).

Relationships and Ties

According to the relationships and ties model, parental relationships are hypothesized to be a potential pathway of neighborhood effects on adolescent development, especially social and emotional well-being. This frame draws heavily from the family stress model developed from research on economic hardship and unemployment in which links between family low income and adolescent outcomes are accounted for by parents' sense of financial strain, depression, and resultant parenting (Conger et al., 1994; Conger et al., 2002; McLoyd, 1990). Parental relationships and support networks are thought to mediate and moderate associations between parents' (and possibly youths') well-being and their behavior. We broaden this model of family economic hardship to neighborhood disadvantage such that neighborhood disadvantage may affect parental well-being and subsequent adolescent outcomes through parental behavior and home environment. Because empirical work exploring whether these individual and family mechanisms transmit neighborhood influences to adolescents is limited, we present relevant work on the different components of the model.

Aspects of parental well-being thought to be associated with neighborhood residence include physical and mental health, efficacy, coping skills, and irritability. At both the individual and neighborhood levels, compelling evidence exists for links between adults' physical and mental health and neighborhood structural conditions, particularly SES (e.g., Cubbin, LeClere, & Smith, 2000; Diez Roux et al., 2001; Roberts, 1997). For example, experimental work indicates that low-income parents who moved from high- to low-poverty neighborhoods reported superior mental and physical health compared with parents who remained in high-poverty neighborhoods (Katz et al., 2001; Leventhal & Brooks-Gunn, in press). Another study based on adolescent reports found that neighborhood disadvantage was positively associated with family stress (after accounting for family SES; Allison et al., 1999). Links between neighborhood structure and parental well-being with parenting practices as well as adolescent outcomes have been found. Among parents of adolescents in disadvantaged neighborhoods, parental efficacy mediated the use of family management strategies among African American parents but not European American parents (Elder et al., 1995). Finally, maternal self-esteem was found to moderate the positive association between the neighborhood dropout rate and adolescent risk-taking behavior such that this association was enhanced for youth with mothers with low self-esteem (Kowaleski-Jones, 2000).

Support networks including access to friends and family and connections within neighborhood may intervene between neighborhood economic resources and adolescent well-being (Cook et al., 1997). These support networks may buffer parents from the stressors of neighborhood violence, disorder, and poverty and subsequently may diminish the adverse effects of low parental functioning on adolescent development (Conger et al., 1994; Elder et al., 1995; McLoyd, 1990; Ross & Jang, 2000). It is unclear whether the density of support networks varies by neighborhood SES and racial-ethnic diversity; support may be strongest in middle-income neighborhoods (compared with low- and high-income neighborhoods) as well as in those with high immigrant concentrations, particularly Latino populations (Klebanov, Brooks-Gunn, & Duncan, 1994; Molnar, Buka, Brennan, Holton, & Earls, 2003; Rosenbaum, Popkin, Kaufman, & Rusin, 1991). For parents, social connections within the community appear to be particularly useful for job referral networks and for monitoring and caring for children when parents are unavailable (Coleman, 1988; Logan & Spitze, 1994). In terms of adolescents' own relationships and ties, in a sample of adolescents receiving social services, adolescents' received support from family and peers appeared to buffer the positive association between reported neighborhood problems and their mental health, especially internalizing problems (Stiffman, Hadley-Ives, Elze, & Johnson, 1999).

Neighborhood conditions—notably poverty, violence, and danger—are hypothesized to be associated with several parenting behaviors—warmth, harshness, and supervision and monitoring—and subsequent adolescent development. Both quantitative and qualitative work on family economic hardship reveals that parental stress and anxiety may have the largest impact on harsh parenting (Conger et al., 1994; McLoyd, 1990). In a quasi-experimental study, adolescents who moved from poor to less poor neighborhoods reported receiving less harsh parenting than did youth who remained in poor neighborhoods (Briggs, 1997). In poor and dangerous neighborhoods, parent-child relationships have been shown to be marked by low warmth and high aggression (Earls, McGuire, & Shay, 1994; Klebanov et al., 1994; Taylor, 2000), which may be linked to adolescent problem behavior (Beyers, Loeber, Wilstrom, & Stouthamer-Loeber, 2001). Several studies have explicitly tested mediation models. One study examining the family stress model among a sample of African American adolescent boys found that neighborhood poverty may indirectly affect violent behavior by means of family stress and conflict and by means of adolescents' feelings of self-worth (however, analyses did not control for individual and family background characteristics; Paschall & Hubbard, 1998). Yet another study found that quality of parenting (monitoring, warmth-support, inductive reasoning, harsh discipline, hostility, and communication), assessed through videotaped parent-child interactions, mediated the positive association between community disadvantage and adolescents' problem behavior (controlling for family SES; Simons et al., 1996).

In the field of neighborhood research, parental supervision and monitoring are thought to be particularly important during the adolescent years by modulating adolescents' exposure to community influences; subsequent outcomes may depend at least in part on neighborhood characteristics (Gonzales, Cauce, Friedman, & Mason, 1996; Lamborn, Dornbusch, & Steinberg, 1996; Pettit, Bates, Dodge, & Meece, 1999). A number of ethnographic researchers have observed that parents in dangerous and impoverished neighborhoods may use restrictive monitoring techniques with their adolescents to limit youths' exposure to negative community influences (Anderson, 1990 Burton, 1990; Burton & Jarrett, 2000; Furstenberg, 1993; Jarrett, 1997). One quasi-experimental study of moving from low- to middle-income neighborhoods supports this finding; parents who moved to advantaged neighborhoods used less restrictive parenting practices than did parents in low-income neighborhoods (Briggs, 1997). In terms of links with adolescent outcomes, parental monitoring of early dating behavior was found to mediate the positive association between neighborhood low SES and teenage childbearing (Hogan & Kitagawa, 1985; c.f. Baumer & South, 2001; South & Baumer, 2000). In addition, two studies reported that among families living in disadvantaged neighborhoods, high parental monitoring in conjunction with high emotional support served as a protective factor for adolescent problem behavior (negative peer affiliation and delinquency; Brody et al., 2001; Gorman-Smith, Tolan, & Henry, 2000).

Several characteristics of the home environment may act as vehicles of neighborhood influences on youth—physical home environment, presence of routines and structure, and exposure to violence. The physical home environment may be most salient for adolescents' health. Neighborhood low income (compared with middle income) is negatively associated with quality of physical home environments (after controlling for family SES; Klebanov et al., 1994). Experimental and nonexperimental evidence reveals that children and adolescents living in poor neighborhoods may be at risk for injury and asthma (Durkin, Davidson, Kuhn, & O'Connor, 1994; Katz et al., 2001). This situation is probably in part due to quality of the physical home environment.

The presence of family routines and structure, such as regular mealtimes and homework times, are thought to be significant for adolescents' social development (Boyce, Jensen, James, & Peacock, 1983; Bradley, 1995). At the theoretical level, it has been hypothesized that such routines may be weak in neighborhoods with high poverty and unemployment, marked violence, and low social cohesion (Leventhal & Brooks-Gunn, 2000; Wilson, 1987; Wilson, 1991). One quasi-experimental study found no effect on adolescents' family routines of moving from poor to less poor neighborhoods; however, this hypothesis remains to be further tested (Fauth, Leventhal, & Brooks-Gunn, 2002).

Finally, exposure to violence (as a witness or a victim) may be a potential pathway for neighborhood effects on adolescents' physical and emotional health in particular (Osofsky, 2000). Living in a poor neighborhood is associated with children's exposure to violence in the community and in the home (Coulton, Korbin, & Su, 1999; Coulton, Korbin, Su, & Chow, 1995; Martinez & Richters, 1993; Richters & Martinez, 1993). Findings are mixed as to whether the intersection of adolescents' exposure to violence in the home and the community is associated with exacerbated mental health problems (see Buka, Stichick, Birdthistle, & Earls, 2001, for a review).

Norms and Collective Efficacy

The norms and collective efficacy model draws heavily from differential social organization and collective efficacy theories (Sampson, 1992; Sampson et al., 1997; Shaw & McKay, 1942). According to these perspectives, collective efficacy—defined as the extent of community-level social connections including mutual trust, shared values among residents, and residents' willingness to intervene on behalf of community—controls the ability of communities to monitor residents' behavior in line with social norms and to maintain public order (Sampson, Morenoff, & Earls, 1999; Sampson et al., 1997). Community formal and informal institutions are thought to act as the regulatory mechanisms, and the capacity of these institutions to monitor residents' behavior—especially peer groups and physical threats, in turn—is hypothesized to be a function of specific community structural characteristics including low SES, racial-ethnic diversity, residential instability, and single parenthood (Coulton et al., 1995; Sampson, 1992; Sampson & Groves, 1989). For instance, in poor, residentially unstable, racially-ethnically diverse neighborhoods with many single parents, social organization is often low, resulting in the promulgation of adolescent problem behaviors such as crime and vandalism. In contrast, when social organization is high, adolescents are less likely to engage in these negative behaviors and may display more prosocial behaviors such as school engagement and civic participation. In the past few years, a number of researchers studying adolescents have tested various components of this model, and much of the work has focused on problem behaviors—delinquency, crime, violence, substance use, and sex. Again, this section reviews research on the different model components.

An important distinction to make is that the social connections described under the norms and collective efficacy model are more diffuse than the social networks discussed under the relationships and ties model and operate primarily at the community level (see Sampson, 1999, for further discussion of this distinction). In the Project on Human Development in Chicago Neighborhoods, collective efficacy and social control (measured by a community survey) were found to be negatively associated with neighborhood socioeconomic disadvantage, level of crime and violence, and observations of physical and social disorder (Raudenbush & Sampson, 1999; Sampson et al., 1999; Sampson et al., 1997; see also Pattilo, 1998). At both the neighborhood and individual levels, community social control of youth is negatively associated with adolescent problem behavior (after accounting for neighborhood structure; Brody et al., 2001; Elliott et al., 1996; Sampson, 1997).

Peer group behavior and norms are a central pathway through which neighborhood structure is anticipated to influence adolescent outcomes, especially social and emotional outcomes. Peer effects are generally hypothesized to be negative because they are exacerbated when community institutions and norms fail to regulate peer group behavior. Living in a socially disadvantaged neighborhood is positively associated with adolescents' affiliation with deviant peers (Brody et al., 2001; Ge, Brody, Conger, Simons, & Murry, 2002; Quane & Rankin, 1998). One study found that the effect of community disadvantage on adolescent childbearing was accounted for by peer attitudes and behavior, as reported by adolescents (controlling for background characteristics; South & Baumer, 2000). Moreover, a lack of formal and informal institutions present to supervise adolescent peer group activities, in turn, has been found to mediate the association between neighborhood SES (and related characteristics) and adolescents' delinquent, criminal, and prosocial behavior (Sampson & Groves, 1989; Shaw & McKay, 1942; Veysey & Messner, 1999). Finally, other work has shown that peer support moderated neighborhood effects on adolescents' antisocial behavior, substance use, and school achievement, such that in high-risk neighborhoods, peer support had more negative effects and in low-risk neighborhoods, peer effects were more beneficial (Dubow, Edwards, & Ippolito, 1997; Gonzales et al., 1996).

Physical threats including the extent of violence, the availability of harmful and illegal substances, and other general threats to well-being are hypothesized to be associated with community mechanisms of control and subsequent adolescent outcomes, especially physical and emotional development. Two housing programs in which low-income families moved from pubic housing in high-poverty neighborhoods to less poor neighborhoods found that parents reported that getting away from drugs and gangs was their primary motivation for wanting to move (Briggs, 1997; Goering et al., 1999). In fact, follow-ups of these program found that children and youth who moved to better neighborhoods were less likely to be exposed to violence than were peers who remained in poor neighborhoods (Fauth et al., 2002; Katz et al., 2001). Youth from poor, urban neighborhoods who are exposed to high levels of community violence have been shown to display internalizing problems as well as physical and psychiatric symptoms (Cooley-Quille, Boyd, Frantz, & Walsh, 2001). In addition, several studies have found that neighborhood danger accounted for links between neighborhood low SES and adolescent outcomes, including emotional problems and timing of first intercourse (Aneshensel & Sucoff, 1996; Pettit et al., 1999; Upchurch, Sucoff, & Levy-Storms, 1999).

Access to illegal and harmful substances has been shown to vary as a function of neighborhood characteristics, with low-income neighborhoods and those with high proportions of African Americans providing adolescents with greater access to alcohol, cigarettes, and cocaine than do higher income neighborhoods and predominately European American neighborhoods (Briggs, 1997; Fauth et al., 2002; Landrine, Klonoff, & Alcaraz, 1997); however, it is unclear if neighborhood availability of substances is associated with adolescent substance use (Ennett et al., 1997). Two studies of disadvantaged youth found that adolescent reports of drug availability in their neighborhoods were adversely linked with youths' offending behavior and likelihood of gang affiliation (Chung, Hill, Hawkins, Gilchrist, & Nagin, 2002; Hill, Howell, Hawkins, & Battin-Pearson, 1999).

POLICY IMPLICATIONS AND FUTURE DIRECTIONS

Adolescence is a period marked by expanding social interactions. Therefore, the goal of this chapter was to examine the influence of one social context on adolescent development—neighborhoods. We took as our starting point that neighborhoods likely play an important role during this phase of the life course. The empirical evidence was reviewed to this end, followed by specification of a framework for studying the pathways of neighborhood influences on developmental outcomes. An overview of methodological issues was also provided. In conclusion, an integration of the empirical, theoretical, and methodological findings is presented in this section, along with policy implications and directions for future research.

Findings from the literature review revealed growing support for neighborhood structural effects on adolescent development, particularly for SES (compared with racial-ethnic diversity and residential instability). Neighborhood SES effects were not restricted to a particular domain; however, the specific aspect of SES that mattered most varied by outcome. Neighborhood high SES was positively associated with adolescents' educational achievement, and neighborhood low SES was adversely associated with their behavioral and social well-being and sexual and fertility outcomes. Findings were generally more consistent for older than for younger adolescents, probably because research on this developmental period was based largely on national samples, whereas research on younger adolescents drew more heavily from city and regional samples. It is also possible that neighborhoods play an increasingly important role in development during the latter half of adolescence as exposure to extrafamilial influences grows. Finally, neighborhood structural effects appeared to be more pronounced for male than for female adolescents—particularly for achievement outcomes—suggesting that boys may be granted greater autonomy by parents and school officials (and therefore may have more contact with neighborhood influences), that boys may be more susceptible to neighborhood influences (particularly peer groups), or both.

Despite consistent patterns of results, the overall size of neighborhood structural effects reported in nonexperimental studies was small to modest, accounting for approximately 5–10% of the variance in adolescent outcomes (after adjusting for child and family background characteristics). In comparison, the limited experimental work suggests rather large neighborhood income effects on adolescent development, at least when low-income youth and their families were given the opportunity to move from high- to low-poverty neighborhoods. Together, these findings suggest that neighborhood influences contribute to adolescents' developmental outcomes and should be incorporated into research on this phase of the life course.

To understand the observed associations between neighborhood structure and adolescent development, however, requires drawing upon our theoretical models—institutional resources, relationships and ties, and norms and collective efficacy. Responding to previous concerns, the models proposed within this framework highlight different underlying mechanisms (individual, family, school, peer, and community), with the utility of each based in part on the outcome under investigation and in part on the age group studied. Accordingly, we use these models to interpret the findings from the literature review in conjunction with relevant research findings examining process models. The association between neighborhood high SES and achievement is best understood in accordance with the institutional resource model. Affluent neighborhoods may have higher quality schools as well as students with more achievement-oriented norms than do less advantaged communities. Economically advantaged neighborhoods also may have more resources that promote learning, such as libraries and educational programs, than do more disadvantaged communities. Some empirical support exists for the premise regarding school quality. Alternatively, family relationships may be at play. High-SES neighborhoods may be conducive to home environments with structure and routines that foster educational attainment; however, little work has examined this hypothesis.

The associations among low-SES neighbors and mental health problems, delinquency, crime, sexual activity, and childbearing are best understood within the rubric of the norms and collective efficacy model. In economically and socially disadvantaged neighborhoods, informal social control of youth may be low, resulting in few institutions to regulate behavior, especially among adolescent peer groups. Compelling evidence exists to support this argument, especially concerning crime and delinquency. According to the institutional resource frame, low-SES neighborhoods may lack social and recreational resources such as after-school and youth programs—circumstances that in turn have adverse effects on adolescents' adjustment. Again, research indicates this situation to be the case. Adolescents in low-SES neighborhoods also may have low expectations about the opportunities available to them, resulting in a disincentive to avoid problem behavior; almost no research addresses this hypothesis. Finally, although findings are mixed, relationship mechanisms, including low parental supervision and monitoring of youth, may be operating. In addition, low-quality parent-child relationship, particularly during early adolescence, may fail to buffer youth from negative community influences.

We can use the theoretical models to interpret the results of the literature review, but much more work remains to be done in conceptually oriented neighborhood research on adolescents. As we have reviewed, an increasing number of researchers are beginning to approach this challenge, and the norms and collective efficacy model has been most widely tested, particularly with respect to problem behavior. In fact, results of these studies indicate that at least half of the variance in neighborhood structural effects on adolescent behavior appears to be accounted for by such processes (Elliott et al., 1996; Sampson, 1997).

Conceptually focused neighborhood research has been hampered by methodological limitations. Specifically, studies that are not designed to study neighborhood effects often lack adequate samples in terms of variation within and between neighborhoods to test theoretical models, nor do these studies measure (or at least measure reliably) neighborhood processes, such as social control and school norms, and individual and family mechanisms, such as parental supervision, necessary for examining theoretical models. To assess neighborhood processes, as discussed under the institutional resource and norms and collective efficacy models, which appear to be especially important during the adolescent years, alternative methodologies are required. The strategies reviewed and recommended include community surveys, systematic social observations, and alternative administrative data sources. The advantage of these approaches is that they provide measures of neighborhood dimensions (beyond structure) obtained from independent sources (as opposed to participant ratings, which are often subject to threats of nonindependence of measurement). Aside from neighborhood-based studies, which typically address these design and measurement limitations, experimental studies are advocated because they overcome problems of selection or omitted variable bias present in nonexperimental neighborhood research.

Testing theoretical models permits an identification of specific underlying mechanisms of neighborhood influences, which is necessary for drawing policy recommendations. The findings presented suggest that the aspect of neighborhood targeted by policy makers depends on the outcome under consideration. If adolescents' educational attainment were the primary outcome of interest, focusing on potential pathways of high SES, such as school quality, would be recommended. Alternatively, if adolescent crime and delinquency were the target, then building community mechanisms of control would be recommended, in addition to providing recreational and social programs for youth. For sexual risk behaviors, similar strategies could be implemented as well as work with families to help parents successfully monitor children and to foster close parent-child relations.

In summary, neighborhoods appear to matter for adolescent development; however, how they matter is only beginning to be elucidated. Process-oriented research is needed to design effective neighborhood-focused programs and policies aimed at enhancing the lives of adolescents and their families.

REFERENCES

Aaronson, D. (1997). Sibling estimates of neighborhood effects. In J. Brooks-Gunn, G. J. Duncan, & J. L. Aber (Eds.), *Neighborhood poverty: Policy implications in studying neighborhoods* (Vol. 2, pp. 80–93). New York: Russell Sage Foundation Press.

Aber, J. L., Gephart, M. A., Brooks-Gunn, J., & Connell, J. P. (1997). Development in context: Implications for studying neighborhood effects. In J. Brooks-Gunn, G. J. Duncan, & J. L. Aber (Eds.), *Neighborhood poverty: Context and consequences for children* (Vol. 1, pp. 44–61). New York: Russell Sage Foundation Press.

Allison, K. W., Burton, L. M., Marshall, S., Perez-Febles, A., Yarrington, J., Kirsh, L. B., & Merriwether-DeVries, C. (1999). Life experiences among urban adolescents: Examining the role of context. *Child Development, 70*(4), 1017–1029.

Anderson, E. (1990). *Streetwise.* Chicago: University of Chicago Press.

Aneshensel, C. S., & Sucoff, C. A. (1996). The neighborhood context of adolescent mental health. *Journal of Health and Social Behavior, 37,* 293–310.

Bachman, J. G., & Schulenberg, J. (1993). How part-time work intensity relates to drug use, problem behavior, time use, and satisfaction among high school seniors: Are these consequences or merely correlates? *Developmental Psychology, 29*(2), 220–235.

Baker, P. C., & Mott, F. L. (1989). *NLSY child handbook 1989: A guide and resource document for the National Longitudinal Survey of Youth 1986 Child Data.* Columbus, OH: Center for Human Resources Research, Ohio State University.

Baumer, E. P., & South, S. J. (2001). Community effects on youth sexual activity. *Journal of Marriage and the Family, 63,* 540–554.

Beyers, J. M., Loeber, R., Wilstrom, P. H., & Stouthamer-Loeber, M. (2001). What predicts adolescent violence in better-off neighborhoods? *Journal of Abnormal Child Psychology, 29*(5), 369–381.

Billy, J. O. G., Brewster, K. L., & Grady, W. R. (1994). Contextual effects of the sexual behavior of adolescent women. *Journal of Marriage and the Family, 56,* 387–404.

Billy, J. O. G., & Moore, D. E. (1992). A multilevel analysis of marital and nonmarital fertility in the U.S. *Social Forces, 70,* 977–1011.

Boyce, W. T., Jensen, E. W., James, S. A., & Peacock, J. L. (1983). The Family Routines Inventory: Theoretical origins. *Social Science and Medicine, 17,* 193–200.

Bradley, R. H. (1995). Environment and parenting. In M. H. Bornstein (Ed.), *Handbook of parenting: Vol. 2. Biology and ecology of parenting* (pp. 235–261). Mahwah, NJ: Erlbaum.

Brewster, K. L. (1994a). Neighborhood context and the transition to sexual activity among young Black women. *Demography, 31,* 603–614.

Brewster, K. L. (1994b). Race differences in sexual activity among adolescent women: The role of neighborhood characteristics. *American Sociological Review, 59,* 408–424.

Brewster, K. L., Billy, J. O. G., & Grady, W. R. (1993). Social context and adolescent behavior: The impact of community on the transition to sexual activity. *Social Forces, 71*(3), 713–740.

Briggs, X. d. S. (Ed.). (1997). *Yonkers revisited: The early impacts of scattered-site public housing on families and neighborhoods.* New York: National Center for Children and Families, Teachers College, Columbia University.

Brody, G. H., Ge, X., Conger, R. D., Gibbons, F. X., Murry, V. M., Gerrard, M., et al. (2001). The influence of neighborhood disadvantage, collective socialization, and parenting on African American children's affiliation with deviant peers. *Child Development, 72*(4), 1231–1246.

Bronfenbrenner, U. (1979). *The ecology of human development.* Cambridge, MA: Harvard University Press.

Brooks-Gunn, J., Duncan, G. J., & Aber, J. L. (Eds.). (1997). *Neighborhood poverty: Vol. 1. Context and consequences for children.* New York: Russell Sage Foundation Press.

Brooks-Gunn, J., Duncan, G. J., Klebanov, P. K., & Sealand, N. (1993). Do neighborhoods influence child and adolescent development? *American Journal of Sociology, 99,* 353–395.

Brooks-Gunn, J., Klebanov, P. K., & Liaw, F. (1995). The learning, physical, and emotional environment of the home in the context of poverty: The Infant Health and Development Program. *Children and Youth Services Review, 17*(1–2), 251–276.

Brooks-Gunn, J., McCormick, M. C., Klebanov, P. K., & McCarton, C. (1998). Health care use of 3 year-old low birthweight premature children: Effects of family and neighborhood poverty. *The Journal of Pediatrics, 132,* 971–975.

Bryk, A. S., & Raudenbush, S. W. (1992). *Hierarchical linear models for social and behavioral research: Applications and data analysis methods.* Newbury Park, CA: Sage.

Buka, S. L., Stichick, T. L., Birdthistle, I., & Earls, F. J. (2001). Youth exposure to violence: Prevalence, risks, and consequences. *American Journal of Orthopsychiatry, 71*(3), 298–310.

Bursik, R. J. (1988). Social disorganization and theories of crime and delinquency: Problems and prospects. *Criminology, 26,* 515–552.

Burton, L. M. (1990). Teenage childbearing as an alternative life-course strategy in multigenerational black families. *Human Nature, 1,* 123–143.

Burton, L. M., & Jarrett, R. L. (2000). In the mix, yet on the margins: The place of families in urban neighborhood and child development research. *Journal of Marriage and the Family, 62*(4), 1114–1135.

Caspi, A., Taylor, A., Moffitt, T. E., & Plomin, R. (2000). Neighborhood deprivation affects children's mental health: Environmental risk identified in a genetic design. *Psychological Science, 11*(4), 338–342.

Chung, I., Hill, K. G., Hawkins, J. D., Gilchrist, L. D., & Nagin, D. S. (2002). Childhood predictors of offense trajectories. *Journal of Research in Crime and Delinquency, 39*(1), 60–90.

Coleman, J. S. (1988). Social capital in the creation of human capital. *American Journal of Sociology, 94,* S95–S120.

Conger, R. D., Ge, X., Elder, G. H., Lorenz, F. O., & Simons, R. L. (1994). Economic stress, coercive family process, and development problems of adolescents. *Child Development, 65,* 541–561.

Conger, R. D., Wallace, L. E., Sun, Y., Simons, R. L., McLoyd, V. C., & Brody, G. H. (2002). Economic pressure in African American families: A replication and extension of the family stress model. *Developmental Psychology, 38*(2), 179–193.

Connell, J. P., & Halpern-Felsher, B. (1997). How neighborhoods affect educational outcomes in middle childhood and adolescence: Conceptual issues and an empirical example. In J. Brooks-Gunn, G. J. Duncan, & J. L. Aber (Eds.), *Neighborhood poverty: Context and consequences for children* (Vol. 2, pp. 174–199). New York: Russell Sage Foundation Press.

Cook, T. D., Shagle, S. C., & Degirmencioglu, S. M. (1997). Capturing social process for testing mediational models of neighborhood effects. In J. Brooks-Gunn, G. J. Duncan, & J. L. Aber (Eds.), *Neighborhood poverty: Policy implications in studying neighborhoods* (Vol. 2, pp. 94–119). New York: Russell Sage Foundation Press.

Cooley-Quille, M., Boyd, R. C., Frantz, E., & Walsh, J. (2001). Emotional and behavioral impact of exposure to community violence in inner-city adolescents. *Journal of Clinical Child Psychology, 30*(1), 199–206.

Coulton, C. J., Korbin, J., Chan, T., & Su, M. (2001). Mapping residents' perceptions of neighborhood boundaries: A methodological note. *American Journal of Community Psychology, 29*(2), 371–383.

Coulton, C. J., Korbin, J. E., & Su, M. (1999). Neighborhoods and child maltreatment: A multilevel study. *Child Abuse and Neglect, 23,* 1019–1040.

Coulton, C. J., Korbin, J. E., Su, M., & Chow, J. (1995). Community level factors and child maltreatment rates. *Child Development, 66,* 1262–1276.

Crane, J. (1991). The epidemic theory of ghettos and neighborhood effects on dropping out and teenage childbearing. *American Journal of Sociology, 96,* 1226–1259.

Cubbin, C., LeClere, F. B., & Smith, G. S. (2000). Socioeconomic status and injury mortality: Individual and neighborhood determinants. *Journal of Epidemiology and Community Health, 54*(7), 517–524.

Diez Roux, A. V., Merkin, S. S., Arnett, D., Chambless, L., Massing, M., Nieto, F. J., et al. (2001). Neighborhood of residence and incidence of coronary heart disease. *The New England Journal of Medicine, 345,* 99–106.

Dornbusch, S. M., Ritter, L. P., & Steinberg, L. (1991). Community influences on the relation of family status to adolescent school performance: Differences between African Americans and non-Hispanic whites. *American Journal of Education, 38*(4), 543–567.

Dubow, E. F., Edwards, S., & Ippolito, M. F. (1997). Life stressors, neighborhood disadvantage, and resources: A focus on inner-city children's adjustment. *Journal of Clinical Child Psychology, 26,* 130–144.

Duncan, G. J. (1994). Families and neighbors as sources of disadvantage in the schooling decisions of white and black adolescents. *American Journal of Education, 103,* 20–53.

Duncan, G. J., Connell, J. P., & Klebanov, P. K. (1997). Conceptual and methodological issues in estimating causal effects of neighborhoods and family conditions on individual development. In J. Brooks-Gunn, G. J. Duncan, & J. L. Aber (Eds.), *Neighborhood poverty: Vol 1. Context and consequences for children* (pp. 219–250). New York: Russell Sage Foundation Press.

Duncan, G. J., & Raudenbush, S. W. (1999). Assessing the effects of context in studies of children and youth development. *Educational Psychologist, 34*(1), 29–41.

Durkin, M. S., Davidson, L. L., Kuhn, L., & O'Connor, P. (1994). Low-income neighborhoods and the risk of severe pediatric injury: A small-area analysis in Northern Manhattan. *American Journal of Public Health, 84*(4), 587–592.

Earls, F., & Buka, S. L. (1997). *Project on Human Development in Chicago Neighborhoods: Technical report.* Rockville, MD: National Institute of Justice.

Earls, F., McGuire, J., & Shay, S. (1994). Evaluating a community intervention to reduce the risk of child abuse: Methodological strategies in conducting neighborhood surveys. *Child Abuse and Neglect, 18,* 473–485.

Elder, G. H., Eccles, J. S., Ardelt, M., & Lord, S. (1995). Inner-city parents under economic pressure: Perspectives on the strategies of parenting. *Journal of Marriage and the Family, 57,* 771–784.

Elliott, D. S., Wilson, W. J., Huizinga, D., Sampson, R. J., Elliott, A., & Rankin, B. (1996). The effects of neighborhood disadvantage on adolescent development. *Journal of Research in Crime and Delinquency, 33,* 389–426.

Ennett, S. T., Flewelling, R. L., Lindrooth, R. C., & Norton, E. C. (1997). School and neighborhoods characteristics associated with school rates of alcohol, cigarette, and marijuana use. *Journal of Health and Social Behavior, 38,* 55–71.

Ensminger, M. E., Lamkin, R. P., & Jacobson, N. (1996). School leaving: A longitudinal perspective including neighborhood effects. *Child Development, 67,* 2400–2416.

Entwisle, D. R., Alexander, K. L., & Olson, L. S. (1994). The gender gap in math: Its possible origins in neighborhood effects. *American Sociological Review, 59,* 822–838.

Evans, W. N., Oates, W. E., & Schwab, R. M. (1992). Measuring peer group effects: A study of teenage behavior. *Journal of Political Economy, 100*(5), 966–991.

Fauth, R. C., Leventhal, T., & Brooks-Gunn, J. (2002). *Moving out, are they moving up? Early impacts of scattered site public housing on low-income youth.* Manuscript submitted for publication.

Foster, E. M., & McLanahan, S. (1996). An illustration of the use of instrumental variables: Do neighborhood conditions affect a young person's chance of finishing high school? *Psychological Methods, 1*(3), 249–260.

Furstenberg, F. F., Jr. (1993). How families manage risk and opportunity in dangerous neighborhoods. In W. J. Wilson (Ed.), *Sociology and the public agenda* (pp. 231–238). Newbury Park, CA: Sage.

Furstenberg, F. F., Jr. (2001). Managing to make it: Afterthoughts. *Journal of Family Issues, 22*(2), 150–162.

Furstenberg, F. F., Jr., Cook, T. D., Eccles, J., Elder, G. H., & Sameroff, A. (Eds.). (1999). *Managing to make it: Urban families and adolescent success.* Chicago: University of Chicago Press.

Galambos, N. L., & Leadbeater, B. (2000). Trends in adolescent research for the new millennium. *International Journal of Behavioral Development, 24*(3), 289–294.

Garner, C. L., & Raudenbush, S. W. (1991). Neighborhood effects on educational attainment: A multilevel analysis. *Sociology of Education, 64,* 251–262.

Ge, X., Brody, G. H., Conger, R. D., Simons, R. L., & Murry, V. M. (2002). Contextual application of pubertal transition effects on deviant peer affiliation and externalizing behavior among African American children. *Developmental Psychology, 38*(1), 42–54.

Gleason, P. M., & Cain, G. G. (1997). *Earnings of black and white youth and their relation to poverty* [Discussion paper No. 1138–1197]. Madison, WI: University of Wisconsin, Institute for Research on Poverty.

Goering, J. (Ed.). (in press). *Choosing a better life? How public housing tenants selected a HUD experiment to improve their lives and those of their children: The Moving to Opportunity Demonstration Program.* Washington, DC: Urban Institute Press.

Goering, J., Kraft, J., Feins, J., McInnis, D., Holin, M. J., & Elhassan, H. (1999, September). *Moving to Opportunity for Fair Housing Demonstration Program: Current status and initial findings.* Washington, DC: U.S. Department of Housing and Urban Development.

Gonzales, N. A., Cauce, A. M., Friedman, R. J., & Mason, C. A. (1996). Family, peer, and neighborhood influences on academic achievement among African-American adolescents: One-year prospective effects. *American Journal of Community Psychology, 24,* 365–387.

Gorman-Smith, D., Tolan, P., & Henry, D. B. (2000). A developmental-ecological model of the relation of family functioning to patterns of delinquency. *Journal of Quantitative Criminology, 16*(2), 169–198.

Halpern-Felsher, B., Connell, J. P., Spencer, M. B., Aber, J. L., Duncan, G. J., Clifford, E., Crichlow, W., Usinger, P., & Cole, S. S. (1997). Neighborhood and family factors predicting educational risk and attainment in African American and white children and adolescents. In J. Brooks-Gunn, G. J. Duncan, & J. L. Aber (Eds.), *Neighborhood poverty: Context and consequences for children* (Vol. 1, pp. 146–173). New York: Russell Sage Foundation Press.

Haveman, R., & Wolfe, B. (1994). *Succeeding generations: On the effects of investments in children.* New York: Russell Sage Foundation Press.

Hernandez, D. J. (1993). *America's children: Resources from family, government, and the economy.* New York: Russell Sage Foundation Press.

Hill, K. G., Howell, J. C., Hawkins, J. D., & Battin-Pearson, S. R. (1999). Childhood risk factors for adolescent gang membership: Results from the Seattle social development project. *Journal of Research in Crime and Delinquency, 36*(3), 300–322.

Hill, M. (1991). *The Panel Study of Income Dynamics: The Sage series guides to major social science data bases* (Vol. 2). Newbury Park, CA: Sage.

Hoffman, J. P. (2002). The community context of family structure and adolescent drug use. *Journal of Marriage and the Family, 64,* 314–330.

Hogan, D. P., & Kitagawa, E. M. (1985). The impact of social status, family structure, and neighborhood on the fertility of Black adolescents. *American Journal of Sociology, 90,* 825–855.

Hughes, M. E., Furstenberg, F. F., & Teitler, J. O. (1995). The impact of an increase in family planning services on the teenage population of Philadelphia. *Family Planning Perspectives, 27,* 60–65.

Jarrett, R. L. (1997). Bringing families back in: Neighborhood effects on child development. In J. Brooks-Gunn, G. J. Duncan, & J. L. Aber (Eds.), *Neighborhood poverty: Policy implications in studying neighborhoods* (Vol. 2, pp. 48–64). New York: Russell Sage Foundation Press.

Jencks, C., & Mayer, S. E. (1990). The social consequences of growing up in a poor neighborhood. In L. Lynn & M. McGeary (Eds.), *Inner-city poverty in the United States* (pp. 111–186). Washington, DC: National Academy Press.

Katz, L. F., Kling, J. R., & Liebman, J. B. (2001). Moving to opportunity in Boston: Early results of a randomized mobility experiment. *Quarterly Journal of Economics, 116,* 607–654.

Kaufman, J., & Rosenbaum, J. (1992). The education and employment of low-income black youth in white suburbs. *Educational Evaluation and Policy Analysis, 14*(3), 229–240.

Klebanov, P. K., Brooks-Gunn, J., & Duncan, G. J. (1994). Does neighborhood and family poverty affect mothers' parenting, mental health, and social support? *Journal of Marriage and the Family, 56,* 441–455.

Kohen, D., Brooks-Gunn, J., Leventhal, T., & Hertzman, C. (2002). Neighborhood income and physical and social disorder in Canada: Associations with young children's competencies. *Child Development, 73*(6), 1844–1860.

Kornhauser, R. (1978). *Social sources of delinquency.* Chicago: University of Chicago Press.

Kowaleski-Jones, L. (2000). Staying out of trouble: Community resources and problem behavior among high-risk adolescents. *Journal of Marriage and the Family, 62,* 449–464.

Ku, L., Sonenstein, F. L., & Pleck, J. H. (1993). Neighborhood, family, and work: Influences on the premarital behaviors of adolescent males. *Social Forces, 72*(2), 479–503.

Lamborn, S. D., Dornbusch, S., & Steinberg, L. (1996). Ethnicity and community context as moderators of the relations between family decision making and adolescent adjustment. *Child Development, 67,* 283–301.

Landrine, H., Klonoff, E. A., & Alcaraz, R. (1997). Racial discrimination in minors' access to tobacco. *Journal of Black Psychology, 23*(2), 135–147.

Larson, R. W., Brown, B. B., & Mortimer, J. T. (2002). Preface to special issue on adolescents' preparation for the future: Perils and promise. *Journal of Research on Adolescence, 12*(1), iii–v.

Leventhal, T., & Brooks-Gunn, J. (2000). The neighborhoods they live in: Effects of neighborhood residence upon child and adolescent outcomes. *Psychological Bulletin, 126,* 309–337.

Leventhal, T., & Brooks-Gunn, J. (2001). Changing neighborhoods and child well-being: Understanding how children may be affected in the coming century. *Advances in Life Course Research, 6,* 263–301.

Leventhal, T., & Brooks-Gunn, J. (2002). *A randomized study of neighborhood effects on low-income children's educational outcomes.* Manuscript submitted for publication.

Leventhal, T., & Brooks-Gunn, J. (2003a). Moving on up: Neighborhood effects on children and families. In M. H. Burnstein & R. H. Bradley (Eds.), *Socioeconomic status, parenting, and child development* (pp. 203–230). Mahwah, NJ: Erlbaum.

Leventhal, T., & Brooks-Gunn, J. (2003b). Neighborhood-based initiatives. In J. Brooks-Gunn, A. S. Fuligni, & L. J. Berln (Eds.), *Early childhood development in the 21st century: Profiles of current research initiatives* (pp. 278–295). New York: Teachers College Press.

Leventhal, T., & Brooks-Gunn, J. (in press). Moving to Opportunity: An experimental study of neighborhood effects on mental health. *American Journal of Public Health.*

Leventhal, T., Graber, J. A., & Brooks-Gunn, J. (2001). Adolescent transitions into employment: When a job is not just a job. *Journal of Research on Adolescence, 11*(3), 297–323.

Loeber, R., & Wikstrom, P.-O. H. (1993). Individual pathways to crime in different types of neighborhoods. In D. P. Farrington, R. J. Sampson, & P.-O. H. Wikstrom (Eds.), *Integrating individual and ecological aspects of crime* (pp. 169–204). Stockholm, Sweden: National Council for Crime Prevention.

Logan, J. R., & Spitze, G. D. (1994). Family neighbors. *American Journal of Sociology, 100*(2), 453–476.

Ludwig, J., Duncan, G. J., & Hirschfield, P. (2001). Urban poverty and juvenile crime: Evidence from a randomized housing-mobility experiment. *Quarterly Journal of Economics, 116,* 665–679.

Ludwig, J., Ladd, H., & Duncan, G. J. (2001). Urban poverty and educational outcomes. In W. G. Gale & J. R. Pack (Eds.), *Brookings-Wharton papers on urban affairs 2001* (pp. 147–201). Washington, DC: Brookings Institution Press.

Martinez, P., & Richters, J. E. (1993). The NIMH Community Violence Project: II. Children's distress symptoms associated with violence exposure. *Psychiatry, 56,* 22–35.

Massey, D. S., & Denton, N. A. (1993). *American apartheid: Segregation and the making of the underclass.* Cambridge: Harvard University Press.
Mayer, S. E., & Jencks, C. (1989). Growing up in poor neighborhoods: How much does it matter? *Science, 243,* 1441–1445.
McLoyd, V. C. (1990). The impact of economic hardship on black families and children: Psychological distress, parenting, and socioemotional development. *Child Development, 61,* 311–346.
Molnar, B. E., Buka, S. L., Brennan , R. T., Holton, J. K., & Earls, F. (2003). A multi-level study of neighborhoods and parent-to-child physical aggression: Results from the Project on Human Development in Chicago Neighborhoods. *Child Maltreatment, 8*(2), 84–97.
Mortimer, J. T., Finch, M. D., Ryu, S., Shanahan, M. J., & Call, K. T. (1996). The effects of work intensity on adolescent mental health, achievement, and behavioral adjustment: New evidence from a prospective study. *Child Development, 67,* 1243–1261.
Newacheck, P. W., Hughes, D. C., & Stoddard, J. J. (1996). Children's access to primary care: Differences by race, income, and insurance status. *Pediatrics, 97,* 26–32.
Newacheck, P. W., Stoddard, J. J., & McManus, M. (1993). Ethnocultural variations in the prevalence and impact of childhood chronic conditions. *Pediatrics, 91,* 1031–1038.
Newman, K. S. (1999). *No shame in my game: The working poor in the inner city.* New York: Knopf and Russell Sage Foundation.
Ogbu, J. U. (1991). Minority coping responses and school experience. *Journal of Psychohistory, 18*(4), 433–456.
Osofsky, J. D. (2000). The impact of violence on children. *Future of Children, 9*(3), 33–49.
Paschall, M. J., & Hubbard, M. L. (1998). Effects of neighborhood and family stressors on African American male adolescents' self-worth and propensity for violent behavior. *Journal of Consulting and Clinical Psychology, 66*(5), 825–831.
Pattilo, M. E. (1998). Sweet mothers and gangbangers: Managing crime in a black middle-class neighborhood. *Social Forces, 76*(3), 747–774.
Paulter, K. J., & Lewko, J. H. (1987). Children's and adolescents' views of the work world in times of economic uncertainty. In J. H. Lewko (Ed.), *How children and adolescents view the world of work* (pp. 21–31). San Francisco: Jossey-Bass.
Peeples, F., & Loeber, R. (1994). Do individual factors and neighborhood context explain ethnic differences in juvenile delinquency. *Journal of Quantitative Criminology, 10,* 141–157.
Pettit, G. S., Bates, J. E., Dodge, K. A., & Meece, D. W. (1999). The impact of after-school peer contact on early adolescent externalizing problems is moderated by parental monitoring, perceived neighborhood safety, and prior adjustment. *Child Development, 70*(3), 768–778.
Plotnick, R. D., & Hoffman, S. D. (1999). The effect of neighborhood characteristics on young adult outcomes: Alternative estimates. *Social Science Quarterly, 80*(1), 1–18.
Quane, J. M., & Rankin, B. H. (1998). Neighborhood poverty, family characteristics, and commitment to mainstream goals: The case of African American adolescents in inner city. *Journal of Family Issues, 19*(6), 769–794.
Ramirez-Valles, J., Zimmerman, M. A., & Juarez, L. (2002). Gender differences of neighborhood and social control processes: A study of the timing of intercourse among low-achieving urban, African-American youth. *Youth and Society, 33*(3), 418–441.
Ramirez-Valles, J., Zimmerman, M. A., & Newcomb, M. D. (1998). Sexual risk behavior among youth: Modeling the influence of prosocial activities and socioeconomic factors. *Journal of Health and Social Behavior, 39,* 237–253.
Raudenbush, S. W., & Sampson, R. J. (1999). Assessing direct and indirect effects in multilevel designs with latent variables. *Sociological Methods and Research, 28,* 123–153.
Raudenbush, S. W., & Sampson, R. J. (1999). Ecometrics: Toward a science of assessing ecological settings, with application to the systematic social observations of neighborhoods. *Sociological Methodology, 29,* 1–41.
Reardon, S. F., Brennan, R., & Buka, S. L. (2002). Estimating multi-level discrete-time hazard models using cross-sectional data: Neighborhood effects on the onset of adolescent cigarette use. *Multivariate Behavioral Research, 37*(3), 297–330.

Reiss, A. (1971). Systematic observations of natural social phenomena. In H. Costner (Ed.), *Sociological methodology* (pp. 3–33). San Francisco: Jossey-Bass.

Richters, J. E., & Martinez, P. (1993). The NIMH Community Violence Project: I. Children as victims of and witnesses to violence. *Psychiatry, 56,* 7–21.

Roberts, E. M. (1997). Neighborhood social environments and the distribution of low birthweight in Chicago. *American Journal of Public Health, 87,* 597–603.

Rosenbaum, J. E., Popkin, S. J., Kaufman, J. E., & Rusin, J. (1991). Social integration of low-income black adults in middle-class white suburbs. *Social Problems, 38*(4), 448–461.

Ross, C. E., & Jang, S. J. (2000). Neighborhood disorder, fear, and mistrust: The buffering role of social ties with neighbors. *American Journal of Community Psychology, 28*(4), 401–420.

Roth, J., & Brooks-Gunn, J. (2000). What do adolescents need for health development?: Implications for youth policy. *Social Policy Report, 14*(1), 3–19.

Roth, J., Brooks-Gunn, J., Murray, L., & Foster, W. (1998). Promoting healthy adolescents: Synthesis of youth development program evaluations. *Journal of Research on Adolescence, 8*(4), 423–459.

Sampson, R. J. (1992). Family management and child development: Insights from social disorganization theory. In J. McCord (Ed.), *Facts, frameworks, and forecasts: Advances in criminological theory* (Vol. 3, pp. 63–93). New Brunswick, NJ: Transaction Books.

Sampson, R. J. (1997). Collective regulation of adolescent misbehavior: Validation results from eighty Chicago neighborhoods. *Journal of Adolescent Research, 12,* 227–244.

Sampson, R. J. (1999). What "community" supplies. In R. F. Ferguson & W. T. Dickens (Eds.), *Urban problems and community development* (pp. 241–292). Washington, DC: Brookings Institution Press.

Sampson, R. J., & Groves, W. B. (1989). Community structure and crime: Testing social-disorganization theory. *American Journal of Sociology, 94,* 774–780.

Sampson, R. J., & Morenoff, J. (1997). Ecological perspectives on the neighborhood context of urban poverty: Past and present. In J. Brooks-Gunn, G. J. Duncan, & J. L. Aber (Eds.), *Neighborhood poverty: Policy implications in studying neighborhoods* (Vol. 2, pp. 1–22). New York: Russell Sage Foundation Press.

Sampson, R. J., Morenoff, J., & Earls, F. (1999). Beyond social capital: Spatial dynamics of collective efficacy for children. *American Sociological Review, 64,* 633–660.

Sampson, R. J., Raudenbush, S. W., & Earls, F. (1997). Neighborhoods and violent crime: A multilevel study of collective efficacy. *Science, 277,* 918–924.

Shaw, C., & McKay, H. (1942). *Juvenile delinquency and urban areas.* Chicago: University of Chicago Press.

Simons, R. L., Johnson, C., Beaman, J. J., Conger, R. D., & Whitbeck, L. B. (1996). Parents and peer group as mediators of the effect of community structure on adolescent behavior. *American Journal of Community Psychology, 24,* 145–171.

South, S. J., & Baumer, E. P. (2000). Deciphering community and race effects on adolescent premarital childbearing. *Social Forces, 78*(4), 1379–1408.

South, S. J., & Baumer, E. P. (2001). Community effects on the resolution of adolescent premarital pregnancy. *Journal of Family Issues, 22*(8), 1025–1043.

South, S. J., & Crowder, K. D. (1999). Neighborhood effects of family formation: Concentrated poverty and beyond. *American Sociological Review, 64,* 113–132.

Spencer, M. B., McDermott, P. A., Burton, L. M., & Kochman, T. J. (1997). An alternative approach to assessing neighborhood effects on early adolescent achievement and problem behavior. In J. Brooks-Gunn, G. J. Duncan, & J. L. Aber (Eds.), *Neighborhood poverty: Vol. 2. Policy implications in studying neighborhoods* (pp. 145–163). New York: Russell Sage Foundation Press.

Steinberg, L., Fegley, S., & Dornbusch, S. M. (1993). Negative impact of part-time work on adolescent adjustment: Evidence from a longitudinal study. *Developmental Psychology, 29*(2), 171–180.

Steinberg, L., & Morris, A. S. (2001). Adolescent development. *Annual Review of Psychology, 52,* 83–110.

Stiffman, A. R., Hadley-Ives, E., Elze, D., & Johnson, S. (1999). Impact of environment on adolescent mental health and behavior. *American Journal of Orthopsychiatry, 69*(1), 73–86.

Sucoff, C. A., & Upchurch, D. M. (1998). Neighborhood context and the risk of childbearing among metropolitan-area black adolescents. *American Sociological Review, 63,* 571–585.

Sullivan, M. L. (1989). *Getting paid: Youth crime and work in the inner city.* Ithaca, NY: Cornell University Press.

Taylor, R. B., Gottfredson, S., & Brower, S. (1984). Block crime and fear: Defensible space, local social ties, and territorial functioning. *Journal of Research in Crime and Delinquency, 21*(4), 303–331.

Taylor, R. D. (2000). An examination of the association of African American mothers' perceptions of their neighborhoods with their parenting and adolescent adjustment. *Journal of Black Psychology, 26*(3), 267–287.

Teitler, J. O., & Weiss, C. C. (2000). Effects of neighborhood and school environments on transitions to first sexual intercourse. *Sociology of Education, 73,* 112–132.

Tienda, M. (1991). Poor people and poor places: Deciphering neighborhood effects on poverty outcomes. In J. Huber (Ed.), *Macro-micro linkages in sociology* (pp. 244–262). Newbury Park, CA: Sage.

Upchurch, D. M., Sucoff, C. A., & Levy-Storms, L. (1999). Neighborhood and family contexts of adolescent sexual activity. *Journal of Marriage and the Family, 61,* 920–933.

Vandell, D. L., & Shumow, L. (1999). After school child care programs. *Future of Children, 9,* 84–90.

Veysey, B. M., & Messner, S. F. (1999). Further testing of social disorganization theory: An elaboration of Sampson and Groves's "community structure and crime." *Journal of Research in Crime and Delinquency, 36*(2), 156–174.

Willis, P. (1977). *Learning to labor: How working-class kids get working-class jobs.* New York: Columbia.

Wilson, W. J. (1987). *The truly disadvantaged: The inner city, the underclass, and public policy.* Chicago: University of Chicago Press.

Wilson, W. J. (1991). Studying inner-city social dislocations: The challenge of public agenda research. *American Sociological Review, 56*(February), 1–14.

Wilson, W. J. (1997). *When work disappears: The world of the new urban poor.* New York: Alfred A. Knopf.

Chapter 16

ADOLESCENTS AND MEDIA

Donald F. Roberts, Lisa Henriksen, and Ulla G. Foehr

A recent report from the Pew Internet and American Life Project opens with a quote from a 17-year-old boy: "I multi-task every single second I am on line. At this very moment I am watching TV, checking my e-mail every two minutes, reading a newsgroup about who shot JFK, burning some music to a CD and writing this message" (Lenhart, Rainie, & Lewis, 2001, p. 10). To the extent that this young man is typical—and he certainly is not atypical—he is probably doing all of this alone in his bedroom. Before day's end, he will spend a quarter of it (6+ hours) using media, and because of multitasking he will encounter more than 7 hours of media messages. His 13-year-old sister will use media for more than 6.5 hours and will read, watch, listen to, or click on about 8 hours of messages (Roberts & Foehr, in press). Either directly or incidentally, those messages describe, depict, and comment on gods and devils, violence and altruism, love and war, friendship and enmity, politics, professions, beauty, sex, drugs—and almost any other dimension of human concern one can imagine. An incessant hymn to consumerism frames most media messages, and they increasingly emanate from channels designed primarily—if not exclusively—for adolescent audiences.

A long history of concern exists about what (if any) effect all those hours of exposure to messages from outside the family and local community have on our youth (Roberts, 2003; Starker, 1989). Concerns about potentially harmful effects of so-called media messages on youth extend back at least to Plato's banning of storytellers from the Republic. Concerns reappear with the emergence of each new communication technology, most recently in the controversy associated with attempts to control the Internet (e.g., the Communications Decency Act; the Child Online Protection Act).

Given the long history of such concerns, it is surprising that researchers concerned with adolescence have paid relatively little attention to mass media. The previous edition of this Handbook makes almost no mention of media, and until recently few textbooks on adolescent development mentioned the role of media in adolescent lives. Although numerous studies of media use and influence have been conducted with *adolescents,* with one exception (Faber, Brown, & McLeod, 1979), examinations of media and *adolescence*—that is, work considering the role of media in adolescent development and how various aspects of adolescent development influence use of and responses to media—have appeared only recently (Arnett, 1995; Larson, 1995; Roberts, 1993; Steele & Brown, 1995).

This chapter surveys a widely scattered empirical literature on media and adolescents. It focuses on youth from roughly 10 through 20 years old and emphasizes research on television, music, movies, magazines, and the new digital communication technologies. The chapter begins with a summary of research on media use patterns. Attention then turns to several theories that have dominated much of the work on media effects. Finally, we briefly summarize research on media effects in topic areas of particular concern to adolescence: violence and aggression, sex, substance use, and body image.

PATTERNS OF ADOLESCENT MEDIA USE

Amount of Media Use

The second decade of life witnesses significant changes in young people's media use—changes in time devoted to media, in how that time is allocated among media, in the social contexts within which media are consumed, and in the motivations for using media. Table 16.1 summarizes age differences in average daily exposure to the media from a comprehensive national sample survey (Roberts & Foehr, in press; Roberts, Foehr, Rideout, & Brodie, 1999).

Media exposure begins early, increasing fairly rapidly until around 12 or 13 years, when it peaks at slightly less than 8 hours daily. It then declines to just more than 7 hours daily as young people's needs and interests change and as transitions from elementary school to middle school and then to high school substantially alter adolescents' activities and discretionary time. Comstock and his colleagues (Comstock, Chaffee, Katzman, McCombs, & Roberts, 1978) noted a similar curvilinear pattern for television exposure in the late 1970s that persists today; viewing peaks around 3.5 hours daily among 11- to 14-year-olds and then declines to less than 2.5 hours among 15- to 18-year-olds (also see Comstock, 1991). Nevertheless, even with the decline, television dominates young people's overall media exposure until late adolescence, and when time devoted to videotapes and movies is folded in, screen media comprise the largest part of the overall media budget throughout adolescence (J. D. Brown, Childers, Bauman, & Koch, 1990; Roberts & Foehr, in press). Among other things, the amount of time devoted to television probably reflects the fact that two thirds of U.S. 8- to 18-year-olds have a television in their bedroom (Roberts, 2000; Roberts & Foehr, in press; Wartella,

Table 16.1. Average Daily Adolescent Leisure-Time Media Use by Age Group

	8–10 years	11–14 years	15–18 years
Television	3:19	3:30	2:23
Videos (rented & self-recorded)	:46	:43	:37
Movies in theaters	:26	:19	:09
Audio media (radio, CDs, tapes)	:55	1:43	2:38
Print media	:54	:42	:37
Videogames	:31	:26	:21
Computer	:23	:31	:26
Total leisure media	7:13	7:55	7:11

Note. Cell entries are means (hh:mm). Adapted from Roberts & Foehr (in press).

Heintz, Aidman, & Mazzarella, 1990) and that much television exposure consists of monitoring rather than attentive viewing (Comstock & Scharrer, 1999).

Several different, age-related patterns emerge for exposure to other media. Most noteworthy is the steady and substantial increase in adolescents' exposure to what for them are primarily music media—radio and recordings. Music exposure climbs from less than an hour among 8- to 10-year-olds to exceed 2.5 hours daily by late adolescence, ultimately comprising the largest segment of older adolescents' media budget. Indeed, the time youths spend with music and their expressed preference for music media have led several researchers to nominate music as the most important medium during late adolescence (Christenson & Roberts, 1998; Larson, Kubey, & Colletti, 1989; Roberts & Henriksen, 1990; Roe, 1987).

Although the likelihood of engaging in leisure reading on any given day is unrelated to age (about 80% of youths from 8 to 18 years report at least 5 minutes daily engaged in leisure reading), both time spent reading and what is read do vary with age. As teens grow older, higher proportions read newspapers and magazines, but substantially lower proportions devote time to books, likely because of increases in reading for school. The result is that average time devoted to leisure reading overall declines steadily from just under an hour daily among 8- to 10-year-olds to a little more than half an hour among 15- to 18-year-olds (Neuman, 1995; Roberts, 2000; Roberts & Foehr, in press). Exposure to video games and videotapes shows minor fluctuations with age, generally accounting for between 20 and 30 minutes daily, with 15- to 18-year-olds tending to report the lowest levels of exposure. Finally, although at one time or another most U.S. adolescents have used a computer (Kaiser Family Foundation, 2001) and about three quarters of U.S. youths between 12 and 17 years currently go on-line (Lenhart et al., 2001), on any given day no more than half of teenagers use a computer (Lenhart et al., 2001; Roberts & Foehr, in press). The high incidence of nonusers results in relatively low estimates of average computer exposure for the total teenage population—from 20 to 30 minutes daily. On the other hand, youths who use computers on a daily basis (typically but not exclusively teenagers who have access to a personal computer in the home) report more than 50 minutes daily use, with 11- to 14-year-olds reporting almost an hour daily on the computer (Roberts & Foehr, in press). In addition to providing access to an extensive array of information and entertainment via the World Wide Web, computers are rapidly becoming both a primary music channel and a means to play DVDs. As computers assume many of the functions of older media and increasingly serve as an important means of interpersonal communication (Lenhart et al., 2001), more and more adolescents nominate computers as their preferred medium (Knowledge Networks, 2002; Roberts et al., 1999).

Adolescent media exposure varies with a number of background characteristics. Although some research found that adolescent girls devote more time than do boys to television and radio (J. D. Brown, Childers, Bauman, & Koch, 1990), recent data indicate that boys spend more time than do girls watching television, but that girls spend substantially more time than do boys listening to music (Roberts & Foehr, in press). Boys use video games and computers more than girls do, and the gender difference for overall computer use is largely due to time boys spend with computer games (Roberts, Foehr, et al., 1999). Except for time spent with computers, overall media exposure tends to be inversely related to indicators of household socioeconomic status. Youth from higher-income households and those whose parents completed college report less time with television, videos, video games, and music than do peers from lower-income or lower-education homes. However, most of the relationships between media use and indicators of socioeconomic status tend to dissipate, if not disappear, among older adolescents (Roberts & Foehr, in press), likely an indication of increasing independence from family influence. Youth from single-parent homes also spend more time with media in general and television in particular, probably because single parents, who may lack the energy or economic resources to provide alternative activities, are less likely to control media use (J. D. Brown, Childers, Bauman, et al., 1990; Medrich, Roizen, Rubin, & Buckley, 1982; Roberts & Foehr, in press). Race or ethnicity also relates to media exposure. Media exposure among African American 8- to 18-year-olds averages just over 9 hours daily, among Hispanic youths over 8 hours, and among White youths about 7 hours. These relationships largely withstand controls for socioeconomic status. Compared to White adolescents, African American adolescents average 1.5 hours more daily exposure to television and videos.

Comstock (1991; Comstock & Scharrer, 1999) notes that "household television centrality" substantially increases the likelihood that children and adolescents are heavy television viewers. Indicators of television centrality include a household television that operates during most waking hours, norms that permit viewing at all hours and occasions (e.g., during meals), absence of rules regulating viewing, and high levels of viewing among adults. Although each of the various indicators tends to occur more frequently in lower socioeconomic households and in African American households, they are by no means limited to these groups. Even when such factors as race or household socioeconomic status are controlled, adolescents from homes in which television plays a major role view significantly more television (Medrich et al., 1982; Roberts & Foehr, in press). Moreover, subsequent to leaving home for college, a setting in which time to view television is presumably constrained, youth from homes where television had been central continue to view more (Kenny, 1985, reported in Comstock & Scharrer, 1999). In other words, household television centrality appears to cultivate lifelong viewing habits.

Averages, of course, conceal a great deal of information. For any given medium on any given day, adolescents' media exposure ranges from 0 to well over 5 hours. Because personal computers have not yet reached saturation levels, it is not surprising that more than half of U.S. 8- to 18-year-olds report no computer use on a given day as opposed to 14% reporting more than 1 hour daily. On the other hand, given that the typical U.S. household contains three television sets and U.S. youths average more than 3 hours of viewing daily, it may be a bit more unexpected that on any given day, one third of 8- to 18-year-olds watch an hour or less, and fully 20% report *no* television exposure. At the other extreme, more than 20% report in excess of 5 hours daily television viewing, with some claiming as much as 8 or 9 hours of viewing on a given day (Roberts & Foehr, in press). It appears that media use begets media use. When youth classified as light, moderate, or heavy users of one medium are compared on exposure to other media (e.g., when light and heavy television viewers' use of all media *except* television is examined), those classified as heavy users of one medium report from 1 to 2 hours more exposure to the remaining media than do those classified as light or moderate users (Roberts &

Foehr, in press). For example, youth who spend less than 5 hours daily watching television spend 4.5 hours daily with other media, whereas those who report 5 or more hours of daily television viewing are exposed to 5.5 hours of other media content. Several earlier studies also found greater than average amounts of reading among teenagers who watch greater than average amounts of television (California Assessment Program, 1980; Morgan, 1980). Morgan (1980) speculates that high television use and high print use may go hand in hand because heavy users are more interested in media in general. The phenomenon may also derive from greater use of escapist reading material by adolescents who watch a lot of TV (Comstock & Scharrer, 1999), material of the sort that may be compatible with viewing television while reading. The value judgment implicit in the term *escapist* gives pause, but the idea that reading and viewing occur at the same time has merit. Like youth who view a great deal of television, those who read or use computers substantially more than average also use all other media more than do light readers or light computer users. For example, youth who report no computer use are exposed to just over 6.5 hours of other media; those who use computers more than 1 hour daily report 9.5 hours of exposure to other media (Roberts & Foehr, in press). We take such reports as evidence of the growing frequency of media multitasking among adolescents. Value judgments about the nature of the content aside, more than any other medium, the computer facilitates use of several channels simultaneously. As evidenced by the quote that opened this chapter, adolescents surf the web as they stream music, play video games, watch television, or all three. Indeed, it strains credulity to think that the remarkably high amounts of overall media exposure reported by some adolescents could be achieved were it not for such multitasking. The issue remaining to be examined is whether and how such multitasking influences information processing, comprehension, and behavior.

Contexts of Use

Historical and age-related changes in the social context of adolescent media use have implications for both the functions that media serve and their possible consequences. As adolescents grow older, increasingly more of their media consumption occurs either in the presence of peers or siblings or while the adolescent is alone—that is, without adult supervision or guidance.

Television is sometimes described as the most family-oriented medium, and the decline in adolescents' television viewing has been characterized as an indicator of young people's attempts to establish independence from or at least to renegotiate parental controls (Kubey & Csikszentmihalyi, 1990; Larson, 1995; Larson & Kubey, 1983; Larson et al., 1990). However, such characterizations are based on data gathered in the 1980s or earlier, when the bulk of viewing typically occurred around a single household television set, and three networks competed for a family audience. The situation today is quite different. The proliferation of television sets within U.S. households, their migration to young peoples' bedrooms (Roberts, 2000), and industry recognition of adolescents' purchasing power (Pecora, 1998; Teenage Research Unlimited, 2001) has led to niche programming aimed at young audiences, rendering obsolete the notion of television as a family medium. Television may remain the medium most likely to be shared with family, but by the beginning of adolescence, parent-child coviewing is more the exception than the rule. Family sharing of music, movies and video, digital media, and print is even less common.

Sheer time spent with age-mates identifies peer groups as an important context of adolescent behavior, including media behavior. From 12 years onward, more than one third of adolescents watch television mainly in the presence of friends or siblings; almost 60% are mainly with friends or siblings when watching movies or videotapes (Roberts et al., 1999). Group viewing of videotapes is the norm for 9th and 10th graders with access to a VCR (Greenberg & Heeter, 1987). These teenagers are more likely to watch television and rented movies (frequently R-rated) with a girlfriend, boyfriend, or other peers than with parents or alone. Similarly, popular music exposure often occurs in the company of friends—at parties and dances, as a background to interactions, and as grist for the conversation mill (Christenson & Roberts, 1998), and Roe (1985) characterizes popular music listening as "essentially a group phenomenon" (p. 355).

By midadolescence, however, the most typical context for media consumption appears to be the solitude of adolescents' bedrooms. Reading, of course, has always been a solitary pastime, but more and more, adolescents engage most other media while alone. Over 60% of 7th–12th graders claim to be alone when they use computers or play video games. By late adolescence, more than one third state they are "mainly alone" when they watch television, and diary data indicate that more than 40% of all viewing time transpires in solitude (Roberts et al., 1999). Although music listening may be a group phenomenon in that it serves various social functions, by early adolescence most exposure to radio and recordings tends to be solitary and personal (Christenson, 1994; Christenson & Roberts, 1998; Larson & Kubey, 1983).

In short, as youth progress through adolescence, television viewing decreases, music listening and computer use increase, and media tend to migrate to adolescents' bedrooms. Media exposure increasingly occurs when young people are alone or with friends or siblings, another indicator of increasing adolescent independence from family and the importance of both peer groups and solitude as contexts for adolescent development (Christenson & Roberts, 1998; Harris, 1998; Kubey & Csikszentmihalyi, 1990; Larson, 1995; Sang, Schmitz, & Tasche, 1992).

Motivations for Media Use

People use media for many reasons. A long tradition of uses and gratifications research has identified an extensive list of specific objectives satisfied by the media. Such objectives include entertainment, tension relief, staying current with popular culture, learning about the world, sensation seeking, escape from loneliness, and many others (for reviews, see Christenson & Roberts, 1998; Dominick, 1996; Rosengren, Wenner, & Palmgreen, 1985; Rubin, 2002). One of several distillations of the literature suggests five categories of uses and gratifications (Dominick, 1996):

1. *Diversion:* Seeking pleasure, relaxation, escape from boredom or worries, and mood management; this is frequently labeled the entertainment function and tends to dominate adolescents' stated reasons for using media.
2. *Cognition:* Seeking or acquiring information, ranging from monitoring current events via news media to learning the alphabet from Sesame Street or norms for

various aspects of human behavior from entertainment content. It is important to note that much of the information acquired is incidental—neither intentionally sought nor produced to teach or inform (e.g., screen portrayals of violence; so-called thin ideal depictions of women).

3. *Social utility:* Facilitating relationships with family, friends, or desired social groups; a social lubricant; a source of "conversational currency" (Dominick, 1996); an outlet for "parasocial interaction" (i.e., establishing vicarious social relationships with media and people in the media; Horton & Wohl, 1956; Rubin, Perse, & Powell, 1985).
4. *Withdrawal:* Establishing barriers between the self and others to avoid conflict, ensure uninterrupted attention and focus, or simply obtain solitude.
5. *Personal identity:* Helping to establish a sense of self through the auditioning of potential roles and identities; building self-confidence; seeking moral guidance, social acceptance, or status. Although this final category might be distributed across the first four, its clear relevance to the developmental tasks of adolescence argue for keeping it separate (Christenson & Roberts, 1998; McQuail, Blumler, & Brown, 1972).

Both the propensity for different media to gratify these needs and characteristics that influence individual media choices vary substantially. Moreover, gratifications obtained from media are not always those that are sought. Although youth may turn on television simply to have fun or to escape boredom, often they incidentally learn about the latest fashion, confirm or disconfirm existing beliefs or values, experience a change in mood, and so forth. When asked directly, adolescents typically say that they use media for pleasure; to fill time; to relieve boredom and loneliness; and to create, change, or maintain certain moods (Arnett, 1995; Christenson & Roberts, 1998; Wells, 1990). The social uses and meanings that media offer also provide an important key to understanding their role in the lives of adolescents. Media in general and music media in particular serve quasi-social functions for adolescents when used to relieve feelings of loneliness by invoking or replacing absent peers (Gantz, Gartenberg, Pearson, & Schiller, 1978; Larson et al., 1989; Roe, 1984). In addition, solitary listening may provide social capital helpful in earning status with peers; pop music experts tend to have more friends and enjoy enhanced social status (Adoni, 1978; R. Brown & O'Leary, 1971).

MEDIA AND ADOLESCENT DEVELOPMENT

Attempts to integrate developmental theory with research on media use and effects generally proceed from either or both of two fundamental concepts. One concerns the importance of an array of tasks or issues that adolescents engage on their way to adulthood. The second views adolescence as a period of psychological fragmentation associated with, among other things, exploration of a variety of potential selves. Ultimately, more or less consciously, adolescents construct their own evolving worldviews and an assortment of attitudes, beliefs, and behaviors that define each individual.

Theories of adolescent development typically recognize a number of tasks or issues that adolescents must resolve (Conger & Peterson, 1985; Feldman & Elliot, 1990; Violato & Holden, 1987) and that may come into focus at different times for different youth (Coleman, 1993). Regardless of when adolescents confront a particular developmental issue, uncertainty associated with the task engenders a need for relevant information. Intense focus on an issue and "lived experience" (i.e., a construct that encompasses the ways in which background variables, developmental status, and other factors "differentiate one person's experience of day-to-day occurrences from that of another"; J. D. Brown, 2000, p. 36) interact to influence how any particular message is interpreted. Thus, depending on the issue with which they are engaged, two teenagers may derive quite different meanings and gratifications from the same entertainment television program. For example, adolescent girls interpreted and responded to sexual media content differently depending on whether they had not yet confronted, were confronting, or had already confronted the issue of sex and sexuality (J. D. Brown, White, & Nikopoulou, 1993).

Central among adolescent tasks is identity formation—that is, defining the self in terms of attributes displayed across multiple roles or personae (e.g., academic, athletic, romantic, sexual, identity in relation to parents, peers, community, etc.; J. D. Brown, 2000; Harter, 1990a, 1990b; Larson, 1995). Each of the myriad decisions adolescents face (e.g., how to behave on a date, whether to study, to take drugs, to go to college, what occupation to pursue) adds to their continually evolving lived experience (J. D. Brown, 2000) and contributes to values, beliefs, and goals that guide future behaviors (Harter, 1999; Marcia, 1980); all of this points to adolescence as a period of rapid change and attendant uncertainty, conditions long associated with increased information seeking (Berlyne, 1965). The uncertainty inherent in adolescence emerges just when parental controls on information seeking in general and media use in particular begin to weaken. Therefore, adolescents increasingly take control of their own information and media choices. Finally, contemporary media often address highly salient topics (i.e., sex, drugs, and the many facets of pop culture) that parents and other adults are likely to ignore, avoid, or know relatively little about. Thus, media emerge, almost by default, as potentially powerful sources of information for adolescents who are self-socializing to the adult world (Arnett, 1995; J. D. Brown, 2000; Christenson & Roberts, 1998; Larson, 1995; Roberts, 1993).

As young people construct their identity, they may use media to relieve anxiety about developmental changes, explore alternative solutions to problems, reinforce the choices they make, or—perhaps most important—reflect on who they are and who they may become. Most exploration of potential selves occurs in solitude, when adolescents explore their private selves. Because much of contemporary Western adolescents' private (solitary) time occurs in the presence of mass media and because media content touches on most adolescent issues and depicts a wide array of potential roles and personae, several scholars argue that media are increasingly important socialization agents for contemporary youth (Arnett, 1995; J. D. Brown, 2000; Larson, 1995; Roberts, 1993; Steele & Brown, 1995; Strouse & Fabes, 1985).

Theoretical Approaches to Media Effects

Regardless of age or developmental status, three theoretical approaches most frequently applied to media effects research are cultivation theory (Gerbner, Gross, Morgan, Signorielli, & Shanahan, 2002); social cognitive theory, particularly as it applies to observational learning (Bandura, 1986, 2002); and various conceptualizations of schematic information processing (Berkowitz, 1990; Berkowitz & Rogers, 1986; Fiske & Taylor, 1991; Shank & Abelson, 1977; Shrum, 2002; Zillmann, 2002).

Cultivation theory posits (a) that mass media systems in general and television in particular present highly uniform pictures of the world that tend to conceal their biased and selective nature (e.g., television's world is more violent than the real world); (b) that most people consume media nonselectively; and (c) that high exposure cultivates acceptance of the media's view of the world (Gerbner et al., 2002; Morgan, 1988). Cultivation research is dominated by correlational studies relating amount of television exposure to beliefs and attitudes characteristic of the television view of the world. For example, subsequent to documenting that television portrays the world as a mean and scary place, Gerbner and his associates found that adolescents who viewed a lot of television were substantially more likely than were light viewers to report being afraid to walk alone in the city at night. Heavy viewers also overestimated both the percentage of people involved in violence and the frequency with which police use violence (Gerbner, Gross, Signorielli, Morgan, & Jackson-Beeck, 1979).

Fundamental questions regarding the legitimacy of many of the causal inferences drawn from cultivation studies have been raised (e.g., Comstock, 1991; Hirsch, 1980, 1981; Potter, 1993; Shrum, 1995). Nevertheless, numerous cultivation studies indicate a strong association between amount of exposure and acceptance of television's worldview even when relevant third variables are controlled, and these studies identify a variety of moderating conditions that influence these consequences (Gerbner, Gross, Morgan, & Signorielli, 1980; Hawkins & Pingree, 1980; Shanahan & Morgan, 1999; Signorielli & Morgan, 1990).

Media research employing social cognitive theory's conceptualization of observational learning focuses on cognitive and psychological processes as they relate to how media portrayals influence learning and performance of observed behavior. According to social cognitive theory, when people pay attention to and think about information from media (or from elsewhere), they acquire new or modify existing mental representations. What is observed, learned, or performed depends in part on characteristics of the modeled display (e.g., Is the behavior rewarded? Is it performed by an attractive model?). The display's influence on learning also depends on characteristics of the observer (e.g., gender, race, preexisting attitudes and experience, current needs and emotional states, etc.). Learned symbolic representations may serve to guide subsequent behavior, depending on a variety of factors (e.g., opportunity, perceived appropriateness, expectations of reinforcement, feelings of self-efficacy, etc.; Bandura, 1986, 2002). Thus, for example, relative to youths who see a model punished for aggressive behavior, those who see aggressive behavior either rewarded or eliciting no consequences subsequently behave more aggressively (Bandura et al., 1963b), depending on subsequent conditions.

Various approaches to schematic information processing concern (a) how the mental representations (schemas, scripts, etc.) people store in memory influence social judgments (Fiske & Taylor, 1991; Shank & Abelson, 1977), (b) factors influencing schema accessibility (Berkowitz, 1990; Sanbonmatsu & Fazio, 1991), and (c) factors implicated in the development of schema, with some recent attention to the role played by media (Roskos-Ewoldsen, Roskos-Ewoldsen, & Carpentier, 2002; Shrum, 2002; Zillmann, 2002). Media scholars have long held that to some degree one's prior mental representation of the world influences interpretation of new information (e.g., Schramm, 1971). Schema theories predict which mental constructs are brought to mind, and the degree to which they influence interpretation and judgment depends on the nature of the portrayal in relation to individual and contextual factors. For example, for one person a depicted knife fight might elicit thoughts primarily associated with violence or aggression, ranging from shouting matches to gunfights to scenes of war. For another person or for the same person under different conditions, the portrayed knife fight might elicit primarily thoughts of pain, fear, flight, and the nature of victims. Interpretation of the portrayal varies depending on the degree to which either of the two schemas is primed—that is, brought into focal awareness and used to interpret the scene. Additionally, the act of attending and interpreting may also influence subsequent accessibility of whatever schema a portrayal implicates. Thus, individuals who see the knife fight scene are more likely than are those who do not to interpret a subsequent, ambiguous scene or event as aggressive (or fearful). To the extent that schemas are primed, judgments about media content are affected; to the extent that media content is attended to, schemas are primed and accessibility of associated schemas is affected.

Although not exclusively and not always explicitly, these general theoretical approaches underlie much of the research about media effects on adolescents' (and others') perceptions, attitudes, and behaviors.

MEDIA EFFECTS ON ADOLESCENTS

The following review briefly summarizes the research literature concerning adolescents and media effects on violence and aggression, sexual beliefs and behavior, body image, and substance use. These topics were chosen because they represent areas of public concern and areas of research that demonstrate the influence of media in adolescent lives.

Violence and Aggression

Although criticisms of content analyses of violent media content abound (Potter, 2002), there is little question that portrayals of violence are a mainstay of media content, particularly for television and film (e.g., Gerbner & Gross, 1976; Gerbner et al., 1979; Gerbner et al., 1980). A recent examination of a representative week of U.S. television programming across 23 channels during each of 3 years (1994–1997), based on approximately 2,700 hours of material each year, found that more than 60% of entertainment programs portray some violence, and that almost a third of those programs feature nine or more violent interactions (Smith et al., 1998). More important is that violence is largely portrayed in ways that experimental research has demonstrated are likely to increase viewers' learning of, desensitization to, and fear of aggressive behavior. For example, television violence is seldom punished, frequently justified, and often performed by attractive characters—all contextual variables demonstrated to affect learning, desensitization, or fear in potentially undesirable ways (Smith et al., 1998).

Concern with effects of media violence on youth dates at least from early 20th-century criticisms of pulp fiction, penny westerns, and silent films (Starker, 1989). Some of the first empirical research on media effects of any sort examined young adolescents' responses to violent motion pictures (Charters, 1933; Peterson & Thurston, 1933). It was not until the early 1960s, however, that two seminal experiments demonstrated that exposure to audiovisual violence increased children's (Bandura et al., 1963a) and adolescents' (Berkowitz & Rawlings, 1963) aggressive responses. These studies sparked a torrent of empirical research on youth and media violence (for reviews, see Comstock, 1991; Comstock & Scharrer, 1999; Potter, 2002; Strasburger & Wilson, 2002). Since that time, numerous laboratory experiments have documented a short-term, causal relationship between young people's exposure to media violence and subsequent aggressiveness, desensitization, and fear (Cline, Croft, & Courrier, 1973; Linz, Donnerstein, & Penrod, 1984, 1988). Additionally, correlational research has consistently shown positive associations between amount of violence viewing, both aggressive attitudes and behaviors (e.g., Belson, 1978; McIntyre & Teevan, 1972), and perceptions of a "mean and scary world" (Gerbner et al., 1979). Although such synchronous correlations preclude causal inferences, several longitudinal studies, at least one of which spanned more than 20 years (Huesmann, 1986; Huesmann & Eron, 1986), have demonstrated that heavy viewing of television violence during the early years predicts subsequent aggressiveness—even criminal behavior—in the adolescent and early adult years. Finally meta-analyses that estimate an effect size from numerous studies report causal links between violence viewing and subsequent aggression accounting for as much as 10% of the variance (Bushman & Anderson, 2001; Hearold, 1986; Paik & Comstock, 1994).

Meta-analyses indicate that that violence viewing produces more pronounced and measurable effects among young children than among adolescents (Comstock & Scharrer, 1999), probably because older youths are more socialized to avoid aggression and have better impulse control. Nevertheless, numerous studies find that exposure to symbolic violence increases adolescents' aggressive beliefs, attitudes, and behaviors. These studies include experimental demonstrations that exposure to violent music videos decreased adolescents' disapproval of violence (Greeson & Williams, 1986; Hansen & Hansen, 1990; Johnson, Jackson, & Gatto, 1995) and that watching a brutal beating portrayed as vengeful increased college students' willingness to administer shocks to another student (Berkowitz & Alioto, 1973), as well as cross-sectional and longitudinal surveys that yield consistently positive associations between adolescents' violence viewing and serious aggressive behavior (Belson, 1978; Huesmann, Eron, Lefkowitz, & Wilder, 1984).

Extensive reviews of the hundreds of empirical studies of youth and media violence (Comstock, 1991; also see Comstock & Scharrer, 1999; Potter, 2002) point to three major generalizations about young people's responses to symbolic violence. First, media depictions of violence affect behavior by influencing the development of cognitive schemas that serve as rough guides to action depending on cues operating in some subsequent situation. Second, susceptibility to a given portrayal varies dramatically as a function of individual experiences, abilities, needs, interests, emotional states, and so forth—a constellation of variables similar to Brown's concept of lived experience (J. D. Brown, 2000; Steele & Brown, 1995). Third, a wide array of message characteristics affect individual interpretations of a given depiction. Comstock (1991) characterizes them as affecting the degree to which a behavior is perceived as efficacious (e.g., is the act rewarded, punished, successful, useful?), normative (e.g., is the act justified or congruent with accepted social norms?), or pertinent (e.g., is the act familiar, useful, important to the viewer, or relevant to conditions the viewer is likely to encounter?).

Recently, violent electronic games have received attention, particularly the highly realistic and graphic games of the past decade. Although electronic games share many of the same attributes as other forms of audiovisual violence, they are different in several important ways. One is the potential to engage players deeply, possibly to the point that immersion in electronic games leads to altered states during which rational thought is suspended and highly arousing aggressive scripts are increasingly likely to be learned (Glickson & Avnon, 1997; Moneta & Csikszentmihalyi, 1996). Another is the extent that rewards for violent behavior in video games are experienced directly rather than vicariously—that is, television viewers witness on-screen characters receive reinforcements for their actions, but game players win points (rewards) contingent on their actions (Provenzo, 1991). Studies of effects of electronic games yield mixed results. Correlational evidence suggests that adolescents with more violent electronic game experience produce more aggressive responses than do youngsters with less experience (Cohn, 1995). Surveys also find that high use of electronic games is related to more delinquent behavior and more aggressive personality styles (Anderson & Dill, 2000), and that game players receive higher teacher ratings of aggressiveness (Fling et al., 1992). Experiments have not demonstrated increased aggressive behavior subsequent to playing violent games, but some evidence suggests that violent games engender increased feelings of aggression and hostility (Anderson & Bushman, 2001; Dill & Dill, 1998), decreased empathy, and stronger proviolence attitudes (Funk, Buchman, Schimming, & Hagen, 1998). From their comprehensive meta-analysis, Anderson and Bushman (2001) conclude that "playing violent video games increases aggression in males and females, in children and adults, in experimental and non-experimental settings" (p. 358).

The conclusions of recent reviews of research on the impact of media violence on youth are chilling. Taken together, hundreds of relevant studies representing different assumptions, different approaches, and different weaknesses and strengths offer convincing evidence of a causal link between exposure to media violence and various antisocial outcomes (i.e., increased aggressiveness, increased acceptance of violence, decreased sensitivity to others' suffering). The connection is as strong for serious delinquent behavior (e.g., violent assault) as for milder acts (e.g., hostile questionnaire responses; Comstock, 1991). Indeed, Bushman and Anderson (2001) show that the strength of the media violence-aggression link is almost as strong as that between smoking and cancer and is stronger than for such largely unquestioned causal linkages as those between condom use and decreased risk of HIV or between amount of homework and academic achievement. In short, although media violence is only one of several contributors to antisocial consequences among adolescents, solid evidence demonstrates that for some adolescents under some conditions, exposure to symbolic violence plays a significant causal role.

It is noteworthy that the more limited research literatures focused on other behavioral domains suggest that key findings on media influence from the violence literature may also apply to a greater or lesser extent to aspects of adolescent socialization related to sex and sexuality, body image, and health-related decisions concerning tobacco, alcohol, and illicit drug use.

Sexual Beliefs and Behavior

Concern about the influence of sex-related information and portrayals competes closely with concern about media violence. One of the major developmental tasks of adolescence is adjusting to sexually maturing bodies and feelings (Simpson, 2001). Intrinsically challenging in itself, the task is further complicated when the sensitive nature of the topic diminishes open communication between adolescents and parents or other adults. The potential for media influence is strengthened—often by default—in the absence of other socializing influences. Today's youth have unprecedented access to entertainment media featuring abundant, widely varied, on-demand information concerning sex and sexual behavior. Adolescents' high levels of exposure make both incidental and intentional learning about sex from media virtually inevitable.

The sheer quantity of sexual themes in mainstream media is noteworthy. Recent content analyses find that sexual media content has become more frequent and more explicit over time (J. D. Brown, Childers, & Waszak, 1990; Buerkel-Rothfuss, 1993). Most analyses of sexual content have focused on television. Recently, more than half of a representative sample of all television shows contained sexual content, and sexual scenes exceeded three per hour (Kunkel et al., 1999). Two thirds of prime-time television shows contained sexual content. However, this study defined sexual content broadly, and much of this content was talk about sex or concerned such behaviors as passionate kissing, flirting, and intimate touching. Sexual intercourse was depicted or strongly implied in just 7% of shows. Many other studies speak to the same point—sex on television is abundant whether one looks at popular teen shows (Cope-Farrar & Kunkel, 2002; Ward, 1995), prime-time television (Kunkel, Cope, & Colvin, 1996; Kunkel et al., 1999), soap operas (Greenberg & Buselle, 1996; Greenberg & Woods, 1999), talk shows (Greenberg, Sherry, Busselle, Hnilo, & Smith, 1997), or music videos (Baxter, De Riemer, Landini, Leslie, & Singletary, 1985; Sherman & Dominick, 1986), but depictions of intercourse are relatively infrequent.

As important as its *quantity* is how sexual content is depicted. Generally, television portrays sex as pleasurable and carefree, rarely referring to associated risks, responsibilities, or consequences (Greenberg & Buselle, 1996; Greenberg & Woods, 1999; Kunkel et al., 1999). Popular teen shows are more likely than others to portray the risks and consequences of sexual activity (Kunkel et al., 1999), but recent work suggests that although programs with teenage characters often depict emotional or social consequences of sex (e.g., humiliation, disappointment, guilt, anxiety, rejection), physical consequences (e.g., unwanted pregnancy, STDs) are far less common (Aubrey, 2002). Female characters are more likely to experience negative consequences than are male characters. Sex on television most often occurs between unmarried partners (Greenberg, Graef, Fernandez-Collado, Korzenny, & Atkin, 1980; Sapolsky & Taberlet, 1991). About half of characters engaging in sexual contact have an established romantic relationship with each other, a quarter know each other but have no romantic relationship, and 16% have just met (Kunkel et al., 1999). Most characters engaging in intercourse are over the age of 25, almost a quarter are young adults (ages 18–24), and 9% are under 18 (Kunkel et al., 1999).

Other media also offer abundant information about sex. A preponderance of stories in women's and teen magazines deal with sexual issues. A study of teen magazines found that among feature articles, stories about interpersonal relations were most frequent and were dominated by topics such as dating and heterosexuality (Evans, Rutberg, Sather, & Turner, 1991). From 1986 to 1996 teen magazines dramatically increased space devoted to sexual content and slightly increased space devoted to sexual health topics (Walsh-Childers, Gotthoffer, & Lepre, 2002). Proportionally, today's teen magazines are about equally likely to feature stories about sex or sexual health. Women's magazines, however, offer more stories about sex than about sexual health.

Over the past few decades, popular music lyrics have emphasized sex over romance and have become increasingly explicit (Carey, 1969; Christenson & Roberts, 1998; Fedler, Hall, & Tanzi, 1982). Music videos in particular contain substantial sexual imagery (Baxter, De Riemer, Landini, Leslie, & Singletary, 1985), and often the sexual images are paired with violence (Sherman & Dominick, 1986). Sexual themes are also prevalent in popular R-rated movies, in which sex acts are more frequent and more explicit than on television (Greenberg et al., 1993).

Although the issue has been the focus of a great deal of public concern, little empirical research exists describing sexual content on the Internet. Cooper (1998) suggests that sex is the most searched topic on the Internet. Of course, *sex* refers to different things in different contexts (e.g., gender, biology, pornography, etc.), confounding researchers' attempts to catalog sexual content. Regardless of the true volume of on-line sexual content, a great deal is readily accessible—even when one is not looking for it. Seventy percent of 15- to 17-year-old computer users reported inadvertently encountering pornographic content on-line (Kaiser Family Foundation, 2001). Whether exposure is intentional or inadvertent and whether exposure is sought for the purpose of acquiring knowledge, exploring alternatives, or experiencing pornography, the Internet has emerged as a significant resource for sex-related content.

Clearly, when adolescents use media, incidental exposure to substantial amounts of information about sex frequently occurs. In addition, media also rank among adolescents' most important sources (along with school health classes, peers, and parents) when they seek sexual information intentionally (Sutton, Brown, Wilson, & Klein, 2002). Research indicates that adolescents seek sexual information from television (J. D. Brown et al., 1993; Greenberg & Linsangan, 1993; Kaiser Family Foundation, MTV, & Teen People, 1999; Kaiser Family Foundation & YM Magazine, 1996; Sutton, Brown, Wilson, & Klein, 2002), magazines (Kaiser Family Foundation & YM Magazine, 1998), and the Internet (Kaiser Family Foundation, 2001). Not only do teens use the Internet to find information about sex, but some adolescent girls are also using their personal home pages as tools for sexual self-expression (Stern, 2002). In short, a growing body of research shows that sexual content is readily available in media messages and that adolescents are exposed to those messages both incidentally and intentionally.

A few studies, most focused on television, movies, or music videos, have examined effects of exposure to such content; for the most part these studies explore the relationship between exposure to various kinds of sexual portrayals and adolescents' sexual attitudes, knowledge, or expectations. Both correlational and experimental studies link exposure to sexual content on television to more insouciant views of sex and sexuality. In one experiment, 13- to 14-year-old boys and girls who watched 15 hours of prime-time shows depicting sexual relations between unmarried partners rated sexual improprieties as significantly less objectionable than did viewers of sexual portrayals between married partners or viewers of nonsexual relationships (Bryant & Rockwell, 1994). Exposure to sexual content has also been related to more permissive attitudes toward premarital sex (Greeson & Williams, 1987; Strouse, Buerkel-Rothfuss, & Long, 1995) and more recreational attitudes toward sex (Ward, 2002; Ward & Rivadeneyra, 1999). Additionally, heavy television viewers are more likely to have negative attitudes toward remaining a virgin (Courtright & Baran, 1980). A few studies have looked at sexual expectations and knowledge in relation to television exposure. They find that specially designed programs led to increased knowledge and acquisition of related terms (Greenberg, Perry, & Covert, 1983) and that television exposure was related to expectations of higher frequency of sexual behaviors in the real world (Buerkel-Rothfuss & Strouse, 1993; Ward & Rivadeneyra, 1999) and in some cases to decreased sexual satisfaction (Baran, 1976). Studies examining the effects of exposure to sexually explicit films report similar results: greater acceptance of sexual infidelity and promiscuity (Zillman, 1994), reduced disapproval of rape (J. D. Brown, Childers, & Waszak, 1990; Zillman & Bryant, 1982), and less satisfaction with intimate partners (Zillman & Bryant, 1988).

The few studies that have attempted to link exposure to sexual media content with sexual behavior have produced mixed results. According to J. D. Brown and Newcomer (1991), teens who watched more sexual television content were more likely to have had sexual intercourse than were teens who watched less sexual content. Other research has identified a positive relationship between viewing sexual content (music videos and soap operas) and reported sexual activity (Strouse et al., 1995; Strouse & Buerkel-Rothfuss, 1993) and between adolescents' reading of sports or music magazines and increased likelihood of engaging in risky behaviors, including sexual intercourse (Klein, Brown, Childers, Oliveri, Porter, & Dykers, 1993). Although television exposure predicts young people's sexual attitudes and expectations, it is not a consistent predictor of sexual behavior (Ward & Rivadeneyra, 1999). Indeed, longitudinal research found that neither amount nor content of television viewed predicted early initiation of intercourse among young adolescents (Peterson, Moore, & Furstenberg, 1991), although the viewing measures have been criticized (Huston, Wartella, & Donnerstein, 1998).

Finally, some work suggests that teens use sexually explicit media acquired through alternative channels (Bryant, 1985; Buerkel-Rothfuss, Strouse, Pettey, & Shatzer, 1993). Research on responses to pornographic content, primarily conducted with college students (over 18 years old), has found serious negative consequences of exposure to sexually explicit content. Zillmann (2000) explored the influence of extended exposure to sexually explicit material and cited such effects as habituation, distorted perceptions of sexual activity in the populace, diminished trust in intimate partners, and evaluation of promiscuity as the natural state.

Although research on media effects regarding sexual content is not as extensive as that on violent content, indications are that media may play a comparatively more important role in shaping adolescents' beliefs about, attitudes toward, and behaviors related to sex. When all media are considered, the amount and variety of content related to sex easily equals and may well surpass the amount related to violence. More important is that there is a period in virtually every adolescent's life when he or she is likely to be intensely focused on information about sex. Furthermore, perhaps most important is that the sensitive nature of the issue and ensuing reluctance of many adults to discuss sex with adolescents, in combination with the ubiquitous and private nature of sexual content available in media, have given media an important role in sexual socialization almost by default.

Body Image

As with other areas in which social concerns have fueled studies of media influence on adolescents, the issue of body image has gained attention because of its importance to adolescents' physical and emotional health and because of the quantity and nature of relevant information to be found in mainstream media. Sociocultural explanations for the development of body image disturbance and eating disorders accord media—particularly television and fashion magazines—an influential role (Cash & Pruzinsky, 2002; Thompson & Smolak, 2001). The media's pervasive and largely unattainable standards of weight and beauty tend to complicate adolescents' task of developing and maintaining a positive body image. Most of the research in this area focuses on young women because they exhibit higher rates of body dissatisfaction and eating disorders than do young men (van Hoeken, Lucas, & Hoek, 1998). However, popular media also convey stereotypes of the ideal male body, with similarly negative consequences for adolescent males (see Labre, 2002).

Much of the concern about media influence on body image focuses on the advertising and editorial content of fashion magazines (Evans, Rutberg, Sather, & Turner, 1991; Malkin, Wornian, & Chrisler, 1999; Nemeroff, Stein, Stiehl, & Smilack, 1994). Not surprisingly, content analyses of body depictions in magazines suggest that thinness and weight loss are highly rewarded (Owen & Laurel-Seller, 2000; Silverstein, Perdue, Peterson, & Kelly, 1986; Wiseman, Gray, Mosimann, & Ahrens, 1992). A thin ideal of feminine beauty also dominates television, where underweight women are overrepresented in comparison to the general population (Fouts & Burggraff, 1999, 2000) and a preponderance of commercials tout the benefits of weight loss and beauty aids (Downs & Harrison, 1985).

Several studies document associations between teenagers' media use and their concerns about weight and body image (for review, see British Medical Association, 2000; Thompson, Heinberg, Altabe, & Tantleff-Dunn, 1999). For example, girls' body dissatisfaction is positively correlated with their watching soap operas, music videos (Tiggemann & Pickering, 1996), and television programs featuring thin main characters (Botta, 1999; Harrison, 2001), as well as with reading fashion magazines at least twice a week (Field et al., 1999) and reading magazines that feature thin models and dieting information (Harrison & Cantor, 1997).

Controlled experiments typically compare the effects of seeing magazine ads with ultrathin or average-size models on ratings of body satisfaction or physical attractiveness. A particularly novel example randomly assigned female undergraduates to wait in a room with either fashion or news magazines to peruse before completing a questionnaire about dieting (Turner, Hamilton, Jacobs, Angood, & Dwyer, 1997). Those who read fashion magazines expressed greater dissatisfaction with their weight and greater fear of getting fat than did those who read news magazines. A meta-analysis of 43 effect sizes gleaned from 25 controlled experiments demonstrated a small but relatively consistent effect on the body image of girls and women, indicating lower body satisfaction after viewing thin media images than after viewing images of average-size models, plus-size models, or inanimate objects (Groesz, Levine, & Murnen, 2002). Such effects were greater among younger women (not yet in college) and among those with initially low levels of body satisfaction.

Considering how much more time adolescents devote to television than to magazines, surprisingly few experiments examine effects of a thin ideal portrayed on television. Five out of six experiments that compared the effects of appearance-related commercials with other commercials reported adverse effects on at least some participants. Girls and women exposed to appearance-related commercials (or commercials that depict women as sex objects) expressed greater anger, anxiety, and depression (Cattarin, Thompson, Thomas, & Williams, 2000; Hargreaves & Tiggemann, 2002; Heinberg & Thompson, 1995); reported lower body satisfaction (Hargreaves & Tiggemann, 2002; Heinberg & Thompson, 1995; Lavine, Sweeney, & Wagner, 1999); rated beauty characteristics as being more important to attract the opposite sex (Tan, 1979); and reported a greater tendency to compare themselves with models in the ads (Cattarin et al., 2000). However, when sorority members were exposed to product commercials rated as either highly body-image or neutral-image oriented, the body-image commercials reduced body size overestimations and made young women feel less depressed (Myers & Biocca, 1992).

Evidence from controlled experiments has been criticized on several counts (Levine & Smolak, 1996; Thompson et al., 1999). The effects of brief exposure on body image may be short-lived and confined to conditions that do not reflect adolescents' everyday experiences with the media. Moreover, the method is ill suited to test the effects of cumulative exposure to thin-ideal media. To address such concerns, Stice and his colleagues randomly assigned adolescent girls to a 15-month subscription for *Seventeen* magazine or to a no-subscription condition (Stice, Spangler, & Agras, 2001). Although the subscribers spent more time reading *Seventeen* than did the comparison group (21 vs. 15 total hours), the study found no main effects for the magazine subscription on any outcome. Among girls who lacked adequate social support, however, the manipulation increased body dissatisfaction, dieting behaviors, and bulimic symptoms, and it increased negative affect among girls with initially high body dissatisfaction. Thus, among particularly vulnerable adolescents, long-term exposure to thin-ideal images in the media may have enduring effects.

Observations of adolescent girls' reactions to the introduction of television to Fiji also provides evidence about the impact of prolonged exposure to television on body image disturbance and eating pathology (Becker, 1995; Becker, Burwell, Gilman, Herzog, & Hamburg, 2002). For example, self-reported vomiting to control weight, which was nonexistent at baseline, increased to 11.3% three years after television was introduced (Becker et al., 2002). Three years after the introduction of television in 1995, the proportion of teen girls with abnormally high scores on a questionnaire about disordered eating more than doubled, and girls who lived in households with a television set were three times more likely to have abnormally high scores than were girls without such access. In stark contrast to a pretelevision norm that endorsed a robust appetite and body size, 74% of girls reported feeling "too big or fat" and 69% said they had dieted to lose weight after television's introduction.

The degree to which individuals accept or internalize socially defined standards for weight and beauty, referred to as thin-ideal internalization, is an important mediator of the relationship between media exposure and disturbances in body image as well as eating-dieting behaviors (Thompson et al., 1999). Various measures of this construct assess the extent to which individuals wish to look like fashion models or media celebrities, compare their own body to media figures, and use the media to learn about what is attractive (Cusamano & Thompson, 2001; Heinberg, Thompson, & Stormer, 1995; Thompson & Stice, 2001). For example, wanting to look like people portrayed in media is among the strongest predictors of adolescents' concerns about weight (Field et al., 2001; Taylor et al., 1998) and greatly increases the odds of becoming a constant dieter (Field et al., 2001). In addition, thin-ideal internalization mediated the relationship between eating disorder symptoms and exposure to ideal body images in magazines and television (Stice, Schupak-Neuberg, Shaw, & Stein, 1994).

Interventions that teach young women to be more critical consumers of media have been effective in reducing thin-ideal internalization (Irving, DuPen, & Berel, 1998; Thompson & Heinberg, 1999) and in mitigating the impact of media images on body dissatisfaction (Posavac, Posavac, & Weigel, 2001). Future research should consider how media education may be tailored to suit the needs of various age, gender, and ethnic groups. In addition, the evidence for media effects on adolescent body image would be strengthened by moving research from cross-sectional, experimental to longitudinal, observational methods. Such data would permit stronger causal inferences about the effect of these messages on adolescents' perceptions, attitudes, and behaviors.

Tobacco, Alcohol, and Illicit Drug Use

Much of the research on media influence on adolescent substance use addresses public concern about widespread promotion of tobacco and alcohol. In 1997, the most recent year for which comparative data are available, the tobacco industry spent $549 million on print and outdoor ads and $432,000 on the Internet (Federal Trade Commission [FTC], 2002); the alcohol industry spent $1.1. billion on traditional advertising (television, radio, print, and outdoor) and $1 million on the Internet (FTC, 1999). Not included in these expenditures are the costs to feature products, logos, or signs in movies, television programs, and music videos. Product placement is forbidden for cigarette manufacturers but commonplace for the alcohol industry. In 1997–1998, the alcohol industry arranged product placements in 233 movies and 181 television series, including 8 of the 15 shows most popular with teens (FTC, 1999).

Although the tobacco and alcohol industries deny targeting consumers who are too young to buy their products, advertising makes smoking and drinking more appealing to youth (for reviews, see U.S. Department of Health and Human Services, 1994; Strasburger, 2002). Advertising accounts for 34% of experimentation with cigarettes (Pierce, Gilpin, & Choi, 1999) and 10–30% of adolescents' alcohol use (Atkin, 1993; Gerbner, 1990). Young people are attracted to tobacco advertising and promotions (Fischer, Schwartz, Richards, Goldstein, & Rojas, 1991; U.S. Department of Health and Human Services, 1994), and the vast majority of adolescent smokers prefer the most heavily advertised brands (Barker, 1994; Pierce et al., 1991; Pierce et al., 1999). Numerous studies reveal that young smokers recognize and know more about cigarette advertisements than do their nonsmoking peers (Aitken & Eadie, 1990; Aitken, Leathar, & O'Hagan, 1985; Aitken, Leathar, O'Hagan, & Squair, 1987; Chapman & Fitzgerald, 1982; Goldstein, Fischer, Richards, & Creten, 1987; Klitzner, Gruenewald, & Bamberger, 1991).

In addition, greater intentions to smoke are associated with exposure to and knowledge of cigarette advertising (Altman, Levine, Coeytaux, Slade, & Jaffe, 1996; E. M. Botvin, Botvin, Michela, Baker, & Filazzola, 1991; G. Botvin, Goldberg, Botvin, & Dusenbury, 1993; Gilpin, Pierce, & Rosbrook, 1997; Unger, Johnson, & Rohrbach, 1995). A few prospective studies demonstrate a causal role for tobacco advertising in the uptake of smoking (Aitken, Eadie, Hastings, & Haywood, 1991; Biener & Siegel, 2000; Dobson, Woodward, & Leeder, 1992; Pierce, Choi, Gilpin, Farkas, & Berry, 1998). For example, adolescents who were never smokers (ages 12–15) who named a favorite cigarette brand and owned a promotional item for cigarettes at baseline were more than twice as likely as other peers to be identified as established smokers 4 years later (Biener & Siegel, 2000). Indeed, several researchers suggest that tobacco advertising exerts greater influence on adolescent smoking than does smoking by peers or family members (Evans, Farkas, Gilpin, Berry, & Pierce, 1995; Pierce et al., 1998; Sargent et al., 2000).

Like cigarette advertising, alcohol ads portray drinking as a socially desirable, normative behavior without harmful consequences for adolescent health (Grube, 1993; Madden & Grube, 1994). The contribution of advertising exposure to adolescents' positive beliefs about drinking has been demonstrated in experiments (Dunn & Yniguez, 1999; Slater & Domenech, 1995) and cross-sectional surveys (Aitken, Eadie, Leathar, McNeill, & Scott, 1988; Austin & Meili, 1994; Grube & Wallack, 1994). The hypothesis that advertising promotes adolescent drinking is supported by positive correlations between ad exposure and self-reported consumption (Atkin, 1993; Atkin, Hocking, & Block, 1984); favorable responses to advertising that precede experimentation with alcohol (Austin & Knaus, 2000; Unger, Johnson, & Rohrbach, 1995); and increased consumption after manipulation of college students' exposure to beer ads (Wilks, Vardanega, & Callan, 1992). Moreover, in longitudinal surveys, boys who recalled more alcohol ads at age 15 reported drinking larger quantities of beer at age 18 (Connolly, Casswell, Zhang, & Silva, 1994), and boys' brand loyalty and favorable responses to beer advertising at age 18 predicted an increase in beer consumption at age 21 (Casswell & Zhang, 1998).

Dramatic changes in the nature of tobacco and alcohol advertising should stimulate new research in this area. Tobacco companies are promoting their charitable works and youth smoking prevention on television for the first time in 30 years, and advertisements for hard liquor are appearing on television for the first time since 1948. Unfortunately, little is known about adolescents' exposure and reactions to such messages (Farrelly et al., 2002; Henriksen & Fortmann, 2002). Smoking in movies is widespread, even in movies made for children. Tobacco appeared in 87% of the top 25 box office hits from 1988 to 1997 (Dalton et al., 2002), in 89% of the 100 most popular movies from 1996 to 1997 (Roberts, Henriksen, et al., 1999), and in 56% of G-rated, animated features (Goldstein, Sobell, & Newman, 1999). Almost as many unrestricted movies as R-rated movies depict tobacco use (Roberts, Henriksen, et al., 1999). Moreover, the rate of tobacco use in movies is increasing, now averaging 10.5 instances per hour (Thumbs Up! Thumbs Down!, 2001; Kacirk & Glantz, 2001). Thus, adolescents—who spend an average of 40 minutes per day watching movies and videotapes (Roberts, Henriksen, et al., 1999)—see approximately 2,500 portrayals of smoking in a single year.

Teens are more likely to smoke if their favorite film star smokes (Distefan, Gilpin, Sargent, & Pierce, 1999; Tickle, Sargent, Dalton, Beach, & Heatherton, 2001). In a survey of approximately five thousand 9- to 15-year-olds, students who reported the greatest exposure to smoking in movies (150 scenes or more) were almost three times more likely to try smoking than were students who report the least exposure (50 or fewer scenes; Sargent et al., 2001). Indeed, seeing smoking in movies fosters more positive attitudes toward the behavior, distorts adolescents' perceptions about its popularity, and may encourage tobacco use (Sargent et al., 2001, 2002).

Drinking is even more prevalent than smoking in popular media, although fewer studies address the influence of such portrayals on youth. Alcohol appeared in 93% of the 200 most popular video rentals in 1996 and 1997—in 94% of R-rated, 97% of PG-13, and 76% of G- or PG-rated movies (Roberts, Henriksen, et al., 1999). More than 70% of 80 top-rated prime-time situation comedies and serial dramas depicted alcohol use; 42% portrayed major characters at a place or event where alcohol was present; and 22% were set in a bar, club, or restaurant where alcohol was served (Christenson, Henriksen, & Roberts, 2000). The presence of alcohol in music videos has increased over time. In a 1994 sample of 518 videos, alcohol appeared in more videos on MTV (27%) and VH1 (25%) than on BET (19%; DuRant et al., 1997). In a 1998 sample of 258 videos, alcohol appeared in 47% of videos on BET and 33% of videos on MTV and VH1 (Roberts, Christenson, Henriksen, & Bandy, 2002). These changes in trends are likely due to the growing popularity of rap music, a genre in which references to luxury brands of champagne and brandy as status symbols are particularly common (Roberts et al., 2002).

At least one study found that exposure to portrayals and promotions of alcohol is a causal factor in the onset of adolescent drinking. In a longitudinal survey of approximately 1,500 ninth graders, the odds of first alcohol use between baseline and 18-month follow-up increased significantly with baseline hours of television and music video viewing (Robinson, Chen, & Killen, 1998).

In spite of the growing concern that mass media glamorize illicit drug use, few empirical studies address this topic. A content analysis of top 20 box-office hits from 1977 to 1988 found more frequent and overt portrayals of illicit drug use in R-rated movies over time (Terre, Drabman, & Speer, 1991). Illicit drugs appeared in 22% of the 200 most popular video rentals in 1996 and 1997—in 20% of R-rated and 17% of PG-13 movies (Roberts, Henriksen, et al., 1999). On television, illicit drugs were mentioned or seen in 20% of the top-rated prime-time situation comedies and serial dramas (Christenson et al., 2000) and in 19% of music videos (Roberts et al., 2002).

Although adolescents identify television as their primary source of information about illicit drugs (Weiss & Moore, 1995; Wright & Pearl, 2000), surprisingly little is known about adolescents' exposure to drug use portrayals. It would be helpful to examine the individual differences that predict which adolescents see and hear references to illicit drugs on television and in other entertainment media. In addition, research is needed to understand how adolescents interpret such portrayals and the consequences for their attitudes and behaviors regarding drug use.

What little is known about the relationship between illicit drug use and media exposure focuses on adolescent preferences for different types of music. The perception that some music subcultures promote drug use dates back at least as far the association of jazz and cocaine in the 1920s (Berridge, 1988). A study of the frequency and nature of drug references in popular music analyzed 1,000 songs from five genres: alternative rock, country-western, Hot-100, heavy metal, and rap. Illicit drugs were mentioned in 63% of rap lyrics and in about 10% of the lyrics from other categories (Roberts, Henriksen, et al., 1999).

A handful of correlational studies confirm higher rates of self-reported drug use among fans of heavy metal (Arnett, 1991; King, 1988; Martin, Clarke, & Pearce, 1993) and rave music (Forsyth, Barnard, & McKeganey, 1997; Pedersen & Skrondal, 1999) but not among fans of rap music (Took & Weiss, 1994). In the largest study to date, subcultural music preferences predicted all illegal drug use patterns reported by a sample of more than 10,000 Norwegian 14- to 17-year-olds (Pedersen & Skrondal, 1999). Students who liked Seattle or grunge rock were almost twice as likely to report using marijuana and amphetamines as other students. Liking house or techno music was associated with a two- to threefold increase in the odds of using ecstasy (MDMA) only and of using ecstasy and amphetamines. Adolescents who never used illegal drugs reported significantly less interest in all kinds of music studied (house or techno, Seattle or grunge, acid jazz, and new age).

Longitudinal research is needed to permit causal inferences about media effects and provide a closer examination of characteristics that may explain why adolescents who favor particular types of music are also more likely to use illicit drugs. Roe (1995) coined the term "media delinquency" to refer to adolescents' affinity for what he calls "disvalued" media and other forms of delinquency, including illicit drug use. Other researchers emphasize the role of sensation seeking, a preference for exciting experiences and stimuli (Arnett, 1991; Litle & Zuckerman, 1986). Future research should examine how myriad aspects of involvement with music—lyric comprehension, concert attendance, magazine subscriptions, and celebrity identification—inform adolescents' attitudes and behaviors regarding illicit drug use.

RETROSPECT AND PROSPECT

Across areas of concern to researchers focused on adolescents, empirical evidence describing media content and patterns of media exposure far outweighs data on the consequences of such exposure. A growing body of research has examined how different characteristics of the adolescent audience (i.e., Brown's lived experience; J. D. Brown, 2000) influence interpretations of media content. However, aside from a few studies that use age as a proxy for developmental status and even fewer studies that use sexual attitudes or experience to infer the status of adolescent sexual development (e.g., J. D. Brown et al., 1993; Thompson et al., 1993), research looks primarily at social and demographic variables (e.g., gender, race, parent-child relations) rather than developmental status. In short, research concerning media effects on adolescents consists largely of studies conducted *with* adolescents, either because of public concern over media influence on youth (typically, negative influence) or because compulsory education renders school-age youth a readily available subject population. Rarely does this work investigate adolescence per se.

Also noteworthy is the problem orientation of most research about adolescents and the media (Roberts & Bachen, 1981); that is, research typically begins with an area of social behavior perceived to be problematic and then looks for theoretical models that can be applied to examine whether and how media influence relevant cognitive, attitudinal, or behavioral outcomes (see, for example, Comstock, 1991; Comstock et al., 1978; Strasburger & Wilson, 2002). Thus, public perceptions (and empirical evidence) of increases in youth violence, sexual activity, substance use, and so on often raise questions about the media's role in such behavior, stimulating systematic examination of media content and of how such content affects beliefs and behavior. Hence, many more studies have examined potentially harmful or antisocial behaviors than helpful or prosocial behaviors.

For the most part, research on adolescents and media falls under one of three general headings: content analyses, media use studies, and effects studies.

A large number of content analyses are relevant to adolescents and most media. One exception is a dearth of systematic information about content available on the World Wide Web. The most relevant content analyses document the quantity and nature of media messages that are particularly germane to adolescent audiences—that is, studies emphasizing perceived or real social problems. Such research has documented how much media portray various problem issues and related behaviors and how such portrayals are framed, identifying the prevalence of numerous message-related variables that have been documented to influence learning and acceptance of any kind of message.

In addition to content analyses, a large and consistent research literature indicates that adolescents spend a substantial part of their time exposed to media messages. Surveys focus on the relationship between various demographic and social variables and media consumption, documenting important age-related and individual differences in the amount, type, and content of media adolescents consume. Two recent trends are important to the understanding of the potential consequences of adolescent media use. First, the preponderance of adolescent media use occurs in solitude, increasing from early to late adolescence. Second, the past decade has witnessed a substantial increase in media channels and content aimed particularly at adolescents, largely due to recognition that adolescents constitute a valuable market for advertisers.

Finally, effects studies shed light on numerous factors that mediate learning from media exposure. Research has identified an extensive list of message- and audience-related variables that influence reception and interpretation of media messages as well as conditions influencing subsequent display of what has been learned from media content. Many of the findings apply to children, adolescents, and adults alike. However, to the extent that adolescent development influences or is influenced by media content, a great many holes in our knowledge remain. The bulk of media effects research consists of either correlational data obtained from surveys or short-term experiments. Comfort levels with both the external validity of and causal inferences from many of the cited studies would be greatly enhanced by more long-term, longitudinal, and observational research.

Unlike effects research concerned with young children, developmental theory has seldom guided research on media effects and adolescents. Indeed, our knowledge about media and adolescence exists because studies of relevant social issues have been conducted with adolescent participants. However, adolescence denotes a much richer concept than the age criterion for research subjects. It is a period of rapid change and attendant uncertainty, during which youth confront an array of developmental tasks that mark the transition to adulthood (e.g., establishing self-identity, sexual identity, independence, etc.). One characterization of adolescent development points to a kind of psychological fragmentation, a process by which young people differentiate a public from a private self, and possibly many private selves from each other. During such fragmentation, adolescents confront identity formation by trying on an array of potential selves. Moreover, it appears that the disequilibrium inherent in confronting a given developmental task likely triggers a need for information about that task and simultaneously implicates related schemas or cognitive categories that serve as frameworks within which new information is processed. In such instances, the same media content may be mainly construed in terms of sexual behavior or independence from authority, depending on which issue a given adolescent confronts.

This view of adolescent development, considered in relation to findings from research on media and adolescents, points to the importance of bridging the gap between the two literatures. Psychological fragmentation may, as Larson (1995) argues, occur largely in solitude. However, it is largely solitude from live sources of information—parents, siblings, peers—not from mediated sources. Today's adolescents withdraw to rooms filled with media offering an array of messages designed to appeal particularly to their age group. To the extent that they confront developmental tasks and explore various potential selves during such private time, media potentially play a central role in adolescent socialization. Media provide content about issues central to development just when adolescents are most likely to be seeking that information. Focus on a given issue increases accessibility to issue-related schemas; these, in turn, influence how media content is interpreted, what view of the world is cultivated, what specific beliefs and behaviors are learned, and to some extent, what view of the emerging self is constructed. In other words, media speak to the unique needs of adolescents when they are highly susceptible to influence from any messages.

Research that integrates theories of adolescent development with theories of media processes and effects is needed. Such integration offers the promise of increasing understanding of how adolescent development affects uses of and responses to media content, and perhaps more important, how media content influences adolescent socialization.

REFERENCES

Adoni, H. (1978). The functions of mass media in the political socialization of adolescents. *Communication Research, 6,* 84–106.

Aitken, P. P., & Eadie, D. R. (1990). Reinforcing effects of cigarette advertising on under-age smoking. *British Journal of Addiction, 85,* 399–412.

Aitken, P. P., Eadie, D. R., Hastings, G. B., & Haywood, A. J. (1991). Predisposing effects of cigarette advertising on children's intentions to smoke when older. *British Journal of Addiction, 86,* 383–390.

Aitken, P. P., Eadie, D. R., Leathar, D. S., McNeill, R. E., & Scott, A. C. (1988). Television advertisements for alcoholic drinks do reinforce under-age drinking. *British Journal of Addiction, 83,* 1399–1419.

Aitken, P. P., Leathar, D. S., & O'Hagan, F. J. (1985). Children's perceptions of advertisements for cigarettes. *Social Science & Medicine, 21,* 785–797.

Aitken, P. P., Leathar, D. S., O'Hagan, F. J., & Squair, S. I. (1987). Children's awareness of cigarette advertisements and brand imagery. *British Journal of Addiction, 82,* 615–622.

Altman, D., Levine, D., Coeytaux, R., Slade, J., & Jaffe, R. (1996). Tobacco promotion and susceptibility to tobacco use among adolescents aged 12 through 17 in a nationally representative sample. *American Journal of Public Health, 86,* 1590–1593.

Anderson, C. A., & Bushman, B. J. (2001). Effects of violent video games on aggressive behavior, aggressive cognition, aggressive affect, physiological arousal, and prosocial behavior: A meta-analytic review of the scientific literature. *Psychological Science, 12,* 353–359.

Anderson, C. A., & Dill, K. E. (2000). Video games and aggressive thoughts, feelings, and behavior in the laboratory and in life. *Journal of Personality and Social Psychology, 78,* 772–790.

Arnett, J. J. (1991). Adolescents and heavy metal music: From the mouths of metalheads. *Youth & Society, 23*(1), 76–98.

Arnett, J. J. (1995). Adolescents' uses of media for self-socialization. *Journal of Youth and Adolescence, 24,* 519–533.

Atkin, C. K. (1993). Effects of media alcohol messages on adolescent audiences. *Adolescent Medicine: State of the Art Reviews, 4,* 527–542.

Atkin, C., Hocking, J., & Block, M. (1984). Teenage drinking: Does advertising make a difference? *Journal of Communication, 34*(2), 157–167.

Aubrey, J. S. (2002, April). *The sexual double standard in teen-oriented programming: A content analysis.* Paper presented at the Society for Research on Adolescence, New Orleans, LA.

Austin, E. W., & Knaus, C. (2000). Predicting the potential for risky behavior among those "too young" to drink as the result of appealing advertising. *Journal of Health Communication, 5*(1), 13–27.

Austin, E. W., & Meili, H. K. (1994). Effects of interpretations of televised alcohol portrayals on children's alcohol beliefs. *Journal of Broadcasting & Electronic Media, 38,* 417–435.

Bandura, A. (1986). *Social foundations of thought and action: A social cognitive theory.* Englewood Cliffs, NJ: Prentice-Hall.

Bandura, A. (2002). Social cognitive theory of mass communication. In J. Bryant & D. Zillmann (Eds.), *Media effects: Advances in theory and research* (2nd ed., pp. 121–153). Mahwah, NJ: Erlbaum.

Bandura, A., Ross, D., & Ross, S. A. (1963a). Imitation of film-mediated aggressive models. *Journal of Abnormal and Social Psychology, 66,* 3–11.

Bandura, A., Ross, D., & Ross, S. A. (1963b). Vicarious reinforcement and imitative learning. *Journal of Abnormal and Social Psychology, 67,* 601–607.

Baran, S. (1976). Sex on TV and adolescent sexual self-image. *Journal of Broadcasting, 20*(1), 61–68.

Barker, D. (1994). Changes in the cigarette brand preferences of adolescent smokers—United States 1989–1993. *Morbidity and Mortality Weekly Report, 43*(32), 577–581.

Baxter, R. L., De Riemer, C., Landini, A., Leslie, L., & Singletary, M. W. (1985). A content analysis of music videos. *Journal of Broadcasting and Electronic Media, 29,* 333–340.

Becker, A. E. (1995). *Body, self, and society: The view from Fiji.* Philadelphia: University of Pennsylvania Press.

Becker, A. E., Burwell, R. A., Herzog, D. B., Hamburg, P., & Gilman, S. E. (2002). Eating behaviours and attitudes following prolonged exposure to television among ethnic Fijian adolescent girls. *British Journal of Psychiatry, 180,* 509–514.

Belson, W. A. (1978). *Television violence and the adolescent boy.* Westmead, England: Saxon House, Teakfield Limited.

Berkowitz, L. (1990). On the formation and regulation of anger and aggression: A cognitive-neoassociationist analysis. *American Psychologist, 45,* 494–503.

Berkowitz, L., & Alioto, J. T. (1973). The meaning of an observed event as a determinant of aggressive consequences. *Journal of Personality and Social Psychology, 28,* 206–217.

Berkowitz, L., & Rawlings, E. (1963). Effects of film violence on inhibitions against subsequent aggression. *Journal of Abnormal and Social Psychology, 66,* 405–412.

Berkowitz, L., & Rogers, K. H. (1986). A priming effect analysis of media influence. In J. Bryant & D. Zillmann (Eds.), *Perspectives on media effects* (pp. 57–81). Hillsdale, NJ: Erlbaum.

Berlyne, D. (1965). *Structure and direction in thinking.* New York: Wiley.

Berridge, V. (1988). The origins of the English drug "scene", 1890–1930. *Medical History, 32*(1), 51–64.
Biener, L., & Siegel, M. (2000). Tobacco marketing and adolescent smoking: More support for a causal inference. *American Journal of Public Health, 90*(3), 407–411.
Botta, R. A. (1999). Television images and adolescent girls' body image disturbance. *Journal of Communication, 49*(2), 22–41.
Botvin, E. M., Botvin, G. J., Michela, J. L., Baker, E., & Filazzola, A. (1991). Adolescent smoking behavior and the recognition of cigarette advertisements. *Journal of Applied Social Psychology, 21*(11), 919–932.
Botvin, G., Goldberg, C., Botvin, E., & Dusenbury, L. (1993). Smoking behavior of adolescents exposed to cigarette advertising. *Public Health Reports, 108,* 217–224.
British Medical Association. (2000). *Eating disorders, body image, and the media.* London: Author.
Brown, J. D. (2000). Adolescents' sexual media diets. *Journal of Adolescent Health,* supplement to *24*(2), 25–40.
Brown, J. D., Childers, K., Bauman, K., & Koch, G. (1990). The influence of new media and family structure on young adolescents' television and radio use. *Communication Research, 17,* 65–82.
Brown, J. D., Childers, K. W., & Waszak, C. S. (1990). Television and adolescent sexuality. *Journal of Adolescent Health Care, 11,* 62–70.
Brown, J. D., & Newcomer, S. F. (1991). Television viewing and adolescents' sexual behavior. *Journal of Homosexuality, 21,* 77–91.
Brown, J. D., White, A. B., & Nikopoulou, L. (1993). Disinterest, intrigue, resistance: Early adolescent girls' use of sexual media content. In B. S. Greenberg, J. D. Brown, & N. L. Buerkel-Rothfuss (Eds.), *Media, sex and the adolescent* (pp. 177–195). Creskill, NJ: Hampton Press.
Brown, R., & O'Leary, M. (1971). Pop music in an English secondary school system. *American Behavioral Scientist, 14,* 401–413.
Bryant, J. (1985). Frequency of exposure, age of initial exposure, and reaction to initial exposure to pornography. In D. Zillmann & J. Bryant (Eds.), *Pornography: Research advances and policy considerations.* Hillsdale, NJ: Erlbaum.
Bryant, J., & Rockwell, S. C. (1994). Effects of massive exposure to sexually oriented prime-time television programming on adolescents' moral judgment. In D. Zillman, J. Bryant, & A. C. Huston (Eds.), *Media, children, and the family: Social scientific, psychodynamic, and clinical perspectives* (pp. 183–195). Hillsdale, NJ: Erlbaum.
Buerkel-Rothfuss, N. L. (1993). Background: What prior research shows. In B. S. Greenberg, J. D. Brown, & N. L. Buerkel-Rothfuss (Eds.), *Media, sex and the adolescent* (pp. 5–18). Creskill, NJ: Hampton Press.
Buerkel-Rothfuss, N. L., & Strouse, J. S. (1993). Media exposure and perceptions of sexual behaviors: The cultivation hypothesis moves to the bedroom. In B. S. Greenberg, J. D. Brown, & N. L. Buerkel-Rothfuss (Eds.), *Media, sex and the adolescent* (pp. 225–247). Creskill, NJ: Hampton Press.
Buerkel-Rothfuss, N. L., Strouse, J. S., Pettey, G., & Shatzer, M. (1993). Adolescents' and young adults' exposure to sexually oriented and sexually explicit media. In B. S. Greenberg, J. D. Brown, & N. L. Buerkel-Rothfuss (Eds.), *Media, sex and the adolescent* (pp. 99–113). Creskill, NJ: Hampton Press.
Bushman, B. J., & Anderson, C. A. (2001). Media violence and the American public: Scientific fact versus media misinformation. *American Psychologist, 56,* 477–489.
California Assessment Program. (1980). *Student achievement in California schools. 1979–1980 annual report: Television and student achievement.* Sacramento, CA: California State Department of Education.
Carey, J. (1969). Changing courtship patterns in the popular song. *American Journal of Sociology, 4,* 720–731.
Cash, T. F., & Pruzinsky, T. (2002). *Body image: A handbook of theory, research, and clinical practice.* New York: Guilford Press.

Casswell, S., & Zhang, J. F. (1998). Impact of liking for advertising and brand allegiance on drinking and alcohol-related aggression: A longitudinal study. *Addiction, 93,* 1209–1217.

Cattarin, J. A., Thompson, J. K., Thomas, C., & Williams, R. (2000). Body image, mood, and televised images of attractiveness: The role of social comparison. *Journal of Social & Clinical Psychology, 19,* 220–239.

Chapman, S., & Fitzgerald, B. (1982). Brand preference and advertising recall in adolescent smokers: Some implications for health promotion. *American Journal of Public Health, 72*(5), 491–494.

Charters, W. W. (1933). *Motion pictures and youth: A summary.* New York: Macmillan.

Christenson, P. G. (1994). Childhood patterns of music use and preferences. *Communication Reports, 7*(2), 136–144.

Christenson, P. G., Henriksen, L., & Roberts, D. F. (2000). *Substance use in popular prime-time television.* Washington, DC: United States Office of National Drug Control Policy.

Christenson, P. G., & Roberts, D. F. (1998). *It's not only rock and roll: Popular music in the lives of adolescents.* Cresskill, NJ: Hampton Press.

Cline, V. B., Croft, R. G., & Courrier, S. (1973). Desensitization of children to television violence. *Journal of Personality and Social Psychology, 27,* 360–365.

Cohn, L. B. (1995). Violent video games: Aggression, arousal, and desensitization in young adolescent boys. *Dissertation Abstracts International, 57*(2-B), 1463. (UMI No. 9616947)

Coleman, J. (1993). Adolescence in a changing world. In S. Jackson & H. Rodrigues-Tome (Eds.), *Adolescence and its social worlds* (pp. 251–268). Hove, England: Erlbaum.

Comstock, G. (1991). *Television and the American child.* San Diego, CA: Academic Press.

Comstock, G., Chaffee, S., Katzman, N., McCombs, M., & Roberts, D. F. (1978). *Television and human behavior.* New York: Columbia University Press.

Comstock, G., & Scharrer, E. (1999). *Television: What's on, who's watching, and what it means.* San Diego, CA: Academic Press.

Conger, J., & Peterson, A. (1984). *Adolescence and youth: Psychological development in a changing world* (3rd ed.). New York: Harper & Row.

Connolly, G. M., Casswell, S., Zhang, J. F., & Silva, P. A. (1994). Alcohol in the mass media and drinking by adolescents: A longitudinal study. *Addiction, 89,* 1255–1263.

Cooper, A. (1998). Sexuality and the Internet: Surfing into the new millennium. *CyberPsychology & Behavior, 1,* 181–187.

Cope-Farrar, K., & Kunkel, D. (2002). Sexual messages in teens' favorite prime-time television programs. In J. D. Brown, J. R. Steele, & K. Walsh-Childers (Eds.), *Sexual teens, sexual media* (pp. 59–75). Mahwah, NJ: Erlbaum.

Courtright, J. A., & Baran, S. J. (1980). The acquisition of sexual information by young people. *Journalism Quarterly, 57,* 107–114.

Cusumano, D. L., & Thompson, J. K. (2001). Media influence and body image in 8–11-year-old boys and girls: A preliminary report on Multidimensional Media Influence Scale. *International Journal of Eating Disorders, 29*(1), 37–44.

Dalton, M. A., Tickle, J. J., Sargent, J. D., Beach, M. L., Ahrens, M. B., & Heatherton, T. F. (2002). The incidence and context of tobacco use in popular movies from 1988 to 1997. *Preventive Medicine, 34,* 516–523.

Dill, K. E., & Dill, J. C. (1998). Video game violence: A review of the empirical literature. *Aggression and Violent Behavior, 3,* 407–428.

Distefan, J. M., Gilpin, E. A., Sargent, J. D., & Pierce, J. P. (1999). Do movie stars encourage adolescents to start smoking? Evidence from California. *Preventive Medicine, 28,* 1–11.

Dobson, A., Woodward, S., & Leeder, S. (1992). Tobacco smoking in response to cigarette advertising. *The Medical Journal of Australia, 156,* 815–816.

Dominick, J. (1996). *The dynamics of mass communication* (5th ed.). New York: McGraw-Hill.

Downs, A. C., & Harrison, S. K. (1985). Embarrassing age spots or just plain ugly? Physical attractiveness stereotyping as an instrument of sexism on American television commercials. *Sex Roles, 13*(1–2), 9–19.

Dunn, M. E., & Yniguez, R. M. (1999). Experimental demonstration of the influence of alcohol advertising on the activation of alcohol expectancies in memory among fourth- and fifth-grade children. *Experimental and Clinical Psychopharmacology, 7,* 473–483.

DuRant, R. H., Rome, E. S., Rich, M., Allred, E., Emans, S. J., & Woods, E. R. (1997). Tobacco and alcohol use behaviors portrayed in music videos: A content analysis [published erratum]. *American Journal of Public Health, 87,* 1131–1135.

Evans, E. D., Rutberg, J. Sather, C., & Turner, C. (1991). Content analysis of contemporary teen magazines for adolescent females. *Youth & Society, 23*(1), 99–120.

Evans, N., Farkas, F., Gilpin, E., Berry, C., & Pierce, J. (1995). Influence of tobacco marketing and exposure to smokers on adolescent susceptibility to smoking. *Journal of the National Cancer Institute, 87,* 1538–1545.

Faber, R., Brown, J., & McLeod, J. (1979). Coming of age in the global village: Television and adolescence. In E. Wartella (Ed.), *Children communicating: Media, and the development of thought, speech, understanding* (pp. 215–249). Beverly Hills, CA: Sage.

Farrelly, M. C., Healton, C. G., Davis, K. C., Messeri, P., Hersey, J. C., & Haviland, M. L. (2002). Getting to the truth: Evaluating national tobacco countermarketing campaigns. *American Journal of Public Health, 92,* 901–907.

Federal Trade Commission. (1999). *Self-regulation in the alcohol industry: A review of industry efforts to avoid promoting alcohol to underage consumers.* Washington, DC: Author.

Federal Trade Commission. (2000). *Marketing violent entertainment to children: A review of self-regulation and industry practices in the motion picture, music recording & electronic game industries.* Washington, DC: Author.

Federal Trade Commission. (2002). *Cigarette report for 2000.* Washington, DC: Author.

Fedler, F., Hall, J., & Tanzi, L. A. (1982). Popular songs emphasize sex, de-emphasize romance. *Mass Communication Review, 9,* 10–15.

Feldman, S. S., & Elliott, G. R. (Eds.). (1990). *At the threshold: The developing adolescent.* Cambridge, MA: Harvard University Press.

Field, A. E., Camargo, C. A., Jr., Taylor, C. B., Berkey, C. S., Roberts, S. B., & Colditz, G. A. (2001). Peer, parent, and media influences on the development of weight concerns and frequent dieting among preadolescent and adolescent girls and boys. *Pediatrics, 107*(1), 54–60.

Field, A. E., Cheung, L., Wolf, A. M., Herzog, D. B., Gortmaker, S. L., & Colditz, G. A. (1999). Exposure to the mass media and weight concerns among girls. *Pediatrics, 103*(3), E36.

Fischer, P. M., Schwartz, M. P., Richards, J. W., Goldstein, A. O., & Rojas, T. H. (1991). Brand logo recognition by children aged 3 to 6 years. *Journal of the American Medical Association, 266,* 3145–3148.

Fiske, S. T., & Taylor, S. E. (1991). *Social cognition* (2nd ed.). New York: McGraw-Hill.

Fling, S., Smith, L., Rodriguez, T., Thornton, D., Atkins, E., & Nixon, K. (1992). Videogames, aggression, and self-esteem: A survey. *Social Behavior and Personality, 20,* 39–46.

Forsyth, A. J., Barnard, M., & McKeganey, N. P. (1997). Musical preference as an indicator of adolescent drug use. *Addiction, 92,* 1317–1325.

Fouts, G., & Burggraf, K. (1999). Television situation comedies: Female body images and verbal reinforcements. *Sex Roles, 40,* 473–481.

Fouts, G., & Burggraf, K. (2000). Television situation comedies: Female weight, male negative comments, and audience reactions. *Sex Roles, 42,* 925–932.

Funk, J. B., Buchman, D. D., Schimming, J. L., & Hagan, J. D. (1998, August). *Attitudes towards violence, empathy, and violent electronic games.* Paper presented at the annual meeting of the American Psychological Association, Washington, DC.

Gantz, W., Gartenberg, H., Pearson, M., & Schiller, S. (1978). Gratifications and expectations associated with popular music among adolescents. *Popular Music and Society, 6,* 81–89.

Gerbner, G. (1990). Stories that hurt: Tobacco, alcohol, and other drugs in the mass media. In H. Resnik (Ed.), *Youth and drugs: Society's mixed messages* (pp. 53–129). Rockville, MD: Office for Substance Use Prevention.

Gerbner. G., & Gross, L. (1976). Living with television: The violence profile. *Journal of Communication, 26*(2), 172–199.

Gerbner, G., Gross, L., Morgan, M., & Signorielli, N. (1980). The "mainstreaming" of America: Violence profile no. 11. *Journal of Communication, 30*(3), 10–29.

Gerbner, G., Gross, L., Morgan, M., Signorielli, N., & Shanahan, J. (2002). Growing up with television: Cultivation processes. In J. Bryant & D. Zillman (Eds.), *Media effects: Advances in theory and research* (2nd ed., pp. 43–67). Mahwah, NJ: Erlbaum.

Gerbner, G., Gross, L., Signorielli, N., Morgan, M., & Jackson-Beeck, M. (1979). The demonstration of power: Violence profile no. 10. *Journal of Communication, 29*(3), 177–201.

Gilpin, E., Pierce, J., & Rosbrook, B. (1997). Are adolescents receptive to current sales promotion practices of the tobacco industry? *Preventive Medicine, 26*(1), 14–21.

Glickson, J., & Avnon, M. (1997). Exploration in virtual reality: Absorption, cognition, and altered state of consciousness. *Imagination, Cognition, and Personality, 17,* 141–151.

Goldstein, A., Fischer, P., Richards, J., & Creten, D. (1987). Relationship between high school student smoking and recognition of cigarette advertisements. *Journal of Pediatrics, 110,* 488–491.

Goldstein, A. O., Sobel, R. A., & Newman, G. R. (1999). Tobacco and alcohol use in G-rated children's animated films. *Journal of the American Medical Association, 281,* 1131–1136.

Greenberg, B. S., & Buselle, R. (1996). Soap operas and sexual activity: A decade later. *Journal of Communication, 46*(4), 153–160.

Greenberg, B. S., Graef, D., Fernandez-Collado, C., Korzenny, F., & Atkin, C. K. (1980). Sexual intimacy on commercial TV during prime time. *Journalism Quarterly, 57,* 211–215.

Greenberg, B., & Heeter, C. (1987). VCRs and young people. *American Behavioral Scientist, 30,* 509–521.

Greenberg, B., & Linsangan, R. (1993). Gender differences in adolescents' media use, exposure to sexual content and parental mediation. In B. S. Greenberg, J. D. Brown, & N. L. Buerkel-Rothfuss (Eds.), *Media, sex and the adolescent* (pp. 134–144). Creskill, NJ: Hampton Press.

Greenberg, B. S., Perry, K. L., & Covert, A. M. (1983). The body human: Sex education, politics and television. *Family Relations, 32,* 419–425.

Greenberg, B. S., Sherry, J. L., Busselle, R. W., Hnilo, L. R., & Smith, S. W. (1997). Daytime television talk shows: Guests, content and interactions. *Journal of Broadcasting & Electronic Media, 41,* 412–426.

Greenberg, B. S., Siemicki, M., Dorfman, S., Heeter, C., Stanley, C., Soderman, A., et al. (1993). Sex content in R-rated films viewed by adolescents. In B.S. Greenberg, J. D. Brown, & N. L. Buerkel-Rothfuss (Eds.), *Media, sex and the adolescent* (p. 45–58). Creskill, NJ: Hampton Press.

Greenberg, B. S., & Woods, M. G. (1999). The soaps: Their sex, gratifications, and outcomes. *The Journal of Sex Research, 36,* 250–257.

Greeson, L., & Williams, R. A. (1986). Social implications of music videos for youth: An analysis of the content and effects of MTV. *Youth and Society, 18,* 177–189.

Groesz, L. M., Levine, M. P., & Murnen, S. K. (2002). The effect of experimental presentation of thin media images on body satisfaction: A meta-analytic review. *International Journal of Eating Disorders, 31*(1), 1–16.

Grube, J. W. (1993). Alcohol portrayals and alcohol advertising on television. *Alcohol Health & Research World, 17,* 61–66.

Grube, J. W., & Wallack, L. (1994). Television beer advertising and drinking knowledge, beliefs, and intentions among schoolchildren. *American Journal of Public Health, 84,* 254–259.

Hansen, C. H., & Hansen, R. D. (1990). Rock music videos and antisocial behavior. *Basic and Applied Social Psychology, 11,* 357–369.

Hargreaves, D., & Tiggemann, M. (2002). The effect of television commercials on mood and body dissatisfaction: The role of appearance-schema activation. *Journal of Social and Clinal Psychology, 21,* 287–308.

Harris, J. R. (1998). *The nurture assumption: Why children turn out the way they do.* New York: The Free Press.

Harrison, K. (2001). Ourselves, our bodies: Thin-ideal media, self-discrepancies, and eating disorder symptomatology in adolescents. *Journal of Social & Clinical Psychology, 20*(3), 289–323.

Harrison, K., & Cantor, J. (1997). The relationship between media consumption and eating disorders. *Journal of Communication, 47*(1), 40–67.

Harter, S. (1990a). Processes underlying adolescent self-concept formation. In R. Montemayor, G. Adams, & T. Gullotta (Eds.), *From childhood to adolescence: A transitional period?* (pp. 205–239). Newbury Park, CA: Sage.

Harter, S. (1990b). Self and identity development. In S. Feldman & G. Elliott (Eds.), *At the threshold: The developing adolescent* (pp. 352–387). Cambridge, MA: Harvard University Press.

Harter, S. (1999). *The construction of the self: a developmental perspective.* New York: Guilford Press.

Hawkins, R. P., & Pingree, S. (1980). Some processes in the cultivation effect. *Communication Research, 7,* 193–226.

Hearold, S. (1986). A synthesis of 1043 effects of television on social behavior. In G. Comstock (Ed.), *Public communication and behavior* (Vol. 1, pp. 65–133). New York: Academic Press.

Heinberg, L. J., & Thompson, J. K. (1995). Body image and televised images of thinness and attractiveness: A controlled laboratory investigation. *Journal of Social & Clinical Psychology, 14,* 325–338.

Heinberg, L. J., Thompson, J. K., & Stormer, S. (1995). Development and validation of the Sociocultural Attitudes Towards Appearance Questionnaire (SATAQ). *International Journal of Eating Disorders, 17*(1), 81–89.

Henriksen, L., & Fortmann, S. P. (2002). Young adults' opinions of Philip Morris and its television advertising. *Tobacco Control, 11*(3), 236–240.

Hirsch, P. (1980). The "scary world" of the nonviewer and other anomalies: A reanalysis of Gerbner et al. Findings on cultivation analysis, part I. *Communication Research, 7,* 403–456.

Hirsch, P. (1981). On not learning from one's own mistakes: A reanalysis of Gerbner et al. Finding on cultivation analysis, part II. *Communication Research, 8,* 3–38.

Horton, D., & Wohl, R. R. (1956). Mass communication and para-social interaction. *Psychiatry, 19,* 215–229.

Huesmann, L. R. (1986). Psychological processes promoting the relation between media violence and aggressive behavior by the viewer. *Journal of Social Issues, 42*(3), 125–139.

Huesmann, L. R., & Eron, L. D. (Eds.). (1986). *Television and the aggressive child: A cross-national comparison.* Hillsdale, NJ: Erlbaum.

Huesmann, L. R., Eron, L. D., Lefkowitz, M. M., & Walder, L. O. (1984). The stability of aggression over time and generations. *Developmental Psychology, 20,* 1120–1134.

Huston, A. C., Wartella, E., & Donnerstein, E. (1998). *Measuring the effects of sexual content in the media.* Menlo Park, CA: Kaiser Family Foundation.

Irving, L. M., DuPen, J., & Berel, S. (1998). A media literacy program for high school females. *Eating Disorders: The Journal of Treatment and Prevention, 6*(2), 119–132.

Johnson, J. D., Jackson, L. A., & Gatto, L. (1995). Violent attitudes and deferred academic aspirations: Deleterious effects of exposure to rap music. *Basic and Applied Social Psychology, 16*(1, 2), 27–41.

Kacirk, K., & Glantz, S. A. (2001). Smoking in movies in 2000 exceeded rates in the 1960s. *Tobacco Control, 10*(4), 397–398.

Kaiser Family Foundation. (2001). *Generation Rx.com: How young people use the Internet for health information.* Menlo Park, CA: Author.

Kaiser Family Foundation, MTV, & *Teen People.* (1999). *What teens know and don't (but should) about sexually transmitted diseases.* Menlo Park, CA: Authors.

Kaiser Family Foundation & *YM Magazine.* (1996). *Kaiser Family Foundation survey on teens and sex.* Menlo Park, CA: Authors.

Kaiser Family Foundation & *YM Magazine.* (1998). *Teens talk about dating, intimacy and their sexual experiences.* Menlo Park, CA: Authors.

Kenny, J. F. (1985). *The family as mediator of television use and the cultivation phenomenon among college students.* Unpublished doctoral dissertation, Syracuse University, Syracuse, NY.

King, P. (1988). Heavy metal music and drug abuse in adolescents. *Postgraduate Medicine, 83*(5), 295–304.

Klein, J. D., Brown, J. D., Childers, K. W., Oliveri, J., Porter, C., & Dykers, C. (1993). Adolescents' risky behavior and mass media use. *Pediatrics, 92*(1), 24–31.

Klitzner, M., Gruenewald, P. J., & Bamberger, E. (1991). Cigarette advertising and adolescent experimentation with smoking. *British Journal of Addiction, 86,* 287–298.

Knowledge Networks. (2002, April). More kids say Internet is the medium they can't live without [Press release]. Westfield, NJ: Author.

Kubey, R., & Czikszentmihalyi, M. (1990). *Television and the quality of life: How viewing shapes everyday experience.* Hillsdale, NJ: Erlbaum.

Kunkel, D., Cope, K. M., & Colvin, C. (1996). *Sexual messages on Family Hour television: Content and context.* Menlo Park, CA: Children Now and Kaiser Family Foundation.

Kunkel, D., Cope, K. M., Farinola, W. M., Biely, E., Rollin, E., & Donnerstein, E. (1999). *Sex on TV.* Menlo Park, CA: Kaiser Family Foundation.

Labre, M. P. (2002). Adolescent boys and the muscular male body ideal. *Journal of Adolescent Health, 30*(4, Suppl.), 233–242.

Larson, R. (1995). Secrets in the bedroom: Adolescents' private use of media. *Journal of Youth and Adolescence, 24,* 535–550.

Larson, R., & Kubey, R. (1983). Television and music: Contrasting media in adolescent life. *Youth and Society, 15,* 13–31.

Larson, R., Kubey, R., & Colletti, J. (1989). Changing channels: Early adolescent media choices and shifting investments in family and friends. *Journal of Youth and Adolescence, 18,* 583–599.

Lavine, H., Sweeney, D., & Wagner, S. H. (1999). Depicting women as sex objects in television advertising: Effects on body dissatisfaction. *Personality & Social Psychology Bulletin, 25,* 1049–1058.

Lenhart, A., Rainie, L., & Lewis, O. (2001). *Teenage life online: The rise of the instant-message generation and the Internet's impact on friendships and family relationships.* Washington, DC: Pew Internet & American Life Project.

Levine, M. P., & Smolak, L. (1996). Media as a context for the development of disordered eating. In L. Smolak, M. P. Levine, & R. Striegel-Moore (Eds.), *The developmental psychopathology of eating disorders: Implications for research, prevention, and treatment.* Mahwah, NJ: Erlbaum.

Linz, D., Donnerstein, E., & Penrod, S. (1984). The effects of multiple exposures to filmed violence against women. *Journal of Communication, 34*(3), 130–147.

Linz, D., Donnerstein, E., & Penrod, S. (1988). Effects of long-term exposure to violent and sexually degrading depictions of women. *Journal of Personality and Social Psychology, 55,* 758–768.

Litle, P., & Zuckerman, M. (1986). Sensation seeking and music preferences. *Personality and Individual Differences, 7,* 575–577.

Madden, P. A., & Grube, J. W. (1994). The frequency and nature of alcohol and tobacco advertising in televised sports, 1990 through 1992. *American Journal of Public Health, 84,* 297–299.

Malkin, A. R., Wornian, K., & Chrisler, J. C. (1999). Women and weight: Gendered messages on magazine covers. *Sex Roles, 40,* 647–655.

Marcia, J. (1980). Identity in adolescence. In J. Adelson (Ed.), *Handbook of adolescent psychology* (pp. 159–187). New York: Wiley.

Martin, G., Clarke, M., & Pearce, C. (1993). Adolescent suicide: Music preference as an indicator of vulnerability. *Journal of the American Academy of Child & Adolescent Psychiatry, 32,* 530–535.

McIntyre, J. J., & Teevan, J. J., Jr. (1972). Television violence and deviant behavior. In G. A. Comstock & E. A. Rubinstein (Eds.), *Television and social behavior: Vol. 3. Television and adolescent aggressiveness* (pp. 239–313). Washington, DC: U.S. Government Printing Office.

McQuail, D., Blumler, J. G., & Brown, J. R. (1972). The television audience: A revised perspective. In D. McQuail (Ed.), *Sociology of mass communications* (pp. 135–165). Harmondsworth, England: Penguin.

Medrich, E. A., Roizen, J. A., Rubin, V., & Buckley, S. (1982). *The serious business of growing up: A study of children's lives outside school.* Berkeley, CA: University of California Press.

Moneta, G. B., & Csikszentmihalyi, M. (1996). The effect of perceived challenges and skills on the quality of subjective experience. *Journal of Personality, 64,* 275–310.

Morgan, M. (1980). Television viewing and reading: Does more equal better? *Journal of Communication, 30*(1), 159–165.

Morgan, M. (1988). Cultivation analysis. In E. Barnouw (Ed.), *International encyclopedia of communication* (Vol. 1, pp. 430–433). New York: Oxford University Press.

Myers, P. N., & Biocca, F. A. (1992). The elastic body image: The effect of television advertising and programming on body image distortions in young women. *Journal of Communication, 42*(3), 108–133.

Nemeroff, C. J., Stein, R. I., Diehl, N. S., & Smilack, K. M. (1994). From the Cleavers to the Clintons: Role choices and body orientation as reflected in magazine article content. *International Journal of Eating Disorders, 16*(2), 167–176.

Owen, P. R., & Laurel-Seller, E. (2000). Weight and shape ideals: Thin is dangerously in. *Journal of Applied Social Psychology, 30,* 979–990.

Paik, H., & Comstock, G. (1994). The effects of television violence on antisocial behavior: A meta-analysis. *Communication Research, 21,* 516–546.

Pecora, N. O. (1998). *The business of children's entertainment.* New York: Guilford Press.

Pedersen, W., & Skrondal, A. (1999). Ecstasy and new patterns of drug use: A normal population study. *Addiction, 94*(11), 1695–1706.

Peterson, J. L., Moore, K. A., & Furstenberg, F. F. (1991). Television viewing and early initiation of sexual intercourse: Is there a link? *Journal of Homosexuality, 21,* 93–119.

Peterson, R. C., & Thurston, L. L. (1933). *Motion pictures and the social attitudes of children.* New York: Macmillan.

Pierce, J., Choi, W., Gilpin, E., Farkas, A., & Berry, C. (1998). Tobacco industry promotion of cigarettes and adolescent smoking. *Journal of the American Medical Association, 279,* 511–515.

Pierce, J. P., Gilpin, E., Burns, D. M., Whalen, E., Rosbrook, B., Shopland, D., et al. (1991). Does tobacco advertising target young people to start smoking? Evidence from California. *Journal of the American Medical Association, 266,* 3154–3158.

Pierce, J. P., Gilpin, E. A., & Choi, W. S. (1999). Sharing the blame: Smoking experimentation and future smoking-attributable mortality due to Joe Camel and Marlboro advertising and promotions. *Tobacco Control, 8*(1), 37–44.

Potter, W. J. (1993). Cultivation theory and research: A conceptual critique. *Human Communication Research, 19,* 564–601.

Potter, W. J. (2002). *The 11 myths of media violence.* Thousand Oaks, CA: Sage.

Posavac, H. D., Posavac, S. S., & Weigel, R. G. (2001). Reducing the impact of media images on women at risk for body image disturbance: Three targeted interventions. *Journal of Social & Clinical Psychology, 20,* 324–340.

Provenzo, E. F. (1991). *Video kids: Making sense of Nintendo.* Cambridge, MA: Harvard University Press.

Roberts, D. F. (1993). Adolescents and the mass media: From "Leave It to Beaver" to "Beverly Hills 90210." *Teachers College Record, 94,* 629–644.

Roberts, D. F. (2000). Media and youth: Access, exposure and privatization. *Journal of Adolescent Health, 24*(Suppl. 2), 8–14.

Roberts, D. F. (2003). Children and the changing media environment: From Plato's Republic to Hillary's village. In R. P. Weissberg, H. J. Walberg, M. V. O'Brien, & C. B. Kuster (Eds.), *Long-term trends in the well-being of children and youth: Issues in children's and families' lives* (pp. 255–276). Washington, DC: Child Welfare League of America Press.

Roberts, D. F., & Bachen, C. M. (1981). Mass communication effects. In M. R. Rozenzweig & L. W. Porter (Eds.), *Annual Review of Psychology* (Vol. 32, pp. 307–356). Palo Alto, CA: Annual Reviews.

Roberts, D. F., Christenson, P., Henriksen, L., & Bandy, E. (2002). *Substance use in popular music videos.* Washington, DC: Office of National Drug Control Policy.

Roberts, D. F., & Foehr, U. G. (in press). *Kids and media in America: Patters of use at the millennium.* New York: Cambridge University Press.

Roberts, D. F., Foehr, U. G., Rideout, V. J., & Brodie, M. (1999). *Kids and media at the new millennium.* Menlo Park, CA: The Henry J. Kaiser Family Foundation.

Roberts, D. F., & Henriksen, L. (1990, June). *Music listening vs. television viewing among older adolescents.* Paper presented at the annual meetings of the International Communication Association, Dublin, Ireland.

Roberts, D. F., Henriksen, L., & Christenson, P. (1999). *Substance use in popular movies and music.* Washington, DC: Office of National Drug Control Policy.

Robinson, T. N., Chen, H. L., & Killen, J. D. (1998). Television and music video exposure and risk of adolescent alcohol use. *Pediatrics, 102*(5), E54.

Roe, K. (1984, August). *Youth and music in Sweden: Results from a longitudinal study of teenagers' music use.* Paper presented at the annual meeting of the International Association of Mass Communication Research, Prague, Czechoslovakia.

Roe, K. (1985). Swedish youth and music: Listening patterns and motivations. *Communication Research, 12,* 353–362.

Roe, K. (1987). The school and music in adolescent socialization. In J. Lull (Ed.), *Popular music and communication* (pp. 212–230). Beverly Hills, CA: Sage.

Roe, K. (1995). Adolescents' use of socially disvalued media: Towards a theory of media delinquency. *Journal of Youth and Adolescence, 24,* 617–631.

Rosengren, K. E., Wenner, L. A., & Palmgreen, P. (Eds.). *Media gratifications research: Current perspectives.* Beverly Hills, CA: Sage.

Roskos-Ewoldsen, D. R., Roskos-Ewoldsen, B., & Carpentier, F. R. D (2002). Media priming: A synthesis. In J. Bryant & D. Zillmann (Eds.), *Media effects: Advances in theory and research* (2nd ed., pp. 97–120). Mahwah, NJ: Erlbaum.

Rubin, A. M. (2002). The uses-and-gratifications perspective of media effects. In J. Bryant & D. Zillmann (Eds.), *Media effects: Advances in theory and research* (2nd ed., pp. 525–548). Mahwah, NJ: Erlbaum.

Rubin, A. M., Perse, E. M., & Powell, R. A. (1985). Loneliness, parasocial interaction, and local television news viewing. *Human Communication Research, 12,* 155–180.

Sanbonmatsu, D. M., & Fazio, R. H. (1991). Construct accessibility: Determinants, consequences, and implications for the media. In J. Bryant & D. Zillmann (Eds.), *Responding to the screen: Reception and reaction processes* (pp. 45–62). Hillsdale, NJ: Erlbaum.

Sang, F., Schmitz, B., & Tasche, K. (1992). Individuation and television coviewing in the family: Developmental trends in the viewing behavior of adolescents. *Journal of Broadcasting and Electronic Media,* 427–441.

Sapolsky, B. S., & Tabarlet, J. O. (1991). Sex in prime time television: 1979 versus 1989. *Journal of Broadcasting and Electronic Media, 35,* 505–516.

Sargent, J. D., Beach, M. L., Dalton, M. A., Mott, L. A., Tickle, J. J., Ahrens, M. B., et al. (2001). Effect of seeing tobacco use in films on trying smoking among adolescents: Cross sectional study. *British Medical Journal, 323*(7326), 1394–1397.

Sargent, J. D., Dalton, M., Beach, M., Bernhardt, A., Heatherton, T., & Stevens, M. (2000). Effect of cigarette promotions on smoking uptake among adolescents. *Preventive Medicine, 30*(4), 320–327.

Sargent, J. D., Dalton, M. A., Beach, M. L., Mott, L. A., Tickle, J. J., Ahrens, M. B., et al. (2002). Viewing tobacco use in movies: Does it shape attitudes that mediate adolescent smoking? *American Journal of Preventive Medicine, 22*(3), 137–145.

Schank, R. C., & Abelson, R. P. (1977). *Scripts, plans, goals, and understanding: An inquiry into human knowledge structures.* Hillsdale, NJ: Erlbaum.

Schramm, W. (1971). The nature of communication between humans. In W. Schramm & D. F. Roberts (Eds.), *The process and effects of mass communication* (pp. 3–53). Urbana: University of Illinois Press.

Shanahan, J., & Morgan, M. (1999). *Television and its viewers: Cultivation theory and research.* Cambridge, England: Cambridge University Press.

Sherman, B. L., & Dominick, J. R. (1986). Violence and sex in music videos: TV and rock 'n' roll. *Journal of Communication, 36*(1), 79–93.

Shrum, L. J. (1995). Assessing the social influence of television: A social cognition perspective on cultivation effects. *Communication Research, 22,* 402–429.

Shrum, L. J. (2002). Media consumption and perceptions of social reality: Effects and underlying processes. In J. Bryand & D. Zillmann (Eds.), *Media effects: Advances in theory and research* (2nd ed., pp. 69–95). Mahwah, NJ: Erlbaum.

Signorielli, N., & Morgan, M. (Eds.). (1990). *Cultivation analysis: New directions in media effects research.* Newbury Park, CA: Sage.

Silverstein, B., Perdue, L., Peterson, B., & Kelly, E. (1986). The role of the mass media in promoting a thin standard of bodily attractiveness for women. *Sex Roles, 14,* 519–532.

Simpson, A. R. (2001). *Raising teens: A synthesis of research and a foundation for action.* Boston: Harvard School of Public Health.

Slater, M. D., & Domenech, M. M. (1995). Alcohol warnings in TV beer advertisements. *Journal of Studies on Alcohol, 56,* 361–367.

Smith, S.L., Wilson, B.J., Kunkel, D., Linz, D., Potter, W.J., Colvin, C., et al. (1998). Violence in television programming overall: University of California, Santa Barbara study. In *National television violence study* (Vol. 3, pp. 5–220). Newbury Park, CA: Sage.

Starker, S. (1989). *Evil influences: Crusades against the mass media.* New Brunswick, CT: Transaction.

Steele, J. R., & Brown, J. D. (1995). Adolescent room culture: Studying media in the context of everyday life. *Journal of Youth and Adolescence, 24,* 551–576.

Stern, S. (2002). Sexual selves on the world wide web: Adolescent girls' home pages as sites for sexual self-expression. In J. D. Brown, J. R. Steele, & K. Walsh-Childers (Eds.), *Sexual teens, sexual media* (pp. 265–285). Mahwah, NJ: Erlbaum.

Stice, E., Schupak-Neuberg E., Shaw, H. E., & Stein, R. I. (1994). Relation of media exposure to eating disorder symptomatology: An examination of mediating mechanisms. *Journal of Abnormal Psychology, 103,* 836–840.

Stice, E., Spangler, D., & Agras, W. S. (2001). Exposure to media-portrayed thin-ideal images adversely affects vulnerable girls: A longitudinal experiment. *Journal of Social & Clinical Psychology, 20,* 270–288.

Strasburger, V. C. (2002). Alcohol advertising and adolescents. *Pediatric Clinics of North America, 49,* 353–376.

Strasburger, V. C., & Wilson, B. J. (2002). *Children, adolescents, & the media.* Thousand Oaks, CA: Sage.

Strouse, J. S., & Buerkel-Rothfuss, N. L. (1993). Media exposure and the sexual attitudes and behaviors of college students. In B. S. Greenberg, J. D. Brown, & N. L. Buerkel-Rothfuss (Eds.), *Media, sex and the adolescent* (pp. 277–292). Creskill, NJ: Hampton Press.

Strouse, J. S., Buerkel-Rothfuss, N., & Long, E. C. (1995). Gender and family as moderators of the relationship between music video exposure and adolescent sexual permissiveness. *Adolescence, 30,* 505–521.

Strouse, J. S., & Fabes, R. A. (1985). Formal vs. informal sources of sex education: Competing forces in the sexual socialization process. *Adolescence, 78,* 251–263.

Sutton, M. J., Brown, J. D., Wison, K. M., & Klein, J. D. (2002). Shaking the tree of knowledge for forbidden fruit: Where adolescents learn about sexuality and contraception. In J. D. Brown, J. R. Steele, & K. Walsh-Childers (Eds.), *Sexual teens, sexual media* (pp. 25–55). Mahwah, NJ: Erlbaum.

Tan, A. S. (1979). TV beauty ads and role expectations of adolescent female viewers. *Journalism Quarterly, 56,* 283–288.

Taylor, C. B., Sharpe, T., Shisslak, C., Bryson, S., Estes, L. S., Gray, N., et al. (1998). Factors associated with weight concerns in adolescent girls. *International Journal of Eating Disorders, 24*(1), 31–42.

Teenage Research Unlimited. (2001). Teens spend $155 billion in 2000 [press release]. Retrieved August 23, 2001, from http//www.teenresearch.com/Prview.cfm?edit_id=75

Terre, L., Drabman, R. S., & Speer, P. (1991). Health-relevant behaviors in media. *Journal of Applied Social Psychology, 21,* 1303–1319.

Thompson, J. K., & Heinberg, L. J. (1999). The media's influence on body image disturbance and eating disorders: We've reviled them, now can we rehabilitate them? *Journal of Social Issues, 55,* 339–353.

Thompson, J. K., & Smolak, L. (2001). *Body image, eating disorders, and obesity in childhood and adolescence.* Washington, DC: American Psychological Association.

Thompson, J. K., & Stice, E. (2001). Thin-ideal internalization: Mounting evidence for a new risk factor for body-image disturbance and eating pathology. *Current Directions in Psychological Science, 10*(5), 181–183.

Thompson, J. K., Heinberg, L. J., Altabe, M., & Tantleff-Dunn, S. (1999). *Exacting beauty: Theory, assessment, and treatment of body image disturbance.* Washington, DC: American Psychological Association.

Thompson, M., Walsh-Childers, K., & Brown, J. D. (1993). The influence of family communication patterns and sexual experience on processing of a movie video. In B. S. Greenberg, J. D. Brown, & N. L. Buerkel-Rothfuss (Eds.), *Media, sex and the adolescent* (pp. 248–263). Creskill, NJ: Hampton Press.

Thumbs Up! Thumbs Down! (2001). *Data summary and comparison of tobacco use in movies.* Sacramento, CA: American Lung Association of Sacramento-Emigrant Trails.

Tickle, J. J., Sargent, J. D., Dalton, M., Beach, M., & Heatherton, T. F. (2001). Favourite movie stars, their tobacco use in contemporary movies, and its association with adolescent smoking. *Tobacco Control, 10*(1), 16–22.

Tiggemann, M., & Pickering, A. S. (1996). Role of television in adolescent women's body dissatisfaction and drive for thinness. *International Journal of Eating Disorders, 20*(2), 199–203.

Took, K. J., & Weiss, D. S. (1994). The relationship between heavy metal and rap music and adolescent turmoil: Real or artifact? *Adolescence, 29*(115), 613–621.

Turner, S. L., Hamilton, H., Jacobs, M., Angood, L. M., & Dwyer, D. H. (1997). The influence of fashion magazines on the body image satisfaction of college women: An exploratory analysis. *Adolescence, 32*(127), 603–614.

Unger, J. B., Johnson, C. A., & Rohrbach, L. A. (1995). Recognition and liking of tobacco and alcohol advertisements among adolescents: Relationships with susceptibility to substance use. *Preventive Medicine, 24,* 461–466.

U.S. Department of Health and Human Services. (1994). *Preventing tobacco use among young people: A report of the Surgeon General, 1994.* Atlanta, GA: Public Health Service, Centers for Disease Control and Prevention, Office on Smoking and Health.

van Hoeken, D., Lucas, A. R., & Hoek, H. W. (1998). Epidemiology. In H. W. Hoek, J. L. Treasure, & M. A. Katzman (Eds.), *Neurobiology in the treatment of eating disorders* (pp. 97–126). New York: Wiley.

Violato, C., & Holden, W. (1987). A confirmatory factory analysis of a four-factory model of adolescent concerns. *Journal of Youth and Adolescence, 17,* 101–113.

Walsh-Childers, K., Gotthoffer, A., & Lepre, C. R. (2002). From "just the facts" to "downright salacious": Teens' and women's magazine coverage of sex and sexual health. In J. D. Brown, J. R. Steele, & K. Walsh-Childers (Eds.), *Sexual teens, sexual media* (pp. 153–171). Mahwah, NJ: Erlbaum.

Ward, L. M. (1995). Talking about sex: Common themes about sexuality in the prime-time television programs children and adolescents view most. *Journal of Youth and Adolescence, 24,* 595–615.

Ward, L. M. (2002). Does television exposure affect emerging adults' attitudes and assumptions about sexual relationships? Correlational and experimental confirmation. *Journal of Youth and Adolescence, 31,* 1–15.

Ward, L. M., & Rivadeneyra, R. (1999). Contribution of Entertainment Television to adolescents' sexual attitudes and expectations: The role of viewing amount versus viewer involvement. *The Journal of Sex Research, 36,* 237–249.

Wartella, E., Heintz, K., Aidman, A., & Mazzarella, S. (1990). Television and beyond: Children's video media in one community. *Communication Research, 17,* 45–64.

Weiss, S., & Moore, M. (1995). Sources of alcohol and drug information among Israeli urban adolescents. *Journal of Drug Education, 25,* 211–222.
Wells, A. (1990). Popular music: Emotional use and management. *Journal of Popular Culture, 24*(1), 105–117.
Wilks, J., Vardanega, A. T., & Callan, V. J. (1992). Effect of television advertising of alcohol on alcohol consumption and intentions to drive. *Drug & Alcohol Review, 11*(1), 15–21.
Wiseman, C. V., Gray, J. J., Mosimann, J. E., & Ahrens, A. H. (1992). Cultural expectations of thinness in women: An update. *International Journal of Eating Disorders, 11*(1), 85–89.
Wright, J. D., & Pearl, L. (2000). Experience and knowledge of young people regarding illicit drug use, 1969–99. *Addiction, 95,* 1225–1235.
Zillmann, D. (2000). Influence of unrestrained access to erotica on adolescents' and young adults' dispositions toward sexuality. *Journal of Adolescent Health, 27,* 41–44.
Zillmann, D. (2002). Exemplification theory of media influence. In J. Bryant & D. Zillmann (Eds.), *Media effects: Advances in theory and research* (2nd ed., pp. 19–41). Mahwah, NJ: Erlbaum.

Chapter 17

THE LEGAL REGULATION OF ADOLESCENCE

Elizabeth S. Scott and Jennifer L. Woolard

The scientific view of the boundaries between childhood and adulthood recognizes adolescence as a discrete developmental period "beginning in biology and ending in society" (Lerner & Galambos, 1998, p. 414). Scientists generally divide the span of adolescence into early (ages 11–14), middle (ages 15–18) and late (ages 18–21) periods (Steinberg, 1999). Few researchers believe that development in all domains track these phases with stage-like consistency but instead consider adolescent development as a series of transitions to maturity, the pace of which varies among adolescents and across contexts within an individual (Steinberg, 1999). Biological, cognitive, and social transitions affect adolescents' capacities to respond to their environment and elicit changing expectations and reactions from the larger social world (Lerner & Galambos, 1998; Steinberg, 1999).

To what extent does legal regulation recognize the developmental reality of adolescence as a discrete stage and distinguish between adolescents and children (and adults)? The answer is not very much at all. Generally, policy makers ignore this transitional developmental stage, classifying adolescents legally either as children or as adults, depending on the issue at hand. Lawmakers have quite a clear image of childhood, and legal regulation is based on this image (Scott, 2000). Children are assumed to be vulnerable and dependent and to lack the capacity to make competent decisions. Thus, not surprisingly, they are not held legally accountable for their choices or behavior. Children also are not accorded most of the legal rights and privileges that adults enjoy, such as voting, driving, drinking, and making their own medical decisions. Finally, children are assumed to be vulnerable and unable to care for themselves. Thus, their parents and the government are obligated to provide services critical to their welfare—care, support, and education that allow them to develop into healthy adults. When children cross the line to legal adulthood, they are considered autonomous citizens responsible for their own conduct, entitled to legal rights and privileges, and no longer entitled to protections.

The simple binary classification of legal childhood and adulthood in fact is more complex than it seems because the boundary between childhood and adulthood varies depending on the policy purpose. For example, for most purposes, children become legal adults on their 18th birthdays, which is the modern "age of majority." However, 20-year-old college students are legally prohibited from drinking alcohol, while youths in elementary school can be subject to the adult justice system when they are charged with crimes. Thus, although legal regulation offers a clear account of the attributes of children, their legal status is complicated by the shifting boundary between childhood and adulthood.

For most purposes, adolescents are described in legal rhetoric as though they were indistinguishable from young children and are subject to paternalistic policies based on assumptions of dependence, vulnerability, and incompetence. For other purposes, teenagers are treated as fully mature adults, who are competent to make decisions, accountable for their choices, and entitled to no special accommodation. The variation is due mostly to the fact that different policy goals are important in different contexts rather than to efforts to attend to variations in developmental maturity in different domains. For example, allowing 16-year-olds to drive gives young persons independence and mobility, while restricting the privilege to buy alcoholic beverages until age 21 protects youths (and the rest of us) from the costs of immature judgment.

Is there a cost to a legal approach that ignores the developmental realities of adolescence? In our view, the binary classification of childhood and adulthood works quite well for most purposes. It has the advantage of simplicity and administrative efficiency, and arguably it promotes parental responsibility by linking parents' support obligation to their children's general status as dependants. Moreover, because adult rights and duties are extended at different ages for different purposes, the transition to adulthood takes place gradually, even without an intermediate stage of legal adolescence. Adolescents may benefit if they are allowed to make some adult decisions but not others. To return to our example, 16-year-olds acquire experience in the adult domain of driving long before they are legally authorized to make other adult choices like drinking. Thus, even though the crude legal categories distort developmental reality, for the most part, the binary classification system is not harmful to the welfare of adolescents or to general social welfare. In fact, in some areas in which legal regulation subjects adolescents to special treatment (different from adults or children), youths would be better served by the standard approach. As we discuss later in this chapter, regulation of adolescent abortion is such a case.

In some contexts, however, categorical assumptions that ignore the transitional stage of adolescence can lead to harmful outcomes. Juvenile justice policy provides a stark example of a failure of the binary approach. This is an arena in which the boundary of childhood shifted dramatically over the course of the 20th century, and strikingly different accounts of young offenders have been deployed in service of the different policy agendas. The juvenile justice system was established at the end of the 19th century with the purpose of providing rehabilitation to young offenders instead of punishment in the criminal justice system. The Progressive reformers who founded the juvenile court were very committed (in their rhetoric, at least) to describing and dealing with young offenders as children (Van Waters, 1926). In recent years, a major law reform movement has transformed this system, such that today preadolescents can be tried as adults for serious crimes in many states (Torbet et al., 1996). Developmental research indicates both portraits are largely fictional; developmental reality is much more complex. Moreover, in our view, both the romanticized vision of youth offered by the early Progressive founders and the harsh account of modern conservatives have been the basis of unsatisfactory policies. In contrast to many other areas of legal regulation, binary classification in the juvenile justice sphere imposes significant costs both on young offenders and on society. In this context, effective legal regulation requires a realistic account of adolescence based on developmental theory and empirical research.

For more than 20 years, social scientists and legal scholars have argued for the need for developmental research on adolescence to inform legal policy and practice (Grisso & Lovinguth, 1982; Melton, 1981; Reppucci, Weithorn, Mulvey, & Monahan, 1984; Wald, 1976). In this chapter we describe and evaluate the extent to which legal regulation recognizes the developmental reality of adolescence and differences between adolescents and either children or adults. First, we present the legal account of childhood, sketching the traits that are assumed to distinguish children from adults and discussing the absence of any clear vision of adolescence. Next, we describe how the legal boundary between childhood and adulthood is determined, and we show that the judgment is determined by policy (and politics) as much as it is by science. Our analysis includes a description of the forces that led to the passage of the 26th Amendment, which extended voting rights to 18-year-olds—an enactment that led states to lower the age of majority for many purposes. We then examine medical decision making and abortion rights, an issue that clarifies the difficulties in creating a special legal status for adolescence. Finally, we examine juvenile justice policy and explain why binary classification has not worked well in this context. We conclude that a justice policy that treats adolescence as a distinct legal category not only will promote youth welfare but will also help reduce the costs of youth crime.

LEGAL ASSUMPTIONS ABOUT CHILDHOOD

Several assumptions undergird the legal regulation of children. Because children are assumed to be incapable of looking out for themselves, they need adult care and protection. Specifically, three interrelated dimensions of immaturity guide legal policy. First, children are dependent beings and must rely on adults to meet their basic needs for survival—food, shelter, clothing—and for education and care to allow them to mature into healthy, productive adults. Children are also presumed to be incapable of making sound decisions, due to cognitive immaturity that limits youthful understanding and reasoning capacities and to immature judgment (because of psychosocial immaturity) that may lead to harmful or risky choices (Scott, 1992; Zimring, 1982). Finally, children are presumed to be malleable, a characteristic that makes them susceptible to influence and vulnerable to harm from others (Van Waters, 1926).

These assumptions about childhood justify the need for adult control over children's lives and clarify why the legal rights, privileges, and duties to which adults are subject are not extended to children. The law accords parents the primary authority and responsibility for rearing children and caring for their needs. Parents have authority to make decisions about all aspects of children's lives, from medical care and education to the most mundane aspects of daily living. In turn, the law charges parents with safeguarding children's welfare and protecting them from harm. The Supreme Court elaborated on the basis of parental authority in *Parham v. J.R* (1979), an opinion that dealt with the commitment of children to state psychiatric hospitals.

> The law's concept of a family rests on a presumption that parents possess what children lack in maturity, experience, and capacity for judgment required to make life's difficult decisions. More importantly, historically it has recognized that natural bonds of affection lead parents to act in the best interests of their children. (p. 602)

Parents do not have blanket authority in making child-rearing decisions, however. When parents fail to fulfill their duties, the consequences redound to the child and to a society interested in a healthy, productive citizenry. When parents abuse or neglect their children, the state intervenes on children's behalf under its *parens patriae* authority to protect the welfare of minors (Rendleman, 1971). The state also preempts parental authority categorically on some matters; thus, parents are subject to child labor and compulsory school attendance laws that remove discretion on these matters (*Prince v. Massachusetts,* 1944).

The unique legal status of children can be seen in several distinct aspects of legal regulation. First, the rights and privileges of children are more restricted than are those of adults. For example, concerns about juvenile crime and victimization led to curfew laws that restrict minors' nighttime freedom in ways that would clearly be unconstitutional if they were applied to adults (*Schleifer v. City of Charlottesville,* 1997). Limitations on free speech (such as censorship of school newspapers) are imposed on youths because of their presumed vulnerability (*Hazelwood School District v. Kuhlmeier,* 1988). Minors are not permitted to vote, drink alcohol, drive a vehicle, or give consent to their own medical treatment.

Second, children are not held accountable for their choices or responsible for their behavior to the same extent as adults because of assumptions about their cognitive and social immaturity and vulnerability to influence. For example, under the infancy doctrine in contract law, minors can avoid liability on their contracts, presumably because they can not be expected to exercise adult-like judgment or to resist a seller's influence when they are considering a purchase (Scott & Kraus, 2002). Youth are also not held to adult standards for their criminal conduct. The juvenile court was created in part out of the recognition that youthful misconduct is in part a product of their immaturity and that young offenders are less culpable than their adult counterparts are (Arenella, 1992; Scott & Steinberg, 2003).

Third, children are accorded special legal protections and entitlements because of their dependency. Parents are required by law to provide the necessities of food, shelter, clothing, and care for their children, and the government subsidizes the provision of these services when parents are financially unable to do so themselves. The public education system guarantees a free education to children in all states. Civil and criminal child maltreatment laws encourage parents to care for their children; failure to do so can result in coercive interventions ranging from parenting assistance to termination of parental rights and criminal conviction.

In summary, assumptions about the vulnerability, incompetence, and dependency of children result in a complex set of regulations that accord children a unique status in law. Minors are provided special legal protections and entitlements, held less accountable for their actions, and accorded fewer rights and privileges than are adults. Policy makers have multiple goals of protecting children, promoting parental responsibility, and ensuring that children mature into productive adults, all of which are grounded in a set of shared assumptions about what it means to be a child.

DRAWING THE LINE BETWEEN LEGAL CHILDHOOD AND ADULTHOOD

Although the law sets varying age boundaries depending upon the domain of interest, the presumptive boundary between childhood and adulthood is the legal age of majority, which currently is age 18. To some extent, this line tracks developmental knowledge; late adolescents are more similar to adults than to children in their physical and cognitive development (Gardner, Scherer, & Tester, 1989; Siegler, 1991). However, childhood has multiple legal boundaries that are reflected in a complex system of age grading. Deviations from the age of majority can be explained in part as justified because different decision-making domains require different maturity levels. For example, greater maturity is required to serve as president than to drive a motor vehicle. However, although assumptions about maturity and immaturity play a role in the legal judgment about when children become adults for different purposes, other considerations factor into the age-grading scheme. Lawmakers balance the competing goals of promoting youth welfare, protecting parental authority, and considering societal benefit. Administrative efficiency also plays a role, as do political controversy and compromise, as is seen most clearly in the debate over minors' access to abortion. In this section, we examine the categorical approach of the age of majority, and we then turn to medical decision making and abortion access to illustrate the complexity of domain-specific variation in the legal view of adolescence. Both of these latter issues have generated interest among researchers interested in evaluating the legal standard by comparing adolescent and adult capacities.

The Age of Majority: The Legal Invisibility of Adolescence

The age of majority functions as the threshold to legal adulthood for many purposes. Upon attaining the age of 18, adolescents are no longer subject to parental authority; parents are no longer responsible for their children, and the state withdraws the services and protections available under its *parens patriae* powers. Eighteen-year-olds have the legal authority to consent to medical treatment; to execute contracts, deeds, and leases; to vote; and to serve on juries (e.g., Va Code Ann. §1-13.42). They are considered responsible, autonomous individuals who bear the consequences—both good and bad—of their actions and choices.

The legal age of majority represents a crude judgment that late adolescents are mature enough to function in society as adults, but it is not tailored to recognize any specific developmental milestone. Life span research confirms that development is by no means complete at age 18; indeed, some have suggested that young adulthood should constitute a new postadolescence phase of development (Arnett, 2000). Differences between late adolescents and adults are a matter of degree rather than kind, yet as with most phases of development individuals vary widely in their capacities (Scott, Reppucci, & Woolard, 1995; Steinberg & Cauffman, 1996).

The categorical age of majority ignores variation among individuals as well as varying maturity demands in different decision domains, but extending legal childhood into late adolescence has some advantages, even though adult privileges and rights likely are often withheld from competent youths (Melton, 1983a). An extended dependency period assures that youths receive protections and support both from their parents and from the government, and it may reinforce parental responsibility (Scott & Scott, 1995). A bright line rule creates certainty regarding expectations for the relationship between youth, parents, and the state. Domain- or decision-specific assessments of adolescents' capacities would undermine that certainty, creating a complex, inefficient, and costly process that is prone to error. Moreover, for most purposes postponement of adult status imposes few costs on adolescents. Thus, even though it sacrifices developmental accuracy, the categorical approach embodied in the age of majority meets most of the legal system's needs with minimal developmental cost to adolescents.

The right to vote has long been a defining marker of legal adulthood, and it has historically been linked to the age of majority. A cornerstone of participatory democracy, the right to vote is withheld from minors because they are presumed less capable of exercising the right through educated, informed understanding (Cultice, 1992). Thus, the question of when individuals are capable of exercising this right is a consideration in the judgment of when the right should be extended. In the 1960s, research suggested that adolescents possess some of the capacities that are important to political participation. For example, abstract understanding of rights, a sense of community, and conception of the individual as part of the larger social contract develop throughout adolescence into adulthood (Adelson & O'Neil, 1966; Haste &Torney-Purta, 1992).

Most of that early work focused on attitudes and perceptions of children and adolescence, rather than the underlying cognitive capacities (Dudley & Gitelson, 2002; Haste & Torney-Purta, 1992). More recent work examines the development of political socialization (Haste, 1992) and cognitive representations of the social order and political system (Torney-Purta, 1992), but empirical data on age differences between adolescents and adults or developmental trajectories are quite limited. Reviews of political socialization research suggest that there is no particular point when persons learn about politics or develop civic engagement (Dudley & Gitelson, 2002). Although several recent journal issues have been devoted to understanding political engagement and civic participation (Flanagan & Sherrod, 1998; Sherrod, Flanagan, & Youniss, 2002), substantial gaps exist in our understanding of these phenomena from a developmental perspective.

Although adolescents may possess the necessary capacities to engage in informed voting behavior, only rarely in our history has attention focused on the age at which the right to vote is extended, and for the most part, few objections have been expressed over withholding this right from minors—in contrast to protest over withholding other constitutionally protected rights, such as the right to make abortion decisions. This situation probably reflects recognition that it would be costly to identify those individual adolescents who are capable of making informed voting decisions. Lawmakers may also assume that adolescents (and society) incur little harm by postponing the exercise of voting rights until age 18.

In the 1960s, these factors were overcome by a substantial and ultimately successful effort to lower the voting age from 21 to 18. The historical record of this important reform, which is embodied in the 26th amendment to the United States Constitution, highlights the importance of the social and political factors in defining adult status and underscores that developmental maturity may not be the core consideration (Cultice, 1992). During the Vietnam War, legal minors, who were not permitted to vote or exercise other adult rights, were being drafted into military service and sent into battle. Moreover, college students were actively engaged in political participation, protesting against the Vietnam War and in support of civil rights. Noting these political facts, the Senate committee that considered the proposal to lower the voting age also documented in its report that this age group already engaged in a number of adult roles as employees, taxpayers, and citizens subject to criminal laws and punishments (S. Rep. No. 92-26, 1971). The report emphasized that for most purposes, psychological maturity is achieved by age 18.

The passage of the 26th amendment offers an interesting account of the forces that influence judgments about when children become legal adults. First, social and political forces in large measure propelled the initiative to shift the boundary of childhood, but legislators also believed that it was important to ground their proposal in substantive developmental claims about the cognitive and psychosocial maturity of 18-year-olds. Another interesting theme is that in defining the boundary of adult status, lawmakers thought that parity should exist between rights and responsibilities. On this view, 18-year-olds were transformed from children into adults with the most important right of citizenship because they were required to bear the must onerous civic responsibility—military service.

Because the right to vote has always been the marker of legal adulthood, the age of majority was lowered to age 18 for most purposes after the passage of the 26th amendment. This took place through sweeping legislative and judicial action at both the state and federal levels that lowered the age of adult status in domains as disparate as medical decision making, contracting, and entitlement to support.

Medical Decision Making: Special Legal Status for Adolescents

In contrast to the sparse empirical foundation for the extension of voting rights to late adolescents, a substantial body of research has focused on adolescents' capacity to consent to medical treatment. Although in general, adolescents are subject to their parents' authority in this realm, the law has granted adolescents the authority to consent to certain types of treatment without involving their parents. Moreover, a complex regulatory scheme governs adolescent decisions to obtain abortion; in this domain lawmakers have adopted the unusual approach of treating adolescence as a category distinct from childhood and adulthood. Although the capacities to consent to different medical procedures may develop comparably, different social and political considerations have shaped legal policies in these contexts. Thus the broad domain of medical decision making offers an interesting case study in how factors other than maturity may determine the boundary between childhood and adulthood.

Medical Treatment: Informed Consent and Mature Minors

Adolescents do not have the legal authority to consent to most medical treatments until they reach the age of majority. Presumed to lack the necessary capacities, they are subject to the decision-making authority of their parents, who are presumed to act in their children's best interests. The basis for parental authority in this area is relatively straightforward. Medical treatment must be based on competent informed consent—otherwise, the treatment provider commits a battery on the patient (e.g., *Younts v. St. Francis Hospital,* 1970). For consent to be informed, it must be knowing, rational, and voluntary (Meisel, Roth, & Lidz, 1977). In general, these legal concepts have been translated to mean that an individual must have a factual understanding of the information provided, utilize a rational process to assimilate information, and make a decision that is not simply the result of coercion or deference to another. Legal regulation gives parents authority to give informed consent to their children's (including adolescents') medical treatment, in part because lawmakers assume that children and adolescents are not competent to do so themselves.

Thus, an interesting threshold question is whether this assumption about adolescents' incompetence is valid. Competence is a legal construct that may differ depending on the context; a finding of competence to consent to one form of medical treatment does not necessarily indicate a generalized competence to consent to all treatments. Nonetheless, basic cognitive capacities known to develop during childhood and adolescence underlie the ability to provide informed consent, regardless of the specific context. Grisso and Vierling (1978) map the legal terms of knowing, intelligent, and voluntary consent onto relevant psychological concepts and developmental considerations. Using their framework, we summarize what is known about adolescents' capacities generally, providing detail from studies of informed consent.

Grisso and Vierling (1978) define *knowing* consent as the match between the meaning of the information provided to the patient and the meaning attached by the patient to that information; this implicates understanding of specific terms as well as ethical and legal concepts such as rights and confidentiality. Research on children's knowledge of rights reports an age-based progression from concrete thinking about what rights can do for an individual to more abstract appraisals of rights and moral implications, typically emerging in adolescence (Melton, 1980, 1983b; Melton & Limber, 1992), although concrete thinking about rights still persists in adolescence (e.g., Ruck, Keating, Abramovitch, & Koegl, 1998).

Intelligent consent refers to the capacity for assimilating and processing the information in a rational manner to reach a decision. Such a process implicates a wide range of abilities for abstract reasoning and logical thinking. Recent reviews conclude that these basic cognitive capacities have developed sufficiently by about midadolescence, although variations exist among individuals and within individuals across decision domains (Steinberg & Cauffman, 1996). Weithorn and Campbell (1982) presented 9-, 14-, 18-, and 21-year-olds with hypothetical dilemmas regarding alternative treatments for two medical conditions (diabetes and epilepsy) and two psychological conditions (depression and enuresis). The 14-year-olds performed comparably to the two adult groups on outcome scores for evidence of choice, reasonableness of outcome (as judged by experts in the field), rationality of reasons, and understanding on three of four dilemmas. In the epilepsy dilemma, however, a higher percentage of adolescents rejected the reasonable treatment, which occasionally had physical side effects that might affect attractiveness. Although 9-year-olds were able to express a reasonable treatment choice, they clearly demonstrated poorer capacities than did adolescents and adults to understand and reason about the information provided.

Voluntary consent is given freely, not as a product of coercion or deference to others. Scherer and colleagues (Scherer, 1991; Scherer & Reppucci, 1998) presented groups of children, adolescents, and adults with three hypothetical treatment dilemmas in which the degree of parental influence varied. Most participants in all groups deferred to parental authority for less serious treatment decisions, but adolescents and young adults were less likely than children were to go along with parental wishes regarding a kidney transplant. Developmental aspects of deference to the authority of medical personnel are not as well known. In this realm, research on consent to treatment is sparse; after treatment decisions have been made, however, adolescents are generally less compliant than adults are, but rates vary by the type of treatment and related factors such as complexity of regime (Cromer & Tarnowski, 1989).

The research corpus on consent to treatment is limited by its reliance on samples of White, middle-class youth responding to hypothetical vignette, but it indicates that by age 14, most adolescents have developed the capacities to meet the threshold requirements for informed consent to medical and mental health treatment. Thus, empirical evidence largely contradicts the legal presumption of minors' incompetence to consent to treatment.

Even if many adolescents are competent to make medical decisions, giving parents legal authority may be a sensible policy for most medical treatments. It obviates the need and cost of individual competence assessments, and it encourages parents to provide for their children's welfare—and to pay their children's medical bills. Moreover, although adolescents may be competent to make medical decisions within the informed consent framework, psychosocial influences on decision making may lead them to make choices that reflect immature judgment. As mentioned, for example, Weithorn and Campbell (1982) found adolescents more reluctant than adults to choose a beneficial treatment with untoward effects on physical appearance—perhaps due to greater youthful sensitivity to peer approval. In general, it seems likely that children and their parents do not have a conflict of interest about most treatment decisions, so the standard approach of giving parents authority generally functions satisfactorily to protect children's interests in this realm.

Most exceptions to the general rule that parents have authority to make medical decisions for their children arise in contexts in which minors' welfare and the general social welfare would be compromised if parental consent were required. The traditional mature minor doctrine allows older competent minors to consent to routine beneficial treatment or treatment in emergency situations when parents would likely consent or are unavailable (Wadlington, 1973). More interesting are statutes in many states that give minors the authority to consent to specific types of medical treatments. Such treatments typically include treatment for sexually transmitted diseases, substance abuse, mental health problems, and contraception and pregnancy (e.g., Va Code § 54.1-2969).

These minor consent statutes presume that adolescents are competent to consent to the designated medical treatments but not on the basis of a judgment about adolescent maturity. Instead, minors are allowed to seek treatment without involving their parents out of concern that the standard requirement of parental consent may expose vulnerable youths to harm. The harm may come from two sources. First, lawmakers may rightly be concerned that for the kinds of treatments targeted by minors' consent statutes, parents, in fact, may have a conflict of interest with their children; if so, the traditional presumption that parents will generally act to promote their children's welfare may not hold. For example, parents may be angry when they learn of their children's sexual activity or drug use. Just as important is that adolescents' fears about the anticipated parental reaction—regardless of whether such fears are accurate—might deter some adolescents from seeking needed treatment. Removing the parental consent barrier to treatment benefits the adolescents themselves as well by encouraging them to seek treatment; it also may reduce the prevalence of these harmful and costly conditions and thus also benefit social welfare.

Access to Abortion: Competing Ideologies and Developmental Capacities

Of the issues in which lawmakers have departed from the standard legal treatment of adolescence, none has generated more controversy than the question of when or if legal minors should have access to abortion. This debate has brought into stark relief conflicting perspectives on adolescents and their capacities. Conservatives depict pregnant teens as children who should be subject to their parents' authority, whereas advocates for youthful self-determination describe them as adults. Moreover, both sides are concerned not only with the developmental capacities and rights of minors but also with the larger contest over abortion rights, regardless of age (Gorney, 1998; Rubin, 1998). Developed against the background of this intense controversy, the legal framework is a complex product of political compromise. Thus, in many states, lawmakers regulating abortion have rejected the conventional binary classification and created a separate legal category for adolescents, classifying teens on a case-by-case basis as either children or adults. We argue that this costly regulatory scheme harms the interests of pregnant teens and offers little in the way of social benefit.

Advocates of adolescent self-determination argue that adolescents should be accorded adult status because the decision to terminate a pregnancy differs in many ways from other types of medical treatment. Because this choice is grounded in constitutionally based privacy and autonomy rights, lawmakers can not ignore evidence that adolescents have the developmental maturity to make this decision. In the last two decades, researchers have struggled to investigate adolescent decision making about abortion in ecologically valid ways. Social scientists have examined many dimensions of the abortion decision, including moral and personal dimensions of reasoning (e.g., Smetana, 1981), patterns of consultation with others (e.g., Finken & Jacobs, 1996; Resnick, Bearlinger, Stark, & Blum, 1994), and the medical and mental health sequelae (Pope, Adler, & Tschann, 2001; Quinton, Major, & Richards, 2001).

The few studies that have focused on this decision context have found few significant differences between the capacities of older adolescents and adults to meet the legal requirements for informed consent to abortion. Lewis interviewed 42 adolescents and adults about their pregnancy decisions and found no age-based differences in decision-making strategy or abstract reasoning. Adolescents did view their decisions as more externally compelled (through pressure from parents) than adults, indirectly implicating the voluntariness prong of competence. Ambuel and Rappaport (1992) interviewed young adolescents (ages 15 and under), older adolescents (ages 16–17), and adults (ages 18–21) awaiting pregnancy test results at a medical clinic. Responses were scored according to four criteria relevant to legal competence: volition of choice, global quality of reasoning, consequences, and richness of reasoning. Overall, these researchers found no age differences in any dimensions of competence. Young adolescents who reported they would not consider abortion as an option scored significantly worse than adults did on volition, consequences, and global quality of reasoning. Although these studies are limited, they are consistent with more general research on decision making in their conclusion that mid- to late adolescents have developed the basic cognitive capacities required to provide valid informed consent.

Those who argue that adolescents should be classified as adults for purposes of abortion decision making do not rely solely on developmental claims or on the constitutional importance of the decision. After all, minors may be competent to exercise constitutional rights in other domains (e.g., voting, jury service) but are not granted the right to do so, in part because no great harm results from postponement. A distinguishing feature of the childbearing decision is that it cannot be postponed and that it has enormous consequences for the individual—often for the course of her future life. Moreover, pregnancy and childbirth pose substantial health risks for teens—and for their children—as well as negative consequences for the future welfare of both young mothers and their children (Furstenburg, Brooks-Gunn, & Chase-Lansdale, 1989). For these reasons, advocates who have little interest in adolescent self-determination per se might well support adolescent access to abortion on paternalistic grounds (Scott, 1992).

The rationale for allowing adolescents to make decisions about abortion without involving their parents is similar in many regards to the rationale that supports the minor consent statutes, as we discussed previously. As with treatment for substance abuse, contraception, and sexually transmitted diseases, the decision about abortion is one on which parents' interests may not be consonant with those of their children. The parents' moral or religious views about abortion or teenage sexual behavior may trump concerns for the health or welfare of their pregnant adolescents. Although substantial research documents parental attitudes, behaviors, and influence on adolescent sexual behavior (Brooks-Gunn & Furstenburg, 1989; Meschke, Bartholomae, & Zentall, 2002), only a few studies have examined parental views or decision making in the abortion context (Henshaw & Kost, 1992; Resnick et al., 1994; Torres, Forrest, & Eisman, 1980).

Abortion is similar to treatments targeted by minors' consent statutes in another way. Even if parents would be supportive of the choices their daughters make, teens might postpone dealing with the pregnancy because they fear their parents' reactions—a consequence with potentially even greater consequences than postponing other treatments. Approximately one half to two thirds of all adolescents do consult their parents about pregnancy; younger adolescents—who may be most in need of parental support and advice—are more likely than are older girls to talk to their parents (Adler, Smith, & Tschann, 1998). Indeed, most adolescents who obtain an abortion consult parents or another adult (Resnick et al., 1994). In a nationally representative sample of unmarried minors having an abortion, 61% had told their parents; the most common reasons for nondisclosure were desires to preserve the relationship with parents (e.g., they might be hurt, disappointed, or angry), to prevent interference with relationships (e.g., parents might prevent relationship with the sexual partner), and to protect parents from additional problems (e.g., parents already had enough stress; Henshaw & Kost, 1992). In a study of women obtaining an elective, first-trimester abortion, adolescents scored significantly higher than adults on perceptions that having an abortion conflicts with how her parents viewed her (Quinton et al., 2001). At 1 month after the abortion, adolescents reported fewer benefits and greater harm from the abortion than did adults, a difference that was explained in part by the significant age difference in parental conflict. Some observers have suggested that adolescents have unrealistically negative views of potential parental reaction to sex-related issues (Newcomer & Udry, 1985), but in large measure the accuracy of their beliefs is less relevant than the impact of those beliefs and concerns on adolescent behavior. In the Henshaw and Kost (1992) study, a substantial proportion of adolescents who did not tell their parents about their abortions reported as the reasons that they had experienced family violence (30%), feared domestic violence, or thought they might be kicked out of the house if their parents found out about the abortion. Thus, standard legal requirements of parental consent to minors' medical treatment may pose a threat to the welfare of pregnant teens.

In one way abortion is different from the treatments targeted by minors consent statutes, but the difference itself arguably points in the direction of adolescent self-determination in this context. Unlike other procedures for which adolescents can provide consent without their parents' involvement, abortion involves a highly contested moral choice. Few dispute that the right choice for adolescents with a drug problem is treatment. However, no consensus exists about the right choice for a pregnant adolescent. Thus, a core issue in classifying pregnant teens as children or as adults is whether parents (or courts) should have the authority to impose their values on a pregnant adolescent or whether her values should determine whether she ends the pregnancy or has a child.

The legal regulation of adolescent access to abortion varies in different states. Some states (e.g., Connecticut, Washington) have shifted the boundary of childhood downward and classified pregnant teens as adults for abortion decisions, adopting the approach of the minor consent statutes. Others have maximized the reach of parental authority to the extent that it is constitutionally permitted, conceptualizing abortion as similar to more routine medical decisions. A series of United States Supreme Court decisions have defined the parameters of state regulation, permitting restrictions that would be unconstitutional for adults while simultaneously preventing states from subjecting adolescents to conventional parental authority. Parental consent cannot be required of mature minors, but states can require that the determination of maturity be the subject of a judicial proceeding (*Bellotti v. Baird,* 1979). Under Supreme Court doctrine, if a minor is found to be immature, the court, exercising the state's *parens patriae* authority, must determine whether an abortion without parental involvement is in her best interest (*Bellotti v. Baird,* 1979; *City of Akron v. Akron Center for Reproductive Health,* 1983). Although parents are not granted veto power over an adolescent's abortion (*Bellotti v. Baird,* 1979; *City of Akron v. Akron Center for Reproductive Health,* 1983; *Planned Parenthood of Central Missouri v. Danforth,* 1976), states can require that parents must be notified of their daughter's intent to obtain abortion (*H.L. v. Matheson,* 1981; *Hodgson v. Minnesota,* 1990; *Ohio v. Akron Center for Reproductive Health,* 1990). Indeed, the Court upheld a parental requirement that *both* parents be notified even if they are divorced (*Hodgson v. Minnesota,* 1990).

Under the scheme of legal regulation that has evolved in response to the Supreme Court's pronouncements, many states require that the maturity of the pregnant adolescent be determined an individualized basis in a judicial bypass hearing, in which a judge evaluates whether the teen is "mature and well enough informed" to make her own abortion decision (*Bellotti v. Baird,* 1979, p. 647). The Court has provided no further guidance to courts making these determinations and studies, and judicial opinions confirm that the indeterminacy of such a standard results in wide variability of bypass hearing outcomes. In some states virtually all petitions are granted with justifications that appear paternalistic rather than autonomy-focused (Mnookin, 1985). In Massachusetts, 1,000 hearings per year resulted in 13 denials over a 10-year period (Mnookin, 1985). Similarly, only 9 minors were deemed immature out of 477 Ohio bypass hearings that lasted an average of 12 minutes (Yates & Pliner, 1988). Other states grant few petitions, and advocates recommended that adolescents go to nearby states to seek an abortion (Lewin, 1992). The capacities those adolescents seeking abortion via judicial bypass (as a distinct subgroup of adolescents seeking abortion) have not been systematically studied; nonetheless, it is highly unlikely that the extreme variation in the outcomes of bypass hearings is a function of accurate competence assessments (i.e., virtually all young women in one state are competent to consent, whereas all in another state are not), particularly given the hearings' limited duration. Much more likely is that the attitudes of courts about abortion, teen pregnancy, and parental authority play an important role in judges' evaluations of maturity.

The legal framework endorsed by the Supreme Court can be understood as an effort to find an acceptable resolution to a highly contested dispute about the boundary of childhood—a dispute that has more to do with conflicting attitudes about abortion itself than with views on the maturity or autonomy interests and capacities of adolescents. In a legal framework that predicates the minor's exercise of her constitutional right of choice on her ability to persuade a court of her maturity, even mature teens are subject to greater regulation than are their adult counterparts. At the same time, however, states are precluded from treating pregnant adolescents as children subject to their parents' authority solely because they are minors. This regulatory scheme eschews the categorical bright-line demarcation of childhood in favor of a special intermediate status for adolescents, albeit through a costly, time-consuming procedure of individualized maturity determinations.

On its face, this exception to the bright-line rule is consistent with recognition of adolescence as a unique developmental period. However, it appears that this regulatory framework that treats adolescence as an intermediate category can be understood as the result of political and moral compromise rather than as an expression of developmentally based legal theory. Although this compromise may remove the controversy from the politically charged legislative arena to the more deliberative setting of the courtroom, the regulatory scheme has little to recommend it. Empirical research has yet to examine the impact of participation in bypass hearings on health and developmental outcomes, but this procedural hurdle may lead pregnant teens to delays that can increase the health risks of abortion. Moreover, there is little reason to believe that the assessment of maturity that is the function of bypass hearings serves any useful purpose. Few studies examine the factors that predict judicial decision making. In some jurisdictions minimal variability in the outcome measure precludes meaningful statistical analysis; in others, judicial attitudes about abortion or teen pregnancy may trump adolescent capacities as an outcome predictor. The upshot is that the creation of an intermediate category of adolescence in this context apparently does little to promote the health of adolescents and the welfare of society or has no obvious advantage over the binary classification found in minors' consent statutes under which adolescents are simply treated as legal adults.

The experience with abortion regulation reinforces the theme with which we began. Although psychologists recognize adolescence as a distinct developmental period, for the most part, the law's tendency to ignore this transitional stage does not seem to have harmful effects. The rather simplistic approach of binary classification, under which the transition to adulthood is effected through a series of bright-line legal rules, seems to serve the collective purpose of facilitating young citizens' development to healthy adulthood. Adolescents can drive at age 16, they can vote and execute contracts at age 18, but they remain children until age 21 for the purposes of purchasing alcohol and (in some states) receiving child support while they attend college. The societal and developmental costs of delaying these rights and responsibilities do not appear to outweigh the benefits of such an approach.

RECOGNIZING ADOLESCENCE IN JUVENILE JUSTICE POLICY

There is one context in which policies that recognize the unique developmental status of adolescence would serve to promote both the interests of youth and of society. In juvenile justice policy, lawmakers have followed the conventional approach, treating young offenders either as children or as adults during different historical periods. As the following account suggests, neither of these approaches has worked satisfactorily.

Evolving Portraits of Adolescent Offenders

The Era of Wayward Children: The Traditional Juvenile Court

At the turn of the 20th century, the establishment of the juvenile court was part of a broader Progressive reform agenda that expanded the boundaries of childhood and dramatically reshaped the relationship between families and the state (Kett, 1977; Levine & Levine, 1970; Tiffin, 1982). With the creation of compulsory school attendance laws, the prohibition of child labor, and the establishment of a child welfare system, government assumed a far more active role in the supervision and even preemption of parental authority in the upbringing of children. Progressive reformers pursued a fundamental objective of improving the experience of childhood and expanding its boundaries, with a goal of shaping youths into productive citizens. In the rhetoric of this era, adolescents were described as children who required the care and protection of their parents—or of the state if parents were not up to the task. A reformer and juvenile court judge, Miriam Van Waters (1926) described the underlying theory of the new juvenile court, which was a core component of the Progressive program, in the following terms:

> The child of the proper age to be under the jurisdiction of the juvenile court is encircled by the arm of the state, which, as a sheltering, wise parent, assumes guardianship and has power to shield the child from the rigors of the common law and from the neglect and depravity of adults. (p. 9)

In an era in which teens often assumed adult roles and responsibilities, reformers used several strategies to create a new image of adolescents. First, as the statement by Van Waters suggests, advocates described the youths who would benefit from Progressive policies in terms that emphasized their vulnerability, innocence, and dependence. For example, dramatic stories of horrendous working conditions in factories bolstered the arguments for the need for protection through compulsory school attendance and child labor laws (Bremner, 1974). The solution to exploitation of children was a government ready to intervene to provide what the Progressives thought parents failed to provide—firm guidance and benevolent protection from harm.

The romantic rhetoric and protectionist agenda was readily accepted as applied to children who were subject to parental maltreatment, but reshaping the image of delinquent youth was more of a challenge. An important focus of Progressive reform was the establishment of a separate court that would respond to the needs of children who were subject to abuse and neglect by their parents and would also deal with juvenile offenders up to 16 or 18 years of age. Young offenders would not be subject to criminal punishment but instead would receive rehabilitative treatment that would guide them on the path to productive adulthood. A second rhetorical strategy employed by the reformers was to downplay distinctions between young offenders and child victims of parental abuse, by arguing that abuse, neglect, and delinquency were *all* manifestations of inadequate parenting (Fox, 1967). Thus, young offenders were portrayed as children whose parents had failed them, and the state's role in both delinquency and maltreatment cases was "to intervene in the spirit of a wise parent" (Van Waters, 1926, p. 11) to provide care and rehabilitation. Advocates and judges related stories of young offenders—boys and girls, younger and older teens, committing minor and more serious offenses—who came before the juvenile court and responded favorably to paternalistic interventions designed only to promote their welfare (Lindsey & O'Higgins, 1909).

Although the child labor and school attendance reforms effectively shifted the boundary of childhood, the Progressive efforts in the area of juvenile justice were far less successful. The romanticized accounts of young offenders as innocent children wronged by their parents ignored the crucial distinction between delinquents and maltreated children—that criminal conduct causes harm to others. Thus, the system's pretense that delinquency proceedings were solely to promote the welfare of the child before the court ignored the state's legitimate interest in protecting society from crime. Moreover, acceptance of the rehabilitative model was likely always premised on the success of rehabilitative interventions in reforming young offenders and protecting society—and over time, confidence in the effectiveness of rehabilitation waned.

Advocates for youths also became disenchanted with the juvenile court (Allen, 1964). Young offenders were processed without the procedural protections and guarantees that were provided in adult criminal court, in exchange for a promise of rehabilitation that was seldom provided (*In re Gault,* 1967; *Kent v. U.S.*, 1966). The traditional model of juvenile justice, in treating (or in claiming to treat) young offenders as children, failed to serve the interests of adolescent offenders, and it failed to serve society's interest. As the 20th century progressed, the myth of the rehabilitative ideal was discredited together with the image of the adolescent offender as an innocent child.

Contemporary Reform and Young Criminals

In sharp contrast to the Progressive depiction of young offenders as children, contemporary conservative reformers argue that youths who commit serious crimes should be tried and punished as adults. This modern reform movement was triggered by substantial increases in violent youth crime in the late 1980s, and it has led to sweeping statutory changes over the past decade or so (Torbet & Szymanski, 1998). The explicit goals of this crusade are public safety and punishment, and little concern is expressed about the welfare of young wrongdoers or hope for their reform. The historical depiction of delinquents as wayward children has been replaced by a modern archetype of the savvy young criminal who is a serious threat to society. Modern advocates of tough policies deny any psychological distinctions between youths and adults that are relevant to criminal responsibility; the mantra of the movement is "adult time for adult crime" (Ellis, 1993; Regnery, 1985).

The contemporary reformers have accomplished the transformation of children charged with crimes into legal adults through several legislative strategies. First, the age at which juveniles can be transferred to adult court has been lowered for many crimes (Torbet et al., 1996). The juvenile court has always used transfer to adult court as a safety valve for youths who are ill suited to its jurisdiction. Traditionally, transfer required a judicial inquiry into a juvenile's appropriateness for juvenile court that considered a broad set of criteria, including the youth's maturity and development. Recent reforms have not only lowered the age of transfer and expanded the range of crimes that can trigger a transfer hearing, but they have also narrowed the scope of the transfer inquiry to focus only on offense seriousness and prior record. In combination, these changes facilitate the transfer of greater numbers of juveniles.

Moreover, reliance on judicial hearings in which transfer decisions are made on a case-by-case basis by judges has yielded in many states to other avenues to criminal court adjudication and punishment of juveniles (Torbet & Szymanski, 1998). Legislative waiver categorically excludes from juvenile court jurisdiction large classes of young offenders, which are usually defined by age and offense category. Thus, a 13-year-old charged with armed robbery may be statutorily defined as an adult and simply not eligible for juvenile court treatment at all. Moreover, *direct file* statutes confer discretion on prosecutors to charge youths as juveniles or as adults for certain crimes. In addition, youths sentenced in juvenile court under blended sentencing schemes serve time in adult facilities after they exceed the age of juvenile corrections jurisdiction. Through these mechanisms, the modern reformers have transformed the legal landscape by lowering the age of adult prosecution and punishment for a broad range of juvenile offenders. Although no national statistics exist, researchers estimate that more than 200,000 youths are tried annually as adults (Sickmund, Snyder, & Poe-Yamagata, 1997).

On one level, these reforms are consistent with some other policies that have lowered the age boundary to define adolescents as adults. Advocates for consent statutes and alcohol restrictions for minors, for example, argue that these policies respond to harmful conduct by adolescents in ways that promote social welfare. Unlike these other policies, however, the modern juvenile justice reforms make little pretense that punishing young offenders as adults will benefit the juveniles themselves. Their advocacy rests solely on a claim that punitive policies will reduce the social costs of youth crime and promote social welfare. In its lack of regard for the welfare of young persons, juvenile justice policy is unique and anomalous in the legal regime of youth regulation. Shortly we review the growing research base that challenges this claim, and we argue that social welfare and youth welfare are undermined by modern juvenile justice reforms.

Enthusiasm for punishing young criminals continues—and cases such as that of the young Washington, DC sniper, John Malvo, reinforce punitive attitudes (Blair, 2003). However, rates of violent juvenile crime have decreased significantly since the mid-1990s (Torbet & Szymanski, 1998) and many people question the wisdom of policies that treat youths as adults for purposes of criminal responsibility when they are deemed vulnerable dependent children for every other legal purpose. A case that captured national attention recently was that of Lionel Tate, a Florida boy who was sentenced to life in prison for killing his 6-year-old neighbor in a wrestling match. Even the prosecutor in that case afterwards expressed regret and discomfort that Lionel had received such harsh punishment (Canedy, 2003). Some critics have argued that the contemporary policies that hold young offenders fully responsible for their crimes violate well-accepted principles that define just punishment in the criminal law (Scott & Steinberg, 2003). In the view of many observers, a reexamination of punitive justice policies is in order (Zimring, 1998, 1999).

Post-Gault Accounts of Adolescent Offenders

Both the history of the traditional juvenile court and the account of contemporary justice policies under which youths are classified as adults suggest that the standard approach to legal regulation of adolescence—binary classification—has not worked well in the context of crime policy. In considering the alternative of a more developmentally based juvenile justice policy, some lessons can be taken from a brief period in the 1970s and 1980s, when reformers and lawmakers took steps to develop a juvenile justice system based on an accurate account of adolescence. The reform period was initiated by the landmark Supreme Court opinion of *In re Gault* in 1967.

In re Gault (1967) exposed the flaws of the rehabilitative model of juvenile justice and the disjunction between the Progressives' rhetoric describing young offenders as innocent children and the harsh reality of juvenile justice interventions. As Justice Fortas described it, juveniles faced the worst of both worlds; they received neither the rehabilitative interventions promised in juvenile court nor the procedural protections guaranteed to adults in the criminal justice system. In *Gault* and a series of Supreme Court opinions that followed in the late 1960s and early 1970s, the Court made clear that juvenile court delinquency proceedings must reform to recognize that youths charged with crimes faced jeopardy and that the state was not simply concerned with their welfare. Juveniles were entitled to be represented by attorneys and they were afforded other procedural rights. At the same time, the Court maintained that the juvenile court was not simply a replica of adult criminal court because its clients were youths and not adults (*McKiever v. Pennsylvania,* 1971).

During the period after *Gault,* several groups proposed reforms based on a developmental account of adolescence (American Bar Association, 1982; Zimring, 1978). These groups rejected the dichotomy of innocent child versus fully responsible adult as the framework for juvenile justice policy. Instead, they posited that young wrongdoers have sufficient capacities of understanding and moral judgment to be held accountable for their offenses but that they were psychologically less mature and thus less blameworthy than were adults. The reformers balanced accountability and immaturity in a framework of diminished responsibility, under which young offenders received shorter sentences for their crimes. The post-*Gault* reforms legitimated the state's interest in public safety and retribution and at the same time acknowledged important developmental differences between adolescents and adults. They also argued that youths should be given "room to reform" because many such youths would mature out of their tendency to commit crimes (Zimring, 1982). Dispositional programs that acknowledged the developmental needs of adolescence and facilitated the transition to productive adulthood were part of the reform vision.

The post-*Gault* reforms led to legislative and policy change during this period. A number of states modified the goals of their juvenile justice systems to incorporate public safety and retribution along with rehabilitation. New sentencing schemes were keyed to offense seriousness and prior record rather than to offender characteristics. However, most statutory reforms of this period also embodied a core premise of the post-*Gault* reforms—that because of their developmental immaturity as compared with adults, young offenders should be dealt with in a separate court and correctional system and should be subject to more lenient punishment than that of their adult counterparts.

Even in the wake of the recent conservative reforms, elements of the developmentally oriented post-*Gault* reforms remain. Some state statutes retain a focus on rehabilitation and offender development in defining the goals of their juvenile justice policy. Pennsylvania, for example, has adopted a "balanced approach" that emphasizes "competency development" (to enable young offenders to become productive adults when they return to society; 42 Pa C.S. § 6301(b), 1999). Moreover, strict sentencing schemes are not always followed by judges who consider immaturity when fashioning dispositions. A Michigan judge recently insisted on sentencing a 13-year-old boy convicted of committing homicide when he was 11 to a juvenile facility, despite a statutory provision encouraging adult penalties (Knott & Brand-Williams, 2000). Moreover, new reform groups have emerged that advocate developmentally based juvenile justice policy, and these groups have undertaken legally relevant development research agendas to inform policy. For example, the MacArthur Foundation has funded a Research Network on Adolescent Development and Juvenile Justice, which over the past decade has undertaken a broad range of ambitious research and policy initiatives in the juvenile justice area.

A Developmental Model of Juvenile Justice Policy

Although the boundary of childhood is drawn in most legal contexts without reference to the transitional developmental stage of adolescence, the conventional approach has failed to produce effective policies in this context. In this section we explain why the law's standard objectives in regulating minors—of promoting youth welfare as well as social welfare—are better served if policy makers recognize that young offenders are neither innocent children nor mature adults.

Traditional juvenile justice policy, although its tone was benign, did more harm than good. Even assuming that the Progressive reformers had pure intentions (an assumption that some have challenged; Platt, 1977), the myth of offenders as vulnerable children was implausible when it was applied to older youths charged with serious crimes. It undermined the credibility of the system, leading many to believe that public safety and accountability did not get adequate attention (Feld, 1999). Moreover, as the Court recognized in *Gault,* young offenders themselves were harmed because the juvenile court operated without the procedural constraints that protect adult criminal defendants, whose interest was always understood to be in conflict with that of the state. Furthermore, because the ostensible purpose of intervention was to rehabilitate rather than punish the child, the court and correctional system had virtually unbridled discretion in fashioning dispositions, unconstrained by the principles limiting criminal punishment (Allen, 1964; Scott & Steinberg, 2003). Thus, because punishment and public protection were important but hidden forces at work in the disposition of young offenders, the reality of the juvenile justice system was that many youths got little rehabilitation in prison-like correctional facilities. A return to traditional juvenile justice policy is not the solution to the excesses of the recent punitive reforms.

Modern reformers make two empirical claims in justifying punitive policies—claims that we challenge in this section. First, they assume that adolescents are not different from adults in any way that is important to criminal responsibility and thus deserve the same punishment for their offenses as their adult counterparts. Second, conservative reformers also assume (and argue) that punishing young offenders as adults is essential to protection of society from juvenile crime. The empirical evidence from developmental psychology and criminology challenges both of these assumptions. First, the evidence indicates that adolescent psychosocial immaturity distinguishes young lawbreakers from adults in ways that are very likely to affect their understanding and judgment in making criminal choices. Thus, holding them fully accountable for their crimes violates the principle of proportionality, which defines fair criminal punishment. Second, it is not clear that tough policies reduce crime or promote social welfare. Recent research on developmental pathways suggests that the majority of adolescent offenders desist from offending as part of their life course development. Moreover, other research comparing youths retained in juvenile court with those prosecuted as adults indicates that harsh policies may aggravate recidivism rates. Thus, policies based on utilitarian goals must consider the long-term consequences of punishment in addition to the direct costs of juvenile crime.

Criminal Responsibility in Adolescence

The criminal law assumes that most offenders make rational autonomous choices to commit crimes and that the legitimacy of punishment is undermined if the criminal decision is coerced, irrational, or based on a lack of understanding about the meaning of the choice (Bonnie, Coughlin, Jeffries, & Low, 1997). Punishment must be proportionate to blameworthiness, which is mitigated if the individual's decision-making capacity is seriously compromised.

Historically, developmental immaturity has been deemed irrelevant to criminal responsibility because juveniles were processed in a separate court and correctional system that ostensibly did not impose punishment at all (Scott & Steinberg, 2003; Walkover, 1984). Thus, the question of how the criminal law should take immaturity into account in deciding fair punishment got little attention. Recently, the role of immaturity in the determination of criminal responsibility has become important as younger and younger offenders are processed in adult court. There is a pressing need for theory and research regarding how developmental immaturity should be considered in determining criminal responsibility and punishment.

Psychological research supports the hypothesis that developmental factors influence youthful judgment and (ultimately) decision making in ways that could be relevant to criminal choices. Several authors have reviewed how aspects of adolescent psychosocial development might implicate youths' capacities as defendants (e.g., Cauffman & Steinberg, 2000; Scott & Grisso, 1997; Scott et al., 1995; Scott & Steinberg, 2003; Steinberg & Cauffman, 1996). First, adolescents tend to have a foreshortened temporal perspective, identifying and emphasizing short-term over long-term consequences (Greene, 1986; Nurmi, 1991). Adolescents may also be less risk averse than are adults. It is well documented that youths tend to engage in risky behaviors more often than adults, and they appear to calculate and weigh risks and benefits differently than do adults (Byrnes, 1998; Furby & Beyth-Marom, 1992; Gardner, 1992). Third, adolescents are more responsive to peer influence than are adults; peer conformity and compliance are powerful influences on adolescent behavior and probably play an important role in delinquent conduct as well (Berndt, 1979; Costanzo & Shaw, 1966). In contrast to adult offending, most juvenile crime occurs in groups, and peer influence may be an important motivating factor (Reiss & Farrington, 1991). Finally, the limited research that exists suggests that adolescents are more impulsive than adults are and that they tend to be subject to more rapid and extreme mood changes—although the relationship between impulsivity and moodiness is unclear (Steinberg & Cauffman, 1996).

Developmental research is consistent with theories about cognitive and psychosocial differences between adolescent offenders and adults, but only a few empirical studies of culpability exist. Fried and Reppucci (2001) evaluated the influence of several psychosocial factors on criminal decision making using videotaped vignettes of a series of decisions resulting in a crime. Age-based differences in psychosocial capacities followed a U-shaped function with midadolescents (ages 15–16) scoring lower on maturity than did their younger (ages 12–14) and older (ages 17–18) counterparts. A possible explanation for this pattern is that the responses of younger teens, who have not yet undergone individuation, may reflect their parents' values. Cauffman and Steinberg (2000) examined age differences between adolescents and adults on a series of hypothetical vignettes describing various criminal behaviors. They also found age differences in psychosocial factors, which in turn predicted decision outcomes. Higher psychosocial maturity was associated with more socially responsible decisions in the vignettes. Age did not remain a significant predictor after psychosocial maturity was taken into account.

Although this research is limited in scope, it provides initial support for the hypothesis that developmental factors contribute to immature judgment in ways that may differentiate adolescent criminal decision making from that of adults. These studies provide the impetus for continued research into developmental capacities that are relevant to legal assessments of culpability. The findings are consistent with the notion that adolescent offenders should be considered less blameworthy than adults but not blameless, as an insane defendant might be. Developmental arguments support adoption of a diminished responsibility standard in which punishment is calibrated to the evolving maturity of adolescents (Feld, 1999; Zimring, 1998, 1999).

Adolescent Development and Social Costs of Crime

Conservative reformers would likely reject a diminished responsibility standard, emphasizing that the developmental differences between adolescents and adults are not large—certainly as compared to the differences between typical adult offenders and insane criminals or young children. Moreover, they might argue that the social costs of youth crime trump any policy or principle favoring consideration of the relatively subtle differences between the criminal choices of adolescents and adults. In this section, we draw on developmental and criminology research to challenge the claim that punitive policies are the best means to achieve public protection and minimize the social cost of youth crime. These ends can better be served by policies that protect the future prospects of young offenders.

The utilitarian argument for tough sanctions has a superficial appeal in that youths who are in prison can not be on the street committing crimes. However, this stance ignores what are likely to be substantial long-term costs of punitive policies, in light of existing knowledge about the developmental patterns of antisocial behavior in adolescence. Rather than reducing crime, prosecuting and sentencing youths as adults may have iatrogenic effects that increase the costs of offending both for individual offenders and for society.

The recent trend toward widespread processing and punishing of adolescents as adults expands the net of social control well beyond the relatively small proportion of offenders that research indicates are on long-term offending trajectories. Many youth engage in some form of delinquency during adolescence (offending rates appear to peak around age 16 or 17) but desist as adulthood approaches (Blumstein & Cohen, 1987; Farrington, 1986; Jessor & Jessor, 1977). Indeed, most teenage males participate in some delinquent behavior—a fact that has led Terrie Moffitt, a developmental psychologist, to conclude that delinquent behavior is "a normal part of teen life"(Moffitt, 1993). Thus, Moffitt, basing her conclusions on her research on developmental trajectories, labels most youthful criminal conduct "adolescence-limited" behavior. Her research, which is supported by many other studies, identifies a relatively small percentage of youthful offenders with stable long-term offending patterns that might fit the notion of a career criminal (D'Unger, Land, McCall, & Nagin, 1998; Moffitt, 1993). A number of factors predict the likelihood of belonging to the group that Moffitt has labeled "life course persistent offenders," but differentiating them from more typical adolescent offenders in a cross-sectional sample of same-aged offenders is an uncertain business and prone to error. Transfer policies driven by age and offense type can not distinguish serious persistent offenders from those likely to desist with maturity.

It seems likely that whether and when typical adolescent offenders will accomplish the transition to conventional adult roles successfully may depend in part on the state's response to their criminal conduct. A policy of imposing adult criminal penalties on young offenders may increase the probability that they will become career criminals, or it may delay desistence. At a minimum, criminal punishment is likely to undermine their future educational and employment prospects and general social productivity as members of society.

Research evidence supports this concern. Prosecution and incarceration in the adult system appear to increase recidivism and limit prospects for a productive future. Young offenders in Florida described the criminal court process and pretrial detainment in very different terms from those used by their youthful counterparts in juvenile court (Bishop & Frazier, 2000; Bishop, Frazier, Lanza-Kaduce, & White, 1998). Offenders perceived juvenile court in relatively favorable terms, describing the court process and resulting punishment as well-intentioned and fair. Transferred offenders believed that court officials (including some defense counsel) were disengaged or hostile to their interests; they found the process confusing and the outcomes unfair. Transferred juveniles felt physically and emotionally threatened by staff and other inmates. They also reported learning about crime from other inmates. Although one might reasonably expect that inmates would view incarceration as a negative experience, the distinctions drawn between the inmates in the juvenile and criminal justice systems are important because the effectiveness of punishment in reducing recidivism likely depends in part on perceptions of its legitimacy (Bishop & Frazier, 2000).

Perhaps more compelling evidence of the harms of incarceration comes from studies that indicate that transfer appears to increase recidivism rates for most offense categories. Studies in Florida (Bishop et al., 1998; Winner et al., 1997) and New York and New Jersey (Fagan, 1996) compared youths adjudicated as adults with those retained in juvenile court for comparable offenses. Both sets of studies used multiple measures of recidivism over short-term and long-term (4–7 years) follow-up periods. Fagan's research found that transfer was associated with higher rearrest and reincarceration among robbery offenders but not among burglary offenders. Using a matching procedure that paired transferred youths and juvenile system youths on demographic and offense variables, the Florida studies found that transferred youths were more likely to reoffend in five of the seven offense categories studied, and they were rearrested more often and more rapidly than their juvenile court counterparts.

Higher recidivism rates are not the only potential social cost of transfer; criminal conviction also harms young offenders' future prospects for productive lives upon release. Incarceration in prison interferes with educational attainment (Austin, Johnson, & Gregariou, 2000; Harlow, 2003). In many states felony convictions must be reported on employment applications and usually result in the loss of civil rights such as voting, eligibility for jury service, and some occupational licensing (Bishop & Frazier, 2000). In comparison to the challenges that face youths leaving the juvenile system, the negative experience of criminal court and prison and the civil effects of criminal conviction create formidable barriers for youths seeking to return to society and make the transition to productive adulthood.

The research on transfer's effects is limited to a few studies in a few states, but the research challenges the presumption that punitive legal policies are the optimal response to juvenile offending. The developmental needs of youthful offenders at best are ignored in adult prison and at worst are severely undermined by criminal punishment. Given the available evidence, there is no reason to be optimistic that society's interest in public safety and crime reduction is promoted by punitive policies.

A policy based on a more realistic account of adolescence would emphasize three features. First, it would embrace the principle of fair and proportionate punishment by adopting a diminished responsibility standard that holds youths accountable for their crimes but recognizes that adolescents are less culpable than adults. Young offenders must learn appropriate lessons about the consequences of their criminal behavior but through more lenient punishments than adults receive. Second, a developmentally based policy would protect adolescents' prospects for a productive future. Ultimate goals of public safety and crime reduction are served if young offenders are able to assume conventional roles in society. Procedures that limit the stigma associated with offending (e.g., closed hearings) and correctional programs that provide opportunities to develop productive skills maximize the prospects that young wrongdoers can become productive adults. Finally, it is important to maintain a separate juvenile justice system that holds offenders accountable but enhances their competent development. Some observers argue that these goals could be incorporated into a unified criminal justice system that provides what has been called a "youth discount" in sentencing (e.g., Feld, 1999). However, the organizational culture and structure of the adult system and the politics surrounding criminal justice combine to make such fundamental change unlikely to succeed. A separate juvenile justice system is more likely to recognize the reduced culpability of young offenders through more lenient sentencing and more likely to invest in programs designed for adolescents.

CONCLUSIONS

Over the course of the last century, lawmakers have tended to ignore adolescence, preferring instead to categorize individuals in this developmental stage as either children or adults depending on the policy context. Presumptions about dependency, vulnerability, and incompetence to make decisions are used to justify a bright-line demarcation between childhood and adulthood. In general, this approach has functioned well, providing adolescents with societal protections at relatively low cost to their developmental autonomy. However, in juvenile justice policy, the binary approach has been a failure. Cast alternately as innocent, wayward children or fully mature predators, juvenile delinquents have been subject to policy initiatives that fail to protect their interests or those of society. A policy approach grounded in a realistic account of adolescence would maximize the likelihood that juvenile offenders could desist from crime and reintegrate successfully into the community.

The 21st century may see policy makers paying attention to this transitional stage in other areas. Although—as we have suggested—this move can be costly and should be taken only when binary categories are inadequate, in some contexts adolescents might benefit from a probationary period in which adult skills can be acquired and with protection from the costs of inexperienced choices. Some states have recently adopted this approach in extending driving privileges to adolescents (Cal. Veh. Code Sect. 12814.6; West, 2000). On issues as varied as liability for contracts and preferences in custody disputes, lawmakers have recently taken tentative steps toward recognizing the uniqueness of this developmental stage (Scott, 2000). Developmental research underscores the notion that adolescents resemble both children and adults in many ways, depending on the context and circumstances. The developmental realities of adolescence alone will never dictate legal regulation, but developmental research and theory can provide the empirical foundation for policies that promote a healthy and productive transition from childhood to adulthood.

REFERENCES

Adelson, J., & O'Neil, R. (1966). The growth of political ideas in adolescence: The sense of community. *Journal of Personality and Social Psychology, 4,* 295–306.

Adler, N. E., Smith, L. B., & Tschann, J. M. (1998). Abortion among adolescents. In L. J. Beckman & S. M. Harvey (Eds.), *The new civil war: The psychology, culture, and politics of abortion* (pp. 285–298). Washington, DC: American Psychological Association.

Allen, F. (1964). *The borderland of criminal justice.* Chicago: University of Chicago Press.
Ambuel, B., & Rappaport, J. (1992). Developmental trends in adolescents' psychological and legal competence to consent to abortion. *Law and Human Behavior, 16,* 129–154.
American Bar Association. (1982). *ABA/IJA juvenile justice standards: Standards relating to dispositions.* Washington, DC: American Bar Association.
Arenella, P. (1992). Convicting the morally blameless. *UCLA Law Review, 39,* 1511–1622.
Arnett, J. J. (2000). Emerging adulthood: A theory of development from the late teens through the twenties. *American Psychologist, 55,* 469–480.
Austin, J., Johnson, K. D., & Gregariou, M. (2000). *Juveniles in adult prisons and jails: A national assessment* (No. NCJ 182503). Washington, DC: Bureau of Justice Assistance, United States Department of Justice.
Bellotti v. Baird, 443 U.S. 622 (1979).
Berndt, T. J. (1979). Developmental changes in conformity to peers and parents. *Developmental Psychology, 15,* 608–616.
Bishop, D. M., & Frazier, C. E. (2000). Consequences of transfer. In J. Fagan & F. Zimring (Eds.), *The changing borders of juvenile justice: Transfer of adolescents to the criminal court* (pp. 227–276). Chicago: University of Chicago Press.
Bishop, D. M., Frazier, C. E., Lanza-Kaduce, L., & White, H. G. (1998). *Juvenile transfers to criminal court study: Phase I final report.* Washington, DC: Office of Juvenile Justice and Delinquency Prevention.
Blair, J. (2003, January 16). Teenager held in sniper case will be tried as adult. *New York Times,* p. A18.
Blumstein, A., & Cohen, J. (1987). Characterizing criminal careers, *Science, 237,* 985–991.
Bonnie, R., Coughlin, A., Jeffries, J., & Low, P. (1997). *Criminal law.* New York: Foundation Press.
Bremner, R. H. (Ed.). (1974). *Children & youth in America: A documentary history* (Vol. 4). Cambridge, MA: Harvard University Press.
Brooks-Gunn, J., & Furstenburg, F., Jr. (1989). Adolescent sexual behavior. *American Psychologist, 44,* 249–257.
Byrnes, J. P. (1998). *The nature and development of decision making.* Mahwah, NJ: Erlbaum.
Canedy, D. (2003, January 5). As Florida boy serves life term, even prosecutor wonders why. *New York Times,* p. 1-1.
Cauffman, E., & Steinberg, L. (2000). (Im)maturity of judgment in adolescence: Why adolescents may be less culpable than adults. *Behavioral Sciences and the Law, 18,* 741–760.
City of Akron v. Akron Center for Reproductive Health, 462 U.S. 416 (1983).
Costanzo, P. R., & Shaw, M. E. (1966). Conformity as a function of age level. *Child Development, 37,* 967–975.
Cromer, B. A., & Tarnowski, K. J. (1989). Noncompliance in adolescents: A review. *Journal of Developmental and Behavioral Pediatrics, 10,* 207–215.
Cultice, W. (1992). *Youth's battle for the ballot: A history of the voting age in America.* Westport, CT: Greenwood Press.
Dudley, R. L, & Gitelson, A. R. (2002). Political literacy, civic education, and civic engagement: A return to political socialization? *Applied Developmental Science, 6,* 175–182.
D'Unger, A. V., Land, K. C., McCall, P. L., & Nagin, D. S. (1998). How many latent classes of delinquent/criminal careers? Results from mixed Poisson regression analyses. *American Journal of Sociology, 103,* 1593–1630.
Ellis, E. (1993, January 15). Lungren to seek lower age for trial as adult. *Los Angeles Times,* p. A3.
Fagan, J. (1996). The comparative advantages of juvenile versus criminal court sanction on recidivism among adolescent felony offenders. *Law and Policy, 18,* 77–112.
Farrington, D. (1986). Age and crime. In M. Tonry & N. Morris (Eds.), *Crime and justice: An annual review of research* (pp. 189–250). Chicago: University of Chicago Press.
Feld, B. (1999). *Bad kids: Race and transformation of the juvenile court.* New York: Oxford University Press.

Finken, L. L., & Jacobs, J. E. (1996). Consultant choice across decision contexts: Are abortion decisions different? *Journal of Adolescent Research, 11,* 235–260.

Flanagan, C. A., & Sherrod, L. R. (1998). Youth political development: An introduction. *Journal of Social Issues, 54,* 447–450.

Fox, S. (1967). *The juvenile court: Its context, problems and opportunities.* Washington, DC: President's Commission on Law Enforcement and Administration of Justice.

Fried, C., & Reppucci, N. D. (2001). Criminal decision making: The development of adolescent judgment, criminal responsibility, and culpability. *Law and Human Behavior, 25,* 45–61.

Furby, L., & Beyth-Marom, R. (1992). Risk taking in adolescence: A decision-making perspective. *Developmental Review, 12,* 1–44.

Furstenburg, F. F., Brooks-Gunn, J., & Chase-Lansdale, L. (1989). Teenaged pregnancy and childbearing. *American Psychologist, 44,* 313–320.

Gardner, W. (1992). A life span theory of risk taking. In N. Bell & R. W. Bell (Eds.), *Adolescent and adult risk taking: The 8th Texas symposium on interfaces in psychology* (pp. 66–83). Thousand Oaks, CA: Sage.

Gardner, W., Scherer, D., & Tester, M. (1989). Asserting scientific authority: Cognitive development and adolescent legal rights. *American Psychologist, 44,* 895–902.

Gorney, C. (1998). *Articles of faith: A frontline history of the abortion wars.* New York: Simon and Schuster.

Greene, A. L. (1986). Future-time perspective in adolescence: The present of things future revisited. *Journal of Youth and Adolescence, 15,* 99–113.

Grisso, T., & Lovinguth, T. (1982). Lawyers and child clients: A call for research. In J. Henning (Ed.), *Children and the law.* Springfield, IL: Charles C. Thomas.

Grisso, T., & Vierling, L. (1978). Minors' consent to treatment: A developmental perspective. *Professional Psychology, 9,* 412–427.

Harlow, C.W. (2003). *Education and correctional populations* (No. NCJ 195670). Washington, DC: Bureau of Justice Statistics, United States Department of Justice.

Haste, H. (1992). Lay social theory: The relation between political, social, and moral understanding. In H. Haste & J. Torney-Purta (Eds.), *The development of political understanding: A new perspective* (pp. 27–38). San Francisco: Jossey-Bass.

Haste, H., & Torney-Purta, J. (1992). Introduction. In H. Haste & J. Torney-Purta (Eds.), *The development of political understanding: A new perspective* (pp. 1–10). San Francisco: Jossey-Bass.

Hazelwood School Dist. v. Kuhlmeier, 484 U.S. 260 (1988).

Henshaw, S. K., & Kost, K. (1992). Parental involvement in minors' abortion decisions. *Family Planning Perspectives, 21,* 85–88.

H. L. v. Matheson, 450 U.S. 398 (1981).

Hodgson v. Minnesota, 497 U.S. 417 (1990).

In re Gault, 387 U.S. 1 (1967).

Jessor, R., & Jessor, S. L. (1977). *Problem behavior and psychosocial development: A longitudinal study of youth.* New York: Academic Press.

Kent v. U.S., 383 U.S. 541 (1966).

Kett, J. (1977). *Rites of passage: Adolescence in America 1790 to the present.* New York: Basic Books.

Knott, L., & Brand-Williams, O. (2000, January 14). Young killer gets juvenile detention: State's get-tough policy blasted by sentencing judge. *The Detroit News,* p. A1.

Lerner, R. M., & Galambos, N. L. (1998). Adolescent development: Challenges and opportunities for research, programs, and policies. *Annual Review of Psychology, 49,* 413–446.

Levine, M., & Levine, A. (1970). *A social history of helping services: Clinic, court, school and community.* New York: Appleton-Century-Crofts.

Lewin, T. (1992, May 28). Parental consent to abortion: How enforcement can vary. *The New York Times,* pp. A1, B8.

Lewis, C. C. (1980). A comparison of minors' and adults' pregnancy decisions. *American Journal of Psychiatry, 50,* 446–453.

Lindsey, B. B., & O'Higgins, H. J. (1909). *The beast.* Seattle: University of Washington Press.
McKeiver v. Pennsylvania, 403 U.S. 528 (1971).
Meisel, A., Roth, L. H., & Lidz, C. W. (1977). Toward a model of the legal doctrine of informed consent. *American Journal of Psychiatry, 134,* 285–289.
Melton, G. B. (1980). Children's concepts of their rights. *Journal of Clinical Child Psychology, 9,* 186–190.
Melton, G. B. (1981). Psycholegal issues in juveniles' competency to waive their rights. *Journal of Clinical Child Psychology, 10,* 59–62.
Melton, G. B. (1983a). *Child advocacy: Psycholegal issues and interventions.* New York: Plenum.
Melton, G. B. (1983b). Toward "personhood" for adolescents: Autonomy and privacy as values in public policy. *American Psychologist, 38,* 99–103.
Melton, G. B., & Limber, S. (1992). What children's rights mean to children: Children's own views. In M. Freeman & P. Veerman (Eds.), *Ideologies of children's rights* (p. 167–187). Dordrecht, Netherlands: Martinus Nijhoff.
Meschke, L. L., Bartholomae, S., & Zentall, S. R. (2002). Adolescent sexuality and parent-adolescent processes: Promoting health teen choices. *Journal of Adolescent Health, 31,* 264–279.
Mnookin, R. (1985). Bellotti v. Baird: A hard case. In R. H. Mnookin (Ed.), *In the interest of children: Advocacy, law reform and public policy* (pp. 150–264). New York: W. H. Freeman.
Moffitt, T. E. (1993). Adolescence-limited and life-course-persistent antisocial behavior: A developmental taxonomy. *Psychological Review, 100,* 674–701.
Newcomer, S. F., & Udry, J. R. (1985). Parent-child communication and adolescent sexual behavior. *Family Planning Perspectives, 17,* 169–174.
Nurmi, J. (1991). How do adolescents see their future: A review of the development of future orientation and planning. *Developmental Review, 11,* 1–59.
Ohio v. Akron Center for Reproductive Health, 497 U.S. 502 (1990).
Parham v. J. R., 442 U.S. 584 (1978).
Pennsylvania Code Section 42-6301 (1999).
Planned Parenthood of Central Missouri v. Danforth, 428 U.S. 52 (1976).
Platt, A. (1977). *The child savers: The invention of delinquency* (2nd ed.). Chicago: University of Chicago Press.
Pope, L. M., Adler, N. E., & Tschann, J. M. (2001). Postabortion psychological adjustment: Are minors at increased risk? *Journal of Adolescent Health, 29,* 2–11.
Prince v. Massachusetts, 321 U.S. 158 (1944).
Quinton, W. J., Major, B., & Richards, C. (2001). Adolescents and adjustment to abortion: Are minors at greater risk? *Psychology, Public Policy, and Law, 7,* 491–514.
Regnery, A. S. (1985). Getting away with murder: Why the juvenile justice system needs an overhaul. *Policy Review, 34,* 65–72.
Reiss, A., Jr., & Farrington, D. (1991). Advancing knowledge about co-offending: Results from a prospective longitudinal survey of London males. *Journal of Criminal Law and Criminology, 82,* 360–395.
Rendleman, D. R. (1971). Parens patriae: From chancery to the juvenile court. *South Carolina Law Review, 23,* 205–259.
Reppucci, N. D., Wiethorn, L. A., Mulvey, E. P., & Monahan, J. (Eds.). (1984). *Children, mental health, and the law.* Beverly Hills, CA: Sage.
Resnick, M. D., Bearinger, L. H., Stark, P., & Blum, R. W. (1994). Patterns of consultation among adolescent minors obtaining an abortion. *American Journal of Orthopsychiatry, 64,* 310–316.
Rubin, E. R. (Ed.). (1998). *The abortion controversy: A documentary history.* Westport, CT: Praeger.
Ruck, M. D., Keating, D. P., Abramovitch, R., & Koegl, C. J. (1998). Adolescents' and children's knowledge about rights: Some evidence for how young people view rights in their own lives. *Journal of Adolescence, 21,* 275–289.
Scherer, D. (1991). The capacities of minors to exercise voluntariness in medical treatment decisions. *Law and Human Behavior, 15,* 431–449.
Scherer, D. G., & Rappucci, N. D. (1988). Adolescents' capacities to provide voluntary informed

consent: The effects of parental influence and medical dilemmas. *Law and Human Behavior, 12,* 123–141.

Schleifer v. City of Charlottesville, 963 F. Supp. 534 (W.D. Va. 1997), *aff'd* 159 F. 3d 843 (4th Cir. 1998).

Scott, E. (1992). Judgment and reasoning in adolescent decisionmaking. *Villanova Law Review, 37,* 1607–1669.

Scott, E. (2000). Criminal responsibility in adolescence: Some lessons from developmental psychology. In T. Grisso & B. Schwartz (Eds.), *Youth on trial* (pp. 291–324). Chicago: University of Chicago Press.

Scott, E., & Grisso, T. (1997). The evolution of adolescence: A developmental perspective of juvenile justice reform. *Journal of Criminal Law and Criminology, 88,* 137–195.

Scott, E. S., Reppucci, N. D., & Woolard, J. L. (1995). Adolescent decision making in legal contexts. *Law and Human Behavior, 19,* 221–244.

Scott, E. S., & Scott, R. (1995). Parents as fiduciaries. *Virginia Law Review, 81,* 2401–2476 .

Scott, E., & Steinberg, L. (2003). Blaming youth. *Texas Law Review, 81,* 799–840.

Scott, R. E., & Kraus, J. S. (2002). *Contract law and theory* (3rd ed.). Newark, NJ: Lexis Nexis.

Sherrod, L.R., Flanagan, C., & Youniss, J. A. (2002). Editors' introduction. *Applied Developmental Science, 6,* 173–174.

Sickmund, M., Snyder, H. N., & Poe-Yamagata, E. (1997). *Juvenile offenders and victims: 1997 update on violence.* Washington, DC: U.S. Department of Justice, Office of Juvenile Justice and Delinquency Prevention.

Siegler, R. S. (1991). *Children's thinking.* Englewood Cliffs, NJ: Prentice-Hall.

Smetana, J. G. (1981). Reasoning in the personal and moral domains: Adolescent and young adult women's decision-making regarding abortion. *Journal of Applied Developmental Psychology, 2,* 211–226.

S. Rep. No. 92-26 (1971).

Steinberg, L. (1999). *Adolescence.* Boston: McGraw-Hill.

Steinberg, L., & Cauffman, E. (1996). Maturity of judgment in adolescence: Psychosocial factors in adolescent decision making. *Law and Human Behavior, 20,* 249–272.

Steinberg, L., & Cauffman, E. S. (1999). The elephant in the courtroom: A developmental perspective on the adjudication of youthful offenders. *Virginia Journal of Social Policy and Law, 6,* 389–417.

Tiffin, S. (1982). *In whose best interest? Child welfare reform in the progressive era.* Westport, CT: Greenwood Press.

Torbet, P., Gable, R., Hurst, H., IV, Montgomery, I., Szymanski, L., & Thomas, D. (1996). *State responses to serious and violent juvenile crime.* Washington DC: Office of Juvenile Justice and Delinquency Prevention, United States Department of Justice.

Torbet, P., & Szymanski, L. (1998). *State legislative responses to violent juvenile crime: 1996–1997 update.* Washington, DC: Office of Juvenile Justice and Delinquency Prevention, United States Department of Justice.

Torney-Purta, J. (1992). Cognitive representations of the political system in adolescents: The continuum from pre-novice to expert. In H. Haste & J. Torney-Purta (Eds.), *The development of political understanding: A new perspective* (pp. 11–25). San Francisco: Jossey-Bass.

Torres, A., Forrest, J. D., & Eisman, S. (1980). Telling parents: Clinic policies and adolescents' use of family planning and abortion services. *Family Planning Perspectives, 12,* 284–292.

Van Waters, M. (1925). *Youth in conflict.* New York: Republic Publishing Co.

VA. Code Ann. § 1-13.42 (Michie 2000).

VA. Code Ann. § 54.1-2969 (Michie 1999).

Wadlington, W. (1973). Minors and health care: The age of consent. *Osgoode Hall Law Journal, 11,* 115–125.

Wald, M. (1976). Legal policies affecting children: A lawyer's request for aid. *Child Development, 46,* 1–5.

Walkover, A. (1984). The infancy defense in the new juvenile court. *UCLA Law Review, 31,* 503–562.

Weithorn, L. A., & Campbell, S. B. (1982). The competency of children and adolescents to make informed treatment decisions. *Child Development, 53,* 1589–1598.
Yates, S., & Pliner, A. J. (1988). Judging maturity in the courts: The Massachusetts consent statute. *American Journal of Public Health, 78,* 646–649.
Younts v. St. Francis Hospital and School of Nursing, Inc., 469 P.2d 300 (Kan. 1970).
Zimring, F. E. (1978). *Twentieth Century Fund Task Force on sentencing policy toward young offenders: Confronting youth crime.* Trumbull, CT: Holmes & Meier.
Zimring, F. E. (1982). *The changing legal world of adolescence.* New York: The Free Press.
Zimring, F. E. (1998). *American youth violence.* New York: Oxford University Press.
Zimring, F. E. (1999). Commentary: The hardest of the hard cases: Adolescent homicide in juvenile and criminal courts. *Virginia Journal of Social Policy and Law, 6,* 437–469.

Part Three

ADOLESCENT CHALLENGES, CHOICES, AND POSITIVE YOUTH DEVELOPMENT

Chapter 18

ADOLESCENT HEALTH FROM AN INTERNATIONAL PERSPECTIVE

Robert W. Blum and Kristin Nelson-Mmari

INTRODUCTION

Over the past 20 years, dramatic social, political, economic shifts, and medical and public health interventions have radically altered the landscape of adolescent health around the world. A generation ago, AIDS was unknown; today, between a quarter and a third of adolescent females in Botswana, South Africa, and Zimbabwe are infected. A generation ago, infectious diseases predominated as the major sources of morbidity and mortality globally; today, social, behavioral, and environmental factors predominate. A generation ago, the age of marriage was significantly lower than it is today. More people lived in rural communities and fewer young people attended school.

These transitions as well as others have had and will continue to have profound impact on the health of youth. This paper briefly reviews the key social transitions that influence adolescent and young adult health globally. Next, the leading causes of morbidity and mortality are discussed. This section is followed by a discussion of health service delivery, health promotion, and our current knowledge of positive youth development. Finally, implications for the future of adolescent health and well-being are identified.

POPULATION AND SOCIAL TRENDS

Today adolescents comprise 20% of the world's population, and more than 85% reside in developing countries. Over the 55-year period between 1970 and 2025, it is estimated that the number of urban youth will increase 600% (World Health Organization, 1997). Table 18.1 presents by region the current and projected populations of young people 10–24 years of age.

Child Survival

Of all the social changes that have had a major impact on adolescent health in the world, none has had as much impact as what has resulted from improved child survival.

This chapter was originally prepared as a background paper for the National Academy of Sciences Panel on Transitions to Adulthood in Developing Countries.

Table 18.1 Population of Young People 10–24 Years by Region

Region	Population 10–24 Years in Millions	
	2000	2025
The World	1,663	1,796
Africa	256	401
Asia	1,031	1,048
North America	64	65
Latin America	155	163
Europe	149	109
Western Pacific	7	8

Note. From Population Reference Bureau, Washington, DC, 2002.

A dramatic increase in the number of young people has resulted from the child survival initiatives implemented in the 1970s and 1980s around the globe, especially in the developing regions of the world. During the 20th century alone the overall population of the world rose from 1.6 billion to over 6.0 billion people, with 80% of that growth occurring after 1950. In less economically developed regions of the world, life expectancy at birth has increased by as much as 20 years over the last half century—from 41 years in 1950 to 64 years in 2000. Between the years 1985 and 2015, it is projected that the world's population of 5- to 14-year-olds will increase from 885 million to 1.2 billion. By 2015, infant and child mortality is predicted to fall from 14.6 million to 7.5 million deaths per year and that of school-age children to decline from 1.6 to 1.3 million deaths annually (Jamison & Mosley, 1991).

Shifting Demographics

As the absolute number of youth changes, so too do the distribution of youth globally continue to drift toward developing countries and especially toward sub-Saharan Africa and Asia. As noted by the United Nations Department of Economic and Social Affairs (1996) of the 77 million people added to the world each year, 97% live in less developed regions. In Africa, the growth is greatest and has a projected population increase from 794 million in 2000, rising to 2.0 billion 50 years from 2003.

The median age in much of sub-Saharan Africa is between 28 and 41 years, in comparison with industrialized countries, where the median age is less than half that figure. In fact, all of the 10 youngest countries of the world are in sub-Saharan Africa (Table 18.2).

International Migration

Cross-national migration has accelerated dramatically over the past 20 years—in part as a function of economic imperatives, war, natural disasters, hunger, and famine. In the 25 years between 1970 and 1995, industrialized countries absorbed 35 million refugees. In 1965, there were 75 million international immigrants—today, more than 125 million. In 2000, the United Nations High Commission on Refugees (UNHCR) es-

Table 18.2 Median Age of Populations in Countries Where It Is the Lowest

Country	Median age of the Population
Yemen	15.0
Nigeria	15.1
Uganda	15.4
Burkina Faso	15.6
D. Republic of the Congo	15.6
Angola	15.9
Somalia	16.0
Burundi	16.0
Zambia	16.5
Benia	16.6

Note. From UN Population Division, 2001.

timated that 22.3 million people are world refugees, returnees, or displaced people—most of whom were women and children. Factors that influence international migration include the following:

- Income disparities between and within regions
- Labor and migration policies of countries
- Political conflicts, natural disasters, and war
- Environmental degradation (e.g., loss of farmland)
- Brain drain

Rural to Urban Migration

Not only is international migration growing, but rural to urban migratory patterns have also shifted. Over the past 20 years, large numbers of rural young women (ages 18–24 years) have come looking for work in major urban areas (Guest, 1999; Singelmann, 1993). The result is that in a number of cities in Latin America and Asia, young adult females outnumber their male counterparts (Guest, 1999; Skeldon, 1990). Elsewhere, the demand (real or perceived) for laborers in the city has resulted in a significant influx of males seeking employment. Youth migration is a major cause of rural to urban migration. It also predisposes to significant behavioral health risks that stem from unemployment and poverty—violence, prostitution, STDs and HIV, and substance use.

More than a decade ago, Over and Piat (1992) identified the interrelationships between economic development, urbanization, high male-to-female ratios, rising prostitution, and HIV and AIDS in 18 sub-Saharan African cities. This "web of causation," coupled with relatively low levels of education among young females, fueled the HIV pandemic. Today, these deadly linkages are played out in many newly industrialized zones of Asia.

The United Nations estimates that during the next 30 years, essentially all population growth will occur in urban areas. The urbanization of the youth population clearly has associated risks, but as Guest notes (1999), it is not without economic benefit as well—especially to rural communities, where the economic rewards of urban employment often accrue (e.g., income of urban workers returning to rural relatives).

Education

One of the trends that has had a major impact on young people over the last 20 years has been the rising value of education, as reflected in government policies around the world. Mensch, Bruce, and Greene (1999) note that nearly half of all countries for which the United Nations Education, Scientific, and Cultural Organization (UNESCO) maintains data ($N = 103$) mandate schooling through at least age 14. The following table reflects the shifts in education over the past 20 years by region of the world (Table 18.3).

As can be seen from Table 18.3, every region of the world has seen dramatic educational gains, and although a gender gap remains, the gap is narrowing. For example, for sub-Saharan Africa in 1980, there was a 9% spread between males and females enrolled in secondary school; most recently it was 6%. In Asia, a 14% gender gap in 1980 narrowed to 11% most recently. Furthermore, most important is that the percent of girls being educated has gone up dramatically since 1980; it has more than doubled for Africa from 15% to 33%, it has gone up from 34% to 51% in Asia, and in Latin America there is essentially no gender gap in schooling through age 18–19 (Mensch et al., 1999).

Many factors influence matriculation rates within a country:

- Government allocations for education
- Urban-rural priorities
- Walking distance to school
- Need for gender-segregated schools
- Family priorities and values for education
- Family economic pressures

Table 18.3 Percent Enrolled in Secondary School by Region: 1980 and Most Recent Available Year

	Percent Enrolled in Secondary School			
	1980		Most recent year	
Region	Males	Females	Males	Females
The World	54	44	63	56
Africa	26	15	38	33
• Sub-Saharan Africa	19	10	29	23
Asia	48	34	62	51
• South Central Asia	38	20	55	37
• Southeast Asia	40	35	53	49
• East Asia	59	45	77	70
North America	91	92	99	98
Latin America	41	43	N/A	N/A
Europe	86	88	97	102

Note. From Population Reference Bureau, Washington, DC, 2002.

- Costs of schooling
- Gender role expectations

Poverty

The International Classification of Diseases codes *extreme poverty* as 795.5. It is the leading cause of disease and death in the world. It is a condition that affects nearly one fifth of the world's population—1.1 billion people. It is what underlies the disparity of life expectancy between industrialized countries (78 years) and developing countries (43 years). The gap continues to widen, and as life expectancy continues to increase in many developed countries, it is declining in many developing nations.

The growing economic disparity among nations is reflected in the following graph that shows trends in per capita income in regions of the world over the last quarter century (Figure 18.1).

There are many factors that influence the trends reflected in Figure 18.1, but despite economic globalization (or perhaps because of it), resources continue to shift from developing to wealthier nations (e.g., loan repayments, economic restructuring). Complicating this picture is the rise of unemployment. As people come to the cities looking for work that is not there, crime, prostitution, and their associated health risks increase.

Evidence suggests that poverty has a disproportionate impact on adolescent girls. Kumar (2002), for example, has noted that due to untreated iron deficiency, girls from impoverished families in India are 12–15 cm shorter than their wealthier peers. Likewise, girls from economically disadvantaged households are significantly more likely than their peers to marry at a young age. Where resources are limited, girls get a lesser share of health, education, and social services as well as goods (Kumar, 2002). So too, most of

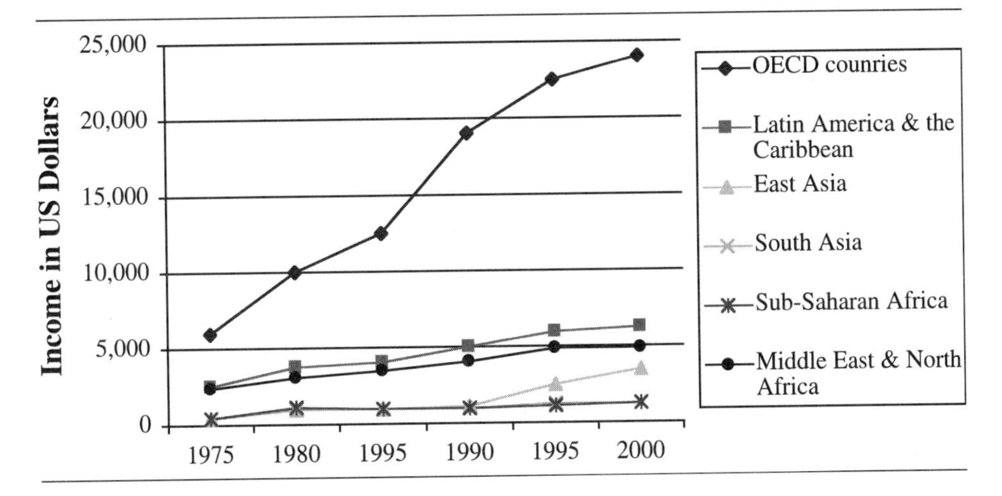

Figure 18.1 Per-capita income by region, 1975 to 2000.

Source. World Bank, World Development Indicators (2000). [CD-ROM].

Note: Per-capita GDP is expressed in international dollars using purchasing power parity (PPP) conversion rates. (Organisation for Economic Co-operation and Development). Reported in UN Department of Economic and Social Affairs, World Population Monitoring (2001).

the maternal mortality of India—estimated by its government to be 430 per 100,000—occurs among those who are the most economically disadvantaged (Kumar, 2002).

And so it is with every cause of adolescent mortality and morbidity. As we look at the trends that follow, we must view them within the economic and social contexts of young people today that suggest that even when there is cause to celebrate, the gap between rich and poor is continuing to widen.

CAUSES OF MORTALITY

Table 18.4 depicts both globally and by region the five leading causes of death for youth and young adults ages 15–29 years. What we see is that unintentional injury is the leading killer of young people in nearly every region of the world, with HIV-AIDS and other infectious diseases still the second leading cause of death in much of the developing world (in most industrialized nations, it is suicide). Homicide, war, and interpersonal violence follow.

Unintentional Injuries

For industrialized countries, unintentional injuries are the number-one killer for those aged 15–29 years, and in developing countries where industry is increasing and infec-

Table 18.4 Five Leading Causes of Mortality in 15- to 29-Year-Olds

	Leading Causes of Death[a]				
World Regions	Unintentional Injuries	AIDS	Other Infectious Causes	Homicide, War, and Other Intentional Injuries	Suicide and Self-Inflicted Injuries
All world regions	1 (531,000)	2 (326,000)	3 (229,000)	4 (227,000)	5 (124,000)
South America and Caribbean	2 (64,000)	5 (11,000)	4 (12,000)	1 (72,000)	3 (14,000)
Africa	4 (56,000)	1 (225,000)	2 (104,000)	3 (66,000)	5 (6,000)
Southeast Asia	1 (178,000)	3 (72,000)	2 (81,000)	5 (33,000)	4 (37,000)
Western Pacific	1 (119,000)	5 (8,000)	3 (19,000)	4 (17,000)	2 (32,000)
Eastern Mediterranean	1 (40,000)	4 (7,000)	2 (21,000)	3 (15,000)	5 (5,000)
Europe	1 (74,000)	5 (2,000)	4 (10,000)	3 (23,000)	2 (30,000)
North America[b]	1	6	5	3	2

[a]Data on maternal mortality among 15 to 29 year olds not available.

[b]In North America cancer is the fourth leading cause of death in the adolescent and young adult years. From WHO Global Burden of Disease, Mortality Tables (2000).

tious diseases are being controlled, unintentional injury will soon become just as great a cause for concern (World Health Organization [WHO], 2001). In a survey of the causes of death among adolescents in South Africa, unintentional injuries were found to account for 57% of all mortality in the 10- to 19-year age group, and similar results have been found in Papua New Guinea, Nigeria, Singapore, and a number of South American countries (WHO, 1995). Within the category of unintentional injuries, traffic-related fatalities are by far the most prevalent in most world regions. For adolescents aged 15–24 years, traffic-related injuries are the leading cause of injury deaths among 11 industrialized countries, ranging from a low of 12 to 15 per 100,000 in England, The Netherlands, Norway, and Israel to a high of 49 deaths per 100,000 in New Zealand (Fingerhut, Cox, & Warner, 1998).

In Taiwan between 1960 and 1977, injuries climbed from the seventh to the third leading cause of death, and the rate of death from traffic accidents rose from 38.9 to 57.2 per 100,000 inhabitants. In Hong Kong, Singapore, and Thailand, traffic accidents and drownings are a major cause of premature death, and traffic accidents are responsible for more potential years of life lost than malaria and tuberculosis combined. In developing countries, where the number of vehicles has been increasing every year, traffic safety conditions are becoming more precarious. In Africa, road traffic mortality increased more than 200%, and in Asia, it increased 150% between 1968 and 1983 (Barker, 2000). In Latin America, an even more alarming increase was found among adolescents. For example, adolescent mortality caused by road traffic accidents increased by 600% in Mexico, 250% in Venezuela, and 210% in Chile, in part because of the increased population density of urban settings and in part because of increased access to vehicles (Maddaleno & Silber, 1993). A review of traffic-related mortality in 83 industrialized and nonindustrialized countries showed that on average, middle-income countries had the highest reported traffic-related mortality per 100,000 population, whereas the poorest countries had the highest traffic-related mortality per registered vehicle (WHO, 1995).

Young men are at most risk for traffic-related mortality. In fact, worldwide, unintentional injury resulting from traffic accidents is the main cause of death among young men; such fatalities are often associated with drug and alcohol use (WHO, 1998). In Thailand, nearly twice as many boys as girls have been involved in a traffic accident, and 48.5% of urban boys report having been in an accident in the last three years (Barker, 2000). Boys are at higher risk of road traffic accidents than are girls for a number of reasons. First, they often spend a larger proportion of their time outside of the home, and they spend more time in or around streets and public thoroughfares. Use of alcohol or other substances combined with reckless use of motor vehicles are behaviors that male peer groups often condone (Barker, 2000).

However, traffic accidents are not the only injuries threatening the lives of young people. Recreational and sports accidents in the developed countries, burns and poisonings in the developing countries, and falls and drownings in every region also represent major risks (WHO, 1993). In Brazil, drowning is second only to traffic accidents as a cause of death in young people aged 10–14 years. Drownings also account for 15% of all adolescent deaths in Uruguay, 10% in Paraguay, 8.3% in Costa Rica, and 7% in Argentina and Mexico (Maddaleno & Silber, 1993). In Asia, drowning is the leading cause of accident mortality in children and young adults, and in many countries of the

Table 18.5 Prevalence of HIV-AIDS by Regions of the World (2000)

Region	Number
Sub-Saharan Africa	25,300,000
Latin America	1,400,000
North America	920,000
Eastern Europe and Central Asia	700,000
Eastern Asia and Pacific	640,000
Australia and New Zealand	390,000
Caribbean	390,000

Source: From UNAIDS (2000).

continent, it accounts for up to 30% of accidental deaths, although some such deaths may be disguised suicides (WHO, 1993).

HIV-AIDS

In addition to deaths due to unintentional injury, the second leading important killer of young people worldwide is HIV-AIDS (see Table 18.5). In Africa, it is the number-one killer of young adults between the ages of 15 and 29 years (WHO, 2001). Globally, in the past 20 years, more than 60 million people have been infected with HIV, half of whom became infected between the ages of 15 and 24 years. Today, nearly 12 million young people are living with HIV-AIDS (Kiragu, 2001). Although prevalence rates demonstrate that young people are frequent victims of HIV-AIDS, the epidemic among youth still remains largely invisible both to young people themselves and to society as a whole (Kiragu, 2001). Young people often carry HIV for years without realizing that they are infected. Consequently, the epidemic spreads beyond high-risk groups to the broader population of young people, making it more difficult to control.

The prevalence of HIV-AIDS among young people varies greatly among regions and countries. Currently, sub-Saharan Africa faces the worst prospects, but portions of the Caribbean are close behind. Although only 10% of the world's youth live in sub-Saharan Africa, the region contained almost 75% of all youth living with HIV-AIDS in 2001, with a total of 8.6 million infected young people (Kiragu, 2001). Even within this region, there are substantial differences in HIV prevalence. Botswana has the highest proportion of infected youth, with an estimated 30% of women ages 15–24 being infected. Other countries in eastern and southern Africa have high prevalence rates as well. In a study conducted in Rwanda, over 25% of pregnant women aged 17 or younger tested positive for HIV (Koontz & Conly, 1994). Similarly, in Zimbabwe, 30% of pregnant girls ages 15–19 were HIV positive (Verkuyl, 1995).

In contrast, HIV prevalence in West Africa is low. Within Asia and the Pacific regions, the only countries that have HIV prevalence rates greater than 1% among youth are Cambodia, Myanmar, and Thailand. Meanwhile, the Caribbean region has some of the most serious AIDS epidemics outside sub-Saharan Africa. At least 2% of young women are infected with HIV in the Bahamas, Dominican Republic, Guyana, and Haiti. In Eastern Europe and Central Asia, HIV prevalence is relatively low. Only in the Ukraine are more than 1% of young men ages 15–24 infected. Similarly, in North Africa and the Near East, HIV infection among young people is rare; however, injection drug use may soon create a new wave of infections in the region (Kiragu, 2001).

Gender differences in patterns of HIV infection among young people vary substantially around the world. In regions where heterosexual transmission of HIV dominates, often more young women than men are infected; this is especially true in sub-Saharan Africa, where HIV infection rates among young women are more than five times higher than among young men. In Kenya, nearly one teenage woman in four is living with HIV, compared to 1 teenage male in 25 (Joint United Nations Programme on HIV/AIDS [UNAIDS], 2000). Likewise, in Botswana, about one third of women ages 15–24 are estimated to be HIV positive, which is twice the proportion of infected men in the same age group. A number of factors—social, cultural, and biological—contribute to the greater vulnerability of girls to HIV. Young women may be at a disadvantage in negotiating condom use or the fidelity of their partners because of age differences, economic disparities, and gender norms. Biologically, the risk of becoming infected with HIV during unprotected sex is two to four times greater for a woman than for a man, and for the young adolescent female the cells of the cervix are still maturing, which predisposes them to infection (Kiragu, 2001). Male-to-female transmission is more likely because during vaginal intercourse, a female has a larger surface area of her genital tract exposed to her partner's sexual secretions than does a man. Also, HIV concentration is generally higher in a man's semen than in a woman's sexual secretions (Kiragu, 2001).

Other Communicable Diseases

Beyond HIV-AIDS, other infectious diseases represent the third leading cause of death in the world and especially in developing countries. The WHO estimates that among children 5–14 years, communicable diseases claim 310,000 deaths annually: 251,000 infectious and parasitic; 47,000 respiratory; and 11,000 due to nutritional deficiencies. Among those 15–29 years old, the burden of infectious diseases rises to an estimated 592,000 deaths per year—most of which are infectious or parasitic (555,000) and the remainder respiratory (29,000) or nutritional (7,000). In adolescents, the following are the leading infectious and parasitic conditions, most of which are not routinely fatal, although many are chronic and debilitating (Blum & Lammers, 1998).

Helminths

The WHO estimates that approximately 400 million school-age young people are infected with intestinal helminths affecting growth, nutritional status, physical fitness, and school performance. The quartet of common helminthic infections include ascariasis, trichuiasis, strongyloidiasis, and hookworm. Hookworms have a peak prevalence during late adolescence and early adulthood. Adolescent females and young adult women appear to be more heavily infected than are males. High "worm burden" is associated with iron deficiency anemia because worms use iron as their source of nutrition. In sub-Saharan Africa in 1991 the estimated prevalence rate for hookworm for women of childbearing age was 32%, with between 7.5 and 7.8 million women both pregnant and infected—a combination highly associated with morbidity.

Schistosomiasis

Schistosomiasis is the second most common parasitic infection after malaria and is endemic in much of Africa, the Eastern Mediterranean, South America, and the Caribbean. Associated symptoms include dysuria, hematuria, or both. Contact with contaminated fresh water is the major source of infection, with the snail serving as the host. Males tend to be more commonly infected than females. Peak prevalence is in the second decade of life. Specifically, at puberty there is a marked increase in prevalence, intensity of infection, and manifestations of morbidity. Not uncommonly the genital lesions associated with this condition are confused with STDs, thereby causing social stigma. In endemic countries, hematuria is considered *the* pubertal rite of passage.

Tuberculosis

The WHO estimates that 1.3 billion people worldwide have tuberculosis, of whom 3 million die annually. Although it is well known to be associated with the immunocompromised host, tuberculosis appears to be more aggressive around the time of puberty. Thus, adolescents who acquire the disease are more likely than younger children to develop cavitary lesions. Such virulence has been attributed to hormonal changes and to altered protein and calcium metabolism associated with adolescent growth. Clearly, the problem is compounded by poverty, crowding, and unsanitary living conditions. Gender distribution appears to be approximately equal until 15 years of age, after which time the risk is higher for males. Bacille Calmette-Guérin (BCG) vaccine is commonly given at birth in many developing countries, but its effectiveness in preventing adult disease remains controversial. For children under 14 years, effectiveness estimates are in the range of 40–70%.

Malaria

Where malaria is fatal, primarily in Africa, mortality associated with malaria tends to be limited primarily to those under 5 years of age. It is, however, the most prevalent tropical disease threatening 40% of the world's population. Males show a higher prevalence of malaria than do females, perhaps due to work exposure.

Pregnant woman have been reported to have an increased susceptibility to *P. falciparum* malaria—the most malignant form of the condition, perhaps secondary to immune depression of pregnancy. Lower resistance to the condition increases the risk especially of *primi gravidae* to death, abruption (tearing of the placenta with associated hemorrhage), abortion, or low birth weight. It may also predispose the infant to persistent anemia.

Homicide and War

Health statistics from many parts of the world confirm that injuries resulting from violence are also among the chief causes of mortality for young people but particularly for adolescent males. Available statistics indicate that the most violent region in the world is the Americas, where homicide rates are highest among young men ages 15–24 years (World Bank, 1997; Pan American Health Organization [PAHO], 1993). According to PAHO, homicide is the second leading cause of death among young males ages 15–24 years in 10 out of 21 countries with populations greater than 1 million, with the highest being in Colombia (267 per 100,000 in 1994), Puerto Rico, Venezuela, and Brazil (72 per 100,000). The United States is considered to have an intermediate adolescent homicide rate in this region; however, at 38 per 100,000 it is four times higher than the next highest rate among the 21 industrialized countries and highest when compared to Western European countries, Canada, Australia, and New Zealand (Fingerhut & Kleinman, 1990; PAHO, 1998).

In the Americas region, one third of all deaths due to homicides are among adolescents aged 10–19 years (PAHO, 1998). In Colombia, between 1991 and 1995, there were 112,000 homicides. Young people accounted for 41,000 deaths; the vast majority was among young males (World Bank, 1997). Between 1977 and 1994, the specific death rate among 15- to 19-year-olds due to homicide increased by 160% in Brazil, and currently homicide is responsible for 30% of all deaths among this age group (Falbo, Buzzetti, & Cattaneo, 2001). In approximately half of all Latin American countries, homicides are included among the five leading causes of death for adolescents, with a peak incidence among 15- to 29-year-old males (Maddaleno & Silber, 1993).

For Latin America, income inequality has been cited as a primary factor associated with homicide (Falbo et al., 2001; Kohn, 2001). To identify the risk and protective factors associated with adolescent homicide, Falbo and colleagues conducted a case-control study in Recife, Brazil. Accordingly, use of illicit drugs and prior police records were two of the more important risk factors, whereas education, religious observance, and having a father in the home were the primary protective factors identified. These findings, along with the fact that most homicides are a result of firearms, provide definable risk and protective factors that can be addressed through public policy and effective programming that target such factors (Falbo et al., 2001; Kohn, 2001).

In other developing country regions, less is known about patterns of violence related to mortality because many of these countries have incomplete vital registration systems. However, from a few small-scale studies that have been conducted, it can be seen that assaults and homicides are becoming an increasingly part of everyday life. For example, a study of the load on primary care services in a South African township found that violence accounted for approximately 26% of casualties in 10- to 14-year-old children and approximately 60% in those aged 15 to 19 years (Forjuoh & Zwi, 1998).

Mortality as a result of war probably claims more adolescent lives in developing countries than do other forms of homicide because young people (aged 10–24 years) are the majority of soldiers in most developing country wars. A 1996 United Nations Children's Fund (UNICEF) report found that adolescents have been used as combatants in many conflicts in countries such as Liberia, Mozambique, Cambodia, Myanmar, and Sierra Leone (UNICEF, 1996). In fact, according to WHO (1998), more than 100 million young people have been involved in armed conflict, either as soldiers, civilians, or refugees. As a result of the recent widespread availability of handheld weapons such as the AK-47 and M-16 rifles, more adolescents have been drawn into battles that previously would have been fought only by men able to carry heavy weaponry. Also, many claim that involving children and adolescents in war is relatively simple to do because they are easier to intimidate, they do not ask for salaries, they are less likely than adults to run away, and they question less what they are expected to do (UNICEF,

1996). However, because monitoring systems are generally weak and records are poorly kept or hidden in wartime, accurate global statistics on child and adolescent casualties related to war are lacking.

Suicide

In most industrialized countries, suicide ranks after injuries as the second leading cause of death among adolescents; globally, however, it ranks fifth as an identifiable cause of death for youth and young adults. Worldwide, between 100,000 and 200,000 young people commit suicide annually, and the rates for young people appear to be rising more quickly than those for all other age groups in both developed and developing countries (Barker, 2000; WHO, 1993). However, suicide rates vary tremendously worldwide, from a high in Hungary and Sri Lanka to a low in Egypt and Kuwait. In general, Arabic and Latin American countries have relatively low rates of suicide, whereas countries of primarily European descent, such as Australia, United States, and Canada, tend to have relatively high rates (Diekstra, 1989). For example, suicides are responsible for 5% of all deaths among adolescents in Chile, Uruguay, Costa Rica, and Ecuador compared with approximately 10% in the United States for the same year (Maddaleno & Silber, 1993).

In most regions of the world, suicide is more common for males than for females. In the United States, where suicide is currently the second leading cause of death among young people ages 13–19 and the third leading cause of death among young people ages 15–24, boys are four times as likely to commit suicide as are girls (National Institute of Mental Health [NIMH], 1998); this is largely explained by the fact that when young men attempt suicide, they are far more likely to use a gun (Miller & Hemenway, 2001). In fact, more people in the United States kill themselves by using guns than by all other methods combined. In 1998, there were approximately 30,000 suicide deaths among Americans, of which 57% were caused by guns (Miller & Hemenway, 2001).

In a review of the prevalence of adolescent suicide, Ryland and Kruisi (1992) concluded that in the past 40 years, there has been a fourfold increase in the rate of adolescent suicide in most Western countries, including the United States, Australia, and New Zealand. In Brazil, India, and Mexico, suicide rates among adolescents also increased from between 5% to 62% over the past two decades (Brown, 2001). It is unclear, though, as to why young people should be so much more likely to kill themselves today than in the past. One possible explanation is that young people have greater access to lethal weapons. Similarly, research has shown that for youth, there is a direct correlation between percent of the population that owns guns and suicide rates. In the United States, for example, among children aged 5–14 the suicide rate was on average twice as high as the suicide rate among other industrialized countries. This twofold increased risk of suicide among U.S. children was accounted for by a U.S. firearm suicide rate that was 10 times higher than firearm suicide rates in other industrialized countries (Miller & Hemenway, 2001).

In other countries, psychiatrists are theorizing that there is an increase in suicide because of the loss of tradition, social cohesion, and spontaneous social support—primarily as the result of globalization. Also, research has shown that young people are at greater risk of committing suicide if they are exposed to certain identified risk factors such as alcohol, other substance abuse, and mental illness (Brown, 2001). For example, the suicide rate associated with alcoholism is between 75 and 85 times greater than the overall suicide rate for the general population, and this is true among all age groups. For substance misuse, the suicide rate appears to be approximately 12 times that of the general population. In Western countries, it has also been shown that individuals with mental health problems, particularly severe depression, underlie 50–90% of suicides (Brown, 2001).

Maternal Mortality

Another prominent cause for mortality among adolescent women, particularly in developing countries, is maternal mortality. Levels of maternal mortality in industrialized and developing countries show a greater disparity than any other public health indicator, far exceeding differences in infant mortality rates, which are most often taken as the measure of comparative disadvantage (AbouZahr, Wardlaw, Stanton, & Hill, 1996). Although there have been significant declines in infant mortality rates in recent years, the same cannot be said for maternal mortality. In fact, women who become pregnant in developing countries face a risk of death due to pregnancy that is 80–600 times higher than women in developed countries (United Nations, 1991). In 1990, the average maternal mortality rate in the developed countries was 27 per 100,000 live births, whereas in countries such as Angola, Bhutan, Chad, Guinea, Nepal, Sierra Leone, and Somalia, the rates were at least 1,500 per 100,000 live births (WHO, 1996).

Young women who have not reached full physical and physiological maturity are almost three times as likely to die from complications in childbirth as are older women. Because of pelvic immaturity, they are much more likely than older women to experience cephalopelvic disproportion, toxemia, and placental abruption leading to hemorrhage and death. Data from studies in several countries consistently show a higher risk of maternal death among teenage girls compared with women aged 20–34 years (WHO, 1993). The risk for very young teenagers (10–14 years) is much greater than even for older teenagers (15–19 years). A study in Bangladesh showed that girls aged 10–14 years had a maternal mortality ratio five times that of women aged 20–24 years, while for 15- to 19-year-olds the rate was twice that of the 20- to 24-year-olds (WHO, 1995). Similarly, in Jamaica and Nigeria, it has been found that pregnant women under age 15 were four to eight times more likely to die during pregnancy and childbirth than those aged 15 to 19 years (WHO, 1993). Also, community-based studies of the age-specific maternal mortality ratio (MMR) in seven developing countries found the MMR to be higher among 15- to 19-year-olds than in 20- to 24-year-olds, with the MMRs in 15- to 19-year-olds ranging from under 50 per 100,000 live births in areas of two Latin American countries to more than 100 per 100,000 live births in areas of two Asian countries (WHO, 1995). These high rates of maternal mortality make a substantial contribution to the overall mortality among these age groups in developing countries. In Bangladesh, for example, the excess of female deaths over those of males in the 15–24 years age group—and even throughout the reproductive period—can be attributed mainly to causes of maternal mortality (WHO, 1995).

The life-threatening complications of pregnancy that women under age 20 face are the same risks that all other women face: hemorrhage, sepsis, pregnancy-induced hypertension, preeclampsia and eclampsia, obstructed labor, complications of unsafe abortion, and iron-deficiency anemia. However, young women face greater risks related to hypertension, obstructed labor, iron-deficiency anemia, and complications related to unsafe abortion. For example, cause-specific maternal mortality rates from Matlab, Bangladesh showed that deaths from hypertensive disorders of pregnancy and abortion were twice as high among teenagers as among women aged 20–34 (Fauveau, Koenig, Chakraborty, & Chowdhury, 1988). Hypertensive disorders, if untreated, can lead to eclampsia, which is also often fatal. In Mozambique, it was found that preeclampsia and eclampsia accounted for almost half of maternal deaths in women younger than 20 years (Granja, Machungo, Gomes, & Bergstrom, 2001). These risks are higher for young women not only because of their age, but also because births to younger women often are first births, which are riskier than second, third, or fourth births. In addition, socioeconomic factors, including poverty, malnutrition, lack of education, and lack of access to prenatal care or emergency obstetrical care can increase a young women's risk of maternal mortality (McCauley & Salter, 1995).

MORBIDITY TRENDS

Reproductive Health Issues

Pregnancy and Early Childbearing

A substantial number of sexually active unmarried young women experience pregnancy, which is typically both unplanned and unwanted. Among females about to be married in Shanghai, 40% admitted experiencing an unwanted pregnancy (Gao, 1998, cited in WHO, 2001); in sites of Botswana, 42% of out-of-school adolescent females had experienced a pregnancy (Kgosidintsi, 1997); and in Jamaica, approximately 40% of women experienced an unwanted pregnancy at least once before they reached the age of 20 (Eggleston, Jackson, & Hardee, 1999). In general, it appears that in-school youth are less likely to experience an unwanted pregnancy than are those from the general population. For example, among students in the final 3 years of secondary school in Buenos Aires, Argentina, only 3% of all females reported a pregnancy and 2% of males reported making a partner pregnant (Mendez Ribas, Necchi, & Schufer, 1995).

Although the majority of adolescents who do give birth are married, a substantial proportion are not. In much of sub-Saharan Africa, one third of births to women aged 15–19 occur among unmarried adolescents; the proportion is quite low (4–6%) in Burkina Faso, Mali, Niger, and Nigeria, but it exceeds three quarters in Botswana and Namibia (Alan Guttmacher Institute [AGI], 1998). Typically in Latin America and the Caribbean, 12–25% of adolescent births are to unmarried women.

As access to education has increased and the benefits of postponing childbearing have become more widely known, adolescent childbearing has declined in some countries where it once was common. Women aged 20–24 in parts of Asia are about 80% as likely as those 40–44 to have had their first child during adolescence; elsewhere in the region, they are only one half to two thirds as likely to have done so. In North Africa and the Middle East, adolescent childbearing has fallen by about one quarter to one half. In contrast, smaller declines have occurred in sub-Saharan Africa; in fact, in some

African countries, adolescents are more likely to give birth than they were a generation ago (AGI, 1998). Typically, adolescent childbearing rates range between 120 to about 160 per 1,000 in most countries in sub-Saharan Africa. At the extreme, annual age-specific fertility rates of more than 200 births per 1,000 women aged 15–19 are found in Mali and Niger. In Latin America and the Caribbean, changes in levels of teenage childbearing have varied. For example, there has been a 37% decline in the Dominican Republic, no change in Bolivia, and a slight increase in Brazil (AGI, 1998).

As a result of teenagers' physiological and social immaturity and their lack of prenatal care, health risks associated with adolescent pregnancies and childbearing are more pronounced than are those among older women (UN, 1989; National Academy of Sciences [NAS], 1996). Hypertension is one such complication. As in other parts of the world, studies conducted in Africa document an increased risk of pregnancy-related complications among young women. Specifically, high blood pressure is one of the primary pregnancy complications that afflict young adolescent mothers (UN, 1989). When high blood pressure is accompanied by proteinuria, edema, or both, after 20 weeks of gestation a patient's condition can worsen to preeclampsia, which (if it is uncontrolled) can progress to extreme hypertension, seizures, convulsions, and cerebral hemorrhage (WHO, 1991; Zabin & Kiragu, 1998). Several studies have examined high blood pressure among young women in Africa. In reviewing more than 21,000 deliveries in Zaria, Nigeria, Harrison (1985) demonstrated that 40% of young women with eclampsia were aged 15 or younger. Similar findings have been documented in Nigeria, Kenya, Cape Verde, and Tanzania (Zabin & Kiragu, 1998).

Also, because of their pelvic immaturity, obstructed labor is another common pregnancy-related complication among young adolescents; this is reflected in the increased proportion of labors in this age group that end in Cesarean section or destructive operations (WHO, 1995). Not uncommonly, obstructed labor leaves women with a vagino-rectal or urethral fistulae. The result is continual leakage of urine or feces, constant irritation, and social ostracism. The incidence of fistula has not been well documented in developing countries but has been estimated from 55 to 100 per 100,000 deliveries in Africa and may be as high as 4% of all deliveries in Afghanistan (Cottingham & Royston, 1991).

Abortion

Data on levels of induced abortion in developing countries are notoriously difficult to gather, either because abortion is clandestine or because the issue is too sensitive. Total estimates of abortions among women under age 20 in developing countries range from 1 million to 4.4 million a year. Worldwide, about 58% of all women having abortions live in Asia, 11% in Africa, and 9% in Latin America and the Caribbean. The remainder live in Europe (17%) and elsewhere in the developed world—Australia, Canada, Japan, New Zealand, and the United States (5%; AGI, 1998). Global estimates suggest that women having legal abortions (estimated at 26 million) outnumber those having illegal abortions (almost 20 million); this is primarily because in two areas of the world in which extremely high numbers of women have abortions—China and Eastern Europe—the procedure is legal. Given that abortion is clandestine in nearly all of Africa and Latin America, negligible numbers of women in these regions obtain legal abortions. Almost half of all legal abortions occur in East Asia (mainly China, but also in Hong Kong and South Korea), 17% in the rest of Asia, 21% in Eastern Europe, 6% in Western Europe, and 9% in the rest of the developed world.

Although abortion is common among adolescents, some demographers argue that the vast majority of abortion clients in many developing countries are married, adult women with children, who want to delay the next birth or terminate childbearing altogether. Conversely, in developed countries, a disproportionate share of abortion clients are adolescents (Mensch et al., 1999). Singh and Henshaw cite data from the United States and England, where about one quarter of abortion clients are under age 20, and data from four Latin American countries (Bolivia, Colombia, Peru, and Venezuela) and India, where respectively 12% and 5% of abortion clients are that young (Singh & Henshaw, 1996, cited in Mensch et al., 1999).

Although abortion rates may be lower for adolescent girls than for older women, available data suggest that young women are much more likely than older women to undergo illegal, unsafe abortions. Also, because of fear, shame, lack of access, or lack of money, young women are more likely to delay seeking medical care if complications arise after abortion (McCauley & Salter, 1995). In developing countries, where most abortions are illegal, many abortions are unsafe and for some result in lifelong disability, infertility, or death (McCauley & Salter, 1995). In fact, in regions where abortion is unsafe, it may be one of the greatest health risks a sexually active young woman can face.

The health risks of unsafe abortion include sepsis (infection) caused by unsanitary instruments or incomplete abortion, hemorrhage, injuries to genital organs (such as cervical laceration or uterine perforation), and toxic reactions to chemicals or drugs used to induce abortion. Hirsch and Barker (1992) compiled abortion data from 27 studies in developing countries (drawn largely from urban, hospital-based samples) and found that adolescent admissions accounted for 60% of females admitted with abortion-related complications in developing countries each year. Several studies conducted in Africa substantiate their findings. For example, it was found in Zambia that 80% of women with induced abortion-related complications admitted to hospitals were under 19 years old (Likwa, 1998). Similarly, in Nairobi, a study found that at Kenyatta National Hospital, abortion was the leading cause of admission to the emergency gynecological ward, and women aged 15–19 accounted for one third of all postabortion care cases admitted. Results from another study conducted in Nigeria indicated that in five hospitals, 55% of postabortion patients were under the age of 20, and 85% of the cases reported were single women (Okagbue, 1990). Latin American studies have also shown that women under age 20 account for more than their share of abortion complications and related deaths. For example, in six Latin American countries, 14% to almost 40% of women hospitalized for abortion complications in the 1980s were under age 20 (AGI, 1994).

STDs

Another major sequela of unprotected sexual activity in adolescence is the acquisition of an STD, often with devastating effects on future fertility. In fact, of the estimated 333 million new STDs that occur in the world every year, at least one third occur in young people under 25 years of age (Advocates for Youth, 2001). According to WHO estimates, 1 in 20 adolescents worldwide acquires an STD each year. Studies conducted in both developed and developing countries have confirmed that STDs are a major public health problem, but in sub-Saharan Africa, the incidence rates are far higher due to poor resources for treating STDs (Wasserheit & Holmes, 1992). As a point of comparison, in one large African city, the incidence rate of gonorrhea was reported to be 3,000 to 10,000 per 100,000 population, whereas a study from the United States reported annual incidence of gonorrhea of 233 per 100,000 population in 1991 and in Sweden, approximately 39 per 100,000 population in 1987 (Kasule et al., 1997)—a difference of 10–30 times. The prevalence of STDs in Ethiopia is among the highest in Africa; one clinic-based study showed that up to 64% of Ethiopian women had at least three separate STDs at the time of diagnosis (Duncan et al., 1994).

Compared with the extensive efforts devoted to research and intervention on HIV and AIDS, very little attention has been paid to other STDs. In particular, there has been limited discussion of the role of young and adult men in the transmission of human papilloma virus (HPV), which can be transmitted even with condom use. An estimated 10 million women, the majority in their late teens and early 20s, have active HPV infections. In parts of Africa and Asia, where regular Pap testing is less common than in industrialized countries, cervical cancer from HPV is the most common cause of cancer-related mortality. HPV is implicated in 95% of cervical cancer. In men, HPV is frequently asymptomatic, and men frequently infect young women without even knowing it (Barker, 2000).

STDs deserve attention not only because of their high prevalence, but also because they frequently go undetected and untreated and can result in serious reproductive morbidity and mortality. However, reporting of STDs is often poor, and the actual prevalence among adolescents may be higher than inadequate figures indicate (Mtimavalye & Belsey, 1987; National Research Council [NRC], 1997). As a result of the underreporting of STDs, their immediate effects on adolescents are not always apparent. In northern Nigeria, Bello (1987) surveyed 1,104 asymptomatic males and females and found that 24% of college females had laboratory evidence of gonorrhea. Moreover, WHO-sponsored research on STDs has found that an increasing number of young men are contracting chlamydia urethritis, which is asymptomatic in up to 80% of cases. Prevalence studies on chlamydial urethritis in Chile with 154 asymptomatic adolescent males found that 3% of sexually active males tested positive (Barker, 2000).

Small-scale studies have shown that for both behavioral and biological reasons, STDs are more prevalent among adolescents than among adults. In Kenya, Orwenyo (1984, cited in Zabin & Kiragu, 1998) found that 36% of pregnant women aged 15–24 years suffered from an STD, compared with only 16% of their older counterparts. In Brazil, nearly 30% of sexually active adolescent males in low-income areas said they have had an STD at least once (Childhope, 1997). A study in Ethiopia showed that young women having first sex before menarche were more likely to acquire an STD than were those who had first sex at later ages (Duncan, 1994). Similarly, in Burkina Faso, a study among adolescent commercial sex workers revealed a higher rate of infection than in older prostitutes, a pattern that has also been shown in the United States (Damiba, Vermund, & Kelley, 1990; Markos, Wade, & Waltzman, 1992).

Adolescents who know that they are infected frequently fail to obtain timely treatment for STDs. Most initial STD infections are associated with annoying but not worrisome local symptoms that do not appear to warrant a clinic visit (Lande, 1993). In

Zambia, young people said that when they had an STD, they used home remedies first and formal health services "as a last resort" (Webb, 1997). Health services in most areas do not accommodate the special needs of adolescents and often discourage attendance even when the need for care is well understood (Senderowitz, 1995). In Zimbabwe, more than half of the health providers interviewed said that parents should be notified if a young, unmarried client comes in for STD treatment (Kim, Maragwanda, & Kols, 1997).

Female Genital Mutilation

Traditional reproductive practices that specifically affect adolescents are common in many developing countries. The most serious of these is female genital cutting or mutilation (FGM), which is a traditional practice that involves cutting away parts of the female external genitalia as a rite of passage for young girls to womanhood and marriage. FGM previously used to be referred to as female circumcision; however, the term has been largely abandoned because it implies an analogy with male circumcision, which results in comparatively little harm (Population Reference Bureau, 2002). FGM is known to be practiced in one form or another in 28 sub-Saharan countries, in a few countries on the Arab Peninsula, among some minority communities in Asia, and among migrants from these areas who have settled in Europe, Australia, and North America (Population Reference Bureau, 2002). The tradition may have originated 2,000 years ago in southern Egypt or northern Sudan, but in many parts of West Africa, the practice began in the 19th or 20th century (Shell-Duncan & Hernlund, 2000).

The availability of reliable figures on the prevalence of FGM has increased greatly in recent years: It is estimated that more than 130 million girls and women worldwide have undergone FGM, and nearly 2 million more girls are at risk each year. National data have now been collected in the Demographic and Health Survey (DHS) program for six countries: the Central African Republic, Ivory Coast, Egypt, Eritrea, Mali, and Sudan. In these countries, from 43% to 97% of reproductive-age women have experienced FGM (Althaus, 1997). Within countries, prevalence may vary across ethnic groups; in Mali, where the overall proportion of women who have undergone FGM is 94%, only 17% of women of Tamachek ethnicity have had it done. Estimates for other countries are generally based on local surveys or anecdotal information. The estimated proportion of women who have undergone FGM in these countries ranges from 5% in Uganda and the Congo to 98% in Djibouti and Somalia (Althaus, 1997).

The WHO has standardized classifications of FGM into four main groupings: Type I (in which part or all of the clitoris is removed); Type II (in which both the clitoris and the labia minora are removed); Type III (commonly referred to as infibulation, in which the clitoris and labia minora are removed and the labia majora stitched to seal the vagina partially); and Type IV (other genital operations that include clitoral piercing, stretching the labia, cauterization, and scraping or cutting of the vagina). Of these four types, WHO estimates that clitoridectomy (Type I) is the most common procedure and accounts for up to 80% of all cases. Meanwhile, infibulation accounts for 15% of all cases.

These procedures are generally performed on girls between the ages of 4 and 12, although they are practiced in some cultures as early as a few days after birth or as late as just prior to marriage, pregnancy, or after the first birth (Population Reference Bureau, 2002). Typically, a traditional birth attendant or an elder village woman with little or no medical training performs the procedure. Instruments used include razor blades, glass, kitchen knives, sharp rocks, scissors, and scalpels. During these procedures, infections such as tetanus occur frequently due to unsanitary conditions and the lack of medical follow-up (Hosken, 1993). Uncontrolled bleeding can also occur if the wound is not well sealed. Long-term consequences include painful intercourse, damage to the urinary system, and scarring of the tissue, which often seals the edges of the wounds together and shrinks the genital passage (Hosken, 1993). Infibulation is particularly likely to cause serious long-term health problems. Because the urethral opening is covered, repeated urinary tract infections are common, and stones may form in the urethra and bladder because of obstruction and infection. If the opening is very small, menstrual flow may be blocked, leading to reproductive tract infections and lowered fertility or sterility. One early study estimated that 20–25% of cases of sterility in northern Sudan could be linked to infibulation (Mustafa, 1966, cited in Althaus, 1997). Without deinfibulation before childbirth, obstructed labor may occur, causing life-threatening complications for both mother and infant. In addition to physical damage resulting from genital mutilation, psychological trauma has been implicated in young women's future emotional functioning (Zabin & Kiragu, 1998). Although such sequelae are difficult to attribute and quantify, they cannot be discounted. They can result from the trauma of the event or occur later when subsequent difficulties arise as a result of the procedure.

VIOLENCE

Sexual Coercion and Abuse

Given the sensitive nature of the topic, nonconsensual sexual activity is difficult to research. The topic is particularly sensitive among youth, the age group in which coercion and abuse is most likely to occur. Accurately estimating the prevalence of sexual coercion and abuse in the world, especially in developing countries, is complicated primarily because there have been relatively few studies to address this issue, and cultural mores against reporting abuse make it difficult to collect from records. However, according to information from justice systems and rape crisis centers in Chile, Peru, Malaysia, Mexico, Panama, Papua New Guinea, and the United States, it has been shown that between one third and two thirds of known sexual assault victims are age 15 or younger (Heise, Ellsberg, & Gottemoello, 1999).

Some studies have used different ways of assessing coercion—in some, force was defined as any sexual activity that was not consensual; in others, a considerable age difference between partners was regarded as an indirect indicator of coercion; and still others defined it more directly to be rape or sex with sugar daddies (males, usually substantially older than their partner who exchange money, gifts, or both for sex; WHO, 2001). The majority of case studies that have examined this issue show that between 5% and 15% of all young females report a forced or coerced sexual experience. In some cases, the figure is even higher. For example, among in- and out-of school adolescents in three cities in Botswana, 21% experienced forced or coerced sex; in Peru, this figure was 20% among secondary school students and 41% among young females attending urban night study centers in Lima (Villanueva, 1992, cited in WHO, 2001). In rural Malawi, 55% of adolescent girls surveyed report that they were often forced to have sex (Advocates for Youth, 2000). In a case study in Manila, Philippines, 6% of unwed mothers report a pregnancy as a result of rape, and another 7% reported that a pregnancy resulted from sex in exchange for money to support a drug habit (Bautista, 1989, cited in WHO, 2001).

The younger a woman is at first intercourse, the more likely that sex is forced. In New Zealand, one girl in four who had intercourse before the age of 14 reported that she was forced to do so, often by a much older man. Similarly, in the United States, 24% of those who had intercourse before age 14 reported having been forced (Heise et al., 1999).

Young girls are particularly vulnerable to coercion into sexual relationships with older men. The sugar daddy phenomenon is frequently cited as a common reason that young girls will have sex against their will. In Botswana, about one in five adolescent females report that it is difficult to refuse sex when money and gifts are offered (Kgosidintsi, 1997, cited in WHO, 2001). Similarly, a study of female adolescents in Kenya revealed that 50% of the girls admitted receiving gifts in the form of money, ornaments, and clothes from their partners when they engaged in sex for the first time (Waju & Radeny, 1995).

Although most studies confirm that girls are more likely to be victims of sexual abuse or coercion, there are also several studies that show that large numbers of boys suffer from sexual abuse. In Kenya, a national survey of youth found that 28% of boys and 22% of girls reported that forced sex was attempted with them. In addition, 31% of boys and 27% of girls reported having been pressured to have sex (Erulkar et al., 1998). In the Caribbean, 7.5% of boys aged 16–18 reported having experienced some kind of sexual abuse (Stewart, Sebastiani, Delgado, & Lopez, 1996). In Zimbabwe, 30% of secondary-study students interviewed reported that they had been sexually abused; half were boys being abused by female perpetrators (Shanler, Heise, Weiss, & Stewart, 1998).

Sexual abuse and coercion can lead to a wide variety of unhealthy consequences, including behavioral and psychological problems, sexual dysfunction, relationship problems, low self-esteem, depression, thoughts of suicide, alcohol and substance abuse, and sexual risk taking (Heise et al., 1999). Victims of sexual coercion and abuse are generally less likely to feel they have power in sexual relationships. A longitudinal comparative study of sexual violence during adolescence in South Africa, Brazil, and the United States found that sexual coercion and abuse in adolescent intimate relationships are associated with lower condom use (WHO, 2001). Sexual violence has also been linked to many serious physical health problems such as injury, chronic pain syndromes, and gastrointestinal disorders (Heise et al., 1999). For example, a variety of studies have found that women suffering from chronic pelvic pain are consistently more likely to have a history of childhood sexual abuse, sexual assault, or sexual abuse by their partners (Heise et al., 1999).

NUTRITION

Body Mass Index and Undernutrition

The nutritional status of adolescents is usually measured in terms of weight for height (body mass index or BMI) rather than weight for age. Although the latter is more useful in measuring overall long-term growth, weight for height is more useful in measuring current health status (WHO, 1993). Undernutrition (low weight) results in poor pregnancy outcomes among adolescent girls. Undernutrition also limits school achievement and work productivity, as has been shown in other age groups (Kurz & Johnson-Welch, 1994). In measurable terms, undernutrition is defined as a BMI that is less than the 5th percentile of the National Center for Health Statistics (NCHS) and WHO reference data (WHO, 1995).

In the studies undertaken by the International Center for Research on Women (ICRW) to measure the nutritional status among adolescent girls, undernutrition was found to be highly prevalent in India (53%), Nepal (36%), and Benin (23%). However, even when prevalence was high, BMI for age tended to improve over the course of adolescence. One reason for this finding could be that the girls started their growth spurts later than the U.S. reference population did, and thus when they appeared to be undernourished at age 12, they could have been growing normally but along a slower trajectory (Kurz & Johnson-Welch, 1994). Similarly, in India a study measuring the growth of adolescent girls in an affluent urban area found that their growth during childhood paralleled that of well-nourished girls in Europe. However, their adolescent growth spurt was of a much smaller magnitude so that despite their affluence, their final height was significantly less than that of their European counterparts (Vir, 1990, cited in WHO, 1995).

Anemia

Iron-deficiency anemia is generally recognized as the greatest nutritional problem among adolescents. During adolescence, iron requirements are increased, reaching a maximum at peak growth, and remaining almost as high in girls after menarche to replace menstrual loss. Adolescent iron requirements are even higher in developing countries because of infectious diseases and parasitic infestations that cause iron loss (Kanani & Poojara, 2000). Approximately 27% of adolescents in developing countries are estimated to be anemic, compared to 6% in developed countries, although figures vary according to country, region, and socioeconomic status. In Africa, 57% of adolescent boys and 45% of girls are anemic; in Latin America, 22% of boys and 12% of girls are anemic; and in Asia the prevalence is 17% for boys and 19% for girls (DeMaeyer & Aiels-Tegman, 1985; Shanler et al., 1998). Adolescent girls have generally been thought to have higher prevalence of anemia than do boys, primarily because the onset of menstrual blood loss coincides with the adolescent growth spurt. However, boys also have high iron requirements because they are developing muscle mass during the adolescent growth spurt. As the growth of adolescents slows, boys' iron status is thought to improve. For instance, it is the norm for older male adolescents and men to have large stores of iron. The functional importance of this transient anemia in adolescent males in many developing countries is not known but may be similar to the nonreproductive consequences for women (Kurz & Johnson-Welch, 1994).

Smaller-scale studies have shown that younger women who are pregnant are much more likely to be anemic than are older women. For example, Adedoyin and Adetoro (1989) found that 60% of 496 teenage mothers were anemic, compared with 15% of 500 women aged 24–30. DeMaeyer and Aiels-Tegman (1985) also found that anemia is almost two times more common among adolescent mothers than among older ones; this is primarily because a teenager's body must compete for nourishment with her fetus, which can further deplete her already low iron and nutrient reserves. Anemia in women has been shown to be associated with reduced levels of energy and productivity, impaired immune function, reproductive failure, and maternal mortality (Levin, Pollitt, Galloway, & McGuire, 1993, cited in WHO, 1995). In addition, anemia was independently associated with lower school achievement in adolescent girls (Delisle, Chandra-Mouli, & de Benoist, 2001).

To understand the response of iron status to intervention, a food intervention was implemented in Guatemala that contained 18 mg of iron, 100% of the recommended daily allowance. Researchers gave supplements and then placebos in alternate 3-month segments over 1 year. The study found that hemoglobin levels increased immediately upon intake of iron supplement but then fell when only the placebo was taken; this suggests that although iron status can improve rapidly with supplementation, additional interventions are needed to maintain improved status (Kurz & Johnson-Welch, 1994).

Obesity and Overweight

The increasing prevalence of obesity among adolescents worldwide—even among those in the lowest income groups—is a fairly recent development in malnutrition. Much of the increase in adolescent obesity can be explained by a nutrition transition to fat-rich diets and a decrease in physical activity, particularly among urban populations (Schneider, 2000). Globalization has made cheap vegetable oils and fats widely available, greatly increasing fat consumption in all nations (Drewnowski & Popkin, 1997, cited in Schneider, 2000). Also, the process of urbanization automatically brings with it changes related to activity patterns, especially involving a greater dependence on public transportation and automobiles. Consequently, the nutrition transition occurs at lower levels of gross national product than ever before, and developing countries are no longer immune to the problems of obesity. In China, for instance, obesity is just emerging, but it is a problem associated with urban living, high income, and adolescence (Delisle et al., 2001). In South Africa, adolescent obesity, particularly among urban African female adolescents, has been documented in a number of publications (Walker, 1980; Walker & Walker, 1977; Walker, Walker, Manetsi, & Tsotetsi, 1990, cited in Cameron & Getz, 1997).

Obesity at adolescence is an important public health issue because it tends to persist into adulthood, and with that comes increased risks to diabetes, heart disease, orthopedic problems, and many other chronic diseases (Braddon, Rodgers, Wadsworth, & Davies, 1986, cited in Andersen, 2000). Dietz (1998) has also cautioned that obese children are much more likely to face both health and psychological challenges related to their childhood and adolescence than are their leaner counterparts. In the United States, pediatricians are increasingly seeing hyperlipidemia, hypertension, and diabetes in their obese patients (Andersen, 2000). Abdominal obesity in particular (high waist-hip ratio) is already associated with adverse blood lipid profiles in adolescents, as was demonstrated in a longitudinal study among children and adolescents in Bogalusa (United States; Freedman, Serdula, Srinavasan, & Berenson, 1999, cited in Delisle et al., 2001).

TOBACCO AND SUBSTANCE USE

Tobacco Use

One of the forms of behavior most damaging to the health of youth in the long term is the use of tobacco. Although the chronic ill health and mortality associated with smoking usually become evident after two or three decades of tobacco use, young smokers are generally less physically fit than their nonsmoking counterparts. Smoking has been found to lower the immune response and is linked to complications related to upper respiratory tract infections (WHO, 1993).

Currently, smoking remains one of the most important preventable causes of death in the world. According to the WHO, approximately 4 million people per year die from tobacco-related illnesses, a figure that is expected to rise to 10 million by the year 2030 (WHO, 1999). By that time, approximately 70% of these deaths will be occurring in developing countries. Tobacco industries will be primarily to blame. Tobacco advertising often links smoking with images of adventure, physical attractiveness, sexual success, and even higher athletic ability—all images designed to have a very powerful effect on young people. Developing countries, as of yet, have fewer restrictions placed on cigarette marketing and distributing than do industrialized countries; consequently, transnational tobacco companies are increasing their operations in many of these countries (Stebbins, 1990). During the 1980s, cigarette companies convinced countries in Asia to open up their markets to imported cigarettes to enact trade sanctions. The results were disastrous. In South Korea, for example, the smoking rate among teenage boys was 18% in 1988; a year later, after cigarette imports were allowed, it rose to 30%.

Studies conducted in industrialized countries indicate that most people begin using tobacco before the age of 18 years (U.S. Department of Health and Human Services, 1994; Secretary of State for Health for Scotland, Wales, and North Ireland, 1999). Recent trends show even an earlier age of initiation and rising smoking prevalence rates among children and adolescents. For example, according to the Global Youth Tobacco Survey, the highest prevalence of early initiation of cigarette smoking is in China, Poland, and Zimbabwe, where nearly one third of the students who ever smoked cigarettes started smoking before the age of 10 years (Warren et al., 2000). Moreover, nearly 70% of students aged 13 to 15 in the Ukraine, Poland, and the Russian Federation have smoked cigarettes at least once (Warren et al., 2000). Generally, in most countries, boys are more likely than girls to use tobacco. However, where this tendency is reversed, there may be a successful advertising campaign by the tobacco industry in making cigarettes look fashionable (Warren et al., 2000).

Notably, most young people who start smoking report that they want to stop, and worldwide, over two thirds of youth between the ages of 13 and 15 have tried to stop smoking (Warren et al., 2000). However, the traditional focus of youth prevention programs has been on preventing youth from starting to smoke. Relatively few have offered smoking cessation programs to those who may already be smoking. Programs that target tobacco use among young people, therefore, need to expand their focus to include both preventing starting and offering smoking cessation programs to youth.

Alcohol and Drug Use

In most industrialized countries, alcohol is generally accessible to everyone, including young people. Although moderate use of alcohol by adults and teenagers is socially accepted in many countries, excessive use is invariably considered to be a problem with severe social and physical consequences (Nace, 1987). In the United States, a large body of literature has demonstrated that alcohol use is significantly associated with road traffic accidents among young people. Heavy adult alcoholic drinkers are also at greater risk for cancer, ulcers, heart disease, muscle wastage, malnutrition, and cirrhosis of the liver, which is a leading cause of death in several countries (WHO, 1993).

Although most young people in industrialized countries try alcohol, the numbers of young people who abuse it are much smaller, and the numbers of those who go on to have an alcohol problem later in life are also relatively small (WHO, 1995). Studies from the United States have indicated that those with the potential for becoming alcoholics are identifiable by environmental, genetic, and social factors, which means that prevention programs can use targeted measures that are more effective than general warnings to the entire population of youth (Tucker, 1987, cited in WHO, 1995).

In Latin America, however, alcohol use and abuse are increasing rapidly among young people. A study in Chile, for example, showed that 80% of 9-year-olds were reported to have drunk alcoholic drinks at least once a week (Coombs & Globetti, 1986). Moreover, among 15- to 19-year-olds, it is estimated that approximately 12% of Chilean youth drink in excess (WHO, 1993). In sub-Saharan Africa, studies among high school students in Kenya, Ghana, and Zambia have shown that between 70% and 80% of students use alcohol, and 10–14% could be classified as abusing it. Patterns of use in these countries are linked to changes in the social context of using alcohol, from being primarily associated with traditional ceremonies to its more widespread use in daily socializing (WHO, 1995). Studies conducted in Nigeria (which revealed that approximately 52% of high school students use alcohol) also link the extensive use of alcohol by youth to the ready availability and lack of sanctions on its production, distribution, and consumption. For instance, there are no age or time restrictions on alcohol use in most parts of the country (Adelekan, 1989). Similar situations can be found in other African countries as well.

Research has also shown important differences between the sexes in regard to alcohol use and the physical effects of alcohol. A national survey of adolescents in the United States found that 20% of males compared to 16% of females report using alcohol 2 days or more per month (Blum & Rinehart, 1997). Studies in developing countries have also demonstrated that females are less likely to use alcohol than are males. Part of the reason for this finding is that alcohol use is frequently part of a constellation of externalizing risk-taking behaviors often associated with males, including interpersonal violence and acting-out behaviors (Harris, Blum, & Resnick, 1991). In many countries, drinking by young men is viewed as reinforcing the male image of courage, toughness, and maturity. In Brazil, for example, alcohol use was associated with having the courage to propose sexual relations (Barker, 2000; Childhope, 1997).

Moreover, physical factors such as body water content make females much more susceptible than males to the effects of alcohol. Consequently, consumption of the same amount of alcohol is likely to result in more serious health effects for females, even when their body weight is taken into account (WHO, 1993).

In addition to alcohol use, there has been a tremendous amount of interest in the use of narcotic drugs among young people. Worldwide, marijuana appears to be the most widely used illicit substance. Fifteen percent of young people in Mexico and Chile and 40% of youth in Brazil report regular use of marijuana. In the United States, almost 60% of youth between the ages of 15 and 18 years have used marijuana at least once, while in the United Kingdom, Canada, and the Netherlands, less than 20% of young people have used marijuana (Lammers & Blum, 1997; WHO, 1993).

Similar to what has been demonstrated concerning tobacco and alcohol use, studies have also shown that more boys than females engage in illicit drug use. For instance, in Ecuador, 80% of narcotic users are men; the majority are in their late teen years to early 20s (United Nations Office on Drugs and Crime [UNDCP] & National Council for the Control of Narcotics and Psychotropic Substances [CONSEP], 1996, cited in WHO, 2000). In Jamaica, lifetime and current usage rates of marijuana for young and adult men are two to three times greater than are usage rates for young women (Wallace & Reid, 1994). In the United States, boys are also more likely than girls to say that they use drugs to be cool (Schoen et al., 1998).

HEALTH SERVICES AND HEALTH PROMOTION

Given the serious health consequences that adolescents currently face, the provision and promotion of health services to adolescents are increasingly being recognized as essential program components to adolescent health. In 1994, during the Cairo International Conference on Population and Development (ICPD), 180 signatory nations in attendance proposed in the Programme of Action that

> countries must ensure that the programs and attitudes of health care providers do not restrict the access of adolescents to appropriate services and the information they need, including on sexually transmitted diseases and sexual abuse. In doing so, and in order to address sexual abuse, these services must safeguard the rights of adolescents to privacy, confidentiality, respect, and informed consent, respecting cultural values and religious beliefs.

However, the delivery of clinical health services to adolescents—particularly that of services related to reproductive health—has been faced by numerous challenges; in part, this is because in the past, reproductive health services have largely addressed older, married women; thus, young people perceive—often correctly—that clinics offering reproductive health services would not welcome them. In a study in Senegal, adolescents complained that when they went to family planning clinics, they encountered negative feelings not only from clinic staff but also from other older clients waiting for services. Many also said that when they asked some of the nurses for contraceptives, they were refused (Katz & Tolley, 1996). Similarly, four studies in Asia found a number of barriers that providers encounter when servicing the sexual health needs of adolescents. In all four sites, despite the recognition of the need to provide information, counseling, and contraceptive services to adolescents, providers' attitudes and perceptions were ambivalent about serving unmarried youth (WHO, 2002). As a consequence of such barriers, adolescents primarily rely on resources outside the formal health service provision system, such as home remedies, provision of contraceptives through friends or relatives, and clandestine abortion and medication purchased without a doctor's prescription from pharmacies or traditional health practitioners.

In an effort to increase adolescents' use of the formal health care sector, many programmers and researchers have begun implementing adolescent- (or youth-) friendly health services. Services are understood to be adolescent friendly if they "have policies and attributes that attract youth to the facility or program, provide a comfortable and appropriate setting for youth, meet the needs of young people and are able to retain their youth clientele for follow up and repeat visits" (Senderowitz, 1999). However, limited evaluation studies on adolescent-friendly service programs have yet to determine whether they can actually improve service utilization among youth. One recent evaluation of a linked school- and health facility-based adolescent sexual-reproductive health program in Salvador, Brazil, found no evidence of increased use of clinic-based reproductive health services among secondary school students over a 30-month period following the introduction of the program in public schools and clinics (Magnani, Gaffikin, & Aquino, 2001). Similarly, in Gweru, Zimbabwe, seven clinics were made more youth friendly by training nurses and creating youth corners, where youth could come to receive information from peer educators about reproductive health issues in a private setting. However, the evaluation revealed that although the youth-friendly service activities helped to increase youth satisfaction with the services received, they did not result in increased adolescent service utilization levels (Moyo, Bond, Williams, & Mueller, 2000). Finally, in Zambia, Mmari and Magnani (in press) found that although service utilization increased at some clinics that implemented youth-friendly services, community acceptance of reproductive health services for adolescents had a larger impact on health care seeking behaviors among the adolescents. Clearly, more studies are needed—especially in developing countries—to examine how health programs can increase service utilization among adolescents.

POSITIVE YOUTH DEVELOPMENT: REFRAMING THE ISSUES GLOBALLY

Although so far this chapter has focused on issues of morbidity and mortality among young people, interest has been growing around the world over the past decade in the risk and protective factors that are associated with and causally linked to the morbidity and mortality we have been discussing. This line of research asks why some who are raised under adverse circumstances appear to live healthy and productive lives while their brothers and sisters experience a range of negative outcomes. These protective factors are seen as the elements of resilience (Garmezy, 1991), assets (Benson, 1997), and more recently positive youth development (Blum, 2003).

When we look at this line of research from around the world, certain protective factors have been repeatedly identified: (a) connectedness to parents, other adults, or both; (b) connectedness to school, school-based peer networks, or both; (c) attendance at school, school completion, or both; (d) parental monitoring and supervision; (e) a personal belief in something beyond one's self (spirituality).

In a nine-country study of the Caribbean, Blum et al. (in press) found that both family connectedness and school attendance were associated with a later age of sexual debut in every country where they were studied except one. So too, suicidality (suicidal thoughts and attempts) was significantly less among youth who reported higher levels of family connectedness. Both family connectedness and school attendance were associated with lower levels of violence across each of the countries in the Caribbean where it was studied; moreover, school performance was either significantly associated with less violence or showed clear trends in that direction. Similar findings were seen for substance use and abuse. When the WHO compiled data across more than 65 countries of the world, they found many of these same factors to be associated with later onset of sexual initiation, less substance use, and lower levels of depression (see Table 18.6).

What we conclude from the WHO analyses is that for each of the outcomes studied, key protective factors included a positive relationship with parents, a positive school environment, and having spiritual beliefs beyond one's self.

CONCLUSIONS

When we look across the world, we can draw a number of conclusions with significant impact on the future of young people. First, in both relative terms and absolute numbers there are more young people now than ever before, the numbers will increase over the next 50 years, and the relative proportion of youth in industrialized countries will decline.

Trends that have and will continue to have a major impact include the decline of infectious causes of mortality; the rise of urban living; increases in secondary school matriculation, education, and the changing role of women in society; and the delay in the age of marriage.

Issues that were not on the global radar for youth a generation ago are of increasing salience: out-of-wedlock births, clandestine abortion, physical and sexual abuse, suicide, homicide, and most important, HIV-AIDS.

These issues and trends have placed adolescent health on the national agendas of developing and developed countries alike. As we have come to better understand the factors that put young people at risk for poor health outcomes, we have also come to a much better understanding than that of a decade ago as to the interventions that hold the greatest promise for reducing harm, especially those that come from social and behavioral etiologies. We know, for example, that information alone is usually not sufficient to change behavior. Also, fear is an insufficient motivator for human behavior change; and risk reduction programs alone often are found to have limited impact.

On the other hand, interventions that include life skills appear to have more positive impact on reducing potentially harmful behaviors of adolescence as well as contributing to positive outcomes. Youth participation also often appears to be an important principle. Programs that link youth with prosocial adults and those that strengthen the social capital in a community also benefit young people.

There is a myth in many quarters that the problems facing young people are of such

Table 18.6 Risk and Protective Factors for Select Behaviors: World Health Organization

	Early Sexual Initiation					Substance Use					Depression				
	Africa	Asia	Caribbean	South America	Americas	Africa	Asia	Caribbean	South America	Americas	Africa	Caribbean	South America	Americas	Asia
Has a positive relationship with parents	P	P	P	P	—	Pns	P	P	P	P	P	P	P	P	P
Has a positive relationship with teachers	P	P	—	P	—	—	—	—	—	—	—	—	—	—	—
Parents provide structure and boundaries	—	—	—	—	—	P	P	—	Pns	Pns	—	—	—	—	—
Parents encourage self-expression	—	—	—	—	—	—	—	—	—	—	P	P	P	P	P
Has friends who are sexually active	R	—	R	R	—	—	—	—	—	—	—	—	—	—	—
Has conflict in the family	—	—	—	—	—	R	R	—	Rns	Rns	R	R	R	R	ns
Engages in other risky behaviors	R	—	R	—	—	—	—	—	—	—	—	—	—	—	—
Has a positive school environment	—	—	—	—	—	P	P	P	P	P	P	P	Pns	P	P
Has friends who use substances	—	—	—	—	—	R	R	—	Rns	Rns	—	—	—	—	—
Has a positive relationship with adults in the community	—	—	—	—	—	—	—	—	—	—	P	P	Pns	Pns	P
Has spiritual beliefs.	—	P	P	—	P	—	P	P	—	P					

Note. — = not measured; P = protective factor; R = risk factor; ns = not significant protective or risk factor.

magnitude or intransigence that nothing can be done; in fact, however, nothing can be further from the truth. From Uganda to Uruguay to Uzbekistan, ample evidence demonstrates that many of the negative trends we have reported in this chapter can be halted or reversed. The question is one of political will and national priority. The issues are significant, but so, too, are the opportunities.

REFERENCES

AbouZahr, C., Wardlaw, T., Stanton, C., & Hill, K. (1996). Maternal mortality. *World Health Statistics Quarterly, 49,* 77–87.

Adedoyin, M., & Adetoro, O. (1989). Pregnancy and its outcome among teenage mothers in Ilorin, Nigeria. *East African Medical Journal, 66,* 448–452.

Adelekan, M. (1989). Self-reported drug use among secondary school students in the Nigerian state of Ogun. *Bulletin on Narcotics, 26,* 109–116.

Advocates for Youth. (2000). *The facts: Sexual abuse and violence in sub-Saharan Africa.* Washington, DC: Author.

Advocates for Youth. (2001). *The facts: The HIV/AIDS pandemic among youth in sub-Saharan Africa.* Washington, DC: Author.

Alan Guttmacher Institute. (1994). *Clandestine abortion: A Latin American reality.* New York: Author.

Alan Guttmacher Institute. (1998). *Into a new world: Young women's sexual and reproductive lives.* New York: Author.

Althaus, F. (1997). Special report: Female circumcision. Rite of passage or violation of rights? *International Family Planning Perspectives, 23,* 130–133.

Andersen, R. (2000). The spread of the childhood obesity epidemic. *Canadian Medical Association Journal, 163,* 1461–1463.

Barker, G. (2000). *What about boys? A literature review on the health and development of adolescent boys.* Geneva, Switzerland: Department of Child and Adolescent Health and Development, World Health Organization.

Bautista, P. (1989). *Young, unwed mothers: Medical, psychosocial, and demographic implications.* Quezon City, Philippines: Management Communication Systems.

Bello, C. (1987). Population screening for gonorrhea in northern Nigeria. *West African Journal of Medicine, 2,* 49–52.

Benson, P. L. (1997). *All kids are our kids: What communities must do to raise caring and responsible children and adolescents.* San Francisco: Jossey Bass.

Blum, R. W. (2003). Positive youth development: A strategy for improving adolescent health. In F. Jacobs, D. Wertlieb, & R. M. Lerner (Eds), *Handbook of applied developmental science, enhancing the life chances of youth and families: Contributions of programs, policies, and service systems* (Vol. 2, pp. 237–252). Thousand Oaks, CA: Sage.

Blum, R. W., & Lammers, C. (1997). International health. In S. B. Friedman, S. K. Schonberg, M. M. Fisher, & E. M. Alderman (Eds.), *Comprehensive adolescent health care* (2nd ed., pp. 17–22). Philadelphia: Mosby.

Blum, R. W., Halcón, L., Beuhring, T., Pate, E., Campell-Forrester, S., & Venema, A. (in press). Adolescent health in the Caribbean: Risk and protective factors. *American Journal of Public Health.*

Blum, R., & Rinehart, P. (1997). *Reducing the risk: Connections that make a difference in the lives of youth.* Bethesda, MD: Add Health.

Braddon, R., Rodgers, B., Wadsworth, M., & Davies, J. (1986). Onset of obesity in a 36-year birth cohort study. *British Medical Journal (Clinical Research Edition), 293,* 299–303.

Brown, P. (2001). Choosing to die: A growing epidemic among the young. *Bulletin of the World Health Organization, 29,* 1175–1177.

Cameron, N., & Getz, B. (1997). Sex differences in the prevalence of obesity in rural African adolescents. *International Journal of Obesity, 21,* 775–782.

Childhope. (1997). *Gender, sexuality, and attitudes related to AIDS among low-income youth and street youth in Rio de Janeiro, Brazil.* New York: Author.
Coombs, D., & Globetti, G. (1986). Alcohol use and alcoholism in Latin America: Changing patterns and sociocultural explanations. *International Journal of Addiction, 21,* 59–81.
Cottingham, J., & Royston, E. (1991). *Obstetric fistulae: A review of available information* [Report prepared for the World Health Organization]. Geneva, Switzerland: World Health Organization.
Damiba, A., Vermund, S., & Kelley, K. (1990). Prevalence of gonorrhea, syphilis, and trichomoniasis in prostitutes in Burkina Faso. *East African Medical Journal, 67,* 473–477.
Delisle, H., Chandra-Mouli, V., & de Benoist, B. (2001). *Should adolescents be specifically targeted for nutrition in developing countries? To address which problems, and how?* Geneva, Switzerland: World Health Organization.
DeMaeyer, E., & Aiels-Tegman, M. (1985). The prevalence of anemia in the world. *World Health Statistics Quarterly, 38,* 302–316.
Diekstra, R. (1989). Suicide and the attempted suicide: An international perspective. *Acta Psychiatry. Scandinavia, 80*(Suppl. 354), 1–24.
Dietz, W. (1998). Childhood weight affects adult morbidity and mortality. *Journal of Nutrition, 128*(Suppl. 2), 411S–414S.
Drewnowski, A., & Popkin, B. (1997). The nutrition transition: New trends in the global diet. *Nutrition Reviews, 55,* 31–43.
Duncan, M., Tibaux, G., Pelzer, A., Mehari, L., Peutherer, J., Young, H., et al. (1994). Teenage obstetric and gynaecological problems in an African city. *Central African Journal of Medicine, 40,* 234–244.
Eggleston, E., Jackson, J., & Hardee, K. (1999). Sexual attitudes and behavior among young adolescents in Jamaica. *International Family Planning Perspectives, 25,* 78–84.
Erulkar, A. S., Karueru, J. P., Kaggwa, G., Kingola, N., Nyagah, F. K., & Ochieng, B. (1998). *Adolescent experiences and lifestyles in Central Province Kenya: A baseline report.* Nairobi, Kenya: Population Council.
Falbo, G., Buzzetti, R., & Cattaneo, A. (2001). Homicide in children and adolescents: A case-control study in Recife, Brazil. *Bulletin of the World Health Organization, 79,* 2–7.
Fauveau, V., Koenig, M. A., Chakraborty, J., & Chowdhury, A. I. (1988). Causes of maternal mortality in rural Bangladesh: 1976–1985. *Bulletin of the World Health Organization, 66,* 643–651.
Fingerhut, L., Cox, C., & Warner, M. (1998). International comparative analysis of injury mortality: Findings from the ice on injury statistics. *Advance Data, 303,* 1–20.
Fingerhut, L., & Kleinman, J. (1990). International and interstate comparisons of homicide among young males. *Journal of the American Medical Association, 263,* 3292–3295.
Forjuoh, S., & Zwi, A. (1998). Violence against children and adolescents: International perspectives. *Pediatric Clinics of North America, 45,* 415–426.
Freedman, D., Serdula, M., Srinavasan, R., & Berenson, G. (1999). Relation of circumferences and skinfold thickness to lipid and insulin concentrations in children and adolescents: The Bogalusa heart study. *American Journal of Clinical Nutrition, 69,* 308–317.
Gao, E. (1998). *Study on the needs and unmet needs for reproductive health care among unmarried women in Shanghai* [Unpublished Final report]. Shanghai, People's Republic of China: Shanghai Institute of Planned Parenthood.
Garmezy, N. (1991). Resilience in children's adaptation to negative life events and stressed environments. *Pediatric Annals, 20*(9), 459–460, 463–466.
Granja, A., Machungo, F., Gomes, A., & Bergstrom, S. (2001). Adolescent maternal mortality in Mozambique. *Journal of Adolescent Health, 28,* 303–306.
Guest, P. (1994). The impact of population change on the growth of mega-cities. *Asia-Pacific Population Journal, 9,* 37–56.
Guest, P. (1999). Mobility transitions within a global system: Migration in the ESCAP region. *Asia-Pacific Population Journal, 14,* 57–72.
Harris, L., Blum, R. W., & Resnick, M. (1991). Teen females in Minnesota: A portrait of quiet disturbance. *Women and Therapy, 11,* 119–135.

Harrison, K. (1985). Child-bearing, health and social priorities: A survey of 22,774 consecutive hospital births in Zaria, Northern Nigeria. *British Journal of Obstetrics and Gynaecology, 5*(Suppl. 5), 111–119.

Heise, L., Ellsberg, M., & Gottemoello, M. (1999). Ending violence against women. In *Population Reports, Series L(11),* 1–6. Baltimore: Johns Hopkins University School of Public Health, Population Information Program.

Hirsch, J., & Barker, G. (1992). *Adolescents and unsafe abortion in developing countries: A preventable tragedy.* Washington, DC: Center for Population Options.

Hosken, F. P. (1993). *The Hosken report: Genital and sexual mutilation of females* (4th ed.). Lexington, MA: Women's International Network News.

Jamison, D. T., & Mosley, W. H. (1991). Disease control priorities in developing countries: Health policy responses to epidemiological change. *American Journal of Public Health, 81,* 15–22.

Joint United Nations Programme on HIV/AIDS. (1996). *Listen, learn, live! World AIDS campaign with children and young people: Facts and figures.* Retrieved June 26, 2001, from http://www.unaids.org/wac/1999/eng/facts-e.pdf

Joint United Nations Programme on HIV/AIDS. (1997). *Report on the global HIV/AIDS epidemic.* Retrieved July 2000, from http://www.unaids.org/epidemic_update/report/index.html

Joint United Nations Programme on HIV/AIDS. (2000). *Young people and HIV/AIDS: UNAIDS briefing paper.* Geneva, Switzerland: Author.

Kanani, S., & Poojara, R. (2000). Symposium: Improving adolescent iron status before childbearing: Supplementation with iron and folic acid enhances growth in adolescent Indian girls. *Journal of Nutrition, 130,* 452S–455S.

Kasule, J., Mbizvo, M. T., Gupta, V., Fusakaniko, S., Mwateba, R., Mpanju-Shumbusho, W., et al. (1997). Zimbabwean teenager's knowledge of AIDS and other sexually transmitted diseases. *East African Medical Journal, 74,* 76–81.

Katz, K., & Tolley, E. (1996). *Measuring access to family planning education and services for young adults in Dakar, Senegal.* Research Triangle, NC: Family Health International.

Kgosidintsi, N. (1997). *Sexual behavior and risk of HIV infection among adolescent females in Botswana* [Final report]. National Institute of Development, Research, and Documentation.

Kim, Y., Maragwanda, C., & Kols, A. (1997). Quality of counseling of young clients in Zimbabwe. *East African Medical Journal, 74,* 514–518.

Kiragu, K. (1995). Female genital mutilation: A reproductive health concern. In *Supplement to Population Reports, Series J(41),* 1–4. Baltimore: Johns Hopkins University School of Public Health, Population Information Program.

Kiragu, K. (2001). Youth and HIV/AIDS: Can we avoid catastrophe? In *Population Reports, Series L., No. 12.* Baltimore: The Johns Hopkins University Bloomberg School of Public Health, Population Information Program.

Kohn, R. (2001). Homicide among adolescents in the Americas: A growing epidemic. *Bulletin of the World Health Organization, 79,* 172.

Koontz, S., & Conly, S. (1994). *Youth at risk: Meeting the sexual health needs of adolescents.* Population Action International.

Kumar, A. (2002). Poverty and adolescent girl health. *The Bihar Times,* pp. 1–5.

Kurz, K., & Johnson-Welch, C. (1994). *The nutrition and lives of adolescents in developing countries: Findings from the nutrition of adolescent girls research program.* New York: International Center for Research on Women.

Lande, R. (1993). Controlling sexually transmitted diseases. In *Population reports, Series L, No. 9,* 424. Baltimore: Johns Hopkins School of Public Health, Population Information Program.

Levin, H., Pollitt, E., Galloway, R., & McGuire, J. (1993). Micronutrient deficiency disorders. In D. Jamison, H. Mosely, A. Measham, & J. Babadilla (Eds.), *Disease control priorities in developing countries.* New York: Oxford University Press.

Likwa, R. (1998). *A pilot study on characteristics of women presenting for abortion and complications of induced abortion at the University Teaching Hospital.* Lusaka, Zambia: Ministry of Health.

Maddaleno, M., & Silber, T. (1993). An epidemiological view of adolescent health in Latin America. *Journal of Adolescent Health, 14,* 595–604.

Magnani, R., Gaffikin, L., & Aquino, E. (2001). *Evaluation of an integrated adolescent sexuality education/health service provider training pilot project in Salvador, Bahia, Brazil.* Washington, DC: Focus on Young Adults Program and Pathfinder International.

Markos, A., Wade, A., & Walzman, M. (1992). The adolescent female prostitute and sexually transmitted diseases. *International Journal of STDs and AIDS, 3,* 92–95.

McCauley, A. P., & Salter, C. (1995). Meeting the needs of young adults. In *Population Reports, Series J, No. 41,* 1–5. Baltimore: Johns Hopkins School of Public Health, Population Information Program.

Mendez Ribas, J., Necchi, S., & Schufer, M. (1995, May). *Risk awareness and sexual protection: Perceptions and behavior among a sexually active population.* Report submitted to the Hospital Clinica, University of Buenos Aires, Buenos Aires, Argentina.

Mensch, B., Bruce, J., & Greene, M. (1999). *The uncharted passage: Girls' adolescence in the developing world.* New York: Population Council.

Miller, M., & Hemenway, D. (2001). Firearm prevalence and the risk of suicide: A review. *Harvard Health Policy Review, 2,* 1–3.

Mmari, K., & Magnani, R. (in press). Does making clinic-based reproductive health services more "youth friendly" increase service utilization by adolescents? Evidence from Lusaka, Zambia. *Journal of Adolescent Health.*

Moyo, I., Bond, K., Williams, T., & Mueller, L. (2000). *Reproductive health antecedents, attitudes, and practices among youth in Gweru, Zimbabwe.* Washington, DC: Focus on Young Adults Program and Pathfinder International.

Mtimavalye, L., & Belsey, M. (1987, October). *Infertility and sexually transmitted diseases: Major problems in maternal and child health and family planning.* Paper presented at the International Conference on Better Health for Women and Children Through Family Planning, Nairobi, Kenya.

Mustafa, A. (1966). Female circumcision and infibulation in the Sudan. *Journal of Obstetrics and Gynaecology of the British Commonwealth, 73,* 302–306.

Nace, E. (1987). Epidemiology of alcoholism. *Pediatrician, 14,* 2–6.

National Academy of Sciences. (1996). *Her lifetime: Female morbidity and mortality in sub-Saharan Africa.* Washington, DC: Author.

National Institute of Mental Health. (1998). *Suicide facts.* Bethesda, MD: NIMH.

National Research Council Committee on Population. (1997). *Reproductive health in developing countries: Expanding dimensions, building solutions.* Washington, DC: National Academy Press.

Okagbue, I. (1990). Pregnancy termination and the law in Nigeria. *Studies in Family Planning, 21,* 197–208.

Orwenyo, J. (1984). *A study of sexually transmitted diseases in pregnant women presenting at the Kenyatta National Hospital, Nairobi, Kenya.* Unpublished master's thesis, University of Nairobi, Nairobi, Kenya.

Over, M., & Piat, P. (1992). HIV infection and other sexually transmitted diseases. In D. T. Jamison & W. H. Mosely (Eds.), *Disease control priorities in developing countries* (pp. 455–527). Oxford, England: Oxford University Press for the World Bank.

Pan American Health Organization. (1993). *Resolution on violence.* Washington, DC: Author.

Pan American Health Organization. (1998). *Health in the Americas.* Washington, DC: Author.

Population Reference Bureau. (2002). *Abandoning female genital cutting: Prevalence, attitudes, and efforts to end the practice.* Washington, DC.

Ryland, D., & Kruesi, M. (1992). Suicide among adolescents. *International Review of Psychiatry, 4,* 185–195.

Schneider, D. (2000). International trends in adolescent nutrition. *Social Science and Medicine, 51,* 955–967.

Schoen, C., Dans, K., Collins, K., Greenberg, K., DesRoches, C., & Abrams, M. (1998). *The health of adolescent boys: Findings from a commonwealth fund survey.* New York: Commonwealth Fund.

Secretary of State for Health and Secretaries of State for Scotland, Wales, and Northern Ireland. (1999). *Smoking kills: A white paper on tobacco.* London: H. M. Stationary Office.

Senderowitz, J. (1995). *Adolescent health: Reassessing the passage to adulthood.* Washington, DC: World Bank.

Senderowitz, J. (1999). *Making reproductive health services youth friendly.* Washington, DC: Focus on Young Adults Program and Pathfinder International.

Shanler, S., Heise, L., Weiss, L., & Stewart, L. (1998). Sexual abuse and young adult reproductive health. In *Focus Series.* Washington, DC: FOCUS on Young Adults Program.

Shell-Duncan, B., & Hernlund, Y. (2000). *Female circumcision in Africa: Culture, controversy, and change.* Boulder, CO: Lynne Rienner.

Singelmann, J. (1993). *Levels and trends of female internal migration in developing countries, 1960–1980: Internal migration of women in developing countries* (pp. 77–93). New York: United Nations.

Singh, S., & Henshaw, S. (1996). *The incidence of abortion: A worldwide overview focusing on methodology and on Latin America.* Paper presented at the International Union for the Scientific Study of Population Seminar on Socio-Cultural and Political Aspects of Abortion From an Anthropological Perspective, Trivandrum, India.

Skeldon, R. (1990). *Population mobility in developing countries: A reinterpretation.* London: Belhaven Press.

Stebbins, K. (1990). Transnational tobacco companies and health in underdeveloped countries: Recommendations for avoiding a smoking epidemic. *Social Science and Medicine, 30,* 227–235.

Stewart, L., Sebastiani, A., Delgado, G., & Lopez, G. (1996). Consequences of sexual abuse of adolescents. *Reproductive Health Matters, 7,* 129–134.

Swanson, E., Aigar, S., Akhlaghi, M., et al. (2000). World Development Indicators 2000 [Computer software]. Development Economics Vice Presidency's Development Data Group, World Bank.

Tucker, L. (1987). Alcohol and adolescents: Who drinks and who doesn't. *Pediatrician, 14,* 32–38.

United Nations. (1989). *Adolescent reproductive behavior: Evidence from developing countries* (Vol. 2). New York: Author.

United Nations. (1991). *The world's women 1970–1990: Trends and statistics.* New York: Author.

United Nations Children's Fund. (1996). *The state of the world's children.* Oxford University Press.

United Nations Department of Economic and Social Affairs. (1996). Temporal trends in population, environment and development. *World Population Monitoring,* 11.

United Nations Office of Drugs and Crime & National Council for the Control of Narcotics and Psychotropic Substances. (1996). Evaluacion rapida sobre el abuso de drogas en las areas urbanus del Ecuador: Quito, Guayaquil y Machala. Informe final investigacion. [Rapid evaluation on drug abuse in urban areas in Ecuador.] Quito, Ecuador: Author.

United Nations Population Division. (2001). *World population prospects: The 2000 revision. Highlights.* New York: Population Division, Department of Economic and Social Affairs, United Nations.

U.S. Department of Health and Human Services. (1994). *Preventing tobacco use among young people: A report of the Surgeon General.* Atlanta, GA: Centers for Disease Control, National Center for Chronic Disease Prevention and Health Promotion, Office of Smoking and Health.

Verkuyl, D. (1995). Practicing obstetrics and gynecology in areas with a high prevalence of HIV infection. *Lancet, 346,* 293–296.

Villanueva, M. (1992). *Pregnancy and reproductive health in students that attend night school.* Lima, Peru: Cayetano Heredia Peruvian University, Institute for Population Studies.

Vir, S. (1990). Adolescent growth in girls: The Indian perspective. *Indian Pediatrics, 27,* 1249–1255.

Waju, W., & Radeny, S. (1995). *Sexuality among adolescents in Kenya, Nairobi.* Nairobi, Kenya: Kenya Association for the Promotion of Adolescent Health.

Walker, A. (1980). The puzzle of obesity in the African black female. *Lancet, 1,* 263.

Walker, A., & Walker, B. (1977). Weight, height, and triceps skinfold in south African black, Indian, and white pupils of 18 years. *Journal of Tropical Medicine Hygiene, 80,* 119–125.

Walker, A., Walker, B., Manetsi, B., & Tsotetsi, N. (1990). Obesity in black women in Soweto, South Africa: Minimal effects on hypertension, hyperlipidaemia, and hyperglycaemia. *Journal of Research on Social Health, 110,* 100–103.

Wallace, J., & Reid, K. (1994). *Country drug abuse profile: 1994. Jamaica.* Paper presented at the Expert Forum on Demand Reduction, Nassau, Bahamas.

Warren, C., Riley, L., Asma, S., Eriksen, M., Green, L., Blanton, C., et al. (2000). Tobacco use by youth: A surveillance report from the global youth tobacco survey project. *Bulletin of the World Health Organization, 78,* 868–876.

Wasserheit, J., & Holmes, K. (1992). Reproductive tract infection: Challenges for international health policy, programmes and research. In A. Germain, K. Holmes, P. Piot, & J. Wasserheit (Eds.), *Reproductive tract infections: Global impact and priorities for women's reproductive health* (pp. 7–33). New York: Plenum Press.

Webb, D. (1997). *Adolescence, sex, and fear: Reproductive health services and young people in urban Zambia.* Lusaka, Zambia: Central Board of Health, and UNICEF.

World Bank. (1997, March). *Crime and violence as development issues in Latin America and the Caribbean.* Paper prepared for the Conference on Urban Crime and Violence in Rio de Janeiro.

World Health Organization. (1991). *Sexual relations among young people in developing countries: Evidence from WHO case studies.* Geneva, Switzerland: Author.

World Health Organization. (1993). *The health of young people: A challenge and a promise.* Geneva, Switzerland: Author.

World Health Organization. (1995). *A picture of health: A review and annotated bibliography of the health of young people in developing countries.* Geneva, Switzerland: Author.

World Health Organization. (1996). *Revised 1990 estimates of maternal mortality: A new approach by WHO and UNICEF.* Geneva, Switzerland: Author.

World Health Organization. (1997). *Fact Sheet No. 186.* Geneva, Switzerland: Author.

World Health Organization. (1998). *World health report 1998.* Geneva, Switzerland: Author.

World Health Organization. (1999). *World health report 1999.* Geneva, Switzerland: Author.

World Health Organization. (2001). *Sexual relations among young people in developing countries: Evidence from WHO case studies.* Geneva, Switzerland: Author.

World Health Organization. (2002). *Research on reproductive health at WHO: Biennial report 2000–2001.* Geneva, Switzerland: Author.

Zabin, L. S., Kiragu, K. (1998). The health consequences of adolescent sexual and fertility behavior in sub-Saharan Africa. *Studies in Family Planning, 29*(2), 210–232.

Chapter 19

INTERNALIZING PROBLEMS DURING ADOLESCENCE

Julia A. Graber

The development of psychopathology during adolescence has been perhaps the single most studied area in the field of adolescence (Steinberg & Morris, 2001). Extensive focus has been on depression, conduct disorder, and related subclinical problems and symptoms that fall under the categories of internalizing and externalizing behaviors. In undertaking the task of reviewing the literatures that fall under the heading of internalizing problems, it was striking to observe how many studies focused on what they called internalizing behaviors or problems and how few actually define the term. Internalizing problems are generally considered to belong to the subgroup of psychopathology that involves disturbances in emotion or mood, whereas externalizing problems have tended to refer to dysregulations in behavior. The affect versus behavior distinction between internalizing and externalizing problems is not clear cut, but the general identification of internalizing problems as focused on emotional components such as sadness, guilt, worry, and so forth is consistent across several definitions. More specifically, depression and anxiety disorders and the subclinical problems in these areas typically comprise discussions of internalizing problems and disorders (see Kovacs & Devlin, 1998, and Zahn-Waxler, Klimes-Dougan, & Slattery, 2000, for recent reviews of internalizing problems and disorders in childhood and adolescence, and the chapter by Farrington in this volume for a discussion of externalizing problems during adolescence).

It is interesting to note that the concept of internalization has been investigated as a core task of early childhood (Kochanska, 1993). One definition of internalization is the incorporation into the self of guiding principles (as values or patterns of culture) through learning or socialization (adapted from a standard dictionary). Stemming from psychoanalytic and social learning theories, internalization is commonly thought of in the context of the regulation of moral behavior or the development of conscience (Kochanska, 1993). Kochanska (1993) suggests that internalization comes about in early childhood through parent-child communication with a focus on developing feelings of empathy, guilt, and prosocial affect such as concern for others, and cause and effect of behaviors as demonstrated in how one's behavior makes others feel. In psychoanalytic theory, anxiety and guilt are the internalized emotions that replace parental control of behavior (Muuss, 1996). In the present usage, *internalizing* refers to problems or disorders of emotion or mood; the dysregulation of emotion might be thought of as

The author was supported by funds from the National Institute of Mental Health.

overinternalization of certain emotions such as guilt or anxiety or as overinvolvement in the emotions of significant others (e.g., the inability to distinguish one's own responsibility for another's emotional state from nonself causes of distress in others).

The notion that changes in mood or emotionality are part of the conceptualization of adolescence both in scientific and nonscientific communities has been held since the first theoretical discussions of adolescence (e.g., Aristotle, Hall, and S. Freud). Whereas the literature based on universal or typical changes in mood or emotion during adolescence has been limited (with a few exceptions, e.g., Larson, Csikszentmihalyi, & Graef, 1980), a vast literature exists on depression during adolescence. Therefore, the goal of this chapter is not to provide a comprehensive review of that literature or even of the etiology of depression (see Birmaher et al., 1996; Compas & Oppedisano, 2000; Garber, 2000; Goodyer, 2001; Lewinsohn, Rohde, & Seeley, 1998; and others for recent reviews). Instead, this discussion provides an overview of internalizing symptoms, problems, and disorders and their etiology throughout the first two to three decades of life. The chapter focuses on models and factors that may be particularly salient to understanding which types of problems become prevalent during adolescence and on areas of investigation that merit further study to illuminate questions such as *Why adolescence?* or *Why more girls?*

DEVELOPMENTAL PERSPECTIVES ON INDIVIDUAL DIFFERENCES

At the time that Steinberg and Morris (2001) suggested that psychopathology was the most common focus of studies of adolescence, they were referring to the published literature over the past 10–15 years. The surge of interest in adolescent development in the 1980s resulted in several longitudinal projects that spanned the middle school and sometimes high school or young adult periods. These studies grew from an interest in understanding the role of transitions on the course of development (e.g., Elder, 1985) as well as specific interest in the combined or transactional influences of biological, social, and psychological processes in determining adjustment pathways (e.g., Lerner & Foch, 1987; Simmons & Blyth, 1987). It could be argued that these initial studies were undertaken to understand the typical or normal problems of adolescence with perhaps greater attention to variations in adjustment (e.g., moodiness, parent-adolescent conflict, academic achievement) rather than the focus on disorder per se. Such projects reported on the range and diversity of normative adolescent development but also delineated the nature of problems experienced by adolescents. A subsequent surge in the 1990s of community- and epidemiology-based studies attempted to determine the severity of these problems by focusing on the assessment and experience of disorder.

From a developmental perspective, several observations can be made about the nature of much of the research on adolescent problems and disorders during the last few decades. First, because there was an absence of information on development during adolescence and even debate as to when or whether disorders such as depression were experienced by children and adolescents (Kovacs & Devlin, 1998), most studies considered development during adolescence itself. Often enrollment of participants was based on year in school or change in school as a starting point (e.g., Petersen, 1984; Simmons & Blyth, 1987). As with any investigation, a window of development to study must be chosen. The continued choice to use such demarcations as year in school, however, means that much of the research does not in fact tap core issues of continuity and change in developmental processes. Most discussions of transitions and the study of adolescence state that behavior and adjustment during these transitions is dependent on the nature of the transitions and how they are navigated as well as developmental experiences prior to making the transitions (Graber & Brooks-Gunn, 1996; Rutter, 1994). In the study of internalizing problems, some studies have examined childhood behaviors in connection with subsequent adjustment or behavior in adolescence, sometimes even accounting for a transitional experience (e.g., Caspi & Moffitt, 1991). More often, however, studies of childhood experiences conclude with suggestions that subsequent influences on adolescent internalizing behaviors would be expected, and studies of adolescence note that preexisting patterns, behaviors, and experiences were undoubtedly factors in who developed problems during adolescence. Although they are conceptually linked, the two lines of investigation are still lacking substantial empirical bases for evaluation of the continuity or discontinuity in developmental processes from childhood to adolescence.

Second, on a related point, after Offer and his colleagues (Offer, 1987; Offer & Offer, 1975) and subsequently others (see the chapter by Benson et al. in this volume) demonstrated that the popular belief that all adolescents would have problems was not true (at least in terms of self-image), the literature focused on issues of what constituted meaningful difficulties and who experienced such difficulties. For example, it became accepted that parent-child conflict would occur in early adolescence or around midpuberty for most adolescents (Paikoff & Brooks-Gunn, 1991; Steinberg, 2001). Thus, conflict is seen as part of a normative process, and perceptions that young adolescents are argumentative with parents are not viewed as signs of disorder or even of significant problems (even if an argumentative adolescent is stressful for parents). Moodiness as well was thought to be expected from young adolescents. As noted, evidence on this point is limited but the seminal work of Larson and his colleagues (1980) finds that adolescents demonstrate more mood changes during the day than do adults. In this case, some moodiness may be normative, but there is limited evidence that such moodiness then results in pervasive symptomatology. In contrast, however, elevated internalizing symptoms such as negative mood—feelings of depression, sadness, or irritability—that persist and begin to interfere with activities such as schoolwork or interactions with peers are not normative and may be indicators of potentially serious psychopathology.

As noted by others in this volume and elsewhere, nearly all youth experience challenges during the transition into adolescence, and often throughout the adolescent decade. As such, either all youth should have dramatic shifts in behavior and potentially damaging effects from the experience of simultaneous and cumulative challenges, or—alternatively—these changes are endemic to the developmental process. In this case, the system develops such that all youth should have the appropriate resources to adapt and sustain adaptive behavioral patterns. In reality, as has been repeated in nearly all discussions of continuity and change (e.g., Cairns, 1998; Kagan, 1980; Lerner, 2002; Rutter, 1994), both stability and change occur in social behaviors during the adolescent period. It may be that the development of internalizing problems or even disorders during adolescence is not about substantial behavioral change or new problems arising but rather is dependent on individual characteristics that existed well before adolescence (Bandura, 1964). The challenges of adolescence may have exacerbated or accentuated these characteristics such that the symptomatology is more problem-like, resulting in decreased functioning and serious dysregulation in mood. In turn, for some youth, internalizing problems may emerge at this time of development in connection with more concurrent or recent experiences. Therefore, the meaningful developmental questions regarding internalizing problems in adolescence must focus on individual differences in development. The important issue regarding continuity and change is not whether the normative transitions of adolescence result in difficulties but rather why they result in difficulties for certain individuals. Prior to a discussion of why some individuals experience internalizing problems and others do not, it is useful to consider the rates of these problems during adolescence.

EPIDEMIOLOGY OF ANXIETY AND DEPRESSION IN ADOLESCENCE

As noted, the general category of internalizing problems or symptoms includes disturbance in emotion or mood. This definition might be all encompassing, but instead the discussion of internalizing problems is usually limited to the investigation of depression or anxiety. Much of the literature has considered depression and anxiety disorders and their respective subclinical problems and symptoms as distinct experiences. In the present discussion, a review of prevalence rates for anxiety and depressive disorders is included along with prevalence rates of subclinical symptoms and problems. Compas and his colleagues (Compas, Ey, & Grant, 1993; Compas & Oppedisano, 2000; Petersen et al., 1993) have developed a framework for viewing depressive disorders and subclinical symptoms that is applicable to internalizing problems more generally. Under this framework, internalizing symptomatology can be classified into three levels or types: disorders as determined by diagnostic criteria, syndromes or subclinical problems, and internalizing moods or dysregulated emotion or moods. Depressed or anxious moods are reports of emotional states that are not assessed in terms of their duration or in connection with other symptoms. Syndromal classifications are based on endorsement of a constellation of symptoms that co-occur in a statistically consistent manner. The experience of internalizing moods or symptoms is quite common during adolescence; fewer youth experience syndromes or problems, and fewer still have disorders.

Zahn-Waxler and her colleagues (2000) note that theories and research on anxiety and depression in childhood and adolescence have often been separate lines of investigation. At the same time, as is evident in the following discussion and in recent investigations (Clark, Watson, & Reynolds, 1995; Compas & Oppedisano, 2000; Krueger, Caspi, Moffitt, & Silva, 1998), the extent to which anxiety and depression are distinct experientially or in the course of development is debatable; that is, there are several reasons to consider joint processes of etiology, not the least of which is the substantial co-occurrence or comorbidity of anxiety and depressive symptoms during childhood and adolescence. As indicated, within studies of psychopathology during adolescence, many more studies have focused on depression. A review of prevalence rates in childhood and adolescence for the anxiety and depressive disorders perhaps makes some of this focus clearer; that is, whereas rates of some anxiety disorders clearly increase from childhood to adolescence, others are confined almost exclusively to early childhood or may be present at any point in development over the life span. In contrast, rates of depression are low in childhood and increase dramatically during adolescence. Examination of rates of both broader groups of disorders and related subclinical symptoms is informative for subsequent discussion of why some problems increase at adolescence.

Prevalence Rates for Disorders

The *Diagnostic and Statistical Manual of Mental Disorders–Fourth Edition–Text Revision* (*DSM-IV-TR;* American Psychiatric Association, 2000) identifies six main subcategories of anxiety disorders that are applicable to children and adolescents: separation anxiety disorder, generalized anxiety disorder (GAD), obsessive-compulsive disorder, posttraumatic and acute stress disorder, and specific phobias. Across investigations and collapsing across anxiety disorders, Costello and Angold (1995) reported that prevalence rates for any anxiety disorder in children and adolescents ranged from 5.7% to 17.7%. Rates showed a slight tendency to increase with age (Costello & Angold, 1995), but such data must be interpreted with caution because they are based on "any anxiety disorder" and some specific disorders may demonstrate variation by age, whereas others do not. Detailed information on symptoms and criteria for diagnosis of disorders are found in the *DSM-IV-TR.* The criteria for diagnosis of GAD are listed here in Table 19.1 because this disorder tends to emerge in late childhood and adolescence. GAD is characterized by excessive feelings of anxiety and worry. Disparities in prevalence rates across studies are in part accounted for by whether the diagnostic criteria used included assessment of functional impairment. When impairment is considered, rates of disorder decrease (Vasey & Ollendick, 2000; Zahn-Waxler et al., 2000) because more children and adolescents report the requisite symptoms of the disorder, but a smaller number indicate significant impairments in functioning along with these disorders.

In addition, girls have higher rates of several of the anxiety disorders, with the possible exception of posttraumatic stress disorder (Vasey & Ollendick, 2000). The gender difference in rates varies by type of anxiety disorder, and for some anxiety disorders data are limited on whether gender differences are consistently demonstrated. For example, separation anxiety, which tends to be found in young children, demonstrates a 3: 1 (girls: boys) gender difference in rates. In contrast, GAD may have equal prevalence rates by gender or higher rates for boys than for girls in childhood, but among adolescents it is more prevalent in girls (Bowen, Offord, & Boyle, 1990; McGee et al., 1990).

Most discussions of depression during adolescence focus on major depressive disorder (MDD) because it is the most commonly diagnosed depressive disorder in childhood and adolescence. Manic-depressive disorder is rarely diagnosed in children or adolescents, although there may be an emerging trend for early onset bipolar disorder (see Post, Leverich, Xing, & Weiss, 2001, for a review of this literature). An overview of the criteria for a major depressive episode is also listed in Table 19.1. A depressive episode is characterized by feelings of depression, sadness, or a loss of pleasure for a period of 2 weeks or more, coupled with a minimum number and frequency of the other symptoms listed. For children and adolescents, irritability rather than depressed mood may be experienced. Prevalence rates of MDD have ranged from 0.4% to 8.3% among adolescents (Birmaher et al., 1996). Estimates of lifetime prevalence for MDD among adolescents range from 15% to 20% (Birmaher et al., 1996; Garber, 2000; Lewinsohn &

Table 19.1 Selected *DSM-IV-TR* Criteria for General Anxiety Disorder and Major Depressive Episode

Symptoms and Criteria for Generalized Anxiety Disorder	
A	Excessive anxiety or worry on most days for 6 months about a number of events or activities
B	Difficulty controlling the worry
C	Anxiety and worry are associated with 3 or more of the following symptoms: 1. Restlessness 2. Easily fatigued 3. Difficulty concentrating 4. Irritability 5. Muscle tension 6. Sleep disturbance
Symptoms and Criteria for a Major Depressive Episode	
A	Depressed mood or loss of interest for a 2-week period (or irritability among children and adolescents)
B	4 or more of the following symptoms in the same 2-week period: 1. Weight loss or weight gain 2. Insomnia or hypersomnia 3. Restlessness or slowness (psychomotor agitation or retardation) 4. Fatigue or loss of energy 5. Feelings of worthlessness or inappropriate guilt 6. Inability to concentrate 7. Recurrent thoughts of death or suicide ideation or plans
Additional Criteria for Both GAD and MDD	
A	Symptoms result in significant impairment in social and occupational functioning.
B	Symptoms are not due to physical illness or drug use.

Note. Criteria are adapted from *DSM-IV-TR* (APA, 2000).

Essau, 2002). MDD is the most commonly occurring disorder among adolescents. Because several longitudinal studies of depression have now followed samples across adolescence into adulthood (e.g., the Oregon Adolescent Depression Project [OADP], the Great Smoky Mountain Study, [GSM], the Dunedin Multidisciplinary Health and Development Study), detailed estimates of lifetime prevalence, 1-year incidence, and rates of recurrence are available in several studies.

As noted, rates of MDD are fairly low in childhood and begin to rise during early adolescence. In the OADP, the mean age of onset was 14.9 (Lewinsohn et al., 1998). This age is consistent with other community-based studies, although studies of clinical samples tend to report earlier ages of onset for first depressive episode (e.g., 11 years of age in Kovacs, Obrosky, Gatsonis, & Richards, 1997).

Studies of variations in rates by subgroups of the population have focused predominantly on gender differences in rates. There has been debate as to the consistency of gender differences in MDD in childhood, with some studies reporting slightly higher rates for boys (Angold & Costello, 2001) and most finding no gender difference prior to adolescence. By age 15, the gender difference in depression is at the adult rate of about 2: 1 (girls: boys). Much less attention has been paid to sociodemographic and cultural effects on rates of disorders in childhood and adolescence. Sampling strategies have frequently not allowed for disentangling race or ethnicity variations in rates from poverty or other demographic factors (e.g., rural versus urban environments). In the GSM, White adolescents (ages 9–17) had higher rates of MDD than did Black youth (Costello, Keeler, & Angold, 2001). Moreover, poverty was predictive of disorder among White but not Black youth. Overall, rates of disorders were comparable in this rural sample to studies of urban and suburban adolescents (Costello et al., 2001).

Thus, in the discussion of the experience of internalizing disorders, depression clearly becomes a significant concern during adolescence; rates may also increase for anxiety—or at least for GAD—during this time period as well. At the same time, both types of disorders appear to be more common in girls than in boys by midadolescence.

Subclinical Problems, Syndrome, or Mood

As indicated, many individuals experience subclinical problems and symptoms of anxiety and depression. Again, Compas and his colleagues (Compas et al., 1993; Compas & Oppedisano, 2000; Petersen et al., 1993) have differentiated the experience of depressed mood or anxious mood from syndromes or problems. Depressed or anxious mood are reports of emotional states that are not assessed in terms of their duration or in connection with other symptoms. Therefore, in studies of adolescent moods or symptoms, rates of depressed mood have fluctuated dramatically; for example, some reports indicated as many as 40% of the sample experienced depressed mood (Compas et al., 1993; Petersen et al., 1993). Similar compilation of rates of anxious mood in different age ranges or across studies has not been made.

Measures of depressive symptoms typically report age and gender differences in elevated symptoms that parallel differences found for disorders (Twenge & Nolen-Hoeksema, 2002). In a recent meta-analysis of the Children's Depression Inventory, Twenge and Nolen-Hoeksema (2002) found no gender difference in scores during childhood but a significant gender difference with higher scores for girls, beginning at age 13. No effects of sociodemographic status were found across studies, although this information was not available for all studies. In addition, no differences in means were found between White and Black children and adolescents. However, Hispanic children were found to have significantly higher scores than were other children. Higher rates of mood disorders have also been reported in Mexican-American adults who were born in the United States (Vega et al., 1998). In general, subclinical symptomatology follows patterns of subgroup prevalence similar to that seen for disorder.

Again, syndromal classifications are based on endorsement of a constellation of symptoms and symptoms that co-occur in a statistically consistent manner. Achenbach (e.g., 1993) has derived a syndrome that taps anxiety and depression and distinguishes referred from nonreferred adolescents. In this approach, about 5–6% of adolescents may report anxious-depressive syndrome as determined by scores above or below a cut point (Compas et al., 1993; Petersen et al., 1993). The assessment of syndrome is based on statistical associations among a checklist of symptoms as rated by several reporters (i.e., parent, teacher, self); in this approach, separate distinct syndromes for depression and anxiety are not found. Rather, these symptoms consistently co-occurred, a point that is salient to the next section.

The syndromal category as defined by Achenbach is one approach to defining a subclinical internalizing problem based on a specific measure of behavior problems. Several other measures have been developed to assess depressive and anxiety symptoms and problems; many have established cutoff scores for identifying potential disorders. Such measures are useful not only in research for comparing the experience of symptoms in the general population of youth but also as screeners for identifying individuals who may have more serious disorders. In this case, individuals scoring above the determined cutoff score are the most likely to have a disorder if a full diagnostic protocol is used. However, such measures and cutoff scores are not identical to diagnostic interview protocols and identify individuals with elevated symptoms who do not have a disorder; that is, individuals may endorse high levels of symptoms and be over an established cutoff point on a screening instrument but may not meet all necessary *DSM-IV-TR* criteria for diagnosis of a disorder. For example, an individual may report all the symptoms of disorder but may not indicate much functional impairment from the symptoms, the symptoms may not have been present for the required duration, many but not all symptoms may be present, and so forth.

It is interesting to note that in the development of the Center for Epidemiological Study Depression scale (CES-D), Radloff (1977, 1991) recommends different cutoff points for adolescents versus adults. For this measure, a lower score identifies the high-risk group of adults and a higher score identifies the comparable high-risk group of adolescents who are likely to have a depressive disorder. Such findings indicate that adolescents report greater numbers and frequency of symptoms of depression than do adults even though the rates of disorder may not vary by mid- to late adolescence to adulthood. In a recent review, Avenevoli and Steinberg (2001) suggested that adolescents have "differential manifestation" of symptoms in comparison to other age groups due to unique developmental experiences of this period. Because symptom measures typically include a range of symptoms related to depression or internalizing problems but not limited to the diagnostic criteria, there is evidence that symptom profiles differ for older versus younger adolescents, at least among girls (Brooks-Gunn, Rock, & Warren, 1989).

The particularly high rates of depressed mood and moderate rates of syndromes or problems have led to questions about the importance of these experiences in terms of predictability to subsequent disorder or concurrent difficulties. Numerous discussions have focused on whether there is merit in considering subclinical symptoms and factors that influence variations in mean scores on symptom and emotion scales. At one point in time, much of the literature was limited to assessments of affect or symptoms and did not include assessment of disorder (see Costello & Angold, 1995). As longitudinal studies that included diagnostic interviews were conducted, the literature base expanded dramatically with extensive information on the predictors of disorder, continuity of disorder, and other related issues. From such studies, it has been suggested that subclinical problems are particularly salient to identifying individuals who may be the youth most likely to develop a subsequent disorder. In the OADP, the best predictor of developing a depressive disorder over a 1-year period was having elevated symptomatology (i.e., scoring over a cutoff on a screener) at the first assessment (Gotlib, Lewinsohn, & Seeley, 1995). Thus, at this end of the spectrum of symptoms, there seems to be greater continuity of symptomatology than for individuals with mid- or low-level symptoms. Moreover, for depressive symptoms (Gotlib et al., 1995) and other problems (e.g., eating problems and disorders; Graber, Tyrka, & Brooks-Gunn, 2002), individuals with elevated symptoms or problems but not disorder tend to have impairment in functioning that is similar to that seen among youth who meet criteria for disorder.

Factors that predict disorder or predict progression on this type of pathway to internalizing disorders are central to the discussion of internalizing problems in adolescence. Factors that influence perturbations or minor changes in emotion or symptoms may hold promise for future investigation but alternatively may not be important in understanding who is at risk for serious dysfunction or who may need treatment.

Comorbidity or Co-occurrence of Anxiety and Depression

As studies of adolescent development incorporated or focused specifically on internalizing disorders and problems, it became clear that internalizing problems do not occur in isolation of other disorders and problems. Single-problem or single-disorder studies had previously failed to account for this phenomenon. With the utilization and development of comprehensive diagnostic interviews that assess multiple disorders for use in research protocols (see McClellan & Werry, 2000, for a special issue on these protocols), rates of co-occurrence or comorbidity of disorders were also assessed. Comorbidity, or occurrence of a second disorder in an individual with an existing disorder, poses a special concern in the study of adolescent psychopathology, especially in any discussion of internalizing disorders and problems. Caron and Rutter (1991) note that failure to identify comorbid conditions leads to two main problems. First, effects associated with the identified condition may be attributable to the other condition; second, the experience of the other condition may influence the course of the first. Identifying comorbid conditions and the correlates of these conditions is essential for understanding the developmental processes of psychopathology across adolescence. Moreover, comorbidity may influence severity or impairment experienced by the individual and certainly affects the course of and outcomes of intervention.

It has been widely demonstrated that depression and depressive symptoms frequently co-occur with other symptoms and disorders (Compas & Hammen, 1994; Kessler et al., 1996; Lewinsohn, Hops, Roberts, Seeley, & Andrews, 1993; Shaffer et al., 1989). Nearly half or even two thirds of all adolescents who meet diagnostic criteria for depression have a comorbid condition (McGee et al., 1990; Rohde, Lewinsohn, & Seeley, 1991). Research also suggests that in most cases the other disorder preceded the depressive episode (Kessler et al., 1996; Rohde et al., 1991). For anxiety disorders, comorbidity is also commonly reported across studies (Kovacs & Devlin, 1998; Zahn-Waxler et al., 2000). Most important is that comorbidity observed for anxiety and depression is quite high, with the OADP reporting a lifetime comorbidity of anxiety with MDD of 73.1% (Lewinsohn, Zinbarg, Seeley, Lewinsohn, & Sack, 1997). In particular, adolescent depression has frequently been preceded by childhood anxiety disorders.

As has been mentioned, there are empirical reasons to question whether childhood and adolescent anxious and depressive symptomatology are distinct. Compas and Oppedisano (2000) further suggest that a lack of discrimination between anxiety and depression may also occur at the diagnostic level; examination of symptoms of MDD and GAD reveal several similarities—restlessness, fatigue, and irritability (see Table 19.1). Children and adolescents with mixed syndromes of anxious and depressive emotions and symptoms may have heightened risk for development of subsequent disorders as well as increased impairment in other areas (e.g., social interactions) than would individuals with only elevated anxious or depressive symptoms.

In an empirical examination of disorders among late adolescents and young adults in the Dunedin study, Krueger and his colleagues (1998) used structural equation modeling (SEM) to test the extent to which specific disorders may actually be indicators of what they termed "stable, underlying core psychopathological processes." A two-factor model of internalizing versus externalizing disorders demonstrated the best fit at ages 18 and 21 years, and individuals demonstrated substantial continuity in their rank position within these latent constructs over time. Such an approach may explain concurrent comorbidity rates within internalizing disorders (i.e., MDD and anxiety disorders) as well as the longitudinal predictions of prior anxiety disorders for subsequent adolescent depressive disorder.

In addition, subclinical internalizing symptoms and problems also demonstrate high rates of co-occurrence with other types of problems. For example, several studies report moderate to high correlations between scores for internalizing and externalizing symptoms (see Zahn-Waxler et al., 2000 for a brief review). In a study of subclinical eating and depression problems (Graber & Brooks-Gunn, 2001), patterns of psychosocial impairment paralleled findings from studies of other disorders. Specifically, individuals with co-occurring depressive and eating problems reported the greatest disturbances in family and peer relationships in comparison to individuals with only one of these problems. Thus, co-occurrence of problems and comorbidity of disorder are fairly normative for adolescent psychopathology. This fact may partially explain why many risk factors for internalizing problems are not found to be specific to internalizing problems but rather are linked to various psychopathologies.

FACTORS ASSOCIATED WITH INTERNALIZING PROBLEMS

There are numerous theories and studies of factors associated with or potentially predictive of internalizing problems or disorders. In general, models tend to be organized around the following categories: genetics; biology, which may include discussions of markers of disorder, neurodevelopment, and hormones; relationships (family and peer); stress; and psychological factors, which may include cognitive processes, personality, and related psychopathology (e.g., Birmaher et al., 1996; Garber, 2000; Petersen et al., 1993). From a developmental perspective, however, such categorizations fall short of viewing the data from integrative, transactional, or biopsychosocial perspectives; for example, genetic and parenting effects on depression are no doubt interactive (Lerner, 2002).

It may also be particularly important to tease apart factors associated with the first episode of disorder or problems versus factors associated with recurrence. Within any particular study of adolescents, the subgroup experiencing an internalizing problem may be experiencing it for the first time or may have a recurrent or persistent problem. Recent longitudinal studies of depression find unique predictors of each (e.g., Lewinsohn et al., 1998). Moreover, some models identify general processes that may lead to elevations in depressed or anxious mood or even disorder but do not specify fully why rates shift dramatically for depression during adolescence. Other models focus on aspects of adolescent development and may or may not be applicable to general processes that lead to depression. For example, puberty is often included in models of increased internalizing problems during adolescence but rarely is mentioned in general process models of depression in adulthood (although more interest in hormonal correlates of internalizing problems has emerged across the life span). Of course, puberty itself is not a singular construct (see the chapter by Susman & Rogol in this volume) but rather may be a heading for types of hormonal influences on affect or an indicator of individual differences in psychosocial experiences that influence internalizing problems. Finally, the most important individual difference to account for in internalizing problems is gender.

In the discussion of factors associated with internalizing problems, the applicability of the model to general processes (e.g., depression for anyone, at any point in the life course), problems during adolescence, and the explanatory role in gender differences are considered. In addition, although reasons to consider internalizing problems as an entity may be compelling, many of the empirical studies of factors predictive of problems during adolescence examine the prediction and correlates of depression (MDD) and depressive symptoms; anxiety is not as extensively examined. The empirical literature on internalizing disorders and symptoms may in some cases report on an internalizing construct, depressive symptoms or disorders, or anxiety symptoms and disorders. The following sections may not include literatures on all three categories of problems because the relevant research may not be available.

Developmental Models for Behavioral Change During Adolescence

Whereas most discussions of internalizing problems and disorders review findings under the core headings of the risk factors listed previously, the adolescent literature has also strongly focused on considering models that incorporate developmental experience in order to explain behavioral change among adolescents (e.g., Graber & Brooks-Gunn, 1996; Petersen et al., 1993). The focus of these models is specifically on explaining person-context interactions or—essentially—individual differences in the experience of adolescence. The models stem from interactional or transactional approaches that might apply to development throughout the life span (e.g., Sameroff, 1975), but in theses cases, particular transitions or experiences of adolescence are focal to understanding adjustment or behavioral change at this time (Graber & Brooks-Gunn, 1996). In terms of application to internalizing problems, three models are frequently discussed and may be particularly salient for understanding why internalizing problems rise during adolescence and why some youth are at greater risk than are others. These models are (a) cumulative or simultaneous events models (Petersen, Sarigiani, & Kennedy,

1991; Simmons & Blyth, 1987), (b) accentuation or diathesis-stress models (Caspi & Moffitt, 1991; see also the chapter by Susman in this volume), and (c) differential sensitivity or vulnerability models (Graber & Brooks-Gunn, 1996; Matthews, 1989).

As noted in this chapter and throughout this volume, adolescence is remarkable as a developmental period because of the confluence of transitions and challenges that occur during this period of development (e.g., Graber, Brooks-Gunn, & Petersen, 1996). Models of cumulative and simultaneous events posit that when individuals experience major events or transitions such as school changes or pubertal development, either in close sequence (cumulatively) or simultaneously, those individuals are more likely to have negative behavioral and emotional outcomes from the confluence of events. In this case, presumably, coping resources are overwhelmed and thus internalizing symptoms increase.

Accentuation models, in turn, posit that major developmental transitions accentuate existing problems, resulting in increased problems and poor outcomes after the transition (Block, 1982; Elder & Caspi, 1990). In refinements of this model, Caspi and Moffitt (1991) have also considered the interaction of prior problems with the type or nature of the transition (e.g., making the transition earlier than one's peers do) in predicting who experiences a worsening of problems during adolescence.

Recently, there has been interest in the extent to which particular developmental periods or processes result in differential or heightened sensitivity to stress, resulting in periods of increased vulnerability for health risks more generally. The heightened sensitivity models have often been based on understanding how women's reproductive transitions (puberty, pregnancy, menopause) result in changes in mental and physical health (e.g., Dorn & Chrousus, 1997; Graber & Brooks-Gunn, 1996). Biological systems may be more sensitive to environmental or contextual influences during times of rapid change, as seen in reproductive transitions. Similarly, models of differential sensitivity—also like accentuation models—suggest that individuals with preexisting characteristics are potentially more sensitive to developmental transitions and challenges. In this case, the transition or challenge need not be biologically based to confer risk; rather, the individual brings to the situation physiological (reactive responses to stress) or psychological (emotion regulation, temperament) characteristics that make the challenges of adolescence more difficult and hence more likely to lead to internalizing problems or disorders during this time.

These models, or groups of models, have often been used to explain the impact of puberty or other transitions on internalizing problems (as well as externalizing problems). These models are revisited in the following sections on specific classes of factors that are predictive of internalizing problems and in discussions in which such models may be useful for framing the literature.

Biological Markers

One goal in the study of internalizing problems—especially disorders—has been to identify how emotional experiences translate into the behavioral and biological dysregulations observed in depressive and anxiety disorders. Investigations on biological mechanisms of disorder first focused on determining which systems differed between disordered and nondisordered individuals. Then, more process-oriented studies considered how experiences influence biological systems and the development of internalizing problems or disorders. In this section, a brief review of debate regarding biological markers of disorders is provided.

Numerous studies of adults have documented biological systems that demonstrate altered or abnormal functioning when comparing individuals with MDD or an anxiety disorder with individuals who do not have disorder or have nonaffective disorders (see Birmaher et al., 1996; Dahl & Ryan, 1996; and Meyer, Chrousos, & Gold, 2001, for reviews). In comparable studies of children and adolescents, it was immediately apparent that several findings were not replicated in preadult samples. Such discrepancies were unsettling because children, adolescents, and adults reported many similar external—or rather symptomalogic—aspects of internalizing disorders; however, internal dysregulations were not consistently observed. These discrepancies resulted in several tangential and occasionally nonproductive discussions as to whether children and adolescents were really depressed if they did not show the biological markers of depression or did not respond to psychopharmacological treatment at the same rate as did adults.

Of course, recent efficacy trials of the effectiveness of the present generation of drugs (i.e., selective serotonin reuptake inhibitors [SSRIs]), indicate that this class of drugs seems to be effective in treating depression in children, adolescents, and adults (Emslie et al., 1997). However, many other discrepancies are not fully accounted for, although they are likely due in part to a variety of methodological factors (Birmaher et al., 1996). In addition, the neuroendocrine system is still undergoing substantial normative development in childhood and adolescence, making it likely that maturational factors account for some differences between adults, children, and adolescents. A comprehensive listing of which markers are or are not found in adolescents versus adults is beyond the scope of this chapter, although several reviews provide detailed analysis of these issues (e.g., Birmaher et al., 1996; Dahl & Ryan, 1996; Meyer et al., 2001). Studies of physiological dysregulation that is concurrent with depression or anxiety in and of itself do not identify predictors of these disorders. Instead, such markers identify factors that need to be explained in the development of a disorder or possible systems that are pathways that link experiences to abnormal functioning of neurological or endocrine systems.

L-HPA and HPG Endocrine Systems

Two hormonal systems, the limbic-hypothalamic-pituitary-adrenal (L-HPA) and the hypothalamic-pituitary-gonadal (HPG), have been implicated in the development of internalizing problems and disorders—in part stemming from studies of biological markers that differentiate disordered from nondisordered individuals and in part from an interest in behavioral change with puberty. Both the L-HPA and the HPG systems are involved in pubertal development. In addition, a literature that seems to grow exponentially on animal and human studies is outlining the neurobiology of the construct of stress. Much of this work has focused on the L-HPA axis of the autonomic nervous system. In terms of understanding changes in emotions or problems at adolescence, this system not only is involved in the experience of stress but also plays a role in pubertal development. In fact, maturation of some functions of the adrenal glands as demonstrated in adrenarche are perhaps the first hormonal changes of puberty, occurring in middle childhood for most individuals (Reiter & Grumbach, 1982). It has been suggested that early adolescence may be an important period of development of the stress response system because the HPA axis matures after puberty (Walker, Walder, & Reynolds, 2001). This maturation may increase the expression of behavioral problems in vulnerable individuals (Walker et al., 2001). Another closely related system, the HPG axis, is activated with the initial changes of puberty. As described by Susman and Rogol (see chapter by these authors in this volume), HPG activity results in substantial changes in several hormones, many of which have been linked to increases in internalizing symptoms among young adolescents.

The L-HPA Axis

An organism's response to stress involves activation of its HPA axis. Individual differences in the L-HPA system in particular in the response to stress may be particularly salient to identifying adolescents who may be vulnerable to developing internalizing problems or disorders. Detailed descriptions of the neurobiology of stress have been provided by McEwen (2000) and Meyer and colleagues (2001). Gunnar and Vazquez (2001) provide the following streamlined but informative overview:

> Activation of the LHPA system entails the increased production and release of hormones within the brain and pituitary gland. Corticotropin releasing hormone (CRH) is the main secretogogue stimulating the pituitary to secrete adrenocorticotropin hormone (ACTH), which in turn acts on the adrenal to secrete cortisol. However, similar to many endocrine hormones, CRH also acts as a neurotransmitter in areas outside the hypothalamus. For example, increased amounts of CRH, particularly in sites such as the central nucleus of the amygdala (CEA, an area associated with fear and anxiety), is believed to play a role in the development of anxiety disorder. Likewise, CRH elevations in the bed nucleus of the stria terminalis (BNST, a relay station from the "emotional limbic brain" to the hypothalamus) is also associated with the development of affective pathology. (p. 516)

Cortisol demonstrates diurnal variation; the highest levels occur just before waking and are followed by a rapid decline, then relatively stable, low levels in the late afternoon and evening, followed by increases during sleep. In addition, cortisol levels tend to increase in response to novelty and stress—especially social stressors—and then decrease as the individual assesses the threat level or copes with the challenge. Acute elevation of glucocorticoids (cortisol in humans) in response to a stressful situation seems to promote cognitive processing of emotions via the formation of memories of the situation (McEwen, 2000). This beneficial effect is differentiated from the experience of chronic production of glucocorticoids, which appear to damage brain structures. Chronic production of cortisol may be the result of a chronic stressor or may be the result of failing to regulate the cortisol response to frequently occurring social stressors. For example, some individuals maintain elevated cortisol levels after a stressful event, whereas most people show physiological adaptation relatively quickly. McEwen (2000) suggests that over time, individuals who do not show adaptation to common stressors may end up chronically exposed to elevated cortisol levels. This type of stress response may explain why major life events lead to increases in internalizing symptoms via daily hassles (e.g., Compas, Howell, Ledoux, Phares, & Williams, 1989). If a major event increases the likelihood that the individual will experience more stressors, the net result is greater exposure to glucocorticoids and their potential damaging effects. Aside from stressful life events, the lives of adolescents are filled with socially challenging situations—meeting new people, trying to fit in with a new group of peers, having a romantic relationship—all of which may elicit stress responses. All of these events may elicit more frequent or prolonged responses in girls or subgroups of girls who are vulnerable to emotional responses to relationship events. One can imagine a girl who feels that having a romantic relationship with her boyfriend is very important and feels socially challenged during several interactions beyond the social challenge of a first date. (See the subsequent discussion of the role romantic relationships play in the development of internalizing problems at adolescence.)

Animal studies and some recent work in humans have demonstrated that early experiences may result in long-term alterations in the L-HPA system. In rodents, studies of maternal separation in early development revealed interesting effects of maternal behavior on the HPA axis (see Boccia & Pedersen, 2001, for a discussion of this literature). Specifically, following a short separation, mothers engaged in increased care of their offspring; when exposed to other stressors, these offspring demonstrated smaller hormonal stress responses and quick recovery to baseline in comparison to nonseparated pups. In contrast, following long maternal separations, mothers decreased care of their offspring; when exposed to stressors, these offspring had higher and prolonged hormonal stress responses and showed greater anxiety and fear. Subsequent studies demonstrated that some mothers provided more or less care in the absence of the experimental separation condition. Comparisons of naturally occurring variations found the same effects on offspring as experimentally induced variations in maternal care. The effects of parenting on the developing HPA system speaks to how physiological vulnerabilities to stress may be established via early experience.

In addition, the seminal work of Suomi and his colleagues (see Suomi, 1999, for a review) have documented the interaction of genetic based vulnerabilities for reactive, particularly high or sustained responses to stress and maternal behavior in rhesus monkeys. In this work, reactive monkeys (those who demonstrate heightened responses to novelty and challenge) reared with less responsive or less nurturant caregivers were likely to develop symptoms and behaviors indicative of depression in response to stressors. In contrast, reactive monkeys who were reared by highly nurturant, patient mothers were likely to excel in the troop social hierarchy, often becoming leaders in the group.

Studies of stress response in adolescents are growing and are including nonclinical samples. These studies should provide a clearer picture of the links between physiological stress responses, experiences of stressful events and adolescent transitions, and increases in internalizing problems and disorders. In one such study of disordered and normal control adolescents, Klimes-Dougan, Hastings, Granger, Usher, and Zahn-Waxler (2001) found that maintaining increased cortisol response to challenge was associated with both internalizing and externalizing symptoms; having a strong decrease in cortisol in response to challenge was also associated with internalizing symptoms. Additional studies on how and why early vulnerabilities may eventually result in the dysregulations observed in depression among adults and whether dysregulations are specific to particular types of problems or disorders are warranted.

HPG and HPA Axis Changes at Puberty

As noted, the HPG and HPA axis are both involved in pubertal development (see Buchanan, Eccles, & Becker, 1992; and the chapter by Susman & Rogol in this volume for reviews). As these systems develop at puberty, hormonal levels increase dramatically, and some hormones are linked to changes in internalizing symptoms and disorders. In particular, much of the literature has focused on adrenal hormones that increase at adrenarche (dehydroepiandrosterone [DHEA] and its sulfate [DHEAS]) and gonadal hormones (testosterone and estradiol), although it should be noted that testosterone is also produced by the adrenal glands at puberty. Because studies of pubertal hormones and internalizing symptoms are reviewed by Susman and Rogol (this volume) and elsewhere (e.g., Brooks-Gunn, Graber, & Paikoff, 1994; Graber, Brooks-Gunn, & Archibald, in press), the specific studies are not reviewed here. In general, effects of pubertal hormones on behavior seem to be more often found with externalizing symptoms and aggression. However, some evidence indicates that rapid increases in hormones as indexed by estradiol are associated with increases in depressive symptoms among girls (Brooks-Gunn & Warren, 1989). Moreover, Angold, Costello, Erkanli, and Worthman (1999) reported that estradiol and testosterone levels during puberty were predictive of MDD in girls such that higher hormonal levels were associated with increased rates of MDD.

One problem with such findings is that ultimately all girls attain the hormonal levels typical of adult reproductive functioning, but not all girls become depressed. Subsequent analyses by Angold in the GSM indicate that other factors (i.e., maternal mental health) moderate these associations (Angold, Worthmare, & Costello, 2003). It may be that depression is less likely to manifest prior to advanced or postpubertal development (at least in girls), an issue that is discussed more fully in the review of the role of genetic factors in internalizing problems. In contrast, it may also be that some individuals do in fact have elevated gonadal hormonal levels after puberty and in adulthood. A few studies (e.g., Lai, Vesprini, Chu, Jernström, & Narod, 2001) have reported that women who experienced menarche at earlier ages may have higher levels of estrogen in adulthood. In this case, elevated estrogen levels may be a pathway to internalizing problems or at least depression over the life course of women.

Interactions between hormonal systems may result in the pubertal transition as a time of heightened sensitivity to environmental events or stressors. For example, in recent work on girls, my colleagues and I have found evidence that aspects of puberty (i.e., pubertal timing) and stress response may be linked, and both may be important for understanding initial changes in internalizing symptoms in the early adolescent years (Graber, Brooks-Gunn, & Warren, in press). In delineating pathways of health risks in general for women, McEwen (1994) points out that gonadal hormones have effects in the brain beyond reproductive systems, including in the hippocampus, where glucocorticoid effects of stress are also observed. Taylor et al. (2000) also identify the "tend-and-befriend" pattern of response to stress that may be more representative of female responses to stress, especially social stressors. Moreover, the physiological mechanisms underlying this response involve female reproductive (gonadal) hormones and oxytocin, a hormone that is often associated with maternal caregiving behaviors.

Advances in understanding gender differences in internalizing problems and disorders may be afforded by considering multiple stress systems and interactions across systems.

Pubertal Factors Other Than Hormonal Change

In addition to the role that hormones at puberty may play in increases in internalizing symptoms or even disorders, an emerging literature suggests that one aspect of pubertal development—specifically, pubertal timing (going through puberty earlier, at about the same time, or later than one's peers)—is associated with several dimensions of psychopathology during adolescence. In particular, earlier maturation among girls has been associated with depressive symptoms and disorders (e.g., Ge, Conger, & Elder, 2001a; Graber, Lewinsohn, Seeley, & Brooks-Gunn, 1997; Hayward et al., 1997; Stice, Presnell, & Bearman, 2001) as well as externalizing (e.g., Graber et al., 1997) and eating disorders and symptoms (e.g., Graber, Brooks-Gunn, Paikoff, & Warren, 1994; Graber et al., 1997).

For boys, timing has more often been linked to elevated symptoms rather than disorders (e.g., Graber et al., 1997). Early maturation in boys has been associated with increased depressive symptoms or internalizing types of psychological distress (e.g., Ge, Conger, & Elder, 2001b; Graber et al., 1997) as well as externalizing behaviors (e.g., Ge et al., 2001b). Late maturation for boys also seems to confer some risk for psychopathology with higher rates of disruptive behavior disorders and increased alcohol use and abuse in young adulthood (Andersson & Magnusson, 1990; Graber, Seeley, Brooks-Gunn, & Lewinsohn, 2003).

Specific links within racial groups between timing and adjustment are just beginning to be studied. Ge, Brody, Conger, Simons, and Murry (2002) report similar effects of early maturation in both boys and girls on internalizing and externalizing behaviors and symptoms in a community sample of African American young adolescents. Although the empirical base is still quite limited, the emerging evidence is that early maturation is a risk for adjustment problems for European American and African American youth and possibly other groups. Clearly, pubertal timing is not a specific predictor for internalizing problems, but understanding how it confers risk for different problems and disorders may be informative to explaining why each problem increases during adolescence. Given the prevalence of effects for early maturing girls, understanding the mechanisms or pathways for these effects may be particularly important in understanding why gender differences in internalizing problems and disorders emerge in adolescence.

The aforementioned tests of simultaneous transition models have found that early maturing girls were at risk for increases in depressive symptoms across adolescence because they were more likely than were boys to experience rapid pubertal change at the same time as a school transition. In addition, two main hypotheses have been the foundation of these studies (Brooks-Gunn, Petersen, & Eichorn, 1985). An early maturation hypothesis suggests that maturing earlier than one's peers results in individuals' entering into more adult-like behaviors commensurate with their physical appearance but prior to developing the skills or competencies needed to negotiate these situations. The result is that early maturers—potentially both girls and boys—may engage in more problem behaviors and experience greater distress during adolescence. It has long been suggested that earlier maturers were at risk specifically because they reached puberty and commensurate social challenges prior to developing the necessary social skills needed to meet these challenges. However, no studies have actually examined this hypothesis; that is, no studies of pubertal timing have intensively assessed social cognitive, social, and emotion regulation skills. Yet, research in other domains suggests that these types of skills are important in the development of internalizing problems.

A separate hypothesis suggests that being out of synch with one's peers results in poor mental health; in this case, early maturing girls and late maturing boys should be at risk for negative outcomes because their development is the most off time, given the relative gender difference in puberty. A caveat of this general hypothesis is that early maturing girls will seek out individuals more like themselves (e.g., older peers) and engage in problem behaviors at young ages (Stattin & Magnusson, 1990). As my colleagues and I have discussed previously (Graber, Archibald, et al., in press), tests of this hypothesis have focused on early maturing girls' associations with deviant peers or associations with boys, presumably romantic partners. Most examinations of this hypothesis have focused on effects on externalizing behaviors and the effects of boys on early maturing girls' behaviors or the effects of deviant peers on early maturing boys and girls (e.g., Ge et al., 2002).

In my own work with colleagues using the OADP sample, I have found that, along with the striking rates of depressive and substance use disorders among early maturing girls, these girls also consistently report lower levels of social support from family and friends in midadolescence and young adulthood (Graber et al., 1997; Graber et al., 2003). Women who had been early maturers had higher rates of traits of antisocial personality disorder at age 24, a disorder associated with serious impairments in interpersonal relationships. Deficits in social interactions may be a pathway for girls to develop internalizing problems and possibly other problems and disorders (see later discussions); early maturation may be one component of this pathway. This hypothesis requires more detailed examinations of the quality of relationships for early maturing girls as well as the type of individuals with whom they have relationships.

Stressful Events

As indicated, the neurobiology of stress responses is a burgeoning field in the study of internalizing problems. Underlying this interest has been the tenet that stressful occurrences or events lead to increases in internalizing symptoms. Garber (2000) defines stressful life events as "circumstances characterized by either the lack or loss of a highly desirable and obtainable goal or the presence of a highly undesirable and inescapable event" (p. 475). The adult and child depression literatures frequently report retrospective associations between the experience of major life events and having a depressive episode. Among adults, 60–70% of individuals with MDD report a major stressful event in the preceding year, usually some type of loss; effects are more modest in studies of depressed children and adolescents (Birmaher et al., 1996). Traumatic loss, such as exposure to suicide, dramatically increases the risk for depression among adults and adolescents (see Birmaher et al., 1996, for a review). Similarly, some evidence indicates that anxiety disorders are preceded by a stressful life event (Vasey & Ollendick, 2000).

The events need not be associated with the anxiety problem directly—as in the case of PTSD, in which a precipitating event leads to the distress response—but instead, other anxiety disorders such as GAD may arise after family relocations, school changes, or other stressful life events (Vasey & Ollendick, 2000).

Links between the experience of stressful life events and internalizing problems or disorders are mediated by several factors such as the individual's coping behaviors, abilities, and social supports when events are experienced. The individual's assessment of the importance of the event, the assessment of how negative the event is or what impact it has on other areas of the individual's life, and whether the event is controllable or uncontrollable are all factors in whether stressful events are associated with increased internalizing problems or disorders (Birmaher et al., 1996; Vasey & Ollendick, 2000). Compas et al. (1989) report that major events in the family tended to increase the number of minor stressful events, or daily hassles, for family members, and more such events led to increased behavior problems (total internalizing and externalizing symptoms) among young adolescents; thus, events in the broader context of an adolescent's life as well as immediately experienced events may be salient to developing internalizing symptoms. Furthermore, individual differences in terms of how events are interpreted or processed cognitively have been linked to onset and maintenance of internalizing problems (Kaslow, Adamson, & Collins, 2000); the role of cognitive factors in the development of internalizing problems is discussed in a subsequent section.

These findings are likely applicable to links between stressful events and internalizing symptoms at any point in the life course. As noted, cumulative or simultaneous event models suggest that increased internalizing symptoms or problems during adolescence are in part due to the likelihood that adolescents will have more stressful life events, given the nature of normative adolescent development; these events include puberty, school change, increased family conflict, changes in peer relationships, and so on. Reports of stressful life events (negative and positive events) have been found to increase during young to midadolescence, potentially peaking around the mid to later stages of puberty (Brooks-Gunn, 1991; Ge, Lorenz, Conger, Elder, & Simons, 1994). Moreover, increases in stressful events have been linked to increases in internalizing symptoms or depressive symptoms in these studies.

In the relatively few studies that have looked at simultaneity or ordering of developmental events or transitions, the occurrence of peak pubertal development (as indexed by rapid change in physical growth) prior to school change was predictive of increased depressive symptoms several years later at 12th grade (Petersen et al., 1991). Notably, this effect was only found for girls; given the normative timing differences in the experience of puberty between girls and boys, with girls starting puberty earlier than boys and the normative grades when young adolescents make school transitions, only girls had significant pubertal changes prior to making a school change. Hence, gender differences in internalizing symptoms over adolescence may in part be explained by the timing of developmental events or transitions.

Girls may also be at greater risk for increases in internalizing symptoms during adolescence not just because of the synchrony in the timing of events and transitions but also because of the types of events that normatively occur for adolescents and how girls respond to them. For example, during the middle school years, adolescents frequently experience changes in their close relationships—involving peer groups, friendships, and family relations. Many of these changes fall under the label of events such as broke up with a friend, had a fight with a parent, and so on. Girls, in comparison to boys, may be more likely to experience negative emotions in response to events in relationships, report more events that are relationship focused, and perseverate on events that have happened with peers (Kessler & McLeod, 1984; Rudolf, 2002). Additional discussion of these issues is presented in a later section in regard to family and peer factors.

Psychological Factors: Cognitions, Emotion Regulation, and Temperament Cognitions

In the prior discussion of stressful life events, it is clear that not all adolescents who experience challenge or stress develop internalizing problems; hence, individual characteristics, skills, and capacities have been identified as salient to differences among individuals in the experience of internalizing symptoms and problems. There is a well-documented literature that cognitive factors such as cognitive styles or attribution biases are associated with depressive symptoms (Kaslow et al., 2000; Nolen-Hoeksema, 1994). Cognitive changes during adolescence are well documented (see the chapter by Keating in this volume) and are considered to be a foundation of subsequent evaluations of the self and processing of the other challenges of adolescence (Harter, 1998). While cognitive abilities increase in several domains during adolescence, allowing for more nuanced reflections on the self, one's future, and the world, one question that remains is the extent to which changes in cognition are predictive of changes in internalizing symptoms and problems or whether cognitive styles or biases are established well before adolescence. In this case, cognitive styles are preexisting factors that interact with the challenges of adolescence or any challenges in the course of development leading to internalizing problems; that is, individuals with these styles of interpreting the world and thinking about themselves are more likely to become depressed or have internalizing problems at any time when increased challenges occur, and adolescence may be the first time in development when cumulative or simultaneous stressors are likely to occur.

Kaslow et al. (2000) identify three primary areas of cognitive processing that are associated with depression in particular. These areas include negative self-schemas (negative views of the self), faulty information processing (attributional biases), and negative expectancies (helplessness and hopelessness). As noted, changes in thinking about the self are part of adolescent development. In addition, self-consciousness seems to increase during early adolescence. In general, measures of self-image or esteem tend to demonstrate moderate to strong associations with internalizing symptoms (Brooks-Gunn, Rock, & Warren, 1989), making it difficult to consider negative self-evaluations separately from these symptoms. Body image concerns may be particularly salient for girls in connection with internalizing symptoms as well as eating disorders and subclinical eating problems (e.g., Allgood-Merten, Lewinsohn, & Hops, 1990; Graber, Petersen, & Brooks-Gunn, 1996; Rierdan, Koff, & Stuffs, 1989). Disturbances in body image are common during early adolescence (or puberty) for both girls and boys, but most youth demonstrate increases in body esteem over adolescence (Graber et al., 1996). However, evidence suggests that the subgroup of girls with recurrent or persistent poor body image during adolescence not only have elevated depressive and eating symptoms during adolescence but also have higher symptomatology in young adulthood (Ohring, Graber, & Brooks-Gunn, 2002). In this study, girls with persistent body dissatisfaction were also more likely to have gone through puberty earlier than their peers were. Thus, negative self-evaluations, in this case, were linked to an aspect of adolescent development—puberty; individual differences in how puberty was experienced were important in determining who had continued negative self-evaluations, at least for body dissatisfaction. In the limited literature on boys' body dissatisfaction, comparable individual differences are not found. Thus, self-evaluations about the body may be an important factor in why more girls and why some girls, in particular, have internalizing problems during adolescence.

The literature on faulty information processing and negative expectancies, in contrast, has pointed more to the notion that cognitive styles are in place prior to adolescence and are moderators of the experience of adolescent challenges in predicting internalizing symptoms. In general, cognitive styles or faulty information processing usually reflect how social information or events are interpreted by the individual. Biases in attributions about events that negative events are attributable to internal, stable, and global causes and that positive events are attributable to external, unstable, and specific causes are linked to elevated depressive symptoms (Kaslow et al., 2000). The interpretation of the controllability of events in one's life has also been linked to anxiety disorders and symptoms (Vasey & Ollendick, 2000). Expectations about one's ability to influence outcomes as outlined by Seligman (1975) show similar associations to internalizing symptoms and problems. In this case, a sense of hopelessness (again, beliefs that events have internal, stable, and global causes that one can do little about) has been linked to depressive symptoms and disorder (Abramson, Metalsky, & Alloy, 1989).

Cognitive styles or attributions consistently differentiate youth with or without disorders and those with elevated versus normative internalizing symptom levels (see Kaslow et al., 2000, for a review). However, a recent meta-analysis did not find that cognitive attributional styles consistently interacted with life events to predict depression as would be expected (Joiner & Wagner, 1995). Much of the research to date on this issue is cross-sectional, making it difficult to determine whether cognitive styles develop or change substantially during adolescence or whether they reflect a preexisting trait-like construct. In recent analyses with the OADP sample, many adolescents demonstrated consistent cognitive styles over a 1-year period, but subgroups of youth demonstrated change (Schwartz, Kaslow, Seeley, & Lewinsohn, 2000). Change in cognitive styles were associated with other cognitive factors; for example, better self-esteem at the initial assessment predicted change from maladaptive to an adaptive cognitive style over time.

Notably, evidence suggests that certain types of attributions or cognitive styles may be more salient to the maintenance and recurrence of depression. For example, Nolen-Hoeksema (1994) has identified a ruminating cognitive style as one in which the individual ruminates on negative emotions; ruminating has been linked to longer and more severe depressive episodes. In particular, Nolen-Hoeksema (1994) suggests that girls are more likely to be ruminators than are boys. In her model, girls are more likely to have an attributional style that is linked to internalizing symptoms, and girls are more likely to experience normative developmental experiences of adolescence in a negative manner—that is, form negative body images in response to challenges of puberty. Such an interactive model would address the question of why more girls become depressed or have elevated internalizing symptoms and problems.

Along with attributions about events and expectations about one's ability to influence events, individuals also have differences in the approaches they use to cope with the events. These areas are often related, as seen with ruminating styles in which the individual focuses on negative emotions and rather than engage in problem solving or a distracting behavior, instead responds to the emotions with continued perseveration on the emotions or events that led to them. More generally, cognitive beliefs about the extent to which one's actions are likely to influence events, what can be done about events, or why they occur are in part the result of attributional biases, but they also lead to subsequent behavioral responses to events and feelings. Hence, coping behaviors and cognitive processing are probably interactive in predicting the development of internalizing behaviors (Compas, Connor, Saltzman, Thomsen, & Wadsworth, 1999).

Emotion Regulation

As noted, internalizing problems are defined as dysregulations in mood and affect and hence by definition are indications of difficulties in regulating negative emotions. Emotion regulation skills tend to develop substantially during early childhood (Zahn-Waxler et al., 2000) but also continue to develop in response to new demands of adolescent emotional experience. Deater-Deckard (2001) identified emotion regulation and social cognitive skills as particularly salient to skills in peer relations of children and adolescents. Among young adolescents, better abilities to understand how others are feeling or their thoughts are associated with greater peer acceptance (Bosacki & Astington, 1999). Poor emotion regulation skills have been linked to early childhood problems, especially anger management and aggression problems (Deater-Deckard, 2001; Rubin, Bukowski, & Parker, 1998).

In some sense, emotion regulation and coping are similar constructs. Zahn-Waxler and her colleagues (2000) have argued that promoting emotion regulation in early childhood may be linked subsequently to poor regulation later in development. In particular, regulating externalizing behaviors is a primary focus in early childhood, but individuals—specifically girls—who learn to regulate these behaviors and emotions effectively may develop dispositions for internalizing emotions such as fear and guilt. Vasey and Ollendick (2000) note that regulation of fear via promoting a sense of control and self-efficacy versus promoting avoidance of the stimuli or situation is important in understanding how parents socialize children to be anxious. Such findings speak to how attributional biases may be established as parents socialize children to develop different beliefs about control and efficacy of their environments (Zahn-Waxler et al., 2000). At the same time, attributions and emotion regulation skills may result from the interaction of biologically based (possibly with a genetic component) factors and socialization.

Temperament

As suggested in the discussion of attributional biases, for many individuals such characteristic approaches to the social world seem to be stable, whereas for certain subgroups change in these constructs may occur across development. It has been suggested that temperament or personality may be one way of conceptualizing consistency in how individuals respond to their environments. A detailed discussion of how personality or temperament may be linked to internalizing problems over the course of development is beyond the scope of this chapter. However, a few brief examples support suggestions that these constructs may be important and under-studied in their role in the development of psychopathology more generally.

Kagan (1998) views temperament as a stable way of responding to the environment—in particular, to unexpected events. Similarly, Block and Block (1980) describe ego resilience and ego control as personality types, which again reflect how an individual responds to environmental stress or frustration. Research based in each system has found that children and adolescents with a particular personality subtype (inhibited temperament or overcontrollers) had higher rates of internalizing problems than did those with other temperament or personality types (e.g., Kagan, 1998, for a review; Robins, John, Caspi, Moffitt, & Stouthamer-Loeber, 1996). Perhaps the most compelling evidence in this area stems from Suomi's animal models of the interaction of temperament and rearing conditions (see Suomi, 1999, for a review) that was previously described in the section on L-HPA activity. Selective breeding produced monkeys with these response patterns; however, rearing experiences had a profound impact on the behavioral adjustment of these monkeys.

Thus, a compelling nonhuman primate model and some evidence in studies of children suggest that temperament or personality may be a vulnerability for internalizing problems, but other factors must mediate or moderate subsequent associations. Such a model does not directly explain why internalizing problems increase at adolescence in humans or why more girls develop these problems, although taken with previously discussed models that account for increased challenges and transitions at adolescence, these factors likely play a role in determining who develops internalizing problems. Furthermore, differential parenting practices by gender with children who are overcontrolled or inhibited-reactive may account in part for the development of particular attributional biases or coping responses in girls versus boys.

Genetic Factors and Family Aggregation

As with many mental and physical disorders, genetic factors have been identified as important as risk factors for depression and internalizing problems. Several studies of adolescent and childhood depressive disorder have considered the impact of genetic factors, either via studies of disorder in offspring of adults with disorders or via studies of family history of disorder in samples of depressed adolescents. Moreover, Birmaher and his colleagues (1996) suggest that looking across twin and adoption studies, about 50% of the variance in mood disorders (e.g., MDD, dysthymic disorder, and bipolar disorder) is accounted for by genetic similarity. The consensus seems to be that children of depressed parents are about three times more likely to have a lifetime history of MDD (Hammen, Burge, Burney, & Adrian, 1990; Weissman et al., 1987), even accounting for differences across study designs (Strober, 2001). Fewer family history, twin, or adoptions studies specific to anxiety problems and disorders in childhood or adolescence have been conducted (Vasey & Ollendick, 2000). Twin studies of adults find that genetic similarity constitutes risk for general and specific anxiety disorders (see Kendler, 2001, for a recent review).

Kovacs and her colleagues (Kovacs, Devlin, Pollock, Richards, & Mukerji, 1997) find that individuals who have the onset of MDD in childhood and adolescence have reports of familial disorder that are higher than what is typically reported among individuals with older onset. In twin studies of adults, familial MDD was associated with longer duration of episodes, increased recurrence, and higher reports of suicidal ideation (Kendler, Gardner, & Prescott, 1999). As indicated, one problem in listing factors associated with disorder or symptoms is that the factors are likely not distinct predictors of the problem but may be associated with increased psychopathology in several areas. In this case, the impact of having depressed parents is not confined to depression among their children and adolescents but rather is also associated with increased rates of anxiety and disruptive disorders in offspring (e.g., Hammen et al., 1990; Weissman, Fendrich, Warner, & Wickramaratne, 1992). Kendler (1995) has hypothesized that such findings may be explained by a genetic vulnerability that is shared by depression and anxiety such that other environmental factors interact with or exacerbate this vulnerability, resulting in one or the other disorder. Again, this inference is consistent with the position that anxiety and depression—subclinically and clinically—may not be distinct aspects of internalizing problems but rather have substantial shared characteristics, both in their symptoms and potentially in their underlying genetics.

The notion that genetic factors play a role in vulnerabilities that then require gene-environment interactions for subsequent expression of symptomatology does not fit with a compartmentalized approach to predictors of depression or anxiety. Environmental influences also have genetic components, especially when the environments include parents. Characteristics of parents, such as their own temperaments or vulnerabilities to environmental stressors, influence not only the parents' likelihood of developing an internalizing problem but also their parenting behaviors. Genetic factors, as yet unidentified, may play a role in the development of internalizing problems and disorders. Whereas one could argue that all behaviors have some genetic component, the statement may be best interpreted via comparisons of estimates of genetic variance for a range of symptoms; that is, the estimate of 50% of the variance accounted for by genetic similarity for childhood and adolescent MDD is less than estimates of genetic similarity on schizophrenia in adults and slightly less than estimates for alcoholism in adults (Kendler, 2001).

The role of familial disorder in childhood and adolescent onset of disorder suggests that genetic similarity or other familial factors are particularly important in onset of disorder prior to adulthood. Family context or parental behaviors may be more salient when individuals live with family members, or genetic similarity may be predictive of a vulnerability that results in earlier development of disorder. One recent study, drawing on the Virginia Twin Study of Adolescent Behavioral Development, differentiated the role of genetic similarity in pre- and postpubertal subclinical symptomatology for depression (Silberg et al., 1999). It is interesting to note that genetic similarity was not important in explaining variance in symptoms in prepubertal children. Rather, genetic similarity was only significant in symptoms of pubertal and postpubertal adolescents.

Furthermore, consistent with other studies, negative life events were predictive of depressive symptoms in both boys and girls. For girls, however, depressive symptoms increased with age, even for girls who did not experience negative life events. Also, genetic similarity accounted for variance in the reporting of negative life events. Thus, genetic similarity was associated with a vulnerability or disposition (e.g., to report or to experience negative life events) that covaried with increased internalizing symptoms—in this case, depressive symptoms. Again, Silberg and her colleagues (1999) only find genetic similarity to be salient to models of symptoms in individuals who are pubertal and postpubertal. Although genetic similarity likely plays a role in depression across the life span, this study points to the salience of such similarity in describing increases in depression at this time and potentially to accounting more for girls' increases at this time. Certainly, additional studies are needed to replicate this finding. Because the study looked at variations in symptom levels among adolescents, it remains to be seen whether comparable findings would be obtained for depressive disorders or anxiety symptoms and disorders. Moreover, it would be most informative to expand our understanding of the characteristics that have been described as vulnerabilities or dispositions that seem to be the process through which genetic similarity is associated with internalizing symptoms and problems (see Collins, Maccoby, Steinberg, Hetherington, & Bornstein, 2000; Lerner, 2002).

Family Relations and Context

Studies of family aggregration implicate family factors other than genetic similarity in the development of internalizing problems. Family relationships, events, interactions, and broader family contextual factors have all been linked to changes in internalizing symptoms in childhood and adolescence. As discussed, socialization behaviors of parents may influence the development of cognitive attributions and emotion regulation. The nature of parent-child interactions and attachments has been the focus of numerous theories of internalizing disorders (Bowlby, 1980; Zahn-Waxler et al., 2000). Freudian psychoanalytic theory identified the source of both anxiety and depression among adults as problems in early childhood relationships with parents.

In the work of Bowlby and Ainsworth on attachment, early parent-child interactions, as tapped by caregiver sensitivity and consistency, shape the child's expectations for the behavior of others in the child's life (see R. A. Thompson, 1998, for a review). These working models of relationships have been linked to the development of internalizing problems in that insecure attachment models are associated with depression in adolescents and adults (Garber, 2000). In this theoretical framework, the attachment relationship in infancy or early childhood shapes the development of the working model, but subsequent changes in parental behaviors also influence the child's working model over the course of development (R. A. Thompson, 1998). Individual differences in working models for relationships could be explanatory of individual differences in who is at risk for internalizing problems during adolescence, but in and of itself, this theoretical perspective would not explain why the problems increase at adolescence; that is, an interaction with other factors would be necessary, but an insecure working model may be a vulnerability for internalizing problems.

Depressive disorders in adolescence have been associated with increased family conflict, lower family warmth, parental rejection, and prior and concurrent maltreatment or abuse (Birmaher et al., 1996). A similar mix of family relational, interactional, and contextual factors have been identified as predictors of increases in internalizing symptoms over the course of early to late adolescence. Notably, Rueter, Scaramella, Wallace, and Conger (1999) examined the impact of parent-child conflict on internalizing symptoms and disorder using SEM and latent growth curve models to test direct and indirect effects over time. Both internalizing symptoms and parent-child conflict in early adolescence (ages 12–13) predicted changes in internalizing symptoms over time and in reports of history of disorder by young adulthood (ages 19–20). Specifically, prior parent-child disagreement influenced internalizing disorders via their indirect effect on subclinical symptoms rather than via a direct path to later disorder. In this study, gender differences in pathways were not assessed, although the rates of anxiety and depressive disorders demonstrated the expected gender difference (Rueter et al., 1999).

Other longitudinal projects have demonstrated that maternal adjustment and marital discord or divorce result in increases in internalizing symptoms over early to late adolescence and in community samples that included rural and urban youth (Crawford, Cohen, Midlarsky, & Brook, 2001; Forehand, Biggar, & Kotchick, 1998). Forehand and his colleagues (1998) looked at the impact of multiple family risk factors (e.g., divorce, maternal depressive symptoms, mother-child relations) and found that when more than three risk factors were present during early adolescence, depressive symptoms were dramatically higher in late adolescence and young adulthood. However, the presence of more than three family risk factors also predicted poorer academic achievement or attainment by young adulthood. Thus, the number of risks was predictive of psychopathology, but risks were not specific to type of problem or domain of functioning. In addition, this study found no consistent patterns of differences in the experience of cumulative risks by gender.

In contrast, Crawford and his colleagues (2001) focused on the effects of maternal distress, as indexed by internalizing symptoms and marital discord, in predicting changes and gender differences in internalizing symptoms at three times in adolescence. Notably, the SEM results suggested that gender differences in internalizing symptoms emerged around ages 13–14 and were predicted by maternal distress. As noted in the discussion of family history of disorder and in other studies of internalizing symptoms and negative emotion (e.g., Eisenberg, Fabes, Shepard, Guthrie, Murphy, & Reiser, 1999), links between parental distress and adolescent internalizing symptoms may be accounted for by genetic similarity. At the same time, the prediction that maternal distress leads to greater increases in internalizing symptoms for girls is suggestive of the role of other factors. Crawford et al. (2001) point to the hypothesis put forward by Kessler and McLeod (1984) that women are more vulnerable than men to network events—that is, stressful events that happen in one's network of close relationships. Of course, these findings are also consistent with the aforementioned finding that the association of genetic similarity with depressive symptoms emerged only among pubertal and postpubertal girls. This association would be consistent with the age when gender differences emerged in the Crawford et al. (2001) study and with the finding that stressful life events influenced depressive symptoms and had a genetic component (Silberg et al., 1999). Perhaps genetic similarity in the disposition to experience or to report stressful events is limited to stressful events within close social networks such as family and friends. Alternatively, vulnerability to network events may in part be associated with who is in one's network, in that adolescent girls who develop internalizing problems or disorders may be more likely to have female network members who share a genetic vulnerability to internalizing problems.

One issue that is repeatedly raised in the discussion of family influences on depression in adolescents is that effects may not be unidirectional. Rather, having an adolescent with serious internalizing symptoms or disorder places additional strains on families and may result in increased conflict between parents and children, changes in expressions of warmth, communication problems among family members, and strain in the marital relationship of parents (Birmaher et al., 1996; Garber, 2000). The aforementioned study of Reuter and her colleagues (1999) also used SEM to test the bidirectional influence hypothesis. In this study, they did not find support for internalizing symptoms' predicting family conflict; however, they did find that conflict had an indirect effect on symptoms and disorder over time. In related work on symptoms of eating disorders, quality of family relations predicted increased symptoms in young adolescents (Archibald, Graber, & Brooks-Gunn, 1999), and increasing eating symptomatology predicted declines in quality of family relations among mid- to late adolescents in separate studies that tested bidirectional effects using SEM (Archibald, Linver, Graber, & Brooks-Gunn, 2002). Quality of family relations may be more salient to younger adolescents or may have a greater impact on internalizing emotions during this period of development. Subsequent research needs to build upon longitudinal investigations that also model simultaneous change in order to determine the role of family interactions and quality of relationships on internalizing problems.

Finally, stemming from ecological models such as that of Bronfenbrenner (1977), studies of family influences on internalizing symptoms and problems during adolescence have also examined the influence of contextual factors that influence children and families. Several studies have found that economic strain or persistent parental unemployment are predictive of internalizing symptoms among rural, White, and urban African American adolescents, usually via effects on parental mental health or parenting behaviors in parent-child interactions (Conger, Ge, Elder, Lorenz, & Simons, 1994; McLoyd, Jayaratne, Ceballo, & Borquez, 1994; Wadsworth & Compas, 2002). Drawing upon McLoyd's prior studies, subsequent studies have also found that the effect of economic hardship need not occur solely via effects on parents but also occur via the perceptions of adolescents (Conger, Conger, Matthews, & Elder, 1999; Wadsworth & Compas, 2002); that is, adolescents who perceive that economic problems exist for the family are more likely to have increasing internalizing symptoms over time (Conger et al., 1999). However, individual characteristics such as more agentic coping strategies or mastery may be protective against perceiving strain in the first place (i.e., mastery predicted the likelihood of perceiving economic hardship; Conger et al., 1999) or may mediate effects of strain and family conflict on internalizing symptoms (Wadsworth & Compas, 2002).

As with other family factors, family contextual events and experiences do not uniformly predict internalizing symptoms in adolescence; rather, other individual characteristics are salient to who responds to such events and experiences with increased distress. Although some studies have found that certain pathways or processes linking economic conditions to adolescent internalizing symptoms demonstrated differences by gender, these studies have more often been explanatory of general effects on symptoms—usually well within the normal range of functioning—and have not shed light on why more girls develop these problems or even why increases happen during adolescence. To clarify, many of these studies have documented factors that predict changes for some individuals but not others in internalizing symptoms during adolescence. However, models might fit equally well in predicting changes in internalizing symptoms in childhood.

Peers

The impact of peer relationships on adjustment has been much less studied in adolescence than in childhood. In addition, much of the focus on peer relationships has been on aggression and externalizing problems. At the same time, withdrawal from social relationships and activities has been viewed as an indicator of impairment among youth experiencing internalizing problems; for example, the diagnostic criteria both for GAD and for MDD in the *DSM-IV-TR* require that the anxious or depressive symptoms result in significant impairment in social or occupational functioning. Thus, it has not always been clear—especially in cross-sectional studies—whether poor peer relationships served as the antecedent or the consequence of internalizing problems.

In childhood, peer rejection resulting from social withdrawal rather than from aggression has been linked to increased depressive symptoms and possibly disorder (Hecht, Inderbitzen, & Bukowski, 1998; Rubin & Burgess, 2001). An extensive cross-sectional literature on bullying and victimization also suggests that children without peer supports who are victimized are more likely to have higher internalizing symptoms (Deater-Deckard, 2001; Hawker & Boulton, 2000). Victimization in and of itself does not necessarily predict internalizing problems. Rather, in this and in other areas, difficulties with peers more generally may be buffered by the effect of having one or a few close friends, depending on the nature of the friends (Deater-Deckard, 2001). However, adolescents seem to associate with peers who have similar levels of internalizing symptoms (Hogue & Steinberg, 1995); in such cases, friends may reward less effective coping strategies for dealing with problems and maintain elevated symptoms or problems.

As noted in this volume (see chapter by Brown) and elsewhere (Berndt, 1996; Cairns & Cairns, 1994, Muuss, 1996), the quality of peer relationships changes during adolescence, and peer relationships and interactions become increasingly important to adolescents. Of investigations that have considered any type of peer component in connection with internalizing problems, often the focus has been on peer events as a domain of stressful life events (e.g., had a fight with a friend, broke up with a friend, made a new friend, etc.). As noted in the discussion of stressful life events, the report of stressful life events increases with age and is predictive of increased internalizing or at least depressive symptoms (Brooks-Gunn, 1991; Ge et al., 1994; Silberg et al., 1999). Peer-related events may account for a significant number of the events that adolescents experience (Brooks-Gunn, 1991) and may be more salient to girls than to boys.

Cairns and Cairns (1994) found that close peer relationships and peer group membership change frequently for many adolescents during the middle school years, with a tendency for greater stability by late high school. The strain of making transitions in peer groups has been linked to decreases in feeling of self-worth among young adolescents (Fenzel, 2000). Way (1996), in an ethnographic study of urban high school students, found that negative experiences with peers often resulted in negative emotions (e.g., distrust) about peers and close relationships. Significant periods of isolation or withdrawal from relationships with peers were also reported by several youth. The turbulence and the quality of peer relationships may play a role in increases in internalizing problems during adolescence, especially in early to midadolescence. As with studies of childhood, better quality of a close friendship may buffer negative effects of having few friends or difficulties in larger peer groups (Berndt, Hawkins, & Jiao, 1999).

Although the literature on adolescent peer relationships is suggestive of why difficulties in this area may lead to increases in internalizing problems, factors underlying the quality of peer relationships likely influence how effectively individuals meet the new demands of peer relationships during adolescence. Prior relationship skills and patterns are certainly likely to influence how well adolescent challenges are met and may help to identify who will have greater difficulties during adolescence. For example, boys who were rejected and aggressive as children demonstrated increases in both externalizing and internalizing symptoms during early and midadolescence (Coie, Terry, Lenox, Lochman, & Hyman, 1995). In contrast, girls who were rejected in childhood regardless of reason for rejection (withdrawal or aggression) had higher reports of internalizing symptoms in childhood and in early and midadolescence. These girls entered adolescence with elevated symptoms and did not show increases in internalizing. Thus, within any group of adolescent girls with elevated internalizing symptoms, some will have had persistent internalizing problems and others will not have had preadolescent difficulties.

As mentioned, emotion regulation or social cognitive skills influence competence in peer relationships and may be one source of individual differences in who does and does not experience internalizing problems or poor peer relationships. Such factors may also influence how peer events are experienced, in that individuals with better skills may have fewer negative peer events (e.g., fight less often) or may deal with the emotional impact of negative events more effectively, either through better regulation skills or the buffering effect of having other positive relationships. Again, the salience of relationships to the emotional experience of adolescent girls coupled with instability of relationships during early adolescence may be important factors in explaining gender differences in internalizing problems (e.g., Rudolf, 2002).

Romantic and Sexual Relationships

The importance of romantic relationships in adolescent development has recently seen a surge of attention both for understanding developmental processes and for understanding problems and challenges faced by adolescents (e.g., Furman, Brown, & Feiring, 1999; Shulman & Collins, 1997). In the case of internalizing problems, the impact of romantic relationships—like that of peer relationships—has often been considered in terms of stressful life events such as breaking up with a girl- or boyfriend, beginning dating, and so on. Experiences such as breaking up with a partner are stressful for adolescents and potentially lead to intensely experienced negative emotions, depressive symptoms, and possibly episodes (Joyner & Udry, 2000; Larson, Clore, & Wood, 1999). At the same time, having a romantic relationship or having several relationships is predictive of increased depressive symptoms over time in both boys and girls (Joyner & Udry, 2000). Joyner and Udry (2000) also found that becoming involved in a relationship had a larger negative effect on girls' depressive symptoms than on boys' depressive symptoms. The negative effects on depressive symptoms were highest for younger girls who had repeated or continuous involvement in relationships. In part, the effect of having a relationship on increased depressive symptoms over time was explained by other factors; for boys, declines in school performance accounted for part of this effect and for girls, decreases in quality of relationship with parents accounted for part of the effect. The number and stability of relationships reported over time were also important in explaining the negative impact of relationships, with more relationships and less stability leading to increases in depressive symptoms.

Although the empirical evidence on the impact of romantic involvements on adolescents is limited, a mostly separate literature on sexual behaviors sheds some light on this issue (see the chapter by Savin-Williams & Diamond in this volume). Actually, an enormous literature has examined the sexual activity of adolescents, but only recently has that literature been linked to relationships or with internalizing problems. Even though it is frequently noted that managing sexual feelings and interactions likely challenges emotion and behavior regulation skills, very little attention has been given to this aspect of sexual behavior. The emotional challenges of regulating sexual feelings and interactions may be embedded within the other emotional challenges of intimate or romantic relationships in some cases. However, it is likely that sexual experiences outside of relationships may also affect emotions and adjustment.

The percentage of adolescents who progress to intercourse increases during mid-adolescence; for example, for girls and boys, respectively, 25% and 27% of 15-year-olds, 39% and 45% of 16-year-olds, and 52% and 59% of 17-year-olds have had intercourse (Alan Guttmacher Institute [AGI], 1994; Terry & Manlove, 1999). Individuals, especially girls, who have intercourse at younger ages are thought to be at greater risk for a number of sexual health related problems and are more likely to transition to the next sexual partner more quickly than are older girls (AGI, 1994). Joyner and Udry (2000) reported that adolescents who had less stability and a higher number of relationships had higher reports of depressive symptoms.

It is not clear whether managing sexuality, relationships, or the interplay of both have a role in increases in depressive symptoms with romantic relationships. For example, is the breakup of a relationship more stressful, eliciting more sadness, if the relationship included intercourse? The romantic relationships of adolescents are increasingly likely to include intercourse, the longer the relationship lasts (Bearman & Bruckner, 2001). Another example of the challenges posed by relationships can be seen in recent studies of adolescent responses to sexual infidelity and betrayal in romantic relationships (Feldman & Cauffman, 1999; S. Thompson, 1994). In some cases, infidelity or betrayal leads to breakups and hence potentially increases in internalizing symptoms. However, not all relationships that involve infidelity or betrayal result in breaking off the relationship. In either situation, many adolescents experience strong negative emotions such as sadness, despondency, and disillusionment in response to infidelities in romantic and sexual relationships (Feldman & Cauffman, 1999; S. Thompson, 1994).

It is important to note that negative emotional responses and fears related to sexual and romantic relationships are not uniform across adolescents. In the narratives of a racially and ethnically diverse sample of girls, S. Thompson (1994) found that girls who idealized romantic relationships described more fear of rejection and despondency at being dumped. Downey and her colleagues (Downey, Bonica, & Rincon, 1999) have identified rejection sensitivity as salient to understanding pathways to unhealthy relationships and subsequent poor adjustment among adolescents. In this model, past childhood experiences of rejection—initially from parents and then from peers—result in heightened sensitivity to rejection from romantic partners. Rejection-sensitive individuals may shy away from romantic involvements out of increased fearfulness about close relationships or may find themselves seeking such involvements in order to gain acceptance that has previously been lacking. Individuals who seek acceptance may be overly willing to acquiesce in the relationship or place high value on it. In addition, rejection-sensitive individuals tend to be highly jealous and hostile in their relationships; these feelings often lead to more conflict in the relationship, which subsequently leads to breakup. Notably, among late adolescents, young women but not young men who were rejection sensitive reported higher depressive symptoms after a relationship breakup (Downey et al., 1999); aggressive feelings were more common for rejection-sensitive young men.

This discussion on the potential impact of romantic and sexual relationships on internalizing problems has been based on findings across several literatures that seem to suggest that these relationships may be a particular challenge to adolescents and may be a source of increased internalizing problems for some youth. Unfortunately, an empirical interest in romantic relationships is fairly recent (e.g., Furman et al., 1999), and many studies of sexual behaviors have focused heavily on teen pregnancy and health risks such as sexually transmitted diseases rather than on psychopathology. However, the importance of these experiences, the new emotion regulation challenges elicited by theses experiences, the dramatic increase of these experiences around the time that internalizing problems increase (especially rates of MDD), and the potential for problems in relationships or relationship patterns to account for gender differences in internalizing problems would all suggest that more nuanced investigations beyond stressful events (e.g., breakups) on how adolescents regulate these relationships are warranted. Models, such as that of Downey on rejection sensitivity, that integrate childhood experiences, development of gender differences in response to these experiences, and the ways in which prior vulnerabilities interact with challenges at adolescence are likely to be informative for understanding who is at risk for increased internalizing problems during adolescence.

IMPLICATIONS AND CONCLUSIONS

In the course of this chapter, the goal has been to consider the nature of internalizing symptoms, problems, and disorders during adolescence, as well as to consider factors or models that explain why internalizing problems occur, why they increase during adolescence, and why more girls than boys experience these problems. As noted previously, it has been questioned whether subclinical problems are of importance. Clearly, in the developmental perspective taken here and elsewhere, subclinical problems are important as a pathway to disorder for some individuals. However, as is evidenced in the present review, the literatures on disorder and subclinical problems are incomplete in several areas. The extent to which findings for subclinical problems also apply to the development of disorder or the extent to which dysregulations observed in disordered individuals also occur to a lesser—or even the same—extent in individuals with subclinical problems has often not been assessed.

Compelling evidence suggests that preexisting biological and psychological vulnerabilities or dispositions are an important factor in who develops internalizing problems during adolescence. Evidence of both socializing experiences and genetic similarity accounts for the establishment of these vulnerabilities. However, why these vulnerabilities are accentuated at adolescence is still not completely clear. Tests of models that specifically explain why rates increase have not been as abundant as studies that identify rate changes or individual differences.

Explaining why more girls experience internalizing problems has long been a focal point in research in this area, and the mechanisms underlying this effect are emerging. Certainly, as Nolen-Hoeksema (1994) has asserted, unique challenges of adolescence and puberty may exist for girls more than for boys. In addition, studies on adolescent relationships have been particularly relevant to the issue of gender differences. Additional studies of relationships, how they are experienced (both psychologically and physiologically), and why some individuals may have particular difficulties with interpersonal relationships (e.g., early maturing girls) would likely illuminate not only why more girls have internalizing problems but also why some boys experience these problems as well.

Across the correlates and possible predictors of internalizing problems that have been discussed, it is clear that recent studies have been more integrative and have included multiple factors. Such approaches have made it feasible to compare relative influences of predictors on internalizing problems and their relative impact on other problems. No single study will be able to examine in depth each of the factors discussed in this review, but focused investigations that study pieces of different models and make comparative tests of models will continue to advance this area of research. Whereas several new findings have emerged in the past few years and certainly since the original studies of adolescence and adolescent disorder were begun, numerous gaps in the literature still remain, especially in terms of integration of constructs.

In conclusion, it is probably useful to highlight what was not considered in this review. This review did not include all studies of internalizing problems and disorders but rather drew from prior reviews and recent studies that seemed to advance the areas of interest here (i.e., those most salient to adolescence and individual differences). More important is that this chapter did not consider issues of prevention or treatment of problems and disorders. Certainly, the primary reason for understanding why these problems occur is to prevent them or treat them more effectively. Although a thorough discussion of treatment and prevention issues is beyond the scope of this chapter, several recent reviews consider the advances that have been made in treatment and prevention (e.g., Garber, 2000; Lewinsohn et al., 1998). Notably, Post and his colleagues (2001) identify several reasons that treatment and prevention of internalizing disorders during adolescence should be a focus in research and practice. First, episodes of MDD are frequently untreated among adolescents. Second, evidence suggests that recurrent episodes of disorder become harder to treat. And finally, early treatment of disorders may be protective against recurrent episodes later in development. Thus, better identification of disordered youth and better access to services for them would substantially improve mental health in subsequent cohorts of adults.

From the wealth of empirical evidence that has amassed in recent years, internalizing problems and disorders are certainly a serious health concern among adolescents, and these problems merit the attention they have been given and will likely continue to receive. At the same time, more focused attention on the individual differences in development that result in internalizing problems for some youth in contrast to factors that promote better adjustment is warranted.

REFERENCES

Abramson, L. Y., Metalsky, G., & Alloy, L. B. (1989). Hopelessness depression: A theory-based subtype of depression. *Psychological Review, 96,* 358–372.

Achenbach, T. M. (1993). *Empirically based taxonomy.* Burlington, VT: University of Vermont Department of Psychiatry.

Alan Guttmacher Institute. (1994). *Sex and America's teenagers.* New York: Author.

Allgood-Merten, B., Lewinsohn, P. M., & Hops, H. (1990). Sex differences and adolescent depression. *Journal of Abnormal Psychology, 99,* 55–63.

American Psychiatric Association. (2000). *Diagnostic and statistical manual of mental disorders* (text revision). Washington, DC: Author.

Andersson, T., & Magnusson, D. (1990). Biological maturation in adolescence and the development of drinking habits and alcohol abuse among young males: A prospective longitudinal study. *Journal of Youth and Adolescence, 19,* 33–41.

Angold, A., & Costello, E. J. (2001). The epidemiology of depression in children and adolescents. In I. M. Goodyer (Ed.), *The depressed child and adolescent* (2nd ed., pp. 143–178). Cambridge, England: Cambridge University Press.

Angold, A., Costello, E. J., Erkanli, A., & Worthman, C. M. (1999). Pubertal changes in hormone levels and depression in girls. *Psychological Medicine, 29,* 1043–1053.

Angold, A., Worthman, C. M., & Costello, E. J. (2003). Puberty and depression. In C. Hayward (Ed.), *Gender differences at puberty.* New York: Cambridge University Press.

Archibald, A. B., Graber, J. A., & Brooks-Gunn, J. (1999). Associations among parent-adolescent relationships, pubertal growth, dieting and body image in young adolescent girls: A short term longitudinal study. *Journal of Research on Adolescence, 9,* 395–415.

Archibald, A. B., Linver, M. R., Graber, J. A., & Brooks-Gunn, J. (2002). Parent-adolescent relationships and girls' unhealthy eating: Testing reciprocal effects. *Journal of Research on Adolescence, 12,* 451–461.

Avenevoli, S., & Steinberg, L. (2001). The continuity of depression across the adolescent transition. In H. Reese & R. Kail (Eds.), *Advances in child development and behavior* (Vol. 28, pp. 139–173). New York: Academic Press.

Bandura, A. (1964). The stormy decade: Fact or fiction? *Psychology in the Schools, 1,* 224–231.

Bearman, P. S., & Bruckner, H. (2001). Promising the future: Virginity pledges and first intercourse. *American Journal of Sociology, 106,* 859–912.

Berndt, T. J. (1996). Transitions in friendship and friends' influence. In J. A. Graber, J. Brooks-Gunn, & A. C. Petersen (Eds.), *Transitions through adolescence: Interpersonal domains and context* (pp. 57–84). Mahwah, NJ: Erlbaum.

Berndt, T. J., Hawkins, J. A., & Jiao, Z. (1999). Influences of friends and friendships on adjustment to junior high school. *Merrill-Palmer Quarterly, 45,* 13–41.

Birmaher, B., Ryan, N. D., Williamson, D. E., Brent, D. A., Kaufman, J., Dahl, R. E., et al. (1996). Childhood and adolescent depression: A review of the past 10 years. Part I. *Journal of the American Academy of Child & Adolescent Psychiatry, 35,* 1427–1439.

Block, J. (1982). Assimilation, accommodation, and the dynamics of personality development. *Child Development, 53,* 281–295.

Block, J. H., & Block, J. (1980). The role of ego-control and ego-resiliency in the organization of behavior. In W. A. Collins (Ed.), *Minnesota symposia on child psychology* (Vol. 13, pp. 39–101). Hillsdale, NJ: Erlbaum.

Boccia, M. L., & Pedersen, C. (2001). Animal models of critical and sensitive periods in social and emotional development. In D. B. Bailey, Jr., J. T. Bruer, F. J. Symons, & J. W. Lichtman (Eds.), *Critical thinking about critical periods* (pp. 107–127). Baltimore, MD: Brookes.

Bosacki, S., & Astington, J. W. (1999). Theory of mind in preadolescence: Relations between social understanding and social competence. *Social Development, 8,* 237–255.

Bowen, R. C., Offord, D. R., & Boyle, M. H. (1990). The prevalence of overanxious disorder and separation anxiety disorder: Results form the Ontario Child Health Study. *Journal of the American Academy of Child & Adolescent Psychiatry, 29,* 753–758.

Bowlby, J. (1980). *Attachment and loss: Vol. 3. Loss, sadness, and depression.* New York: Basic Books.

Bronfenbrenner, U. (1977). Toward an experimental ecology of human development. *American Psychologist, 32,* 513–531.

Brooks-Gunn, J. (1991). How stressful is the transition to adolescence in girls? In M. E. Colten & S. Gore (Eds.), *Adolescent stress: Causes and consequences* (pp. 131–149). Hawthorne, NY: Aldine de Gruyter.

Brooks-Gunn, J., Graber, J. A., & Paikoff, R. L. (1994). Studying links between hormones and negative affect: Models and measures. *Journal of Research on Adolescence, 4*(4), 469–486.

Brooks-Gunn, J., Petersen, A. C., & Eichorn, D. (1985). The study of maturational timing effects in adolescence. *Journal of Youth and Adolescence, 14*(3), 149–161.

Brooks-Gunn, J., Rock, D., & Warren, M. P. (1989). Comparability of constructs across the adolescent years. *Developmental Psychology, 25*(1), 51–60.

Brooks-Gunn, J., & Warren, M. P. (1989). Biological contributions to affective expression in young adolescent girls. *Child Development, 60,* 372–385.

Buchanan, C. M., Eccles, J. S., & Becker, J. B. (1992). Are adolescents the victims of raging hormones: Evidence for activational effects of hormones on moods and behavior at adolescence. *Psychological Bulletin, 111,* 62–107.

Cairns, R. B. (1998). Developmental plasticity and continuity in social interactions: Attachment and aggression. In National Institute of Mental Health (Ed.), *Advancing research on developmental plasticity: Integrating the behavioral science and neuroscience of mental health* (NIH Publication No. 98-4338; pp. 153–163). Bethesda, MD: National Institute of Health.

Cairns, R. B., & Cairns, B. D. (1994). *Lifelines and risks: Pathways of youth in our time.* New York: Cambridge University Press.

Caron, C., & Rutter, M. (1991). Comorbidity in child psychopathology: Concepts, issues and research strategies. *Journal of Child Psychology and Psychiatry, 32*(7), 1063–1080.

Caspi, A., & Moffitt, T. E. (1991). Individual differences are accentuated during periods of social change: The sample case of girls at puberty. *Journal of Personality and Social Psychology, 61,* 157–168.

Clark, L. A., Watson, D., & Reynolds, S. (1995). Diagnosis and classification of psychopathology: Challenges to the current system and future directions. *Annual Review of Psychology, 46,* 121–153.

Coie, J., Terry, R., Lenox, K., Lochman, J., & Hyman, C. (1995). Childhood peer rejection and aggression as predictors of stable patterns of adolescent disorder. *Development & Psychopathology, 7,* 697–713.

Collins, W. A., Maccoby, E. E., Steinberg, L., Hetherington, E. M., & Bornstein, M. H. (2000). Contemporary research on parenting: The case for nature and nurture. *American Psychologist, 55,* 218–232.

Compas, B. E., Connor, J. K., Saltzman, H., Thomsen, A. H., & Wadsworth, M. (1999). Getting specific about coping: Effortful and involuntary responses to stress in development. In M. Lewis & D. Ramsay (Eds.), *Soothing and stress* (pp. 229–256). Mahwah, NJ: Erlbaum.

Compas, B. E., Ey, S., & Grant, K. E. (1993). Taxonomy, assessment, and diagnosis of depression during adolescence. *Psychological Bulletin, 114*(2), 323–344.

Compas, B. E., & Hammen, C. L. (1994). Child and adolescent depression: Covariation and comorbidity in development. In R. J. Haggerty, L. R. Sherrod, N. Garmezy, & M. Rutter (Eds.), *Stress, risk, and resilience in children and adolescents: Process, mechanisms, and interventions* (pp. 225–267). New York: Cambridge University Press.

Compas, B. E., Howell, D. C., Ledoux, N., Phares, V., & Williams, R. A. (1989). Parent and child stress and symptoms: An integrative analysis. *Developmental Psychology, 25,* 550–559.

Compas, B. E., & Oppedisano, G. (2000). Mixed anxiety/depression in childhood and adolescence. In A. J. Sameroff, M. Lewis, & S. M. Miller (Eds.), *Handbook of developmental psychopathology* (2nd ed., pp. 531–548). New York: Plenum Press.

Conger, R. D., Conger, K. J., Matthews, L. S., & Elder, G. H., Jr. (1999). Pathways of economic influence on adolescent adjustment. *American Journal of Community Psychology, 27,* 519–541.

Conger, R. D., Ge, X., Elder, G. H., Jr., Lorenz, F. O., & Simons, R. L. (1994). Economic stress, coercive family process, and developmental problems of adolescence. *Child Development, 65,* 541–561.

Costello, E. J., & Angold, A. (1995). Epidemiology. In J. S. March (Ed.), *Anxiety disorders in children and adolescents* (pp. 109–124). New York: Guilford Press.

Costello, E. J., Keeler, G. P., & Angold, A. (2001). Poverty, race/ethnicity, and psychiatric disorder: A study of rural children. *American Journal of Public Health, 91,* 1494–1498.

Crawford, T. N., Cohen, P., Midlarsky, E., & Brook, J. S. (2001). Internalizing symptoms in adolescents: Gender differences in vulnerability to parental distress and discord. *Journal of Research on Adolescence, 11,* 95–118.

Dahl, R. E., & Ryan, N. D. (1996). The psychobiology of adolescent depression. In D. Cicchetti & S. L. Toth (Eds.), *Rochester symposium on developmental psychopathology: Vol. 7. Adolescence: Opportunities and challenges* (pp. 197–232). Rochester, NY: University of Rochester Press.

Deater-Deckard, K. (2001). Annotation: Recent research examining the role of peer relationships in the development of psychopathology. *Journal of Child Psychology and Psychiatry, 42,* 565–579.

Dorn, L. D., & Chrousos, G. P. (1997). The neurobiology of stress: Understanding regulation of affect during female biological transitions. *Seminars in Reproductive Endocrinology, 15,* 19–35.

Downey, G., Bonica, C., & Rincon, C. (1999). Rejection sensitivity and adolescent romantic relationships. In W. Furman, B. B. Brown, & C. Feiring (Eds.), *Contemporary perspectives on adolescent relationships* (pp. 148–174). New York: Cambridge University Press.

Eisenberg, N., Fabes, R. A., Shepard, S. A., Guthrie, I. K., Murphy B. C., & Reiser, M. (1999). Parental reactions to children's negative emotions: Longitudinal relations to quality of children's social functioning. *Child Development, 70,* 513–534.

Elder, G. H., Jr. (1985). Perspectives on the life course. In G. H. Elder, Jr. (Ed.), *Life course dynamics: Trajectories and transitions, 1968–1980* (pp. 23–49). Ithaca, NY: Cornell University Press.

Elder, G. H., Jr., & Caspi, A. (1990). Studying lives in a changing society: Sociological and personological explorations. In A. I. Rabin, R. A. Zucker, S. Frank, & R. A. Emmons (Eds.), *Studying persons and lives* (pp. 201–247). New York: Springer.

Emslie, G. J., Rush, J. A., Weinberg, W. A., Kowatch, R. A., Hughes, C. W., Carnody, T., et al. (1997). A double-blind, randomized, placebo-controlled trial of fluoxetine in children and adolescents with depression. *Archives of General Psychiatry, 54,* 1031–1037.

Feldman, S. S., & Cauffman, E. (1999). Sexual betrayal among late adolescents: Perspectives of the perpetrator and the aggrieved. *Journal of Youth and Adolescence, 28,* 235–258.

Fenzel, L. M. (2000). Prospective study of changes in global self-worth and strain during the transition to middle school. *Journal of Early Adolescence, 20,* 93–116.

Forehand, R., Biggar, H., & Kotchick, B. A. (1998). Cumulative risk across family stressors: Short- and long-term effects for adolescents. *Journal of Abnormal Child Psychology, 26,* 119–128.

Furman, W., Brown, B. B., & Feiring, C. (Eds.). (1999). *Contemporary perspectives on adolescent relationships.* New York: Cambridge University Press.

Garber, J. (2000). Development and depression. In A. J. Sameroff, M. Lewis, & S. M. Miller (Eds.), *Handbook of developmental psychopathology* (2nd ed., pp. 467–490). New York: Plenum Press.

Ge, X., Brody, G. H., Conger, R. D., Simons, R. L., & Murry, V. M. (2002). Contextual amplification of pubertal transition effects on deviant peer affiliation and externalizing behavior among African American children. *Developmental Psychology, 38,* 42–54.

Ge, X., Conger, R. D., & Elder, G. H., Jr. (2001a). Pubertal transition, stressful life events, and the emergence of gender differences in adolescent depressive symptoms. *Developmental Psychology, 37,* 404–417.

Ge, X., Conger, R. D., & Elder, G. H., Jr. (2001b). The relationship between puberty and psychological distress in adolescent boys. *Journal of Research on Adolescence, 11,* 49–70.

Ge, X., Lorenz, F. O., Conger, R. D., Elder, G. H., Jr., & Simons, R. L. (1994). Trajectories of stressful life events and depressive symptoms during adolescence. *Developmental Psychology, 30,* 467–483.

Goodyer, I. M. (Ed.). (2001) *The depressed child and adolescent* (2nd ed.). Cambridge, England: Cambridge University Press.

Gotlib, I. H., Lewinsohn, P. M., & Seeley, J. R. (1995). Symptoms versus a diagnosis of depression: Differences in psychosocial functioning. *Journal of Consulting and Clinical Psychology, 63,* 90–100.

Graber, J. A., & Brooks-Gunn, J. (1996). Transitions and turning points: Navigating the passage from childhood through adolescence. *Developmental Psychology, 32*(4), 768–776.

Graber, J. A., & Brooks-Gunn, J. (2001). Co-occurring eating and depressive problems: An 8-year study of adolescent girls. *International Journal of Eating Disorders, 30*(3), 37–47.

Graber, J. A., Brooks-Gunn, J., & Archibald, A. B. (in press). Links between puberty and externalizing and internalizing behaviors in girls: Moving from demonstrating effects to identifying pathways. In D. M. Stoff & E. J. Susman (Eds.), *Developmental psychobiology of aggression.* New York: Cambridge University Press.

Graber, J. A., Brooks-Gunn, J., Paikoff, R. L., & Warren, M. P. (1994). Prediction of eating problems: An eight year study of adolescent girls. *Developmental Psychology, 30,* 823–834.

Graber, J. A., Brooks-Gunn, J., & Petersen, A. C. (Eds.). (1996). *Transitions through adolescence: Interpersonal domains and context.* Mahwah, NJ: Erlbaum.

Graber, J. A., Brooks-Gunn, J., & Warren, M. P. (in press). Pubertal effects on adjustment in girls: Moving from demonstrating effects to identifying pathways. *Journal of Youth & Adolescence.*

Graber, J. A., Lewinsohn, P. M., Seeley, J. R., & Brooks-Gunn, J. (1997). Is psychopathology associated with the timing of pubertal development? *Journal of the American Academy of Child and Adolescent Psychiatry, 36,* 1768–1776.

Graber, J. A., Petersen, A. C., & Brooks-Gunn, J. (1996). Pubertal processes: Methods, measures, and models. In J. A. Graber, J. Brooks-Gunn, & A. C. Petersen (Eds.), *Transitions through adolescence: Interpersonal domains and context* (pp. 23–53). Mahwah, NJ: Erlbaum.

Graber, J. A., Seeley, J. R., Brooks-Gunn, J., & Lewinsohn, P. M. (2003). *Pubertal timing and psychopathology: Are effects maintained in young adulthood*? Manuscript submitted for publication.

Graber, J. A., Tyrka, A. R., & Brooks-Gunn, J. (2002). How similar are correlates of different subclinical eating problems and Bulimia Nervosa? *Journal of Child Psychology and Psychiatry, 43,* 1–12.

Gunnar, M. R., & Vazquez, D. M. (2001). Low cortisol and flattening of expected daytime rhythm: Potential indices of risk in human development. *Development and Psychopathology, 13,* 515–538.

Hammen, C., Burge, D., Burney, E., & Adrian, C. (1990). Longitudinal study of diagnoses in children of women with unipolar and bipolar affective disorder. *Archives of General Psychiatry, 47,* 1112–1117.

Harter, S. (1998). The development of self-representations. In W. Damon (Series Ed.), & N. Eisenberg (Vol. Ed.), *Handbook of child psychology: Vol. 4. Social, emotional, and personality development* (pp. 553–617). New York: Wiley.

Hawker, D. S. J., & Boulton, M. J. (2000). Twenty years' research on peer victimization and psychosocial maladjustment: A meta-analytic review of cross-sectional studies. *Journal of Child Psychology and Psychiatry, 41,* 441–455.

Hayward, C., Killen, J. D., Wilson, D. M., Hammer, L. D., Litt, I. F., Kraemer, H. C., et al.

(1997). Psychiatric risk associated with early puberty in adolescent girls. *Journal of the American Academy of Child & Adolescent Psychiatry, 36,* 255–262.

Hecht, D. B., Inderbitzen, H. M., & Bukowski, A. L. (1998). The relationship between peer status and depressive symptoms in children and adolescents. *Journal of Abnormal Child Psychology, 26,* 153–160.

Hogue, A., & Steinberg, L. (1995). Homophily of internalizing distress in adolescent peer groups. *Developmental Psychology, 31,* 897–906.

Joiner, T. E., & Wagner, K. D. (1995). Attributional style and depression in children and adolescents: A meta-analytic review. *Clinical Psychology Review, 15,* 777–798.

Joyner, K., & Udry, J. R. (2000). You don't bring me anything but down: Adolescent romance and depression. *Journal of Health and Social Behavior, 41,* 369–391.

Kagan, J. (1980). Perspectives on continuity. In O. G. Brim, Jr., & J. Kagan (Eds.), *Constancy and change in human development* (pp. 26–74). Cambridge, MA: Harvard University Press.

Kagan, J. (1998). Biology and the child. In W. Damon (Series Ed.) & N. Eisenberg (Vol. Ed.), *Handbook of child psychology: Vol. 4. Social, emotional, and personality development* (pp. 177–236). New York: Wiley.

Kaslow, N. J., Adamson, L. B., & Collins, M. H. (2000). A developmental psychopathology perspective on the cognitive components of child and adolescent depression. In A. J. Sameroff, M. Lewis, & S. M. Miller (Eds.), *Handbook of developmental psychopathology* (2nd ed., pp. 491–510). New York: Plenum Press.

Kendler, K. S. (1995). Genetic epidemiology in psychiatry: Taking both genes and environment seriously. *Archives of General Psychiatry, 52,* 895–899.

Kendler, K. S. (2001). Twin studies of psychiatric illness. *Archives of General Psychiatry, 58,* 1005–1014.

Kendler, K. S., Gardner, C. O., & Prescott, C. A. (1999). Clinical characteristics of major depression that predict risk of depression in relatives. *Archives of General Psychiatry, 56,* 322–327.

Kessler, R. C., & McLeod, J. D. (1984). Sex differences in vulnerability to undesirable life events. *American Sociological Review, 49,* 620–631.

Kessler, R. C., Nelson, C. B., McGonagle, K. A., Liu, J., Swartz, M., & Blazer, D. G. (1996). Comorbidity of *DSM-III-R* major depressive disorder in the general population: Results from the U.S. National Comorbidity Survey. *British Journal of Psychiatry, 168*(Suppl. 30), 17–30.

Klimes-Dougan, B., Hastings, P. D., Granger, D. A., Usher, B. A., & Zahn-Waxler, C. (2001). Adrenocorticol activity in at-risk and normally developing adolescents: Individual differences in salivary cortisol basal levels, diurnal variation, and responses to social challenges. *Development and Psychopathology, 13,* 695–719.

Kochanska, G. (1993). Toward a synthesis of parental socialization and child temperament in early development of conscience. *Child Development, 64,* 325–347.

Kovacs, M., & Devlin, B. (1998). Internalizing disorders in childhood. *Journal of Child Psychology & Psychiatry, 39,* 47–63.

Kovacs, M., Devlin, B., Pollock, M., Richards, C., & Mukerji, P. (1997). A controlled family history study of childhood-onset depressive disorder. *Archives of General Psychiatry, 54,* 613–623.

Kovacs, M., Obrosky, D. S., Gatsonis, C., & Richards, C. (1997). First episode major depressive and dysthymic disorder in childhood: Clinical and sociodemographic factors in recovery. *Journal of the American Academy of Child & Adolescent Psychiatry, 36,* 777–784.

Krueger, R. F., Caspi, A., Moffitt, T. E., & Silva, P. A. (1998). The structure and stability of common mental disorders *(DSM-III-R):* A longitudinal-epidemiological study. *Journal of Abnormal Psychology, 107,* 216–227.

Lai, J., Vesprini, D., Chu, W., Jernström, H., & Narod, S. A. (2001). CYP gene polymorphisms and early menarche. *Molecular Genetics and Metabolism, 74,* 449–457.

Larson, R. W., Clore, G. L., & Wood, G. A. (1999). The emotions of romantic relationships: Do they wreak havoc on adolescents? In W. Furman, B. B. Brown, & C. Feiring (Eds.), *Contemporary perspectives on adolescent relationships* (pp. 19–49). New York: Cambridge University Press.

Larson, R. W., Csikszentmihalyi, M., & Graef, R. (1980). Mood variability and psychosocial adjustment of adolescents. *Journal of Youth and Adolescence, 9,* 469–490.

Lerner, R. M. (2002). *Concepts and theories of human development* (3rd ed.). Mahwah, NJ: Erlbaum.

Lerner, R. M., & Foch, T. T. (Eds.). (1987). *Biological-psychosocial interactions in early adolescence.* Hillsdale, NJ: Erlbaum.

Lewinsohn, P. M., & Essau, C. A. (2002). Depression in adolescents. In I. Gotlib & C. Hammen (Eds.), *Handbook of depression* (pp. 541–559). New York: Guilford Press.

Lewinsohn, P. M., Hops, H., Roberts, R. E., Seeley, J. R., & Andrews, J. A. (1993). Adolescent psychopathology: I. Prevalence and incidence of depression and other *DSM-III-R* disorders in high school students. *Journal of Abnormal Psychology, 102,* 133–144.

Lewinsohn, P. M., Rohde, P., & Seeley, J. R. (1998). Major depressive disorder in older adolescents: Prevalence, risk factors, and clinical implications. *Clinical Psychology Review, 18,* 765–794.

Lewinsohn, P. M., Zinbarg, R., Seeley, J. R., Lewinsohn, M., & Sack, W. H. (1997). Lifetime comorbidity among anxiety disorders and between anxiety disorders and other mental disorders in adolescents. *Journal of Anxiety Disorders, 11,* 377–394.

Matthews, K. A. (1989). Interactive effects of behavior and reproductive hormones on sex differences in risk for coronary heart disease. *Health Psychology, 8,* 373–387.

McClellan, J. M., & Werry, J. S. (Eds.). (2000). Research psychiatric diagnostic interviews for children and adolescents [Special issue]. *Journal of the American Academy of Child & Adolescent Psychiatry, 39*(1).

McEwen, B. S. (1994). How do sex and stress hormones affect nerve cells? *Annals of the New York Academy of Sciences, 743,* 1–18.

McEwen, B. S. (2000). The neurobiology of stress: From serendipity to clinical relevance. *Brain Research, 886,* 172–189.

McGee, R., Fehan, M., Williams, S., Partridge, F., Silva, P. A., & Kelly, J. (1990). *DSM-III* disorders in a large sample of adolescents. *Journal of the American Academy of Child & Adolescent Psychiatry, 29,* 611–619.

McLoyd, V. C., Jayaratne, T. E., Ceballo, R., & Borquez, J. (1994). Unemployment and work interruption among African American single mothers: Effects on parenting and adolescent socioemotional functioning. *Child Development, 65,* 562–589.

Meyer, S. E., Chrousos, G. P., & Gold, P. W. (2001). Major depression and the stress system: A life span perspective. *Development and Psychopathology, 13,* 565–580.

Muuss, R. E. (1996). *Theories of adolescence.* New York: McGraw-Hill Companies.

Nolen-Hoeksema, S. (1994). An interactive model for the emergence of gender differences in depression in adolescence. *Journal of Research on Adolescence, 4,* 519–534.

Offer, D. (1987). In defense of adolescents. *Journal of the American Medical Association, 257,* 3407–3408.

Offer, D., & Offer, J. B. (1975). *From teenage to young manhood.* New York: Basic Books.

Ohring, R., Graber, J. A., & Brooks-Gunn, J. (2002). Girls' recurrent and concurrent body dissatisfaction: Correlates and consequences over 8 years. *International Journal of Eating Disorders, 31,* 404–415.

Paikoff, R., & Brooks-Gunn, J. (1991). Do parent-child relationships change during puberty? *Psychological Bulletin, 110*(1), 47–66.

Petersen, A. C. (1984). The early adolescence study: An overview. *Journal of Early Adolescence, 4,* 103–106.

Petersen, A. C., Compas, B., Brooks-Gunn, J., Stemmler, M., Ey, S., & Grant, K. (1993). Depression in adolescence. *American Psychologist, 48*(2), 155–168.

Petersen, A. C., Sarigiani, P. A., & Kennedy, R. E. (1991). Adolescent depression: Why more girls? *Journal of Youth and Adolescence, 20,* 247–271.

Post, R. M., Leverich, G. S., Xing, G., & Weiss, S. R. B. (2001). Developmental vulnerabilities to the onset and course of bipolar disorder. *Development and Psychopathology, 13,* 581–598.

Radloff, L. S. (1977). The CES-D scale: A self-report depression scale for research in the general population. *Applied Psychological Measurement, 1,* 385–401.

Radloff, L. S. (1991). The use of the Center for Epidemiologic Studies Depression Scale in adolescents and young adults. *Journal of Youth and Adolescence, 20,* 149–166.

Reiter, E. O., & Grumbach, M. M. (1982). Neuroendocrine control mechanisms and the onset of puberty. *Annual Review of Physiology, 44,* 595–613.

Rierdan, J., Koff, E., & Stubbs, M. L. (1989). A longitudinal analysis of body image as a predictor of the onset and persistence of adolescent girls' depression. *Journal of Early Adolescence, 9,* 454–466.

Robins, R. W., John, O. P., Caspi, A., Moffitt, T. E., & Stouthamer-Loeber, M. (1996). Resilient, overcontrolled, and undercontrolled boys: Three replicable personality types. *Journal of Personality and Social Psychology, 70,* 157–171.

Rohde, P., Lewinsohn, P. M., & Seeley, J. R. (1991). The comorbidity of unipolar depression: II. Comorbidity with other mental disorders in adolescents and adults. *Journal of Abnormal Psychology, 100,* 214–222.

Rubin, K. H., Bukowski, W., & Parker, J. G. (1998). Peer interactions, relationships, and groups. In W. Damon (Series Ed.), & N. Eisenberg (Vol. Ed.), *Handbook of child psychology: Vol. 4. Social, emotional, and personality development* (pp. 619–700). New York: Wiley.

Rubin, K. H., & Burgess, K. (2001). Social withdrawal and anxiety. In M. W. Vasey & M. R. Dadds (Eds.), *The developmental psychopathology of anxiety* (pp. 407–434). London: Oxford University Press.

Rudolf, K. D. (2002). Gender differences in emotional responses to interpersonal stress during adolescence. *Journal of Adolescent Health, 30*(Issue 4, Suppl. 1), 3–13.

Rueter, M. A., Scaramella, L., Wallace, L. E., & Conger, R. D. (1999). First onset of depressive or anxiety disorders predicted by the longitudinal course of internalizing symptoms and parent-adolescent disagreement. *Archives of General Psychiatry, 56,* 726–732.

Rutter, M. (1994). Continuities, transitions and turning points in development. In M. Rutter & D. F. Hay (Eds.), *Development through life: A handbook for clinicians* (pp. 1–25). London: Blackwell Scientific Publications.

Sameroff, A. (1975). Transactional models in early social relationships. *Human Development, 18,* 65–79.

Schwartz, J. A., Kaslow, N. J., Seeley, J. R., & Lewinsohn, P. M. (2000). Psychological, cognitive, and interpersonal correlates of attributional change in adolescents. *Journal of Clinical Child Psychology, 29,* 188–198.

Seligman, M. E. P. (1975). *Helplessness: On depression, development, and death.* San Francisco: Freeman.

Shaffer, D., Campbell, M., Cantwell, D., Bradley, S., Carlson, G., Cohen, D., et al. (1989). Child and adolescent psychiatric disorders in *DSM-IV:* Issues facing the working group. *Journal of the American Academy of Child and Adolescent Psychiatry, 28,* 830–835.

Shulman, S., & Collins, W. A. (Vol. Eds.). (1997). *New directions for child development: Vol. 78. Romantic relationships in adolescence: Developmental perspectives.* San Francisco, CA: Jossey-Bass.

Silberg, J., Pickles, A., Rutter, M., Hewitt, J., Simonoff, E., Maes, H., et al. (1999). The influence of genetic factors and life stress on depression among adolescent girls. *Archives of General Psychiatry, 56,* 225–232.

Simmons, R. G., & Blyth, D. A. (1987). *Moving into adolescence: The impact of pubertal change and school context.* New York: Aldine.

Stattin, H., & Magnusson, D. (1990). *Paths through life: Vol. 2. Pubertal maturation in female development.* Hillsdale, NJ: Erlbaum.

Steinberg, L. (2001). We know some things: Parent-adolescent relationships in retrospect and prospect. *Journal of Research on Adolescence, 11,* 1–19.

Steinberg, L., & Morris, A. S. (2001). Adolescent development. *Annual Review of Psychology, 52,* 83–110.

Stice, E., Presnell, K., & Bearman, S. K. (2001). Relation of early menarche to depression, eating disorders, substance abuse, and comorbid psychopathology among adolescent girls. *Developmental Psychology, 37,* 608–619.

Strober, M. (2001). Family-genetic aspects of juvenile affective disorders. In I. M. Goodyer (Ed.), *The depressed child and adolescent* (2nd ed., pp. 179–203). Cambridge, England: Cambridge University Press.

Suomi, S. J. (1999). Attachment in Rhesus monkeys. In J. Cassidy & P. R. Shaver (Eds.), *Handbook of attachment: Theory, research, and clinical applications* (pp. 181–197). New York: Guilford Press.

Taylor, S. E., Klein, L. C., Lewis, B. P., Gruenewald, T. L., Gurung, R. A. R., & Updegraff, J. A. (2000). Biobehavioral responses to stress in females: Tend-and-befriend, not fight-or-flight. *Psychological Review, 107,* 411–429.

Terry, E., & Manlove, J. (1999). Trends in sexual activity and contraceptive use among teens. *Child Trends Research Briefs.* Retrieved November 9, 2000, from http://www.childtrends.org/PDF/teentrends.pdf

Thompson, R. A. (1998). Early sociopersonality development. In W. Damon (Series Ed.) & N. Eisenberg (Vol. Ed.), *Handbook of child psychology: Vol. 4. Social, emotional, and personality development* (pp. 25–104). New York: Wiley.

Thompson, S. (1994). Changing lives, changing genres: Teenage girls' narratives about sex and romance, 1978–1986. In A. S. Rossi (Ed.), *Sexuality across the life course. The John D. and Catherine T. MacArthur Foundation series on mental health and development: Studies on successful midlife development* (pp. 209–232). Chicago: University of Chicago Press.

Twenge, J. M., & Nolen-Hoeksema, S. (2002). Age, gender, race, socioeconomic status, and birth cohort differences on the Children's Depression Inventory: A meta-analysis. *Journal of Abnormal Psychology, 111,* 578–588.

Vasey, M. W., & Ollendick, T. H. (2000). Anxiety. In A. J. Sameroff, M. Lewis, & S. M. Miller (Eds.), *Handbook of developmental psychopathology* (2nd ed., pp. 511–529). New York: Plenum Press.

Vega, W. A., Kolody, B., Aguilar-Gaxiola, S., Alderete, E., Catalano, R., & Caraveo-Anduaga, J. (1998). Lifetime prevalence of *DSM-III-R* psychiatric disorders among urban and rural Mexican Americans in California. *Archives of General Psychiatry, 55,* 771–778.

Wadsworth, M. E., & Compas, B. E. (2002). Coping with family conflict and economic strain: The adolescent perspective. *Journal of Research on Adolescence, 12,* 243–274.

Walker, E. F., Walder, D. J., & Reynolds, F. (2001). Developmental changes in cortisol secretion in normal and at-risk youth. *Development and Psychopathology, 13,* 721–732.

Way, N. (1996). Between experiences of betrayal and desire: Close friendships among urban adolescents. In B. J. R. Leadbeater & N. Way (Eds.), *Urban girls: Resisting stereotypes, creating identities* (pp. 173–192). New York: New York University Press.

Weissman, M. M., Fendrich, M., Warner, V., & Wickramaratne, P. (1992). Incidence of psychiatric disorder in offspring at high and low risk for depression. *Journal of the American Academy of Child & Adolescent Psychiatry, 31,* 640–648.

Weissman, M. M., Gammon, G. D., John, K., Merikangas, K. R., Prusoff, B. A., & Sholomskas, D. (1987). Children of depressed parents: Increased psychopathology and early onset of major depression. *Archives of General Psychiatry, 44,* 847–853.

Zahn-Waxler, C., Klimes-Dougan, B., & Slattery, M. J. (2000). Internalizing problems of childhood and adolescence: Prospects, pitfalls, and progress in understanding the development of anxiety and depression. *Development and Psychopathology, 12,* 443–466.

Chapter 20

CONDUCT DISORDER, AGGRESSION, AND DELINQUENCY

David P. Farrington

Within the limits of a short chapter, it is obviously impossible to provide an exhaustive review of all aspects of conduct disorder, aggression, and delinquency in adolescence. Many extensive book-length reviews have examined these topics (e.g. Connor, 2002; Hill & Maughan, 2001; Rutter, Giller, & Hagell, 1998). In this chapter, I am very selective in focusing on what seem to me the most important findings obtained in the highest quality studies. I particularly focus on risk factors discovered in prospective longitudinal surveys and on successful interventions demonstrated in randomized experiments. (For descriptions of longitudinal surveys, see Kalb, Farrington, & Loeber, 2001; for reviews of risk factors, see Hawkins et al., 1998; for reviews of intervention studies, see Farrington & Welsh, in press.) My emphasis is mainly on young people aged 10–17 and on research carried out in North America, Great Britain, or similar Western democracies. Most research has been carried out with males, but studies of females are included when they are applicable (Moffitt, Caspi, Rutter, & Silva, 2001). My focus is on substantive results rather than methodological and theoretical issues.

In general, all types of antisocial behavior tend to coexist and are intercorrelated. I have chosen to concentrate on conduct disorder, aggression, and delinquency because they are the most important types of adolescent antisocial behaviors studied in different fields: conduct disorder in clinical psychology and in child and adolescent psychiatry, aggression in developmental psychology, and delinquency in criminology and sociology. Although there is sometimes inadequate communication between different fields, it should be borne in mind that these behaviors are logically and empirically related, so that risk factors and successful interventions that apply to one of these types of antisocial behavior are also likely to apply to the other two types. Before reviewing risk factors and successful interventions, I briefly review the definition, measurement, and epidemiology of each type of antisocial behavior.

CONDUCT DISORDER

Definition and Measurement

Robins (1999) has traced the development of conduct disorder (CD) definitions over time. According to the *Diagnostic and Statistical Manual of Mental Disorders–Fourth*

Edition (*DSM–IV;* American Psychiatric Association, 1994, p. 85), the essential feature of CD is a repetitive and persistent pattern of behavior in which the basic rights of others or major age-appropriate societal norms are violated. Also, the disturbance of behavior must cause clinically significant impairment in social, academic, or occupational functioning. According to the *DSM-IV* diagnostic criteria, 3 or more out of 15 specified behaviors, including aggression to people or animals, property destruction, stealing or lying, and violating rules (e.g. truanting, running away), must be present for CD to be diagnosed. The prevalence of CD is lower if evidence of impairment is required as well as specified behaviors (Romano, Tremblay, Vitaro, Zoccolillo, & Pagani, 2001). Frequent, serious, persistent behaviors that are shown in several different settings are most likely to be defined as symptoms of a disorder.

CD can be diagnosed by a clinician in a psychiatric interview with a child and the parents, or it can be assessed using a structured interview administered by a nonclinician, such as the Diagnostic Interview Schedule for Children (DISC; Shaffer et al., 1996). Childhood antisocial behavior can also be assessed using rating scales or behavior problem checklists such as the Child Behavior Checklist (CBCL), typically completed by a parent, and its associated Teacher Report Form (TRF) and Youth Self-Report (YSR; Achenbach, 1993). These tests yield broadband scales such as externalizing behavior and more specific scales of aggression, delinquency, and hyperactivity, with impressive cross-cultural replicability (Achenbach, Verhulst, Baron, & Althaus, 1987). The aggression and delinquency scales are highly correlated (Pakiz, Reinherz, & Frost, 1992). The delinquency scale of the CBCL is closely related to the diagnosis of CD on the DISC (Kasius, Ferdinand, van den Berg, & Verhulst, 1997).

Prevalence, Onset, and Continuity

Nottelman and Jensen (1995) have usefully summarized findings obtained in epidemiological studies of CD. One problem in interpreting prevalence results concerns the time period to which they refer, which may be 6 months, 12 months, or cumulatively over a period of years. Prevalence rates are greater for males than for females and vary at different ages. Also, prevalence rates change as the *DSM* definitions change (Lahey et al., 1990). Space here is not sufficient to review measurement issues or changes in prevalence over time (e.g. Achenbach, Dumenci, & Rescorla, 2003).

The instantaneous (as opposed to cumulative) prevalence of CD is about 6–16% of adolescent boys and about 2–9% of adolescent girls (Mandel, 1997). For example, in the Ontario Child Health Study in Canada, the 6-month prevalence of CD at age 12–16 was 10% for boys and 4% for girls (Offord et al., 1987). In the New York State longitudinal study, the 12-month prevalence of CD for boys was 16% at both ages 10–13 and 14–16 (Cohen, Cohen, & Kasen, 1993). For girls, it was 4% at age 10–13 and 9% at age 14–16. Zoccolillo (1993) suggested that CD criteria may be less applicable to the behavior of girls than to the behavior of boys and hence that gender-specific CD criteria should be developed.

It is not entirely clear how the prevalence of CD varies over the adolescent age range, and this variation may depend on how CD is measured. For example, in the MECA study, which was a cross-sectional survey of 1,285 adolescents aged 9–17, the DISC was completed by parents and by adolescents (Lahey et al., 2000). The prevalence of CD (in the previous 6 months) did not vary significantly over this age range according to parents, but it increased with age according to adolescent self-reports. According to adolescents, the prevalence of CD increased for boys from 1.3% at age 9–11 to 6% at age 12–14 and 11% at age 15–17. For girls, prevalence increased from 0.5% at age 9–11 to 3% at age 12–14 and 4% at age 15–17. Hence, the male: female ratio for CD was greatest at age 15–17.

In the longitudinal Great Smoky Mountains Study of Youth, Maughan, Pickles, Rowe, Costello, and Angold (2000) investigated developmental trajectories of aggressive and nonaggressive conduct problems. They found that there were three categories of adolescents between ages 9 and 16, with stable high conduct problems, stable low conduct problems, and decreasing conduct problems. Boys were more likely to have stable high or decreasing conduct problems over time, whereas girls were more likely to have stable low conduct problems over time.

DSM-IV has classified CD into childhood-onset versus adolescent-onset types. Childhood-onset CD typically begins with the emergence of oppositional defiant disorder (ODD), characterized by temper tantrums and defiant, irritable, argumentative, and annoying behavior (Hinshaw, Lahey, & Hart, 1993). Mean or median ages of onset for specific CD symptoms have been provided by various researchers, but they depend on the age of the child at measurement and the consequent cumulative prevalence of the symptoms. Retrospectively in the Epidemiological Catchment Area project, Robins (1989) reported that the mean age of onset (before 15) for stealing was 10 for males and females, and for vandalism it was 11 for males and females. However, ages of onset were generally later for girls than for boys.

Although exact onset ages varied, some CD symptoms consistently appeared before others. This observation led Loeber et al. (1993) to postulate a model of three developmental pathways in disruptive childhood behavior. The overt pathway began with minor aggression (e.g. bullying) and progressed to physical fighting and eventually serious violence. The covert pathway began with minor nonviolent behavior (e.g. shoplifting) and progressed to vandalism and eventually serious property crime. The authority conflict pathway began with stubborn behavior and progressed to defiance and eventually authority avoidance (e.g. running away). Typically, progression in the overt pathway was accompanied by simultaneous progression in the covert pathway. Tolan and Gorman-Smith (1998) found that the hypothesized pathways were largely confirmed in the U.S. National Youth Survey and the Chicago Youth Development Study.

There is considerable continuity or stability in CD, at least over a few years. In the Ontario Child Health Study, 45% of children aged 4–12 who were CD in 1983 still had CD 4 years later, compared with only 5% of those who had no disorder in 1983 (Offord et al., 1992). CD was more stable than ADHD or emotional disorder. Also, stability was greater for children aged 8–12 (60% persisting) than for children aged 4–7 (25% persisting). However, the interpretation of results was complicated by comorbidity; 35% of those with CD in 1983 had ADHD 4 years later, and conversely 34% of those with ADHD in 1983 had CD 4 years later. In a Dutch follow-up study using the CBCL, Verhulst and van der Ende (1995) found a significant correlation (.54) between externalizing scores over an 8-year period spanning adolescence.

Similar results have been reported by other researchers. In their New York State study, Cohen, Cohen, and Brook (1993) found that 43% of CD children aged 9–18 were still CD 2.5 years later (compared with 10% of non-CD children). There were no significant age or gender differences in stability, but stability increased with the severity of CD. In the Developmental Trends Study, Lahey et al. (1995) reported that half of CD boys aged 7–12 still had CD 3 years later. Persistence was predicted by parental antisocial personality disorder and by the boy's low verbal IQ, but not by age, socioeconomic status (SES), or ethnicity.

AGGRESSION

Definition and Measurement

Aggression is defined as behavior that is intended to and actually harms another person (Coie & Dodge, 1998). Many different types of aggression have been distinguished, including physical versus verbal aggression, reactive versus proactive aggression, and hostile versus instrumental aggression. Bullying is one of the most clearly defined types of aggression, and it has usually been studied in schools (Farrington, 1993b). Its definition typically includes physical, verbal, or psychological attack or intimidation that is intended to cause fear, distress, or harm to a victim; an imbalance of power, with the more powerful child oppressing the less powerful one; and repeated incidents between the same children over a prolonged time period. Aggression is measured in a variety of ways, including self-reports, parent reports, teacher ratings, peer ratings, and school records. Systematic observation is also used (e.g. Pepler & Craig, 1995). It is important to investigate the concordance of results obtained by these different methods, but these types of measurement issues are generally not discussed in this chapter. Many aggressive acts committed by adolescents are not witnessed by teachers, parents, or peers. For example, in a Dublin study, O'Moore and Hillery (1989) found that teachers identified only 24% of self-reported bullies. In an observational study in Canada, Craig, Pepler, and Atlas (2000) discovered that the frequency of bullying was twice as high in the playground as in the classroom. However, Stephenson and Smith (1989) in England reported that teacher and peer nominations of which children were involved in bullying were highly correlated (.8).

Prevalence, Onset, and Continuity

The incidence of physical aggression (hitting) increases up to age 2 and then decreases between ages 2 and 4, when verbal aggression increases (Coie & Dodge, 1998). Most aggression at the preschool ages is directed against siblings or peers. The incidence of physical aggression continues to decrease in the elementary school years; as language and abstract thinking improve, children increasingly use words rather than aggressive actions to resolve conflicts, and internal inhibitions and the ability to delay gratification also improve.

In a cross-sectional survey of a large representative sample of Canadian children, Tremblay et al. (1999) found that the prevalence of hitting, kicking, and biting (as reported by mothers) decreased steadily from age 2 to age 11. Furthermore, in the

Montreal longitudinal study, the prevalence of teacher-rated physical aggression of boys decreased steadily from age 6 to age 15. Nagin and Tremblay (1999) identified four different trajectories of aggression in the Montreal sample: consistently high, consistently low, high-decreasing, and moderate-decreasing. It is interesting to note that in a cross-sectional survey of a large sample of American children (Fitzpatrick, 1997), the prevalence of self-reported physical fighting decreased from Grade 3 (age 8) to Grade 12 (age 17). Also, in the Pittsburgh Youth Study, the prevalence of parent-rated physical aggression of boys decreased between ages 10 and 17 (Loeber & Hay, 1997). Of course, it is possible that the seriousness of aggression (e.g. according to injuries to participants) may increase between ages 10 and 17. Criminal violence is discussed in the delinquency section.

The prevalence of bullying is often very high. For example, in the Dublin study of O'Moore and Hillery (1989), 58% of boys and 38% of girls said that they had ever bullied someone. The prevalence is lower when bullying is restricted to sometimes or more often this term. With this definition, 11% of boys and 2.5% of girls were bullies in secondary schools in Norway (Olweus, 1991); and 8% of boys and 4% of girls were bullies in secondary schools in Sheffield, England (Whitney & Smith, 1991). The prevalence of bullying decreases with age from elementary to secondary schools.

Gender differences in aggression are not very great in infancy and toddlerhood (Loeber & Hay, 1997), but they increase from the preschool years onwards. Boys use more physical and verbal aggression, both hostile and instrumental. However, indirect or relational aggression—spreading malicious rumors, not talking to other children, excluding peers from group activities—is more characteristic of girls (Bjorkvist, Lagerspetz, & Kaukiainen, 1992; Crick & Grotpeter, 1995). Gender differences in aggression tend to increase in adolescence, as female physical aggression decreases more than male physical aggression.

There is significant continuity in aggression over time. In a classic review, Olweus (1979) found that the average stability coefficient (correlation) for male aggression was .68 in 16 surveys covering time periods of up to 21 years. Huesmann, Eron, Lefkowitz, and Walder (1984) in New York State reported that peer-rated aggression at age 8 significantly predicted peer-rated aggression at age 18 and self-reported aggression at age 30. Female aggression is also significantly stable over time; stability coefficients were similar for males and females in the Carolina Longitudinal Study (Cairns & Cairns, 1994, p. 63). However, Loeber and Stouthamer-Loeber (1998) pointed out that a high (relative) stability of aggressiveness was not incompatible with high rates of desistance from physical aggression (absolute change) from childhood to adulthood.

Olweus (1979) argued that aggression was a stable personality trait. However, recent theories of aggression place most emphasis on cognitive processes. For example, Huesmann and Eron (1989) put forward a cognitive-script model, in which aggressive behavior depends on stored behavioral repertoires (cognitive scripts) that have been learned during early development. In response to environmental cues, possible cognitive scripts are retrieved and evaluated. The choice of aggressive scripts, which prescribe aggressive behavior, depends on the past history of rewards and punishments and on the extent to which adolescents are influenced by immediate gratification as opposed to long-term consequences. According to this theory, the persisting trait of aggressiveness is a collection of well-learned aggressive scripts that are resistant to change. A similar theory was proposed by Dodge (1991). There is not space here to discuss other cognitive or decision-making theories of antisocial behavior.

DELINQUENCY

Definition and Measurement

Delinquency is defined according to acts prohibited by the criminal law, such as theft, burglary, robbery, violence, vandalism, and drug use. There are many problems in using legal definitions of delinquency. For example, the boundary between what is legal and what is illegal may be poorly defined and subjective, as when school bullying gradually escalates into criminal violence. Legal categories may be so wide that they include acts that are behaviorally quite different, as when robbery ranges from armed bank holdups carried out by gangs of masked men to thefts of small amounts of money perpetrated by one schoolchild on another. Legal definitions rely on the concept of intent, which is difficult to measure reliably and validly, rather than on the behavioral criteria preferred by social scientists. Also, legal definitions change over time. However, their main advantage is that because they have been adopted by most delinquency researchers, their use makes it possible to compare and summarize results obtained in different projects.

Delinquency is commonly measured either using official records of arrests or convictions or using self-reports of offending. The advantages and disadvantages of official records and self-reports are to some extent complementary. In general, official records include the worst offenders and the worst offenses, whereas self-reports include more of the normal range of delinquent activity. The worst offenders may be missing from samples interviewed in self-report studies (Cernkovich, Giordano, & Pugh, 1985). Self-reports have the advantage of including undetected offenses but the disadvantages of concealment and forgetting. By normally accepted psychometric criteria of validity, self-reports are valid (Junger-Tas & Marshall, 1999). For example, self-reported delinquency predicted later convictions among undetected boys in the Cambridge Study in Delinquent Development, which is a prospective longitudinal survey of 400 London boys (Farrington, 1989b). In the Pittsburgh Youth Study, the seriousness of self-reported delinquency predicted later court referrals (Farrington, Loeber, Stouthamer-Loeber, van Kammen, & Schmidt, 1996). However, predictive validity was enhanced by combining self-report, parent, and teacher information about offending.

The key issue is whether the same results are obtained with both self-reports and official records. For example, if both show a link between parental supervision and delinquency, it is likely that supervision is related to delinquent behavior (rather than to any biases in measurement). Generally, the worst offenders according to self-reports (taking account of frequency and seriousness) tend also to be the worst offenders according to official records (Huizinga & Elliott, 1986). In the Cambridge Study, the predictors and correlates of official and self-reported delinquency were very similar (Farrington, 1992c).

Prevalence, Onset, and Continuity

Even when measured by convictions, the cumulative prevalence of delinquency is substantial. In the Cambridge Study, 20% of males were convicted before age 17. The annual prevalence of convictions increased to a peak at age 17 and then declined (Farrington, 1992a). It was 1.5% at age 10, 5% at age 13, 11% at age 17, 6% at age 22, and 3% at age 30. According to national figures for England and Wales (Prime, White, Liriano, & Patel, 2001), about 15% of males and 3% of females born in 1953–1963 were convicted up to age 17 for a standard list offense (i.e., more serious offense; e.g., excluding traffic infractions and drunkenness).

Cumulative prevalence is also substantial in the United States. In a longitudinal study of more than 27,000 persons born in Philadelphia in 1958, Tracy, Wolfgang, and Figlio (1985) found that 33% of males and 14% of females were arrested before age 18 for nontraffic offenses. The male: female ratio was greater for more serious (crime index) offenses: 18% of males versus 4% of females.

National U.S. figures show that in 2001, the male: female ratio for arrests of persons under 18 was 4.5 for index violence and 2.1 for index property offenses (Federal Bureau of Investigation [FBI], 2002, Table 33). The peak age for male index property offenses was about 16–18, whereas male index violence peaked a little later, at ages 18–19 (FBI, 2002, Table 39). The peak age for female index property offenses was about 15–17, whereas female index violence peaked later, at ages 19–21 (FBI, 2002, Table 40). The male: female ratio for crime index offenses increased from 2.1 at age 13–14 to 2.8 at age 17.

The prevalence of delinquency according to self-reports is even higher, of course. In the large-scale Denver, Rochester, and Pittsburgh longitudinal studies, the annual prevalence of street crimes (burglary, serious theft, robbery, aggravated assault, etc.) increased from less than 15% at age 11 to almost 50% at age 17 (Huizinga, Loeber, & Thornberry, 1993). Similarly, in the U.S. National Youth Survey, the annual prevalence of self-reported violence increased to a peak of 28% of males at age 17 and 12% of females at ages 15–17 (Elliott, 1994). Annual prevalence rates for specific acts have been provided by Loeber, Farrington, Stouthamer-Loeber, and van Kammen (1998, p. 94). For example, shoplifting increased from 10% of boys at age 10 to 19% at age 13. Carrying a weapon increased from 12% of boys at age 10 to 23% at age 13.

The age distributions of CD, aggression, and delinquency seem somewhat inconsistent. Although the incidence of physical aggression (hitting and kicking) decreases from age 10 to age 17, the prevalence of CD and violent and property offenses generally increases over this age range. It may be that most children grow out of minor types of antisocial behavior, perhaps because of increasing internal inhibitions inculcated by parents, but that more serious types increase during adolescence, perhaps because of the increasing importance of peer influence (Farrington, 1986).

Criminal career research using official records of delinquency generally shows a peak age of onset between 13 and 16. In the Cambridge study, the peak age of onset was at 14; 5% of the males were first convicted at that age (Farrington, 1992a). The onset curves up to age 25 of working-class males in London and Stockholm were quite similar (Farrington & Wikström, 1994). Sequences of onsets were studied for Montreal delinquents by LeBlanc and Frechette (1989). They discovered that shoplifting and vandalism tended to occur before adolescence (average age of onset = 11), burglary and motor vehicle theft in adolescence (average onset 14–15), and sex offenses and drug trafficking in the later teenage years (average onset 17–19).

In the Cambridge Study, the males first convicted at the earliest ages (10–13) tended to become the most persistent offenders, committing an average of nine offenses that led to convictions in an average criminal career lasting 12 years up to age 40 (Farrington, Lambert, & West, 1998). Similarly, Farrington and Wikström (1994), using official records in Stockholm, and LeBlanc and Frechette (1989) in Montreal, using both self-reports and official records, showed that the duration of criminal careers decreased with increasing age of onset. It is generally true that an early age of onset of antisocial behavior predicts a long and serious antisocial career (Loeber & LeBlanc, 1990).

Moffitt (1993a) distinguished between "life-course-persistent" offenders, who had an early onset and a long criminal career, and "adolescence-limited" offenders, who started later and had a short criminal career. Her analyses in the Dunedin (New Zealand) study generally confirmed the features of her postulated model (Moffitt, Caspi, Dickson, Silva, & Stanton, 1996). Childhood- and adolescent-onset cases differed in temperament as early as three years of age. Life-course-persistent and adolescence-limited offenders were identified using conviction records in the Cambridge study (Nagin, Farrington, & Moffitt, 1995). According to self-reports, however, the apparent reformation of the adolescence-limited offenders was less than complete. At age 32, they continued to drink heavily, use drugs, get into fights, and commit criminal acts.

Several researchers have investigated factors that predict early- versus late-onset offending. In the Cambridge study, the strongest predictors were rarely spending leisure time with the father, troublesome school behavior, authoritarian parents, and psychomotor impulsivity (Farrington & Hawkins, 1991). In the Pittsburgh Youth Study, the strongest correlates of early onset were physical aggression, ODD, ADHD, truancy, peer delinquency, and poor parental supervision (Loeber, Stouthamer-Loeber, van Kammen, & Farrington, 1991). A great deal of criminological research has been conducted on other criminal career features such as desistance, duration of careers, escalation, and deescalation (Farrington, 1997a), but space is not sufficient to review them here.

Generally, there is significant continuity between delinquency in one age range and delinquency in another. In the Cambridge study, nearly three quarters (73%) of those convicted as juveniles at age 10–16 were reconvicted at age 17–24, in comparison with only 16% of those not convicted as juveniles (Farrington, 1992a). Nearly half (45%) of those convicted as juveniles were reconvicted at age 25–32, in comparison with only 8% of those not convicted as juveniles. Furthermore, this continuity over time did not merely reflect continuity in police reaction to delinquency. For 10 specified offenses, the significant continuity between offending in one age range and offending in a later age range held for self-reports as well as for official convictions (Farrington, 1989b).

Other studies show similar continuity in delinquency. For example, Sweden, Stattin and Magnusson (1991) reported that nearly 70% of males registered for crime before age 15 were registered again between ages 15 and 20, and nearly 60% were registered between ages 21 and 29. Also, the number of juvenile offenses is an effective predictor of the number of adult offenses (Wolfgang, Thornberry, & Figlio, 1987). There was considerable continuity in offending between the ages of 10 and 25 in both London and Stockholm (Farrington & Wikström, 1994).

COMORBIDITY AND VERSATILITY

In general, CD adolescents tend also to be aggressive and delinquent. In the Christchurch study in New Zealand, Fergusson and Horwood (1995) reported that 90% of children with three or more CD symptoms at age 15 were self-reported frequent offenders at age 16 (compared with only 17% of children with no CD symptoms). In the Denver Youth Survey, Huizinga and Jakob-Chien (1998) found that about half of male and female self-reported violent offenders had a large number of externalizing symptoms on the CBCL.

Numerous studies show that aggression in childhood and adolescence predicts later delinquency and crime. For example, Pulkkinen (1987) in Finland followed up nearly 400 children between ages 8 and 20 and found that offensive aggression (attacking or teasing without reason) at age 14 predicted officially recorded violent crimes up to age 20. In the Cambridge study, teacher ratings of aggression at ages 12–14 (disobedient, difficult to discipline, unduly rough, quarrelsome and aggressive, overcompetitive) significantly predicted self-reported violence at age 16–18 (physical fighting) and convictions for violence up to age 32 (Farrington, 1991).

Generally, delinquents are versatile rather than specialized in their offending. In the Cambridge study, 86% of violent offenders also had convictions for nonviolent offenses (Farrington, 1991). Violent and nonviolent but equally frequent offenders were very similar in their childhood and adolescent features in the Oregon Youth Study (Capaldi & Patterson, 1996). Studies of transition matrices summarizing the probability of one type of offense following another show that a small degree of specificity is superimposed on a great deal of generality in juvenile delinquency (Farrington, Synder, & Finnegan, 1988).

The Cambridge study shows that delinquency is associated with many other types of antisocial behavior. The boys who were convicted before age 18 (most commonly for offenses of dishonesty, such as burglary and theft) were significantly more antisocial than were the nondelinquents on almost every factor that was investigated at that age (West & Farrington, 1977). The convicted delinquents drank more beer, they got drunk more often, and they were more likely to say that drink made them violent. They smoked more cigarettes, they had started smoking at an earlier age, and they were more likely to be heavy gamblers. They were more likely to have been convicted for minor motoring offenses, to have driven after drinking at least 10 units of alcohol (e.g. 5 pints of beer), and to have been injured in road accidents.

The delinquents were more likely to have taken prohibited drugs such as marijuana or LSD, although few of them had convictions for drug offenses. Also, they were more likely to have had sexual intercourse—especially with a variety of different girls and especially beginning at an early age—but they were less likely to use contraceptives. The delinquents were more likely to go out in the evenings and were especially likely to spend time hanging about on the street. They tended to go around in groups of four or more and were more likely to be involved in group violence or vandalism. They were much more likely to have been involved in physical fights, to have started fights, to have carried weapons, and to have used weapons in fights. They were also more likely to express aggressive and antiestablishment attitudes on a questionnaire (negative to police, school, rich people, and civil servants).

Because CD, aggression, and delinquency are overlapping problems, they tend to have the same risk factors, and interventions that are effective in reducing one of these types of antisocial behavior tend also to be effective in reducing the other two types.

RISK FACTORS

Longitudinal data are required to establish the time ordering of risk factors and antisocial behavior. It is extremely difficult in correlational or cross-sectional studies to draw valid conclusions about cause and effect. Similarly, because of the difficulty of establishing causal effects of factors that vary only between individuals (e.g., gender and ethnicity) and because such factors have no practical implications for intervention (e.g., it is not practicable to change males into females), unchanging variables are not reviewed here. In any case, their effects on offending are usually explained by reference to other modifiable factors. For example, gender differences in offending have been explained on the basis of different socialization methods used by parents with boys and girls or of different opportunities for offending of males and females. According to Rowe, Vazsonyi, and Flannery (1995), risk factors for delinquency are similar for boys and girls, but boys are generally exposed to more risk factors or higher levels of risk factors.

Risk factors are discussed one by one; additive, interactive, independent, or sequential effects are not exhaustively reviewed, although these issues are important. Protective factors and resilience are not discussed because they are covered in the chapter by Bruce Compas. Because of limitations of space and because of their limited relevance for psychosocial interventions, biological factors are not reviewed. For example, one of the most replicable findings in the literature is that antisocial and violent adolescents tend to have low resting heart rates (Raine, 1993, p.167). In the Cambridge study, resting heart rate at age 18 was significantly related to convictions for violence and to self-reported violence, independently of all other variables (Farrington, 1997b). Little space is also here to review theories of the causal mechanisms by which risk factors might have their effects on antisocial behavior.

It is plausible to suggest that risk factors influence the potential for aggression and antisocial behavior and that whether this potential becomes the actuality in any situation depends on immediate situational factors such as opportunities and victims. In other words, antisocial acts depend on the interaction between the individual and the environment (Farrington, 1998). However, space is not sufficient here to review immediate situational influences or situational crime prevention (Clarke, 1995).

Temperament and Personality

Personality traits such as sociability or impulsiveness describe broad predispositions to respond in certain ways, and temperament is basically the childhood equivalent of personality. Temperament is clearly influenced by biological factors but is not itself a biological variable like heart rate (in my view). The modern study of child temperament began with the New York longitudinal study of Chess and Thomas (1984). Children in their first 5 years of life were rated on temperamental dimensions by their parents, and these dimensions were combined into three broad categories of easy, difficult, and "slow to warm up" temperament. Having a difficult temperament at ages 3–4 (frequent irritability, low amenability and adaptability, irregular habits) predicted poor psychiatric adjustment at ages 17–24.

Unfortunately, it was not very clear exactly what a difficult temperament meant in practice, and this method of categorization risked tautological conclusions (e.g., because the criteria for difficult temperament and ODD were overlapping). Later researchers have used more specific dimensions of temperament. For example, Kagan (1989) in Boston classified children as inhibited (shy or fearful) or uninhibited at age 21 months and found that they remained significantly stable on this classification up to age 7 years. Furthermore, the uninhibited children at age 21 months significantly tended to be identified as aggressive at age 13 years, according to self and parent reports (Schwartz, Snidman, & Kagan, 1996).

Important results on the link between childhood temperament and later offending have been obtained in the Dunedin longitudinal study in New Zealand (Caspi, 2000). Temperament at age 3 years was rated by observing the child's behavior during a testing session. The most important dimension of temperament was being undercontrolled (restless, impulsive, with poor attention), and this characteristic predicted aggression, self-reported delinquency, and convictions at ages 18–21.

Studies using classic personality inventories such as the Minnesota Multiphasic Personality Inventory (MMPI) and California Psychological Inventory (CPI; Wilson & Herrnstein, 1985, pp. 186–198) often seem to produce essentially tautological results, such as that delinquents are low on socialization. The Eysenck personality questionnaire has yielded more promising results (Eysenck, 1996). In the Cambridge study, those high on both Extraversion and Neuroticism tended to be juvenile self-reported delinquents, adult official offenders, and adult self-reported offenders, but not juvenile official delinquents (Farrington, Biron, & LeBlanc, 1982). Furthermore, these relationships held independently of other variables such as low family income, low intelligence, and poor parental child-rearing behavior. However, when individual items of the personality questionnaire were studied, it was clear that the significant relationships were caused by the items measuring impulsiveness (e.g., doing things quickly without stopping to think).

Impulsiveness

Impulsiveness is the most crucial personality dimension that predicts antisocial behavior (Lipsey & Derzon, 1998). Unfortunately, a bewildering number of constructs refer to a poor ability to control behavior. They include impulsiveness, hyperactivity, restlessness, clumsiness, failure to consider consequences before acting, a poor ability to plan ahead, short time horizons, low self-control, sensation seeking, risk taking, and a poor ability to delay gratification.

Many studies show that hyperactivity predicts later offending. In the Copenhagen Perinatal Project, hyperactivity (restlessness and poor concentration) at ages 11–13 significantly predicted arrests for violence up to age 22, especially among boys experiencing delivery complications (Brennan, Mednick, & Mednick, 1993). Similarly, in the Orebro longitudinal study in Sweden, hyperactivity at age 13 predicted police-recorded violence up to age 26. The highest rate of violence was among males with both motor restlessness and concentration difficulties (15%), compared to 3% of the remainder (Klinteberg, Andersson, Magnusson, & Stattin, 1993).

In the Cambridge study, boys nominated by teachers as lacking in concentration or restless; those nominated by parents, peers, or teachers as the most daring or taking most risks; and those who were the most impulsive on psychomotor tests at age 8–10 all tended to become offenders later in life. Daring behavior, poor concentration, and restlessness all predicted both official convictions and self-reported delinquency, and daring behavior was consistently one of the best independent predictors (Farrington, 1992c). It is interesting to note that Farrington, Loeber, and van Kammen (1990) found that hyperactivity predicted juvenile offending independently of conduct problems. Lynam (1996) proposed that boys with both hyperactivity and CD were most at risk of chronic offending and psychopathy, and Lynam (1998) presented evidence in favor of this hypothesis from the Pittsburgh Youth Study.

The most extensive research on different measures of impulsiveness was carried out in the Pittsburgh Youth Study by White et al. (1994). The measures that were most strongly related to self-reported delinquency at ages 10 and 13 were teacher-rated impulsiveness (e.g., acts without thinking), self-reported impulsiveness, self-reported undercontrol (e.g., is unable to delay gratification), motor restlessness (from videotaped observations), and psychomotor impulsiveness (on the Trail Making Test). Generally, the verbal behavior rating tests produced stronger relationships with offending than did the psychomotor performance tests, suggesting that cognitive impulsiveness was more relevant than was behavioral impulsiveness (based on test performance). Tests measuring future time perception and delay of gratification were only weakly related to self-reported delinquency. Lynam and Moffitt (1995) concluded that low IQ and impulsiveness were independent risk factors for delinquency.

Low IQ and Low Educational Achievement

Low IQ and low school achievement are important predictors of CD, delinquency, and adolescent antisocial behavior (Moffitt, 1993b). In an English epidemiological study of 13-year-old twins, low IQ of the child predicted conduct problems independently of social class and of the IQ of parents (Goodman, Simonoff, & Stevenson, 1995). Low school achievement was a strong correlate of CD in the Pittsburgh Youth Study (Loeber et al., 1998). In both the Ontario Child Health Study (Offord, Boyle, & Racine, 1989) and the New York State longitudinal study (Velez, Johnson, & Cohen, 1989), failing a grade predicted CD. Underachievement, defined according to a discrepancy between IQ and school achievement, is also characteristic of CD children, as Frick et al. (1991) reported in the Developmental Trends Study.

Low IQ and low school achievement also predict youth violence. In the Philadelphia Biosocial project (Denno, 1990), low verbal and performance IQ at ages 4 and 7 and low scores on the California Achievement Test at age 13–14 (vocabulary, comprehension, math, language, spelling) all predicted arrests for violence up to age 22. In Project

Metropolitan in Copenhagen, low IQ at age 12 significantly predicted police-recorded violence between ages 15 and 22. The link between low IQ and violence was strongest among lower-class boys (Hogh & Wolf, 1983).

Low IQ measured in the first few years of life predicts later delinquency. In a prospective longitudinal survey of about 120 Stockholm males, low IQ measured at age 3 significantly predicted officially recorded offending up to age 30 (Stattin & Klackenberg-Larsson, 1993). Frequent offenders (with 4 or more offenses) had an average IQ of 88 at age 3, whereas nonoffenders had an average IQ of 101. All of these results held up after controlling for social class. Similarly, low IQ at age 4 predicted arrests up to age 27 in the Perry preschool project (Schweinhart, Barnes, & Weikart, 1993) and court delinquency up to age 17 in the Collaborative Perinatal Project (Lipsitt, Buka, & Lipsitt, 1990).

In the Cambridge study, twice as many of the boys scoring 90 or less on a nonverbal IQ test (Raven's Progressive Matrices) at ages 8–10 were convicted as juveniles as were the remainder (West & Farrington, 1973). However, it was difficult to disentangle low IQ from low school achievement because they were highly intercorrelated and because both predicted delinquency. Low nonverbal IQ predicted juvenile self-reported delinquency to almost exactly the same degree as it predicted juvenile convictions (Farrington, 1992c), suggesting that the link between low IQ and delinquency was not caused by the less intelligent boys' having a greater probability of being caught. Also, low IQ and low school achievement predicted offending independently of other variables such as low family income and large family size (Farrington, 1990) and were important predictors of bullying (Farrington, 1993b).

Low IQ may lead to delinquency through the intervening factor of school failure. The association between school failure and delinquency has been demonstrated repeatedly in longitudinal surveys. In the Pittsburgh Youth Study, Lynam, Moffitt, and Stouthamer-Loeber (1993) concluded that low verbal IQ led to school failure and subsequently to self-reported delinquency, but only for African-American boys. Another plausible explanatory factor underlying the link between low IQ and delinquency is the ability to manipulate abstract concepts. Children who are lacking in this skill tend to do badly in IQ tests and in school achievement, and they also tend to commit offenses, mainly because of their poor ability to foresee the consequences of their offending. Delinquents often do better on nonverbal performance IQ tests, such as object assembly and block design, than they do on verbal IQ tests (Moffitt, 1993b), suggesting that they find it easier to deal with concrete objects than with abstract concepts. Similarly, Rogeness (1994) concluded that CD children had deficits in verbal IQ but not in performance IQ.

Impulsiveness, attention problems, low IQ, and low school achievement could all be linked to deficits in the executive functions of the brain, located in the frontal lobes. These executive functions include sustaining attention and concentration, abstract reasoning, concept formation, goal formulation, anticipation and planning, programming and initiation of purposive sequences of motor behavior, effective self-monitoring and self-awareness of behavior, and inhibition of inappropriate or impulsive behaviors (Moffitt & Henry, 1991). It is interesting to note that in the Montreal longitudinal-experimental study, a measure of executive functioning based on cognitive-neuropsychological tests at age 14 was the strongest neuropsychological discriminator between violent and nonviolent boys (Seguin, Pihl, Harden, Tremblay, & Boulerice, 1995). This relationship held independently of a measure of family adversity (based on parental age at first birth, parental education level, broken family, and low SES).

Child Rearing and Child Abuse

In the Pittsburgh Youth Study, poor parental supervision was an important risk factor for CD (Loeber et al., 1998). Poor maternal supervision and low persistence in discipline predicted CD in the Developmental Trends Study (Frick et al., 1992) but not independently of parental antisocial personality disorder. Rothbaum and Weisz (1994) carried out a meta-analysis and concluded that parental reinforcement, parental reasoning, parental punishments, and parental responsiveness to the child were all related to externalizing child behavior.

Of all child-rearing factors, poor parental supervision is the strongest and most replicable predictor of delinquency (Smith & Stern, 1997), and harsh or punitive discipline (involving physical punishment) is also an important predictor (Haapasalo & Pokela, 1999). The classic longitudinal studies by McCord (1979) in Boston and Robins (1979) in St. Louis show that poor parental supervision, harsh discipline, and a rejecting attitude all predict delinquency. Similar results were obtained in the Cambridge study. Harsh or erratic parental discipline; cruel, passive, or neglecting parental attitudes; and poor parental supervision—all measured at age 8—all predicted later juvenile convictions and self-reported delinquency (West & Farrington, 1973). Generally, the presence of any of these adverse family background features doubled the risk of a later juvenile conviction.

Steinberg, Lamborn, Dornbusch, and Darling (1992) distinguished an authoritarian style of parenting (punitively emphasizing obedience) from an authoritative style (granting autonomy with good supervision). In the Cambridge study (Farrington, 1994), having authoritarian parents was the second most important predictor of convictions for violence (after hyperactivity and poor concentration). It is interesting to note that having authoritarian parents was the most important childhood risk factor that discriminated between violent offenders and frequently convicted nonviolent offenders (Farrington, 1991). An authoritarian, punitive parenting style is also related to child bullying (Baldry & Farrington, 1998).

Aggressive and violent behavior seems to be transmitted from parents to children, as Widom (1989) found in a study of abused children in Indianapolis. Children who were physically abused up to age 11 were significantly likely to become violent offenders in the next 15 years (Maxfield & Widom, 1996). Similarly, in the Rochester Youth Development Study, Smith and Thornberry (1995) showed that recorded child maltreatment under age 12 predicted self-reported violence between ages 14 and 18, independently of gender, ethnicity, SES, and family structure. The extensive review by Malinosky-Rummell and Hansen (1993) confirms that being physically abused as a child predicts later violent and nonviolent offending.

Possible causal mechanisms linking childhood victimization and adolescent antisocial behaviors have been reviewed by Widom (1994). First, childhood victimization may have both immediate and long-lasting consequences (e.g., shaking may cause brain injury). Second, childhood victimization may cause bodily changes (e.g., desensitization to pain) that encourage later aggression. Third, child abuse may lead to impulsive or dissociative coping styles that in turn lead to poor problem-solving skills or poor school performance. Fourth, victimization may cause changes in self-esteem or in social information-processing patterns that encourage later aggression. Fifth, child abuse may lead to changed family environments (e.g., being placed in foster care) that have deleterious effects. Sixth, juvenile justice practices may label victims, isolate them from prosocial peers, and encourage them to associate with delinquent peers.

Parental Conflict and Disrupted Families

There is no doubt that parental conflict and interparental violence predict adolescent antisocial behavior, as the meta-analysis of Buehler et al. (1997) shows. Also, parental conflict is related to childhood externalizing behavior, regardless of whether the information about both comes from parents or children (Jenkins & Smith, 1991). In the Pittsburgh Youth Study, CD boys tended to have parents who had unhappy relationships (Loeber et al., 1998). Parental conflict also predicts delinquency (West & Farrington, 1973).

In the Christchurch Study in New Zealand, children who witnessed violence between their parents were more likely to commit both violent and property offenses, according to their self-reports (Fergusson & Horwood, 1998). Witnessing father-initiated violence was still predictive after controlling for other risk factors such as parental criminality, parental substance abuse, parental physical punishment, a young mother, and low family income.

Parental separation and single-parent families predict CD children. In the Christchurch Study, separations from parents in the first 5 years of a child's life (especially) predicted CD at age 15 (Fergusson, Horwood, & Lynskey, 1994). In the New York StateLongitudinal Study, CD was predicted by parental divorce but far more strongly by having a never-married lone mother (Velez et al., 1989). In the Ontario Child Health Study, coming from a single-parent family predicted CD, but this feature was highly related to poverty and dependence on welfare benefits (Blum, Boyle, & Offord, 1988).

In the Dunedin Study in New Zealand, boys from single-parent families disproportionately tended to be convicted; 28% of violent offenders were from single-parent families, compared with 17% of nonviolent offenders and 9% of unconvicted boys (Henry, Caspi, Moffitt, & Silva, 1996). Based on analyses of four surveys (including the Cambridge study), Morash and Rucker (1989) concluded that the combination of teenage childbearing and a single-parent, female-headed household was especially conducive to the development of offending in children. Later analyses of the Cambridge study showed that teenage childbearing combined with a large number of children particularly predicted offending by the children (Nagin, Pogarsky, & Farrington, 1997).

Many studies show that broken homes or disrupted families predict delinquency (Wells & Rankin, 1991). In the Newcastle (England) Thousand-Family Study, Kolvin, Miller, Fleeting, and Kolvin (1988) reported that marital disruption (divorce or separation) in a boy's first 5 years predicted his later convictions up to age 32. Similarly, in the Dunedin study in New Zealand, Henry, Moffitt, Robins, Earls, and Silva (1993) found that children who were exposed to parental discord and many changes of the primary caretaker tended to become antisocial and delinquent.

Most studies of broken homes have focused on the loss of the father rather than of the mother, simply because the loss of a father is much more common. McCord (1982) in Boston carried out an interesting study of the relationship between homes broken by loss of the natural father and later serious offending of the children. She found that the prevalence of offending was high for boys reared in broken homes without affectionate mothers (62%) and for those reared in united homes characterized by parental conflict (52%), regardless of whether they had affectionate mothers. The prevalence of offending was low for those reared in united homes without conflict (26%) and—it is important to note—equally low for boys from broken homes with affectionate mothers (22%). These results suggest that it is not so much the broken home that is criminogenic as the parental conflict that often causes it and that a loving mother might in some sense be able to compensate for the loss of a father.

In the Cambridge study, both permanent and temporary separations from a biological parent before age 10 (usually from the father) predicted convictions and self-reported delinquency, providing that they were not caused by death or hospitalization (Farrington, 1992c). However, homes broken at an early age (under age 5) were not unusually criminogenic (West & Farrington, 1973). Separation before age 10 predicted both juvenile and adult convictions (Farrington, 1992b) and predicted convictions up to age 32 independently of all other factors such as low family income or poor school attainment (Farrington, 1993a).

Explanations of the relationship between disrupted families and delinquency fall into three major classes. Trauma theories suggest that the loss of a parent has a damaging effect on a child, most commonly because of the effect on attachment to the parent. Life course theories focus on separation as a sequence of stressful experiences and on the effects of multiple stressors such as parental conflict, parental loss, reduced economic circumstances, changes in parent figures, and poor child-rearing methods. Selection theories argue that disrupted families produce delinquent children because of preexisting differences from other families in risk factors such as parental conflict, criminal or antisocial parents, low family income, or poor child-rearing methods.

Hypotheses derived from the three theories were tested in the Cambridge study (Juby & Farrington, 2001). Although boys from broken homes (permanently disrupted families) were more delinquent than were boys from intact homes, they were not more delinquent than were boys from intact high-conflict families. Overall, the most important factor was the postdisruption trajectory. Boys who remained with their mother after the separation had the same delinquency rate as did boys from intact low-conflict families. Boys who remained with their father, with relatives, or with others (e.g., foster parents) had high delinquency rates. It was concluded that the results favored life course theories rather than trauma or selection theories.

Antisocial Parents and Large Families

It is clear that antisocial parents tend to have antisocial children (Lipsey & Derzon, 1998). In the Developmental Trends Study, parental antisocial personality disorder was the best predictor of childhood CD (Frick et al., 1992), and parental substance use was an important predictor of the onset of CD (Loeber, Green, Keenan, & Lahey, 1995). Similarly, in the New York State Longitudinal Study, parental antisocial personality disorder was a strong predictor of externalizing child behavior (Cohen, Brook, Cohen,

Velez, & Garcia, 1990). In the Pittsburgh Youth Study, parents with behavior problems and substance use problems tended to have CD boys (Loeber et al., 1998).

In their classic longitudinal studies, McCord (1977) and Robins, West, and Herjanic (1975) showed that criminal parents tended to have delinquent sons. In the Cambridge study, the concentration of offending in a small number of families was remarkable. Less than 6% of the families were responsible for half of the criminal convictions of all members (fathers, mothers, sons, and daughters) of all 400 families (Farrington, Barnes, & Lambert, 1996). Having a convicted mother, father, brother, or sister significantly predicted a boy's own convictions. Same-sex relationships were stronger than were opposite-sex relationships, and older siblings were stronger predictors than were younger siblings. Furthermore, convicted parents and delinquent siblings were related to a boy's self-reported as well as official offending (Farrington, 1979). CD symptoms also tend to be concentrated in families, as shown in the Ontario Child Health Study (Szatmari, Boyle, & Offord, 1993).

Similar results were obtained in the Pittsburgh Youth Study. Arrests of fathers, mothers, brothers, sisters, uncles, aunts, grandfathers, and grandmothers all predicted the boy's own delinquency (Farrington, Jolliffe, Loeber, Stouthamer-Loeber, & Kalb, 2001). The most important relative was the father; arrests of the father predicted the boy's delinquency independently of all other arrested relatives. Only 8% of families accounted for 43% of arrested family members.

Farrington et al. (2001) reviewed six different explanations for why offending and antisocial behavior were concentrated in families and transmitted from one generation to the next. First, there may be intergenerational continuities in exposure to multiple risk factors such as poverty, disrupted families, and living in deprived neighborhoods. Second, assortative mating (the tendency of antisocial females to choose antisocial males as partners) facilitates the intergenerational transmission of offending. Third, family members may influence each other (e.g., older siblings may encourage younger ones to be antisocial). Fourth, the effect of a criminal parent on a child's offending may be mediated by environmental mechanisms such as poor parental supervision and inconsistent discipline. Fifth, intergenerational transmission may be mediated by genetic mechanisms. Sixth, labeling and police bias may occur against known criminal families.

Many studies show that large families predict delinquency (Fischer, 1984). For example, in the English National Survey of Health and Development, Wadsworth (1979) found that the percentage of boys who were officially delinquent increased from 9% for families containing one child to 24% for families containing four or more children. The Newsons in their Nottingham study also concluded that large family size was one of the most important predictors of delinquency (Newson, Newson, & Adams, 1993). Large family size also predicts adolescent self-reported violence (Farrington, 2000).

In the Cambridge study, if a boy had four or more siblings by his 10th birthday, his risk of being convicted as a juvenile was doubled (West & Farrington, 1973). Large family size predicted self-reported delinquency as well as convictions (Farrington, 1979) and adult as well as juvenile convictions (Farrington, 1992b). Also, large family size was the most important independent predictor of convictions up to age 32 in a logistic regression analysis (Farrington, 1993a). Large family size was similarly important in the Cambridge and Pittsburgh studies, even though families were on average smaller in Pittsburgh in the 1990s than in London in the 1960s (Farrington & Loeber, 1999).

Brownfield and Sorenson (1994) reviewed several possible explanations for the link between large families and delinquency, including those focusing on features of the parents (e.g., criminal parents, teenage parents), those focusing on parenting (e.g., poor supervision, disrupted families) and those focusing on socioeconomic deprivation or family stress. Another interesting theory suggested that the key factor was birth order: Large families include more later-born children, who tend to be more delinquent. Using an analysis of self-reported delinquency in a Seattle survey, they concluded that the most plausible intervening causal mechanism was exposure to delinquent siblings. In the Cambridge study, co-offending by brothers was surprisingly common; about 20% of boys who had brothers close to them in age were convicted for a crime committed with their brother (Reiss & Farrington, 1991, p. 386).

Socioeconomic Factors

It is clear that antisocial children disproportionately come from low-SES families. In the Ontario Child Health Study, CD children tended to come from low-income families with unemployed parents who were living in subsidized housing and dependent on welfare benefits (Offord, Alder, & Boyle, 1986). In the New York State longitudinal study, low SES, low family income, and low parental education predicted CD children (Velez et al., 1989). In the Developmental Trends Study, low SES predicted the onset of CD (Loeber et al., 1995); moreover, in the Pittsburgh Youth Study, family dependence on welfare benefits was characteristic of CD boys (Loeber et al., 1998).

In general, coming from a low-SES family predicts adolescent violence. For example, in the U.S. National Youth Survey, the prevalence of self-reported assault and robbery was about twice as high among lower-class youth as among middle-class ones (Elliott, Huizinga, & Menard, 1989). In Project Metropolitan in Stockholm (Wikström, 1985) and in the Dunedin study in New Zealand (Henry et al., 1996), the SES of a boy's family—based on the father's occupation—predicted his later violent crimes. Several researchers have suggested that the link between a low-SES family and adolescent antisocial behavior is mediated by family socialization practices. For example, Dodge, Pettit, and Bates (1994) found that about half of the effect of SES on peer-rated aggression and teacher-rated externalizing problems was accounted for by family socialization.

Low SES is a less consistent predictor of delinquency. However, much depends on whether it is measured by income and housing or by occupational prestige. In the Cambridge study, low family income and poor housing predicted official and self-reported juvenile and adult delinquency, but low parental occupational prestige predicted only self-reported delinquency (Farrington, 1992b, 1992c). Low family income was a strong predictor of self-reported violence (Farrington, 2000), and having an unemployed father was one of the strongest predictors of convictions for violence (Farrington, 1994).

Peer Influences

It is well established that having delinquent friends is an important predictor of delinquency (Lipsey & Derzon, 1998). What is less clear is how far antisocial peers encourage and facilitate adolescent antisocial behavior or whether it is merely that birds of a feather flock together. Delinquents may have delinquent friends because of co-offending, which is particularly common in persons under age 21 (Reiss & Farrington, 1991). However, using structural equation modeling in the Oregon Youth Study, Patterson, Capaldi, and Bank (1991) concluded that having delinquent friends predicted delinquency. Also, Elliott and Menard (1996) in the U.S. National Youth Survey concluded that delinquent friends influenced an adolescent's own delinquency and that the reverse was also true: More delinquent adolescents were more likely to have delinquent friends. In the Pittsburgh Youth Study, Keenan, Loeber, Zhang, Stouthamer-Loeber, and van Kammen (1995) discovered that having antisocial friends predicted the later onset of a boy's antisocial behavior.

There is no doubt that highly aggressive children tend to be rejected by most of their peers (Coie, Dodge, & Kupersmidt, 1990). However, it is unclear how far peer rejection causes later aggression. Low popularity was only a marginal predictor of adolescent aggression and teenage violence in the Cambridge study (Farrington, 1989a). Coie and Miller-Johnson (2001) found that the boys who were both aggressive and rejected by their classmates became the self-reported and official delinquents. However, although aggressive children are rejected by conventional peers, they can be popular with other aggressive children (Cairns, Cairns, Neckerman, Gest, & Gariepy, 1988).

School and Community Influences

It is also well established that delinquents disproportionately attend high-delinquency-rate schools, which have high levels of distrust between teachers and students, low commitment to the school by students, and unclear and inconsistently enforced rules (Graham, 1988). In the Cambridge study, attending a high-delinquency-rate school at age 11 significantly predicted a boy's own delinquency (Farrington, 1992c). However, what is less clear is how far the schools themselves influence antisocial behavior by their organization, climate, and practices and how far the concentration of offenders in certain schools is mainly a function of their intakes. In the Cambridge study, most of the variation between schools in their delinquency rates could be explained by differences in their intakes of troublesome boys at age 11 (Farrington, 1972). However, reviews of American research show that schools with clear, fair, and consistently enforced rules tend to have low rates of student misbehavior (Gottfredson, 2001; Herrenkohl, Hawkins, Chung, Hill, & Battin-Pearson, 2001).

Many studies show that boys living in urban areas are more violent than those living in rural ones. In the U.S. National Youth Survey, the prevalence of self-reported assault and robbery was considerably higher among urban youth (Elliott et al., 1989). Within urban areas, boys living in high-crime neighborhoods are more violent than are those living in low-crime neighborhoods. In the Rochester Youth Development Study, living in a high crime neighborhood significantly predicted self-reported violence (Thornberry, Huizinga, & Loeber, 1995). Similarly, in the Pittsburgh Youth Study, living in a bad neighborhood (either as rated by the mother or based on census measures of poverty, unemployment, and female-headed households) significantly predicted official and reported violence (Farrington, 1998).

It is clear that offenders disproportionately live in inner-city areas characterized by physical deterioration, neighborhood disorganization, and high residential mobility (Shaw & McKay, 1969). Again, however, it is difficult to determine how far the areas themselves influence antisocial behavior and how far it is merely the case that antisocial people tend to live in deprived areas (e.g., because of their poverty or public housing allocation policies). It is interesting to note that both neighborhood researchers such as Gottfredson, McNeil, and Gottfredson (1991) and developmental researchers such as Rutter (1981) have concluded that neighborhoods have only indirect effects on antisocial behavior via their effects on individuals and families. However, Sampson, Raudenbush, and Earls (1997) argued that a low degree of collective efficacy (i.e., a low degree of informal social control) in a neighborhood caused high crime rates.

SUCCESSFUL INTERVENTIONS

I focus here especially on results obtained in randomized experiments with reasonably large samples because the effect of any intervention on antisocial behavior can be demonstrated most convincingly in such experiments (Farrington, 1983). For more extensive reviews of the effects of interventions, see Wasserman and Miller (1998) and Catalano, Arthur, Hawkins, Berglund, and Olson (1998). Most interventions target risk factors and aim to prevent antisocial behavior. However, it is equally important to strengthen protective factors and promote healthy adolescent development (Catalano, Hawkins, Berglund, Pollard, & Arthur, 2002).

Early Home Visiting

Adolescent delinquency can be prevented by intensive home-visiting programs. For example, in the state of New York, Olds, Henderson, Chamberlain, and Tatelbaum (1986) randomly allocated 400 mothers either to receive home visits from nurses during pregnancy, to receive visits both during pregnancy and during the first 2 years of life, or to receive no visits (control group). The home visitors gave advice about prenatal and postnatal care of the child, about infant development, and about the importance of proper nutrition and avoiding smoking and drinking during pregnancy.

The results of this experiment showed that the postnatal home visits caused a decrease in recorded child physical abuse and neglect during the first 2 years of life, especially by poor unmarried teenage mothers; 4% of visited versus 19% of nonvisited mothers of this type were guilty of child abuse or neglect This last result is important because (as mentioned previously) children who are physically abused or neglected tend to become violent offenders later in life. In a 15-year follow-up, the main focus was on lower-class unmarried mothers. Among these high-risk mothers, those who received prenatal and postnatal home visits had fewer arrests than did those who received prenatal visits or no visits (Olds et al., 1997). Also, children of these mothers who received prenatal home visits, postnatal home visits, or both had less than half as many arrests as did children of mothers who received no visits (Olds et al., 1998). According to Aos, Phipps, Barnoski, and Lieb (2001a), the benefit-cost ratio for high risk mothers was 3.1, based on savings to crime victims and criminal justice.

Preschool Programs

One of the most successful early prevention programs has been the Perry preschool project carried out in Michigan by Schweinhart and Weikart (1980). This project was essentially a Head Start program targeted on disadvantaged African American children. The experimental children attended a daily preschool program backed up by weekly home visits usually lasting 2 years (covering ages 3–4). The aim of the plan-do-review program was to provide intellectual stimulation, to increase thinking and reasoning abilities, and to increase later school achievement.

As demonstrated in several other Head Start projects, the experimental group showed gains in intelligence that were rather short-lived. However, they were significantly better in elementary school motivation, school achievement at age 14, teacher ratings of classroom behavior at ages 6–9, self-reports of classroom behavior at age 15, and self-reports of offending at age 15. A later follow-up of the Perry sample (Berrueta-Clement, Schweinhart, Barnett, Epstein, & Weikart, 1984) showed that at age 19 the experimental group was more likely to be employed, more likely to have graduated from high school, more likely to have received college or vocational training, and less likely to have been arrested. By age 27, the experimental group had accumulated only half as many arrests on average as the controls had (Schweinhart et al., 1993). Also, they had significantly higher earnings and were more likely to be home owners. Hence, this preschool intellectual enrichment program led to decreases in school failure, in delinquency, and in other undesirable outcomes. For every $1 spent on the program, $7 were saved in the long run.

Like the Perry project, the Child Parent Center (CPC) in Chicago provided disadvantaged children with a high-quality, active-learning preschool supplemented with family support (Reynolds, Temple, Robertson, & Mann, 2001). However, unlike Perry, CPC continued to provide the children with the educational enrichment component into elementary school, up to age 9. Just focusing on the effect of the preschool intervention, the study found that compared to a control group, those who received the program were less likely to be arrested for both nonviolent and violent offenses by the time they were 18. The CPC program also produced other benefits for those in the experimental compared to the control group, such as a higher rate of high school completion.

Parent Training

Parent training is also an effective method of preventing delinquency. Many different types of parent training have been used (Kazdin, 1997), but the behavioral parent management training developed by Patterson (1982) in Oregon is one of the most promising approaches. His careful observations of parent-child interaction showed that parents of antisocial children were deficient in their methods of child rearing. These parents failed to tell their children how they were expected to behave, failed to monitor their children's behavior to ensure that it was desirable, and failed to enforce rules promptly and unambiguously with appropriate rewards and penalties. The parents of antisocial children used more punishment (such as scolding, shouting, or threatening) but failed to make it contingent on the child's behavior.

Patterson attempted to train these parents in effective child-rearing methods—namely, noticing what a child is doing, monitoring behavior over long periods, clearly stating house rules, making rewards and punishments contingent on behavior, and negotiating disagreements so that conflicts and crises did not escalate. His treatment was shown to be effective in reducing child stealing and antisocial behavior over short periods in small-scale studies (Dishion, Patterson, & Kavanagh, 1992; Patterson, Chamberlain, & Reid, 1982; Patterson, Reid, & Dishion, 1992).

Another parenting intervention, termed functional family therapy, was evaluated in Utah by Alexander and Parsons (1973). This intervention aimed to modify patterns of family interaction by modeling, prompting, and reinforcement to encourage clear communication of requests and solutions between family members and to minimize conflict. Essentially, all family members were trained to negotiate effectively, to set clear rules about privileges and responsibilities, and to use techniques of reciprocal reinforcement with each other. This technique halved the recidivism rate of minor delinquents in comparison with other approaches (client-centered or psychodynamic therapy). Its effectiveness with more serious delinquents was confirmed in a replication study using matched groups (Gordon, 1995).

The multidimensional treatment foster care (MTFC) program, evaluated in Oregon by Chamberlain and Reid (1998), also produced desirable results. Participants (young males with a history of serious and chronic offending and their parents) in the MTFC program received individual (e.g., skills in problem solving) and family (e.g., parent management training) therapy, while controls went to the usual community-based group care facility. One year after the completion of the program, MTFC cases were less likely than controls to have engaged in further criminal activity as measured by police arrests.

Skills Training

The set of techniques variously termed cognitive-behavioral interpersonal social skills training have proved to be successful (Lipsey & Wilson, 1998). For example, the Reasoning and Rehabilitation program developed by Ross and Ross (1995) in Ottawa, Canada aimed to modify the impulsive, egocentric thinking of delinquents to teach them to stop and think before acting, to consider the consequences of their behavior, to conceptualize alternative ways of solving interpersonal problems, and to consider the impact of their behavior on other people, especially their victims. It included social skills training, lateral thinking (to teach creative problem solving), critical thinking (to teach logical reasoning), values education (to teach values and concern for others), assertiveness training (to teach nonaggressive, socially appropriate ways to obtain desired outcomes), negotiation skills training, interpersonal cognitive problem-solving training (to teach thinking skills for solving interpersonal problems), social perspective training (to teach how to recognize and understand other people's feelings), role playing and modeling (demonstration and practice of effective and acceptable interpersonal behavior). This program led to a large decrease in reoffending in a small sample of delinquents.

Jones and Offord (1989) implemented a skills training program in an experimental public housing complex in Ottawa and compared it with a control complex. The program centered on nonschool skills, both athletic (e.g., swimming and hockey) and non-athletic (e.g., guitar and ballet). The aim of developing skills was to increase self-esteem, to encourage children to use time constructively, and to provide desirable role models. Participation rates were high; about three quarters of age-eligible children in the experimental complex took at least one course in the first year. The program was successful; delinquency rates decreased significantly in the experimental complex compared to the control complex. The benefit-cost ratio, based on savings to taxpayers, was 2.5.

Peer Programs

No outstanding examples of effective intervention programs for antisocial behavior targeted on peer risk factors have emerged. The most promising programs involve using high-status conventional peers to teach children ways of resisting peer pressure; such programs are effective in reducing drug use (Tobler, Lessard, Marshall, Ochshorn, & Roona, 1999). Also, in a randomized experiment in St. Louis, Feldman, Caplinger, and Wodarski (1983) showed that placing antisocial adolescents in activity groups dominated by prosocial adolescents led to a reduction in their antisocial behavior (compared with antisocial adolescents placed in antisocial groups). This study suggests that the influence of prosocial peers can be harnessed to reduce antisocial behavior.

The most important intervention program whose success seems to be based mainly on reducing peer risk factors is the Children at Risk program (Harrell, Cavanagh, Harmon, Koper, & Sridharan, 1997), which targeted high-risk adolescents (average age 12) in poor neighborhoods of five cities across the United States. Eligible youths were identified in schools and randomly assigned to experimental or control groups. The program was a comprehensive community-based prevention strategy targeting risk factors for delinquency, including case management and family counseling, family skills training, tutoring, mentoring, participating in after-school activities, and community policing. The program was different in each neighborhood.

The initial results of the program were disappointing, but a 1-year follow-up showed that (according to self-reports) experimental youths were less likely to have committed violent crimes and to have used or sold drugs (Harrell, Cavanagh, & Sridharan, 1999). The process evaluation showed that the greatest change was in peer risk factors. Experimental youths associated less often with delinquent peers, felt less peer pressure to engage in delinquency, and had more positive peer support. In contrast, there were few changes in individual, family, or community risk factors, possibly because of the low participation of parents in parent training and of youths in mentoring and tutoring (Harrell et al., 1997, p. 87). In other words, problems linked to the serious and multiple needs and problems of the families arose in the implementation of the program.

School Programs

An important school-based prevention experiment was carried out in Seattle by Hawkins, von Cleve, and Catalano (1991). This study combined parent training, teacher training, and skills training. About 500 first-grade children (age 6) were randomly assigned to be in experimental or control classes. The children in the experimental classes received special treatment at home and school that was designed to increase their attachment to their parents and their bonding to the school, on the assumption that delinquency was inhibited by the strength of social bonds. Their parents were trained to notice and reinforce socially desirable behavior in a program called "Catch them being good." Their teachers were trained in classroom management—for example, to provide clear instructions and expectations to children, to reward children for participation in desired behavior, and to teach children prosocial (socially desirable) methods of solving problems.

In an evaluation of this program 18 months later, when the children were in different classes, Hawkins et al. (1991) found that according to teacher ratings, the boys who received the experimental program were significantly less aggressive than were the control boys. This difference was particularly marked for White boys versus African-American boys. The experimental girls were not significantly less aggressive, but they were less self-destructive, anxious, and depressed. In the latest follow-up, Hawkins, Catalano, Kosterman, Abbott, and Hill (1999) found that at age 18, the full-intervention group (those receiving the intervention from Grades 1–6) admitted less violence, less alcohol abuse, and fewer sexual partners than did the late intervention group (Grades 5–6 only) or the controls. The benefit-cost ratio of this program according to Aos et al. (2001a) was 4.3. Other school-based programs have also been successful in reducing antisocial behavior (Catalano et al., 1998).

Antibullying Programs

Several school-based programs have been designed to decrease bullying. The most famous of these programs was implemented by Olweus (1994) in Norway. It aimed to increase awareness and knowledge of teachers, parents, and children about bullying and to dispel myths about it. A 30-page booklet was distributed to all schools in Norway describing what was known about bullying and recommending what steps schools and teachers could take to reduce it. Also, a 25-min video about bullying was made available to schools. Simultaneously, the schools distributed to all parents a four-page folder containing information and advice about bullying. In addition, anonymous self-report questionnaires about bullying were completed by all children.

The program was evaluated in Bergen. Each of the 42 participating schools received feedback information from the questionnaire about the prevalence of bullies and victims in a specially arranged school conference day. Also, teachers were encouraged to develop explicit rules about bullying (e.g., do not bully, tell someone when bullying happens, bullying will not be tolerated, try to help victims, try to include children who are being left out) and to discuss bullying in class, using the video and role-playing exercises. Also, teachers were encouraged to improve monitoring and supervision of children, especially in the playground. The program was successful in reducing the prevalence of bullying by half.

A similar program was implemented in England in 23 Sheffield schools by Smith and Sharp (1994). The core program involved establishing a whole-school antibullying policy, raising awareness of bullying and clearly defining roles and responsibilities of teachers and students so that everyone knew what bullying was and what they should do about it. In addition, optional interventions were tailored to particular schools—curriculum work (e.g., reading books, watching videos), direct work with students (e.g., assertiveness training for those who were bullied) and playground work (e.g., training lunchtime supervisors). This program was successful in reducing bullying (by 15%) in primary schools, but had relatively small effects (a 5% reduction) in secondary schools.

Multimodal Programs

Multimodal programs including both skills training and parent training are more effective than either alone (Wasserman & Miller, 1998). An important multimodal program was implemented by Tremblay, Pagani-Kurtz, Vitaro, Masse, and Pihl (1995) in Montreal, Canada. They identified about 250 disruptive (aggressive-hyperactive) boys at age 6 for a prevention experiment. Between ages 7 and 9, the experimental group received training to foster social skills and self-control. Coaching, peer modeling, role playing, and reinforcement contingencies were used in small group sessions on such topics as how to help, what to do when you are angry, and how to react to teasing. Also, their parents were trained using the parent management training techniques developed by Patterson (1982).

This prevention program was quite successful. By age 12, the experimental boys committed less burglary and theft, were less likely to get drunk, and were less likely to be involved in fights than were the controls. Also, the experimental boys had higher school achievement. At every age from 10 to 15, the experimental boys had lower self-reported delinquency scores than did the control boys. It is interesting to note that the differences in antisocial behavior between experimental and control boys increased as the follow-up progressed.

Intervention programs that tackle several of the major risk factors for CD and delinquency are likely to be particularly effective. Henggeler, Melton, Smith, Schoenwald, and Hanley (1993) in South Carolina evaluated multisystemic therapy (MST) for juvenile offenders, tackling family, peer, and school risk factors simultaneously in individualized treatment plans tailored to the needs of each family. MST was compared with the usual Department of Youth Services treatment involving out-of-home placement in the majority of cases. In a randomized experiment with delinquents, MST was followed by fewer arrests, lower self-reported delinquency, and less peer-oriented aggression. Borduin et al. (1995) also showed that MST was more effective in decreasing arrests and antisocial behavior than was individual therapy. According to Aos, Phipps, Barnoski, and Lieb (2001b), MST has one of the highest benefit-cost ratios of any program; for every $1 spent on it, $13.45 were saved in victim and criminal justice costs.

The results were somewhat less favorable in a real-world implementation of MST using therapists recruited and trained in each site. Previous experiments had been implemented and closely monitored by MST experts. Henggeler, Melton, Brondino, Scherer, and Hanley (1997) randomly allocated chronic and violent juvenile offenders either to MST or to the usual services (which in this case mainly involved probation and restitution). MST led to a decrease in arrests, self-reported delinquency, and antisocial behavior, but only when treatment fidelity was high. The researchers concluded that in real world applications, therapist adherence to MST principles was a crucial factor. Worrying results were also obtained in a large-scale independent evaluation of MST in Canada by Leschied and Cunningham (2002). More than 400 youths who were either offenders or at risk of offending were randomly assigned to receive either MST or the usual services (typically, probation supervision). Six months after treatment, 28% of the MST group had been reconvicted compared with 31% of the control group, a non-significant difference.

CONCLUSIONS

A great deal is known about adolescent antisocial behavior. First, males are more antisocial than are females. Second, all types (including CD, aggression, and delinquency) tend to coexist and are intercorrelated. Third, the most antisocial adolescents at one age tend also to be the most antisocial at a later age. Fourth, an early onset of antisocial behavior predicts a long and serious antisocial career. However, both the prevalence and the age of onset of antisocial behavior can vary dramatically according to its definition and how it is measured. Research is needed on a wider range of features of antisocial careers—not only prevalence and onset but also frequency, seriousness, duration, escalation, deescalation, desistance, remission, motivation, and situational influences. More studies are needed with multiple informants and frequent measurements.

How the prevalence and incidence of antisocial behavior vary between ages 10 and 17 is less well understood. The existing evidence suggests that the incidence of physical aggression decreases, but the prevalence of CD and delinquency increase. More research is needed on the age distribution of different types of antisocial behavior in order to explain these findings. Also, more research is needed on different types of developmental pathways and trajectories during this age range.

A great deal is known about the key risk factors for adolescent antisocial behavior, which include impulsiveness, low IQ and low school achievement, poor parental supervision, child physical abuse, punitive or erratic parental discipline, cold parental attitude, parental conflict, disrupted families, antisocial parents, large family size, low family income, antisocial peers, high delinquency-rate schools, and high-crime neighborhoods. However, the causal mechanisms linking these risk factors with antisocial outcomes are less well established. Larger developmental theories that explain all the results need to be formulated and tested (Lahey, Moffitt, & Caspi, 2003). More research is needed on risk factors for persistence or escalation of antisocial behavior. How far risk factors are the same for males and females, for different ethnic groups, or at different ages needs to be investigated. More cross-cultural comparisons of risk factors and more studies of protective factors are needed.

The comorbidity and versatility of antisocial behavior pose a major challenge to understanding. It is important to investigate how far all results are driven by a minority of multiple-problem adolescents or chronic delinquents. Often, multiple risk factors lead to multiple-problem boys (Loeber et al., 2001). How far any given risk factor generally predicts a variety of different outcomes (as opposed to specifically predicting one or two outcomes) and how far each outcome is generally predicted by a variety of different risk factors (as opposed to being specifically predicted by only one or two risk factors) are unclear. An increasing number of risk factors seems to lead to an increasing probability of antisocial outcomes—almost regardless of the particular risk factors included in the prediction measure—but more research is needed on this issue. Space in this chapter was insufficient to review theories explaining the links between risk factors and antisocial outcomes, but these theories have to be based on knowledge about the additive, independent, interactive, and sequential effects of risk factors.

There are many examples of successful intervention programs, including general parent education in home visiting programs, preschool intellectual enrichment programs, parent management training, cognitive-behavioral skills training, antibullying programs, and multimodal programs including individual and family interventions. However, many experiments are based on small samples and short follow-up periods. The challenge to researchers is to transport carefully monitored small-scale programs implemented by high-quality university personnel into routine large-scale use without losing their effectiveness. Often, multimodal programs are the most successful, making it difficult to identify the active ingredient. Successful multimodal programs should be followed by more specific experiments targeting single risk factors, which could be very helpful in establishing which risk factors have causal effects.

More efforts are needed to tailor types of interventions to types of adolescents. Ideally, an intervention should be preceded by a screening or needs assessment to determine which problems need to be rectified and which adolescents are most likely to be amenable to treatment. It is important to establish how far interventions are successful with the most antisocial adolescents in order to identify where the benefits will be greatest in practice. Also, more cost-benefit analyses are needed to show how much money is saved by successful programs. Saving money is a powerful argument to convince policy makers and practitioners to implement intervention programs.

A great deal has been learned about adolescent antisocial behavior in the last 25 years, especially from longitudinal and experimental studies. More investment in these kinds of studies is needed in the next 25 years in order to advance knowledge about and decrease these troubling social problems.

REFERENCES

Achenbach, T. M. (1993). *Empirically based taxonomy: How to use syndromes and profile types derived from the CBCL4-18, TRF and YSR.* Burlington, VT: University of Vermont Department of Psychiatry.

Achenbach, T. M., Dumenci, L., & Rescorla, L. A. (2003). Are American children's problems still getting worse? A 23-year comparison. *Journal of Abnormal Child Psychology, 31,* 1–11.

Achenbach, T. M., Verhulst, F. C., Baron, G. D., & Althaus, M. (1987). A comparison of syndromes derived from the child behavior checklist for American and Dutch boys aged 6–11 and 12–16. *Journal of Child Psychology and Psychiatry, 28,* 437–453.

Alexander, J. F., & Parsons, B. V. (1973). Short-term behavioral intervention with delinquent families: Impact on family process and recidivism. *Journal of Abnormal Psychology, 81,* 219–225.

American Psychiatric Association. (1994). *Diagnostic and statistical manual of mental disorders* (4th ed.). Washington, DC: Author.

Aos, S., Phipps, P., Barnoski, R., & Lieb, R. (2001a). *The comparative costs and benefits of programs to reduce crime.* Olympia, WA: Washington State Institute for Public Policy.

Aos, S., Phipps, P., Barnoski, R., & Lieb, R. (2001b). The comparative costs and benefits of programs to reduce crime: A review of research findings with implications for Washington State. In B. C. Welsh, D. P. Farrington, & L. W. Sherman (Eds.), *Costs and benefits of preventing crime* (pp. 149–175). Boulder, CO: Westview Press.

Baldry, A. C., & Farrington, D. P. (1998). Parenting influences on bullying and victimization. *Legal and Criminological Psychology, 3,* 237–254.

Berrueta-Clement, J. R., Schweinhart, L. J., Barnett, W. S., Epstein, A. S., & Weikart, D. P. (1984). *Changed lives.* Ypsilanti, MI: High/Scope.

Bjorkvist, K., Lagerspetz, K. M. J., & Kaukiainen, A. (1992). Do girls manipulate and boys fight? Developmental trends in regard to direct and indirect aggression. *Aggressive Behavior, 18,* 117–127.

Blum, H. M., Boyle, M. H., & Offord, D. R. (1988). Single-parent families: Child psychiatric disorder and school performance. *Journal of the American Academy of Child and Adolescent Psychiatry, 27,* 214–219.

Borduin, C. M., Mann, B. J., Cone, L. T., Henggeler, S. W., Fucci, B. R., Blaske, D. M., et al. (1995). Multisystemic treatment of serious juvenile offenders: Long-term prevention of criminality and violence. *Journal of Consulting and Clinical Psychology, 63,* 569–578.

Brennan, P. A., Mednick, B. R., & Mednick, S. A. (1993). Parental psychopathology, congenital factors, and violence. In S. Hodgins (Ed.), *Mental disorder and crime* (pp. 244–261). Newbury Park, CA: Sage.

Brownfield, D., & Sorenson, A. M. (1994). Sibship size and sibling delinquency. *Deviant Behavior, 15,* 45–61.

Buehler, C., Anthony, C., Krishnakumar, A., Stone, G., Gerard, J., & Pemberton, S. (1997). Interparental conflict and youth problem behaviors: A meta-analysis. *Journal of Child and Family Studies, 6,* 233–247.

Cairns, R. B., & Cairns, B. D. (1994). *Lifelines and risks: Pathways of youth in our time.* Cambridge, England: Cambridge University Press.

Cairns, R. B., Cairns, B. D., Neckerman, H. J., Gest, S. D., & Gariepy, J-L. (1988). Social networks and aggressive behavior: Peer support or peer rejection? *Developmental Psychology, 24,* 815–823.

Capaldi, D. M., & Patterson, G. R. (1996). Can violent offenders be distinguished from frequent offenders? Prediction from childhood to adolescence. *Journal of Research in Crime and Delinquency, 33,* 206–231.

Caspi, A. (2000) The child is father of the man: Personality continuities from childhood to adulthood. *Journal of Personality and Social Psychology, 78,* 158–172.

Catalano, R. F., Arthur, M. W., Hawkins, J. D., Berglund, L., & Olson, J. J. (1998). Comprehensive community and school based interventions to prevent antisocial behavior. In R. Loeber & D. P. Farrington (Eds.), *Serious and violent juvenile offenders: Risk factors and successful interventions* (pp. 248–283). Thousand Oaks, CA: Sage.

Catalano, R. F., Hawkins, J. D., Berglund, L., Pollard, J. A., & Arthur, M. W. (2002). Prevention science and positive youth development: Competitive or cooperative frameworks? *Journal of Adolescent Health, 31,* 230–239.

Cernkovich, S. A., Giordano, P. C., & Pugh, M. D. (1985). Chronic offenders: The missing cases in self-report delinquency research. *Journal of Criminal Law and Criminology, 76,* 705–732.

Chamberlain, P., & Reid, J. B. (1998). Comparison of two community alternatives to incarceration for chronic juvenile offenders. *Journal of Consulting and Clinical Psychology, 66,* 624–633.

Chess, S., & Thomas, A. (1984). *Origins and evolution of behavior disorders: From infancy to early adult life.* New York: Brunner/Mazel.

Clarke, R. V. (1995). Situational crime prevention. In M. Tonry & D. P. Farrington (Eds.), *Building a safer society: Strategic approaches to crime prevention* (pp. 91–150). Chicago: University of Chicago Press.

Cohen, P., Brook, J. S., Cohen, J., Velez, C. N., & Garcia, M. (1990). Common and uncommon pathways to adolescent psychopathology and problem behavior. In L. N. Robins & M. Rutter (Eds.), *Straight and devious pathways from childhood to adulthood* (pp. 242–258). Cambridge, England: Cambridge University Press.

Cohen, P., Cohen, J., & Brook, J. (1993). An epidemiological study of disorders in late childhood and adolescence: II. Persistence of disorders. *Journal of Child Psychology and Psychiatry, 34,* 869–877.

Cohen, P., Cohen, J., Kasen, S., Velez, C. N., Hartmark, C., Johnson, J., et al. (1993). An epidemiological study of disorders in late childhood and adolescence: I. Age and gender-specific prevalence. *Journal of Child Psychology and Psychiatry, 34,* 851–867.

Coie, J. D., & Dodge, K. A. (1998). Aggression and antisocial behavior. In W. Damon & N. Eisenberg (Eds.), *Handbook of child psychology: Vol. 3. Social, emotional and personality development* (pp. 779–862). New York: Wiley.

Coie, J. D., Dodge, K. A., & Kupersmidt, J. (1990). Peer group behavior and social status. In S. R. Asher & J. D. Coie (Eds.), *Peer rejection in childhood* (pp. 17–59). Cambridge, England: Cambridge University Press.

Coie, J. D., & Miller-Johnson, S. (2001). Peer factors and interventions. In R. Loeber & D. P. Farrington (Eds.), *Child delinquents: Development, intervention, and service needs* (pp. 191–209). Thousand Oaks, CA: Sage.

Connor, D. F. (2002). *Aggression and antisocial behavior in children and adolescents.* New York: Guilford Press.

Craig, W. M., Pepler, D., & Atlas, R. (2000). Observations of bullying in the playground and in the classroom. *School Psychology International, 21,* 22–36.

Crick, N. R., & Grotpeter, J. K. (1995). Relational aggression, gender, and social-psychological adjustment. *Child Development, 66,* 710–722.

Denno, D. W. (1990). *Biology and violence: From birth to adulthood.* Cambridge, England: Cambridge University Press.

Dishion, T. J., Patterson, G. R., & Kavanagh, K. A. (1992). An experimental test of the coercion model: Linking theory, measurement and intervention. In J. McCord & R. Tremblay (Eds.), *Preventing antisocial behavior* (pp. 253–282). New York: Guilford.

Dodge, K. A. (1991). The structure and function of reactive and proactive aggression. In D. J. Pepler & K. H. Rubin (Eds.), *The development and treatment of childhood aggression* (pp. 201–218). Hillsdale, NJ: Erlbaum.

Dodge, K. A., Pettit, G. S., & Bates, J. E. (1994). Socialization mediators of the relation between socioeconomic status and child conduct problems. *Child Development, 65,* 649–665.

Elliott, D. S. (1994). Serious violent offenders: Onset, developmental course, and termination. *Criminology, 32,* 1–21.

Elliott, D. S., Huizinga, D., & Menard, S. (1989). *Multiple problem youth: Delinquency, substance use, and mental health problems.* New York: Springer-Verlag.

Elliott, D. S., & Menard, S. (1996). Delinquent friends and delinquent behavior: Temporal and developmental patterns. In J. D. Hawkins (Ed.), *Delinquency and crime: Current theories* (pp. 28–67). Cambridge, England: Cambridge University Press.

Eysenck, H. J. (1996). Personality and crime: Where do we stand? *Psychology, Crime and Law, 2,* 143–152.

Farrington, D. P. (1972). Delinquency begins at home. *New Society, 21,* 495–497.

Farrington, D. P. (1979). Environmental stress, delinquent behavior, and convictions. In I. G. Sarason & C. D. Spielberger (Eds.), *Stress and anxiety* (Vol. 6, pp. 93–107). Washington, DC: Hemisphere.

Farrington, D. P. (1983). Randomized experiments on crime and justice. In M. Tonry & N. Morris (Eds.), *Crime and justice* (Vol. 4, pp. 257–308). Chicago: University of Chicago Press.

Farrington, D. P. (1986). Age and crime. In M. Tonry & N. Morris (Eds.), *Crime and justice* (Vol. 7, pp. 189–250). Chicago: University of Chicago Press.

Farrington, D. P. (1989a). Early predictors of adolescent aggression and adult violence. *Violence and Victims, 4,* 79–100.

Farrington, D. P. (1989b). Self-reported and official offending from adolescence to adulthood. In M. W. Klein (Ed.), *Cross-national research in self-reported crime and delinquency* (pp. 399–423). Dordrecht, Netherlands: Kluwer.

Farrington, D. P. (1990). Implications of criminal career research for the prevention of offending. *Journal of Adolescence, 13,* 93–113.

Farrington, D. P. (1991). Childhood aggression and adult violence: Early precursors and later life outcomes. In D. J. Pepler & K. H. Rubin (Eds.), *The development and treatment of childhood aggression* (pp. 5–29). Hillsdale, NJ: Erlbaum.

Farrington, D. P. (1992a). Criminal career research in the United Kingdom. *British Journal of Criminology, 32,* 521–536.

Farrington, D. P. (1992b). Explaining the beginning, progress and ending of antisocial behavior from birth to adulthood. In J. McCord (Ed.), *Facts, frameworks and forecasts: Advances in criminological theory* (Vol. 3, pp. 253–286). New Brunswick, NJ: Transaction.

Farrington, D. P. (1992c). Juvenile delinquency. In J. C. Coleman (Ed.), *The school years* (2nd ed., pp. 123–163). London: Routledge.

Farrington, D. P. (1993a). Childhood origins of teenage antisocial behavior and adult social dysfunction. *Journal of the Royal Society of Medicine, 86,* 13–17.

Farrington, D. P. (1993b). Understanding and preventing bullying. In M. Tonry & N. Morris (Eds.), *Crime and justice* (Vol. 17, pp. 381–458). Chicago: University of Chicago Press.

Farrington, D. P. (1994). Childhood, adolescent and adult features of violent males. In L. R. Huesman (Ed.), *Aggressive behavior: Current perspectives* (pp. 215–240). New York: Plenum.

Farrington, D. P. (1997a). Human development and criminal careers. In M. Maguire, R. Morgan, & R. Reiner (Eds.), *The Oxford handbook of criminology* (2nd ed., pp. 361–408). Oxford, England: Clarendon Press.

Farrington, D. P. (1997b). The relationship between low resting heart rate and violence. In A. Raine, P. A. Brennan, D. P. Farrington, & S. A. Mednick (Eds.), *Biosocial bases of violence* (pp. 89–105). New York: Plenum.

Farrington, D. P. (1998). Predictors, causes and correlates of male youth violence. In M. Tonry & M. H. Moore (Eds.), *Youth violence* (pp. 421–475). Chicago: University of Chicago Press.

Farrington, D. P. (2000). Adolescent violence: Findings and implications from the Cambridge Study. In G. Boswell (Ed.), *Violent children and adolescents: Asking the question why* (pp. 19–35). London: Whurr.

Farrington, D. P., Barnes, G., & Lambert, S. (1996a). The concentration of offending in families. *Legal and Criminological Psychology, 1,* 47–63.

Farrington, D. P., Biron, L., & LeBlanc, M. (1982). Personality and delinquency in London and Montreal. In J. Gunn & D. P. Farrington (Eds.), *Abnormal offenders, delinquency, and the criminal justice system* (pp. 153–201). Chichester, England: Wiley.

Farrington, D. P., & Hawkins, J. D. (1991). Predicting participation, early onset, and later persistence in officially recorded offending. *Criminal Behavior and Mental Health, 1,* 1–33.

Farrington, D. P., Jolliffe, D., Loeber, R., Stouthamer-Loeber, M., & Kalb, L. M. (2001). The concentration of offenders in families, and family criminality in the prediction of boys' delinquency. *Journal of Adolescence, 24,* 579–596.

Farrington, D. P., Lambert, S., & West, D. J. (1998). Criminal careers of two generations of family members in the Cambridge Study in Delinquent Development. *Studies on Crime and Crime Prevention, 7,* 85–106.

Farrington, D. P., & Loeber, R. (1999). Transatlantic replicability of risk factors in the development of delinquency. In P. Cohen, C. Slomkowski, & L. N. Robins (Eds.), *Historical and geographical influences on psychopathology* (pp. 299–329). Mahwah, NJ: Erlbaum.

Farrington, D. P., Loeber, R., Stouthamer-Loeber, M. S., van Kammen, W., & Schmidt, L. (1996). Self-reported delinquency and a combined delinquency seriousness scale based on boys, mothers and teachers: Concurrent and predictive validity for African Americans and Caucasians. *Criminology, 34,* 493–517.

Farrington, D. P., Loeber, R., & van Kammen, W. B. (1990). Long-term criminal outcomes of hyperactivity-impulsivity-attention deficit and conduct problems in childhood. In L. N. Robins & M. Rutter (Eds.), *Straight and devious pathways from childhood to adulthood* (pp. 62–81). Cambridge, England: Cambridge University Press.

Farrington, D. P., Snyder, H. N., & Finnegan, T. A. (1988). Specialization in juvenile court careers. *Criminology, 26,* 461–487.

Farrington, D. P., & Welsh, B. C. (in press). Family-based prevention of offending: A meta-analysis. *Australian and New Zealand Journal of Criminology.*

Farrington, D. P., & Wikström, P-O. H. (1994). Criminal careers in London and Stockholm: A cross-national comparative study. In E. G. M. Weitekamp & H. J. Kerner (Eds.), *Cross-*

national longitudinal research on human development and criminal behavior (pp. 65–89). Dordrecht, Netherlands: Kluwer.

Federal Bureau of Investigation. (2002). *Crime in the United States, 2001.* Washington DC: Author.

Feldman, R. A., Caplinger, T. E., & Wodarski, J. S. (1983). *The St. Louis conundrum.* Englewood Cliffs, NJ: Prentice-Hall.

Fergusson, D. M., & Horwood, L. J. (1995). Predictive validity of categorically and dimensionally scored measures of disruptive childhood behaviors. *Journal of the American Academy of Child and Adolescent Psychiatry, 34,* 477–485.

Fergusson, D. M., & Horwood, L. J. (1998). Exposure to interparental violence in childhood and psychosocial adjustment in young adulthood. *Child Abuse and Neglect, 22,* 339–357.

Fergusson, D. M., Horwood, J., & Lynskey, M. T. (1994). Parental separation, adolescent psychopathology, and problem behaviors. *Journal of the American Academy of Child and Adolescent Psychiatry, 33,* 1122–1131.

Fischer, D. G. (1984). Family size and delinquency. *Perceptual and Motor Skills, 58,* 527–534.

Fitzpatrick, K. M. (1997). Fighting among America's youth: A risk and protective factors approach. *Journal of Health and Social Behavior, 38,* 131–148.

Frick, P. J., Kamphaus, R. W., Lahey, B. B., Loeber, R., Christ, M. A. G., Hart, E. L., et al. (1991). Academic underachievement and the disruptive behavior disorders. *Journal of Consulting and Clinical Psychology, 59,* 289–294.

Frick, P. J., Lahey, B. B., Loeber, R., Stouthamer-Loeber, M., Christ, M. A. G., & Hanson, K. (1992). Familial risk factors to oppositional defiant disorder and conduct disorder: Parental psychopathology and maternal parenting. *Journal of Consulting and Clinical Psychology, 60,* 49–55.

Goodman, R., Simonoff, E., & Stevenson, J. (1995). The impact of child IQ, parent IQ and sibling IQ on child behavioral deviance scores. *Journal of Child Psychology and Psychiatry, 36,* 409–425.

Gordon, D. A. (1995). Functional family therapy for delinquents. In R. R. Ross, D. H. Antonowicz, & G. K. Dhaliwal (Eds.), *Going straight: Effective delinquency prevention and offender rehabilitation* (pp. 163–178). Ottawa, Canada: Air Training and Publications.

Gottfredson, D. C. (2001). *Schools and delinquency.* Cambridge, England: Cambridge University Press.

Gottfredson, D. C., McNeil, R. J., & Gottfredson, G. D. (1991). Social area influences on delinquency: A multilevel analyses. *Journal of Research in Crime and Delinquency, 28,* 197–226.

Graham, J. (1988). *Schools, disruptive behaviour and delinquency.* London: Her Majesty's Stationery Office.

Haapasalo, J., & Pokela, E. (1999). Child-rearing and child abuse antecedents of criminality. *Aggression and Violent Behavior, 1,* 107–127.

Harrell, A. V., Cavanagh, S. E., Harmon, M. A., Koper, C. S., & Sridharan, S. (1997). *Impact of the Children at Risk program: Comprehensive final report* (Vol. 2). Washington, DC: The Urban Institute.

Harrell, A. V., Cavanagh, S. E., & Sridharan, S. (1999). *Evaluation of the Children at Risk program: Results one year after the program.* Washington, DC: U.S. National Institute of Justice.

Hawkins, J. D., Catalano, R. F., Kosterman, R., Abbott, R., & Hill, K. G. (1999). Preventing adolescent health risk behaviors by strengthening protection during childhood. *Archives of Pediatrics and Adolescent Medicine, 153,* 226–234.

Hawkins, J. D., von Cleve, E., & Catalano, R. F. (1991). Reducing early childhood aggression: Results of a primary prevention program. *Journal of the American Academy of Child and Adolescent Psychiatry, 30,* 208–217.

Hawkins, J. D., Herrenkohl, T., Farrington, D. P., Brewer, D., Catalano, R. F., & Harachi, T. W. (1998). A review of predictors of youth violence. In R. Loeber & D. P. Farrington (Eds.), *Serious and violent juvenile offenders: Risk factors and successful interventions* (pp. 106–146). Thousand Oaks, CA: Sage.

Henggeler, S. W., Melton, G. B., Brondino, M. J., Scherer, D. G., & Hanley, J. H. (1997). Multisystemic therapy with violent and chronic juvenile offenders and their families: The role of treatment fidelity in successful dissemination. *Journal of Consulting and Clinical Psychology, 65,* 821–833.

Henggeler, S. W., Melton, G. B., Smith, L. A., Schoenwald, S. K., & Hanley, J. H. (1993). Family preservation using multisystemic treatment: Long-term follow-up to a clinical trial with serious juvenile offenders. *Journal of Child and Family Studies, 2,* 283–293.

Henry, B., Caspi, A., Moffitt, T. E., & Silva, P. A. (1996). Temperamental and familial predictors of violent and nonviolent criminal convictions: Age 3 to age 18. *Developmental Psychology, 32,* 614–623.

Henry, B., Moffitt, T., Robins, L., Earls, F., & Silva, P. (1993). Early family predictors of child and adolescent antisocial behavior: Who are the mothers of delinquents? *Criminal Behavior and Mental Health, 2,* 97–118.

Herrenkohl, T. I., Hawkins, J. D., Chung, I-J., Hill, K. G., & Battin-Pearson, S. (2001). School and community risk factors and interventions. In R. Loeber & D. P. Farrington (Eds.), *Child delinquents: Development, intervention and service needs* (pp. 211–246). Thousand Oaks, CA: Sage.

Hill, J., & Maughan, B. (Eds.). (2001). *Conduct disorders in childhood and adolescence.* Cambridge, England: Cambridge University Press.

Hinshaw, S. P., Lahey, B. B., & Hart, E. L. (1993). Issues of taxonomy and comorbidity in the development of conduct disorder. *Development and Psychopathology, 5,* 31–49.

Hogh, E., & Wolf, P. (1983). Violent crime in a birth cohort: Copenhagen 1953–1977. In K. T. van Dusen & S. A. Mednick (Eds.), *Prospective studies of crime and delinquency* (pp. 249–267). Boston: Kluwer-Nijhoff.

Huesmann, L. R., & Eron, L. D. (1989). Individual differences and the trait of aggression. *European Journal of Personality, 3,* 95–106.

Huesmann, L. R., Eron, L. D., Lefkowitz, M. M., & Walder, L. O. (1984). Stability of aggression over time and generations. *Developmental Psychology, 20,* 1120–1134.

Huizinga, D., & Elliott, D. S. (1986). Reassessing the reliability and validity of self-report measures. *Journal of Quantitative Criminology, 2,* 293–327.

Huizinga, D., & Jakob-Chien, C. (1998). The contemporaneous co-occurrence of serious and violent juvenile offending and other problem behaviors. In R. Loeber & D. P. Farrington (Eds.), *Serious and violent juvenile offenders: Risk factors and successful interventions* (pp. 47–67). Thousand Oaks, CA: Sage.

Huizinga, D., Loeber, R., & Thornberry, T. P. (1993). Longitudinal study of delinquency, drug use, sexual activity and pregnancy among children and youth in three cities. *Public Health Reports, 108,* 90–96.

Jenkins, J. M., & Smith, M. A. (1991). Marital disharmony and children's behavior problems: Aspects of a poor marriage that affect children adversely. *Journal of Child Psychology and Psychiatry, 32,* 793–810.

Jones, M. B., & Offord, D. R. (1989). Reduction of antisocial behavior in poor children by nonschool skill-development. *Journal of Child Psychology and Psychiatry, 30,* 737–750.

Juby, H., & Farrington, D. P. (2001). Disentangling the link between disrupted families and delinquency. *British Journal of Criminology, 41,* 22–40.

Junger-Tas, J., & Marshall, I. H. (1999). The self-report methodology in crime research. In M. Tonry (Ed.), *Crime and justice* (Vol. 25, pp. 291–367). Chicago: University of Chicago Press.

Kagan, J. (1989). Temperamental contributions to social behavior. *American Psychologist, 44,* 668–674.

Kalb, L. M., Farrington, D. P., & Loeber, R. (2001). Leading longitudinal studies on delinquency, substance use, sexual behavior, and mental health problems with childhood samples. In R. Loeber & D. P. Farrington (Eds.), *Child delinquents: Development, intervention, and service needs* (pp. 415–423). Thousand Oaks, CA: Sage.

Kasius, M. C., Ferdinand, R. F., van den Berg, H., & Verhulst, F. C. (1997). Associations between different diagnostic approaches for child and adolescent psychopathology. *Journal of Child Psychology and Psychiatry, 38,* 625–632.

Kazdin, A. E. (1997). Parent management training: Evidence, outcomes and issues. *Journal of the American Academy of Child and Adolescent Psychiatry, 36,* 1349–1356.

Keenan, K., Loeber, R., Zhang, Q., Stouthamer-Loeber, M., & van Kammen, W. B. (1995). The influence of deviant peers on the development of boys' disruptive and delinquent behavior: A temporal analysis. *Development and Psychopathology, 7,* 715–726.

Klinteberg, B. A., Andersson, T., Magnusson, D., & Stattin, H. (1993). Hyperactive behavior in childhood as related to subsequent alcohol problems and violent offending: A longitudinal study of male subjects. *Personality and Individual Differences, 15,* 381–388.

Kolvin, I., Miller, F. J. W., Fleeting, M., & Kolvin, P. A. (1988). Social and parenting factors affecting criminal-offence rates: Findings from the Newcastle Thousand Family Study (1947–1980). *British Journal of Psychiatry, 152,* 80–90.

Lahey, B. B., Loeber, R., Hart, E. L., Frick, P. J., Applegate, B., Zhang, Q., et al. (1995). Four-year longitudinal study of conduct disorder in boys: Patterns and predictors of persistence. *Journal of Abnormal Psychology, 104,* 83–93.

Lahey, B. B., Loeber, R., Stouthamer-Loeber, M., Christ, M. A. G., Green, S., Russo, M. F., et al. (1990). Comparison of *DSM-III* and *DSM-III-R* diagnoses for prepubertal children: Changes in prevalence and validity. *Journal of the American Academy of Child and Adolescent Psychiatry, 29,* 620–626.

Lahey, B. B., Moffitt, T. E., & Caspi, A. (Eds.). (2003). *The causes of conduct disorder and serious juvenile delinquency.* New York: Guilford Press.

Lahey, B. B., Schwab-Stone, M., Goodman, S. H., Waldman, I. D., Canino, G., Rathouz, P. J., et al. (2000). Age and gender differences in oppositional behavior and conduct problems: A cross-sectional household study of middle childhood and adolescence. *Journal of Abnormal Psychology, 109,* 488–503.

LeBlanc, M., & Frechette, M. (1989). *Male criminal activity from childhood through youth.* New York: Springer-Verlag.

Leschied, A., & Cunningham A. (2002). *Seeking effective interventions for serious young offenders: Interim results of a four-year randomized study of multisystemic therapy in Ontario, Canada.* London, Ontario, Canada: London Family Court Clinic.

Lipsey, M. W., & Derzon, J. H. (1998). Predictors of violent or serious delinquency in adolescence and early adulthood: A synthesis of longitudinal research. In R. Loeber & D. P. Farrington (Eds.), *Serious and violent juvenile offenders: Risk factors and successful interventions* (pp. 86–105). Thousand Oaks, CA: Sage.

Lipsey, M. W., & Wilson, D. B. (1998). Effective intervention for serious juvenile offenders: A synthesis of research. In R. Loeber & D. P. Farrington (Eds.), *Serious and violent juvenile offenders: Risk factors and successful interventions* (pp. 313–345). Thousand Oaks, CA: Sage.

Lipsitt, P. D., Buka, S. L., & Lipsitt, L. P. (1990). Early intelligence scores and subsequent delinquency: A prospective study. *American Journal of Family Therapy, 18,* 197–208.

Loeber, R., Farrington, D. P., Stouthamer-Loeber, M., Moffitt, T. E., Caspi, A., & Lynam, D. (2001). Male mental health problems, psychopathy, and personality traits: Key findings from the first 14 years of the Pittsburgh Youth Study. *Clinical Child and Family Psychology Review, 4,* 273–297.

Loeber, R., Farrington, D. P., Stouthamer-Loeber, M., & van Kammen, W. B. (1998). *Antisocial behavior and mental health problems: Explanatory factors in childhood and adolescence.* Mahwah, NJ: Erlbaum.

Loeber, R., Green, S. M., Keenan, K., & Lahey, B. B. (1995). Which boys will fare worse? Early predictors of the onset of conduct disorder in a six-year longitudinal study. *Journal of the American Academy of Child and Adolescent Psychiatry, 34,* 499–509.

Loeber, R., & Hay, D. F. (1997). Key issues in the development of aggression and violence from childhood to early adulthood. *Annual Review of Psychology, 48,* 371–410.

Loeber, R., & LeBlanc, M. (1990). Toward a developmental criminology. In M. Tonry & N. Morris (Eds.), *Crime and justice* (Vol. 12, pp. 375–473). Chicago: University of Chicago Press.

Loeber, R., & Stouthamer-Loeber, M. (1998). Development of juvenile aggression and violence: Some common misconceptions and controversies. *American Psychologist, 53,* 242–259.

Loeber, R., Stouthamer-Loeber, M., van Kammen, W. B., & Farrington, D. P. (1991). Initiation, escalation and desistance in juvenile offending and their correlates. *Journal of Criminal Law and Criminology, 82,* 36–82.

Loeber, R., Wung, P., Keenan, K., Giroux, B., Stouthamer-Loeber, M., & van Kammen, W. B. (1993). Developmental pathways in disruptive child behavior. *Development and Psychopathology, 5,* 101–132.

Lynam, D. (1996). Early identification of chronic offenders: Who is the fledgling psychopath? *Psychological Bulletin, 120,* 209–234.

Lynam, D. R. (1998). Early identification of the fledgling psychopath: Locating the psychopathic child in the current nomenclature. *Journal of Abnormal Psychology, 107,* 566–575.

Lynam, D. R., & Moffitt, T. E. (1995). Delinquency and impulsivity and IQ: A reply to Block (1995). *Journal of Abnormal Psychology, 104,* 399–401.

Lynam, D., Moffitt, T. E., & Stouthamer-Loeber, M. (1993). Explaining the relation between IQ and delinquency: Class, race, test motivation, school failure or self-control? *Journal of Abnormal Psychology, 102,* 187–196.

Malinosky-Rummell, R., & Hansen, D. J. (1993). Long-term consequences of childhood physical abuse. *Psychological Bulletin, 114,* 68–79.

Mandel, H. P. (1997). *Conduct disorder and underachievement.* New York: Wiley.

Maughan, B., Pickles, A., Rowe, R., Costello, E. J., & Angold, A. (2000). Developmental trajectories of aggressive and nonaggressive conduct problems. *Journal of Quantitative Criminology, 16,* 199–221.

Maxfield, M. G., & Widom, C. S. (1996). The cycle of violence revisited six years later. *Archives of Pediatrics and Adolescent Medicine, 150,* 390–395.

McCord, J. (1977). A comparative study of two generations of native Americans. In R. F. Meier (Ed.), *Theory in criminology* (pp. 83–92). Beverly Hills, CA: Sage.

McCord, J. (1979). Some child-rearing antecedents of criminal behavior in adult men. *Journal of Personality and Social Psychology, 37,* 1477–1486.

McCord, J. (1982). A longitudinal view of the relationship between paternal absence and crime. In J. Gunn & D. P. Farrington (Eds.), *Abnormal offenders, delinquency, and the criminal justice system* (pp. 113–128). Chichester, England: Wiley.

Moffitt, T. E. (1993a). Adolescence-limited and life-course-persistent antisocial behavior: A developmental taxonomy. *Psychological Review, 100,* 674–701.

Moffitt, T. E. (1993b). The neuropsychology of conduct disorder. *Development and Psychopathology, 5,* 135–151.

Moffitt, T. E., Caspi, A., Dickson, N., Silva, P., & Stanton, W. (1996). Childhood-onset versus adolescent-onset antisocial conduct problems in males: Natural history from ages 3 to 18 years. *Development and Psychopathology, 8,* 399–424.

Moffitt, T. E., Caspi, A., Rutter, M., & Silva, P. A. (2001). *Sex differences in antisocial behavior.* Cambridge, England: Cambridge University Press.

Moffitt, T. E., & Henry, B. (1991). Neuropsychological studies of juvenile delinquency and juvenile violence. In J. S. Milner (Ed.), *Neuropsychology of aggression* (pp. 131–146). Boston: Kluwer.

Morash, M., & Rucker, L. (1989). An exploratory study of the connection of mother's age at childbearing to her children's delinquency in four data sets. *Crime and Delinquency, 35,* 45–93.

Nagin, D. S., Farrington, D. P., & Moffitt, T. E. (1995). Life-course trajectories of different types of offenders. *Criminology, 33,* 111–139.

Nagin, D. S., Pogarsky, G., & Farrington, D. P. (1997). Adolescent mothers and the criminal behavior of their children. *Law and Society Review, 31,* 137–162.

Nagin, D. S., & Tremblay, R. E. (1999). Trajectories of boys' physical aggression, opposition, and hyperactivity on the path to physically violent and nonviolent juvenile delinquency. *Child Development, 70,* 1181–1196.

Newson, J., Newson, E., & Adams, M. (1993). The social origins of delinquency. *Criminal Behavior and Mental Health, 3,* 19–29.

Nottelman, E. D., & Jensen, P. S. (1995). Comorbidity of disorders in children and adolescents: Developmental perspectives. In T. H. Ollendick & R. J. Prinz (Eds.), *Advances in clinical child psychology* (Vol. 17, pp. 109–155). New York: Plenum.

Offord, D. R., Alder, R. J., & Boyle, M. H. (1986). Prevalence and sociodemographic correlates of conduct disorder. *American Journal of Social Psychiatry, 6,* 272–278.

Offord, D. R., Boyle, M. H., & Racine, Y. (1989). Ontario Child Health Study: Correlates of disorder. *Journal of the American Academy of Child and Adolescent Psychiatry, 28,* 856–860.

Offord, D. R., Boyle, M. H., Racine, Y. A., Fleming, J. E., Cadman, D. T., Blum, H. M., et al. (1992). Outcome, prognosis and risk in a longitudinal follow-up study. *Journal of the American Academy of Child and Adolescent Psychiatry, 31,* 916–923.

Offord, D. R., Boyle, M. H., Szatmari, P., Rae-Grant, N. I., Links, P. S., Cadman, D. T., et al. (1987). Ontario Child Health Study: II. Six-month prevalence of disorder and rates of service utilization. *Archives of General Psychiatry, 44,* 832–836.

Olds, D. L., Eckenrode, J., Henderson, C. R., Kitzman, H., Powers, J., Cole, R., et al. (1997). Long-term effects of home visitation on maternal life course and child abuse and neglect. *Journal of the American Medical Association, 278,* 637–643.

Olds, D. L., Henderson, C. R., Chamberlain, R., & Tatelbaum, R. (1986). Preventing child abuse and neglect: A randomized trial of nurse home visitation. *Pediatrics, 78,* 65–78.

Olds, D. L., Henderson, C. R., Cole, R., Eckenrode, J., Kitzman, H., Luckey, D., et al. (1998). Long-term effects of nurse home visitation on children's criminal and antisocial behavior: 15-year follow-up of a randomized controlled trial. *Journal of the American Medical Association, 280,* 1238–1244.

Olweus, D. (1979) Stability of aggressive reaction patterns in males: A review. *Psychological Bulletin, 86,* 852–875.

Olweus, D. (1991). Bully/victim problems among school children: Basic facts and effects of a school based intervention program. In D. J. Pepler & K. H. Rubin (Eds.), *The development and treatment of childhood aggression* (pp. 411–448). Hillsdale, NJ: Erlbaum.

Olweus, D. (1994). Bullying at school: Basic facts and effects of a school based intervention program. *Journal of Child Psychology and Psychiatry, 35,* 1171–1190.

O'Moore, A. M., & Hillery, B. (1989). Bullying in Dublin schools. *Irish Journal of Psychology, 10,* 426–441.

Pakiz, B., Reinherz, H. Z., & Frost, A. K. (1992). Antisocial behavior in adolescence: A community study. *Journal of Early Adolescence, 12,* 300–313.

Patterson, G. R. (1982). *Coercive family process.* Eugene, OR: Castalia.

Patterson, G. R., Capaldi, D., & Bank, L. (1991). An early starter model for predicting delinquency. In D. J. Pepler & K. H. Rubin (Eds.), *The development and treatment of childhood aggression* (pp. 139–168). Hillsdale, NJ: Erlbaum.

Patterson, G. R., Chamberlain, P., & Reid, J. B. (1982). A comparative evaluation of a parent training program. *Behavior Therapy, 13,* 638–650.

Patterson, G. R., Reid, J. B., & Dishion, T. J. (1992). *Antisocial boys.* Eugene, OR: Castalia.

Pepler, D. J., & Craig, W. M. (1995). A peek behing the fence: Naturalistic observations of aggressive children with remote audiovisual recording. *Developmental Psychology, 31,* 548–553.

Prime, J., White, S., Liriano, S., & Patel, K. (2001). *Criminal careers of those born between 1953 and 1978* (Statistical Bulletin 4/01). London: Home Office.

Pulkkinen, L. (1987). Offensive and defensive aggression in humans: A longitudinal perspective. *Aggressive Behavior, 13,* 197–212.

Raine, A. (1993). *The psychopathology of crime.* San Diego, CA: Academic Press.

Reiss, A. J., & Farrington, D. P. (1991). Advancing knowledge about co-offending: Results from a prospective longitudinal survey of London males. *Journal of Criminal Law and Criminology, 82,* 360–395.

Reynolds, A. J., Temple, J. A., Robertson, D. L., & Mann, E. A. (2001). Long-term effects of an early childhood intervention on educational achievement and juvenile arrest: A 15-year follow-up of low-income children in public schools. *Journal of the American Medical Association, 285,* 2339–2346.

Robins, L. N. (1979). Sturdy childhood predictors of adult outcomes: Replications from longitudinal studies. In J. E. Barrett, R. M. Rose, & G. L. Klerman (Eds.), *Stress and mental disorder* (pp. 219–235). New York: Raven Press.

Robins, L. N. (1989). Epidemiology of antisocial personality. In J. O. Cavenar (Ed.), *Psychiatry* (Vol. 3, pp. 1–14). Philadelphia: Lippincott.

Robins, L. N. (1999). A 70-year history of conduct disorder: Variations in definition, prevalence and correlates. In P. Cohen, C. Slomkowski, & L. N. Robins (Eds.), *Historical and geographical influences on psychopathology* (pp. 37–56). Mahwah, NJ: Erlbaum.

Robins, L. N., West, P. J., & Herjanic, B. L. (1975). Arrests and delinquency in two generations: A study of black urban families and their children. *Journal of Child Psychology and Psychiatry, 16,* 125–140.

Rogeness, G. A. (1994). Biologic findings in conduct disorder. *Child and Adolescent Psychiatric Clinics of North America, 3,* 271–284.

Romano, E., Tremblay, R. E., Vitaro, F., Zoccolillo, M., & Pagani, L. (2001). Prevalence of psychiatric diagnoses and the role of perceived impairment: Findings from an adolescent community sample. *Journal of Child Psychology and Psychiatry, 42,* 451–461.

Ross, R. R., & Ross, R. D. (Eds.). (1995). *Thinking straight: The reasoning and rehabilitation program for delinquency prevention and offender rehabilitation.* Ottawa, Ontario, Canada: Air Training and Publications.

Rothbaum, F., & Weisz, J. R. (1994). Parental caregiving and child externalizing behavior in nonclinical samples: A meta-analysis. *Psychological Bulletin, 116,* 55–74.

Rowe, D. C., Vaszonyi, A. T., & Flannery, D. J. (1995). Sex differences in crime: Do means and within-sex variation have similar causes? *Journal of Research in Crime and Delinquency, 32,* 84–100.

Rutter, M. (1981). The city and the child. *American Journal of Orthopsychiatry, 51,* 610–625.

Rutter, M., Giller, H., & Hagell, A. (1998) *Antisocial behavior in young people.* Cambridge, England: Cambridge University Press.

Sampson, R. J., Raudenbush, S. W., & Earls, F. (1997). Neighborhoods and violent crime: A multilevel study of collective efficacy. *Science, 277,* 918–924.

Schwartz, C. E., Snidman, N., & Kagan, J. (1996). Early childhood temperament as a determinant of externalizing behavior in adolescence. *Development and Psychopathology, 8,* 527–537.

Schweinhart, L. J., Barnes, H. V., & Weikart, D. P. (1993). *Significant benefits.* Ypsilanti, MI: High/Scope.

Schweinhart, L. J., & Weikart, D. P. (1980). *Young children grow up.* Ypsilanti, MI: High/Scope.

Seguin, J., Pihl, R. O., Harden, P. W., Tremblay, R. E., & Boulerice, B. (1995). Cognitive and neuropsychological characteristics of physically aggressive boys. *Journal of Abnormal Psychology, 104,* 614–624.

Shaffer, D., Fisher, P., Dulcan, M. K., Davies, M., Piacentini, J., Schwab-Stone, M. E., et al. (1996). The NIMH Diagnostic Interview Schedule for Children, version 2.3 (DISC-2.3): Description, acceptability, prevalence rates and performance in the MECA Study. *Journal of the American Academy of Child and Adolescent Psychiatry, 35,* 865–877.

Shaw, C. R., & McKay, H. D. (1969). *Juvenile delinquency and urban areas* (Rev. ed.). Chicago: University of Chicago Press.

Smith, C. A., & Stern, S. B. (1997). Delinquency and antisocial behavior: A review of family processes and intervention research. *Social Service Review, 71,* 382–420.

Smith, C. A., & Thornberry, T. P. (1995). The relationship between childhood maltreatment and adolescent involvement in delinquency. *Criminology, 33,* 451–481.

Smith, P. K., & Sharp, S. (1994). *School bullying: Insights and perspectives.* London: Routledge.

Stattin, H., & Klackenberg-Larsson, I. (1993). Early language and intelligence development and their relationship to future criminal behavior. *Journal of Abnormal Psychology, 102,* 369–378.

Stattin, H., & Magnusson, D. (1991). Stability and change in criminal behavior up to age 30. *British Journal of Criminology, 31,* 327–346.

Steinberg, L., Lamborn, S. D., Dornbusch, S. M., & Darling, N. (1992). Impact of parenting practices on adolescent achievement: Authoritative parenting, school involvement and encouragement to succeed. *Child Development, 63,* 1266–1281.

Stephenson, P., & Smith, D. (1989). Bullying in the junior school. In D. Tattum & D. Lane (Eds.), *Bullying in schools.* Stoke-on-Trent, England: Trentham.

Szatmari, P., Boyle, M. H., & Offord, D. R. (1993). Familial aggregation of emotional and behavioral problems of childhood in the general population. *American Journal of Psychiatry, 150,* 1398–1403.

Thornberry, T. P., Huizinga, D., & Loeber, R. (1995). The prevention of serious delinquency and violence: Implications from the program of research on the causes and correlates of delinquency. In J. C. Howell, B. Krisberg, J. D. Hawkins, & J. J. Wilson (Eds.), *Sourcebook on serious, violent and chronic juvenile offenders* (pp. 213–237). Thousand Oaks, CA: Sage.

Tobler, N. S., Lessard, T., Marshall, D., Ochshorn, P., & Roona, M. (1999). Effectiveness of school-based drug prevention programs for marijuana use. *School Psychology International, 20,* 105–137.

Tolan, P. H., & Gorman-Smith, D. (1998). Development of serious and violent offending careers. In R. Loeber & D. P. Farrington (Eds.), *Serious and violent juvenile offenders: Risk factors and successful interventions* (pp. 68–85). Thousand Oaks, CA: Sage.

Tracy, P. E., Wolfgang, M. E., & Figlio, R. M. (1985). *Delinquency in two birth cohorts.* Washington, DC: U.S. Office of Juvenile Justice and Delinquency Prevention.

Tremblay, R. E., Japel, C., Perusse, D., McDuff, P., Boivin, M., Zoccolillo, M., et al. (1999). The search for the age of onset of physical aggression: Rousseau and Bandura revisited. *Criminal Behavior and Mental Health, 9,* 8–23.

Tremblay, R. E., Pagani-Kurtz, L., Vitaro, F., Masse, L. C., & Pihl, R. D. (1995). A bimodal preventive intervention for disruptive kindergarten boys: Its impact through mid-adolescence. *Journey of Consulting and Clinical Psychology, 63,* 560–568.

Velez, C. N., Johnson, J., & Cohen, P. (1989). A longitudinal analysis of selected risk factors for childhood psychopathology. *Journal of the American Academy of Child and Adolescent Psychiatry, 28,* 861–864.

Verhulst, F. C., & van der Ende, J. (1995). The eight-year stability of problem behavior in an epidemiologic sample. *Pediatric Research, 38,* 612–617.

Wadsworth, M. (1979). *Roots of delinquency.* London: Martin Robertson.

Wasserman, G. A., & Miller, L. S. (1998). The prevention of serious and violent juvenile offending. In R. Loeber & D. P. Farrington (Eds.), *Serious and violent juvenile offenders: Risk factors and successful interventions* (pp. 197–247). Thousand Oaks, CA: Sage.

Wells, L. E., & Rankin, J. H. (1991). Families and delinquency: A meta-analysis of the impact of broken homes. *Social Problems, 38,* 71–93.

West, D. J., & Farrington, D. P. (1973). *Who becomes delinquent?* London: Heinemann.

West, D. J., & Farrington, D. P. (1977). *The delinquent way of life.* London: Heinemann.

White, J. L., Moffitt, T. E., Caspi, A., Bartusch, D. J., Needles, D. J., & Stouthamer-Loeber, M. (1994). Measuring impulsivity and examining its relationship to delinquency. *Journal of Abnormal Psychology, 103,* 192–205.

Whitney, I., & Smith, P. K. (1991). *A survey of the nature and extent of bullying in junior/middle and secondary schools* [Final report to the Gulbenkian Foundation]. Sheffield, England: University of Sheffield, Department of Psychology.

Widom, C. S. (1989). The cycle of violence. *Science, 244,* 160–166.

Widom, C. S. (1994). Childhood victimization and adolescent problem behaviors. In R. D. Ketterlinus & M. E. Lamb (Eds.), *Adolescent problem behaviors* (pp. 127–164). Hillsdale, NJ: Erlbaum.

Wikström, P-O. H. (1985). *Everyday violence in contemporary Sweden.* Stockholm: National Council for Crime Prevention.
Wilson, J. Q., & Herrnstein, R. J. (1985). *Crime and human nature.* New York: Simon and Schuster.
Wolfgang, M. E., Thornberry, T. P., & Figlio, R. M. (1987). *From boy to man, from delinquency to crime.* Chicago: University of Chicago Press.
Zoccolillo, M. (1993). Gender and the development of conduct disorder. *Development and Psychopathology, 5,* 65–78.

Chapter 21

ADOLESCENT SUBSTANCE USE

Laurie Chassin, Andrea Hussong, Manuel Barrera, Jr., Brooke S.G. Molina, Ryan Trim, and Jennifer Ritter

Adolescence is often described as a time of experimentation with risky or problem behaviors (Arnett, 2000), and substance use is one such behavior that is initiated during this age period. Substance use and addictive disorders are topics of considerable importance both because of their significance for adolescent development and because of their public health impact. For example, considering both adults and adolescents, recent estimates are that the use and abuse of alcohol, nicotine, and illegal drugs cost the United States approximately $257 billion per year, exceeding the costs associated with heart disease or cancer (Institute of Medicine, 1994a). Surprisingly, given its importance, adolescent substance use as a research area is relatively new, although it has seen rapid and significant expansion in the past three decades.

This chapter describes the prevalence and predictors of adolescent substance use and substance use problems, with particular emphasis on their relation to the developmental issues of adolescence. The chapter is not intended to be comprehensive; for example, we do not consider issues of treatment (see Deas & Thomas, 2001) or prevention (see Bukoski, 1997; Substance Abuse & Mental Health Services Administration [SAMHSA], 1999). Rather, we selectively emphasize recent empirical work and studies that illustrate important general themes in adolescent substance use research.

In this chapter, we include studies of substances that are legal if consumed by adults (cigarettes and alcohol) as well as illegal drugs. Moreover, we include studies of substance use (i.e., the quantity and frequency of consumption) and studies of substance use problems or formal diagnoses of substance use disorders. The standard diagnostic taxonomy (*Diagnostic and Statistical Manual of Mental Disorders–Fourth Edition [DSM-IV];* American Psychiatric Association, 1994) includes two different substance use disorders, substance dependence, and substance abuse. Although the adequacy of these diagnoses has been questioned in terms of their appropriateness for adolescent populations (Deas, Riggs, Langenbucher, Goldman, & Brown, 2000; Fulkerson, Harrison, & Beebe, 1999; Martin, Kaczynski, Maisto, Bukstein, & Moss, 1995), current practice is to diagnose adolescents with the same criteria that are used for adults. According to the *DSM-IV,* substance dependence is a maladaptive pattern of substance use that includes tolerance (needing increased amounts of the substance to achieve intoxication or experiencing reduced effects from the same amount of consumption), withdrawal (cognitive and physiological changes upon discontinuing use), and compulsive use reflecting psychological dependence (e.g., unsuccessful efforts to cut down).

In contrast, substance abuse, which is considered less severe, involves repeated negative consequences of substance use, including failure to fulfill obligations at work, school, or home and use of substances in situations that are physically hazardous. Researchers have suggested that the antecedents of adolescent substance use differ from those of substance use problems or disorders (Colder & Chassin, 1999; Shedler & Block, 1990). Thus, we include both studies of adolescent substance use and substance use disorders and note the distinctions between them.

PREVALENCE OF ADOLESCENT SUBSTANCE USE AND SUBSTANCE USE DISORDERS

Epidemiological studies and most other studies of adolescent drug use rely on adolescents' self-reports because parents are unlikely to be aware of their adolescents' use. Indeed, parent and adolescent reports show low levels of agreement (Cantwell, Lewinsohn, Rohde, & Seeley, 1997). Although it is beyond the scope of this chapter, a large literature has addressed the validity (and threats to validity) of these adolescent self-reports, including their validation with biological measures (e.g., Dolcini, Adler, & Ginsberg, 1996). In general, these data suggest that self-reports can be valid if they are obtained under conditions of anonymity and privacy and when there is little motivation to distort responses. For example, data from a 1990 National Household Survey on Drug Abuse (NHSDA) field test sample suggest that self-administered methods substantially improve reporting, compared to interviewer-style questioning (Rogers, Miller, & Turner, 1998).

Data from the Monitoring the Future (MTF) study, a national school-based survey, show that adolescent substance use is relatively common by the end of the high school years (Johnston, O'Malley, & Bachman, 2002). For example, in 2001 approximately 54% of 12th graders used some illegal drug in their lifetimes, with 25.7% using in the past month (a common definition of current use). Marijuana is the most frequently used illegal drug, with 49% of 12th graders reporting some lifetime use and 5.8% using daily in 2001 (Johnston et al., 2002). The use of substances that are legal for adults (i.e., alcohol and tobacco) is even more common, with 73.3% of high school seniors reporting drinking in the past year and 49.8% reporting drinking in the past month (Johnston et al., 2002). Sixty-one percent of high school seniors report some experience with cigarette smoking, and 19% were daily smokers in 2001 (Johnston et al., 2002). The use of different drugs is highly interrelated in both epidemiological and clinical samples of adolescents (Johnston, O'Malley, & Bachman, 2000). For example, in the 1985 NHSDA data, 24% of illicit drug users used multiple drugs simultaneously within the past year, and 43% had used alcohol along with an illicit drug (Clayton, 1992).

The MTF data also reveal interesting patterns of change over time. In general, adolescent substance use involvement reached a peak in the mid-1970s and early 1980s and then declined. Substance use rose again in the early 1990s but has since leveled off. Specific drugs show marked increases and decreases in use over time. For example, cocaine use among 12th graders peaked in the late 1970s, showed dramatic declines between 1986 and 1992 (to about one fourth the rate), but then began to increase again until

2000. As of 2002, there were declining trends for cigarettes, LSD, inhalants, and heroin use without a needle but increasing trends for ecstasy (MDMA) and steroids (Johnston et al., 2002). Johnston et al. (2000) note that as older drugs wane in popularity, new drugs replace them. For example, PCP showed a rapid rise in the 1970s, crack and cocaine in the 1980s, and Rohypnol and ecstasy in the 1990s. It is interesting to note that the popularity of specific drugs often revives after a period of low use. Johnston et al. (2000) suggest that the use of particular drugs may make such a comeback because knowledge of its risks and negative effects gets lost from the adolescent culture after a period of nonuse. They refer to this phenomenon as "generational forgetting."

Substantial numbers of adolescents who use alcohol or drugs also report some problem associated with their substance use. For example, in a community sample, Zoccolillo, Vitaro, and Tremblay (1999) found that of those using alcohol more than five times in their lives, 70% of boys and 53% of girls reported experiencing at least one alcohol-related problem (e.g., going to school high), and 20% of boys and 11% of girls reported three or more problems. Of those who had used drugs more than five times, 94% of boys and 85% of girls reported at least one drug-related problem, and 68% of boys and 52% of girls reported three or more problems. However, the prevalence of diagnosable substance use disorders among adolescents is markedly lower, with point prevalences of 3–4% for alcohol disorders and 2–3% for drug use disorders among younger adolescents (13–16 years of age). For example, Fergusson, Horwood, and Lynskey (1993) found that 5.5% of their New Zealand birth cohort of 15-year-olds could be diagnosed with a lifetime history of substance use disorder (1.7% for illegal drugs and 3.5% for alcohol). In a school-based sample of high school students, Lewinsohn, Hops, Roberts, Seeley, and Andrews (1993) found lifetime prevalence rates of 4.6% for alcohol abuse or dependence and 6.3% for drug abuse or dependence. In an older sample (17- to 20-year-olds) Cohen et al. (1993) found that 14.9% met criteria for alcohol abuse or dependence, and 4% met criteria for drug abuse or dependence.

DEMOGRAPHIC CORRELATES OF USE, ABUSE, AND DEPENDENCE

Gender

Studies have documented gender differences in substance use such that girls use fewer drugs with less frequency than do boys (Johnston et al., 2000). For example, MTF data show that 12th-grade males report substantially higher prevalence rates in the annual use of heroin, LSD, steroids, and smokeless tobacco, as well as in the daily use of marijuana and alcohol. At younger grades, however, males and females show similar rates for many drugs, and females have higher rates of annual use of inhalants, tranquilizers, and amphetamines in 8th grade. A similar accentuation of gender differences at older ages has been reported for substance use disorders (Cohen et al., 1993).

Males and females may also use drugs for different reasons. For example, males report stronger social and enhancement motives for drinking than do females (Cooper, 1994). Younger females report stronger coping and conformity motives for drinking than do males, although this gender difference reverses at older ages (Cooper, 1994).

Studies of tobacco use have found that females report stronger weight regulation and anxiety reduction motives than do males (Grunberg, Winders, & Wewers, 1991).

Ethnicity

Several analyses of epidemiological data have concluded that there are ethnic differences in adolescent substance use (see Barrera, Castro, & Biglan, 1999; and Kandel, 1995, for reviews). Kandel's (1995) broad conclusion from 14 epidemiological studies was that American Indian adolescents show the highest lifetime prevalence of use and Asian Americans the lowest use. Of the other major ethnic groups, non-Hispanic Caucasians report the highest use, followed by Hispanics and African Americans, in that order.

The MTF study showed that African American high school seniors have the lowest prevalence rates for all drugs as compared to White and Hispanic high school seniors (Johnston et al., 2000). In 6th and 8th grades, Hispanic students report more use than do non-Hispanic Caucasians, but this difference reverses at 12th grade. Whites may start using drugs later in adolescence and eventually overtake the prevalence rates of Hispanics (Johnston et al., 2000), although this crossover may also be caused by the comparatively high dropout rate of Hispanics. American Indian adolescents also show high rates of use (Plunkett & Mitchell, 2000), although their levels of use vary by geographic location and tribal affiliation (Stubben, 1997). Ethnic differences have also been found in the prevalence of diagnosed adolescent substance use disorders. Costello, Farmer, Angold, Burns, and Erkanli (1997) reported that American Indian adolescents were significantly more likely to receive a substance use disorder diagnosis than were Caucasian adolescents. Results from the Methods for the Epidemiology of Childhood and Adolescent Mental Disorders (MECA) study (Kandel et. al. 1997) showed that Caucasian and African American adolescents were more likely to be diagnosed with a substance use disorder than were Hispanic adolescents. It is important to note that although rates of adolescent substance use vary by ethnicity, the previous conclusion may oversimplify a more complex picture in that interactions of gender and ethnicity might influence prevalence rates (Griesler & Kandel, 1998), and the correlated effects of ethnicity and SES are difficult to disaggregate.

In addition to ethnic group differences in prevalence rates, there have been some reports of ethnic differences in the correlates of adolescent substance use (see reviews by Newcomb, 1995; Resnicow, Soler, Braithwaite, Ahluwalia, & Butler, 2000). For example, Resnicow et al. (2000) concluded that peers have a greater influence on the smoking of Hispanic and White youth than they do on the smoking of African Americans. They also concluded that parental influence on smoking is greater for African American youth than it is for Whites. However, several large studies show more ethnic similarities than differences in the developmental processes underlying adolescent substance use. For example, Barrera, Biglan, Ary, and Li (2001) showed that adolescent substance use is correlated with antisocial behaviors and poor academic performance to form a problem behavior construct that is comparable for Latino, American Indian, and Caucasian adolescents. This same study supported the ethnic equivalence of a model of family and peer influences on adolescent problem behavior. Other studies with large samples of adolescents from several different ethnic groups have also shown ethnic similarities in the relation of alcohol use to risk and protective factors (Costa, Jessor, & Turbin, 1999) and to separation and individuation (Bray, Getz, & Baer, 2000).

AGE-RELATED TRAJECTORIES OF ADOLESCENT SUBSTANCE USE: RELATIONS TO DEVELOPMENTAL TRANSITIONS

Both substance use and substance use disorders show systematic age-related patterns from adolescence to adulthood that have led some researchers to view substance abuse and dependence as developmental disorders (Sher & Gotham, 1999; Tarter & Vanukov, 1994). Substance use is typically initiated in adolescence. For example, MTF data suggest that the typical time for alcohol use onset as well as for first intoxication is between 7th and 10th grades (Johnston et al., 2000). Adolescent substance use typically begins with the use of legal drugs (tobacco and alcohol), and rates of illegal drug use onset peak in the high school years (Johnston et al., 2000; Kandel, 1975). Given that adolescent substance use typically onsets between 7th and 10th grade, it is interesting to speculate about its link with the developmental transitions to middle school and to high school. These transitions involve a complex set of changes in the academic and social contexts of adolescents' lives, including less personal and positive student-teacher relationships and changes in the peer environment (Eccles, Lord, Roeser, Barber, & Jozefowicz, 1997). However, the link between these school transitions and adolescent substance use is complex. For example, Eccles et al. (1997) found that among low-achieving adolescents, those whose self-esteem increased during the transition to middle school showed the most substance use in high school. However, among high-achieving adolescents, those whose self-esteem decreased during the transition to middle school showed increased substance use. Eccles et al. (1997) suggest that low-achieving adolescents whose self-esteem increased might have disengaged from academics and formed deviant peer affiliations that promoted substance use.

Adolescent substance use has also been associated with the pubertal transition—specifically to early puberty among adolescent girls (Dick, Rose, Viken, & Kaprio, 2000; Stattin & Magnusson, 1990; Stice, Presnell, & Bearman, 2001). Girls who enter puberty earlier than do their age-peers show an earlier onset of alcohol use and cigarette smoking (Stattin & Magnusson, 1990), whereas late-maturing girls are more likely to abstain from substance use (Aro & Taipale, 1987). It is important to note that these findings have been replicated in a sample of adolescent twin girls who were discordant for pubertal timing (Dick et al., 2000). This study is important because it demonstrates an effect of early pubertal timing on adolescent substance use even after controlling for confounding between-family factors that are associated with early maturation. Moreover, although studies show a catch-up effect in which the effects of early pubertal timing are reduced by late adolescence and early adulthood (Dick et al., 2000), longer-term effects can still be detected. For example, Graber, Lewinsohn, Seeley, and Brooks-Gunn (1997) found a relation between early maturation and substance use disorders in the high school years, and Stattin and Magnusson (1990) found that late-maturing girls were still more likely than were early maturing girls to be abstainers at age 25.

The association between early maturation and substance use in adolescent girls has been hypothesized to be caused by their associations with older peers who provide models and opportunities for substance use. However, evidence for this mediating mechanism is not consistent and was not found in within-family analyses of a twin sample (Dick et al., 2000). It is interesting to note that Dick et al. (2000) found that the relation between early maturation and substance use was moderated by whether the family lived in an urban versus a rural environment, such that early maturation was related to substance use only for those who lived in an urban environment. The authors suggest that families in rural environments might have stronger parental influences, less access to substances, or both, so that the effects of early maturation are negated (Dick et al., 2000). These findings illustrate the importance of contextual influences as moderators of the relations between developmental transitions and adolescent substance use.

Substance use also changes in relation to role transitions, including transitions to higher education, work, and romantic relationships. However, the ways in which these transitions are related to adolescent substance use involve multiple processes that Yamaguchi and Kandel (1985) term "role socialization" and "role selection." Role selection refers to the fact that not all individuals select (or are selected into) the roles of work, higher education, and romantic relationships. Role selection encompasses the effects of adolescent substance use on role occupancy as well as the fact that characteristics associated with both adolescent drug use and social roles may explain the relation between them. For example, adolescents who use substances are less likely to go on to college (Bachman, Wadsworth, O'Malley, Johnston, & Schulenberg, 1997; Newcomb & Bentler, 1988a); this may be because their substance use is performance-impairing, because adolescents who are less motivated to succeed academically are also more likely to use drugs, or both. In contrast, role socialization refers the reverse direction of effect—that is, the effect of role responsibilities on substance use behavior. Because the demands and norms of adult roles are generally incompatible with substance use, adult role occupancy typically reduces alcohol and drug use.

The combination of role selection and role socialization processes produces complex relations between substance use and role occupancy that can vary with age. For work roles, high school students who work more hours also report more substance use (Bachman & Schulenberg, 1993; Steinberg & Dornbusch, 1991). However, in young adulthood, those who enter adult work roles decrease their substance use, perhaps because of the demands of adult roles as predicted by role socialization (Bachman et al., 1997).

Adolescents' transitions into dating and romantic relationships has also been associated with substance involvement. During the middle and high school years, adolescents who begin dating earlier than their peers (Levy, 2002; Wright, 1982) and—among girls—those who select older or substance-using partners (Levy, 2002) report greater substance use. However, these findings are cross-sectional, and the independence of these effects from personality characteristics has not been established. Thus, both selection into dating relationships (role selection) and the effects of the dating relationship (role socialization) may influence adolescent substance use. During young adulthood, the assumption of marital roles is associated with reductions in substance use (Bachman et al., 1997).

Finally, although higher educational attainment is generally associated with reduced adolescent substance use (Hawkins, Catalano, & Miller, 1992), an exception occurs during the transition to college. Data from the MTF Study (Bachman et al., 1997) show that college-bound high school seniors drank less than did their peers who were not college bound (consistent with a role selection effect). After the transition to college, however, those who were college students drank at higher levels than did their peers who did not attend college. Bachman et al. (1997) attribute this pattern to the new freedoms of college life, including living arrangements independent of parental supervision and social norms that promote alcohol use.

In general, then, over the adolescent years, alcohol and drug use increase in quantity and frequency, peaking between ages 18–25. The prevalence of diagnosed substance abuse and dependence also peaks in this age period (e.g., Grant et al., 1994). In the mid- to late 20s, the consumption of alcohol and illegal drugs begins to decline, perhaps in response to the demands of newly acquired adult roles such as marriage, work, and parenthood (Bachman et al., 1997; Yamaguchi & Kandel, 1985). Substance use disorders that decline in young adulthood have been referred to as developmentally limited (Zucker, 1987).

These findings describe an overall age-related trajectory of adolescent onset, late adolescent escalation, and adult decline in substance use. However, recent evidence suggests that it is useful to distinguish among multiple age-related trajectories. Because some type of substance use during adolescence is developmentally and statistically normative, it is necessary to distinguish developmental trajectories of substance use that are relatively benign from those that result in clinical impairment or diagnosable substance use disorders. Several studies have suggested that an early age of substance use onset is one predictor of subsequent course and clinical impairment. For example, alcohol use initiation before age 14 (Grant & Dawson, 1997) and illegal drug use before age 15 (Robins & Pryzbeck, 1985) are associated with elevated risk for the development of alcohol and drug disorders.

Recent developments in statistical techniques of mixture modeling (Muthen & Shedden, 1999; Nagin, 1999) have allowed researchers to empirically identify multiple developmental trajectories of substance use. The few studies that have used this method have identified a subgroup in which early age of onset is associated with a steeply escalating course of use and with the most problematic outcomes (including diagnosed abuse or dependence); this has been found both for cigarette smoking (Chassin, Presson, Pitts, & Sherman, 2000) and heavy drinking (Chassin, Pitts, & Prost, 2002; K. Hill, White, Chung, Hawkins, & Catalano, 2000). Moreover, studies of these early-escalating subgroups have shown them to be associated with a family history of substance use and with high levels of conduct problems (Chassin et al., 2002; Costello, Erkanli, Federman, & Angold, 1999; S. Hill, Shen, Lowers, & Locke, 2000; Loeber, Stouthamer-Loeber, & White, 1999).

Conversely, studies have also identified a late-onset subgroup (at least late in the adolescent age period) whose smoking or heavy drinking does not begin until after high school (Chassin et al., 2000; Chassin et al., 2002). For these adolescents, substance use initiation may be associated with decreases in parental supervision, perhaps during the transition out of the parental home. Adolescent substance use that begins after the high school years has been relatively neglected by researchers, and most prevention programs have been targeted at younger age groups. Thus, relatively little is known about the late-onset subgroup, which represents an important target for future research.

CONSEQUENCES OF ADOLESCENT SUBSTANCE USE

Adolescent substance use itself may affect the course of adolescent development and create significant consequences for later adult outcomes. In general, the immediate, short-term effects of substance use are related to its impact on judgment and performance. For example, even a single episode of heavy drinking has been associated with a risk for morbidity and mortality from impaired driving, accidents, and risky sexual behavior (Murgraff, Parrott, & Bennett, 1999). However, long-term effects are less clear. For example, Jessor, Donovan, and Costa (1991) found little impact of adolescent alcohol use on adult outcomes unless the alcohol use persisted into adulthood. Moreover, it is difficult methodologically to disentangle the unique impact of adolescent substance use on developmental outcomes because substance use itself is correlated with numerous other risk factors, including conduct problems, poor parenting, and high-risk temperament, all of which are important determinants of later outcomes. For example, drinking among college students is correlated with educational attainment, but this relationship is attenuated when preexisting measures of high school aptitude and achievement are considered (Wood, Sher, Erickson, & DeBord, 1997).

Longitudinal studies suggest that the long-term consequence most consistently related to adolescent substance use is the continued use of the same substance (Kandel, Davies, Karus, & Yamaguchi, 1986). In addition, studies have shown that adolescent substance use is associated with lowered levels of educational attainment and less occupancy of conventional adult roles such as worker, spouse, and parent (Chassin, Presson, Sherman, & Edwards, 1992; Yamaguchi & Kandel, 1985). Newcomb and Bentler (1988a) suggest that because drug-using adolescents enter adult roles prematurely (foreshortening educational attainment), without having the requisite social, emotional, and cognitive skills, their role performance is less successful, and they show less stability in their role occupancy. Newcomb and Bentler (1988a) refer to this pattern as pseudomaturity because adolescent substance use produces the superficial appearance of adult role status without the actual adult maturity that is necessary for success in these roles. This interpretation is consistent with Jessor and Jessor's (1977) hypothesis that adolescent substance use is motivated in part by a drive to prematurely attain adult status.

Adolescent substance use may also impact the experience of leaving the family home. Although few studies have examined predictors of leaving home transitions, girls' early transitions out of the parental home have been associated with a history of substance use during adolescence (O'Connor, Allen, Bell, & Hauser, 1996; Stattin & Magnusson, 1996). Similarly, Hussong and Chassin (2002) found that adolescent risk behaviors, including substance use, predicted both earlier departures from home and greater difficulties in this transition, such as leaving because of perceived unhappiness and leaving with less parental consultation.

Adolescent substance use has also been linked to later adult psychological distress and mental health problems. Johnson et al. (2000) found that those who smoked more than a pack of cigarettes a day at age 16 were more likely to be diagnosed with anxiety disorders at age 22 (controlling for age, sex, temperament, other adolescent drug use, and adolescent anxiety and depressive disorders). Newcomb and Bentler (1988b) found that illegal drug use and cigarette smoking had negative effects on emotional distress 8 years later.

It is interesting to note that adolescent alcohol use may be an exception to this conclusion. Newcomb and Bentler (1988b) found that adolescent alcohol use was associated with enhanced positive self-feelings and improved social relationships in young adulthood. Leifman, Kuhlhorn, Allebeck, Andreasson, and Romelsjo (1995) also reported that those who were light drinkers in late adolescence had better psychological status and sociability than did abstainers. The association between adolescent drinking and improved mood and social relationships may be related to the instrumental use of alcohol to obtain valued social goals in adolescence (Maggs, 1997).

If adolescent drug use has negative impact on adult outcomes, it is important to identify the mechanisms underlying these effects. First, the pharmacological effects of consumption might be performance impairing—for example, interfering with studying or performing on a job. Second, to the extent that adolescent substance use develops into physical and psychological dependence, then impaired functioning will result. Third, adolescent substance use may influence adult psychosocial outcomes by influencing emerging developmental competency. Baumrind and Moselle (1985) suggested that adolescent substance use can produce a false sense of reality that interferes with the ability to evaluate and respond to environmental demands while also permitting an avoidance of these demands; this will impair the development of effective coping. Similarly, Baumrind and Moselle (1985) proposed that adolescent drug use can create a false sense of autonomy and also undermine the development of intimate relationships. Baumrind's hypothesis that drug use during adolescence impairs emerging developmental competencies is important but has had few empirical tests. Chassin, Pitts, and DeLucia (1999) found that adolescents' illegal drug use predicted lowered autonomy and less competence in positive activities in young adulthood (above and beyond earlier adolescent symptomatology). Moreover, drug-using adolescents have low levels of behavioral coping (Wills, 1986). However, whether adolescent drug use impairs emerging developmental competencies is largely unknown.

THEORETICAL MODELS

Theoretical models of adolescent substance use consider variables ranging from the intrapersonal to the macroenvironmental level (Hawkins et al., 1992; Petraitis, Flay, & Miller, 1995). Given the heterogeneity of substance use, it is unlikely that any one factor or etiological pathway could explain the development of substance use or substance use disorders; rather, there are likely to be multiple pathways and multiple subtypes of substance use and substance use disorders.

Some of the earliest theories consider adolescent substance use within a broader framework of behavioral deviance (e.g., Elliott, Huizinga, & Ageton, 1985; Hirschi, 1969; Jessor & Jessor, 1977). These theories draw upon the strong correlations between adolescent substance use and a broad range of other nonconventional behaviors that range from low aspirations for academic achievement and staying out past curfew to theft and violence. Elliott's social control theory (Elliott et al., 1985) emphasizes the causal role of weak bonds to conventional society, including institutions (e.g., school, religion) and values, as well as lack of attachment to conventional role models (e.g., parents and teachers). Role strain, or poor fit between an adolescent's aspirations and perceptions of available resources to achieve the desired goals, is one contributor to the weak bonding with societal convention. As with Jessor and Jessor's problem behavior theory (1977), attachment to like-minded peers results, and socialization into unconventional behavior, including substance use and abuse, follows. Empirical support for these general deviance models is plentiful (for a review, see Petraitis et al., 1995).

Although risk factors for substance use and problem behaviors overlap substantially (e.g., Fergusson, Lynsky, & Horwood, 1996a), it is not clear that substance use and other deviant behaviors reflect a single underlying construct of adolescent deviance. Recent longitudinal data suggest that variability in substance use and delinquent behavior in adolescence is due to both shared and behavior-specific variance (Mason & Windle, 2002). Some studies have shown specificity in the predictors of different problem behaviors (Maggs & Hurrelman, 1998; White, Pandina, & LaGrange; 1987). For example, Erickson, Crosnoe, and Dornbusch (2000) found stronger prospective prediction from social bonding variables (e.g., parent attachment, educational commitment) to substance use than to delinquent behavior. Loeber et al. (1999) found that bad neighborhoods predicted delinquency and aggression better than they predicted substance use. Although studies have not identified a consistent pattern of unique predictors of substance use compared to delinquency, the most prudent conclusion at this time is that substance use is both strongly related to, yet distinct in some ways from, other conduct problems.

Although much variability in substance use is explained by general deviance theories, these models do not directly address genetic and biological vulnerability toward substance use (Cloninger, 1987; Tarter, Alterman, & Edwards, 1985; Zucker, 1987). A particularly useful integration of theoretical models has been provided by Sher (1991), who identifies three (interrelated) pathways to substance use involvement and substance use disorders (a deviance-proneness pathway, a negative affect pathway, and an enhanced reinforcement pathway). Sher's models are particularly useful because they incorporate genetic and environmental risk; they link early childhood antecedents to later adult substance use disorders, and they respect the reality of transactional influences that may exacerbate risk (e.g., reciprocal influences between parenting behavior and personality). Sher's models were originally formulated to explain why individuals with a family history of substance use disorder are at elevated risk for substance use disorders. However, it is important to note that these same processes are hypothesized to produce substance use and substance use disorders among adolescents in general. They do not apply only to those with family history risk. Thus, our review is organized according to Sher's proposed pathways, after first describing family history of substance abuse or dependence use as a risk factor.

Family History of Substance Abuse or Dependence

Adults with a family history of alcoholism are themselves at elevated risk for alcohol abuse or dependence (McGue, 1994; Russell, 1990), although the magnitude of the risk varies substantially across studies (from risk ratios of 2–3 in community samples to 9 in severely antisocial samples, McGue, 1994; Russell, 1990). There is also elevated risk (up to eightfold) for drug disorders among relatives of probands with drug disorders (Merikangas et al., 1998).

In adolescence, family history risk is associated with an early onset of substance use (Chassin et al., 2000; Costello et al., 1999) and with the persistence of substance use over time (Chassin et al., 2000). Twin studies suggest that this family history risk has both heritable and environmental mediators and that the magnitude of heritability may vary for different substances (Merikangas & Avenevoli, 2000). For example, in a study of 17-year-old twins, McGue, Elkins, and Iacono (2000) found that heritability for use and abuse of illegal drugs was 25%, whereas heritability for tobacco use and dependence was more powerful (40–60%). Similarly, Han, McGue, and Iacono (1999) reported varying magnitudes of heritability estimates for tobacco (59%), alcohol (60%), and drug use (33%) in male adolescents, again suggesting that the importance of genetic and environmental influences may vary by the type of substance that is used. On the other hand, because there was also significant covariation among these heritability estimates, some aspects of liability toward adolescent substance use may be common across different forms of use. Studies of the molecular genetics of substance abuse and dependence have proposed many possibilities for candidate genes (see Nestler, 2000; Reich, Hinrichs, Culverhouse, & Bierut, 1999; Uhl, 1999).

Although twin and adoption studies indicate significant heritability for substance use and abuse in adolescence, family history risk can also exert influence through fetal exposure. Baer, Barr, Bookstein, Sampson, and Streissguth (1998) found that prenatal exposure to alcohol raised risk for adolescent alcohol use and use-related negative consequences above and beyond a family history of alcoholism. Similarly, Cornelius, Leech, Goldschmidt, and Day (2000) found that prenatal tobacco exposure raised risk for offspring tobacco use in childhood. Prenatal exposure may raise risk for adolescent substance use either through its effect on receptors, which then make the child more biologically sensitive to the effects of the substance, or by raising risk for temperamental underregulation and conduct problems, which are themselves risk factors for adolescent substance use (Cornelius et al., 2000). Finally, as noted earlier, family history may influence risk for adolescent substance use through deviance proneness, negative affect regulation, and substance use effects pathways.

DEVIANCE PRONENESS MODELS

Sher's (1991) deviance proneness submodel suggests that the development of substance disorders occurs within a broader context of conduct problems and antisociality. Adolescents at risk for substance disorders are thought to be temperamentally difficult and prone to cognitive deficits, including verbal skill deficits and executive functioning deficits that contribute to a lack of self-regulation. In addition, high-risk children are thought to receive inadequate parenting, and this combination of temperamental, cognitive, and environmental risk factors sets the stage for failure at school and ejection from the mainstream peer group; this results in affiliation with deviant peers who provide opportunities, models, and approval for alcohol and drug use. Because these theories consider substance use within the broader context of antisocial behavior, they are quite similar to theories that attempt to explain the etiology of conduct problems more generally (e.g, see Patterson, 1986). Empirical evidence for each of these links is reviewed in the following section.

Temperament and Personality

A host of studies report that temperamental and personality traits reflecting behavioral undercontrol and poor self-regulation are associated with adolescent substance use problems. The personality characteristics most consistently associated with adolescent substance use include unconventionality, low ego control, sensation seeking, aggression, impulsivity, and an inability to delay gratification (Hawkins et al., 1992).

Longitudinal research has demonstrated that childhood temperamental characteristics reflecting undercontrolled behavior are predictive of later substance use problems. For instance, Block, Block, and Keyes (1988) found that adolescents who used marijuana at least weekly were characterized as children by heightened levels of behavioral undercontrol and interpersonal alienation, and these traits were observable as early as 3–4 years of age. Similarly, Caspi, Moffitt, Newman, and Silva (1996) found that 3-year-old boys described by others as impulsive, restless, and distractible were at increased risk for a diagnosis of drug dependence by age 21. Lerner and Vicary (1984) found that 5-year-old children with difficult temperamental profiles, including high levels of behavioral reactivity, emotionality, and slow adaptability were more likely than were nondifficult children to use substances in adolescence and young adulthood.

Several biobehavioral markers of behavioral undercontrol and risk for adolescent substance use problems have been identified. One is a diminished P3 component in event-related brain potentials. Reductions in P3 amplitude have been reported for several forms of undercontrolled behaviors, including antisocial personality disorder, ADHD, and aggression, as well as substance use disorders (Begleiter & Porjesz, 1999; Iacono, Carlson, Taylor, Elkins, & McGue, 1999). Moreover, young children of alcoholics also show reduced P3 amplitude even before the onset of drinking (Begleiter & Porjesz, 1999), and reduced P3 amplitude predicts drinking onset in this population (S. Hill et al., 2000; Iacono et al., 1999). Other candidate biobehavioral markers for behavioral undercontrol and risk for substance use include neurochemical and neuroendocrine response and ability to modulate autonomic nervous system reactivity (Iacono et al., 1999; Tarter et al., 1999).

Data from twin studies further suggest that indicators of behavioral undercontrol have substantial heritability and may serve to increase risk for substance use problems in adolescents, particularly in the context of familial alcoholism. The Minnesota Family Twin Study (Iacono et al., 1999) has found substantial heritability for a variety of indices of undercontrol, including reduced constraint, poor psychophysiological modulation in response to stress, and high levels of externalizing behavior. These traits were also more likely to characterize children with a family history of alcoholism. In turn, these risk factors were strongly associated with a diagnosis of adolescent substance dependence, even after controlling for effects of paternal alcoholism. Taken together, these findings support a genetic diathesis model for adolescent substance use problems, with the diathesis consisting of heritable individual differences in behavioral undercontrol.

Although they are rarely empirically tested, the effects of temperament on substance use are also presumed to be modified by the environment—particularly by the family environment. Wills, Sandy, Yaeger, and Shinar (2001) and Stice and Gonzales (1998) examined moderating effects of temperament and parenting on adolescent substance use and found that parental risk factors and parenting behaviors differentially affected risk for substance use among adolescents with differing temperaments. Thus, despite their heritable bases, the effects of temperamental characteristics on substance use outcomes may be either exacerbated or buffered by the type of parenting that the adolescent receives.

Cognitive Functioning

Additional evidence for deficient self-regulation as a risk factor for adolescent substance use and abuse may be found in studies of cognitive functioning. Specifically, adolescents with substance use problems are characterized by lower levels of executive functioning—that is, higher-order cognitive processes that allow for future goal-oriented behavior. These processes include planning, organizational skills, selective attention, hypothesis generation, cognitive flexibility, maintenance of cognitive-set, decision making, judgment, inhibitory control, and self-regulation (Lezak, 1995). These deficits make it difficult for children to create strategic and goal-oriented responses to environmental stimuli and to use feedback to modify their behavior in response to environmental events (Peterson & Pihl, 1990). Such cognitive difficulties then produce heightened levels of behavioral undercontrol, such as impulsive and externalizing behavior, which raise risk for substance use and substance use disorders (Peterson & Pihl, 1990).

Deficits in cognitive function have been well documented in studies of adults with substance use disorders (Rourke & Loberg, 1996; Sher, Martin, Wood, & Rutledge, 1997), and emerging research suggests that these findings may also apply to adolescents with substance use problems. For example, Brown and colleagues reported that relative to youth without alcohol problems, a sample of alcohol-dependent adolescents were characterized by poorer retention of verbal and nonverbal information, poorer attentional capacities, and deficits in visual-spatial planning (Tapert & Brown, 1999). Similarly, Giancola and colleagues (Giancola, Mezzich, & Tarter, 1998) found that adolescent girls with a substance use disorder exhibited poorer executive functioning relative to controls.

Although these cross-sectional studies cannot determine whether executive functioning deficits are a cause or effect of substance use, other data suggest that executive functioning deficits are found in children of alcoholics, even at early ages, before alcohol problems have developed (e.g., Drejer, Theilgard, Teasdale, Schulsinger, & Goodwin, 1985; Giancola, Martin, Tarter, Pelham, & Moss, 1996; Harden & Pihl, 1995; Peterson, Finn, & Pihl, 1992).These data suggest that executive functioning may be an antecedent risk factor rather than a result of alcohol consumption in this population. Moreover, Deckel and Hesselbrock (1996) found that children of alcoholics with poorer executive functioning showed greater increases in alcohol consumption over a 3-year period than did children of alcoholics with higher levels of executive functioning, suggesting that executive functioning was a prospective predictor of substance use among high-risk adolescents.

Although these findings suggest that executive functioning impairments play a role in the development of substance use—particularly among those with parental alcoholism—not all studies have replicated these findings. Some studies fail to find executive functioning deficits in children of alcoholics (a population at heightened risk for substance use and substance use disorders; e.g., Bates & Pandina, 1992; Wiers, Gunning, & Sargeant, 1998). Moreover, executive function deficits have been well-documented in children with conduct problems (e.g., Moffitt, 1993), so executive functioning deficits among substance-abusing adolescents may be related to externalizing symptomatology rather than specific to substance use (Giancola & Mezzich, 2000).

Parenting and Socialization

Variations in several aspects of parenting, including nurturance, discipline, monitoring, and conflict are related to adolescent substance use. Parenting that combines high levels of nurturance with consistent discipline has been associated with a lowered risk of adolescent substance use (see Hawkins et al., 1992, for a review). Stice and Barrera (1995) found that low levels of parental social support and discipline prospectively predicted increases in adolescent substance use over time. Similarly, low levels of parental monitoring have been shown to prospectively predict both the onset of substance use and of heavy drinking in adolescence (Reifman, Barnes, Dintcheff, Farrell, & Uhteg, 1998; Steinberg, Fletcher, & Darling, 1994). Finally, high levels of family conflict (Webb & Baer, 1995), lack of family cohesion (Duncan, Tildesley, Duncan, & Hops, 1995), and parental divorce and single-parent families (Duncan, Duncan, & Hops, 1998) have been associated with higher levels of adolescent substance use.

Not only is adolescent substance use related to general parenting style, family climate, and parent-adolescent relationships, but data also suggest that adolescent substance use may be related to parents' specific socialization about the use of substances. Not only do parents set general rules and expectations for adolescent behavior, but they also set rules and policies about the use of tobacco, alcohol, and other drugs; they may discuss reasons not to use these substances, and they may punish substance use behavior. Cross-sectional studies have suggested that socialization that is specific to substance use may also deter adolescents' substance use behavior (Chassin, Presson, Todd, Rose, & Sherman, 1998; Jackson & Henrickson, 1997).

Thus, available data suggest that parent socialization either in the form of general parenting and parent-adolescent relationships or in the form of specific attempts to deter substance use may influence the development of adolescent substance use behavior. Moreover, although data are not extensive, several mediational models suggest that the effects of parenting on adolescent substance use may be mediated through the effects of parenting on affiliations with deviant peer networks as specified in deviance proneness models (Chassin, Curran, Hussong, & Colder, 1996; Dishion, Patterson, & Reid, 1988). Finally, parenting can have important influences on adolescents' connections to broader social-contextual resources such as participation in after-school sports, religious organizations, and clubs which, in turn, can influence substance use outcomes (Scaramella & Keyes, 2001).

There are important limitations to existing data on parental influences. First, most of these studies examine adolescent substance use rather than substance use disorders. Second, the relation between parenting and adolescent substance use may be explained by other characteristics of the adolescent; that is, adolescents who are rebellious, externalizing, and poorly regulated may be difficult to monitor and discipline, and they may also evoke parental rejection (Ge et al., 1996). It may be these adolescent characteristics that raise risk for substance use rather than the parenting behavior per se. Reciprocal relations between adolescent problem behavior and parenting must be considered. Third, because parents provide both genetic and environmental influences, the correlations between parenting and adolescent substance use that are reported in the literature may inflate the magnitude of what appears to be environmental influence. For example, McGue, Sharma, and Benson (1996) reported only relatively small correlations between adolescent alcohol involvement and family functioning in adoptive families compared to biological families, suggesting that the magnitude of family environmental influences on adolescent alcohol use might be relatively modest. Finally, it is not known how the role of parenting and family environment factors might differentially affect adolescent substance abuse and dependence across different ethnic or cultural groups. Despite evidence for generalizability of familial influences across ethnic groups (Barrera et al., 2001), other studies have reported differential magnitudes of correlations between parenting and substance use across ethnicity (e.g., see Griesler & Kandel, 1998, for tobacco use) or that the relations between authoritative parenting and adolescent deviance proneness might vary as a function of ethnicity and community context (Lamborn, Dornbusch, & Steinberg, 1996).

School Failure and Academic Aspirations

Children who are temperamentally poorly regulated, who receive poor parental nurturance and involvement and deficient parental monitoring and discipline, and who have cognitive deficits in executive and verbal functioning are at heightened risk for school failure (Patterson, 1986). Moreover, school failure itself may further elevate risk for the onset of adolescent substance use through several mechanisms. First, school failure is a source of stress and negative affect, which can raise risk for substance use to regulate that affect. Second, school failure can weaken school attachment (e.g., aspirations for higher education, values placed on academic success, participation in mainstream school activities). Estrangement from conventional mainstream social institutions makes adolescents more vulnerable to engaging in problem behaviors, including drug use, because they feel less bound by conventional social norms and values. Moreover, adolescents who are not committed to academic success will experience less role conflict between the demands of academic roles and the impairment produced by substance use, so that they have less reason to refrain from substance use. Third, school failure can increase risk for adolescent drug use because it raises risk for adolescents' rejection from a mainstream peer group, particularly if the school failure is associated with aggressive or underregulated behavior (Dishion, Patterson, Stoolmiller, & Skinner, 1991). Adolescents who are rejected from a mainstream peer group are more likely to affiliate with deviant peers who model and approve of substance use behavior. Consistent with these mechanisms, available empirical evidence suggests that adolescents with poor grades (Duncan, Duncan, Biglan, & Ary, 1998; Kandel, 1978), low educational aspirations (e.g., Paulson, Combs, & Richardson, 1990), and low value and expectations for attaining educational success (Jessor & Jessor, 1977) are more likely to use alcohol or drugs. Moreover, MTF data showed that poor school achievement prospectively predicted substance use (in this case, tobacco use) across ethnic groups for both boys and girls (Bryant, Schulenberg, Bachman, O'Malley, & Johnston, 2000).

Peer Influences

A robust, widely-replicated finding is that adolescent alcohol and drug use can be predicted from the alcohol and drug use behavior of their friends (Hawkins et al., 1992; Kandel, 1978), both close friends and larger friendship groups (Urberg, Degirmencioglu, & Pilgrim, 1997). Affiliation with a drug-using peer group elevates risk for adolescent substance use by providing models and opportunities for engaging in drug use as well as norms that approve of drug use behavior. Drug use is also related to membership in different adolescent cliques (e.g., preppies, jocks, etc.; Sussman, Dent, & McCullar, 2000), and it may serve to communicate particular social images that are characteristic of these peer groups (Barton, Chassin, Presson, & Sherman, 1982). Moreover, substance use by peers within each type of peer context (i.e., close friendships, peer groups, and social groups) contributes uniquely to adolescent substance use, and the presence of non-drug-using peers in one context (e.g., within close friendships) can offset risk associated with the presence of substance-using peers in another context (e.g., within larger peer groups, Hussong, in press). Finally, siblings can constitute an important source of peer influence on adolescent drug use (Brook, Nomura, & Cohen, 1989). Correlations have been found between adolescent alcohol use and sibling alcohol use in both biological and adoptive sibling pairs, suggesting an environmental transmission mechanism (McGue et al., 1996).

However, even though peer use is typically the strongest predictor of adolescent substance use, researchers have also questioned the interpretation of this relation. Because most studies have the adolescent report on both his or her own use and the behavior of his or her friends, the magnitude of the correlation between peer use and adolescent use is inflated because adolescents who themselves use drugs systematically overestimate their friends' use (Bauman & Ennett, 1996). Correlations between adolescent and friends' drug use are lower (although still significant) when peers are surveyed directly (Kandel, 1978). Moreover, cross-sectional correlations reflect the contribution of two different processes: peer selection (in which drug-using adolescents seek out similar friends) and peer influence (in which drug-using peers influence adolescents' behavior). The contribution of peer selection further inflates the magnitude of the association between peer use and adolescent use (Bauman & Ennett, 1996), although longitudinal data suggest that both peer selection and peer influence processes are operative (Curran, Stice, & Chassin, 1997; Kandel, 1978).

Childhood Conduct Problems

A central assumption of the deviance proneness model is that adolescent substance use disorders are related to the broader development of conduct problems and antisociality—an assumption with robust empirical support (Hawkins et al., 1992). Conduct problems and aggression predict adolescent substance use (Henry et al., 1993; Kellam, Brown, Rubin, & Ensminger, 1983), escalations in use over time (K. Hill et al., 2000; Hussong, Curran, & Chassin, 1998), and later substance abuse and dependence diagnoses (Chassin, DeLucia, & Todd, 1999) among both boys and girls (Chassin, DeLucia, & Todd, 1999; Costello et al., 1999; Disney, Elkins, McGue, & Iacono, 1999). The magnitude of the association with conduct problems is strongest for illicit drug use and substance use disorders as opposed to licit substance use (Disney et al., 1999); this may reflect the fact that licit drug use in adolescence can be normative and socially enhancing (Maggs & Hurrelmann, 1998).

Whether attention deficit/hyperactivity disorder (ADHD) contributes to risk for substance use in adolescence is unclear. A strong comorbidity between conduct disorder and ADHD complicates interpretation of findings. Childhood ADHD symptoms or diagnosis predict adolescent substance use and substance use disorder in clinic-referred (Barkley et al., 1990; Molina & Pelham, 2003) and in some nonclinic samples (Disney et al., 1999; Lynsky & Fergusson, 1995) but not all (Costello et al., 1999). However, these effects usually diminish to nonsignificance once conduct disorder or conduct problems are controlled; this may indicate that the relation between ADHD and substance use is spurious (due to conduct disorder as an underlying third variable). Alternatively, it may indicate a mediated process in which ADHD symptoms cause the development of later conduct problems that in turn increase the likelihood of adolescent substance use. It is interesting to note that ADHD may confer unique risk for tobacco use above and beyond the development of conduct problems (Burke et al., 2001; Disney et al., 1999; Milberger, Biederman, Faraone, Chen, & Jones, 1997; Molina & Pelham, 2003). Given the well-established beneficial effects of nicotine on attention in adults (Levin et al., 1998), adolescents with ADHD may smoke cigarettes as a way to self-medicate their attentional deficits.

STRESS AND NEGATIVE AFFECT PATHWAYS

Theories about the role of stress and negative affect hypothesize that adolescents who are at risk for substance disorders experience a high level of stress and resulting negative affect and use alcohol or drugs as a way to decrease this negative affect (i.e., as a form of self-medication). Although this model is intuitively appealing, it has not enjoyed widespread empirical support and remains controversial in the adolescent literature.

Life Stress

Consistent findings indicate that adolescents who experience high levels of life stress are more likely to use alcohol or drugs and to escalate the quantity and frequency of their use over time (Chassin et al., 1996; Wills, Vaccaro, McNamara, & Hirky, 1996). However, the literature on the stress-substance use relation in adolescence may overestimate the effects of stress because some measures of stress include items that may reflect the adolescents' conduct problems (e.g., items like *conflicts with teachers*). However, even studies that restrict their stress items to uncontrollable life events still report significant prediction of adolescent substance use (e.g., Chassin et al., 1996; Newcomb & Harlow, 1986).

Adolescents who are at risk for substance use may not only be exposed to heightened levels of stress, but they may also be characterized by abnormal stress responses. Adult children of alcoholics have been reported to exhibit elevated psychophysiological response to stress in the laboratory compared to those without parental alcoholism (Conrod, Peterson, & Pihl, 1997). Similar findings have been obtained with a small sample of boys whose families had multiple alcoholic members (Harden & Pihl, 1995). These young boys showed greater heart rate increases and peripheral vasoconstriction during a mental arithmetic task than did boys without a family history of alcoholism, suggesting that substance use may provide a way to regulate stress response. In contrast, however, Moss, Vanyukov, Yao, and Irillova (1999) found that sons whose fathers had a substance use disorder had a decreased salivary cortisol response to an anticipated stressor and that those boys with lower cortisol responses also showed more marijuana use. Moss et al. (1999) suggest that hyporeactivity in these boys may represent an adaptation to chronic exposure to high levels of stress. Finally, Iacono et al. (1999) suggest that adolescents at risk for substance use problems show poor modulation of stress responses, as reflected in an ability to control psychophysiological arousal in predictable versus unpredictable exposures to a laboratory stressor. Although the possibility that high-risk adolescents show abnormalities in stress response is potentially of great etiological importance, very few empirical studies (particularly of girls) have examined this, so conclusions must remain preliminary at this point.

The Role of Emotional Distress

The relation of emotional distress to adolescent substance use and substance use disorders has not been consistently upheld. Many studies have reported cross-sectional correlations between negative affect and adolescent substance use (Chassin, Pillow, Curran, Molina, & Barrera, 1993; Cooper, Frone, Russell, & Mudar, 1995), as well as substantial comorbidity between clinically diagnosed depression and adolescent nicotine dependence (Fergusson, Lynsky, & Horwood, 1996b), alcoholism (Rohde, Lewinsohn, & Seeley, 1996), and drug abuse or dependence (Deykin, Buka, & Zeena, 1992). However, other researchers have argued that negative affectivity has only weak relations to adolescent substance use compared to factors such as peer affiliations and that effects of emotional distress are weak and indirect (Swaim, Oetting, & Beauvais, 1989). Moreover, studies considering the role of negative affect have often failed to consider the effects of externalizing symptoms and conduct problems. Because there is considerable covariation between internalizing and externalizing symptoms, it has not been clearly established that negative affect has a unique relation to adolescent substance use (above and beyond co-occurring conduct problems).

Perhaps most important is that longitudinal studies have not consistently confirmed that negative affectivity prospectively predicts the onset or escalation of adolescent substance use or the development of substance abuse and dependence (Hansell & White, 1991). For example, Hussong et al. (1998) found that internalizing symptoms did not prospectively predict growth over time in alcohol use, and K. Hill et al. (2000) found that internalizing symptoms did not prospectively predict trajectories of heavy drinking from adolescence to young adulthood. In fact, anxiety has been associated with delayed onset of gateway drug use such as cigarette smoking (Costello et al., 1999). Regarding clinical disorders, Chassin, Pitts, DeLucia, and Todd (1999) found that adolescent internalizing symptoms did not prospectively predict young adult alcohol and drug diagnoses, and Rohde et al. (1996) did not find that depressive disorder preceded the development of adolescent alcohol abuse and dependence. This pattern of cross-sectional but not prospective relations between negative affect and adolescent substance use suggests that negative affect might be a result rather than a cause of adolescent substance use and substance use problems.

Despite the inconsistent prospective findings, it might be premature to dismiss the role of negative affect in the development of adolescent substance use disorders for several reasons. First, some studies do find prospective effects (e.g., Windle & Windle, 2001). Second, the time lag of measurement in most longitudinal studies (often a year or more) is not optimal for detecting self-medication effects, which should occur much more proximally to the occurrence of negative affect. Microanalytic techniques, such as experience sampling methods, might reveal different findings (Hussong, Hicks, Levy, & Curran, 2001).

In addition, conflicting findings might be due to variation in the type of negative affect that is assessed. Support has been stronger for depression, irritability, and anger as prospective predictors of adolescent substance use than for anxiety (Block et al., 1988; Swaim et al., 1989). In prospective analyses, Kaplow, Curran, Angold, and Costello (2001) showed that generalized anxiety disorder predicted substance use initiation, whereas separation anxiety disorder decreased the likelihood of initiation. Anxious adolescents who fear social interaction and parental separation may be less likely to select into (or to be selected into) peer contexts that promote substance use, thus decreasing risk for substance use, whereas those anxious adolescents with more generalized fears may initiate substance use to self-medicate. However, because other researchers suggest that clinically diagnosed social phobia increases risk for substance use (Merikangas & Avenevoli, 2000), further studies of social phobia are warranted. In short, variations in both the type of negative affect (depression, anger, irritability vs. anxiety) and the severity of the distress (e.g., symptomatology versus actual clinical diagnosis) might produce differing findings.

Related to the distinction between the roles of anxiety and depression is the role of positive affect. Recent conceptualizations of the distinction between anxiety and depression suggest that anxiety may co-occur with positive affect, whereas depression is more likely correlated with low levels of positive affect (Watson, Clark, & Carey, 1988). Indeed, a motivation to use substances in order to increase positive affect has also been posited within affect regulation models (Cooper et al., 1995), although it has not been as widely studied as the motivation to reduce negative affect. Some researchers have suggested that adolescents who use substances to maintain or enhance positive affect may use at moderate levels of quantity and frequency, whereas those who use substances to relieve negative affect may show higher consumption (Labouvie, Pandina, White, & Johnson, 1990). Data also suggest that low levels of positive affect are particularly associated with adolescent substance use for those adolescents who are also highly impulsive (Colder & Chassin, 1997). Thus, affect regulation models should consider multiple states, including depression, anxiety, general distress, and positive affect.

Finally, the lack of consistent relations between negative affect and adolescent substance use may reflect the presence of moderator variables, such that negative affectivity produces risk for substance use under only certain circumstances. In Sher's (1991) submodel, one important potential moderator variable is coping style. Theoretically, adolescents should not react to emotional distress by turning to substance use if other, more adaptive coping mechanisms are available to them. Some data suggest that behavioral coping (e.g., make a plan and follow it) may serve such an adaptive function (Wills, 1986) but that disengagement coping (e.g., coping through anger, hanging out with friends) may actually amplify the effects of life stress events on growth over time in adolescent substance use (Wills, Sandy, Yaeger, Cleary, & Shinar, 2001). Similarly, Sher (1991) suggests that the relation between stress or emotional distress and substance use should be stronger for those who expect substance use to relieve their emotional distress, and this hypothesis has received some empirical support (Kushner, Sher, Wood, & Wood, 1994).

Individual differences may also moderate the relation between negative affectivity and adolescent substance use. For example, research in social development has suggested that low levels of temperamental self-regulation will amplify the relation between reactivity (a propensity to experience intense affective states) and conduct problems (Eisenberg et al., 2000). Thus, adolescents who are highly emotionally reactive may show particularly heightened risk for substance use, abuse, or dependence when they also show low levels of temperamental self-regulation. It is interesting to note that some laboratory data also suggest that individuals who are temperamentally underregulated may derive the strongest psychophysiological stress response dampening benefits from consuming alcohol (Levenson, Oyama, & Meek, 1987). If behaviorally undercontrolled individuals derive greater stress response dampening effects from consuming alcohol and drugs, then this would be consistent with stronger links between stress or negative affect and substance use for individuals who are low in self-regulation. This notion of self-regulation as a moderator variable in the relation between negative affect and substance use can serve to bridge deviance proneness models of adolescent substance use with stress and negative affect models of adolescent substance use. Although these two models have typically been conceptualized and studied in isolation of each other, the relation between these two pathways is worthy of future study. Finally, both gender and age may moderate the relation between negative affectivity and substance use disorders. Negative affect and self-medication motives may be more strongly linked to substance abuse and dependence that have late onset (later in adulthood) and that occur among females (Cloninger, 1987).

MODELS OF SUBSTANCE USE EFFECTS

The discussion of deviance proneness and stress and negative affect models serves to illustrate the importance of considering the functions that substance use might serve for adolescents. Deviance proneness models highlight the fact that adolescent substance use occurs in a broader social context of low behavioral constraint and drug use–promoting peer networks. Within these contexts, substance use may serve to communicate a social image of toughness and precocity and express an adolescent's actual or ideal self-concept (Barton et al., 1982; Jessor & Jessor, 1977; Sussman et al., 2000). Stress and negative affect models highlight the affect-regulating functions that alcohol and drug use might serve for adolescents. It is important to remember that alcohol and drug consumption produces reinforcing pharmacological effects and to consider these effects within etiological models of adolescent substance use and abuse. In substance use effects models, risk for substance disorders is thought to be associated with individual differences in sensitivity to the pharmacological effects of alcohol and other drugs (as well as with temperamental and cognitive variables discussed earlier). As individuals experience different effects of their alcohol and drug use, these experiences then influence their expectancies about the effects of future consumption, which, in turn, influence future substance use.

A large literature on substance use effects has examined the impact of alcohol and drug self-administration in both human and animal laboratory studies, and this literature is beyond the scope of the current chapter. Moreover, for ethical reasons, laboratory studies of self- administration have been largely confined to adult participants. Researchers who are interested in child and adolescent populations have studied beliefs or expectancies about substance use effects more often than they have studied actual effects in the laboratory. These expectancies can be measured in young children even before substance use begins, become increasingly complex with age (Dunn & Goldman, 1996), and predict adolescent drug use (Aarons, Brown, Stice, & Coe, 2001; Smith, Goldman, Greenbaum, & Christiansen, 1995; Stacy, Newcomb, & Bentler, 1991).

Although laboratory studies have been largely confined to adult samples, they are certainly important for etiological theories of substance use. For example, these studies suggest that individuals with family histories of alcoholism derive greater cardiovascular stress response dampening benefits from consuming alcohol in anticipation of a laboratory stressor (Levenson et al., 1987) and show greater increases in resting heart rate after drinking (which has been interpreted as reflecting greater reinforcement from the psychostimulant effects of alcohol; Conrod et al., 1997). Thus, high-risk individuals may derive more reinforcement from drinking than do their low-risk peers, and this characteristic might explain their greater alcohol involvement. Similarly, high-risk men experience less negative impact of alcohol consumption than do their low-risk peers (e.g., less body sway and less perceived intoxication), and a lowered response to the negative effects of alcohol prospectively predicts the development of alcohol use disorders 15 years later (Schuckit & Smith, 2000). Individuals who experience little negative impact of drinking will have little reason to curtail their intake, thus raising their risk for high levels of consumption and subsequent alcohol use disorders. Taken together, these data suggest that positive or negative pharmacological effects of consumption may motivate future use and thus influence risk for developing substance use disorders.

Macrolevel Influences: Neighborhoods and Schools

Sher's (1991) models do not focus on social influences that are broader than peer and family environments. However, some efforts have been made to understand the ways in which broader macrolevel factors such as school environments, neighborhoods, and state policies might influence adolescent substance use and substance use disorders. These factors could influence risk for substance use and abuse by providing social norms about the acceptability of use, affecting ease of access to substances, and providing punishment or sanctions for use.

The status of neighborhoods is often assessed with indicators of neighborhoods' socioeconomic status (SES), ethnic composition, and residential mobility (Leventhal & Brooks-Gunn, 2000). Surprisingly, although disadvantaged neighborhoods show more adolescent conduct problems and delinquency than do advantaged neighborhoods, the opposite has been found for adolescent substance use (Leventhal & Brooks-Gunn, 2000). For example, higher rates of adolescent substance use have been reported for neighborhoods with higher SES (Skager & Fisher, 1989), low rates of residential instability, high neighborhood attachment, low density (Ennett, Flewelling, Lindrooth, & Norton, 1997), and higher prevalences of residents with professional or managerial occupations (Luthar & Cushing, 1999). However, findings are not entirely consistent. Smart, Adlaf, and Walsh (1994) found an inverse relation between neighborhood SES and adolescent substance use. More research is necessary to identify the mechanisms underlying these neighborhood effects and also to examine ways in which they interrelate with other etiological factors such as personality characteristics and family environment. Although some research suggests that neighborhood influences serve to moderate the effects of personality characteristics on juvenile offending (Lynam et al.,

2000) and that neighborhood influences on adolescent problem behaviors are mediated through family environment effects (Scaramella & Keyes, 2001; Simons, Johnson, Beamans, Conger, & Whitbeck, 1996), these types of analyses have not been applied to studies of adolescent substance use disorders as specific outcomes.

In addition to social disadvantage, researchers have suggested that schools and neighborhoods in which norms are more favorable to use and in which there are greater availability and access to substances are associated with higher use rates. For example, school norms have been related to adolescent substance use (Allison et al., 1999), and density of alcohol outlets has been related to alcohol use at the community level (Scribner, Cohen, & Fisher, 2000). For legal drugs such as alcohol and tobacco, findings such as these have been used to support public policies that aim to decrease adolescents' access to substances and change community norms (e.g., raising drinking ages, reducing sales to minors, increasing tobacco taxes, restricting advertising) as ways of reducing adolescent substance use (e.g., see Institute of Medicine, 1994b, for a review). An analysis of state policies directed at adolescents' access to tobacco showed a significant negative relation between the extensiveness of a state's tobacco control policies and the prevalence of youth smoking within the state (Luke, Stamatakis, & Brownson, 2000), although this relation was undermined in tobacco-producing states.

CONCLUSIONS AND FUTURE DIRECTIONS

As illustrated by the previous discussion, much is known about the nature of adolescent substance use and substance use disorders and their developmental antecedents. A large and diverse literature has produced consensus that a family history of substance abuse, childhood conduct problems, temperamental traits reflecting behavioral undercontrol, and affiliations with drug-using peers all raise risk for substance use and substance use disorders.

However, many unanswered questions and areas for future research remain. Basic descriptive studies are needed to distinguish among multiple trajectories of substance use in adolescence, to determine whether some are relatively benign, and to determine whether there are differential antecedents for trajectories that result in clinical impairment and addictive disorders. Studies are needed to examine the impact of adolescent substance use on emerging developmental competencies and coping abilities. Regarding etiology, although the role of family history risk is well established, much less is known about the mechanisms underlying the intergenerational transmission of risk or about the protective factors that might buffer this risk. Moreover, stress and negative affect regulation models of adolescent substance use disorders are in need of further study. Further research is needed to clarify the roles of different types of negative affect and the importance of moderating variables such as coping or behavioral undercontrol. Rather than consider affect regulation pathways and deviance proneness pathways in isolation, it may be more useful to focus on behavioral undercontrol and underregulation as moderators of the relation between negative affect and substance use outcomes. Regarding the deviance proneness pathway, more research is needed to identify variables that are related specifically to substance use outcomes rather than to conduct problems in general.

Across all the developmental models, more data are needed on ways in which existing findings might vary across particular gender and ethnic subgroups. Moreover, this topic is in need of stronger theory development that would help guide our interpretations of why particular risk or protective factors might operate in particular ways within certain gender or ethnic subgroups. Research is also needed to study the effects of neighborhood, school, and social policy influences as they interact with individual, family, and peer factors.

It is unlikely that a single etiological pathway will be capable of explaining the development of adolescent substance use disorders. Thus, we are in need of studies and methods that are capable of differentiating among multiple pathways that might underlie different trajectories of substance use. Achieving this goal requires studies that are multilevel and multidisciplinary and that embed studies of substance use and substance use disorders within a broader developmental perspective. Given the clinical and public health importance of adolescent substance use and substance use disorders, it is essential that the field continues to expand in these future directions.

REFERENCES

Aarons, G., Brown, S., Stice, E., & Coe, M. (2001). Psychometric evaluation of the marijuana and stimulant effect expectancy questionnaires for adolescents. *Addictive Behaviors, 26,* 219–236.

Allison, K.W., Crawford, I., Leone, P., Trickett, E., Perez-Febles, A., Burton, L., et al. (1999). Adolescent substance use: Preliminary examinations of school and neighborhood context. *American Journal of Community Psychology, 27,* 111–141.

American Psychiatric Association. (1994). *The diagnostic and statistical manual of mental disorders* (4th ed.). Washington, DC: Author.

Arnett, J. J. (2000). Emerging adulthood: A theory of development from the late teens through the twenties. *American Psychologist, 55,* 469–480.

Aro, H., & Taipale, V. (1987). The impact of timing of puberty on psychosomatic symptoms among fourteen to sixteen-year old Finnish girls. *Child Development, 58,* 261–268.

Bachman, J.G., & Schulenberg, J. (1993). How part-time work intensity relates to drug use, problem behavior, time use, and satisfaction among high school seniors: Are these consequences or merely correlates? *Developmental Psychology, 29,* 220–235.

Bachman, J.G., Wadsworth, K., O'Malley, P., Johnston, L., & Schulenberg, J. (1997). *Smoking, drinking, and drug use in young adulthood: The impact of new freedoms and new responsibilities.* Mahwah, NJ: Erlbaum.

Baer, J.S., Barr, H., Bookstein, F., Sampson, P., & Streissguth, A. (1998). Prenatal alcohol exposure and family history of alcoholism in the etiology of adolescent alcohol problems. *Journal of Studies on Alcohol, 59,* 533–543.

Barkley, R.A., Fischer, M., Edelbrock, C. S., & Smallish, L. (1990). The adolescent outcome of hyperactive children diagnosed by research criteria: I. An 8-year prospective follow-up study. *Journal of the American Academy of Child and Adolescent Psychiatry, 29,* 546–557.

Barrera, M., Jr., Biglan, A., Ary, D., & Li, F. (2001). Modeling parental and peer influences on problem behavior of American Indian, Hispanic, and non-Hispanic Caucasian youth. *Journal of Early Adolescence, 21,* 133–156.

Barrera, M.B., Castro, F. G., & Biglan, A. (1999). Ethnicity, substance use, and development: Exemplars for exploring group differences and similarities. *Development and Psychopathology, 11,* 805–822.

Barton, J., Chassin, L., Presson, C., & Sherman, S.J. (1982). Social image factors as motivators of smoking initiation in early and middle adolescents. *Child Development, 53,* 1499–1511.

Bates, M., & Pandina, R. (1992). Familial alcoholism and premorbid cognitive deficit: A failure to replicate subtype differences. *Journal of Studies on Alcohol, 53,* 320–327.

Bauman, K. E., & Ennett, S. T. (1996). On the importance of peer influence for adolescent drug use: Commonly neglected considerations. *Addiction, 91,* 185–198.

Baumrind, D., & Moselle, K. (1985). A developmental perspective on adolescent drug abuse. *Advances in alcohol and substance abuse, 4,* 41–67.

Begleiter, H., & Porjesz, B. (1999). What is inherited in the predisposition toward alcoholism: A proposed model. *Alcoholism: Clinical and Experimental Research, 23,* 1125–1135.

Block, J., Block, H., & Keyes, S. (1988). Longitudinally foretelling drug usage in adolescence: Early childhood personality and environmental precursors. *Child Development, 59,* 336–355.

Bray, J. H., Getz, J. G., & Baer, P. E. (2000). Adolescent individuation and alcohol use in multiethnic youth. *Journal of Studies on Alcohol, 61,* 588–597.

Brook, J.S., Nomura, C., & Cohen, P. (1989). A network of influences on adolescent drug involvement: Neighborhood, school, peer, and family. *Genetic, Social and General Psychology Monographs, 115,* 125–145.

Bryant, A., Schulenberg, J., Bachman, J., O'Malley, P., & Johnston, L. (2000). Understanding the links among school misbehavior, academic achievement and cigarette use: A national panel study of adolescents. *Prevention Science, 1,* 71–87.

Bukoski, N. (1997). *Meta-analysis of drug abuse prevention programs* (NIDA Research Monograph No. 170). Washington, DC: National Institute on Drug Abuse.

Burke, J., Loeber, R., & Lahey, B. (2001). Which aspects of ADHD are associated with tobacco use in early adolescence? *Journal of Child Psychology and Psychiatry and Allied Disciplines, 42,* 493–502.

Cantwell, D., Lewinsohn, P., Rohde, P., & Seeley, J.R. (1997). Correspondence between adolescent report and parent report of psychiatric diagnostic data. *Journal of the American Academy of Child and Adolescent Psychiatry, 36,* 610–619.

Caspi, A., Moffitt, T., Newman, D., & Silva, P. (1996). Behavioral observations at age 3 predict adult psychiatric disorders. *Archives of General Psychiatry, 53,* 1033–1039.

Chassin, L., Curran, P.J., Hussong, A.M., & Colder, C.R. (1996). The relation of parent alcoholism to adolescent substance use: A longitudinal follow-up study. *Journal of Abnormal Psychology, 105,* 70–80.

Chassin, L., Pillow, D.R., Curran, P.J., Molina, B.S.G., & Barrera, Jr., M. (1993). Relation of parental alcoholism to early adolescent substance use: A test of three mediating mechanisms. *Journal of Abnormal Psychology, 102,* 3–19.

Chassin, L., Pitts, S., & DeLucia, C. (1999). The relation of adolescent substance use to young adult autonomy, positive activity involvement, and perceived competence. *Development and Psychopathology, 11,* 915–932.

Chassin, L., Pitts, S., DeLucia, C., & Todd, M. (1999). A longitudinal study of children of alcoholics: Predicting young adult substance use disorders, anxiety and depression. *Journal of Abnormal Psychology, 108,* 106–119.

Chassin, L., Pitts, S., & Prost, J. (2002). Heavy drinking trajectories from adolescence to young adulthood in a high risk sample: Predictors and substance abuse outcomes. *Journal of Consulting and Clinical Psychology, 70,* 67–78.

Chassin, L., Presson, C.C., Sherman, S.J., & Edwards, D. (1992). The natural history of cigarette smoking and young adult social roles. *Journal of Health and Social Behavior, 33,* 328–347.

Chassin, L., Presson, C.C., Pitts, S., & Sherman, S.J. (2000). The natural history of cigarette smoking from adolescence to adulthood in a midwestern community sample: Multiple trajectories and their psychosocial correlates. *Health Psychology, 19,* 223–231.

Chassin, L., Presson, C.C., Todd, M., Rose, J., & Sherman, S.J. (1998). Maternal socialization of adolescent smoking: The intergenerational transmission of parenting and smoking. *Developmental Psychology, 34,* 1189–1201.

Clayton, R. (1992). Transitions in drug use: Risk and protective factors. In M. Glantz & R. Pickens (Eds.), *Vulnerability to drug abuse* (pp. 15–51). Washington, DC: American Psychological Association.

Cloninger, C. R. (1987). Neurogenetic adaptive mechanisms in alcoholism. *Science, 236,* 410–416.

Cohen, P., Cohen, J., Kassen, S., Velez, C., Hartmark, C., Johnson, J., et al. (1993). An epidemiologic study of disorders in late childhood and adolescence: I. Age-specific and gender-specific prevalence. *Journal of Child Psychology and Psychiatry and Allied Disciplines, 34,* 851–867.

Colder, C., & Chassin, L. (1997). Affectivity and impulsivity: Temperament risk for adolescent alcohol involvement. *Psychology of Addictive Behaviors, 11,* 83–97.

Colder, C., & Chassin, L. (1999). The psychosocial characteristics of alcohol users vs. problem users: Data from a student of adolescents at risk. *Development and Psychopathology, 11,* 321–348.

Conrod, P., Petersen, J., & Pihl, R.O. (1997). Disinhibited personality and sensitivity to alcohol reinforcement: Independent correlates of drinking behavior in sons of alcoholics. *Alcoholism: Clinical and Experimental Research, 21,* 1320–1332.

Cooper, M. L. (1994). Motivations for alcohol use among adolescents: Development and validation of a four-factor model. *Psychological Assessment, 6,* 117–128.

Cooper, M. L., Frone, M. R., Russell, M., & Mudar, P. (1995). Drinking to regulate positive and negative emotions: A motivational model of alcohol use. *Journal of Personality and Social Psychology, 69,* 990–1005.

Cornelius, M., Leech, S., Goldschmidt,. L., & Day, N. (2000). Prenatal tobacco exposure: Is it a risk factor for early tobacco experimentation? *Nicotine and Tobacco Research, 2,* 45–52.

Costa, F. M., Jessor, R., & Turbin, M. S. (1999). Transition into adolescent problem drinking: The role of psychosocial risk and protective factors. *Journal of Studies on Alcohol, 60,* 480–490.

Costello, E.J., Erkanli, A., Federman, E., & Angold, A. (1999). Development of psychiatric comorbidity with substance abuse in adolescents: Effects of timing and sex. *Journal of Clinical Child Psychology, 28,* 298–311.

Costello, E. J., Farmer, E. M. Z., Angold, A., Burns, B. J., & Erkanli, A. (1997). Psychiatric disorders among American Indian and white youth in Appalachia: The Great Smoky Mountains Study. *American Journal of Public Health, 87,* 827–832.

Curran, P.J., Stice, E., & Chassin, L. (1997). The relation between adolescent alcohol use and peer alcohol use: A longitudinal random coefficients model. *Journal of Consulting and Clinical Psychology, 65,* 130–140.

Deas, D., Riggs, P., Langenbucher, J., Goldman, M., & Brown, S. (2000). Adolescents are not adults: Developmental considerations in alcohol users. *Alcoholism: Clinical and Experimental Research, 24,* 232–237.

Deas, D., & Thomas, S. (2001). An overview of controlled studies of adolescent substance abuse treatment. *American Journal of the Addictions, 10,* 178–189.

Deckel, A.W., & Hesselbrock, V. (1996). Behavioral and cognitive measurements predict scores on the MAST: A 3-year prospective study. *Alcoholism: Clinical and Experimental Research, 20,* 1173–1178.

Deykin, E., Buka, S., & Zeena, T. (1992). Depressive illness among chemically dependent adolescents. *American Journal of Psychiatry, 149,* 1341–1347.

Dick, D. M., Rose, R.J., Viken, R., & Kaprio, J. (2000). Pubertal timing and substance use: Associations between and within families across late adolescence. *Developmental Psychology, 36,* 180–189.

Dishion, T., Patterson, G.R., & Reid, J.R. (1988). Parent and peer factors associated with drug sampling in early adolescence: Implications for treatment. *NIDA Research Monograph, 77,* 69–93.

Dishion, T., Patterson, G.R., Stoolmiller, M., & Skinner, M. (1991). Family, school, and behavioral antecedents to early adolescent involvement with antisocial peers. *Developmental Psychology, 27,* 127–180.

Disney, E., Elkins, I., McGue, M., & Iacono, W. (1999). Effects of ADHD, conduct disorder, and gender on substance use and abuse in adolescence. *American Journal of Psychiatry, 156,* 1515–1521.

Dolcini, M., Adler, N., & Ginsberg, D. (1996). Factors influencing agreement between self-reports and biological measures of smoking among adolescents. *Journal of Research on Adolescence, 6,* 515–542.

Drejer, K., Theilgard, A., Teasdale, T. W., Schulsinger, F., & Goodwin, D. W. (1985). A prospective study of young men at high risk for alcoholism: Neuropsychological assessment. *Alcoholism: Clinical and Experimental Research, 9,* 498–502.

Duncan, S. C., Duncan, T. E., Biglan, A., & Ary, D. (1998). Contributions of the social context to the development of adolescent substance use: A multivariate latent growth modeling approach. *Drug and Alcohol Dependence, 50,* 57–71.

Duncan, T. E., Duncan, S. C., & Hops, H. (1998). Latent variable modeling of longitudinal and multilevel alcohol use data. *Journal of Studies on Alcohol, 59,* 399–408.

Duncan, T. E., Tildesley, E., Duncan, S. C., & Hops, H. (1995). The consistency of family and peer influences on the development of substance use in adolescence. *Addiction, 90,* 1647–1660.

Dunn, M., & Goldman, M. (1996). Empirical modeling of an alcohol expectancy network in elementary-school children as a function of grade. *Experimental and Clinical Psychopharmacology, 4,* 209–217.

Eccles, J. S., Lord, S. E., Roeser, R. W., Barber, B. L., & Jozefowicz, D. (1997). The association of school transitions in early adolescence with developmental trajectories through high school. In J. Schulenberg, J. Maggs, & K. Hurrelmann (Eds.), *Health risks and developmental transitions during adolescence* (pp 283–320). Cambridge, England: Cambridge University Press.

Eisenberg, N., Guthrie, I., Fabes, S., Shepard, S., Losoya, S., Murphy, B., et al. (2000). Prediction of elementary school children's externalizing problem behaviors from attentional and behavioral regulation and negative emotionality. *Child Development, 71,* 1367–1382.

Elliott, D. S., Huizinga, D., & Ageton, S. (1985). *Explaining delinquency and drug use.* Beverly Hills, CA: Sage.

Ennett, S., Flewelling, R., Lindrooth, R., & Norton, E. (1997). School and neighborhood characteristics associated with school rates of alcohol, cigarette, and marijuana use. *Journal of Health and Social Behavior, 38,* 55–71.

Erickson, K., Crosnoe, R., & Dornbusch, S. (2000). A social process model of adolescent deviance: Combining social control and differential association perspectives. *Journal of Youth and Adolescence, 29,* 395–425.

Fergusson, D. M., Horwood, L. J., & Lynskey, M. T. (1993). Prevalence and comorbidity of *DSM-III-R* diagnoses in a birth cohort of 15 year olds. *Journal of the American Academy of Child and Adolescent Psychiatry, 32,* 1127–1134.

Fergusson, D. M., Lynsky, M., & Horwood, L. J. (1996). Alcohol misuse and juvenile offending in adolescence. *Addiction, 91,* 483–494.

Fergusson, D. M., Lynsky, M., & Horwood, L. J. (1996). Comorbidity between depressive disorders and nicotine dependence in a cohort of 16 year olds. *Archives of General Psychiatry, 53,* 1043–1047.

Fulkerson, J. A., Harrison, P. A., & Beebe, T. J. (1999). *DSM-IV* substance abuse and dependence: Are there really two dimensions of substance use problems in adolescents. *Addiction, 94,* 495–506.

Ge, X., Conger, R., Cadoret, R., Neiderheiser, J., Yates, W., Troughton, E., et al. (1996). The developmental interface between nature and nurture: A mutual influence model of child antisocial behavior and parent behavior. *Developmental Psychology, 32,* 574–589.

Giancola, P. R., Martin, C. S., Tarter, R. E., Pelham, W., & Moss, H. B. (1996). Executive cognitive functioning and aggressive behavior in preadolescent boys at high risk for substance abuse/dependence. *Journal of Studies on Alcohol, 57,* 352–359.

Giancola, P. R., & Mezzich, A. C. (2000). Neuropsychological deficits in female adolescents with a substance use disorder: Better accounted for by conduct disorder. *Journal of Studies on Alcohol, 61,* 809–817.

Giancola, P. R., Mezzich, A. C., & Tarter, R. E. (1998). Disruptive, delinquent and aggressive behavior in female adolescents with a psychoactive substance use disorder: Relation to executive cognitive functioning. *Journal of Studies on Alcohol, 59,* 560–567.

Graber, J., Lewinsohn, P., Seeley, J., & Brooks-Gunn, J. (1997). Is psychopathology associated with the timing of pubertal development? *Journal of the American Academy of Child and Adolescent Psychiatry, 36,* 1768–1776.

Grant, B. F., & Dawson, D. A. (1997). Age at onset of alcohol use and its association with *DSM-IV* alcohol abuse and dependence: Results from the National Longitudinal Epidemiologic Survey. *Journal of Substance Abuse, 9,* 103–110.

Grant, B. F., Harford, T., Dawson, D. A., Chou, P. Dufour, M., & Pickering, K. (1994). Prevalence of *DSM-IV* alcohol abuse and dependence. *Alcohol, Health, and Research World, 18,* 243–248.

Griesler, P. C., & Kandel, D. B. (1998). Ethnic differences in the correlates of adolescent cigarette smoking. *Journal of Adolescent Health, 23,* 167–180.

Grunberg, N., Winders, S., & Wewers, M. (1991). Gender differences in tobacco use. *Health Psychology, 10,* 143–153.

Han, C., McGue, M., & Iacono, W. (1999). Lifetime tobacco, alcohol, and other substance use in adolescent Minnesota twins: Univariate and multivariate behavior genetic analyses. *Addiction, 94,* 981–983.

Hansell, S., & White, H. R. (1991). Adolescent drug use, psychological distress, and physical symptoms. *Journal of Health and Social Behavior, 32,* 288–301.

Harden, P., & Pihl, R. (1995). Cognitive function, cardiovascular reactivity, and behavior in boys at high risk for alcoholism. *Journal of Abnormal Psychology, 104,* 94–103.

Hawkins, J. D., Catalano, R., & Miller, J. (1992). Risk and protective factors for alcohol and other drug problems in adolescence and early adulthood: Implications for substance abuse prevention. *Psychological Bulletin, 112,* 64–105.

Henry, B., Feehan, M., McGee, R., Stanton, W., Moffitt, T., & Silva, P. (1993). The importance of conduct problems and depressive symptoms in predicting adolescent substance use. *Journal of Abnormal Child Psychology, 21,* 469–480.

Hill, K., White, H. R., Chung, I-J., Hawkins, J. D., & Catalano, R. F. (2000). Early adult outcomes of adolescent binge drinking: Person- and variable-centered analyses of binge drinking trajectories. *Alcoholism: Clinical and Experimental Research, 24,* 892–901.

Hill, S., Shen, S., Lowers, L., & Locke, J. (2000). Factors predicting the onset of adolescent drinking in families at high risk for developing alcoholism. *Biological Psychiatry, 48,* 265–275.

Hirschi, T. (1969). *Causes of delinquency.* Berkeley, CA: University of California Press.

Hussong, A. M. (in press). Differentiating peer contexts and risk for adolescent substance use. *Journal of Youth and Adolescence.*

Hussong, A., & Chassin, L. (2002). Parent alcoholism and the leaving home transition. *Development and Psychopathology, 14,* 139–157.

Hussong, A., Curran, P., & Chassin, L. (1998). Pathways of risk for accelerated heavy alcohol use among adolescent children of alcoholic parents. *Journal of Abnormal Child Psychology, 26,* 453–466.

Hussong, A., Hicks, R., Levy, S., & Curran, P. (2001). Specifying the relations between affect and heavy alcohol use among young adults. *Journal of Abnormal Psychology, 110,* 449–461.

Iacono, W. G., Carlson, S. R., Taylor, J., Elkins, I. J., & McGue, M. (1999). Behavioral disinhibition and the development of substance-use disorders: Findings from the Minnesota Twin Family Study. *Development and Psychopathology, 11,* 869–900.

Institute of Medicine. (1994a). *Pathways of addiction: Opportunities in drug abuse research.* Washington, DC: National Academy Press.

Institute of Medicine. (1994b). *Growing up tobacco free: Preventing nicotine addiction in children and youths.* Washington, DC: National Academy Press.

Jackson, C., & Henriksen, L. (1997). Do as I say: Parent smoking, antismoking socialization, and smoking onset among children. *Addictive Behaviors, 22,* 107–114.

Jessor, R., Donovan, J., & Costa, F. (1991). *Beyond adolescence: Problem behavior and young adult development.* Cambridge, England: Cambridge University Press.

Jessor, R., & Jessor, S. (1977). *Problem behavior and psychosocial development: A longitudinal study of youth.* New York: Academic Press.

Johnson, J.G., Cohen, P., Pine, D., Klein, D., Kasen, S., & Brook, J. (2000). Association between cigarette smoking and anxiety disorders during adolescence and early adulthood. *Journal of the American Medical Association, 284,* 2348–2351.

Johnston, L., O'Malley, P., & Bachman, J. (2000). *Monitoring the future: National survey results on drug use, 1975–1999* (NIH Publication No. 00-4802). Bethesda, MD: National Institute on Drug Abuse.

Johnston, L., O'Malley, P., & Bachman, J. (2002). *Monitoring the future: National results on adolescent drug use: Overview of key findings, 2001* (NIH Publication No. 02-5105). Bethesda, MD: National Institute on Drug Abuse.

Kandel, D. B. (1975). Stages in adolescent involvement in drug use. *Science, 165,* 912–914.

Kandel, D. B. (1978). Convergences in prospective longitudinal surveys of drug use in normal populations. In D. B. Kandel (Ed.), *Longitudinal research on drug use: Empirical findings and methodological issues* (pp. 3–40). New York: Wiley.

Kandel, D. B. (1995). Ethnic differences in drug use: Patterns and paradoxes. In G. J. Botvin, S. Schinke, & M. Orlandi (Eds.), *Drug abuse prevention with multi-ethnic youth* (pp. 81–104). Thousand Oaks, CA: Sage.

Kandel, D. B., Davies, M., Karus, D., & Yamaguchi, K. (1986). The consequences in young adulthood of adolescent drug involvement. *Archives of General Psychiatry, 43,* 746–754.

Kandel, D. B., Johnson, J. G., Bird, H. R., Canino, G., Goodman, S., Lahey, B., et al. (1997). Psychiatric disorders associated with substance use among children and adolescents: Findings from the Methods for the Epidemiology of Child and Adolescent Mental Disorders (MECA) study. *Journal of Abnormal Child Psychology, 25,* 121–132.

Kaplow, J. B., Curran, P. J., Angold, A., & Costello, E. J. (2001). The prospective relation between dimensions of anxiety and the initiation of adolescent alcohol use. *Journal of Clinical Child Psychology, 30,* 316–326.

Kellam, S., Brown, C., Rubin, B., & Ensminger, M. (1983). Paths leading to teenage psychiatric symptoms and substance use: Developmental epidemiological studies in Woodlawn. In S. B. Guze, J. Earls, & J. Barrett (Eds.), *Childhood psychopathology and development* (pp. 17–52), New York: Norton.

Kushner, M., Sher, K. J., Wood, M., & Wood, P. (1994). Anxiety and drinking behavior: Moderating effects of tension-reduction expectancies. *Alcoholism: Clinical and Experimental Research, 18,* 852–860.

Labouvie, E., Pandina, R. J., White, J. R., & Johnson, V. (1990). Risk factors of adolescent drug use: An affect-based interpretation. *Journal of Substance Abuse, 2,* 262–285.

Lamborn, S. D., Dornbursch, S. M., & Steinberg, L. (1996). Ethnicity and community context as moderators of the relations between family decision-making and adolescent adjustment. *Child Development, 67,* 283–301.

Leifman, H., Kuhlhorn, E., Allebeck, P., Andreasson, S., & Romelsjo, A. (1995). Abstinence in late adolescence: Antecedents to and covariates of a sober lifestyle and its consequences. *Social Science and Medicine, 41,* 113–121.

Lerner, J. V., & Vicary, J. R. (1984). Difficult temperament and drug use: Analyses from the New York Longitudinal Study. *Journal of Drug Education, 14,* 1–8.

Levenson, R., Oyama, O., & Meek, P. (1987). Greater reinforcement from alcohol for those at risk: Parental risk, personality risk, and sex. *Journal of Abnormal Psychology, 96,* 247–253.

Leventhal, T., & Brooks-Gunn, J. (2000). The neighborhoods they live in: The effects of neighborhood residence on child and adolescent outcomes. *Psychological Bulletin, 126,* 309–337.

Levin, E., Connors, C., Silva, D., Hinton, S., Meek, W., March, J., et al. (1998). Transdermal nicotine effects on attention. *Psychopharmacology, 140,* 135–141.

Levy, S. A. (2002). *Dating behaviors and adolescent substance use.* Unpublished masters thesis, University of North Carolina, Chapel Hill.

Lewinsohn, P., Hops, H., Roberts, R., Seeley, J., & Andrews, J. (1993). Adolescent psychopathology I: Prevalence and incidence of depression and other *DSM-III-R* disorders in high school students. *Journal of Abnormal Psychology, 102,* 133–144.

Lezak, M. D. (1995). *Neuropsychological assessment (3rd ed.).* New York: Oxford University Press.

Loeber, R., Stouthamer-Loeber, M., & White, H. R. (1999). Developmental aspects of delinquency and internalizing problems and their association with persistent juvenile substance use between ages 7 and 18. *Journal of Clinical Child Psychology, 28,* 322–332.

Luke, D. A., Stamatakis, K. A., & Brownson, R. C. (2000). State youth-access tobacco control policies and youth smoking behavior in the United States. *American Journal of Preventive Medicine, 19,* 180–187.

Luthar, S. S., & Cushing, G. (1999). Neighborhood influences and child development: A prospective study of substance abusers' offspring. *Development and Psychopathology, 11,* 763–784.

Lynam, D. , Caspi, A., Moffitt, T., Wikstrom, P-O., Loeber, R., & Novak, S. (2000). The interaction between impulsivity and neighborhood context on offending: The effects of impulsivity are stronger in poorer neighborhoods. *Journal of Abnormal Psychology, 109,* 563–574.

Lynsky, M. T., & Fergusson, D. M. (1995). Childhood conduct problems, attention deficit behaviors, and adolescent alcohol, tobacco and illicit drug use. *Journal of Abnormal Child Psychology, 23,* 281–302.

Maggs, J. L. (1997). Alcohol use and binge drinking as goal-directed action during the transition to post-secondary education. In J. Schulenberg, J. L. Maggs, & K. Hurrelmann (Eds.), *Health risks and developmental transitions during adolescence* (pp. 345–371). Cambridge, England: Cambridge University Press.

Maggs, J. L., & Hurrelmann, K. (1998). Do substance use and delinquency have differential associations with adolescents' peer relations? *International Journal of Behavioral Development, 22,* 367–388.

Martin, C. S., Kaczynski, N. A., Maisto, S. A., Bukstein, O. M., & Moss, H. B. (1995). Patterns of DSM-IV alcohol abuse and dependence in adolescent drinkers. *Journal of Studies on Alcohol, 56,* 672–680.

Mason, W., & Windle, M. (2002). Reciprocal relations between adolescent substance use and delinquency: A longitudinal latent variable analysis. *Journal of Abnormal Psychology, 111,* 63–76.

McGue, M. (1994). Genes, environment, and the etiology of alcoholism. In R. Zucker, G. Boyd, & J. Howard (Eds.), *The development of alcohol problems: Exploring the biopsychosocial matrix of risk* (NIAAA Research Monograph 26, pp. 1–40). Washington, DC: U.S. Government Printing Office.

McGue, M., Elkins, I., & Iacono, W. (2000). Genetic and environmental influences on adolescent substance use and abuse. *American Journal of Medical Genetics, 96,* 671–677.

McGue, M., Sharma, A., & Benson, P. (1996). Parent and sibling influences on adolescent alcohol use and misuse: Evidence from a U.S. adoption cohort. *Journal of Studies on Alcohol, 57,* 8–18.

Merikangas, K., & Avenevoli, S. (2000). Implications of genetic epidemiology for the prevention of substance use disorders. *Addictive Behaviors, 25,* 807–820.

Merikangas, K., Stolar, M., Stevens, D., Goulet, J., Preisign, M., Fenton, B., et al. (1998). Familial transmission of substance use disorders. *Archives of General Psychiatry, 55,* 973–979.

Milberger, S., Biederman, J., Faraone, S., Chen, L., & Jones, J. (1997). ADHD is associated with early initiation of cigarette smoking in children and adolescents. *Journal of the American Academy of Child and Adolescent Psychiatry, 36,* 37–44.

Moffitt, T. E. (1993). Adolescence-limited and life-course-persistent antisocial behavior: a developmental taxonomy. *Psychological Review, 100,* 674–701.

Molina, B. S. G., & Pelham, W. E. (2003). *Childhood predictors of adolescent substance use in a longitudinal study of children with ADHD. Journal of Abnormal Psychology.*

Moss, H. B., Vanyukov, M., Yao, J., & Irillova, G. (1999). Salivary cortisol responses in prepubertal boys: The effects of parental substance abuse and association with drug use behavior during adolescence. *Biological Psychiatry, 45,* 1293–1299.

Murgraff, V., Parrott, A., & Bennett, P. (1999). Risky single-occasion drinking among young people—definition, correlates, policy, and intervention: A broad overview of research findings. *Alcohol and Alcoholism, 34,* 3–14.

Muthen, B., & Shedden, K. (1999). Finite mixture modeling with mixture outcomes using the EM algorithm. *Biometrics, 55,* 463–469.
Nagin, D. (1999). Analyzing developmental trajectories: A semi-parametric group-based approach. *Psychological Methods, 4,* 139–157.
Nestler, E. (2000). Genes and addiction. *Nature Genetics, 26,* 277–281.
Newcomb, M. D. (1995). Drug use etiology among ethnic minority adolescents: Risk and protective factors. In G. J. Botvin, S. Schinke, & M. A. Orlandi (Eds.), *Drug abuse prevention with multiethnic youth* (pp. 105–129). Thousand Oaks, CA: Sage.
Newcomb, M., & Bentler, P. (1988a). *Consequences of adolescent drug use: Impact on the lives of young adults.* Newbury Park, CA: Sage.
Newcomb, M., & Bentler, P. (1988b). Impact of adolescent drug use and social support on problems of young adults: A longitudinal study. *Journal of Abnormal Psychology, 97,* 64–75.
Newcomb, M., & Harlow, L. (1986). Life events and substance use among adolescents: Mediating effects of perceived loss of control and meaninglessness in life. *Journal of Personality and Social Psychology, 51,* 564–577.
O'Connor, T. G., Allen, J. P., Bell, K. L., & Hauser, S. T. (1996). Adolescent-parent relationships and leaving home in young adulthood. In J. A. Graver & J. S. Dubas (Eds.), *Leaving home: Understanding the transition to adulthood: Vol. 71. New directions for child development,* (pp. 39–52). San Francisco: Jossey-Bass.
Patterson, G. R. (1986). Performance models for antisocial boys. *American Psychologist, 41,* 432–444.
Paulson, M., Combs, R., & Richardson, M. (1990). School performance, educational aspirations, and drug use among children and adolescents. *Journal of Drug Education, 20,* 289–303.
Peterson, J. B., Finn, P. R., & Pihl, R. O. (1992). Cognitive dysfunction and the inherited predisposition to alcoholism. *Journal of Studies on Alcohol, 53,* 154–160.
Petraitis, J. Flay, B., & Miller, T. (1995). Reviewing theories of adolescent substance use: Organizing pieces in the puzzle. *Psychological Bulletin, 117,* 76–86.
Peterson, J. B., & Pihl, R. O. (1990). Information processing, neuropsychological function, and the inherited predisposition to alcoholism. *Neuropsychological Review, 1,* 343–369.
Plunkett, M., & Mitchell, C. (2000). Substance use rates among American Indian adolescents: Regional comparisons with Monitoring the Future High School Seniors. *Journal of Drug Issues, 30,* 593–620.
Reich, T., Hinrichs, A., Culverhouse, R., & Bierut, L. (1999). Genetic studies of alcoholism and substance dependence. *American Journal of Human Genetics, 65,* 599–605.
Reifman, A., Barnes, G. M., Dintcheff, B. A., Farrell, M. P., & Uhteg, L. (1998). Parental and peer influences on the onset of heavier drinking among adolescents. *Journal of Studies on Alcohol, 59,* 311–317.
Resnicow, K., Soler, R., Braithwaite, R. L., Ahluwalia, J. S., & Butler, J. (2000). Cultural sensitivity in substance use prevention. *Journal of Community Psychology, 28,* 271–290.
Robins, L. N., & Pryzbeck, T. R. (1985). *Age of onset of drug use as a factor in drug and other disorders* (NIDA Research Monograph No. 56, pp.178–192). Washington, DC: National Institute on Drug Abuse.
Rogers, S., Miller, H., & Turner, C. (1998). Effects of interview mode on bias in survey measurement of drug use: Do respondent characteristics make a difference? *Substance Use and Misuse, 33,* 2179–2220.
Rohde, P., Lewinsohn, P., & Seeley, J. (1996). Psychiatric comorbidity with problematic alcohol use in high school students. *Journal of the American Academy of Child and Adolescent Psychiatry, 35,* 101–109.
Rourke, S. B., & Loberg, T. (1996). Neurobehavioral correlates of alcoholism. In I. Grant & K.M. Adams (Eds.), *Neuropsychological assessment of neuropsychiatric disorders* (2nd ed., pp. 423–485). New York: Oxford University Press.
Russell, M. (1990). Prevalence of alcoholism among children of alcoholics. In M. Windle & J. Searles (Eds.), *Children of alcoholics: Critical perspectives* (pp. 9–38). New York: Guilford.
Substance Abuse & Mental Health Services Administration [SAMHSHA]. (1999). *Understanding*

substance abuse prevention: Toward the 21st century: A primer on effective programs (DHHS Publication No. (SMA) 99-3301). Washington, DC: U.S. Government Printing Office.

Scaramella, L. V., & Keyes, A. W. (2001). The social contextual approach and rural adolescent substance use: Implications for prevention in rural settings. *Clinical Child and Family Psychology Review, 4,* 231–251.

Schuckit, M. A., & Smith, T. L. (2000). The relationships of a family history of alcohol dependence, a low level of response to alcohol and six domains of life functioning to the development of alcohol use disorders. *Journal of Studies on Alcohol, 61,* 827–835.

Scribner, R., Cohen, D., & Fisher, W. (2000). Evidence of a structural effect for alcohol outlet density: A multilevel analysis. *Alcoholism: Clinical and Experimental Research, 24,* 188–196.

Shedler, J., & Block, J. (1990). Adolescent drug use and psychological health: A longitudinal inquiry. *Psychological Bulletin, 45,* 612–630.

Sher, K. J. (1991). *Children of alcoholics: A critical appraisal of theory and research.* Chicago: University of Chicago Press.

Sher, K. J., & Gotham, J. J. (1999). Pathological alcohol involvement: A developmental disorder of young adulthood. *Development and Psychopathology, 11,* 933–956.

Sher, K. J., Martin, E. D., Wood, P. K., & Rutledge, P. C. (1997). Alcohol use disorders and neuropsychological functioning in first-year undergraduates. *Experimental and Clinical Psychopharmacology, 5,* 304–315.

Simons, R., Johnson, C., Beamans, J., Conger, R., & Whitbeck, L. (1996). Parents and peer group as mediators of the effect of community structure on adolescent problem behavior. *American Journal of Community Psychology, 24,* 145–171.

Skager, R., & Fisher, D. (1989). Substance use among high schoolers in relation to school characteristics. *Addictive Behaviors, 14,* 129–138.

Smart, R. G., Adlaf, E. M., & Walsh, G. W. (1994). Neighborhood socio-economic factors in relation to student drug use and programs. *Journal of Child and Adolescent Substance Abuse, 3,* 37–46.

Smith, G. T., Goldman, M. S., Greenbaum, P. E., & Christiansen, B. A. (1995). Expectancy for social facilitation from drinking: The divergent paths of high-expectancy and low-expectancy adolescents. *Journal of Abnormal Psychology, 104,* 32–40.

Stacy, A., Newcomb, M., & Bentler, P. (1991). Cognitive motivation and problem drug use: A 9 year longitudinal study. *Journal of Abnormal Psychology, 100,* 502–515.

Stattin, H., & Magnusson, D. (1990). *Pubertal maturation in female development: Vol 2. Paths through life.* Hillsdale, NJ: Erlbaum.

Stattin, H., & Magnusson, D. (1996). Leaving home at an early age among females. In J. A. Graver & J. S. Dubas (Eds.), *Leaving home: Understanding the transition to adulthood: Vol. 71. New directions for child development* (pp. 53–70). San Francisco: Jossey-Bass.

Steinberg, L., & Dornbusch, S. M. (1991). Negative correlates of part-time employment during adolescence: Replication and elaboration, *Developmental Psychology, 29,* 171–180.

Steinberg, L., Fletcher, A., & Darling, N. (1994). Parental monitoring and peer influences on adolescent substance use. *Pediatrics, 93,* 1060–1064.

Stice, E., & Barrera, M. (1995). A longitudinal examination of the reciprocal relations between perceived parenting and adolescents' substance use and externalizing behaviors. *Developmental Psychology, 33,* 322–334.

Stice, E., & Gonzales, N. (1998). Adolescent temperament moderates the relationship of parenting to antisocial behavior. *Journal of Adolescent Research, 13,* 5–31.

Stice, E., Presnell, K., & Bearman, S. (2001). Relation of early menarche to depression, eating disorders, substance abuse, and comorbid psychopathology among adolescent girls. *Developmental Psychology, 37,* 608–619.

Stubben, J. (1997). Culturally competent substance abuse prevention research among rural American Indian communities. In E. B. Robertson, Z. Sloboda, G. M. Boyd, L. Beatty, & N. J. Kozel (Eds.), *Rural substance abuse: State of knowledge and issues* (NIDA Research Monograph No. 168, pp. 459–483). Rockville, MD: National Institute on Drug Abuse.

Sussman, S., Dent, C., & McCullar, W. (2000). Group self-identification as a prospective pre-

dictor of drug use and violence in high-risk youth. *Psychology of Addictive Behaviors, 14,* 192–196.
Swaim, R., Oetting, E., Beauvais, F. (1989). Links from emotional distress to adolescent drug use: A path model. *Journal of Consulting and Clinical Psychology, 57,* 227–231.
Tapert, S. F., & Brown, S. A. (1999). Neuropsychological correlates of adolescent substance use: Four-year outcomes. *Journal of the International Neuropsychological Society, 5,* 481–493.
Tarter, R. E., Alterman, A. I., & Edwards, K. L. (1985). Vulnerability to alcoholism in men: A behavior-genetic perspective. *Journal of Studies on Alcohol, 46,* 329–356.
Tarter, R., & Vanyukov, M. (1994). Alcoholism: A developmental disorder. *Journal of Consulting and Clinical Psychology, 62,* 1096–2007.
Tarter, R., Vanukov, M., Giancola, P., Dawes, M, Blackson, T., Mezzich, A., et al. (1999). Etiology of early age onset substance use disorder: A maturational perspective. *Development and Psychopathology, 11,* 657–683.
Uhl, G. R. (1999). Molecular genetics of substance abuse vulnerability: A current approach. *Neuropsychopharmacology, 20,* 3–9.
Urberg, K. A., Degirmencioglu, S. M., & Pilgrim, C. (1997). Close friend and group influence on adolescent cigarette smoking and alcohol use. *Developmental Psychology, 33,* 834–844.
Watson, D., Clark, L. A., & Carey, G. (1988). Positive and negative affectivity and their relation to anxiety and depressive disorders. *Journal of Abnormal Psychology, 97,* 346–353.
Webb, J. A., & Baer, P. E. (1995). Influence of family disharmony and parental alcohol use on adolescent social skills, self-efficacy and alcohol use. *Addictive Behaviors, 20,* 127–135.
White, H. R., Pandina, R. J., & LaGrange, R. L. (1987). Longitudinal predictors of serious substance use and delinquency. *Criminology, 25,* 715–739.
Wiers, R. W., Gunning, W. B., & Sergeant, J. A. (1998). Is a mild deficit in executive function in boys related to childhood ADHD or to parental multigenerational alcoholism? *Journal of Abnormal Child Psychology, 26,* 415–430.
Wills, T. A. (1986). Stress and coping in early adolescence: Relationships to substance use in urban school samples. *Health Psychology, 5,* 503–529.
Wills, T., & Cleary, S. (1997). The validity of self-reports of smoking: Analyses by race/ethnicity in a school sample of urban adolescents. *American Journal of Public Health, 87,* 56–61.
Wills, T. A., Sandy, J., Yaeger, A., Cleary, S., & Shinar, O. (2001). Coping dimensions, life stress, and adolescent substance use: A latent growth analysis. *Journal of Abnormal Psychology, 110,* 309–323.
Wills, T. A., Sandy, J. M., Yaeger, A., & Shinar, O. (2001). Family risk factors and adolescent substance use: Moderation effects for temperament dimensions. *Developmental Psychology, 37,* 283–297.
Wills, T. A., Vaccaro, D., McNamara, G., & Hirky, A. (1996). Escalated substance use: A longitudinal grouping analysis from early to middle adolescence. *Journal of Abnormal Psychology, 105,* 166–180.
Windle, M., & Windle, R. (2001). Depressive symptoms and cigarette smoking among middle adolescents: Prospective associations and intrapersonal and interpersonal influences. *Journal of Consulting and Clinical Psychology, 69,* 215–226.
Wood, P., Sher, K. J., Erickson, D., & DeBord, K. (1997). Predicting academic problems in college from freshman alcohol involvement. *Journal of Studies on Alcohol, 58,* 200–210.
Wright, L. S. (1982). Parental permission to date and its relationship to drug use and suicidal thought among adolescents. *Adolescence, 66,* 409–417.
Yamaguchi, K., & Kandel, D. B. (1985). On the resolution of role incompatibility: A life event history analysis of family roles and marijuana use. *American Journal of Sociology, 90,* 1284–1325.
Zoccolillo, M., Vitaro, F., & Tremblay, R. (1999). Problem drug and alcohol use in a community sample of adolescents. *Journal of the American Academy of Child and Adolescent Psychiatry, 38,* 900–907.
Zucker, R. A. (1987). The four alcoholisms: A developmental account of the etiologic process. In P. C. Rivers (Ed.), *Nebraska symposium on motivation, 1986: Alcohol and addictive behavior* (pp. 27–83). Lincoln: University of Nebraska Press.

Chapter 22

ADOLESCENTS WITH DEVELOPMENTAL DISABILITIES AND THEIR FAMILIES

Penny Hauser-Cram and Marty Wyngaarden Krauss

This preparation of this manuscript was partially support by grant R40 MC 00177 from the Maternal and Child Health Bureau (Title V, Social Security Act), Health Resources and Services Administration, Department of Health and Human Services.

This chapter explores the adolescent period for individuals with developmental disabilities and their families. The inclusion of this chapter in a volume that focuses predominantly on typically developing adolescents attests to the increased visibility of and concern for persons with various types of disabilities in our society. Although the research base studying the adolescent period among children with developmental disabilities is comparatively sparse, there is a considerable public policy interest in maximizing the developmental potential of children and adolescents with developmental disabilities, as is evident by the mandates of the Individuals with Disabilities Education Act (IDEA) and the Americans with Disabilities Act. In addition, although longitudinal studies of the development of children with developmental disabilities are few in number, they are yielding important theoretical and applied knowledge regarding the utility of mainstream developmental theories, such as developmental systems theory (Lerner, 2002b), to our understanding of the relation between biological and environmental influences on their development. Thus, there is an increased interest in integrating the unique and common concerns of youth with developmental disabilities in scholarly reviews of adolescent development, such as the present volume.

The period of adolescence is traditionally defined not in terms of a specific span of years, but rather in terms of what occurs during this life phase: the transition from childhood to adulthood (Modell & Goodman, 1990). As noted by Zahn-Waxler (1996), adulthood is characterized by the internalization of societal norms, economic independence, formation of viable family units, and acceptance of responsibility for oneself and for others. For individuals with developmental disabilities, there may be notable constraints on the extent to which some of these adult roles are achieved, particularly with respect to economic independence and formation of family units. The biological, cognitive, psychological, and social changes that characterize the transition from the adolescent period to adulthood, however, are as challenging for individuals with developmental disabilities (and their families) as they are for typically developing individuals. Unlike typically developing adolescents, however, adolescents with developmental disabilities may chronologically reach adulthood without the same degree of personal independence and autonomy that generally defines the adult stage of development. However, as Graber and Brooks-Gunn (1996) note, "understanding how individuals navigate developmental transitions is at the crux of understanding risk and resilience across the life span" (p. 768).

Our review of the adolescent period for individuals with developmental disabilities addresses four main topics: (a) a discussion of developmental theories with applicability to persons with developmental disabilities, (b) an analysis of the literature on the major developmental tasks associated with adolescence and how such tasks are affected by developmental disabilities, (c) a discussion of the role and functioning of the families of adolescents with developmental disabilities, and (d) a proposed research agenda required to fill in the many missing pieces of our understanding of this critical life stage. We begin with a brief description of the definition of developmental disabilities.

DEFINITION OF DEVELOPMENTAL DISABILITIES

The term *developmental disabilities* was codified in Public Law (PL) 95-682, the Developmental Disabilities Bill of Rights Act of 1978. It is defined as a condition attributable to a mental or physical impairment that begins before age 22, is likely to continue indefinitely, and results in substantial functional limitation in three or more areas of major life activity. The scope of major life activities include self-care, receptive and expressive language, learning, mobility, self-direction, capacity for independent living, and economic self-sufficiency. Among the most common conditions included within the label of developmental disabilities are autism, cerebral palsy, epilepsy, mental retardation, and other neurological impairments. The rates of documented disability during childhood and adolescence have increased substantially over the last decade (Fujiura & Yamaki, 2000); current estimates indicate that approximately 12% of youth receive special services because of a developmental disability (U.S. Department of Education, 2001).

THEORETICAL MODELS OF ADOLESCENT DEVELOPMENT: IMPLICATIONS FOR ADOLESCENTS WITH DISABILITIES

Developmental theories about adolescence for typically developing children have been fundamental to the construction of a knowledge base about this life phase, yet few theorists have applied their models explicitly to adolescents with developmental disabilities. Such application would provide empirical information that could assist in constructing appropriate services as well as expand our knowledge about the extent to which developmental theories apply broadly. In this section, we discuss three theoretical perspectives with regard to their potential application to adolescents with developmental disabilities: psychosocial models, developmental compensation models, and developmental systems models.

Perhaps the most cited work on adolescent development is Erikson's psychosocial model (Erikson, 1950, 1968). Although he delineates stages in the development of the ego from infancy through the elder years, identity and its epigenetic development forms the core of this theory applied to the adolescent period. Accordingly, Erikson features the adolescent period as a time of strife in which the individual ideally constructs an identity formed through the development of a set of personal ideals and belief systems while developing an orientation toward a future role deemed appropriate by society. The next period—the transition from adolescence to young adulthood—is also marked by strivings but focused on forming intimate relationships. This life phase is characterized by the engagement in mutual interchanges, which provide the individual with a deeper understanding of the emotions, psychological processes, and belief systems of a partner.

Although clearly generated from a psychoanalytic framework, Erikson based his view of the epigenetic model on principles of interaction between the individual and the society. He considered that individuals interact with a widening "social radius" (Erikson, 1950, p. 270)—that is, adolescents increasingly relate to a variety of social systems as they respond to society's expectations. Society, according to Erikson, ideally both safeguards and encourages transitions at appropriate times in the individual's life cycle.

Erikson's model is presumed to relate to all youth, although he does not address questions about the extent to which these central adolescent developmental transitions—the development of identity and the construction of intimate relationships—apply to adolescents with developmental disabilities. Nevertheless, there is reason to believe that such transitions and the strivings inherent in them occur for all adolescents, including those with disabilities. The strife may be even greater for those with disabilities, however, because of the adolescent's limited skills (such as in motor skills required to participate in athletic activities with friends) or because of society's restricted view of appropriate opportunities (in areas such as independent living, employment, postsecondary education). Adolescents with disabilities may also experience a delay in the timing of developmental transitions, so many may confront identity issues at a later chronological age than do their typically developing peers. Additionally, youth with severe levels of cognitive impairment or with particular types of disability, such as autism, may be constrained in ways that make the depth of identity formation and intimacy more compromised than that of typically developing individuals.

In contrast to Erikson's emphasis on the development of the ego, action psychologists focus on ways in which the individual is an agent of his or her own development. Individuals construct developmental pathways through their unique capacities to have intentions, act on them, and evaluate the intention-action cycle (Brandtstädter, 1998). The action perspective is exemplified by Baltes and colleagues (Baltes, 1997; Baltes, Lindenberger, & Staudinger, 1998; Freund, Li, & Baltes, 1999), who delineate three intersecting processes that foster development: selection, optimization, and compensation. These processes include how an individual selects a certain goal, persists in learning the skills or brings resources to bear on that goal (i.e., optimization), and compensates for limitations that prevent goal optimization. Although this model has been applied empirically primarily to development during the aging process, it has value in understanding the development of individuals during other life stages, especially adolescence (Lerner, 2002a). From this perspective, the adolescent is viewed as an agentic being, capable of setting goals and of developing strategies, including ones that compensate for organic or acquired limitations, to achieve those goals.

The importance of compensation for adolescents with developmental disabilities was addressed specifically by Vygotsky (Rieber & Carton, 1993) in his study of "defectology," the Russian term in the 1920s for the study of disabilities. Vygotsky maintained that children with developmental disabilities adopt compensation processes along a "roundabout path" (p. 126); that is, they adapt to developmental challenges by constructing different approaches or developing different goals. In this way, the individual with a disability "transforms the minus of the handicap into the plus of compensation" (p. 34). Youth vary in the range of compensatory strategies they have available to them, based only partially on the nature and severity of their disability. According to Vygotsky, the reserve of compensatory forces are less a property of the child's motivation or personality and more a product of the "social-collective life of the child" (p. 127). Thus, the opportunities provided to those with disabilities are related to the type of compensatory behaviors and strategies that can be employed. From this perspective, the availability of opportunities for the adolescent with developmental disabilities to enhance appropriate compensatory strategies is central to optimal development.

Developmental systems models expand a view of development beyond the psychosocial and motivational realms by considering the multiple and changing contexts in which adolescents develop, learn, act, and are nurtured. According to Bronfenbrenner and Morris (1998), adolescents are affected by their own psychological processes and the immediate settings in which they interact, such as the family and the school. Moreover, adolescent development is also affected by systems that influence these proximal settings, including government policies and cultural ideologies. Lerner's (2002b) depiction of developmental contextualism emphasizes the bidirectional relations among the adolescent and the multiple interacting systems, each influencing the other in complex patterns. Such models have important implications for adolescents with developmental disabilities because they posit that even though particular adolescents may be limited cognitively, motorically, or both by biological factors, their development influences and is influenced by sets of interacting and intersecting systems. Some of those systems affect them directly, such as their family and school, but others influence their immediate contexts through government policy (e.g., IDEA) and through societal views of appropriate behavior, goals, and opportunities for individuals with disabilities. Furthermore, the adolescent's own ability to be an agent of change emerges from these approaches (Brandtstädter, 1998); an adolescent's development may expand beyond that predicted by societal expectations. Such agency is potentially important to the development of youth with developmental disabilities as well, although possibly more difficult for some adolescents to access.

In summary, all three theoretical perspectives on the development of typical adolescents offer valuable ways of framing research on youth with disabilities. These perspectives are similar in their view that the adolescent's development is promoted through interaction with others and through activities in the social world. According to the psychosocial model, adolescents are striving to understand their own identity and to develop intimate relationships with others. Developmental compensatory approaches emphasize the way that adolescents with disabilities can promote the development of alternative pathways to goal attainment. The developmental systems perspective offers a broad model of adolescents engaged in and affected by multiple interacting systems, which determine the opportunities they are provided, the way others perceive them, and their own sense of agency. All three approaches have similarities in their assumptions about the importance of social interaction and family-community contexts to the promotion of optimal development but differ in terms of emphasis of one feature over another. All three also assume that the adolescent acts to varying extents as an agent of his or her own development.

In this chapter we maintain that similar principles exist for adolescents with developmental disabilities. We propose that the timing of developmental changes often are delayed chronologically for youth with disabilities and that some adolescents with serious cognitive limitations may only partially make the transition into the adolescent phase. Nevertheless, the majority of adolescents with developmental disabilities will be faced with challenges during this period similar to those of other adolescents.

THE TASKS OF THE ADOLESCENT PERIOD: APPLICATIONS TO ADOLESCENTS WITH DEVELOPMENTAL DISABILITIES

Adolescence is a time of transition, transformation, and realignment for adolescents, their parents, and their siblings. Among typically developing adolescents, becoming socially competent adults engenders several important tasks: autonomy, relatedness, and competence (Connell & Wellborn, 1991). These tasks clearly emerge from the developmental theory in that all require a sense of both identity and agency as well as require the developing adolescent to negotiate multiple interacting social systems. These tasks present unique but relatively unstudied challenges to adolescents with developmental disabilities (Glidden & Zetlin, 1992). These developmental accomplishments require individuation, which involves the disengagement from emotional dependence on adults and the development of a set of distinct views and belief systems (Steinberg & Silverberg, 1986) while maintaining connectedness to family and others (Grotevant & Cooper, 1986). Three small but growing knowledge bases related to the developmental endeavors of this phase exist on adolescents with disabilities: the formation of supportive peer relationships, the development of autonomy, and successful transitions in relationships with parents.

The Construction of Supportive Peer Networks

Constructing a supportive peer network is an important part of adaptive social adjustment. Indeed, poor social adjustment during adolescence is a predictor of adult psychopathology (East et al, 1992). Data indicate that most adolescents spend much more time with their peer network than with family members (Brown, 1990). From a psychosocial perspective, peer networks help the adolescent develop a sense of self and prepare for the development and maintenance of long-term intimate relationships.

In contrast to the complex and growing social networks of typically developing adolescents, studies of adolescents with developmental disabilities consistently point to high rates of social isolation (Richardson, Koller, & Katz, 1985). Anderson and Clarke (1982) conducted an extensive study in the United Kingdom of 119 adolescents with either cerebral palsy or spina bifida. They found that 31% reported seeing no friends outside of school hours (in contrast to 3% of their typically developing peers) and concluded that social isolation is the most common source of stress among this group of adolescents. Such isolation is not restricted to adolescents with severe cognitive or physical limitations because those with learning disabilities also experience high rates of peer rejection (Zetlin & Turner, 1985) and fewer, less stable, and more conflict-ridden friendships (Zetlin & Murtaugh, 1988). Swanson and Malone (1992) conducted a meta-analysis of 39 studies of the social skills of children with learning disabilities. They concluded that on average, children with learning disabilities were reported to be at the 18th percentile in peer acceptance and at the 78th percentile for peer rejection.

Social isolation may be attributed to several factors. The social skills of many adolescents with developmental disabilities may be either unusual or delayed; this is likely because social and cognitive functioning, although they are not isomorphic, are integrated processes. In a study of 64 adolescents with moderate mental retardation, Siperstein and Bak (1989) found that those with higher cognitive performance were more frequently nominated to be friends by their peers. Leffert and Siperstein (2002) maintain that many aspects of social-cognitive processing critical to positive peer relationships are challenging for individuals with intellectual disabilities. These aspects include the encoding and interpretation of cues (e.g., reading facial expressions), consideration of goals (e.g., relinquishing an immediate goal to attain a long-term goal), and the generation and evaluation of strategies (e.g., determining alternative ways to enter a social group and selecting one that fits the group's purpose).

Social perspective-taking is an important aspect of development that continues to be transformed during adolescence and appears to be reliant on sophisticated cognitive processes. Selman (1980; Selman, Beardslee, Schultz, Krupa, & Poderefsky, 1986) posits that during the adolescent period, self-reflection grows into mutual reflection and—eventually—to an understanding of a network of perspectives that support reciprocity, loyalty, and self-disclosure in friendships. Adolescents with certain disabilities, such as autism, have pronounced difficulty with social perspective-taking and thus tend to be limited in their ability to perceive the world through the eyes of others. This deficit has been attributed to an impairment in the theory of mind (i.e., in the ability to impute mental states to oneself and others, and thus to make inferences regarding the thought processes of others; Baron-Cohen, 1995). In contrast to adolescents with autism, those with other types of developmental disabilities, such as Down syndrome, may have limitations in other aspects of social interaction, such as communication, (Sigman & Ruskin, 1999), that affect their skills of social engagement. Thus, adolescents with different biologically based developmental disabilities may have distinct patterns of strengths and deficits related to social interaction, an observation that has been noted in studies of younger children (Hodapp, 1997).

In addition to unusual or delayed patterns of social cognitive processing, adolescents with disabilities may exhibit maladaptive behaviors that interfere with the construction of positive peer relationships. In a review of the social competence of students with mild disabilities, Gresham and MacMillan (1997) concluded that those who have difficulty regulating their own behavior also have the poorest social relationships (Merrell, Johnson, Merz, & Ring, 1992). Tonge (1999) noted that behavior problems are three to four times more likely to occur in children with developmental disabilities in comparison to other children. Furthermore, behavior problems in individuals with developmental disabilities appear to increase dramatically during the adolescent period (Jacobson, 1990). Thus, many adolescents with disabilities are hampered by either excessive withdrawal from others or excessive forms of acting-out behaviors that may diminish the desires of other adolescents to interact with them.

Furthermore, high rates of hospitalization and health care needs are characteristic of adolescents with severe intellectual disabilities and thus limit opportunities for social interaction with peers. Birenbaum and Cohen (1993) reported that children and young adults with severe mental retardation were hospitalized at eight times the national rate. Adolescents who are hospitalized or unable to attend school for long periods of time have the additional challenges of attempting reentry into peer groups that may have changed or realigned during their absence. The relation between health status and social competence of adolescents with disabilities has been seldom examined, however.

The Development of Autonomy

A second important task of adolescence, the development of autonomy, is receiving increasing attention among those studying adolescents with developmental disabilities. The development of autonomy may be a difficult task for such adolescents because of their compromised capacity to perform at a level consistent with their chronological age, coupled with restricted opportunities for exercising independence (Turnbull & Turnbull, 1985). Nevertheless, the development of a sense of personal agency, or self-determination, appears to be as critical to their psychological well-being and personal growth as it is for other adolescents (Wehmeyer, 1994).

Autonomy implies the ability to act according to one's preferences, interests, and abilities, and therefore it involves a knowledge of self (Wehmeyer, 1994). How do adolescents with developmental disabilities regard themselves? Given current interest in issues of autonomy and self-determination, it is surprising that so few studies have been conducted on identity development in adolescents or young adults with developmental disabilities. In one of the few investigations on this topic, Davies and Jenkins (1997) conducted interviews with 53 young adults with intellectual impairments and their caregivers. They found that only 8 participants understood the terms traditionally applied to their disability (e.g., mental handicap) and that most parents and other caregivers reported choosing not to discuss the meaning of such terms with the young adults. Nevertheless, many of these young adults incorporated a sense of diminished personal agency and of many societal limitations into their view of self, created through their daily experiences with adults, including caregivers, parents, and employers, who had power over them.

Halpern (1985) proposed that success for the young adult with developmental disabilities involves the following: (a) employment, (b) living independently or with a friend, (c) paying at least a portion of living expenses, and (d) involvement in leisure pursuits. These activities all involve autonomous behavior and presume the development of optimal levels of independence during the adolescent period. The importance of self-agency, which is required for autonomous behavior, is a growing theme in the literature on children with developmental disabilities. In a longitudinal study of children with Down syndrome, motor impairment, or developmental delay (Hauser-Cram et al., 2001), we found that those who had higher levels of mastery motivation during the preschool years had greater development in the acquisition of skills of daily living (e.g., dressing, bathing, and self-care) through middle childhood. Thus, children's early strivings for agency predict their adaptive skill development. Children and adolescents need to have varied opportunities for continued skill development, yet parents and other caregivers may limit such opportunities unknowingly. For example, Anderson and Clarke (1982) found that only 21% of adolescents with disabilities were given household chores compared to 69% of typically developing adolescents.

Wehmeyer and Schwartz (1998) reported that adolescents with developmental disabilities who had higher levels of self-determination had more positive adult outcomes, including higher rates of employment. Employment offers one opportunity for increased autonomy because through employment adolescents often develop a sense of responsibility, increased self-reliance, and expanded social networks. The majority of adolescents in the United States engage in employment opportunities (Mortimer, Shanahan, & Ryu, 1994), and in many communities some employment options exist for adolescents with developmental disabilities.

Indeed, more has been written about employment than about any other aspect of this phase of life for adolescents and young adults with developmental disabilities. Findings from the National Longitudinal Transition Study (Blackorby & Wagner, 1996) indicate that only slightly more than one third of youth with intellectual disabilities are employed within 5 years of exiting secondary school. Employment tends to be at poverty-level wages but varies by ethnicity and gender. African American or Hispanic youth with disabilities are less likely to be employed than are their European American peers, and females are less likely to be employed than males. Although employment options may be limited for those with intellectual disabilities, postsecondary educational opportunities for such youth are even more restricted. The opportunity to attend college and possibly live away from home in a somewhat protected environment does not exist for most adolescents with developmental disabilities.

Involvement in other types of postsecondary programs, however, tends to be increasing. In a survey of community adjustment of former special education students in Iowa, Frank and Sitlington (2000) note a trend toward increasing attendance at community colleges and job training or apprenticeship programs. The need for such postsecondary programs is likely to grow in the next decade as adolescents with developmental disabilities who have experienced education in what Public Law 99-457 mandates as the least restrictive setting emerge from high schools and push for a range of future opportunities.

Transition in Relationships with Parents

Although self-determination is one dimension of autonomy, separation of emotional dependence from parents is another. Steinberg and Silverberg (1986) have conceptualized emotional autonomy as including individuation, nondependency, deidealization of parents, and perceptions of parents as people. Because several of these constructs require sophisticated cognitive processes, adolescents with developmental disabilities may be less well equipped to develop optimal levels of emotional autonomy. Therefore, it is not surprising that Zetlin and Turner's (1985) retrospective study of adolescents with developmental disabilities indicated that although more than one half reported having struggles with parents over issues of independence, only a third achieved emotional autonomy.

Examining the relation between the development of emotional autonomy and the climate of parental support is essential in predicting positive adolescent development (Lamborn & Steinberg, 1993). Developing autonomy and self-reliance but also maintaining connected relationships to parents is important to the well-being of typically developing adolescents (Grotevant & Cooper, 1986; Youniss & Smollar, 1985) and also critical for those with disabilities (Field, Hoffman, & Posch, 1997). In a study of adults with mild mental retardation living independently, Winik, Zetlin, and Kaufman (1985) found that those with the greatest independence and self-esteem had parents who had promoted independence and autonomy.

Because adolescents with disabilities, in comparison to their peers, have fewer friendships and higher levels of behavior problems (Glidden & Zetlin, 1992), parents may become more rather than less protective during the adolescent period. Such protection may limit immediate opportunities for independence but may serve an intermediate function that in turn promotes autonomy. For example, Dixon and Reddacliff (2001) found that parental behaviors that protected a son or daughter from difficulties and exploitation led to more successful employment outcomes of young adults with mild intellectual disabilities. The nature of parental protection and how it is enacted warrants careful study.

Furthermore, many adolescents with developmental disabilities will continue to live with their parents for many years (Fujiura & Braddock, 1992; Seltzer & Krauss, 1994). In a study of individuals with mild handicaps who had attended special education programs in Maryland, Scuccimarra and Speece (1990) found that the majority resided with their parents, although more than 75% of those individuals said they would prefer to live independently. Parents and other family members serve as a potentially strong support network for individuals with developmental disabilities but may also substitute for friends. McGrew, Johnson, and Bruininks (1994) studied young adults with mild to severe disabilities and reported that an inverse relation occurs between the number of family and nonfamily members in their social networks. Therefore, the parent-child relationship, although it is always complex, becomes increasingly so for adolescents with developmental disabilities, especially for those who rely on parents for many aspects of their daily living and social activities.

FAMILIES OF ADOLESCENTS WITH DEVELOPMENTAL DISABILITIES

Until recently, most theorists of adolescent development focused on the conflict between parents and their adolescent children, especially in relation to the adolescent tasks of identity and autonomy (Schutze, 1989). As a consequence, the role of the family was conceptualized as one of departure (Douvan & Adelson, 1966), in order to give way to the dominating influence of peer groups, to accommodate to the adolescent's sexual maturity, and to permit autonomous behavior. More contemporary studies have focused on factors affecting parenting competence during the adolescent period, suggesting that parents can exert an active (rather than departing) influence on how their adolescent child develops.

For example, Bogenschneider, Small, and Tsay (1997), drawing from Belsky's (1984) research on parenting competence in the early childhood period, examined the role of parent characteristics, contextual sources of support, and adolescent characteristics on parenting competence during the adolescent period among typically developing youth. Whereas Belsky (1984; Belsky, Robins, & Gamble, 1984) found that *parent* characteristics were most influential in predicting parenting competence in the early childhood period, Bogenschneider et al. (1997) found that during adolescence, adolescent characteristics (e.g., adolescent openness to parental socialization, parent-child stress, and support from the social network) were the most important predictors of parenting competence. Clearly, recognition is emerging that the interactions among family members during the adolescent period constitute a fertile ground for understanding both adolescent and parental outcomes and that there are changing dynamics in the influence of parents on their children and children on their parents.

Although there is a paucity of research on the interactions and reciprocal influences of parents on their adolescents with developmental disabilities, there is a broader literature available on the life span impacts on families of having a child with a developmental disability. Research on the role of the family for individuals with developmental disabilities acknowledges that the family occupies a central and enduring role over the life course and that taking a life span perspective reveals both undeniable stresses on parental well-being and health, as well as positively regarded accommodations to family life and values (Heller, Hsieh, & Rowitz, 1997; Krauss & Seltzer, 1994).

It is widely acknowledged that the adolescent period for typically developing children is often accompanied by heightened turmoil for their families, who must cope with the effects of the biological, cognitive, social, and psychological maturation of their adolescent. Part of the transition from childhood to adulthood includes the push and pull of relinquishing parental roles of protectiveness, close supervision, and authority and adopting parenting styles that respect the adolescent's emerging needs for autonomy, independence, and more egalitarian relationships with the parents. When the adolescent has a developmental disability, however, the normative tasks of adolescence and the normative tasks of parents during this period may be experienced in ways that are both similar and distinct in comparison to families of typically developing adolescents. As Zetlin and Turner (1985) note, "although retarded individuals experience the same biological changes and drives as nonretarded youngsters, the issues associated with adolescence—emancipation, self concept, sexuality—are exacerbated by the presence of their handicap" (p. 571).

There has been a surge of research in the last several decades on the influence of children with developmental disabilities on their families and the influence of families on the development of children with developmental disabilities (e.g., Hauser-Cram et al., 2001; Keogh, Garnier, Bernheimer, & Gallimore, 2000; Mink, Nihira, & Meyers, 1983; Seltzer & Heller, 1997). This body of research has roots in transactional theories of human development (Lerner, 2002b; Sameroff & Fiese, 2000), models of the ecology of human development (Bronfenbrenner, 1979), family systems theory (Olson, Russell, & Sprenkle, 1983), and family life cycle theory (Carter & McGoldrick, 1980). Common to all these theoretical roots are three core propositions. First, individual development is shaped by both the biological attributes of the individual and the multiple and complex environmental contexts over the life course in which the individual exists. Second, changes in the individual and his or her environment affect other members of the individual's environment in reciprocal and iterative ways. Third, there are predictable stages in human and family development that shape the tasks, functions, and behaviors of individuals and other family members. Although this chapter focuses on a particular life stage for individuals with developmental disabilities and—by extension—of their families, much of what conditions the development of the adolescent and his or her family during this protracted period is linked to prior periods of individual development and family patterns and is affected by the anticipated outcomes for the adolescent during adulthood.

Family Life Cycle Theory

In order to provide a context for considering the family environment of adolescents with developmental disabilities, a brief discussion of family life cycle theory is provided. Family life cycle theory posits that just as individuals have stages of development, families as a collective unit pass through predictable stages over the life course. These stages are typically defined by the employment status of the head of the household, the entry into and exit of family members from the family, and the age of the oldest child in the family. Theorists of the family life cycle posit variable number of stages, from as few as seven (Duvall, 1957) to as many as 24 (Rodgers, 1960). The most commonly used set of stages include the following: couple, childbearing, school age, adolescence, launching, postpubertal, and aging (Olson et al., 1984). Within each stage, there are specific tasks and functions that families perform, including economic, physical, rest and recuperation, socialization, self-definition, affection, guidance, educational, and vocational (Turnbull, Summers, & Brotherson, 1986). For each stage, the priorities of these different functions vary and the roles that individual family members assume in the conduct of these functions reflects their individual developmental capabilities and needs. Particular functions may be heavily influenced by the age of the child.

For example, during the adolescent period, there is usually less emphasis by parents on the physical care of their child and greater emphasis on the child's vocational preparation. In contrast to the childbearing stage when physical affection and contact is a dominant feature of the parent-child relationship, during the adolescent stage, there is a greater emphasis on letting go and in reducing child dependency.

Challenges for Families During the Adolescent Period

Turnbull et al. (1986) articulated the major stressors arising from different family life course stages and the transitions across them for families of children with developmental disabilities. With respect to the adolescent period, they enumerated the following stressors:

- Adjusting emotionally to the chronicity of the handicapping condition
- Identifying issues surrounding emerging sexuality
- Dealing with peer isolation and rejection
- Making role adjustments based on skill development
- Future planning for vocational development

- Arranging for leisure-time activities
- Participating in individualized education planning (IEP) conferences
- Dealing with physical and emotional changes of puberty

Although some of these stressors are applicable to all families of adolescents (e.g., issues surrounding emerging sexuality, dealing with physical and emotional changes of puberty), some are relatively distinctive features of parenting a child with a developmental disability (e.g., future planning for vocational development, arranging for leisure-time activities, participation in IEP meetings). Indeed, as discussed later in this chapter, parental roles in the transition of adolescents with developmental disabilities from school to work is one of the major areas of research on parental involvement during this life stage.

Substantial evidence indicates that the adolescent period has particular and specific stressful content for parents of children with developmental disabilities. The stressful content seems to span various dimensions, including sobering appraisals of the child's developmental status, awareness of the potential for continued dependence (rather than independence) on the family, and trepidation over the end of federally guaranteed rights to services as children leave the special education system.

Baine, McDonald, Wilgosh, and Mellon (1993) conducted quantitative and qualitative research on families of adolescents with severe disabilities. Their research included the development of major categories of family stress and, within those categories, subthemes that identified the general and unique stressors reported by parents. The most stressful issues were a mixture of characteristics of the adolescent (i.e., dependency, lack of autonomy, individual vulnerability, physical size, severity of disability) and aspects of the service systems that support these individuals (i.e., transition from school to adult services, eligibility for government assistance, residential costs). The least stressful aspects were related to family interpersonal dynamics (i.e., between adolescents with disabilities and their siblings, parental philosophy).

Follow-up interviews with a subsample of the families participating in the quantitative portion of their research revealed a deeper and wider range of concerns than were evident in the numerical ratings of the areas of potential stress. The authors summarized parental concerns about individual characteristics of their adolescents with developmental disabilities as follows:

> The parents expressed particular concerns about long-term, family life-planning related to chronic dependency of the persons with disabilities; physical management problems related to the increasing size and strength of the individual; concerns related to cleanliness, grooming, aggression, and inappropriate age and gender related behavior (e.g., expression of affection), and the amount of care required ("we must plan everything around his needs"). Baine et al. (1993, p. 185)

With respect to stressors for the family, the qualitative information revealed concerns about the costs of long-term care, often requiring family sacrifices, parental tension regarding the role or level of involvement of fathers, and the strain on parents of having to organize or create a social, educational, and supportive world for their adolescent child.

Harris, Glasberg, and Delmolino (1998) note that for families of children with developmental disabilities, adolescence may signify the end of illusion. Parental aspirations and dreams about dramatic changes in their child's functional abilities may be tempered by a more clearly viewed awareness of the child's developmental horizon. Bristol and Schopler (1983), for example, note that parents of adolescents with autism have a greater sense of realism and pessimism about their child's development in comparison to parents of younger children with this disorder.

Wikler (1986) notes that there is a cyclical quality to family stress over different developmental stages. Her research indicates that stress is highest in families of a child with developmental disabilities who is just entering early adolescence or early adulthood, as compared to stress among families whose child with disabilities is in later adolescence or further into young adulthood. Her work supports the idea that transition periods are particularly problematic for families. One explanation for the increased stress for families of adolescents with disabilities was attributed to the degree of community acceptance offered to children with developmental disabilities at different life stages.

DeMyer and Goldberg (1983) and Bristol (1984) note that as children with developmental disabilities age, their behaviors are less well tolerated by society and they are less socially acceptable than younger children who, despite their disabilities, may be seen as cute or whose atypical behaviors are less deviant from the range of behaviors of typically developing children. The lack of community acceptance for adolescents with developmental disabilities may translate into greater social isolation of their families and may instill a greater rigidity of family routines, in comparison to families of typically developing adolescents, for whom social acceptance issues are less pressing and for whom more relaxed family routines often emerge as a consequence of the increasing independence of their adolescent.

Parent-Child and Sibling Relationships in the Adolescent Period

For many parents of children with developmental disabilities, there is a complex mixture of gratification and frustration encountered in the parenting experience, leading to what Larson (1998) calls the "embrace of paradox." Based on a study of Latina mothers of children with developmental disabilities, Larson explained this phenomenon as follows:

> Despite what would appear as multiple limitations in their daily lives due to the caretaking of a child with disability, these mothers shared hopeful maternal visions and profound personal growth that emerged because of this experience. What surfaced . . . was a life metaphor, the embrace of paradox, that was central to the mothers' maternal work. The embrace of paradox was the management of the internal tension of opposing forces between loving the child as he or she was and wanting to erase the disability, between dealing with the incurability while pursuing solutions, and between maintaining hopefulness for the child's future while being given negative information and battling their own fears. (p. 873)

Parental narratives of their lives with children with developmental disabilities echo Larson's description—particularly during the adolescent period, when the realignment of parental roles in the face of their child's efforts towards independence and autonomy constitutes a compelling family challenge (e.g., Kaufman, 1999; Park, 2001).

Zetlin and Turner (1985) conducted an ethnographic study of 25 young adults with mild mental retardation about their adolescence. The study included in-depth participant observation and interviews with the young adults and extensive interviewing of their parents. Their results provide insights into the interactions between parents and adolescents with mental retardation during a stage of life when, for some, the social consequences of their disabilities become painfully manifest. They concluded that

> it appears that both parents and sample members viewed the adolescent experience as more problematic than either the childhood period or the adult years and generally agreed on the nature of the adolescent conflicts. For the most part, these retarded adolescents were concerned with the same issues that preoccupy nonretarded adolescents—personal identity and autonomy. They interpreted parental attitudes and practices as nonsupportive and issues of competence and self-definition as sources of frustration and self-conflict . . . The implications of their handicapped status as well as their limitations were salient concerns for the first time, and many of their experiences—parental restrictiveness, peer rejection, expectancy-performance discrepancies—contributed to their uneasiness and discontent. (p. 578)

Although sibling relationships during adolescence between brothers and sisters without disabilities and their siblings with disabilities have been studied less extensively, there is evidence that this can be a period in which new social and emotional strains develop (McHugh, 1999). Krauss and Seltzer (2001) report that siblings of brothers and sisters with disabilities often experience issues that are unique to their family situation and that may set them apart from their friends who do not have a sibling with a disability. For example, nondisabled siblings worry about what their future role will be regarding the care and support of their brother or sister with a disability. Furthermore, embarrassment about odd behaviors of a sibling with a developmental disability may result in avoidance of public social activities and greater social isolation for nondisabled adolescent siblings.

Many have hypothesized that siblings of children with disabilities are exposed to extra demands for caregiving (serving as aides to their parents), to expectations for greater emotional sensitivity, and to higher levels of social involvement with their brother or sister with a disability (Grissom & Borkowski, 2002; Lobato, 1983; McHale & Gamble, 1987). Nixon and Cummings (1999) studied whether young adolescent brothers and sisters who have a sibling with a disability evidence greater emotional distress and behavioral reactivity to family conflicts. They found that siblings of children with developmental disabilities were more sensitive to family stress, utilized more active coping strategies, and had lower thresholds of conflict intensity for responding in comparison to siblings of children without disabilities. They concluded that "children growing up with a disabled sibling may be exposed to learning histories that sensitize them to conflict in multiple social contexts . . . These children have learned to become alert to potential problems in family dynamics and are inclined to do something about it" (p. 282).

The durability of the sibling relationship has also been noted in empirical studies (Krauss, Seltzer, Gordon, & Friedman, 1996). In a survey of adult siblings of persons with mental retardation, about a quarter indicated that they planned to coreside with their brother or sister when their parents could no longer take care of the family member. In addition, despite having experienced increased interpersonal turmoil during the adolescent period (based on retrospective assessments), the vast majority described their experiences as "mostly positive" and noted the valuable lessons of compassion, tolerance, respect for differences, and patience that they had learned. Indeed, the majority of studies on sibling relationships when one sibling has a disability have found them to be more positive and nurturing than relationships between typically developing siblings (Stoneman, 2001).

Parental Tasks in the Adolescent Period

As noted earlier, one of the markers of the end of the adolescent period is the assumption of adult roles, including employment, self-sufficiency, and formation of independent family units. For many individuals with developmental disabilities, these roles are particularly problematic. Because of the ongoing and heightened responsibilities of parents in planning for the future of their adolescents with disabilities, parental involvement in shaping the future may be far more extensive than is the case among families of typically developing adolescents. A recent study examined the most common dilemmas reported by parents of adolescents with developmental disabilities (Thorin, Yovanoff, & Irvin, 1996). The six most common dilemmas were the following:

- Wanting to create opportunities for independence for the young adult and wanting to assure that health and safety needs are met
- Wanting a life separate from the young adult and wanting to do whatever is necessary to assure a good life for him or her
- Wanting to provide stability and predictability in the family life and wanting to meet the changing needs of the young adult and family
- Wanting to create a separate social life for the young adult and wanting to have less involvement in his or her life
- Wanting to avoid burnout and wanting to do everything possible for the young adult
- Wanting to maximize the young adult's growth and potential and wanting to accept the young adult as he or she is

This enumeration of parental dilemmas underscores the fact that for many families of adolescents with developmental disabilities, the parental role intensifies rather than diminishes during the period of transition to adulthood. Parental involvement occurs in regard to fundamental issues of protecting their child's health and safety, to constructing or arranging environments in which their child's social and economic life can be supported, and to providing a context in which their child's capabilities are maximized. These tasks constitute an atypical agenda in comparison to the tasks of parents of typically developing adolescents.

One of the unique tasks facing families of adolescents with developmental disabilities is planning for their adolescent's transition from special education services to adulthood. Considerable evidence indicates that the prospect of losing the mandated educational and related services guaranteed by IDEA when a child with a disability reaches the age of 22 is one of the most stressful aspects of the adolescent period for parents (Thorin & Irvin, 1992). Recent estimates suggest that more than 5 million children ages 6–21 receive special education services under IDEA (U.S. Department of Education, 2001). Of these children, approximately 200,000 exit the school system each year and enter the adult world (Wehman, 1996).

A component of IDEA requires that no later than age 16, an individualized transition plan be crafted as part of a student's IEP that identifies needed transition services. The scope of the plan may include instruction, community experiences, development of employment and other postschool adult living objectives, and acquisition of daily living skills and functional vocational evaluation, where appropriate. The planning process is undertaken by a team of individuals, including the student, his or her parents, and personnel from community and adult service agencies who will be involved when the adolescent becomes an adult (Frank & Sitlington, 2000).

Studies of the transition process from school to work have found that parents of children with disabilities are significantly less involved in transition planning than they desire to be (McNair & Rusch, 1991), although it appears that parental involvement increases as the severity of the child's disability increases (Kraemer & Blacher, 2001). Because a hallmark of being an adult is being employed (leading to economic self-sufficiency), and because of the many social benefits attributed to being employed, there is a great deal of attention in the practice and research literature on efforts by parents and service systems to enhance the future employability of adolescents with developmental disabilities. Parental expectations for the future vocational activities of their adolescents with disabilities are an important factor in such transition plans. In a recent study, almost two thirds of parents of children with severe mental retardation expected their child to work, most commonly in a day activity center or sheltered workshop (Kraemer & Blacher, 2001). Parent roles in achieving desired vocational outcomes were examined in a qualitative study that identified the following important family characteristics: moral support, practical assistance, role models of appropriate work ethic, protection from difficulties and exploitation, and family cohesion (Dixon & Reddacliff, 2001). Clearly, parents occupy a critical position in the lives of youth with developmental disabilities, and parents' engagement in planning activities for the adult life of their adolescent constitutes a major family task of the adolescent period.

CONCLUSIONS: SETTING A RESEARCH AGENDA FOR THE NEXT DECADE

Despite the increased visibility of individuals with disabilities in our society, knowledge about their development—especially during the adolescent phase—is meager. This limited knowledge base exists in contrast to the growing sophisticated and complex knowledge about adolescent development more generally. Although research on parental adaptation to raising a child with disabilities has been informed by theoretical models of family systems and the family life cycle, studies on the development of adolescents with disabilities have been for the most part descriptive in nature. Furthermore, most studies have failed to consider the multiple bidirectional relations among adolescents with disabilities and their parents, siblings, and other family members. Finally, studies have not focused on the multiple contexts in which adolescents develop and learn. Descriptive studies are important for foundational knowledge, but theories of adolescent development and family change can lend valuable perspectives that will help the knowledge base grow in ways that reflect the complexity of the human experience.

The tasks of the adolescent period are particularly challenging for many adolescents with developmental disabilities and their families, and empirical knowledge guided by theoretical perspectives can be applied to those challenges. Psychosocial models of development emphasize the importance of identity development during the adolescent period, yet few researchers have undertaken work on identity development in youth with disabilities. Researchers operating from the narrative tradition (e.g., Davies & Jenkins, 1997; Kaufman, 1999) report that youth with intellectual impairments, like all youth, develop a sense of self through activities they find meaningful and through positive social relationships with others. Research could offer an even richer analysis of the various paths to identity development among youth with disabilities.

In contrast to the paucity of studies on identity development, investigations on social relationships of youth with disabilities are increasing. Models of social cognition have stimulated a deeper understanding of the limitations unique to specific disabilities, such as autism, which may thwart the construction of a supportive peer network. Therefore, further research on the development of social cognition in adolescents with varying disabilities is particularly important and may lead to the construction of interventions that assist with the development and maintenance of friendships. Although some interventions are promising in this area, especially for school-age children (e.g., Campbell & Siperstein, 1994), few have been developed for adolescents. A greater understanding is needed of the mechanisms by which social cognitive functioning advances during the adolescent period as well as how such functioning differs by type of disability, level of cognitive impairment, and types of supports provided by families, schools, and communities. Investigations guided by the selection, optimization, and compensation model of Baltes and colleagues (Baltes et al., 1998) could add a valuable perspective to our understanding of the development of social relationships in youth with disabilities by focusing attention on how such adolescents can optimize social functioning.

Compensation models do not necessarily imply that the individual alone is responsible for creating novel approaches. Vygotskian perspectives suggest that we also should focus on how the social community can support alternative developmental routes for youth with disabilities. In terms of educational goals, this view is currently being advanced by those who advocate the use of universal design for learning (Rose & Meyer, 2002). They maintain that barriers to learning are not inherently within the student but rather reside in our methods of providing instruction. For example, students who have difficulty with comprehension can have purposefully designed prompts built into complex text material provided digitally on a computer, just as youth who are visually impaired can have text augmented or read to them through the computer. From a developmental systems perspective, it is also important that research on children with developmental disabilities and their families pay much greater attention to the increasing ethnic and cultural diversity of American society (Hauser-Cram & Howell, 2003). There is a stunning lack of attention in the literature on adolescence and developmental disabilities to the impact of cultural beliefs and norms. Particularly given the prominence of contextual influences in most contemporary theoretical approaches to the study of development, it is surprising that culture is not used as an organizing principle of development (Valsiner, 1989). As Garcia Coll and Magnuson (2000) note, most interventions and programs for children with developmental disabilities are permeated with the values and goals of mainstream European American culture and are insensitive to the differing world views, parenting practices, social views, and belief systems of other cultures. Given the prominence of the family as an enduring context in which adolescents with developmental disabilities live, more focused research on the experiences of families and adolescents from various ethnic and cultural groups is a critical challenge for the future.

Another essential area of research involves the examination of adolescent-parent relationships. Adolescents with developmental disabilities in general are more reliant on their parents for a range of support features, including sometimes that of the sole source of friendship. At this time the adolescent may be striving toward greater self-determination and autonomy and his or her parents may be recognizing that their life cycle as parents differs from that of their family and friends. The task of developing independence within a connected relationship may take on different forms for adolescents with developmental disabilities, depending on their type of disability and level of adaptive functioning. Furthermore, research on the bidirectional effects of the parent-child relationship and their changes during the transition from childhood to adulthood among youth with disabilities are unstudied. Such research would yield important information about the extent to which models based on typically developing adolescents apply more broadly.

It is also imperative that research designs include adolescents with developmental disabilities as key informants about their lives. A variety of methodologies have been successful in including persons with developmental disabilities, including participant observation, in-depth and over-time interviewing, and ethnographic techniques. These individuals have much to teach us about how they view their own development socially and emotionally and about how their relationships with their parents, siblings, and peers change (for better or for worse) during this critical life stage.

In sum, the adolescent period for individuals with developmental disabilities is an understudied area but one that may be critical for our understanding of the continuities and discontinuities of their development over time. As is true for all adolescents, this period is fraught with enormous challenges as youngsters move towards greater individuation, increasing independence from their parents, more autonomy, and deeper capacities to form complex interpersonal relationships. For adolescents with developmental disabilities, these tasks are also prominent, but may be more difficult to master in light of their biological and cognitive impairments. The role of the family is thus increasingly important and—in contrast to families of typically developing adolescents—may become more intensified and consequential in shaping the future of their adolescent with a disability. As inquiries about the full range of human development—including that of persons with developmental disabilities—proceed, the opportunity to deepen our knowledge by including consideration of both typical and atypical development during adolescence should be seized.

REFERENCES

Anderson, E. M., & Clarke, L. (1982). *Disability in adolescence.* London: Methuen.

Baine, D., McDonald, L., Wilgosh, L., & Mellon, S. (1993). Stress experienced by families of older adolescents or young adults with severe disability. *Australia and New Zealand Journal of Developmental Disabilities, 18,* 177–188.

Baltes, P. B. (1997). On the incomplete architecture of human ontology: Selection, optimization, and compensation as foundation of developmental theory. *American Psychologist, 52,* 366–380.

Baltes, P. B., Lindenberger, U., & Staudinger, U. M. (1998). Life-span theory in developmental psychology. In W. Damon (Series Ed.) & R. M. Lerner (Vol. Ed.), *Handbook of child psychology: Vol 1. Theoretical models of human development* (5th ed., pp. 1029–1144). New York: Wiley.

Baron-Cohen, S. (1995). *Mindblindness: An essay on autism and theory of mind.* Cambridge, MA: Bradford Books, MIT Press.

Belsky, J. (1984). The determinants of parenting: A process model. *Child Development, 55,* 83–96.

Belsky, J., Robins, E., & Gamble, W. (1984). The determinants of parental competence: Toward a contextual theory. In M. Lewis (Ed.), *Beyond the dyad* (pp. 251–279). New York: Plenum Press.

Birenbaum, A., & Cohen, H. J. (1993). On the importance of helping families: Policy implications from a national study. *Mental Retardation, 31,* 67–74.

Blackorby, J., & Wagner, M. (1996). Longitudinal postschool outcomes of youth with disabilities: Findings from the National Longitudinal Transition Study. *Exceptional Children, 62,* 399–413.

Bogenschneider, K., Small, S. A., & Tsay, J. C. (1997). Child, parent, and contextual influences on perceived parenting competence among parents of adolescents. *Journal of Marriage and the Family, 59,* 345–362.

Brandtstädter, J. (1998). Action perspectives on human development. In W. Damon (Series Ed.) & R. M. Lerner (Vol. Ed.), *Handbook of child psychology: Vol. 1. Theoretical models of human development* (5th ed., pp. 807–863). New York: Wiley.

Bristol, M. M. (1984). Family resources and successful adaptation to autistic children. In E. Schopler & G. B. Mesibov (Eds.), *Issues in autism: Vol. III. The effects of autism on the family* (pp. 289–310). New York: Plenum.

Bristol, M. M., & Schopler, E. (1983). Stress and coping in families of autistic adolescents. In E. Schopler & G. B. Mesibov (Eds.), *Autism in adolescents and adults* (pp. 251–278). New York: Plenum.

Bronfenbrenner, U. (1979). *The ecology of human development.* Cambridge, MA: Harvard University Press.

Bronfenbrenner, U., & Morris, P. A. (1998). The ecology of developmental process. In W. Damon (Series Ed.) & R. M. Lerner (Vol. Ed.), *Handbook of child psychology: Vol. 1. Theoretical models of human development* (5th ed., pp. 993–1028). New York: Wiley.

Brown, B. B. (1990). Peer groups and peer cultures. In S. Feldman & G. R. Elliott (Eds.), *At the threshold: The developing adolescent* (pp. 171–196). Cambridge, MA: Harvard University Press.

Campbell, P., & Siperstein, G. N. (1994). *Improving social competence: A resource guide for elementary school teachers.* Needham Heights, MA: Allyn and Bacon, Simon and Schuster Education Group.

Carter, E., & McGoldrick, M. (Eds.). (1980). *The family life cycle: A framework for family therapy.* New York: Gardner Press.

Connell, J. P., & Wellborn, J. G. (1991). Competence, autonomy, and relatedness: A motivational analysis of self-system processes. In M. R. Gunnar & L. A. Sroufe (Eds.), *Minnesota symposium on child psychology: Vol. 23. Self processes in development* (pp. 43–77). Hillsdale, NJ: Erlbaum.

Davies, C. A., & Jenkins, R. (1997). "She has different fits to me": How people with learning difficulties see themselves. *Disability and Society, 12,* 95–105.

DeMyer, M. K, & Goldberg, P. (1983). Family needs of the autistic adolescent. In E. Schopler & G. B. Mesibov (Eds.), *Autism in adolescents and adults* (pp. 225–250). New York: Plenum.

Dixon, R. M., & Reddacliff, C. A. (2001). Family contribution to the vocational lives of vocationally competent young adults with intellectual disabilities. *International Journal of Disability, Development and Education, 48,* 193–206.

Douvan, E., & Adelson, J. (1966). *The adolescent experience.* New York: Wiley.

Duvall, E. (1957). *Family development.* Philadelphia: J. B. Lippencott.

East, P. L., Lerner, R. M., Lerner, J. V., Talwar-Soni, R., Ohannessian, C. M., & Jacobson, L. P. (1992). Early adolescent-peer group fit, peer relations, and psychosocial competence: A short term longitudinal study. *Journal of Early Adolescence, 12,* 132–152.

Erikson, E. H. (1950). *Childhood and society.* New York: Norton.

Erikson, E. H. (1968). *Identity, youth and crisis.* New York: Norton.

Field, S., Hoffman, A., & Posch, M. (1997). Self-determination during adolescence: A developmental perspective. *Remedial and Special Education, 18,* 285–293.

Frank, A. R., & Sitlington, P. L. (2000). Young adults with mental disabilities: Does transition planning make a difference? *Education and Training in Mental Retardation and Developmental Disabilities, 35,* 119–134.

Freund, A. M., Li, K. Z. H., & Baltes, P. B. (1999). Successful development and aging: The role of selection, optimization, and compensation. In J. Brandstadter & R. M. Lerner (Eds.), *Action and self-development: Theory and research throughout the life-span* (pp. 401–434). Thousand Oaks, CA: Sage.

Fujiura, G. T., & Braddock, D. (1992). Fiscal and demographic trends in mental retardation services: The emergence of the family. In L. Rowitz (Ed.), *Mental retardation in the year 2000* (pp. 316–338). New York: Springer-Verlag.

Fujiura, G. T., & Yamaki, K. (2000). Trends in demography of childhood poverty and disability. *Exceptional Children, 66,* 187–199.

Garcia Coll, C. T., & Magnuson, K. (2000). Cultural differences as sources of developmental vulnerabilities and resources. In J. P. Shonkoff & S. J. Meisels (Eds.), *Handbook of early childhood intervention* (2nd ed., pp. 94–144). New York: Cambridge University Press.

Glidden, L. M., & Zetlin, A. G. (1992). Adolescence and community adjustment. In L. Rowitz (Ed.), *Mental retardation in the year 2000* (pp. 101–114). New York: Springer-Verlag.

Graber, J. A., & Brooks-Gunn, J. (1996). Transitions and turning points: Navigating the passage from childhood through adolescence. *Developmental Psychology, 32,* 768–776.

Gresham, F. M., & MacMillan, D. L. (1997). Social competence and affective characteristics of students with mild disabilities. *Review of Educational Research, 67,* 377–415.

Grissom, M. O., & Borkowski, J. G. (2002). Self-efficacy in adolescents who have siblings with or without disabilities. *American Journal on Mental Retardation, 107,* 79–90.

Grotevant, H. D., & Cooper, C. R. (1986). Individuation in family relationships. *Human Development, 29,* 82–100.

Halpern, A. (1985). Transition: A look at the foundation. *Exceptional Children, 51,* 479–486.

Harris, S. L., Glasberg, B., & Delmolino, L. (1998). Families and the developmentally disabled adolescent. In U. B. VanHassert & M. Hereson (Eds.), *Handbook of psychological treatment problems for children and adolescents* (pp. 519–548). Mahwah, NJ: Erlbaum.

Hauser-Cram, P., & Howell, A. (2003). The development of young children with disabilities and their families: Implications for policies and programs. In R. M. Lerner, F. Jacobs, & D. Wertlieb (Eds.), *Handbook of applied developmental science* (Vol. 1, pp. 259–279). Thousand Oaks, CA: Sage.

Hauser-Cram, P., Warfield, M. E., Shonkoff, J. S., Krauss, M. W., Sayer, A., & Upshur, C. C. (2001). Children with disabilities: A longitudinal study of child development and parent well-being. *Monographs of the Society for Research in Child Development*, *66*(3, Serial No. 266).

Heller,T., Hsieh, K., & Rowitz, L. (1997). Maternal and paternal caregiving of persons with mental retardation across the lifespan. *Family Relations, 46,* 407–415.

Hodapp, R. (1997). Direct and indirect behavioral effects of different genetic disorders of mental retardation. *American Journal on Mental Retardation, 102,* 67–79.

Jacobson, J. W. (1990). Do some mental disorders occur less frequently among
persons with mental retardation? *American Journal on Mental Retardation, 94,* 596–602.

Kaufman, S. Z. (1999). *Retarded isn't stupid, mom.* Baltimore, MD: Paul H. Brookes.

Keogh, B. K., Garnier, H. E., Bernheimer, L. P., & Gallimore, R. (2000). Models of child-family interaction for children with developmental delays: Child-driven or transactional? *American Journal on Mental Retardation, 105,* 32–46.

Kraemer, B. R., & Blacher, J. (2001). Transition for young adults with severe mental retardation: School preparation, parent expectations, and family involvement. *Mental Retardation, 39,* 423–435.

Krauss, M. W., & Seltzer, M. M. (1994). Taking stock: Expected gains from a life-span developmental perspective on mental retardation. In M. M. Seltzer, M. W. Krauss, & M. Janicki (Eds.), *Life course perspectives on adulthood and old age* (pp. 213–220). Washington, DC: American Association on Mental Retardation.

Krauss, M. W., & Seltzer, M. M. (2001). Having a sibling with mental retardation. In J. V. Lerner, R. M. Lerner, & J. Finkelstein (Eds.), *Adolescence in America: An encyclopedia* (pp. 436–440). Santa Barbara, CA: ABC–CLIO, Inc.

Krauss, M. W., Seltzer, M. M., Gordon, R., & Friedman, D. (1996). Binding ties: The roles of adult siblings of persons with mental retardation. *Mental Retardation, 34,* 83–03.

Lamborn, S. D., & Steinberg, L. (1993). Emotional autonomy redux: Revisiting Ryan and Lynch. *Child Development, 64,* 483–499.

Larson, E. (1998). Reframing the meaning of disability to families: The embrace of paradox. *Social Science and Medicine, 47,* 865–875.

Leffert, J. S., & Siperstein, G. N. (2002). Social cognition: A key to understanding adaptive behavior in individuals with mild mental retardation. *International Review of Research in Mental Retardation, 25,* 135–181.

Lerner, R. M. (2002a). *Adolescence: Development, diversity, context, and application.* Upper Saddle River, NJ: Prentice Hall.

Lerner, R. M. (2002b). *Concepts and theories of human development* (3rd ed.). Mahwah, NJ: Erlbaum.

Lobato, D. (1983). Siblings of handicapped children: A review. *Journal of Autism and Developmental Disorders, 13,* 347–363.

McGrew, K. S., Johnson, D. R., & Bruininks, R. H. (1994). Factor analysis of community adjustment outcome measures for young adults with mild to severe disabilities. *Journal of Psychoeducational Assessment, 12,* 55–66.

McHale, S., & Gamble, W. (1987). Sibling relationships and adjustment of children with disabled brothers and sisters. *Journal of Children in Contemporary Society, 19,* 131–158.

McHugh, M. (1999). *Special siblings: Growing up with someone with a disability.* New York: Hyperion.

McNair, J., & Rusch, F. R. (1991). Parent involvement in transition programs. *Mental Retardation, 29,* 93–101.

Merrell, K., Johnson, E., Merz, J., & Ring, E. (1992). Social competence of students with mild handicaps and low achievement: A comparative study. *School Psychology Review, 21,* 125–137.

Mink, I., Nihira, C., & Meyers, C. (1983). Taxonomy of family life styles: I. Homes with TMR children. *American Journal of Mental Deficiency, 87,*484–497.

Modell, J., & Goodman, M. (1990). Historical perspectives. In S. Feldman & G. Elliott (Eds.), *At the threshold: The developing adolescent* (pp. 93–122). Cambridge, MA: Harvard University Press.

Mortimer, J. T., Shanahan, M., & Ryu, S. (1994). The effects of adolescent employment on school-related orientation and behavior. In R. K. Silbereisen & E. Todt (Eds.), *Adolescence in context: The interplay of family, school, peers, and work in adjustment* (pp. 304–326). New York: Springer-Verlag.

Nixon, C. L., & Cummings, E. M. (1999). Sibling disability and children's reactivity to conflicts involving family members. *Journal of Family Psychology, 13,* 274–285.

Olson, D. H., McCubbin, H. I., Barnes, H., Larsen, A., Muxen, M., & Wilson, M. (1984). *One thousand families: A national survey.* Beverly Hills, CA: Sage.

Olson, D. H., Russell, C. S., & Sprenkle, D. H. (1983). Circumplex model VI: Theoretical update. *Family Process, 22,* 69–83.

Park, C. C. (2001). *Exiting Nirvana.* Boston: Little, Brown & Co.
Richardson, S. A., Koller, H., & Katz, M. (1985). Relationship of upbringing to later behavior disturbance of mildly mentally retarded young people. *American Journal of Mental Deficiency, 90,* 1–8.
Rieber, R. W., & Carton, A. S. (Eds.) (1993). *The collected works of L. S. Vygotsky: Vol. 2. The fundamentals of defectology (Abnormal psychology and learning disabilities).* New York: Plenum Press.
Rodgers, R. (1960, August). *Proposed modifications of Duvall's family life cycle stages.* Paper presented at the American Sociological Association Meeting, New York, NY.
Rose, D. H., & Meyer, A. (2002). *Teaching every student in the digital age: Universal design for learning.* Alexandria, VA: Association for Supervision and Curriculum Development.
Sameroff, A. J., & Fiese, B. H. (2000). Transactional regulation: The developmental ecology of early intervention. In J. P. Shonkoff & S. J. Meisels (Eds.), *Handbook of early childhood intervention* (2nd ed., pp. 135–159). New York: Cambridge University Press.
Schutze, Y. (1989). Adolescents and their families. In K. Kreppner & R. M. Lerner (Eds.), *Family systems and life-span development* (pp. 367–380). Hillsdale, NJ: Erlbaum.
Scuccimarra, D. J., & Speece, D. L. (1990). Employment outcomes and social integration of students with mild handicaps: The quality of life two years after high school. *Journal of Learning Disabilities, 23,* 213–219.
Selman, R. L. (1980). *The growth of interpersonal understanding.* New York: Academic Press.
Selman, R. L., Beardslee, W., Schultz, L. H., Krupa, M., & Poderefsky, D. (1986). Assessing adolescent interpersonal negotiation strategies: Toward the integration of structural and functional models. *Developmental Psychology, 22,* 450–459.
Seltzer, M. M., & Heller, T. (1997). Families and caregiving across the life course: Research advances on the influence of context. *Family Relations, 46,* 321–323.
Seltzer, M. M., & Krauss, M. W. (1994). Aging parents and coresident adult children: The impact of lifelong caregiving. In M. M. Seltzer, M. W. Krauss, & M. P. Janicki (Eds.), *Life course perspectives on adulthood and old age* (pp. 3–18). Washington, DC: American Association on Mental Retardation.
Sigman, M., & Ruskin, E. (1999). Continuity and change in the social competence of children with autism, Down syndrome, and developmental delays. *Monographs of the Society for Research in Child Development, 64*(1, Serial No. 256).
Siperstein, G. N., & Bak, J. J. (1989). Social relationships of adolescents with moderate mental retardation. *Mental Retardation, 27,* 5–10.
Steinberg, L., & Silverberg, S. B. (1986). The vicissitudes of autonomy in early adolescence. *Child Development, 57,* 841–851.
Stoneman, Z. (2001). Supporting positive sibling relationships during childhood. *Mental Retardation and Developmental Disabilities Research Reviews, 7,* 134–142.
Swanson, H. L., & Malone, S. (1992). Social skills and learning disabilities: A meta-analysis of the literature. *School Psychology Review, 22,* 427–443.
Thorin, E. J., & Irvin, L. K. (1992). Family stress associated with transition to adulthood of young people with severe disabilities. *Journal of the Association for Persons with Severe Handicaps, 17,* 31–39.
Thorin, E., Yovanoff, P., & Irvin, L. (1996). Dilemmas faced by families during their young adults' transitions to adulthood: A brief report. *Mental Retardation, 34,* 117–120.
Tonge, B. (1999). Psychopathology of children with developmental disabilities. In N. Bouras (Ed.), *Psychiatric and behavioral disorders in developmental disabilities and mental retardation* (pp. 157–174). New York: Cambridge University Press.
Turnbull, A. P., Summers, J. A., & Brotherson, M. J. (1986). Family life cycle: Theoretical and empirical implications and future directions for families with mentally retarded members. In J. J. Gallagher & P. Vietze (Eds.), *Families of handicapped persons: Research, programs, and policy issues* (pp. 45–66). Baltimore: Brookes.
Turnbull, A. P., & Turnbull, H. R. (1985). Developing independence. *Journal of Adolescent Health Care, 6,* 108–119.

U.S. Department of Education. (2001). *Twenty-third annual report to Congress on the implementation of the Individuals with Disabilities Education Act.* Washington, DC: U.S. Department of Education.

Valsiner, J. (1989). From group comparisons to group knowledge: Lessons from cross-cultural psychology. In J. P. Forgas & J. M. Innes (Eds.), *Recent advances in social psychology: An international perspective* (pp. 501–510). Amsterdam: North-Holland.

Wehman, P. (1996). *Life beyond the classroom: Transition strategies for young people with disabilities* (2nd ed.). Baltimore: Brookes.

Wehmeyer, M. L. (1994). Perceptions of self-determination and psychological empowerment of adolescents with mental retardation. *Education and Training in Mental Retardation and Developmental Disabilities, 29,* 9–21.

Wehmeyer, M. L., & Schwartz, M. (1998). The relationship between self-determination and quality of life for adults with mental retardation. *Education and Training in Mental Retardation and Developmental Disabilities, 33,* 3–12.

Wikler, L. M. (1986). Family stress theory and research on families of children with mental retardation. In J. J. Gallagher & P. Vietze (Eds.), *Families of handicapped persons: Research, programs, and policy issues* (pp. 167–196). Baltimore: Brookes.

Winik, L., Zetlin, A. G., & Kaufman, S. Z. (1985). Adult mildly retarded persons and their parents: The relationship between involvement and adjustment. *Applied Research in Mental Retardation, 6,* 409–419.

Youniss, J., & Smollar, J. (1985). *Adolescent relations with mothers, fathers, and friends.* Chicago: University of Chicago Press.

Zahn-Waxler, C. (1996). Environment, biology, and culture: Implications for adolescent development. *Developmental Psychology, 32,* 571–573.

Zetlin, A. G., & Murtaugh, M. (1988). Friendship patterns of mildly learning handicapped high school students. *American Journal on Mental Retardation, 92,* 447–457.

Zetlin, A. G., & Turner, J. L. (1985). Transition from adolescence to adulthood: Perspectives of mentally retarded individuals and their families. *American Journal of Mental Deficiency, 89,* 570–579.

Chapter 23

VOLUNTEERISM, LEADERSHIP, POLITICAL SOCIALIZATION, AND CIVIC ENGAGEMENT

Constance A. Flanagan

The topics that comprise this chapter fall under the umbrella of political socialization and refer to those practices whereby younger generations are incorporated as full members of the polity or public sphere of society (Flanagan & Gallay, 1995). Although individuals are guaranteed rights by virtue of their status as citizens, it is through the exercise of those rights that they assume membership and have a voice in defining the polity and through their civic engagement that citizens sustain their rights (Walzer, 1989).

There has been an increasing interest of late in scholarship on young people's civic engagement, motivated in large measure out of concerns that it is on the decline. But this is not the first time that attention has been paid to the developmental roots of political theories, attitudes, and knowledge. In this chapter I first summarize three earlier approaches to this topic (political socialization, cognitive developmental, and generational theories). Following that section I synthesize the contemporary work, drawing from studies of youth participating in community-based organizations and service learning programs. In the concluding section I discuss elements of a new developmental theory.

POLITICAL SOCIALIZATION THEORY

Interest in the psychological mechanisms underlying political stability motivated early political socialization studies in the aftermath of World War II. Political scientists and developmental psychologists in this tradition focused on the early years as formative of political loyalties and held that maturation in later adolescence "crystallizes and internalizes patterns established during the preadolescent period" (Dawson & Prewitt, 1969, p. 51). According to this theory, loyalty to civic leaders and the polity they represented flowed from the young child's sense of basic trust in the benevolence of those leaders—that is, his or her belief that they ruled with the child's best interests in mind (Easton & Dennis, 1969). Knowledge about the specifics would come later but was based on this affective foundation.

Although political socialization theory fell out of favor due to rather modest empirical results, its recognition of an early emotional basis for patriotism was an important contribution. However, several critiques are also in order. First is the focus on elected leaders. Not only does political development concern more than partisan politics but the public's trust in elected leaders waxes and wanes with the times. Although it increased significantly after September 11, 2002, it declined precipitously after Watergate, a trend that was true for children as well as adults. Young people may feel patriotic about their nation and its symbols, but that attachment is probably at best minimally associated with their confidence in particular leaders.

A second critique of political socialization theory concerns its emphasis on the social integration of younger generations into an extant political system and their assimilation of system norms (Hyman, 1959). In this vertical model it was assumed that adult agents passed on to the younger generation a set of principles that sustained the system. Relatively little attention was paid to politics as a contestation of views, to reasons why marginalized groups would buy into a system in which they might feel excluded, or to the role of peers in political development. In fact, change—whether in individuals or in society—was given short shrift. The focus on childhood eclipsed attention to the adolescent years and the ways in which growth in understanding the political system might also be related to an increase in political cynicism. The active role of younger generations in interpreting the principles of their social order—of stabilizing the system by making those principles their own—was not part of the models of human development in that period. Instead, political socialization drew from a replication model in which older generations passed an intact system on to younger generations. As generational replacement theorists have subsequently shown, engagement of younger generations and replacement of their elders in the political process is a source of political change (Delli Carpini, 1989).

COGNITIVE DEVELOPMENTAL THEORY

In the early 1960s, adolescents' political theories were explored in a series of studies with 11- 18-year-olds in the United States, Great Britain, and Germany (Adelson & O'Neil, 1966; Gallatin, 1980). Less interested in intergenerational stability, cognitive developmentalists looked instead at how adolescents' conception of the political domain changed as they matured. How did early versus late adolescents conceive of the law and authority? What did they understand about systems of governance or social institutions, about the rights and obligations of citizens and the state? To shed light on these issues, Adelson and his colleagues used a semistructured interview, asking young people to imagine that a group of 1,000 people who were dissatisfied with their government had taken it upon themselves to move to an island (Adelson & O'Neil, 1966). Participants were asked to imagine how they would organize this new society. Interviewers then probed how older and younger adolescents reasoned about the political domain—that is, what form of government they would choose and why, what was the purpose of leadership or laws in a society. The investigators noted a shift in conceptualization of the political domain in midadolescence, around 13 or 14. Whereas younger adolescents had more benevolent views of leaders and were more willing to follow even an autocratic leader, older adolescents felt more committed to the representation of the people's voices in decision making and noted that some leaders would abuse their power. With respect to laws, younger adolescents tended towards a law-and-order orientation, feeling that laws were necessary to restrict individual freedom. Among older adolescents, there was a more nuanced understanding of laws: the dangers of restricting individual freedom were raised, as was the importance of laws to protect the public good. In summary, growth in political thinking included greater concern for individual rights, for the community at large, and for the distinction between the legitimate and the arbitrary (Gallatin, 1980).

This theory provided an important tool by focusing on age-related shifts in conceptions of the political domain. However, it did not explain the mechanisms underlying these transitions. Nor could it account for certain contradictions in adolescents' thinking. For example, despite an increase in hypothetical reasoning, pessimism about the possibilities of eliminating social problems such as poverty or crime increased with age (Leahy, 1983). Although late adolescents were aware that social systems could be changed, they were not very adept at imagining alternatives to the status quo.

However, this may reflect more about the average adolescent's exposure to alternative political systems than about their capacities. One recent study comparing the political views of adolescents in four security-based societies in which the state plays a major social welfare role with their peers in two opportunity-based societies in which individuals shoulder more responsibility for their basic needs concluded that normative beliefs about the proper relationship between states and citizens reflect the social contracts to which the youth are accustomed (Flanagan & Campbell, in press). Other work suggests that exposure to alternative systems can broaden adolescents' political perspectives. Using a simulation exercise, Torney-Purta (1992) has demonstrated that adolescents' schemas about international politics accommodate when they assume the roles of different nations and share perspectives on political issues as seen from different nations' points of view.

THE GENERATIONAL MODEL

Whereas political socialization theory focused on intergenerational stability in political loyalties, the generational perspective concentrated on the role of historical events in distinguishing generations and on young people as actors, engaged in rather than merely reacting to social change. Theorists in this tradition contended that the late adolescent and early adult period was a watershed in the development of a political ideology. Drawing from Mannheim (1952), they held that this was a stage when an individual was not yet saddled with social roles and could have a fresh contact with his or her society (i.e., could view it from a new perspective). At this stage of transition to adulthood, many young people are in settings away from their families where they are exposed to different lifestyles, norms, and perspectives on social issues and would potentially form new reference groups (Alwin, Cohen, & Newcomb, 1991). For example, longitudinal comparisons of high school seniors who attended college in the late 1960s with their peers who did not attend college revealed that political attitudes were shaken up by the college experience but that once crystallized, the attitudes of those who went to college were more stable thereafter (Jennings, 1993).

Consolidating political views is part of the process of consolidating identity. Thus, the way an individual grapples with and resolves the salient social issues of the period when he or she comes of age becomes an integral part of personality thereafter (Stewart & Healy, 1989). In fact, longitudinal work shows that it is not the historical events per se but the way that different generational units deal with those events that predicts their subsequent political positions (Jennings, 2002). Notably, it is not simple exposure or even interest in the salient political issues during one's coming of age but rather how actively one grapples with and is affected by those issues that is formative of identity thereafter.

McAdam (1988) has argued that engaging in intense political activism during the transition to adulthood transforms identity in fundamental ways. He compared young adults who participated in the Mississippi Freedom Summer voter registration drives with a group of their peers who volunteered to go but in the end did not participate. Although the period of time was short, the actions in which these volunteers were engaged were highly contested and their lives were on the line. According to McAdam, these facts, combined with the collective identity they experienced as part of a group powerfully committed to a cause, fundamentally transformed their identities and also disrupted subsequent life trajectories.

By focusing on the transition to adulthood as a politically defining period, less attention was paid in generational theory to the formative role of family values in the development of political views. Longitudinal studies that followed students of the 1960s and their parents showed that the political positions of activists and their parents were more liberal than were those of their age-mates during the height of student activism as well as 15 years later (Dunham & Bengston, 1992). Likewise, a study conducted in the 1990s found that college students' attitudes towards the Persian Gulf war were similar to the attitudes that the students' parents had held toward the Vietnam War in their college years (Duncan & Stewart, 1995). Not surprisingly, concordance of political attitudes is higher in those families in which political issues are salient topics of discussion and action (Jennings, 2002).

Not one of these three theories that attended to the developmental antecedents of politics in adulthood was grounded in the everyday lives of adolescents. However, many of the skills and motivations associated with adult political engagement are learned in the formative years. Moreover, political views, like other aspects of social cognition, are rooted in social relations. Among other things, they concern the way we think about our membership in society, our rights, responsibilities, and relationships with others in society. Such views are formulated as adolescents theorize about society and their role in it and as significant adults in their lives share their views of the world and the values that matter to them (Flanagan & Tucker, 1999). In the next section I synthesize relevant contemporary work arguing for a new theory of youth political development, grounded in the everyday experiences of young people. I have summarized this work by attending to two themes: adolescents' *experiences of membership* in local community organizations and institutions and the *exercise of rights and assumption of responsibilities* in these groups—which I have taken from Michael Walzer's (1989, p. 211) definition of a citizen as one who ". . . is most simply, a *member* of a political community, entitled to whatever *prerogatives* and encumbered with whatever *responsibilities* are attached to membership."

THE ROLE OF VOLUNTARY ASSOCIATIONS IN SUSTAINING DEMOCRACY

As theorists in the political socialization tradition argued, affective ties to the polity develop before one fully understands the system (Easton & Dennis, 1969). Those ties are the basis for patriotism and the foundation for political stability. But what are the developmental mechanisms whereby affection for the polity evolves? One likely source is the kind of experiences adolescents have to participate in the institutions of their communities.

In particular, membership in community-based youth organizations (CBYOs) and extracurricular activities at school may be a developmental foundation for later civic engagement because it is in such experiences that youth develop an affection for the polity. In CBYOs youth learn what it means to belong and to matter to fellow members of their community (Eccles & Gootman, 2001). In a phrase, they appreciate the meaning of a sense of place. An excellent example is provided in the practice of the Quantum Opportunities Program (Hahn, Leavitt, & Aaron, 1994, cited in Eccles & Gootman, 2001) when staff acted on the motto, "Once in QOP, always in QOP" by contacting those youth who dropped out of the program to remind them that they were still part of the QOP family. In contrast, when youth do not hear messages that they belong, they feel disaffected, lacking an emotional bond to fellow community members. Affection for the polity and engagement in community affairs are logical extensions of the sense of connection youth develop from involvement in community based organizations. Longitudinal analyses of eighth graders from the National Educational Longitudinal Survey revealed that extensive connections to others through family, religious institutions, and extracurricular activities were significantly related to political and civic involvement in young adulthood (Smith, 1999).

Likewise, according to several retrospective studies, participation in community-based clubs and organizations and extracurricular activities during the adolescent years is related to civic and political participation in adulthood (Van Horn, Flanagan, & Willits, 2003; Verba, Schlozman, & Brady, 1995; Youniss, McLellan, & Yates, 1997), although these relationships may be most pronounced in midlife when people have set down roots in a community and have a vested interest in community affairs. In their national three-generation panel study, Jennings and Stoker (2001) found that participation in voluntary associations peaked during the high school years, dropped off in early adulthood, and increased again at midlife. That high schools typically offer a wide range of extracurricular options and that students are expected to join are probably implicated in the high levels of organizational participation in late adolescence (Jennings & Stoker, 2001). Norms of engagement in high school also are likely to serve a socially integrative function. Hilles and Kahle (1985) found that across social class groups, high school students' perceptions that teachers and administrators expected them to be involved in extracurricular activities was correlated with their social integration, role commitment, and academic achievement.

Political Roles of Voluntary Youth Associations

Like other institutions of socialization, community-based youth organizations are both normative and mediating institutions. They help to stabilize societies by integrating youth into prosocial reference groups, but they also contribute to social change by providing spaces where younger generations can contest the status quo and devise alternatives. The practices of these organizations shape the dispositions of younger generations. Character traits of loyalty, duty, and honor are reinforced in the Boy Scout pledge, and service to my club, community, country, and world is the standard that a 4-H member promises he or she will strive to achieve. Although their function is typically to develop the traits of good citizens by acting as a prosocial reference group, the political role of these organizations is more palpable in specific historical epochs. For example, during the height of the Cold War in the 1950s, the Young Pioneers and Comsomol organizations in Central and Eastern Europe openly encouraged youth to demonstrate their patriotism. During the 1960s and 1970s as Cold War tensions thawed, their political role was less overt; the organization was known primarily for sponsoring camping and environmental reclamation projects (Flanagan, Bowes, Jonsson, Csapo, & Sheblanova, 1998). Likewise, during the two world wars, the 4-H organization was called into service for its country. As older youth were recruited off of the farm and into the military or defense industries, younger 4-H members stepped forward to serve their country by raising victory gardens. Food for Freedom was their war slogan, and it was estimated that from 1943 until the end of World War II, 4-H club members produced enough food to feed a million soldiers serving in the American armed forces (Van Horn, Flanagan, & Thomson, 1998). In less politically charged times, these groups assume a more subtle role but one that still benefits the social order. They serve a socially integrative function by providing structure for free time, a prosocial peer reference group, and adult mentors who are volunteering their own time to a community organization.

Youth who are involved in organized community groups are less likely to be involved in antisocial activities or substance abuse (Allen, Kuperminc, Philliber, & Herre, 1997; Larson, 1992), although sports may be an exception to this rule (Eccles & Barber, 1999). However, the civic role of these organizations transcends their diversionary function. In the next section I argue that the structure and practices of voluntary community-based youth organizations benefit democracy by developing the democratic dispositions and civic identities of young people.

GROUP SOLIDARITY, CIVIC ENGAGEMENT, AND TRUST

Because political socialization was originally framed as an intergenerational process, the importance of peer relationships was underestimated in the early theory. However, peer relationships in CBYOs are key to developing a democratic social order because their structure is more egalitarian than that of the other institutions of socialization (families and schools). In CBYOs youth can exercise their voice, test out ideas, disagree with each other, and make meaningful contributions to their communities (Heath & McLaughlin, 1993). These groups also play a role in the development of social trust, a social good that undergirds democracy.

Trust is a belief in the goodwill of others, a belief that they share with us a commitment to a common good. Interpersonal or thick trust is rooted in and reinforced by regular contact and dense networks with people we know. Social trust, which is thinner, extends the boundaries of those we consider fair, helpful, and trustworthy to a wider circle of fellow citizens or humanity more generally (Putnam, 2000). The reciprocal relationship between civic engagement and social trust has been referred to as a virtuous circle: Adults who are more trusting are more likely to get engaged in civic affairs, and levels of social trust are increased by such engagement (Brehm & Rahn, 1997; Putnam, 2000; Verba et al., 1995), although this is mainly the case for organizations with diverse membership and those engaged in charitable work (Uslaner, 2002). Likewise, adolescents who are involved in community-based or extracurricular activities have higher levels of trust and more positive views of others in their communities when compared to peers who are uninvolved in such groups (Flanagan, Gill, & Gallay, in press). Why?

First, whereas acceptance and membership in families typically are assumed, membership and trust among one's peers are earned by working together toward goals defined in common, by working through differences that could otherwise divide the group. In the process, adolescents can see how their individual effort contributes to the group and how the collective efforts of several people can produce a better product (Youniss et al., 1997). Therefore, participation in these organizations is an opportunity for young people to develop a collective identity.

Second, by virtue of their nonhierarchical structure, community organizations afford opportunities for young people to exercise their voice and practice leadership in the context of a collective. In contrast to families and schools, in which relationships of power and authority are essentially asymmetrical, in youth groups the status of the members is the same. In principle, this level playing field means that members can gain experience in admitting and resolving differences of opinion in an atmosphere in which the consequences of disagreeing are the same for everyone in the group. Thus, ownership of the projects and identification with the organization and its goals increases and members are more likely to feel accountable to the group because they are an integral part of it.

To the extent that a young person identifies with an organization or group, he or she should feel a sense of solidarity with others in the group; this is important because political goals are rarely achieved by individuals acting alone, and feelings of solidarity are related to civic engagement. Among adults a sense of collective identity motivates action on behalf of the group (Klandermans, Sabucedo, Rodriguez, & de Weerd, 2002) and among adolescents feelings of peer solidarity are associated with commitments to public interest goals such as serving one's community, nation, and people in need (Flanagan, Bowes, et al., 1998).

To achieve collective goals, individual members typically have to forego some personal preferences. In the give-and-take of peer group negotiations, young people learn that people (fellow citizens and members of the public) have different perspectives. They learn that (as in community affairs and in politics) resolving differences of opinion may require bargaining and compromise. Perhaps for these reasons, Alexis de Tocqueville (1848/1969), an early observer of American mores, referred to such voluntary community associations as the "schools of democracy" where the ties one felt to fellow citizens served to moderate the individual's commitment to narrow self-interest.

Citizens in democracies are expected to make autonomous decisions free from control or interference by the state. Thus, younger generations need opportunities to practice skills of information gathering, deliberation, discussion, and debate, which are the bases for making informed political judgments. Opportunities for opinion formation in classroom discussion and debate are correlated in cross-national studies with students' civic knowledge and commitments to civic goals (Torney-Purta, Lehmann, Oswald, & Schulz, 2001), and opportunities to have a meaningful voice in organizational decisions are consistently identified as an essential factor for effective CBYOs (Camino & Zeldin, 2002; Heath, 1999) and service learning projects (Billig, 2000). Indeed, the infusion of youth into CBOs often results in restructuring of the organization itself and of the communities with which it collaborates. Relationships within the organization improve as adults accommodate their stereotypes and become more trusting of young people (Zeldin, McDaniel, Topitzes, & Calvert, 2000). In fact, both the attitudes of adults and the dynamics of the organization change when young people's voice is seriously infused in the organization. Zeldin et al. (2000) found that as adults became more aware of young people's competence and contributions, their stereotypes decreased and their comfort level in working with youth increased. Youths' energy, enthusiasm, and even their willingness to take risks (which is often framed as a problem in the literature on adolescence) reinvigorated the organization and its ties to the community. Perhaps because adolescents are so insistent on authenticity, their involvement brought both the adults and the organization back to its core values.

We know that other institutions (families and schools) offer more opportunities for opinion formation, discourse, cooperative learning, and debate to mainstream and middle-class youth (Oakes, 1985; Slomczynski, Miller, & Kohn, 1981). Thus, opportunities in CBYOs for the social inclusion of otherwise marginalized groups are especially important. Work by Kahne and his colleagues is important in this regard. They found that African American male teens felt more at home in out-of-school programs (felt more respected by adults, more comfortable with and trusting of peers, and generally more accepted) than they did in the school setting (Kahne et al., 2001).

UNEQUAL OPPORTUNITIES FOR ENGAGEMENT IN COMMUNITY-BASED YOUTH ORGANIZATIONS

In practice, opportunities to belong to CBYOs are unevenly distributed across communities in the United States. National studies indicate that 29% of early adolescents are not reached by community youth programs at all (U.S. Department of Education, 1990) and that in disadvantaged communities, resources are not ample to sustain programs (Carnegie Council on Adolescent Development, 1992). Because socially advantaged communities often have both the financial resources as well as a larger pool of adults available to serve as volunteers, young people in these communities are more likely to be involved in CBYOs. And such involvement is typically a venue for youth engagement in community service (Hart & Atkins, 2002). Adolescents also are more likely to be involved in CBYOs and extracurricular activities when their parents are involved in civic or political affairs or reinforce their children's involvement (Fletcher, Elder, & Mekos, 2000; Van Horn et al., 2003).

Among adults in the United States, social class and political participation are stubbornly linked. Those who are better educated, better paid, and better connected are more likely to participate, in part because schools and jobs are settings in which people get recruited into civic activities (Verba et al., 1995). Opportunities via faith-based groups to practice organizational and leadership skills and to be recruited into civic action are one of the few ways that citizens overcome these class disparities (Verba et al., 1995). Similar opportunities for youth from less advantaged communities to practice civic, organizational, and leadership skills might help to redress socioeconomic inequities in adults' political participation. However, longitudinal work suggests that social disparities in the pathways to civic participation begin in childhood. Children (especially males) from single-parent families are less likely to be connected as teens to religious institutions in their communities and less likely as adults to be engaged in community voluntarism (Lichter, Shanahan, & Gardner, 2002). Class disparities in voting as a young adult can be traced to similar disparities in participation in extracurricular activities as early as the eighth grade (Lopez, 2002).

Even when community-based organizations are available, their practices may actually marginalize some young people by insisting that they assimilate to a majority culture. Such experiences of exclusion convey information about how the social contract—the tie that binds states and citizens together—works and how its tenets apply to people "like us" (Flanagan & Campbell, in press; Flanagan, Ingram, Gallay, & Gallay, 1997; Flanagan & Tucker, 1999). For example, for sexual minority youth, school policies that ban student organizations such as Gay Straight Alliances (GSAs) foreshadow civil rights issues they will face as adults such as the U.S. military's "Don't ask, don't tell" policy or the bans on same sex civil unions in the policies of many states (Russell, 2002). But young people who feel that they cannot be authentic in extant CBYOs can form their own voluntary associations. Like other groups who have been marginalized by mainstream institutions, they can claim a free space in which—without fears of reprisals—they can share information, debate ideas, and define a collective identity and political agenda (Evans & Boyte, 1992).

EMERGING MODELS OF YOUTH CIVIC ENGAGEMENT

In fact, a new model of CBYOs has been evolving, which extends the civic aspects of the positive youth development framework (Lerner, Fisher, & Weinberg, 2000) and responds specifically to young people who have been marginalized by more mainstream organizations. These grassroots community-based organizations are led by youth and often engage them in activism for social change (Brown et al., 2001; Checkoway, 1998; Cutler & Edwards, 2002; Finn & Checkoway, 1998; Irby, Ferber, & Pittman, 2001; Schensul, 1998; Wheeler, 2000). Many include a commitment to social justice as an integral part of their mission.

Across programs and sites, consistent features of effective models emerge. First is an emphasis on the collective rather than the individual nature of youth agency and leadership and on the coconstruction of products. Commitment to the group also is the basis on which young people hold leaders accountable. According to Roach et al. (1999), young leaders evolve in close concert with the organization and with the good of the group in the forefront of attention. Otherwise, peers will censure them for acting in their own self-interest. Youth leaders emerge through a process in which identification with and dedication to the group is the key ingredient. As Roach et al. (1999) point out, this process model is a more developmental conceptualization of leadership, which contrasts with that in the literature on adult leaders, in which the focus is on the unique traits and abilities of leaders that distinguish them from fellow members of their organization.

Second, effective youth organizations provide opportunities for all members to practice a range of roles. As a result, individuals gain competencies and broaden their perspectives. In addition, the organization is more democratic because no single or small group of individuals is in charge (Dewey, 1916), and the fate of the organization does not depend on a small group. Furthermore, leadership can be distributed across a broad pool of talent and expertise. Because there are graduated responsibilities in the organization, membership—especially of older and more experienced youth—is sustained (McLaughlin, 2000). By implication, age integration via cross-age programming is characteristic of these organizations (Roach et al., 1999; Stoneman, 2002; Wheeler, 2000).

Third, striking the right balance between freedom and structure also is key to organizational success (Eccles & Gootman, 2001). Effective organizations are not run in a laissez-faire fashion but are structured with a small set of rules collectively generated by the members. Typically, rules emphasize the equal status of members and hold all members accountable. The structure of rules adds an element of predictability and provides young people with the security of a free space where they can test out ideas and make revisions based on learning from their mistakes (Rogoff, Baker-Sennett, Lacasa, & Goldsmith, 1995).

Fourth, young people's role in organizational governance is more than titular or symbolic. In the YouthBuild program, for example, the young people who learn skills in the building trades also are in charge of the assets of the program and make decisions about who will get contracts to train them (Stoneman, 2002). Youth-led community organizations are one example of the ways that young people are exercising a voice in the affairs of society. Other venues where they can be heard include public policy consultation on youth issues, community coalitions for youth development, the decisions of nonprofit organizations, and school-based service learning programs (Camino & Zeldin, 2002).

It would appear that including the voice of young people in community decision-making is an idea whose time has come. International human rights treaties such as the United Nations Convention on the Rights of the Child (which nongovernment organizations [NGOs] are using to hold signatory states accountable) emphasize children's rights to care and nurturance but also to self-determination (Limber & Flekkoy, 1995). The last of the venues listed above (service) is an example of the final feature of effective youth-led community programs, i.e., that young participants themselves provide benefits, tangible service or products to the broader community. Perhaps the best example is the affordable housing units that the YouthBuild program provides to the community's residents (Stoneman, 2002).

Youth-led organizations imply a new role for adults in CBYOs. Rather than leading, adults need to be in the background—monitoring, mentoring, facilitating, but not being in charge; this does not mean that adults are unimportant to the enterprise. In fact, young people want support from adults in the form of providing dialogue, coaching, and connections to sources of institutional, community, and political power (Camino & Zeldin, 2002; Heath, 1999). However, youth envision these roles for adults within a partnering framework in which there is equality and mutual respect between the parties and in which adults and youth alike play by the rules (Heath, 1994). The ways in which adults interpret their authority and the rules of governance are important to the success of the organization (Camino, 2000) and also help to foster democratic dispositions in the youth with whom they work. When adolescents feel that adults in positions of authority hold the same high standards for and respect the ideas of everyone in the group and insist on respect and tolerance as basic rules of peer interaction, the youth themselves are more committed to serving their community, serving their country, and working to improve intergroup relations (Flanagan & Faison, 2001; Flanagan, Gallay, & Gill, 2003).

Easton (1953) described politics as the "authoritative allocation of values" (p. 129), referring to the power of political ideas and policies to shape widespread beliefs and values. Politics does guide the goals and practices of formative institutions (schools, community-based organizations) and children's social theories incorporate the norms, values, and beliefs emphasized in these environments (Goodnow, Miller, & Kessel, 1995). Political stability is assured as each new generation adopts as their own the core values of their polity. However, schools and community-based organizations are mediating institutions, settings where the principles of the social contract between states and citizens are interpreted and negotiated. Thus, the core values of the polity are redefined in each new generation and collectively, the choices of people in these formative institutions give meaning to the broader tenets that bind citizens of the polity together (Flanagan & Campbell, in press).

VOLUNTEERISM AND CIVIC ENGAGEMENT

Service to the community has always been part of the civic mission and training of mainstream CBYOs. Their pledges and practices emphasize loyalty to the organization and the polity via service in the local community. Service also is part of the ethos of faith-based organizations. Thus, it is not surprising that prior to the institutionalization of community service in public education, the Independent Sector reported that 75% of young people who belonged to a youth group and 80% of those who were active in a religious organization had done volunteer work in their communities.

Voluntary community service is a more normative expectation for adolescents in the United States when compared to their peers in 27 other nations (Torney-Purta et al., 2001), and females are more likely than are their male peers to report that they engage in service (Flanagan, Jonsson, et al., 1998; Niemi, Hepburn, & Chapman, 2000). Family factors associated with greater civic involvement include religiosity (Hunsberger, 1999) and parents' own engagement in civic and political affairs (Chan & Elder, 2001; Van Horn et al., 2003).

Trends in the last decade show how rapidly service learning programs are becoming a normative part of public education (Sagawa, 1998). In 1993, federal support for community service was written into law in the National and Community Service Trust Act, with administrative responsibilities for the programs entrusted to the Corporation for National and Community Service (CNCS). Service learning, as outlined in the legislation, combines meaningful community service with a formal educational curriculum and structured time for reflection, distinguishing its purported educational benefits from less structured community service opportunities. Adolescents and young adults are the age groups targeted in several of the CNCS programs: Learn and Serve America, which links education with service for grades K–16; youth corps modeled after the Civilian Conservation Corps (CCC) of the 1930s; and AmeriCorps.

In the late 1990s 64% of all public schools and 83% of public high schools provided some form of community service programs, and nearly a third of all schools had service learning programs in place (Billig, 2000). Adolescents are more likely to engage in behaviors that they perceive as normative (Brown, 1990), and national studies of college freshmen suggest that community service has become such a norm: Fully 81% of the college freshman class of 2000 reported that they had done some form of volunteer work (Kellogg, 2001). What do youth learn by engaging in service?

Outcomes of Service Learning

Although most studies are correlational, several short-term longitudinal studies now have found positive benefits during the program but more mixed evidence for lasting effects. The most consistent findings are that young people feel efficacious and good about their engagement and that an ethic of service develops—that is, there is an increase in concern for others, in a sense of social responsibility, and in motivational and behavioral indicators of continued service after initial involvement (see reviews by Billig, 2000, and Perry & Katula, 2001). In their large national study of college students, Astin, Sax, and Avalos (1999) found effects of high school students' service a decade later, controlling for service while in college. Similarly, among high school students, engagement in service in the ninth grade was related to a transformation in students' priorities by the end of high school (Johnson, Beebe, Mortimer, & Snyder, 1998). Not only were these youth likely to be involved in service, but—regardless of selection factors—they became less concerned with their own careers, became more concerned with the social and altruistic rewards of work, and placed greater value on involvement in their communities.

Besides the ethic of service, evidence suggests that participation is associated with increases in tolerance, commitments to equal opportunity, and cultural diversity, and reductions in stereotyping, prejudice, and the inclination to blame the victim for his or her condition (Eyler & Giles, 1999; Markus, Howard, & King, 1993; Melchior, 1999; Metz, 2002). How enduring effects are depends on how long the program lasts (Eyler & Giles, 1997; Shumer, 1997). Many programs engage youth for so few hours of actual community work that measurable change would be surprising to say the least. A national evaluation of middle- and high-school students in state of the art Learn and Serve America programs found increases during the program year in students' acceptance of cultural diversity, service leadership, and engagement with school, although a year later effects were only found for students who continued in service during the subsequent year (Melchior, 1999).

Relatively little attention has been paid to the developmental timing or sequence of different types of service experiences or to the match between program characteristics and the developmental competencies and needs of the participants. However, community service has been identified as a particularly important component of community-based programs for 15- to 18-year-olds (Eccles & Gootman, 2002), and the evaluation of Learn and Serve America did find that changes were more pronounced for high school students when compared to middle-school students (Melchior, 1999). Such results raise intriguing questions about the match between program characteristics and developmental readiness. Although developmental stage has typically been ignored in designs, certain features of effective programs have been identified, including student involvement in selecting, designing, and implementing the project; communication between school and community partners; challenging tasks; reflection on the experience; and regular assessment of program efficacy (Billig, 2000).

Caution is warranted before deciding that service learning is a magic bullet of civic reform in schools. Some studies have found no results associated with service. For example, Hamilton and Zeldin's (1987) study of high school students who did internships in local government found that compared to their peers in conventional civics classes, interns' knowledge of local government increased, although their image of local government did not become more positive. Service learning has been criticized for what might be termed its philanthropic, charity, or noblesse oblige orientation—that is, that the privileged give back to a society who has treated them well but forgotten whole groups of fellow citizens (Sullivan, 2002). Noticeably absent from most discussions of service is the question of privilege and whose community is being served. However, the institutionalization of service in public education does mean that youth across different communities will be doing service, which opens up possibilities for research on how the service experience may vary by the social class of the participants and the relationship of the participants to the community being served.

Service learning programs also have been criticized for diverting attention from the political bases of many of the problems (homelessness, hunger, literacy, environmental degradation) that the voluntary sector is addressing (Walker, 2002). This question is an empirical one, however, because psychological rather than political outcomes typically have been measured. One study of Canadian youth that did look at adolescents' involvement in campaigning and politics was able to distinguish a cluster of youth who engaged in community service but not in the political arena and another who engaged in both (Pancer, Pratt, & Hunsberger, 2000). Compared to their uninvolved peers and those who helped others when asked to, the two community-involved clusters had higher identity achievement scores, were more likely to have mothers who were also active in the community, and were more likely to discuss political issues with parents, although the politically active group had a more distant relationship with their parents. Although only 8% of the sample in this large study were in the political activist cluster, they were the most active youth who also sustained the highest levels of community involvement over time.

The institutionalization of community service has turned a lens on the learning component of this form of experiential education. Because it is classroom based, service learning is more likely than is community service to generate discussions between students (Astin, Vogelgesang, Ikeda, & Yee, 2000), a fact that is important for connecting the experience to broader public issues. Classroom discussions that encourage students to question the deeper roots of social problems are associated for some students with gains in empathy for the persons served by the program and in appreciation of the multiple dimensions of social problems (Batchelder & Root, 1994; Yates & Youniss, 1997).

Some studies find that the benefits of engaging in service are more marked for those youth whose backgrounds place them at risk (Blyth, Saito, & Berkas, 1999). For example, as an alternative to detention for late adolescents in the juvenile justice system, service has been shown to significantly reduce the likelihood of arrest in early adulthood (Uggen & Janikula, 1999). In the Teen Outreach Program (TOP), classroom discussions of adolescents' community service experience helped participants develop self-discipline and build their social and assertiveness skills and ultimately their self-confidence (Allen et al., 1994). The TOP also found that those students who did more hours of service were more likely to pass their academic courses. Although it is speculative, one explanation for these results is that service offers youth an opportunity to make a meaningful contribution to their community and that this opportunity adds a new sense of purpose to life for youth growing up in challenging settings.

Of course, youth who engage in service do so with their own predispositions. A sizable body of research documents individual differences among adolescents and adults in values such as social responsibility, civic commitment, loyalty, and patriotism, and these differences are related to the likelihood of being involved in community service and in the civic and political affairs of one's community (Flanagan, in press). Personal motivations vary; in one study of undergraduates, altruistic versus egoistic motivations were concordant with the political orientation (liberal vs. conservative) of the volunteer (Sherrod, 2002). Sustaining a commitment to service may depend on how well matched the work is to the motivation to serve (Clary & Snyder, 1999). Openness to new experiences is another predisposing factor. At least one study found that those who were open to the experience and felt they learned something had higher levels of social trust—that is, significantly more positive views of fellow citizens—when compared to peers who did not learn from their experience (Flanagan et al., in press).

Compared to other voluntary pursuits such as extracurricular activities or clubs that are interest-based and thus tend to have a homogeneous membership, community service has more potential for exposing adolescents to a heterogeneous range of people and issues in their communities (Flanagan et al., in press). According to two national studies of undergraduates involved in a broad range of service learning programs, students report that they gained new insights into their relationship and responsibility for other members of their society as a result of their experience in service (Eyler & Giles, 1999). Youniss and Yates (1999) explain this as a transformation of civic-moral identity and argue that as young people engage in service with people in need, their awareness of humanity and the circle of others to which they feel responsible is enlarged. National panel studies of adults suggest that the practice does shape the person—formal volunteering has a positive impact on the likelihood that one will engage in informal helping such as lending a hand to a neighbor, whereas the latter (informal helping) does not predict formal volunteering (Wilson & Musick, 1997).

Methodological Recommendations for the Field of Service Learning

As noted earlier, evaluations of service learning programs have yielded mixed results. As in any new area of research, methods are improving as the field matures. As part of this evolution, it will be important that tighter linkages be made between the specific practices of a service program and measurable change in participants. Operational definitions of *service* too often mix functionary work with direct service to people, when these two kinds of practice have very different implications for adolescent development (McLellan & Youniss, 2002). Short-term longitudinal designs are known to miss sleeper effects (Jennings & Stoker, 2001; Kagan & Moss, 1962), and—as already noted—the duration of involvement affects the likelihood of lasting effects. Many of the desirable outcomes may already be high when they are measured as baseline indicators, leaving relatively little room for gains associated with the program. When one considers the years of learning that occurred and habits and attitudes consolidated prior to an adolescent's involvement in these programs, a lasting impact or even a significant change beyond baseline measures is quite a high standard for what are primarily short term programs.

Future work in this field should frame service learning as a developmental opportunity for gaining civic practice and relate it to other forms of civic/political engagement. Within such a framework, one could test whether there are unique advantages of service for later involvement in community affairs and political activism over other opportunities such as civic education or community-based youth groups. In past generations community work was often a bridge to politics, but there is some concern that young people today see it as an alternative (National Association of Secretaries of State, 2000). They certainly feel more effective in the service as compared to the political arena, which many consider corrupt and ineffectual (Galston, 2001). Compared to other nations, voluntary community associations have always played an integral role in how democracy works in the United States (Tocqueville, 1848/1969). Insofar as opportunities for civic engagement via CBYOs vary by the community's socioeconomic status (Hart & Atkins, 2002), it would seem that the institutionalization of service learning into public schools might equalize opportunities for civic practice.

CONCLUSION: BUILDING A THEORY OF YOUTH CIVIC DEVELOPMENT

In recent years there has been progress on several fronts that collectively hold promise for moving the agenda of youth civic engagement forward. First is a shift in the field of adolescence, away from a youth-at-risk to a youth-as-asset paradigm. Youth civic engagement is a logical extension of this framework that focuses on the contributions adolescents make to communities (Flanagan & Van Horn, 2003). By insisting that young people should have a voice in community decisions, the assets approach reframes political socialization from an emphasis on preparing for the day when they are old enough to exercise the franchise to enabling adolescents to act in the here and now as citizens.

A second front is the seamless connection between scholarship and practice in the field of community youth development, which increases the likelihood that scholarship will focus on the issues that matter to young people. Finally, in recent years there has been marked progress in defining youth civic engagement as a cross-disciplinary field and in engaging political scientists and developmental psychologists in joint discussions (Sherrod, Flanagan, & Youniss, 2002). However, theory will move forward only if scientists move beyond the boundaries of their disciplines.

Political scientists will have to acknowledge that voting and its correlates (knowledge about and interest in electoral politics and current events) makes for a narrow definition of politics in the context of adolescents' lives. Even theorists in the early political socialization tradition decried the fact that this narrow framing of the domain obscured the very processes that gave meaning to political participation (Hyman, 1959). Rather than focusing on conventional political outcomes, we have to raise questions such as the following: What are the practices in developmental settings that promote engagement with the political process? If democracies depend on people with "democratic dispositions" (Elshtain, 1995, p. 2), what experiences in the formative years nurture political conviction, respect for the views of others, and a passion for the public good that transcends narrow self-interest?

Developmentalists may understand more about the formation of democratic dispositions. However, they have to link the development of personalities to participation in the polity and its affairs. When adults vote with a political party, they do so in part because they identify with that party—that is, their worldviews and values are condordant with that party's attributions for and solutions to social or economic issues. As we have argued in our program of work on adolescents' interpretations of the social contract, these political views develop in concert with the identity process (Flanagan & Tucker, 1999; Flanagan, Bowes, et al., 1998).

Identity is considered a definitive task of the adolescent and young adult years. As young people reflect on who they are and the future to which they aspire, they will also take stock of their societies. Political views are taking shape as part of this process, although youth may not refer to them as such if politics connotes only conventional activity to them. But politics reflecting an individual's worldview, politics as a language for explaining social problems is forming in these years, although it is probably well into the third decade of life before these views crystallize (Jennings, 1989).

Values are standards we use to assess our personal behavior but are also a basis for organizing our political views and positions on public policies (Jennings, 1991). Adults make sense of political issues by developing theories about the underlying cause of the problem (Kinder & Fiske, 1986). Research on adolescents' theories about inequality suggests that their evolving political views are concordant with their own values and worldviews and with those emphasized in their families: Those holding individuals accountable for being poor, homeless, or unemployed are more materialistic and believe in the logic of opportunity, whereas those endorsing the systemic or structural roots of inequality are more altruistic and report that compassion is emphasized in their families (Flanagan & Tucker, 1999). These relationships were strongest among youth who held firm ideological positions.

More than 150 years ago, Tocqueville (1848/1969) observed that to sustain democracy, it was important to develop particular habits or customs in citizens. Echoing this claim, Sullivan and Transue (1999) contend that two psychological orientations in the people are necessary to make democracy work. The first is an ethos of political participation and the attitudes and values that promote it, and the second is tolerance for the views of those with whom we fundamentally disagree and a commitment to their right to voice their views. In this concluding section I address the question, "What kinds of opportunities and practices increase the likelihood of such traits in younger generations?"

An Ethic of Civic Participation

First, an ethic of civic/political participation implies a passion for and identification with the public good. In this chapter, I have argued that when young people feel a sense of place in their communities, they come to see that their interests are realized in the interests of the whole. By extension, as adults, contributing to the community isn't an option. It is simply the right thing to do (Flanagan, 2003).

As political socialization theorists contended, there is an affective basis for civic participation. When we label some adolescents *disaffected,* we imply that emotional ties to the community are lacking, revealing how fundamental we consider social bonds between young people and their communities. However, theorists in the political socialization tradition argued that confidence or trust in the benevolence of leaders was the foundation for system support. In contrast, developmental research points to the key role that respect plays in the likelihood that adolescents will feel an emotional bond to their communities and buy into the system. Youth development work suggests that trust in and commitment to the system develops from regular and repeated experiences of respect from adults in positions of authority (Camino & Zeldin, 2002; Flanagan et al., in press). Adolescents are also more likely to pay attention to the news if programs respect rather than talk down to the audience (Buckingham, 2000). If commitment to the organization is a standard to which adolescents hold their own leaders accountable (Roach et al., 1999), we might expect that their assessments of public officials would be based on similar standards—that is, whether they genuinely respect and are accountable to the public. Political cynicism should increase with age as youth realize that not all public servants are so responsive and that the system is not perfect, an awareness that might occur earlier among marginalized groups. But even cynicism about politicians can be moderated by face-to-face experiences with candidates running for office and a civic education program (such as the Annenberg Student Voices project), which teaches students that they have a right to hold elected officials accountable (Romer, 2002).

Second, as already noted, a reciprocal relationship exists between political participation and social trust. Opportunities during the adolescent years to participate in organizations should nurture trusting dispositions in younger generations and thereby initiate the virtuous circle of participation and social trust. Participation in organizations develops trusting and trustworthy dispositions in young citizens who are likely to continue their participation as adults. However, not all associations are alike in these civic benefits. As Portes (1998) has argued, social capital has its downsides when the strong internal bonds of trust within an organization or group are maintained at the expense of including newcomers or outsiders. In this regard, Dewey (1916) pointed to two characteristics of groups that make them democratic. First, to the extent that the interests of the members are numerous and varied, it should be more likely that everyone would play an integral role in the group and less likely that only a few people would take charge. The ideal organization is thus one in which there are multiple opportunities for different young people to assume leadership roles. Second, to the extent that interactions with others outside the group were full and free, the group would be less likely to be isolationist and exclusive. Thus, to nurture a democratic ethic, organizations should ensure that their members have heterogeneous encounters and are exposed to perspectives that differ from their own.

Developing a participatory ethic in youth also implies a belief that politics is controversial, that it matters to have an opinion, and that it is okay—even a good thing—to be skeptical about the status quo. Convergent evidence from several different lines of work suggests that an awareness that political issues are controversial is correlated with political engagement. Jennings (2002) found that adults at midlife who had participated in political protest as youth were more likely than were their uninvolved peers to be engaged in conventional politics and to encourage a civic ethic, including volunteer work, in their children.

Other work shows that participating in discussion and debate at school is correlated with high school students'—especially African American students' (Niemi & Junn, 1998)—political knowledge (Torney-Purta et al., 2001) and with young adults' knowledge of and attention to politics (Keeter, Zukin, Andolina, & Jenkins, 2002). Families also nurture a participatory ethic when they engage in political debate. Their children are more knowledgeable about and interested in politics (McLeod, 2000) and are more likely to participate in political protest (Haan, Smith, & Block, 1968).

Tolerance

Tolerance is the second trait that Sullivan and Transue contend democracies need in their citizens. They distinguish tolerance from apathy, noting that it is not indifference to the views of others but a commitment to the civil liberties of those whose ideologies we oppose. Characteristics of personality that are positively related to tolerance include openness to new experiences, optimism, and trust. The stronger one's commitment to democratic norms (the rights of minorities, freedom of speech and assembly, etc.), the stronger is one's commitment to tolerance (Sullivan & Transue, 1999). However, among adults and teens alike, support of a group's free speech is qualified by whether the group promotes violence, by concerns about the harm to others that might result, and by a desire to hear both sides of an issue (Avery, 2002; Sullivan & Transue, 1999). Insofar as tolerance is not a natural proclivity, democratic societies may have to be proactive in socializing this trait. Nonetheless, adolescence is an ideal time to foster tolerance.

Autonomy is considered a hallmark of the adolescent years. Thus, principles of self-determination and of civil liberties including tolerance for dissent should have a particular resonance. During adolescence, there are significant changes in the way in which rights and liberties are conceived with older adolescents, and their mothers more likely than early adolescents and their mothers to endorse rights to self-determination (Ruck, Peterson-Badali, & Day, 2002). Compared to early adolescents and even to their own parents, late adolescents are more likely to defend the rights of speech and assembly of extremists on the right and the left of the political spectrum (Owen & Dennis, 1987). Free speech is less likely to be defended by early adolescents when its exercise would result in the exclusion of some groups, whereas older adolescents and college students are more inclined to support the civil liberties of all groups regardless of the message they espouse (Helwig, 1995).

What kinds of developmental opportunities increase the likelihood that tolerance will develop? The first answer is interactions with others whose life experiences and viewpoints differ from one's own. For example, tolerance of dissenting views is higher among adolescents who debate current events with parents who listen to and respect their opinions (Owen & Dennis, 1987; Santoloupo & Pratt, 1994). Likewise, open classroom climates in which exchange of divergent opinion is encouraged are likely to increase young people's exposure to different viewpoints. At the least, such practices make young people aware that there can be multiple perspectives on a social issue. Developmental studies indicate that it is typically not until late adolescence that adolescents learn to integrate and resolve different points of view (Selman, Watts, & Schultz, 1997), which may be an artifact of age-grading trends and the homogenization of adolescents' experience in the United States.

Second, we need to cultivate the natural proclivities of human beings to empathize with others, which Hoffman (2000) contends can evolve in early adolescence into compassion for disenfranchised groups. Research with activists in the civil rights and antiwar movements of the 1950s and 1960s (Dunham & Bengston, 1992) and of those who sheltered Holocaust survivors during World War II (Oliner & Oliner, 1988) confirm that compassion and social responsibility were core family values that motivated their actions. These family values also are implicated in the extent to which public service figures in an adolescent's value priorities. In one comparative study, it was significantly related to the likelihood that adolescents in all seven nations would be involved in community work and to the importance they attached to serving their country (Flanagan, Bowes, et al., 1998).

Compassion has not been investigated as a correlate of tolerance. However, compassion reflects an openness toward and concern for others. According to cross-cultural work, values that are oriented towards others' needs are antipodal to values which focus on the self (Schwartz, 1996). Among high school and college students, the latter (i.e., self-interest) is associated with negative stereotypes of African Americans (Katz & Hass, 1988), with antiforeigner attitudes among German students (Boehnke, Hagan, & Hefler, 1998), and with antiimmigrant attitudes among American youth (Flanagan & Gallay, 1999). In fact, self-interest in the form of materialist values seems to erode adolescents' trust in humanity in general. High school students who hold such values are less likely to believe that people generally are fair, helpful, and trustworthy (Rahn & Transue, 1998).

In *Bowling Alone,* Robert Putnam (2000) points to the parallels between the conditions of life in the United States today and those at the turn of the last century. These parallels include disparities in wealth; growing corporate power; waves of immigration; massive change in the demographics of the population; new forms of technology, commerce, and communication; and a restructured workplace. At the turn of the last century, optimism about the potential for social change was balanced by pessimism about seemingly intractable social ills. However, the civic culture was revitalized as Americans created and joined an unprecedented number of voluntary associations, not the least of which were new youth organizations. In less than a decade (1901–1910) most of the nationwide youth organizations that were to dominate the 20th century were founded—the Boy and Girl Scouts; Campfire Girls; 4-H, Boys Clubs, and Girls Clubs; Big Brothers and Big Sisters; and the American Camping Association (Putnam, 2000, p. 393). Similar signs of civic inventiveness can be seen in new directions today in youth-led community-based programs (Flanagan & Faison, 2001).

The participation of younger generations in community-based organizations is a foundation on which western democracies are built. It is within such "schools of democracy" that young people develop the social allegiances and democratic dispositions and learn the political skills that guarantee the transfer of democracy to a new generation.

As volunteerism, leadership, and civic engagement gain currency as legitimate topics of research, youth civic-political development may finally take its place as a domain of adolescent development.

REFERENCES

Adelson, J., & O'Neil, R. (1966). The development of political thought in adolescence: A sense of community. *Journal of Personality and Social Psychology, 4,* 295–308.

Allen, J. P., Kuperminc, G., Philliber, S., & Herre, K. (1994). Programmatic prevention of adolescent problem behaviors: The role of autonomy, relatedness, and volunteer service in the teen outreach program. *American Journal of Community Psychology, 22,* 617–638.

Alwin, D. F., Cohen, R. L., & Newcomb, T. M. (1991). *Political attitudes over the life span: The Bennington Women after fifty years.* Madison: University of Wisconsin Press.

Astin, W. A., Sax, L. J., & Avalos, J. (1999). Long-term effects of volunteerism during the undergraduate years. *The Review of Higher Education, 22*(2), 187–202.

Astin, A.W., Vogelgesang, L. J., Ikeda, E. K., & Yee, J. A. (2000, January). *How service learning affects students.* Los Angeles, CA: Higher Education Research Institute, UCLA.

Avery, P. G. (2002). Teaching tolerance: What research tells us. *Social Education, 66*(5), 270–275.

Batchelder, T. H., & Root, S. (1994). Effects of an undergraduate program to integrate academic learning and service. *Journal of Adolescence, 17*(4), 341–355.

Billig, S. H. (2000). Research on K-12 school based service learning: The evidence builds. *Phi Delta Kappan, May,* 658–664.

Blyth, D. A., Saito, R., & Berkas, T. (1997). A quantitative study of the impact of service-learning programs. In A. S. Waterman (Ed.), *Service-learning: Applications from the research* (pp. 39–56). Mahwah, NJ: Erlbaum.

Boehnke, K., Hagan, J., & Hefler, G. (1998). On the development of xenophobia in Germany: The adolescent years. *Journal of Social Issues, 54*(3), 585–602.

Brehm, J., & Rahn, W. (1997). Individual-level evidence for the causes and consequences of social capital. *American Journal of Political Science, 41,* 999–1023.

Brown, B. B. (1990). Peer groups and peer cultures. In S. S. Feldman & G. R. Elliott (Eds.), *At the threshold: The developing adolescent* (pp. 171–196). Cambridge, MA: Harvard University Press.

Brown, K. M., Forthofer, M. S., Bryant, C. A., Eaton, D. K., Merritt, T., Landis, D. E. C. et al. (2001). Developing youth capacity for community-based research: The Sarasota County Demonstration Project. *Journal of Public Health Management Practice, 7*(2), 53–60.

Buckingham, D. (2000). *The making of citizens: Young people, news, and politics.* New York: Routledge.

Camino, L. A. (2000). Youth-adult partnerships: Entering new territory in community work and research. *Applied Developmental Science, 4*(S1), 11–20.

Camino, L. A., & Zeldin, S. (2002). Everyday lives in communities: Discovering citizenship through youth-adult partnerships. *Applied Developmental Science, 6*(4), 213–220.

Carnegie Council on Adolescent Development. (1992). *A matter of time: Risk and opportunity in the nonschool hours.* New York: Carnegie Corporation of New York.

Chan, C. G., & Elder, Jr., G. H. (2001). Family influences on the social participation of youth: The effects of parental social involvement and farming. *Rural Sociology, 66,* 22–42.

Checkoway, B. (1998). Involving young people in neighborhood development. *Children's and Youth Services Review, 20,*(9, 10), 765–795.

Clary, E. G., & Snyder, M. (1999). The motivations to volunteer: Theoretical and practical considerations. *Current Directions in Psychological Science, 8,* 156–159.

Cutler, I. M., & Edwards, S. L. (2002). Linking youth and community development: Ideas from the community youth development initiative. *CYD Journal, 3*(1), 16–33.

Dawson, R. E., & Prewitt, K. (1969). *Political socialization.* Boston: Little, Brown, and Company.

Delli Carpini, M. X. (1989). Age and history: Generations and sociopolitical change. In R. Sigel (Ed.), *Political learning in adulthood: A sourcebook of theory and research* (pp. 11–55). Chicago: University of Chicago Press.

Dewey, J. (1916). *Democracy and education: An introduction to the philosophy of education.* New York: The Free Press.

Duncan, L. E., & Stewart, A. J. (1995). Still bringing the Vietnam war home: Sources of contemporary student activism. *Personality and Social Psychology Bulletin, 18,* 147–158.

Dunham, C., & Bengston, V. (1992). The long-term effects of political activism on intergenerational relations. *Youth and Society, 24,* 31–51.

Easton, D. (1953). *The political system: An inquiry into the state of political science.* New York: Knopf.

Easton, D. (1965). *A systems analysis of political life.* New York: Wiley.

Easton, D., & Dennis, J. (1969). *Children in the political system.* New York: McGraw Hill.

Eccles, J. S., & Barber, B. L. (1999). Student council, volunteering, basketball, or marching band: What kind of extracurricular involvement matters? *Journal of Adolescent Research, 14,* 10–43.

Eccles, J. S., & Gootman, J.A. (Eds.). (2002). *Community programs to promote youth development.* Washington, DC: National Academy Press.

Elshtain, J. B. (1995). *Democracy on trial.* New York: Basic Books.

Evans, S. M., & Boyte, H. C. (1992). *Free spaces: The sources of democratic change in America.* Chicago: University of Chicago Press.

Eyler, J., & Giles, D. (1997). The importance of program quality in service-learning. In A. Waterman (Ed.), *Service learning: Applications from he research* (pp. 57–76). Mahwah, NJ: Erlbaum.

Eyler, J., & Giles, D. E. (1999). *Where's the learning in service-learning?* San Francisco: Jossey-Bass.

Finn, J. L., & Checkoway, B. (1998). Young people as competent community builders: A challenge to social work. *Social Work, 43*(4), 335–345.

Flanagan, C. A. (in press). Citizenship/Social Responsibility/Loyalty/Teamwork. In M. E. Seligman & C. Peterson (Eds.), *Values in action classification.*

Flanagan, C. A. (2003). Trust, identity, and civic hope. In L. Wagener & J. Furrow (Eds.), Beyond the self: Perspectives on transcendence and identity development [Special issue of *Applied Developmental Science*].

Flanagan, C. A., Bowes, J., Jonsson, B., Csapo, B., & Sheblanova, E. (1998). Ties that bind: Correlates of adolescents' civic commitments in seven countries. *Journal of Social Issues, 54*(3), 457–475.

Flanagan, C. A., & Campbell, B. (in press). Social class and adolescents' beliefs about justice in different social orders. *Journal of Social Issues.*

Flanagan, C. A., & Faison, N. (2001). Youth civic development: Implications of research for social policy and programs. *Social Policy Report* (Vol. 15, no. 1). Ann Arbor, MI: Society for Research in Child Development.

Flanagan, C. A., & Gallay, L. S. (1999, March). What does it mean to be an American? Views of tolerance, opportunity, and justice from youth in different cultures and communities. Paper invited for presentation at the international conference, Right-wing extremism, Nationalism, and Xenophobia: Hazards to Democracy and Life Course Development in Germany and North America, University of Toronto Institute for Human Development, Life Course, and Aging, Toronto, Canada.

Flanagan, C. A., Gallay, L., & Gill, S. (2003). *Adolescents' beliefs in America and commitment to democratic values: Processes for different racial/ethnic groups.* Unpublished manuscript.

Flanagan, C. A., Gill, S., & Gallay, L. S. (in press). Social participation and social trust in adolescence: The importance of heterogeneous encounters. In A. Omoto (Ed.), *Social participation in processes of community change and social action* (Vol. 19).

Flanagan, C., Ingram, P., Gallay, E. M., & Gallay, E. E. (1997). Why are people poor? Social conditions and adolescents' interpretation of the "social contract." In R. D. Taylor & M. C. Wang (Eds.), *Social and emotional adjustment and family relations in ethnic minority families* (pp. 53–62). Mahwah, NJ: Erlbaum.

Flanagan, C. A., Jonsson, B., Botcheva, L., Csapo, B., Bowes, J., Macek, P., et al. (1998). Adolescents and the "Social Contract": Developmental roots of citizenship in seven countries. In M. Yates & J. Youniss (Eds.), *Community service and civic engagement in youth: International perspectives* (pp. 135–155). New York: Cambridge University Press.
Flanagan, C .A., & Tucker, C. J. (1999). Adolescents' explanations for political issues: Concordance with their views of self and society. *Developmental Psychology, 35*(5), 1198–1209.
Flanagan, C. A., & Van Horn, B. (2003). Youth civic development: A logical next step in community youth development. In F. A. Villarruel, D. F. Perkins, L. M. Borden, & J. G. Keith (Eds.), *Community youth development: Practice, policy, and research* (pp. 273–297). Thousand Oaks, CA: Sage.
Fletcher, A. C., Elder, G. H., & Mekos, D. (2000). Parental influences on adolescent involvement in community activities. *Journal of Research on Adolescence, 10*(1), 29–48.
Gallatin, J. (1980). Political thinking in adolescence. In J. Adelson (Ed.), *Handbook of adolescent psychology* (pp. 344–382). New York: Wiley.
Galston, W. A. (2001). Political knowledge, political engagement, and civic education. *Annual Review of Political Science, 4,* 217–234.
Goodnow, J. J., Miller, P. J., & Kessel, F. (1995). Cultural practices as contexts for development. *New Directions for Child Development, 67,* 1–12.
Haan, N., Smith, M. B., & Block, J. (1968). Moral reasoning of young adults: Political-social behavior, family background, and personality correlates. *Journal of Personality and Social Psychology, 10,* 183–201.
Hahn, A., Leavitt, T., & Aaron, P. (1994). *Evaluation of the Quantum Opportunity Program (QOP): Did the program work?* Waltham, MA: Brandeis University, Heller Graduate School.
Hamilton, S. F., & Zeldin, R. S. (1987). Learning civics in the community. *Curriculum Inquiry, 17*(4), 407–420.
Hart, D., & Atkins, R. (2002). Civic competence in urban youth. *Applied Developmental Science, 6*(4), 227–236.
Heath, S. B. (1994). The project of learning from the inner-city youth perspective. *New Directions for Child Development, 63,* 25–34.
Heath, S. B. (1999). Dimensions of language development: Lessons from older children. In A. Masten (Ed.), *Cultural processes in child development: The Minnesota symposium on child psychology* (Vol. 29, pp. 59–75). Mahwah, NY: Erlbaum.
Heath, S. B., & McLaughlin, M. W. (Eds.). (1993). *Identity and inner-city youth: Beyond ethnicity and gender.* New York: Teachers College Press.
Helwig, C. C. (1995). Adolescents' and young adults' conceptions of civil liberties: Freedom of speech and religion. *Child Development, 66,* 152–166.
Hilles, W. S., & Kahle, L. R. (1985). Social contract and social integration in adolescent development. *Journal of Personality and Social Psychology, 49,* 1114–1121.
Hoffman, M. L. (2000). *Empathy and moral development: Implications for caring and justice.* Cambridge, England: Cambridge University Press.
Hyman, H. H. (1959). *Political socialization: A study in the psychology of political behavior.* Glencoe, NY: The Free Press.
Irby, M., Ferber, T., & Pittman, K. (2001). *Youth action: Youth contributing to communities, communities supporting youth* (Vol. 6). Takoma Park, MD: The Forum for Youth Investment, International Youth Foundation.
Jennings, M. K. (1989). The crystallization of orientations. In M. K. Jennings & J. van Deth (Eds.), *Continuities in political action* (pp. 313–348). Berlin, Germany: DeGruyter.
Jennings, M. K. (1991). Thinking about social injustice. *Political Psychology,12,* 187–204.
Jennings, M. K. (1993). Education and political development among young adults. *Politics and the Individual, 3,* 1–24.
Jennings, M. K. (2002). Generation units and the student protest movement in the United States: An intra- and intergenerational analysis. *Political Psychology, 23,* 303–324.
Jennings, M. K., & Stoker, L. (2001, August). *Generations and civic engagement: A longitudinal*

multiple-generation analysis. Paper presented at the 2001 annual meeting of the American Political Science Association, San Francisco, CA.

Johnson, M. K., Beebe, T., Mortimer, J. T., & Snyder, M. (1998). Volunteerism in adolescence: A process perspective. *Journal of Research on Adolescence, 8,* 309–332.

Kagan, J., & Moss, H. A. (1962). *Birth to maturity.* New York: Wiley.

Kahne, J., Nagaoka, J., Brown, A., O'Brien, J., Quinn, T., & Thiede, K. (2001). Assessing after-school programs as settings for youth development. *Youth and Society, 32*(4), 421–446.

Katz, I., & Hass, R. G. (1988). Racial ambivalence and American value conflict: Correlational and priming studies of dual cognitive structures. *Journal of Personality and Social Psychology, 55,* 893–905.

Keeter, S., Zukin, C., Andolina, M., & Jenkins, K. (2002). *The civic and political health of the nation: A generational portrait.* College Park: Center for Information and Research on Civic Learning and Engagement (CIRCLE), University of Maryland.

Kellogg, A. (2001, January 26). Looking inward, freshmen care less about politics and more about money. *The Chronicle of Higher Education,* A 47–A 49.

Kinder, D. R., & Fiske, S. T. (1986). Presidents in the public mind. In M. G. Hermann (Ed.), *Political psychology* (pp. 193–218). San Francisco: Jossey-Bass.

Klandermans, B., Sabucedo, J. M., Rodriguez, M., & de Weerd, M. (2002). Identity processes in collective action participation: Farmers' identity and farmers' protest in the Netherlands and Spain. *Political Psychology, 23*(2), 235–251.

Larson, R. W. (2000). Toward a psychology of positive youth development. *American Psychologist, 55,* 170–183.

Leahy, R. L. (1983). The development of the conception of economic inequality: II. Explanations, justifications, and conceptions of social mobility and social change. *Developmental Psychology, 19,* 111–125.

Lerner, R. M., Fisher, C. B., & Weinberg, R. A. (2000). Toward a science for and of the people: Promoting civil society through the application of developmental science. *Child Development, 71*(1), 11–20.

Lichter, D. T., Shanahan, M. J., & Gardner, E. L. (2002). Helping others? The effects of childhood poverty and family instability on pro social behavior. *Youth and Society, 34*(1), 89–119.

Limber, S. P., & Flekkoy, M. G. (1995). The U.N. Convention on the Rights of the Child: Its relevance for social scientists. *Social Policy Report, IX*(2), 1–15.

Lopez, M. H. (2002, December 5–6). *Precursors to civic/political engagement in the young adult years: Evidence from the National Educational Longitudinal Survey.* Paper presented at meetings sponsored by the MacArthur Network on the Transition to Adulthood, Washington, DC.

Mannheim, K. (1952). The problem of generations. In P. Kecshevich (Ed.), *Essays on the sociology of knowledge* (pp. 276–322). London: Routledge & Kegan Paul. (Original work published 1928)

Markus, G. B., Howard, J. P., & King, D. C. (1993). Integrating community service and classroom instruction enhances learning: Results from an experiment. *Educational Evaluation and Policy Analysis, 15,* 410–419.

McAdam, D. (1988). *Freedom summer.* New York: Oxford University Press.

McLaughlin, M. (2000). *Community counts: How youth organizations matter for youth development.* Washington, DC: Public Education Network.

McLellan, J. A., & Youniss, J. (2003). Two systems of youth service: Determinants of voluntary and required community service. *Journal of Youth and Adolescence, 32,* 47–58.

McLeod, J. M. (2000). Media and civic socialization of youth. *Journal of Adolescent Health, 27*(2), 45–51.

Melchior, A. (1999). *Summary report: National evaluation of Learn and Serve America.* Waltham, MA: Center for Human Resources, Brandeis University.

Metz, E. (2002, April). *Linking background factors and community service experiences to high school students' concern for poverty issues.* Paper presented at Biennial Meeting of the Society for Research on Adolescence, New Orleans, LA.

National Association of Secretaries of State. (2000). *New millennium project, Part I: American youth attitudes on politics, citizenship, government, and voting.* Lexington, KY: Author.

Niemi, R. G., Hepburn, M., & Chapman, C. (2000). Community service by high school students: A cure for civic ills? *Political Behavior, 21*(1), 45–69.

Niemi, R. G., & Junn, J. (1998). *Civic education: What makes students learn.* New Haven, CT: Yale University Press.

Oakes, J. (1985). *Keeping track: How schools structure inequality.* New Haven, CT: Yale University Press.

Oliner, S., & Oliner, P. (1988). *The altruistic personality.* New York: Free Press.

Owen, D., & Dennis, J. (1987). Preadult development of political tolerance. *Political Psychology, 8,* 547–561.

Pancer, M., Pratt, M., & Hunsberger, B. (2000, July). *The roots of community and political involvement in Canadian youth.* Paper presented at the XVI biennial meetings of the International Society for the Study of Behavioral Development, Beijing, China.

Perry, J. L., & Katula, M. C. (2001). Does service affect citizenship? *Administration and Society, 33*(3), 330–365.

Portes, A. (1998). Social capital: Its origins and applications in modern sociology. *Annual Review of Sociology, 24,* 1–24.

Putnam, R. D. (2000). *Bowling alone: The collapse and revival of American community.* New York: Simon & Schuster.

Rahn, W. M., & Transue, J. E. (1998). Social trust and value change: The decline of social capital in American youth, 1976–1995. *Political Psychology, 19,* 545–565.

Roach, A. A., Wyman, L. T., Brookes, H., Chavez, C., Heath, S. B., & Valdes, G. (1999). Leadership giftedness: Models revisited. *Gifted Child Quarterly, 43*(1), 13–24.

Rogoff, B., Baker-Sennett, J., Lacasa, P., & Goldsmith, D. (1995). Development through participation in sococultural activity. *Cultural practices as contexts for development: New directions for child development, 67*(Spring), 45–65.

Romer, D. (2002, March). *Evaluation of student voices: What have we learned and what are we going to do?* Presentation for the Student Voices Advisory Board meeting, March 16, Grand Cayman, British West Indies.

Ruck, M. D., Peterson-Badali, M., & Day, D. M. (2002). Adolescents' and mothers' understanding of children's rights in the home. *Journal of Research on Adolescence, 12*(3), 373–398.

Russell, S. T. (2002). Citizenship for sexual minority youth: Challenges and emerging opportunities. *Applied Developmental Science, 6*(4), 258–263.

Sagawa, S. (1998). Ten years of youth in service to America. In S. Halperin (Ed.), *The forgotten half revisited: American youth and young families, 1988–2008* (pp. 137–158). Washington, DC: American Youth Policy Forum.

Santoloupo, S., & Pratt, M. (1994). Age, gender, and parenting style in mother-adolescent dialogues and adolescent reasoning. *Journal of Adolescent Research, 9,* 241–261.

Schensul, J. J. (1998). Community-based risk prevention with urban youth. *School Psychology Review, 27*(2), 233–245.

Schwartz, S. (1996). Value priorities and behavior: Applying a theory of integrated value systems. In C. Seligman, J. M. Olson, & M. P. Zanna (Eds.), *The psychology of values: The Ontario symposium* (Vol. 8, pp. 1–24). Mahwah, NJ: Erlbaum.

Selman, R. L., Watts, C. L., & Schultz, L. H. (1997). *Fostering friendship: Pair therapy and prevention.* New York: Aldine de Gruyter.

Sherrod, L. (2002, April). *Community service and youth's political views.* Paper presented at the Biennial Meeting of the Society for Research on Adolescence, New Orleans, LA.

Sherrod, L., Flanagan, C., & Youniss, J. (Eds.). (2002). Dimensions of citizenship and opportunities for youth development: The what, why, when, where and who of citizenship development. *Applied Developmental Science, 6*(4), 264–272.

Shumer, R. D. (1997). Learning from qualitative research. In A. Waterman (Ed.), *Service learning: Applications from the research* (pp. 25–38). Mahwah, NJ: Erlbaum.

Slomczynski, K. M., Miller, J., & Kohn, M. L. (1981). Stratification, work, and values: A Polish-United States comparison. *American Sociological Review, 46,* 720–744.

Smith, E. S. (1999). Effects of investment in the social capital of youth on political and civic behavior in young adulthood: A longitudinal analysis. *Political Psychology, 20*(3), 553–580.

Stewart, A. J., & Healy, J. M. (1989). Linking individual development and social changes. *American Psychologist, 44,* 30–42.

Stoneman, D. (2002). The role of youth programming in the development of civic engagement. *Applied Developmental Science, 6*(4), 221–226.

Sullivan, L. (2002). The state of youth organizing: 1990–2000. In *The state of philanthropy, 2002* (pp. 25–30). Washington, DC: National Committee for Responsive Philanthropy.

Sullivan, J. L., & Transue, J. E. (1999). The psychological underpinnings of democracy: A selective review of research on political tolerance, interpersonal trust, and social capital. *Annual Review of Psychology, 50,* 625–650.

Tocqueville, A. (1969). *Democracy in America.* J. P. Mayer, (Ed.), G. Lawrence, trans., Garden City, NY: Doubleday. (Original work published 1848)

Torney-Purta, J. (1992). Cognitive representations of the political system in adolescents: The continuum from pre-novice to expert. *New Directions for Child Development, 56,* 11–25.

Torney-Purta, J., Lehmann, R., Oswald, H., & Schulz, W. (2001). *Citizenship and education in twenty-eight countries: Civic knowledge and engagement at age fourteen.* Amsterdam: International Association for the Evaluation of Educational Achievement (IEA).

Uggen, C., & Janikula, J. (1999). Volunteerism and arrest in the transition to adulthood. *Social Forces, 78*(1), 331–362.

U.S. Department of Education, Office of Educational Research and Improvement, National Center for Education Statistics. (1990). *National education longitudinal study of 1988: A profile of the American eighth grader* (pp. 50–54). Washington, DC: U.S. Government Printing Office.

Uslaner, E. M. (2002). *The moral foundations of trust.* Cambridge, England: Cambridge University Press.

Van Horn, B., Flanagan, C., & Thomson, J. (1998, December). Changes and challenges in 4-H. Part 1. *Journal of Extension.*

Van Horn, B., Flanagan, C. A., & Willits, F. K. (2002). *Youth, family and club experiences and adult civic engagement.* Manuscript submitted for publication.

Verba, S., Schlozman, K. L., & Brady, H. E. (1995). *Voice and equality: Civic voluntarism in American politics.* Cambridge, MA: Cambridge Harvard University Press.

Walker, T. (2002). Service as a pathway to political participation: What research tells us. *Applied Developmental Science, 6*(4), 183–188.

Walzer, M. (1989). Citizenship. In T. Ball, J. Farrand, & R. Hanson (Eds.), *Political innovation and conceptual change* (pp. 211–219). New York: Cambridge University Press.

Wheeler, W. (2000). Emerging organizational theory and the youth development organization. *Applied Developmental Science, 4*(S1), 47–54.

Wilson, J., & Musick, M. (1997). Who cares? Toward an integrated theory of volunteer work. *American Sociological Review, 62*(October), 694–713.

Yates, M., & Youniss, J. (1997). Community service and political-moral identity in adolescents. *Journal of Research on Adolescence, 6,* 271–284.

Youniss, J., McLellan, J. A., & Yates, M. (1997). What we know about engendering civic identity. *American Behavioral Scientist, 40,* 620–631.

Youniss, J., & Yates, M. (1999). Youth service and moral-civic identity: A case for everyday morality. *Educational Psychology Review, 11*(4), 363–378.

Zeldin, S., McDaniel, A. K., Topitzes, D., & Calvert, M. (2000). *Youth in decision-making: A study on the impacts of youth on adults and organizations.* Chevy Chase, MD: National 4-H Council.

Chapter 24

APPLYING DEVELOPMENTAL SCIENCE: METHODS, VISIONS, AND VALUES

Lonnie R. Sherrod, Nancy A. Busch-Rossnagel, and Celia B. Fisher

The final consortium of sponsor organizations for the National Task Force on Applied Developmental Science included: the American Psychological Association's (APA) divisions of Developmental Psychology (Division 7), Adult Development and Aging (Division 20),and Child, Youth, and Family Services (Division 37); the Gerontological Society of America; the International Society for Infant Studies; the National Black Child Development Institute; the National Council on Family Relations; the Society for Research on Adolescence; and the Society for Research in Child Development. Major financial support for the conference was provided by the Foundation for Child Development and the William T. Grant Foundation. Generous contributions were also received from the APA Science Directorate, the Jennifer Corn Carter Family Philanthropic Fund, the A.L. Mailman Foundation, Ablex Publishing Corporation, Lawrence Erlbaum Associates. McGraw-Hill College Division, the Psychological Corporation, and Fordham University.

INTRODUCTION

In this chapter, we describe the methods, visions, and values that have come to distinguish applied developmental science (ADS). Simply distinguishing ADS from other developmental sciences is, however, too narrow. ADS is a unique integration of science, application, and practice, and this integration distinguishes it from most other sciences. For example, it is different from basic developmental science because of its primary focus on understanding the correlates and consequences of practical problems facing individuals across the lifespan. It is different from community psychology and the study of social policy and programs in its emphasis on continuity and change and on the interactions that occur between life stage and socially constructed interventions. It is different from clinical psychology and psychiatry in its emphasis on normative development, prevention, resilience, and the promotion of positive development across the life span. The purpose of this chapter is to explicate these unique characteristics of ADS. Its singular character is reflected in its methods, and these methods are what in large part give ADS its distinctive vision and values. Methods go hand in hand with values and both frame vision.

In this paper, we first describe the origins and history of ADS as an important perspective to guide research. We review prior theories and perspectives, notably the life span approach and biosocial orientation that paved the way for ADS, and we discuss some general contributions of ADS to developmental research. Thereafter we explicate the methods of ADS because they are so integral to its character; we describe the areas of assessment and early intervention, evaluation research, multiculturalism, and dissemination. Following descriptions of these methods around which training in ADS should be organized, we review the core elements of training. Next we consider the unique vision of ADS, reflecting the uses of the previously described methods. This vision currently consists of attention to ethics, using research to evaluate and inform social policies, pursuing prevention and promotion, and fostering university-community partnerships.

Origins and History of ADS

ADS arose in part from the National Conference on Graduate Education in the Applications of Developmental Science Across the Life Span (Fisher et al., 1993). In 1990 representatives from several national scholarly organizations with an interest in human development met because they were concerned with the interface (or lack thereof) between developmental science and the then-current challenges to positive development. These representatives recognized the need for a national consensus on the definition of competencies necessary to apply the developmental science knowledge base to social problems facing individuals at all points along the life course. The National Conference on Graduate Education in the Applications of Developmental Science Across the Life Span was convened at Fordham University on October 10–12, 1991. The aim of the conference was to create a living document that would define the scope, methodologies, knowledge base, and field experiences necessary to conduct applied developmental science activities (Fisher et al., 1993; Fisher & Murray, 1996).

Conference participants emphasized three conjoint aspects defining the scope of ADS. The applied aspect represents the goal of synthesizing knowledge from research and from applications in order to describe and explain developmental phenomena; this synthesis then allows one to intervene and to design preventive interventions that enhance the uses of knowledge about human development. The developmental aspect represents the focus on systematic and successive changes (as well as stabilities) within and between individuals, families, and social systems. The science aspect represents the application of a broad range of research methods required to test the validity of theory and application and to highlight the reciprocal interaction between theory and application.

Five broad categories of applied developmental science activities were identified at the conference: (a) testing the validity of developmental theories and professional practices in real world contexts; (b) investigating the developmental causes, consequences, and correlates of societal problems; (c) constructing, administering, and interpreting developmentally and culturally sensitive assessment instruments to identify protective factors and vulnerabilities of individuals at developmental risk; (d) designing, implementing, and evaluating developmental interventions; and (e) disseminating knowledge about developmental processes to professionals and organizations engaged in helping individuals and families at different points along the life span.

Additionally, four broad domains of competency for the conduct of applied developmental science were identified: (a) expertise in developmental theory and content, including cultural diversity and normative and atypical biological, physical, and social processes; (b) quantitative and qualitative research techniques necessary to evaluate change over time and to construct psychometrically sound developmental assessment instruments; (c) methods to understand and enhance individual and family development, including psychosocial assessment and program design and evaluation; and (d) ethical, legal, social policy, and professional knowledge necessary to understand and assist organizations and communities to serve individuals and families.

To illustrate, the program in developmental psychology at Fordham University was organized around this vision following the conference; its graduate curriculum and training program reflect these values and teach these methods—it is an applied developmental program. For a detailed description, see Fisher et al. (1993); Higgins-D'Alessandro, Hamilton, and Fisher (1998); and Fisher and Osofsky (1997). The point is that it is possible to structure a field including training in that field around the particular components that define ADS. We believe that it represents the future of developmental science. Certainly the generation of current graduate students, the future leaders of the field, in organizations such as the Society for Research in Child Development (SRCD) keenly embrace this vision, respect the values, and hunger for the methods (Sussman-Stillmann & Brown, 1997).

THEORETICAL FOUNDATIONS

Because the methods of ADS are so closely tied to theoretical origins, it is useful to briefly review this foundation.

Life Span Perspective

A life span approach first and foremost advocates that the potential for growth and change continues throughout the full life span, unlike the grand theories of development as offered by Piaget (1960) or Freud (1964), who present development as ending in early adolescence. Second, a life span approach allows for both multiple paths and multiple endpoints in development, again in contrast to the grand theories that articulate a single path to a single endpoint. Third, a life span approach argues for multiple influences on development: age-graded ones that are typically studied by developmentalists; history-graded ones, which reflect the impact of living in a particular place and time; and nonnormative events, or the chance occurrences that happen throughout life. Finally, the recognition of multiple influences implies that the field must be multidisciplinary; psychology does not own developmental science (Baltes & Reese, 1984; Sorensen, Weinert, & Sherrod, 1986). One of the important areas of growth of ADS since the conference in 1991 is its increasing expansion to multiple disciplines in the social and behavioral sciences (Lerner, 1995; Lerner & Galambos, 1998).

The life span approach has also been instrumental in inventing new methods to guide developmental research, such as testing-the-limits (Baltes, Lindenberger, & Staudinger, 1998) and cohort sequential designs (Baltes & Reese, 1984). Cohort sequential designs not only allow for examination of history-graded influences and the impact of sociopolitical factors on development, but they also provide cost efficient means of studying development longitudinally (Baltes & Reese, 1994). Testing the limits approaches borrowed from medical studies of cardiac stress allow examination of individual potential, not just of expressed performance (Baltes et al., 1998; Baltes & Reese, 1984). ADS exploits both methods, extending them in applied directions.

Biosocial Orientation

A biosocial approach builds on evolutionary science. Recognizing that biology changes more slowly than the environment, it emphasizes that we carry a genetic heritage selected for earlier and much different environments. As a result, it is imperative that we consider the organism's range of reaction to its current environments (Lancaster, Altmann, Rossi, & Sherrod, 1987).

One of the best examples of this viewpoint is the historical development of the female reproductive lifeline. In our ancestors—as represented in for example the !Kung—females became reproductively capable in their late teens, had a short period before marriage of subfertility, and then lactate for 4–5 years after each birth, which builds in natural birth control, so that across their life span females have four to five births, each separated by 4–5 years (Lancaster, 1986). This life course may be contrasted with the reproductive lifeline of contemporary females, in which reproductive capacity is typically acquired in early adolescence, with first birth typically at least a decade later. These females then have two to three births across their life spans with minimal lactation so that no natural birth control ensues. As a result, such a female faces a lifetime of artificial birth control and a tenfold increase in experienced menstrual periods. The biosocial approach now asks what is the range of reaction of human reproductive biology to this dramatic change in reproductive lifeline—in regard to health issues, for example, such as cervical or breast cancer or displeasure from menstrual periods (Lancaster, 1986).

Again, ADS expands such thought in applied directions, asking about changes in the environment and possible social policy responses to them. We know, for example, that childcare does not compromise the infant's development of an attachment to his or her major caregivers (Clarke-Stewart & Allhusen, 2002). Yet, what is the infant's range of reactions to the number of different caregivers he or she can experience in early life? This question applies to high-quality care in the form of nannies, which show turnover, as well as to center-based care.

UNIQUE CONTRIBUTIONS OF ADS

Since the 1991 Conference, the theoretical foundations and scope of applied developmental science has been broadened to include a more diverse approach to research, a new vision of program evaluation, and community-university partnerships (Fisher & Lerner, 1994; Fisher, Murray, & Sigel, 1996; Fisher & Osofsky, 1997; Lerner, 1995; Lerner & Galambos, 1998). Sherrod (2002) has argued that by recognizing the importance of context and culture, emphasizing developmental appropriateness, and focusing on continuity and change even in regard to prevention and intervention, ADS bridges the gap between research and practice, and promotes both as appropriate for collaborations (Fisher & Lerner, 1994).

One important contribution that ADS has made during the past 10 years is that it blurs the distinction between applied and basic research. We have long believed this distinction to be artificial. The two types of research are differentiated by the source of their question and the time frame for the relevance of the results, but both can be useful in our quest to understand the core developmental process linking person and context and to improve the social good. Research on self-efficacy (Bandura, 1992) is an example of originally basic research that has proven extremely useful in the battle to prevent HIV infection (Sherrod, 1998). Because social problems arise more quickly than science can generate information to deal with them (Prewitt, 1980), we need some information on the shelves to pull off as new problems arise. The research on self-efficacy served this purpose in regard to the AIDS epidemic.

Similarly, applied research is complex. Huston (2002) has differentiated two types of applied research: policy-relevant research such as studies of the mechanisms by which poverty affects child development and policy analyses or studies of actual social programs and policies such as welfare reform. Psychologists have not typically been involved in the latter type of research, which is unfortunate because most program and policies deal at some level with behavior change (Sherrod, 2002). ADS aims to correct this situation by training psychologists specifically to do policy-relevant research as well as policy analysis and to recognize when basic research has a contribution to make to policy. It thereby blurs the distinction between types of research by emphasizing that all are equally necessary to our science of human development.

The second contribution of applied developmental science during the past decade is its perspective on program evaluations. Black-box evaluations, based on clinical drug trials, are not necessarily appropriate for studies of social programs and policies. Although experimental designs with random assignment to control and program groups are desirable because they allow attribution of causality, social programs and policies are complex, multivariate endeavors that affect and are affected by numerous micro- and macrofactors. They are not single-variable drugs. Hence, it is questionable how appropriate the experimental design may in fact be for evaluations of social programs and policies (Hollister & Hill, 1995). It is more important to note, however, that other approaches should be explored; something as simple as examining the relationship between program participation variables and outcome variables could be useful. Sherrod (1997) has argued that for disadvantaged children and youth, programs and policies are as important to their development as schools and families and should be studied as contexts for development. Hence, evaluation research is not a separate, different type of research to be pursued by contract evaluators. It becomes a routine form of learning about phenomena, a different method or approach to use as circumstances dictate the need for it.

Third, perhaps the most important contribution of ADS, is its recognition that the communication between researchers and others must be bidirectional; both researchers and community participants, for example, have lessons to learn from each other (Lerner & Fisher, 1994; Lerner & Simon, 1998; Sherrod, 1998). Nonacademicians can learn how to evaluate and critique information from scientists, and researchers can learn what information the community needs and how it can be effectively communicated to laypersons. Such communication between researchers and community participants serves not only to improve research but is also critical to maintaining a public commitment to science. This approach has perhaps the greatest impact on the way that research is actually done. It relieves the researcher of full control of his or her enterprise and makes research a collaborative process between researcher and participant. One of the mistakes made in the current educational reform effort is its failure to recognize the need for a new three *R*s in education—reasoning, responsibility, and relationships (B. Hamburg, 1993)—given the demands of today's jobs. These three *R*s are also needed in contemporary developmental science. Investigators must know how to build relationships with participants, must recognize their social responsibility to participants and to society at large, and must acknowledge the complex reasoning processes necessary to both. ADS recognizes the need for these three *R*s in its training of researchers; they are as important as is an understanding of traditional research methods and statistics.

METHODS

The descriptions of methods in the following section illustrate the particular contributions of ADS reviewed previously, but they also review other contributions of ADS in assessment and intervention, multiculturalism, and dissemination. Finally we consider the training of the applied developmental scientist.

Assessment and Early Intervention

Assessment has become a fact of life for today's infants, children, and adolescents, often as a result of state or federal mandates. These mandates represent a traditional one-size-fits-all approach that can provide an assessment of minimum competencies but is ill suited to understanding the complexities of individual human development or of changes as a result of educational reforms. The perspective of ADS suggests a different approach, one based on best practices for assessment.

Best Practices for Assessment First, to be applied, assessment should have purpose and utility. There are several different reasons for assessment, most of them related to the well-being of the person or group being assessed. The first step is usually screening to identify individuals at risk for poorer developmental outcomes and thus to reduce the number of individuals who receive more in-depth assessment. Traditionally, this in-depth assessment provides information for diagnosis, but in the ADS perspective, diagnosis is replaced by creation of a conceptual framework for the problem or issue. This conceptual framework then leads to the identification of an intervention through program planning. The intervention should include program evaluation at both the individual level (monitoring changes) and at the group level.

Consistent with the bidirectional nature of communication within the ADS perspective, assessment also has utility for the ADS professional. Assessment provides us with a scheme of normative development and of context effects, which are often best identified by testing the limits. A technique of theory-guided practice on specific skills or test items, the testing-the-limits technique modifies the context of assessment to observe what individuals can do under ideal conditions (Kliegl, Smith, & Baltes, 1989). In addition to contextual normative information, assessment provides information about the range of individual differences.

Within the ADS perspective, assessment should also be developmental. Developmental assessment has traditionally referred to normative, age-graded assessment (e.g., the establishment of major developmental milestones). However, the biosocial orientation of ADS clearly shows that chronological age may not be the best marker for time-related changes, especially after infancy. Instead, developmental assessment should be characterized by recognition of individual differences and by plasticity—that is, the potential for systematic change across the life span.

Finally, for assessment to be consistent with ADS, it should be a process rather than being equated with testing. A test is "a set of tasks or questions intended to elicit particular types of behaviors when presented under standardized conditions and to yield scores that have desired psychometric properties" (American Psychological Association, American Educational Research Associate, and National Council on Measurement in Education, 1974, p. 2). In other words, for a test, the end product is the score. Assessment is a larger process that may—or may not—include tests but that does examine behavior in a variety of settings, the meaning of the performance on the test or the behavior in general in terms of an individual's functioning, and the likely explanation for that functioning (the conceptual framework).

That assessment is not equated with testing does not mean that ADS is free to ignore psychometric principles. The contrary is in fact true—additional attention to the psychometric qualities of tests, observations, and so forth in different contexts should be a hallmark of the ADS approach. In this way we can discriminate bias and random error.

Cultural Equivalence in Assessment Because of its attention to multicultural issues, the ADS perspective is particularly suited to identify issues associated with the lack of cultural equivalence of measures. The issue of cultural equivalence is easily exemplified by the issue of language used for assessment (Busch-Rossnagel, 2002). Most assessment is based on measures available just in English. The ADS professional who wants to obtain information from a non–English-speaking population (here, we use the example of Spanish) is faced with creating measures that are linguistically equivalent. This process usually starts with a simple translation, done by an individual with fluency in both languages. Because translation is not a one-to one mapping, the process may include asking several bilingual individuals to undertake the translation to achieve a consensus. However, the result may be flowing Spanish that is not true to the intent of the English measure because of the lack of precision in the original English version. The most precise words are often less commonly used in everyday interactions, so their use in a psychological measure increases the required reading level—and hence the difficulty—of the measure.

A second way of approaching translation is through the process of back translation, which is also known as double translation. In this process, a bilingual person translates an English version into Spanish, and then this Spanish translation is translated back into English by a second bilingual person. This process completes the back or double translation. The back translation (which is in English) is compared with the original English text. If the two versions are different, the Spanish version is altered to more closely approximate the original English. The altered Spanish version is subjected to another back translation to English. Such an iterative process, going through several rounds of translation, usually improves the comparability of the Spanish and the English versions (Marín & Marín, 1991; Werner & Campbell, 1970).

Back translation through several iterations is usually seen as the best practice to develop linguistically equivalent versions of measures. However, because only the Spanish version is modified and the English version is not changed, back translation has limitations. When the original, English measure is standardized and cannot be modified without jeopardizing the psychometric information gathered on the standardized measure, then iterative back translation must suffice to protect the standardization.

However, when both versions of the instruments are being developed simultaneously, a better option is available. This process is called *decentering* (Werner & Campbell, 1970). On the surface, the process of decentering is the same as the iterative process of back translation. However, when comparing Spanish and English versions, either version may be modified to enhance the match between the two. Where discrepancies exist between the two versions, bilingual individuals can discuss the intent of the English item, rewrite the item for clarification, and then translate and back translate again. In other words, each round of translation informs the development process for both versions of the questionnaire and often has the effect of clarifying the focus of the items. Decentering is likely to affect the development of a measure because it clarifies the linguistic boundaries of the constructs.

Linguistic equivalence does not mean psychological equivalence. It is necessary to examine the pattern of relationships for the two versions with other measures to see whether they are psychologically equivalent (Busch-Rossnagel, 1992, 1998). Psychological equivalence is particularly important when assessing interaction or social processes, such as parenting, because these processes may have different meanings in different ethnic and cultural contexts (Vargas & Busch-Rossnagel, 2000; Zayas & Solari, 1994). As with any type of psychometric effort, linguistic and psychological equivalence are never proven; we just continue to gather more evidence.

The ADS Utilitarian Perspective on Assessment What is necessary for an assessment to be valid from the ADS perspective? First, consistent with current testing standards, an assessment (or a test) is not valid in and of itself; rather, there is valid use of assessment. From this utilitarian, applied perspective, valid use first depends on the qualifications of the examiner. Like traditional testing standards, ADS assumes that the examiner is skilled, that the he or she is able to establish rapport with the individual(s), and that any standardized assessments are administered, scored, and interpreted correctly. However, the bidirectional nature of communication within ADS changes the role of the examiner from the expert to a colleague. The participants in the assessment (and the guardians for children and youth) are equals in determining the validity of the assessment. Most important is that the participants are the ones who determine whether assessment should occur and who evaluate the utility of the information obtained. In other words, the participants help to establish the referral questions that define the assessment process.

In addition to a skilled examiner who respects the participants as contributors to the assessment process, the validity of assessment rests with an adequate understanding-examination of the context—at all the possible levels. What is the effect of the context in the assessment if the examiner is African American and the participant is non-Hispanic White? What is the effect of having parent permission when the assessment is of the sexual behavior of adolescents? What is the physical context effect when advanced placement exams are interrupted by a bomb scare in a high school? Use of multiple contexts during the assessment process will help identify the effects of context. In other words, context should be treated as one of the variables to be examined in the assessment process.

Validity of use also requires an understanding of lack of perfect prediction from the assessment result. Whereas current behavior-performance-functioning may be observed, future behavior is only inferred. And that inference occurs within the conceptual framework created by the assessment process. If the ADS professional has a thorough grounding in research methods, then the conceptual framework may be a series of competing hypotheses for which this assessment process is looking for disconfirmation. Research methods teach us that we cannot confirm the null hypothesis—so we phrase our research questions to reject the null hypothesis. Unfortunately, many traditional assessment methods, especially projective tests (Anastasi, 1988), approach the assessment process in the opposite way—looking for evidence to support the hypothesis. What the process should be doing is taking that hypothesis and actively seeking information that would refute it.

The utility of assessment rests with communication of the results, and here again the ADS perspective is different from traditional practice. In traditional practice the result of the assessment is a series of scores, usually standardized (e.g., an IQ score or the results of the SATs), so that they have meaning for the experts. Mental health professionals are socialized to write assessment reports for other professionals, so that the reports are dense with jargon that may have little meaning and even less utility for the participants. Such reports are often focused on weaknesses, the areas of poor functioning that originally brought the participant in to the assessment process.

In contrast, the bidirectionality of communication involved in ADS suggests that the participants should shape the method of communication of results. For some participants, a standardized score may be understandable, but for many participants and guardians, the most understandable quantitative score is the percentile rank. Quantitative information should be contextualized by identifying strengths as well as weaknesses because strengths may help identify ideas for improvement or enhancement. Reports of observations of the performance will also suggest strengths and ideas for promotion of positive behaviors. When we carefully observed the reactions of Puerto Rican children to the standardized method of assessing mastery motivation, we noted that the Puerto Rican children showed much more social referencing that the Anglo toddlers tested before (Busch-Rossnagel, Vargas, Knauf, & Planos, 1993). Social referencing occurs when the young child looks to a more knowledgeable partner to interpret a situation, and we have used this observation about the proclivity of Puerto Rican youth to engage in this behavior to develop measures of social mastery motivation (Busch-Rossnagel, 1998).

Early Intervention

The need to communicate assessment results that include ideas for the promotion of development returns us to the heart of the assessment process for ADS. The goal of assessment, at whatever level should be to provide information that is useful to modify or optimize development. The life span perspective that underlies the ADS approach highlights that the potential for growth exists throughout the life course, but because of changes in the potential of plasticity across life, it suggests the importance of early intervention to facilitate change most effectively (Baltes, Lindenberger, & Standinger, 1998).

For example, research in the decade of the brain—the 1990s—demonstrated that the brain has greater potential for neural development from age 3 years to age 10 years (Kotulak, 1996). During the period, the brain is densely wired, with an oversupply of synapses between brain cells. Those connections that are used—that receive stimulation—are reinforced and continue to exist, whereas those that are unstimulated are likely to be eliminated. This process facilitates the acquisition of a wide range of skills in childhood; humans certainly continue to learn after this period, but change and particularly remediation become more difficult as the network of synapses diminishes in density.

Early invention is not defined simply by age. The life span perspective notes that there are multiple influences on developmental processes. Although age-graded ones have been the focus of most developmental study (as noted previously), chronological age may not be the most appropriate indicator of ontogenetic change. In adolescence, a marker of pubertal maturity may be better, so that early intervention for girls would occur earlier than for boys.

History-graded and nonnormative influences may also be targets for early intervention. One survey found that 10% of New York City schoolchildren had some symptoms of posttraumatic stress syndrome (PTSD) after the attacks of September 11. Rather than waiting for diagnoses of PTSD in adolescents who experienced the attacks at close range (e.g., the students at Stuyvesant High School, who were two blocks away from the World Trade Center), mental health professionals intervened early with the goal of preventing PTSD. Later surveys suggest that prompt intervention was useful—rates of probable PTSD dropped by about two thirds between October of 2001 and January of 2002.

Evaluation Research

Evaluations of social programs and interventions are one explicit form of directly applied research and are therefore integral to ADS. O'Connor (1995) describes the history of evaluation research in this country since its origins around midcentury. Early efforts in particular emphasized a black-box approach, reflecting the experimental paradigm prevalent at that time. In the standard experimental paradigm, individuals are randomly assigned to groups. One group receives the intervention, one functions as a control receiving no intervention, and selected outcomes are measured in the two groups. Group comparisons then ask whether there are statistically significant differences on any of the outcomes. If such differences are found, then causality for the difference in outcomes can be attributed to the intervention because presumably that was the only difference between the groups, due to random assignment. To some extent, this paradigm persists, at least in terms of the purported gold standard to which the evaluator should aspire. This paradigm is also mandatory in drug trials that aim for FDA approval so that policy makers then expect the same standard to apply before they are willing to pass laws.

Several issues remain, however, in regard to applying this paradigm to community-based social interventions. Random assignment is frequently not possible, so that one must then resort to a quasi-experimental design; there are several such possibilities but none is without problems (Rossi, Freeman, & Lipsey, 1999). Random assignment also often raises ethical problems about withholding an intervention from individuals who need it; such problems are often more serious if the intervention is for children. Perhaps most important is that community-based social interventions are more complex in multivariate ways than is the case with drugs. Therefore, it is not clear that random assignment works in the same way. Many factors other than the social intervention may account for outcomes (Hollister & Hill, 1995). Finally, in large social program evaluations, it is possible for statistical significance to be found for differences that in fact are too small to be meaningful in the lives of individuals. In summary, although experimentation is desirable because it does allow assignment of casualty, it is not an ideal method for evaluation of social policies and community-based social interventions. Therefore, other approaches should also be utilized.

Much of what we know about child development is based on correlational, not experimental research. Children are not assigned to good and bad parents, but we think we know something about what constitutes effective parenting. We think we know something about the impact of child abuse, and yet children are not randomly assigned to abusive and nonabusive parents. Correlational and regression techniques can also be useful to evaluations. In many cases, it is just as useful to know how much of the variance in an outcome is explained by the intervention as it is to know if there is a group difference.

Furthermore, many programs and interventions are not designed as experiments. They are established to help, to heal, or to promote the well-being of their participants. Hence, it is often assumed that no learning is possible in such efforts, and no evaluation is attempted; yet all such interventions are in fact social experiments. The program developers have in mind that if they do something, their actions will lead to some outcomes; this is the basic experimental model relating independent to dependent variables. Hence, a first step in designing an evaluation is to articulate this theory of change. Then the evaluation becomes theory-based research testing this theory of change (Connell, Aber, & Walker, 1995). From this perspective, the evaluation then not only evaluates the intervention, but it also can offer basic information about the phenomena addressed by the intervention.

In this way, the evaluation then becomes an opportunity for learning more generally. Sherrod (1997) has made the point that interventions and community programs are a large part of the context in which disadvantaged children grow up—probably as important as schools and families, for example. Hence, such community-based actions merit study not only in terms of whether they work, but also as phenomena with importance as developmental influences. In short, ADS brings this broadened perspective to evaluation research, pursuing multiple methods to investigate the effectiveness of interventions, but also using interventions and programs as opportunities to study developmental phenomena.

Multiculturalism

The centrality of context for research and application is a substantive assumption of the applied developmental science perspective (Fisher et al., 1993; Fisher & Lerner,

1994; Fisher & Osofsky, 1997; Higgins-D'Alessandro, Hamilton, & Fisher, 1998; Lerner, 1995; Lerner, Fisher, & Weinberg, 2000a, 2000b; Lerner, Sparks, & McCubbin, 2000). Integral to the successful application of the developmental science base to the practical problems of individuals and families is an understanding of how diversity, plurality, multiculturalism, and multilingualism shape developmental phenomena. Developmental theory, research designs, and interventions formulated around an understanding of normative (but possibly different) cultural paths of development is essential to establish an empirical foundation about which service delivery and social policy can contribute in positive ways to ethnically diverse communities (Fisher, Hatashita-Wong, & Isman, 1999). An applied developmental science that reflects the multicultural demographic landscape of America, that goes beyond conceptualizing members from different ethnic groups as minorities, and that moves toward understanding the unique developmental trajectories of racial and ethnic minorities is essential for creating sound theoretically and empirically based social programs (Fisher, Jackson, & Villarruel, 1997). In this section we highlight three areas critical to the construction of sound multicultural theory and application.

Definitions of Race and Ethnicity

In scientific and public discourse, the terms *race* and *ethnicity* have been used categorically in the absence of clear definitions of what these terms mean (Jensen & Hoagwood, 1997; Yee, Fairchild, Weizman, & Wyatt, 1993). Racial definitions represent a fluid social phenomenon, continuously shaped and redefined by social, economic, and political forces (Chan & Hune, 1995; Omi & Winant, 1986). All too often these meanings—when applied to ethnic minority populations in the United States—carry connotations of lives characterized by lower socioeconomic status and urban life and mask an understanding of the complexities of intraindividual differences within racial, ethnic, and cultural groups and the significance of these terms for the individual, the public, and the scientific establishment (Cocking, 1994; Heath, 1997; Helms, 1996; Oboler, 1995; Ogbu, 1994; Stanfield, 1993; Zuckerman, 1990). For example, racial categorizations are used to define groups that are socially constructed on the basis of physical similarities assumed to reflect phenotypic expressions of shared genotypes; therefore, they may have little psychological meaning outside of studying reactions to how one is treated by others on the basis of racial characteristics (Oboler, 1995; Phinney, 1996; Ragin & Hein, 1993). Similarly, the term *ethnicity* refers to groups that are socially constructed on the basis of assumed cultural, linguistic, religious, and historical similarities (Cross, 1991; Fisher et al, 1997; Padilla, 1995). However, ethnic membership is not a static quality; rather, it is a dynamic process of communities that individuals may choose to identify with or from which to exclude themselves (Dennis, 1993; Gimenéz, 1992).

To ensure that the construction of programs and policies based upon developmental research will address the needs of all individuals and families, applied developmental scientists need to move away from the use of static definitions of race and ethnicity and begin to explore the contextual and dynamic aspects of these dimensions of groups and individuals. When designing and describing research and interventions, applied developmental scientists need to carefully consider and explicitly describe the theoretical, empirical, and social frameworks upon which their definitions of race and ethnicity are used to identify participant populations and to allow their research findings to be evaluated within the context of continuously changing scientific and societal conceptions of these definitions (Fisher et al., 2002).

Sensitivity to Within-Group Differences and Individual Factors In addition to reconceptualizing definitions of the terms *race* and *ethnicity,* applied developmental scientists face challenges in their efforts to define the ethnic group membership of individuals and families whose development they seek to understand and promote. The unfortunate tendency to categorize participants into broad panethnic labels (e.g., Black, Hispanic, Asian, or American Indian rather than Caribbean or African American, Puerto Rican or Colombian, Korean or Japanese, Navajo or Sioux) dilutes and obscures moderating effects of national origin, immigration history, acculturation, religion, and tradition on normative and maladaptive development (Fisher et al., 1997; Fisher et al., 2002; LaFromboise, Hardin, Coleman, & Gerton, 1993; Rumbaut, 1991; Spencer, Swanson, & Cunningham, 1991). The use of panethnic terms also can produce overgeneralizations about the nature of ethnic minority development, which neglects the unique differences among individuals within various racial, ethnic, and cultural groups and masks the influence on mental health of racial, ethnic, mixed-race, or bicultural self-identification (Mio, Trimble, Arredondo, Cheatham, & Sue, 1999; Oboler, 1995; Ogbu, 1994; Root, 1992; Trimble, 1990).

A corollary to overgeneralizations caused by panethnic categorizations is the tendency to ignore the role of race and ethnicity in development. A social characteristics model of development erroneously assumes that intergroup ethnic differences can be explained by variations in demographic factors such as income, education, and employment status . Such an approach ignores the independent historical and contemporary role of culture and minority group status and identification on development and obscures influences on positive development of stressors associated with immigration, acculturation, intergenerational cultural conflict, and exposure to racial and ethnic discrimination (Biafora et al., 1993; Chun, 1995; Fishbein, 2002; Fisher et al., 2000; Klonoff et al., 1999; Slonim-Nevo, 1992; Spencer, 1995; Steele, 1997; Terrell, Terrell, & Miller, 1993)

Moving Away From Comparative and Deficit Approaches to Ethnic Minority Development To produce knowledge that will best serve the needs of ethnic minority individuals and families, applied developmental scientists move away from the historical use of comparative research designs in which the developmental patterns of non-Hispanic White or other ethnic majority groups serve as the standard of mental health and in which ethnic differences are interpreted as group deficits (Busch-Rossnagel, 1992; Graham, 1992; Heath, 1997; McAdoo, 1990; Padilla, 1995; Takanishi, 1994). When such an approach is applied to policies directed at medical, economic, and mental health disparities between ethnic minority and majority groups, interventions may be inappropriately geared to unproven genetic, familial, or cultural factors ignoring the destructive influence of discriminatory public policies on the quality of schools, access to drugs, employment opportunities, exposure to violence, and inequities in criminal justice proceedings in the lives of American ethnic minority groups (Fisher et al., 2002).

Social policies and development promoting programs will benefit from applied developmental science's incorporation of noncomparative methodologies that stress the careful documentation of demographic parameters (e.g., language, community networks, the role of extended and fictive kin) conducted through interviews in an individual's language of preference (e.g., Diaz-Soto, 1989). Such an approach shifts the lens of applied developmental science toward the documentation of assets, strengths, and resiliencies that exist in individuals, families, and the environments in which they interact so that the characteristics associated with normative and positive development can be utilized in the formation of developmental theory, programs, and policies (Connell, Spencer, & Aber, 1994; Fisher et al., 1997; Scales, Benson, Leffert, & Blyth, 2000; Spencer, 1995).

Dissemination: Giving Child Development Knowledge Away

As the situation of children has deteriorated across the past decades (D. Hamburg, 1992; Hernandez, 1993; Lerner, 1995), organizations committed to helping children and families have increasingly realized that efforts—if they are to be maximally effective—must be based in what we know about child and youth development and about the impact of different types of influences on the development of children from diverse backgrounds and of different ages. At the same time, scientists—even those who do so-called basic research—have also recognized the deteriorating plight of America's children and as a result have begun to assume some responsibility for ensuring that their research results are disseminated to policy makers, service providers, and other nonacademic audiences. Consequently, there has been and continues to be growth in the United States in recent years in the numbers and types of projects committed to using information from research to improve the lives of children, youth, and families.

ADS fully emphasizes the importance of the dissemination of research information to nonacademic audiences. All dissemination efforts are based on the idea that research on child development provides much critically useful information of relevance to parenting and family decision-making and to the design and evaluation of programs and policies serving children and families. Yet, such information is too frequently relegated to academic journals and is not disseminated to the public, to the staff of programs serving children, to evaluators of such programs, to policy makers, to funders, or to others who work on children's behalf. Such dissemination not only has the potential to improve the work that is done on children's behalf, but it is also critical to maintaining a firm and substantial national commitment to funding research on child development.

Researchers are concerned with the quality of information. The purpose of academics in pursuing dissemination is to make information available to the full array of constituencies—public and private—that are concerned with the well-being of children and to policy makers and funders who set priorities and funding levels for scientific research. Because researchers' dissemination efforts do not proceed from a partisan special interest and because they do not advocate for particular partisan purposes or positions, they maintain a political neutrality that does not always characterize other dissemination efforts. For this reason, dissemination—giving child development knowledge away—as former chair of the SRCD's Committee on Child Development, Public Policy, and Public Information, Richard A. Weinberg, described it, is a particularly useful service for applied researchers to undertake to complement their primary concern with research and education (Sherrod, 1999).

Broad-based dissemination—especially through the various media—requires both specific expertise and a network of relevant contacts (McCall, 1992). ADS training is designed to equip the future researcher with the expertise to work with the media, to testify before congress, and to establish the necessary contacts to pursue these ends. Several lessons about the media are noteworthy.

First, even in a time of heightened legislative activity, the media are primarily interested in research information that is new and groundbreaking in some way. Relevance of known facts to policy decisions and implications of what we know for legislative directions are not sufficient to engage the media's attention. This situation indicates the need to educate the media, the public, and legislators about the general importance of research-based information. Information may not be the only factor influencing legislation or the public will, but it should make a contribution. This orientation of the media indicates the need to help nonscientists understand the nature of research and to increase their interest in basic research as well as research immediately relevant to policies. Information should be valued because of its relevance for the issues at hand, not just because it is new or groundbreaking. Old information can be just as useful as the new.

Second, researchers must be trained to serve as spokespersons to the media in specific, specialized fields, and they must be willing to do so. The media are interested in personal contact with the relevant researchers, and local media are particularly interested in local researchers' perspectives. The field of developmental research needs a resource network of researchers who are ready and capable of communicating with the media and with legislators. Researchers need training in interacting with the various forms of the media. ADS pursues these ends by considering dissemination and developing expertise in dissemination as important as statistics and research methods. Universities can be mobilized to attend to dissemination because they are interested in publicity. Moreover, researchers with appropriate training, as provided by ADS, are able to assemble what is known in specific areas in a clear, communicable fashion; that is, ADS researchers have an interest in dissemination because they have learned how to communicate effectively outside their fields.

Several years ago, the social policy committee (Committee on Child Development, Public Policy, and Public Information) of SRCD prepared the Directory of Organizations Concerned with Public Information of Relevance to Child Development (Rosenberg & Sherrod, 1994). More than 60 such efforts across the country were identified and one-page summaries provided. That directory is now out of print, but attention to dissemination in the field has continued to grow (Sherrod, 1999). ADS is of course not the only contributor to this growth in dissemination in the field, but it has made a contribution. More important is that it elevates dissemination to a necessary, important, and respectful undertaking for researchers. Researchers accept interaction with the media for what it is. They do not fear misrepresentation. They do their part to disseminate the information from their research.

The methods of ADS, which have been described, generate unique contributions to research on development across the life span. Attention to assessment and early intervention, evaluation research, multiculturalism, and dissemination are as critical to ADS as research methods and statistics are to psychology generally. Because these methods are such an integral part of the field, training in ADS also must have a special quality. In the next section, we describe the nature of training graduate students in

ADS. The training program in Applied Development Psychology at Fordham University exemplifies the characteristics described in the next section.

TRAINING

What are the criteria that mark distinguished training programs in ADS? We believe that the recommendations from the National Conference on Graduate Education in the Applications of Developmental Science Across the Life Span (Fisher et al., 1993) are still valid today. The curriculum outlined there proposes the development of competence in four domains—development theory and content, research methods, application strategies, and professional issues—and notes that field experiences are one criterion for discriminating applied developmental programs from traditional developmental programs.

The recommendations concluded with the recognition that the ADS perspective requires a multidisciplinary emphasis, which might lead some to believe that training must occur in settings freed from disciplinary constraints. Given the nature of the academic enterprise, most training is still done—and is likely to continue to be done—within discipline-delineated departments and schools. The breadth of the discipline may vary from the traditional arts and sciences departments, such as psychology and sociology with multiple specializations, to the applications of the disciplines, such as departments or schools of education or social work, to fields that pride themselves on their multidisciplinary nature, such as child development or human ecology.

An understanding of the several issues affecting higher education is necessary if these discipline-based departments are to implement efficiently the recommendations for training in ADS. The first issue is that change within a single academic unit (e.g., a department) is usually easier than change among multiple academic units. Thus, training programs should identify in which of the four curricular domains the academic unit can provide training within itself. We suggest that by definition, a discipline-delineated department can and should be providing training in the theory and content of development. Likewise, the mastery of the basic research methods for a discipline should be the first step in this domain. For psychology, this process would include understanding of the classic experiment with random assignment to condition. With such a basis, the applied developmental psychologist can then gain the understanding as to how the experiment may be limited for the understanding of the complexity of human development. Because we cannot randomly assign majority or minority status or cultural background, our research designs do not control the potential confounding variables, such as languages, education, income level, and so forth. Such comparisons do little to enhance our understanding of the role that psychological processes underlying culture play in development (Busch-Rossnagel, 1992). However, without a discipline-based foundation in basic research methods, we ignore the advances of science and run the risk of common-sense errors such as proving the null hypothesis or attributing causality to correlated events. A final area in which to begin with discipline-delineated training is for assessment and intervention techniques, whose validities are closely tied to discipline-based research methods.

Exposure to multiple disciplines can help applied development scientists in training to understand the limits of the basic research methods of their discipline. In addition, such exposure is critical for training in program evaluation, which must recognize the complexities of our biosocial existence, the economic realities of intervention (or of failure to intervene), and the policies affecting all applications of ADS.

Likewise, multidisciplinary understanding is the foundation of field experiences, which are the distinguishing element of ADS training (Fisher et al., 1993). Consistent with bidirectional communication, identification of the status of students as individuals in training must be an inherent aspect of ADS field experiences, particularly those involving service delivery. Although this issue may be a source of continuing discussion in other fields (Miller & Rodwell, 1997), the ADS approach clearly calls for communities—particularly those of society's more vulnerable populations—to be a part of the training process. We suggest, then, that in ADS field experiences, the in-training status of students be clearly labeled, for instance, with terms such as intern.

Negotiating University Support

McCall (1990) suggested the identification of an integrating theme as one of the first steps in establishing a unit for interdisciplinary education and research. The integrating theme should be an issue that can be addressed from the perspective of many different discipline-based departments; an example would be children, youth, and families or university-community partnerships. We note that themes (or at least the buzzwords that sell them) may come and go, but the areas of educational degrees should have staying power. Thus, we suggest that degrees from identifiable disciplines are more marketable than are fields that require an explanation. However, higher education is rapidly embracing certificates, which usually require a less tedious approval process and thus might be based on a theme.

The issue of marketability highlights a primary issue affecting all of higher education. Gone are the days when adequate justifications for a program were faculty interest and expertise. Today program development requires consideration of a series of questions. Is there a population of individuals interested in training in this area? What will be the value-added result of training in this area? ADS professionals often have a good understanding of the needs of children, adolescents, and families, but the way in which training in ADS will meet those needs may require changes in public policy (e.g., more funding for youth and family initiatives). Thus, administrators are likely to challenge not the societal need for skilled professionals in this area, but the needs of the marketplace and the opportunities currently available as student outcomes. In addition, ADS professionals need to articulate how proposals for new courses, certificates, or degrees will affect the status quo. Will new courses reduce the availability of senior faculty for other needs, such as introductory courses for undergraduates? Will new certificates or degrees cannibalize students from other programs, such as clinical or community psychology?

McCall (1990) also noted that building a base of support and securing funding were necessary first steps for interdisciplinary initiatives, and these efforts are likely to bring to light the key issues underlying the planning at the institution providing the training program. Education is becoming more businesslike as universities adopt revenue and cost allocation models and unit- (school- or college-) based budgeting. These models emphasize educational units, such as schools or colleges as being at the heart of the educational enterprise. Therefore, they identify all revenue and costs as being generated or associated with a particular unit. For direct revenues and costs, such as tuition revenue and the faculty salaries associated with instruction, the identity of the unit that generated the revenue or cost is usually straightforward.

However, many activities conducted by universities are not directly tied to a particular unit, and the revenues or costs of these activities are allocated to the unit by some agreed-upon formula. Thus, the cost of the human resources office might be allocated on the percent of employees in a given unit out of the total number of employees. The revenue generated by the football team (or the costs associated with the team if the balance is negative) might be allocated on the basis of the percentage of undergraduate students in and alumni from the unit, under the assumption that it is the undergraduate students and alumni who benefit from or support the presence of football on campus. The cost of the office supporting research might be allocated on the basis of the percentage of faculty and graduate students to indicate that the research process is most associated with faculty development and graduate study. Such models apparently inhibit cross-unit collaboration by assigning costs for activities conducted outside the unit. However, in a valid unit-based budgeting model, revenues and costs are consistently associated with the unit—or multiple units—that generate them, and this practice facilitates planning and longer-term budget projections and commitments.

Building a base of support for the long-term viability of training programs may require adjustments in the faculty reward system. For example, how do team-taught courses count both for faculty workload and for personnel decisions such as tenure, promotion, and merit awards? McCall's notion of an independent coordinator may be applied here, particularly for the benefit of junior faculty. An individual, often an administrator, who is committed to ADS training may be necessary to propose compromises that will facilitate the multidisciplinary training.

Thus, ADS training in the four curricular areas begins in discipline-based departments but must branch out to provide the multidisciplinary exposure that is at the heart of ADS. Multidisciplinary work in turn requires new patterns of collaboration within universities that might include awarding certificates, explicit statements of revenue, and cost allocation models, and faculty rewards. In the end, McCall's proposal to market, not sell will be the key to the long-term viability of training programs. If the vision and the values of ADS are operationalized in a program that attracts students and funding, the results speak for themselves and will change the universities in which they are found

VISION AND VALUES

The vision inherent in ADS and the values it promotes derive from its methods. Vision and values represent the application of methods to important issues in developmental research in the real world. In the following section, we review the vision and values of ADS by describing its approach to ethical issues in research, the design of social policies for children and families, the prevention of problems and the promotion of positive development, and the facilitation of university-community partnerships.

Ethical Issues in Applied Developmental Science

ADS raises distinctive ethical issues. The developmental perspective raises questions about the age at which interventions should be initiated and whether an intervention at any one point in the life span is sufficient to sustain desired outcomes (Fisher & Tryon, 1990; Fisher, 1993; Lerner & Tubman, 1990). The emphasis in ADS on individual differences and within-person change challenges applied developmental scientists consulting to the courts or policy makers to distinguish knowledge based upon mean group differences from the ability to predict the developmental trajectory of any one person. Applied developmental scientists must also guard against personal and societal biases that may shape research design and data interpretation to fit contemporary norms rather than the actual experience of individuals and families studied (Fisher, 2002; Fisher et al., 2002; Fisher & Wallace, 2000).

The ethical concerns of applied developmental scientists reflect the moral values of beneficence, nonmaleficence, autonomy, and justice. Applied developmental scientists strive to design studies and intervention programs that maximize good outcomes and minimize harm, respect the autonomy and privacy rights of individuals and families, and provide equal access to the benefits of research and social policies. In this section we highlight just some of the ethical challenges of applied developmental science.

Maximizing Benefits and Minimizing Risks of Applied Developmental Science

When developmental science is applied to practical problems facing individuals and families, the potential to promote human welfare increases along with the potential to inflict harm. Both positive and negative results of research examining the correlates of social problems as well as the design and evaluation of development enhancing programs can have long-lasting impact on social attitudes and social policy. For example, one problem for the ADS investigator is that research rarely yields the single-factor, cause-and-effect statements that practitioners and policy makers want to hear. Another problem is that in responding to policy makers' desire to implement least-cost interventions, applied developmental scientists may test social programs in their weakest form, thus risking rejection of potentially valuable interventions or stigmatization of members of the vulnerable populations who were the focus of the intervention (Fisher & Wallace, 2000; Lewis, 1994). Applied developmental scientists must resist pressures to make statements that go beyond the data, to design developmental interventions that compromise maximal enrichment, or conduct program evaluations biased toward intervention failure.

The cultural and economic diversity of the American population poses the risk that a developmental intervention that has proved successful with one segment of population will be assumed by policy makers to work for a different segment, when in fact it may be ineffective or harmful; thus, applied developmental scientists must be mindful that measures of psychological constructs or interventions designed to promote positive development for one group may or may not have the same or even similar psychometric properties or patterns of effectiveness for other groups differing in developmental level, socioeconomic status, geographic setting, ethnicity, or culture (CNPAAEMI, 2000; Knight & Hill, 1998; Laosa, 1990; Parron, 1997).

To avoid contributing to the implementation of ineffective social policies, the misapplication of developmental principles to real-world problems, and an erroneous public understanding of self and others, applied developmental scientists must strive to (a) conduct research and select program outcome measures that are as close as possible to the phenomena addressed, (b) ensure the reliability and the developmental and cultural equivalence of assessment instruments, (c) ensure that intervention methods are monitored and reliably applied, and (d) obtain an appropriate balance between good experimental design and the obligation to provide fair access to research and intervention (Fisher et al., 2002; Fisher & Tryon, 1990).

Informed Consent

In research and intervention, informed consent is viewed as a primary means of protecting research participants' autonomy and welfare. Applied developmental scientists must provide individuals and (when appropriate) their guardians with information about research procedures, assessments, or interventions that might influence their willingness to participate themselves or allow their children to participate. Such information typically includes a description of the nature and goals of the procedures, foreseeable risks or benefits of participation, the extent as well as limits of confidentiality, and the voluntary nature of participation. Vulnerable families seeking services in community mental health or medical centers may be concerned that failure to consent would result in discontinuation of services. To protect the voluntary nature of consent to participate in intervention research or program evaluation, applied developmental scientists should inform individuals and families about the experimental nature of the intervention, services that will or will not be available to the control group(s), how assignment to treatment and control groups will be made, and available services if an individual does not wish to participate or wishes to withdraw after a program has begun.

Federal regulations and state law require the permission of a guardian when minors are involved in research or treatment. With a few exceptions (e.g., mature or emancipated minors), children under the age of 18 do not have the legal capacity to consent and—depending on their age and the complexity of the research or intervention context—may lack the cognitive capacity to comprehend the nature of their participation and rights (Abramovitch, Freedman, Thoden, & Nikolich, 1991; Bruzzese & Fisher, 2003; Ruck, Abramovitch, & Keating, 1998; Weithorn, 1983). However, out of respect for children's developing autonomy, in addition to guardian permission, federal regulations and professional codes of conduct require a minor's affirmative agreement (assent) unless participation provides the possibility of direct benefit not available elsewhere (American Psychological Association, 2002; Department of Health and Human Services [DHHS], 1991).

The guardian permission requirement assumes that children come from a reasonably secure and loving family. However, the high-risk conditions that bring children to the attention of applied developmental scientists (e.g., child abuse, health-compromising sexual behaviors, runaway youth) may make obtaining consent from identified guardians difficult, place the child in jeopardy, or violate a teenager's privacy rights (Brooks-Gunn & Rotheram-Borus, 1994). Thus, federal and state laws allow the waiver of guardian permission for research and intervention when such waivers would afford greater child protection (DHHS, 1991; Fisher et al., 1999). When such permission is waived, applied developmental scientists must ensure that an independent-consent advocate for the minor is present during recruitment to verify the minor's understanding of the research or intervention, to support his or her preferences, and to ensure that participation is voluntary (Fisher, Hoagwood, & Jensen, 1996).

Difficulties in acquiring guardian consent from at-risk youth have led in recent years to renewed debate over the use of passive consent (asking parents to respond only if they do not wish their children to participate) as a means of increasing research participation of underrepresented populations. An implicit assumption underlying advocacy for passive consent is that a caring and knowledgeable guardian would perceive the research as important and desirable and that parents who do not return consent forms either lack the knowledge to appreciate the importance of the research or are unconcerned about their children's welfare. The ethical dangers of passive consent are illustrated in the narratives of parents and children who view the procedure as a deceptive means of undermining the purpose of parental permission and of coercing and encouraging children to deceive their parents (Fisher, 2002).

Confidentiality and Disclosure

Applied developmental scientists conducting research or program evaluation related to risk and resilience in vulnerable populations often uncover confidential information about illegal behaviors, mental health problems, and health-compromising behaviors that may be unknown to family members or others concerned with a participant's welfare (Fisher, Hoagwood, et al., 1996). In some instances, disclosure is required by law. All 50 states have laws requiring mental health professionals to report suspected child abuse or neglect, and at least 13 states require researchers, as members of the general citizenry, to do the same (Liss, 1994). Following the case of *Tarasoff v. Regents of the University of California* (1976), a number of states have duty-to-protect laws that require health professionals to inform a third party of the prospect of being harmed by a client. Although there has yet to be case law in the area of research, applied developmental scientists need to give appropriate consideration to whether their relationship to a research participant meets the duty to protect (Appelbaum & Rosenbaum, 1989).

Decisions regarding whether to disclose confidential information when reporting is not required by law are more ethically complex. During the course of a study or program evaluation, some individuals without documented mental disorders may reveal suicidal ideation or other self-harming behaviors. Applied developmental scientists need to be knowledgeable about procedures for determining and managing suicidal intent (Pearson, Stanley, King, & Fisher, 2001) and criteria to determine whether other self-endangering behaviors that might be anticipated to arise during the course of research or program evaluation (e.g., use of a toxic inhalant to get high) require action and whether such actions involve disclosing the information to other concerned adults or assisting the participant in obtaining appropriate treatment (Fisher, 2002).

Research procedures and assessments for program evaluation may reveal additional dangerous but not life-threatening behaviors such as substance abuse, delinquency, truancy, or high-risk sexual behaviors. In these situations disclosures to school counselors or child protection agencies regarding risk behaviors may harm participants or their families if those informed react punitively, react incompetently, or entangle the family in criminal proceedings. In these situations routine procedures for assuring confidentiality may not be sufficient to protect participants from subpoena stemming from criminal investigations or custody disputes. An applied developmental scientist can apply for a certificate of confidentiality under 301(d) of the Public Health Service Act, which provides immunity from any government or civil order to disclose identifying information contained in research records (Hoagwood, 1994; Melton, 1990).

The extent to which keeping information about participant risk confidential or disclosing it to others is further clouded by emerging evidence that a significant proportion of teenagers and their parents want investigators to actively assist them in obtaining help for problems revealed during the course of research (Fisher, 2002; Fisher, Higgins-D'Alessandro, et al., 1996; O'Sullivan & Fisher, 1997). Ethical decision making in such circumstances requires that the applied developmental scientist (a) consider the possible risks that might be uncovered during the course of a study or intervention, the legal obligations, and the reporting expectations of prospective participants; (b) clarify the extent to which information obtained is derived from reliable and valid measures of risk; (c) identify resources that can best serve the interests of participants in need of referral or direct intervention; (d) based on the prior considerations, determine an appropriate confidentiality and disclosure policy; and (e) during informed consent, share with prospective participants and their guardians the policy that the investigator will follow (Fisher, 2000, 2002).

Design of Social Policies for Children and Families

It is essential that psychologists be present at the policy-making table. Much policy is oriented toward changing human behavior—reducing high-risk sexual behavior, preventing teenage pregnancy, improving school performance, or reducing substance abuse. Hence, it is unfortunate that America's policy making has been disproportionately driven by economists and scholars other than psychologists who study behavior. Not only is it appropriate for psychologists to be involved in policy making, but they also have an important contribution to make. Their knowledge of human behavior and development is indispensable. If we are to design policies that improve the lives of people, it is critical that psychologists who understand behavior and developmentalists who study children and families be involved (Sherrod, 2002).

Furthermore, policies and programs are part of the ecology in which people live and hence are critical areas for psychological research. As we have already noted, it is important to study programs as contexts for youth development (Sherrod, 1997). Bronfenbrenner and Morris (1998) have provided psychologists with the critically important ideas derived from ecological systems theory that describe the importance of different levels of this policy context. For example, there are macrosystem variables of culture and social norms, exosystem variables involving social institutions, mesosystem variables involving family and schools, and microsystem variables reflecting the world of the individual child.

Psychological research, because of its focus on individual behavior, has disproportionately concerned itself with proximal rather than distal variables, with the microsystem and mesosystem in Bronfenbrenner's scheme. That focus has changed to some extent during the past decade as attention to context and culture has increased. However, it is time that policies and programs be included as part of the mesosystem and macrosystem studied by developmentalists, along with families and schools as social institutions that have an important influence on socialization and development.

From this perspective, policy work is not substantially different from clinical attention; it is just focused at a macrolevel rather than trying to solve individual problems. It might be viewed as a developmental extension of community psychology. Hence, it is logical and perfectly consistent with its field goals that psychology include policy making in the areas to which it attends. Psychology programs such as the applied developmental program at Fordham University includes such curricula as part of their mission, but the importance is too great to be limited to a few select programs. Policy making should be as core to the field as are research methods and statistics. If policy makers are to develop effective policies and programs, it is essential that psychologists be involved, and policies and programs provide important areas for psychological research.

To some extent, it is easier to involve psychology in the policy making process than it is to include research. Although psychology is a science, it also has a practitioner element, which increases its relevance to policy. Clinical psychology, forensics, and industrial-organizational psychology are applied branches of psychology, although they tend to function at an individual rather than a systems level. However, theoretically, there is no substantive reason that policy making should not be added to this array (Sherrod, 1997).

Although it should be obvious that information from research should be useful to policy making, that usefulness is in fact too frequently not recognized. First, other factors such as ideology or cost outweigh information. Second, it is frequently difficult for research to provide the clear, direct singular-answer type of guidance that is needed for policy making. Third, we have noted that social problems change faster than our ability to generate information to address them (Prewitt, 1995). Hence, pressure is relatively constant against using research to guide policy; thus, the need to base policy making in research must be always on the agenda of the applied researcher (Zigler & Hall, 2000; Zigler, Kagan, & Hall, 1996).

Perhaps at no point in the history of the United States has it been more important to direct effective policy solutions to such problems. There are a variety of serious social problems confronting children, youth, and families today that require our immediate and concerted efforts. Too often, however, policies and programs are based on ideology, misguided efforts, or solutions designed with too little information. Therefore, the importance of building and maintaining substantial connections between research and policy has never been more important.

Elsewhere, Sherrod (2002) outlined and elaborated seven points about developing and maintaining a close interaction between research and policy. These points included the following:

1. It is necessary to use both demographic information summarizing the problem and research study findings that address the underlying causes and consequences of the problem. Both basic and applied research are needed.
2. Developmental appropriateness and developmental continuity are crucial considerations; that is, interventions must be designed to target the developmental needs of the age period for which they are focused, and it is also important to at-

tend to the developmental mechanisms by which interventions my generate effects that would be expected to last long beyond the end of the program. Furthermore, it would be interesting to ask about the cumulative impact across the life span of interventions experienced at different ages.

3. There are no magic bullets; that is, there are no interventions that are going to solve all the problems faced by disadvantaged children and youth. Short-lived interventions can be expected to help, not to fix lives. Sustained social commitment is required to help those children and families with needs.
4. It is essential that we adopt a diverse approach to the design of policies and to their assessment and evaluation. We have to be creative about solutions to social problems and open to different forms of evaluative research so that the method suits the question.
5. Dissemination is also a key ingredient of the research-policy interaction, but the target of dissemination must be clear and varies by both the problem being addressed and the policy being proposed.
6. Cost-benefit analyses and recommended means of achieving costs have to be part of the efforts to help children and families; otherwise, failure is assured.
7. Regardless of how well one pursues the goal of using research to guide policy formation, even while attending to all the points made herein, research will be only one of many factors driving policy. The research practitioner has to recognize this fact, do the best he or she can, and not despair.

Most researchers today who are interested in policy found their interest through some indirect route because psychology programs do not currently devote much attention to policy. The younger generation of researchers is, however, very interested in research-policy connections; there is, for example, an SRCD social policy network for students (Susman-Stillman and Brown, 1997). We must exploit this interest by developing institutional mechanisms for young scholars to follow a career path that allows them to use research to guide policy. One such route is fellowships such as the Congressional Science Fellowships of SRCD. ADS and training programs such as the one at Fordham University offer another such mechanism. Attention to the prevention of problems and the promotion of development (covered in the next section) offers one avenue for eliciting the interest of developmental scientists seeking an applied orientation.

Prevention and Promotion

In recent years, a new approach has arisen in the youth development field. This approach moves beyond treatment and even beyond prevention to the promotion of development. This focus on the positive development of youth moves beyond fixing problems or eliminating defects. For several decades, research and policy have been devoted to identifying and correcting problems of youth: high-risk sexual behavior, teenage pregnancy, school failure and dropout, substance use and abuse, violence, and crime. It was from this focus that the emphasis on risk factors became prominent. Because not all youth succumb equally to risks, the concept of resiliency emerged, and prevention efforts were developed. Although these efforts have enjoyed some success in reducing risks and health-compromising behaviors, their achievement is constrained by limited funding and by the limited evidence of sustained behavior change after the program has ended (Benson, Scales, Leffert, & Roehlkkepartain, 1999; Scales et al., 2000).

A focus on promoting the positive development of youth rather than on fixing problems leads to the development-promoting qualities of families and communities and to policies that make up for the shortfalls of the environments. If we provide the supports that youth need, all have the potential to beat the odds (Larsen, 2000).

This approach is based on the contributions of several groups such as the Search Institute, the International Youth Foundation, and the Youth Policy Forum (Benson, Leffert, Scales, & Blyth, 1998). Both external and internal assets of youth have been identified and correlated with environmental and individual resiliency factors. Internal factors include commitment to learning, positive values, social competencies, and positive identity. Broad categories of external factors include family and community supports, empowerment, boundaries and expectations, and constructive use of time. The presence of risk behaviors is inversely correlated with assets. These assets, of course, interact in complex ways and vary substantially by community (Benson et al., 1998; Scales et al., 2000). However, this approach demonstrates how providing the means to meet youth's multiple developmental needs by ensuring protection, support, and opportunities across these important contexts is a preferred focus for intervention.

The interest in positive youth development has focused primarily on adolescents. The National Research Council of the Institute of Medicine (2000) recently outlined a set of the key ingredients in strengths-based programs that promote effective development and support family coping (Tolan, Sherrod, Gorman-Smith, & Henry, 2003):

1. Programs must have clear goals and intended outcomes.
2. The content or focus is age appropriate but challenging.
3. The involvement is based on active learning processes.
4. The program provides a positive and safe environment.
5. There are adequate materials and facilities to conduct the program.
6. The staff is well prepared, supported, and stable.
7. The staff is culturally competent and conducts outreach to diverse groups.
8. The program or approach should be related to and work with parents and existing community groups and organizations.
9. The program elicits, supports, and promotes parental involvement and does not separate youth needs from family or parental needs but rather integrates them.
10. The program or approach is conducted within a learning organization; the organization is willing to adapt, improve, and develop as the setting, youth needs, and opportunities shift.

This focus on the promotion of positive development is, however, relevant to all periods of the life span. ADS applies it equally from conception to the end of life (e.g., see Baltes et al., 1998).

Another critical aspect of the ADS vision is university-community partnerships, which have arisen in recent years to promote a new kind of relationship between researchers, their study participants, and the communities that may benefit from research.

University-Community Partnerships

In recent years, resulting in part from perspectives and principles inherent in ADS, a new approach to research has arisen. In this approach, researchers do not set themselves up as experts to study subjects in the form of community residents, schoolchildren, or participants in youth programs. Instead, the research project is established as a partnership between the researcher and the participants in his or her study. In fact, certain universities, especially the land-grant ones, have established partnerships with the communities in which they reside (Kellogg Commission, 1999). Individual research projects then exist in the context of these partnerships. Universities share their expertise and other resources, and community institutions and residents share their perspectives, their local wisdom, and their willingness to cooperate with research (Fisher, 2002; Lerner & Fisher, 1994; Lerner & Simon, 1998a, b; Sherrod, 1998a). These partnerships between typical academic institutions and community organizations and community residents carry many implications for research and for the functioning of the university. Universities adopting this stance to their communities have been described as outreach universities (Lerner & Simon, 1998a).

These outreach universities carry the full array of characteristics of ADS. They blur the distinction between basic and applied research. They bring a new perspective on evaluation research, one that uses programs and policies to generate new information about children and youth. They contribute to the dissemination of science, thereby increasing its usefulness to policy and programs. Finally—and perhaps most important—these university-community collaborations contribute to the reciprocity of communication between academics and others; too often academics have assumed a unidirectional flow of information from them to others. A bidirectional flow increases the chances that anyone will listen to academics and increases the usefulness of the communication to them. It becomes a learning endeavor for all involved parties (Sherrod, 1998b).

The outreach university orientation carries an equal number of implications for the nature of institutions of higher learning. First, by reaching out to precollegiate schools in their communities, universities can contribute to the reform of precollegiate education. Mentorship and internship programs are one vehicle, for example. Second, it can contribute to the reform of higher education. Although most of our attention to educational reform has been at the precollegiate level, collegiate education is also in need of review and revision. For example, compared to the widespread concern for high school dropout, almost no attention has been paid to dropout from college. Yet dropping out of college can have equally serious consequences for the dropout, and minorities are at particularly high risk for dropout. Third, in this historical moment of rapid and extensive social change in technology, medicine, and most other domains, lifelong learning becomes essential. Certainly, universities are the vehicle to lifelong learning, beginning with their approach to collegiate education. Finally, universities can extend their reach to serve community residents such as individuals now required to move off welfare, as well as the more typical young adult college student population (Sherrod, 1998a).

We have also previously argued that the outreach university provides a means of reconnecting philanthropy and science (Sherrod, 1998a). When philanthropy originated early in this century, science was seen as a means of identifying the core causes of social problems so that appropriate strategies could be devised to effectively address such problems. As philanthropy has increasingly turned its attention to systematic social reform during the latter half of the century (Wisely, 1998), science has been viewed to be less relevant, and a broad chiasm has developed between philanthropy and research. The outreach university has the potential to readdress this relationship and reforge connections that could prove useful to both constituencies (Sherrod, 1998a).

Thus, the potential contributions and impacts of the university partnerships are many and varied. The number of such efforts has increased substantially in recent years; they are a core ingredient of ADS.

CONCLUSIONS

In this chapter we have used descriptions of the methods, values, and vision of ADS to illustrate its unique contributions to developmental science. Although all developmental science need not be applied, we believe that ADS has a very important and original contribution to make; that is why we have devoted our program at Fordham University to it and why we have devoted our research careers to its furtherance.

The methods of ADS—assessment and early intervention, evaluation research, multiculturalism, and dissemination—provide tools as important and as generally useful as research methods and statistics in the broader field of psychology. These methods lead to concerns for ethics in research, to the design of social policies, to prevention and promotion, and to university-community partnerships, which when taken together define values and create a vision that define a truly unique new approach to developmental science. The implications for training are of course profound, but the existence of an applied developmental training program at Fordham University for now more than 10 years demonstrate that it is doable.

Furthermore, developmental science has a place for many approaches; basic research is needed as well as policy-relevant research and policy analysis. But it is fully possible that programs could devote a track to ADS without reorienting their whole program, and we believe the younger generation of researchers are ripe for this approach. We are committed to the field and believe that the future of developmental research will be significantly enhanced by the relatively new approach represented in ADS.

REFERENCES

Abramovitch, R., Freedman, J. L., Thoden, K., & Nikolich, C. (1991). Children's capacity to consent to participation in psychological research: Empirical findings. *Child Development, 62,* 1100–1109.

American Psychological Association. (2002). Ethical principles of psychologists and code of conduct. *American Psychologist.*

American Psychological Association, American Educational Research Associate, & National Council on Measurement in Education. (1974). *Standards for educational and psychological tests.* Washington, DC: American Psychological Association.

Anastasi, A. (1988). *Psychological testing.* New York: Macmillan.

Appelbaum, P. S., & Rosenbaum, A. (1989). Tarasoff and the researcher: Does the duty to protect apply in the research setting? *American Psychologist, 44,* 885–894.

Baltes, P., Lindenberger, U., & Staudinger, U. M. (1998) Life-span theory in developmental psychology. In W. Damon (Series Ed.) & R. M. Lerner (Vol. Ed.), *Handbook of child psychology: Vol. 1. Theoretical models of human development* (5th ed., pp. 1029–1144). New York: Wiley.

Baltes, P., & Reese, H. (1984). The life-span perspective in developmental psychology. In M. Bornstein & M. Lamb (Eds.), *Developmental psychology: An advanced textbook.* Hillsdale, NJ: Erlbaum.

Bandura, A. (1992). A social cognitive approach to the exercise of control over AIDS infection. In R. J. DiClemente (Ed.), *Adolescents and AIDS: A generation in jeopardy.* Newbury Park, CA: Sage.

Benson, P., Scales, P., Leffert, N., & Roehlkkepartain, E. (1999) *A fragile foundation: The state of developmental assets among American youth.* Minneapolis, MN: Search Institute.

Benson, P., Leffert, N., Scales, P., & Blyth, D. (1998). Beyond the village rhetoric: Creating healthy communities for children and adolescents. *Applied Developmental Science, 2,* 138–159.

Biafora, F. A., Jr., Warheit, G. J., Zimmerman, R. S., Gil, A. G., Apospori, E., & Taylor, D. (1993). Racial mistrust and deviant behaviors among ethnically diverse African American adolescent boys. *Journal of Applied Social Psychology, 23,* 891–910.

Bronfenbrenner, U., & Morris, P. A. (1998). The ecology of developmental processes. In W. Damon (Series Ed.) & R. M. Lerner (Vol. Ed.), *Handbook of child psychology: Vol. 1. Theoretical models of human development* (pp. 993–1028). New York: Wiley.

Brooks-Gunn, J., & Rotheram-Borus, M. J. (1994). Rights to privacy in research: Adolescents versus parents. *Ethics & Behavior, 4,* 109–121.

Bruzzese, J. M., & Fisher, C. B. (2003). Assessing and enhancing the research consent capacity of children and youth. *Applied Developmental Science, 7,* 13–26.

Busch-Rossnagel, N. A. (1992). Commonalities between test validity and external validity in basic research on Hispanics. In K. F. Geisinger (Ed.), *Psychological testing of Hispanics* (pp. 195–214). Washington, DC: American Psychological Association.

Busch-Rossnagel, N. A. (1998). *Development in Puerto Rican and Dominican toddlers* (Final Progress Report, Grant HD30590, National Institute of Child Health and Development).

Busch-Rossnagel, N. A. (2002). Creating culturally and community-sensitive measures of development. In A. Higgins (Ed.), *Influential lives: New directions for child and adolescent development.* San Francisco: Jossey-Bass.

Busch-Rossnagel, N. A., Vargas, M., Knauf, D. E., & Planos, R. (1993). Mastery motivation in ethnic minority groups: The sample case of Hispanics. In D. Messer (Ed.), *Mastery motivation in early childhood: Development, measurement and social processes* (pp. 132–148). London: Routledge.

Chan, K. S., & Hune, S. (1995). Racialization and panethnicity: From Asians in America to Asian Americans. In W. D. Hawley & A. W. Jackson (Eds.), *Toward a common destiny: Improving race and ethnic relations in America* (pp. 205–236). San Francisco: Jossey-Bass.

Chun, K. (1995). The myth of Asian American success and its educational ramifications. In D. Nakanishi & T. Nishida (Eds.), *The Asian American educational experience* (pp. 95–112). New York: Routledge.

Clarke-Stewart, A. K., & Allhusen, V. (2002). Nonparental caregiving. In M. Bornstein (Ed.), *Handbook of parenting* (2nd ed.). Newbury Park, CA: Sage.

Connell, J., Aber, J. L., & Walker, G. (1995). How do urban communities affect youth: Using social science research to inform the design and evaluation of comprehensive community initiatives. In J. Connell, A. Kubisch, L. Schorr, & C. Weiss (Eds.), *New approaches to evaluating community initiatives.* New York: The Aspen Institute.

Connell, J. P., Spencer, M. B., & Aber, J. L. (1994). Educational risk and resilience in African American youth: Context, self, action, and outcomes in school. *Child Development, 65,* 493–506.

Council of National Psychological Associations for the Advancement of Ethnic Minority Interests. (2000). *Guidelines for research in ethnic minority communities.* Washington, DC: American Psychological Association.

Cross, W. E. (1991). *Shades of black: Diversity in African-American identity.* Philadelphia: Temple University Press.

Dennis, R. M. (1993). Studying across difference: Race, class and gender in qualitative research. In J. H. Stanfield III & R. M. Dennis (Eds), *Race and ethnicity in research methods* (pp. 53–74). Newbury Park, CA: Sage.

Department of Health and Human Services. (1991, August). Title 45 Public Welfare, Part 46, *Code of Federal Regulations, Protection of Human Subjects.*

Diaz Soto, L. (1989). Relationship between home environment and intrinsic and extrinsic orientation of high achieving and low achieving Puerto Rican children. *Education Research Quarterly, 13,* 22–36.

Fisher, C. B. (1993). Integrating science and ethics in research with high-risk children & youth. *Society for Research in Child Development Public Policy Report, 7,* 1–26.

Fisher, C. B. (2000). Relational ethics in psychological research: One feminist's journey. In M. Brabeck (Ed.), *Practicing feminist ethics in psychology* (pp. 125–142) Washington, DC: American Psychological Association.

Fisher, C. B. (2002). Participant consultation: Ethical insights into parental permission and confidentiality procedures for policy relevant research with youth. In R. M. Lerner, F. Jacobs, & D. Wertlieb (Eds.), *Handbook of applied developmental science* (Vol. 4, pp. 371–396). Thousand Oaks, CA: Sage.

Fisher, C. B., Hatashita-Wong, M., & Isman, L. (1999). Ethical and legal issues in clinical child psychology. In W. K. Silverman & T. H. Ollendick (Eds.), *Developmental issues in the clinical treatment of children and adolescents* (pp. 470–486). Boston: Allyn & Bacon.

Fisher, C. B., Higgins-D'Allesandro, A., Rau, J. M. B., Kuther, T., & Belanger, S. (1996). Reporting and referring research participants: The view from urban adolescents. *Child Development, 67,* 2086–2099.

Fisher, C. B., Hoagwood, K., Duster, T., Grisso, T., Frank, D. A, Macklin, R., et al. (2002). Research ethics for mental health science involving ethnic minority children and youth. *American Psychologist, 57,* 1024–1040.

Fisher, C. B., Hoagwood, K., & Jensen, P. (1996). Casebook on ethical issues in research with children and adolescents with mental disorders. In K. Hoagwood, P. Jensen, & C. B. Fisher (Eds.), *Ethical issues in research with children and adolescents with mental disorders* (pp. 135–238). Hillsdale, NJ: Erlbaum.

Fisher, C, B., Jackson, J., & Villarruel, F. (1997). The study of African American and Latin American children and youth. In W. Damon (Series Ed.) & R. M. Lerner (Ed.), *Handbook of child psychology: Theoretical models of human development* (5th ed., pp. 1145–1207). New York: Wiley.

Fisher, C. B., & Lerner, R. (1994). *Applied developmental psychology.* New York: McGraw-Hill.

Fisher, C. B., & Murray, J. P. (1996). Applied developmental science comes of age. In C. B. Fisher, J. P. Murray, & W. E. Sigel (Eds.), *Graduate training in applied developmental science for diverse disciplines and educational settings* (pp. 1–22). Norwood, NJ: Ablex.

Fisher, C. B., Murray, J. P., & Sigel, I. E. (Eds.). (1996). *Graduate training in applied developmental science for diverse disciplines and educational settings.* Norwood, NJ: Ablex.

Fisher, C. B., & Osofsky, J. (1997) Training the applied developmental scientist for prevention and practice: Two current examples. In *Social policy report.* Chicago: Society for Research in Child Development.

Fisher, C. B., Murray, J. P., Dill, J. R., Hagen, J. W., Hogan, M. J., Lerner, R. M., et al. (1993). The national conference on graduate education in the applications of developmental science across the life span. *Journal of Applied Developmental Psychology, 14,* 1–10.

Fisher, C. B., & Tryon, W. W. (1990). Emerging ethical issues in an emerging field. In C. B. Fisher & W. W. Tryon (Eds.), *Ethics in applied developmental psychology: Emerging issues in an emerging field* (pp. 1–14). Norwood, NJ: Ablex.

Fisher, C. B., & Wallace, S. A. (2000). Through the community looking glass: Re-evaluating the ethical and policy implications of research on adolescent risk and psychopathology. *Ethics & Behavior, 10,* 99–118.

Fisher, C. B., Wallace, S. A., & Fenton, R. E. (2000). Discrimination distress during adolescence. *Journal of Youth and Adolescence, 29,* 679–695.

Freud, S. (1964). *An outline of psychoanalysis: Vol. 23. The standard edition of the complete psychological works of Sigmund Freud* (James Strachey, Ed. & Trans.). London: Hogarth Press. (Original work published 1940)

Gimenéz, M. E. (1992). U.S. ethnic politics: Implications for Latin Americans. *Latin American Perspectives, 19,* 7–17.

Graham, S. (1992). "Most of the subjects were white and middle class": Trends in published research on African Americans in selected APA journals, 1970–1989. *American Psychologist, 47,* 629–639.

Hamburg, B. A. (1993). *President's report: New futures for the "forgotten half." Realizing unused potential for learning and productivity: Annual report of the William T. Grant Foundation.* New York: William T. Grant Foundation.

Hamburg, D. (1992). *Today's children: Creating a future for a generation in crisis.* New York: Time.

Heath, S. B. (1997). Culture: Contested realm in research on children and youth. *Applied Developmental Science, 1,* 113–123.

Helms, J. E. (1996). Toward a methodology for measuring and assessing racial as distinguished from ethnic identity. In G. R. Sodowsky & J. C. Impara (Eds.), *Multicultural assessment in counseling and clinical psychology* (pp. 143–192). Lincoln, NE: Buros Institute of Mental Measurement.

Hernandez, D. (1993). *America's children: Resources from family, government, and the economy.* New York: Russell Sage Foundation.

Higgins-D'Allesandro, A., Hamilton, M., & Fisher, C. B. (1998). Educating the applied developmental psychologist for community partnerships: The Fordham model. In R. M. Lerner & L. A. K. Simon (Eds), *Outreach universities for America's youth and families: Building community collaborations for the 21st century.* Garland.

Hoagwood, K. (1994). The Certificate of confidentiality at NIMH: Applications and implications for service research with children. *Ethics & Behavior, 4,* 123–121.

Hollister, R., & Hill, J. (1995). Problems in the evaluation of community-wide initiatives. In J. Connell, A. Kubisch, L. Schor, & C. Weiss (Eds.), *New approaches to evaluating community initiatives: Concepts, methods, contexts.* Washington, DC: The Aspen Institute.

Huston, A. (2002). From research to policy: Choosing questions and interpreting the answers. In A. Higgins-D'Alessandro and K. Jankowski (Eds.), *Science and society: New directions of child development.* San Francisco, CA: Jossey–Bass.

Jensen, P. S., & Hoagwood, K. (1997). Developmental psychopathology and the notion of culture: Introduction to the special issue on the fusion of cultural horizons. Cultural influences on the assessment of psychopathology in children and adolescents. *Applied Developmental Science, 1,* 108–112.

Kellogg Commission. (1999). *Returning to our roots: The engaged institution.* Washington, DC: National Association of State Universities and Land-Grant Colleges.

Kliegl, R., Smith, J., & Baltes, P. B. (1989). Testing-the-limits and the study of adult age differences in cognitive plasticity of a mnemonic skill. *Developmental Psychology, 25,* 247–256.

Klonoff, E. A., Landrine, H., & Ullman, J. B. (1999). Racial discrimination and psychiatric symptoms among blacks. *Cultural Diversity and Ethnic Minority Psychology, 5,* 329–339.

Knight, G. P., & Hill, N. E. (1998). Measurement equivalence in research involving minority adolescents. In V. C. McLoyd & L. Steinberg (Eds.), *Studying minority adolescents: Conceptual, methodological, and theoretical issues* (pp. 183–211). Mahwah, NJ: Erlbaum.

Kotulak, R. (1996). *Inside the brain: Revolutionary discoveries of how the mind works.* Kansas City, MO: Andres and McNeel.

LaFromboise, T., Hardin, L., Coleman, K., & Gerton, J. (1993). Psychological impact of biculturalism: Evidence and theory. *Psychological Bulletin, 114,* 395–412.

Lancaster, J. (1986). Human adolescence and reproduction: An evolutionary perspective. In J. Lancaster & B. Hamburg (Eds.), *School-age pregnancy and parenthood: Biosocial dimensions* (pp. 17–38). New York: Aldine de Gruyter.

Lancaster, J., Altmann, J., Rossi, A., & Sherrod, L. (1987). Introduction. In J. Lancaster, J. Altmann, A. Rossi, & L. Sherrod (Eds.), *Parenting across the life span: Biosocial dimensions* (pp. 1–12). New York: Aldine de Gruyter.

Laosa, L. M. (1990). Population generalizability, cultural sensitivity, and ethical dilemmas. In C. B. Fisher & W. W. Tyron (Eds), *Ethics in applied developmental psychology: Emerging issues in an emerging field* (pp. 227–252). Norwood, NJ: Ablex.

Larsen, R. (2000). Toward a psychology of positive youth development. *American Psychologist, 55,* 170–183.

Lerner, R. M. (1995). *America's youth in crisis: Challenges and options for programs and policies.* Thousand Oaks, CA: Sage.

Lerner, R. M., & Fisher, C. B. (1994). From applied developmental psychology to applied developmental science: Community coalitions and collaborative careers. In C. B. Fisher & R. M. Lerner (Eds.), *Applied developmental psychology* (pp. 503–522). New York: McGraw-Hill.

Lerner, R. M., Fisher, C. B., & Weinberg, R. A. (2000a). Applying developmental science in the twenty-first century: International scholarship for our times. *International Journal of Behavioral Development, 24,* 24–29.

Lerner, R. M., Fisher, C. B., & Weinberg, R. A. (2000b). Towards a science for and of the people: Promoting civil society through the application of developmental science. *Child Development, 71,* 11–20.

Lerner, R. M., & Galambos, N. (1998). Adolescent development: Challenges and opportunities for research, programs, and policies. In J. T. Spence (Ed.), *Annual review of psychology* (Vol. 49, pp. 413–446). Palo Alto, CA: Annual Reviews

Lerner, R. M., & Simon, L. A. K. (1998a). The new American outreach university: Challenges and options. In R. M. Lerner & L. A. K. Simon (Eds.), *University-community collaborations for the twenty-first century: Outreach scholarship for youth and families* (pp. 3–23). New York: Garland.

Lerner, R. M., & Simon, L. A. K. (Eds.). (1998b). *University-community collaborations for the twenty-first century: Outreach scholarship for youth and families.* New York: Garland.

Lerner, R. M., Sparks, E. S., & McCubbin, L. (2000). Family diversity and family policy. In D. Demo, K. Allen, & M. Fine (Eds.), *Handbook of family diversity* (pp. 380–401). New York: Oxford University Press.

Lerner, R. M., & Tubman, J. G. (1990). Plasticity in development: Ethical implications for developmental interventions. In C. B. Fisher & W. W. Tryon (Eds.), *Ethics in applied developmental psychology: Emerging issuer in an emerging field* (pp. 113–132). Norwood, NJ: Ablex.

Liss, M. (1994). State and federal laws governing reporting for researchers. *Ethics & Bheavior, 4,* 133–146.

Marín, G., & Marín, B. V. (1991). *Research with Hispanic populations.* Newbury Park, CA: Sage.

McAdoo, H. P. (1990). The ethics of research and intervention with ethnic minority parents and their children. In C. B. Fisher & W. W. Tyron (Eds), *Ethics in applied developmental psychology: Emerging issues in an emerging field.* (pp. 273–284). Norwood, NJ: Ablex.

McCall, R. B. (1990). Promoting interdisciplinary and faculty-service-provider relations. *American Psychologist, 45,* 1319–1324.

McCall, R. B. (1992). A guide to communicating through the media. In K. McCartney & D. Phillips (Eds.), *An insider's guide to providing expert testimony before Congress.* Ann Arbor, MI: Society for Research in Child Development .

Melton, G. H. (1990). Certificates of confidentiality under the public health service act: Strong protection but not enough. *Violence & Victims, 5,* 67–71.

Miller, J., & Rodwell, M. K. (1997). Disclosure of student status in agencies: Do we still have a secret? *Families in Society, 78,* 72–83.

Mio, J., Trimble, J., Arredondo, P., Cheatham, H., & Sue, D. (Eds). (1999). *Keywords in multicultural interventions: A dictionary.* Westport, CT: Greenwood.

National Research Council of the Institute of Medicine. (2000). *After school programs to promote child and adolescent development: Summary of a workshop.* Washington, DC: National Academy Press.

Oboler, S. (1995). *Ethnic labels, Latino lives: Identity and the politics of (re)presentation in the United States.* Minneapolis: University of Minnesota Press.

O'Connor, A. (1995). Evaluating comprehensive community initiatives: A view from history. In J. Connell, A. Kubisch, L. Schorr, & C. Weiss (Eds.), *New approaches to evaluating community initiatives.* Washington, DC: The Aspen Institute.

Ogbu, J. U. (1994). From cultural differences to differences in cultural frame of reference. In P. M. Greenfield & R. R. Cocking (Eds.), *Cross-cultural roots of minority child development* (pp. 365–392). Mahwah, NJ: Erlbaum.

Omi, M., & Winant, H. (1986). *Racial formation in the United States.* New York: Routledge & Kegan Paul.

O'Sullivan, C., & Fisher, C. B. (1997). The effect of confidentiality and reporting procedures on parent-child agreement to participate in adolescent risk research. *Applied Developmental Science, 1*(4), 185–197.

Padilla, A. M. (1995). *Hispanic psychology: Critical issues in theory and research.* Thousand Oaks, CA: Sage.

Parron, D. L. (1997). The fusion of cultural horizons: Cultural influences on the assessment of psychopathology on children. *Applied Developmental Science, 1,* 156–159.

Pearson, J. L., Stanley, B., King, C., & Fisher, C. B. (2001). Intervention research for persons at high risk for suicidality: Safety and ethical considerations. *Journal of Clinical Psychiatry Supplement, 62,* 17–26.

Piaget, J. (1960). *The child's conception of the world.* London: Routledge.

Phinney, J. S. (1996). When we talk about American ethnic groups, what do we mean? *American Psychologist, 51,* 918–927.

Prewitt, K. (1980). The council and the usefulness of the social sciences. *Annual Report of the President, 1979–1980.* New York: Social Science Research Council.

Prewitt, K. (1995). *Social sciences and private philanthropy: The quest for social* (Essays on Philanthropy, No. 15, Series on Foundations and their role in American life). Indiana University Center on Philanthropy.

Ragin, C. C., & Hein, J. (1993). The comparative study of ethnicity: Methodological and conceptual issues. In J. H. Stanfield III & R. M. Dennis (Eds), *Race and ethnicity in research methods* (pp. 254–272). Newbury Park, CA: Sage.

Root, M. (1992). *Racially mixed people in American.* Newbury Park, CA: Sage.

Rosenberg, S., & Sherrod, L. R. (1994). *Directory of organizations concerned with public information of relevance to children.* New York: William T. Grant Foundation.

Rossi, P. H., Freeman, H. E., and Lispsey, M. W. (1999). *Evolution: A Systematic Approach.* Thousand Oaks, CA: Sage.

Ruck, M. D., Abramovitch, R., & Keating, D. P. (1998). Children's and adolescents' understanding of rights: Balancing nurturance and self-determination. *Child Development, 64,* 404–417.

Rumbaut, R. (1991). The agony of exile: A study of migration and adaptation of Indochinese refugee adults and children. In F. L. Ahean Jr. & J. L. Athey (Eds), *Refugee children: Theory, research, and services.* Baltimore: John Hopkins University Press.

Scales, P. C., Benson, P. L., Leffert, N., & Blyth, D. A. (2000). Contribution of developmental assets to the prediction of thriving among adolescents. *Applied Developmental Science, 4,* 27–46.

Seráfica, F. C. (1997). Psychopathology and resilience in Asian American children and adolescents. *Applied Developmental Science, 1,* 145–155.

Sherrod, L. (1997). Promoting youth development through research-based policies. *Applied Developmental Science, 1,* 17–27.

Sherrod, L. R. (1998a). The common pursuits of modern philanthropy and the proposed outreach university: Enhancing research and education. In R. M. Lerner & L. A. Simon (Eds.), *University-community collaborations for the twenty-first century.* New York: Garland.

Sherrod, L. R. (1998b). Funding opportunities for applied developmental science. In P. A. Ralston, R. Lerner, A. Mullis, C. Simerly, & J. Murray (Eds.), *Social change, public policy, and community collaboration: Training human development professionals for the twenty-first century.* MA: Kluwer

Sherrod, L. R. (1999). Giving child development knowledge away: Using university-community partnerships to disseminate research on children, youth and families. *Applied Developmental Science, 3,* 228–234.

Sherrod, L. R. (2002). The role of psychology in setting a policy agenda for children and families. In A. Higgins-D'Alessandro & K. Jankowski (Eds.), *Science and Policy: New directions for child development.* San Francisco, CA: Jossey-Bass.

Sorensen, A., Weinert, F., & Sherrod, L. (Eds.). (1986). *Human development and the life course.* Hillsdale, NJ: Erlbaum.

Slonim-Nevo, V. (1992). First premarital intercourse among Mexican American and Anglo American adolescent women: Interpreting ethnic differences. *Journal of Adolescent Research, 7(*3), 332–351.

Spencer, M. B. (1995). Old issues and new theorizing about African-American youth: A phenomenological variant of ecological systems theory. In. R. L. Taylor (Ed.), *Black youth: Perspectives on their status in the United States* (pp. 37–70). Westport, CT: Praeger.

Spencer, M. B., Swanson, D. P., & Cunningham, M. (1991). Ethnicity, ethnic identity, and competence formation: Adolescent transition and cultural transformation. *Journal of Negro Education, 60,* 366–387.

Stanfield, J. H. (1993). Epistemological considerations. In J. H. Stanfield & R. M. Dennis (Eds.), *Race and ethnicity in research methods* (pp. 16–36). Newbury Park, CA: Sage.

Steele, C. M. (1997). A threat in the air: How stereotypes shape intellectual identity and performance. *American Psychologist, 52,* 613–629.

Susman-Stillman, A., & Brown, J. (1997). Building research and policy connections: Training and career options for developmental scientists. In *Social Policy Reports.* Chicago: Society for Research in Child Development.

Takanishi, R. (1994). Continuities and discontinuities in the cognitive socialization of Asian-originated children: The case of Japanese Americans. In P. M. Greenfield & R. R. Cocking (Eds.), *Cross-cultural roots of minority child development* (pp. 351–362). Mahwah, NJ: Erlbaum.

Terrell, F., Terrell, S. L., & Miller, F. (1993). Level of cultural mistrust as a function of educational and occupational expectations among African American students. *Adolescence, 28*(11), 573–578.

Tolan, P., Sherrod, L., Gorman-Smith, D., & Henry, D. (2002). Building protection and opportunity for inner city children and youth and their families. In K. Maton, C. Schellenbach, & B. Leadbeater (Eds.), *Fostering resilient children, youth, families and communities: Strength based research and policy.* Washington, DC: American Psychological Association.

Trimble, J. E. (1990). Ethnic specification, validation prospects and future of drug abuse research. *International Journal of the Addictions, 25,* 149–169.

Vargas, M., & Busch-Rossnagel, N. A. (2000). Authority plus affection: Latino parenting during adolescence. In M. M. Montero-Sieburth & F. A. Villarruel (Eds.), Making invisible Latino adolescents visible: A critical approach to Latino diversity (pp. 265–287) New York: Garland.

Weithorn, L. A. (1983). Children's capacities to decide about participation in research. *IRB: A Review of Human Subjects Research, 5,* 1–5.

Werner, O., & Campbell, D. T. (1970). Translating, working through interpreters and the problem of decentering. In R. Cohen (Ed.), *A handbooks of methods in cultural anthropology.* New York: American Museum of Natural History.

Wisely, D. S. (1997–1998). The pursuit of a virtuous people. *Advancing Philanthropy* (Winter), 14–20.

Yee, A. H., Fairchild, H. H., Weizmann, F., & Wyatt, G. E. (1993). Addressing psychology's problem with race. *American Psychologist, 49,* 748–754.
Zayas, L. H., & Solari, F. (1994). Early childhood socialization in Hispanic families: Context, culture, and practice implications. *Professional Psychoogy, 25,* 200–206.
Zigler, E., & Hall, N. (2000). *Child development and social policy.* New York: McGraw-Hill.
Zigler, E., Kagan, S., & Hall, N. (1996). *Children, families, and government: Preparing for the 21st century.* Cambridge, England: University of Cambridge Press.
Zuckerman, M. (1990). Some dubious premises in research and theory on racial differences: Scientific, social, and ethical issues. *American Psychologist, 45*(12), 1297–1303.

Chapter 25

YOUTH DEVELOPMENT, DEVELOPMENTAL ASSETS, AND PUBLIC POLICY

Peter L. Benson, Marc Mannes, Karen Pittman, and Thaddeus Ferber

This chapter examines the interrelationships among the evolving field of youth development, Search Institute's developmental asset framework, and public policy for youth. The chapter describes the strength-based youth development approach in large part by comparing it to and contrasting it with the deficit-based orientation to successful development. It also discusses the theoretical and empirical basis of the developmental asset framework as a prime exemplar of positive youth development, a comprehensive conceptualization of developmental well-being, and a generator of knowledge regarding the developmental pathways of young people. We identify relevant social and cultural dynamics affecting youth, consider their implication for youth development policy, and highlight a number of public policies from around the country that reflect the tenets and unfolding wisdom of healthy youth development. The chapter concludes by assessing the sociopolitical prospects for developmental principles and knowledge to actually inform and shape public policy for young people.

According to Burt, Zweig, and Roman (2002), public policy is regularly blind to adolescents, except on occasions when their actions make adults uneasy. Consequently, when the issue of adolescent health has surfaced on the national policy agenda over the last four decades, it has typically been in response to problem behaviors and expressions of psychopathology. Takanishi (1993) argues that since the 1960s, national youth policy has been driven by a developmental deficit orientation, due in part to the high visibility of escalating rates of developmental threats and health-compromising behavior, as documented in numerous national studies in the closing decades of the 20th century. These prevailing circumstances need to be juxtaposed with a more recent resurgence in adolescent development research in the 1980s and 1990s that—when combined with studies of the daily experience of adolescents—raised two additional issues for policy makers to consider. First, many of the supports and opportunities youth need to effectively navigate through the second decade of life were becoming less accessible (Brown, Larson, & Saraswathi, 2002). Second, the massive technological, economic, and social changes that had transpired since 1960 required a reassessment of the kinds of supports and opportunities youth need to transition successfully from adolescence to adulthood (Benson, 2003; Pittman, Irby, & Ferber, 2001; Zaslow & Takanishi, 1993). A growing body of research on the limited success of programs targeted at reducing or preventing risk behaviors (Dougherty, 1993; Gambone, 1993) and several highly influential reports on the developmental needs of middle school and high school youth (Carnegie Corporation of New York, 1992, 1995), combined to fuel new interest in more strength-based developmental approaches to promoting youth well-being. Accordingly, a more common refrain in many policy discussions is that public investment for adolescence should increasingly be guided by a youth development perspective (Hahn, 2002; Sherrod, 1997).

COMPARING APPROACHES TO DEVELOPMENTAL SUCCESS

Some have claimed that the science and application of promoting developmental strengths in young people represents a significant paradigm shift (Roth & Brooks-Gunn, 2000). This newer orientation is more fully understood by contrasting it with an alternative framework that has a much longer history and a more dominant influence on youth studies, policies, and services. The traditional deficit orientation has been largely organized around the identification, reduction, and prevention of factors that are understood as undermining healthy development (e.g., physical and sexual abuse, racism and related forms of exclusion, violence in families and neighborhoods, access to alcohol and other substances, media violence), as well as the reduction and prevention of unhealthy behavior (e.g., alcohol use, tobacco use, substance use, adolescent pregnancy, violence, school dropout, and antisocial behavior). A focus on the concept of risk lies at the heart of the traditional deficit paradigm addressing youth. Seligman and Csikszentmihalyi (2000) make the case that the field of psychology has been singularly focused on the investigation, treatment, prevention, and reduction of pathology and its symptoms. Fisher and Wallace's (2000) research identifies the enormous challenges to conducting socially and ethically responsible research on adolescent risk and psychopathology in the absence of a true investigative partnership actively involving community members. They call for community consultations between researchers and community participants to employ culturally sensitive lenses and gauge the risks and benefits of particular studies.

Philosophical, scientific, social, and political critiques of the deficit approach and its emphasis on risks have been made. Beck (1992) conducted a social analysis of the permeation of risk throughout all aspects of advanced modern Western society and judged it to be a natural and regrettable consequence of technical-scientific hegemony with worrisome global implications. According to Beck, the social production of both wealth and risk are inextricably linked in postmodern civilization by virtue of ecological devaluations, economic insecurities, political uncertainties, health hazards, and social heteronomy resulting from scientific discoveries and technological innovation. Valencia (1997) identifies the racial and class biases at the core of the evolution and application of the deficit approach in education. Swadener and Lubeck (1995) posit that the pervasiveness of the children-and-families-at-risk construct in America has decidedly political overtones in the way it is used to sidestep the inequitable distribution of social and economic resources and avoid critical analysis of the power of privilege.

This historically dominant deficit orientation, akin to the medical model in medicine, has been strongly imprinted on social policy and virtually reified in related fields of practice. It should come then as no surprise that a number of national youth policy initiatives during the last 30 years have borne the label *war*—on teen pregnancy, drugs, and violence, to name a few (Goleman, 1995). It is also not surprising, once again consistent with the medical model, that health in general (and adolescent health in particular) continue to routinely be defined as the absence of symptom, maladjustment, or health-compromising behaviors (Miringhoff & Miringhoff, 1999). The field of prevention—with its implied interest in eliminating the onset of problems or minimizing their adverse consequences—has consistently grown and become institutionalized in terms of policy formulation and programmatic funding. With nearly all federal research funding across the social and life sciences emphasizing disease and pathology, young scholars with the intellectual curiosity to investigate health and well-being are likely to be dissuaded by insufficient revenue from building a respectable and sustainable research career. A recent notable departure is the effort by the W.T. Grant Foundation to concentrate its grant making on understanding the contexts that can foster positive development (Hein, 2002). Many of the national barometers used to monitor and report trends in child and adolescent health that inform policy makers and practitioners focus on risks and problem behavior, with success interpreted as the lack of their manifestation (Benson, 1997; Pittman & Irby, 1998).

By way of comparison, the field of youth development adopts more of a wellness perspective, places particular emphasis on the existence of healthy conditions, and expands the concept of health to include the skills, prosocial behaviors, and competencies needed to succeed in employment, education, and civic life. It moves beyond the eradication of risk and deliberately argues for the promotion of well-being. Accordingly, a common refrain in youth development circles is "problem-free is not fully prepared" (Pittman et al., 2001). This perspective builds on an expanding trend in the study of adolescence and youth work to employ a strength-based orientation, focus on understanding, and foster the developmental experiences and resources that enhance educational, social, and health outcomes.

Hamilton (1999) characterizes positive youth development as three interconnected ideas: (a) youth have an inherent capacity to grow toward optimal development if given appropriate opportunity and supportive developmental ecologies; (b) youth programs orchestrate at the community level a range of developmentally appropriate supports and opportunities that build on and enhance the strengths of youth; and (c) youth programs are designed to emphasize competency, skill building, youth participation, and inclusion.

The building blocks of successful development have variously been called supports and opportunities, developmental assets, and developmental nutrients (Benson, Scales, & Mannes, 2003). Closely aligned with this growing line of inquiry is the study of resilience and its identification of the processes and sources of successful adaptation in the face of high exposure to developmental threats (Garmezy, 1985; Masten & Curtis, 2000). This interest in successful development and the pathways that promote it are gradually exerting a degree of influence on research and practice in many fields (e.g., psychology, evaluation, social work, public health), and are becoming recurrent discussion themes in youth policy forums.

In actuality, the history of youth policy defies easy characterization. Some evidence suggests that although the prevention, treatment, and reduction of youth problem behavior characterize the primary worldviews and mindsets driving policy makers, researchers, and practitioners, a comparatively smaller but continuous, parallel stream of activity can be characterized as the youth development approach. A government report released in 1996 claims that "focusing on young people's strengths rather than their failings is the underlying principle of the youth development construct and has been the driving force behind the U.S. Department of Health and Human Services' youth-related programs for over two decades" (U.S. Department of Health and Human Services [DHHS], 1996, p. 3). The report argues that the Youth Development and Delinquency Prevention Administration's investment, dating back to 1970, encouraged a delinquency prevention strategy based on promoting "a sense of competence, a sense of usefulness, a sense of helping, a sense of power" (DHHS, 1996, p. 4). Another more recent policy initiative aligned with youth development principles is service learning and community service, buoyed in part by the 1990 National and Community Service Act (Stukas, Clary, & Snyder, 1999). The developmental strengths approach experienced even greater legitimacy by the release of a major National Research Council report called *Community Programs to Promote Youth Development* (National Research Council & Institute of Medicine, 2002) and the new focus of the W.T. Grant Foundation on youth as resources (Hein, 2002).

A more reasonable conclusion to draw at this point in time is that *reducing and preventing developmental deficits* and *promoting developmental strengths* are parallel, unique, and complementary tracks. They both have informed youth policy during the last 40 years, with the former clearly ascendant and the latter gaining momentum and a heightened measure of recognition. Figure 25.1 illustrates the relationship between the deficit- and strength-based policy orientations in terms of how each paradigm defines healthy developmental ends and specifies means to secure those ends. The figure illuminates the ways in which there are conceptual and operational arenas of distinctiveness and overlap between the two orientations and depicts their increasing interplay.

First, Figure 25.1 contrasts two general ways of thinking about the outcomes associated with successful development. The first emphasizes preventing or reducing health-compromising behavior (Cell C) such as alcohol, tobacco, and illicit drug use; adolescent pregnancy; violence; antisocial behavior; depression; and suicide. The second attends to promoting behaviors demonstrating caring, competence, and thriving (Cell D) that are beneficial to self and society. Given that the first of these two outcome domains has driven the vast majority of policy initiatives and related program evaluations as well as scientific studies having to do with adolescent development (Benson, 1997), the conceptualization and measurement of Cell D lags behind that of Cell C. Still, several attempts to render definition to the thriving and well-being space in the past decade are worth highlighting. Pittman and Irby (1996) proposed a four-part taxonomy for capturing the major tasks of successful adolescent development: developing competence, confidence, character, and connections. Lerner (2002) added a fifth *c:* caring (or compassion). Connell and his colleagues suggested a framework involving the concepts of learning to be productive, learning to connect, and learning to navigate (Connell, Gambone, & Smith, 2002). Several scholars have begun to delineate and measure the concept of thriving, which includes multiple behaviors postulated to promote both the individual and social good (Lerner, 2002; Scales, Benson, Leffert, & Blyth, 2000). Among these activities are academic success, the affirmation of diversity, leadership skill, and civic engagement.

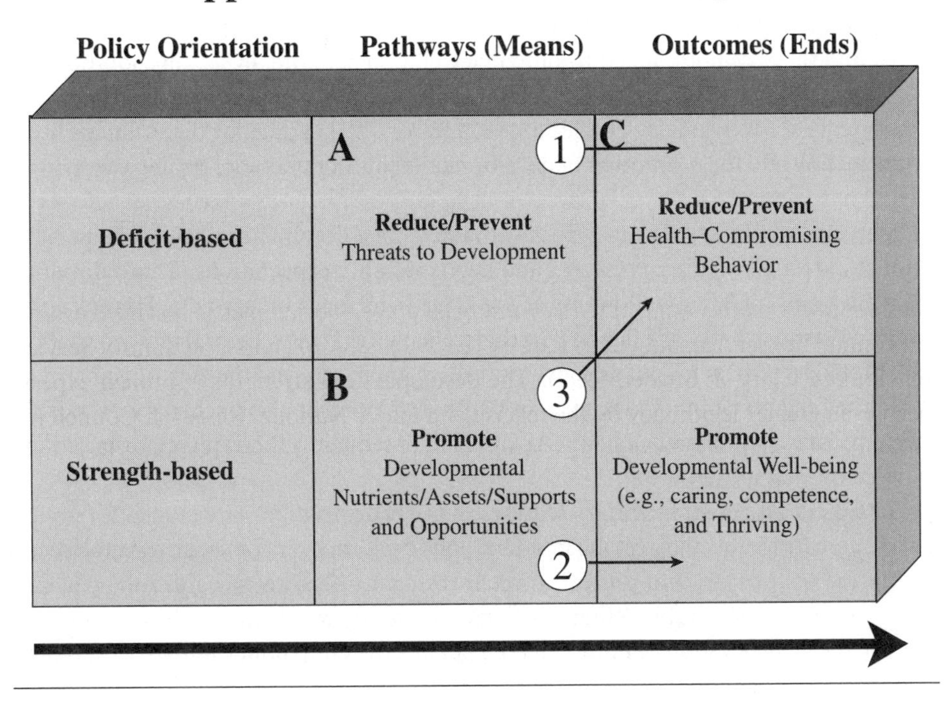

Figure 25.1 **Approaches to Successful Development**

The dominant deficit paradigm—variously labeled the risk reduction, the problem behavior, or prevention approach—tends to pay more of its attention to the outcomes essentially represented in Cell C, even though it also has to consider the means in Cell A by which those outcomes can be accomplished. Arrow 1 represents this traditional emphasis of the deficit-based paradigm. In contrast, the youth development perspective has tended to concentrate more on the pathways of promoting developmental nutrients (Cell B) and only secondarily on the positive outcomes themselves (Cell D). As one recent definition put it, "youth development mobilizes programs, organizations, systems, and communities to build developmental strengths in order to promote health and well-being" (Benson & Saito, 2001, p. 144). Arrow 2 represents the usual emphasis of the strength-based paradigm.

Each paradigm has a particular emphasis and reflects a theoretically distinct pathway for improving the lives of young people. Yet, over time, the two approaches have become increasingly conceptually interwoven by model developers and practitioners who see them as inherently complementary in real-world applications (Benson, 1997; Hawkins & Catalano, 1992). For example, the field called prevention science parts company with the traditional deficit-based paradigm. In prevention science, the driving organizing principle of producing the reduction-prevention of negative outcomes by reducing-preventing threats to development has been broadened to also attend to developmental nutrients that are labeled as protective factors and are also seen as important to minimizing or curtailing negative outcomes. So, for example, an initiative to reduce adolescent alcohol use might combine efforts to reduce the supply of alcohol available to youth within a community and promote more equitable access to quality after-school programs. Each of the two strategies is seen as having alcohol prevention utility, and they are both linked to outcome Cell C. Therefore, in seeking solutions to risk-taking behavior, the central theories and models in the prevention science approach (e.g., see Hawkins & Catalano, 1992; Jessor, 1991) argue for the utility of both risk reduction and the promotion of developmental nutrients as core strategies (Arrows 1 and 3 in Figure 25.1).

Interconnections are also spawned by the sustained dominance of the deficit orientation and related funding pressures and accountability expectations. Youth development programs, policies, and practices are clearly the focus of Arrow 2. However, the sustained pervasiveness of a deficit paradigm, the fact that most federal and foundation fund providers remain locked into that prevailing approach, and the lack of viable metrics for healthy development means that youth development also becomes inextricably tied to reducing problem behavior (Arrow 3). Consequently, both policy orientations share an interest in Arrow 3.

The unique and complimentary features of the two paradigms are crucial for policy makers to consider as they establish intent and forge strategy for securing adolescent health. Public, private, and philanthropic investments need to recognize the genuine contributions of the complimentary pathways to youth health and well-being and encourage the incorporation of both outcome perspectives into policy initiatives and programmatic interventions.

THE SCIENCE AND APPLICATION OF THE DEVELOPMENTAL ASSET FRAMEWORK

The foundations of the developmental asset framework advanced by Search Institute are rooted in an integration of multiple lines of inquiry designed to identify the building blocks of healthy development (Benson, Leffert, Scales, & Blyth, 1998; Scales & Leffert, 1999).The framework is grounded in major developmental strength concepts such as resiliency and competence (Garmezy, 1985; Masten et al., 1995), protective factors (Hawkins, Catalano, & Miller, 1992; Jessor , Turbin, & Costa,1998), and connectedness (Scales & Gibbons, 1996; Resnick et al., 1997). In addition to drawing upon theory and research in these core developmental strengths, the framework has incorporated the findings of many studies within child and adolescent developmental psychology.

The framework emphasizes primary socialization contexts and processes for youth across the middle and high school years. The breadth of the framework's purview allows it to override the warning of Connell et al. (2002) that too often practice arenas for the youth development perspective are confined to after-school programs or add-on programs within school settings and "excludes key settings in which youth develop" (p. 292). They charge the youth development field to conceptualize with greater clarity the multiple community settings in which supports and opportunities can emerge.

The framework places a premium on the universe of ecologies (Bronfenbrenner, 1979) that have a particular and collective social responsibility in fostering positive development. The socializing systems of family (Simpson, 2001), school (Starkman,

Scales, & Roberts, 1999), neighborhood (Sampson, Morenoff, & Earls, 1999; Sampson, Raudenbush, & Earls, 1997), youth-serving organizations (Larson, 2000; Wynn, 1997), and religion (Paragment & Park, 1995; Resnick et al., 1997; Werner & Smith, 1992; Youniss, McLellan, & Yates, 1999) are among the prime settings and sources contributing to youth development. The ability of these developmental contexts to facilitate connection, regulation, and autonomy has been identified by a number of researchers as fundamental to healthy adolescent functioning (Barber & Olsen, 1997; Eccles, Early, Frasier, Belansky, & McCarthy, 1997). The framework's interest in and respect for the developmental dynamics that transpire among these ecologies is especially noteworthy, given the uncommonness of approaches that consider reciprocal and transactional encounters across social settings and sources as vital to healthy development (Bronfenbrenner, 1979; Scales & Leffert, 1999). By virtue of its concern for interactive and redundant developmental processes, the developmental asset framework articulates the kinds of relationships, social experiences, social environments, and patterns of interaction, norms, and competencies over which a community of people—through its socializing systems—has considerable control.

The relativity of developmental strength concepts and the expression of developmental dynamics must be kept in mind. Brown et al. (2002) posit that middle-class youth in India, Southeast Asia, and Europe have much more in common with each other than with their economically poorer counterparts in their own nations. Masten and Curtis (2000) remind us that what is viewed as resilient, competent, protective, or even connected is also culturally and historically bound. In America, autonomy for youth meant something very different 100 years ago and will likely have a different connotation in the 22nd century. Whereas stricter parenting seems to be related to better outcomes among African American children living in more urban or high-risk neighborhoods (Furstenburg, 1993), it is related to poorer outcomes among White children in less stressed and high-risk environments (Steinberg, Mounts, Lamborn, & Dornbusch, 1991).

Even though these developmental concepts and dynamics may manifest themselves in diverse ways across transnational social classes and time periods as well as within a particular country's racial, ethnic, and socioeconomic subcultures, they are best appreciated as the kinds of foundational developmental task accomplishments that secure the health and well-being of youth and ultimately make optimal development possible (Benson, 2003). The developmental asset framework is also stimulating pioneering attempts by scholars and practitioners to move beyond normal development and consider optimal development along with the contributions various socialization settings make to maximizing development (Lerner, Brentano, Dowling, & Anderson, 2002).

Scales and Leffert's (1999) research synthesis undergirding the framework focused on integrating developmental experiences that have been shown to contribute to (a) the prevention of high-risk behaviors, (b) the enhancement of thriving outcomes, and (c) the capacity to function adequately in the face of adversity. The other intent of the synthesis was to identify developmental factors that appear to be particularly robust in predicting health outcomes across sex, race-ethnicity, and family income.

Forty developmental assets have been specified and then subdivided into two groups: 20 external assets (i.e., health-promoting features of the environment) and 20 internal assets (e.g., commitments, values, and competencies). The external assets are grouped into four categories: (a) support, (b) empowerment, (c) boundaries and expectations, and (d) constructive use of time. The internal assets are grouped into the four categories of (a) commitment to learning, (b) positive values, (c) social competencies, and (d) positive identity.

In 1989 Search Institute began conducting studies of 6th–12th grade students in public and private schools throughout the nation. Then in 1996 the Institute developed a 156-item survey instrument, *Search Institute Profiles of Student Life: Attitudes and Behaviors.* From 1989 through 2001, more than 2,500 communities and more than 1,800,000 adolescents have completed the instrument. The instrument measures each of the 40 developmental assets, along with other constructs that include developmental deficits, high-risk behaviors consonant with federally funded research studies, and thriving indicators. The specific assets comprising the developmental asset framework and the set of developmental deficits, high-risk behaviors, and thriving indicators are presented in Table 25.1.

The survey is administered anonymously in a classroom setting with standardized instructions. Routinely, these school district oriented studies serve as a complete census of all 6th- to 12th-grade students attending school on the day the survey is administered and renders a developmental profile of youth. Conducting the survey is typically part of a community strategy to mobilize around the developmental asset framework. The report developed for and delivered to a city or town often becomes a widely shared public document catalyzing a community-wide call to action on behalf of youth development.

Aggregate reports on the national sample completing the survey during particular years have been published periodically (Benson, 1990; Benson, Scales, Leffert, & Roehlkepartain, 1999). The latest data set is composed of slightly more than 217,000 youth who completed the survey during the 1999–2000 school year. These reports, along with the most recent data set, have served as the basis for a line of inquiry that has analyzed the promotional and protective value of the developmental assets and examined their cumulative benefits and predictive power.

Evidence exists to make a case that the number of developmental assets in young people's lives (a measure of the developmental richness of a young person's total ecology) and clusters of assets (often operating in specific contexts for specific outcomes of interest for particular young people) promote healthy behavior (Scales, Benson, Leffert, & Blyth, 2000), prevent unhealthy behavior (Leffert et al., 1998; Taylor et al., 2002), and help us better understand patterns of risk and thriving among adolescents (Benson et al., 1999).

The developmental assets appear to provide what can be thought of as beneficial vertical and horizontal pile-up effects. Vertical pile-up effects can manifest and be measured in several different ways. The total number of assets young people experience at any one time, the clustering or co-occurrence of risks and assets, and the accumulation over time of the effects of a young person's developmental history are all examples. What we call horizontal pile-up effects are represented and measured as the interactions among the developmental assets as a result of experiencing complimentary developmental strengths across contexts and social networks within one's total ecology and experiencing clusters of assets that are particularly related to specific developmental outcomes.

Benson (1990) reported on an early Search Institute study of more than 47,000 6th–

Table 25.1 The Developmental Asset Framework

40 Developmental Assets	
External Assets	
Support	1. Family support—Family life provides high levels of love and support.
	2. Positive family communication—Young person and her or his parent(s) communicate positively, and young person is willing to seek parent(s) advice and counsel.
	3. Other adult relationships—Young person receives support from three or more nonparent adults.
	4. Caring neighborhood—Young person experiences caring neighbors.
	5. Caring school climate—School provides a caring, encouraging environment.
	6. Parent involvement in schooling—Parent(s) are actively involved in helping young person succeed in school.
Empowerment	7. Community values youth—Young person perceives that community adults value youth.
	8. Youth as resources—Young people are given useful roles in the community.
	9. Service to others—Young person serves in the community one hour or more per week.
	10. Safety—Young person feels safe at home, at school, and in the neighborhood.
Boundaries and Expectations	11. Family boundaries—Family has clear rules and consequences, and monitors the young person's whereabouts.
	12. School boundaries—School provides clear rules and consequences.
	13. Neighborhood boundaries—Neighbors take responsibility for monitoring young people's behavior.
	14. Adult role models—Parent(s) and other adults model positive, responsible behavior.
	15. Positive peer influence—Young person's best friends model positive, responsible behavior.
	16. High expectations—Both parents and teachers encourage the young person to do well.
Constructive Use of Time	17. Creative activities—Young person spends three or more hours per week in lessons or practice in music, theater, or other arts.
	18. Youth programs—Young person spends three hours or more per week in sports, clubs, or organizations at school, and/or in the community.
	19. Religious community—Young person spends one or more hours per week in activities in a religious institution.
	20. Time at home—Young person is out with friends "with nothing special to do" two or fewer nights per week.

(continued)

Table 25.1 *(Continued)*

Internal Assets	
Commitment to Learning	21. Achievement motivation—Young person is motivated to do well in school.
	22. School engagement—Young person is actively engaged in learning
	23. Homework—Young person reports doing at least one or more hours of homework every school day.
	24. Bonding to school—Young person cares about her or his school.
	25. Reading for pleasure—Young person reads for pleasure 3 or more hours per week.
Positive Values	26. Caring—Young person places high value on helping other people.
	27. Equality and social justice—Young person places high value on promoting equality and reducing hunger and poverty.
	28. Integrity—Young person acts on convictions and stands up for her or his beliefs.
	29. Honesty—Young person "tells the truth even when it is not easy."
	30. Responsibility—Young person accepts and takes personal responsibility.
	31. Restraint—Young person believes it is important not to be sexually active or to use alcohol or other drugs.
Social Competencies	32. Planning and decision making—Young person knows how to plan ahead and make choices.
	33. Interpersonal competence—Young person has empathy, sensitivity, and friendship skills.
	34. Cultural competence—Young person has knowledge of and comfort with people of different cultural/racial/ethnic backgrounds.
	35. Resistance skills—Young person can resist negative peer pressure and dangerous situations.
	36. Peaceful conflict resolution—Young person seeks to resolve conflict nonviolently.
Positive Identity	37. Personal power—Young person feels he or she has control over "things that happen to me."
	38. Self-esteem—Young person reports having high self-esteem.
	39. Sense of purpose—Young person reports "my life has a purpose."
	40. Positive view of personal future—Young person is optimistic about her or his personal future.

Table 25.1 *(Continued)*

Developmental Deficits	
Alone at home	Spends two hours or more per school day alone at home.
TV overexposure	Watches television or videos three or more hours per school day.
Physical abuse	Reports one or more incidents of physical abuse in lifetime.
Victim of violence	Reports being a victim of violence one or more times in the past two years.
Drinking parties	Reports attending one or more parties in the last year "where other kids your age were drinking."
High-Risk Behavior	
Problem alcohol use	Has used alcohol three or more times in the past month or got drunk one or more times in the past two weeks.
Tobacco use	Smokes one or more cigarettes every day or frequently uses chewing tobacco.
Illicit drug use	Has used illicit drugs three or more times in the past 12 months
Sexual intercourse	Has had sexual intercourse three or more times in lifetime.
Depression and suicide	Is frequently depressed and/or has attempted suicide.
Violence	Has engaged in three or more acts of fighting, hitting, injuring a person, carrying or using a weapon, or threatening physical harm in the past 12 months.
Antisocial behavior	Has been involved in three or more incidents of shoplifting, trouble with police, or vandalism in the past year.
School problems	Has skipped school two or more days in the past four weeks and/or has below a C average.
Gambling	Has gambled three or more times in the past 12 months.
Thriving Indicators	
Succeeds in school	Gets mostly A's on report card.
Helps others	Helps friends or neighbors one or more hours each week
Values diversity	Places high importance on getting to know people of other racial/ethnic groups
Maintains good health	Pays attention to healthy nutrition and exercise.
Exhibits leadership	Has been a leader of a group or organization in the past 12 months.
Resists danger	Avoids doing things that are dangerous.
Delays gratification	Saves money for something special rather than spending it all right away.
Overcomes adversity	Does not give up when things get difficult.

Note. Reprinted with permission from Search Institute (Minneapolis, MN: Search Institute). ©1997. www.search-institute.org

12th graders that showed that youth who experience a horizontal pile-up of assets via engagement in four developmentally rich settings (family, school, structured youth activity, and faith community) report six times fewer risk behaviors than do other adolescents. This finding is reinforced through Sanders' (1998) study of more than 800 urban African American students in the 8th grade, which lends additional support for the hypothesis that strengths piling up across ecological domains magnify the protective and thriving effects of positive experiences in single contexts. Sanders suggested that "when students receive support from the family, church, and school simultaneously, the effects on their attitudes about self and the importance of schooling are magnified" (p. 402).

The protective and promotional significance of the developmental assets is best illustrated by studies showing how risk *and* thriving patterns co-occur as a function of varying categories of asset levels. On the protective side, the average number of 10 high-risk behavior patterns reported by young people drops sharply—by half or more—with each successive shift to a higher quartile of reported assets (Benson et al., 1999). Consistent with the findings of other researchers (e.g., Jessor & Jessor, 1977; Ketterlinus, Lamb, Nitz, & Elster, 1992), Benson et al. (1999) also reported that risk behaviors tend to co-occur. Analysis based on the data set of approximately 100,000 youth who completed the survey during the 1996–1997 school year suggested that students who engage in any of those risk patterns are more than four times as likely as are other students to engage in at least three additional risk behavior patterns.

Moreover, Benson et al. (1999) identified a consistent pattern of assets helping to explain the prevention of typical high-risk behaviors. In a different analysis of the same sample, Leffert et al., (1998) found that certain clusters of developmental assets explained a considerable proportion of the variance associated with those high-risk behavior patterns. Although slightly different clusters of assets were meaningful in explaining different outcomes, the total models (with demographic variables) accounted for 21–41% of the variance, and the assets contributed 16–35%.

Benson et al. (1999) demonstrated that relationship between developmental assets and thriving indicators is the same as with high-risk behavior patterns. From a promotional perspective the data reveals that asset-rich youth are six times more likely to experience indicators of thriving.

In terms of academic achievement, research reviewed in Scales and Leffert (1999) and Starkman et al. (1999) consistently shows that the assets are related to and may well help contribute to students' academic success. Benson et al. (1999) found that asset-rich students are 2.5 times more likely to report getting mostly As in school than are students who have only an average level of the assets. Leffert, Scales, Vraa, Libbey, and Benson (forthcoming) find that students experiencing higher levels of developmental assets generally had higher actual grades in English, science, social studies, and mathematics; higher cumulative GPAs; and higher class ranks. In addition, high levels of assets seemed to be related to the narrowing of traditional gender equity gaps as reflected by GPAs and math grades.

More extensive descriptions of the framework's development, the measurement of assets, and the predictive power of the framework can be found in a series of publications (Benson, 1997; Benson, 2003; Benson et al.,1998; Leffert et al., 1998; Scales et al., 2000).

The developmental asset framework attributes salient roles and responsibilities to multiple socialization settings for fostering positive youth development. Therefore, it is imperative that significant social and economic forces affecting these developmental contexts are identified and better understood in order to establish a more informed basis for generating public policies.

YOUTH DEVELOPMENT AND PUBLIC POLICY: THE CULTURAL CONTEXT

Dramatic changes in family composition, family mobility, media exposure, the nature and demands of work, the rapid migration of women into the outside-of-home workforce, and the isolation of families from community supports have complicated and even altered pathways to developmental success for youth (Fukuyama, 1999; Hernandez, 1994; National Research Council and Institute of Medicine, 2000, 2002). According to social historians such as Fukuyama (1999), during such times of rapid social change, societies tend to experience an upswing in problem behaviors such as substance use and violence. Fukuyama associates this consequence in America with two co-occurring processes: the lessening of social restraints and the expansion of individualism as the referent point for identity. Yankelovich (1998) reinforces this cultural assessment by noting several significant value shifts in American society over the last several decades. He argues that the concept of duty has been transformed, with less value being placed on what one owes to others as a matter of moral obligation. Respectability has also undergone a change in the sense that less value is placed on symbols of correct behavior for a person of a particular social class. Social morality has experienced a decline, with less value being attributed to observing society's rules. Finally, Yankelovich suggests that the importance and emphasis of sacrifice have been recalibrated and reoriented. Less value is placed on sacrifice as a moral good, and the very idea of sacrifice has been tied to more pragmatic economic criteria.

The cumulative weight of social change dynamics, problem behavior issues, and value shifts needs to be considered against the backdrop of one of the more discussed phenomena influencing contemporary cultural life—"the disappearance of social capital and civic engagement in America" (Putnam, 1996, p. 34). Healthy society—at least in Western terms—requires the mobilization of social networks and social norms to support the pursuit of shared goals (social capital) and the meaningful participation of citizens in building and being community (civic engagement). McKnight (1995) rails against the evolution of the American human service industry and its unintended consequence of suppressing community social capital and engagement. The implication is that an overemphasis on professionalized services unintentionally fuels—or is a correlate of—downward trends in forms of community participation particularly crucial for child and adolescent socialization (Benson et al., 1998).

Both the intrinsic benevolence of social capital and the downward trends in social relations and civic participation are open to skepticism. American writers as far back as Sinclair Lewis have generally mocked and penned disdain for the cautiousness, conformity, and regimentation associated with at least the small-town version of civic and associational life. Moreover, other data exist to draw a less gloomy picture than the one sketched by Putnam (Keeter, Zukin, Andolina, & Jenkins, 2002; Ladd, 1996). Nonetheless, in political science and public affairs the suppression of social capital and civic engagement continue to be widely discussed as possible explanations for historical downturns in voting behavior and seen as stemming from rising levels of social mistrust, social isolation, and the cultural cache surrounding the ethos of individualism (Benson, 1997).

Accepting the assumption that rapid change does indeed produce problematic youth behaviors, as those problem behaviors are subjected to persistent media attention (Gilliam & Bales, 2001; Scales, 2001), they are likely to create an environment in which action is demanded or expected of elected officials. Gilliam and Bales (2001) demonstrate how the media consistently frames youth in a negative light and portrays them as dangerous and self-absorbed. The prevalence of this frame may feed a tendency by policy makers to legislate programs and initiatives designed to reduce harm.

The form and substance of policy options and responses is also invariably tied to highly subjective assessments and interpretation of the causes and nature of the problems themselves (Garbarino, 1993). Garbarino makes clear that adolescent behavioral problems can be seen as "ice cubes," which suggests that they are tied to individual development and emanate from individual and family flaws, or "icebergs," in which the roots of problems lie beyond and below the individual in broad social and cultural forces. More than likely because of the strong societal bias towards individualism, the tendency in American policy making is to make policy choices and produce programs that view the adolescent behavioral situation as one of ice cubes, absent the broader recognition that individual-level changes quite often depend on modifications in the larger social ecology (Goodman, Wandersman, Chinman, Imm, & Morrissey, 1996). Consequently, incentives are in place for the government to inexorably build social indicators and monitoring systems to track problem behaviors. Subsequent research and practice are steered to naming, counting, and reducing the incidence of environmental developmental risks (e.g., family violence, poverty, family disintegration) and health-compromising behaviors (e.g., substance use, adolescent pregnancy, interpersonal violence, school dropout).

Widespread faith in and respect for science, with its philosophical grounding in logical positivism and its emphasis on detached inquiry, along with the splits between basic research and application and the splits between expert and practitioner, may also make a contribution to policy rooted in resolving and reconciling deficiencies. According to Giddens (1991), the inherent reflexivity of science interjects doubt into the world and makes a major contribution to the anxieties and insecurities of the postmodern world. For Boyte (2000), positivism structures patterns of theory evaluation, assessment, and outcome measures around fixing social problems. Benson (2003) argues that an overreliance on this organizing frame supports the creation of elaborate and expensive service and program delivery infrastructures, creates a dependence on professional experts, and encourages an ethos of fear. It derogates, ignores, and interferes with the natural and inherent capacity of communities to be community.

Whereas the aforementioned philosophical and intellectual currents fuel investments in deficit-reducing approaches, a new line of inquiry is beginning to focus attention on the widespread societal depletion of developmental supports and opportunities. In an important overview of development in the United States, Bronfenbrenner and Morris (1998) identify a growing chaos in traditional socializing systems. The social and cultural forces discussed in this section have dramatically altered youth access to sources of support, empowerment, connection, modeling, and value transmission over the last 40 years (Benson et al., 1998). Pervasive age segregation contributes to the deep disconnect adolescents have from long-term, sustained relationships with multiple adults (Benson, 1997). The issue of socialization inconsistency that now typifies the journey of human development in most communities results in many youths experiencing a dissonance in core messages they receive about boundaries, expectations, and values (Damon, 1995). In examining the contemporary American social landscape, we discover that fundamental developmental support mechanisms are relatively uncommon (Benson et al., 1999). Nagging and ample data support the conclusion that the human development infrastructure—if not outright chaotic—is particularly fragile and perhaps even ruptured in far too many American communities (e.g., Benson, 1997; Benson et al., 1998). Quantitative support for this conclusion emerges from aggregated community-level studies utilizing Search Institute's developmental asset framework mentioned earlier. In survey-based profiles of hundreds and hundreds of suburban, rural, and urban communities, we discover that these developmental assets are relatively uncommon (Benson et al., 1999). Only a minority of American 6th- to 12th-grade youth report access to such critical developmental resources as caring neighborhood, intergenerational relationships, adult role models, a caring school climate, and creative (art, music, drama) activities (e.g., see Benson et al., 1999). To be more precise, a 1997 aggregated sample of 99,000 middle school and high school students in 213 communities across the country yielded these percentages of youth who possess the following developmental assets: nonrelated adult relationships, 41%; caring neighborhood, 40%; a caring school climate, 25%. Furthermore, subgroup analyses of student reports reveal that this nonnormatic access to these kinds of developmental resources hold across gender, grade, parental education, and race-ethnicity (Benson et al., 1999). A year-2000 aggregated sample of 217,000 youth from 318 communities in 33 states, although it was able to show slight percentage improvement, still demonstrated similar results.

This information is especially disturbing in light of the data showing that opportunities for youth to have sustained relationships with nonrelated adults, their ability to live in places where adults know and interact with them, and their experience of schools as places of care, support, and intellectual stimulation are understood to be predictive of significant adolescent health outcomes (Scales & Leffert, 1999). Although some young people are indeed faring better than others in terms of social environments conducive to and supportive of healthy development, most young people report that they do not experience these connections and supports. A low level of access to fundamental developmental resources is normative for youth across gender, grade level, parental education, and race-ethnicity.

Results from two Gallup Polls conducted in 2000 with a representative sample of American adults and in 2002 with adults and youth offer some insights regarding the social norms for adult engagement with adolescents (Scales et al., 2001). Both adult samples reveal that even though a strong majority of adults consider it very important to communicate and enforce a common set of beliefs and behavioral expectations to youth, they routinely tend not to take personal action and view other adults as even less likely to act. A lack of social expectations, pressure, permission, and support may account for a wide gap between consensus on the importance of engagement and actually engaging in activity to bring it about (Scales, Benson, & Mannes, 2003).

A major question that emerges from this cultural assessment is, *what effects and implications do all of these events and circumstances have on policy responses to youth development?* One effect is youth development advocates' motivation to increasingly propose youth engagement and youth participation as key strategies in preparing youth for adulthood.

A second major effect is a deeper appreciation for and understanding of the ways in which the environments of the many life settings that touch the lives of youth can nurture developmental nutrients (Benson, Scales, & Mannes, 2003; Pittman et al., 2001); this includes delineating the key features that all settings must exhibit to secure developmental objectives. The recent National Research Council (2002) report entitled *Community Programs to Promote Youth Development* identified these developmentally attentive features as follows: physical and psychological safety; appropriate structure; supportive relationships; opportunities to belong; positive social norms; support for efficacy and mattering; opportunities for skill building; and coordination among family, school, and community efforts.

A third major effect is the more prominent embrace of community as a locus of action for mobilizing multiple actors. Community is increasingly understood as an important means for integrating the contexts that shape positive adolescent development as well as an arena for comprehensive, citywide initiatives promoting child and adolescent well-being (Benson, 1997; Blyth & Leffert, 1995; Damon, 1997; National Research Council and Institute of Medicine, 2000, 2002). The idea of developmentally attentive community flows naturally out of this recognition and provides a potentially useful conceptual framework for exploring and positing optimal configurations of resources, opportunities, experiences, and relationships across many institutional and sector ecologies. At its core, developmentally attentive community reenergizes community sources of developmental strengths for youth in the following five ways: (a) mobilizing adults, (b) engaging youth, (c) transforming sectors, (d) strengthening programs, and (e) unleashing supports for change (Benson & Libbey, 2001; Benson, Scales, & Mannes, 2003).

Moreover, the idea of developmentally attentive community links to several relevant intellectual currents. It is a concrete way to operationalize Bronfenbrenner's (1979) pioneering ecological model of human development by articulating both the independent and synergistic roles community residents and sectors play in constructing an optimal environment for positive child and youth development. A developmentally attentive community activates the strength-building capacity of its residents (both adults and youth) and promotes collective action for purposes of transforming developmental settings and sources that constitute the community infrastructure (Mannes, Benson, Kretzmann, & Norris, 2003). From the field of community organizing, it serves as the basis for Tilly's (1973) notion of collective action—that is, that a community's pooled resources need to be applied by a critical mass of community members to advance the common good; this entails resurrecting the role of nonprofessional citizens as potential generators of developmental nutrients and necessitates rejuvenating civic engagement (Benson, 1997). A developmentally attentive community orchestrates the flow of positive developmental energy emanating from an organized and active citizenry so that youth acquire as many developmental assets as possible. It ensures that youth experience multiple developmentally rich ecologies and that all youth—not just those deemed to be at risk and served by standard prevention or risk-reduction programs—

are the intended beneficiaries. In general, developmentally attentive communities are also characterized by more indirect influences that support and sustain these more direct resident and sector influences through social norms that promote adult engagement with the young and financial resources to bring developmental well-being to fruition. This idea is consistent with Damon's (1995) understanding of the developmental necessity of communities mobilizing around a unified consensus of core values that begins to concretize the definition of the common good.

Based upon this all-too-brief cultural review that has sought to surface germane social and political circumstances within which the youth development paradigm has emerged, an overriding challenge is to determine how policy can be used to strengthen social capacity and build sensible and appropriate pathways to developmental success for youth.

DEVELOPMENTALLY ATTENTIVE YOUTH PUBLIC POLICY

Progress in securing developmentally attentive community is in part tied to promulgating developmentally attentive public policies for youth. Developmentally attentive youth public policy would meet two primary conditions. First, such policy would be congruent with the organizing frame of youth development and help codify the tenets of the field. There would be movement beyond negative outcomes and academic success to encompass both positive and nonacademic outcomes (Pittman, Diversi, & Ferber, 2002). A broad range of services, supports, and opportunities would be made available to young people and would prominently feature their voices and actions as agents of positive change (Pittman, Yohalem, & Irby, 2003). Second, applied youth development knowledge would be woven into youth policy. In other words, policies would be grounded in what is empirically known and understood about healthy development. Roth & Brooks-Gunn (2000) provide policy makers with a brief and user-friendly cataloguing of the existing knowledge base. Unfortunately, neither of these two primary conditions are routinely met at the federal level (Hahn, 2002), and the same can be said for other governmental units responsible for generating youth policy.

Securing developmentally attentive youth policy must also contend with the issue of whether the United States has a singular youth policy or possesses an assemblage of policies that for convenience can be clustered under a wide youth policy umbrella. Pittman et al.(2003) argue that America has a plethora of policies affecting youth, including the more obvious ones that are developed in the education, juvenile justice, child welfare, and social service spheres. There are also a trove of policies that may seem less obvious but have just as direct an impact on youth, such as health insurance coverage, tax credits, tax cuts, and school vouchers (Zigler, Kagan, & Hall, 1996). Pittman et al. (2003) determine that the United States lacks a unified and coherent policy agenda for youth that is cognizant of the dynamics of youth development, incorporates developmental insights, and is decidedly strength based in its approach. At the federal level, neither policies nor policy mechanisms currently exist that are capable of shepherding young people through the complicated and challenging developmental transitions from childhood through adolescence and on into adulthood.

Hahn (2002) takes a much more circumscribed perspective on what actually constitutes American youth policy and suggests it has primarily focused on school reform, out-of-school youth, and programming during nonschool hours. He also acknowledges the relatively modest reach of those existing forms of youth programs to only approximately 12% of eligible youth. At the state government level, Hahn suggests youth policy can be characterized as "young, underdeveloped, and inconsistent," even though there are a growing number of positive examples in specific states, many of which are presented later in this section. The viewpoint that interprets school reform, out-of-school youth, and programming during nonschool hours as viable and significant youth policy makes the case for the relevance to youth of what can be thought of as "micro public policies," which are typically created by school boards, community-based organizations, and foundations.

Developmentally attentive youth policy would help engender the formation of social capital by primarily building upon Macedo's (2002) distinction between the relative merits of its bridging and bonding forms. He asserts that the bridging aspect of social capital is far more important than the bonding version because the former builds ties within a pluralistic society, whereas the latter maintains sharp social and economic distinctions between insiders and outsiders. A developmentally attentive public policy for youth would affirm that associations and interrelationships across diverse social contexts can actually make meaningful contributions to positive development and would recognize the family, neighborhood, school, youth organization, places of work, and congregations as policy intervention points. Transforming schools into more developmentally rich settings, building linkages across multiple socializing institutions, mobilizing citizens, launching community-wide initiatives organized around a shared vision of strength building, and expanding funding for quality of out-of-school programs can all be seen as features of youth development policy initiatives. Moreover, enlightened youth public policy would actually create incentives for the formation of bridging social capital in order to promote human and operational relationships across diverse developmental settings. Clearly, public policy framed with a youth development orientation, based on developmental knowledge, and emphasizing bridging social capital introduces the need for many interlocking strategies cultivating youth access to and utilization of developmental opportunities and supports. Although it is unreasonable to expect any more than a modicum of coherence resulting from diverse policy expressions channeled through multiple outlets, a dispersive strategy can still help create a more hospitable zeitgeist for developmentally attentive public policy.

The advancement of developmentally attentive public policy is also dependent upon the degree of success in dealing with several classic dimensions of the policy-making process. The first dimension deals with the multiple factors associated with policy agenda setting (Kingdon, 1984). Building an asset-oriented youth public policy agenda is predicated upon articulating issues that need to be on the agenda and formulating policy options that seem reasonable and capable of resolving those issues. Pittman et al.'s (2001) enunciation of youth development concerns are instructive for crafting a youth policy agenda. Items such as moving beyond prevention, quick fixes, and basic services can certainly serve to guide agenda-setting thinking, and Pittman et al. (2001) have gone on to suggest ways in which those concerns can be translated into constructing a policy agenda. A large part of agenda setting entails consciousness raising, education, and advocacy to foster a more enlightened and motivated developmentally attentive policy climate among the general public and elected officials.

The second dimension of policy making addresses policy enactment and entails diverse strategies and tactics (Bardach, 1972; Dear & Patti, 1981) that in this instance would be associated with moving a piece of developmentally attuned legislation from inception to executive signing. Major activities involve seeking sponsorship for legislation, contributing ideas to and writing the actual content of statutes, forging coalitions to lobby and ensure passage, and all the while monitoring and maintaining vigilance as potential policies grind their way through the legislative process. The third dimension focuses on the actual implementation of policy by taking into account a host of human and organizational factors integral to the various contexts in which developmentally attentive policies are carried out (Pressman & Wildavsky, 1974). Here, particular attention is paid to elements that give policies their distinctive implementation tone, character, and influence as they play out in the real world. These elements, which are essential to policy-based interventions and programs, include the status of interorganizational and intergovernmental relations, the political tenor of organizational networks, the infrastructure of delivery systems, and agencies at the point of service delivery and individuals involved in providing the service (Mannes et al., 2003).

Next, we consider the role of these three core dimensions of policy making in attaining developmentally attentive public policies for youth at different governmental levels, as well as in the micropolicy category. A number of examples are included for illustrative purposes.

Setting the Policy Agenda

During the 1960s, developmental knowledge was key to conceptualizing Head Start and other early childhood policy initiatives (Zigler & Anderson, 1979). Yet, similar circumstances have never arisen with regard to adolescent policy, perhaps because of the prevailing supremacy of the risk reduction policy approach. Policy makers' thin understanding of strength-based child and youth development also compromises the inclusion of developmental content (Rickel & Becker, 1997). A study by Zero to Three (2000) showed that the general public also has a very limited and often incorrect knowledge of early child development, and it is likely they would fare the same if they were assessed on their understanding of adolescent development. The lack of adequate grounding in the basics of development undercuts efforts to have the public demand and rally in support of a policy agenda that is based on what is actually known about applied development research and practice.

A lack of coherence around actual agenda content is also seen as a liability. This incoherence stems largely from various advocates' inability to reach common ground around goals, objectives, and methods. As the State Legislative Leaders Foundation (1995) reports, "Building a coherent message on children's policy is challenging, however, because there is no clearly discernable legislative agenda for children and families; rather, a multitude of individuals and organizations with different agendas are sending mixed messages about what is best for children" (p. 42).

Constituencies with the most expertise on the subject of development are likely to be government employees with either expertise in or passion for youth development and housed in agencies at various units of government, professionals in organizations serving youth, and advocates from child and youth policy organizations. Although each of these groups' policy power has limits, they can still play crucial roles and perform essential activities, and they should be seen as valuable allies in moving progressive youth policy forward.

Ferber, Pittman, and Marshall (2002) focus on the state level and identify several of the most important tasks associated with agenda setting: (a) vision and issue framing; (b) marketing, messages, and communication; and (c) making the case to funders. Regarding the first task, the Louisiana Youth Policy Network has created a vision and guiding set of principles targeting local investment for youth education and employment. The initiative will be evaluated using a set of core indicators around the themes of ensuring that children and families get a healthy start, helping children and youth succeed in school, improving the life chances of youth and young adults, and strengthening the positive development of youth.

Agenda setting for marketing, messages, and communication must confront the general public's largely held negative views of young people (Scales, 2001). Gilliam and Bales (2001) attribute the viewpoint to the cumulative impact of mainstream media news and entertainment that produces a public narrative of youth as self-absorbed, amoral, violent, and experimenters with risky behaviors. Certain states such as Oregon, through its campaign entitled Get Real: Connect With Youth, are engaged in the second critical task of seeking to change public consciousness by developing clear messages and communications to promote a more accurate, positive view of young people as a basis for launching positive development public policies (Ferber et al., 2002). For several years a citywide asset-building initiative in Portland entitled Take the Time conducted a similar scope of work (Mannes, Lewis, Hintz, Foster, & Nakkula., 2002).

According to Ferber et al. (2002), the policy agenda-setting task of justifying investments on behalf of youth demands policy makers' active involvement in informing and influencing key decision points in legislative budget cycles and leveraging foundation and corporate revenue in support of young people. The Connecticut Office for Community Youth Development's Funders Connection, convened by the state Office of Policy and Management, is but one example of collaboration among 11 state agencies, family and community foundations, corporate giving offices, and United Ways in the state. The project encourages representatives from multiple organizations underwriting initiatives to find common ground on key elements of a policy agenda that will translate into cost efficiencies, greater impact, and better outcomes for youth.

Membership associations for office holders such as the National League of Cities through its Institute for Youth, Education, and Families helps mayors and city council members determine how they create a policy climate in which strength-based solutions are conceived and feasible policy options to secure those solutions attain legitimacy. In a similar vein, the National Governors Association has established a Youth Policy Network to help shape agenda setting.

The developmental asset framework has become a resource for policy agenda setting. Elected officials from around the country, including mayors in Cary, North Carolina and Boise, Idaho have helped coalesce an asset-oriented policy agenda by establishing a vision, crafting policy messages, designing policy communication strategies, and establishing youth appointments on commissions and boards with voting rights (Melby, 2001). School boards and superintendents use developmental assets as a cornerstone for school reform policy. In Portage County, Ohio the framework is employed to guide the work of the continuous improvement committee's emphasis on instructional and educational services. In the Traverse Bay area of northwest Michigan, GiveEm40 24.7, an asset-building community initiative, the top administrators of the five-county school system utilize the framework as an agenda setter for improving school climate and enhancing teacher and student performance.

Enacting Strength-Based Policy

Takanishi (1996) specifies three axioms essential to youth policy enactment: (a) establish universal requirements for healthy adolescent development; (b) focus on life transitions as critical opportunities for interventions, and (c) target many pivotal institutions (the sources and settings of developmental strengths and asset building cited earlier) that cumulatively can alter the pathway toward healthy development.

As discussed earlier, attempts to enact a cohesive youth policy have remained stubbornly beyond reach. Hahn (2002) reminds us that a Young Americans Act was passed by Congress in 1988–1989 but in the absence of an appropriation did not materialize and that a Youth Development Block Grant, attempted in the 1994–1995 legislative session, also failed to become law. In the early years of the 21st century Congress has before it two complementary policy proposals intimating that the heretofore elusive national youth policy is possible. The first, the Younger Americans Act (YAA) is viewed by many professionals and advocates as the legislative umbrella that can put youth development on the map by spelling out clear principles, establishing a national coordinating body and local youth councils, and creating a flexible block grant state funding stream for community-based youth services. The legislative intent is to assure that youth have access to programs and services providing them with the competencies and character they need to fully meet their future responsibilities as adults and citizens. The campaign is bolstered by a large grassroots advocacy campaign, a centerpiece of which is endorsements from more than 250 national and local youth-serving organizations. A version was introduced in both legislative chambers in 2001 with solid bipartisan support, and revised versions are likely to be introduced in future sessions.

The other policy blueprint is the Children's Defense Fund's (CDF's) creation of an omnibus bill that packages a multitude of separate pieces of child and youth legislation that have been introduced or are up for reauthorization. The omnibus bill spans the full range of policy issues—health, child development, child care, education, income support, nutrition, housing, family stability, juvenile justice, gun safety, and youth development (defined as after-school programs—i.e., 21st Century Community Learning Centers), funding for community-based programs through the YAA and programs for older youth, including YouthBuild, Job Corps, and the Workforce Investment Act.

Differences in the scope of the two bills underscore several fault lines in the attempt to enact youth policy. Whereas the YAA is more circumscribed, tightly linked to youth development, and preferred by certain professional groups and lobbyists, the broader CDF proposed legislation is consistent with a view held by a number of national organizations and funding entities that youth development policies and programs should not be separated from child development, family support, and community development. Reconciling the dilemmas associated with a more unilateral youth development policy approach versus one wherein youth development is nested within child, family, and community interests has significant implications for the form and substance of policy prescriptions.

The lack of an American national youth policy is striking in comparison with many other nations' ability to formulate a unified and coherent youth policy agenda, produce expressions of collective policy, and determine the mechanics of implementation. According to Ferber et al. (2002), in 1995 the Commonwealth Youth Ministers reached agreement that all of their member countries should formulate specific national youth policies and develop national action plans. Australia, Namibia, Zambia, the Republic of Seychelles, and New Zealand (among others) have all forged youth policy mission statements to guide policy design and operation.

Youth policy enactment at the state level may lack a long and well-established history, but more has been achieved there than at the federal level. Ferber et al. (2002) show how state policy makers have been laying the groundwork for broad-based enactment by developing cross-cutting initiatives and model policies. States are developing requests for proposals (RFPs) and memorandums of understanding (MOUs) that create the justification and protocols for how various departments and agencies—both inside and outside of government and across service delivery systems—can work together collaboratively. In Massachusetts, policy has been enacted that grants tuition waivers at any one of Massachusetts' 29 state and community colleges and universities for youth aging out of the foster care system.

Ferber et al. (2002) also specify the critical enactment task of making sure there is genuine and meaningful youth and community involvement. Foster youth played an active role in developing the proposal, lobbying key decision makers, testifying before the Board of Higher Education, and implementing a media campaign in support of the Massachusetts foster care youth policy initiative. The Iowa Collaboration for Youth Development's (ICYD's) primary objective is to increase youth involvement in state and local level planning, policy discussions, and decision making. The developmental asset framework also fosters youth engagement in policy enactment. At the municipal level, in Alexandria, Virginia, the Youth Policy Commission created a committee to conduct background research and then plan a community-wide asset-building initiative.

Still, without adequate legislative appropriations, enacting developmentally attentive policy at the macro- or microlevel is a hollow victory. Newman, Smith, and Murphy (2001) have calculated that it would cost approximately $144 billion dollars to provide youth development supports and opportunities to all school-age children and youth in America. Although the mathematical exercise has merit, tabulating the magnitude of the investment is not likely to create a more hospitable policy environment or win political converts.

At a more pragmatic and practical level, governmental appropriation sources need to remember that in addition to playing a role in policy agenda setting, they also can make sure policy enactment has some teeth by providing revenue to ensure a basis for policy action. Fortunately, there are examples of micro-public-level policies that are changing the opportunities and resources available to youth in local settings. A number of local United Ways are employing developmental asset criteria as the basis for making appropriations to community-based agencies to ensure that they will work with youth in strength-based ways.

Implementing Youth Development Policy

With the gradual emergence of more youth-development-friendly policy at the state level, more attention is being paid to implementation issues. State policy makers are taking into account organizations, alliances, and networks operating in neighborhoods, in communities, and throughout their entire areas of jurisdiction to see that strength-based policies take root and produce beneficial consequences. State attention is devoted to the orchestration and oversight of programs representing the application of enacted policies.

Ferber et al. (2002) identify several significant tasks state-level policy makers are engaged in to buttress implementation. The first deals with creating inter- and intracoordinating bodies to link youth development activities across state and community systems. These coordinating entities tend to function as design and administrative support structures for planning, collaboration, and funding. They vary in terms of their charge, where they are housed within state government, how they are staffed, how they came into being, and how permanent they are, along with the amount of resources, responsibility, and power they have been granted. Despite structural and operational distinctions, these bodies have the potential to fill a critical void in choreographing state policy efforts for youth.

In Massachusetts the Executive Office of Health and Human Services created an Office of Youth Development with an Advisory Council in 1999 to forge statewide youth policy and establish and support effective youth development programs at the state and local levels. The Kentucky Youth Development Partnership has brought together a group of 18 national, state, and local youth-serving organizations to foster collaboration of youth services at the state and local levels and to promote positive youth development. Similar efforts are being conducted at the county and municipal levels with the developmental asset framework instrumental to progress. In Butler County, Ohio, a comprehensive strategy that embraces the asset approach is bringing agencies together for purposes of strengthening youth. The Denver Comprehensive Plan 2000 was established to foster a citywide response to the needs of its children and youth, and its design was informed by the developmental assets.

A second critical state policy task relates to the intersection of implementation and accountability. A number of states are working to specify outcomes and indicators and then to go on to collect, analyze, and disseminate data in ways that promote a shared sense of accountability for youth policies and programs. Given the dominance of the deficit-oriented policy paradigm, states are confronted with an uphill struggle to incorporate promotional indicators that measure and track positive attitudes and behaviors. Vermont, however, has succeeded in including youth assets data in its annual outcome and indicators publication, the Agency of Human Services' Community Profiles, by adding in 2001 developmental asset oriented questions to its state Youth Risk Behavior Survey. This is administered biannually to most students in Grades 8–12, and taping strength-based data from the Search Institute survey, Profiles of Student Life: Attitudes & Behaviors, that has been completed by more than 15,000 of the state's youth.

Ferber et al. (2002) also conveys how states are enhancing implementation related capacity for asset-oriented initiatives and interventions by creating demonstration projects, fortifying the capabilities of professionals and volunteers, and revamping multiple facets of the service delivery infrastructure. Curricula are being developed, training sessions conducted, resources disseminated through workshops and conferences, and partnerships between state agencies and regions and communities encouraged and honored.

Several specific asset-building policy implementation efforts are worth mentioning. Alaska-ICE is a 6-year statewide youth development initiative emphasizing the shared responsibility for preparing Alaska's children and youth for the future (including their academic success, civil behavior, racial tolerance, and reduction of risk behaviors). It is based on the vision set forth by the Association of Alaska School Board's 1991 long-range plan and the book *Helping Kids Succeed—Alaskan Style,* created in partnership with Alaska Department of Health and Social Services in 1998. This book, which provides tools and suggestions for building assets among Alaskan youth, is based on the Search Institute's developmental asset framework and ideas for action provided by thousands of citizens. Alaska-ICE provides local, regional, and statewide training; technical assistance; demonstration projects; and coaching and resources to schools, community organizations, parent groups, and faith communities. The Association of Alaska School Boards was able to obtain a direct congressional appropriation to support their long-term objective of raising healthy children and youth. The Commission on Youth in the Commonwealth of Virginia funded pilot asset-building community projects in three sites. The New York State Office of Child and Family Services through its Integrated County Planning Initiative is building a blueprint with its field force to blend the developmental asset framework with other youth models in order to advance youth development on a cross-system basis.

The compilation of evidence in this section implies that American society is in a formative stage of agenda setting, enactment, and implementation efforts with regard to developmentally attentive youth policies. Even with comparatively less progress on the federal front, the expanding breadth of activity at the state and microlevel offers initial instruction on how such public policies for youth can become more easily formulated and put into practice.

YOUTH DEVELOPMENT POLICY AS A MORAL IMPERATIVE AND PUBLIC IDEA

Several strategies can assist public officials in their role as policy makers, public servants in their role as policy shapers and enforcers, and the general public in their role as the ultimate policy arbiters to become more fully engaged in developmentally attentive public policies for youth. All three groups need to expand and hone their repertoire of policy agenda setting, enacting, and implementing skills to make change. There is no doubt that greater adeptness and agility with developmental domains, desired outcomes, key inputs, service delivery, and management strategies is essential to helping them deal with the mechanics of youth development policy. Accountability metrics comprised of national indicators of health and developmental well-being to augment the existing edifice of deficit-driven measurement systems will be of great use in bringing balance into national reporting system and set the stage for multipronged youth policy responses. Quality longitudinal research looking at interrelationships among interventions designed to reduce threats to development, promote developmental nutrients, reduce health-compromising behaviors, and promote well-being will interject wisdom into the creation of viable youth development policy options. Practical tools will be invaluable in helping government, the academy, the nonprofit sector, and main street chart a positive path for American youth.

Still, at the end of the legislative session, board meeting, or community gathering, success is as much—if not more—about capturing the hearts and minds of Americans as it is about more efficiently and effectively completing a set of technical policy-related activities. How might this be accomplished? For one thing, public officials, public servants, and the general public can choose to increasingly vocalize the importance of devising policies that can transform the social settings that touch the lives of youth into developmentally rich ecologies because they believe in the innate value of development. Additionally, they can become more articulate in specifying policies that can weave those rich ecologies woven into a developmentally attentive social fabric because they understand the resultant societal benefits. These insights lead Benson and Pittman (2001) to surface the moral concerns at the core of youth development and asset-oriented policies, programs, and practices for youth and lead Pittman et al. (2001) to discuss how youth policy can be transformed into an idea that has palpable cultural currency. Real progress is substantially tied to public officials, public servants, and the general public embracing the moral imperative of developmentally healthy youth and committing to the good life for youth as a public idea that resonates in civic life. It would also require recognizing young people as what economists refer to as a public good, which thereby helps justify public support for their optimal development (England & Folbre, 2002). The path will not be an easy one.

Skocpol and Dickert (2001) describe how advocacy for children and families in civic America has changed over the last 50 years from locally rooted membership federations at the center of American public life to professionally run and nationally focused advocacy groups. They point to the lack of substantive bridges linking local groups and nationally organized professional groups and caution that the lack of linkages stymies effective policy agenda setting and subsequent action. These factors likely further exacerbate state legislative leaders' perception of an incoherent children's policy agenda. Imig (2001) paints a bleak picture of our society's ability to persuade parents and communities to mobilize around child and youth policy issues.

Mentoring and after-school initiatives stand out in contrast to this general situation. But, even with the general public and public policy supportive of mentoring and after-school programming, Walker (2001) concedes that the emphasis remains on preventing or reducing negative behavior that retards or impairs youths' reaching their potential, and there is very little acknowledgement of the need to actually foster healthy development. The stark dimensions of the social dilemma helping Americans recognize the important distinction between a deficit and a positive orientation is readily apparent in the results of a Gallup Poll released in March 2001 that indicated that a majority of Americans concentrate on their weaknesses and try to fix them as opposed to building on their strengths (Buckingham, 2001). Similar results were obtained in a number of countries around the world, which indicates the global reach of human allegiance to remediation as a way of being. According to Buckingham, Ben Franklin described wasted strengths as "sundials in the shade," and the Gallup research indicates that many individuals, families, and organizations in America keep their sundials in the shade.

As a result of informal conversations with about two dozen Americans, Walker (2001) came to the conclusion that few had much confidence that public policy could make any difference in the lives of youth. Because according to Walker the policy climate is "rooted largely in the opinions and common sense of ordinary citizens" (p.78), the suspicions and doubts that surfaced complicate the possibility of progress on the developmental front for youth. His experiences only serve to reinforce a prevailing social perspective that policy-based solutions have limited merit.

Despite the challenges, youth development policy remains worth seeking because the good life for youth and the revitalization and refurbishment of civil society are increasingly seen as vitally interconnected, and emphasizing their interrelationship only serves to elevate their public presence. Lerner, Fisher, and Weinberg (2000) affirm that civil society will grow and prosper as public policies provide youth with the opportunities for caring-compassion, competence, character, connection, and confidence. In the broadest sense, civil society represents the social contract among the people occupying a political jurisdiction. For Walzer (1998), civil society "names the space of uncoerced human association and also the set of relational networks—formed for the sake of family, faith, interest, and ideology—that fill this space" (pp. 291–292). Walzer's definition of civil society is consonant with Putnam's (1993) assertion of social capital as essential to the vitality of democratic society and with major points made by models and framework in youth development, including the developmental asset framework. Energizing the voluntary associational nature of the various settings and source of development, as well as firming connections among them, is essential to realizing developmentally rich ecologies and is harmonious with how developmentally attentive community can be attained (Lerner & Benson, 2003).

In Walzer's (1998) review of 19th- and 20th-century social thought on strengthening civil society in order to ensure that citizens—young and old—can attain the good life, two lines of thinking are particularly germane to the current state of youth and their development. One approach affirms that the good life is secured through the marketplace and attained primarily through personal choice. Freedom itself is predicated upon one's ability to choose among product and service options. Living well primarily entails focusing on consumer choices and only secondarily deals with public affairs and policy. Youth reach their full human potential as competitive and private creatures engaged in rational economic choice. Walzer, however, raises concerns that the celebration of autonomy inherent in the marketplace actually undermines the basis for social solidarity. Moreover, he asserts that the market works strenuously to avoid entanglement with government policy because of its penchant for a minimalist state.

A second perspective defines the good life as engaged citizens of a public community fully participating in political affairs and policy matters. This affirmation of civic republicanism hails political activity, collective involvement with fellow citizens, and the mutual fabrication of policy. Youth reach their full human potential as public figures—active and engaged citizens caught up in proposing, debating, and deciding. In this second category, contemporary America is often found wanting. Fisher and Karger (1997) note the evolution of a more private contemporary world, the hallmarks of which are an emphasis on the private rights of individuals, the expansion of private spaces, and the expanded power of private institutions. They raise concerns about the impact of these trends on social life and the public good. These kinds of shortcomings likely stimulate the impulses behind initiatives such as youth activism, service-learning, and community service that are designed to get youth more meaningfully involved with and contributing to civic culture (Zeldin, 2000).

Zimmerman (1992) investigated the relationship among state political culture, the level of public investments for well-being, and negatively framed indicators of well-being such as divorce, suicide, poverty, and teen pregnancy. She was able to show that states adhering to a more individualistic political culture—meaning that they emphasized private concerns over public ones and high value was placed on keeping public interventions minimal—did less to mediate connections among people and had poorer results on those individual and family well-being indicators; this was contrasted with states that were less individualistic, did more to mediate connections, and had better results for the individual and family indicators of well-being.

In terms of moral imperatives, Etzioni (2001) questions whether a more robust civil society and the good life for all people—including youth—can be attained without specifying the moral characteristics of the good society. He chooses to draw distinctions between the civil and the good society and by tapping rich legacies of social philosophy and political theory charts differing pathways to reaching the good. Etzioni posits that the liberal theory's approach to a strong civil society is predisposed to reject social formulations of the good by either the state or society based upon adherence to a position of moral pluralism. He goes on to suggest that in marked contrast to the reluctance of liberal political theory, both communitarian and conservative theorists are eager to specify what is good. Conservative thought is committed to specifying the good and very comfortable with state enforcement of sanctioned moral behavior. The impetus for contemporary conservative thought and action come from the belief that moral relativism ignited by the 1960s and moral irresponsibility stoked by the welfare state have engendered a loss of social virtue and foisted moral anarchy on the culture. Similar to conservatives, communitarians take exception with the value neutrality of liberal thought. Even though communitarian theorists share conservative interest in delineating the good, they differ from conservative theorists by remaining resistant to an articulation of morality by the state. Instead, communitarians believe that the public itself needs to negotiate and promote a shared understanding of appropriate morality.

Although a discussion of social philosophy and political theory may seem highly irrelevant to youth policy, Lakoff (1996) argues that policy positions reflect moral worldviews. More to the point is that these divergent orientations to articulating the good are routinely the contentious grist of social bickering and policy squabbles. An especially acrimonious argumentative tone in political and policy circles over distinct moral worldviews in more recent time has led to widespread public alienation and estrangement from many policy matters (Elshtain, 1996).

For those who are at ease with expressions of the good, Zeldin (2000) enunciates the moral indicators of optimal community for the full development of youth: an equitable infrastructure, communitas (spirit, good feelings, and creativity), emotional attachment, and caritas (adult attitudinal and behavioral demonstration of caring and confidence in youth).

The concept of social citizenship offers citizens a way to go about establishing that optimal community for youth. Marshall (1964) identified social citizenship as a next stage of citizenship to emerge in the 20th century after first civil and then political citizenship had been secured in the two previous 100-year periods. Social citizenship calls for full access to a society's social heritage and the right to live a life according to prevailing social standards. It affirms the social rights citizens possess, and the responsibilities they have to the well-being of their fellow citizens.

Fraser and Gordon (1998) examine the political economy in America and take the position that an emphasis on civil society and civil rights that is property centered and contract based actually serves as an impediment to the expression of social citizenship. Even in accepting the significant obstacles America's "cultural mythology of civil citizenship" (Fraser & Gordon, 1998, p.125) places in the way of a robust social citizenship, the idea remains meaningful for developmentally attentive youth policy. Notwithstanding Imig's (2001) overall sense of disappointment in the lack of stalwart advocacy for the well-being of young people, he is still able to recognize the Academy for Educational Development, the Asset-Based Community Development Institute, and Search Institute for their community organizing work around strength-based development. Although the work of these organizations advances the cause of social citizenship, one is left to ask what else can be done to advance community members' acceptance of, responsibility for, and willingness to take action to promulgate progressive youth public policy. Mannes (2002) proposes that as a start, human development be understood and accepted as a basic social right.

One has the sense that developmentally attentive youth policy is more easily realized in a culture and an epoch in which social citizenship is valued and vibrant. An activated sense of social citizenship in the United States would help affirm the moral legitimacy of developmentally healthy young people and marshal public will behind producing developmental strengths for all youth. It would offer professional, political, and lay audiences a sense of purpose, hope, and optimism that development can be the touchstone of public policy for youth. Then America could honestly be heralded as the land of developmental opportunity.

REFERENCES

Barber, B. K., & Olsen, J. A. (1997). Socialization in context: Connection, regulation, and autonomy in the family, school, neighborhood, and with peers. *Journal of Adolescent Research, 12,* 287–315.

Bardach, E. (1972). *The skill factor in politics.* Berkeley, CA: University of California Press.

Beck, U. (1992). *Risk society: Towards a new modernity.* Thousand Oaks, CA: Sage.

Benson, P. L. (1990). *The troubled journey: A portrait of 6th-12th grade youth.* Minneapolis, MN: Search Institute.

Benson, P. L. (1997). *All kids are our kids: What communities must do to raise caring and responsible children and adolescents.* San Francisco, CA: Jossey-Bass.

Benson, P. L. (2003). Developmental assets and asset-building community: Conceptual and empirical foundations. In R. M. Lerner & P. L. Benson (Eds.), *Developmental assets and asset-building communities: Implications for research, policy and practice* (pp.19–64). Boston: Kluwer Academic/Plenum.

Benson, P. L., Leffert, N., Scales, P. C., & Blyth, D. A. (1998). Beyond the "village" rhetoric: Cre-

ating healthy communities for children and adolescents. *Applied Developmental Science, 2*(3), 138–159.
Benson, P. L., & Libbey, H. (2001). Minneapolis Promise: Reflections on the journey. *The Center* (Summer), 54–67.
Benson, P. L., & Pittman, K. (2001). Moving the youth development message: Turning a vague idea into a moral imperative. In P. L. Benson & K. J. Pittman (Eds.), *Trends in youth development: visions, realities, and challenges* (pp. vii–xii). Norwell, MA: Kluwer Academic.
Benson, P. L., & Saito, R. N. (2001). The scientific foundations of youth development. In P. L. Benson & K. J. Pittman (Eds.), *Trends in youth development: Visions, realities, and challenges* (pp. 135–154). Norwell, MA: Kluwer Academic.
Benson, P. L., Scales, P. C., Leffert, N., & Roehlkepartain, E. C. (1999). *A fragile foundation: The state of developmental assets among American youth.* Minneapolis, MN: Search Institute.
Benson, P. L., Scales, P. C., & Mannes, M. (2003). Developmental strengths and their sources: Implications for the study and practice of community building. In R. M. Lerner, F. Jacobs, & D. Wertlieb (Eds.), *Handbook of applied developmental science: Promoting positive child, adolescent, and family development through research, policies and programs: Vol. 1. Applying developmental science for youth and families: Historical and theoretical foundations* (pp. 369–406). Newbury Park, CA: Sage.
Blyth, D. A., & Leffert, N. (1995). Communities as contexts for adolescent development: An empirical analysis. *Journal of Adolescent Research, 10*(1), 64–87.
Borenstein, M. H. (2000). Contemporary research on parenting: The case for nature and nurture. *American Psychologist, 55,* 218–232.
Boyte, H. C. (2000). The struggle against positivism. *Academe, 86*(4), 46–51.
Bronfenbrenner, U. (1979). *The ecology of human development.* Cambridge, MA: Harvard University Press.
Bronfenbrenner, U., & Morris, P. A. (1998). The ecology of developmental processes. In R. M. Lerner & W. Damon (Eds.), *Handbook of child psychology* (Vol. 1, 5th ed., pp. 993–1028). New York: Wiley.
Brown, B. B., Larson, R. W., & Saraswathi, T. S. (2002). *The world's youth: Adolescence in eight regions of the globe.* New York: Cambridge University Press.
Buckingham, M. (2001). *Focus on your strengths or fix your weaknesses?* Princeton, NJ: The Gallup Organization.
Burt, M. R., Zweig, J. M., & Roman, J. (2002). Modeling the payoffs of interventions to reduce adolescent vulnerability. *Journal of Adolescent Health, 31*(1S), 40–57.
Carnegie Corporation of New York. (1992). *A matter of time: Risk and opportunity in the nonschool hours.* Waldorf, MD: Carnegie Council on Adolescent Development.
Carnegie Corporation of New York. (1995). *Great transitions: Preparing adolescents for a new century.* Waldorf, MD: Carnegie Council on Adolescent Development.
Connell, J. P., Gambone, M. A., & Smith, T. J. (2002). Youth development in community settings: Challenges to our field and our approach. In P. L. Benson & K. Pittman (Eds.), *Trends in youth development: Vision, realities and challenges.* Boston: Kluwer Academic.
Damon, W. (1995). *Greater expectations: Overcoming the culture of indulgence in America's homes and schools.* New York: Free Press.
Damon, W. (1997). *The youth charter: How communities can work together to raise standards for all our children.* New York: Free Press.
Damon, W., & Gregory, A. (1997). The youth charter: Towards the formation of adolescent moral identity. *Journal of Moral Education, 26,* 117–130.
Dear, R., & Patti, R. (1981). Legislative advocacy: Seven effective tactics. *Social Work, 26,* 289–297.
Dougherty, D. M. (1993). Adolescent health: Reflections on a report to the U.S. Congress. *American Psychologist, 48,* 193–201.
Eccles, J. S., Early, D., Frasier, K., Belansky, E., & McCarthy, K. (1997). The relation of connection, regulation, and support for autonomy to adolescents' functioning. *Journal of Adolescent Research, 12,* 263–286.

Elshtain, J. B. (1996). Democracy at century's end. *Social Service Review, 70*(4), 507–515.
England, P., & Folbre, N. (2002). Reforming the social family contract: Public support for child rearing in the United States. In G. J. Duncan & P. L. Chase-Lansdale (Eds.), *For better and for worse: Welfare reform and the well-being of children and families* (pp. 290–323). New York: Russell Sage Foundation.
Etzioni, A. (2001). *The monochrome society.* Princeton, NJ: Princeton University Press.
Ferber, T., Pittman, K., & Marshall, T. (2002). *State youth policy: Helping all youth to grow up fully prepared and fully engaged.* Takoma Park, MD: The Forum for Youth Investment.
Fisher, C. B., & Wallace, S. A. (2000). Through the community looking glass: Reevaluating the ethical and policy implications of research on adolescent risk and psychopathology. *Ethics and Behavior, 10*(2), 99–118.
Fisher, R., & Karger, H. J. (1997). *Social work and community in a private world: Getting out in public.* New York: Longman.
Fraser, N., & Gordon, L. (1998). Contract versus charity: Why is there no social citizenship in the United States? In G. Shafir (Ed.), *The citizenship debates: A reader* (pp. 113–127). Minneapolis: University of Minnesota Press.
Fukuyama, F. (1999). *The great disruption: Human nature and the reconstitution of the social order.* New York: Simon & Schuster.
Furstenberg, F. F. (1993). How families manage risk and opportunity in dangerous neighborhoods. In W. J. Wilson (Ed.), *Sociology and the public agenda* (pp. 231–258). Newbury Park, CA: Sage.
Gambone, M. (1993). *Strengthening programs for youth: Promoting adolescent development in the JTPA system.* Philadelphia: Public/Private Ventures.
Garbarino, J. (1993). Enhancing adolescent development through social policy. In P. H. Tolan & B. J. Cohler (Eds.), *Handbook of clinical research and practice with adolescents* (pp. 469–488). Oxford, England: Wiley.
Garmezy, N. (1985). Stress resistant children: The search for protective factors. In J. E. Stevenson (Ed.), *Recent research in developmental psychopathology: Journal of Child Psychology and Psychiatry book supplement no. 4* (pp. 213–233). Oxford, England: Pergamon.
Giddens, A. (1991). *Modernity and self-identity: Self and society in the late modern age.* Stanford, CA: Stanford University Press.
Gilliam, F. D., & Bales, S. N. (2001). Strategic frame analysis: Reframing America's youth. *Social Policy Report, 15*(3), 1–14.
Goleman, D. (1995). *Emotional intelligence.* New York: Bantam Books.
Goodman, R. M., Wandersman, A., Chinman, M., Imm, P., & Morrissey, E. (1996). An ecological assessment of community-based interventions for prevention and health promotion: Approaches to measuring community coalitions. *American Journal of Community Psychology 24*(1), 33–61.
Hahn, A. B. (2002). *Youth development policy: What American foundations can do to promote policy in support of the emerging field of youth development.* Kansas City, MO: Ewing Marion Kauffman Foundation.
Hamilton, S. (1999). *A three-part definition of youth development.* Unpublished manuscript, Cornell University College of Human Ecology, Ithaca, NY.
Hawkins, J. D., & Catalano, R. F. (1992). *Communities that care: Action for drug abuse prevention.* San Francisco: Jossey-Bass.
Hawkins, J. D., Catalano, R. F., & Miller, J. Y. (1992). Risk and protective factors for alcohol and other drug problems in adolescence and early adulthood: Implications for substance abuse prevention. *Psychological Bulletin, 112,* 64–105.
Hein, K. (2002). Enhancing assets for positive youth development: The vision, values, and action agenda of the W.T. Grant Foundation. In R. M. Lerner & P. L. Benson (Eds.), *Developmental assets and asset-building community: Implications for research*. Boston: Kluwer Academic.
Hernandez, D. J. (1994). Children's changing access to resources: A historical perspective. *Social Policy Report, 8*(1), 1–23.
Imig, D. (2001). Mobilizing parents and communities for children. In C. J. DeVita & R. M.

Williams (Eds.), *Who speaks for America's children? The role of child advocates in public policy* (pp. 191–207). Washington, DC: Urban Institute Press.

Jessor, R. (1991). Risk behavior in adolescence: A psychosocial framework for understanding and action. *Journal of Adolescent Health, 12,* 597–605.

Jessor, R., & Jessor, S. (1977). *Problem behavior and psychosocial development: A longitudinal study of youth.* New York: Academic.

Jessor, R., Turbin, M. S., & Costa, F. M. (1998). Risk and protection in successful outcomes among disadvantaged adolescents. *Applied Developmental Science, 2,* 194–208.

Keeter, S., Zukin, C., Andolina, M., & Jenkins, K. (2002). *The civic and political health of the nation: A generational portrait. A report to the Pew Charitable Trusts.* College Park, MD: Center for Information and Research on Civic Learning and Engagement (CIRCLE).

Ketterlinus, R. D., Lamb, M. E., Nitz, K., & Elster, A. B. (1992). Adolescent nonsexual and sex-related problem behaviors. *Journal of Adolescent Research, 7,* 431–456.

Kingdon, J. (1984). *Agendas, alternatives, and public policies.* Boston: Little, Brown.

Ladd, E. C. (1996). The data just don't show erosion of America's "social capital." *The Public Perspective, 7*(June/July), 1–22.

Lakoff, G. (1996). *Moral politics: What conservatives know that liberals don't.* Chicago: University of Chicago Press.

Larson, R. W. (2000). Toward a psychology of positive youth development. *American Psychologist, 55,* 170–183.

Leffert, N., Benson, P. L., Scales, P. C., Sharma, A. R., Drake, D. R., & Blyth, D. A. (1998). Developmental assets: Measurement and prediction of risk behaviors among adolescence. *Applied Developmental Science, 2*(4), 209–230.

Leffert, N., Scales, P. C., Vraa, R., Libbey, H., & Benson, P. L. (forthcoming). *The role of developmental assets in the academic achievement of adolescents.* Manuscript submitted for publication.

Lerner, R. M. (2002). *Concepts and theories of human development* (3rd ed.). Mahwah, NJ: Erlbaum.

Lerner, R. M., & Benson, P. L. (2003). *Developmental assets and asset-building communities: Implications for research, policy, and practice.* New York: Kluwer Academic/Plenum.

Lerner, R. M., Brentano, C., Dowling, E. M., & Anderson, P. M. (2002). Positive youth development: Thriving as the basis of personhood and civil society. *New Directions for Youth Development, 95,* 11–33.

Lerner, R. M., Fisher, C. B., & Weinberg, R. A. (2000). Toward a science for and of the people: Promoting civil society through the application of developmental science. *Child Development, 71,* 11–20.

Macedo, S. (2002). The trouble with bonding. *The Responsive Community; Rights and Responsibilities, 12*(4), 16–27.

Mannes, M. (2002). Search Institute's evolving approach to community-based human development and the role of service learning. In M. E. Kenny, L. A. K. Simon, K. Kiley-Brabeck, & R. M. Lerner (Eds.), *Learning to serve: Promoting civil society through service learning* (pp. 423–441). Norwell, MA: Kluwer Academic.

Mannes, M., Benson, P. L., Kretzmann, J., & Norris, T. (2003). The American tradition of community development: Implications for guiding community engagement in youth development. In R. M. Lerner, F. Jacobs, & D. Wertlieb (Eds.), *Handbook of applied developmental science: Promoting positive child, adolescent, and family development through research, policies and programs, Vol. 1. Applying developmental science for youth and families: Historical and theoretical foundations.* Newbury Park, CA: Sage.

Mannes, M., Lewis, S., Hintz, N., Foster, K., & Nakkula, M. (2002). *Cultivating developmentally attentive communities: A report on the First Wave of the national Asset-Building Case Study Project.* Minneapolis: Search Institute.

Marshall, T. H. (1964). Citizenship and social class. In T. H. Marshall (Ed.), *Class, citizenship and social development*. Garden City, NY: Doubleday.

Masten, A. S., Coatsworth, J. D., Neeman, J., Gest, S. D., Tellehn, A., & Garmezy, N. (1995).

The structure and coherence of competence from childhood through adolescence. *Child Development, 66,* 1635–1659.

Masten, A. S., & Curtis, W. J. (2000). Integrating competence and psychopathology: Pathways toward a comprehensive science of adaption in development. *Development and Psychopathology, 12*(3), 529–550.

McKnight, J. (1995). *The careless society: Community and its counterfeits.* New York: Basic Books.

Melby, T. (2001). In teens we trust: Youth take a seat in local government. *Assets* (Spring),12–13.

Miringoff, M., & Miringoff, M.-L. (1999). *The social health of the nation: How America is really doing.* New York: Oxford University Press.

National Research Council and Institute of Medicine. (2000). *From neurons to neighborhoods: The science of early child development.* Washington, DC: National Academy Press.

National Research Council and Institute of Medicine. (2002). *Community programs to promote youth development.* Washington, DC: National Academy Press.

Newman, R. P., Smith, S. M., & Murphy, R. (2001). A matter of money: The cost and financing of youth development. In P. L. Benson & K. J. Pittman (Eds.), *Trends in youth development: Visions, realities and challenges* (pp. 91–134). Boston: Kluwer Academic.

Paragment, K. I., & Park, C. L. (1995). Merely a defense? The variety of religious means and ends. *Journal of Social Issues, 51*(2), 13–32.

Pittman, K., Diversi, M., & Ferber, T. (2002). Social policy supports for adolescence in the twenty-first century: Framing questions. *Journal of Research on Adolescence, 12*(1), 149–158.

Pittman, K., & Irby, M. (1996). *Preventing problems or promoting development: Competing priorities or inseparable goals?* Baltimore: International Youth Foundation.

Pittman, K., & Irby, M. (1998). Reflections on a decade of promoting youth development. In S. Halperin (Ed.), *The forgotten half revisited: American youth and young families, 1988–2008* (pp. 159–169). Washington, DC: American Youth Policy Forum.

Pittman, K., Irby, M., & Ferber, T. (2001). Unfinished business: Further reflections on a decade of promoting youth development. In P. L. Benson & K. Pittman (Eds.), *Trends in youth development: visions, realities and challenges* (pp. 3–5). Boston: Kluwer Academic.

Pittman, K., Irby, M., Tolman, J., Yohalem, N., & Ferber, T. (2002). *Preventing problems, promoting development, encouraging engagement: Competing priorities or inseparable goals?* Takoma Park, MD: The Forum for Youth Investment.

Pittman, K., Yohalem, N., & Irby, M. (2003). Exploring youth policy in the U.S.: Options for progress. In R. M. Lerner, F. Jacobs, & D. Wertlieb, *Handbook of applied developmental science: Promoting positive child, adolescent, and family development through research, policies and programs. Vol. 2: Enhancing the life chances of youth and families. Contributions of programs, policies, and service systems* (pp. 563–583). Newbury Park, CA: Sage.

Pressman, J. L., & Wildavsky, A. (1974). *Implementation.* Berkeley, CA: University of California Press.

Putnam, R.D. (1993). *Making democracy work: Civic traditions in modern Italy.* Princeton, NJ: Princeton University Press.

Putnam, R. D. (1996). The strange disappearance of civic America. *The American Prospect, 24,* 34–50.

Resnick, M. D., Bearman, P. S., Blum, R. W., Bauman, K. E., Harris, K. M., Jones, J., et al. (1997). Protecting adolescents from harm: Findings from the National Longitudinal Study on Adolescent Health. *Journal of the American Medical Association, 278*(10), 823–832.

Rickel, A. U., & Becker, E. (1997). *Keeping children from harm's way: How national policy affects psychological development.* Washington, DC: American Psychological Association.

Roth, J., & Brooks-Gunn, J. (2000). What do adolescents need for healthy development? Implications for youth policy. *Social Policy Report, 14*(1), 3–19.

Sampson, R. J., Morenoff, J. D., & Earls, F. (1999). Beyond social capital: Spatial dynamics of collective efficacy for children. *American Sociological Review, 64,* 633–660.

Sampson, R. J., Raudenbush, S. W., & Earls, F. C. (1997). Neighborhoods and violent crime: A multilevel study of collective efficacy. *Science, 277,* 918–924.

Sanders, M. G. (1998). The effects of school, family, and community support on the academic achievement of African American adolescents. *Urban Education, 33,* 385–409.

Scales, P. C. (2001). The public image of adolescents. *Social Science and Modern Society, 38*(4), 64–70.

Scales, P. C., Benson, P. L., Leffert, N., & Blyth, D. A. (2000). Contribution of developmental assets to the prediction of thriving among adolescents. *Applied Developmental Science, 4*(1), 27–46.

Scales, P. C., Benson, P. L., & Mannes, M. (2003). Grading grown-ups 2002: How do American kids and adults relate? Findings from a national study. [Unpublished report, Search Institute, Minneapolis, MN. Report available from Search Institute and accessible at http://www.search-institute.org]

Scales, P. C., Benson, P. L., Roehlkepartain, E. C., Hintz, N. R., Sullivan, T. K., Mannes, M., et al. (2001). The role of neighborhood and community in building developmental assets for children and youth: A national study of social norms among American adults. *Journal of Community Psychology, 29*(6), 703–727.

Scales, P. C., & Gibbons, J. L. (1996). Extended family members and unrelated adults in the lives of young adolescents: A research agenda. *Journal of Early Adolescence, 16*(4), 365–389.

Scales, P. C., & Leffert, N. (1999). *Developmental assets: A synthesis of the scientific research on adolescent development.* Minneapolis, MN: Search Institute.

Seligman, M. E. P., & Csikszentmihalyi, M. (2000). Positive psychology: An introduction. *American Psychologist, 55*(1), 5–14.

Sherrod, L. R. (1997). Promoting youth development through research-based policies. *Applied Developmental Science, 1,* 17–27.

Simpson, A. R. (2001). *Raising teens: A synthesis of research and foundation for action.* Boston: Harvard School of Public Health.

Skocpol, T., & Dickert, J. (2001). Speaking for families and children in a changing civic America. In C. J. DeVita & R. Mosher-Williams (Eds.), *Who speaks for America's children? The role of child advocates in public policy* (pp. 137–164). Washington, DC: Urban Institute Press.

Starkman, N., Scales, P. C., & Roberts, C. (1999). *Great places to learn: How asset building schools help students succeed.* Minneapolis, MN: Search Institute.

State Legislative Leaders Foundation. (1995). *Keys to effective legislation for children and families.* Centerville, MA: Author.

Steinberg, L., Mounts, N. S., Lamborn, S. D., & Dornbusch, S. M. (1991). Authoritative parenting and adolescent adjustment across varied ecological niches. *Journal of Research on Adolescence, 1,* 19–36.

Stukas, A. A., Clary, E. G., & Snyder, M. (1999). Service learning: Who benefits and why. *Social Policy Report, 12*(1–19).

Swadener, B. B., & Lubeck, S. (1995). The social construction of children and families "at risk": An introduction. In B. B. Swadener, & S. Lubeck (Eds.), *Children and families at promise: Deconstructing the discourse of risk* (pp. 1–14). Albany, NY: State University of New York.

Takanishi, R. (1993). The opportunities of adolescence—research, interventions and policy. *American Psychologist, 48,* 85–87.

Takanishi, R. (1996). Changing images of adolescents: Rethinking our policies. In E. F. Zigler, S. L. Kagan, & N. W. Hall (Eds.), *Children, families, and government: Preparing for the twenty-first century* (pp. 256–267). Cambridge, England: Cambridge University Press.

Taylor, C. S., Lerner, R. M., von Eye, A., Balsano, A. B., Dowling, E. M., Anderson, P. M., et al. (2002). Individual and ecological assets and positive developmental trajectories among gang and community-based organizations for youth. *New Directions for Youth Development, 95,* 57–72.

Tilly, C. (1973). Do communities act? *Sociological Inquiry, 43,* 209–240.

U.S. Department of Health and Human Services. (1996). *Reconnecting youth and community: A youth development approach.* Washington, DC: U.S. Department of Health and Human Services.

Valencia, R. R. (1997). *The evolution of deficit thinking: Educational thought and practice.* Washington, DC: Taylor and Francis.

Walker, G. (2001). The policy climate for early adolescent initiatives. In P. L. Benson & K. J. Pittman (Eds.), *Trends in youth development: Visions, realities and challenges*. Boston: Kluwer Academic.

Walzer, M. (1998). The civil society argument. In G. Shafir (Ed.), *The citizenship debates: A reader* (pp. 291–308). Minneapolis: University of Minnesota Press.

Werner, E., & Smith, R. (1992). *Overcoming the odds: High-risk children from birth to adulthood.* Ithaca, NY: Cornell University Press.

Wynn, J. (1997). *Primary supports, schools, and other sects: Implications for learning and civic life.* Paper prepared for the Harvard Project on Schooling and Children, Chapin Hall Center for Children, Chicago.

Yankelovich, D. (1998). How American individualism is evolving. *The Public Perspective, 9,* 3–6.

Youniss, J., McLellan, J. A., & Yates, M. (1999). Religion, community service, and identity in American youth. *Journal of Adolescence, 22,* 243–253.

Zaslow, M. J., & Takanishi, R. (1993). Priorities for research on adolescent development. *American Psychologist, 48,* 185–192.

Zeldin, S. (2000). Integrating research and practice to understand and strengthen communities for adolescent development: An introduction to the special issue and current issues. *Applied Developmental Science, 4*(Suppl. 1), 2–10.

Zero to Three. (2000). *What grown-ups understand about child development: A national benchmark survey.* Washington, DC: Author.

Zigler, E., & Anderson, K. (1979). An idea whose time had come: The intellectual and political climate for Head Start. In E. Zigler & J. Valentine (Eds.), *Project Head Start: A legacy of the war on poverty* (pp. 3–19). New York: Free Press.

Zigler, E. F., Kagan, S. L., & Hall, N. W. (1996). *Children, families and government: Preparing for the twenty-first century.* Cambridge, England: Cambridge University Press.

Zimmerman, S. L. (1992). *Family policies and family well-being: The role of political culture*. Newbury Park, CA: Sage.

Afterword: On the Future Development of Adolescent Psychology

Beatrix Hamburg and David Hamburg

This second edition of the *Handbook of Adolescent Psychology* documents and elucidates the coming of age of the field of adolescent development. Many of the remarkable achievements over the past 25 years in cognitive neuroscience, genetics, other biomedical sciences and the behavioral and social sciences are represented in the contributions of the interdisciplinary group of authors. This assembled body of knowledge provides impressive evidence of the web of factors that interact to determine pathways of adolescent development. Their chapters also reflect the importance of advances in multilevel research designs and sophisticated data analytic strategies for addressing the complexity of sorting out the impacts of multiple interacting influences.

The editors remind us that adolescence, as a distinctive and lengthy developmental period, is a modern invention linked to the social changes of the successes of industrialization about 100 years ago. Over the course of the last half of the twentieth century there were rapid, continuing, new major social changes that compelled us to reassess priorities and look anew at the tasks and challenges for adolescents in the twenty-first century. As the field looks to the future, it is clear that there is much that is already known and can be readily translated into policy and practice. There is also a strong foundation of scientific inquiry, collaboration, and rigorous methodology to buttress ongoing basic and applied research. Before focusing on the highlights of the major social changes and critical events of the latter part of the last century and beginning of the current one that are significant for a future agenda, it may be useful to put the heritage that we bring to our modern world into a brief evolutionary framework.

Although primates have existed for at least 50 million years, there is evidence that early man as a district hominid primate existed and began evolving 2 to 3 million years ago. Our own species, Homo sapiens, has existed for 50,000 to 100,000 years with very little change. During most of this time, our earliest ancestors were hunter-gatherers with primitive tools. They lived in small groups whose social organization was based on intense and persistent attachments between the group members. There are ancient and powerful links between in-group attachment and survival. The advent of agriculture was about 10,000 years ago. It is believed that its worldwide adoption, in effective form, took several thousand years. Agriculture is still prominent in many parts of the world as a family or small group enterprise characterized by strong in-group attachment bonds and mutual support. Although the evolutionary dating is murky, the historical record does clearly document that aggressive behavior directed against strangers and out-groups has also been a consistent aspect of human behavior. This learned behavior is facilitated by a pervasive human propensity for harsh dichotomizing between the positively valued "us" and the negatively valued "them."

The Industrial Revolution was initiated about 200 years ago. Although the full impact has not yet been realized on a worldwide basis, the Western world has had an industrial society for several generations, about 100 years. During the past 50 years, the post-industrial high-technology and current information-technology eras have emerged. We are experiencing an explosion of the biological science breakthroughs, most notably in the neurosciences and the mapping of the human genome. Weapons of war have gone from clubs, arrows, and simple guns to atomic bombs and biological weapons. Clearly change has been a feature of the human experience, but the rate of change has been notably accelerating, and recent key changes have truly transformed the world of our adolescents.

Over the span of evolutionary time, natural selection has favored structural and behavioral attributes that enhance adaptability to environmental and social change. Across time, the human species has coped with significant change. Humans have radiated to all parts of the globe and have adapted to the most diverse ecological niches and environmental changes. This uniquely powerful learning and adaptive capacity is the salient difference that sets us apart from other creatures. There is strong evidence that youngsters and adolescents, in particular, are attracted to novelty. They enjoy exploratory behavior that can also include deliberate risk-taking. These attributes can be useful. In fact, over time, adolescents have introduced substantial innovation into their environments. However, in the modern world, adolescents engage in behaviors or make decisions that can lead to adverse immediate and long-term consequences that affect their health, significant relationships, academic success, or life options. Much has been done in this area, but there is continuing need to give priority to mounting systematic and integrated programs to assure that all or most adolescents can deal constructively with these fateful decisions.

Throughout human history and across cultures, most families have been able to meet the basic needs of their members for survival, growth, protection, and successful adaptation to the cultural norms. Equally important has been the family role in carrying out the education and socialization of the children for their future roles as workers, parents, and valued members of their community group. Prior to industrialization and related urbanization, families lived in small supportive communities with relatives and friends who were well known to each other and had shared values. Many modern families are single-parent or two-working-parent households. Time and energy to fulfill the parenting roles have diminished. Due to mobility, there is much more isolation of the small family. Families used to live in contexts that had high predictability across generations. Now, for the first time, in modern families there is an awareness that parents must try to prepare their children for an unknowable and unpredictable future. There are no reliable societal substitutes to provide the parents with the lost web of support, and there is no provision of new ways to meet the socialization needs of the children. Instead of experiencing the stability of a small community with shared values, youngsters today are bombarded by a strident array of media messages, enticing advertising, rock music and videos, and Internet lures that include chat rooms on all topics, including pornography and hate group web sites. Violence is the most popular component of interactive computer games. Perhaps even more important is the real-world violence that has been escalating and is prevalent in homes, schools, and neighborhoods. The stunning images of the 9-11 bombing of the World Trade Towers have left children and adolescents with unforgettable awareness of hatred, destruction, and vulnerability, not just here in the United States but around the world. Nelson Mandela has expressed it well:

> The twentieth century will be remembered as a century marked by violence. It burdens us with a legacy of mass destruction, of violence inflicted on a scale never seen and never possible before in human history. But this legacy—the result of new technology in the service of ideologies of hate—is not the only one we carry, or that we must face up to.
>
> Less visible, but even more widespread, is the legacy of day-to-day, individual suffering. It is the pain of children who are abused by people who should protect them, women injured or humiliated by violent partners, elderly persons maltreated by their caregivers, youths who are bullied by other youths, and people of all ages who inflict violence upon themselves. This suffering—and there are many other examples that I could give—is a legacy that reproduces itself as new generations learn from the violence of generations past, as victims learn from victimizers, and as the social conditions that nurture violence are allowed to continue. No country, no city, no community is immune. But neither are we powerless. (Mandela, 2002)

In a world so full of hatred and violence, past and present, human conflict and its resolution are subjects that deserve major research, educational, policy, and program efforts—not only in schools and universities, but in community organizations, religious institutions, and the media. To this day, however, these institutions often retain ethnocentric and prejudicial orientations to differing degrees. In some cases, they are extreme and take on an overriding significance. In many places and in many generations, we have seen that it is possible to shape young people in hateful ways, and in extreme cases to prepare them for large-scale killing—even at the expense of their own lives.

We need to know much more about how young people can learn to adopt more positive orientations toward those outside their own group while maintaining the values, alliance, and security of their primary group. High priority must be given to the task of educating and socializing for prosocial behavior. It must begin in early life and continue through adolescence. It is important to learn much more about the developmental pathways that instill and reinforce prosocial, affiliative, and tolerant behaviors in developmentally appropriate ways at each stage of the life span. In this regard, little systematic attention has been paid to the influences of the large and increasingly diverse peer populations that are now prominent in schools and neighborhoods. These issues may have particular salience for adolescents as they seek to define their identity. There may be intergenerational differences between parents and young persons that affect the adoption of empathic and tolerant attitudes toward those perceived as different or alien. Even parents who had been accepting of a mix of childhood friendships may become far less tolerant during the adolescent period of dating and deep friendships. In all of these areas there is much to be learned by reviewing our own extant basic and applied research as well as by making a comparable review of the international literature on intergroup relations among adolescents. Furthermore, studying these issues in exchanges and collaborations with colleagues across the globe will also be intrinsically desirable. Through such study, new, useful research paradigms and model programs for further study will emerge. The very fact of global collaborations will have the additional benefit of strengthening ties with scientists and their students across a wide range of cultures. This enhanced understanding and respect for colleagues in other parts of the world will have its own role in dispelling stereotypes and ethnocentrism in the international scholarly community.

There are no quick or easy answers to the major new challenges to the entire society posed by the profound transformations in the latter part of the past century. We must find different ways to meet the essential requirements for effective child and adolescent development. Pivotal institutions of society can assume new roles that will supplement and support the burdened modern family. Unquestionably, schools are first among these institutions. The changes of today's world have fundamentally altered the requirements for the appropriate education of contemporary children and youth. There is now a consensus that a modern nation must fully develop the talents of its entire student population if it is to be socially cohesive, economically vigorous, and globally competitive. The norm should be expectations of high academic achievement for all students. In the transformed, and still changing, high-technology information age, there is an increasing recognition that, college-bound or not, all children will need to acquire a solid knowledge base, critical thinking skills, social competencies, and respect for others.

Developmental and educational needs are closely meshed from early childhood throughout adolescence. Powerful links in early childhood between socioemotional well-being, school readiness, and learning proficiency have been well established. The same nexus deserves further study in the critical transition to the larger school context of junior high or middle school. This transition occurs at the time of puberty, with its drastic bodily changes and significant maturational change in the brain. Which learning formats or teaching strategies are most appropriate for this very special developmental phase? Just as kindergarten does not resemble the third grade, should middle school or junior high be closely modeled on high school? With the intense interest that adolescents have in their own physical changes at puberty, this is a time of great opportunity to focus on human biology and links to the health and behavior issues. It is also the time when fateful health choices are being considered but, for most, not yet acted upon. Throughout most of human history the physical changes of puberty and resulting adult physique marked the end of childhood and entry into the adult world of work. In many cultures there are important rituals to mark this entry in adulthood. It is only in the past century and in the post-industrial societies that postpubertal young people have not been assigned meaningful, contributory social roles. In agrarian societies their strength and energy was a valued asset. For those youth, their contribution was a source of self-worth and identification as a valued member of a valued group. Modern adolescents are role-less for the most part. They are our leisure class. They often seek their group identification and self-worth in teams, cliques, and gangs. Community service can play a major role in giving modern youth a valued role. When community service is linked to schools as service learning, it can also serve a range of academic goals. Supervised community service provides adolescents with supportive, nonparental mentors. American children and youth spend less time in school than their counterparts in other modern societies. As a result of the attenuated school year and short school days, they have substantial, unstructured after-school leisure time. There are youth-serving agencies that meet the after-school needs of some of the youth, but for the youngsters most at risk, constructive community resources are least likely to be available.

The world is rapidly moving into a higher state of interdependency driven by technological advances, economic opportunities, intellectual curiosity, and personal contacts. There is more movement across national boundaries than ever before of people, money, information, ideas, and images. We live together with billions of people, mostly strangers; we need them and they need us—to make a living, to travel, to cope with widespread problems like infectious diseases and terrorism, and to assure our safe supplies of food and water, a clean environment, and physical protection.

So now we must, of necessity, find better ways to interact with strangers, move beyond stereotypes, and—to the extent possible—turn strangers into familiar people, even turn adversaries into friends.

All research-based knowledge of human conflict, the diversity of our species, and the paths to mutual accommodation must become integrated into education, conveying both the facts of human diversity and the common humanity we all share. We can convey the fascination of other cultures, making understanding and respect a core attribute of our outlook on the world, including the capacity to interact effectively in the emerging world economy. At the same time, we must enhance the capacity of each culture to protect human rights and minimize violence.

Deeper understanding is essential to achieve peaceful living and cope with the unprecedented destructive capacities of the human species. Scientific and scholarly professions must engage in interdisciplinary, systematic research on the conditions under which violent behaviors are likely to occur, the conditions under which human conflict can be effectively resolved, and the conditions under which just peace can be maintained on an enduring basis.

Efforts by the pivotal institutions to improve relations among diverse peoples require a strong knowledge base derived from research. This will clarify ways in which young people can reduce intergroup tensions and cope with expressions of ethnic, cultural, religious, or nationalistic intolerance among their peers. Research will find new kinds of interventions to improve the school and community climate for group interaction and elucidate which practices within schools can create an atmosphere of mutual respect and positive relations among peers as well as between students and teachers. This handbook points the way to such fundamental advances.

REFERENCE

Mandela, N. (2002). Foreword. In World Health Organization, *World Report on Violence and Health.* Geneva: World Health Organization.

Author Index

Subject Index